Texas Rules of Court

Volume I – State

2016

THOMSON REUTERS™

Mat#41778593

ISBN 978–0–314–68216–1

PREFACE

Designed for use in the office or courtroom, this pamphlet contains the Texas state rules.

WHAT'S NEW

Texas Rules of Court Volume I–State 2016, includes rules and associated material governing practice before the Texas state courts. It is current with amendments received through February 1, 2016.

CONTACT US

For additional information or research assistance, call the reference attorneys at 1-800-REF-ATTY (1-800-733-2889). Contact our U.S. legal editorial department directly with your questions and suggestions by e-mail at editors.us-legal@tr.com.

Thank you for subscribing to this product. Should you have any questions regarding this product please contact Customer Service at 1-800-328-4880 or by fax at 1-800-340-9378. If you would like to inquire about related publications, or to place an order, please contact us at 1-800-344-5009 or visit us online.

THE PUBLISHER

March 2016

TABLE OF CONTENTS

TEXAS RULES OF CIVIL PROCEDURE

Effective September 1, 1941

Including Amendments Received Through February 1, 2016

Research Note

See Vernon's Texas Rules Annotated, *Volumes 1 to 6 for judicial constructions and other research aids.*

SECTION 9. EVIDENCE AND DISCOVERY

A. EVIDENCE

B. DISCOVERY

SECTION 10. THE JURY IN COURT

SECTION 11. TRIAL OF CAUSES

A. APPEARANCE AND PROCEDURE

B. CONTINUANCE AND CHANGE OF VENUE

C. THE TRIAL

PUBLISHER'S NOTE

Supreme Court Orders have directed that the notes and comments which follow the rules are incomplete, are included only for the convenience of the bench and bar, and are not a part of the rules.

The Supreme Court Order signed and entered August 15, 1997, which finally approved amendments to Rule 166a effective September 1, 1997, provides in part: "The comment appended to these changes, unlike other notes and comments in the rules, is intended to inform the construction and application of the rule."

The Supreme Court Order signed and entered November 9, 1998, which finally approved revisions to the Rules of Civil Procedure governing discovery effective January 1, 1999, provides in part: "The notes and comments appended to these revisions, unlike some other notes and comments in the rules, are intended to inform the construction and application of these rules by both courts and practitioners."

PART I

GENERAL RULES

Rule 1. Objective of Rules

The proper objective of rules of civil procedure is to obtain a just, fair, equitable and impartial adjudication of the rights of litigants under established principles of substantive law. To the end that this objective may be attained with as great expedition and dispatch and at the least expense both to the litigants and to the state as may be practicable, these rules shall be given a liberal construction.

Oct. 29, 1940, eff. Sept. 1, 1941.

Historical Notes

Source

New rule.

Rule 2. Scope of Rules

These rules shall govern the procedure in the justice, county, and district courts of the State of Texas in all actions of a civil nature, with such exceptions as may be hereinafter stated. Where any statute in effect immediately prior to September 1, 1941, prescribed a rule of procedure in lunacy, guardianship, or estates of decedents, or any other probate proceedings in the county court differing from these Rules, and not included in the "List of Repealed Statutes," such statute shall apply; and where any statute in effect immediately prior to September 1, 1941, and not included in the "List of Repealed Statutes," prescribed a rule of procedure in any special statutory proceeding differing from these rules, such statute shall apply. All statutes in effect immediately prior to September 1, 1941, prescribing rules of procedure in bond or recognizance forfeitures in criminal cases are hereby continued in effect as rules of procedure governing such cases, but where such statutes prescribed no rules of procedure in such cases, these rules shall apply. All statutes in effect immediately prior to September 1, 1941, prescribing rules of procedure in tax suits are hereby continued in effect as rules of procedure governing such cases, but where such statutes prescribed no rules of procedure in such cases, these rules shall apply; provided, however, that Rule 117a shall control with respect to citation in tax suits.

Oct. 29, 1940, eff. Sept. 1, 1941. Amended by orders of Sept. 20, 1941, eff. Dec. 31, 1941; June 16, 1943, eff. Dec. 31, 1943; Aug. 18, 1947, eff. Dec. 31, 1947; April 10, 1986, eff. Sept. 1, 1986.

Historical Notes

Source

Federal Rule 1, adapted to Texas practice.

Rule 3. Construction of Rules

Unless otherwise expressly provided, the past, present or future tense shall each include the other; the masculine, feminine, or neuter gender shall each include the other; and the singular and plural number shall each include the other.

Oct. 29, 1940, eff. Sept. 1, 1941.

Historical Notes

Source

Vernon's Ann.Civ.St. art. 10, subds. 2 to 4.

Rule 3a. Local Rules

Each administrative judicial region, district court, county court, county court at law, and probate court may make and amend local rules governing practice before such courts, provided:

(1) that any proposed rule or amendment shall not be inconsistent with these rules or with any rule of the administrative judicial region in which the court is located;

(2) no time period provided by these rules may be altered by local rules;

(3) any proposed local rule or amendment shall not become effective until it is submitted and approved by the Supreme Court of Texas;

(4) any proposed local rule or amendment shall not become effective until at least thirty days after its publication in a manner reasonably calculated to bring it to the attention of attorneys practicing before the court or courts for which it is made;

(5) all local rules or amendments adopted and approved in accordance herewith are made available upon request to the members of the bar;

(6) no local rule, order, or practice of any court, other than local rules and amendments which fully comply with all requirements of this Rule 3a, shall ever be applied to determine the merits of any matter.

Oct. 29, 1940, eff. Sept. 1, 1941. Amended by order of June 10, 1980, eff. Jan. 1, 1981; renumbered from former Rule 817 and amended by order of Dec. 5, 1983, eff. April 1, 1984; amended by orders of April 10, 1986, eff. Sept. 1, 1986; July 15, 1987, eff. Jan. 1, 1988; April 24, 1990, eff. Sept. 1, 1990.

Comment—1990

To make Texas Rules of Civil Procedure timetables mandatory and to preclude use of unpublished local rules or other "standing" orders or local practices to determine issues of substantive merit.

Historical Notes

Source

Federal Rule 83.

Rule 4. Computation of Time

In computing any period of time prescribed or allowed by these rules, by order of court, or by any applicable statute, the day of the act, event, or default after which the designated period of time begins to run is not to be included. The last day of the period so computed is to be included, unless it is a Saturday, Sunday, or legal holiday, in which event the period runs until the end of the next day which is not a Saturday, Sunday, or legal holiday. Saturdays, Sundays, and legal holidays shall not be counted for any purpose in any time period of five days or less in these rules, except that Saturdays, Sundays, and legal holidays shall be counted for purpose of the three-day periods in Rules 21 and 21a, extending other periods by three days when service is made by mail.

Oct. 29, 1940, eff. Sept. 1, 1941. Amended by orders of July 26, 1960, eff. Jan. 1, 1961; April 24, 1990, eff. Sept. 1, 1990; Dec. 11, 2013, eff. Jan. 1, 2014.

Comment—1990

Amended to omit counting Saturdays, Sundays and legal holidays in all periods of less than five days with certain exceptions.

Historical Notes

Source

Federal Rule 6(a), omitting the Federal provision excluding intermediate Sundays or holidays when the period of time is less than seven days and the Federal reference to half-holidays.

2013 Amendment

The order dated December 11, 2013 substituted "made by mail" for "made by registered or certified mail, or by telephonic document transfer, and for purposes of the five-day periods provided for under Rules 748, 749, 749a, 749b, and 749c", and made other nonsubstantive changes.

Rule 5. Enlargement of Time

When by these rules or by a notice given thereunder or by order of court an act is required or allowed to be done at or within a specified time, the court for cause shown may, at any time in its discretion (a) with or without motion or notice, order the period enlarged if application therefor is made before the expiration of the period originally prescribed or as extended by a previous order; or (b) upon motion permit the act to be done after the expiration of the specified period where good cause is shown for the failure to act. The court may not enlarge the period for taking any action under the rules relating to new trials except as stated in these rules.

If any document is sent to the proper clerk by first-class United States mail in an envelope or wrapper properly addressed and stamped and is deposited in the mail on or before the last day for filing same, the same, if received by the clerk not more than ten days tardily, shall be filed by the clerk and be deemed filed in time. A legible postmark affixed by the United States Postal Service shall be prima facie evidence of the date of mailing.

Oct. 29, 1940, eff. Sept. 1, 1941. Amended by orders of Oct. 12, 1949, eff. March 1, 1950; July 21, 1970, eff. Jan. 1, 1971; Oct. 3, 1972, eff. Feb. 1, 1973; July 22, 1975, eff. Jan. 1, 1976; April 10, 1986, eff. Sept. 1, 1986; April 24, 1990, eff. Sept. 1, 1990.

Comment—1990

To make the last date for mailing under Rule 5 coincide with the last date for filing.

Historical Notes

Source

Federal rule 6(b), with minor textual changes.

Rule 6. Suits Commenced on Sunday

No civil suit shall be commenced nor process issued or served on Sunday, except in cases of injunction, attachment, garnishment, sequestration, or distress proceedings; provided that citation by publication published on Sunday shall be valid.

Oct. 29, 1940, eff. Sept. 1, 1941. Amended by order of Oct. 3, 1972, eff. Feb. 1, 1973.

Historical Notes

Source

Vernon's Ann.Civ.St. art. 1974, unchanged.

Rule 7. May Appear by Attorney

Any party to a suit may appear and prosecute or defend his rights therein, either in person or by an attorney of the court.

Oct. 29, 1940, eff. Sept. 1, 1941.

Historical Notes

Source

Vernon's Ann.Civ.St. art. 1993, unchanged.

Rule 8. Attorney in Charge

On the occasion of a party's first appearance through counsel, the attorney whose signature first appears on the initial pleadings for any party shall be the attorney in charge, unless another attorney is specifically designated therein. Thereafter, until such designation is changed by written notice to the court and all other parties in accordance with Rule 21a, said attorney in charge shall be responsible for the suit as to such party.

All communications from the court or other counsel with respect to a suit shall be sent to the attorney in charge.

Oct. 29, 1940, eff. Sept. 1, 1941. Amended by order of July 15, 1987, eff. Jan. 1, 1988.

Historical Notes

Source

District and County Court Rule 45, unchanged.

Rule 9. Number of Counsel Heard

Not more than two counsel on each side shall be heard on any question or on the trial, except in important cases, and upon special leave of the court.

Oct. 29, 1940, eff. Sept. 1, 1941.

Historical Notes

Source

District and County Court Rule 44, unchanged.

Rule 10. Withdrawal of Attorney

An attorney may withdraw from representing a party only upon written motion for good cause shown. If another attorney is to be substituted as attorney for the party, the motion shall state: the name, address, telephone number, telecopier number, if any, and State Bar of Texas identification number of the substitute attorney; that the party approves the substitution; and that the withdrawal is not sought for delay only. If another attorney is not to be substituted as attorney for the party, the motion shall state: that a copy of the motion has been delivered to the party; that the party has been notified in writing of his right to object to the motion; whether the party consents to the motion; the party's last known address and all pending settings and deadlines. If the motion is granted, the withdrawing attorney shall immediately notify the party in writing of any additional settings or deadlines of which the attorney has knowledge at the time of the withdrawal and has not already notified the party. The Court may impose further conditions upon granting leave to withdraw. Notice or delivery to a party shall be either made to the party in person or mailed to the party's last known address by both certified and regular first class mail. If the attorney in charge withdraws and another attorney remains or becomes substituted, another attorney in charge must be designated of record with notice to all other parties in accordance with Rule 21a.

Oct. 29, 1940, eff. Sept. 1, 1941. Amended by orders of July 15, 1987, eff. Jan. 1, 1988; April 24, 1990, eff. Sept. 1, 1990.

Comment—1990

The amendment repeals the present rule and clarifies the requirements for withdrawal.

Comment—1988

The amendment repeals the present rule and makes provision for withdrawal of counsel, setting forth the requirements for withdrawal and withdrawal with substitution of counsel. The amendment also carries forward the requirements of amended Rule 8 regarding designation of attorney in charge.

Historical Notes

Source

District and County Court Rule 46, unchanged.

Rule 11. Agreements To Be in Writing

Unless otherwise provided in these rules, no agreement between attorneys or parties touching any suit pending will be enforced unless it be in writing, signed and filed with the papers as part of the record, or unless it be made in open court and entered of record.

Oct. 29, 1940, eff. Sept. 1, 1941. Amended by order of July 15, 1987, eff. Jan. 1, 1988.

Comment—1988

The amendment makes it clear that Rule 11 is subject to modification by any other rule of Civil Procedure.

Historical Notes

Source

District and County Court Rule 47, unchanged.

Rule 12. Attorney to Show Authority

A party in a suit or proceeding pending in a court of this state may, by sworn written motion stating that he believes the suit or proceeding is being prosecuted or defended without authority, cause the attorney to be cited to appear before the court and show his authority to act. The notice of the motion shall be served upon the challenged attorney at least ten days before the hearing on the motion. At the hearing on the motion, the burden of proof shall be upon the challenged attorney to show sufficient authority to prosecute or defend the suit on behalf of the other party. Upon his failure to show such authority, the court shall refuse to permit the attorney to appear in the cause, and shall strike the pleadings if no person who is authorized to prosecute or defend appears. The motion may be heard and determined at any time before the parties have announced ready for trial, but the trial shall not be unnecessarily continued or delayed for the hearing.

Oct. 29, 1940, eff. Sept. 1, 1941. Amended by order of June 10, 1980, eff. Jan. 1, 1981.

Historical Notes

Source

Vernon's Ann.Civ.St. art. 320. Rule 12 made minor textual change in art. 320 and added the requirement that notice be served at least ten days before the trial of the motion.

Rule 13. Effect of Signing of Pleadings, Motions and Other Papers; Sanctions

The signatures of attorneys or parties constitute a certificate by them that they have read the pleading, motion, or other paper; that to the best of their knowledge, information, and belief formed after reasonable inquiry the instrument is not groundless and brought in bad faith or groundless and brought for the purpose of harassment. Attorneys or parties who shall bring a fictitious suit as an experiment to get an opinion of the court, or who shall file any fictitious pleading in a cause for such a purpose, or shall make statements in pleading which they know to be groundless and false, for the purpose of securing a delay of the trial of the cause, shall be held guilty of a contempt. If a pleading, motion or other paper is signed in violation of this rule, the court, upon motion or upon its own initiative, after notice and hearing, shall impose an appropriate sanction available under Rule 215,[1] upon the person who signed it, a represented party, or both.

Courts shall presume that pleadings, motions, and other papers are filed in good faith. No sanctions under this rule may be imposed except for good cause, the particulars of which must be stated in the sanction order. "Groundless" for purposes of this rule means no basis in law or fact and not warranted by good faith argument for the extension, modification, or reversal of existing law. A general denial does not constitute a violation of this rule. The amount requested for damages does not constitute a violation of this rule.

Oct. 29, 1940, eff. Sept. 1, 1941. Amended by orders of July 15, 1987, eff. Jan. 1, 1988; April 24, 1990, eff. Sept. 1, 1990.

1 Probably Vernon's Ann.Rules Civ.Proc., rule 215.2(b).

Comment—1990

To require notice and hearing before a court determines to impose sanctions, to specify that any sanction imposed be appropriate, and to eliminate the 90–day "grace" period provided in the former version of the rule.

Historical Notes

Source

District and County Court Rule 51, unchanged.

Rule 14. Affidavit by Agent

Whenever it may be necessary or proper for any party to a civil suit or proceeding to make an affidavit, it may be made by either the party or his agent or his attorney.

Oct. 29, 1940, eff. Sept. 1, 1941.

Historical Notes

Source

Vernon's Ann.Civ.St. art. 24, unchanged.

Rule 14a. Repealed by Order of April 10, 1986, eff. Sept. 1, 1986

Historical Notes

The repealed rule, which provided that the provisions of Rules 430 and 437 were to apply to appellate procedure in all other courts of the state, was added by order dated Oct. 10, 1945.

Rule 14b. Return or Other Disposition of Exhibits

The clerk of the court in which the exhibits are filed shall retain and dispose of the same as directed by the Supreme Court.

Jan. 1, 1967, eff. Jan. 1, 1967. Amended by order of July 15, 1987, eff. Jan. 1, 1988.

Supreme Court Order Relating to Retention and Disposition of Exhibits

In compliance with the provisions of Rule 14b, the Supreme Court hereby directs that exhibits offered or admitted into evidence shall be retained and disposed of by the clerk of the court in which the exhibits are filed upon the following basis.

This order shall apply only to: (1) those cases in which judgment has been rendered on service of process by publication and in which no motion for new trial was filed within two years after judgment was signed; and, (2) all other cases in which judgment has been signed for one year and in which no appeal was perfected or in which a perfected appeal was dismissed or concluded by a final judgement as to all parties and the issuance of the appellate court's mandate such that the case is no longer pending on appeal or in the trial court.

The party who offered an exhibit may withdraw it from the clerk's office within thirty days of the later of (1) a case becoming subject to this order, or (2) the effective date of this order. The clerk, unless otherwise directed by the court, may dispose of any exhibits remaining after such time period.

Rule 14c. Deposit in Lieu of Surety Bond

Wherever these rules provide for the filing of a surety bond, the party may in lieu of filing the bond deposit cash or other negotiable obligation of the government of the United States of America or any agency thereof, or with leave of court, deposit a negotiable obligation of any bank or savings and loan association chartered by the government of the United States of America or any state thereof that is insured by the government of the United States of America or any agency thereof, in the amount fixed for the surety bond, conditioned in the same manner as would be a surety bond for the protection of other parties. Any interest thereon shall constitute a part of the deposit.

June 10, 1980, eff. Jan. 1, 1981.

PART II

RULES OF PRACTICE IN DISTRICT AND COUNTY COURTS

SECTION 1. GENERAL RULES

Rule 15. Writs and Process

The style of all writs and process shall be "The State of Texas"; and unless otherwise specially provided by law or these rules every such writ and process shall be directed to any sheriff or any constable within the State of Texas, shall be made returnable on the Monday next after expiration of twenty days from the date of service thereof, and shall be dated and attested by the clerk with the seal of the court impressed thereon; and the date of issuance shall be noted thereon.

Oct. 29, 1940, eff. Sept. 1, 1941.

Historical Notes

Source

Vernon's Ann.Civ.St. art. 2286. Rule 15 modified prior provisions in that it permitted writs and process to be directed "to any sheriff or any constable within the State of Texas" rather than "to the sheriff or any constable of the proper county." Rule 15 also substituted provision making writs and process "returnable on the Monday next after expiration of twenty days from the date of service thereof" for prior provision making them "returnable on the first day of the next term of the court after the issuance thereof."

Rule 16. Shall Endorse all Process

Every officer or authorized person shall endorse on all process and precepts coming to his hand the day and hour on which he received them, the manner in which he executed them, and the time and place the process was served and shall sign the returns officially.

Oct. 29, 1940, eff. Sept. 1, 1941. Amended by order of July 15, 1987, eff. Jan. 1, 1988.

Comment—1988

Article 3926a, effective September 1, 1981, authorizes the commissioner's court of each county to set a "reasonable" fee for service of process; mileage is no longer an authorized expense for serving process.

Historical Notes

Source

Vernon's Ann.Civ.St. art. 6875, with minor textual change.

Rule 17. Officer to Execute Process

Except where otherwise expressly provided by law or these rules, the officer receiving any process to be executed shall not be entitled in any case to demand his fee for executing the same in advance of such execution, but his fee shall be taxed and collected as other costs in the case.

Oct. 29, 1940, eff. Sept. 1, 1941.

Historical Notes

Source

Vernon's Ann.Civ.St. art. 3911, adding "Except where otherwise expressly provided by law or these rules".

Rule 18. When Judge Dies During Term, Resigns or is Disabled

If the judge dies, resigns, or becomes unable to hold court during the session of court duly convened for the term, and the time provided by law for the holding of said court has not expired, such death, resignation, or inability on the part of the judge shall not operate to adjourn said court for the term, but such court shall be deemed to continue in session. If a successor to such judge shall qualify and assume office during the term, or if a judge be transferred to said district from some other judicial district, he may continue to hold said court for the term provided, and all motions undisposed of shall be heard and determined by him, and statements of facts and bills of exception shall be approved by him. If the time for holding such court expires before a successor shall qualify, and before a judge can be transferred to said district from some other judicial district, then all motions pending, including those for new trial, shall stand as continued in force until such successor has qualified and assumed office, or a judge has been transferred to said district who can hold said court, and thereupon such judge shall have power to act thereon at the succeeding term, or on an earlier day in vacation, on notice to all parties to the motion, and such orders shall have the same effect as if rendered in term time. The time for allowing statement of facts and bills of exception from such orders shall date from the time the motion was decided.

Oct. 29, 1940, eff. Sept. 1, 1941. Amended by order of June 16, 1943, eff. Dec. 31, 1943.

Historical Notes

Source

Vernon's Ann.Civ.St. art. 2288.

Rule 18a. Recusal and Disqualification of Judges

(a) *Motion; Form and Contents.* A party in a case in any trial court other than a statutory probate court or justice court may seek to recuse or disqualify a judge who is sitting in the case by filing a motion with the clerk of the court in which the case is pending. The motion:

(1) must be verified;

(2) must assert one or more of the grounds listed in Rule 18b;

(3) must not be based solely on the judge's rulings in the case; and

(4) must state with detail and particularity facts that:

(A) are within the affiant's personal knowledge, except that facts may be stated on information and belief if the basis for that belief is specifically stated;

(B) would be admissible in evidence; and

(C) if proven, would be sufficient to justify recusal or disqualification.

(b) *Time for Filing Motion.*

(1) Motion to Recuse. A motion to recuse:

(A) must be filed as soon as practicable after the movant knows of the ground stated in the motion; and

(B) must not be filed after the tenth day before the date set for trial or other hearing unless, before that day, the movant neither knew nor reasonably should have known:

(i) that the judge whose recusal is sought would preside at the trial or hearing; or

(ii) that the ground stated in the motion existed.

(2) Motion to Disqualify. A motion to disqualify should be filed as soon as practicable after the movant knows of the ground stated in the motion.

(c) *Response to Motion.*

(1) By Another Party. Any other party in the case may, but need not, file a response to the motion. Any response must be filed before the motion is heard.

(2) By the Respondent Judge. The judge whose recusal or disqualification is sought should not file a response to the motion.

(d) *Service of Motion or Response.* A party who files a motion or response must serve a copy on every other party. The method of service must be the same as the method of filing, if possible.

(e) *Duty of the Clerk.*

(1) Delivery of a Motion or Response. When a motion or response is filed, the clerk of the court must immediately deliver a copy to the respondent judge and to the presiding judge of the administrative judicial region in which the court is located ("the regional presiding judge").

(2) Delivery of Order of Recusal or Referral. When a respondent judge signs and files an order of recusal or referral, the clerk of the court must immediately deliver a copy to the regional presiding judge.

(f) *Duties of the Respondent Judge; Failure to Comply.*

(1) Responding to the Motion. Regardless of whether the motion complies with this rule, the respondent judge, within three business days after the motion is filed, must either:

(A) sign and file with the clerk an order of recusal or disqualification; or

(B) sign and file with the clerk an order referring the motion to the regional presiding judge.

(2) Restrictions on Further Action.

(A) Motion Filed Before Evidence Offered at Trial. If a motion is filed before evidence has been offered at trial, the respondent judge must take no further action in the case until the motion has been decided, except for good cause stated in writing or on the record.

(B) Motion Filed After Evidence Offered at Trial. If a motion is filed after evidence has been offered at trial, the respondent judge may proceed, subject to stay by the regional presiding judge.

(3) Failure to Comply. If the respondent judge fails to comply with a duty imposed by this rule, the movant may notify the regional presiding judge.

(g) *Duties of Regional Presiding Judge.*

(1) Motion. The regional presiding judge must rule on a referred motion or assign a judge to rule. If a party files a motion to recuse or disqualify the regional presiding judge, the regional presiding judge may still assign a judge to rule on the original, referred motion. Alternatively, the regional presiding judge may sign and file with the clerk an order referring the second motion to the Chief Justice for consideration.

(2) Order. The ruling must be by written order.

(3) Summary Denial for Noncompliance.

(A) Motion to Recuse. A motion to recuse that does not comply with this rule may be denied without an oral hearing. The order must state the nature of the noncompliance. Even if the motion is amended to correct the stated noncompliance, the motion will count for purposes of determining whether a tertiary recusal motion has been filed under the Civil Practice and Remedies Code.

(B) Motion to Disqualify. A motion to disqualify may not be denied on the ground that it was not filed or served in compliance with this rule.

(4) Interim Orders. The regional presiding judge or judge assigned to decide the motion may issue interim or ancillary orders in the pending case as justice may require.

(5) Discovery. Except by order of the regional presiding judge or the judge assigned to decide the motion, a subpoena or discovery request may not issue to the respondent judge and may be disregarded unless accompanied by the order.

(6) Hearing.

(A) Time. The motion must be heard as soon as practicable and may be heard immediately after it is referred to the regional presiding judge or an assigned judge.

(B) Notice. Notice of the hearing must be given to all parties in the case.

(C) By Telephone. The hearing may be conducted by telephone on the record. Documents submitted by facsimile or email, otherwise admissible under the rules of evidence, may be considered.

(7) Reassignment of Case if Motion Granted. If the motion is granted, the regional presiding judge must transfer the case to another court or assign another judge to the case.

(h) *Sanctions.* After notice and hearing, the judge who hears the motion may order the party or attorney who filed the motion, or both, to pay the reasonable attorney fees and expenses incurred by other parties if the judge determines that the motion was:

(1) groundless and filed in bad faith or for the purpose of harassment, or

(2) clearly brought for unnecessary delay and without sufficient cause.

(i) *Chief Justice.* The Chief Justice of the Supreme Court of Texas may assign judges and issue any orders permitted by this rule or pursuant to statute.

(j) *Appellate Review.*

(1) Order on Motion to Recuse.

(A) Denying Motion. An order denying a motion to recuse may be reviewed only for abuse of discretion on appeal from the final judgment.

(B) Granting Motion. An order granting a motion to recuse is final and cannot be reviewed by appeal, mandamus, or otherwise.

(2) Order on Motion to Disqualify. An order granting or denying a motion to disqualify may be reviewed by mandamus and may be appealed in accordance with other law.

June 10, 1980, eff. Jan. 1, 1981. Amended by orders of Dec. 15, 1983, eff. April 1, 1984; April 10, 1986, eff. Sept. 1, 1986; July 15, 1987, eff. Jan. 1, 1988; April 24, 1990, eff. Sept. 1, 1990; July 5, 2011, and July 22, 2011, eff. Aug. 1, 2011.

Comment—2011

Rule 18a governs the procedure for recusing or disqualifying a judge sitting in any trial court other than a statutory probate court, justice court, or municipal court. Chapter 25 of the Government Code governs statutory probate courts, Rule 528 governs justice courts, and Chapter 29 of the Government Code governs municipal courts. Under Rule 18a, a judge's rulings may not be the sole basis for a motion to recuse or disqualify the judge. But when one or more sufficient other bases are raised, the judge hearing the motion may consider evidence of rulings when considering whether to grant the motion. For purposes of this rule, the term "rulings" is not meant to encompass a judge's statements or remarks about a case.

The amendments to Rule 18b are not intended to be substantive.

Rule 18b. Grounds for Recusal and Disqualification of Judges

(a) *Grounds for Disqualification.* A judge must disqualify in any proceeding in which:

(1) the judge has served as a lawyer in the matter in controversy, or a lawyer with whom the judge previously practiced law served during such association as a lawyer concerning the matter;

(2) the judge knows that, individually or as a fiduciary, the judge has an interest in the subject matter in controversy; or

(3) either of the parties may be related to the judge by affinity or consanguinity within the third degree.

(b) *Grounds for Recusal.* A judge must recuse in any proceeding in which:

(1) the judge's impartiality might reasonably be questioned;

(2) the judge has a personal bias or prejudice concerning the subject matter or a party;

(3) the judge has personal knowledge of disputed evidentiary facts concerning the proceeding;

(4) the judge or a lawyer with whom the judge previously practiced law has been a material witness concerning the proceeding;

(5) the judge participated as counsel, adviser, or material witness in the matter in controversy, or expressed an opinion concerning the merits of it, while acting as an attorney in government service;

(6) the judge knows that the judge, individually or as a fiduciary, or the judge's spouse or minor child residing in the judge's household, has a financial interest in the subject matter in controversy or in a party to the proceeding, or any other interest that could be substantially affected by the outcome of the proceeding;

(7) the judge or the judge's spouse, or a person within the third degree of relationship to either of them, or the spouse of such a person:

(A) is a party to the proceeding or an officer, director, or trustee of a party;

(B) is known by the judge to have an interest that could be substantially affected by the outcome of the proceeding; or

(C) is to the judge's knowledge likely to be a material witness in the proceeding.

(8) the judge or the judge's spouse, or a person within the first degree of relationship to either of them, or the spouse of such a person, is acting as a lawyer in the proceeding.

(c) *Financial Interests.* A judge should inform himself or herself about personal and fiduciary financial interests, and make a reasonable effort to inform himself or herself about the personal financial interests of his or her spouse and minor children residing in the household.

(d) *Terminology and Standards.* In this rule:

(1) "proceeding" includes pretrial, trial, or other stages of litigation;

(2) the degree of relationship is calculated according to the civil law system;

(3) "fiduciary" includes such relationships as executor, administrator, trustee, and guardian;

(4) "financial interest" means ownership of a legal or equitable interest, however small, or a relationship as director, adviser, or other active participant in the affairs of a party, except that:

(A) ownership in a mutual or common investment fund that holds securities is not a "financial interest" in such securities unless the judge participates in the management of the fund;

(B) an office in an educational, religious, charitable, fraternal, or civic organization is not a "financial interest" in securities held by the organization;

(C) the proprietary interest of a policyholder in a mutual insurance company, of a depositor in a mutual savings association, or a similar proprietary interest, is a "financial interest" in the organization only if the outcome of the proceeding could substantially affect the value of the interest;

(D) ownership of government securities is a "financial interest" in the issuer only if the outcome of the proceeding could substantially affect the value of the securities;

(E) an interest as a taxpayer or utility ratepayer, or any similar interest, is not a "financial interest" unless the outcome of the proceeding could substantially affect the liability of the judge or a person related to him within the third degree more than other judges.

(e) *Waiving a Ground for Recusal.* The parties to a proceeding may waive any ground for recusal after it is fully disclosed on the record.

(f) *Discovery and Divestiture.* If a judge does not discover that the judge is recused under subparagraphs (b)(6) or (b)(7)(B) until after the judge has devoted substantial time to the matter, the judge is not required to recuse himself or herself if the judge or the person related to the judge divests himself or herself of the interest that would otherwise require recusal.

July 15, 1987, eff. Jan. 1, 1988. Amended by orders of April 24, 1990, eff. Sept. 1, 1990; July 5, 2011, and July 22, 2011, eff. Aug. 1, 2011.

Comment—2011

Rule 18a governs the procedure for recusing or disqualifying a judge sitting in any trial court other than a statutory probate court, justice court, or municipal court. Chapter 25 of the Government Code governs statutory probate courts, Rule 528 governs justice courts, and Chapter 29 of the Government Code governs municipal courts. Under Rule 18a, a judge's rulings may not be the sole basis for a motion to recuse or disqualify the judge. But when one or more sufficient other bases are raised, the judge hearing the motion may consider evidence of rulings when considering whether to grant the motion. For purposes of this rule, the term "rulings" is not meant to encompass a judge's statements or remarks about a case.

The amendments to Rule 18b are not intended to be substantive.

Comment—1990

The grounds for a judge's mandatory recusal have been expanded from those in prior Rule 18b(2).

Historical Notes

A former rule 18b, relating to recusal or disqualification of justices of Courts of Appeals or the Supreme Court, was added by order of Dec. 5, 1983, and was repealed by order of April 10, 1986, eff. Sept. 1, 1986. See, now, Rules App.Proc., rule 16.3.

Rule 18c. Recording and Broadcasting of Court Proceedings

A trial court may permit broadcasting, televising, recording, or photographing of proceedings in the courtroom only in the following circumstances:

(a) in accordance with guidelines promulgated by the Supreme Court for civil cases, or

(b) when broadcasting, televising, recording, or photographing will not unduly distract participants or impair the dignity of the proceedings and the parties have consented, and consent to being depicted or recorded is obtained from each witness whose testimony will be broadcast, televised, or photographed, or

(c) the broadcasting, televising, recording, or photographing of investiture, or ceremonial proceedings.

April 24, 1990, eff. Sept. 1, 1990.

Comment—1990

New rule. To provide for guidelines for broadcasting, televising, recording, and photographing court proceedings.

Rule 19. Non-Adjournment of Term

Every term of court shall commence and convene by operation of law at the time fixed by statute without any act, order, or formal opening by a judge or other official thereof, and shall continue to be open at all times until and including the last day of the term unless sooner adjourned by the judge thereof.

Oct. 29, 1940, eff. Sept. 1, 1941. Amended by order of June 16, 1943, eff. Dec. 31, 1943.

Historical Notes

Source

Vernon's Ann.Civ.St. art. 1922.

Rule 20. Minutes Read and Signed

On the last day of the session, the minutes shall be read, corrected and signed in open court by the judge. Each special judge shall sign the minutes of such proceedings as were had by him.

Oct. 29, 1940, eff. Sept. 1, 1941.

Historical Notes

Source

Vernon's Ann.Civ.St. art. 1918, modified by deleting the requirement that minutes be read daily, and by extending the rule's provision to judges of both district and county courts.

Rule 21. Filing and Serving Pleadings and Motions

(a) *Filing and Service Required.* Every pleading, plea, motion, or application to the court for an order, whether in the form of a motion, plea, or other form of request, unless presented during a hearing or trial, must be filed with the clerk of the court in writing, must state the grounds therefor, must set forth the relief or order sought, and at the same time a true copy must be served on all other parties, and must be noted on the docket.

(b) *Service of Notice of Hearing.* An application to the court for an order and notice of any hearing thereon, not presented during a hearing or trial, must be served upon all other parties not less than three days before the time specified for the hearing, unless otherwise provided by these rules or shortened by the court.

(c) *Multiple Parties.* If there is more than one other party represented by different attorneys, one copy of each pleading must be served on each attorney in charge.

(d) *Certificate of Service.* The party or attorney of record, must certify to the court compliance with this rule in writing over signature on the filed pleading, plea, motion, or application.

(e) *Additional Copies.* After one copy is served on a party, that party may obtain another copy of the same pleading upon tendering reasonable payment for copying and delivering. Tx. Supreme Court Misc. Dkt. No. 13–9165 Court of Criminal Appeals Misc. Dkt. No. 13–003

(f) *Electronic Filing.*

(1) Requirement. Except in juvenile cases under Title 3 of the Family Code and truancy cases under Title 3A of the Family Code, attorneys must electronically file documents in courts where electronic filing has been mandated. Attorneys practicing in courts where electronic filing is available but not mandated and unrepresented parties may electronically file documents, but it is not required.

(2) Email Address. The email address of an attorney or unrepresented party who electronically files a document must be included on the document.

(3) Mechanism. Electronic filing must be done through the electronic filing manager established by the Office of Court Administration and an electronic filing service provider certified by the Office of Court Administration.

(4) Exceptions.

(A) Wills are not required to be filed electronically.

(B) The following documents must not be filed electronically:

(i) documents filed under seal or presented to the court in camera; and

(ii) documents to which access is otherwise restricted by law or court order.

(C) For good cause, a court may permit a party to file other documents in paper form in a particular case.

(5) Timely Filing. Unless a document must be filed by a certain time of day, a document is considered timely filed if it is electronically filed at any time before midnight (in the court's time zone) on the filing deadline. An electronically filed document is deemed filed when transmitted to the filing party's electronic filing service provider, except:

(A) if a document is transmitted on a Saturday, Sunday, or legal holiday, it is deemed filed on the next day that is not a Saturday, Sunday, or legal holiday; and

(B) if a document requires a motion and an order allowing its filing, the document is deemed filed on the date that the motion is granted.

(6) Technical Failure. If a document is untimely due to a technical failure or a system outage, the filing party may seek appropriate relief from the court. If the missed deadline is one imposed by these rules, the filing party must be given a reasonable extension of time to complete the filing.

(7) Electronic Signatures. A document that is electronically served, filed, or issued by a court or clerk is considered signed if the document includes:

(A) a "/s/" and name typed in the space where the signature would otherwise appear, unless the document is notarized or sworn; or

(B) an electronic image or scanned image of the signature.

(8) Format. An electronically filed document must:

(A) be in text-searchable portable document format (PDF);

(B) be directly converted to PDF rather than scanned, if possible;

(C) not be locked; and

(D) otherwise comply with the Technology Standards set by the Judicial Committee on Information Technology and approved by the Supreme Court.

(9) Paper Copies. Unless required by local rule, a party need not file a paper copy of an electronically filed document.

(10) Electronic Notices From the Court. The clerk may send notices, orders, or other communications about the case to the party electronically. A court seal may be electronic.

(11) Non–Conforming Documents. The clerk may not refuse to file a document that fails to conform with this rule. But the clerk may identify the error to be corrected and state a deadline for the party to resubmit the document in a conforming format.

(12) Original Wills. When a party electronically files an application to probate a document as an original will, the original will must be filed with the clerk within three business days after the application is filed.

(13) Official Record. The clerk may designate an electronically filed document or a scanned paper document as the official court record. The clerk is not required to keep both paper and electronic versions of the same document unless otherwise required by local rule. But the clerk must retain an

original will filed for probate in a numbered file folder.

Oct. 29, 1940, eff. Sept. 1, 1941. Amended by orders of Sept. 20, 1941, eff. Dec. 31, 1941; Aug. 18, 1947, eff. Dec. 31, 1947; July 11, 1977, eff. Jan. 1, 1978; June 10, 1980, eff. Jan. 1, 1981; April 24, 1990, eff. Sept. 1, 1990; Dec. 11, 2013, eff. Jan. 1, 2014; Aug. 28, 2015, eff. Sept. 1, 2015.

Comment—2013

Rule 21 is revised to incorporate rules for electronic filing, in accordance with the Supreme Court's order—Misc. Docket No. 12–9206, amended by Misc. Docket Nos. 13–9092 and 13–9164—mandating electronic filing in civil cases beginning on January 1, 2014. The mandate will be implemented according to the schedule in the order and will be completed by July 1, 2016. The revisions reflect the fact that the mandate will only apply to a subset of Texas courts until that date.

Comment—1990

To require filing and service of all pleadings and motions on all parties and to consolidate notice and service Rules 21, 72 and 73.

Historical Notes

Source

Vernon's Ann.Civ.St. art. 2291.

2013 Amendment

The order dated December 11, 2013 inserted the present subsection (a) to (e) designations and headings, and in those subsecs. substituted "must" for "shall" throughout; in subsec. (c) substituted "each pleading must be served on each" for "such pleading shall be served on delivered or mailed to each"; and added subsec. (f).

2015 Amendment

The order dated August 28, 2015, in subd. (f)(1) inserted "and truancy cases under Title 3A of the Family Code".

Rule 21a. Methods of Service

(a) *Methods of Service.* Every notice required by these rules, and every pleading, plea, motion, or other form of request required to be served under Rule 21, other than the citation to be served upon the filing of a cause of action and except as otherwise expressly provided in these rules, may be served by delivering a copy to the party to be served, or the party's duly authorized agent or attorney of record in the manner specified below:

(1) Documents Filed Electronically. A document filed electronically under Rule 21 must be served electronically through the electronic filing manager if the email address of the party or attorney to be served is on file with the electronic filing manager. If the email address of the party or attorney to be served is not on file with the electronic filing manager, the document may be served on that party or attorney under subparagraph (2).

(2) Documents Not Filed Electronically. A document not filed electronically may be served in person, mail, by commercial delivery service, by fax, by email, or by such other manner as the court in its discretion may direct.

(b) *When Complete.*

(1) Service by mail or commercial delivery service shall be complete upon deposit of the document, postpaid and properly addressed, in the mail or with a commercial delivery service.

(2) Service by fax is complete on receipt. Service completed after 5:00 p.m. local time of the recipient shall be deemed served on the following day.

(3) Electronic service is complete on transmission of the document to the serving party's electronic filing service provider. The electronic filing manager will send confirmation of service to the serving party.

(c) *Time for Action After Service.* Whenever a party has the right or is required to do some act within a prescribed period after the service of a notice or other paper upon him and the notice or paper is served upon him by mail, three days shall be added to the prescribed period.

(d) *Who May Serve.* Notice may be served by a party to the suit, an attorney of record, a sheriff or constable, or by any other person competent to testify.

(e) *Proof of Service.* The party or attorney of record shall certify to the court compliance with this rule in writing over signature and on the filed instrument. A certificate by a party or an attorney of record, or the return of the officer, or the affidavit of any other person showing service of a notice shall be prima facie evidence of the fact of service. Nothing herein shall preclude any party from offering proof that the document was not received, or, if service was by mail, that the document was not received within three days from the date that it was deposited in the mail, and upon so finding, the court may extend the time for taking the action required of such party or grant such other relief as it deems just.

(f) *Procedures Cumulative.* These provisions are cumulative of all other methods of service prescribed by these rules.

Aug. 18, 1947, eff. Dec. 31, 1947. Amended by orders of July 21, 1970, eff. Jan. 1, 1971; Oct. 3, 1972, eff. Feb. 1, 1973; July 11, 1977, eff. Jan. 1, 1978; June 10, 1980, eff. Jan. 1, 1981; Dec. 5, 1983, eff. April 1, 1984; April 24, 1990, eff. Sept. 1, 1990; Dec. 11, 2013, eff. Jan. 1, 2014.

Comment—2013

Rule 21a is revised to incorporate rules for electronic service in accordance with the Supreme Court's order—Misc. Docket No. 12–9206, amended by Misc. Docket Nos. 13–9092 and 13–9164—mandating electronic filing in civil cases beginning on January 1, 2014.

Comment—1990

To allow for service by current delivery means and technologies.

Historical Notes

2013 Amendment

The order dated December 11, 2013 rewrote the rule, which prior thereto read:

"Every notice required by these rules, and every pleading, plea, motion, or other form of request required to be served under Rule 21, other than the citation to be served upon the filing of a cause of action and except as otherwise expressly provided in these rules, may be served by delivering a copy to the party to be served, or the party's duly authorized agent or attorney of record, as the case may be, either in person or by agent or by courier receipted delivery or by certified or registered mail, to the party's last known address, or by telephonic document transfer to the recipient's current telecopier number, or by such other manner as the court in its discretion may direct. Service by mail shall be complete upon deposit of the paper, enclosed in a postpaid, properly addressed wrapper, in a post office or official depository under the care and custody of the United States Postal Service. Service by telephonic document transfer after 5:00 p.m. local time of the recipient shall be deemed served on the following day. Whenever a party has the right or is required to do some act within a prescribed period after the service of a notice or other paper upon him and the notice or paper is served upon by mail or by telephonic document transfer, three days shall be added to the prescribed period. Notice may be served by a party to the suit, an attorney of record, a sheriff or constable, or by any other person competent to testify. The party or attorney of record shall certify to the court compliance with this rule in writing over signature and on the filed instrument. A certificate by a party or an attorney of record, or the return of an officer, or the affidavit of any person showing service of a notice shall be prima facie evidence of the fact of service. Nothing herein shall preclude any party from offering proof that the notice or instrument was not received, or, if service was by mail, that it was not received within three days from the date of deposit in a post office or official depository under the care and custody of the United States Postal Service, and upon so finding, the court may extend the time for taking the action required of such party or grant such other relief as it deems just. The provisions hereof relating to the method of service of notice are cumulative of all other methods of service prescribed by these rules."

Rule 21b. Sanctions for Failure to Serve or Deliver Copy of Pleadings and Motions

If any party fails to serve on or deliver to the other parties a copy of any pleading, plea, motion, or other application to the court for an order in accordance with Rules 21 and 21a, the court may in its discretion, after notice and hearing, impose an appropriate sanction available under Rule 215–2b.[1]

April 24, 1990, eff. Sept. 1, 1990.

[1] Probably Vernon's Ann.Rules Civ.Proc., rule 215.2(b).

Comment—1990

New rule. Repealed provisions of Rule 73, to the extent same are to remain operative, are moved to this new Rule 21b to provide sanctions for the failure to serve any filed documents on all parties.

Historical Notes

A former rule 21b relating to notice by certified mail was repealed by order of Dec. 5, 1983, eff. April 1, 1984. See, now, rule 21a.

Rule 21c. Privacy Protection for Filed Documents

(a) *Sensitive Data Defined.* Sensitive data consists of:

(1) a driver's license number, passport number, social security number, tax identification number, or similar government-issued personal identification number;

(2) a bank account number, credit card number, or other financial account number; and

(3) a birth date, home address, and the name of any person who was a minor when the underlying suit was filed.

(b) *Filing of Documents Containing Sensitive Data Prohibited.* Unless the inclusion of sensitive data is specifically required by a statute, court rule, or administrative regulation, an electronic or paper document, except for wills and documents filed under seal, containing sensitive data may not be filed with a court unless the sensitive data is redacted.

(c) *Redaction of Sensitive Data: Retention Requirement.* Sensitive data must be redacted by using the letter "X" in place of each omitted digit or character or by removing the sensitive data in a manner indicating that the data has been redacted. The filing party must retain an unredacted version of the filed document during the pendency of the case and any related appellate proceedings filed within six months of the date the judgment is signed.

(d) *Notice to Clerk.* If a document must contain sensitive data, the filing party must notify the clerk by:

(1) designating the document as containing sensitive data when the document is electronically filed; or

(2) if the document is not electronically filed, by including, on the upper left-hand side of the first page, the phrase: "NOTICE: THIS DOCUMENT CONTAINS SENSITIVE DATA."

(e) *Non–Conforming Documents.* The clerk may not refuse to file a document that contains sensitive data in violation of this rule. But the clerk may identify the error to be corrected and state a deadline for the party to resubmit a redacted, substitute document.

(f) *Restriction on Remote Access.* Documents that contain sensitive data in violation of this rule must not be posted on the Internet.

Added by order of Dec. 11, 2013, eff. Jan. 1, 2014.

Comment—2013

Rule 21c is added to provide privacy protection for documents filed in civil cases.

Historical Notes

A former rule 21c, which related to extensions of time on appeal, was repealed by order of April 10, 1986, eff. Sept. 1, 1986.

SECTION 2. INSTITUTION OF SUIT

Rule 22. Commenced by Petition

A civil suit in the district or county court shall be commenced by a petition filed in the office of the clerk.

Oct. 29, 1940, eff. Sept. 1, 1941.

Historical Notes

Source

Vernon's Ann.Civ.St. art. 1971 with minor textual change.

Rule 23. Suits To Be Numbered Consecutively

It shall be the duty of the clerk to designate the suits by regular consecutive numbers, called file numbers, and he shall mark on each paper in every case the file number of the cause.

Oct. 29, 1940, eff. Sept. 1, 1941.

Historical Notes

Source

District and County Court Rule 82, modified by deleting "In preparing the court docket".

Rule 24. Duty of Clerk

When a petition is filed with the clerk he shall indorse thereon the file number, the day on which it was filed and the time of filing, and sign his name officially thereto.

Oct. 29, 1940, eff. Sept. 1, 1941.

Historical Notes

Source

Vernon's Ann.Civ.St. art. 1972, modified by adding "and the time of filing".

Rule 25. Clerk's File Docket

Each clerk shall keep a file docket which shall show in convenient form the number of the suit, the names of the attorneys, the names of the parties to the suit, and the nature thereof, and, in brief form, the officer's return on the process, and all subsequent proceedings had in the case with the dates thereof.

Oct. 29, 1940, eff. Sept. 1, 1941.

Historical Notes

Source

Vernon's Ann.Civ.St. art. 1973, with minor textual change.

Rule 26. Clerk's Court Docket

Each clerk shall also keep a court docket in a permanent record that shall include the number of the case and the names of parties, the names of the attorneys, the nature of the action, the pleas, the motions, and the ruling of the court as made.

Oct. 29, 1940, eff. Sept. 1, 1941. Amended by order of April 24, 1990, eff. Sept. 1, 1990.

Historical Notes

Source

District and County Court Rule 79, with minor textual change.

Rule 27. Order of Cases

The cases shall be placed on the docket as they are filed.

Oct. 29, 1940, eff. Sept. 1, 1941.

Historical Notes

Source

District and County Court Rule 80, unchanged.

SECTION 3. PARTIES TO SUITS

Rule 28. Suits in Assumed Name

Any partnership, unincorporated association, private corporation, or individual doing business under an assumed name may sue or be sued in its partnership, assumed or common name for the purpose of enforcing for or against it a substantive right, but on a motion by any party or on the court's own motion the true name may be substituted.

Oct. 29, 1940, eff. Sept. 1, 1941. Amended by order of July 21, 1970, eff. Jan. 1, 1971.

Historical Notes

Source

Federal Rule 17(b), modified to permit suit by or against "an individual doing business under an assumed name."

Rule 29. Suit On Claim Against Dissolved Corporation

When no receiver has been appointed for a corporation which has dissolved, suit may be instituted on any claim against said corporation as though the same had not been dissolved, and service of process may be obtained on the president, directors, general manager, trustee, assignee, or other person in charge of the affairs of the corporation at the time it was dissolved, and judgment may be rendered as though the corporation had not been dissolved.

Oct. 29, 1940, eff. Sept. 1, 1941.

Historical Notes

Source

Vernon's Ann.Civ.St. art. 1391, with minor textual change.

Rule 30. Parties to Suits

Assignors, endorsers and other parties not primarily liable upon any instruments named in the chapter of the Business and Commerce Code, dealing with commercial paper, may be jointly sued with their principal obligors, or may be sued alone in the cases provided for by statute.

Oct. 29, 1940, eff. Sept. 1, 1941. Amended by order of July 15, 1987, eff. Jan. 1, 1988.

Historical Notes

Source

Vernon's Ann.Civ.St. art. 572, with minor textual change.

Rule 31. Surety Not To Be Sued Alone

No surety shall be sued unless his principal is joined with him, or unless a judgment has previously been rendered against his principal, except in cases otherwise provided for in the law and these rules.

Oct. 29, 1940, eff. Sept. 1, 1941.

Historical Notes

Source

Vernon's Ann.Civ.St. art. 6251, modified by substituting "except in cases otherwise provided for in the law and these rules" for "except in the cases otherwise provided for in the laws relating to parties to suits."

Rule 32. May Have Question of Suretyship Tried

When any suit is brought against two or more defendants upon any contract, any one or more of the defendants being surety for the other, the surety may cause the question of suretyship to be tried and determined upon the issue made for the parties defendant at the trial of the cause, or at any time before or after the trial or at a subsequent term. Such proceedings shall not delay the suit of the plaintiff.

Oct. 29, 1940, eff. Sept. 1, 1941.

Historical Notes

Source

Vernon's Ann.Civ.St. art. 6246, unchanged.

Rule 33. Suits By or Against Counties

Suits by or against a county or incorporated city, town or village shall be in its corporate name.

Oct. 29, 1940, eff. Sept. 1, 1941.

Historical Notes

Source

Vernon's Ann.Civ.St. art. 1980, unchanged.

Rule 34. Against Sheriff, etc.

Whenever a sheriff, constable, or a deputy or either has been sued for damages for any act done in his official character, and has taken an indemnifying bond for the acts upon which the suit is based, he may make the principal and surety on such bond parties defendant in such suit, and the cause may be continued to obtain service on such parties.

Oct. 29, 1940, eff. Sept. 1, 1941.

Historical Notes

Source

Vernon's Ann.Civ.St. art. 1988, unchanged.

Rule 35. On Official Bonds

In suits brought by the State or any county, city, independent school district, irrigation district, or other political subdivision of the State, against any officer who has held an office for more than one term, or against any depository which has been such depository for more than one term, or has given more than one official bond, the sureties on each and all such bonds may be joined as defendants in the same suit whenever it is difficult to determine when the default sued for occurred and which set of sureties on such bonds is liable therefor.

Oct. 29, 1940, eff. Sept. 1, 1941. Amended by order of June 16, 1943, eff. Dec. 13, 1943.

Historical Notes

Source

Vernon's Ann.Civ.St. art. 1989, unchanged.

Rule 36. Different Officials and Bondsmen

In suits by the State upon the official bond of a State officer, any subordinate officer who has given bond, payable either to the State or such superior officer, to cover all or part of the default sued for, together with the sureties on his official bond, may be joined as defendants with such superior officer and his bondsmen whenever it is alleged in the petition that both of such officers are liable for the money sued for.

Oct. 29, 1940, eff. Sept. 1, 1941.

Historical Notes

Source

Vernon's Ann.Civ.St. art. 1990, unchanged.

Rule 37. Additional Parties

Before a case is called for trial, additional parties necessary or proper parties to the suit, may be brought in, either by the plaintiff or the defendant, upon such terms as the court may prescribe; but not at a time nor in a manner to unreasonably delay the trial of the case.

Oct. 29, 1940, eff. Sept. 1, 1941.

Historical Notes

Source

Vernon's Ann.Civ.St. art. 1992, unchanged.

Rule 38. Third-Party Practice

(a) When defendant may bring in third party. At any time after commencement of the action a defending party, as a third-party plaintiff, may cause a citation and petition to be served upon a person not a party to the action who is or may be liable to him or to the plaintiff for all or part of the plaintiff's claim against him. The third-party plaintiff need not obtain leave to make the service if he files the third-party petition not later than thirty (30) days after he serves his original answer. Otherwise, he must obtain leave on motion upon notice to all parties to the action. The person served, hereinafter called the third-party defendant, shall make his defenses to the third-party plaintiff's claim under the rules applicable to the defendant, and his counterclaims against the third-party plaintiff and cross-claims against other third-party defendants as provided in Rule 97. The third-party defendant may assert against the plaintiff any defenses which the third-party plaintiff has to the plaintiff's claim. The third-party defendant may also assert any claim against the plaintiff arising out of the transaction or occurrence that is the subject matter of the plaintiff's claim against the third-party plaintiff. The plaintiff may assert any claim against the third-party defendant arising out of the transaction or occurrence that is the subject matter of the plaintiff's claim against the third-party plaintiff, and the third-party defendant thereupon shall assert his defenses and his counterclaims and cross-claims. Any party may move to strike the third-party claim, or for its severance or separate trial. A third-party defendant may proceed under this rule against any person not a party to the action who is or who may be liable to him or to the third-party plaintiff for all or part of the claim made in the action against the third-party defendant.

(b) When plaintiff may bring in third party. When a counterclaim is asserted against a plaintiff, he may cause a third party to be brought in under circumstances which under this rule would entitle a defendant to do so.

(c) This rule shall not be applied, in tort cases, so as to permit the joinder of a liability or indemnity insurance company, unless such company is by statute or contract liable to the person injured or damaged.

(d) This rule shall not be applied so as to violate any venue statute, as venue would exist absent this rule.

Oct. 29, 1940, eff. Sept. 1, 1941. Amended by orders of March 31, 1941, eff. Sept. 1, 1941; Dec. 5, 1983, eff. April 1, 1984.

Historical Notes

Source

Federal Rule 14 with minor textual changes.

Rule 39. Joinder of Persons Needed for Just Adjudication

(a) Persons to be Joined if Feasible. A person who is subject to service of process shall be joined as a party in the action if (1) in his absence complete relief cannot be accorded among those already parties, or (2) he claims an interest relating to the subject of the action and is so situated that the disposition of the action in his absence may (i) as a practical matter impair or impede his ability to protect that interest or (ii) leave any of the persons already parties subject to a substantial risk of incurring double, multiple, or otherwise inconsistent obligations by reason of his claimed interest. If he has not been so joined, the court shall order that he be made a party. If he should join as a plaintiff but refuses to do so, he may be made a defendant, or, in a proper case, an involuntary plaintiff.

(b) Determination by Court Whenever Joinder Not Feasible. If a person as described in subdivision (a)(1)–(2) hereof cannot be made a party, the court shall determine whether in equity and good conscience the action should proceed among the parties before it, or should be dismissed, the absent person being thus regarded as indispensable. The factors to be considered by the court include: first, to what extent a judgment rendered in the person's absence might be prejudicial to him or those already parties; second, the extent to which, by protective provisions in the judgment, by the shaping of relief, or other measures, the prejudice can be lessened or avoided; third, whether a judgment rendered in the person's absence will be adequate; fourth, whether the plaintiff will have an adequate remedy if the action is dismissed for non-joinder.

(c) Pleading Reasons for Nonjoinder. A pleading asserting a claim for relief shall state the names, if known to the pleader, of any persons as described in subdivision (a)(1)–(2) hereof who are not joined, and the reasons why they are not joined.

(d) Exception of Class Actions. This rule is subject to the provisions of Rule 42.

Oct. 29, 1940, eff. Sept. 1, 1941. Amended by order of July 21, 1970, eff. Jan. 1, 1971.

Historical Notes

Source

Federal Rule 19 with textual change.

Rule 40. Permissive Joinder of Parties

(a) Permissive Joinder. All persons may join in one action as plaintiffs if they assert any right to relief jointly, severally, or in the alternative in respect of or arising out of the same transaction, occurrence, or series of transactions or occurrences and if any question of law or fact common to all of them will arise in the action. All persons may be joined in one action as defendants if there is asserted against them jointly, severally, or in the alternative any right to relief in respect of or arising out of the same transaction, occurrence, or series of transactions or occurrences and if any question of law or fact common to all of them will arise in the action. A plaintiff or defendant need not be interested in obtaining or defending against all the relief demanded. Judgment may be given for one or more of the plaintiffs according to their respective rights to relief, and against one or more defendants according to their respective liabilities.

(b) Separate Trials. The court may make such orders as will prevent a party from being embarrassed, delayed, or put to expense by the inclusion of a party against whom he asserts no claim and who asserts no claim against him, and may order separate trials or make other orders to prevent delay or prejudice.

Oct. 29, 1940, eff. Sept. 1, 1941.

Historical Notes

Source

Federal Rule 20, unchanged.

Rule 41. Misjoinder and Non-Joinder of Parties

Misjoinder of parties is not ground for dismissal of an action. Parties may be dropped or added, or suits filed separately may be consolidated, or actions which have been improperly joined may be severed and each ground of recovery improperly joined may be docketed as a separate suit between the same parties, by order of the court on motion of any party or on its own initiative at any stage of the action, before the time of submission to the jury or to the court if trial is without a jury, on such terms as are just. Any claim against a party may be severed and proceeded with separately.

Oct. 29, 1940, eff. Sept. 1, 1941. Amended by order of March 31, 1941, eff. Sept. 1, 1941.

Historical Notes

Source

Federal Rule 21, modified by addition of provision for adding and dropping parties and for consolidation of suits and for severing actions in case of misjoinder of parties or causes.

Rule 42. Class Actions

(a) Prerequisites to a Class Action. One or more members of a class may sue or be sued as representative parties on behalf of all only if (1) the class is so numerous that joinder of all members is impracticable, (2) there are questions of law, or fact common to the class, (3) the claims or defenses of the representative parties are typical of the claims or defenses of the class, and (4) the representative parties will fairly and adequately protect the interests of the class.

(b) Class Actions Maintainable. An action may be maintained as a class action if the prerequisites of subdivision (a) are satisfied, and in addition:

(1) the prosecution of separate actions by or against individual members of the class would create a risk of

(A) inconsistent or varying adjudications with respect to individual members of the class which would establish incompatible standards of conduct for the party opposing the class, or

(B) adjudications with respect to individual members of the class which would as a practical matter be dispositive of the interests of the other members not parties to the adjudications or substantially impair or impede their ability to protect their interests; or

(2) the party opposing the class has acted or refused to act on grounds generally applicable to the class, thereby making appropriate final injunctive relief or corresponding declaratory relief with respect to the class as a whole; or

(3) the questions of law or fact common to the members of the class predominate over any questions affecting only individual members, and a class action is superior to other available methods for the fair and efficient adjudication of the controversy. The matters pertinent to these issues include:

(A) the interest of members of the class in individually controlling the prosecution or defense of separate actions;

(B) the extent and nature of any litigation concerning the controversy already commenced by or against members of the class;

(C) the desirability or undesirability of concentrating the litigation of the claims in the particular forum; and

(D) the difficulties likely to be encountered in the management of a class action.

(c) Determining by Order Whether to Certify a Class Action; Notice and Membership in Class.

(1)(A) When a person sues or is sued as a representative of a class, the court must—at an early practicable time—determine by order whether to certify the action as a class action.

(B) An order certifying a class action must define the class and the class claims, issues, or defenses, and must appoint class counsel under Rule 42 (g).

(C) An order under Rule 42(c)(1) may be altered or amended before final judgment. The court may order the naming of additional parties in order to insure the adequacy of representation.

(D) An order granting or denying certification under Rule 42(b)(3) must state:

(i) the elements of each claim or defense asserted in the pleadings;

(ii) any issues of law or fact common to the class members;

(iii) any issues of law or fact affecting only individual class members;

(iv) the issues that will be the object of most of the efforts of the litigants and the court;

(v) other available methods of adjudication that exist for the controversy;

(vi) why the issues common to the members of the class do or do not predominate over individual issues;

(vii) why a class action is or is not superior to other available methods for the fair and efficient adjudication of the controversy; and

(viii) if a class is certified, how the class claims and any issues affecting only individual members, raised by the claims or defenses asserted in the pleadings, will be tried in a manageable, time efficient manner.

(2)(A) For any class certified under Rule 42(b)(1) or (2), the court may direct appropriate notice to the class.

(B) For any class certified under Rule 42(b)(3), the court must direct to class members the best notice practicable under the circumstances, including individual notice to all members who can be identified through reasonable effort. The notice must concisely and clearly state in plain, easily understood language:

(i) the nature of the action;

(ii) the definition of the class certified;

(iii) the class claims, issues, or defenses;

(iv) that a class member may enter an appearance through counsel if the member so desires;

(v) that the court will exclude from the class any member who requests exclusion, stating when and how members may elect to be excluded; and

(vi) the binding effect of a class judgment on class members under Rule 42 (c)(3).

(3) The judgment in an action maintained as a class action under subdivision (b)(1) or (b)(2), whether or not favorable to the class, shall include and describe those whom the court finds to be members of the class. The judgment in an action maintained as a class action under subdivision (b)(3), whether or not favorable to the class, shall include and specify or describe those to whom the notice provided in subdivision (c)(2) was directed, and who have not requested exclusion, and whom the court finds to be members of the class.

(d) Actions Conducted Partially as Class Actions; Multiple Classes and Subclasses. When appropriate (1) an action may be brought or maintained as a class action with respect to particular issues, or (2) a class may be divided into subclasses and each subclass treated as a class, and the provisions of this rule shall then be construed and applied accordingly.

(e) Settlement, Dismissal or Compromise.

(1)(A) The court must approve any settlement, dismissal, or compromise of the claims, issues, or defenses of a certified class.

(B) Notice of the material terms of the proposed settlement, dismissal or compromise, together with an explanation of when and how the members may elect to be excluded from the class, shall be given to all members in such manner as the court directs.

(C) The court may approve a settlement, dismissal, or compromise that would bind class members only after a hearing and on finding that the settlement, dismissal, or compromise is fair, reasonable, and adequate.

(2) The parties seeking approval of a settlement, dismissal, or compromise under Rule 42(e)(1) must file a statement identifying any agreement made in connection with the proposed settlement, dismissal, or compromise.

(3) In an action previously certified as a class action under Rule 42(b)(3), the court may not approve a settlement unless it affords a new opportunity to

request exclusion to individual class members who had an earlier opportunity to request exclusion but did not do so.

(4)(A) Any class member may object to a proposed settlement, dismissal, or compromise that requires court approval under Rule 42(e)(1)(A).

(B) An objection made under Rule 42(e)(4)(A) may be withdrawn only with the court's approval.

(f) Discovery. Unnamed members of a class action are not to be considered as parties for purposes of discovery.

(g) Class Counsel.

(1) Appointing Class Counsel.

(A) Unless a statute provides otherwise, a court that certifies a class must appoint class counsel.

(B) An attorney appointed to serve as class counsel must fairly and adequately represent the interests of the class.

(C) In appointing class counsel, the court

(i) must consider:

the work counsel has done in identifying or investigating potential claims in the action;

counsel's experience in handling class actions, other complex litigation, and claims of the type asserted in the action;

counsel's knowledge of the applicable law; and

the resources counsel will commit to representing the class;

(ii) may consider any other matter pertinent to counsel's ability to fairly and adequately represent the interests of the class;

(iii) may direct potential class counsel to provide information on any subject pertinent to the appointment and to propose terms for attorney fees and nontaxable costs; and

(iv) may make further orders in connection with the appointment.

(2) Appointment Procedure.

(A) The court may designate interim counsel to act on behalf of the putative class before determining whether to certify the action as a class action.

(B) When there is one applicant for appointment as class counsel, the court may appoint that applicant only if the applicant is adequate under Rule 42(g)(1)(B) and (C). If more than one adequate applicant seeks appointment as class counsel, the court must appoint the applicant or applicants best able to represent the interests of the class.

(C) The order appointing class counsel may include provisions about the award of attorney fees or nontaxable costs under Rule 42(h) and (i).

(h) Procedure for determining Attorney Fees Award. In an action certified as a class action, the court may award attorney fees in accordance with subdivision (i) and nontaxable costs authorized by law or by agreement of the parties as follows:

(1) Motion for Award of Attorney Fees. A claim for an award of attorney fees and nontaxable costs must be made by motion, subject to the provisions of this subdivision, at a time set by the court. Notice of the motion must be served on all parties and, for motions by class counsel, directed to class members in a reasonable manner.

(2) Objections to Motion. A class member, or a party from whom payment is sought, may object to the motion.

(3) Hearing and Findings. The court must hold a hearing in open court and must find the facts and state its conclusions of law on the motion. The court must state its findings and conclusions in writing or orally on the record.

(i) Attorney's fees award.

(1) In awarding attorney fees, the court must first determine a lodestar figure by multiplying the number of hours reasonably worked times a reasonable hourly rate. The attorney fees award must be in the range of 25% to 400% of the lodestar figure. In making these determinations, the court must consider the factors specified in Rule 1.04(b), TEX. DISCIPLINARY R. PROF. CONDUCT.

(2) If any portion of the benefits recovered for the class are in the form of coupons or other noncash common benefits, the attorney fees awarded in the action must be in cash and noncash amounts in the same proportion as the recovery for the class.

(j) Effective date. Rule 42(i) applies only in actions filed after September 1, 2003.

Oct. 29, 1940, eff. Sept. 1, 1941. Amended by orders of Sept. 20, 1941, eff. Dec. 31, 1941; May 9, 1977, eff. Sept. 1, 1977; Dec. 5, 1983, eff. April 1, 1984; Oct. 9, 2003, eff. Jan. 1, 2004.

Comment—2003

The second paragraph of subdivision (a) regarding derivative suits has been deleted because it is redundant of Article 5.14 of the Business Corporation Act, which sets forth detailed procedures for derivative suits.

Subparagraph (b)(3) is omitted as unnecessary.

The requirement that certification be decided "at an early practicable time" is a change from the previous Texas rule 42 (c)(1) and federal rule 23 (c)(1), which required the trial court to decide the certification issue "as soon as practicable after the commencement of [the suit]." The amended language is not intended to permit undue delay or permit excessive discovery unrelated to certification, but is designed to encourage good practices in making certification decisions only after receiving the information necessary to decide whether certification should be granted or denied and how to define the class if certification is granted.

Historical Notes

Source

Federal rule 23.

Rule 43. Interpleader

Persons having claims against the plaintiff may be joined as defendants and required to interplead when their claims are such that the plaintiff is or may be exposed to double or multiple liability. It is not ground for objection to the joinder that the claims of the several claimants or the titles on which their claims depend do not have a common origin or are not identical but are adverse to and independent of one another, or that the plaintiff avers that he is not liable in whole or in part to any or all of the claimants. A defendant exposed to similar liability may obtain such interpleader by way of cross-claim or counterclaim. The provisions of this rule supplement and do not in any way limit the joinder of parties permitted in any other rules.

Oct. 29, 1940, eff. Sept. 1, 1941.

Historical Notes

Source

Federal Rule 22(1), with minor textual change.

Rule 44. May Appear by Next Friend

Minors, lunatics, idiots, or persons non compos mentis who have no legal guardian may sue and be represented by "next friend" under the following rules:

(1) Such next friend shall have the same rights concerning such suits as guardians have, but shall give security for costs, or affidavits in lieu thereof, when required.

(2) Such next friend or his attorney of record may with the approval of the court compromise suits and agree to judgments, and such judgments, agreements and compromises, when approved by the court, shall be forever binding and conclusive upon the party plaintiff in such suit.

Oct. 29, 1940, eff. Sept. 1, 1941.

Historical Notes

Source

Vernon's Ann.Civ.St. art. 1994, subds. 1 and 2, unchanged.

SECTION 4. PLEADING

A. GENERAL

Rule 45. Definition and System

Pleadings in the district and county courts shall

(a) be by petition and answer;

(b) consist of a statement in plain and concise language of the plaintiff's cause of action or the defendant's grounds of defense. That an allegation be evidentiary or be of legal conclusion shall not be grounds for an objection when fair notice to the opponent is given by the allegations as a whole; and

(c) contain any other matter which may be required by any law or rule authorizing or regulating any particular action or defense.

Pleadings that are not filed electronically must be in writing, on paper measuring approximately 8 1/2 inches by 11 inches, and signed by the party or his attorney. The use of recycled paper is strongly encouraged.

All pleadings shall be construed so as to do substantial justice.

Oct. 29, 1940, eff. Sept. 1, 1941. Amended by orders of July 15, 1987, eff. Jan. 1, 1988; April 24, 1990, eff. Sept. 1, 1990; Sept. 4, 1990; Dec. 11, 2013, eff. Jan. 1, 2014.

Comment—1990

To provide for filing of pleadings having either original or copies of signatures and verifications including documents telephonically transferred.

Historical Notes

Source

Vernon's Ann.Civ.St. art. 1997, substituting the first sentence of (b) for subd. 2, which read: "Consist of a statement in logical and legal form of the facts constituting the plaintiff's cause of action or the defendant's ground of defense"; and adding the second sentence of (b). Rule 45 embraces former District and County Court Rules 1 (pleading by petition and answer) and 32 (fatally defective pleadings). The "substantial justice" provision of Rule 45 followed Federal Rule 8(f).

2013 Amendment

The order dated December 11, 2013 rewrote the rule, which prior thereto had read:

"Pleadings in the district and county courts shall

"(a) be by petition and answer;

"(b) consist of a statement in plain and concise language of the plaintiff's cause of action or the defendant's grounds of defense. That an allegation be evidentiary or be of legal conclusion shall not be grounds for objection when fair notice to the opponent is given by the allegations as a whole;

"(c) contain any other matter which may be required by any law or rule authorizing or regulating any particular action or defense;

"(d) be in writing, on paper measuring approximately 8 1/2 inches by 11 inches, and signed by the party or his attorney, and either the signed original together with any verification or a copy of said original and copy of any such verification shall be filed with the court. The use of recycled paper is strongly encouraged.

"When a copy of the signed original is tendered for filing, the party or his attorney filing such copy is required to maintain the signed original for inspection by the court or any party incident to the suit, should a question be raised as to its authenticity.

"All pleadings shall be construed so as to do substantial justice."

Rule 46. Petition and Answer; Each One Instrument of Writing

The original petition, first supplemental petition, second supplemental petition, and every other, shall each be contained in one instrument of writing, and so with the original answer and each of the supplemental answers.

Oct. 29, 1940, eff. Sept. 1, 1941.

Historical Notes

Source

District and County Court Rule 9, unchanged.

Rule 47. Claims for Relief

An original pleading which sets forth a claim for relief, whether an original petition, counterclaim, cross-claim, or third party claim, shall contain:[1]

(a) a short statement of the cause of action sufficient to give fair notice of the claim involved;

(b) a statement that the damages sought are within the jurisdictional limits of the court;

(c) except in suits governed by the Family Code, a statement that the party seeks:

(1) only monetary relief of $100,000 or less, including damages of any kind, penalties, costs, expenses, pre-judgment interest, and attorney fees; or

(2) monetary relief of $100,000 or less and non-monetary relief; or

(3) monetary relief over $100,000 but not more than $200,000; or

(4) monetary relief over $200,000 but not more than $1,000,000; or

(5) monetary relief over $1,000,000; and

(d) a demand for judgment for all the other relief to which the party deems himself entitled.

Relief in the alternative or of several different types may be demanded; provided, further, that upon special exception the court shall require the pleader to amend so as to specify the maximum amount claimed. A party that fails to comply with (c) may not conduct discovery until the party's pleading is amended to comply.

Oct. 29, 1940, eff. Sept. 1, 1941. Amended by order of July 11, 1977, eff. Jan. 1, 1978; April 24, 1990, eff. Sept. 1, 1990; Feb. 12, 2013, eff. March 1, 2013.

[1] See Appendix to Rules of Civil Procedure for form.

Comment—2013

Rule 47 is amended to require a more specific statement of the relief sought by a party. The amendment requires parties to plead into or out of the expedited actions process governed by Rule 169, added to implement section 22.004(h) of the Texas Government Code. Except in a in a suit governed by the Family Code, the Property Code, the Tax Code, or Chapter 74 of the Civil Practice & Remedies Code, a suit in which the original petition contains the statement in paragraph (c)(1) is governed by the expedited actions process. The further specificity in paragraphs (c)(2)–(5) is to provide information regarding the nature of cases filed and does not affect a party's substantive rights.

Historical Notes

Source

Federal Rule 8(a), modified by substituting "petition" for "claim," by substituting (a) for the federal requirement of "a short and plain statement of the claim showing that the pleader is entitled to relief," by omission of the federal requirement of a "statement of the grounds upon which the court's jurisdiction depends, unless the court already has jurisdiction," and by other minor textual change.

2013 Amendment

The order dated February 12, 2013, in subsec. (b) substituted "a" for "in all claims for unliquidated damages only the"; inserted present subsec. (c) and renumbered former subsec. (c) as present subsec. (d); and in the last undesignated paragraph added the last sentence.

Rule 48. Alternative Claims for Relief

A party may set forth two or more statements of a claim or defense alternatively or hypothetically, either in one count or defense or in separate counts or defenses. When two or more statements are made in the alternative and one of them if made independently would be sufficient, the pleading is not made insufficient by the insufficiency of one or more of the alternative statements. A party may also state as many separate claims or defenses as he has regardless of consistency and whether based upon legal or equitable grounds or both.

Oct. 29, 1940, eff. Sept. 1, 1941.

Historical Notes

Source

Federal Rule 8(e), in part, unchanged.

Rule 49. Where Several Counts

Where there are several counts in the petition, and entire damages are given, the verdict or judgment, as the case may be, shall be good, notwithstanding one or more of such counts may be defective.

Oct. 29, 1940, eff. Sept. 1, 1941.

Historical Notes

Source

Vernon's Ann.Civ.St. art. 2213, unchanged.

Rule 50. Paragraphs, Separate Statements

All averments of claim or defense shall be made in numbered paragraphs, the contents of each of which shall be limited as far as practicable to a statement of a single set of circumstances; and a paragraph may be referred to by number in all succeeding pleadings, so long as the pleading containing such paragraph has not been superseded by an amendment as provided by Rule 65. Each claim founded upon a separate transaction or occurrence and each defense other than denials shall be stated in a separate count or defense whenever a separation facilitates the clear presentation of the matters set forth.

Oct. 29, 1940, eff. Sept. 1, 1941.

Historical Notes

Source

Federal Rule 10(b) modified by adding "so long as the pleading containing such paragraph has not been superseded by an amendment as provided by Rule 65."

Rule 51. Joinder of Claims and Remedies

(a) Joinder of Claims. The plaintiff in his petition or in a reply setting forth a counterclaim and the defendant in an answer setting forth a counterclaim may join either as independent or as alternate claims as many claims either legal or equitable or both as he may have against an opposing party. There may be a like joinder of claims when there are multiple parties if the requirements of Rules 39, 40, and 43 are satisfied. There may be a like joinder of cross claims or third-party claims if the requirements of Rules 38 and 97, respectively, are satisfied.

(b) Joinder of Remedies. Whenever a claim is one heretofore cognizable only after another claim has been prosecuted to a conclusion, the two claims may be joined in a single action; but the court shall grant relief in that action only in accordance with the relative substantive rights of the parties. This rule shall not be applied in tort cases so as to permit the joinder of a liability or indemnity insurance company, unless such company is by statute or contract directly liable to the person injured or damaged.

Oct. 29, 1940, eff. Sept. 1, 1941. Amended by orders of Sept. 20, 1941, eff. Dec. 31, 1941; July 26, 1960, eff. Jan. 1, 1961.

Historical Notes

Source

Federal Rule 18, modified by omitting reference to right of plaintiff to join an action upon a claim for money and an action to set aside a fraudulent conveyance.

Rule 52. Alleging a Corporation

An allegation that a corporation is incorporated shall be taken as true, unless denied by the affidavit of the adverse party, his agent or attorney, whether such corporation is a public or private corporation and however created.

Oct. 29, 1940, eff. Sept. 1, 1941.

Historical Notes

Source

Vernon's Ann.Civ.St. art. 1999, substituting "is incorporated" for "was duly incorporated."

Rule 53. Special Act or Law

A pleading founded wholly or in part on any private or special act or law of this State or of the Republic of Texas need only recite the title thereof, the date of its approval, and set out in substance so much of such act or laws as may be pertinent to the cause of action or defense.

Oct. 29, 1940, eff. Sept. 1, 1941.

Historical Notes

Source

Vernon's Ann.Civ.St. art. 2000, unchanged.

Rule 54. Conditions Precedent

In pleading the performance or occurrence of conditions precedent, it shall be sufficient to aver generally that all conditions precedent have been performed or have occurred. When such performances or occurrences have been so plead, the party so pleading same shall be required to prove only such of them as are specifically denied by the opposite party.

Oct. 29, 1940, eff. Sept. 1, 1941. Amended by order of March 31, 1941, eff. Sept. 1, 1941.

Historical Notes

Source

Federal Rule 9(c), substituting "it shall be" for "it is".

Rule 55. Judgment

In pleading a judgment or decision of a domestic or foreign court, judicial or quasi-judicial tribunal, or of a board or officer, it shall be sufficient to aver the judgment or decision without setting forth matter showing jurisdiction to render it.

Oct. 29, 1940, eff. Sept. 1, 1941.

Historical Notes

Source

Federal Rule 9(e), substituting "it shall be" for "it is."

Rule 56. Special Damage

When items of special damage are claimed, they shall be specifically stated.

Oct. 29, 1940, eff. Sept. 1, 1941.

Historical Notes

Source

Federal Rule 9(g), unchanged.

Rule 57. Signing of Pleadings

Every pleading of a party represented by an attorney shall be signed by at least one attorney of record in his individual name, with his State Bar of Texas identification number, address, telephone number, email address, and if available, fax number. A party not represented by an attorney shall sign his pleadings, state his address, telephone number, email address, and, if available, fax number.

Oct. 29, 1940, eff. Sept. 1, 1941. Amended by orders of June 10, 1980, eff. Jan. 1, 1981; April 24, 1990, eff. Sept. 1, 1990; Dec. 11, 2013, eff. Jan. 1, 2014.

Comment—1990

To supply attorney telecopier information with other identifying information on pleadings. Documents telephonically transferred are permitted to be filed under changes in Rule 45.

Historical Notes

Source

Federal Rule 11, first two sentences, unchanged.

2013 Amendment

The order dated December 11, 2013, after "telephone number," inserted "email address," in two places, and substituted "fax" for "telecopier" in two places.

Rule 58. Adoption by Reference

Statements in a pleading may be adopted by reference in a different part of the same pleading or in another pleading or in any motion, so long as the pleading containing such statements has not been superseded by an amendment as provided by Rule 65.

Oct. 29, 1940, eff. Sept. 1, 1941.

Historical Notes

Source

Federal Rule 10(c), first sentence, modified by adding "so long as the pleading containing such amendments has not been superseded by an amendment as provided by Rule 65."

Rule 59. Exhibits and Pleading

Notes, accounts, bonds, mortgages, records, and all other written instruments, constituting, in whole or in part, the claim sued on, or the matter set up in defense, may be made a part of the pleadings by copies thereof, or the originals, being attached or filed and referred to as such, or by copying the same in the body of the pleading in aid and explanation of the allegations in the petition or answer made in reference to said instruments and shall be deemed a part thereof for all purposes. Such pleadings shall not be deemed defective because of the lack of any allegations which can be supplied from said exhibit. No other instrument of writing shall be made an exhibit in the pleading.

Oct. 29, 1940, eff. Sept. 1, 1941.

Historical Notes

Source

District and County Court Rule 19, eliminating certain provisions and adding provisions for copying an exhibit into the body of the pleading and making an exhibit a part of the pleading for all purposes and for supplying allegations from an exhibit.

Rule 60. Intervenor's Pleadings

Any party may intervene by filing a pleading, subject to being stricken out by the court for sufficient cause on the motion of any party.

Oct. 29, 1940, eff. Sept. 1, 1941. Amended by order of April 24, 1990, eff. Sept. 1, 1990.

Comment—1990

Rules 21 and 21a control notice and service of pleadings of intervenors.

Historical Notes

Source

Vernon's Ann.Civ.St. art. 1998, modified to authorize intervention without leave of court whether court is in session or in vacation.

Rule 61. Trial: Intervenors: Rules Apply to All Parties

These rules of pleading shall apply equally, so far as it may be practicable to intervenors and to parties, when more than one, who may plead separately.

Oct. 29, 1940, eff. Sept. 1, 1941.

Historical Notes

Source

Vernon's Ann.Civ.St. art. 1998, with minor textual change; District and County Court Rule 30, unchanged.

Rule 62. Amendment Defined

The object of an amendment, as contra-distinguished from a supplemental petition or answer, is to add something to, or withdraw something from, that which has been previously pleaded so as to perfect that which is or may be deficient, or to correct that which has been incorrectly stated by the party making the amendment, or to plead new matter, additional to that formerly pleaded by the amending party, which constitutes an additional claim or defense permissible to the suit.

Oct. 29, 1940, eff. Sept. 1, 1941.

Historical Notes

Source

District and County Court Rules 12 and 15, combined with minor textual change.

Rule 63. Amendments and Responsive Pleadings

Parties may amend their pleadings, respond to pleadings on file of other parties, file suggestions of death and make representative parties, and file such other pleas as they may desire by filing such pleas with the clerk at such time as not to operate as a surprise to the opposite party; provided, that any pleadings, responses or pleas offered for filing within seven days of the date of trial or thereafter, or after such time as may be ordered by the judge under Rule 166, shall be filed only after leave of the judge is obtained, which leave shall be granted by the judge unless there is a showing that such filing will operate as a surprise to the opposite party.

Oct. 29, 1940, eff. Sept. 1, 1941. Amended by orders of July 26, 1960, eff. Jan. 1, 1961; April 24, 1990, eff. Sept. 1, 1990.

Comment—1990

To require that all trial pleadings of all parties, except those permitted by Rule 66, be on file at least seven days before trial unless leave of court permits later filing.

Historical Notes

Source

Vernon's Ann.Civ.St. art. 2001, subds. 1 and 2, modified to authorize amendment without leave when filed at least seven days before trial date and to require leave thereafter, granted by judge rather than by court.

Rule 64. Amended Instrument

The party amending shall point out the instrument amended, as "original petition," or "plaintiff's first supplemental petition," or as "original answer," or "defendant's first supplemental answer" or other instrument filed by the party and shall amend by filing a substitute therefor, entire and complete in itself, indorsed "amended original petition," or "amended first supplemental petition," or "amended original answer," or "amended first supplemental answer," accordingly as said instruments of pleading are designated.

Oct. 29, 1940, eff. Sept. 1, 1941.

Historical Notes

Source

District and County Court Rule 13, omitting requirement that amendment point out date of instrument amended and making minor textual changes.

Rule 65. Substituted Instrument Takes Place of Original

Unless the substituted instrument shall be set aside on exceptions, the instrument for which it is substituted shall no longer be regarded as a part of the pleading in the record of the cause, unless some error of the court in deciding upon the necessity of the amendment, or otherwise in superseding it, be complained of, and exception be taken to the action of the court, or unless it be necessary to look to the superseded pleading upon a question of limitation.

Oct. 29, 1940, eff. Sept. 1, 1941.

Historical Notes

Source

District and County Court Rule 14, with minor textual change.

Rule 66. Trial Amendment

If evidence is objected to at the trial on the ground that it is not within the issues made by the pleading, or if during the trial any defect, fault or omission in a pleading, either of form or substance, is called to the attention of the court, the court may allow the pleadings to be amended and shall do so freely when the presentation of the merits of the action will be subserved thereby and the objecting party fails to satisfy the court that the allowance of such amendment would prejudice him in maintaining his action or defense upon the merits. The court may grant a postponement to enable the objecting party to meet such evidence.

Oct. 29, 1940, eff. Sept. 1, 1941. Amended by order of March 31, 1941, eff. Sept. 1, 1941.

Historical Notes

Source

Federal Rule 15(b), last two sentences, adding "or if during the trial any defect, fault or omission in a pleading, either of form or substance, is called to the attention of the trial court"; substituting "allowance of such amendment" for "admission of such evidence"; and substituting "postponement" for "continuance."

Rule 67. Amendments to Conform to Issues Tried Without Objection

When issues not raised by the pleadings are tried by express or implied consent of the parties, they shall be treated in all respects as if they had been raised in the pleadings. In such case such amendment of the pleadings as may be necessary to cause them to conform to the evidence and to raise these issues may be made by leave of court upon motion of any party at any time up to the submission of the case to the Court or jury, but failure so to amend shall not affect the result of the trial of these issues; provided that written pleadings, before the time of submission, shall be necessary to the submission of questions, as is provided in Rules 277 and 279.

Oct. 29, 1940, eff. Sept. 1, 1941. Amended by orders of March 31, 1941, eff. Sept. 1, 1941; April 24, 1990, eff. Sept. 1, 1990.

Historical Notes

Source

Federal Rule 15(b), first two sentences, unchanged.

Rule 68. Court May Order Repleader

The court, when deemed necessary in any case, may order a repleader on the part of one or both of the parties, in order to make their pleadings substantially conform to the rules.

Oct. 29, 1940, eff. Sept. 1, 1941.

Historical Notes

Source

District and County Court Rule 29, unchanged.

Rule 69. Supplemental Petition or Answer

Each supplemental petition or answer, made by either party, shall be a response to the last preceding pleading by the other party, and shall not repeat allegations formerly pleaded further than is necessary as an introduction to that which is stated in the pleading then being drawn up. These instruments, to wit, the original petition and its several supplements, and the original answer and its several supplements, shall respectively, constitute separate and distinct parts of the pleadings of each party; and the position and identity, by number and name, with the indorsement of each instrument, shall be preserved throughout the pleadings of either party.

Oct. 29, 1940, eff. Sept. 1, 1941.

Historical Notes

Source

District and County Court Rule 10, omitting requirement that allegations be of "facts".

Rule 70. Pleading: Surprise: Cost

When either a supplemental or amended pleading is of such character and is presented at such time as to take the opposite party by surprise, the court may charge the continuance of the cause, if granted, to the party causing the surprise if the other party satisfactorily shows that he is not ready for trial because of the allowance of the filing of such supplemental or amended pleading, and the court may, in such event, in its discretion require the party filing such pleading to pay to the surprised party the amount of reasonable costs and expenses incurred by the other party as a result of the continuance, including attorney fees, or make such other order with respect thereto as may be just.

Oct. 29, 1940, eff. Sept. 1, 1941. Amended by order of June 10, 1980, eff. Jan. 1, 1981.

Historical Notes

Source

District and County Court Rule 16, with minor textual change.

Rule 71. Misnomer of Pleading

When a party has mistakenly designated any plea or pleading, the court, if justice so requires, shall treat the plea or pleading as if it had been properly designated. Pleadings shall be docketed as originally designated and shall remain identified as designated, unless the court orders redesignation. Upon court order filed with the clerk, the clerk shall modify the docket and all other clerk records to reflect redesignation.

Oct. 29, 1940, eff. Sept. 1, 1941. Amended by order of July 15, 1987, eff. Jan. 1, 1988.

Historical Notes

Source

Federal Rule 8(c), last sentence, extending the federal provision as to defenses and counterclaims to any misnamed plea or pleading.

Rule 72. Repealed by Order of April 24, 1990, eff. Sept. 1, 1990

Historical Notes

Former Rule 72, which related to the filing of pleadings, was added by Order dated Oct. 29, 1940 and was amended by Orders of July 11, 1977; Dec. 5, 1983; and July 15, 1987.

See, now, Vernon's Ann.Rules Civ.Proc., Rule 21.

Rule 73. Repealed by Order of April 24, 1990, eff. Sept. 1, 1990

Historical Notes

Former Rule 73, which related to failure to furnish a copy of pleadings to the adverse party, was added by Order of Oct. 29, 1940 and was amended by Order of June 10, 1980.

See, now, Vernon's Ann.Rules Civ.Proc., Rule 21b.

Rule 74. Filing with the Court Defined

The filing of pleadings, other papers and exhibits as required by these rules shall be made by filing them with the clerk of the court, except that the judge may permit the papers to be filed with him, in which event he shall note thereon the filing date and time and forthwith transmit them to the office of the clerk.

Oct. 29, 1940, eff. Sept. 1, 1941. Amended by order of July 20, 1966, eff. Jan. 1, 1967.

Historical Notes

Source

Federal Rule 5(e), adding "and time," and making minor textual change.

Rule 75. Filed Pleadings; Withdrawal

All filed pleadings shall remain at all times in the clerk's office or in the court or in custody of the clerk, except that the court may by order entered on the minutes allow a filed pleading to be withdrawn for a limited time whenever necessary, on leaving a certified copy on file. The party withdrawing such pleading shall pay the costs of such order and certified copy.

Oct. 29, 1940, eff. Sept. 1, 1941.

Historical Notes

Source

Vernon's Ann.Civ.St. art. 2002a, last sentence, unchanged.

Rule 75a. Filing Exhibits: Court Reporter to File with Clerk

The court reporter or stenographer shall file with the clerk of the court all exhibits which were admitted in evidence or tendered on bill of exception during the course of any hearing, proceeding, or trial.

July 20, 1966, eff. Jan. 1, 1967.

Rule 75b. Filed Exhibits: Withdrawal

All filed exhibits admitted in evidence or tendered on bill of exception shall, until returned or otherwise disposed of as authorized by Rule 14b, remain at all times in the clerk's office or in the court or in the custody of the clerk except as follows:

(a) The court may by order entered on the minutes allow a filed exhibit to be withdrawn by any party only upon such party's leaving on file a certified, photo, or other reproduced copy of such exhibit. The party withdrawing such exhibit shall pay the costs of such order and copy.

(b) The court reporter or stenographer of the court conducting the hearing, proceedings, or trial in which exhibits are admitted or offered in evidence, shall have the right to withdraw filed exhibits, upon giving the clerk proper receipt therefor, whenever necessary for the court reporter or stenographer to transmit such original exhibits to an appellate court under the provisions of Rule 379 or to otherwise discharge the duties imposed by law upon said court reporter or stenographer.

July 20, 1966, eff. Jan. 1, 1967.

Rule 76. May Inspect Papers

Each attorney at law practicing in any court shall be allowed at all reasonable times to inspect the papers and records relating to any suit or other matter in which he may be interested.

Oct. 29, 1940, eff. Sept. 1, 1941.

Historical Notes

Source

Vernon's Ann.Civ.St. art. 318, omitting provision for a descriptive receipt of withdrawn instruments.

Rule 76a. Sealing Court Records

1. Standard for Sealing Court Records. Court records may not be removed from court files except as permitted by statute or rule. No court order or opinion issued in the adjudication of a case may be sealed. Other court records, as defined in this rule, are presumed to be open to the general public and may be sealed only upon a showing of all of the following:

(a) a specific, serious and substantial interest which clearly outweighs:

(1) this presumption of openness;

(2) any probable adverse effect that sealing will have upon the general public health or safety;

(b) no less restrictive means than sealing records will adequately and effectively protect the specific interest asserted.

2. Court Records. For purposes of this rule, court records means:

(a) all documents of any nature filed in connection with any matter before any civil court, except:

(1) documents filed with a court in camera, solely for the purpose of obtaining a ruling on the discoverability of such documents;

(2) documents in court files to which access is otherwise restricted by law;

(3) documents filed in an action originally arising under the Family Code.

(b) settlement agreements not filed of record, excluding all reference to any monetary consideration, that seek to restrict disclosure of information concerning matters that have a probable adverse effect upon the general public health or safety, or the administration of public office, or the operation of government.

(c) discovery, not filed of record, concerning matters that have a probable adverse effect upon the general public health or safety, or the administration of public office, or the operation of government, except discovery in cases originally initiated to preserve bona fide trade secrets or other intangible property rights.

3. Notice. Court records may be sealed only upon a party's written motion, which shall be open to public inspection. The movant shall post a public notice at the place where notices for meetings of county governmental bodies are required to be posted, stating: that a hearing will be held in open court on a motion to seal court records in the specific case; that any person may intervene and be heard concerning the sealing of court records; the specific time and place of the hearing; the style and number of the case; a brief but specific description of both the nature of the case and the records which are sought to be sealed; and the identity of the movant. Immediately after posting such notice, the movant shall file a verified copy of the posted notice with the clerk of the court in which the case is pending and with the Clerk of the Supreme Court of Texas.

4. **Hearing.** A hearing, open to the public, on a motion to seal court records shall be held in open court as soon as practicable, but not less than fourteen days after the motion is filed and notice is posted. Any party may participate in the hearing. Non-parties may intervene as a matter of right for the limited purpose of participating in the proceedings, upon payment of the fee required for filing a plea in intervention. The court may inspect records in camera when necessary. The court may determine a motion relating to sealing or unsealing court records in accordance with the procedures prescribed by Rule 120a.

5. **Temporary Sealing Order.** A temporary sealing order may issue upon motion and notice to any parties who have answered in the case pursuant to Rules 21 and 21a upon a showing of compelling need from specific facts shown by affidavit or by verified petition that immediate and irreparable injury will result to a specific interest of the applicant before notice can be posted and a hearing held as otherwise provided herein. The temporary order shall set the time for the hearing required by paragraph 4 and shall direct that the movant immediately give the public notice required by paragraph 3. The court may modify or withdraw any temporary order upon motion by any party or intervenor, notice to the parties, and hearing conducted as soon as practicable. Issuance of a temporary order shall not reduce in any way the burden of proof of a party requesting sealing at the hearing required by paragraph 4.

6. **Order on Motion to Seal Court Records.** A motion relating to sealing or unsealing court records shall be decided by written order, open to the public, which shall state: the style and number of the case; the specific reasons for finding and concluding whether the showing required by paragraph 1, has been made; the specific portions of court records which are to be sealed; and the time period for which the sealed portions of the court records are to be sealed. The order shall not be included in any judgment or other order but shall be a separate document in the case; however, the failure to comply with this requirement shall not affect its appealability.

7. **Continuing Jurisdiction.** Any person may intervene as a matter of right at any time before or after judgment to seal or unseal court records. A court that issues a sealing order retains continuing jurisdiction to enforce, alter, or vacate that order. An order sealing or unsealing court records shall not be reconsidered on motion of any party or intervenor who had actual notice of the hearing preceding issuance of the order, without first showing changed circumstances materially affecting the order. Such circumstances need not be related to the case in which the order was issued. However, the burden of making the showing required by paragraph 1, shall always be on the party seeking to seal records.

8. **Appeal.** Any order (or portion of an order or judgment) relating to sealing or unsealing court records shall be deemed to be severed from the case and a final judgment which may be appealed by any party or intervenor who participated in the hearing preceding issuance of such order. The appellate court may abate the appeal and order the trial court to direct that further public notice be given, or to hold further hearings, or to make additional findings.

9. **Application.** Access to documents in court files not defined as court records by this rule remains governed by existing law. This rule does not apply to any court records sealed in an action in which a final judgment has been entered before its effective date. This rule applies to cases already pending on its effective date only with regard to:

(a) all court records filed or exchanged after the effective date;

(b) any motion to alter or vacate an order restricting access to court records, issued before the effective date.

April 24, 1990, eff. Sept. 1, 1990.

Comment—1990

New rule to establish guidelines for sealing certain court records in compliance with Government Code § 22.010.

Rule 77. Lost Records and Papers

When any papers or records are lost or destroyed during the pendency of a suit, the parties may, with the approval of the judge, agree in writing on a brief statement of the matters contained therein; or either party may supply such lost records or papers as follows:

a. After three days' notice to the adverse party or his attorney, make written sworn motion before the court stating the loss or destruction of such record or papers, accompanied by certified copies of the originals if obtainable, or by substantial copies thereof.

b. If, upon hearing, the court be satisfied that they are substantial copies of the original, an order shall be made substituting such copies or brief statement for the originals.

c. Such substituted copies or brief statement shall be filed with the clerk, constitute a part of the cause, and have the force and effect of the originals.
Oct. 29, 1940, eff. Sept. 1, 1941. Amended by order of June 16, 1943, eff. Dec. 31, 1943.

Historical Notes

Source

Vernon's Ann.Civ.St. art. 2289, unchanged.

B. PLEADINGS OF PLAINTIFF

Rule 78. Petition; Original and Supplemental; Indorsement

The pleading of plaintiff shall consist of an original petition, and such supplemental petitions as may be necessary in the course of pleading by the parties to the suit. The original petition and the supplemental petitions shall be indorsed, so as to show their respective positions in the process of pleading, as "original petition," "plaintiff's first supplemental petition," "plaintiff's second supplemental petition," and so on, to be successively numbered, named, and indorsed.
Oct. 29, 1940, eff. Sept. 1, 1941.

Historical Notes

Source

District and County Court Rule 3, omitting "to enable the plaintiff to state all the facts presenting his cause of action, and such other facts as may be required to rebut the facts that may be stated in the original and supplemental petitions as pleaded by the defendant," at end of first sentence.

Rule 78a. Case Information Sheet

(a) *Requirement*. A civil case information sheet, in the form promulgated by the Supreme Court of Texas [1], must accompany the filing of:

(1) an original petition or application; and

(2) a post-judgment petition for modification or motion for enforcement in a case arising under the Family Code.

(b) *Signature*. The civil case information sheet must be signed by the attorney for the party filing the pleading or by the party.

(c) *Enforcement*. The court and clerk must take appropriate measures to enforce this rule. But the clerk may not reject a pleading because the pleading is not accompanied by a civil case information sheet.

(d) *Limitation on Use*. The civil case information sheet is for data collection for statistical and administrative purposes and does not affect any substantive right.

(e) *Applicability*. The civil case information sheet is not required in cases filed in justice courts or small-claims courts, or in cases arising under Title 3 of the Family Code.
Added by orders of May 3, 2010 and Aug. 16, 2010, eff. Sept. 1, 2010.

[1] See Appendix to Rules of Civil Procedure for form.

Comment

Rule 78a is added to require the submission of a civil case information sheet to collect data for statistical and administrative purposes, *see, e.g.*, Tex. Gov't Code § 71.035. A civil case information sheet is not a pleading. Rule 78a is placed with other rules regarding pleadings because civil case information sheets must accompany pleadings.

Rule 79. The Petition

The petition shall state the names of the parties and their residences, if known, together with the contents prescribed in Rule 47 above.
Oct. 29, 1940, eff. Sept. 1, 1941.

Historical Notes

Source

New rule.

Rule 80. Plaintiff's Supplemental Petition

The plaintiff's supplemental petitions may contain special exceptions, general denials, and the allegations of new matter not before alleged by him, in reply to those which have been alleged by the defendant.
Oct. 29, 1940, eff. Sept. 1, 1941.

Historical Notes

Source

District and County Court Rule 5, with minor textual change.

Rule 81. Defensive Matters

When the defendant sets up a counter claim, the plaintiff may plead thereto under rules prescribed for pleadings of defensive matter by the defendant, so far as applicable. Whenever the defendant is required to plead any matter of defense under oath, the plaintiff shall be required to plead such matters under oath when relied on by him.
Oct. 29, 1940, eff. Sept. 1, 1941.

Historical Notes

Source

Vernon's Ann.Civ.St. art. 2004, unchanged.

Rule 82. Special Defenses

The plaintiff need not deny any special matter of defense pleaded by the defendant, but the same shall be regarded as denied unless expressly admitted.
Oct. 29, 1940, eff. Sept. 1, 1941.

Historical Notes

Source

Vernon's Ann.Civ.St. art. 2005, unchanged.

C. PLEADINGS OF DEFENDANT

Rule 83. Answer; Original and Supplemental; Indorsement

The answer of defendant shall consist of an original answer, and such supplemental answers as may be necessary, in the course of pleading by the parties to the suit. The original answer and the supplemental answers shall be indorsed, so as to show their respective positions in the process of pleading, as "original answer," "defendant's first supplemental answer," "defendant's second supplemental answer," and so on, to be successively numbered, named and indorsed.
Oct. 29, 1940, eff. Sept. 1, 1941.

Historical Notes

Source

District and County Court Rule 6, omitting "to enable the defendant to state all of the exceptions and facts presenting his defense as contained in his original answer, and such other facts as may be required to rebut the facts that may be stated in the original and supplemental petitions as pleaded by the plaintiff," at the end of the first sentence.

Rule 84. Answer May Include Several Matters

The defendant in his answer may plead as many several matters, whether of law or fact, as he may think necessary for his defense, and which may be pertinent to the cause, and such matters shall be heard in such order as may be directed by the court, special appearance and motion to transfer venue, and the practice thereunder being excepted herefrom.
Oct. 29, 1940, eff. Sept. 1, 1941. Amended by orders of Oct. 12, 1949, eff. March 1, 1950; April 12, 1962, eff. Sept. 1, 1962; June 15, 1983, eff. Sept. 1, 1983.

Historical Notes

Source

Vernon's Ann.Civ.St. arts. 2006, in part, and 2012, combined with minor textual change.

Rule 85. Original Answer; Contents

The original answer may consist of motions to transfer venue, pleas to the jurisdiction, in abatement, or any other dilatory pleas; of special exceptions, of general denial, and any defense by way of avoidance or estoppel, and it may present a cross-action, which to that extent will place defendant in the attitude of a plaintiff. Matters in avoidance and estoppel may be stated together, or in several special pleas, each presenting a distinct defense, and numbered so as to admit of separate issues to be formed on them.
Oct. 29, 1940, eff. Sept. 1, 1941. Amended by order of June 15, 1983, eff. Sept. 1, 1983.

Historical Notes

Source

District and County Court Rule 7, eliminating "other facts in" between "any" and "defense"; eliminating "the same being pleaded in the due order of pleading as required by statute" after "avoidance or estoppel"; substituting "Matters" for "Facts"; and making minor textual change.

Rule 86. Motion to Transfer Venue

1. **Time to File.** An objection to improper venue is waived if not made by written motion filed prior to or concurrently with any other plea, pleading or motion except a special appearance motion provided for in Rule 120a. A written consent of the parties to transfer the case to another county may be filed with the clerk of the court at any time. A motion to transfer venue because an impartial trial cannot be had in the county where the action is pending is governed by the provisions of Rule 257.

2. **How to File.** The motion objecting to improper venue may be contained in a separate instrument filed concurrently with or prior to the filing of a movant's first responsive pleading or the motion may be combined with other objections and defenses and included in the movant's first responsive pleading.

3. **Requisites of Motion.** The motion, and any amendments to it, shall state that the action should be transferred to another specified county of proper venue because:

(a) The county where the action is pending is not a proper county; or

(b) Mandatory venue of the action in another county is prescribed by one or more specific statutory provisions which shall be clearly designated or indicated.

The motion shall state the legal and factual basis for the transfer of the action and request transfer of the action to a specific county of mandatory or proper venue. Verification of the motion is not required. The motion may be accompanied by supporting affidavits as provided in Rule 87.

4. Response and Reply. Except as provided in paragraph 3(a) of Rule 87, a response to the motion to transfer is not required. Verification of a response is not required.

5. Service. A copy of any instrument filed pursuant to Rule 86 shall be served in accordance with Rule 21a.

Oct. 29, 1940, eff. Sept. 1, 1941. Amended by orders of March 31, 1941, eff. Sept. 1, 1941; June 16, 1943, eff. Dec. 31, 1943; July 20, 1954, eff. Jan. 1, 1955; April 12, 1962, eff. Sept. 1, 1962; June 15, 1983, eff. Sept. 1, 1983.

Historical Notes

Source

Vernon's Ann.Civ.St. art. 2007, modified, inter alia, to require statement of post office address of defendant or his attorney and to increase from five to ten days the time for filing a controverting affidavit.

Rule 87. Determination of Motion to Transfer

1. Consideration of Motion. The determination of a motion to transfer venue shall be made promptly by the court and such determination must be made in a reasonable time prior to commencement of the trial on the merits. The movant has the duty to request a setting on the motion to transfer. Except on leave of court each party is entitled to at least 45 days notice of a hearing on the motion to transfer.

Except on leave of court, any response or opposing affidavits shall be filed at least 30 days prior to the hearing of the motion to transfer. The movant is not required to file a reply to the response but any reply and any additional affidavits supporting the motion to transfer must, except on leave of court, be filed not later than 7 days prior to the hearing date.

2. Burden of Establishing Venue.

(a) *In General.* A party who seeks to maintain venue of the action in a particular county in reliance upon Section 15.001 (General Rule), Sections 15.011–15.017 (Mandatory Venue), Sections 15.031–15.040 (Permissive Venue), or Sections 15.061 and 15.062 (Multiple Claims), Civil Practice and Remedies Code, has the burden to make proof, as provided in paragraph 3 of this rule, that venue is maintainable in the county of suit. A party who seeks to transfer venue of the action to another specified county under Section 15.001 (General Rule), Sections 15.011–15.017 (Mandatory Venue), Sections 15.031–15.040 (Permissive Venue), or Sections 15.061 and 15.062 (Multiple Claims), Civil Practice and Remedies Code, has the burden to make proof, as provided in paragraph 3 of this rule, that venue is maintainable in the county to which transfer is sought. A party who seeks to transfer venue of the action to another specified county under Sections 15.011–15.017, Civil Practice and Remedies Code on the basis that a mandatory venue provision is applicable and controlling has the burden to make proof, as provided in paragraph 3 of this rule, that venue is maintainable in the county to which transfer is sought by virtue of one or more mandatory venue exceptions.

(b) *Cause of Action.* It shall not be necessary for a claimant to prove the merits of a cause of action, but the existence of a cause of action, when pleaded properly, shall be taken as established as alleged by the pleadings. When the defendant specifically denies the venue allegations, the claimant is required, by prima facie proof as provided in paragraph 3 of this rule, to support such pleading that the cause of action taken as established by the pleadings, or a part of such cause of action, accrued in the county of suit. If a defendant seeks transfer to a county where the cause of action or a part thereof accrued, it shall be sufficient for the defendant to plead that if a cause of action exists, then the cause of action or part thereof accrued in the specific county to which transfer is sought, and such allegation shall not constitute an admission that a cause of action in fact exists. But the defendant shall be required to support his pleading by prima facie proof as provided in paragraph 3 of this rule, that, if a cause of action exists, it or a part thereof accrued in the county to which transfer is sought.

(c) *Other Rules.* A motion to transfer venue based on the written consent of the parties shall be determined in accordance with Rule 255. A motion to transfer venue on the basis that an impartial trial cannot be had in the county where the action is pending shall be determined in accordance with Rules 258 and 259.

3. Proof.

(a) *Affidavits and Attachments.* All venue facts, when properly pleaded, shall be taken as true unless specifically denied by the adverse party. When a venue fact is specifically denied, the party pleading the venue fact must make prima facie proof of that venue fact; provided, however, that no party shall ever be required for venue purposes to support by prima facie proof the existence of a cause of action or part thereof, and at the hearing the pleadings of the parties shall be taken as conclusive on the issues of existence of a cause of action. Prima facie proof is made when the venue facts are properly pleaded and an affidavit, and any duly proved attachments to the affidavit, are filed fully and specifically setting forth the facts supporting such pleading. Affidavits shall be made on personal knowledge, shall set forth specific facts as would be admissible in evidence, and shall show affirmatively that the affiant is competent to testify.

(b) *The Hearing.* The court shall determine the motion to transfer venue on the basis of the pleadings, any stipulations made by and between the parties and such affidavits and attachments as may be filed by the parties in accordance with the preceding subdivision of this paragraph 3 or of Rule 88.

(c) If a claimant has adequately pleaded and made prima facie proof that venue is proper in the county of suit as provided in subdivision (a) of paragraph 3, then the cause shall not be transferred but shall be retained in the county of suit, unless the motion to transfer is based on the grounds that an impartial trial cannot be had in the county where the action is pending as provided in Rules 257–259 or on an established ground of mandatory venue. A ground of mandatory venue is established when the party relying upon a mandatory exception to the general rule makes prima facie proof as provided in subdivision (a) of paragraph 3 of this rule.

(d) In the event that the parties shall fail to make prima facie proof that the county of suit or the specific county to which transfer is sought is a county of proper venue, then the court may direct the parties to make further proof.

4. No Jury. All venue challenges shall be determined by the court without the aid of a jury.

5. Motion for Rehearing. If venue has been sustained as against a motion to transfer, or if an action has been transferred to a proper county in response to a motion to transfer, then no further motions to transfer shall be considered regardless of whether the movant was a party to the prior proceedings or was added as a party subsequent to the venue proceedings, unless the motion to transfer is based on the grounds that an impartial trial cannot be had under Rules 257–259 or on the ground of mandatory venue, provided that such claim was not available to the other movant or movants.

Parties who are added subsequently to an action and are precluded by this rule from having a motion to transfer considered may raise the propriety of venue on appeal, provided that the party has timely filed a motion to transfer.

6. There shall be no interlocutory appeals from such determination.

Oct. 29, 1940, eff. Sept. 1, 1941. Amended by orders of Sept. 20, 1941, eff. Dec. 31, 1941; June 16, 1943, eff. Dec. 31, 1943; Aug. 18, 1947, eff. Dec. 13, 1947; June 15, 1983, eff. Sept. 1, 1983; July 15, 1987, eff. Jan. 1, 1988; April 24, 1990, eff. Sept. 1, 1990.

Comment—1990

To clarify that no proof of any kind is required of any party to establish any element of a cause of action or part thereof; proof is restricted to place, if any, and the pleadings establish all other elements and may not be controverted for venue purposes as to the existence of a cause of action or part thereof.

Historical Notes

Source

Vernon's Ann.Civ.St. art. 2008, in part, modified, inter alia, to permit service of notice of controverting plea by registered mail.

Rule 88. Discovery and Venue

Discovery shall not be abated or otherwise affected by pendency of a motion to transfer venue. Issuing process for witnesses and taking depositions shall not constitute a waiver of a motion to transfer venue, but depositions taken in such case may be read in evidence in any subsequent suit between the same parties concerning the same subject matter in like manner as if taken in such subsequent suit. Deposition transcripts, responses to requests for admission, answers to interrogatories and other discovery products containing information relevant to a determination of proper venue may be considered by the court in making the venue determination when they are attached to, or incorporated by reference in, an affidavit of a party, a witness or an attorney who has knowledge of such discovery.

Oct. 29, 1940, eff. Sept. 1, 1941. Amended by orders of June 15, 1983, eff. Sept. 1, 1983; July 15, 1987, eff. Jan. 1, 1988.

Historical Notes

Source

Vernon's Ann.Civ.St. art. 2018, unchanged.

Rule 89. Transferred If Motion Is Sustained

If a motion to transfer venue is sustained, the cause shall not be dismissed, but the court shall transfer said cause to the proper court; and the costs incurred prior to the time such suit is filed in the court to which said cause is transferred shall be taxed against the plaintiff. The clerk shall make up a transcript of all the orders made in said cause, certifying thereto officially under the seal of the court, and send it with the original papers in the cause to the clerk of the court to which the venue has been changed. Provided, however, if the cause be severable as to parties defendant and shall be ordered transferred as to one or more defendants but not as to all, the clerk, instead of sending the original papers, shall make certified copies of such filed papers as directed by the court and forward the same to the clerk of the court to which the venue has been changed. After the cause has been transferred, as above provided for the clerk of the court to which the cause has been transferred shall mail notification to the plaintiff or his attorney that transfer of the cause has been completed, that the filing fee in the proper court is due and payable within thirty days from the mailing of such notification, and that the case may be dismissed if the filing fee is not timely paid; and if such filing fee is timely paid, the cause will be subject to trial at the expiration of thirty days after the mailing of notification to the parties or their attorneys by the clerk that the papers have been filed in the court to which the cause has been transferred; and if the filing fee is not timely paid, any court of the transferee county to which the case might have been assigned, upon its own motion or the motion of a party, may dismiss the cause without prejudice to the refiling of same.

Oct. 29, 1940, eff. Sept. 1, 1941. Amended by orders of June 16, 1943, eff. Dec. 31, 1943; June 15, 1983, eff. Sept. 1, 1983.

Historical Notes

Source

Vernon's Ann.Civ.St. arts. 2019 and 2020, combined with minor textual change.

Rule 90. Waiver of Defects in Pleading

General demurrers shall not be used. Every defect, omission or fault in a pleading either of form or of substance, which is not specifically pointed out by exception in writing and brought to the attention of the judge in the trial court before the instruction or charge to the jury or, in a non-jury case, before the judgment is signed, shall be deemed to have been waived by the party seeking reversal on such account; provided that this rule shall not apply as to any party against whom default judgment is rendered.

Oct. 29, 1940, eff. Sept. 1, 1941. Amended by order of June 10, 1980, eff. Jan. 1, 1981.

Historical Notes

Source

New rule.

Rule 91. Special Exceptions

A special exception shall not only point out the particular pleading excepted to, but it shall also point out intelligibly and with particularity the defect, omission, obscurity, duplicity, generality, or other insufficiency in the allegations in the pleading excepted to.

Oct. 29 1940, eff. Sept. 1, 1941. Amended by order of March 31, 1941, eff. Sept. 1, 1941.

Historical Notes

Source

District and County Court Rule 18, modified by omitting last sentence, requiring "particularity," and making minor textual changes.

Rule 91a. Dismissal of Baseless Causes of Action

91a.1 Motion and Grounds. Except in a case brought under the Family Code or a case governed by Chapter 14 of the Texas Civil Practice and Remedies Code, a party may move to dismiss a cause of action on the grounds that it has no basis in law or fact. A cause of action has no basis in law if the allegations, taken as true, together with inferences reasonably drawn from them, do not entitle the claimant to the relief sought. A cause of action has no basis in fact if no reasonable person could believe the facts pleaded.

91a.2 Contents of Motion. A motion to dismiss must state that it is made pursuant to this rule, must identify each cause of action to which it is addressed, and must state specifically the reasons the cause of action has no basis in law, no basis in fact, or both.

91a.3 Time for Motion and Ruling. A motion to dismiss must be:

(a) filed within 60 days after the first pleading containing the challenged cause of action is served on the movant;

(b) filed at least 21 days before the motion is heard; and

(c) granted or denied within 45 days after the motion is filed.

91a.4 Time for Response. Any response to the motion must be filed no later than 7 days before the date of the hearing.

91a.5 Effect of Nonsuit or Amendment; Withdrawal of Motion.

(a) The court may not rule on a motion to dismiss if, at least 3 days before the date of the hearing, the respondent files a nonsuit of the challenged cause of action, or the movant files a withdrawal of the motion.

(b) If the respondent amends the challenged cause of action at least 3 days before the date of the hearing, the movant may, before the date of the hearing, file a withdrawal of the motion or an amended motion directed to the amended cause of action.

(c) Except by agreement of the parties, the court must rule on a motion unless it has been withdrawn or the cause of action has been nonsuited in accordance with (a) or (b). In ruling on the motion, the court must not consider a nonsuit or amendment not filed as permitted by paragraphs (a) or (b).

(d) An amended motion filed in accordance with (b) restarts the time periods in this rule.

91a.6 Hearing; No Evidence Considered. Each party is entitled to at least 14 days' notice of the hearing on the motion to dismiss. The court may, but is not required to, conduct an oral hearing on the motion. Except as required by 91a.7, the court may not consider evidence in ruling on the motion and must decide the motion based solely on the pleading of the cause of action, together with any pleading exhibits permitted by Rule 59.

91a.7 Award of Costs and Attorney Fees Required. Except in an action by or against a governmental entity or a public official acting in his or her official capacity or under color of law, the court must award the prevailing party on the motion all costs and reasonable and necessary attorney fees incurred with respect to the challenged cause of action in the trial court. The court must consider evidence regarding costs and fees in determining the award.

91a.8 Effect on Venue and Personal Jurisdiction. This rule is not an exception to the pleading requirements of Rules 86 and 120a, but a party does not, by filing a motion to dismiss pursuant to this rule or obtaining a ruling on it, waive a special appearance or a motion to transfer venue. By filing a motion to dismiss, a party submits to the court's jurisdiction only in proceedings on the motion and is bound by the court's ruling, including an award of attorney fees and costs against the party.

91a.9 Dismissal Procedure Cumulative. This rule is in addition to, and does not supersede or affect, other procedures that authorize dismissal.

Adopted by order of Feb. 12, 2013, eff. March 1, 2013.

Comment—2013

Rule 91a is a new rule implementing section 22.004(g) of the Texas Government Code, which was added in 2011 and calls for rules to provide for the dismissal of causes of action that have no basis in law or fact on motion and without evidence. A motion to dismiss filed under this rule must be ruled on by the court within 45 days unless the motion, pleading, or cause of action is withdrawn, amended, or nonsuited as specified in 91a.5. If an amended motion is filed in response to an amended cause of action in accordance with 91a.5(b), the court must rule on the motion within 45 days of the filing of the amended motion and the respondent must be given an opportunity to respond to the amended motion. The term "hearing" in the rule includes both submission and an oral hearing. Attorney fees awarded under 91a.7 are limited to those associated with challenged cause of action, including fees for preparing or responding to the motion to dismiss.

Historical Notes

Source

New Rule.

Rule 92. General Denial

A general denial of matters pleaded by the adverse party which are not required to be denied under oath, shall be sufficient to put the same in issue. When the defendant has pleaded a general denial, and the plaintiff shall afterward amend his pleading, such original denial shall be presumed to extend to all matters subsequently set up by the plaintiff.

When a counterclaim or cross-claim is served upon a party who has made an appearance in the action, the party so served, in the absence of a responsive pleading, shall be deemed to have pleaded a general denial of the counterclaim or cross-claim, but the party shall not be deemed to have waived any special appearance or motion to transfer venue. In all other respects the rules prescribed for pleadings of defensive matter are applicable to answers to counterclaims and cross-claims.

Oct. 29, 1940, eff. Sept. 1, 1941. Amended by orders of Dec. 5, 1983, eff. April 1, 1984; Dec. 19, 1984, eff. April 1, 1985.

Historical Notes

Source

Vernon's Ann.Civ.St. arts. 2006, last sentence with minor textual change, and 2011, combined.

Rule 93. Certain Pleas to Be Verified

A pleading setting up any of the following matters, unless the truth of such matters appear of record, shall be verified by affidavit.

1. That the plaintiff has not legal capacity to sue or that the defendant has not legal capacity to be sued.

2. That the plaintiff is not entitled to recover in the capacity in which he sues, or that the defendant is not liable in the capacity in which he is sued.

3. That there is another suit pending in this State between the same parties involving the same claim.

4. That there is a defect of parties, plaintiff or defendant.

5. A denial of partnership as alleged in any pleading as to any party to the suit.

6. That any party alleged in any pleading to be a corporation is not incorporated as alleged.

7. Denial of the execution by himself or by his authority of any instrument in writing, upon which any pleading is founded, in whole or in part and charged to have been executed by him or by his authority, and not alleged to be lost or destroyed. Where such instrument in writing is charged to have been executed by a person then deceased, the affidavit shall be sufficient if it states that the affiant has reason to believe and does believe that such instru-

ment was not executed by the decedent or by his authority. In the absence of such a sworn plea, the instrument shall be received in evidence as fully proved.

8. A denial of the genuineness of the indorsement or assignment of a written instrument upon which suit is brought by an indorsee or assignee and in the absence of such a sworn plea, the indorsement or assignment thereof shall be held as fully proved. The denial required by this subdivision of the rule may be made upon information and belief.

9. That a written instrument upon which a pleading is founded is without consideration, or that the consideration of the same has failed in whole or in part.

10. A denial of an account which is the foundation of the plaintiff's action, and supported by affidavit.

11. That a contract sued upon is usurious. Unless such plea is filed, no evidence of usurious interest as a defense shall be received.

12. That notice and proof of loss or claim for damage has not been given as alleged. Unless such plea is filed such notice and proof shall be presumed and no evidence to the contrary shall be admitted. A denial of such notice or such proof shall be made specifically and with particularity.

13. In the trial of any case appealed to the court from the Industrial Accident Board [1] the following, if pleaded, shall be presumed to be true as pleaded and have been done and filed in legal time and manner, unless denied by verified pleadings:

(a) Notice of injury.

(b) Claim for compensation.

(c) Award of the Board.

(d) Notice of intention not to abide by the award of the Board.

(e) Filing of suit to set aside the award.

(f) That the insurance company alleged to have been the carrier of the workers' compensation insurance at the time of the alleged injury was in fact the carrier thereof.

(g) That there was good cause for not filing claim with the Industrial Accident Board [1] within the one year period provided by statute.

(h) Wage rate.

A denial of any of the matters set forth in subdivisions (a) or (g) of paragraph 13 may be made on information and belief.

Any such denial may be made in original or amended pleadings; but if in amended pleadings the same must be filed not less than seven days before the case proceeds to trial. In case of such denial the things so denied shall not be presumed to be true, and if essential to the case of the party alleging them, must be proved.

14. That a party plaintiff or defendant is not doing business under an assumed name or trade name as alleged.

15. In the trial of any case brought against an automobile insurance company by an insured under the provisions of an insurance policy in force providing protection against uninsured motorists, an allegation that the insured has complied with all the terms of the policy as a condition precedent to bringing the suit shall be presumed to be true unless denied by verified pleadings which may be upon information and belief.

16. Any other matter required by statute to be pleaded under oath.

Oct. 29, 1940, eff. Sept. 1, 1941. Amended by orders of March 31, 1941, eff. Sept. 1, 1941; Sept. 20, 1941, eff. Dec. 31, 1941; June 16, 1943, eff. Dec. 31, 1943; Oct. 12, 1949, eff. March 1, 1950; July 21, 1970, eff. Jan. 1, 1971; July 22, 1975, eff. Jan. 1, 1976; June 15, 1983, eff. Sept. 1, 1983; Dec. 5, 1983, eff. April 1, 1984.

1 The name of the Industrial Accident Board was changed to the Texas Workers' Compensation Commission pursuant to Acts 1989, 71st Leg., 2nd C.S., ch. 1, § 17.01. The Texas Workers' Compensation Commission was abolished and the Workers' Compensation Division of the Texas Department of Insurance was established pursuant to Acts 2005, 79th Leg., ch. 265, § 1.003.

Historical Notes

Source

Vernon's Ann.Civ.St. arts. 2010 and 5074. Article 2010, which included subds. (a) to (*l*) originally pertained to defendant's pleadings, and was broadened to encompass verified pleas generally. The last sentence of subd. (h) was added. Subdivision (i) was rewritten. Minor textual changes were made.

The second sentence of subd. (*l*), adapted from art. 5074, was added.

Adoption of Rule 93 effected the repeal of Vernon's Ann. Civ.St. art. 1999, alleging a corporation, now covered in subd. (g); Vernon's Ann.Civ.St. art. 3734, execution of written instruments, now covered in subd. (h); Vernon's Ann.Civ.St. art. 573, plea of forgery, now covered in subd. (i); Vernon's Ann.Civ.St. art. 574, failure of consideration, now covered in subd. (j); and arts. 2010 and 5074.

Rule 94. Affirmative Defenses

In pleading to a preceding pleading, a party shall set forth affirmatively accord and satisfaction, arbitration and award, assumption of risk, contributory negligence, discharge in bankruptcy, duress, estoppel, failure of consideration, fraud, illegality, injury by fellow servant, laches, license, payment, release, res judicata, statute of frauds, statute of limitations, waiver, and any other matter constituting an avoidance or affirmative defense. Where the suit is on an insurance contract which insures against certain general hazards, but contains other provisions limiting such general liability, the party suing on such contract shall never be required to allege that the loss was not due to a risk or cause coming within any of the exceptions specified in the contract, nor shall the insurer be allowed to raise such issue unless it shall specifically allege that the loss was due to a risk or cause coming within a particular exception to the general liability; provided that nothing herein shall be construed to change the burden of proof on such issue as it now exists.

Oct. 29, 1940, eff. Sept. 1, 1941. Amended by order of March 31, 1941, eff. Sept. 1, 1941.

Historical Notes

Source

Federal Rule 8(c), first sentence, unchanged.

Rule 95. Pleas of Payment

When a defendant shall desire to prove payment, he shall file with his plea an account stating distinctly the nature of such payment, and the several items thereof; failing to do so, he shall not be allowed to prove the same, unless it be so plainly and particularly described in the plea as to give the plaintiff full notice of the character thereof.

Oct. 29, 1940, eff. Sept. 1, 1941.

Historical Notes

Source

Vernon's Ann.Civ.St. art. 2014, omitting references to counterclaim and set-off.

Rule 96. No Discontinuance

Where the defendant has filed a counterclaim seeking affirmative relief, the plaintiff shall not be permitted by a discontinuance of his suit, to prejudice the right of the defendant to be heard on such counterclaim.

Oct. 29, 1940, eff. Sept. 1, 1941.

Historical Notes

Source

Vernon's Ann.Civ.St. art. 2016, unchanged.

Rule 97. Counterclaim and Cross-Claim

(a) Compulsory Counterclaims. A pleading shall state as a counterclaim any claim within the jurisdiction of the court, not the subject of a pending action, which at the time of filing the pleading the pleader has against any opposing party, if it arises out of the transaction or occurrence that is the subject matter of the opposing party's claim and does not require for its adjudication the presence of third parties of whom the court cannot acquire jurisdiction; provided, however, that a judgment based upon a settlement or compromise of a claim of one party to the transaction or occurrence prior to a disposition on the merits shall not operate as a bar to the continuation or assertion of the claims of any other party to the transaction or occurrence unless the latter has consented in writing that said judgment shall operate as a bar.

(b) Permissive Counterclaims. A pleading may state as a counterclaim any claim against an opposing party whether or not arising out of the transaction or occurrence that is the subject matter of the opposing party's claim.

(c) Counterclaim Exceeding Opposing Claim. A counterclaim may or may not diminish or defeat the recovery sought by the opposing party. It may claim relief exceeding in amount or different in kind from that sought in the pleading of the opposing party, so long as the subject matter is within the jurisdiction of the court.

(d) Counterclaim Maturing or Acquired After Pleading. A claim which either matured or was acquired by the pleader after filing his pleading may be presented as a counterclaim by amended pleading.

(e) Cross-Claim Against Co-Party. A pleading may state as a cross-claim any claim by one party against a co-party arising out of the transaction or occurrence that is the subject matter either of the original action or of a counterclaim therein. Such cross-claim may include a claim that the party against whom it is asserted is or may be liable to the cross-claimant for all or part of a claim asserted in the action again the cross-claimant.

(f) Additional Parties. Persons other than those made parties to the original action may be made parties to a third party action, counterclaim or cross-claim in accordance with the provisions of Rules 38, 39 and 40.

(g) Tort shall not be the subject of set-off or counterclaim against a contractual demand nor a contractual demand against tort unless it arises out of or is incident to or is connected with same.

(h) Separate Trials; Separate Judgments. If the court orders separate trials as provided in Rule 174, judgment on a counterclaim or cross-claim may be rendered when the court has jurisdiction so to do, even if the claims of the opposing party have been dismissed or otherwise disposed of.

Oct. 29, 1940, eff. Sept. 1, 1941. Amended by orders of March 31, 1941, eff. Sept. 1, 1941; July 21, 1970, eff. Jan. 1, 1971; Dec. 5, 1983, eff. April 1, 1984.

Historical Notes

Source

Federal Rule 13, modified as follows:

In subd. (a), "within the jurisdiction of the court" has been added;

In subd. (b), "whether or" has been added;

In subd. (c), "so long as the subject matter is within the jurisdiction of the court" has been added;

Subds. (d) and (f) of the federal rule, pertaining respectively to counterclaims against the United States and to omitted counterclaims, have been omitted, and the remaining provisions relettered accordingly.

In subd. (d), Federal Rule 13(e), "filing" has been substituted for "serving," "amended" has been substituted for "supplemental," and "with the permission of the court" has been deleted after "may".

Subd. (e) follows Federal Rule 13(g), unchanged.

Subd. (f), first sentence, follows Federal Rule 13(h), unchanged.

Subd. (g), pertaining to separate trial, follows Federal Rule 13(i) with minor textual change.

Rule 98. Supplemental Answers

The defendant's supplemental answers may contain special exceptions, general denial, and the allegations of new matter not before alleged by him, in reply to that which has been alleged by the plaintiff.

Oct. 29, 1940, eff. Sept. 1, 1941. Amended by order of March 31, 1941, eff. Sept. 1, 1941.

Historical Notes

Source

District and County Court Rule 8.

SECTION 5. CITATION

Rule 99. Issuance and Form of Citation

a. Issuance. Upon the filing of the petition, the clerk, when requested, shall forthwith issue a citation and deliver the citation as directed by the requesting party. The party requesting citation shall be responsible for obtaining service of the citation and a copy of the petition. Upon request, separate or additional citations shall be issued by the clerk. The clerk must retain a copy of the citation in the court's file.

b. Form. The citation shall (1) be styled "The State of Texas," (2) be signed by the clerk under seal of court, (3) contain name and location of the court, (4) show date of filing of the petition, (5) show date of issuance of citation, (6) show file number, (7) show names of parties, (8) be directed to the defendant, (9) show the name and address of attorney for plaintiff, otherwise the address of plaintiff, (10) contain the time within which these rules require the defendant to file a written answer with the clerk who issued citation, (11) contain address of the clerk, and (12) shall notify the defendant that in case of failure of defendant to file an answer, judgment by default may be rendered for the relief demanded in the petition. The citation shall direct the defendant to file a written answer to the plaintiff's petition on or before 10:00 a.m. on the Monday next after the expiration of twenty days after the date of service thereof. The requirement of subsections 10 and 12 of this section shall be in the form set forth in section c of this rule.

c. Notice. The citation shall include the following notice to the defendant: "You have been sued. You may employ an attorney. If you or your attorney do not file a written answer with the clerk who issued this citation by 10:00 a.m. on the Monday next following the expiration of twenty days after you were served this citation and petition, a default judgment may be taken against you."

d. Copies. The party filing any pleading upon which citation is to be issued and served shall furnish the clerk with a sufficient number of copies thereof for use in serving the parties to be served, and when copies are so furnished the clerk shall make no charge for the copies.

Oct. 29, 1940, eff. Sept. 1, 1941. Amended by orders of Oct. 10, 1945, eff. Feb. 1, 1946; July 15, 1987, eff. Jan. 1, 1988; Dec. 12, 2011, eff. Jan. 1, 2012.

Historical Notes

Source

Vernon's Ann.Civ.St. art. 2021, modified to authorize clerk to issue as many citations as plaintiff requests, without delay of securing a return on any prior citation.

2011 Amendment

The order dated December 12, 2011, in subsec. a. added the last sentence.

Rules 100 to 102. Repealed by Order of July 15, 1987, eff. Jan. 1, 1988

Historical Notes

Former Rules 100 to 102, which related to other process, requisites of the citation, and territorial limits of effective service, were added by order of Oct. 29, 1940.

Rule 103. Who May Serve

Process—including citation and other notices, writs, orders, and other papers issued by the court—may be served anywhere by (1) any sheriff or constable or other person authorized by law, (2) any person authorized by law or by written order of the court who is not less than eighteen years of age, or (3) any person certified under order of the Supreme Court. Service by registered or certified mail and citation by publication must, if requested, be made by the clerk of the court in which the case is pending. But no person who is a party to or interested in the outcome of a suit may serve any process in that suit, and, unless otherwise authorized by a written court order, only a sheriff or constable may serve a citation in an action of forcible entry and detainer, a writ that requires the actual taking of possession of a person, property or thing, or process requiring that an enforcement action be physically enforced by the person delivering the process. The order authorizing a person to serve process may be made without written motion and no fee may be imposed for issuance of such order.

Oct. 29, 1940, eff. Sept. 1, 1941. Amended by orders of June 10, 1980, eff. Jan. 1, 1981; July 15, 1987, eff. Jan. 1, 1988; June 29, 2005, eff. July 1, 2005.

Comment—1988

The amendment makes clear that the courts are permitted to authorize persons other than Sheriffs or Constables to serve Citation. Further, Sheriffs or Constables are not restricted to service in their county. The last sentence is added to avoid the necessity of motions and fees.

Comment—2005

The rule is amended to include among the persons authorized to effect service those who meet certification requirements promulgated by the Supreme Court and to prohibit private individuals from serving certain types of process unless, in rare circumstances, a court authorizes an individual to do so.

Historical Notes

2007 Publisher's Note:

Another Supreme Court Order of September 20, 2007 provides: "In addition to the civil process service courses named in Misc. Docket No. 06-9142, and in accordance with the standards described in paragraph seven of that order, the following courses are approved for training to achieve certification by the Process Server Review Board to serve process in any state court in Texas as provided by Tex. R. Civ. P. 103 as amended effective July 1, 2005:

"the 'Texas Civil Process' course offered by the Process Servers Network of Texas; and

"the 'Texas Process Server' course offered by Neff and Neff Associates."

Source

New rule.

Rule 104. Repealed by order of July 15, 1987, eff. Jan. 1, 1988

Historical Notes

Former Rule 104, which related to situations where there is no officer qualified to serve process, was added by order of Oct. 29, 1940.

See, now, Rule 103.

Rule 105. Duty of Officer or Person Receiving

The officer or authorized person to whom process is delivered shall endorse thereon the day and hour on which he received it, and shall execute and return the same without delay.

Oct. 29, 1940, eff. Sept. 1, 1941. Amended by orders of July 11, 1978, eff. Jan. 1, 1978; July 15, 1987, eff. Jan. 1, 1988.

Historical Notes

Source

Vernon's Ann.Civ.St. art. 2025, unchanged.

Rule 106. Method of Service

(a) Unless the citation or an order of the court otherwise directs, the citation shall be served by any person authorized by Rule 103 by

(1) delivering to the defendant, in person, a true copy of the citation with the date of delivery endorsed thereon with a copy of the petition attached thereto, or

(2) mailing to the defendant by registered or certified mail, return receipt requested, a true copy of the citation with a copy of the petition attached thereto.

(b) Upon motion supported by affidavit stating the location of the defendant's usual place of business or usual place of abode or other place where the defendant can probably be found and stating specifically the facts showing that service has been attempted under either (a)(1) or (a)(2) at the location named in such affidavit but has not been successful, the court may authorize service

(1) by leaving a true copy of the citation, with a copy of the petition attached, with anyone over sixteen years of age at the location specified in such affidavit, or

(2) in any other manner that the affidavit or other evidence before the court shows will be reasonably effective to give the defendant notice of the suit.

Oct. 29, 1940, eff. Sept. 1, 1941. Amended by orders of Aug. 18, 1947, eff. Dec. 31, 1947; July 22, 1975, eff. Jan. 1, 1976; July 11, 1977, eff. Jan. 1, 1978; June 10, 1980, eff. Jan. 1, 1981; July 15, 1987, eff. Jan. 1, 1988; April 24, 1990, eff. Sept. 1, 1990.

Comment—1988

Conforms to amendment to Rule 103.

Historical Notes

Source

Vernon's Ann.Civ.St. art. 2026, modified to require endorsement of date of delivery, and by deleting requirement that copy of petition be certified.

Rule 107. Return of Service

(a) The officer or authorized person executing the citation must complete a return of service. The return may, but need not, be endorsed on or attached to the citation.

(b) The return, together with any document to which it is attached, must include the following information:

(1) the cause number and case name;

(2) the court in which the case is filed;

(3) a description of what was served;

(4) the date and time the process was received for service;

(5) the person or entity served;

(6) the address served;

(7) the date of service or attempted service;

(8) the manner of delivery of service or attempted service;

(9) the name of the person who served or attempted to serve the process;

(10) if the person named in (9) is a process server certified under order of the Supreme Court, his or her identification number and the expiration date of his or her certification; and

(11) any other information required by rule or law.

(c) When the citation was served by registered or certified mail as authorized by Rule 106, the return by the officer or authorized person must also contain the return receipt with the addressee's signature.

(d) When the officer or authorized person has not served the citation, the return shall show the diligence used by the officer or authorized person to execute the same and the cause of failure to execute it, and where the defendant is to be found, if ascertainable.

(e) The officer or authorized person who serves or attempts to serve a citation must sign the return. If the return is signed by a person other than a sheriff, constable, or the clerk of the court, the return must either be verified or be signed under penalty of perjury. A return signed under penalty of perjury must contain the statement below in substantially the following form:

"My name is __________ (First) __________ (Middle) __________ (Last), my date of birth is __________, and my address is __________ (Street), __________ (City), __________ (State), __________ (Zip Code), and __________ (Country). I declare under penalty of perjury that the foregoing is true and correct.

Executed in __________ County, State of __________, on the ___ day of __________ (Month), ___ (Year).

____

Declarant"

(f) Where citation is executed by an alternative method as authorized by Rule 106, proof of service shall be made in the manner ordered by the court.

(g) The return and any document to which it is attached must be filed with the court and may be filed electronically or by facsimile, if those methods of filing are available.

(h) No default judgment shall be granted in any cause until proof of service as provided by this rule or by Rules 108 or 108a, or as ordered by the court in the event citation is executed by an alternative method under Rule 106, shall have been on file with the clerk of the court ten days, exclusive of the day of filing and the day of judgment.

Oct. 29, 1940, eff. Sept. 1, 1941. Amended by orders of July 11, 1977, eff. Jan. 1, 1978; June 10, 1980, eff. Jan. 1, 1981; July 15, 1987, eff. Jan. 1, 1988; April 24, 1990, eff. Sept. 1, 1990; Dec. 12, 2011, eff. Jan. 1, 2012.

Comment—1988

Amendments are made to conform to changes in Rule 103.

Comment—1990

To state more directly that a default judgment can be obtained when the defendant has been served with process in a foreign country pursuant to the provisions of Rules 108 or 108a.

Historical Notes

Source

Vernon's Ann.Civ.St. arts. 2034, 2036.

Rule 108. Service in Another State

Where the defendant is absent from the State, or is a nonresident of the State, the form of notice to such defendant of the institution of the suit shall be the same as prescribed for citation to a resident defendant; and such notice may be served by any disinterested person who is not less than eighteen years of age, in the same manner as provided in Rule 106 hereof. The return of service in such cases shall be completed in accordance with Rule 107. A defendant served with such notice shall be required to appear and answer in the same manner and time and under the same penalties as if he had been personally served with a citation within this State to the full extent that he may be required to appear and answer under the Constitution of the United States in an action either in rem or in personam.

Oct. 29, 1940, eff. Sept. 1, 1941. Amended by order of July 22, 1975, eff. Jan. 1, 1976; Dec. 12, 2011, eff. Jan. 1, 2012.

Historical Notes

2011 Amendment

The order dated December 12, 2011 substituted "who is not less than eighteen years of age," for "competent to make oath of the fact", after "in such cases" deleted "shall be endorsed on or attached to the original notice, and", after "in accordance with" deleted "the form provided in", and after "Rule 107" deleted ", and be signed and sworn to by the party making such service before some officer authorized by the laws of this State to take affidavits, under the hand and official seal of such officer".

Source

Vernon's Ann.Civ.St. arts. 2037, 2038, changed to permit same form of citation and method of service as provided for resident defendants.

Rule 108a. Service of Process in Foreign Countries

(1) Manner. Service of process may be effected upon a party in a foreign country if service of the citation and petition is made: (a) in the manner prescribed by the law of the foreign country for service in that country in an action in any of its courts of general jurisdiction; or (b) as directed by the foreign authority in response to a letter rogatory or a letter of request; or (c) in the manner provided by Rule 106; or (d) pursuant to the terms and provisions of any applicable treaty or convention; or (e) by diplomatic or consular officials when authorized by the United States Department of State; or (f) by any other means directed by the court that is not prohibited by the law of the country where service is to be made. The method for service of process in a foreign country must be reasonably calculated, under all of the circumstances, to give actual notice of the proceedings to the defendant in time to answer and defend. A defendant served with process under this rule shall be required to appear and answer in the same manner and time and under the same penalties as if he had been personally served with citation within this state to the full extent that he may be required to appear and answer under the Constitution of the United States or under any applicable convention or treaty in an action either in rem or in personam.

(2) Return. Proof of service may be made as prescribed by the law of the foreign country, by order of the court, by Rule 107, or by a method provided in any applicable treaty or convention.

Dec. 5, 1983, eff. April 1, 1984.

Rule 109. Citation by Publication

When a party to a suit, his agent or attorney, shall make oath that the residence of any party defendant is unknown to affiant, and to such party when the affidavit is made by his agent or attorney, or that such defendant is a transient person, and that after due diligence such party and the affiant have been unable to locate the whereabouts of such defendant, or that such defendant is absent from or is a nonresident of the State, and that the party applying for the citation has attempted to obtain personal service of nonresident notice as provided for in Rule 108, but has been unable to do so, the clerk shall issue citation for such defendant for service by publication. In such cases it shall be the duty of the court trying the case to inquire into the sufficiency of the diligence exercised in attempting to ascertain the residence or whereabouts of the defendant or to obtain service of nonresident notice, as the case may be, before granting any judgment on such service.

Oct. 29, 1940, eff. Sept. 1, 1941. Amended by orders of Oct. 10, 1945, eff. Feb. 1, 1946; July 22, 1975, eff. Jan. 1, 1976; Dec. 5, 1983, eff. April 1, 1984.

Historical Notes

Source

Vernon's Ann.Civ.St. art. 2039, with minor textual change.

Rule 109a. Other Substituted Service

Whenever citation by publication is authorized, the court may, on motion, prescribe a different method of substituted service, if the court finds, and so recites in its order, that the method so prescribed would be as likely as publication to give defendant actual notice. When such method of substituted service is authorized, the return of the officer executing the citation shall state particularly the manner in which service is accomplished, and shall attach any return receipt, returned mail, or other evidence showing the result of such service. Failure of defendant to respond to such citation shall not render the service invalid. When such substituted service has been obtained and the defendant has not appeared, the provisions of Rules 244 and 329 shall apply as if citation had been served by publication.

July 22, 1975, eff. Jan. 1, 1976.

Rule 110. Effect of Rules on Other Statutes

Where by statute or these rules citation by publication is authorized and the statute or rules do not specify the requisites of such citation or the method of service thereof, or where they direct that such citation be issued or served as in other civil actions, the provisions of these rules shall govern. Where, however, the statute authorizing citation by publication provides expressly for requisites of such citation or service thereof, or both, differing from the provisions of Rules 114, 115, and 116, these rules shall not govern, but the special statutory procedure shall continue in force; provided, however, that Rule 117a shall control with respect to citation in tax suits.

Oct. 29, 1940, eff. Sept. 1, 1941. Amended by order of Aug. 18, 1947, eff. Dec. 31, 1947.

Historical Notes

Source

New rule.

Rule 111. Citation by Publication in Action Against Unknown Heirs or Stockholders of Defunct Corporations

If the plaintiff, his agent, or attorney, shall make oath that the names of the heirs or stockholders against whom an action is authorized by Section 17.004, Civil Practice and Remedies Code, are unknown to the affiant, the clerk shall issue a citation for service by publication. Such citation shall be addressed to the defendants by a concise description of their classification, as "the Unknown Heirs of A.B., deceased," or "Unknown Stockholders of ______ Corporation," as the case may be, and shall contain the other requisites prescribed in Rules 114 and 115 and shall be served as provided by Rule 116.

Oct. 29, 1940, eff. Sept. 1, 1941. Amended by order of July 15, 1987, eff. Jan. 1, 1988.

Historical Notes

Source

Vernon's Ann.Civ.St. art. 2040, last two sentences, revised.

Rule 112. Parties to Actions Against Unknown Owners or Claimants of Interest in Land

In suits authorized by Section 17.005, Civil Practice and Remedies Code, all persons claiming under such conveyance whose names are known to plaintiff shall be made parties by name and cited to appear, in the manner now provided by law as in other suits; all other persons claiming any interest in such land under such conveyance may be made parties to the suit and cited by publication under the designation "all persons claiming any title or interest in land under deed heretofore given to ___ of ___ as grantee" (inserting in the blanks the name and residence of grantee as given in such conveyance). It shall be permissible to join in one suit all persons claiming under two or more conveyances affecting title to the same tract of land.

Oct. 29, 1940, eff. Sept. 1, 1941. Amended by order of July 15, 1987, eff. Jan. 1, 1988.

Historical Notes

Source

Vernon's Ann.Civ.St. art. 2041a, § 2 and last sentence of § 3, unchanged.

Rule 113. Citation by Publication in Actions Against Unknown Owners or Claimants of Interest in Land

In suits authorized by Section 17.005, Civil Practice and Remedies Code, plaintiff, his agent or attorney shall make and file with the clerk of the court an affidavit, stating

(a) the name of the grantee as set out in the conveyance constituting source of title of defendants, and

(b) stating that affiant does not know the names of any persons claiming title or interest under such conveyance other than as stated in plaintiff's petition and

(c) if the conveyance is to a company or association name as grantee, further stating whether grantee is incorporated or unincorporated, if such fact is known, and if such fact is unknown, so stating.

Said clerk shall thereupon issue a citation for service upon all persons claiming any title or interest in such land under such conveyance. The citation in such cases shall contain the requisites and be served in the manner provided by Rules 114, 115 and 116.

Oct. 29, 1940, eff. Sept. 1, 1941. Amended by orders of July 20, 1954, eff. Jan. 1, 1955; July 15, 1987, eff. Jan. 1, 1988; April 24, 1990, eff. Sept. 1, 1990.

Historical Notes

Source

Vernon's Ann.Civ.St. art. 2041a, § 3, except last sentence which has been incorporated in rule 112.

Rule 114. Citation by Publication; Requisites

Where citation by publication is authorized by these rules, the citation shall contain the requisites prescribed by Rules 15 and 99, in so far as they are not inconsistent herewith, provided that no copy of the plaintiff's petition shall accompany this citation, and the citation shall be styled "The State of Texas" and shall be directed to the defendant or defendants by name, if their names are known, or to the defendant or defendants as designated in the petition, if unknown, or such other classification as may be fixed by any statute or by these rules. Where there are two or more defendants or classes of defendants to be served by publication, the citation may be directed to all of them by name and classification, so that service may be completed by publication of the one citation for the required number of times. The citation shall contain the names of the parties, a brief statement of the nature of the suit (which need not contain the details and particulars of the claim) a description of any property involved and of the interest of the named or unknown defendant or defendants, and, where the suit involves land, the requisites of Rule 115. If issued from the district or county court, the citation shall command such parties to appear and answer at or before 10 o'clock a.m. of the first Monday after the expiration of 42 days from the date of issuance thereof, specifying the day of the week, the day of the month, and the time of day the defendant is required to answer. If issued from the justice of the peace court, such citation shall command such parties to appear and answer on or before the first day of the first term of court which convenes after the expiration of 42 days from the date of issue thereof, specifying the day of the week, and the day of the month, that such term will meet.

Oct. 29, 1940, eff. Sept. 1, 1941. Amended by orders of Sept. 20, 1941, eff. Dec. 31, 1941; Dec. 16, 1987, eff. Jan. 1, 1988.

Historical Notes

Source

Vernon's Ann.Civ.St. arts. 2041, 2092(6).

Rule 115. Form of Published Citation in Actions Involving Land

In citations by publication involving land, it shall be sufficient in making the brief statement of the claim in such citation to state the kind of suit, the number of acres of land involved in the suit, or the number of the lot and block, or any other plat description that may be of record if the land is situated in a city or town, the survey on which and the county in which the land is situated, and any special pleas which are relied upon in such suit.

Oct. 29, 1940, eff. Sept. 1, 1941.

Historical Notes

Source

Vernon's Ann.Civ.St. art. 2041, with minor textual change.

Rule 116. Service of Citation by Publication

The citation, when issued, shall be served by the sheriff or any constable of any county of the State of Texas or by the clerk of the court in which the case is pending, by having the same published once each week for four (4) consecutive weeks, the first publication to be at least twenty-eight (28) days before the return day of the citation. In all suits which do not involve the title to land or the partition of real estate, such publication shall be made in the county where the suit is pending, if there be a newspaper published in said county, but if not, then in an adjoining county where a newspaper is published. In all suits which involve the title to land or partition of real estate, such publication shall be made in the county where the land, or a portion thereof, is situated, if there be a newspaper in such county, but if not, then in an adjoining county to the county where the land or a part thereof is situated, where a newspaper is published.

Oct. 29, 1940, eff. Sept. 1, 1941. Amended by order of Dec. 5, 1983, eff. April 1, 1984.

Historical Notes

Source

Vernon's Ann.Civ.St. arts. 2039, 2042, 2092(6).

Rule 117. Return of Citation by Publication

The return of the officer executing such citation shall show how and when the citation was executed, specifying the dates of such publication, be signed by him officially and shall be accompanied by a printed copy of such publication.

Oct. 29, 1940, eff. Sept. 1, 1941. Amended by order of Dec. 12, 2011, eff. Jan. 1, 2012.

Historical Notes

2011 Amendment

The order dated December 12, 2011, after "such citation shall" deleted "be indorsed or attached to the same, and".

Source

Vernon's Ann.Civ.St. art. 2043, unchanged.

Rule 117a. Citation in Suits for Delinquent Ad Valorem Taxes

In all suits for collection of delinquent ad valorem taxes, the rules of civil procedure governing issuance and service of citation shall control the issuance and service of citation therein, except as herein otherwise specially provided.

1. Personal Service: Owner and Residence Known, Within State:

Where any defendant in a tax suit is a resident of the State of Texas and is not subject to citation by publication under subdivision 3 below, the process shall conform substantially to the form hereinafter set out for personal service and shall contain the essential elements and be served and returned and otherwise regulated by the provisions of Rules 99 to 107, inclusive.

2. Personal Service: Owner and Residence Known, Out of State:

Where any such defendant is absent from the State or is a non-resident of the State and is not subject to citation by publication under subdivision 3 below, the process shall conform substantially to the form hereinafter set out for personal service and shall contain the essential elements and be served and returned and otherwise regulated by the provisions of Rule 108.

3. Service by Publication: Nonresident, Absent from State, Transient, Name Unknown, Residence Unknown, Owner Unknown, Heirs Unknown, Corporate Officers, Trustees, Receivers or Stockholders Unknown, Any Other Unknown Persons Owing or Claiming or Having an Interest:

Where any defendant in a tax suit is a nonresident of the State, or is absent from the State, or is a transient person, or the name or the residence of any owner of any interest in any property upon which a tax lien is sought to be foreclosed, is unknown to the attorney requesting the issuance of process or filing the suit for the taxing unit, and such attorney shall make affidavit that such defendant is a nonresident of the State, or is absent from the State, or is a transient person, or that the name or residence of such owner is unknown and cannot be ascertained after diligent inquiry, each such person in every such class above mentioned, together with any and all other persons, including adverse claimants, owning or claiming or having any legal or equitable interest in or lien upon such property, may be cited by publication. All unknown owners of any interest in any property upon which any taxing unit seeks to foreclose a lien for taxes, including stockholders of corporations—defunct or otherwise—their successors, heirs, and assigns, may be joined in such suit under the designation of "unknown owners" and citation be had upon them as such; provided, however, that record owners of such property or of any apparent interest therein, including, without limitation, record lien holders, shall not be included in the designation of "unknown owners"; and provided further that where any record owner has rendered the property involved within five years before the tax suit is filed, citation on such record owner may not be had by publication or posting unless citation for personal service has been issued as to such record owner, with a notation thereon setting forth the same address as is contained on the rendition sheet made within such five years, and the sheriff or other person to whom citation has been delivered makes his return thereon that he is unable to locate the defendant. Where any attorney filing a tax suit for a taxing unit, or requesting the issuance of process in such suit, shall make affidavit that a corporation is the record owner of any interest in any property upon which a tax lien is sought to be foreclosed, and that he does not know, and after diligent inquiry has been unable to ascertain, the location of the place of business, if any, of such corporation, or the name or place of residence of any officer of such corporation upon whom personal service may be had, such corporation may be cited by publication as herein provided. All defendants of the classes enumerated above may be joined in the same citation by publication.

An affidavit which complies with the foregoing requirements therefor shall be sufficient basis for the citation above mentioned in connection with it but shall be held to be made upon the criminal responsibility of affiant.

Such citation by publication shall be directed to the defendants by names or by designation as hereinabove provided, and shall be issued and signed by the clerk of the court in which such tax suit is pending. It shall be sufficient if it states the file number and style of the case, the date of the filing of the petition, the names of all parties by name or by designation as hereinabove provided, and the court in which the suit is pending; shall command such parties to appear and defend such suit at or before 10 o'clock a.m. of the first Monday after the expiration of forty-two days from the date of the issuance thereof, specifying such date when such parties are required to answer; shall state the place of holding the court, the nature of the suit, and the date of the issuance of the citation; and shall be signed and sealed by the clerk.

The citation shall be published in the English language one time a week for two weeks in some newspaper published in the county in which the property is located, which newspaper must have been in general circulation for at least one year immediately prior to the first publication and shall in every respect answer the requirements of the law applicable to newspapers which are employed for such a purpose, the first publication to be not less than twenty-eight days prior to the return day fixed in the citation; and the affidavit of the editor or publisher of the newspaper giving the date of publication, together with a printed copy of the citation as published, shall constitute sufficient proof of due publication when returned and filed in court. If there is no newspaper published in the county, then the publication may be made in a newspaper in an adjoining county, which newspaper shall in every respect answer the requirements of the law applicable to newspapers which are employed for such a purpose. The maximum fee for publishing the citation shall be the lowest published word or line rate of that newspaper for classified advertising. If the publication of the citation cannot be had for this fee, chargeable as costs and payable upon sale of the property, as provided by law, and this fact is supported by the affidavit of the attorney for the plaintiff or the attorney requesting the issuance of the process, then service of the citation may be made by posting a copy at the courthouse door of the county in which the suit is pending, the citation to be posted at least twenty-eight days prior to the return day fixed in the citation. Proof of the posting of the citation shall be made by affidavit of the attorney for the plaintiff, or of the person posting it. When citation is served as here provided it shall be sufficient, and no other form of citation or notice to the named defendants therein shall be necessary.

4. Citation in Tax Suits: General Provisions:

Any process authorized by this rule may issue jointly in behalf of all taxing units who are plaintiffs or intervenors in any tax suit. The statement of the nature of the suit, to be set out in the citation, shall be sufficient if it contains a brief general description of the property upon which the taxes are due and the amount of such taxes, exclusive of interest, penalties, and costs, and shall state, in substance, that in such suit the plaintiff and all other taxing units who may set up their claims therein seek recovery of the delinquent ad valorem taxes due on said property, and the (establishment and foreclosure) of liens, if any, securing the payment of same, as provided by law; that in addition to the taxes all interest, penalties, and costs allowed by law up to and including the day of judgment are included in the suit; and that all parties to the suit, including plaintiff, defendants, and intervenors, shall take notice that claims for any taxes on said property becoming delinquent subsequent to the filing of the suit and up to the day of judgment, together with all interest, penalties, and costs allowed by law thereon, may, upon requests therefor, be recovered therein without further citation or notice to any parties thereto. Such citation need not be accompanied by a copy of plaintiff's petition and no such copy need be served. Such citation shall also show the names of all taxing units which assess and collect taxes on said property not made parties to such suit, and shall contain, in substance, a recitation that each party to such suit shall take notice of, and plead and answer to, all claims and pleadings then on file or thereafter filed in said cause by all other parties therein, or who may intervene therein and set up their respective tax claims against said property. After citation or notice has been given on behalf of any plaintiff or intervenor taxing unit, the court shall have jurisdiction to hear and determine the tax claims of all taxing units who are parties plaintiff, intervenor or defendant at the time such process is issued and of all taxing units intervening after such process is issued, not only for the taxes, interest, penalties, and costs which may be due on said property at the time the suit is filed, but those becoming delinquent thereon at any time thereafter up to and including the day of judgment, without the necessity of further citation or notice to any party to said suit; and any taxing unit having a tax claim against said property may, by answer or intervention, set up and have determined its tax claim without the necessity of further citation or notice to any parties to such suit.

5. Form of Citation by Publication or Posting:

The form of citation by publication or posting shall be sufficient if it is in substantially the following form, with proper changes to make the same applicable to personal property, where necessary, and if the suit includes or is for the recovery of taxes assessed on personal property, a general description of such personal property shall be sufficient:

THE STATE OF TEXAS)
COUNTY OF ________)

In the name and by the authority of the State of Texas

Notice is hereby given as follows:

To ____

____

and any and all other persons, including adverse claimants, owning or having or claiming any legal or equitable interest in or lien upon the following described property delinquent to Plaintiff herein, for taxes, to-wit:

____

____

Which said property is delinquent to Plaintiff for taxes in the following amounts:

$________, exclusive of interest, penalties, and costs, and there is included in this suit in addition to the taxes all said interest, penalties, and costs thereon, allowed by law up to and including the day of judgment herein.

You are hereby notified that suit has been brought by ________ as Plaintiffs, against ________ as Defendants, by petition filed on the ___ day of ________, 19___, in a certain suit styled ________ v. ________ for collection of the taxes on said property and that said suit is now pending in the District Court of ________ County, Texas, ___ Judicial District, and the file number of said suit is ________, that the names of all taxing units which assess and collect taxes on the property hereinabove described, not made parties to this suit, are ________.

Plaintiff and all other taxing units who may set up their tax claims herein seek recovery of delinquent ad valorem taxes on the property hereinabove described, and in addition to the taxes all interest, penalties, and costs allowed by law thereon up to and including the day of judgment herein, and the establishment and foreclosure of liens, if any, securing the payment of same, as provided by law.

All parties to this suit, including plaintiff, defendants, and intervenors, shall take notice that claims not only for any taxes which were delinquent on said property at the time this suit was filed but all taxes becoming delinquent thereon at any time thereafter up to the day of judgment, including all interest, penalties, and costs allowed by law thereon, may, upon request therefor, be recovered herein without further citation or notice to any parties herein, and all said parties shall take notice of and plead and answer to all claims and pleadings now on file and which may hereafter be filed in said cause by all other parties herein, and all of those taxing units above named who may intervene herein and set up their respective tax claims against said property.

You are hereby commanded to appear and defend such suit on the first Monday after the expiration of forty-two (42) days from and after the date of issuance hereof, the same being the ________ day of ________, A.D., 19___ (which is the return day of such citation), before the honorable District Court of

__________ County, Texas, to be held at the courthouse thereof, then and there to show cause why judgment shall not be rendered for such taxes, penalties, interest, and costs, and condemning said property and ordering foreclosure of the constitutional and statutory tax liens thereon for taxes due the plaintiff and the taxing units parties hereto, and those who may intervene herein, together with all interest, penalties, and costs allowed by law up to and including the day of judgment herein, and all costs of this suit.

Issued and given under my hand and seal of said court in the City of __________, __________ County, Texas, this __________ day of __________, A.D., 19___.

____

Clerk of the District Court.
__________ County, Texas,
__________ Judicial District.

6. Form of Citation by Personal Service in or out of State:

The form of citation for personal service shall be sufficient if it is in substantially the following form, with proper changes to make the same applicable to personal property, where necessary, and if the suit includes or is for the recovery of taxes assessed on personal property, a general description of such personal property shall be sufficient:

THE STATE OF TEXAS

To __________, Defendant ___,

GREETING:

YOU ARE HEREBY COMMANDED to appear and answer before the Honorable District Court, __________ Judicial District, __________ County, Texas, at the Courthouse of said county in __________, Texas, at or before 10 o'clock a. m. of the Monday next after the expiration of 20 days from the date of service of this citation, then and there to answer the petition of __________, Plaintiff, filed in said Court on the ___ day of __________, A.D., 19___, against __________, Defendant ___, said suit being number __________ on the docket of said Court, the nature of which demand is a suit to collect delinquent ad valorem taxes on the property hereinafter described.

The amount of taxes due Plaintiff, exclusive of interest, penalties, and costs, is the sum of $__________, said property being described as follows, to-wit: __________

____

The names of all taxing units which assess and collect taxes on said property, not made parties to this suit, are:

____

Plaintiff and all other taxing units who may set up their tax claims herein seek recovery of delinquent ad valorem taxes on the property hereinabove described, and in addition to the taxes all interest, penalties, and costs allowed by law thereon up to and including the day of judgment herein, and the establishment and foreclosure of liens securing the payment of same, as provided by law.

All parties to this suit, including plaintiff, defendants, and intervenors, shall take notice that claims not only for any taxes which were delinquent on said property at the time this suit was filed but all taxes becoming delinquent thereon at any time thereafter up to the day of judgment, including all interest, penalties, and costs allowed by law thereon, may, upon request therefor, be recovered herein without further citation or notice to any parties herein, and all said parties shall take notice of and plead and answer to all claims and pleadings now on file and which may hereafter be filed in this cause by all other parties hereto, and by all of those taxing units above named, who may intervene herein and set up their respective tax claims against said property.

If this citation is not served within 90 days after the date of its issuance, it shall be returned unserved.

The officer executing this return shall promptly serve the same according to the requirements of law and the mandates hereof and make due return as the law directs.

Issued and given under my hand and seal of said Court at __________, Texas this the __________ day of __________, A.D., 19___.

____

Clerk of the District Court of
__________ County, Texas.
By __________, Deputy.

Aug. 18, 1947, eff. Dec. 31, 1947. Amended by orders of May 4, 1948, eff. Oct. 1, 1948; July 17, 1950, eff. Dec. 1, 1950; July 15, 1987, eff. Jan. 1, 1988.

Comment—1988

This amendment updates the fee schedule for service of citation of publications to an acceptable fee level for both litigants and the publications.

Rule 118. Amendment

At any time in its discretion and upon such notice and on such terms as it deems just, the court may allow any process or proof of service thereof to be amended, unless it clearly appears that material prejudice would result to the substantial rights of the party against whom the process issued.

Oct. 29, 1940, eff. Sept. 1, 1941.

Historical Notes

Source

Federal Rule 4(h), modified by adding "and upon such notice" and by minor textual change.

Rule 119. Acceptance of Service

The defendant may accept service of process, or waive the issuance or service thereof by a written memorandum signed by him, or by his duly authorized agent or attorney, after suit is brought, sworn to before a proper officer other than an attorney in the case, and filed among the papers of the cause, and such waiver or acceptance shall have the same force and effect as if the citation had been issued and served as provided by law. The party signing such memorandum shall be delivered a copy of plaintiff's petition, and the receipt of the same shall be acknowledged in such memorandum. In every divorce action such memorandum shall also include the defendant's mailing address.

Oct. 29, 1940, eff. Sept. 1, 1941. Amended by orders of Sept. 20, 1941, eff. Dec. 31, 1941; July 20, 1954, eff. Jan. 1, 1955; July 26, 1960, eff. Jan. 1, 1961.

Historical Notes

Source

Vernon's Ann.Civ.St. art. 2045, adding "sworn to before a proper officer."

Rule 119a. Copy of Decree

The district clerk shall forthwith mail a certified copy of the final divorce decree or order of dismissal to the party signing a memorandum waiving issuance or service of process. Such divorce decree or order of dismissal shall be mailed to the signer of the memorandum at the address stated in such memorandum or to the office of his attorney of record.

July 20, 1954, eff. Jan. 1, 1955.

Rule 120. Entering Appearance

The defendant may, in person, or by attorney, or by his duly authorized agent, enter an appearance in open court. Such appearance shall be noted by the judge upon his docket and entered in the minutes, and shall have the same force and effect as if the citation had been duly issued and served as provided by law.

Oct. 29, 1940, eff. Sept. 1, 1941.

Historical Notes

Source

Vernon's Ann.Civ.St. art. 2046, unchanged.

Rule 120a. Special Appearance

1. Notwithstanding the provisions of Rules 121, 122 and 123, a special appearance may be made by any party either in person or by attorney for the purpose of objecting to the jurisdiction of the court over the person or property of the defendant on the ground that such party or property is not amenable to process issued by the courts of this State. A special appearance may be made as to an entire proceeding or as to any severable claim involved therein. Such special appearance shall be made by sworn motion filed prior to motion to transfer venue or any other plea, pleading or motion; provided however, that a motion to transfer venue and any other plea, pleading, or motion may be contained in the same instrument or filed subsequent thereto without waiver of such special appearance; and may be amended to cure defects. The issuance of process for witnesses, the taking of depositions, the serving of requests for admissions, and the use of discovery processes, shall not constitute a waiver of such special appearance. Every appearance, prior to judgment, not in compliance with this rule is a general appearance.

2. Any motion to challenge the jurisdiction provided for herein shall be heard and determined before a motion to transfer venue or any other plea or pleading may be heard. No determination of any issue of fact in connection with the objection to jurisdiction is a determination of the merits of the case or any aspect thereof.

3. The court shall determine the special appearance on the basis of the pleadings, any stipulations made by and between the parties, such affidavits and attachments as may be filed by the parties, the results of discovery processes, and any oral testimony. The affidavits, if any, shall be served at least seven days before the hearing, shall be made on personal knowledge, shall set forth specific facts as would be admissible in evidence, and shall show affirmatively that the affiant is competent to testify.

Should it appear from the affidavits of a party opposing the motion that he cannot for reasons stated present by affidavit facts essential to justify his opposition, the court may order a continuance to permit affidavits to be obtained or depositions to be taken or discovery to be had or may make such other order as is just.

Should it appear to the satisfaction of the court at any time that any of such affidavits are presented in violation of Rule 13, the court shall impose sanctions in accordance with that rule.

4. If the court sustains the objection to jurisdiction, an appropriate order shall be entered. If the objection to jurisdiction is overruled, the objecting party may thereafter appear generally for any purpose. Any such special appearance or such general appearance shall not be deemed a waiver of the objection to jurisdiction when the objecting party or

subject matter is not amenable to process issued by the courts of this State.

April 12, 1962, eff. Sept. 1, 1962. Amended by orders of July 22, 1975, eff. Jan. 1, 1976; June 15, 1983, eff. Sept. 1, 1983; April 24, 1990, eff. Sept. 1, 1990.

Comment—1990

To provide for proof by affidavit at special appearance hearings, with safeguards to responding parties. These amendments preserve Texas prior practice to place the burden of proof on the party contesting jurisdiction.

Rule 121. Answer is Appearance

An answer shall constitute an appearance of the defendant so as to dispense with the necessity for the issuance or service of citation upon him.

Oct. 29, 1940, eff. Sept. 1, 1941.

Historical Notes

Source

Vernon's Ann.Civ.St. art. 2047, unchanged.

Rule 122. Constructive Appearance

If the citation or service thereof is quashed on motion of the defendant, such defendant shall be deemed to have entered his appearance at ten o'clock a. m. on the Monday next after the expiration of twenty (20) days after the day on which the citation or service is quashed, and such defendant shall be deemed to have been duly served so as to require him to appear and answer at that time, and if he fails to do so, judgment by default may be rendered against him.

Oct. 29, 1940, eff. Sept. 1, 1941.

Historical Notes

Source

Vernon's Ann.Civ.St. art. 2093, § 8, applicable to certain districts, unchanged. The former general statute, Art. 2048, was repealed.

Rule 123. Reversal of Judgment

Where the judgment is reversed on appeal or writ of error for the want of service, or because of defective service of process, no new citation shall be issued or served, but the defendant shall be presumed to have entered his appearance to the term of the court at which the mandate shall be filed.

Oct. 29, 1940, eff. Sept. 1, 1941.

Historical Notes

Source

Vernon's Ann.Civ.St. art. 2049, with minor textual change.

Rule 124. No Judgment Without Service

In no case shall judgment be rendered against any defendant unless upon service, or acceptance or waiver of process, or upon an appearance by the defendant, as prescribed in these rules, except where otherwise expressly provided by law or these rules.

When a party asserts a counterclaim or a cross-claim against another party who has entered an appearance, the claim may be served in any manner prescribed for service of citation or as provided in Rule 21(a).

Oct. 29, 1940, eff. Sept. 1, 1941. Amended by order of Dec. 5, 1983, eff. April 1, 1984.

Historical Notes

Source

Vernon's Ann.Civ.St. art. 2050, with minor textual change.

SECTION 6. COSTS AND SECURITY THEREFOR

Rule 125. Parties Responsible

Each party to a suit shall be liable to the officers of the court for all costs incurred by himself.

Oct. 29, 1940, eff. Sept. 1, 1941.

Historical Notes

Source

Vernon's Ann.Civ.St. art. 2051, first sentence, unchanged.

Rule 126. Fee for Execution of Process, Demand

No sheriff or constable shall be compelled to execute any process in civil cases coming from any county other than the one in which he is an officer, unless the fees allowed him by law for the service of such process shall be paid in advance; except when affidavit is filed, as provided by law or these rules. The clerk issuing the process shall indorse thereon the words "pauper oath filed," and sign his name officially below them; and the officer in whose hands such process is placed for service shall serve the same.

Oct. 29, 1940, eff. Sept. 1, 1941.

Historical Notes

Source

Vernon's Ann.Civ.St. art. 2051, second sentence, with minor textual change.

Rule 127. Parties Liable for Other Costs

Each party to a suit shall be liable for all costs incurred by him. If the costs cannot be collected from the party against whom they have been adjudged, execution may issue against any party in such suit for the amount of costs incurred by such party, but no more.

Oct. 29, 1940, eff. Sept. 1, 1941.

Historical Notes

Source

Vernon's Ann.Civ.St. art. 2052, unchanged.

Rule 128. Repealed by Order of Dec. 5, 1983, eff. April 1, 1984

Historical Notes

Former Rule 128, which authorized officers to demand payment of costs, was added by order of Oct. 29, 1940.

Rule 129. How Costs Collected

If any party responsible for costs fails or refuses to pay the same within ten days after demand for payment, the clerk or justice of the peace may make certified copy of the bill of costs then due, and place the same in the hands of the sheriff or constable for collection. All taxes imposed on law proceedings shall be included in the bill of costs. Such certified bill of costs shall have the force and effect of an execution. The removal of a case by appeal shall not prevent the issuance of an execution for costs.

Oct. 29, 1940, eff. Sept. 1, 1941. Amended by order of Dec. 5, 1983, eff. April 1, 1984.

Historical Notes

Source

Vernon's Ann.Civ.St. art. 2054, unchanged.

Rule 130. Officer to Levy

The sheriff or constable upon demand and failure to pay said bill of costs, may levy upon a sufficient amount of property of the person from whom said costs are due to satisfy the same, and sell such property as under execution. Where such party is not a resident of the county where such suit is pending, the payment of such costs may be demanded of his attorney of record; and neither the clerk nor justice of the peace shall be allowed to charge any fee for making out such certified bill of costs, unless he is compelled to make a levy.

Oct. 29, 1940, eff. Sept. 1, 1941.

Historical Notes

Source

Vernon's Ann.Civ.St. art. 2055, with minor textual change.

Rule 131. Successful Party to Recover

The successful party to a suit shall recover of his adversary all costs incurred therein, except where otherwise provided.

Oct. 29, 1940, eff. Sept. 1, 1941.

Historical Notes

Source

Vernon's Ann.Civ.St. art. 2056, unchanged.

Rule 132. Repealed by Order of Dec. 5, 1983, eff. April 1, 1984

Historical Notes

Former Rule 132, which limited the allowance of fees to no more than two witnesses, was added by order dated Oct. 29, 1940.

Rule 133. Costs of Motion

The court may give or refuse costs on motions at its discretion, except where otherwise provided by law or these rules.

Oct. 29, 1940, eff. Sept. 1, 1941.

Historical Notes

Source

Vernon's Ann.Civ.St. art. 2058, with minor textual change.

Rules 134, 135. Repealed by Order of Dec. 5, 1983, eff. April 1, 1984

Historical Notes

Former Rules 134 and 135, which related to costs when exceptions on pleadings are sustained and costs when several suits against the same defendant for causes of action which should have been joined, were added by order dated Oct. 29, 1940.

Rule 136. Demand Reduced by Payments

Where the plaintiff's demand is reduced by payment to an amount which would not have been within the jurisdiction of the court, the defendant shall recover his costs.

Oct. 29, 1940, eff. Sept. 1, 1941.

Historical Notes

Source

Vernon's Ann.Civ.St. art. 2061, unchanged.

Rule 137. In Assault and Battery, etc.

In civil actions for assault and battery, slander and defamation of character, if the verdict or judgment shall be for the plaintiff, but for less than twenty dollars, the plaintiff shall not recover his costs, but each party shall be taxed with the costs incurred by him in such suit.

Oct. 29, 1940, eff. Sept. 1, 1941.

Historical Notes

Source

Vernon's Ann.Civ.St. art. 2062, unchanged.

Rule 138. Cost of New Trials

The costs of new trials may either abide the result of the suit or may be taxed against the party to whom the new trial is granted, as the court may adjudge when he grants such new trial.

Oct. 29, 1940, eff. Sept. 1, 1941.

Historical Notes

Source

Vernon's Ann.Civ.St. art. 2063, unchanged.

Rule 139. On Appeal and Certiorari

When a case is appealed, if the judgment of the higher court be against the appellant, but for less amount than the original judgment, such party shall recover the costs of the higher court but shall be adjudged to pay the costs of the court below; if the judgment be against him for the same or a greater amount than in the court below, the adverse party shall recover the costs of both courts. If the judgment of the court above be in favor of the party appealing and for more than the original judgment, such party shall recover the costs of both courts; if the judgment be in his favor, but for the same or a less amount than in the court below, he shall recover the costs of the court below, and pay the costs of the court above.

Oct. 29, 1940, eff. Sept. 1, 1941.

Historical Notes

Source

Vernon's Ann.Civ.St. art. 2065, unchanged.

Rule 140. No Fee for Copy

No fee for a copy of a paper not required by law or these rules to be copied shall be taxed in the bill of costs.

Oct. 29, 1940, eff. Sept. 1, 1941.

Historical Notes

Source

Vernon's Ann.Civ.St. art. 3906, with minor textual change.

Rule 141. Court May Otherwise Adjudge Costs

The court may, for good cause, to be stated on the record, adjudge the costs otherwise than as provided by law or these rules.

Oct. 29, 1940, eff. Sept. 1, 1941.

Historical Notes

Source

Vernon's Ann.Civ.St. art. 2066, with minor textual change.

Rule 142. Security for Costs

The clerk shall require from the plaintiff fees for services rendered before issuing any process unless filing is requested pursuant to Rule 145 of these rules.

Oct. 29, 1940, eff. Sept. 1, 1941. Amended by orders of March 31, 1941, eff. Sept. 1, 1941; July 15, 1987, eff. Jan. 1, 1988.

Historical Notes

Source

Vernon's Ann.Civ.St. art. 2067, unchanged, and District and County Court Rule 50.

Rule 143. Rule for Costs

A party seeking affirmative relief may be ruled to give security for costs at any time before final judgment, upon motion of any party, or any officer of the court interested in the costs accruing in such suit, or by the court upon its own motion. If such rule be entered against any party and he failed to comply therewith on or before twenty (20) days after notice that such rule has been entered, the claim for affirmative relief of such party shall be dismissed.

Oct. 29, 1940, eff. Sept. 1, 1941. Amended by order of July 21, 1970, eff. Jan. 1, 1971.

Historical Notes

Source

Vernon's Ann.Civ.St. art. 2068, substituting 20-day period for reference to next term of court.

Rule 143a. Costs on Appeal to County Court

If the appellant fails to pay the costs on appeal from a judgment of a justice of the peace or small claims court within twenty (20) days after being notified to do so by the county clerk, the appeal shall be deemed not perfected and the county clerk shall return all papers in said cause to the justice of the peace having original jurisdiction and the justice of the peace shall proceed as though no appeal had been attempted.

July 22, 1975, eff. Jan. 1, 1976.

Rule 144. Judgment on Cost Bond

All bonds given as security for costs shall authorize judgment against all the obligors in such bond for the said costs, to be entered in the final judgment of the cause.

Oct. 29, 1940, eff. Sept. 1, 1941.

Historical Notes

Source

Vernon's Ann.Civ.St. art. 2069, unchanged.

Rule 145. Affidavit on Indigency

(a) *Affidavit.* In lieu of paying or giving security for costs of an original action, a party who is unable to afford costs must file an affidavit as herein described. A "party who is unable to afford costs" is defined as a person who is presently receiving a governmental entitlement based on indigency or any other person who has no ability to pay costs.

Upon the filing of the affidavit, the clerk must docket the action, issue citation and provide such other customary services as are provided any party.

(b) *Contents of Affidavit.* The affidavit must contain complete information as to the party's identity, nature and amount of governmental entitlement income, nature and amount of employment income, other income, (interest, dividends, etc.), spouse's income if available to the party, property owned (other than homestead), cash or checking account, dependents, debts, and monthly expenses. The affidavit shall contain the following statements: "I am unable to pay the court costs. I verify that the statements made in this affidavit are true and correct." The affidavit shall be sworn before a notary public or other officer authorized to administer oaths. If the party is represented by an attorney on a contingent fee basis, due to the party's indigency, the attorney may file a statement to that effect to assist the court in understanding the financial condition of the party.

(c) *IOLTA Certificate.* If the party is represented by an attorney who is providing free legal services, without contingency, because of the party's indigency and the attorney is providing services either directly or by referral from a program funded by the Interest on Lawyers Trust Accounts (IOLTA) program, the attorney may file an IOLTA certificate confirming that the IOLTA-funded program screened the party for income eligibility under the IOLTA income guidelines. A party's affidavit of inability accompanied by an attorney's IOLTA certificate may not be contested.

(d) *Contest.* The defendant or the clerk may contest an affidavit that is not accompanied by an IOLTA certificate by filing a written contest giving notice to all parties and, in an appeal under Texas Government Code, section 28.052, notice to both the small claims court and the county clerk. A party's affidavit of inability that attests to receipt of government entitlement based on indigency may be contested only with respect to the veracity of the attestation. Temporary hearings will not be continued pending the filing of the contest. If the court finds at the first regular hearing in the course of the action that the party (other than a party receiving a governmental entitlement based on indigency) is able to afford costs, the party must pay the costs of the action. Reasons for such a finding must be contained in an order. Except with leave of court, no further steps in the action will be taken by a party who is found able to afford costs until payment is made. If the party's action results in monetary award, and the court finds sufficient monetary award to reimburse costs, the party must pay the costs of the action. If the court finds that another party to the suit can pay the costs of the action, the other party must pay the costs of the action.

(e) *Attorney's Fees and Costs.* Nothing herein will preclude any existing right to recover attorney's fees, expenses or costs from any other party.

Oct. 29, 1940, eff. Sept. 1, 1941. Amended by orders of Dec. 5, 1983, eff. April 1, 1984; July 15, 1987, Jan. 1, 1988; Sept. 19, 2005, eff. Dec. 1, 2005.

Comment—1988

The purpose of this rule is to allow indigents to file suit and have citation issued based solely on an affidavit of indigency filed with the suit.

Comment—2005

The Rule is amended to prohibit the contest of an affidavit that is accompanied by an attorney's IOLTA certificate.

Historical Notes

2005 Amendment

The order dated Sept. 19, 2005 rewrote the rule, which prior thereto read:

"Affidavit of Inability

"In lieu of filing security for costs of an original action, a party who is unable to afford said costs shall file an affidavit as herein described. A "party who is unable to afford costs" is defined as a person who is presently receiving a governmental entitlement based on indigency or any other person who has no ability to pay costs. Said affidavit, and the party's action, shall be processed by the clerk in the manner prescribed by this rule.

"1. Procedure. Upon the filing of the affidavit, the clerk shall docket the action, issue citation and provide such other customary services as are provided any party. After service of citation, the defendant may contest the affidavit by filing a written contest giving notice to all parties, provided that temporary hearings will not be continued pending the filing of the contest. If the court shall find at the first regular hearing in the course of the action that the party (other than a party receiving a governmental entitlement) is able to afford costs, the party shall pay the costs of the action. Reasons for such a finding shall be contained in an order. Except with leave of court, no further steps in the action will be taken by a party who is found able to afford costs until payment is made. If the party's action results in monetary award, and the court finds sufficient monetary award to reimburse costs, the party shall pay the costs of the action. If the court finds that another party to the suit can pay the costs of the action, the other party shall pay the costs of the action.

"2. Affidavit. The affidavit shall contain complete information as to the party's identity, nature and amount of governmental entitlement income, nature and amount of employment income, other income, (interest, dividends, etc.), spouse's income if available to the party, property owned (other than homestead), cash or checking account, dependents, debts, and monthly expenses. The affidavit shall contain the following statements: 'I am unable to pay the court costs. I verify that the statements made in this affidavit are true and correct.' The affidavit shall be sworn before a Notary Public.

"3. Attorney's Certification. If the party is represented by an attorney who is providing free legal services, without contingency, because of the party's indigency, said attorney may file an affidavit to that effect to assist the court in understanding the financial condition of the party."

The order dated Sept. 19, 2005 also added a comment and provided: "Comments appended to these rules are intended to inform their construction and application."

Source

Vernon's Ann.Civ.St. art. 2070, substituting "Such contest may be tried before the trial of the cause, at such time as the court may fix, at the term of court at which the affidavit is filed, after notice thereof has been given to the opposite party or his attorney of record" for "Such contest may be tried before the trial of the cause, at such time as the court may fix, and notice thereof shall be given by noting it on the docket at the term of court at which the affidavit is filed."

The sentence beginning "In the court a contest is filed" has been added.

Rule 146. Deposit for Costs

In lieu of a bond for costs, the party required to give the same may deposit with the clerk of court or the justice of the peace such sum as the court or justice from time to time may designate as sufficient to pay the accrued costs.

Oct. 29, 1940, eff. Sept. 1, 1941.

Historical Notes

Source

Vernon's Ann.Civ.St. art. 2071, with minor textual change.

Rule 147. Applies to Any Party

The foregoing rules as to security and rule for costs shall apply to any party who seeks a judgment against any other party.

Oct. 29, 1940, eff. Sept. 1, 1941. Amended by order of Dec. 5, 1983, eff. April 1, 1984.

Historical Notes

Source

Vernon's Ann.Civ.St. art. 2073, substituting "or any other party upon a cross-action or counterclaim" for "on a counterclaim after the plaintiff has discontinued his suit"; and with minor textual change.

Rule 148. Secured by Other Bond

No further security shall be required if the costs are secured by the provisions of an attachment or other bond filed by the party required to give security for costs.

Oct. 29, 1940, eff. Sept. 1, 1941.

Historical Notes

Source

Vernon's Ann.Civ.St. art. 2074, unchanged.

Rule 149. Execution for Costs

When costs have been adjudged against a party and are not paid, the clerk or justice of the court in which the suit was determined may issue execution, accompanied by an itemized bill of costs, against such party to be levied and collected as in other cases; and said officer, on demand of any party to whom any such costs are due, shall issue execution for costs at once. This rule shall not apply to executors, administrators or guardians in cases where costs are adjudged against the estate of a deceased person or of a ward. No execution shall issue in any case for costs until after judgment rendered therefor by the court.

Oct. 29, 1940, eff. Sept. 1, 1941.

Historical Notes

Source

Vernon's Ann.Civ.St. art. 2077, with minor textual change.

SECTION 7. ABATEMENT AND DISCONTINUANCE OF SUIT

Rule 150. Death of Party

Where the cause of action is one which survives, no suit shall abate because of the death of any party thereto before the verdict or decision of the court is rendered, but such suit may proceed to judgment as hereinafter provided.

Oct. 29, 1940, eff. Sept. 1, 1941.

Historical Notes

Source

Vernon's Ann.Civ.St. art. 2078, first sentence, unchanged.

Rule 151. Death of Plaintiff

If the plaintiff dies, the heirs, or the administrator or executor of such decedent may appear and upon suggestion of such death being entered of record in open court, may be made plaintiff, and the suit shall proceed in his or their name. If no such appearance and suggestion be made within a reasonable time after the death of the plaintiff, the clerk upon the application of defendant, his agent or attorney, shall issue a scire facias for the heirs or the administrator or executor of such decedent, requiring him to appear and prosecute such suit. After service of such scire facias, should such heir or administrator or executor fail to enter appearance within the time provided, the defendant may have the suit dismissed.

Oct. 29, 1940, eff. Sept. 1, 1941. Amended by order of Dec. 5, 1983, eff. April 1, 1984.

Historical Notes

Source

Vernon's Ann.Civ.St. arts. 2078, except first sentence, and 2079, unchanged.

Rule 152. Death of Defendant

Where the defendant shall die, upon the suggestion of death being entered of record in open court, or upon petition of the plaintiff, the clerk shall issue a scire facias for the administrator or executor or heir requiring him to appear and defend the suit and upon the return of such service, the suit shall proceed against such administrator or executor or heir.

Oct. 29, 1940, eff. Sept. 1, 1941.

Historical Notes

Source

Vernon's Ann.Civ.St. art. 2080, unchanged.

Rule 153. When Executor, Etc., Dies

When an executor or administrator shall be a party to any suit, whether as plaintiff or as defendant, and shall die or cease to be such executor or administrator, the suit may be continued by or against the person succeeding him in the administration, or by or against the heirs, upon like proceedings being had as provided in the two preceding rules, or the suit may be dismissed, as provided in Rule 151.

Oct. 29, 1940, eff. Sept. 1, 1941. Amended by order of Dec. 5, 1983, eff. April 1, 1984.

Historical Notes

Source

Vernon's Ann.Civ.St. art. 2081, with minor textual change.

Rule 154. Requisites of Scire Facias

The scire facias and returns thereon, provided for in this section, shall conform to the requisites of citations and the returns thereon, under the provisions of these rules.

Oct. 29, 1940, eff. Sept. 1, 1941.

Historical Notes

Source

Vernon's Ann.Civ.St. art. 2091, with minor textual change.

Rule 155. Surviving Parties

Where there are two or more plaintiffs or defendants, and one or more of them die, upon suggestion of such death being entered upon the record, the suit shall at the instance of either party proceed in the name of the surviving plaintiffs or against the surviving defendants, as the case may be.

Oct. 29, 1940, eff. Sept. 1, 1941.

Historical Notes

Source

Vernon's Ann.Civ.St. art. 2082, unchanged.

Rule 156. Death After Verdict or Close of Evidence

When a party in a jury case dies between verdict and judgment, or a party in a non-jury case dies after the evidence is closed and before judgment is pronounced, judgment shall be rendered and entered as if all parties were living.

Oct. 29, 1940, eff. Sept. 1, 1941. Amended by order of July 11, 1977, eff. Jan. 1, 1978.

Historical Notes

Source

Vernon's Ann.Civ.St. art. 2083, unchanged.

Rule 157. Repealed by Order of July 15, 1987, eff. Jan. 1, 1988

Historical Notes

Former Rule 157, which provided that marriage would not abate a suit, was added by order dated Oct. 29, 1940.

Rule 158. Suit for the Use of Another

When a plaintiff suing for the use of another shall die before verdict, the person for whose use such suit was brought, upon such death being suggested on the record in open court, may prosecute the suit in his own name, and shall be as responsible for costs as if he brought the suit.

Oct. 29, 1940, eff. Sept. 1, 1941.

Historical Notes

Source

Vernon's Ann.Civ.St. art. 2085, unchanged.

Rule 159. Suit for Injuries Resulting in Death

In cases arising under the provisions of the title relating to injuries resulting in death, the suit shall not abate by the death of either party pending the suit, but in such case, if the plaintiff dies, where there is only one plaintiff, some one or more of the parties entitled to the money recovered may be substituted and the suit prosecuted to judgment in the name of such party or parties, for the benefit of the person entitled; if the defendant dies, his executor, administrator or heir may be made a party, and the suit prosecuted to judgment.

Oct. 29, 1940, eff. Sept. 1, 1941.

Historical Notes

Source

Vernon's Ann.Civ.St. art. 2086, unchanged.

Rule 160. Dissolution of Corporation

The dissolution of a corporation shall not operate to abate any pending suit in which such corporation is a defendant, but such suit shall continue against such corporation and judgment shall be rendered as though the same were not dissolved.

Oct. 29, 1940, eff. Sept. 1, 1941.

Historical Notes

Source

Vernon's Ann.Civ.St. art. 1390, part, unchanged. The last clause of Article 1390 was deemed substantive and not repealed. Article 1390 was superseded by V.A.T.S. Bus. Corp.Act, art. 6.05.

Rule 161. Where Some Defendants Not Served

When some of the several defendants in a suit are served with process in due time and others are not so served, the plaintiff may either dismiss as to those not so served and proceed against those who are, or he may take new process against those not served, or may obtain severance of the case as between those served and those not served, but no dismissal shall be allowed as to a principal obligor without also dismissing the parties secondarily liable except in cases provided by statute. No defendant against whom any suit may be so dismissed shall be thereby exonerated from any liability, but may at any time be proceeded against as if no such suit had been brought and no such dismissal ordered.

Oct. 29, 1940, eff. Sept. 1, 1941. Amended by orders of Dec. 5, 1983, eff. April 1, 1984; April 24, 1984, eff. Oct. 1, 1984; July 15, 1987, eff. Jan. 1, 1988.

Historical Notes

Source

Vernon's Ann.Civ.St. art. 2087, deleting "continue the suit until the next term of the court and" after "or he may".

Rule 162. Dismissal or Non-Suit

At any time before the plaintiff has introduced all of his evidence other than rebuttal evidence, the plaintiff may dismiss a case, or take a non-suit, which shall be entered in the minutes. Notice of the dismissal or non-suit shall be served in accordance with Rule 21a on any party who has answered or has been served with process without necessity of court order.

Any dismissal pursuant to this rule shall not prejudice the right of an adverse party to be heard on a pending claim for affirmative relief or excuse the payment of all costs taxed by the clerk. A dismissal under this rule shall have no effect on any motion for sanctions, attorney's fees or other costs, pending at the time of dismissal, as determined by the court. Any dismissal pursuant to this rule which terminates the case shall authorize the clerk to tax court costs against dismissing party unless otherwise ordered by the court.

Oct. 29, 1940, eff. Sept. 1, 1941. Amended by orders of Dec. 5, 1983, eff. April 1, 1984; July 15, 1987, eff. Jan. 1, 1988.

Comment—1988

The purpose of this rule is to fix a definite time after which a party may not voluntarily dismiss or non-suit the cause of action. In addition, these amendments will not disturb any pending motions for sanctions or attorney's fees that were filed before the motion for non-suit or dismissal.

Historical Notes

Source

Vernon's Ann.Civ.St. art. 2089, unchanged.

Rule 163. Dismissal As To Parties Served, Etc.

When it will not prejudice another party, the plaintiff may dismiss his suit as to one or more of several parties who were served with process, or who have answered, but no such dismissal shall in any case, be allowed as to a principal obligor, except in the cases provided for by statute.

Oct. 29, 1940, eff. Sept. 1, 1941. Amended by orders of Dec. 5, 1983, eff. April 1, 1984; July 15, 1987, eff. Jan. 1, 1988.

Historical Notes

Source

Vernon's Ann.Civ.St. art. 2090, with minor textual change.

Rule 164. Repealed by Order of July 15, 1987, eff. Jan. 1, 1988

Historical Notes

Former Rule 164, which related to nonsuits, was added by order dated Oct. 29, 1940, and was amended by order dated July 22, 1975.

Rule 165. Abandonment

A party who abandons any part of his claim or defense, as contained in the pleadings, may have that fact entered of record, so as to show that the matters therein were not tried.

Oct. 29, 1940, eff. Sept. 1, 1941.

Historical Notes

Source

District and County Court Rule 33, omitting reference to costs.

Rule 165a. Dismissal for Want of Prosecution

1. **Failure to Appear.** A case may be dismissed for want of prosecution on failure of any party seeking affirmative relief to appear for any hearing or trial of which the party had notice. Notice of the court's intention to dismiss and the date and place of the dismissal hearing shall be sent by the clerk to each attorney of record, and to each party not represented by an attorney and whose address is shown on the docket or in the papers on file, by posting same in the United States Postal Service. At the dismissal hearing, the court shall dismiss for want of prosecution unless there is good cause for the case to be maintained on the docket. If the court determines to maintain the case on the docket, it shall render a pretrial order assigning a trial date for the case and setting deadlines for the joining of new parties, all discovery, filing of all pleadings, the making of a response or supplemental responses to discovery and other pretrial matters. The case may be continued thereafter only for valid and compelling reasons specifically determined by court order. Notice of the signing of the order of dismissal shall be given as provided in Rule 306a. Failure to mail notices as required by this rule shall not affect any of the periods mentioned in Rule 306a except as provided in that rule.

2. **Non-Compliance With Time Standards.** Any case not disposed of within time standards promulgated by the Supreme Court under its Administrative Rules may be placed on a dismissal docket.

3. **Reinstatement.** A motion to reinstate shall set forth the grounds therefor and be verified by the movant or his attorney. It shall be filed with the clerk within 30 days after the order of dismissal is signed or within the period provided by Rule 306a. A copy of the motion to reinstate shall be served on each attorney of record and each party not represented by an attorney whose address is shown on the docket or in the papers on file. The clerk shall deliver a copy of the motion to the judge, who shall set a hearing on the motion as soon as practicable. The court shall notify all parties or their attorneys of record of the date, time and place of the hearing.

The court shall reinstate the case upon finding after a hearing that the failure of the party or his attorney was not intentional or the result of conscious indifference but was due to an accident or mistake or that the failure has been otherwise reasonably explained.

In the event for any reason a motion for reinstatement is not decided by signed written order within seventy-five days after the judgment is signed, or, within such other time as may be allowed by Rule 306a, the motion shall be deemed overruled by operation of law. If a motion to reinstate is timely filed by any party, the trial court, regardless of whether an appeal has been perfected, has plenary power to reinstate the case until 30 days after all such timely filed motions are overruled, either by a written and signed order or by operation of law, whichever occurs first.

4. **Cumulative Remedies.** This dismissal and reinstatement procedure shall be cumulative of the rules and laws governing any other procedures available to the parties in such cases. The same reinstatement procedures and timetable are applicable to all dismissals for want of prosecution including cases which are dismissed pursuant to the court's inherent power, whether or not a motion to dismiss has been filed.

Oct. 3, 1972, eff. Feb. 1, 1973. Amended by order of July 22, 1975, eff. Jan. 1, 1976; Dec. 5, 1983; July 15, 1987, eff. Jan. 1, 1988.

SECTION 8. PRE-TRIAL PROCEDURE

Rule 166. Pre-trial Conference

In an appropriate action, to assist in the disposition of the case without undue expense or burden to the parties, the court may in its discretion direct the attorneys for the parties and the parties or their duly authorized agents to appear before it for a conference to consider:

(a) All pending dilatory pleas, motions and exceptions;

(b) The necessity or desirability of amendments to the pleadings;

(c) A discovery schedule;

(d) Requiring written statements of the parties' contentions;

(e) Contested issues of fact and simplification of the issues;

(f) The possibility of obtaining stipulations of fact;

(g) The identification of legal matters to be ruled on or decided by the court;

(h) The exchange of a list of direct fact witnesses, other than rebuttal or impeaching witnesses the necessity of whose testimony cannot reasonably be anticipated before the time of trial, who will be called to testify at trial, stating their address and telephone number, and the subject of the testimony of each such witness;

(i) The exchange of a list of expert witnesses who will be called to testify at trial, stating their address and telephone number, and the subject of the testimony and opinions that will be proffered by each expert witness;

(j) Agreed applicable propositions of law and contested issues of law;

(k) Proposed jury charge questions, instructions, and definitions for a jury case or proposed findings of fact and conclusions of law for a nonjury case;

(*l*) The marking and exchanging of all exhibits that any party may use at trial and stipulation to the authenticity and admissibility of exhibits to be used at trial;

(m) Written trial objections to the opposite party's exhibits, stating the basis for each objection;

(n) The advisability of a preliminary reference of issues to a master or auditor for findings to be used as evidence when the trial is to be by jury;

(*o*) The settlement of the case, and to aid such consideration, the court may encourage settlement;

(p) Such other matters as may aid in the disposition of the action.

The court shall make an order that recites the action taken at the pretrial conference, the amendments allowed to the pleadings, the time within which same may be filed, and the agreements made by the parties as to any of the matters considered, and which limits the issues for trial to those not disposed of by admissions, agreements of counsel, or rulings of the court; and such order when issued shall control the subsequent course of the action, unless modified at the trial to prevent manifest injustice. The court in its discretion may establish by rule a pretrial calendar on which actions may be placed for consideration as above provided and may either confine the calendar to jury actions or extend it to all actions.

Pretrial proceedings in multidistrict litigation may also be governed by Rules 11 and 13 of the Rules of Judicial Administration.

Oct. 29, 1940, eff. Sept. 1, 1941. Amended by order of July 26, 1960, eff. Jan. 1, 1961; April 24, 1990, eff. Sept. 1, 1990; Aug. 29, 2003, eff. Sept. 1, 2003.

Comment—1990

To broaden the scope of the rule and to confirm the ability of the trial courts at pretrial hearings to encourage settlement

Historical Notes

The order dated August 29, 2003 added the last paragraph.

Source

Federal Rule 16, modified by adding "and the parties or their duly authorized agents" in first sentence; by adding subd. (a); by redesignating subds. (1) through (6) of Federal Rule 16 subds. (b) through (g); by adding "or auditor" in subd. (f); by deleting "or to non-jury actions" after "to jury actions" in last sentence; and by minor textual change.

Rule 166a. Summary Judgment

(a) For Claimant. A party seeking to recover upon a claim, counterclaim, or cross-claim or to obtain a declaratory judgment may, at any time after the adverse party has appeared or answered, move with or without supporting affidavits for a summary judgment in his favor upon all or any part thereof. A summary judgment, interlocutory in character, may be rendered on the issue of liability alone although there is a genuine issue as to amount of damages.

(b) For Defending Party. A party against whom a claim, counterclaim, or cross-claim is asserted or a declaratory judgment is sought may, at any time, move with or without supporting affidavits for a summary judgment in his favor as to all or any part thereof.

(c) Motion and Proceedings Thereon. The motion for summary judgment shall state the specific grounds therefor. Except on leave of court, with notice to opposing counsel, the motion and any supporting affidavits shall be filed and served at least twenty-one days before the time specified for hearing. Except on leave of court, the adverse party, not later than seven days prior to the day of hearing may file and serve opposing affidavits or other written response. No oral testimony shall be received at the hearing. The judgment sought shall be rendered forthwith if (i) the deposition transcripts, interrogatory answers, and other discovery responses referenced or set forth in the motion or response, and (ii) the pleadings, admissions, affidavits, stipulations of the parties, and authenticated or certified public records, if any, on file at the time of the hearing, or filed thereafter and before judgment with permission of the court, show that, except as to the amount of damages, there is no genuine issue as to any material fact and the moving party is entitled to judgment as a matter of law on the issues expressly set out in the motion or in an answer or any other response. Issues not expressly presented to the trial court by written motion, answer or other response shall not be considered on appeal as grounds for reversal. A summary judgment may be based on uncontroverted testimonial evidence of an interested witness, or of an expert witness as to subject matter concerning which the trier of fact must be guided solely by the opinion testimony of experts, if the evidence is clear, positive and direct, otherwise credible and free from contradictions and inconsistencies, and could have been readily controverted.

(d) Appendices, References and Other Use of Discovery Not Otherwise on File. Discovery products not on file with the clerk may be used as summary judgment evidence if copies of the material, appendices containing the evidence, or a notice containing specific references to the discovery or specific references to other instruments, are filed and served on all parties together with a statement of intent to use the specified discovery as summary judgment proofs: (i) at least twenty-one days before the hearing if such proofs are to be used to support the summary judgment; or (ii) at least seven days before the hearing if such proofs are to be used to oppose the summary judgment.

(e) Case not Fully Adjudicated on Motion. If summary judgment is not rendered upon the whole case or for all the relief asked and a trial is necessary, the judge may at the hearing examine the pleadings and the evidence on file, interrogate counsel, ascertain what material fact issues exist and make an order specifying the facts that are established as a matter of law, and directing such further proceedings in the action as are just.

(f) Form of Affidavits; Further Testimony. Supporting and opposing affidavits shall be made on personal knowledge, shall set forth such facts as would be admissible in evidence, and shall show affirmatively that the affiant is competent to testify to the matters stated therein. Sworn or certified copies of all papers or parts thereof referred to in an affidavit shall be attached thereto or served therewith. The court may permit affidavits to be supplemented or opposed by depositions or by further affidavits. Defects in the form of affidavits or attachments will not be grounds for reversal unless specifically pointed out by objection by an opposing party with opportunity, but refusal, to amend.

(g) When Affidavits Are Unavailable. Should it appear from the affidavits of a party opposing the motion that he cannot for reasons stated present by affidavit facts essential to justify his opposition, the court may refuse the application for judgment or may order a continuance to permit affidavits to be obtained or depositions to be taken or discovery to be had or may make such other order as is just.

(h) Affidavits Made in Bad Faith. Should it appear to the satisfaction of the court at any time that any of the affidavits presented pursuant to this rule are presented in bad faith or solely for the purpose of delay, the court shall forthwith order the party employing them to pay to the other party the amount of the reasonable expenses which the filing of the affidavits caused him to incur, including reasonable attorney's fees, and any offending party or attorney may be adjudged guilty of contempt.

(i) No-Evidence Motion. After adequate time for discovery, a party without presenting summary judgment evidence may move for summary judgment on the ground that there is no evidence of one or more essential elements of a claim or defense on which an adverse party would have the burden of proof at trial. The motion must state the elements as to which there is no evidence. The court must grant the motion unless the respondent produces summary judgment evidence raising a genuine issue of material fact.

Oct. 12, 1949, eff. March 1, 1950. Amended by orders of Oct. 1, 1951, eff. March 1, 1952; July 20, 1966, eff. Jan. 1, 1967; July 21, 1970, eff. Jan. 1, 1971; July 11, 1977, eff. Jan. 1, 1978; June 10, 1980, eff. Jan. 1, 1981; Dec. 5, 1983, eff. April 1, 1984; July 15, 1987, eff. Jan. 1, 1988; April 24, 1990, eff. Sept. 1, 1990; Aug. 15, 1997, eff. Sept. 1, 1997.

Comment—1990

This amendment provides a mechanism for using previously non-filed discovery in summary judgment practice. Such proofs must all be filed in advance of the hearing in accordance with Rule 166a. Paragraphs (d) through (g) are renumbered (e) through (h).

Comment—1997

This comment is intended to inform the construction and application of the rule. Paragraph (i) authorizes a motion for summary judgment based on the assertion that, after adequate opportunity for discovery, there is no evidence to support one or more specified elements of an adverse party's claim or defense. A discovery period set by pretrial order should be adequate opportunity for discovery unless there is a showing to the contrary, and ordinarily a motion under paragraph (i) would be permitted after the period but not before. The motion must be specific in challenging the evidentiary support for an element of a claim or defense; paragraph (i) does not authorize conclusory motions or general no-evidence challenges to an opponent's case. Paragraph (i) does not apply to ordinary motions for summary judgment under paragraphs (a) or (b), in which the movant must prove it is entitled to judgment by establishing each element of its own claim or defense as a matter of law or by negating an element of the respondent's claim or defense as a matter of law. To defeat a motion made under paragraph (i), the respondent is not required to marshal its proof; its response need only point out evidence that raises a fact issue on the challenged elements. The existing rules continue to govern the general requirements of summary judgment practice. A motion under paragraph (i) is subject to sanctions provided by existing law (Tex Civ.Prac. & Rem. Code §§ 9.001–10.006) and rules (Tex.R.Civ.P. 13). The denial of a motion under paragraph (i) is no more reviewable by appeal or mandamus than the denial of a motion under paragraph (c).

Historical Notes

Source

Federal Rule 56, substituting, in subd. (a) "adverse party has appeared or answered" for "pleading in answer thereto has been served." Rule 166-A became effective March 1, 1950.

Rule 166b. Repealed by Order of Aug. 5, 1998, and Nov. 9, 1998, eff. Jan. 1, 1999

Historical Notes

See, now, Vernon's Ann.Rules Civ.Proc., rules 192.1 et seq., 193.5, 195.1 et seq.

Rule 166c. Repealed by Order of Aug. 5, 1998, and Nov. 9, 1998, eff. Jan. 1, 1999

Historical Notes

The repealed rule, relating to stipulations regarding discovery procedure, was derived from order of July 15, 1987. See, now, Vernon's Ann.Rules Civ.Proc., Rule 191.1.

Rule 167. Offer of Settlement; Award of Litigation Costs

Historical Notes

2003 Amendment

The order issued October 9, 2003 provided that the rule [rules 167 to 167.7] is effective January 1, 2004, only in cases filed on or after that date.

A former rule 167, relating to discovery and production of documents and things for inspection, copying or photographing, was repealed by order of Aug. 5, 1998, and Nov. 9, 1998, eff. Jan. 1, 1999. See, now, Vernon's Ann.Rules Civ.Proc., rules 196.1 et seq.

2011 Amendment

The order dated September 9, 2011 provided that the rule amendments adopted by the Order "apply only to cases commenced on or after September 1, 2011."

167.1. Generally

Certain litigation costs may be awarded against a party who rejects an offer made substantially in accordance with this rule to settle a claim for monetary damages - including a counterclaim, crossclaim, or third-party claim - except in:

(a) a class action;

(b) a shareholder's derivative action;

(c) an action by or against the State, a unit of state government, or a political subdivision of the State;

(d) an action brought under the Family Code;

(e) an action to collect workers' compensation benefits under title 5, subtitle A of the Labor Code; or

(f) an action filed in a justice of the peace court or small claims court.

Oct. 9, 2003, eff. Jan. 1, 2004.

167.2. Settlement Offer

(a) *Defendant's declaration a prerequisite; deadline.* A settlement offer under this rule may not be made until a defendant - a party against whom a claim for monetary damages is made - files a declaration invoking this rule. When a defendant files such a declaration, an offer or offers may be made under this rule to settle only those claims by and against that defendant. The declaration must be filed no later than 45 days before the case is set for conventional trial on the merits.

(b) *Requirements of an offer.* A settlement offer must:

(1) be in writing;

(2) state that it is made under Rule 167 and Chapter 42 of the Texas Civil Practice and Remedies Code;

(3) identify the party or parties making the offer and the party or parties to whom the offer is made;

(4) state the terms by which all monetary claims - including any attorney fees, interest, and costs that would be recoverable up to the time of the offer - between the offeror or offerors on the one hand and the offeree or offerees on the other may be settled;

(5) state a deadline - no sooner than 14 days after the offer is served - by which the offer must be accepted;

(6) be served on all parties to whom the offer is made.

(c) *Conditions of offer.* An offer may be made subject to reasonable conditions, including the execution of appropriate releases, indemnities, and other documents. An offeree may object to a condition by written notice served on the offeror before the deadline stated in the offer. A condition to which no such objection is made is presumed to have been reasonable. Rejection of an offer made subject to a condition determined by the trial court to have been unreasonable cannot be the basis for an award of litigation costs under this rule.

(d) *Non-monetary and excepted claims not included.* An offer must not include non-monetary claims and other claims to which this rule does not apply.

(e) *Time limitations.* An offer may not be made:

(1) before a defendant's declaration is filed;

(2) within 60 days after the appearance in the case of the offeror or offeree, whichever is later;

(3) within 14 days before the date the case is set for a conventional trial on the merits, except that an offer may be made within that period if it is in response to, and within seven days of, a prior offer.

(f) *Successive offers.* A party may make an offer after having made or rejected a prior offer. A rejection of an offer is subject to imposition of litigation costs under this rule only if the offer is more favorable to the offeree than any prior offer.

Oct. 9, 2003, eff. Jan. 1, 2004.

167.3. Withdrawal, Acceptance, and Rejection of Offer

(a) *Withdrawal of offer.* An offer can be withdrawn before it is accepted. Withdrawal is effective when written notice of the withdrawal is served on the offeree. Once an unaccepted offer has been withdrawn, it cannot be accepted or be the basis for awarding litigation costs under this rule.

(b) *Acceptance of offer.* An offer that has not been withdrawn can be accepted only by written notice served on the offeror by the deadline stated in the offer. When an offer is accepted, the offeror or offeree may file the offer and acceptance and may move the court to enforce the settlement.

(c) *Rejection of offer.* An offer that is not withdrawn or accepted is rejected. An offer may also be rejected by written notice served on the offeror by the deadline stated in the offer.

(d) *Objection to offer made before an offeror's joinder or designation of responsible third party.* An offer made before an offeror joins another party or designates a responsible third party may not be the basis for awarding litigation costs under this rule against an offeree who files an objection to the offer within 15 days after service of the offeror's pleading or designation.

Oct. 9, 2003, eff. Jan. 1, 2004.

167.4. Awarding Litigation Costs

(a) *Generally.* If a settlement offer made under this rule is rejected, and the judgment to be awarded on the monetary claims covered by the offer is significantly less favorable to the offeree than was the offer, the court must award the offeror litigation costs against the offeree from the time the offer was rejected to the time of judgment.

(b) *"Significantly less favorable" defined.* A judgment award on monetary claims is significantly less favorable than an offer to settle those claims if:

(1) the offeree is a claimant and the judgment would be less than 80 percent of the offer; or

(2) the offeree is a defendant and the judgment would be more than 120 percent of the offer.

(c) *Litigation costs.* Litigation costs are the expenditures actually made and the obligations actually incurred—directly in relation to the claims covered by a settlement offer under this rule—for the following:

(1) court costs;

(2) reasonable deposition costs, in cases filed on or after September 1, 2011;

(3) reasonable fees for not more than two testifying expert witnesses; and

(4) reasonable attorney fees.

(d) *Limits on litigation costs.*

(1) In cases filed before September 1, 2011, the litigation costs that may be awarded under this rule must not exceed the following amount:

(A) the sum of the noneconomic damages, the exemplary or additional damages, and one-half of the economic damages to be awarded to the claimant in the judgment; minus

(B) the amount of any statutory or contractual liens in connection with the occurrences or incidents giving rise to the claim.

(2) In cases filed on or after September 1, 2011, the litigation costs that may be awarded to any party under this rule must not exceed the total amount that the claimant recovers or would recover before adding an award of litigation costs under this rule in favor of the claimant or subtracting as an offset an award of litigation costs under this rule in favor of the defendant.

(e) *No double recovery permitted.* A party who is entitled to recover attorney fees and costs under another law may not recover those same attorney fees and costs as litigation costs under this rule.

(f) *Limitation on attorney fees and costs recovered by a party against whom litigation costs are awarded.* A party against whom litigation costs are awarded may not recover attorney fees and costs under another law incurred after the date the party rejected the settlement offer made the basis of the award.

(g) *Litigation costs to be awarded to defendant as a setoff.* Litigation costs awarded to a defendant must be made a setoff to the claimant's judgment against the defendant.

Oct. 9, 2003, eff. Jan. 1, 2004. Amended by order of Sept. 9, 2011, eff. Sept. 1, 2011.

Historical Notes

2011 Amendment

The order dated September 1, 2011, in subsec. (c)(2) inserted "reasonable deposition costs, in cases filed on or after September 1, 2011;" and renumbered former subsecs. (c)(2) and (c)(3) as (c)(3) and (c)(4), respectively; added the present subsec. (d)(1) designation, and in newly designated subsec. (d)(1) inserted "In cases filed before September 1, 2011,"; renumbered former subsecs. (d)(1) and (d)(2) as (d)(1)(A) and (d)(1)(B), respectfully; and added present subsec. (d)(2).

167.5. Procedures

(a) *Modification of time limits.* On motion, and for good cause shown, the court may - by written order made before commencement of trial on the merits - modify the time limits for filing a declaration under Rule 167.2(a) or for making an offer.

(b) *Discovery permitted.* On motion, and for good cause shown, a party against whom litigation costs are to be awarded may conduct discovery to ascertain the reasonableness of the costs requested. If the court determines the costs to be reasonable, it must order the party requesting discovery to pay all attorney fees and expenses incurred by other parties in responding to such discovery.

(c) *Hearing required.* The court must, upon request, conduct a hearing on a request for an award of litigation costs, at which the affected parties may present evidence.

Oct. 9, 2003, eff. Jan. 1, 2004.

167.6. Evidence Not Admissible

Evidence relating to an offer made under this rule is not admissible except for purposes of enforcing a settlement agreement or obtaining litigation costs. The provisions of this rule may not be made known to the jury by any means.

Oct. 9, 2003, eff. Jan. 1, 2004.

167.7. Other Settlement Offers Not Affected

This rule does not apply to any offer made in a mediation or arbitration proceeding. A settlement offer not made in compliance with this rule, or a settlement offer not made under this rule, or made in an action to which this rule does not apply, cannot be the basis for awarding litigation costs under this rule as to any party. This rule does not limit or affect a party's right to make a settlement offer that does not comply with this rule, or in an action to which this rule does not apply.

Oct. 9, 2003, eff. Jan. 1, 2004. Amended by order of Sept. 9, 2011, eff. Sept. 1, 2011.

Rule 167a. Repealed by Order of Aug. 5, 1998, and Nov. 9, 1998, eff. Jan. 1, 1999

Historical Notes

See, now, Vernon's Ann.Rules Civ.Proc., rules 204.1 to 204.5.

Rule 168. Permission to Appeal

On a party's motion or on its own initiative, a trial court may permit an appeal from an interlocutory

order that is not otherwise appealable, as provided by statute. Permission must be stated in the order to be appealed. An order previously issued may be amended to include such permission. The permission must identify the controlling question of law as to which there is a substantial ground for difference of opinion, and must state why an immediate appeal may materially advance the ultimate termination of the litigation.
Sept. 1, 2011, eff. Sept. 1, 2011.

Comment—2011

Rule 168 is a new rule, added to implement amendments to section 51.014(d)–(f) of the Texas Civil Practice and Remedies Code. Rule 168 applies only to cases filed on or after September 1, 2011. Rule 168 clarifies that the trial court's permission to appeal should be included in the order to be appealed rather than in a separate order. Rule of Appellate Procedure 28.3 sets out the corollary requirements for permissive appeals in the courts of appeals.

Rule 169. Expedited Actions

(a) *Application.*

(1) The expedited actions process in this rule applies to a suit in which all claimants, other than counter-claimants, affirmatively plead that they seek only monetary relief aggregating $100,000 or less, including damages of any kind, penalties, costs, expenses, pre-judgment interest, and attorney fees.

(2) The expedited actions process does not apply to a suit in which a party has filed a claim governed by the Family Code, the Property Code, the Tax Code, or Chapter 74 of the Civil Practice & Remedies Code.

(b) *Recovery.* In no event may a party who prosecutes a suit under this rule recover a judgment in excess of $100,000, excluding post-judgment interest.

(c) *Removal from Process.*

(1) A court must remove a suit from the expedited actions process:

(A) on motion and a showing of good cause by any party; or

(B) if any claimant, other than a counter-claimant, files a pleading or an amended or supplemental pleading that seeks any relief other than the monetary relief allowed by (a)(1).

(2) A pleading, amended pleading, or supplemental pleading that removes a suit from the expedited actions process may not be filed without leave of court unless it is filed before the earlier of 30 days after the discovery period is closed or 30 days before the date set for trial. Leave to amend may be granted only if good cause for filing the pleading outweighs any prejudice to an opposing party.

(3) If a suit is removed from the expedited actions process, the court must reopen discovery under Rule 190.2(c).

(d) *Expedited Actions Process.*

(1) Discovery. Discovery is governed by Rule 190.2.

(2) Trial Setting; Continuances. On any party's request, the court must set the case for a trial date that is within 90 days after the discovery period in Rule 190.2(b)(1) ends. The court may continue the case twice, not to exceed a total of 60 days.

(3) Time Limits for Trial. Each side is allowed no more than eight hours to complete jury selection, opening statements, presentation of evidence, examination and cross-examination of witnesses, and closing arguments. On motion and a showing of good cause by any party, the court may extend the time limit to no more than twelve hours per side.

(A) The term "side" has the same definition set out in Rule 233.

(B) Time spent on objections, bench conferences, bills of exception, and challenges for cause to a juror under Rule 228 are not included in the time limit.

(4) Alternative Dispute Resolution.

(A) Unless the parties have agreed not to engage in alternative dispute resolution, the court may refer the case to an alternative dispute resolution procedure once, and the procedure must:

(i) not exceed a half-day in duration, excluding scheduling time;

(ii) not exceed a total cost of twice the amount of applicable civil filing fees; and

(iii) be completed no later than 60 days before the initial trial setting.

(B) The court must consider objections to the referral unless prohibited by statute.

(C) The parties may agree to engage in alternative dispute resolution other than that provided for in (A).

(5) Expert Testimony. Unless requested by the party sponsoring the expert, a party may only challenge the admissibility of expert testimony as an objection to summary judgment evidence under Rule 166a or during the trial on the merits. This paragraph does not apply to a motion to strike for late designation.

Adopted by order of Feb. 12, 2013, eff. March 1, 2013.

Comment—2013

1. Rule 169 is a new rule implementing section 22.004(h) of the Texas Government Code, which was added in 2011 and calls for rules to promote

the prompt, efficient, and cost-effective resolution of civil actions when the amount in controversy does not exceed $100,000.

2. The expedited actions process created by Rule 169 is mandatory; any suit that falls within the definition of 169(a)(1) is subject to the provisions of the rule.

3. In determining whether there is good cause to remove the case from the process or extend the time limit for trial, the court should consider factors such as whether the damages sought by multiple claimants against the same defendant exceed in the aggregate the relief allowed under 169(a)(1), whether a defendant has filed a compulsory counterclaim in good faith that seeks relief other than that allowed under 169(a)(1), the number of parties and witnesses, the complexity of the legal and factual issues, and whether an interpreter is necessary.

4. Rule 169(b) specifies that a party who prosecutes a suit under this rule cannot recover a judgment in excess of $100,000. Thus, the rule in *Greenhalgh v. Service Lloyds Ins. Co.*, 787 S.W.2d 938 (Tex. 1990), does not apply if a jury awards damages in excess of $100,000 to the party. The limitation in 169(b) does not apply to a counterclaimant that seeks relief other than that allowed under 169(a)(1).

5. The discovery limitations for expedited actions are set out in Rule 190.2, which is also amended to implement section 22.004(h) of the Texas Government Code.

Historical Notes

Source

New rule.

Rule 170. Repealed by Order of Dec. 5, 1983, eff. April 1, 1984

Historical Notes

See, now, Vernon's Ann.Rules Civ.Proc., rule 215.1 et seq.

Rule 171. Master in Chancery

The court may, in exceptional cases, for good cause appoint a master in chancery, who shall be a citizen of this State, and not an attorney for either party to the action, nor related to either party, who shall perform all of the duties required of him by the court, and shall be under orders of the court, and have such power as the master of chancery has in a court of equity.

The order of reference to the master may specify or limit his powers, and may direct him to report only upon particular issues, or to do or perform particular acts, or to receive and report evidence only and may fix the time and place for beginning and closing the hearings, and for the filing of the master's report. Subject to the limitations and specifications stated in the order, the master has and shall exercise the power to regulate all proceedings in every hearing before him and to do all acts and take all measures necessary or proper for the efficient performance of his duties under the order. He may require the production before him of evidence upon all matters embraced in the reference, including the production of books, papers, vouchers, documents and other writings applicable thereto. He may rule upon the admissibility of evidence, unless otherwise directed by the order of reference and has the authority to put witnesses on oath, and may, himself, examine them, and may call the parties to the action and examine them upon oath. When a party so requests, the master shall make a record of the evidence offered and excluded in the same manner as provided for a court sitting in the trial of a case.

The clerk of the court shall forthwith furnish and master with a copy of the order of reference.

The parties may procure the attendance of witnesses before the master by the issuance and service of process as provided by law and these rules.

The court may confirm, modify, correct, reject, reverse or recommit the report, after it is filed, as the court may deem proper and necessary in the particular circumstances of the case. The court shall award reasonable compensation to such master to be taxed as costs of suit.

Oct. 29, 1940, eff. Sept. 1, 1941. Amended by order of Sept. 20, 1941, eff. Dec. 31, 1941.

Historical Notes

Source

Vernon's Ann.Civ.St., art. 2320, and Federal Rule 53. The first paragraph of Rule 171 was adapted from Art. 2320; Federal Rule 53(b) included a like provision. The second paragraph was based on Federal Rule 53(c). The third paragraph was based on Federal Rule 53(d)(1); the fourth on Federal Rule 53(d)(2); and the fifth on Federal Rule 53(e)(2).

Rule 172. Audit

When an investigation of accounts or examination of vouchers appears necessary for the purpose of justice between the parties to any suit, the court shall appoint an auditor or auditors to state the accounts between the parties and to make report thereof to the court as soon as possible. The auditor shall verify his report by his affidavit stating that he has carefully examined the state of the account between the parties, and that his report contains a true statement thereof, so far as the same has come within his knowledge. Exceptions to such report or of any item thereof must be filed within 30 days of the filing of such report. The court shall award reasonable compensation to such auditor to be taxed as costs of suit.

Oct. 29, 1940, eff. Sept. 1, 1941. Amended by order of July 15, 1987, eff. Jan. 1, 1988.

Historical Notes

Source

Vernon's Ann.Civ.St. art. 2292, unchanged.

Rule 173. Guardian Ad Litem

Historical Notes

Source

Vernon's Ann.Civ.St. art. 2159, modified by addition of provision for appointment of guardian ad litem whenever the minor is represented by one having an adverse interest.

173.1. Appointment Governed by Statute or Other Rules

This rule does not apply to an appointment of a guardian ad litem governed by statute or other rules.

June 16, 1943, eff. Dec. 31, 1943. Amended by order of Jan. 27, 2005, eff. Feb. 1, 2005.

Comment—2004

See comments following Rule 173.7.

173.2. Appointment of Guardian ad Litem

(a) *When Appointment Required or Prohibited.* The court must appoint a guardian ad litem for a party represented by a next friend or guardian only if:

(1) the next friend or guardian appears to the court to have an interest adverse to the party, or

(2) the parties agree.

(b) *Appointment of the Same Person for Different Parties.* The court must appoint the same guardian ad litem for similarly situated parties unless the court finds that the appointment of different guardians ad litem is necessary.

June 16, 1943, eff. Dec. 31, 1943. Amended by order of Jan. 27, 2005, eff. Feb. 1, 2005.

Comment—2004

See comments following Rule 173.7.

173.3. Procedure

(a) *Motion Permitted But Not Required.* The court may appoint a guardian ad litem on the motion of any party or on its own initiative.

(b) *Written Order Required.* An appointment must be made by written order.

(c) *Objection.* Any party may object to the appointment of a guardian ad litem.

June 16, 1943, eff. Dec. 31, 1943. Amended by order of Jan. 27, 2005, eff. Feb. 1, 2005.

Comment—2004

See comments following Rule 173.7.

173.4. Role of Guardian ad Litem

(a) *Court Officer and Advisor.* A guardian ad litem acts as an officer and advisor to the court.

(b) *Determination of Adverse Interest.* A guardian ad litem must determine and advise the court whether a party's next friend or guardian has an interest adverse to the party.

(c) *When Settlement Proposed.* When an offer has been made to settle the claim of a party represented by a next friend or guardian, a guardian ad litem has the limited duty to determine and advise the court whether the settlement is in the party's best interest.

(d) *Participation in Litigation Limited.* A guardian ad litem:

(1) may participate in mediation or a similar proceeding to attempt to reach a settlement;

(2) must participate in any proceeding before the court whose purpose is to determine whether a party's next friend or guardian has an interest adverse to the party, or whether a settlement of the party's claim is in the party's best interest;

(3) must not participate in discovery, trial, or any other part of the litigation unless:

(A) further participation is necessary to protect the party's interest that is adverse to the next friend's or guardian's, and

(B) the participation is directed by the court in a written order stating sufficient reasons.

June 16, 1943, eff. Dec. 31, 1943. Amended by order of Jan. 27, 2005, eff. Feb. 1, 2005.

Comment—2004

See comments following Rule 173.7.

173.5. Communications Privileged

Communications between the guardian ad litem and the party, the next friend or guardian, or their attorney are privileged as if the guardian ad litem were the attorney for the party.

June 16, 1943, eff. Dec. 31, 1943. Amended by order of Jan. 27, 2005, eff. Feb. 1, 2005.

Comment—2004

See comments following Rule 173.7.

173.6. Compensation

(a) *Amount.* If a guardian ad litem requests compensation, he or she may be reimbursed for reasonable and necessary expenses incurred and may be paid a reasonable hourly fee for necessary services performed.

(b) *Procedure.* At the conclusion of the appointment, a guardian ad litem may file an application for compensation. The application must be verified and must detail the basis for the compensation requested. Unless all parties agree to the application, the court must conduct an evidentiary hearing to determine the total amount of fees and expenses that are reasonable and necessary. In making this determination, the court must not consider compensation as a percentage of any judgment or settlement.

(c) *Taxation as Costs.* The court may tax a guardian ad litem's compensation as costs of court.

(d) *Other Benefit Prohibited.* A guardian ad litem may not receive, directly or indirectly, anything of value in consideration of the appointment other than as provided by this rule.

June 16, 1943, eff. Dec. 31, 1943. Amended by order of Jan. 27, 2005, eff. Feb. 1, 2005.

Comment—2004

See comments following Rule 173.7.

173.7. Review

(a) Right of Appeal. Any party may seek mandamus review of an order appointing a guardian ad litem or directing a guardian ad litem's participation in the litigation. Any party and a guardian ad litem may appeal an order awarding the guardian ad litem compensation.

(b) Severance. On motion of the guardian ad litem or any party, the court must sever any order awarding a guardian ad litem compensation to create a final, appealable order.

(c) No Effect on Finality of Settlement or Judgment. Appellate proceedings to review an order pertaining to a guardian ad litem do not affect the finality of a settlement or judgment.

June 16, 1943, eff. Dec. 31, 1943. Amended by order of Jan. 27, 2005, eff. Feb. 1, 2005.

Comment—2004

1. The rule is completely revised.

2. This rule does not apply when the procedures and purposes for appointment of guardians ad litem (as well as attorneys ad litem) are prescribed by statutes, such as the Family Code and the Probate Code, or by other rules, such as the Parental Notification Rules.

3. The rule contemplates that a guardian ad litem will be appointed when a party's next friend or guardian appears to have an interest adverse to the party because of the division of settlement proceeds. In those situations, the responsibility of the guardian ad litem as prescribed by the rule is very limited, and no reason exists for the guardian ad litem to participate in the conduct of the litigation in any other way or to review the discovery or the litigation file except to the limited extent that it may bear on the division of settlement proceeds. See *Jocson v. Crabb*, 133 S.W.3d 268 (Tex. 2004) (per curiam). A guardian ad litem may, of course, choose to review the file or attend proceedings when it is unnecessary, but the guardian ad litem may not be compensated for unnecessary expenses or services.

4. Only in extraordinary circumstances does the rule contemplate that a guardian ad litem will have a broader role. Even then, the role is limited to determining whether a party's next friend or guardian has an interest adverse to the party that should be considered by the court under Rule 44. In no event may a guardian ad litem supervise or supplant the next friend or undertake to represent the party while serving as guardian ad litem.

5. As an officer and advisor to the court, a guardian ad litem should have qualified judicial immunity.

6. Though an officer and adviser to the court, a guardian ad litem must not have *ex parte* communications with the court. See Tex. Code Jud. Conduct, Canon 3.

7. Because the role of guardian ad litem is limited in all but extraordinary situations, and any risk that might result from services performed is also limited, compensation, if any is sought, should ordinarily be limited.

8. A violation of this rule is subject to appropriate sanction.

Rule 174. Consolidation; Separate Trials

(a) Consolidation. When actions involving a common question of law or fact are pending before the court, it may order a joint hearing or trial of any or all the matters in issue in the actions; it may order all the actions consolidated; and it may make such orders concerning proceedings therein as may tend to avoid unnecessary costs or delay.

(b) Separate Trials. The court in furtherance of convenience or to avoid prejudice may order a separate trial of any claim, cross-claim, counterclaim, or third-party claim, or of any separate issue or of any number of claims, cross-claims, counterclaims, third-party claims, or issues.

Oct. 29, 1940, eff. Sept. 1, 1941.

Historical Notes

Source

Federal Rule 42, unchanged. Rule 174 superseded Vernon's Ann.Civ.St. art. 2160, Consolidation of suits.

Rule 175. Issue of Law and Dilatory Pleas

When a case is called for trial in which there has been no pretrial hearing as provided by Rule 166, the issues of law arising on the pleadings, all pleas in abatement and other dilatory pleas remaining undisposed of shall be determined; and it shall be no cause for postponement of a trial of the issues of law that a party is not prepared to try the issues of fact.

Oct. 29, 1940, eff. Sept. 1, 1941.

Historical Notes

Source

Vernon's Ann.Civ.St. art. 2166, with minor textual change.

SECTION 9. EVIDENCE AND DISCOVERY

A. EVIDENCE

Rule 176. Subpoenas

Historical Notes

Former rule 176 was repealed by order effective January 1, 1999. For subject matter of former rule 176, see, now, rule 176.3.

176.1. Form

Every subpoena must be issued in the name of "The State of Texas" and must:

(a) state the style of the suit and its cause number;

(b) state the court in which the suit is pending;

(c) state the date on which the subpoena is issued;

(d) identify the person to whom the subpoena is directed;

(e) state the time, place, and nature of the action required by the person to whom the subpoena is directed, as provided in Rule 176.2;

(f) identify the party at whose instance the subpoena is issued, and the party's attorney of record, if any;

(g) state the text of Rule 176.8(a); and

(h) be signed by the person issuing the subpoena.

Aug. 5, 1998 and Nov. 9, 1998, eff. Jan. 1, 1999.

Historical Comments—1999

See comments following 176.8.

Historical Notes

Source:

Former rule 177.

176.2. Required Actions

A subpoena must command the person to whom it is directed to do either or both of the following:

(a) attend and give testimony at a deposition, hearing, or trial;

(b) produce and permit inspection and copying of designated documents or tangible things in the possession, custody, or control of that person.

Aug. 5, 1998 and Nov. 9, 1998, eff. Jan. 1, 1999.

Historical Comments—1999

See comments following 176.8.

Historical Notes

Source:

Former rule 177a.

176.3. Limitations

(a) *Range.* A person may not be required by subpoena to appear or produce documents or other things in a county that is more than 150 miles from where the person resides or is served. However, a person whose appearance or production at a deposition may be compelled by notice alone under Rules 199.3 or 200.2 may be required to appear and produce documents or other things at any location permitted under Rules 199.2(b)(2).

(b) *Use for Discovery.* A subpoena may not be used for discovery to an extent, in a manner, or at a time other than as provided by the rules governing discovery.

Aug. 5, 1998 and Nov. 9, 1998, eff. Jan. 1, 1999.

Historical Comments—1999

See comments following 176.8.

Historical Notes

Source:

Former rule 176.

176.4. Who May Issue

A subpoena may be issued by:

(a) the clerk of the appropriate district, county, or justice court, who must provide the party requesting the subpoena with an original and a copy for each witness to be completed by the party;

(b) an attorney authorized to practice in the State of Texas, as an officer of the court; or

(c) an officer authorized to take depositions in this State, who must issue the subpoena immediately on a request accompanied by a notice to take a deposition under Rules 199[1] or 200,[2] or a notice under Rule 205.3, and who may also serve the notice with the subpoena.

Aug. 5, 1998 and Nov. 9, 1998, eff. Jan. 1, 1999.

[1] Vernon's Ann.Rules Civ.Proc., rule 199.1 et seq.

[2] Vernon's Ann.Rules Civ.Proc., rule 200.1 et seq.

Historical Comments—1999

See comments following 176.8.

176.5. Service

(a) *Manner of Service.* A subpoena may be served at any place within the State of Texas by any sheriff or constable of the State of Texas, or any person who is not a party and is 18 years of age or older. A subpoena must be served by delivering a copy to the witness and tendering to that person any fees required by law. If the witness is a party and is represented by an attorney of record in the proceeding, the subpoena may be served on the witness's attorney of record.

(b) *Proof of Service.* Proof of service must be made by filing either:

(1) the witness's signed written memorandum attached to the subpoena showing that the witness accepted the subpoena; or

(2) a statement by the person who made the service stating the date, time, and manner of service, and the name of the person served.

Aug. 5, 1998 and Nov. 9, 1998, eff. Jan. 1, 1999.

Historical Comments—1999

See comments following 176.8.

Historical Notes

Source:

Former rule 178.

176.6. Response

(a) *Compliance Required.* Except as provided in this subdivision, a person served with a subpoena must comply with the command stated therein unless discharged by the court or by the party summoning such witness. A person commanded to appear and give testimony must remain at the place of deposition, hearing, or trial from day to day until discharged by the court or by the party summoning the witness.

(b) *Organizations.* If a subpoena commanding testimony is directed to a corporation, partnership, association, governmental agency, or other organization, and the matters on which examination is requested are described with reasonable particularity, the organization must designate one or more persons to testify on its behalf as to matters known or reasonably available to the organization.

(c) *Production of Documents or Tangible Things.* A person commanded to produce documents or tangible things need not appear in person at the time and place of production unless the person is also commanded to attend and give testimony, either in the same subpoena or a separate one. A person must produce documents as they are kept in the usual course of business or must organize and label them to correspond with the categories in the demand. A person may withhold material or information claimed to be privileged but must comply with Rule 193.3. A nonparty's production of a document authenticates the document for use against the nonparty to the same extent as a party's production of a document is authenticated for use against the party under Rule 193.7.

(d) *Objections.* A person commanded to produce and permit inspection or copying of designated documents and things may serve on the party requesting issuance of the subpoena—before the time specified for compliance—written objections to producing any or all of the designated materials. A person need not comply with the part of a subpoena to which objection is made as provided in this paragraph unless ordered to do so by the court. The party requesting the subpoena may move for such an order at any time after an objection is made.

(e) *Protective Orders.* A person commanded to appear at a deposition, hearing, or trial, or to produce and permit inspection and copying of designated documents and things, and any other person affected by the subpoena, may move for a protective order under Rule 192.6(b)—before the time specified for compliance—either in the court in which the action is pending or in a district court in the county where the subpoena was served. The person must serve the motion on all parties in accordance with Rule 21a. A person need not comply with the part of a subpoena from which protection is sought under this paragraph unless ordered to do so by the court. The party requesting the subpoena may seek such an order at any time after the motion for protection is filed.

(f) *Trial Subpoenas.* A person commanded to attend and give testimony, or to produce documents or things, at a hearing or trial, may object or move for protective order before the court at the time and place specified for compliance, rather than under paragraphs (d) and (e).

Aug. 5, 1998 and Nov. 9, 1998, eff. Jan. 1, 1999.

Historical Comments—1999

See comments following 176.8.

Historical Notes

Source:

Former rule 179, 201.

176.7. Protection of Person from Undue Burden and Expense

A party causing a subpoena to issue must take reasonable steps to avoid imposing undue burden or expense on the person served. In ruling on objections or motions for protection, the court must provide a person served with a subpoena an adequate time for compliance, protection from disclosure of privileged material or information, and protection from undue burden or expense. The court may impose reasonable conditions on compliance with a subpoena, including compensating the witness for undue hardship.

Aug. 5, 1998 and Nov. 9, 1998, eff. Jan. 1, 1999.

Historical Comments—1999

See comments following 176.8.

176.8. Enforcement of Subpoena

(a) *Contempt.* Failure by any person without adequate excuse to obey a subpoena served upon that person may be deemed a contempt of the court from which the subpoena is issued or a district court in the county in which the subpoena is served, and may be punished by fine or confinement, or both.

(b) *Proof of Payment of Fees Required for Fine or Attachment.* A fine may not be imposed, nor a person served with a subpoena attached, for failure to comply with a subpoena without proof by affidavit of the party requesting the subpoena or the party's attorney of record that all fees due the witness by law were paid or tendered.

Aug. 5, 1998 and Nov. 9, 1998, eff. Jan. 1, 1999.

Historical Comments—1999

1. This rule combines the former rules governing subpoenas for trial and discovery. When a subpoena is used for discovery, the protections from undue burden and expense apply, just as with any discovery.

2. Rule 176.3(b) prohibits the use of a subpoena to circumvent the discovery rules. Thus, for example, a deposition subpoena to a party is subject to the procedures of Rules 196, 199, and 200, and a deposition subpoena to a nonparty is subject to the procedures of Rule 205.

Historical Notes

Source:

Former rule 203.

Rule 177. Repealed by Order of Aug. 5, 1998, and Nov. 9, 1998, eff. Jan. 1, 1999

Historical Notes

See, now, Vernon's Ann.Rules Civ.Proc., rule 176.1.

Rule 177a. Repealed by Order of Aug. 5, 1998, and Nov. 9, 1998, eff. Jan. 1, 1999

Historical Notes

The repealed rule, relating to subpoena for production of documentary evidence, was derived from Federal Rule 45(b) and was added by order of March 19, 1957. See, now, Vernon's Ann.Rules Civ.Proc., rule 176.2(b).

Rule 178. Repealed by Order of Aug. 5, 1998, and Nov. 9, 1998, eff. Jan. 1, 1999

Historical Notes

See, now, Vernon's Ann.Rules Civ.Proc., rule 176.5.

Rule 179. Repealed by Order of Aug. 5, 1998, and Nov. 9, 1998, eff. Jan. 1, 1999

Historical Notes

The repealed rule, relating to attendance of witness, was derived from Vernon's Ann.Civ.St. art. 3707. See, now, Vernon's Ann.Rules Civ.Proc., rule 176.6(a).

Rule 180. Refusal to Testify

Any witness refusing to give evidence may be committed to jail, there to remain without bail until such witness shall consent to give evidence.

Oct. 29, 1940, eff. Sept. 1, 1941.

Historical Notes

Source

Vernon's Ann.Civ.St. art. 3709, as amended by Acts 1939, 46th Leg., p. 323, § 5, unchanged.

Rule 181. Party As Witness

Either party to a suit may examine the opposing party as a witness, and shall have the same process to compel his attendance as in the case of any other witness.

Oct. 29, 1940, eff. Sept. 1, 1941.

Historical Notes

Source

Vernon's Ann.Civ.St. art. 3711, as amended by Acts 1939, 46th Leg., p. 323, § 6, unchanged.

Rule 182. Repealed by Order of July 15, 1987, eff. Jan. 1, 1988

Historical Notes

The repealed rule, relating to testimony of adverse parties in civil suits, was derived from Vernon's Ann.Civ.St. art. 3769c. For the subject matter of former rule 182 see, now, Vernon's Ann. Rules of Evidence, rules 607, 611(c).

Rule 182a. Repealed by Order of July 15, 1987, eff. Jan. 1, 1988

Historical Notes

Prior to repeal, rule 182a, relating to instruction to the jury on the deadman's statute, was amended by order of Dec. 5, 1983. See, now, Vernon's Texas Rules of Evidence, rule 601(b).

Rule 183. Interpreters

The court may appoint an interpreter of its own selection and may fix the interpreter's reasonable compensation. The compensation shall be paid out of funds provided by law or by one or more of the parties as the court may direct, and may be taxed ultimately as costs, in the discretion of the court.

Oct. 29, 1940, eff. Sept. 1, 1941. Amended by order of April 24, 1990, eff. Sept. 1, 1990.

Comment—1990

To adopt procedures for the appointment and compensation of interpreters. Source: Fed. R.Civ.P. 43(f). The provision regarding summoning interpreters and their conduct is deleted because it is covered by Rule 604, Texas Rules of Civil Evidence.

Historical Notes

Source

Vernon's Ann.Civ.St. art. 3712, unchanged.

Rule 184. Repealed by Order of April 24, 1990, eff. Sept. 1, 1990

Historical Notes

See, now, Vernon's Ann.Rules Evidence, rule 202.

Rule 184a. Repealed by Order of April 24, 1990, eff. Sept. 1, 1990

Historical Notes

See, now, Vernon's Ann.Rules Evidence, rule 203.

Rule 185. Suit on Account

When any action or defense is founded upon an open account or other claim for goods, wares and merchandise, including any claim for a liquidated money demand based upon written contract or founded on business dealings between the parties, or is for personal service rendered, or labor done or labor or materials furnished, on which a systematic record has been kept, and is supported by the affidavit of the party, his agent or attorney taken before some officer authorized to administer oaths, to the effect that such claim is, within the knowledge of affiant, just and true, that it is due, and that all just and lawful offsets, payments and credits have been allowed, the same shall be taken as prima facie evidence thereof, unless the party resisting such claim shall file a written denial, under oath. A party resisting such a sworn claim shall comply with the rules of pleading as are required in any other kind of suit, provided, however, that if he does not timely file a written denial, under oath, he shall not be permitted to deny the claim, or any item therein, as the case may be. No particularization or description of the nature of the component parts of the account or claim is necessary unless the trial court sustains special exceptions to the pleadings.

Oct. 29, 1940, eff. Sept. 1, 1941. Amended by orders of Oct. 12, 1949, eff. March 1, 1950; July 21, 1970, eff. Jan. 1, 1971; Dec. 5, 1983, eff. April 1, 1984.

Historical Notes

Source

Vernon's Ann.Civ.St. art. 3736, unchanged.

B. DISCOVERY

Rules 186 to 186b. Repealed by Order of Dec. 5, 1983, eff. April 1, 1984

Historical Notes

For subject matter of former rule 186, see, now, Vernon's Ann.Rules Civ.Proc., rules 187, 200, 208 and 252.

For subject matter of former rules 186a and 186b, see, now, Vernon's Ann.Rules Civ.Proc., rule 166b.

Rule 187. Repealed by Order of Aug. 5, 1998, and Nov. 9, 1998, eff. Jan. 1, 1999

Historical Notes

See, now, Vernon's Ann.Rules Civ.Proc., rules 202.1 et seq.

Rule 188. Repealed by Order of Aug. 5, 1998, and Nov. 9, 1998, eff. Jan. 1, 1999

Historical Notes

Former rule 188, relating to Depositions in Foreign Jurisdiction, was derived from orders of Dec. 5, 1983 and July 15, 1987. See, now, Vernon's Ann.Rules Civ.Proc., rule 201.1.

A former rule 188, relating to Taking of the Deposition of the Adverse Party, repealed by order of July 20, 1966, was derived from Vernon's Civ.St.Art. 3769 and order of October 12, 1949.

Rule 189. Repealed by Order of Dec. 5, 1983, eff. April 1, 1984

Historical Notes

See, now, Vernon's Ann.Rules Civ.Proc., rule 208.

Rule 190. Discovery Limitations

190.1. Discovery Control Plan Required

Every case must be governed by a discovery control plan as provided in this Rule. A plaintiff must allege in the first numbered paragraph of the original petition whether discovery is intended to be conducted under Level 1, 2, or 3 of this Rule.

Aug. 5, 1998 and Nov. 9, 1998, eff. Jan. 1, 1999.

Comment—1999

See comments following Rule 190.6.

Historical Notes

The order of Nov. 9, 1998 provides that the rule applies to all cases filed on or after Jan. 1, 1999, but a court may adopt an appropriate discovery control plan in previously filed cases.

190.2. Discovery Control Plan—Expedited Actions and Divorces Involving $50,000 or Less (Level 1)

(a) *Application.* This subdivision applies to:

(1) any suit that is governed by the expedited actions process in Rule 169; and

(2) unless the parties agree that Rule 190.3 should apply or the court orders a discovery control plan under Rule 190.4, any suit for divorce not involving children in which a party pleads that the value of the marital estate is more than zero but not more than $50,000.

(b) *Limitations.* Discovery is subject to the limitations provided elsewhere in these rules and to the following additional limitations:

(1) Discovery Period. All discovery must be conducted during the discovery period, which begins

when the suit is filed and continues until 180 days after the date the first request for discovery of any kind is served on a party.

(2) Total Time for Oral Depositions. Each party may have no more than six hours in total to examine and cross-examine all witnesses in oral depositions. The parties may agree to expand this limit up to ten hours in total, but not more except by court order. The court may modify the deposition hours so that no party is given unfair advantage.

(3) Interrogatories. Any party may serve on any other party no more than 15 written interrogatories, excluding interrogatories asking a party only to identify or authenticate specific documents. Each discrete subpart of an interrogatory is considered a separate interrogatory.

(4) Requests for Production. Any party may serve on any other party no more than 15 written requests for production. Each discrete subpart of a request for production is considered a separate request for production.

(5) Requests for Admissions. Any party may serve on any other party no more than 15 written requests for admissions. Each discrete subpart of a request for admission is considered a separate request for admission.

(6) Requests for Disclosure. In addition to the content subject to disclosure under Rule 194.2, a party may request disclosure of all documents, electronic information, and tangible items that the disclosing party has in its possession, custody, or control and may use to support its claims or defenses. A request for disclosure made pursuant to this paragraph is not considered a request for production.

(c) Reopening Discovery. If a suit is removed from the expedited actions process in Rule 169 or, in a divorce, the filing of a pleading renders this subdivision no longer applicable, the discovery period reopens, and discovery must be completed within the limitations provided in Rules 190.3 or 190.4, whichever is applicable. Any person previously deposed may be redeposed. On motion of any party, the court should continue the trial date if necessary to permit completion of discovery.

Aug. 5, 1998 and Nov. 9, 1998, eff. Jan. 1, 1999. Amended by order of Feb. 12, 2013, eff. March 1, 2013.

Comment—1999

See comments following Rule 190.6.

Comment—2013

See comments following Rule 190.5.

Historical Notes

The order of Nov. 9, 1998 provides that the rule applies to all cases filed on or after Jan. 1, 1999, but a court may adopt an appropriate discovery control plan in previously filed cases.

2013 Amendment

The order dated February 12, 2013, rewrote the section, which formerly read:

"(a) *Application.* This subdivision applies to:

"(1) any suit that is governed by the expedited actions process in Rule 169, and

"(2) any suit for divorce not involving children in which a party pleads that the value of the marital estate is more than zero but not more than $50,000.

"(b) *Limitations.* Discovery is subject to the limitations provided elsewhere in these rules and to the following additional limitations:

"(1) Discovery Period. All discovery must be conducted during the discovery period, which begins when the suit is filed and continues until 180 days after the date the first request for discovery of any kind is served on a party.

"(2) Total Time for Oral Depositions. Each party may have no more than six hours in total to examine and cross-examine all witnesses in oral depositions. The parties may agree to expand this limit up to ten hours in total, but not more except by court order. The court may modify the deposition hours so that no party is given unfair advantage.

"(3) Interrogatories. Any party may serve on any other party no more than 15 written interrogatories, excluding interrogatories asking a party only to identify or authenticate specific documents. Each discrete subpart of an interrogatory is considered a separate interrogatory.

"(4) Requests for Production. Any party may serve on any other party no more than 15 written requests for production. Each discrete subpart of a request for production is considered a separate request for production.

"(5) Requests for Admissions. Any party may serve on any other party no more than 15 written requests for admissions. Each discrete subpart of a request for admission is considered a separate request for admission.

"(6) Requests for Disclosure. In addition to the content subject to disclosure under Rule 194.2. a party may request disclosure of all documents, electronic information, and tangible items that the disclosing party has in its possession, custody, or control and may use to support its claims or defenses. A request for disclosure made pursuant to this paragraph is not considered a request for production.

"(c) *Reopening Discovery.* If a suit is removed from the expedited actions process in Rule 169 or, in a divorce, the filing of a pleading renders this subdivision no longer applicable, the discovery period reopens, and discovery must be completed within the limitations provided in Rules 190.3 or 190.4, whichever is applicable. Any person previously deposed may be redeposed. On motion of any party, the court should continue the trial date if necessary to permit completion of discovery."

190.3. Discovery Control Plan—By Rule (Level 2)

(a) *Application.* Unless a suit is governed by a discovery control plan under Rules 190.2 or 190.4, discovery must be conducted in accordance with this subdivision.

(b) *Limitations.* Discovery is subject to the limitations provided elsewhere in these rules and to the following additional limitations:

(1) Discovery Period. All discovery must be conducted during the discovery period, which begins when suit is filed and continues until:

(A) 30 days before the date set for trial, in cases under the Family Code; or

(B) in other cases, the earlier of

(i) 30 days before the date set for trial, or

(ii) nine months after the earlier of the date of the first oral deposition or the due date of the first response to written discovery.

(2) Total Time for Oral Depositions. Each side may have no more than 50 hours in oral depositions to examine and cross-examine parties on the opposing side, experts designated by those parties, and persons who are subject to those parties' control. "Side" refers to all the litigants with generally common interests in the litigation. If one side designates more than two experts, the opposing side may have an additional six hours of total deposition time for each additional expert designated. The court may modify the deposition hours and must do so when a side or party would be given unfair advantage.

(3) Interrogatories. Any party may serve on any other party no more than 25 written interrogatories, excluding interrogatories asking a party only to identify or authenticate specific documents. Each discrete subpart of an interrogatory is considered a separate interrogatory.

Aug. 5, 1998, Nov. 9, 1998 and Dec. 31, 1998, eff. Jan. 1, 1999.

Comment—1999

See comments following Rule 190.6.

Historical Notes

The order of Nov. 9, 1998 provides that the rule applies to all cases filed on or after Jan. 1, 1999, but a court may adopt an appropriate discovery control plan in previously filed cases.

The Order dated December 31, 1998, made technical corrections.

190.4. Discovery Control Plan—By Order (Level 3)

(a) *Application.* The court must, on a party's motion, and may, on its own initiative, order that discovery be conducted in accordance with a discovery control plan tailored to the circumstances of the specific suit. The parties may submit an agreed order to the court for its consideration. The court should act on a party's motion or agreed order under this subdivision as promptly as reasonably possible.

(b) *Limitations.* The discovery control plan ordered by the court may address any issue concerning discovery or the matters listed in Rule 166, and may change any limitation on the time for or amount of discovery set forth in these rules. The discovery limitations of Rule 190.2, if applicable, or otherwise of Rule 190.3 apply unless specifically changed in the discovery control plan ordered by the court. The plan must include:

(1) a date for trial or for a conference to determine a trial setting;

(2) a discovery period during which either all discovery must be conducted or all discovery requests must be sent, for the entire case or an appropriate phase of it;

(3) appropriate limits on the amount of discovery; and

(4) deadlines for joining additional parties, amending or supplementing pleadings, and designating expert witnesses.

Aug. 5, 1998 and Nov. 9, 1998, eff. Jan. 1, 1999.

Comment—1999

See comments following Rule 190.6.

Historical Notes

The order of Nov. 9, 1998 provides that the rule applies to all cases filed on or after Jan. 1, 1999, but a court may adopt an appropriate discovery control plan in previously filed cases.

190.5. Modification of Discovery Control Plan

The court may modify a discovery control plan at any time and must do so when the interest of justice requires. Unless a suit is governed by the expedited actions process in Rule 169, the court must allow additional discovery:

(a) related to new, amended or supplemental pleadings, or new information disclosed in a discovery response or in an amended or supplemental response, if:

(1) the pleadings or responses were made after the deadline for completion of discovery or so nearly before that deadline that an adverse party does not have an adequate opportunity to conduct discovery related to the new matters, and

(2) the adverse party would be unfairly prejudiced without such additional discovery;

(b) regarding matters that have changed materially after the discovery cutoff if trial is set or postponed so that the trial date is more than three months after the discovery period ends.

Aug. 5, 1998 and Nov. 9, 1998, eff. Jan. 1, 1999. Amended by order of Feb. 12, 2013, eff. March 1, 2013.

Comment—1999

See comments following Rule 190.6.

Comment—2013

Rule 190 is amended to implement section 22.004(h) of the Texas Government Code, which calls for rules to promote the prompt, efficient, and cost-effective resolution of civil actions when the amount in controversy does not exceed $100,000. Rule 190.2 now applies to expedited actions, as defined by Rule 169. Rule 190.2 continues to apply to divorces not involving children in which the value of the marital estate is not more than $50,000, which are otherwise exempt from the expedited actions process. Amended Rule 190.2(b) ends the discovery period 180 days after the date the first discovery request is served; imposes a fifteen limit maximum on interrogatories, requests for production, and requests for admission; and allows for additional disclosures. Although expedited actions are not subject to mandatory additional discovery under amended Rule 190.5, the court may still allow additional discovery if the conditions of Rule 190.5(a) are met.

Historical Notes

2013 Amendment

The order dated February 12, 2013, in the first undesignated paragraph inserted "Unless a suit is governed by the expedited actions process in Rule 169,"

The order of Nov. 9, 1998 provides that the rule applies to all cases filed on or after Jan. 1, 1999, but a court may adopt an appropriate discovery control plan in previously filed cases.

190.6. Certain Types of Discovery Excepted

This rule's limitations on discovery do not apply to or include discovery conducted under Rule 202[1] ("Depositions Before Suit or to Investigate Claims"), or Rule 621a ("Discovery and Enforcement of Judgment"). But Rule 202 cannot be used to circumvent the limitations of this rule.

Aug. 5, 1998 and Nov. 9, 1998, eff. Jan. 1, 1999.

[1] Vernon's Ann.Rules Civ.Proc., rule 202.1 et seq.

Comment—1999

1. This rule establishes three tiers of discovery plans and requires that every case be in one at all times. A case is in Level 1 if it is pleaded by the plaintiff so as to invoke application Level 1, as provided by Rule 190.2(a). If a plaintiff does not or cannot plead the case in compliance with Rule 190.2(a) so as to invoke the application of Level 1, the case is automatically in Level 2. A case remains in Level 1 or Level 2, as determined by the pleadings, unless and until it is moved to Level 3. To be in Level 3, the court must order a specific plan for the case, either on a party's motion or on the court's own initiative. The plan may be one agreed to by the parties and submitted as an agreed order. A Level 3 plan may simply adopt Level 1 or Level 2 restrictions. Separate Level 3 plans for phases of the case may be appropriate. The initial pleading required by Rule 190.1 is merely to notify the court and other parties of the plaintiff's intention; it does not determine the applicable discovery level or bind the court or other parties. Thus, a plaintiff's failure to state in the initial pleading that the case should be in Level 1, as provided in Rule 190.1, does not alone make the case subject to Level 2 because the discovery level is determined by Rule 190.2. Likewise, a plaintiff's statement in the initial paragraph of the petition that the case is to be governed by Level 3 does not make Level 3 applicable, as a case can be in Level 3 only by court order. A plaintiff's failure to plead as required by Rule 190.1 is subject to special exception.

2. Rule 190.2 does not apply to suits for injunctive relief or divorces involving children. The requirement of an affirmative pleading of limited relief (e.g.: "Plaintiff affirmatively pleads that he seeks only monetary relief aggregating $50,000 or less, excluding costs, pre-judgment interest and attorneys' fees") does not conflict with other pleading requirements, such as Rule 47 and Tex. Rev. Civ. Stat. Ann. art. 4590i, § 5.01. In a suit to which Rule 190.2 applies, the relief awarded cannot exceed the limitations of Level 1 because the purpose of the rule, unlike Rule 47, is to bind the pleader to a maximum claim. To this extent, the rule in *Greenhalgh v. Service Lloyds Ins. Co.*, 787 S.W.2d 938 (Tex. 1990), does not apply.

3. "Discrete subparts" of interrogatories are counted as single interrogatories, but not every separate factual inquiry is a discrete subpart. See Fed. R. Civ. P. 33(a). While not susceptible of precise definition, *see Braden v. Downey*, 811 S.W.2d 922, 927-928 (Tex. 1991), a "discrete subpart" is, in general, one that calls for information that is not logically or factually related to the primary interrogatory. The number of sets of interrogatories is no longer limited to two.

4. As other rules make clear, unless otherwise ordered or agreed, parties seeking discovery must serve requests sufficiently far in advance of the end of the discovery period that the deadline for responding will be within the discovery period. The court may order a deadline for sending discovery requests in lieu of or in addition to a deadline for completing discovery.

5. Use of forms of discovery other than depositions and interrogatories, such as requests for disclosure, admissions, or production of documents, are not restricted in Levels 1 and 2. But depositions on written questions cannot be used to circumvent the limits on interrogatories.

6. The concept of "side" in Rule 190.3(b)(2) borrows from Rule 233, which governs the allocation of peremptory strikes, and from Fed. R. Civ. P. 30(a)(2). In most cases there are only two sides—plaintiffs and defendants. In complex cases, however, there may be more than two sides, such as when defendants have sued third parties not named by plaintiffs, or when defendants have sued each other. As an example, if P1 and P2 sue D1, D2, and D3, and D1 sues D2 and D3, Ps would together be entitled to depose Ds and others per-

mitted by the rule (*i.e.,* Ds' experts and persons subject to Ds' control) for 50 hours, and Ds would together be entitled to depose Ps and others for 50 hours. D1 would also be entitled to depose D2 and D3 and others for 50 hours on matters in controversy among them, and D2 and D3 would together be entitled to depose D1 and others for 50 hours.

7. Any matter listed in Rule 166 may be addressed in an order issued under Rule 190.4. A pretrial order under Rule 166 may be used in individual cases regardless of the discovery level.

8. For purposes of defining discovery periods, "trial" does not include summary judgment.

Historical Notes

The order of Nov. 9, 1998 provides that the rule applies to all cases filed on or after Jan. 1, 1999, but a court may adopt an appropriate discovery control plan in previously filed cases.

Rule 191. Modifying Discovery Procedures and Limitations; Conference Requirement; Signing Disclosures, Discovery Requests, Responses, and Objections; Filing Requirements

191.1. Modification of Procedures

Except where specifically prohibited, the procedures and limitations set forth in the rules pertaining to discovery may be modified in any suit by the agreement of the parties or by court order for good cause. An agreement of the parties is enforceable if it complies with Rule 11 or, as it affects an oral deposition, if it is made a part of the record of the deposition.

Aug. 5, 1998 and Nov. 9, 1998, eff. Jan. 1, 1999.

Comment—1999

See comments following Rule 191.5.

Historical Notes

Source:

Former rule 166c.

191.2. Conference

Parties and their attorneys are expected to cooperate in discovery and to make any agreements reasonably necessary for the efficient disposition of the case. All discovery motions or requests for hearings relating to discovery must contain a certificate by the party filing the motion or request that a reasonable effort has been made to resolve the dispute without the necessity of court intervention and the effort failed.

Aug. 5, 1998 and Nov. 9, 1998, eff. Jan. 1, 1999.

Comment—1999

See comments following Rule 191.5.

191.3. Signing of Disclosures, Discovery Requests, Notices, Responses, and Objections

(a) *Signature Required.* Every disclosure, discovery request, notice, response, and objection must be signed:

(1) by an attorney, if the party is represented by an attorney, and must show the attorney's State Bar of Texas identification number, address, telephone number, and fax number, if any; or

(2) by the party, if the party is not represented by an attorney, and must show the party's address, telephone number, and fax number, if any.

(b) *Effect of Signature on Disclosure.* The signature of an attorney or party on a disclosure constitutes a certification that to the best of the signer's knowledge, information, and belief, formed after a reasonable inquiry, the disclosure is complete and correct as of the time it is made.

(c) *Effect of Signature on Discovery Request, Notice, Response, or Objection.* The signature of an attorney or party on a discovery request, notice, response, or objection constitutes a certification that to the best of the signer's knowledge, information, and belief, formed after a reasonable inquiry, the request, notice, response, or objection:

(1) is consistent with the rules of civil procedure and these discovery rules and warranted by existing law or a good faith argument for the extension, modification, or reversal of existing law;

(2) has a good faith factual basis;

(3) is not interposed for any improper purpose, such as to harass or to cause unnecessary delay or needless increase in the cost of litigation; and

(4) is not unreasonable or unduly burdensome or expensive, given the needs of the case, the discovery already had in the case, the amount in controversy, and the importance of the issues at stake in the litigation.

(d) *Effect of Failure to Sign.* If a request, notice, response, or objection is not signed, it must be stricken unless it is signed promptly after the omission is called to the attention of the party making the request, notice, response, or objection. A party is not required to take any action with respect to a request or notice that is not signed.

(e) *Sanctions.* If the certification is false without substantial justification, the court may, upon motion or its own initiative, impose on the person who made the certification, or the party on whose behalf the request, notice, response, or objection was made, or both, an appropriate sanction as for a frivolous pleading or motion under Chapter 10 of the Civil Practice and Remedies Code.

Aug. 5, 1998 and Nov. 9, 1998, eff. Jan. 1, 1999.

Comment—1999

See comments following Rule 191.5.

191.4. Filing of Discovery Materials

(a) *Discovery Materials Not to Be Filed.* The following discovery materials must not be filed:

(1) discovery requests, deposition notices, and subpoenas required to be served only on parties;

(2) responses and objections to discovery requests and deposition notices, regardless on whom the requests or notices were served;

(3) documents and tangible things produced in discovery; and

(4) statements prepared in compliance with Rule 193.3(b) or (d).

(b) *Discovery Materials to Be Filed.* The following discovery materials must be filed:

(1) discovery requests, deposition notices, and subpoenas required to be served on nonparties;

(2) motions and responses to motions pertaining to discovery matters; and

(3) agreements concerning discovery matters, to the extent necessary to comply with Rule 11.

(c) *Exceptions.* Notwithstanding paragraph (a)—

(1) the court may order discovery materials to be filed;

(2) a person may file discovery materials in support of or in opposition to a motion or for other use in a court proceeding; and

(3) a person may file discovery materials necessary for a proceeding in an appellate court.

(d) *Retention Requirement for Persons.* Any person required to serve discovery materials not required to be filed must retain the original or exact copy of the materials during the pendency of the case and any related appellate proceedings begun within six months after judgment is signed, unless otherwise provided by the trial court.

(e) *Retention Requirement for Courts.* The clerk of the court shall retain and dispose of deposition transcripts and depositions upon written questions as directed by the Supreme Court.

Aug. 5, 1998 and Nov. 9, 1998, eff. Jan. 1, 1999.

Comment—1999

See comments following Rule 191.5.

Historical Notes

Supreme Court order of Jan. 27, 2005 provided:

"As provided by Rule 191.4(e), Texas Rules of Civil Procedure, the Supreme Court hereby directs that deposition transcripts and depositions upon written questions be retained and disposed of by the clerk of the court in which the same are filed on the following basis.

"The order shall apply only to: (1) those cases in which judgment has been rendered on service of process by publication and in which no motion for new trial was filed within two years after judgment was signed; and (2) all other cases in which judgment has been signed for one year and in which no appeal was perfected or in which a perfected appeal was dismissed or concluded by a final judgment as to all parties and the issuance of the appellate court's mandate such that the case is no longer pending on appeal or in the trial court.

"The party who offered a deposition transcript or deposition upon written questions may withdraw it from the clerk's office within thirty days of the later of (1) a case becoming subject to this order, or (2) the effective date of this order. The clerk, unless otherwise directed by the court, may dispose of any deposition transcript or deposition upon written questions remaining after such time period."

"This order is effective June 1, 2005."

Source:

Former rule 209.

191.5. Service of Discovery Materials

Every disclosure, discovery request, notice, response, and objection required to be served on a party or person must be served on all parties of record.

Added Nov. 9, 1998, eff. Jan. 1, 1999.

Comment—1999

1. Rule 191.1 preserves the ability of parties by agreement and trial courts by order to adapt discovery to different circumstances. That ability is broad but not unbounded. Parties cannot merely by agreement modify a court order without the court's concurrence. Trial courts cannot simply "opt out" of these rules by form orders or approve or order a discovery control plan that does not contain the matters specified in Rule 190.4, but trial courts may use standard or form orders for providing discovery plans, scheduling, and other pretrial matters. In individual instances, courts may order, or parties may agree, to use discovery methods other than those prescribed in these rules if appropriate. Because the general rule is stated here, it is not repeated in each context in which it applies. Thus, for example, parties can agree to enlarge or shorten the time permitted for a deposition and to change the manner in which a deposition is conducted, notwithstanding Rule 199.5, although parties could not agree to be abusive toward a witness.

2. Rule 191.2 expressly states the obligation of parties and their attorneys to cooperate in conducting discovery.

3. The requirement that discovery requests, notices, responses, and objections be signed also applies to documents used to satisfy the purposes of such instruments. An example is a statement that privileged material or information has been withheld, which may be separate from a response

to the discovery request but is nevertheless part of the response.

Rule 192. Permissible Discovery: Forms and Scope; Work Product; Protective Orders; Definitions

Historical Notes

Source:

Former rule 166b.

192.1. Forms of Discovery

Permissible forms of discovery are:

(a) requests for disclosure;

(b) requests for production and inspection of documents and tangible things;

(c) requests and motions for entry upon and examination of real property;

(d) interrogatories to a party;

(e) requests for admission;

(f) oral or written depositions; and

(g) motions for mental or physical examinations.

Aug. 5, 1998 and Nov. 9, 1998, eff. Jan. 1, 1999.

Comment—1999

See comments following Rule 192.7.

192.2. Sequence of Discovery

The permissible forms of discovery may be combined in the same document and may be taken in any order or sequence.

Aug. 5, 1998 and Nov. 9, 1998, eff. Jan. 1, 1999.

Comment—1999

See comments following Rule 192.7.

192.3. Scope of Discovery

(a) *Generally.* In general, a party may obtain discovery regarding any matter that is not privileged and is relevant to the subject matter of the pending action, whether it relates to the claim or defense of the party seeking discovery or the claim or defense of any other party. It is not a ground for objection that the information sought will be inadmissible at trial if the information sought appears reasonably calculated to lead to the discovery of admissible evidence.

(b) *Documents and Tangible Things.* A party may obtain discovery of the existence, description, nature, custody, condition, location, and contents of documents and tangible things (including papers, books, accounts, drawings, graphs, charts, photographs, electronic or videotape recordings, data, and data compilations) that constitute or contain matters relevant to the subject matter of the action. A person is required to produce a document or tangible thing that is within the person's possession, custody, or control.

(c) *Persons with Knowledge of Relevant Facts.* A party may obtain discovery of the name, address, and telephone number of persons having knowledge of relevant facts, and a brief statement of each identified person's connection with the case. A person has knowledge of relevant facts when that person has or may have knowledge of any discoverable matter. The person need not have admissible information or personal knowledge of the facts. An expert is "a person with knowledge of relevant facts" only if that knowledge was obtained first-hand or if it was not obtained in preparation for trial or in anticipation of litigation.

(d) *Trial Witnesses.* A party may obtain discovery of the name, address, and telephone number of any person who is expected to be called to testify at trial. This paragraph does not apply to rebuttal or impeaching witnesses the necessity of whose testimony cannot reasonably be anticipated before trial.

(e) *Testifying and Consulting Experts.* The identity, mental impressions, and opinions of a consulting expert whose mental impressions and opinions have not been reviewed by a testifying expert are not discoverable. A party may discover the following information regarding a testifying expert or regarding a consulting expert whose mental impressions or opinions have been reviewed by a testifying expert:

(1) the expert's name, address, and telephone number;

(2) the subject matter on which a testifying expert will testify;

(3) the facts known by the expert that relate to or form the basis of the expert's mental impressions and opinions formed or made in connection with the case in which the discovery is sought, regardless of when and how the factual information was acquired;

(4) the expert's mental impressions and opinions formed or made in connection with the case in which discovery is sought, and any methods used to derive them;

(5) any bias of the witness;

(6) all documents, tangible things, reports, models, or data compilations that have been provided to, reviewed by, or prepared by or for the expert in anticipation of a testifying expert's testimony;

(7) the expert's current resume and bibliography.

(f) *Indemnity and Insuring Agreements.* Except as otherwise provided by law, a party may obtain discovery of the existence and contents of any indemnity or insurance agreement under which any person may be liable to satisfy part or all of a judgment rendered in the action or to indemnify or reimburse for payments made to satisfy the judgment. Information concerning the indemnity or insurance agreement is not by reason of disclosure admissible in evidence at trial.

(g) *Settlement Agreements.* A party may obtain discovery of the existence and contents of any relevant portions of a settlement agreement. Information concerning a settlement agreement is not by reason of disclosure admissible in evidence at trial.

(h) *Statements of Persons with Knowledge of Relevant Facts.* A party may obtain discovery of the statement of any person with knowledge of relevant facts—a "witness statement"—regardless of when the statement was made. A witness statement is (1) a written statement signed or otherwise adopted or approved in writing by the person making it, or (2) a stenographic, mechanical, electrical, or other type of recording of a witness's oral statement, or any substantially verbatim transcription of such a recording. Notes taken during a conversation or interview with a witness are not a witness statement. Any person may obtain, upon written request, his or her own statement concerning the lawsuit, which is in the possession, custody or control of any party.

(i) *Potential Parties.* A party may obtain discovery of the name, address, and telephone number of any potential party.

(j) *Contentions.* A party may obtain discovery of any other party's legal contentions and the factual bases for those contentions.

Aug. 5, 1998 and amended Nov. 9, 1998, eff. Jan. 1, 1999.

Comment—1999

See comments following Rule 192.7.

192.4. Limitations on Scope of Discovery

The discovery methods permitted by these rules should be limited by the court if it determines, on motion or on its own initiative and on reasonable notice, that:

(a) the discovery sought is unreasonably cumulative or duplicative, or is obtainable from some other source that is more convenient, less burdensome, or less expensive; or

(b) the burden or expense of the proposed discovery outweighs its likely benefit, taking into account the needs of the case, the amount in controversy, the parties' resources, the importance of the issues at stake in the litigation, and the importance of the proposed discovery in resolving the issues.

Aug. 5, 1998 and Nov. 9, 1998, eff Jan. 1, 1999.

Comment—1999

See comments following Rule 192.7.

192.5. Work Product

(a) *Work Product Defined.* Work product comprises:

(1) material prepared or mental impressions developed in anticipation of litigation or for trial by or for a party or a party's representatives, including the party's attorneys, consultants, sureties, indemnitors, insurers, employees, or agents; or

(2) a communication made in anticipation of litigation or for trial between a party and the party's representatives or among a party's representatives, including the party's attorneys, consultants, sureties, indemnitors, insurers, employees, or agents.

(b) *Protection of Work Product.*

(1) Protection of Core Work Product–Attorney Mental Processes. Core work product—the work product of an attorney or an attorney's representative that contains the attorney's or the attorney's representative's mental impressions, opinions, conclusions, or legal theories—is not discoverable.

(2) Protection of Other Work Product. Any other work product is discoverable only upon a showing that the party seeking discovery has substantial need of the materials in the preparation of the party's case and that the party is unable without undue hardship to obtain the substantial equivalent of the material by other means.

(3) Incidental Disclosure of Attorney Mental Processes. It is not a violation of subparagraph (1) if disclosure ordered pursuant to subparagraph (2) incidentally discloses by inference attorney mental processes otherwise protected under subparagraph (1).

(4) Limiting Disclosure of Mental Processes. If a court orders discovery of work product pursuant to subparagraph (2), the court must—insofar as possible—protect against disclosure of the mental impressions, opinions, conclusions, or legal theories not otherwise discoverable.

(c) *Exceptions.* Even if made or prepared in anticipation of litigation or for trial, the following is not work product protected from discovery:

(1) information discoverable under Rule 192.3 concerning experts, trial witnesses, witness statements, and contentions;

(2) trial exhibits ordered disclosed under Rule 166 or Rule 190.4;

(3) the name, address, and telephone number of any potential party or any person with knowledge of relevant facts;

(4) any photograph or electronic image of underlying facts (e.g., a photograph of the accident scene)

or a photograph or electronic image of any sort that a party intends to offer into evidence; and

(5) any work product created under circumstances within an exception to the attorney-client privilege in Rule 503(d) of the Rules of Evidence.

(d) *Privilege.* For purposes of these rules, an assertion that material or information is work product is an assertion of privilege.

Aug. 5, 1998, Nov. 9, 1998 and Dec. 31, 1998, eff. Jan. 1, 1999.

Comment—1999

See comments following Rule 192.7.

Historical Notes

The Order dated December 31, 1998, made technical corrections.

192.6. Protective Orders

(a) *Motion.* A person from whom discovery is sought, and any other person affected by the discovery request, may move within the time permitted for response to the discovery request for an order protecting that person from the discovery sought. A person should not move for protection when an objection to written discovery or an assertion of privilege is appropriate, but a motion does not waive the objection or assertion of privilege. If a person seeks protection regarding the time or place of discovery, the person must state a reasonable time and place for discovery with which the person will comply. A person must comply with a request to the extent protection is not sought unless it is unreasonable under the circumstances to do so before obtaining a ruling on the motion.

(b) *Order.* To protect the movant from undue burden, unnecessary expense, harassment, annoyance, or invasion of personal, constitutional, or property rights, the court may make any order in the interest of justice and may—among other things—order that:

(1) the requested discovery not be sought in whole or in part;

(2) the extent or subject matter of discovery be limited;

(3) the discovery not be undertaken at the time or place specified;

(4) the discovery be undertaken only by such method or upon such terms and conditions or at the time and place directed by the court;

(5) the results of discovery be sealed or otherwise protected, subject to the provisions of Rule 76a.

Aug. 5, 1998 and Nov. 9, 1998, eff. Jan. 1, 1999.

Comment—1999

See comments following Rule 192.7.

192.7. Definitions

As used in these rules—

(a) *Written Discovery* means requests for disclosure, requests for production and inspection of documents and tangible things, requests for entry onto property, interrogatories, and requests for admission.

(b) *Possession, Custody, or Control* of an item means that the person either has physical possession of the item or has a right to possession of the item that is equal or superior to the person who has physical possession of the item.

(c) A *Testifying Expert* is an expert who may be called to testify as an expert witness at trial.

(d) A *Consulting Expert* is an expert who has been consulted, retained, or specially employed by a party in anticipation of litigation or in preparation for trial, but who is not a testifying expert.

Aug. 5, 1998 and amended Nov. 9, 1998, eff. Jan. 1, 1999.

Comment—1999

1. While the scope of discovery is quite broad, it is nevertheless confined by the subject matter of the case and reasonable expectations of obtaining information that will aid resolution of the dispute. The rule must be read and applied in that context. *See In re American Optical Corp.*, 988 S.W.2d 711 (Tex. 1998) (per curiam); *K-Mart v. Sanderson*, 937 S.W.2d 429 (Tex. 1996) (per curiam); *Dillard Dept. Stores v. Hall*, 909 S.W.2d 491 (Tex. 1995) (per curiam); *Texaco, Inc. v. Sanderson*, 898 S.W.2d 813 (Tex. 1995) (per curiam); *Loftin v. Martin*, 776 S.W.2d 145, 148 (Tex. 1989).

2. The definition of documents and tangible things has been revised to clarify that things relevant to the subject matter of the action are within the scope of discovery regardless of their form.

3. Rule 192.3(c) makes discoverable a "brief statement of each identified person's connection with the case." This provision does not contemplate a narrative statement of the facts the person knows, but at most a few words describing the person's identity as relevant to the lawsuit.

For instance: "treating physician," "eyewitness," "chief financial officer," "director," "plaintiff's mother and eyewitness to accident." The rule is intended to be consistent with *Axelson v. McIlhany*, 798 S.W.2d 550 (Tex. 1990).

4. Rule 192.3(g) does not suggest that settlement agreements in other cases are relevant or irrelevant.

5. Rule 192.3(j) makes a party's legal and factual contentions discoverable but does not require more than a basic statement of those contentions and does not require a marshaling of evidence.

6. The sections in former Rule 166b concerning land and medical records are not included in this rule. They remain within the scope of discovery and are discussed in other rules.

7. The court's power to limit discovery based on the needs and circumstances of the case is expressly stated in Rule 192.4. The provision is taken from Rule 26(b)(2) of the Federal Rules of Civil Procedure. Courts should limit discovery under this rule only to prevent unwarranted delay and expense as stated more fully in the rule. A court abuses its discretion in unreasonably restricting a party's access to information through discovery.

8. Work product is defined for the first time, and its exceptions stated. Work product replaces the "attorney work product" and "party communication" discovery exemptions from former Rule 166b.

9. Elimination of the "witness statement" exemption does not render all witness statements automatically discoverable but subjects them to the same rules concerning the scope of discovery and privileges applicable to other documents or tangible things.

Rule 193. Written Discovery: Response; Objection; Assertion of Privilege; Supplementation and Amendment; Failure to Timely Respond; Presumption of Authenticity

193.1. Responding to Written Discovery; Duty to Make Complete Response

A party must respond to written discovery in writing within the time provided by court order or these rules. When responding to written discovery, a party must make a complete response, based on all information reasonably available to the responding party or its attorney at the time the response is made. The responding party's answers, objections, and other responses must be preceded by the request to which they apply.

Aug. 5, 1998 and Nov. 9, 1998, eff. Jan. 1, 1999.

Comment—1999

See comments following Rule 193.7.

193.2. Objecting to Written Discovery

(a) *Form and Time for Objections.* A party must make any objection to written discovery in writing—either in the response or in a separate document—within the time for response. The party must state specifically the legal or factual basis for the objection and the extent to which the party is refusing to comply with the request.

(b) *Duty to Respond When Partially Objecting; Objection to Time or Place of Production.* A party must comply with as much of the request to which the party has made no objection unless it is unreasonable under the circumstances to do so before obtaining a ruling on the objection. If the responding party objects to the requested time or place of production, the responding party must state a reasonable time and place for complying with the request and must comply at that time and place without further request or order.

(c) *Good Faith Basis for Objection.* A party may object to written discovery only if a good faith factual and legal basis for the objection exists at the time the objection is made.

(d) *Amendment.* An objection or response to written discovery may be amended or supplemented to state an objection or basis that, at the time the objection or response initially was made, either was inapplicable or was unknown after reasonable inquiry.

(e) *Waiver of Objection.* An objection that is not made within the time required, or that is obscured by numerous unfounded objections, is waived unless the court excuses the waiver for good cause shown.

(f) *No Objection to Preserve Privilege.* A party should not object to a request for written discovery on the grounds that it calls for production of material or information that is privileged but should instead comply with Rule 193.3. A party who objects to production of privileged material or information does not waive the privilege but must comply with Rule 193.3 when the error is pointed out.

Aug. 5, 1998 and Nov. 9, 1998, eff. Jan. 1, 1999.

Comment—1999

See comments following Rule 193.7.

193.3. Asserting a Privilege

A party may preserve a privilege from written discovery in accordance with this subdivision.

(a) *Withholding Privileged Material or Information.* A party who claims that material or information responsive to written discovery is privileged may withhold the privileged material or information from the response. The party must state—in the response (or an amended or supplemental response) or in a separate document—that:

(1) information or material responsive to the request has been withheld,

(2) the request to which the information or material relates, and

(3) the privilege or privileges asserted.

(b) *Description of Withheld Material or Information.* After receiving a response indicating that material or information has been withheld from production, the party seeking discovery may serve a written request that the withholding party identify the information and material withheld. Within 15 days of service of that request, the withholding party must serve a response that:

(1) describes the information or materials withheld that, without revealing the privileged informa-

tion itself or otherwise waiving the privilege, enables other parties to assess the applicability of the privilege, and

(2) asserts a specific privilege for each item or group of items withheld.

(c) *Exemption.* Without complying with paragraphs (a) and (b), a party may withhold a privileged communication to or from a lawyer or lawyer's representative or a privileged document of a lawyer or lawyer's representative—

(1) created or made from the point at which a party consults a lawyer with a view to obtaining professional legal services from the lawyer in the prosecution or defense of a specific claim in the litigation in which discovery is requested, and

(2) concerning the litigation in which the discovery is requested.

(d) *Privilege Not Waived by Production.* A party who produces material or information without intending to waive a claim of privilege does not waive that claim under these rules or the Rules of Evidence if—within ten days or a shorter time ordered by the court, after the producing party actually discovers that such production was made—the producing party amends the response, identifying the material or information produced and stating the privilege asserted. If the producing party thus amends the response to assert a privilege, the requesting party must promptly return the specified material or information and any copies pending any ruling by the court denying the privilege.

Aug. 5, 1998 and Nov. 9, 1998, eff. Jan. 1, 1999.

Comment—1999

See comments following Rule 193.7.

193.4. Hearing and Ruling on Objections and Assertions of Privilege

(a) *Hearing.* Any party may at any reasonable time request a hearing on an objection or claim of privilege asserted under this rule. The party making the objection or asserting the privilege must present any evidence necessary to support the objection or privilege. The evidence may be testimony presented at the hearing or affidavits served at least seven days before the hearing or at such other reasonable time as the court permits. If the court determines that an in camera review of some or all of the requested discovery is necessary, that material or information must be segregated and produced to the court in a sealed wrapper within a reasonable time following the hearing.

(b) *Ruling.* To the extent the court sustains the objection or claim of privilege, the responding party has no further duty to respond to that request. To the extent the court overrules the objection or claim of privilege, the responding party must produce the requested material or information within 30 days after the court's ruling or at such time as the court orders. A party need not request a ruling on that party's own objection or assertion of privilege to preserve the objection or privilege.

(c) *Use of Material or Information Withheld Under Claim of Privilege.* A party may not use—at any hearing or trial—material or information withheld from discovery under a claim of privilege, including a claim sustained by the court, without timely amending or supplementing the party's response to that discovery.

Aug. 5, 1998, Nov. 9, 1998 and Dec. 31, 1998, eff. Jan. 1, 1999.

Comment—1999

See comments following Rule 193.7.

193.5. Amending or Supplementing Responses to Written Discovery

(a) *Duty to Amend or Supplement.* If a party learns that the party's response to written discovery was incomplete or incorrect when made, or, although complete and correct when made, is no longer complete and correct, the party must amend or supplement the response:

(1) to the extent that the written discovery sought the identification of persons with knowledge of relevant facts, trial witnesses, or expert witnesses, and

(2) to the extent that the written discovery sought other information, unless the additional or corrective information has been made known to the other parties in writing, on the record at a deposition, or through other discovery responses.

(b) *Time and Form of Amended or Supplemental Response.* An amended or supplemental response must be made reasonably promptly after the party discovers the necessity for such a response. Except as otherwise provided by these rules, it is presumed that an amended or supplemental response made less than 30 days before trial was not made reasonably promptly. An amended or supplemental response must be in the same form as the initial response and must be verified by the party if the original response was required to be verified by the party, but the failure to comply with this requirement does not make the amended or supplemental response untimely unless the party making the response refuses to correct the defect within a reasonable time after it is pointed out.

Aug. 5, 1998 and Nov. 9, 1998, eff. Jan. 1, 1999.

Comment—1999

See comments following Rule 193.7.

Historical Notes

Source:

Former rule 166b.

193.6. Failing to Timely Respond—Effect on Trial

(a) *Exclusion of Evidence and Exceptions.* A party who fails to make, amend, or supplement a discovery response in a timely manner may not introduce in evidence the material or information that was not timely disclosed, or offer the testimony of a witness (other than a named party) who was not timely identified, unless the court finds that:

(1) there was good cause for the failure to timely make, amend, or supplement the discovery response; or

(2) the failure to timely make, amend, or supplement the discovery response will not unfairly surprise or unfairly prejudice the other parties.

(b) *Burden of Establishing Exception.* The burden of establishing good cause or the lack of unfair surprise or unfair prejudice is on the party seeking to introduce the evidence or call the witness. A finding of good cause or of the lack of unfair surprise or unfair prejudice must be supported by the record.

(c) *Continuance.* Even if the party seeking to introduce the evidence or call the witness fails to carry the burden under paragraph (b), the court may grant a continuance or temporarily postpone the trial to allow a response to be made, amended, or supplemented, and to allow opposing parties to conduct discovery regarding any new information presented by that response.

Aug. 5, 1998 and Nov. 9, 1998, eff. Jan. 1, 1999.

Comment—1999

See comments following Rule 193.7.

Historical Notes

The order of Nov. 9, 1998 provides that a response to a discovery request, an objection to a discovery request, an assertion of privilege, or an amendment or supplementation to a discovery response made before Jan. 1, 1999 need not comply with the new rule.

193.7. Production of Documents Self-Authenticating

A party's production of a document in response to written discovery authenticates the document for use against that party in any pretrial proceeding or at trial unless—within ten days or a longer or shorter time ordered by the court, after the producing party has actual notice that the document will be used—the party objects to the authenticity of the document, or any part of it, stating the specific basis for objection. An objection must be either on the record or in writing and must have a good faith factual and legal basis. An objection made to the authenticity of only part of a document does not affect the authenticity of the remainder. If objection is made, the party attempting to use the document should be given a reasonable opportunity to establish its authenticity.

Aug. 5, 1998 and amended Nov. 9, 1998, eff. Jan. 1, 1999.

Comment—1999

1. This rule imposes a duty upon parties to make a complete response to written discovery based upon all information reasonably available, subject to objections and privileges.

2. An objection to written discovery does not excuse the responding party from complying with the request to the extent no objection is made. But a party may object to a request for "all documents relevant to the lawsuit" as overly broad and not in compliance with the rule requiring specific requests for documents and refuse to comply with it entirely. *See Loftin v. Martin,* 776 S.W.2d 145 (Tex. 1989). A party may also object to a request for a litigation file on the ground that it is overly broad and may assert that on its face the request seeks only materials protected by privilege. *See National Union Fire Ins. Co. v. Valdez,* 863 S.W.2d 458 (Tex. 1993). A party who objects to production of documents from a remote time period should produce documents from a more recent period unless that production would be burdensome and duplicative should the objection be overruled.

3. This rule governs the presentation of all privileges including work product. It dispenses with objections to written discovery requests on the basis that responsive information or materials are protected by a specific privilege from discovery. Instead, the rule requires parties to state that information or materials have been withheld and to identify the privilege upon which the party relies. The statement should not be made prophylactically, but only when specific information and materials have been withheld. The party must amend or supplement the statement if additional privileged information or material is found subsequent to the initial response. Thus, when large numbers of documents are being produced, a party may amend the initial response when documents are found as to which the party claims privilege. A party need not state that material created by or for lawyers for the litigation has been withheld as it can be assumed that such material will be withheld from virtually any request on the grounds of attorney-client privilege or work product. However, the rule does not prohibit a party from specifically requesting the material or information if the party has a good faith basis for asserting that it is discoverable. An example would be material or information described by Rule 503(d)(1) of the Rules of Evidence.

4. Rule 193.3(d) is a new provision that allows a party to assert a claim of privilege to material or

information produced inadvertently without intending to waive the privilege. The provision is commonly used in complex cases to reduce costs and risks in large document productions. The focus is on the intent to waive the privilege, not the intent to produce the material or information. A party who fails to diligently screen documents before producing them does not waive a claim of privilege. This rule is thus broader than Tex. R. Evid. 511 and overturns *Granada Corp. v. First Court of Appeals*, 844 S.W.2d 223 (Tex. 1992), to the extent the two conflict. The ten-day period (which may be shortened by the court) allowed for an amended response does not run from the production of the material or information but from the party's first awareness of the mistake. To avoid complications at trial, a party may identify prior to trial the documents intended to be offered, thereby triggering the obligation to assert any overlooked privilege under this rule. A trial court may also order this procedure.

5. This rule imposes no duty to supplement or amend deposition testimony. The only duty to supplement deposition testimony is provided in Rule 195.6.

6. Any party can request a hearing in which the court will resolve issues brought up in objections or withholding statements. The party seeking to avoid discovery has the burden of proving the objection or privilege.

7. The self-authenticating provision is new. Authentication is, of course, but a condition precedent to admissibility and does not establish admissibility. *See* Tex. R. Evid. 901(a). The ten-day period allowed for objection to authenticity (which period may be altered by the court in appropriate circumstances) does not run from the production of the material or information but from the party's actual awareness that the document will be used. To avoid complications at trial, a party may identify prior to trial the documents intended to be offered, thereby triggering the obligation to object to authenticity. A trial court may also order this procedure. An objection to authenticity must be made in good faith.

Rule 194. Requests for Disclosure

194.1. Request

A party may obtain disclosure from another party of the information or material listed in Rule 194.2 by serving the other party—no later than 30 days before the end of any applicable discovery period—the following request: "Pursuant to Rule 194, you are requested to disclose, within 30 days of service of this request, the information or material described in Rule [state rule, e.g., 194.2, or 194.2(a), (c), and (f), or 194.2(d)-(g)]."

Aug. 5, 1998 and Nov. 9, 1998, eff. Jan. 1, 1999.

Comment—1999

See comments following Rule 194.6.

194.2. Content

A party may request disclosure of any or all of the following:

(a) the correct names of the parties to the lawsuit;

(b) the name, address, and telephone number of any potential parties;

(c) the legal theories and, in general, the factual bases of the responding party's claims or defenses (the responding party need not marshal all evidence that may be offered at trial);

(d) the amount and any method of calculating economic damages;

(e) the name, address, and telephone number of persons having knowledge of relevant facts, and a brief statement of each identified person's connection with the case;

(f) for any testifying expert:

(1) the expert's name, address, and telephone number;

(2) the subject matter on which the expert will testify;

(3) the general substance of the expert's mental impressions and opinions and a brief summary of the basis for them, or if the expert is not retained by, employed by, or otherwise subject to the control of the responding party, documents reflecting such information;

(4) if the expert is retained by, employed by, or otherwise subject to the control of the responding party:

(A) all documents, tangible things, reports, models, or data compilations that have been provided to, reviewed by, or prepared by or for the expert in anticipation of the expert's testimony; and

(B) the expert's current resume and bibliography;

(g) any indemnity and insuring agreements described in Rule 192.3(f);

(h) any settlement agreements described in Rule 192.3(g);

(i) any witness statements described in Rule 192.3(h);

(j) in a suit alleging physical or mental injury and damages from the occurrence that is the subject of the case, all medical records and bills that are reasonably related to the injuries or damages asserted or, in lieu thereof, an authorization permitting the disclosure of such medical records and bills;

(k) in a suit alleging physical or mental injury and damages from the occurrence that is the subject of the case, all medical records and bills obtained by the responding party by virtue of an authorization furnished by the requesting party;

(*l*) the name, address, and telephone number of any person who may be designated as a responsible third party.

Aug. 5, 1998, Nov. 9, 1998 and Dec. 31, 1998, eff. Jan. 1, 1999. Amended by order of March 3, 2004, eff. March 3, 2004.

Comment—1999

See comments following Rule 194.6.

Historical Notes

The Order dated March 3, 2004 provides:

"Rule 194.2(*l*) is added as required by changes in chapter 33 of the Texas Civil Practice and Remedies Code. The amendment applies in all cases filed on or after July 1, 2003, in which a request under Rule 194.1 is made after May 1, 2004."

194.3. Response

The responding party must serve a written response on the requesting party within 30 days after service of the request, except that:

(a) a defendant served with a request before the defendant's answer is due need not respond until 50 days after service of the request, and

(b) a response to a request under Rule 194.2(f) is governed by Rule 195.[1]

Aug. 5, 1998 and Nov. 9, 1998, eff. Jan. 1, 1999.

[1] Vernon's Ann.Rules Civ.Proc., rule 195.1 et seq.

Comment—1999

See comments following Rule 194.6.

194.4. Production

Copies of documents and other tangible items ordinarily must be served with the response. But if the responsive documents are voluminous, the response must state a reasonable time and place for the production of documents. The responding party must produce the documents at the time and place stated, unless otherwise agreed by the parties or ordered by the court, and must provide the requesting party a reasonable opportunity to inspect them.

Aug. 5, 1998 and Nov. 9, 1998, eff. Jan. 1, 1999.

Comment—1999

See comments following Rule 194.6.

194.5. No Objection or Assertion of Work Product

No objection or assertion of work product is permitted to a request under this rule.

Aug. 5, 1998 and Nov. 9, 1998, eff. Jan. 1, 1999.

Comment—1999

See comments following Rule 194.6.

194.6. Certain Responses Not Admissible

A response to requests under Rule 194.2(c) and (d) that has been changed by an amended or supplemental response is not admissible and may not be used for impeachment.

Aug. 5, 1998 and Nov. 9, 1998, eff. Jan. 1, 1999.

Comment—1999

1. Disclosure is designed to afford parties basic discovery of specific categories of information, not automatically in every case, but upon request, without preparation of a lengthy inquiry, and without objection or assertion of work product. In those extremely rare cases when information ordinarily discoverable should be protected, such as when revealing a person's residence might result in harm to the person, a party may move for protection. A party may assert any applicable privileges other than work product using the procedures of Rule 193.3 applicable to other written discovery. Otherwise, to fail to respond fully to a request for disclosure would be an abuse of the discovery process.

2. Rule 194.2(c) and (d) permit a party further inquiry into another's legal theories and factual claims than is often provided in notice pleadings. So-called "contention interrogatories" are used for the same purpose. Such interrogatories are not properly used to require a party to marshal evidence or brief legal issues. Paragraphs (c) and (d) are intended to require disclosure of a party's basic assertions, whether in prosecution of claims or in defense. Thus, for example, a plaintiff would be required to disclose that he or she claimed damages suffered in a car wreck caused by defendant's negligence in speeding, and would be required to state how loss of past earnings and future earning capacity was calculated, but would not be required to state the speed at which defendant was allegedly driving. Paragraph (d) does not require a party, either a plaintiff or a defendant, to state a method of calculating non-economic damages, such as for mental anguish. In the same example, defendant would be required to disclose his or her denial of the speeding allegation and any basis for contesting the damage calculations.

3. Responses under Rule 194.2(c) and (d) that have been amended or supplemented are inadmissible and cannot be used for impeachment, but other evidence of changes in position is not likewise barred.

Rule 195. Discovery Regarding Testifying Expert Witnesses

Comment—1999

1. This rule does not limit the permissible methods of discovery concerning consulting experts whose mental impressions or opinions have been reviewed by a testifying expert. See Rule 192.3(e). Information concerning purely consulting experts, of course, is not discoverable.

2. This rule and Rule 194 do not address depositions of testifying experts who are not retained by, employed by, or otherwise subject to the control of the responding party, nor the production of the materials identified in Rule 192.3(e)(5) and (6) relating to such experts. Parties may obtain this discovery, however, through Rules 176 and 205.

3. In scheduling the designations and depositions of expert witnesses, the rule attempts to minimize unfair surprise and undue expense. A party seeking affirmative relief must either produce an expert's report or tender the expert for deposition before an opposing party is required to designate experts. A party who does not wish to incur the expense of a report may simply tender the expert for deposition, but a party who wishes an expert to have the benefit of an opposing party's expert's opinions before being deposed may trigger designation by providing a report. Rule 191.1 permits a trial court, for good cause, to modify the order or deadlines for designating and deposing experts and the allocation of fees and expenses.

Historical Notes

A former rule 195 was derived from Vernon's Ann.Civ.St. art. 3747 and repealed by order of March 19, 1957, eff. Sept. 1, 1957.

Source:

Former rule 166b.

195.1. Permissible Discovery Tools

A party may request another party to designate and disclose information concerning testifying expert witnesses only through a request for disclosure under Rule 194[1] and through depositions and reports as permitted by this rule.

Aug. 5, 1998 and Nov. 9, 1998, eff. Jan. 1, 1999.

1 Vernon's Ann.Rules Civ.Proc., rule 194.1 et seq.

Comment—1999

See comments following Rule 195.7.

195.2. Schedule for Designating Experts

Unless otherwise ordered by the court, a party must designate experts—that is, furnish information requested under Rule 194.2(f)—by the later of the following two dates: 30 days after the request is served, or—

(a) with regard to all experts testifying for a party seeking affirmative relief, 90 days before the end of the discovery period;

(b) with regard to all other experts, 60 days before the end of the discovery period.

Aug. 5, 1998 and Nov. 9, 1998, eff. Jan. 1, 1999.

Comment—1999

See comments following Rule 195.7.

195.3. Scheduling Depositions

(a) *Experts for Party Seeking Affirmative Relief.* A party seeking affirmative relief must make an expert retained by, employed by, or otherwise in the control of the party available for deposition as follows:

(1) If no report furnished. If a report of the expert's factual observations, tests, supporting data, calculations, photographs, and opinions is not produced when the expert is designated, then the party must make the expert available for deposition reasonably promptly after the expert is designated. If the deposition cannot—due to the actions of the tendering party—reasonably be concluded more than 15 days before the deadline for designating other experts, that deadline must be extended for other experts testifying on the same subject.

(2) If report furnished. If a report of the expert's factual observations, tests, supporting data, calculations, photographs, and opinions is produced when the expert is designated, then the party need not make the expert available for deposition until reasonably promptly after all other experts have been designated.

(b) *Other Experts.* A party not seeking affirmative relief must make an expert retained by, employed by, or otherwise in the control of the party available for deposition reasonably promptly after the expert is designated and the experts testifying on the same subject for the party seeking affirmative relief have been deposed.

Aug. 5, 1998 and Nov. 9, 1998, eff. Jan. 1, 1999.

Comment—1999

See comments following Rule 195.7.

195.4. Oral Deposition

In addition to disclosure under Rule 194,[1] a party may obtain discovery concerning the subject matter on which the expert is expected to testify, the expert's mental impressions and opinions, the facts known to the expert (regardless of when the factual information was acquired) that relate to or form the basis of the testifying expert's mental impressions and opinions, and other discoverable matters, including documents not produced in disclosure, only by oral deposition of the expert and by a report prepared by the expert under this rule.

Aug. 5, 1998 and Nov. 9, 1998, eff. Jan. 1, 1999.

1 Vernon's Ann.Rules Civ.Proc., rule 194.1 et seq.

Comment—1999

See comments following Rule 195.7.

195.5. Court-Ordered Reports

If the discoverable factual observations, tests, supporting data, calculations, photographs, or opinions of an expert have not been recorded and reduced to tangible form, the court may order these matters reduced to tangible form and produced in addition to the deposition.

Aug. 5, 1998 and Nov. 9, 1998, eff. Jan. 1, 1999.

Comment—1999

See comments following Rule 195.7.

195.6. Amendment and Supplementation

A party's duty to amend and supplement written discovery regarding a testifying expert is governed by Rule 193.5. If an expert witness is retained by, employed by, or otherwise under the control of a party, that party must also amend or supplement any deposition testimony or written report by the expert, but only with regard to the expert's mental impressions or opinions and the basis for them.

Aug. 5, 1998, Nov. 9, 1998 and Dec. 31, 1998, eff. Jan. 1, 1999.

Comment—1999

See comments following Rule 195.7.

195.7. Cost of Expert Witnesses

When a party takes the oral deposition of an expert witness retained by the opposing party, all reasonable fees charged by the expert for time spent in preparing for, giving, reviewing, and correcting the deposition must be paid by the party that retained the expert.

Aug. 5, 1998 and Nov. 9, 1998, eff. Jan. 1, 1999.

Comment—1999

1. This rule does not limit the permissible methods of discovery concerning consulting experts whose mental impressions or opinions have been reviewed by a testifying expert. See Rule 192.3(e). Information concerning purely consulting experts, of course, is not discoverable.

2. This rule and Rule 194 do not address depositions of testifying experts who are not retained by, employed by, or otherwise subject to the control of the responding party, nor the production of the materials identified in Rule 192.3(e)(5) and (6) relating to such experts. Parties may obtain this discovery, however, through Rules 176 and 205.

3. In scheduling the designations and depositions of expert witnesses, the rule attempts to minimize unfair surprise and undue expense. A party seeking affirmative relief must either produce an expert's report or tender the expert for deposition before an opposing party is required to designate experts. A party who does not wish to incur the expense of a report may simply tender the expert for deposition, but a party who wishes an expert to have the benefit of an opposing party's expert's opinions before being deposed may trigger designation by providing a report. Rule 191.1 permits a trial court, for good cause, to modify the order or deadlines for designating and deposing experts and the allocation of fees and expenses.

Rule 196. Requests for Production and Inspection to Parties; Requests and Motions for Entry Upon Property

Historical Notes

Source:

Former rule 167.

A former rule 196 was repealed by order of Dec. 5, 1983, eff. April 1, 1984.

196.1. Request for Production and Inspection to Parties

(a) *Request.* A party may serve on another party—no later than 30 days before the end of the discovery period—a request for production or for inspection, to inspect, sample, test, photograph and copy documents or tangible things within the scope of discovery.

(b) *Contents of Request.* The request must specify the items to be produced or inspected, either by individual item or by category, and describe with reasonable particularity each item and category. The request must specify a reasonable time (on or after the date on which the response is due) and place for production. If the requesting party will sample or test the requested items, the means, manner and procedure for testing or sampling must be described with sufficient specificity to inform the producing party of the means, manner, and procedure for testing or sampling.

(c) *Requests for Production of Medical or Mental Health Records Regarding Nonparties.*

(1) Service of Request on Nonparty. If a party requests another party to produce medical or mental health records regarding a nonparty, the requesting party must serve the nonparty with the request for production under Rule 21a.

(2) Exceptions. A party is not required to serve the request for production on a nonparty whose medical records are sought if:

(A) the nonparty signs a release of the records that is effective as to the requesting party;

(B) the identity of the nonparty whose records are sought will not directly or indirectly be disclosed by production of the records; or

(C) the court, upon a showing of good cause by the party seeking the records, orders that service is not required.

(3) Confidentiality. Nothing in this rule excuses compliance with laws concerning the confidentiality of medical or mental health records.

Aug. 5, 1998 and Nov. 9, 1998, eff. Jan. 1, 1999.

Comments—1999

See comments following Rule 196.7.

196.2. Response to Request for Production and Inspection

(a) *Time for Response.* The responding party must serve a written response on the requesting party within 30 days after service of the request, except that a defendant served with a request before the defendant's answer is due need not respond until 50 days after service of the request.

(b) *Content of Response.* With respect to each item or category of items, the responding party must state objections and assert privileges as required by these rules, and state, as appropriate, that:

(1) production, inspection, or other requested action will be permitted as requested;

(2) the requested items are being served on the requesting party with the response;

(3) production, inspection, or other requested action will take place at a specified time and place, if the responding party is objecting to the time and place of production; or

(4) no items have been identified—after a diligent search—that are responsive to the request.

Aug. 5, 1998 and Nov. 9, 1998, eff. Jan. 1, 1999.

Comments—1999

See comments following Rule 196.7.

196.3. Production

(a) *Time and Place of Production.* Subject to any objections stated in the response, the responding party must produce the requested documents or tangible things within the person's possession, custody or control at either the time and place requested or the time and place stated in the response, unless otherwise agreed by the parties or ordered by the court, and must provide the requesting party a reasonable opportunity to inspect them.

(b) *Copies.* The responding party may produce copies in lieu of originals unless a question is raised as to the authenticity of the original or in the circumstances it would be unfair to produce copies in lieu of originals. If originals are produced, the responding party is entitled to retain the originals while the requesting party inspects and copies them.

(c) *Organization.* The responding party must either produce documents and tangible things as they are kept in the usual course of business or organize and label them to correspond with the categories in the request.

Aug. 5, 1998 and Nov. 9, 1998, eff. Jan. 1, 1999.

Comments—1999

See comments following Rule 196.7.

196.4. Electronic or Magnetic Data

To obtain discovery of data or information that exists in electronic or magnetic form, the requesting party must specifically request production of electronic or magnetic data and specify the form in which the requesting party wants it produced. The responding party must produce the electronic or magnetic data that is responsive to the request and is reasonably available to the responding party in its ordinary course of business. If the responding party cannot—through reasonable efforts—retrieve the data or information requested or produce it in the form requested, the responding party must state an objection complying with these rules. If the court orders the responding party to comply with the request, the court must also order that the requesting party pay the reasonable expenses of any extraordinary steps required to retrieve and produce the information.

Aug. 5, 1998 and Nov. 9, 1998, eff. Jan. 1, 1999.

Comments—1999

See comments following Rule 196.7.

196.5. Destruction or Alteration

Testing, sampling or examination of an item may not destroy or materially alter an item unless previously authorized by the court.

Aug. 5, 1998 and Nov. 9, 1998, eff. Jan. 1, 1999.

Comments—1999

See comments following Rule 196.7.

196.6. Expenses of Production

Unless otherwise ordered by the court for good cause, the expense of producing items will be borne by the responding party and the expense of inspecting, sampling, testing, photographing, and copying items produced will be borne by the requesting party.

Aug. 5, 1998 and Nov. 9, 1998, eff. Jan. 1, 1999.

Comments—1999

See comments following Rule 196.7.

196.7. Request or Motion for Entry Upon Property

(a) *Request or Motion.* A party may gain entry on designated land or other property to inspect, measure, survey, photograph, test, or sample the property or any designated object or operation thereon by serving—no later than 30 days before the end of any applicable discovery period—

(1) a request on all parties if the land or property belongs to a party, or

(2) a motion and notice of hearing on all parties and the nonparty if the land or property belongs to a nonparty. If the identity or address of the nonparty is unknown and cannot be obtained through

reasonable diligence, the court must permit service by means other than those specified in Rule 21a that are reasonably calculated to give the nonparty notice of the motion and hearing.

(b) *Time, Place, and Other Conditions.* The request for entry upon a party's property, or the order for entry upon a nonparty's property, must state the time, place, manner, conditions, and scope of the inspection, and must specifically describe any desired means, manner, and procedure for testing or sampling, and the person or persons by whom the inspection, testing, or sampling is to be made.

(c) *Response to Request for Entry.*

(1) Time to Respond. The responding party must serve a written response on the requesting party within 30 days after service of the request, except that a defendant served with a request before the defendant's answer is due need not respond until 50 days after service of the request.

(2) Content of Response. The responding party must state objections and assert privileges as required by these rules, and state, as appropriate, that:

(A) entry or other requested action will be permitted as requested;

(B) entry or other requested action will take place at a specified time and place, if the responding party is objecting to the time and place of production; or

(C) entry or other requested action cannot be permitted for reasons stated in the response.

(d) *Requirements for Order for Entry on Nonparty's Property.* An order for entry on a nonparty's property may issue only for good cause shown and only if the land, property, or object thereon as to which discovery is sought is relevant to the subject matter of the action.

Aug. 5, 1998, Nov. 9, 1998 and Dec. 31, 1998, eff. Jan. 1, 1999.

Comments—1999

1. "Document and tangible things" are defined in Rule 192.3(b).

2. A party requesting sampling or testing must describe the procedure with sufficient specificity to enable the responding party to make any appropriate objections.

3. A party requesting production of magnetic or electronic data must specifically request the data, specify the form in which it wants the data produced, and specify any extraordinary steps for retrieval and translation. Unless ordered otherwise, the responding party need only produce the data reasonably available in the ordinary course of business in reasonably usable form.

4. The rule clarifies how the expenses of production are to be allocated absent a court order to the contrary.

5. The obligation of parties to produce documents within their possession, custody or control is explained in Rule 192.3(b).

6. Parties may request production and inspection of documents and tangible things from nonparties under Rule 205.3.

7. Rule 196.3(b) is based on Tex. R. Evid. 1003.

8. Rule 196.1(c) is merely a notice requirement and does not expand the scope of discovery of a nonparty's medical records.

Historical Notes

The Order dated December 31, 1998, made technical corrections.

Rule 197. Interrogatories to Parties

Historical Notes

Source:

Former rule 168.

A former Rule 197 was repealed by order of Dec. 5, 1983, eff. April 1, 1984.

197.1. Interrogatories

A party may serve on another party—no later than 30 days before the end of the discovery period—written interrogatories to inquire about any matter within the scope of discovery except matters covered by Rule 195.[1] An interrogatory may inquire whether a party makes a specific legal or factual contention and may ask the responding party to state the legal theories and to describe in general the factual bases for the party's claims or defenses, but interrogatories may not be used to require the responding party to marshal all of its available proof or the proof the party intends to offer at trial.

Aug. 5, 1998 and Nov. 9, 1998, eff. Jan. 1, 1999.

[1] Vernon's Ann.Rules Civ.Proc., rule 195.1 et seq.

Comment—1999

See comments following Rule 197.3.

197.2. Response to Interrogatories

(a) *Time for Response.* The responding party must serve a written response on the requesting party within 30 days after service of the interrogatories, except that a defendant served with interrogatories before the defendant's answer is due need not respond until 50 days after service of the interrogatories.

(b) *Content of Response.* A response must include the party's answers to the interrogatories and may include objections and assertions of privilege as required under these rules.

(c) *Option to Produce Records.* If the answer to an interrogatory may be derived or ascertained from public records, from the responding party's business records, or from a compilation, abstract or summary of the responding party's business records, and the burden of deriving or ascertaining the answer is substantially the same for the requesting party as for the responding party, the responding party may answer the interrogatory by specifying and, if applicable, producing the records or compilation, abstract or summary of the records. The records from which the answer may be derived or ascertained must be specified in sufficient detail to permit the requesting party to locate and identify them as readily as can the responding party. If the responding party has specified business records, the responding party must state a reasonable time and place for examination of the documents. The responding party must produce the documents at the time and place stated, unless otherwise agreed by the parties or ordered by the court, and must provide the requesting party a reasonable opportunity to inspect them.

(d) *Verification Required; Exceptions.* A responding party—not an agent or attorney as otherwise permitted by Rule 14—must sign the answers under oath except that:

(1) when answers are based on information obtained from other persons, the party may so state, and

(2) a party need not sign answers to interrogatories about persons with knowledge of relevant facts, trial witnesses, and legal contentions.

Aug. 5, 1998, Nov. 9, 1998 and Dec. 31, 1998, eff. Jan. 1, 1999.

Comment—1999

See comments following Rule 197.3.

Historical Notes

The Order dated December 31, 1998, made technical corrections.

197.3. Use

Answers to interrogatories may be used only against the responding party. An answer to an interrogatory inquiring about matters described in Rule 194.2(c) and (d) that has been amended or supplemented is not admissible and may not be used for impeachment.

Aug. 5, 1998 and Nov. 9, 1998, eff. Jan. 1, 1999.

Comment—1999

1. Interrogatories about specific legal or factual assertions—such as, whether a party claims a breach of implied warranty, or when a party contends that limitations began to run—are proper, but interrogatories that ask a party to state all legal and factual assertions are improper. As with requests for disclosure, interrogatories may be used to ascertain basic legal and factual claims and defenses but may not be used to force a party to marshal evidence. Use of the answers to such interrogatories is limited, just as the use of similar disclosures under Rule 194.6 is.

2. Rule 191's requirement that a party's attorney sign all discovery responses and objections applies to interrogatory responses and objections. In addition, the responding party must sign some interrogatory answers under oath, as specified by the rule. Answers in amended and supplemental responses must be signed by the party under oath only if the original answers were required to be signed under oath. The failure to sign or verify answers is only a formal defect that does not otherwise impair the answers unless the party refuses to sign or verify the answers after the defect is pointed out.

Rule 198. Requests for Admissions

Historical Notes

Source:

Former rule 169.

A former Rule 198 was repealed by order of Dec. 5, 1983, eff. April 1, 1984.

198.1. Request for Admissions

A party may serve on another party—no later than 30 days before the end of the discovery period—written requests that the other party admit the truth of any matter within the scope of discovery, including statements of opinion or of fact or of the application of law to fact, or the genuineness of any documents served with the request or otherwise made available for inspection and copying. Each matter for which an admission is requested must be stated separately.

Aug. 5, 1998 and Nov. 9, 1998, eff. Jan. 1, 1999.

198.2. Response to Requests for Admissions

(a) *Time for Response.* The responding party must serve a written response on the requesting party within 30 days after service of the request, except that a defendant served with a request before the defendant's answer is due need not respond until 50 days after service of the request.

(b) *Content of Response.* Unless the responding party states an objection or asserts a privilege, the responding party must specifically admit or deny the request or explain in detail the reasons that the responding party cannot admit or deny the request. A response must fairly meet the substance of the request. The responding party may qualify an answer, or deny a request in part, only when good faith requires. Lack of information or knowledge is not a proper response unless the responding party states that a reasonable inquiry was made but that the information known or easily obtainable is insufficient to enable the responding party to admit or deny. An assertion that the request presents an issue for trial is not a proper response.

(c) *Effect of Failure to Respond.* If a response is not timely served, the request is considered admitted without the necessity of a court order.

Aug. 5, 1998 and Nov. 9, 1998, eff. Jan. 1, 1999.

198.3. Effect of Admissions; Withdrawal or Amendment

Any admission made by a party under this rule may be used solely in the pending action and not in any other proceeding. A matter admitted under this rule is conclusively established as to the party making the admission unless the court permits the party to withdraw or amend the admission. The court may permit the party to withdraw or amend the admission if:

(a) the party shows good cause for the withdrawal or amendment; and

(b) the court finds that the parties relying upon the responses and deemed admissions will not be unduly prejudiced and that the presentation of the merits of the action will be subserved by permitting the party to amend or withdraw the admission.

Aug. 5, 1998 and Nov. 9, 1998, eff. Jan. 1, 1999.

Rule 199. Depositions Upon Oral Examination

Historical Notes

Source:

Former rules 200, 201.

A former Rule 199 was repealed by order of Dec. 5, 1983, eff. April 1, 1984.

199.1. Oral Examination; Alternative Methods of Conducting or Recording

(a) *Generally.* A party may take the testimony of any person or entity by deposition on oral examination before any officer authorized by law to take depositions. The testimony, objections, and any other statements during the deposition must be recorded at the time they are given or made.

(b) *Depositions by Telephone or Other Remote Electronic Means.* A party may take an oral deposition by telephone or other remote electronic means if the party gives reasonable prior written notice of intent to do so. For the purposes of these rules, an oral deposition taken by telephone or other remote electronic means is considered as having been taken in the district and at the place where the witness is located when answering the questions. The officer taking the deposition may be located with the party noticing the deposition instead of with the witness if the witness is placed under oath by a person who is present with the witness and authorized to administer oaths in that jurisdiction.

(c) *Nonstenographic Recording.* Any party may cause a deposition upon oral examination to be recorded by other than stenographic means, including videotape recording. The party requesting the nonstenographic recording will be responsible for obtaining a person authorized by law to administer the oath and for assuring that the recording will be intelligible, accurate, and trustworthy. At least five days prior to the deposition, the party must serve on the witness and all parties a notice, either in the notice of deposition or separately, that the deposition will be recorded by other than stenographic means. This notice must state the method of nonstenographic recording to be used and whether the deposition will also be recorded stenographically. Any other party may then serve written notice designating another method of recording in addition to the method specified, at the expense of such other party unless the court orders otherwise.

Aug. 5, 1998 and Nov. 9, 1998, eff. Jan. 1, 1999.

Comment—1999

See comments following Rule 199.6.

Historical Notes

Source:

Former rule 202.

199.2. Procedure for Noticing Oral Deposition

(a) *Time to Notice Deposition.* A notice of intent to take an oral deposition must be served on the witness and all parties a reasonable time before the deposition is taken. An oral deposition may be taken outside the discovery period only by agreement of the parties or with leave of court.

(b) *Content of Notice.*

(1) Identity of Witness; Organizations. The notice must state the name of the witness, which may be either an individual or a public or private corporation, partnership, association, governmental agency, or other organization. If an organization is named as the witness, the notice must describe with reasonable particularity the matters on which examination is requested. In response, the organization named in the notice must—a reasonable time before the deposition—designate one or more individuals to testify on its behalf and set forth, for each individual designated, the matters on which the individual will testify. Each individual designated must testify as to matters that are known or reasonably available to the organization. This subdivision does not preclude taking a deposition by any other procedure authorized by these rules.

(2) Time and Place. The notice must state a reasonable time and place for the oral deposition. The place may be in:

(A) the county of the witness's residence;

(B) the county where the witness is employed or regularly transacts business in person;

(C) the county of suit, if the witness is a party or a person designated by a party under Rule 199.2(b)(1);

(D) the county where the witness was served with the subpoena, or within 150 miles of the place of service, if the witness is not a resident of Texas or is a transient person; or

(E) subject to the foregoing, at any other convenient place directed by the court in which the cause is pending.

(3) Alternative Means of Conducting and Recording. The notice must state whether the deposition is to be taken by telephone or other remote electronic means and identify the means. If the deposition is to be recorded by nonstenographic means, the notice may include the notice required by Rule 199.1(c).

(4) Additional Attendees. The notice may include the notice concerning additional attendees required by Rule 199.5(a)(3).

(5) Request for Production of Documents. A notice may include a request that the witness produce at the deposition documents or tangible things within the scope of discovery and within the witness's possession, custody, or control. If the witness is a nonparty, the request must comply with Rule 205[1] and the designation of materials required to be identified in the subpoena must be attached to, or included in, the notice. The nonparty's response to the request is governed by Rules 176[2] and 205. When the witness is a party or subject to the control of a party, document requests under this subdivision are governed by Rules 193 and 196.[3]

Aug. 5, 1998 and Nov. 9, 1998, eff. Jan. 1, 1999.

1 Vernon's Ann.Rules Civ.Proc., rule 205.1 et seq.

2 Vernon's Ann.Rules Civ.Proc., rule 176.1 et seq.

3 Vernon's Ann.Rules Civ.Proc., rule 193.1 et seq. and rule 196.1 et seq.

Comment—1999

See comments following Rule 199.6.

199.3. Compelling Witness to Attend

A party may compel the witness to attend the oral deposition by serving the witness with a subpoena under Rule 176. If the witness is a party or is retained by, employed by, or otherwise subject to the control of a party, however, service of the notice of oral deposition upon the party's attorney has the same effect as a subpoena served on the witness.

Aug. 5, 1998 and Nov. 9, 1998, eff. Jan. 1, 1999.

Comment—1999

See comments following Rule 199.6.

199.4. Objections to Time and Place of Oral Deposition

A party or witness may object to the time and place designated for an oral deposition by motion for protective order or by motion to quash the notice of deposition. If the motion is filed by the third business day after service of the notice of deposition, an objection to the time and place of a deposition stays the oral deposition until the motion can be determined.

Aug. 5, 1998 and Nov. 9, 1998, eff. Jan. 1, 1999.

Comment—1999

See comments following Rule 199.6.

199.5. Examination, Objection, and Conduct During Oral Depositions

(a) *Attendance.*

(1) Witness. The witness must remain in attendance from day to day until the deposition is begun and completed.

(2) Attendance by Party. A party may attend an oral deposition in person, even if the deposition is taken by telephone or other remote electronic means. If a deposition is taken by telephone or other remote electronic means, the party noticing the deposition must make arrangements for all persons to attend by the same means. If the party noticing the deposition appears in person, any other party may appear by telephone or other remote electronic means if that party makes the necessary arrangements with the deposition officer and the party noticing the deposition.

(3) Other Attendees. If any party intends to have in attendance any persons other than the witness, parties, spouses of parties, counsel, employees of counsel, and the officer taking the oral deposition, that party must give reasonable notice to all parties, either in the notice of deposition or separately, of the identity of the other persons.

(b) *Oath; Examination.* Every person whose deposition is taken by oral examination must first be placed under oath. The parties may examine and cross-examine the witness. Any party, in lieu of participating in the examination, may serve written questions in a sealed envelope on the party noticing the oral deposition, who must deliver them to the deposition officer, who must open the envelope and propound them to the witness.

(c) *Time Limitation.* No side may examine or cross-examine an individual witness for more than six hours. Breaks during depositions do not count against this limitation.

(d) *Conduct During the Oral Deposition; Conferences.* The oral deposition must be conducted in the same manner as if the testimony were being obtained in court during trial. Counsel should cooperate with and be courteous to each other and to the witness. The witness should not be evasive and should not unduly delay the examination. Private conferences between the witness and the witness's attorney during the actual taking of the deposition are improper except for the purpose of determining whether a privilege should be asserted. Private conferences may be held, however, during agreed recesses and adjournments. If the lawyers and witnesses do not comply with this rule, the court may allow in evidence at trial statements, objections, discussions, and other occurrences during the oral deposition that reflect upon the credibility of the witness or the testimony.

(e) *Objections.* Objections to questions during the oral deposition are limited to "Objection, leading" and "Objection, form." Objections to testimony during the oral deposition are limited to "Objection, nonresponsive." These objections are waived if not stated as phrased during the oral deposition. All other objections need not be made or recorded during the oral deposition to be later raised with the court. The objecting party must give a clear and concise explanation of an objection if requested by the party taking the oral deposition, or the objection is waived. Argumentative or suggestive objections or explanations waive objection and may be grounds for terminating the oral deposition or assessing costs or other sanctions. The officer taking the oral deposition will not rule on objections but must record them for ruling by the court. The officer taking the oral deposition must not fail to record testimony because an objection has been made.

(f) *Instructions Not to Answer.* An attorney may instruct a witness not to answer a question during an oral deposition only if necessary to preserve a privilege, comply with a court order or these rules, protect a witness from an abusive question or one for which any answer would be misleading, or secure a ruling pursuant to paragraph (g). The attorney instructing the witness not to answer must give a concise, nonargumentative, nonsuggestive explanation of the grounds for the instruction if requested by the party who asked the question.

(g) *Suspending the Deposition.* If the time limitations for the deposition have expired or the deposition is being conducted or defended in violation of these rules, a party or witness may suspend the oral deposition for the time necessary to obtain a ruling.

(h) *Good Faith Required.* An attorney must not ask a question at an oral deposition solely to harass or mislead the witness, for any other improper purpose, or without a good faith legal basis at the time. An attorney must not object to a question at an oral deposition, instruct the witness not to answer a question, or suspend the deposition unless there is a good faith factual and legal basis for doing so at the time.

Aug. 5, 1998 and Nov. 9, 1998, eff. Jan. 1, 1999.

Comment—1999

See comments following Rule 199.6.

Historical Notes

Source:

Former rule 204.

199.6. Hearing on Objections

Any party may, at any reasonable time, request a hearing on an objection or privilege asserted by an instruction not to answer or suspension of the deposition; provided the failure of a party to obtain a ruling prior to trial does not waive any objection or privilege. The party seeking to avoid discovery must present any evidence necessary to support the objection or privilege either by testimony at the hearing or by affidavits served on opposing parties at least seven days before the hearing. If the court determines that an in camera review of some or all of the requested discovery is necessary to rule, answers to the deposition questions may be made *in camera*, to be transcribed and sealed in the event the privilege is sustained, or made in an affidavit produced to the court in a sealed wrapper.

Aug. 5, 1998 and Nov. 9, 1998, eff. Jan. 1, 1999.

Comment—1999

1. Rule 199.2(b)(5) incorporates the procedures and limitations applicable to requests for production or inspection under Rule 196, including the 30-day deadline for responses, as well as the procedures and duties imposed by Rule 193.

2. For purposes of Rule 199.5(c), each person designated by an organization under Rule 199.2(b)(1) is a separate witness.

3. The requirement of Rule 199.5(d) that depositions be conducted in the same manner as if the testimony were being obtained in court is a limit on the conduct of the lawyers and witnesses in the deposition, not on the scope of the interrogation permitted by Rule 192.

4. An objection to the form of a question includes objections that the question calls for speculation, calls for a narrative answer, is vague, is confusing, or is ambiguous. Ordinarily, a witness must answer a question at a deposition subject to the objection. An objection may therefore be inadequate if a question incorporates such unfair assumptions or is worded so that any answer would necessarily be misleading. A witness should

not be required to answer whether he has yet ceased conduct he denies ever doing, subject to an objection to form (i.e., that the question is confusing or assumes facts not in evidence) because any answer would necessarily be misleading on account of the way in which the question is put. The witness may be instructed not to answer. Abusive questions include questions that inquire into matters clearly beyond the scope of discovery or that are argumentative, repetitious, or harassing.

Rule 200. Depositions Upon Written Questions

Historical Notes

Source:

Former rule 208.

Former rule 200 was repealed by order effective January 1, 1999. For subject matter of former rule 200, see, now, rule 199.1 et seq.

200.1. Procedure for Noticing Deposition Upon Written Questions

(a) *Who May Be Noticed; When.* A party may take the testimony of any person or entity by deposition on written questions before any person authorized by law to take depositions on written questions. A notice of intent to take the deposition must be served on the witness and all parties at least 20 days before the deposition is taken. A deposition on written questions may be taken outside the discovery period only by agreement of the parties or with leave of court. The party noticing the deposition must also deliver to the deposition officer a copy of the notice and of all written questions to be asked during the deposition.

(b) *Content of Notice.* The notice must comply with Rules 199.1(b), 199.2(b), and 199.5(a)(3). If the witness is an organization, the organization must comply with the requirements of that provision. The notice also may include a request for production of documents as permitted by Rule 199.2(b)(5), the provisions of which will govern the request, service, and response.

Aug. 5, 1998 and Nov. 9, 1998, eff. Jan. 1, 1999.

Comment—1999

See comments following Rule 200.4.

200.2. Compelling Witness to Attend

A party may compel the witness to attend the deposition on written questions by serving the witness with a subpoena under Rule 176. If the witness is a party or is retained by, employed by, or otherwise subject to the control of a party, however, service of the deposition notice upon the party's attorney has the same effect as a subpoena served on the witness.

Aug. 5, 1998 and Nov. 9, 1998, eff. Jan. 1, 1999.

Comment—1999

See comments following Rule 200.4.

200.3. Questions and Objections

(a) *Direct Questions.* The direct questions to be propounded to the witness must be attached to the notice.

(b) *Objections and Additional Questions.* Within ten days after the notice and direct questions are served, any party may object to the direct questions and serve cross-questions on all other parties. Within five days after cross-questions are served, any party may object to the cross-questions and serve redirect questions on all other parties. Within three days after redirect questions are served, any party may object to the redirect questions and serve recross questions on all other parties. Objections to recross questions must be served within five days after the earlier of when recross questions are served or the time of the deposition on written questions.

(c) *Objections to Form of Questions.* Objections to the form of a question are waived unless asserted in accordance with this subdivision.

Aug. 5, 1998 and Nov. 9, 1998, eff. Jan. 1, 1999.

Comment—1999

See comments following Rule 200.4.

200.4. Conducting the Deposition Upon Written Questions

The deposition officer must: take the deposition on written questions at the time and place designated; record the testimony of the witness under oath in response to the questions; and prepare, certify, and deliver the deposition transcript in accordance with Rule 203. The deposition officer has authority when necessary to summon and swear an interpreter to facilitate the taking of the deposition.

Aug. 5, 1998, Nov. 9, 1998 and Dec. 31, 1998, eff. Jan. 1, 1999.

Comment—1999

1. The procedures for asserting objections during oral depositions under Rule 199.5(e) do not apply to depositions on written questions.

2. Section 20.001 of the Civil Practice and Remedies Code provides that a deposition on written questions of a witness who is alleged to reside or to be in this state may be taken by a clerk of a district court, a judge or clerk of a county court, or a notary public of this state.

Historical Notes

The Order dated December 31, 1998, made technical corrections.

Rule 201. Depositions in Foreign Jurisdictions for Use in Texas Proceedings; Depositions in Texas for Use in Foreign Proceedings

Historical Notes

Former rule 201 was repealed by order effective January 1, 1999. For subject matter of former rule 201, see, now, rules 176.6, 199.

201.1. Depositions in Foreign Jurisdictions for Use in Texas Proceedings

(a) *Generally.* A party may take a deposition on oral examination or written questions of any person or entity located in another state or a foreign country for use in proceedings in this State. The deposition may be taken by:

(1) notice;

(2) letter rogatory, letter of request, or other such device;

(3) agreement of the parties; or

(4) court order.

(b) *By Notice.* A party may take the deposition by notice in accordance with these rules as if the deposition were taken in this State, except that the deposition officer may be a person authorized to administer oaths in the place where the deposition is taken.

(c) *By Letter Rogatory.* On motion by a party, the court in which an action is pending must issue a letter rogatory on terms that are just and appropriate, regardless of whether any other manner of obtaining the deposition is impractical or inconvenient. The letter must:

(1) be addressed to the appropriate authority in the jurisdiction in which the deposition is to be taken;

(2) request and authorize that authority to summon the witness before the authority at a time and place stated in the letter for examination on oral or written questions; and

(3) request and authorize that authority to cause the witness's testimony to be reduced to writing and returned, together with any items marked as exhibits, to the party requesting the letter rogatory.

(d) *By Letter of Request or Other Such Device.* On motion by a party, the court in which an action is pending, or the clerk of that court, must issue a letter of request or other such device in accordance with an applicable treaty or international convention on terms that are just and appropriate. The letter or other device must be issued regardless of whether any other manner of obtaining the deposition is impractical or inconvenient. The letter or other device must:

(1) be in the form prescribed by the treaty or convention under which it is issued, as presented by the movant to the court or clerk; and

(2) must state the time, place, and manner of the examination of the witness.

(e) *Objections to Form of Letter Rogatory, Letter of Request, or Other Such Device.* In issuing a letter rogatory, letter of request, or other such device, the court must set a time for objecting to the form of the device. A party must make any objection to the form of the device in writing and serve it on all other parties by the time set by the court, or the objection is waived.

(f) *Admissibility of Evidence.* Evidence obtained in response to a letter rogatory, letter of request, or other such device is not inadmissible merely because it is not a verbatim transcript, or the testimony was not taken under oath, or for any similar departure from the requirements for depositions taken within this State under these rules.

(g) *Deposition by Electronic Means.* A deposition in another jurisdiction may be taken by telephone, videoconference, teleconference, or other electronic means under the provisions of Rule 199.[1]

Aug. 5, 1998 and Nov. 9, 1998, eff. Jan. 1, 1999.

1 Vernon's Ann.Rules Civ.Proc., rule 199.1 et seq.

Comments—1999

See comments following Rule 201.2.

Historical Notes

Source:

Former rule 188.

201.2. Depositions in Texas for Use in Proceedings in Foreign Jurisdictions

If a court of record of any other state or foreign jurisdiction issues a mandate, writ, or commission that requires a witness's oral or written deposition testimony in this State, the witness may be compelled to appear and testify in the same manner and by the same process used for taking testimony in a proceeding pending in this State.

Aug. 5, 1998 and Nov. 9, 1998, eff. Jan. 1, 1999.

Comments—1999

1. Rule 201.1 sets forth procedures for obtaining deposition testimony of a witness in another state or foreign jurisdiction for use in Texas court proceedings. It does not, however, address whether any of the procedures listed are, in fact, permitted or recognized by the law of the state or foreign jurisdiction where the witness is located. A party must first determine what procedures are permitted by the jurisdiction where the witness is located before using this rule.

2. Section 20.001 of the Civil Practice and Remedies Code provides a nonexclusive list of persons who are qualified to take a written deposition in Texas and who may take depositions (oral or written) in another state or outside the United States.

3. Rule 201.2 is based on Section 20.002 of the Civil Practice and Remedies Code.

Rule 202. Depositions Before Suit or to Investigate Claims

Historical Notes

Former rule 202 was repealed by order effective January 1, 1999. For subject matter of former rule 202, see, now, rules 199.1, 203.6.

202.1. Generally

A person may petition the court for an order authorizing the taking of a deposition on oral examination or written questions either:

(a) to perpetuate or obtain the person's own testimony or that of any other person for use in an anticipated suit; or

(b) to investigate a potential claim or suit.

Aug. 5, 1998 and Nov. 9, 1998, eff. Jan. 1, 1999.

Comments—1999

See comments following Rule 202.5.

202.2. Petition

The petition must:

(a) be verified;

(b) be filed in a proper court of any county:

(1) where venue of the anticipated suit may lie, if suit is anticipated; or

(2) where the witness resides, if no suit is yet anticipated;

(c) be in the name of the petitioner;

(d) state either:

(1) that the petitioner anticipates the institution of a suit in which the petitioner may be a party; or

(2) that the petitioner seeks to investigate a potential claim by or against petitioner;

(e) state the subject matter of the anticipated action, if any, and the petitioner's interest therein;

(f) if suit is anticipated, either:

(1) state the names of the persons petitioner expects to have interests adverse to petitioner's in the anticipated suit, and the addresses and telephone numbers for such persons; or

(2) state that the names, addresses, and telephone numbers of persons petitioner expects to have interests adverse to petitioner's in the anticipated suit cannot be ascertained through diligent inquiry, and describe those persons;

(g) state the names, addresses and telephone numbers of the persons to be deposed, the substance of the testimony that the petitioner expects to elicit from each, and the petitioner's reasons for desiring to obtain the testimony of each; and

(h) request an order authorizing the petitioner to take the depositions of the persons named in the petition.

Aug. 5, 1998 and Nov. 9, 1998, eff. Jan. 1, 1999.

Comments—1999

See comments following Rule 202.5.

202.3. Notice and Service

(a) *Personal Service on Witnesses and Persons Named.* At least 15 days before the date of the hearing on the petition, the petitioner must serve the petition and a notice of the hearing—in accordance with Rule 21a—on all persons petitioner seeks to depose and, if suit is anticipated, on all persons petitioner expects to have interests adverse to petitioner's in the anticipated suit.

(b) *Service by Publication on Persons Not Named.*

(1) Manner. Unnamed persons described in the petition whom the petitioner expects to have interests adverse to petitioner's in the anticipated suit, if any, may be served by publication with the petition and notice of the hearing. The notice must state the place for the hearing and the time it will be held, which must be more than 14 days after the first publication of the notice. The petition and notice must be published once each week for two consecutive weeks in the newspaper of broadest circulation in the county in which the petition is filed, or if no such newspaper exists, in the newspaper of broadest circulation in the nearest county where a newspaper is published.

(2) Objection to Depositions Taken on Notice by Publication. Any interested party may move, in the proceeding or by bill of review, to suppress any deposition, in whole or in part, taken on notice by publication, and may also attack or oppose the deposition by any other means available.

(c) *Service in Probate Cases.* A petition to take a deposition in anticipation of an application for probate of a will, and notice of the hearing on the petition, may be served by posting as prescribed by Section 33(f)(2) of the Probate Code. The notice and petition must be directed to all parties interested in the testator's estate and must comply with the requirements of Section 33(c) of the Probate Code insofar as they may be applicable.

(d) *Modification by Order.* As justice or necessity may require, the court may shorten or lengthen the notice periods under this rule and may extend the notice period to permit service on any expected adverse party.

Aug. 5, 1998 and Nov. 9, 1998, eff. Jan. 1, 1999.

Comments—1999

See comments following Rule 202.5.

202.4. Order

(a) *Required Findings.* The court must order a deposition to be taken if, but only if, it finds that:

(1) allowing the petitioner to take the requested deposition may prevent a failure or delay of justice in an anticipated suit: or

(2) the likely benefit of allowing the petitioner to take the requested deposition to investigate a potential claim outweighs the burden or expense of the procedure.

(b) *Contents.* The order must state whether a deposition will be taken on oral examination or written questions. The order may also state the time and place at which a deposition will be taken. If the order does not state the time and place at which a deposition will be taken, the petitioner must notice the deposition as required by Rules 199[1] or 200.[2] The order must contain any protections the court finds necessary or appropriate to protect the witness or any person who may be affected by the procedure.

Aug. 5, 1998 and Nov. 9, 1998, eff. Jan. 1, 1999.

1 Vernon's Ann.Rules Civ.Proc., rule 199.1 et seq.

2 Vernon's Ann.Rules Civ.Proc., rule 200.1 et seq.

Comments—1999

See comments following Rule 202.5.

202.5. Manner of Taking and Use

Except as otherwise provided in this rule, depositions authorized by this rule are governed by the rules applicable to depositions of nonparties in a pending suit. The scope of discovery in depositions authorized by this rule is the same as if the anticipated suit or potential claim had been filed. A court may restrict or prohibit the use of a deposition taken under this rule in a subsequent suit to protect a person who was not served with notice of the deposition from any unfair prejudice or to prevent abuse of this rule.

Aug. 5, 1998 and Nov. 9, 1998, eff. Jan. 1, 1999.

Comments—1999

1. This rule applies to all discovery before suit covered by former rules governing depositions to perpetuate testimony and bills of discovery.

2. A deposition taken under this rule may be used in a subsequent suit as permitted by the rules of evidence, except that a court may restrict or prohibit its use to prevent taking unfair advantage of a witness or others. The bill of discovery procedure, which Rule 202 incorporates, is equitable in nature, and a court must not permit it to be used inequitably.

Historical Notes

Source:

Former rule 187, 737.

Rule 203. Signing, Certification and Use of Oral and Written Depositions

Historical Notes

Former rule 203 was repealed by order effective January 1, 1999. For subject matter of former rule 203, see, now, rules 176.8, 215.

Source:

Former rules 205, 206, 207.

203.1. Signature and Changes

(a) *Deposition Transcript to be Provided to Witness.* The deposition officer must provide the original deposition transcript to the witness for examination and signature. If the witness is represented by an attorney at the deposition, the deposition officer must provide the transcript to the attorney instead of the witness.

(b) *Changes by Witness; Signature.* The witness may change responses as reflected in the deposition transcript by indicating the desired changes, in writing, on a separate sheet of paper, together with a statement of the reasons for making the changes. No erasures or obliterations of any kind may be made to the original deposition transcript. The witness must then sign the transcript under oath and return it to the deposition officer. If the witness does not return the transcript to the deposition officer within 20 days of the date the transcript was provided to the witness or the witness's attorney, the witness may be deemed to have waived the right to make the changes.

(c) *Exceptions.* The requirements of presentation and signature under this subdivision do not apply:

(1) if the witness and all parties waive the signature requirement;

(2) to depositions on written questions; or

(3) to nonstenographic recordings of oral depositions.

Aug. 5, 1998 and Nov. 9, 1998, eff. Jan. 1, 1999.

203.2. Certification

The deposition officer must file with the court, serve on all parties, and attach as part of the deposition transcript or nonstenographic recording of an oral deposition a certificate duly sworn by the officer stating:

(a) that the witness was duly sworn by the officer and that the transcript or nonstenographic recording of the oral deposition is a true record of the testimony given by the witness;

(b) that the deposition transcript, if any, was submitted to the witness or to the attorney for the witness for examination and signature, the date on which the transcript was submitted, whether the witness returned the transcript, and if so, the date on which it was returned.

(c) that changes, if any, made by the witness are attached to the deposition transcript;

(d) that the deposition officer delivered the deposition transcript or nonstenographic recording of an oral deposition in accordance with Rule 203.3;

(e) the amount of time used by each party at the deposition;

(f) the amount of the deposition officer's charges for preparing the original deposition transcript, which the clerk of the court must tax as costs; and

(g) that a copy of the certificate was served on all parties and the date of service.

Aug. 5, 1998 and Nov. 9, 1998, eff. Jan. 1, 1999.

203.3. Delivery

(a) *Endorsement; To Whom Delivered.* The deposition officer must endorse the title of the action and "Deposition of (name of witness)" on the original deposition transcript (or a copy, if the original was not returned) or the original nonstenographic recording of an oral deposition, and must return:

(1) the transcript to the party who asked the first question appearing in the transcript, or

(2) the recording to the party who requested it.

(b) *Notice.* The deposition officer must serve notice of delivery on all other parties.

(c) *Inspection and Copying; Copies.* The party receiving the original deposition transcript or nonstenographic recording must make it available upon reasonable request for inspection and copying by any other party. Any party or the witness is entitled to obtain a copy of the deposition transcript or nonstenographic recording from the deposition officer upon payment of a reasonable fee.

Aug. 5, 1998 and Nov. 9, 1998, eff. Jan. 1, 1999.

203.4. Exhibits

At the request of a party, the original documents and things produced for inspection during the examination of the witness must be marked for identification by the deposition officer and annexed to the deposition transcript or nonstenographic recording. The person producing the materials may produce copies instead of originals if the party gives all other parties fair opportunity at the deposition to compare the copies with the originals. If the person offers originals rather than copies, the deposition officer must, after the conclusion of the deposition, make copies to be attached to the original deposition transcript or nonstenographic recording, and then return the originals to the person who produced them. The person who produced the originals must preserve them for hearing or trial and make them available for inspection or copying by any other party upon seven days' notice. Copies annexed to the original deposition transcript or nonstenographic recording may be used for all purposes.

Aug. 5, 1998 and Nov. 9, 1998, eff. Jan. 1, 1999.

203.5. Motion to Suppress

A party may object to any errors and irregularities in the manner in which the testimony is transcribed, signed, delivered, or otherwise dealt with by the deposition officer by filing a motion to suppress all or part of the deposition. If the deposition officer complies with Rule 203.3 at least one day before the case is called to trial, with regard to a deposition transcript, or 30 days before the case is called to trial, with regard to a nonstenographic recording, the party must file and serve a motion to suppress before trial commences to preserve the objections.

Aug. 5, 1998 and Nov. 9, 1998, eff. Jan. 1, 1999.

203.6. Use

(a) *Nonstenographic Recording; Transcription.* A nonstenographic recording of an oral deposition, or a written transcription of all or part of such a recording, may be used to the same extent as a deposition taken by stenographic means. However, the court, for good cause shown, may require that the party seeking to use a nonstenographic recording or written transcription first obtain a complete transcript of the deposition recording from a certified court reporter. The court reporter's transcription must be made from the original or a certified copy of the deposition recording. The court reporter must, to the extent applicable, comply with the provisions of this rule, except that the court reporter must deliver the original transcript to the attorney requesting the transcript, and the court reporter's certificate must include a statement that the transcript is a true record of the nonstenographic recording. The party to whom the court reporter delivers the original transcript must make the transcript available, upon reasonable request, for inspection and copying by the witness or any party.

(b) *Same Proceeding.* All or part of a deposition may be used for any purpose in the same proceeding in which it was taken. If the original is not filed, a certified copy may be used. "Same proceeding" includes a proceeding in a different court but involving the same subject matter and the same parties or their representatives or successors in interest. A deposition is admissible against a party joined after the deposition was taken if:

(1) the deposition is admissible pursuant to Rule 804(b)(1) of the Rules of Evidence, or

(2) that party has had a reasonable opportunity to redepose the witness and has failed to do so.

(c) *Different Proceeding.* Depositions taken in different proceedings may be used as permitted by the Rules of Evidence.

Aug. 5, 1998 and Nov. 9, 1998, eff. Jan. 1, 1999.

Historical Notes

Source:

Former rule 202.

Rule 204. Physical and Mental Examination

Historical Notes

Former rule 204 was repealed by order effective January 1, 1999. For subject matter of former rule 204, see, now, rule 199.5.

Source:

Former rule 167a.

204.1. Motion and Order Required

(a) *Motion.* A party may—no later than 30 days before the end of any applicable discovery period—move for an order compelling another party to:

(1) submit to a physical or mental examination by a qualified physician or a mental examination by a qualified psychologist; or

(2) produce for such examination a person in the other party's custody, conservatorship or legal control.

(b) *Service.* The motion and notice of hearing must be served on the person to be examined and all parties.

(c) *Requirements for Obtaining Order.* The court may issue an order for examination only for good cause shown and only in the following circumstances:

(1) when the mental or physical condition (including the blood group) of a party, or of a person in the custody, conservatorship or under the legal control of a party, is in controversy; or

(2) except as provided in Rule 204.4, an examination by a psychologist may be ordered when the party responding to the motion has designated a psychologist as a testifying expert or has disclosed a psychologist's records for possible use at trial.

(d) *Requirements of Order.* The order must be in writing and must specify the time, place, manner, conditions, and scope of the examination and the person or persons by whom it is to be made.

Aug. 5, 1998 and Nov. 9, 1998, eff. Jan. 1, 1999.

204.2. Report of Examining Physician or Psychologist

(a) *Right to Report.* Upon request of the person ordered to be examined, the party causing the examination to be made must deliver to the person a copy of a detailed written report of the examining physician or psychologist setting out the findings, including results of all tests made, diagnoses and conclusions, together with like reports of all earlier examinations of the same condition. After delivery of the report, upon request of the party causing the examination, the party against whom the order is made must produce a like report of any examination made before or after the ordered examination of the same condition, unless the person examined is not a party and the party shows that the party is unable to obtain it. The court on motion may limit delivery of a report on such terms as are just. If a physician or psychologist fails or refuses to make a report the court may exclude the testimony if offered at the trial.

(b) *Agreements; Relationship to Other Rules.* This subdivision applies to examinations made by agreement of the parties, unless the agreement expressly provides otherwise. This subdivision does not preclude discovery of a report of an examining physician or psychologist or the taking of a deposition of the physician or psychologist in accordance with the provisions of any other rule.

Aug. 5, 1998 and Nov. 9, 1998, eff. Jan. 1, 1999.

204.3. Effect of No Examination

If no examination is sought either by agreement or under this subdivision, the party whose physical or mental condition is in controversy must not comment to the court or jury concerning the party's willingness to submit to an examination, or on the right or failure of any other party to seek an examination.

Aug. 5, 1998 and Nov. 9, 1998, eff. Jan. 1, 1999.

204.4. Cases Arising Under Titles II or V, Family Code

In cases arising under Family Code Titles II or V, the court may—on its own initiative or on motion of a party—appoint:

(a) one or more psychologists or psychiatrists to make any and all appropriate mental examinations of the children who are the subject of the suit or of any other parties, and may make such appointment irrespective of whether a psychologist or psychiatrist has been designated by any party as a testifying expert;

(b) one or more experts who are qualified in paternity testing to take blood, body fluid, or tissue samples to conduct paternity tests as ordered by the court.

Aug. 5, 1998 and Nov. 9, 1998, eff. Jan. 1, 1999.

204.5. Definition

For the purpose of this rule, a psychologist is a person licensed or certified by a state or the District of Columbia as a psychologist.

Aug. 5, 1998 and Nov. 9, 1998, eff. Jan. 1, 1999.

Rule 205. Discovery from Nonparties

Historical Notes

Former rule 205, related to submission to witness, changes and signing, was repealed by order effective January 1, 1999. For subject matter of former rule 205, see, now, Vernon's Ann.Rules Civ.Proc., rule 203.1 et seq.

205.1. Forms of Discovery; Subpoena Requirement

A party may compel discovery from a nonparty—that is, a person who is not a party or subject to a party's control—only by obtaining a court order under Rules 196.7, 202, or 204, or by serving a subpoena compelling:

(a) an oral deposition;

(b) a deposition on written questions;

(c) a request for production of documents or tangible things, pursuant to Rule 199.2(b)(5) or Rule 200.1(b), served with a notice of deposition on oral examination or written questions; and

(d) a request for production of documents and tangible things under this rule.

Aug. 5, 1998, Nov. 9, 1998 and Dec. 31, 1998, eff. Jan. 1, 1999.

Comments—1999

See comments following Rule 205.3.

Historical Notes

The Order dated December 31, 1998, made technical corrections.

205.2. Notice

A party seeking discovery by subpoena from a nonparty must serve, on the nonparty and all parties, a copy of the form of notice required under the rules governing the applicable form of discovery. A notice of oral or written deposition must be served before or at the same time that a subpoena compelling attendance or production under the notice is served. A notice to produce documents or tangible things under Rule 205.3 must be served at least 10 days before the subpoena compelling production is served.

Aug. 5, 1998, Nov. 9, 1998 and Dec. 31, 1998, eff. Jan. 1, 1999.

Comments—1999

See comments following Rule 205.3.

Historical Notes

The Order dated December 31, 1998, made technical corrections.

205.3. Production of Documents and Tangible Things Without Deposition

(a) *Notice; Subpoena.* A party may compel production of documents and tangible things from a nonparty by serving—a reasonable time before the response is due but no later than 30 days before the end of any applicable discovery period—the notice required in Rule 205.2 and a subpoena compelling production or inspection of documents or tangible things.

(b) *Contents of Notice.* The notice must state:

(1) the name of the person from whom production or inspection is sought to be compelled;

(2) a reasonable time and place for the production or inspection; and

(3) the items to be produced or inspected, either by individual item or by category, describing each item and category with reasonable particularity, and, if applicable, describing the desired testing and sampling with sufficient specificity to inform the nonparty of the means, manner, and procedure for testing or sampling.

(c) *Requests for Production of Medical or Mental Health Records of Other Nonparties.* If a party requests a nonparty to produce medical or mental health records of another nonparty, the requesting party must serve the nonparty whose records are sought with the notice required under this rule. This requirement does not apply under the circumstances set forth in Rule 196.1(c)(2).

(d) *Response.* The nonparty must respond to the notice and subpoena in accordance with Rule 176.6.

(e) *Custody, Inspection and Copying.* The party obtaining the production must make all materials produced available for inspection by any other party on reasonable notice, and must furnish copies to any party who requests at that party's expense.

(f) *Cost of Production.* A party requiring production of documents by a nonparty must reimburse the nonparty's reasonable costs of production.

Aug. 5, 1998, Nov. 9, 1998 and Dec. 31, 1998, eff. Jan. 1, 1999.

Comments—1999

Under this rule, a party may subpoena production of documents and tangible things from nonparties without need for a motion or oral or written deposition.

Rule 206. Repealed by Order of Aug. 5, 1998 and Nov. 9, 1998, eff. Jan. 1, 1999

Historical Notes

See, now, Vernon's Ann.Rules Civ.Proc., Rules 203.1 et seq.

Repealed rule 206, relating to Certification by Officer; Exhibits; Copies; Notice of Delivery, was derived from orders of Dec. 5, 1983, July 15, 1987, and April 24, 1990.

A former rule 206 was incorporated into rule 204 by the 1983 order; this rule was derived from former rules 208, 208a, and 210.

Rule 207. Repealed by Order of Aug. 5, 1998 and Nov. 9, 1998, eff. Jan. 1, 1999

Historical Notes

See, now, Vernon's Ann.Rules Civ.Proc., rules 203.1 et seq.

Repealed rule 207, relating to Use of Deposition Transcripts in Court Proceedings, was derived from orders of Dec. 5, 1983 and July 15, 1987.

A former rule 207 was incorporated into rule 204 by the 1983 order.

Rule 208. Repealed by Order of Aug. 5, 1998 and Nov. 9, 1998, eff. Jan. 1, 1999

Historical Notes

See, now, Vernon's Ann.Rules Civ.Proc., Rules 200.1 to 200.4.

Former rule 208, relating to Depositions Upon Written Questions, was derived from orders of Dec. 5, 1983, July 15, 1987, and April 24, 1990.

A former rule 208 was incorporated into rule 206 by the 1983 order.

Rule 208a. Repealed by Order of Dec. 5, 1983, eff. April 1, 1984

Historical Notes

Former rule 208a, relating to Certification of Charges, was derived from order of July 22, 1975.

For subject matter of the repealed rule, see, now, Vernon's Ann.Rules Civ.Proc., rule 203.1 et seq.

Rule 209. Repealed by Order of Aug. 5, 1998 and Nov. 9, 1998, eff. Jan. 1, 1999

Historical Notes

For subject matter of the repealed rule, see, now, rule 191.4(e).

Former rule 209, relating to Retention and Disposition of Deposition Transcripts and Depositions Upon Written Questions, was added by order of July 15, 1987.

A former rule 209, relating to submission of depositions to witnesses, was repealed by order of Dec. 5, 1983, eff. April 1, 1984.

Rules 210 to 214. Repealed by Order of Dec. 5, 1983, eff. April 1, 1984

Historical Notes

For subject matter of former rules 211 to 213, see, now, rule 207.

Rule 215. Abuse of Discovery; Sanctions

Historical Notes

Source:

Former rule 203.

215.1. Motion for Sanctions or Order Compelling Discovery

A party, upon reasonable notice to other parties and all other persons affected thereby, may apply for sanctions or an order compelling discovery as follows:

(a) *Appropriate Court.* On matters relating to a deposition, an application for an order to a party may be made to the court in which the action is pending, or to any district court in the district where the deposition is being taken. An application for an order to a deponent who is not a party shall be made to the court in the district where the deposition is being taken. As to all other discovery matters, an application for an order will be made to the court in which the action is pending.

(b) *Motion.*

(1) If a party or other deponent which is a corporation or other entity fails to make a designation under Rules 199.2(b)(1) or 200.1(b); or

(2) If a party, or other deponent, or a person designated to testify on behalf of a party or other deponent fails:

(A) to appear before the officer who is to take his deposition, after being served with a proper notice; or

(B) to answer a question propounded or submitted upon oral examination or upon written questions; or

(3) if a party fails:

(A) to serve answers or objections to interrogatories submitted under Rule 197,[1] after proper service of the interrogatories; or

(B) to answer an interrogatory submitted under Rule 197; or

(C) to serve a written response to a request for inspection submitted under Rule 196,[2] after proper service of the request; or

(D) to respond that discovery will be permitted as requested or fails to permit discovery as requested in response to a request for inspection submitted under Rule 196;

the discovering party may move for an order compelling a designation, an appearance, an answer or answers, or inspection or production in accordance with the request, or apply to the court in which the action is pending for the imposition of any sanction authorized by Rule 215.2(b) without the necessity of first having obtained a court order compelling such discovery.

When taking a deposition on oral examination, the proponent of the question may complete or adjourn the examination before he applies for an order.

If the court denies the motion in whole or in part, it may make such protective order as it would have been empowered to make on a motion pursuant to Rule 192.6.

(c) *Evasive or Incomplete Answer.* For purposes of this subdivision an evasive or incomplete answer is to be treated as a failure to answer.

(d) *Disposition of Motion to Compel: Award of Expenses.* If the motion is granted, the court shall, after opportunity for hearing, require a party or deponent whose conduct necessitated the motion or the party or attorney advising such conduct or both of them to pay, at such time as ordered by the court, the moving party the reasonable expenses incurred in obtaining the order, including attorney fees, unless the court finds that the opposition to the motion was substantially justified or that other circumstances make an award of expenses unjust. Such an order shall be subject to review on appeal from the final judgment.

If the motion is denied, the court may, after opportunity for hearing, require the moving party or attorney advising such motion to pay to the party or deponent who opposed the motion the reasonable expenses incurred in opposing the motion, including attorney fees, unless the court finds that the making of the motion was substantially justified or that other circumstances make an award of expenses unjust.

If the motion is granted in part and denied in part, the court may apportion the reasonable expenses incurred in relation to the motion among the parties and persons in a just manner.

In determining the amount of reasonable expenses, including attorney fees, to be awarded in connection with a motion, the trial court shall award expenses which are reasonable in relation to the amount of work reasonably expended in obtaining an order compelling compliance or in opposing a motion which is denied.

(e) *Providing Person's Own Statement.* If a party fails to comply with any person's written request for the person's own statement as provided in Rule 192.3(h), the person who made the request may move for an order compelling compliance. If the motion is granted, the movant may recover the expenses incurred in obtaining the order, including attorney fees, which are reasonable in relation to the amount of work reasonably expended in obtaining the order.

Oct. 29, 1940, eff. Sept. 1, 1941. Amended by orders of Aug. 5, 1998, and Nov. 9, 1998, eff. Jan. 1, 1999.

1 Vernon's Ann.Rules Civ.Proc., rule 197.1 et seq.

2 Vernon's Ann.Rules Civ.Proc., rule 196.1 et seq.

Comment—1999

See comments following Rule 215.6.

215.2. Failure to Comply with Order or with Discovery Request

(a) *Sanctions by Court in District Where Deposition is Taken.* If a deponent fails to appear or to be sworn or to answer a question after being directed to do so by a district court in the district in which the deposition is being taken, the failure may be considered a contempt of that court.

(b) *Sanctions by Court in Which Action is Pending.* If a party or an officer, director, or managing agent of a party or a person designated under Rules 199.2(b)(1) or 200.1(b) to testify on behalf of a party fails to comply with proper discovery requests or to obey an order to provide or permit discovery, including an order made under Rules 204[1] or 215.1, the court in which the action is pending may, after notice and hearing, make such orders in regard to the failure as are just, and among others the following:

(1) an order disallowing any further discovery of any kind or of a particular kind by the disobedient party;

(2) an order charging all or any portion of the expenses of discovery or taxable court costs or both against the disobedient party or the attorney advising him;

(3) an order that the matters regarding which the order was made or any other designated facts shall be taken to be established for the purposes of the action in accordance with the claim of the party obtaining the order;

(4) an order refusing to allow the disobedient party to support or oppose designated claims or defenses, or prohibiting him from introducing designated matters in evidence;

(5) an order striking out pleadings or parts thereof, or staying further proceedings until the order is obeyed, or dismissing with or without prejudice the action or proceedings or any part thereof, or rendering a judgment by default against the disobedient party;

(6) in lieu of any of the foregoing orders or in addition thereto, an order treating as a contempt of court the failure to obey any orders except an order to submit to a physical or mental examination;

(7) when a party has failed to comply with an order under Rule 204 requiring him to appear or produce another for examination, such orders as are listed in paragraphs (1), (2), (3), (4) or (5) of this subdivision, unless the person failing to comply shows that he is unable to appear or to produce such person for examination.

(8) In lieu of any of the foregoing orders or in addition thereto, the court shall require the party failing to obey the order or the attorney advising him, or both, to pay, at such time as ordered by the court, the reasonable expenses, including attorney fees, caused by the failure, unless the court finds that the failure was substantially justified or that

other circumstances make an award of expenses unjust. Such an order shall be subject to review on appeal from the final judgment.

(c) *Sanction Against Nonparty For Violation of Rules 196.7 or 205.3.* If a nonparty fails to comply with an order under Rules 196.7 or 205.3, the court which made the order may treat the failure to obey as contempt of court.

Oct. 29, 1940, eff. Sept. 1, 1941. Amended by orders of Aug. 5, 1998, and Nov. 9, 1998, eff. Jan. 1, 1999.

1 Vernon's Ann.Rules Civ.Proc., rule 204.1 et seq.

Comment—1999

See comments following Rule 215.6.

215.3. Abuse of Discovery Process in Seeking, Making, or Resisting Discovery

If the court finds a party is abusing the discovery process in seeking, making or resisting discovery or if the court finds that any interrogatory or request for inspection or production is unreasonably frivolous, oppressive, or harassing, or that a response or answer is unreasonably frivolous or made for purposes of delay, then the court in which the action is pending may, after notice and hearing, impose any appropriate sanction authorized by paragraphs (1), (2), (3), (4), (5), and (8) of Rule 215.2(b). Such order of sanction shall be subject to review on appeal from the final judgment.

Oct. 29, 1940, eff. Sept. 1, 1941. Amended by orders of April 24, 1990, eff. Sept. 1, 1990; Aug. 5, 1998, and Nov. 9, 1998, eff. Jan. 1, 1999.

Comment—1999

See comments following Rule 215.6.

Comment—1990

To require notice and hearing before an imposition of sanctions under paragraph 3, and to specify that such sanctions be appropriate.

215.4. Failure to Comply with Rule 198

(a) *Motion.* A party who has requested an admission under Rule 198 may move to determine the sufficiency of the answer or objection. For purposes of this subdivision an evasive or incomplete answer may be treated as a failure to answer. Unless the court determines that an objection is justified, it shall order that an answer be served. If the court determines that an answer does not comply with the requirements of Rule 198,[1] it may order either that the matter is admitted or that an amended answer be served. The provisions of Rule 215.1(d) apply to the award of expenses incurred in relation to the motion.

(b) *Expenses on Failure to Admit.* If a party fails to admit the genuineness of any document or the truth of any matter as requested under Rule 198 and if the party requesting the admissions thereafter proves the genuineness of the document or the truth of the matter, he may apply to the court for an order requiring the other party to pay him the reasonable expenses incurred in making that proof, including reasonable attorney fees. The court shall make the order unless it finds that (1) the request was held objectionable pursuant to Rule 193,[2] or (2) the admission sought was of no substantial importance, or (3) the party failing to admit had a reasonable ground to believe that he might prevail on the matter, or (4) there was other good reason for the failure to admit.

Oct. 29, 1940, eff. Sept. 1, 1941. Amended by orders of Aug. 5, 1998, and Nov. 9, 1998, eff. Jan. 1, 1999.

1 Vernon's Ann.Rules Civ.Proc., rule 198.1 et seq.

2 Vernon's Ann.Rules Civ.Proc., rule 193.1 et seq.

Comment—1999

See comments following Rule 215.6.

215.5. Failure of Party or Witness to Attend or to Serve Subpoena; Expenses

(a) *Failure of Party Giving Notice to Attend.* If the party giving the notice of the taking of an oral deposition fails to attend and proceed therewith and another party attends in person or by attorney pursuant to the notice, the court may order the party giving the notice to pay such other party the reasonable expenses incurred by him and his attorney in attending, including reasonable attorney fees.

(b) *Failure of Witness to Attend.* If a party gives notice of the taking of an oral deposition of a witness and the witness does not attend because of the fault of the party giving the notice, if another party attends in person or by attorney because he expects the deposition of that witness to be taken, the court may order the party giving the notice to pay such other party the reasonable expenses incurred by him and his attorney in attending, including reasonable attorney fees.

Oct. 29, 1940, eff. Sept. 1, 1941. Amended by orders of Aug. 5, 1998, and Nov. 9, 1998, eff. Jan. 1, 1999.

Comment—1999

See comments following Rule 215.6.

215.6. Exhibits to Motions and Responses

Motions or responses made under this rule may have exhibits attached including affidavits, discovery pleadings, or any other documents.

Oct. 29, 1940, eff. Sept. 1, 1941. Amended by orders of Aug. 5, 1998, and Nov. 9, 1998, eff. Jan. 1, 1999.

Comment—1999

The references in this rule to other discovery rules are changed to reflect the revisions in those rules, and former Rule 203 is added as Rule 215.5 in place of the former provision, which is superseded by Rule 193.6.

Rules 215a to 215c. Repealed by Order of Dec. 5, 1983, eff. April 1, 1984

Historical Notes

For subject matter of rules 215a, 215b and 215c, see, now, rules 215.1 et seq., 203.1 et seq., and 202.1 et seq., respectively.

SECTION 10. THE JURY IN COURT

Rule 216. Request and Fee for Jury Trial

a. Request. No jury trial shall be had in any civil suit, unless a written request for a jury trial is filed with the clerk of the court a reasonable time before the date set for trial of the cause on the non-jury docket, but not less than thirty days in advance.

b. Jury Fee. Unless otherwise provided by law, a fee of ten dollars if in the district court and five dollars if in the county court must be deposited with the clerk of the court within the time for making a written request for a jury trial. The clerk shall promptly enter a notation of the payment of such fee upon the court's docket sheet.

Oct. 29, 1940, eff. Sept. 1, 1941. Amended by orders of March 31, 1941, eff. Sept. 1, 1941; Sept. 20, 1941, eff. Dec. 31, 1941; Oct. 12, 1949, eff. March 1, 1950; July 15, 1987, eff. Jan. 1, 1988; April 24, 1990, eff. Sept. 1, 1990.

Historical Notes

Source

Vernon's Ann.Civ.St. arts. 2124 and 2125.

Rule 217. Oath of Inability

The deposit for a jury fee shall not be required when the party shall within the time for making such deposit, file with the clerk his affidavit to the effect that he is unable to make such deposit, and that he can not, by the pledge of property or otherwise, obtain the money necessary for that purpose; and the court shall then order the clerk to enter the suit on the jury docket.

Oct. 29, 1940, eff. Sept. 1, 1941.

Historical Notes

Source

Vernon's Ann.Civ.St. art. 2127, unchanged.

Rule 218. Jury Docket

The clerks of the district and county courts shall each keep a docket, styled, "The Jury Docket," in which shall be entered in their order the cases in which jury fees have been paid or affidavit in lieu thereof has been filed as provided in the two preceding rules.

Oct. 29, 1940, eff. Sept. 1, 1941.

Historical Notes

Source

Vernon's Ann.Civ.St. art. 2128, modified to require placing cases on jury docket upon payment of fee, rather than when jury trial has been ordered by court.

Rule 219. Jury Trial Day

The court shall designate the days for taking up the jury docket and the trial of jury cases. Such order may be revoked or changed in the court's discretion.

Oct. 29, 1940, eff. Sept. 1, 1941. Amended by order of Dec. 5, 1983, eff. April 1, 1984.

Historical Notes

Source

Vernon's Ann.Civ.St. art. 2129, eliminating requirement that order be entered upon minutes.

Rule 220. Withdrawing Cause from Jury Docket

When any party has paid the fee for a jury trial, he shall not be permitted to withdraw the cause from the jury docket over the objection of the parties adversely interested. If so permitted, the court in its discretion may by an order permit him to withdraw also his jury fee deposit. Failure of a party to appear for trial shall be deemed a waiver by him of the right to trial by jury.

Oct. 29, 1940, eff. Sept. 1, 1941. Amended by orders of Aug. 18, 1947, eff. Dec. 31, 1947; July 21, 1970, eff. Jan. 1, 1971.

Historical Notes

Source

Vernon's Ann.Civ.St. art. 2130, with minor textual change.

Rule 221. Challenge to the Array

When the jurors summoned have not been selected by jury commissioners or by drawing the names from a jury wheel, any party to a suit which is to be tried by a jury may, before the jury is drawn challenge the array upon the ground that the officer summoning the jury has acted corruptly, and has wilfully summoned jurors known to be prejudiced against the party challenging or biased in favor of the adverse party. All such challenges must be in writing setting forth distinctly the grounds of such challenge and supported by the affidavit of the party or some other credible person. When such challenge is made, the court shall hear evidence and decide without delay whether or not the challenge shall be sustained.

Oct. 29, 1940, eff. Sept. 1, 1941.

Historical Notes

Source

Vernon's Ann.Civ.St. art. 2131, with minor textual change.

Rule 222. When Challenge Is Sustained

If the challenge be sustained, the array of jurors summoned shall be discharged, and the court shall order other jurors summoned in their stead, and shall direct that the officer who summoned the persons so discharged, and on account of whose misconduct the challenge has been sustained, shall not summon any other jurors in the case.

Oct. 29, 1940, eff. Sept. 1, 1941.

Historical Notes

Source

Vernon's Ann.Civ.St. art. 2132, unchanged.

Rule 223. Jury List in Certain Counties

In counties governed as to juries by the laws providing for interchangeable juries, the names of the jurors shall be placed upon the general panel in the order in which they are randomly selected, and jurors shall be assigned for service from the top thereof, in the order in which they shall be needed, and jurors returned to the general panel after service in any of such courts shall be enrolled at the bottom of the list in the order of their respective return; provided, however, after such assignment to a particular court, the trial judge of such court, upon the demand prior to voir dire examination by any party or attorney in the case reached for trial in such court, shall cause the names of all members of such assigned jury panel in such case to be placed in a receptacle, shuffled, and drawn, and such names shall be transcribed in the order drawn on the jury list from which the jury is to be selected to try such case. There shall be only one shuffle and drawing by the trial judge in each case.

Oct. 29, 1940, eff. Sept. 1, 1941. Amended by order of April 24, 1990, eff. Sept. 1, 1990.

Comment—1990

To provide uniformity in jury shuffles.

Historical Notes

Source

Vernon's Ann.Civ.St. art. 2138, unchanged.

Rule 224. Preparing Jury List

In counties not governed as to juries by the laws providing for interchangeable juries, when the parties have announced ready for trial the clerk shall write the name of each regular juror entered of record for that week on separate slips of paper, as near the same size and appearance as may be, and shall place the slips in a box and mix them well. The clerk shall draw from the box, in the presence of the court, the names of twenty-four jurors, if in the district court, or so many as there may be, if there be a less number in the box; and the names of twelve jurors if in the county court, or so many as there may be, and write the names as drawn upon two slips of paper and deliver one slip to each party to the suit or his attorney.

Oct. 29, 1940, eff. Sept. 1, 1941.

Historical Notes

Source

Vernon's Ann.Civ.St. arts. 2139 and 2140, unchanged.

Rule 225. Summoning Talesman

When there are not as many as twenty-four names drawn from the box, if in the district court, or as many as twelve, if in the county court, the court shall direct the sheriff to summon such number of qualified persons as the court deems necessary to complete the panel. The names of those thus summoned shall be placed in the box and drawn and entered upon the slips as provided in the preceding rules.

Oct. 29, 1940, eff. Sept. 1, 1941.

Historical Notes

Source

Vernon's Ann.Civ.St. art. 2141, modified by substituting "twenty-four" for "twelve," and "twelve" for "six."

Rule 226. Oath to Jury Panel

Before the parties or their attorneys begin the examination of the jurors whose names have thus been listed, the jurors shall be sworn by the court or under its direction, as follows: "You, and each of you, do solemnly swear that you will true answers give to all questions propounded to you concerning your qualifications as a juror, so help you God."

Oct. 29, 1940, eff. Sept. 1, 1941.

Historical Notes

Source

New rule.

Rule 226a. Instructions to Jury Panel and Jury

The court must give instructions to the jury panel and the jury as prescribed by order of the Supreme Court under this rule.

Oct. 29, 1940, eff. Sept. 1, 1941. Added by order of July 20, 1966, eff. Jan. 1, 1967. Amended by order of Jan. 27, 2005, eff. Feb. 1, 2005.

Comment—2005

The rule is clarified. With these amendments, the Supreme Court has ordered changes in the prescribed jury instructions consistent with Act of June 2, 2003, 78th Leg., R.S., ch. 204, § 13.04, 2003 Tex. Gen. Laws 847, 888, codified as Tex. Civ. Prac. & Rem. Code § 41.003.

Historical Notes

2005 Amendment

An order dated January 27, 2005, which amended part III of the approved jury instructions, provided:

"These amendments take effect on February 1, 2005, in all cases filed on or after September 1, 2003... Comments appended to these rules are intended to inform their construction and application."

Jury Instructions Prescribed by Order Under Rule 226a

Pursuant to the provisions of Rule 226a, Texas Rules of Civil Procedure, it is ordered [July 20, 1966] by the Supreme Court of Texas effective January 1, 1967; January 1, 1971; February 1, 1973; December 5, 1983, effective April 1, 1984; July 15, 1987, eff. Jan. 1, 1988; March 15, 2011, eff. April 1, 2011; April 13, 2011, eff. April 13, 2011.

I.

That the following oral instructions, with such modifications as the circumstances of the particular case may require, shall be given by the court to the members of the jury panel after they have been sworn in as provided in Rule 226 and before the voir dire examination:

Members of the Jury Panel [or Ladies and Gentlemen of the Jury Panel]:

Thank you for being here. We are here to select a jury. Twelve [six] of you will be chosen for the jury. Even if you are not chosen for the jury, you are performing a valuable service that is your right and duty as a citizen of a free country.

Before we begin: Turn off all phones and other electronic devices. While you are in the courtroom, do not communicate with anyone through any electronic device. [For example, do not communicate by phone, text message, email message, chat room, blog, or social networking websites such as Facebook, Twitter, or Myspace.] [I will give you a number where others may contact you in case of an emergency.] Do not record or photograph any part of these court proceedings, because it is prohibited by law.

If you are chosen for the jury, your role as jurors will be to decide the disputed facts in this case. My role will be to ensure that this case is tried in accordance with the rules of law.

Here is some background about this case. This is a civil case. It is a lawsuit that is not a criminal case. The parties are as follows: The plaintiff is __________, and the defendant is __________. Representing the plaintiff is __________, and representing the defendant is __________. They will ask you some questions during jury selection. But before their questions begin, I must give you some instructions for jury selection.

Every juror must obey these instructions. You may be called into court to testify about any violations of these instructions. If you do not follow these instructions, you will be guilty of juror misconduct, and I might have to order a new trial and start this process over again. This would waste your time and the parties' money, and would require the taxpayers of this county to pay for another trial.

These are the instructions.

1. To avoid looking like you are friendly with one side of the case, do not mingle or talk with the lawyers, witnesses, parties, or anyone else involved in the case. You may exchange casual greetings like "hello" and "good morning." Other than that, do not talk with them at all. They have to follow these instructions too, so you should not be offended when they follow the instructions.

2. Do not accept any favors from the lawyers, witnesses, parties, or anyone else involved in the case, and do not do any favors for them. This includes favors such as giving rides and food.

3. Do not discuss this case with anyone, even your spouse or a friend, either in person or by any other means [including by phone, text message, email message, chat room, blog, or social networking websites such as Facebook, Twitter, or Myspace]. Do not allow anyone to discuss the case with you or in your hearing. If anyone tries to discuss the case with you or in your hearing, tell me immediately. We do not want you to be influenced by something other than the evidence admitted in court.

4. The parties, through their attorneys, have the right to ask you questions about your background, experiences, and attitudes. They are not trying to meddle in your affairs. They are just being thorough and trying to choose fair jurors who do not have any bias or prejudice in this particular case.

5. Remember that you took an oath that you will tell the truth, so be truthful when the lawyers ask you questions, and always give complete answers. If you do not answer a question that applies to you, that violates your oath. Sometimes a lawyer will ask a question of the whole panel instead of just one person. If the question applies to you, raise your hand and keep it raised until you are called on.

Do you understand these instructions? If you do not, please tell me now.

The lawyers will now begin to ask their questions.

II.

That the following oral and written instructions, with such modifications as the circumstances of the particular case may require, shall be given by the court to the jury immediately after the jurors are selected for the case:

Members of the Jury [or Ladies and Gentlemen]:

You have been chosen to serve on this jury. Because of the oath you have taken and your selection for the jury, you become officials of this court and active participants in our justice system.

[Hand out the written instructions.]

You have each received a set of written instructions. I am going to read them with you now. Some of them you have heard before and some are new.

1. Turn off all phones and other electronic devices. While you are in the courtroom and while you are deliberating, do not communicate with anyone through any electronic device. [For example, do not communicate by phone, text message, email message, chat room, blog, or social networking websites such as Facebook, Twitter, or Myspace.] [I will give you a number where others may contact you in case of an emergency.] Do not post information about the case on the Internet before these court proceedings end and you are released from jury duty. Do not record or photograph any part of these court proceedings, because it is prohibited by law.

2. To avoid looking like you are friendly with one side of the case, do not mingle or talk with the lawyers, witnesses, parties, or anyone else involved in the case. You may exchange casual greetings like "hello" and "good morning." Other than that, do not talk with them at all. They have to

follow these instructions too, so you should not be offended when they follow the instructions.

3. Do not accept any favors from the lawyers, witnesses, parties, or anyone else involved in the case, and do not do any favors for them. This includes favors such as giving rides and food.

4. Do not discuss this case with anyone, even your spouse or a friend, either in person or by any other means [including by phone, text message, email message, chat room, blog, or social networking websites such as Facebook, Twitter, or Myspace]. Do not allow anyone to discuss the case with you or in your hearing. If anyone tries to discuss the case with you or in your hearing, tell me immediately. We do not want you to be influenced by something other than the evidence admitted in court.

5. Do not discuss this case with anyone during the trial, not even with the other jurors, until the end of the trial. You should not discuss the case with your fellow jurors until the end of the trial so that you do not form opinions about the case before you have heard everything.

After you have heard all the evidence, received all of my instructions, and heard all of the lawyers' arguments, you will then go to the jury room to discuss the case with the other jurors and reach a verdict.

6. Do not investigate this case on your own. For example, do not:

a. try to get information about the case, lawyers, witnesses, or issues from outside this courtroom;

b. go to places mentioned in the case to inspect the places;

c. inspect items mentioned in this case unless they are presented as evidence in court;

d. look anything up in a law book, dictionary, or public record to try to learn more about the case;

e. look anything up on the Internet to try to learn more about the case; or

f. let anyone else do any of these things for you.

This rule is very important because we want a trial based only on evidence admitted in open court. Your conclusions about this case must be based only on what you see and hear in this courtroom because the law does not permit you to base your conclusions on information that has not been presented to you in open court. All the information must be presented in open court so the parties and their lawyers can test it and object to it. Information from other sources, like the Internet, will not go through this important process in the courtroom. In addition, information from other sources could be completely unreliable. As a result, if you investigate this case on your own, you could compromise the fairness to all parties in this case and jeopardize the results of this trial.

7. Do not tell other jurors about your own experiences or other people's experiences. For example, you may have special knowledge of something in the case, such as business, technical, or professional information. You may even have expert knowledge or opinions, or you may know what happened in this case or another similar case. Do not tell the other jurors about it. Telling other jurors about it is wrong because it means the jury will be considering things that were not admitted in court.

8. Do not consider attorneys' fees unless I tell you to. Do not guess about attorneys' fees.

9. Do not consider or guess whether any party is covered by insurance unless I tell you to.

10. During the trial, if taking notes will help focus your attention on the evidence, you may take notes using the materials the court has provided. Do not use any personal electronic devices to take notes. If taking notes will distract your attention from the evidence, you should not take notes. Your notes are for your own personal use. They are not evidence. Do not show or read your notes to anyone, including other jurors.

You must leave your notes in the jury room or with the bailiff. The bailiff is instructed not to read your notes and to give your notes to me promptly after collecting them from you. I will make sure your notes are kept in a safe, secure location and not disclosed to anyone.

[You may take your notes back into the jury room and consult them during deliberations. But keep in mind that your notes are not evidence. When you deliberate, each of you should rely on your independent recollection of the evidence and not be influenced by the fact that another juror has or has not taken notes. After you complete your deliberations, the bailiff will collect your notes.]

When you are released from jury duty, the bailiff will promptly destroy your notes so that nobody can read what you wrote.

11. I will decide matters of law in this case. It is your duty to listen to and consider the evidence and to determine fact issues that I may submit to you at the end of the trial. After you have heard all the evidence, I will give you instructions to follow as you make your decision. The instructions also will have questions for you to answer. You will not be asked and you should not consider which side will win. Instead, you will need to answer the specific questions I give you.

Every juror must obey my instructions. If you do not follow these instructions, you will be guilty of juror misconduct, and I may have to order a new trial and start this process over again. This would waste your time and the parties' money, and would require the taxpayers of this county to pay for another trial.

Do you understand these instructions? If you do not, please tell me now.

Please keep these instructions and review them as we go through this case. If anyone does not follow these instructions, tell me.

III.

COURT'S CHARGE

Before closing arguments begin, the court must give to each member of the jury a copy of the charge, which must include the following written instructions, with such modifications as the circumstances of the particular case may require:

Members of the Jury [or Ladies & Gentlemen of the Jury]:

After the closing arguments, you will go to the jury room to decide the case, answer the questions that are attached, and reach a verdict. You may discuss the case with other jurors only when you are all together in the jury room.

Remember my previous instructions: Do not discuss the case with anyone else, either in person or by any other means. Do not do any independent investigation about the case or conduct any research. Do not look up any words in dictionaries or on the Internet. Do not post information about the case on the Internet. Do not share any special knowledge or experiences with the other jurors. Do not use your phone or any other electronic device during your deliberations for any reason. [I will give you a number where others may contact you in case of an emergency.]

[Any notes you have taken are for your own personal use. You may take your notes back into the jury room and consult them during deliberations, but do not show or read your notes to your fellow jurors during your deliberations. Your notes are not evidence. Each of you should rely on your independent recollection of the evidence and not be influenced by the fact that another juror has or has not taken notes.]

[You must leave your notes with the bailiff when you are not deliberating. The bailiff will give your notes to me promptly after collecting them from you. I will make sure your notes are kept in a safe, secure location and not disclosed to anyone. After you complete your deliberations, the bailiff will collect your notes. When you are released from jury duty, the bailiff will promptly destroy your notes so that nobody can read what you wrote.]

Here are the instructions for answering the questions.

1. Do not let bias, prejudice, or sympathy play any part in your decision.

2. Base your answers only on the evidence admitted in court and on the law that is in these instructions and questions. Do not consider or discuss any evidence that was not admitted in the courtroom.

3. You are to make up your own minds about the facts. You are the sole judges of the credibility of the witnesses and the weight to give their testimony. But on matters of law, you must follow all of my instructions.

4. If my instructions use a word in a way that is different from its ordinary meaning, use the meaning I give you, which will be a proper legal definition.

5. All the questions and answers are important. No one should say that any question or answer is not important.

6. Answer "yes" or "no" to all questions unless you are told otherwise. A "yes" answer must be based on a preponderance of the evidence [unless you are told otherwise]. Whenever a question requires an answer other than "yes" or "no," your answer must be based on a preponderance of the evidence [unless you are told otherwise].

The term "preponderance of the evidence" means the greater weight of credible evidence presented in this case. If you do not find that a preponderance of the evidence supports a "yes" answer, then answer "no." A preponderance of the evidence is not measured by the number of witnesses or by the number of documents admitted in evidence. For a fact to be proved by a preponderance of the evidence, you must find that the fact is more likely true than not true.

7. Do not decide who you think should win before you answer the questions and then just answer the questions to match your decision. Answer each question carefully without considering who will win. Do not discuss or consider the effect your answers will have.

8. Do not answer questions by drawing straws or by any method of chance.

9. Some questions might ask you for a dollar amount. Do not agree in advance to decide on a dollar amount by adding up each juror's amount and then figuring the average.

10. Do not trade your answers. For example, do not say, "I will answer this question your way if you answer another question my way."

11. [Unless otherwise instructed] The answers to the questions must be based on the decision of at least 10 of the 12 [5 of the 6] jurors. The same 10 [5] jurors must agree on every answer. Do not agree to be bound by a vote of anything less than 10 [5] jurors, even if it would be a majority.

As I have said before, if you do not follow these instructions, you will be guilty of juror misconduct, and I might have to order a new trial and start this process over again. This would waste your time and the parties' money, and would require the taxpayers of this county to pay for another trial. If a juror breaks any of these rules, tell that person to stop and report it to me immediately.

[Definitions, questions, and special instructions given to the jury will be transcribed here. If exemplary damages are sought against a defendant, the jury must unanimously find, with respect to that defendant, (i) liability on at least one claim for actual damages that will support an award of exemplary damages, (ii) any additional conduct, such as malice or gross negligence, required for an award of exemplary damages, and (iii) the amount of exemplary damages to be awarded. The jury's answers to questions regarding (ii) and (iii) must be conditioned on a unanimous finding regarding (i), except in an extraordinary circumstance when the conditioning instruction would be erroneous. The jury need not be unanimous in finding the amount of actual damages. Thus, if questions regarding (ii) and (iii) are submitted to the jury for defendants D1 and D2, instructions in substantially the following form must immediately precede such questions:

Preceding question (ii):

Answer Question (ii) for D1 only if you unanimously answered "Yes" to Question[s] (i) regarding D1. Otherwise, do not answer Question (ii) for D1. [Repeat for D2.]

You are instructed that in order to answer "Yes" to [any part of] Question (if), your answer must be unanimous. You may answer "No" to [any part off Question (ii) only upon a vote of 10 [5] or more jurors. Otherwise, you must not answer [that part of] Question (ii).

Preceding question (iii):

Answer Question (iii) for D1 only if you answered "Yes" to Question (ii) for D1. Otherwise, do not answer Question (in) for D1. [Repeat for D2.]

You are instructed that you must unanimously agree on the amount of any award of exemplary damages.

These examples are given by way of illustration.]

Presiding Juror:

1. When you go into the jury room to answer the questions, the first thing you will need to do is choose a presiding juror.

2. The presiding juror has these duties:

a. have the complete charge read aloud if it will be helpful to your deliberations;

b. preside over your deliberations, meaning manage the discussions, and see that you follow these instructions;

c. give written questions or comments to the bailiff who will give them to the judge;

d. write down the answers you agree on;

e. get the signatures for the verdict certificate; and

f. notify the bailiff that you have reached a verdict.

Do you understand the duties of the presiding juror? If you do not, please tell me now.

Instructions for Signing the Verdict Certificate:

1. [Unless otherwise instructed] You may answer the questions on a vote of 10 [5] jurors. The same 10 [5] jurors must agree on every answer in the charge. This means you may not have one group of 10 [5] jurors agree on one answer and a different group of 10 [5] jurors agree on another answer.

2. If 10 [5] jurors agree on every answer, those 10 [5] jurors sign the verdict.

If 11 jurors agree on every answer, those 11 jurors sign the verdict.

If all 12 [6] of you agree on every answer, you are unanimous and only the presiding juror signs the verdict.

3. All jurors should deliberate on every question. You may end up with all 12 [6] of you agreeing on some answers, while only 10 [5] or 11 of you agree on other answers. But when you sign the verdict, only those 10 [5] who agree on every answer will sign the verdict.

4. [Added if the charge requires some unanimity] There are some special instructions before Questions ___ explaining how to answer those questions. Please follow the instructions. If all 12 [6] of you answer those questions, you will need to complete a second verdict certificate for those questions.

Do you understand these instructions? If you do not, please tell me now.

____

Judge Presiding

Verdict Certificate

Check one:

___Our verdict is unanimous. All 12 [6] of us have agreed to each and every answer. The presiding juror has signed the certificate for all 12 [6] of us.

____________________	____________________
Signature of Presiding Juror	Printed Name of Presiding Juror

___Our verdict is not unanimous. Eleven of us have agreed to each and every answer and have signed the certificate below.

___Our verdict is not unanimous. Ten [Five] of us have agreed to each and every answer and have signed the certificate below.

	SIGNATURE	NAME PRINTED
1.	___________	___________
2.	___________	___________
3.	___________	___________
4.	___________	___________
5.	___________	___________
6.	___________	___________
7.	___________	___________
8.	___________	___________
9.	___________	___________
10.	___________	___________
11.	___________	___________

If you have answered Question No. ___ [the exemplary damages amount], then you must sign this certificate also.

Additional Certificate

[Used when some questions require unanimous answers]

I certify that the jury was unanimous in answering the following questions. All 12 [6] of us agreed to each of the answers. The presiding juror has signed the certificate for all 12 [6] of us.

[Judge to list questions that require a unanimous answer, including the predicate liability question.]

____________________	____________________
Signature of Presiding Juror	Printed Name of Presiding Juror

IV.

That the following oral instructions shall be given by the court to the jury after the verdict has been accepted by the court and before the jurors are released from jury duty:

Thank you for your verdict.

I have told you that the only time you may discuss the case is with the other jurors in the jury room. I now release you from jury duty. Now you may discuss the case with anyone. But you may also choose not to discuss the case; that is your right.

After you are released from jury duty, the lawyers and others may ask you questions to see if the jury followed the instructions, and they may ask you to give a sworn statement. You are free to discuss the case with them and to give a sworn statement. But you may choose not to discuss the case and not to give a sworn statement; that is your right.

Rule 227. Challenge to Juror

A challenge to a particular juror is either a challenge for cause or a peremptory challenge. The court shall decide without delay any such challenge, and if sustained, the juror shall be discharged from the particular case. Either such challenge may be made orally on the formation of a jury to try the case.

Oct. 29, 1940, eff. Sept. 1, 1941.

Historical Notes

Source

Vernon's Ann.Civ.St. art. 2142, unchanged.

Rule 228. "Challenge for Cause" Defined

A challenge for cause is an objection made to a juror, alleging some fact which by law disqualifies him to serve as a juror in the case or in any case, or which in the opinion of the court, renders him an unfit person to sit on the jury. Upon such challenge the examination is not confined to the answers of the juror, but other evidence may be heard for or against the challenge.

Oct. 29, 1940, eff. Sept. 1, 1941.

Historical Notes

Source

Vernon's Ann.Civ.St. art. 2144, unchanged.

Rule 229. Challenge for Cause

When twenty-four or more jurors, if in the district court, or twelve or more, if in the county court, are drawn, and the lists of their names delivered to the parties, if either party desires to challenge any juror for cause, the challenge shall then be made. The name of a juror challenged and set aside for cause shall be erased from such lists.

Oct. 29, 1940, eff. Sept. 1, 1941.

Historical Notes

Source

Vernon's Ann.Civ.St. art. 2143, substituting "twenty-four" for "twelve," and "twelve" for "six".

Rule 230. Certain Questions Not To Be Asked

In examining a juror, he shall not be asked a question the answer to which may show that he has been convicted of an offense which disqualifies him, or that he stands charged by some legal accusation with theft or any felony.

Oct. 29, 1940, eff. Sept. 1, 1941.

Historical Notes

Source

Vernon's Ann.Civ.St. art. 2145, unchanged.

Rule 231. Number Reduced by Challenges

If the challenges reduce the number of jurors to less than twenty-four, if in the district court, or to less than twelve, if in the county court, the court shall order other jurors to be drawn from the wheel or from the central jury panel or summoned, as the practice may be in the particular county, and their names written upon the list instead of those set aside for cause. Such jurors so summoned may likewise be challenged for cause.

Oct. 29, 1940, eff. Sept. 1, 1941.

Historical Notes

Source

Vernon's Ann.Civ.St. art. 2146, modified by substituting "twenty-four" for "twelve," and "twelve" for "six".

Rule 232. Making Peremptory Challenges

If there remain on such lists not subject to challenge for cause, twenty-four names, if in the district court, or twelve names, if in the county court, the parties shall proceed to make their peremptory challenges. A peremptory challenge is made to a juror without assigning any reason therefor.

Oct. 29, 1940, eff. Sept. 1, 1941.

Historical Notes

Source

Vernon's Ann.Civ.St. art. 2147, modified by substituting "twenty-four" for "twelve," and "twelve" for "six".

Rule 233. Number of Peremptory Challenges

Except as provided below, each party to a civil action is entitled to six peremptory challenges in a case tried in the district court, and to three in the county court.

Alignment of the Parties. In multiple party cases, it shall be the duty of the trial judge to decide whether any of the litigants aligned on the same side of the docket are antagonistic with respect to any issue to be submitted to the jury, before the exercise of peremptory challenges.

Definition of Side. The term "side" as used in this rule is not synonymous with "party," "litigant," or "person." Rather, "side" means one or more litigants who have common interests on the matters with which the jury is concerned.

Motion to Equalize. In multiple party cases, upon motion of any litigant made prior to the exercise of peremptory challenges, it shall be the duty of the trial judge to equalize the number of peremptory challenges so that no litigant or side is given unfair advantage as a result of the alignment of the litigants and the award of peremptory challenges to each litigant or side. In determining how the challenges should be allocated the court shall consider any matter brought to the attention of the trial judge concerning the ends of justice and the elimination of an unfair advantage.

Oct. 29, 1940, eff. Sept. 1, 1941. Amended by order of Dec. 5, 1983, eff. April 1, 1984.

Historical Notes

Source

Vernon's Ann.Civ.St. art. 2148, unchanged.

Rule 234. Lists Returned to the Clerk

When the parties have made or declined to make their peremptory challenges, they shall deliver their lists to the clerk. The clerk shall, if the case be in the district court, call off the first twelve names on the lists that have not been erased; and if the case be in the county court, he shall call off the first six names on the lists that have not been erased; those whose names are called shall be the jury.

Oct. 29, 1940, eff. Sept. 1, 1941.

Historical Notes

Source

Vernon's Ann.Civ.St. art. 2149, unchanged.

Rule 235. If Jury is Incomplete

When by peremptory challenges the jury is left incomplete, the court shall direct other jurors to be drawn or summoned to complete the jury; and such other jurors shall be impaneled as in the first instance.

Oct. 29, 1940, eff. Sept. 1, 1941.

Historical Notes

Source

Vernon's Ann.Civ.St. art. 2150, unchanged.

Rule 236. Oath to Jury

The jury shall be sworn by the court or under its direction, in substance as follows: "You, and each of you, do solemnly swear that in all cases between

parties which shall be to you submitted, you will a true verdict render, according to the law, as it may be given you in charge by the court, and to the evidence submitted to you under the rulings of the court. So help you God."
Oct. 29, 1940, eff. Sept. 1, 1941.

Historical Notes

Source

Vernon's Ann.Civ.St. arts. 2151 and 2179, with minor textual change.

SECTION 11. TRIAL OF CAUSES

A. APPEARANCE AND PROCEDURE

Rule 237. Appearance Day

If a defendant, who has been duly cited, is by the citation required to answer on a day which is in term time, such day is appearance day as to him. If he is so required to answer on a day in vacation, he shall plead or answer accordingly, and the first day of the next term is appearance day as to him.
Oct. 29, 1940, eff. Sept. 1, 1941. Amended by orders of March 31, 1941, eff. Sept. 1, 1941; July 20, 1954, eff. Jan. 1, 1955.

Historical Notes

Source

Vernon's Ann.Civ.St. art. 2152, modified to make appearance day, where answer is to be filed during term, dependent upon date of service rather than on term of court.

Rule 237a. Cases Remanded From Federal Court

When any cause is removed to the Federal Court and is afterwards remanded to the state court, the plaintiff shall file a certified copy of the order of remand with the clerk of the state court and shall forthwith give written notice of such filing to the attorneys of record for all adverse parties. All such adverse parties shall have fifteen days from the receipt of such notice within which to file an answer. No default judgment shall be rendered against a party in a removed action remanded from federal court if that party filed an answer in federal court during removal.
July 20, 1954, eff. Jan. 1, 1955. Amended by orders of Dec. 5, 1983, eff. April 1, 1984; July 15, 1987, eff. Jan. 1, 1988; April 24, 1990, eff. Sept. 1, 1990.

Comment—1990

To expressly provide, consistent with existing law, that a default judgment cannot be taken in a case remanded from federal court if an answer was filed in federal court during removal.

Rule 238. Call of Appearance Docket

On the appearance day of a particular defendant and at the hour named in the citation, or as soon thereafter as may be practicable, the court or clerk in open court shall call, in their order, all the cases on the docket in which such day is appearance day as to any defendant, or, the court or clerk failing therein, any such case shall be so called on request of the plaintiff's attorney.
Oct. 29, 1940, eff. Sept. 1, 1941.

Historical Notes

Source

Vernon's Ann.Civ.St. art. 2153, modified by directing the call of the appearance docket on the appearance day for the particular case, rather than once each term of court; and by authorizing the clerk to make the call.

Rule 239. Judgment by Default

Upon such call of the docket, or at any time after a defendant is required to answer, the plaintiff may in term time take judgment by default against such defendant if he has not previously filed an answer, and provided that the return of service shall have been on file with the clerk for the length of time required by Rule 107.
Oct. 29, 1940, eff. Sept. 1, 1941. Amended by order of April 12, 1962, eff. Sept. 1, 1962; Dec. 12, 2011, eff. Jan. 1, 2012.

Historical Notes

2011 Amendment

The order dated December 12, 2011, after "provided that the" substituted "return of service" for "citation with the officer's return thereon".

Source

Vernon's Ann.Civ.St. art. 2154, modified by adding "in term time" and by minor textual change.

Rule 239a. Notice of Default Judgment

At or immediately prior to the time an interlocutory or final default judgment is rendered, the party taking the same or his attorney shall certify to the clerk in writing the last known mailing address of the party against whom the judgment is taken, which certificate shall be filed among the papers in the cause. Immediately upon the signing of the judgment, the clerk shall mail written notice thereof to the party against whom the judgment was rendered at the address shown in the certificate, and note the fact of such mailing on the docket. The notice shall state the number and style of the case, the court in which the case is pending, the names of the parties in whose favor and against whom the judgment was rendered, and the date of the signing of the judgment. Failure to comply with the provisions of this rule shall not affect the finality of the judgment.

July 20, 1966, eff. Jan. 1, 1967. Amended by order of July 15, 1987, eff. Jan. 1, 1988.

Rule 240. Where Only Some Answer

Where there are several defendants, some of whom have answered or have not been duly served and some of whom have been duly served and have made default, an interlocutory judgment by default may be entered against those who have made default, and the cause may proceed or be postponed as to the others.

Oct. 29, 1940, eff. Sept. 1, 1941.

Historical Notes

Source

Vernon's Ann.Civ.St. art. 2155.

Rule 241. Assessing Damages on Liquidated Demands

When a judgment by default is rendered against the defendant, or all of several defendants, if the claim is liquidated and proved by an instrument in writing, the damages shall be assessed by the court, or under its direction, and final judgment shall be rendered therefor, unless the defendant shall demand and be entitled to a trial by jury.

Oct. 29, 1940, eff. Sept. 1, 1941. Amended by order of Dec. 5, 1983, eff. April 1, 1984.

Historical Notes

Source

Vernon's Ann.Civ.St. art. 2156, modified by substituting "claim" for "cause of action."

Rule 242. Repealed by Order of Sept. 20, 1941, eff. Dec. 31, 1941

Rule 243. Unliquidated Demands

If the cause of action is unliquidated or be not proved by an instrument in writing, the court shall hear evidence as to damages and shall render judgment therefor, unless the defendant shall demand and be entitled to a trial by jury in which case the judgment by default shall be noted, a writ of inquiry awarded, and the cause entered on the jury docket.

Oct. 29, 1940, eff. Sept. 1, 1941. Amended by order of March 31, 1941, eff. Sept. 1, 1941.

Historical Notes

Source

Vernon's Ann.Civ.St. art. 2157, unchanged.

Rule 244. On Service by Publication

Where service has been made by publication, and no answer has been filed nor appearance entered within the prescribed time, the court shall appoint an attorney to defend the suit in behalf of the defendant, and judgment shall be rendered as in other cases; but, in every such case a statement of the evidence, approved and signed by the judge, shall be filed with the papers of the cause as a part of the record thereof. The court shall allow such attorney a reasonable fee for his services, to be taxed as part of the costs.

Oct. 29, 1940, eff. Sept. 1, 1941.

Historical Notes

Source

Vernon's Ann.Cit.St. art. 2158, with minor textual change.

Rule 245. Assignment of Cases for Trial

The Court may set contested cases on written request of any party, or on the court's own motion, with reasonable notice of not less than forty-five days to the parties of a first setting for trial, or by agreement of the parties; provided, however, that when a case previously has been set for trial, the Court may reset said contested case to a later date on any reasonable notice to the parties or by agreement of the parties. Noncontested cases may be tried or disposed of at any time whether set or not, and may be set at any time for any other time.

A request for trial setting constitutes a representation that the requesting party reasonably and in good faith expects to be ready for trial by the date requested, but no additional representation concerning the completion of pretrial proceedings or of current readiness for trial shall be required in order to obtain a trial setting in a contested case.

Oct. 29, 1940, eff. Sept. 1, 1941. Amended by orders of July 22, 1975, eff. Jan. 1, 1976; Dec. 5, 1983, eff. April 1, 1984; April 24, 1990, eff. Sept. 1, 1990.

Comment—1990

First paragraph, to harmonize a first time nonjury setting with the time for jury demand, and to set a more realistic notice for trial. Second paragraph, to standardize the readiness requirement to obtain a trial setting.

Historical Notes

Source

Federal Rule 40, with minor textual change. Former articles 2161, Suits called in order, and 2163, Day set for jury docket, were repealed.

Rule 246. Clerk to Give Notice of Settings

The clerk shall keep a record in his office of all cases set for trial, and it shall be his duty to inform any non-resident attorney of the date of setting of any case upon request by mail from such attorney, accom-

panied by a return envelope properly addressed and stamped. Failure of the clerk to furnish such information on proper request shall be sufficient ground for continuance or for a new trial when it appears to the court that such failure has prevented the attorney from preparing or presenting his claim or defense.
Oct. 29, 1940, eff. Sept. 1, 1941.

Historical Notes

Source

New rule.

Rule 247. Tried When Set

Every suit shall be tried when it is called, unless continued or postponed to a future day or placed at the end of the docket to be called again for trial in its regular order. No cause which has been set upon the trial docket of the court shall be taken from the trial docket for the date set except by agreement of the parties or for good cause upon motion and notice to the opposing party.
Oct. 29, 1940, eff. Sept. 1, 1941. Amended by order of Dec. 5, 1983, eff. April 1, 1984.

Historical Notes

Source

Vernon's Ann.Civ.St. art. 2162. The second sentence of Rule 247 is new.

Rule 248. Jury Cases

When a jury has been demanded, questions of law, motions, exceptions to pleadings, and other unresolved pending matters shall, as far as practicable, be heard and determined by the court before the trial commences, and jurors shall be summoned to appear on the day so designated.
Oct. 29, 1940, eff. Sept. 1, 1941. Amended by orders of Dec. 5, 1983, eff. April 1, 1984; April 24, 1990, eff. Sept. 1, 1990.

Comment—1990

To encourage resolution of matters prior to trial.

Historical Notes

Source

Vernon's Ann.Civ.St. art. 2164, modified by substituting "motions" for "demurrers".

Rule 249. Call of Non-Jury Docket

The non-jury docket shall be taken up at such times as not unnecessarily to interfere with the dispatch of business on the jury docket.
Oct. 29, 1940, eff. Sept. 1, 1941.

Historical Notes

Source

Vernon's Ann.Civ.St. art. 2165, unchanged.

Rule 250. Repealed by Order of Sept. 20, 1941, eff. Dec. 31, 1941

B. CONTINUANCE AND CHANGE OF VENUE

Rule 251. Continuance

No application for a continuance shall be heard before the defendant files his defense, nor shall any continuance be granted except for sufficient cause supported by affidavit, or by consent of the parties, or by operation of law.
Oct. 29, 1940, eff. Sept. 1, 1941.

Historical Notes

Source

Vernon's Ann.Civ.St. art. 2167, unchanged.

Rule 252. Application for Continuance

If the ground of such application be the want of testimony, the party applying therefor shall make affidavit that such testimony is material, showing the materiality thereof, and that he has used due diligence to procure such testimony, stating such diligence, and the cause of failure, if known; that such testimony cannot be procured from any other source; and, if it be for the absence of a witness, he shall state the name and residence of the witness, and what he expects to prove by him; and also state that the continuance is not sought for delay only, but that justice may be done; provided that, on a first application for a continuance, it shall not be necessary to show that the absent testimony cannot be procured from any other source.

The failure to obtain the deposition of any witness residing within 100 miles of the courthouse of the county in which the suit is pending shall not be regarded as want of diligence when diligence has been used to secure the personal attendance of such witness under the rules of law, unless by reason of age, infirmity or sickness, or official duty, the witness will be unable to attend the court, or unless such witness is about to leave, or has left, the State or county in which the suit is pending and will not probably be present at the trial.
Oct. 29, 1940, eff. Sept. 1, 1941. Amended by order of Dec. 5, 1983, eff. April 1, 1984.

Historical Notes

Source

Vernon's Ann.Civ.St. art. 2168, unchanged.

Rule 253. Absence of Counsel as Ground for Continuance

Except as provided elsewhere in these rules, absence of counsel will not be good cause for a continuance or postponement of the cause when called for trial, except it be allowed in the discretion of the court, upon cause shown or upon matters within the knowledge or information of the judge to be stated on the record.

Oct. 29, 1940, eff. Sept. 1, 1941.

Historical Notes

Source

District and County Court Rule 49, modified by adding "Except as provided elsewhere in these rules,".

Rule 254. Attendance on Legislature

In all civil actions, including matters of probate, and in all matters ancillary to such suits which require action by or the attendance of an attorney, including appeals but excluding temporary restraining orders, at any time within thirty days of a date when the legislature is to be in session, or at any time the legislature is in session, or when the legislature sits as a Constitutional Convention, it shall be mandatory that the court continue the cause if it shall appear to the court, by affidavit, that any party applying for continuance, or any attorney for any party to the cause, is a member of either branch of the legislature, and will be or is in actual attendance on a session of the same. If the member of the legislature is an attorney for a party to the cause, his affidavit shall contain a declaration that it is his intention to participate actively in the preparation and/or presentation of the case. Where a party to any cause, or an attorney for any party to a cause, is a member of the legislature, his affidavit need not be corroborated. On the filing of such affidavit, the court shall continue the cause until thirty days after adjournment of the legislature and the affidavit shall be proof of the necessity for the continuance, and the continuance shall be deemed one of right and shall not be charged against the movant upon any subsequent application for continuance.

The right to a continuance shall be mandatory, except only where the attorney was employed within ten days of the date the suit is set for trial, the right to continuance shall be discretionary.

Oct. 29, 1940, eff. Sept. 1, 1941. Amended by order of June 10, 1980, eff. Jan. 1, 1981.

Historical Notes

Source

Vernon's Ann.Civ.St. art. 2168a, with minor textual change.

Rule 255. Change of Venue by Consent

Upon the written consent of the parties filed with the papers of the cause, the court, by an order entered on the minutes, may transfer the same for trial to the court of any other county having jurisdiction of the subject matter of such suit.

Oct. 29, 1940, eff. Sept. 1, 1941.

Historical Notes

Source

Vernon's Ann.Civ.St. art. 2169, unchanged.

Rule 256. Repealed by Order of March 31, 1941, eff. Sept. 1, 1941

Rule 257. Granted on Motion

A change of venue may be granted in civil causes upon motion of either party, supported by his own affidavit and the affidavit of at least three credible persons, residents of the county in which the suit is pending, for any following cause:

(a) That there exists in the county where the suit is pending so great a prejudice against him that he cannot obtain a fair and impartial trial.

(b) That there is a combination against him instigated by influential persons, by reason of which he cannot expect a fair and impartial trial.

(c) That an impartial trial cannot be had in the county where the action is pending.

(d) For other sufficient cause to be determined by the court.

Oct. 29, 1940, eff. Sept. 1, 1941. Amended by order of June 15, 1983, eff. Sept. 1, 1983.

Historical Notes

Source

Vernon's Ann.Civ.St. art. 2170, unchanged.

Rule 258. Shall Be Granted

Where such motion to transfer venue is duly made, it shall be granted, unless the credibility of those making such application, or their means of knowledge or the truth of the facts set out in the said application are attacked by the affidavit of a credible person; when thus attacked, the issue thus formed shall be tried by the judge; and the application either granted or refused. Reasonable discovery in support of, or in opposition to, the application shall be permitted, and such discovery as is relevant, including deposition testimony on file, may be attached to, or incorporated by reference in, the affidavit of a party, a witness, or an attorney who has knowledge of such discovery.

Oct. 29, 1940, eff. Sept. 1, 1941. Amended by order of June 15, 1983, eff. Sept. 1, 1983.

Historical Notes

Source

Vernon's Ann.Civ.St. art. 2171, unchanged.

Rule 259. To What County

If the motion under Rule 257 is granted, the cause shall be removed:

(a) If from a district court, to any county of proper venue in the same or an adjoining district;

(b) If from a county court, to any adjoining county of proper venue;

(c) If (a) or (b) are not applicable, to any county of proper venue;

(d) If a county of proper venue (other than the county of suit) cannot be found, then if from

(1) A district court, to any county in the same or an adjoining district or to any district where an impartial trial can be had;

(2) A county court, to any adjoining county or to any district where an impartial trial can be had;

but the parties may agree that venue shall be changed to some other county, and the order of the court shall conform to such agreement.

Oct. 29, 1940, eff. Sept. 1, 1941. Amended by order of June 15, 1983, eff. Sept. 1, 1983.

Historical Notes

Source

Vernon's Ann.Civ.St. art. 2172, modified by eliminating requirement that venue be changed to adjoining county with the courthouse nearest to the courthouse in the county where the suit is pending.

Rule 260. Repealed by Order of April 24, 1990, eff. Sept. 1, 1990

Rule 261. Transcript on Change

When a change of venue has been granted, the clerk shall immediately make out a correct transcript of all the orders made in said cause, certifying thereto officially under the seal of the court, and send the same, with the original papers in the cause, to the clerk of the court to which the venue has been changed.

Oct. 29, 1940, eff. Sept. 1, 1941.

Historical Notes

Source

Vernon's Ann.Civ.St. art. 2174, unchanged.

C. THE TRIAL

Rule 262. Trial by the Court

The rules governing the trial of causes before a jury shall govern in trials by the court in so far as applicable.

Oct. 29, 1940, eff. Sept. 1, 1941.

Historical Notes

Source

Vernon's Ann.Civ.St. art. 2176, unchanged. Art. 2175, obsolete procedure, was repealed.

Rule 263. Agreed Case

Parties may submit matters in controversy to the court upon an agreed statement of facts filed with the clerk, upon which judgment shall be rendered as in other cases; and such agreed statement signed and certified by the court to be correct and the judgment rendered thereon shall constitute the record of the cause.

Oct. 29, 1940, eff. Sept. 1, 1941.

Historical Notes

Source

Vernon's Ann.Civ.St. art. 2177, unchanged.

Rule 264. Videotape Trial

By agreement of the parties, the trial court may allow that all testimony and such other evidence as may be appropriate be presented at trial by videotape. The expenses of such videotape recordings shall be taxed as costs. If any party withdraws agreement to a videotape trial, the videotape costs that have accrued will be taxed against the party withdrawing from the agreement.

July 15, 1987, eff. Jan. 1, 1988.

Historical Notes

A former rule 264 relating to appeals tried de novo was repealed effective January 1, 1988 by order of the Supreme Court dated July 15, 1987.

Rule 265. Order of Proceedings on Trial by Jury

The trial of cases before a jury shall proceed in the following order unless the court should, for good cause stated in the record, otherwise direct:

(a) The party upon whom rests the burden of proof on the whole case shall state to the jury briefly the nature of his claim or defense and what said party expects to prove and the relief sought. Immediately thereafter, the adverse party may make a similar statement, and intervenors and other parties will be accorded similar rights in the order determined by the court.

(b) The party upon whom rests the burden of proof on the whole case shall then introduce his evidence.

(c) The adverse party shall briefly state the nature of his claim or defense and what said party expects to prove and the relief sought unless he has already done so.

(d) He shall then introduce his evidence.

(e) The intervenor and other parties shall make their statement, unless they have already done so, and shall introduce their evidence.

(f) The parties shall then be confined to rebutting testimony on each side.

(g) But one counsel on each side shall examine and cross-examine the same witness, except on leave granted.

Oct. 29, 1940, eff. Sept. 1, 1941. Amended by orders of March 31, 1941, eff. Sept. 1, 1941; July 20, 1966, eff. Jan. 1, 1967; July 11, 1977, eff. Jan. 1, 1978.

Historical Notes

Source

Vernon's Ann.Civ.St. art. 2180.

Rule 266. Open and Close—Admission

Except as provided in Rule 269 the plaintiff shall have the right to open and conclude both in adducing his evidence and in the argument, unless the burden of proof on the whole case under the pleadings rests upon the defendant, or unless the defendant or all of the defendants, if there should be more than one, shall, after the issues of fact are settled and before the trial commences, admit that the plaintiff is entitled to recover as set forth in the petition, except so far as he may be defeated, in whole or in part, by the allegations of the answer constituting a good defense, which may be established on the trial; which admission shall be entered of record, whereupon the defendant, or the defendants, if more than one, shall have the right to open and conclude in adducing the evidence and in the argument of the cause. The admission shall not serve to admit any allegation which is inconsistent with such defense, which defense shall be one that defendant has the burden of establishing, as for example, and without excluding other defenses: accord and satisfaction, adverse possession, arbitration and award, contributory negligence, discharge in bankruptcy, duress, estoppel, failure of consideration, fraud, release, res judicata, statute of frauds, statute of limitations, waiver, and the like.

Oct. 29, 1940, eff. Sept. 1, 1941.

Historical Notes

Source

District and County Court Rule 31, modified by adding reference to Rule 269 and by substituting "is entitled to recover" for "has a good cause of action," and "allegations" for "facts." The last sentence was added.

Rule 267. Witnesses Placed Under Rule

a. At the request of either party, in a civil case, the witnesses on both sides shall be sworn and removed out of the courtroom to some place where they cannot hear the testimony as delivered by any other witness in the cause. This is termed placing witnesses under the rule.

b. This rule does not authorize exclusion of (1) a party who is a natural person or the spouse of such natural person, or (2) an officer or employee of a party that is not a natural person and who is designated as its representative by its attorney, or (3) a person whose presence is shown by a party to be essential to the presentation of the cause.

c. If any party be absent, the court in its discretion may exempt from the rule a representative of such party.

d. Witnesses, when placed under Rule 614 of the Texas Rules of Civil Evidence, shall be instructed by the court that they are not to converse with each other or with any other person about the case other than the attorneys in the case, except by permission of the court, and that they are not to read any report of or comment upon the testimony in the case while under the rule.

e. Any witness or other person violating such instructions may be punished for contempt of court.

Oct. 29, 1940, eff. Sept. 1, 1941. Amended by order of July 15, 1987, eff. Jan. 1, 1988.

Historical Notes

Source

Sentence beginning "At the request of either party": Vernon's Ann.C.C.P. of 1925, art. 644, now art. 36.03, modified by adding "in a civil case", by deleting provision for placing witnesses in the custody of an officer. Sentence beginning "This is termed" is derived unchanged from art. 644, now art. 3603. Sentences beginning "Neither party," "Where a corporation," and "If any party" are new. Sentence beginning "Witnesses, when placed under rule," follows Vernon's Ann. C.C.P. of 1925, art. 647, now art. 36.06, first sentence. Sentence beginning "Any person" is derived from Vernon's Ann.C.C.P. of 1925, art. 647, now art. 36.06, second sentence.

Rule 268. Motion for Instructed Verdict

A motion for directed verdict shall state the specific grounds therefor.

Oct. 29, 1940, eff. Sept. 1, 1941.

Historical Notes

Source

Federal Rule 50(a), last sentence, unchanged.

Rule 269. Argument

(a) After the evidence is concluded and the charge is read, the parties may argue the case to the jury. The party having the burden of proof on the whole case, or on all matters which are submitted by the charge, shall be entitled to open and conclude the argument; where there are several parties having separate claims or defenses, the court shall prescribe the order of argument between them.

(b) In all arguments, and especially in arguments on the trial of the case, the counsel opening shall present his whole case as he relies on it, both of law and facts, and shall be heard in the concluding argument only in reply to the counsel on the other side.

(c) Counsel for an intervenor shall occupy the position in the argument assigned by the court according to the nature of the claim.

(d) Arguments on questions of law shall be addressed to the court, and counsel should state the substance of the authorities referred to without reading more from books than may be necessary to verify the statement. On a question on motions, exceptions to the evidence, and other incidental matters, the counsel will be allowed only such argument as may be necessary to present clearly the question raised, and refer to authorities on it, unless further discussion is invited by the court.

(e) Arguments on the facts should be addressed to the jury, when one is impaneled in a case that is being tried, under the supervision of the court. Counsel shall be required to confine the argument strictly to the evidence and to the arguments of opposing counsel. Mere personal criticism by counsel upon each other shall be avoided, and when indulged in shall be promptly corrected as a contempt of court.

(f) Side-bar remarks, and remarks by counsel of one side, not addressed to the court, while the counsel on the other side is examining a witness or arguing any question to the court, or addressing the jury, will be rigidly repressed by the court.

(g) The court will not be required to wait for objections to be made when the rules as to arguments are violated; but should they not be noticed and corrected by the court, opposing counsel may ask leave of the court to rise and present his point of objection. But the court shall protect counsel from any unnecessary interruption made on frivolous and unimportant grounds.

(h) It shall be the duty of every counsel to address the court from his place at the bar, and in addressing the court to rise to his feet; and while engaged in the trial of a case, he shall remain at his place in the bar.

Oct. 29, 1940, eff. Sept. 1, 1941. Amended by orders of March 31, 1941, eff. Sept. 1, 1941; April 24, 1990, eff. Sept. 1, 1990.

Historical Notes

Source

Vernon's Ann.Civ.St. art. 2183.

Rule 270. Additional Testimony

When it clearly appears to be necessary to the due administration of justice, the court may permit additional evidence to be offered at any time; provided that in a jury case no evidence on a controversial matter shall be received after the verdict of the jury.

Oct. 29, 1940, eff. Sept. 1, 1941. Amended by order of Dec. 5, 1983, eff. April 1, 1984.

D. CHARGE TO THE JURY

Rule 271. Charge to the Jury

Unless expressly waived by the parties, the trial court shall prepare and in open court deliver a written charge to the jury.

Oct. 29, 1940, eff. Sept. 1, 1941. Amended by orders of May 25, 1973, eff. Sept. 1, 1973; July 15, 1987, eff. Jan. 1, 1988.

Historical Notes

Source

Vernon's Ann.Civ.St. art. 2184: "Unless expressly waived by the parties, the judge shall prepare and in open court deliver a written charge to the jury on the law of the case, or if the case is submitted on special issues, he shall submit the issues of fact to the jury."

Rule 271 deleted "on the law of the case, or" and inserted at that point the sentence beginning "if the case is submitted on a general charge." The last part of Art. 2184 was retained as a separate sentence.

Rule 272. Requisites

The charge shall be in writing, signed by the court, and filed with the clerk, and shall be a part of the record of the cause. It shall be submitted to the respective parties or their attorneys for their inspection, and a reasonable time given them in which to examine and present objections thereto outside the presence of the jury, which objections shall in every instance be presented to the court in writing, or be dictated to the court reporter in the presence of the court and opposing counsel, before the charge is read to the jury. All objections not so presented shall be considered as waived. The court shall announce its rulings thereon before reading the charge to the jury and shall endorse the rulings on the objections if written or dictate same to the court reporter in the presence of counsel. Objections to the charge and the court's rulings thereon may be included as a part of any transcript or statement of facts on appeal and, when so included in either, shall constitute a sufficient bill of exception to the rulings of the court thereon. It shall be presumed, unless otherwise noted in the record, that the party making such objections presented the same at the proper time and excepted to the ruling thereon.

Oct. 29, 1940, eff. Sept. 1, 1941. Amended by orders of Sept. 20, 1941, eff. Dec. 31, 1941; May 25, 1973, eff. Sept. 1, 1973; July 22, 1975, eff. Jan. 1, 1976; July 15, 1987, eff. Jan. 1, 1988.

Historical Notes

Source

Vernon's Ann.Civ.St. art. 2185, modified by addition of third sentence, beginning "When written objections have been so made and presented," by addition of requirement that objections to charge be presented "in writing," and by minor textual change.

Rule 273. Jury Submissions

Either party may present to the court and request written questions, definitions, and instructions to be given to the jury; and the court may give them or a part thereof, or may refuse to give them, as may be proper. Such requests shall be prepared and presented to the court and submitted to opposing counsel for examination and objection within a reasonable time after the charge is given to the parties or their attorneys for examination. A request by either party for any questions, definitions, or instructions shall be made separate and apart from such party's objections to the court's charge.

Oct. 29, 1940, eff. Sept. 1, 1941. Amended by orders of Oct. 12, 1949, eff. March 1, 1950; July 15, 1987, eff. Jan. 1, 1988.

Historical Notes

Source

Vernon's Ann.Civ.St. art. 2186, modified by inserting, in first sentence, "and request" and "special issues, definitions, or explanatory instructions," and by substituting therein "same" for "such instructions"; and by substituting, in second sentence, "requests" for "instructions".

Rule 274. Objections and Requests

A party objecting to a charge must point out distinctly the objectionable matter and the grounds of the objection. Any complaint as to a question, definition, or instruction, on account of any defect, omission, or fault in pleading, is waived unless specifically included in the objections. When the complaining party's objection, or requested question, definition, or instruction is, in the opinion of the appellate court, obscured or concealed by voluminous unfounded objections, minute differentiations or numerous unnecessary requests, such objection or request shall be untenable. No objection to one part of the charge may be adopted and applied to any other part of the charge by reference only.

Oct. 29, 1940, eff. Sept. 1, 1941. Amended by orders of Sept. 20, 1941, eff. Dec. 31, 1941; July 15, 1987, eff. Jan. 1, 1988.

Historical Notes

Source

New rule.

Rule 275. Charge Read Before Argument

Before the argument is begun, the trial court shall read the charge to the jury in the precise words in which it was written, including all questions, definitions, and instructions which the court may give.

Oct. 29, 1940, eff. Sept. 1, 1941. Amended by order of July 15, 1987, eff. Jan. 1, 1988.

Historical Notes

Source

Vernon's Ann.Civ.St. art. 2187, substituting "requested instructions, special issues, definitions, and explanatory instructions" for "special charges".

Rule 276. Refusal or Modification

When an instruction, question, or definition is requested and the provisions of the law have been complied with and the trial judge refuses the same, the judge shall endorse thereon "Refused," and sign the same officially. If the trial judge modifies the same the judge shall endorse thereon "Modified as follows: (stating in what particular the judge has modified the same) and given, and exception allowed" and sign the same officially. Such refused or modified instruction, question, or definition, when so endorsed shall constitute a bill of exceptions, and it shall be conclusively presumed that the party asking the same presented it at the proper time, excepted to its refusal or modification, and that all the requirements of law have been observed, and such procedure shall entitle the party requesting the same to have the action of the trial judge thereon reviewed without preparing a formal bill of exceptions.

Oct. 29, 1940, eff. Sept. 1, 1941. Amended by order of July 15, 1987, eff. Jan. 1, 1988.

Historical Notes

Source

Vernon's Ann.Civ.St. art. 2188, modified by substituting "an instruction, special issue, definition, or explanatory instruction" for "a special instruction" in first sentence; by substituting "the same" for "a special charge," and "same" for "charge" in second sentence; and by substituting "instruction, special issue, definition or explanatory instruction" for "charge," "the same presented it" for "said charge presented the same," "such procedure" for "the same," and "the same" for "such charge" in third sentence.

Rule 277. Submission to the Jury

In all jury cases the court shall, whenever feasible, submit the cause upon broad-form questions. The court shall submit such instructions and definitions as shall be proper to enable the jury to render a verdict.

Inferential rebuttal questions shall not be submitted in the charge. The placing of the burden of proof may be accomplished by instructions rather than by inclusion in the question.

In any cause in which the jury is required to apportion the loss among the parties the court shall submit a question or questions inquiring what percentage, if any, of the negligence or causation, as the case may be, that caused the occurrence or injury in question is attributable to each of the persons found to have been culpable. The court shall also instruct the jury to answer the damage question or questions without any reduction because of the percentage of negligence or causation, if any, of the person injured. The court may predicate the damage question or questions upon affirmative findings of liability.

The court may submit a question disjunctively when it is apparent from the evidence that one or the other of the conditions or facts inquired about necessarily exists.

The court shall not in its charge comment directly on the weight of the evidence or advise the jury of the effect of their answers, but the court's charge shall not be objectionable on the ground that it incidentally constitutes a comment on the weight of the evidence or advises the jury of the effect of their answers when it is properly a part of an instruction or definition.

Oct. 29, 1940, eff. Sept. 1, 1941. Amended by orders of March 31, 1941, eff. Sept. 1, 1941; May 25, 1973, eff. Sept. 1, 1973; Dec. 5, 1983, eff. April 1, 1984; July 15, 1987, eff. Jan. 1, 1988.

Comment—1988

The amendment to paragraph one of Rule 277 would unify the practice of submitting broad form questions to the jury in the form approved by *Lemos v. Montez*, 680 S.W.2d 798 (Tex.1984).

The amendment to the third paragraph includes a textual change and recognizes that damage issues may be predicted on affirmative liability findings.

Historical Notes

Source

Vernon's Ann.Civ.St. art. 2189, modified by addition of new matter.

Rule 278. Submission of Questions, Definitions, and Instructions

The court shall submit the questions, instructions and definitions in the form provided by Rule 277, which are raised by the written pleadings and the evidence. Except in trespass to try title, statutory partition proceedings, and other special proceedings in which the pleadings are specially defined by statutes or procedural rules, a party shall not be entitled to any submission of any question raised only by a general denial and not raised by affirmative written pleading by that party. Nothing herein shall change the burden of proof from what it would have been under a general denial. A judgment shall not be reversed because of the failure to submit other and various phases or different shades of the same question. Failure to submit a question shall not be deemed a ground for reversal of the judgment, unless its submission, in substantially correct wording, has been requested in writing and tendered by the party complaining of the judgment; provided, however, that objection to such failure shall suffice in such respect if the question is one relied upon by the opposing party. Failure to submit a definition or instruction shall not be deemed a ground for reversal of the judgment unless a substantially correct definition or instruction has been requested in writing and tendered by the party complaining of the judgment.

July 15, 1987, eff. Jan. 1, 1988.

Comment—1988

Formerly a part of Rule 279.

Rule 279. Omissions From the Charge

Upon appeal all independent grounds of recovery or of defense not conclusively established under the evidence and no element of which is submitted or requested are waived. When a ground of recovery or defense consists of more than one element, if one or more of such elements necessary to sustain such ground of recovery or defense, and necessarily referable thereto, are submitted to and found by the jury, and one or more of such elements are omitted from the charge, without request or objection, and there is factually sufficient evidence to support a finding thereon, the trial court, at the request of either party, may after notice and hearing and at any time before the judgment is rendered, make and file written findings on such omitted element or elements in support of the judgment. If no such written findings are made, such omitted element or elements shall be deemed found by the court in such manner as to support the judgment. A claim that the evidence was legally or factually insufficient to warrant the submission of any question may be made for the first time after verdict, regardless of whether the submission of such question was requested by the complainant.

Oct. 29, 1940, eff. Sept. 1, 1941. Amended by orders of March 31, 1941, eff. Sept. 1, 1941; July 15, 1987, eff. Jan. 1, 1988; Dec. 16, 1987, eff. Jan. 1, 1988.

Comment—1988

First paragraph transferred to Rule 278.

Historical Notes

Source

Vernon's Ann.Civ.St. art. 2190, with new material added.

E. CASE TO THE JURY

Rule 280. Presiding Juror of Jury

Each jury shall appoint one of their body presiding juror.

Oct. 29, 1940, eff. Sept. 1, 1941. Amended by order of Dec. 5, 1983, eff. April 1, 1984.

Historical Notes

Source

Vernon's Ann.Civ.St. art. 2192, unchanged.

Rule 281. Papers Taken to Jury Room

With the court's permission, the jury may take with them to the jury room any notes they took during the trial. In addition, the jury may, and on request shall, take with them in their retirement the charges and instructions, general or special, which were given and read to them, and any written evidence, except the depositions of witnesses, but shall not take with them any special charges which have been refused. Where only part of a paper has been read in evidence, the jury shall not take the same with them, unless the part so read to them is detached from that which was excluded.

Oct. 29, 1940, eff. Sept. 1, 1941. Amended by orders of Dec. 5, 1983, eff. April 1, 1984; Dec. 13, 2010, and March 15, 2011, eff. April 1, 2011.

Historical Notes

2011 Amendment

The order dated March 15, 2011 rewrote the rule, which prior thereto read:

"The jury may, and on request shall, take with them in their retirement the charges and instructions, general or special, which were given and read to them, and any written evidence, except the depositions of witnesses, but shall not take with them any special charges which have been refused. Where part only of a paper has been read in evidence, the jury shall not take the same with them, unless the part so read to them is detached from that which was excluded."

Source

Vernon's Ann.Civ.St. art. 2193, unchanged.

Rule 282. Jury Kept Together

The jury may either decide a case in court or retire for deliberation. If they retire, they shall be kept together in some convenient place, under the charge of an officer, until they agree upon a verdict or are discharged by the court; but the court in its discretion may permit them to separate temporarily for the night and at their meals, and for other proper purposes.

Oct. 29, 1940, eff. Sept. 1, 1941.

Historical Notes

Source

Vernon's Ann.Civ.St. art. 2194, unchanged.

Rule 283. Duty of Officer Attending Jury

The officer in charge of the jury shall not make nor permit any communication to be made to them, except to inquire if they have agreed upon a verdict, unless by order of the court; and he shall not before their verdict is rendered communicate to any person the state of their deliberations or the verdict agreed upon.

Oct. 29, 1940, eff. Sept. 1, 1941.

Historical Notes

Source

Vernon's Ann.Civ.St. art. 2195, unchanged.

Rule 284. Judge to Caution Jury

Immediately after jurors are selected for a case, the court must instruct them to turn off their phones and other electronic devices and not to communicate with anyone through any electronic device while they are in the courtroom or while they are deliberating. The court must also instruct them that, while they are serving as jurors, they must not post any information about the case on the Internet or search for any information outside of the courtroom, including on the Internet, to try to learn more about the case.

If jurors are permitted to separate before they are released from jury duty, either during the trial or after the case is submitted to them, the court must instruct them that it is their duty not to communicate with, or permit themselves to be addressed by, any other person about any subject relating to the case.

Oct. 29, 1940, eff. Sept. 1, 1941. Amended by orders of Dec. 13, 2010, and March 15, 2011, eff. April 1, 2011.

Historical Notes

2011 Amendment

The order dated March 15, 2011 rewrote the rule, which prior thereto read:

"If permitted to separate, either during the trial or after the case is submitted to them, the jury shall be admonished by the court that it is their duty not to converse with, or permit themselves to be addressed by any other person, on any subject connected with the trial."

Source

Vernon's Ann.Civ.St. art. 2196, unchanged.

Rule 285. Jury May Communicate With Court

The jury may communicate with the court by making their wish known to the officer in charge, who shall inform the court, and they may then in open court, and through their presiding juror, communicate with the court, either verbally or in writing. If the communication is to request further instructions, Rule 286 shall be followed.

Oct. 29, 1940, eff. Sept. 1, 1941. Amended by order of Dec. 5, 1983, eff. April 1, 1984.

Historical Notes

Source

Vernon's Ann.Civ.St. art. 2197, unchanged; the second sentence was new.

Rule 286. Jury May Receive Further Instructions

After having retired, the jury may receive further instructions from the court touching any matter of law, either at their request or upon the court's own motion. For this purpose they shall appear before the judge in open court in a body, and if the instruction is being given at their request, they shall through their presiding juror state to the court, in writing, the particular question of law upon which they desire further instruction. The court shall give such instruction in writing, but no instruction shall be given except in conformity with the rules relating to the charge. Additional argument may be allowed in the discretion of the court.

Oct. 29, 1940, eff. Sept. 1, 1941. Amended by orders of Dec. 5, 1983, eff. April 1, 1984; July 15, 1987, eff. Jan. 1, 1988.

Historical Notes

Source

Vernon's Ann.Civ.St. art. 2198, modified by authorizing court to give additional instructions on its own motion, by requiring jury to make request in writing, and by permitting additional argument at discretion of court.

Rule 287. Disagreement As to Evidence

If the jury disagree as to the statement of any witness, they may, upon applying to the court, have read to them from the court reporter's notes that part of such witness' testimony on the point in dispute; but, if there be no such reporter, or if his notes cannot be read to the jury, the court may cause such witness to be again brought upon the stand and the judge shall direct him to repeat his testimony as to the point in dispute, and no other, as nearly as he can in the language used on the trial; and on their notifying the court that they disagree as to any portion of a deposition or other paper not permitted to be carried with them in their retirement, the court may, in like manner, permit such portion of said deposition or paper to be again read to the jury.

Oct. 29, 1940, eff. Sept. 1, 1941.

Historical Notes

Source

Vernon's Ann.Civ.St. art. 2199, as amended by Acts 1939, 46th Leg., p. 213, § 1.

Rule 288. Court Open for Jury

The court, during the deliberations of the jury, may proceed with other business or recess from time to time, but shall be deemed open for all purposes connected with the case before the jury.

Oct. 29, 1940, eff. Sept. 1, 1941.

Historical Notes

Source

Vernon's Ann.Civ.St. art. 2201, substituting "recess" for "adjourn."

Rule 289. Discharge of Jury

The jury to whom a case has been submitted may be discharged by the court when they cannot agree and the parties consent to their discharge, or when they have been kept together for such time as to render it altogether improbable that they can agree, or when any calamity or accident may, in the opinion of the court, require it, or when by sickness or other cause their number is reduced below the number constituting the jury in such court.

The cause shall again be placed on the jury docket and shall again be set for trial as the court directs.

Oct. 29, 1940, eff. Sept. 1, 1941. Amended by order of Dec. 5, 1983, eff. April 1, 1984.

Historical Notes

Source

Vernon's Ann.Civ.St. art. 2200, reworded with minor textual change.

F. VERDICT

Rule 290. Definition and Substance

A verdict is a written declaration by a jury of its decision, comprehending the whole or all the issues submitted to the jury, and shall be either a general or special verdict, as directed, which shall be signed by the presiding juror of the jury.

A general verdict is one whereby the jury pronounces generally in favor of one or more parties to the suit upon all or any of the issues submitted to it. A special verdict is one wherein the jury finds the facts only on issues made up and submitted to them under the direction of the court.

A special verdict shall, as between the parties, be conclusive as to the facts found.

Oct. 29, 1940, eff. Sept. 1, 1941. Amended by order of Dec. 5, 1983, eff. April 1, 1984.

Historical Notes

Source

Vernon's Ann.Civ.St. art. 2202, reworded.

Rule 291. Form of Verdict

No special form of verdict is required, and the judgment shall not be arrested or reversed for mere want of form therein if there has been substantial compliance with the requirements of the law in rendering a verdict.

Oct. 29, 1940, eff. Sept. 1, 1941. Amended by order of Oct. 3, 1972, eff. Feb. 1, 1973.

Historical Notes

Source

Vernon's Ann.Civ.St. art. 2203, unchanged.

Rule 292. Verdict by Portion of Original Jury

(a) Except as provided in subsection (b), a verdict may be rendered in any cause by the concurrence, as to each and all answers made, of the same ten or more members of an original jury of twelve or of the same five or more members of an original jury of six. However, where as many as three jurors die or be disabled from sitting and there are only nine of the jurors remaining of an original jury of twelve, those remaining may render and return a verdict. If less than the original twelve or six jurors render a verdict, the verdict must be signed by each juror concurring therein.

(b) A verdict may be rendered awarding exemplary damages only if the jury was unanimous in finding liability for and the amount of exemplary damages.

Oct. 29, 1940, eff. Sept. 1, 1941. Amended by order of Oct. 3, 1972, eff. Feb. 1, 1973; Oct. 7, 2004, eff. Feb. 1, 2005; Jan. 27, 2005, eff. Feb. 1, 2005.

Comment—2005

The rule is divided into two subsections. Subsection (a) is clarified. Subsection (b) is added to make the rule consistent with Act of June 2, 2003, 78th Leg., R.S., ch. 204, § 13.04, 2003 Tex. Gen. Laws 847, 888, codified as Tex. Civ. Prac. & Rem. Code § 41.003.

Historical Notes

The order dated Oct. 7, 2004 rewrote the section, which prior thereto read:

"A verdict may be rendered in any cause by the concurrence, as to each and all answers made, of the same ten members of an original jury of twelve or of the same five members of an original jury of six. However, where as many as three jurors die or be disabled from sitting and there are only nine of the jurors remaining of an original jury of twelve, those remaining may render and return a verdict. If less than the original twelve or six jurors render a verdict, the verdict must be signed by each juror concurring therein."

The order dated Jan. 27, 2005 also added a comment and provided:

"These amendments take effect...on February 1, 2005 in all cases filed on or after September 1, 2003 ... Comments appended to these rules are intended to inform their construction and application."

Source

Vernon's Ann.Civ.St. art. 2204, unchanged.

Rule 293. When the Jury Agree

When the jury agree upon a verdict, they shall be brought into court by the proper officer, and they shall deliver their verdict to the clerk; and if they state that they have agreed, the verdict shall be read aloud by the clerk. If the verdict is in proper form, no juror objects to its accuracy, no juror represented as agreeing thereto dissents therefrom, and neither party requests a poll of the jury, the verdict shall be entered upon the minutes of the court.

Oct. 29, 1940, eff. Sept. 1, 1941. Amended by order of Oct. 3, 1972, eff. Feb. 1, 1973.

Historical Notes

Source

Vernon's Ann.Civ.St. art. 2205, modified by eliminating requirement that jurors' names be called by clerk.

Rule 294. Polling the Jury

Any party shall have the right to have the jury polled. A jury is polled by reading once to the jury collectively the general verdict, or the questions and answers thereto consecutively, and then calling the name of each juror separately and asking the juror if it is the juror's verdict. If any juror answers in the negative when the verdict is returned signed only by the presiding juror as a unanimous verdict, or if any juror shown by the juror's signature to agree to the verdict should answer in the negative, the jury shall be retired for further deliberation.

Oct. 29, 1940, eff. Sept. 1, 1941. Amended by orders of Oct. 3, 1972, eff. Feb. 1, 1973; Dec. 5, 1983, eff. April 1, 1984; April 24, 1990, eff. Sept. 1, 1990.

Historical Notes

Source

Vernon's Ann.Civ.St. art. 2206, modified by adding first clause of second sentence and by minor textual change.

Rule 295. Correction of Verdict

If the purported verdict is defective, the court may direct it to be reformed. If it is incomplete, or not responsive to the questions contained in the court's charge, or the answers to the questions are in conflict, the court shall in writing instruct the jury in open court of the nature of the incompleteness, unresponsiveness, or conflict, provide the jury such additional instructions as may be proper, and retire the jury for further deliberations.

Oct. 29, 1940, eff. Sept. 1, 1941. Amended by order of July 15, 1987, eff. Jan. 1, 1988.

Comment—1988

The amendment makes it clear that the court may direct a complete yet defective verdict to be reformed. The amendment also makes it clear that in the event the verdict is incomplete or otherwise improper, the court is limited to giving the jury additional instructions in writing.

Historical Notes

Source

Vernon's Ann.Civ.St. art. 2207, modified by adding "or contains conflicting findings" and "in writing," and by minor textual change.

G. FINDINGS BY THE COURT

Rule 296. Requests for Findings of Facts and Conclusions of Law

In any case tried in the district or county court without a jury, any party may request the court to state in writing its findings of fact and conclusions of law. Such request shall be entitled "Request for Findings of Fact and Conclusions of Law" and shall be filed within twenty days after judgment is signed with the clerk of the court, who shall immediately call such request to the attention of the judge who tried the case. The party making the request shall serve it on all other parties in accordance with Rule 21a.

Oct. 29, 1940, eff. Sept. 1, 1941. Amended by orders of March 19, 1957, eff. Sept. 1, 1957; June 10, 1980, eff. Jan. 1, 1981; Dec. 5, 1983, eff. April 1, 1984; April 24, 1990, eff. Sept. 1, 1990.

Comment—1990

To revise the practice and times for findings of fact and conclusions of law. See also Rules 297 and 298.

Historical Notes

Source

Vernon's Ann.Civ.St. art. 2208, unchanged.

Rule 297. Time to File Findings of Fact and Conclusions of Law

The court shall file its findings of fact and conclusions of law within twenty days after a timely request is filed. The court shall cause a copy of its findings and conclusions to be mailed to each party in the suit.

If the court fails to file timely findings of fact and conclusions of law, the party making the request shall, within thirty days after filing the original request, file with the clerk and serve on all other parties in accordance with Rule 21a a "Notice of Past Due Findings of Fact and Conclusions of Law" which shall be immediately called to the attention of the court by the clerk. Such notice shall state the date the original request was filed and the date the findings and conclusions were due. Upon filing this notice, the time for the court to file findings of fact and conclusions of law is extended to forty days from the date the original request was filed.

Oct. 29, 1940, eff. Sept. 1, 1941. Amended by orders of June 10, 1980, eff. Jan. 1, 1981; Dec. 5, 1983, eff. April 1, 1984; April 24, 1990, eff. Sept. 1, 1990.

Comment—1990

To revise the practice and times for findings of fact and conclusions of law. See also Rules 296 and 298.

Historical Notes

Source

Vernon's Ann.Civ.St. art. 2247, unchanged.

Rule 298. Additional or Amended Findings of Fact and Conclusions of Law

After the court files original findings of fact and conclusions of law, any party may file with the clerk of the court a request for specified additional or amended findings or conclusions. The request for these findings shall be made within ten days after the filing of the original findings and conclusions by the court. Each request made pursuant to this rule shall be served on each party to the suit in accordance with Rule 21a.

The court shall file any additional or amended findings and conclusions that are appropriate within ten days after such request is filed, and cause a copy to be mailed to each party to the suit. No findings or conclusions shall be deemed or presumed by any failure of the court to make any additional findings or conclusions.

Oct. 29, 1940, eff. Sept. 1, 1941. Amended by orders of March 19, 1957, eff. Sept. 1, 1957; April 24, 1990, eff. Sept. 1, 1990.

Historical Notes

Source

Vernon's Ann.Civ.St. art. 2247a, unchanged.

Rule 299. Omitted Findings

When findings of fact are filed by the trial court they shall form the basis of the judgment upon all grounds of recovery and of defense embraced therein. The judgment may not be supported upon appeal by a presumed finding upon any ground of recovery or defense, no element of which has been included in the findings of fact; but when one or more elements thereof have been found by the trial court, omitted unrequested elements, when supported by evidence, will be supplied by presumption in support of the judgment. Refusal of the court to make a finding requested shall be reviewable on appeal.

Oct. 29, 1940, eff. Sept. 1, 1941. Amended by orders of Sept. 20, 1941, eff. Dec. 31, 1941; April 24, 1990, eff. Sept. 1, 1990.

Historical Notes

Source

New rule.

Rule 299a. Findings of Fact To Be Separately Filed and Not Recited in a Judgment

Findings of fact shall not be recited in a judgment. If there is a conflict between findings of fact recited in a judgment in violation of this rule and findings of fact made pursuant to Rules 297 and 298, the latter findings will control for appellate purposes. Findings of fact shall be filed with the clerk of the court as a document or documents separate and apart from the judgment.

April 24, 1990, eff. Sept. 1, 1990.

Comment—1990

To require that findings of fact be separate from the judgment and that such separate findings of fact are controlling on appeal.

H. JUDGMENTS

Rule 300. Court to Render Judgment

Where a special verdict is rendered, or the conclusions of fact found by the judge are separately stated the court shall render judgment thereon unless set aside or a new trial is granted, or judgment is rendered notwithstanding verdict or jury finding under these rules.

Oct. 29, 1940, eff. Sept. 1, 1941.

Historical Notes

Source

Vernon's Ann.Civ.St. art. 2209, with minor textual change.

Rule 301. Judgments

The judgment of the court shall conform to the pleadings, the nature of the case proved and the verdict, if any, and shall be so framed as to give the party all the relief to which he may be entitled either in law or equity. Provided, that upon motion and reasonable notice the court may render judgment non obstante veredicto if a directed verdict would have been proper, and provided further that the court may, upon like motion and notice, disregard any jury finding on a question that has no support in the evidence. Only one final judgment shall be rendered in any cause except where it is otherwise specially provided by law. Judgment may, in a proper case, be given for or against one or more of several plaintiffs, and for or against one or more of several defendants or intervenors.

Oct. 29, 1940, eff. Sept. 1, 1941. Amended by order of July 15, 1987, eff. Jan. 1, 1988.

Historical Notes

Source

Vernon's Ann.Civ.St. art. 2211.

Rule 302. On Counterclaim

If the defendant establishes a demand against the plaintiff upon a counterclaim exceeding that established against him by the plaintiff, the court shall render judgment for defendant for such excess.

Dec. 5, 1983, eff. April 1, 1984.

Historical Notes

Source

Vernon's Ann.Civ.St. art. 2215, unchanged.

Rule 303. On Counterclaim For Costs

When a counterclaim is pleaded, the party in whose favor final judgment is rendered shall also recover the costs, unless it be made to appear on the trial that the counterclaim of the defendant was acquired after the commencement of the suit, in which case, if the plaintiff establishes a claim existing at the commencement of the suit, he shall recover his costs.

Dec 5, 1983, eff. April 1, 1984.

Historical Notes

Source

Vernon's Ann.Civ.St. art. 2216, with minor textual change.

Rule 304. Judgment Upon Record

Judgments rendered upon questions raised upon citations, pleadings, and all other proceedings, constituting the record proper as known at common law, must be entered at the date of each term when pronounced.

Historical Notes

Source

District and County Court Rule 65, unchanged.

Rule 305. Proposed Judgment

Any party may prepare and submit a proposed judgment to the court for signature.

Each party who submits a proposed judgment for signature shall serve the proposed judgment on all other parties to the suit who have appeared and remain in the case, in accordance with Rule 21a.

Failure to comply with this rule shall not affect the time for perfecting an appeal.

Amended by order of April 24, 1990, eff. Sept. 1, 1990.

Comment—1990

To clarify the practice for proposed judgments and notice to other parties.

Historical Notes

1990 Amendment

Rewrote heading and rule.

Source

District and County Court Rule 48, unchanged.

Rule 306. Recitation of Judgment

The entry of the judgment shall contain the full names of the parties, as stated in the pleadings, for and against whom the judgment is rendered. In a suit for termination of the parent-child relationship or a suit affecting the parent-child relationship filed by a governmental entity for managing conservatorship, the judgment must state the specific grounds for termination or for appointment of the managing conservator.

July 21, 1970, eff. Jan. 1, 1971. Amended by order of Feb. 13, 2012, eff. March 1, 2012.

Historical Notes

Source

District and County Court Rules 63 and 64, unchanged except for merger.

2012 Amendment

The order dated February 13, 2012 added the last sentence.

Rule 306a. Periods to Run From Signing of Judgment

1. **Beginning of periods.** The date of judgment or order is signed as shown of record shall determine the beginning of the periods prescribed by these rules for the court's plenary power to grant a new trial or to vacate, modify, correct or reform a judgment or order and for filing in the trial court the various documents that these rules authorize a party to file within such periods including, but not limited to, motions for new trial, motions to modify judgment, motions to reinstate a case dismissed for want of prosecution, motions to vacate judgment and requests for findings of fact and conclusions of law; but this rule shall not determine what constitutes rendition of a judgment or order for any other purpose.

2. **Date to be shown.** Judges, attorneys and clerks are directed to use their best efforts to cause all judgments, decisions and orders of any kind to be reduced to writing and signed by the trial judge with the date of signing stated therein. If the date of signing is not recited in the judgment or order, it may be shown in the record by a certificate of the judge or otherwise; provided, however, that the absence of a showing of the date in the record shall not invalidate any judgment or order.

3. **Notice of judgment.** When the final judgment or other appealable order is signed, the clerk of the court shall immediately give notice to the parties or their attorneys of record by first-class mail advising that the judgment or order was signed. Failure to comply with the provisions of this rule shall not affect the periods mentioned in paragraph (1) of this rule, except as provided in paragraph (4).

4. **No notice of judgment.** If within twenty days after the judgment or other appealable order is signed, a party adversely affected by it or his attorney has neither received the notice required by paragraph (3) of this rule nor acquired actual knowledge of the order, then with respect to that party all the periods mentioned in paragraph (1) shall begin on the date that such party or his attorney received such notice or acquired actual knowledge of the signing, whichever occurred first, but in no event shall such periods begin more than ninety days after the original judgment or other appealable order was signed.

5. **Motion, notice and hearing.** In order to establish the application of paragraph (4) of this rule, the party adversely affected is required to prove in the trial court, on sworn motion and notice, the date on which the party or his attorney first either received a notice of the judgment or acquired actual knowledge of the signing and that this date was more than twenty days after the judgment was signed.

6. **Nunc pro tunc order.** When a corrected judgment has been signed after expiration of the court's plenary power pursuant to Rule 316, the periods mentioned in paragraph (1) of this rule shall run from the date of signing the corrected judgment with respect to any complaint that would not be applicable to the original document.

7. **When process served by publication.** With respect to a motion for new trial filed more than thirty days after the judgment was signed pursuant to Rule 329 when process has been served by publication, the periods provided by paragraph (1) shall be computed as if the judgment were signed on the date of filing the motion.

June 16, 1943, eff. Dec. 31, 1943. Amended by orders of Oct. 10, 1945, eff. Feb. 1, 1946; June 10, 1980, eff. Jan. 1, 1981; Dec. 5, 1983, eff. April 1, 1984; April 10, 1986, eff. Sept. 1, 1986; July 15, 1987, eff. Jan. 1, 1988.

Comment—1988

Amended to reflect repeal of Rule 317.

Historical Notes

1986 Amendment

In par. 1 substituted "that these rules authorize a party to file within such periods" for "in connection with an appeal,", substituted ", motions" for "an original or amended motion" following "not limited to", and substituted "motions to modify judgment, motions to reinstate a case dismissed for want of prosecution, motions to vacate judgment and requests for findings of fact and conclusions of law" for "an appeal bond, certificate of cash deposit, or notice of affidavit in lieu thereof, and bills of exception, and for filing of the petition for writ of error if review is sought by writ of error, and for filing in the appellate court of the transcript and statement of facts"; in par. 4 deleted "except the period for filing a petition for writ, of error" preceding "shall begin on"; in par. 7 substituted "on" for "thirty days before".

1988 Amendment

In par. 6 deleted a reference to repealed rule 317 as it relates to the court's plenary power.

Original rule

"Judges are directed to cause, and attorneys and clerks are directed to use their efforts to cause, the dates upon which judgments, decisions, and orders of any kind are rendered to be stated respectively within such judgments, decisions, and orders; but absence of any such showing shall not invalidate any such judgment or order or any such paper, step, or proceeding."

Rule 306b. Repealed by Order of Dec. 5, 1983, eff. April 1, 1984

Historical Notes

Prior to repeal this rule was amended by order of June 10, 1980.

See, now, Vernon's Ann.Rules Civ.Proc., rule 306a, par. 6.

Rule 306c. Prematurely Filed Documents

No motion for new trial or request for findings of fact and conclusions of law shall be held ineffective because prematurely filed; but every such motion shall be deemed to have been filed on the date of but subsequent to the time of signing of the judgment the motion assails, and every such request for findings of fact and conclusions of law shall be deemed to have been filed on the date of but subsequent to the time of signing of the judgment.

Oct. 10, 1945, eff. Feb. 1, 1946. Amended by orders of April 12, 1962, eff. Sept. 1, 1962; July 22, 1975, eff. Jan. 1, 1976; Dec. 5, 1983, eff. April 1, 1984; April 10, 1986, eff. Sept. 1, 1986; April 24, 1990, eff. Sept. 1, 1990.

Historical Notes

1986 Amendment

Substituted a comma for "or" following "for new trial", deleted ", appeal bond or affidavit in lieu thereof, notice of appeal, or notice of limitations of appeal" preceding "shall be held", deleted "and every such appeal bond or affidavit or notice of appeal or notice of limitation of appeal" following "such request for findings of fact and conclusions of law", and deleted "or the date of the overruling of motion for new trial, if such a motion is filed" at the end.

1990 Amendment

Substituted "time" for "date" twice.

Rule 306d. Repealed by Order of Dec. 5, 1983, eff. April 1, 1984

Historical Notes

See, now, Vernon's Ann.Rules Civ.Proc., rule 306a, par. 3.

Rule 307. Exceptions, etc., Transcript

In non-jury cases, where findings of fact and conclusions of law are requested and filed, and in jury cases, where a special verdict is returned, any party claiming that the findings of the court or the jury, as the case may be, do not support the judgment, may have noted in the record an exception to said judgment and thereupon take an appeal or writ of error, where such writ is allowed, without a statement of facts or further exceptions in the transcript, but the transcript in such cases shall contain the conclusions of law and fact or the special verdict and the judgment rendered thereon.

Historical Notes

Source

Vernon's Ann.Civ.St. art. 2210, redrafted.

Rule 308. Court Shall Enforce Its Decrees

The court shall cause its judgments and decrees to be carried into execution; and where the judgment is for personal property, and it is shown by the pleadings and evidence and the verdict, if any, that such property has an especial value to the plaintiff, the court may award a special writ for the seizure and delivery of such property to the plaintiff; and in such case may enforce its judgment by attachment, fine and imprisonment.

Historical Notes

Source

Vernon's Ann.Civ.St. art. 2217, unchanged.

Rule 308a. In Suits Affecting the Parent–Child Relationship

When the court has ordered child support or possession of or access to a child and it is claimed that the order has been violated, the person claiming that a violation has occurred shall make this known to the court. The court may appoint a member of the bar to investigate the claim to determine whether there is reason to believe that the court order has been violated. If the attorney in good faith believes that the order has been violated, the attorney shall take the necessary action as provided under Chapter 14,[1] Family Code. On a finding of a violation, the court may enforce its order as provided in Chapter 14,[1] Family Code.

Except by order of the court, no fee shall be charged by or paid to the attorney representing the claimant. If the court determines that an attorney's fee should be paid, the fee shall be adjudged against the party who violated the court's order. The fee may be assessed as costs of court, or awarded by judgment, or both.

Oct. 12, 1949, eff. March 1, 1950. Amended by orders of Oct. 10, 1951, eff. March 1, 1952; July 15, 1987, eff. Jan. 1, 1988; April 24, 1990, eff. Sept. 1, 1990.

[1] Repealed; see, generally, V.T.C.A., Family Code Chapter 151 et seq.

Comment—1990

This rule has been completely rewritten and designed to broaden its application to cover problems dealing with possession and access to a child as well as support.

Historical Notes

1990 Amendment

Rewrote heading and rule which prior thereto read:

"Rule 308a. In Child Support Cases

"In cases where the court has ordered periodical payments for the support of a child or children, as provided in the statutes relating to divorce, and it is claimed that such order has been disobeyed, the person claiming that such disobedience has occurred shall make same known to the judge of the court ordering such payments. Such judge may thereupon appoint a member of the bar of that court to advise with and represent said claimant. It shall be the duty of said attorney, if the attorney in good faith believes that said order has been contemptuously disobeyed, to file with the clerk of said court a written statement, verified by the affidavit of said claimant, describing such claimed disobedience. Upon the filing of such statement, or upon its own motion, the court may issue a show cause order to the person alleged to have disobeyed such support order, commanding that person to appear and show cause why they should not be held in contempt of court. Notice of such order shall be served on the respondent in such proceedings in the manner provided in Rule 21a, not less than ten days prior to the hearing on such order to show cause. The hearing on such order may be held either in term time or in vacation. No further written pleadings shall be required. The court, the parties and the attorneys may call and question witnesses to ascertain whether such support order has been disobeyed. Upon a finding of such disobedience, the court may enforce its judgment by orders as in other cases of civil contempt.

"Except with the consent of the court, no fee shall be charged by or paid to the attorney representing the claimant for any services. If the court shall be of the opinion that an attorney's fee shall be paid, the same shall be assessed against the party in default and collected as costs."

Original rule

"In cases where the court has ordered periodical payments for the support of a child or children, as provided in the statutes relating to divorce, and it is claimed that such order has been disobeyed the person claiming that such disobedience has occurred may file with the clerk of the court a written statement describing such claimed disobedience, which statement need not be verified. Upon the filing of such statement, the court may issue a show cause order to the person alleged to have disobeyed such support order, commanding him to appear and show cause why he should not be held in contempt of court. Notice of such order shall be served on the respondent in such proceedings in the manner provided in Rule 21a, not less than ten days prior to the hearing on such order to show cause. The hearing on such order may be held either in term time or vacation. No further written pleadings shall be required. The court may call and question witnesses to ascertain whether such support order has been disobeyed. Upon a finding of such disobedience the court may enforce its judgment by orders as in other cases of civil contempt."

Rule 309. In Foreclosure Proceedings

Judgments for the foreclosure of mortgages and other liens shall be that the plaintiff recover his debt, damages and costs, with a foreclosure of the plaintiff's lien on the property subject thereto, and, except in judgments against executors, administrators and guardians, that an order of sale shall issue to any sheriff or any constable within the State of Texas, directing him to seize and sell the same as under execution, in satisfaction of the judgment; and, if the property cannot be found, or if the proceeds of such sale be insufficient to satisfy the judgment, then to take the money or any balance thereof remaining unpaid, out of any other property of the defendant, as in case of ordinary executions.

July 20, 1966, eff. Jan. 1, 1967.

Historical Notes

Source

Vernon's Ann.Civ.St. art. 2218, modified to provide for directing order of sale to the sheriff or any constable of any county, rather than the county where the property was located.

Rule 310. Writ of Possession

When an order foreclosing a lien upon real estate is made in a suit having for its object the foreclosure of such lien, such order shall have all the force and effect of a writ of possession as between the parties to the foreclosure suit and any person claiming under the defendant to such suit by any right acquired pending such suit; and the court shall so direct in the judgment providing for the issuance of such order. The sheriff or other officer executing such order of sale shall proceed by virtue of such order of sale to place the purchaser of the property sold thereunder in possession thereof within thirty days after the day of sale.

Historical Notes

Source

Vernon's Ann.Civ.St. art. 2219, unchanged.

Rule 311. On Appeal From Probate Court

Judgment on appeal or certiorari from any county court sitting in probate shall be certified to such county court for observance.

Historical Notes

Source

Vernon's Ann.Civ.St. art. 2220, unchanged.

Rule 312. On Appeal From Justice Court

Judgments on appeal or certiorari from a justice court shall be enforced by the county or district court rendering the judgment.

Historical Notes

Source

Vernon's Ann.Civ.St. art. 2221, modified by adding "or district [court] rendering the judgment" to cover situations where county court jurisdiction is transferred to the district court.

Rule 313. Against Executors, etc.

A judgment for the recovery of money against an executor, administrator or guardian, as such, shall state that it is to be paid in the due course of administration. No execution shall issue thereon, but it shall be certified to the county court, sitting in matters of probate, to be there enforced in accordance with law, but judgment against an executor appointed and acting under a will dispensing with the action of the county court in reference to such estate shall be enforced against the property of the testator in the hands of such executor, by execution, as in other cases.

Historical Notes

Source

Vernon's Ann.Civ.St. art. 2222, unchanged.

Rule 314. Confession of Judgment

Any person against whom a cause of action exists may, without process, appear in person or by attorney, and confess judgment therefor in open court as follows:

(a) A petition shall be filed and the justness of the debt or cause of action be sworn to by the person in whose favor the judgment is confessed.

(b) If the judgment is confessed by attorney, the power of attorney shall be filed and its contents be recited in the judgment.

(c) Every such judgment duly made shall operate as a release of all errors in the record thereof, but such judgment may be impeached for fraud or other equitable cause.

Historical Notes

Source

Vernon's Ann.Civ.St. art. 2225, unchanged.

I. REMITTITUR AND CORRECTION

Rule 315. Remittitur

Any party in whose favor a judgment has been rendered may remit any part thereof in open court, or by executing and filing with the clerk a written remittitur signed by the party or the party's attorney of record, and duly acknowledged by the party or the party's attorney. Such remittitur shall be a part of the record of the cause. Execution shall issue for the balance only of such judgment.

July 15, 1987, eff. Jan. 1, 1988.

Historical Notes

1988 Amendment

Rewrote the rule.

Source

Vernon's Ann.Civ.St. art. 2227, unchanged.

Rule 316. Correction of Clerical Mistakes in Judgment Record

Clerical mistakes in the record of any judgment may be corrected by the judge in open court according to the truth or justice of the case after notice of the motion therefor has been given to the parties interested in such judgment, as provided in Rule 21a, and thereafter the execution shall conform to the judgment as amended.

June 16, 1943, eff. Dec. 31, 1943. Amended by order of July 15, 1987, eff. Jan. 1, 1988.

Historical Notes

1988 Amendment

Rewrote the rule heading and the rule.

Source

Vernon's Ann.Civ.St. art. 2228, unchanged.

Rules 317 to 319. Repealed by Order of July 15, 1987, eff. Jan. 1, 1988

J. NEW TRIALS

Rule 320. Motion and Action of Court Thereon

New trials may be granted and judgment set aside for good cause, on motion or on the court's own motion on such terms as the court shall direct. New trials may be granted when the damages are manifestly too small or too large. When it appears to the court that a new trial should be granted on a point or points that affect only a part of the matters in controversy and that such part is clearly separable without unfairness to the parties, the court may grant a new trial as to that part only, provided that a separate trial on unliquidated damages alone shall not be ordered if liability issues are contested. Each motion for new trial shall be in writing and signed by the party or his attorney.

July 20, 1954, eff. Jan. 1, 1955. Amended by orders of July 22, 1975, eff. Jan. 1, 1976; July 11, 1977, eff. Jan. 1, 1978; June 10, 1980, eff. Jan. 1, 1981; Dec. 5, 1983, eff. April 1, 1984; July 15, 1987, eff. Jan. 1, 1988.

Historical Notes

1988 Amendment

Inserted the second sentence.

Source

District and County Court Rule 67, unchanged.

Rule 321. Form

Each point relied upon in a motion for new trial or in arrest of judgment shall briefly refer to that part of the ruling of the court, charge given to the jury, or charge refused, admission or rejection of evidence, or other proceedings which are designated to be complained of, in such a way that the objection can be clearly identified and understood by the court.

June 10, 1980, eff. Jan. 1, 1981.

Historical Notes

Source

District and County Court Rule 67, unchanged.

Rule 322. Generality To Be Avoided

Grounds of objections couched in general terms—as that the court erred in its charge, in sustaining or overruling exceptions to the pleadings, and in excluding or admitting evidence, the verdict of the jury is contrary to law, and the like—shall not be considered by the court.

Historical Notes

Source

District and County Court Rule 68, unchanged.

Rule 323. Repealed by Order of July 11, 1977, eff. Jan. 1, 1978

Rule 324. Prerequisites of Appeal

(a) Motion for New Trial Not Required. A point in a motion for new trial is not a prerequisite to a complaint on appeal in either a jury or a nonjury case, except as provided in subdivision (b).

(b) Motion for New Trial Required. A point in a motion for new trial is a prerequisite to the following complaints on appeal:

(1) A complaint on which evidence must be heard such as one of jury misconduct or newly discovered evidence or failure to set aside a judgment by default;

(2) A complaint of factual insufficiency of the evidence to support a jury finding;

(3) A complaint that a jury finding is against the overwhelming weight of the evidence;

(4) A complaint of inadequacy or excessiveness of the damages found by the jury; or

(5) Incurable jury argument if not otherwise ruled on by the trial court.

(c) Judgment Notwithstanding Findings; Cross-Points

When judgment is rendered non obstante veredicto or notwithstanding the findings of a jury on one or more questions, the appellee may bring forward by cross-point contained in his brief filed in the Court of Appeals any ground which would have vitiated the verdict or would have prevented an affirmance of the judgment had one been rendered by the trial court in harmony with the verdict, including although not limited to the ground that one or more of the jury's findings have insufficient support in the evidence or are against the overwhelming preponderance of the evidence as a matter of fact, and the ground that the verdict and judgment based thereon should be set aside because of improper argument of counsel.

The failure to bring forward by cross-points such grounds as would vitiate the verdict shall be deemed a waiver thereof; provided, however, that if a cross-point is upon a ground which requires the taking of evidence in addition to that adduced upon the trial of the cause, it is not necessary that the evidentiary hearing be held until after the appellate court determines that the cause be remanded to consider such a cross-point.

March 31, 1941, eff. Sept. 1, 1941. Amended by orders of Sept. 20, 1941, eff. Dec. 31, 1941; July 20, 1954, eff. Jan. 1, 1955; March 19, 1957, eff. Sept. 1, 1957; April 12, 1962, eff. Sept. 1, 1962; July 11, 1977, eff. Jan. 1, 1978; June 10, 1980, eff. Jan. 1, 1981; Dec. 5, 1983, eff. April 1, 1984; July 15, 1987, eff. Jan. 1, 1988.

Historical Notes

Source

District and County Court Rule 71a, modified by elimination of reference to fundamental error as exceptional situation not requiring motion for new trial, and by additional of proviso.

Rule 325. Repealed by Order of July 11, 1977, eff. Jan. 1, 1978

Rule 326. Not More Than Two

Not more than two new trials shall be granted either party in the same cause because of insufficiency or weight of the evidence.

Historical Notes

Source

Vernon's Ann.Civ.St. art. 2233, substituting "because of insufficiency or weight of the evidence" for "except when the jury have erred in matter of law or been guilty of misconduct."

Rule 327. For Jury Misconduct

a. When the ground of a motion for new trial, supported by affidavit, is misconduct of the jury or of the officer in charge of them, or because of any communication made to the jury, or that a juror gave an erroneous or incorrect answer on voir dire examination, the court shall hear evidence thereof from the jury or others in open court, and may grant a new trial if such misconduct proved, or the communication made, or the erroneous or incorrect answer on voir dire examination, be material, and if it reasonably appears from the evidence both on the hearing of the motion and the trial of the case and from the record as a whole that injury probably resulted to the complaining party.

b. A juror may not testify as to any matter or statement occurring during the course of the jury's deliberations or to the effect of anything upon his or any other juror's mind or emotions as influencing him to assent to or dissent from the verdict concerning his mental processes in connection therewith, except that a juror may testify whether any outside influence was improperly brought to bear upon any juror. Nor may his affidavit or evidence of any statement by him concerning a matter about which he would be precluded from testifying be received for these purposes.

July 20, 1954, eff. Jan. 1, 1955. Amended by order of Dec. 5, 1983, eff. April 1, 1984.

Historical Notes

Source

Vernon's Ann.Civ.St. art. 2234, modified by adding "and if it reasonably appears from the evidence both on the hearing of the motion and the trial of the case and from the record as a whole that injury probably resulted to the complaining party."

Rule 328. Repealed by Order of July 15, 1987, eff. Jan. 1, 1988

Historical Notes

See, now, Vernon's Ann.Rules App.Proc., Rule 85(b).

Rule 329. Motion for New Trial on Judgment Following Citation by Publication

In cases in which judgment has been rendered on service of process by publication, when the defendant has not appeared in person or by attorney of his own selection:

(a) The court may grant a new trial upon petition of the defendant showing good cause, supported by affidavit, filed within two years after such judgment was signed. The parties adversely interested in such judgment shall be cited as in other cases.

(b) Execution of such judgment shall not be suspended unless the party applying therefor shall give a good and sufficient bond payable to the plaintiff in the judgment, in an amount fixed in accordance with Appellate Rule 47[1] relating to supersedeas bonds, to be approved by the clerk, and conditioned that the party will prosecute his petition for new trial to effect and will perform such judgment as may be rendered by the court should its decision be against him.

(c) If property has been sold under the judgment and execution before the process was suspended, the defendant shall not recover the property so sold, but shall have judgment against the plaintiff in the judgment for the proceeds of such sale.

(d) If the motion is filed more than thirty days after the judgment was signed, the time period shall be computed pursuant to Rule 306a(7).

June 10, 1980, eff. Jan. 1, 1981. Amended by orders of Dec. 5, 1983, eff. April 1, 1984; July 15, 1987, eff. Jan. 1, 1988.

1 See, now, Vernon's Ann.Rules App.Proc., rule 24.1 et seq.

Historical Notes

1988 Amendment

In subd. (b), substituted a reference to Appellate Rule 47 for a reference to Rule 364 and, in subd. (d), changed how the time period was computed if the motion was filed more than thirty days after the judgment was signed.

Source

Vernon's Ann.Civ.St. art. 2236, subd. (6) modified by requiring amount of bond to be fixed in accordance with rule pertaining to supersedeas bonds, rather than in amount double that of value of property or judgment.

Rule 329a. County Court Cases

If a case or other matter is on trial or in the process of hearing when the term of the county court expires, such trial, hearing or other matter may be proceeded with at the next or any subsequent term of court and no motion or plea shall be considered as waived or overruled, because not acted upon at the term of court at which it was filed, but may be acted upon at any time the judge may fix or at which it may have been postponed or continued by agreement of the parties with leave of the court. This subdivision is not applicable to original or amended motions for new trial which are governed by Rule 329b.

July 20, 1954 eff. Jan. 1, 1955. Amended by orders of March 19, 1957, eff. Sept. 1, 1957; July 26, 1960, eff. Jan. 1, 1961.

Historical Notes

Source

New rule, effective Jan. 1, 1955, derived from rule 320, subds. (a) and (d) prior to 1955 amendment of rule 320. The proviso was derived from rule 324 prior to its amendment in 1955.

Rule 329b. Time for Filing Motions

The following rules shall be applicable to motions for new trial and motions to modify, correct, or reform judgments (other than motions to correct the record under Rule 316) in all district and county courts:

(a) A motion for new trial, if filed, shall be filed prior to or within thirty days after the judgment or other order complained of is signed.

(b) One or more amended motions for new trial may be filed without leave of court before any preceding motion for new trial filed by the movant is overruled and within thirty days after the judgment or other order complained of is signed.

(c) In the event an original or amended motion for new trial or a motion to modify, correct or reform a judgment is not determined by written order signed within seventy-five days after the judgment was signed, it shall be considered overruled by operation of law on expiration of that period.

(d) The trial court, regardless of whether an appeal has been perfected, has plenary power to grant a new trial or to vacate, modify, correct, or reform the judgment within thirty days after the judgment is signed.

(e) If a motion for new trial is timely filed by any party, the trial court, regardless of whether an appeal has been perfected, has plenary power to grant a new trial or to vacate, modify, correct, or reform the judgment until thirty days after all such timely-filed motions are overruled, either by a written and signed order or by operation of law, whichever occurs first.

(f) On expiration of the time within which the trial court has plenary power, a judgment cannot be set aside by the trial court except by bill of review for sufficient cause, filed within the time allowed by law; provided that the court may at any time correct a clerical error in the record of a judgment and render judgment nunc pro tunc under Rule 316, and may also sign an order declaring a previous judgment or order to be void because signed after the court's plenary power had expired.

(g) A motion to modify, correct, or reform a judgment (as distinguished from motion to correct the record of a judgment under Rule 316), if filed, shall be filed and determined within the time prescribed by this rule for a motion for new trial and shall extend the trial court's plenary power and the time for perfecting an appeal in the same manner as a motion for new trial. Each such motion shall be in writing and signed by the party or his attorney and shall specify the respects in which the judgment should be modified, corrected, or reformed. The overruling of such a motion shall not preclude the filing of a motion for new trial, nor shall the overruling of a motion for new trial preclude the filing of a motion to modify, correct, or reform.

(h) If a judgment is modified, corrected or reformed in any respect, the time for appeal shall run from the time the modified, corrected, or reformed judgment is signed, but if a correction is made pursuant to Rule 316 after expiration of the period of plenary power provided by this rule, no complaint shall be heard on appeal that could have been presented in an appeal from the original judgment.

July 20, 1954, eff. Jan. 1, 1955. Amended by orders of July 26, 1960, eff. Jan. 1, 1961; July 20, 1966, eff. Jan. 1, 1967; Oct. 3, 1972, eff. Feb. 1, 1973; July 11, 1977, eff. Jan. 1, 1978; June 10, 1980, eff. Jan. 1, 1981; Dec. 5, 1983, eff. April 1, 1984; July 15, 1987, eff. Jan. 1, 1988.

Comment—1988

Amended to conform with repeal of Rule 317.

Historical Notes

1988 Amendment

Deleted references to Rule 317 following references to Rule 316 throughout the rule.

Source

Derived from Rules 330(j), 330(k), 330(*l*), prior to 1955 repeal thereof.

Original rule

"The following rules shall be applicable to motions for new trial filed in all district courts:

"1. A motion for new trial when required shall be filed within ten (10) days after the judgment or other order complained of is rendered.

"2. An original motion for new trial filed within said ten (10) day period may be amended by leave of the court. Said amended motion shall be filed before the original motion is acted upon and within twenty (20) days after the original motion for new trial is filed. Not more than one amended motion for new trial may be filed.

"3. All motions and amended motions for new trial must be determined within not exceeding forty-five (45) days after the original or amended motion is filed, unless by written agreement of the parties in the case, the decision of the motion is postponed to a later date.

"4. It shall be the duty of the proponent of an original or amended motion for new trial to present the same to the court within thirty (30) days after the same is filed. However, at the discretion of the district judge an original motion or amended motion for new trial may be presented or hearing thereon completed after such thirty (30) day period. Such delayed hearing shall not operate to extend the time within which the original or amended motion must be determined, unless such time be extended by agreement as provided for in the preceding subdivision of this Rule. In the event an original motion or amended motion for new trial be not presented within thirty (30) days after the date of the filing thereof, and the district judge in his discretion refuses to consider the same or refuses to hear evidence relating thereto, such motion will be overruled by operation of law forty-five (45) days after the same is filed, unless disposed of by an order rendered before said date.

"5. Judgments in the district court shall become final after the expiration of thirty (30) days after the date of rendition of judgment or order overruling an original or amended motion for new trial. After the expiration of thirty (30) days from the date the judgment is rendered or motion for new trial is overruled, the judgment cannot be set aside except by bill of review for sufficient cause, filed within the time allowed by law. The failure of a party to file a motion for new trial within the ten (10) day period prescribed in subdivision (1) of this rule shall not deprive the district court of jurisdiction to set aside a judgment rendered by it, provided such action be taken within thirty (30) days after the judgment is rendered. The filing of a motion for new trial after ten (10) days have expired and before thirty (30) days have expired since the rendition of the judgment shall not operate to extend the district court's jurisdiction over the judgment for a period of more than thirty days from the date of the rendition of judgment.

"6. In district courts having continuous terms, that is, successive terms in a county throughout the year, without more than two days intervening between any such terms, the following rules shall apply:

"(a) A motion for new trial filed during one term of court may be heard and acted upon at the next term of court.

"(b) No motion for new trial shall be considered as waived or overruled because not acted upon at the term of court at which it was filed, but may be acted upon at any time within the next term of court agreeable to the provisions of this Rule 329-b.

"(c) Judgments of such courts shall become as final after the expiration of thirty (30) days after the date of judgment or after a motion for new trial is overruled as if the term of court had expired.

"7. In district courts which do not have continuous terms as defined above, the following provisions shall apply:

"(a) Whenever a judgment is rendered and the remaining portion of the term does not extend for a period of thirty (30) days after such date of rendition, the term of said court insofar as the case in which the judgment is rendered is concerned shall be automatically extended for a period of thirty (30) days from and after the date of rendition of judgment.

"(b) If original or amended motions for new trial be timely filed in accordance with this Rule 329-b, then the term of court, insofar as the particular case is concerned, shall be further automatically extended until the expiration of thirty (30) days after the time such motion for new trial shall have been disposed of in accordance with the provisions of this Rule."

K. CERTAIN DISTRICT COURTS

Rule 330. Rules of Practice and Procedure in Certain District Courts

The following rules of practice and procedure shall govern and be followed in all civil actions in district courts in counties where the only district court of said county vested with civil jurisdiction, or all the district courts thereof having civil jurisdiction, have successive terms in said county throughout the year, without more than two days intervening between any of such terms, whether or not any one or more of such district courts include one or more other counties within its jurisdiction.

(a) Appealed Cases

In cases appealed to said district courts from inferior courts, the appeal, including transcript, shall be filed in the district court within thirty (30) days after the rendition of the judgment or order appealed from, and the appellee shall enter his appearance on the docket or answer to said appeal on or before ten o'clock a. m. of the Monday next after the expiration of twenty (20) days from the date the appeal is filed in the district court.

Comment

The following statutes are listed as repealed:

Article 2093a. Rules of practice and procedure in district courts in counties wherein sit three district courts.

Article 2093b. Additional return and appearance days in districts composed of two or more counties.

Article 2093b, being Acts 1939, 46th Legislature, p. 218, Sec. 1, became effective April 14, 1939.

Article 2092, the source of Rule 330, was amended by Acts 1939, 46th Legislature, p. 205, effective June 7, 1939. The purpose of the amendment was to make Article 2092 applicable to all counties having five or more district courts with either civil or criminal jurisdiction or both. The amendment of 1939 did not change any of the subdivisions of Article 2092 which are the source of Rule 330.

The Rule Making Act, Article 1731a, was likewise passed by the 46th Legislature and became effective May 15, 1939, prior to the effective date of Article 2092, as amended. See Garrett v. Mercantile Bank at Dallas, 1943, 140 T. 394, 168 S.W.2d 636, for the effect of procedural legislation passed by the 46th Legislature.

(b) Repealed by order of July 22, 1975, eff. Jan. 1, 1976

(c) Postponement or Continuance

Cases may be postponed or continued by agreement with the approval of the court, or upon the court's own motion or for cause. When a case is called for trial and only one party is ready, the court may for good cause either continue the case for the term or postpone and reset it for a later day in the same or succeeding term.

(d) Cases May Be Reset

A case that is set and reached for trial may be postponed for a later day in the term or continued and reset for a day certain in the succeeding term on the same grounds as an application for continuance would be granted in other district courts. After any case has been set and reached in its due order and called for trial two (2) or more times and not tried, the court may dismiss the same unless the parties agree to a postponement or continuance but the court shall respect written agreements of counsel for postponement and continuance if filed in the case when or before it is called for trial unless to do so will unreasonably delay or interfere with other business of the court.

(e) Exchange and Transfer

Where in such county there are two or more district courts having civil jurisdiction, the judges of such courts may, in their discretion, exchange benches or districts from time to time, and may transfer cases and other proceedings from one court to another, and any of them may in his own courtroom try and determine any case or proceeding pending in another court without having the case transferred, or may sit in any other of said courts and there hear and determine any case there pending, and every judgment and order shall be entered in the minutes of the court in which the case is pending and at the time the judgment or order is rendered, and two (2) or more judges may try different cases in the same court at the same time, and each may occupy his own courtroom or the room of any other court. The judge of any such court may issue restraining orders and injunctions returnable to any other judge or court, and any judge may transfer any case or proceeding pending in his court to any other of said courts, and the judge of any court to which a case or proceeding is transferred shall receive and try the same, and in turn shall have power in his discretion to transfer any such case to any other of said courts and any other judge may in his courtroom try any case pending in any other of such courts.

(f) Cases Transferred to Judges Not Occupied

Where in such counties there are two or more district courts having civil jurisdiction, when the judge of any such court shall become disengaged, he shall notify the presiding judge, and the presiding judge shall transfer to the court of the disengaged judge the next case which is ready for trial in any of said courts. Any judge not engaged in his own court may try any case in any other court.

(g) Judge May Hear Only Part of Case

When in such counties there are two or more district courts having civil jurisdiction, any judge may hear any part of any case or proceeding pending in any of said courts and determine the same, or may hear and determine any question in any case, and any other judge may complete the hearing and render judgment in the case.

(h) Any Judge May Hear Dilatory Pleas

Where in such county there are two or more district courts having civil jurisdiction, any judge may hear and determine motions, petitions for injunction, applications for appointment of receivers, interventions, pleas of privilege, pleas in abatement, all dilatory pleas and special exceptions, motions for a new trial and all preliminary matters, questions and proceedings and may enter judgment or order thereon in the court in which the case is pending without having the case transferred to the court of the judge acting, and the judge in whose court the case is pending may thereafter proceed to hear, complete and determine the case or other matter, or any part thereof, and render final judgment therein. Any judgment rendered or action taken by any judge in any of said courts in the county shall be valid and binding.

(i) Acts in Succeeding Terms

If a case or other matter is on trial, or in the process of hearing when the term of court expires, such trial, hearing or other matter may be proceeded with at the next or any subsequent term of court and no motion or plea shall be considered as waived or overruled, because not acted upon at the term of court at which it was filed, but may be acted upon at any time the judge may fix or at which it may have been postponed or continued by agreement of the parties with leave of the court. This subdivision is not applicable to original or amended motions for new trial which are governed by Rule 329b.

(j) Relettered to (i)

(k), (*l*) Repealed by order of July 20, 1954, eff. Jan. 1, 1955

July 20, 1954, eff. Jan. 1, 1955. Amended by orders of July 26, 1960, eff. Jan. 1, 1961; Oct. 3, 1972, eff. Feb. 1, 1973; July 22, 1975, eff. Jan. 1, 1976.

Historical Notes

Source

Vernon's Ann.Civ.St. art. 2092. Subd. (a), sec. 13. Subd. (6), sec. 18, unchanged. Subd. (c), sec. 19, unchanged. Subd. (d), sec. 20, unchanged. Subd. (e), sec. 21, with minor textual change. Subd. (f), sec. 22, with minor textual change. Subd. (g), sec. 24, with minor textual change. Subd. (h), sec. 25, with minor textual change. Subd. (i), sec. 26, unchanged. Subd. (j), sec. 28, unchanged. Subd. (k), sec. 29, with minor textual change. Subd. (*l*), sec. 30.

Rule 331. Repealed by Order of July 15, 1987, eff. Jan. 1, 1988

Historical Notes

Source

Vernon's Ann.Civ.St. art. 2093, reworded and extended to all exceptional District and County Courts.

SECTION 12. REVIEW BY DISTRICT COURTS OF COUNTY COURT RULINGS

Rules 332 to 351. Repealed by Order of July 22, 1975, eff. Jan. 1, 1976

Historical Notes

The repealed rules related to review by district courts of county court rulings in cases involving guardianships and estates of decedents and in cases involving certiorari to county courts.

Prior to repeal, these rules were amended as follows: rule 332, by order of Aug. 18, 1947 and order of April 12, 1962; rules 333 and 334, by order of June 16, 1943 and order of April 12, 1962; and rules 335 to 339, by order of April 12, 1962.

Rules 340 to 343 were repealed by order of April 12, 1962.

Rule 351 was amended by order of Oct. 12, 1949.

The amendment to Const. Art. 5, § 8 and the enactment of Acts 1975, 64th Leg., p. 2196, ch. 701, amending V.A.T.S. Probate Code, §§ 3, 5, 28, 313, and 355, rendered these rules unnecessary.

PART III

RULES OF PROCEDURE FOR THE COURTS OF APPEALS [REPEALED]

NOTE

Part III is repealed. The substance of those former rules within Part III is now contained in the Texas Rules of Appellate Procedure.

SECTION 1. PERFECTING APPEAL

Rules 352 to 358. Repealed by Order of April 10, 1986, eff. Sept. 1, 1986

Historical Notes

For subject matter of former rule 352, see, now, Rules App.Proc., Rules 3.1, 3.2.

For subject matter of former rules 353, 355, and 357, see, now, Rules App.Proc., Rules 20.1, 25.1, and 25.2.

For subject matter of former rule 356, see, now, Rules App.Proc., Rules 20.1, 25.1, 25.2, 26.1 et seq., and 27.1.

For subject matter of former rule 358, see, now, Rules App.Proc., Rules 7.1 and 7.2.

Rule 359. Repealed by Order of Dec. 5, 1983, eff. April 1, 1984

Historical Notes

The repealed rule, relating to petition for writ of error, was adopted by order of October 29, 1940, effective September 1, 1941.

See, now, rule 360.

Rule 360. Repealed by Order of April 10, 1986, eff. Sept. 1, 1986

Rules 361, 362. Repealed by Order of Dec. 5, 1983, eff. April 1, 1984

Historical Notes

The repealed rules, relating to cost bond on writ of error and notice of petition for writ of error, respectively, were adopted by order of October 29, 1940, effective September 1, 1941.

See, now, rule 360.

Rules 363 to 369a. Repealed by Order of April 10, 1986, eff. Sept. 1, 1986

Historical Notes

For subject matter of former rule 363, see, now, Rules App.Proc., Rules 20.1, 25.1, and 25.2.

For subject matter of former rules 364 and 368, see, now, Rules App.Proc., Rule 24.1 et seq.

For subject matter of former rules 365, 366, and 367, see, now, Rules App.Proc., Rule 24.4.

For subject matter of former rule 369a, see, now, Rules App.Proc., Rules 7.1 and 7.2.

SECTION 2. RECORD ON APPEAL

Rule 370. Repealed by Order of June 10, 1980, eff. Jan. 1, 1981

Rules 371 to 373. Repealed by Order of April 10, 1986, eff. Sept. 1, 1986

Historical Notes

For subject matter of former rule 371, see, now, Rules App.Proc., rule 34.1 et seq.

For subject matter of former rules 372 and 373, see, now, Rules App.Proc., Rules 33.1, 33.2.

Rule 374. Repealed by Order of July 11, 1977, eff. Jan. 1, 1978

Rules 375 to 382. Repealed by Order of April 10, 1986, eff. Sept. 1, 1986

Historical Notes

For subject matter of former rules 375 and 378, see, now, Rules App.Proc., rule 34.1 et seq.

For subject matter of former rule 376, see, now, Rules App.Proc., Rules 33.1, 33.2, 34.5, and 34.6.

For subject matter of former rule 376b, see, now, Rules App.Proc., Rule 13.1, 13.5, and 13.6.

For subject matter of former rule 376c, see, now, Rules App.Proc., Rules 13.3, 13.4, and 35.3.

For subject matter of former rule 377, see, now, Rules App.Proc., Rules 20.1, 20.2, 34.5, and 34.6.

For subject matter of former rule 377a, see, now, Rules App.Proc., Rules 27.2 and 27.3.

For subject matter of former rule 379, see, now, Rules App.Proc., Rules 34.5 and 34.6.

For subject matter of former rule 380, see, now, Rules App.Proc., Rules 20.1, 20.2, and 34.6.

For subject matter of former rule 381, see, now, Rules App.Proc., Rules 33.1, 33.2, and 34.1 et seq.

SECTION 3. PROCEEDINGS IN THE COURTS OF APPEALS

Rules 383 to 389a. Repealed by Order of April 10, 1986, eff. Sept. 1, 1986

Historical Notes

For subject matter of former rule 383, see, now, Rules App.Proc., Rules 5, 9.3, 9.5, 12.6, and 52.1 et seq.

For subject matter of former rule 383a, see, now, Rules App.Proc., rules 9.5, 12.6, and 52.1 et seq.

For subject matter of former rule 385, see, now, Rules App.Proc., Rules 26.1, 28.1 et seq., 35.1, and 38.6.

For subject matter of former rule 385a, see, now, Rules App.Proc., Rule 17.1 et seq.

For subject matter of former rule 385b, see, now, Rules App.Proc., Rules 18.6, 18.7, 29.1 et seq., 31.1 et seq., and 49.4.

For subject matter of former rule 386, see, now, Rules App.Proc., Rules 35.1 and 35.2.

For subject matter of former rule 387, see, now, Rules App.Proc., Rules 42.3 and 42.4.

For subject matter of former rule 387a, see, now, Rules App.Proc., Rules 42.1 and 42.2.

For subject matter of former rules 388, 389, and 389a, see, now, Rules App.Proc., Rule 37.2.

For subject matter of former rule 388a, see, now, Rules App.Proc., Rules 5 and 20.1.

Rule 390. Repealed by Order of Dec. 5, 1983, eff. April 1, 1984

Rule 391. Repealed by Order of Oct. 12, 1949, eff. March 1, 1950

Rule 392. Repealed by Order of Dec. 5, 1983, eff. April 1, 1984

Rules 393 to 414. Repealed by Order of April 10, 1986, eff. Sept. 1, 1986

Historical Notes

For subject matter of former rules 393 and 395 to 398, see, now, Rules App.Proc., Rule 12.1 et seq.

For subject matter of former rule 394, see, now, Rules App.Proc., Rule 15.1 et seq.

For subject matter of former rule 401, see, now, Rules App.Proc., Rule 9.6.

For subject matter of former rule 402, see, now, Rules App.Proc., Rules 6.2, 12.2.

For subject matter of former rule 402a, see, now, Rules App.Proc., Rules 6.1(c) and 6.5.

For subject matter of former rule 403, see, now, Rules App.Proc., Rules 6.6.

For subject matter of former rule 404, see, now, Rules App.Proc., Rule 10.5(a).

For subject matter of former rule 407, see, now, Rules App.Proc., Rule 10.5(c).

For subject matter of former rules 408 and 409, see, now, Rules App.Proc., Rules 6.2, 10.1 et seq.

For subject matter of former rule 410, see, now, Rules App.Proc., Rule 40.1.

For subject matter of former rule 411, see, now, Rules App.Proc., Rule 40.1.

For subject matter of former rule 413, see, now, Rules App.Proc., Rule 34.1.

For subject matter of former rule 414, see, now, Rules App.Proc., Rules 9.1 et seq. and 38.1 et seq.

Rules 415 to 417. Repealed by Order of Dec. 5, 1983, eff. April 1, 1984

Historical Notes

Former rules 415 and 416, relating to dismissal of appeal for failure to file brief and the filing of appellee's brief when appellant filed no brief, respectively, were adopted by order of October 29, 1940, effective September 1, 1941.

Former rule 417, relating to typing or writing of briefs, was adopted by order of October 29, 1940, effective September 1, 1941, and was amended by order of October 10, 1945, effective Feb. 1, 1946.

See, now, rule 414.

Rule 418. Repealed by Order of April 24, 1984, eff. Oct. 1, 1984

Historical Notes

Former rule 418, relating to the contents of the briefs, was amended by orders of March 31, 1941; September 20, 1941; July 11, 1977; and June 10, 1980.

See, now, rule 414.

Rules 419, 420. Repealed by Order of April 10, 1986, eff. Sept. 1, 1986

Historical Notes

See, now, Rules App.Proc., Rules 74.1 to 74.10.

Rule 421. Repealed by Order of June 10, 1980, eff. Jan. 1, 1981

Historical Notes

Prior to repeal, this rule, which required an index to briefs, was amended by order of March 31, 1941.

See, now, rule 414.

Rules 422, 423. Repealed by Order of April 10, 1986, eff. Sept. 1, 1986

Historical Notes

For subject matter of repealed rules, see, now, Rules App.Proc., Rules 74.1 to 74.10 and 75.1 to 75.3, respectively.

Rules 424 to 427. Repealed by Order of Dec. 5, 1983, eff. April 1, 1984

Historical Notes

The repealed rules, which related to the subject matter of and time allowed for argument, provided that counsel was expected to answer questions of the court and provided for argument where one party filed brief, were adopted by order of October 29, 1940, effective September 1, 1941.

See, now, rule 423.

Rules 428, 429. Repealed by Order of April 10, 1986, eff. Sept. 1, 1986

Historical Notes

See, now, Rules App.Proc., Rules 55.1 to 55.9.

Rules 430 to 432. Repealed by Order of Dec. 5, 1983, eff. April 1, 1984

Historical Notes

Former rules 430 to 432, which related to amendment of the appeal bond, amendment of briefs, and reporter's access to records, were adopted by order of October 29, 1940, effective September 1, 1941.

For subject matter of former rules 430 and 431, see, now, rules 363a and 414, respectively.

SECTION 4. JUDGMENT

Rules 433 to 442. Repealed by Order of April 10, 1986, eff. Sept. 1, 1986

Historical Notes

For subject matter of former rule 433, see, now, Rules App.Proc., rule 43.1.

For subject matter of former rule 434, see, now, Rules App.Proc., rule 44.1 et seq.

For subject matter of former rule 435, see, now, Rules App.Proc., rule 43.4, 43.5.

For subject matter of former rule 436, see, now, Rules App.Proc., rule 51.1, 51.2.

For subject matter of former rule 437, see, now, Rules App.Proc., rule 44.3.

For subject matter of former rule 438, see, now, Rules App.Proc., rule 45.

For subject matter of former rules 439 to 441, see, now, Rules App.Proc., rule 46.1 et seq.

For subject matter of former rule 442, see, now, Rules App.Proc., rule 18.1 et seq.

Rules 443, 444. Repealed by Order of Dec. 5, 1983, eff. April 1, 1984

Historical Notes

Former rule 443, relating to payment of costs, was adopted by order of October 29, 1940, effective September 1, 1941 and amended by orders of October 3, 1972, July 1, 1977, and June 10, 1980.

Former rule 444, providing for affidavit of inability to pay costs, was adopted by order of October 29, 1940, effective September 1, 1941.

See, now, rule 442.

Rule 445. Repealed by Order of July 11, 1977, eff. Jan. 1, 1978

Rules 446 to 448. Repealed by Order of April 10, 1986, eff. Sept. 1, 1986

Historical Notes

For subject matter of former rule 446, see, now, Rules App.Proc., rule 18.1 et seq.

For subject matter of former rules 447 and 448, see, now, Rules App.Proc., rules 51.1 and 43.4, respectively.

Rules 449, 450. Repealed by Order of Dec. 5, 1983, eff. April 1, 1984

Historical Notes

Former rules 449 and 450, relating to return of execution, and officers failing to make return, respectively, were added by order of October 29, 1940, effective September 1, 1941.

See, now, rule 447.

SECTION 5. OPINIONS

Rules 451, 452. Repealed by Order of April 10, 1986, eff. Sept. 1, 1986

Historical Notes

See, now, Vernon's Ann.Rules App.Proc., Rule 47.1 et seq.

Rules 453 to 455. Repealed by Order of Dec. 5, 1983, eff. April 1, 1984

Rules 456, 457. Repealed by Order of April 10, 1986, eff. Sept. 1, 1986

Historical Notes

For subject matter of former rule 456, see, now, Rules App.Proc., rule 48.1 et seq.

For subject matter of former rule 457, see, now, Rules App.Proc., rule 4.1 et seq., 12.6.

SECTION 6. REHEARING

Rule 458. Repealed by Order of April 10, 1986, eff. Sept. 1, 1986

Historical Notes

For subject matter of repealed rule, see, now, Rules App.Proc., rule 49.1 et seq.

Rule 459. Repealed by Order of Sept. 20, 1941, eff. Dec. 31, 1941

Rule 460. Repealed by Order of April 10, 1986, eff. Sept. 1, 1986

Historical Notes

Source

New rule.

SECTION 7. CERTIFICATION OF QUESTIONS

Rules 461, 462. Repealed by Order of April 10, 1986, eff. Sept. 1, 1986

Rules 463, 464. Repealed by Order of Dec. 5, 1983, eff. April 1, 1984

Rule 465. Renumbered as rule 462 by order of Dec. 5, 1983, eff. April 1, 1984

Rule 466. Repealed by Order of April 10, 1986, eff. Sept. 1, 1986

Historical Notes

Source

Supreme Court Rule 15.

SECTION 8. APPLICATION FOR WRIT OF ERROR

Rule 467. Repealed by Order of Dec. 5, 1983, eff. April 1, 1984

Historical Notes

The repealed rule, relating to reviewing of judgments when good cause was shown, was adopted by order of October 29, 1940, effective September 1, 1941.

See, now, rule 468.

Rules 468 to 470. Repealed by Order of April 10, 1986, eff. Sept. 1, 1986

Historical Notes

For subject matter of former rule 468, see, now, Rules App.Proc., rules 9.3(b), 53.1, and 53.7.

For subject matter of former rule 469, see, now, Rules App.Proc., Rules 9.1 et seq., 53.2, 53.6, 53.8, and 53.9.

Rule 471. Repealed by Order of Dec. 5, 1983, eff. April 1, 1984

Historical Notes

Prior to repeal, this rule which related to service on respondent, was amended by orders of June 16, 1943, and March 19, 1957.

See, now, rule 469(h).

Rule 472. Repealed by Order of April 10, 1986, eff. Sept. 1, 1986

Historical Notes

See, now, Rules App.Proc., rule 54.1 et seq.

Source

Vernon's Ann.Civ.St. art. 1883.

Rule 473. Repealed by Order of Dec. 5, 1983, eff. April 1, 1984

Historical Notes

The repealed rule, amended by order of Oct. 12, 1949, related to petition with record.

See, now, rule 472.

PART IV

RULES OF PRACTICE FOR THE SUPREME COURT [REPEALED]

NOTE

Part IV is now repealed. The substance of those former rules within Part IV is now contained in the Texas Rules of Appellate Procedure.

Rules 474 to 481. Repealed by Order of April 10, 1986, eff. Sept. 1, 1986

Historical Notes

For subject matter of former rule 474, see, now, Rules App.Proc., rules 5, 9.3, 9.5, 12.6, 52.1, 52.2, and 52.3.

For subject matter of former rule 475, see, now, Rules App.Proc., rules 9.5, 12.6, and 52.1 et seq.

For subject matter of former rule 480, see, now, Rules App.Proc., rule 54.1 et seq.

For subject matter of former rule 480a, see, now, Rules App.Proc., rule 9.1 et seq.

For subject matter of former rule 481, see, now, Rules App.Proc., rules 9.5 and 53.2 et seq.

Rule 482. Repealed by Order of Dec. 5, 1983, eff. April 1, 1984

Rules 483 to 486. Repealed by Order of April 10, 1986, eff. Sept. 1, 1986

Historical Notes

For subject matter of former rule 483, see, now, Rules App.Proc., Rules 52.8, 54.1 et seq., 56.1, and 56.2.

For subject matter of former rule 484, see, now, Rules App.Proc., Rule 56.5.

For subject matter of former rule 485, see, now, Rules App.Proc., Rules 5 and 20.1.

For subject matter of former rule 486, see, now, Rules App.Proc., Rules 5, 9.3, 9.5, 12.6, 52.1 et seq., and 56.4.

Rule 487. Repealed by Order of Oct. 10, 1945, eff. Feb. 1, 1946

Rules 488 to 493. Repealed by Order of April 10, 1986, eff. Sept. 1, 1986

Historical Notes

For subject matter of former rule 488, see, now, Rules App.Proc., Rules 15.1 seq.

For subject matter of former rule 490, see, now, Rules App.Proc., Rules 12.1 et seq.

For subject matter of former rule 492, see, now, Rules App.Proc., Rules 9.1 et seq.

For subject matter of former rule 493, see, now, Rules App.Proc., rule 59.2.

Rule 494. Repealed by Order of Oct. 10, 1945, eff. Feb. 1, 1946

Rules 495 to 499a. Repealed by Order of April 10, 1986, eff. Sept. 1, 1986

Historical Notes

For subject matter of former rule 496, see, now, Rules App.Proc., rules 9.5, 11, and 53.3 to 53.8.

For subject matter of former rule 497, see, now, Rules App.Proc., rules 59.1 and 59.2.

For subject matter of former rule 498, see, now, Rules App.Proc., rules 59.4 to 59.6.

For subject matter of former rule 499, see, now, Rules App.Proc., rule 9.6.

For subject matter of former rule 499a, see, now, Rules App.Proc., rule 57.1 et seq.

PART V

RULES OF PRACTICE IN JUSTICE COURTS

Rule 500. General Rules

Rule 500.1. Construction of Rules

Unless otherwise expressly provided, in Part V of these Rules of Civil Procedure:

(a) the past, present, and future tense each includes the other;

(b) the term "it" includes a person of either gender or an entity; and

(c) the singular and plural each includes the other.

Adopted by order of April 15, 2013, eff. Aug. 31, 2013.

Rule 500.2. Definitions

In Part V of these Rules of Civil Procedure:

(a) "Answer" is the written response that a party who is sued must file with the court after being served with a citation.

(b) "Citation" is the court-issued document required to be served upon a party to inform the party that it has been sued.

(c) "Claim" is the legal theory and alleged facts that, if proven, entitle a party to relief against another party in court.

(d) "Clerk" is a person designated by the judge as a justice court clerk, or the judge if there is no clerk available.

(e) "Counterclaim" is a claim brought by a party who has been sued against the party who filed the lawsuit, for example, a defendant suing a plaintiff.

(f) "County court" is the county court, statutory county court, or district court in a particular county with jurisdiction over appeals of civil cases from justice court.

(g) "Cross-claim" is a claim brought by one party against another party on the same side of a lawsuit. For example, if a plaintiff sues two defendants, the defendants can seek relief against each other by means of a cross-claim.

(h) "Default judgment" is a judgment awarded to a plaintiff when the defendant fails to answer and dispute the plaintiff's claims in the lawsuit.

(i) "Defendant" is a party who is sued, including a plaintiff against whom a counterclaim is filed.

(j) "Defense" is an assertion by a defendant that the plaintiff is not entitled to relief from the court.

(k) "Discovery" is the process through which parties obtain information from each other in order to prepare for trial or enforce a judgment. The term does not refer to any information that a party is entitled to under applicable law.

(*l*) "Dismissed without prejudice" means a case has been dismissed but has not been finally decided and may be refiled.

(m) "Dismissed with prejudice" means a case has been dismissed and finally decided and may not be refiled.

(n) "Judge" is a justice of the peace.

(*o*) "Judgment" is a final order by the court that states the relief, if any, a party is entitled to or must provide.

(p) "Jurisdiction" is the authority of the court to hear and decide a case.

(q) "Motion" is a request that the court make a specified ruling or order.

(r) "Notice" is a document prepared and delivered by the court or a party stating that something is required of the party receiving the notice.

(s) "Party" is a person or entity involved in the case that is either suing or being sued, including all plaintiffs, defendants, and third parties that have been joined in the case.

(t) "Petition" is a formal written application stating a party's claims and requesting relief from the court. It is the first document filed with the court to begin a lawsuit.

(u) "Plaintiff" is a party who sues, including a defendant who files a counterclaim.

(v) "Pleading" is a written document filed by a party, including a petition and an answer, that states a claim or defense and outlines the relief sought.

(w) "Relief" is the remedy a party requests from the court, such as the recovery of money or the return of property.

(x) "Serve" and "service" are delivery of citation as required by Rule 501.2, or of a document as required by Rule 501.4.

(y) "Sworn" means signed in front of someone authorized to take oaths, such as a notary, or signed under penalty of perjury. Filing a false sworn document can result in criminal prosecution.

(z) "Third party claim" is a claim brought by a party being sued against someone who is not yet a party to the case.

Adopted by order of April 15, 2013, eff. Aug. 31, 2013.

Rule 500.3. Application of Rules in Justice Court Cases

(a) *Small Claims Case.* A small claims case is a lawsuit brought for the recovery of money damages, civil penalties, personal property, or other relief allowed by law. The claim can be for no more than $10,000, excluding statutory interest and court costs but including attorney fees, if any. Small claims cases are governed by Rules 500–507 of Part V of the Rules of Civil Procedure.

(b) *Debt Claim Case.* A debt claim case is a lawsuit brought to recover a debt by an assignee of a claim, a debt collector or collection agency, a financial institution, or a person or entity primarily engaged in the business of lending money at interest. The claim can be for no more than $10,000, excluding statutory interest and court costs but including attorney fees, if any. Debt claim cases injustice court are governed by Rules 500–507 and 508 of Part V of the Rules of Civil Procedure. To the extent of any conflict between Rule 508 and the rest of Part V, Rule 508 applies.

(c) *Repair and Remedy Case.* A repair and remedy case is a lawsuit filed by a residential tenant under Chapter 92, Subchapter B of the Texas Property Code to enforce the landlord's duty to repair or remedy a condition materially affecting the physical health or safety of an ordinary tenant. The relief sought can be for no more than $ 10,000, excluding statutory interest and court costs but including attorney fees, if any. Repair and remedy cases are governed by Rules 500–507 and 509 of Part V of the Rules of Civil Procedure. To the extent of any conflict between Rule 509 and the rest of Part V, Rule 509 applies.

(d) *Eviction Case.* An eviction case is a lawsuit brought to recover possession of real property under Chapter 24 of the Texas Property Code, often by a landlord against a tenant. A claim for rent may be joined with an eviction case if the amount of rent due and unpaid is not more than $10,000, excluding statutory interest and court costs but including attorney fees, if any. Eviction cases are governed by Rules 500–507 and 510 of Part V of the Rules of Civil Procedure. To the extent of any conflict between Rule 510 and the rest of Part V, Rule 510 applies.

(e) *Application of Other Rules.* The other Rules of Civil Procedure and the Rules of Evidence do not apply except:

(1) when the judge hearing the case determines that a particular rule must be followed to ensure that the proceedings are fair to all parties; or

(2) when otherwise specifically provided by law or these rules.

(f) *Examination of Rules.* The court must make the Rules of Civil Procedure and the Rules of Evidence available for examination, either in paper form or electronically, during the court's business hours.

Adopted by order of April 15, 2013, eff. Aug. 31, 2013.

Rule 500.4. Representation in Justice Court Cases

(a) *Representation of an Individual.* An individual may:

(1) represent himself or herself;

(2) be represented by an authorized agent in an eviction case; or

(3) be represented by an attorney.

(b) *Representation of a Corporation or Other Entity.* A corporation or other entity may:

(1) be represented by an employee, owner, officer, or partner of the entity who is not an attorney;

(2) be represented by a property manager or other authorized agent in an eviction case; or

(3) be represented by an attorney.

(c) *Assisted Representation.* The court may, for good cause, allow an individual representing himself or herself to be assisted in court by a family member or other individual who is not being compensated.

Adopted by order of April 15, 2013, eff. Aug. 31, 2013.

Rule 500.5. Computation of Time; Timely Filing

(a) *Computation of Time.* To compute a time period in these rules:

(1) exclude the day of the event that triggers the period;

(2) count every day, including Saturdays, Sundays, and legal holidays; and

(3) include the last day of the period, but

(A) if the last day is a Saturday, Sunday, or legal holiday, the time period is extended to the next day that is not a Saturday, Sunday, or legal holiday; and

(B) if the last day for filing falls on a day during which the court is closed before 5:00 p.m., the time period is extended to the court's next business day.

(b) *Timely Filing by Mail.* Any document required to be filed by a given date is considered timely filed if deposited in the U.S. mail on or before that date, and received within 10 days of the due date. A legible postmark affixed by the United States Postal Service is evidence of the date of mailing.

(c) *Extensions.* The judge may, for good cause shown, extend any time period under these rules except those relating to new trial and appeal.

Adopted by order of April 15, 2013, eff. Aug. 31, 2013.

Rule 500.6. Judge to Develop the Case

In order to develop the facts of the case, a judge may question a witness or party and may summon any person or party to appear as a witness when the judge considers it necessary to ensure a correct judgment and a speedy disposition.

Adopted by order of April 15, 2013, eff. Aug. 31, 2013.

Rule 500.7. Exclusion of Witnesses

The court must, on a party's request, or may, on its own initiative, order witnesses excluded so that they cannot hear the testimony of other witnesses. This rule does not authorize the exclusion of:

(a) a party who is a natural person or the spouse of such natural person;

(b) an officer or employee designated as a representative of a party who is not a natural person; or

(c) a person whose presence is shown by a party to be essential to the presentation of the party's case.

Adopted by order of April 15, 2013, eff. Aug. 31, 2013.

Rule 500.8. Subpoenas

(a) *Use.* A subpoena may be used by a party or the judge to command a person or entity to attend and give testimony at a hearing or trial. A person may not be required by subpoena to appear in a county that is more than 150 miles from where the person resides or is served.

(b) *Who Can Issue.* A subpoena may be issued by the clerk of the justice court or an attorney authorized to practice in the State of Texas, as an officer of the court.

(c) *Form.* Every subpoena must be issued in the name of the "State of Texas" and must:

(1) state the style of the suit and its case number;

(2) state the court in which the suit is pending;

(3) state the date on which the subpoena is issued;

(4) identify the person to whom the subpoena is directed;

(5) state the date, time, place, and nature of the action required by the person to whom the subpoena is directed;

(6) identify the party at whose instance the subpoena is issued, and the party's attorney of record, if any;

(7) state that "Failure by any person without adequate excuse to obey a subpoena served upon that person may be deemed a contempt of court from which the subpoena is issued and may be punished by fine or confinement, or both"; and

(8) be signed by the person issuing the subpoena.

(d) *Service: Where, By Whom, How.* A subpoena may be served at any place within the State of Texas by any sheriff or constable of the State of Texas, or by any person who is not a party and is 18 years of age or older. A subpoena must be served by delivering a copy to the witness and tendering to that person any fees required by law. If the witness is a party and is represented by an attorney of record in the proceeding, the subpoena may be served on the witness's attorney of record. Proof of service must be made by filing either:

(1) the witness's signed written memorandum attached to the subpoena showing that the witness accepted the subpoena; or

(2) a statement by the person who made the service stating the date, time, and manner of service, and the name of the person served.

(e) *Compliance Required.* A person commanded by subpoena to appear and give testimony must remain at the hearing or trial from day to day until discharged by the court or by the party summoning the witness. If a subpoena commanding testimony is directed to a corporation, partnership, association, governmental agency, or other organization, and the matters on which examination is requested are described with reasonable particularity, the organization must designate one or more persons to testify on its behalf as to matters known or reasonably available to the organization.

(f) *Objection.* A person commanded to attend and give testimony at a hearing or trial may object or move for a protective order before the court at or before the time and place specified for compliance. A party causing a subpoena to issue must take reasonable steps to avoid imposing undue burden or expense on the person served. In ruling on objections or motions for protection, the court must provide a person served with a subpoena an adequate time for compliance and protection from undue burden or expense. The court may impose reasonable conditions on compliance with a subpoena, including compensating the witness for undue hardship.

(g) *Enforcement.* Failure by any person without adequate excuse to obey a subpoena served upon that person may be deemed a contempt of the court from which the subpoena is issued or of a district court in the county in which the subpoena is served, and may be punished by fine or confinement, or both. A fine may not be imposed, nor a person served with a subpoena attached, for failure to comply with a subpoena without proof of service and proof by affidavit of the party requesting the subpoena or the party's attorney of record that all fees due the witness by law were paid or tendered.

Adopted by order of April 15, 2013, eff. Aug. 31, 2013.

Rule 500.9. Discovery

(a) *Pretrial Discovery.* Pretrial discovery is limited to that which the judge considers reasonable and necessary. Any requests for pretrial discovery must be presented to the court for approval by written motion. The motion must be served on the responding party. Unless a hearing is requested, the judge may rule on the motion without a hearing. The discovery request must not be served on the responding party unless the judge issues a signed order approving the request. Failure to comply with a discovery order can result in sanctions, including dismissal of the case or an order to pay the other party's discovery expenses.

(b) *Post-judgment Discovery.* Post-judgment discovery is not required to be filed with the court. The party requesting discovery must give the responding party at least 30 days to respond to a post-judgment discovery request. The responding party may file a written objection with the court within 30 days of receiving the request. If an objection is filed, the judge must hold a hearing to determine if the request is valid. If the objection is denied, the judge must order the party to respond to the request. If the objection is upheld, the judge may reform the request or dismiss it entirely.

Adopted by order of April 15, 2013, eff. Aug. 31, 2013.

Rule 501. Citation and Service

Rule 501.1. Citation

(a) *Issuance.* When a petition is filed with a justice court to initiate a suit, the clerk must promptly issue a citation and deliver the citation as directed by the plaintiff. The plaintiff is responsible for obtaining service on the defendant of the citation and a copy of the petition with any documents filed with the petition. Upon request, separate or additional citations must be issued by the clerk. The clerk must retain a copy of the citation in the court's file.

(b) *Form.* The citation must:

(1) be styled "The State of Texas";

(2) be signed by the clerk under seal of court or by the judge;

(3) contain the name, location, and address of the court;

(4) show the date of filing of the petition;

(5) show the date of issuance of the citation;

(6) show the file number and names of parties;

(7) be directed to the defendant;

(8) show the name and address of attorney for plaintiff, or if the plaintiff does not have an attorney, the address of plaintiff; and

(9) notify defendant that if the defendant fails to file an answer, judgment by default may be rendered for the relief demanded in the petition.

(c) *Notice.* The citation must include the following notice to the defendant in boldface type: "You have been sued. You may employ an attorney to help you in defending against this lawsuit. But you are not required to employ an attorney. You or your attorney must file an answer with the court. Your answer is due by the end of the 14th day after the day you were served with these papers. If the 14th day is a Saturday, Sunday, or legal holiday, your answer is due by the end of the first day following the 14th day that is not a Saturday, Sunday, or legal holiday. Do not ignore these papers. If you do not file an answer by the due date, a default judgment may be taken against you. For further information, consult Part V of the Texas Rules of Civil Procedure, which is available online and also at the court listed on this citation."

(d) *Copies.* The plaintiff must provide enough copies to be served on each defendant. If the plaintiff fails to do so, the clerk may make copies and charge the plaintiff the allowable copying cost.

Adopted by order of April 15, 2013, eff. Aug. 31, 2013.

Rule 501.2. Service of Citation

(a) *Who May Serve.* No person who is a party to or interested in the outcome of the suit may serve citation in that suit, and, unless otherwise authorized by written court order, only a sheriff or constable may serve a citation in an eviction case, a writ that requires the actual taking of possession of a person, property or thing, or process requiring that an enforcement action be physically enforced by the person delivering the process. Other citations may be served by:

(1) a sheriff or constable;

(2) a process server certified under order of the Supreme Court;

(3) the clerk of the court, if the citation is served by registered or certified mail; or

(4) a person authorized by court order who is 18 years of age or older.

(b) *Method of Service.* Citation must be served by:

(1) delivering a copy of the citation with a copy of the petition attached to the defendant in person, after endorsing the date of delivery on the citation; or

(2) mailing a copy of the citation with a copy of the petition attached to the defendant by registered or certified mail, restricted delivery, with return receipt or electronic return receipt requested.

(c) *Service Fees.* A plaintiff must pay all fees for service unless the plaintiff has filed a sworn statement of inability to pay the fees with the court. If the plaintiff has filed a sworn statement of inability to pay, the plaintiff must arrange for the citation to be served by a sheriff, constable, or court clerk.

(d) *Service on Sunday* A citation cannot be served on a Sunday except in attachment, garnishment, sequestration, or distress proceedings.

(e) *Alternative Service of Citation.* If the methods under (b) are insufficient to serve the defendant, the plaintiff, or the constable, sheriff, process server certified under order of the Supreme Court, or other person authorized to serve process, may make a request for alternative service. This request must include a sworn statement describing the methods attempted under (b) and stating the defendant's usual place of business or residence, or other place where the defendant can probably be found. The court may authorize the following types of alternative service:

(1) mailing a copy of the citation with a copy of the petition attached by first class mail to the defendant at a specified address, and also leaving a copy of the citation with petition attached at the defendant's residence or other place where the defendant can probably be found with any person found there who is at least 16 years of age; or

(2) mailing a copy of the citation with a copy of the petition attached by first class mail to the defendant at a specified address, and also serving by any other method that the court finds is reasonably likely to provide the defendant with notice of the suit.

(f) *Service by Publication.* In the event that service of citation by publication is necessary, the process is governed by the rules in county and district court.

Adopted by order of April 15, 2013, eff. Aug. 31, 2013.

Rule 501.3. Duties of Officer or Person Receiving Citation; Return of Service

(a) *Endorsement; Execution; Return.* The officer or authorized person to whom process is delivered must:

(1) endorse on the process the date and hour on which he or she received it;

(2) execute and return the same without delay; and

(3) complete a return of service, which may, but need not, be endorsed on or attached to the citation.

(b) *Contents of Return.* The return, together with any document to which it is attached, must include the following information:

(1) the case number and case name;

(2) the court in which the case is filed;

(3) a description of what was served;

(4) the date and time the process was received for service;

(5) the person or entity served;

(6) the address served;

(7) the date of service or attempted service;

(8) the manner of delivery of service or attempted service;

(9) the name of the person who served or attempted service;

(10) if the person named in (9) is a process server certified under Supreme Court Order, his or her identification number and the expiration date of his or her certification; and

(11) any other information required by rule or law.

(c) *Citation by Mail.* When the citation is served by registered or certified mail as authorized by Rule 501.2(b)(2), the return by the officer or authorized person must also contain the receipt with the addressee's signature.

(d) *Failure to Serve.* When the officer or authorized person has not served the citation, the return must show the diligence used by the officer or authorized person to execute the same and the cause of failure to execute it, and where the defendant is to be found, if ascertainable.

(e) *Signature.* The officer or authorized person who serves or attempts to serve a citation must sign the return. If the return is signed by a person other than a sheriff, constable, or clerk of the court, the return must either be verified or be signed under penalty of perjury. A return signed under penalty of perjury must contain the statement below in substantially the following form:

"My name is (First) (Middle) (Last), my date of birth is (Month) (Day), (Year), and my address is (Street), (City), (State) (Zip Code), (Country). I declare under penalty of perjury that the foregoing is true and correct.

Executed in ________ County, State of ________, on the ___ day of (Month), (Year).

____

Declarant"

(f) *Alternative Service.* Where citation is executed by an alternative method as authorized by 501.2(e), proof of service must be made in the manner ordered by the court.

(g) *Filing Return.* The return and any document to which it is attached must be filed with the court and may be filed electronically or by fax, if those methods of filing are available.

(h) *Prerequisite for Default Judgment.* No default judgment may be granted in any case until proof of service as provided by this rule, or as ordered by the court in the event citation is executed by an alternative method under 501.2(e), has been on file with the clerk of the court 3 days, exclusive of the day of filing and the day of judgment.

Adopted by order of April 15, 2013, eff. Aug. 31, 2013.

Rule 501.4. Service of Papers Other Than Citation

(a) *Method of Service.* Other than a citation or oral motions made during trial or when all parties are present, every notice required by these rules, and every pleading, plea, motion, application to the court for an order, or other form of request, must be served on all other parties in one of the following ways:

(1) In person. A copy may be delivered to the party to be served, or the party's duly authorized agent or attorney of record, in person or by agent.

(2) Mail or courier. A copy may be sent by courier-receipted delivery or by certified or registered mail, to the party's last known address. Service by certified or registered mail is complete when the document is properly addressed and deposited in the United States mail, postage prepaid.

(3) Fax. A copy may be faxed to the recipient's current fax number. Service by fax after 5:00 p.m. local time of the recipient will be deemed to have been served on the following day.

(4) Email. A copy may be sent to an email address expressly provided by the receiving party, if the party has consented to email service in writing. Service by email after 5:00 p.m. local time of the recipient will be deemed to have been served on the following day.

(5) Other. A copy may be delivered in any other manner directed by the court.

(b) *Timing.* If a document is served by mail, 3 days will be added to the length of time a party has to respond to the document. Notice of any hearing requested by a party must be served on all other parties not less than 3 days before the time specified for the hearing.

(c) *Who May Serve.* Documents other than a citation may be served by a party to the suit, an attorney of record, a sheriff or constable, or by any other person competent to testify.

(d) *Certificate of Service.* The party or the party's attorney of record must include in writing on all documents filed a signed statement describing the manner in which the document was served on the other party or parties and the date of service. A certificate by a party or the party's attorney of record, or the return of the officer, or the sworn statement of any other person showing service of a notice is proof of service.

(e) *Failure to Serve.* A party may offer evidence or testimony that a notice or document was not received, or, if service was by mail, that it was not received within 3 days from the date of mailing, and upon so finding, the court may extend the time for taking the action required of the party or grant other relief as it deems just.

Adopted by order of April 15, 2013, eff. Aug. 31, 2013.

Rule 502. Institution of Suit

Rule 502.1. Pleadings and Motions must be Written, Signed, and Filed

Except for oral motions made during trial or when all parties are present, every pleading, plea, motion, application to the court for an order, or other form of request must be written and signed by the party or its attorney and must be filed with the court. A document may be filed with the court by personal or commercial delivery, by mail, or electronically, if the court allows electronic filing. Electronic filing is governed by Rule 21.

Adopted by order of April 15, 2013, eff. Aug. 31, 2013. Amended by order of Dec. 11, 2013, eff. Jan. 1, 2014.

Historical Notes

2013 Amendment

The order dated December 11, 2013 added "Electronic filing is governed by Rule 21.".

Rule 502.2. Petition

(a) *Contents.* To initiate a lawsuit, a petition must be filed with the court. A petition must contain:

(1) the name of the plaintiff;

(2) the name, address, telephone number, and fax number, if any, of the plaintiffs attorney, if applicable, or the address, telephone number, and fax number, if any, of the plaintiff;

(3) the name, address, and telephone number, if known, of the defendant;

(4) the amount of money, if any, the plaintiff seeks;

(5) a description and claimed value of any personal property the plaintiff seeks;

(6) a description of any other relief reqested [1];

(7) the basis for the plaintiff's claim against the defendant; and

(8) if the plaintiff consents to email service of the answer and any other motions or pleadings, a statement consenting to email service and email contact information.

(b) *Justice Court Civil Case Information Sheet.* A justice court civil case information sheet, in the form promulgated by the Supreme Court of Texas, must accompany the filing of a petition and must be signed by the plaintiff or the plaintiff's attorney.[2] The justice court civil case information sheet is for data collection for statistical and administrative purposes and does not affect any substantive right. The court may not reject a pleading because the pleading is not accompanied by a justice court civil case information sheet.

Adopted by order of April 15, 2013, eff. Aug. 31, 2013.

1 So in original.

2 See Appendix to Rules of Civil Procedure for form.

Rule 502.3. Fees; Inability to Pay

(a) *Fees and Statement of Inability to Pay.* On filing the petition, the plaintiff must pay the appropriate filing fee and service fees, if any, with the court. A plaintiff who is unable to afford to pay the fees must file a sworn statement of inability to pay. Upon filing the statement, the clerk must docket the action, issue citation, and provide any other customary services.

(b) *Contents of Statement of Inability to Pay.*

(1) The statement must contain complete information as to the party's identity, nature and amount of governmental entitlement income, nature and amount of employment income, other income (interest, dividends, etc.), spouse's income if available to the party, property owned (other than homestead), cash or checking account, dependents, debts, and monthly expenses.

(2) The statement must contain the following: "I am unable to pay court fees. I verify that the statements made in this statement are true and correct." The statement must be sworn before a notary public or other officer authorized to administer oaths or be signed under penalty of perjury.

(c) *IOLTA Certificate.* If the party is represented by an attorney who is providing free legal services because of the party's indigence, without contingency, and the attorney is providing services either directly or by referral from a program funded by the Interest on Lawyers Trust Accounts (IOLTA) program, the attorney may file an IOLTA certificate confirming that the IOLTA funded program screened the party for income eligibility under the IOLTA income guidelines. A party's statement of inability to pay accompanied by an attorney's IOLTA certificate may not be contested under (d).

(d) *Contest.* Unless an IOLTA certificate is filed, the defendant may file a contest of the statement of inability to pay at any time within 7 days after the day the defendant's answer is due. If the statement attests to receipt of government entitlement based on indigence, the statement may only be contested with regard to the veracity of the attestation. If contested, the judge must hold a hearing to determine the plaintiff's ability to pay. At the hearing, the burden is on the party who filed the statement to prove its inability to pay. The judge may, regardless of whether the defendant contests the statement, examine the statement and conduct a hearing to determine the plaintiff's ability to pay. If the judge determines that the plaintiff is able to afford the fees, the judge must enter a written order listing the reasons for the determination, and the plaintiff must pay the fees in the time specified in the order or the case will be dismissed without prejudice.

Adopted by order of April 15, 2013, eff. Aug. 31, 2013.

Rule 502.4. Venue—Where a Lawsuit May Be Brought

(a) *Applicable Law.* Laws specifying the venue—the county and precinct where a lawsuit may be brought—are found in Chapter 15, Subchapter E of the Texas Civil Practice and Remedies Code, which is available online and for examination during the court's business hours.

(b) *General Rule.* Generally, a defendant in a small claims case as described in Rule 500.3(a) or a debt claim case as described in Rule 500.3(b) is entitled to be sued in one of the following venues:

(1) the county and precinct where the defendant resides;

(2) the county and precinct where the incident, or the majority of incidents, that gave rise to the claim occurred;

(3) the county and precinct where the contract or agreement, if any, that gave rise to the claim was to be performed; or

(4) the county and precinct where the property is located, in a suit to recover personal property.

(c) *Non–Resident Defendant; Defendant's Residence Unknown.* If the defendant is a non-resident of Texas, or if defendant's residence is unknown, the plaintiff may file the suit in the county and precinct where the plaintiff resides.

(d) *Motion to Transfer Venue.* If a plaintiff files suit in an improper venue, a defendant may challenge the venue selected by filing a motion to transfer venue. The motion must be filed before trial, no later than 21 days after the day the defendant's answer is filed, and must contain a sworn statement that the venue chosen by the plaintiff is improper and a specific county and precinct of proper venue to which transfer is sought. If the defendant fails to name a county and precinct, the court must instruct the defendant to do so and allow the defendant 7 days to cure the defect. If the defendant fails to correct the defect, the motion will be denied, and the case will proceed in the county and precinct where it was originally filed.

(1) *Procedure.*

(A) Judge to Set Hearing. If a defendant files a motion to transfer venue, the judge must set a hearing on the motion.

(B) Response. A plaintiff may file a response to a defendant's motion to transfer venue.

(C) Hearing. The parties may present evidence at the hearing. A witness may testify at a hearing, either in person or, with permission of the court, by means of telephone or an electronic communication system.

(D) Judge's Decision. If the motion is granted, the judge must sign an order designating the court to which the case will be transferred. If the motion is denied, the case will be heard in the court in which the plaintiff initially filed suit.

(E) Review. Motions for rehearing and interlocutory appeals of the judge's ruling on venue are not permitted.

(F) Time for Trial of the Case. No trial may be held until at least the 14th day after the judge's ruling on the motion to transfer venue.

(G) Order. An order granting a motion to transfer venue must state the reason for the transfer and the name of the court to which the transfer is made. When such an order of transfer is made, the judge who issued the order must immediately make out a true and correct transcript of all the entries made on the docket in the case, certify the transcript, and send the transcript, with a certified copy of the bill of costs and the original papers in the case, to the court in the precinct to which the case has been transferred. The court receiving the case must then notify the plaintiff that the case has been received and, if the case is transferred to a different county, that the plaintiff has 14 days after receiving the notice to pay the filing fee in the new court, or file a sworn statement of inability to pay. The plaintiff is not entitled to a refund of any fees already paid. Failure to pay the fee or file a sworn statement of inability to pay will result in dismissal of the case without prejudice.

(e) *Fair Trial Venue Change.* If a party believes it cannot get a fair trial in a specific precinct or before a specific judge, the party may file a sworn motion stating such, supported by the sworn statements of two other credible persons, and specifying if the party is requesting a change of location or a change of judge. Except for good cause shown, this motion must be filed no less than 7 days before trial. If the party seeks a change of judge, the judge must exchange benches with another qualified justice of the peace, or if no judge is available to exchange benches, the county judge must appoint a visiting judge to hear the case. If the party seeks a change in location, the case must be transferred to the nearest justice court in the county that is not subject to the same or some other disqualification. If there is only one justice of the peace precinct in the county, then the judge must exchange benches with another qualified justice of the peace, or if no judge is available to exchange benches, the county judge must appoint a visiting judge to hear the case. In cases where exclusive jurisdiction is within a specific precinct, as in eviction cases, the only remedy available is a change of judge. A party may apply for relief under this rule only one time in any given lawsuit.

(f) *Transfer of Venue by Consent.* On the written consent of all parties or their attorneys, filed with the court, venue must be transferred to the court of any

other justice of the peace of the county, or any other county.
Adopted by order of April 15, 2013, eff. Aug. 31, 2013.

Rule 502.5. Answer

(a) *Requirements.* A defendant must file with the court a written answer to a lawsuit as directed by the citation and must also serve a copy of the answer on the plaintiff. The answer must contain:

(1) the name of the defendant;

(2) the name, address, telephone number, and fax number, if any, of the defendant's attorney, if applicable, or the address, telephone number, and fax number, if any, of the defendant; and

(3) if the defendant consents to email service, a statement consenting to email service and email contact information.

(b) *General Denial.* An answer that denies all of the plaintiff's allegations without specifying the reasons is sufficient to constitute an answer or appearance and does not bar the defendant from raising any defense at trial.

(c) *Answer Docketed.* The defendant's appearance must be noted on the court's docket.

(d) *Due Date.* Unless the defendant is served by publication, the defendant's answer is due by the end of the 14th day after the day the defendant was served with the citation and petition, but

(1) if the 14th day is a Saturday, Sunday, or legal holiday, the answer is due on the next day that is not a Saturday, Sunday, or legal holiday; and

(2) if the 14th day falls on a day during which the court is closed before 5:00 p.m., the answer is due on the court's next business day.

(e) *Due Date When Defendant Served by Publication.* If a defendant is served by publication, the defendant's answer is due by the end of the 42nd day after the day the citation was issued, but

(1) if the 42nd day is a Saturday, Sunday, or legal holiday, the answer is due on the next day that is not a Saturday, Sunday, or legal holiday; and

(2) if the 42nd day falls on a day during which the court is closed before 5:00 p.m., the answer is due on the court's next business day.

Adopted by order of April 15, 2013, eff. Aug. 31, 2013.

Rule 502.6. Counterclaim; Cross–Claim; Third Party Claim

(a) *Counterclaim.* A defendant may file a petition stating as a counterclaim any claim against a plaintiff that is within the jurisdiction of the justice court, whether or not related to the claims in the plaintiff's petition. The defendant must file a counterclaim petition as provided in Rule 502.2, and must pay a filing fee or provide a sworn statement of inability to pay the fees. The court need not generate a citation for a counterclaim and no answer to the counterclaim need be filed. The defendant must serve a copy of the counterclaim as provided by Rule 501. 4.

(b) *Cross–Claim.* A plaintiff seeking relief against another plaintiff, or a defendant seeking relief against another defendant may file a cross-claim. The filing party must file a cross-claim petition as provided in Rule 502.2, and must pay a filing fee or provide a sworn statement of inability to pay the fees. A citation must be issued and served as provided by Rule 501.2 on any party that has not yet filed a petition or an answer, as appropriate. If the party filed against has filed a petition or an answer, the filing party must serve the cross-claim as provided by Rule 501.4.

(c) *Third Party Claim.* A defendant seeking to bring another party into a lawsuit who may be liable for all or part of the plaintiff's claim against the defendant may file a petition as provided in Rule 502.2, and must pay a filing fee or provide a sworn statement of inability to pay the fees. A citation must be issued and served as provided by Rule 501.2.
Adopted by order of April 15, 2013, eff. Aug. 31, 2013.

Rule 502.7. Amending and Clarifying Pleadings

(a) *Amending Pleadings.* A party may withdraw something from or add something to a pleading, as long as the amended pleading is filed and served as provided by Rule 501.4 not less than 7 days before trial. The court may allow a pleading to be amended less than 7 days before trial if the amendment will not operate as a surprise to the opposing party.

(b) *Insufficient Pleadings.* A party may file a motion with the court asking that another party be required to clarify a pleading. The court must determine if the pleading is sufficient to place all parties on notice of the issues in the lawsuit, and may hold a hearing to make that determination. If the court determines a pleading is insufficient, the court must order the party to amend the pleading and set a date by which the party must amend. If a party fails to comply with the court's order, the pleading may be stricken.
Adopted by order of April 15, 2013, eff. Aug. 31, 2013.

Rule 503. Default Judgment; Pre–Trial Matters; Trial

Rule 503.1. If Defendant Fails to Answer

(a) *Default Judgment.* If the defendant fails to file an answer by the date stated in Rule 502.5, the judge must ensure that service was proper, and may hold a hearing for this purpose. If it is determined that service was proper, the judge must render a default judgment in the following manner:

(1) *Claim Based on Written Document.* If the claim is based on a written document signed by the defendant, and a copy of the document has been filed with the court and served on the defendant, along with a sworn statement from the plaintiff that this is a true and accurate copy of the document and the relief sought is owed, and all payments, offsets or credits due to the defendant have been accounted for, the judge must render judgment for the plaintiff in the requested amount, without any necessity for a hearing. The plaintiff's attorney may also submit affidavits supporting an award of attorney fees to which the plaintiff is entitled, if any.

(2) *Other Cases.* Except as provided in (1), a plaintiff who seeks a default judgment against a defendant must request a hearing, orally or in writing. The plaintiff must appear at the hearing and provide evidence of its damages. If the plaintiff proves its damages, the judge must render judgment for the plaintiff in the amount proven. If the plaintiff is unable to prove its damages, the judge must render judgment in favor of the defendant. With the permission of the court, a party may appear at a hearing by means of telephone or an electronic communication system.

(b) *Appearance.* If a defendant files an answer or otherwise appears in a case before a default judgment is signed by the judge, the judge must not enter a default judgment and the case must be set for trial as described in Rule 503.3.

(c) *Post–Answer Default.* If a defendant who has answered fails to appear for trial, the court may proceed to hear evidence on liability and damages and render judgment accordingly.

(d) *Notice.* The plaintiff requesting a default judgment must provide to the clerk in writing the last known mailing address of the defendant at or before the time the judgment is signed. When a default judgment is signed, the clerk must immediately mail written notice of the judgment to the defendant at the address provided by the plaintiff, and note the fact of such mailing on the docket. The notice must state the number and style of the case, the court in which the case is pending, the names of the parties in whose favor and against whom the judgment was rendered, and the date the judgment was signed. Failure to comply with the provisions of this rule does not affect the finality of the judgment.

Adopted by order of April 15, 2013, eff. Aug. 31, 2013.

Rule 503.2. Summary Disposition

(a) *Motion.* A party may file a sworn motion for summary disposition of all or part of a claim or defense without a trial. The motion must set out all supporting facts. All documents on which the motion relies must be attached. The motion must be granted if it shows that:

(1) there are no genuinely disputed facts that would prevent a judgment in favor of the party;

(2) there is no evidence of one or more essential elements of a defense which the defendant must prove to defeat the plaintiff's claim; or

(3) there is no evidence of one or more essential elements of the plaintiff's claim.

(b) *Response.* The party opposing the motion may file a sworn written response to the motion.

(c) *Hearing.* The court must not consider a motion for summary disposition until it has been on file for at least 14 days. The judge may consider evidence offered by the parties at the hearing. By agreement of the parties, the judge may decide the motion and response without a hearing.

(d) *Order.* The judge may enter judgment as to the entire case or may specify the facts that are established and direct such further proceedings in the case as are just.

Adopted by order of April 15, 2013, eff. Aug. 31, 2013.

Rule 503.3. Settings and Notice; Postponing Trial

(a) *Settings and Notice.* After the defendant answers, the case will be set on a trial docket at the discretion of the judge. The court must send a notice of the date, time, and place of this setting to all parties at their address of record no less than 45 days before the setting date, unless the judge determines that an earlier setting is required in the interest of justice. Reasonable notice of all subsequent settings must be sent to all parties at their addresses of record.

(b) *Postponing Trial.* A party may file a motion requesting that the trial be postponed. The motion must state why a postponement is necessary. The judge, for good cause, may postpone any trial for a reasonable time.

Adopted by order of April 15, 2013, eff. Aug. 31, 2013.

Rule 503.4. Pretrial Conference

(a) *Conference Set; Issues.* If all parties have appeared in a lawsuit, the court, at any party's request or on its own, may set a case for a pretrial conference.

Reasonable notice must be sent to all parties at their addresses of record. Appropriate issues for the pretrial conference include:

(1) discovery;

(2) the amendment or clarification of pleadings;

(3) the admission of facts and documents to streamline the trial process;

(4) a limitation on the number of witnesses at trial;

(5) the identification of facts, if any, which are not in dispute between the parties;

(6) mediation or other alternative dispute resolution services;

(7) the possibility of settlement;

(8) trial setting dates that are amenable to the court and all parties;

(9) the appointment of interpreters, if needed;

(10) the application of a Rule of Civil Procedure not in Part V or a Rule of Evidence; and

(11) any other issue that the court deems appropriate.

(b) *Eviction Cases.* The court must not schedule a pretrial conference in an eviction case if it would delay trial.

Adopted by order of April 15, 2013, eff. Aug. 31, 2013.

Rule 503.5. Alternative Dispute Resolution

(a) *State Policy.* The policy of this state is to encourage the peaceable resolution of disputes through alternative dispute resolution, including mediation, and the early settlement of pending litigation through voluntary settlement procedures. For that purpose, the judge may order any case to mediation or another appropriate and generally accepted alternative dispute resolution process.

(b) *Eviction Cases.* The court must not order mediation or any other alternative dispute resolution process in an eviction case if it would delay trial.

Adopted by order of April 15, 2013, eff. Aug. 31, 2013.

Rule 503.6. Trial

(a) *Docket Called.* On the day of the trial setting, the judge must call all of the cases set for trial that day.

(b) *If Plaintiff Fails to Appear.* If the plaintiff fails to appear when the case is called for trial, the judge may postpone or dismiss the suit.

(c) *If Defendant Fails to Appear.* If the defendant fails to appear when the case is called for trial, the judge may postpone the case, or may proceed to take evidence. If the plaintiff proves its case, judgment must be awarded for the relief proven. If the plaintiff fails to prove its case, judgment must be rendered against the plaintiff.

Adopted by order of April 15, 2013, eff. Aug. 31, 2013.

Rule 504. Jury

Rule 504.1. Jury Trial Demanded

(a) *Demand.* Any party is entitled to a trial by jury. A written demand for a jury must be filed no later than 14 days before the date a case is set for trial. If the demand is not timely, the right to a jury is waived unless the late filing is excused by the judge for good cause.

(b) *Jury Fee.* Unless otherwise provided by law, a party demanding a jury must pay a fee of $22.00 or must file a sworn statement of inability to pay the fee at or before the time the party files a written request for a jury.

(c) *Withdrawal of Demand.* If a party who demands a jury and pays the fee withdraws the demand, the case will remain on the jury docket unless all other parties present agree to try the case without a jury. A party that withdraws its jury demand is not entitled to a refund of the jury fee.

(d) *No Demand.* If no party timely demands a jury and pays the fee, the judge will try the case without a jury.

Adopted by order of April 15, 2013, eff. Aug. 31, 2013.

Rule 504.2. Empaneling the Jury

(a) *Drawing Jury and Oath.* If no method of electronic draw has been implemented, the judge must write the names of all prospective jurors present on separate slips of paper as nearly alike as may be, place them in a box, mix them well, and then draw the names one by one from the box. The judge must list the names drawn and deliver a copy to each of the parties or their attorneys.

(b) *Oath.* After the draw, the judge must swear the panel as follows: "You solemnly swear or affirm that you will give true and correct answers to all questions asked of you concerning your qualifications as a juror."

(c) *Questioning the Jury.* The judge, the parties, or their attorneys will be allowed to question jurors as to their ability to serve impartially in the trial but may not ask the jurors how they will rule in the case. The judge will have discretion to allow or disallow specific questions and determine the amount of time each side will have for this process.

(d) *Challenge for Cause.* A party may challenge any juror for cause. A challenge for cause is an objection made to a juror alleging some fact, such as a bias or prejudice, that disqualifies the juror from serving in the case or that renders the juror unfit to sit on the jury. The challenge must be made during jury questioning. The party must explain to the judge why the juror should be excluded from the jury. The judge must evaluate the questions and answers given and either grant or deny the challenge. When a challenge for cause has been sustained, the juror must be excused.

(e) *Challenges Not for Cause.* After the judge determines any challenges for cause, each party may select up to 3 jurors to excuse for any reason or no reason at all. But no prospective juror may be excused for membership in a constitutionally protected class.

(f) *The Jury.* After all challenges, the first 6 prospective jurors remaining on the list constitute the jury to try the case.

(g) *If Jury Is Incomplete.* If challenges reduce the number of prospective jurors below 6, the judge may direct the sheriff or constable to summon others and allow them to be questioned and challenged by the parties as before, until at least 6 remain.

(h) *Jury Sworn.* When the jury has been selected, the judge must require them to take substantially the following oath: "You solemnly swear or affirm that you will render a true verdict according to the law and the evidence presented."

Adopted by order of April 15, 2013, eff. Aug. 31, 2013.

Rule 504.3. Jury Not Charged

The judge must not charge the jury.

Adopted by order of April 15, 2013, eff. Aug. 31, 2013.

Rule 504.4. Jury Verdict for Specific Articles

When the suit is for the recovery of specific articles and the jury finds for the plaintiff, the jury must assess the value of each article separately, according to the evidence presented at trial.

Adopted by order of April 15, 2013, eff. Aug. 31, 2013.

Rule 505. Judgment; New Trial

Rule 505.1. Judgment

(a) *Judgment Upon Jury Verdict.* Where a jury has returned a verdict, the judge must announce the verdict in open court, note it in the court's docket, and render judgment accordingly. The judge may render judgment on the verdict or, if the verdict is contrary to the law or the evidence, judgment notwithstanding the verdict.

(b) *Case Tried by Judge.* When a case has been tried before the judge without a jury, the judge must announce the decision in open court, note the decision in the court's docket, and render judgment accordingly.

(c) *Form.* A judgment must:

(1) clearly state the determination of the rights of the parties in the case;

(2) state who must pay the costs;

(3) be signed by the judge; and

(4) be dated the date of the judge's signature.

(d) *Costs.* The judge must award costs allowed by law to the successful party.

(e) *Judgment for Specific Articles.* Where the judgment is for the recovery of specific articles, the judgment must order that the plaintiff recover such specific articles, if they can be found, and if not, then their value as assessed by the judge or jury with interest at the prevailing post-judgment interest rate.

Adopted by order of April 15, 2013, eff. Aug. 31, 2013.

Rule 505.2. Enforcement of Judgment

Justice court judgments are enforceable in the same method as in county and district court, except as provided by law. When the judgment is for personal property, the court may award a special writ for the seizure and delivery of such property to the plaintiff, and may, in addition to the other relief granted in such cases, enforce its judgment by attachment or fine.

Adopted by order of April 15, 2013, eff. Aug. 31, 2013.

Rule 505.3. Motion to Set Aside; Motion to Reinstate; Motion for New Trial

(a) *Motion to Reinstate after Dismissal.* A plaintiff whose case is dismissed may file a motion to reinstate the case no later than 14 days after the dismissal order is signed. The plaintiff must serve the defendant with a copy of the motion no later than the next business day using a method approved under Rule 501.4. The court may reinstate the case for good cause shown.

(b) *Motion to Set Aside Default.* A defendant against whom a default judgment is granted may file a motion to set aside the judgment no later than 14 days after the judgment is signed. The defendant must serve the plaintiff with a copy of the motion no later than the next business day using a method approved under Rule 501.4. The court may set aside the judgment and set the case for trial for good cause shown.

(c) *Motion for New Trial.* A party may file a motion for a new trial no later than 14 days after the judgment is signed. The party must serve all other parties with a copy of the motion no later than the next business day using a method approved under Rule 501.4. The judge may grant a new trial upon a showing that justice was not done in the trial of the case. Only one new trial may be granted to either party.

(d) *Motion Not Required.* Failure to file a motion under this rule does not affect a party's right to appeal the underlying judgment.

(e) *Motion Denied as a Matter of Law.* If the judge has not ruled on a motion to set aside, motion to reinstate, or motion for new trial, the motion is automatically denied at 5:00 p.m. on the 21st day after the day the judgment was signed.

Adopted by order of April 15, 2013, eff. Aug. 31, 2013.

Rule 506. Appeal

Rule 506.1. Appeal

(a) *How Taken; Time.* A party may appeal a judgment by filing a bond, making a cash deposit, or filing a sworn statement of inability to pay with the justice court within 21 days after the judgment is signed or the motion to reinstate, motion to set aside, or motion for new trial, if any, is denied.

(b) *Amount of Bond; Sureties; Terms.* A plaintiff must file a $500 bond. A defendant must file a bond in an amount equal to twice the amount of the judgment. The bond must be supported by a surety or sureties approved by the judge. The bond must be payable to the appellee and must be conditioned on the appellant's prosecution of its appeal to effect and payment of any judgment and all costs rendered against it on appeal.

(c) *Cash Deposit in Lieu of Bond.* In lieu of filing a bond, an appellant may deposit with the clerk of the court cash in the amount required of the bond. The deposit must be payable to the appellee and must be conditioned on the appellant's prosecution of its appeal to effect and payment of any judgment and all costs rendered against it on appeal.

(d) *Sworn Statement of Inability to Pay.*

(1) Filing. An appellant who cannot furnish a bond or pay a cash deposit in the amount required may instead file a sworn statement of inability to pay. The statement must meet the requirements of Rule 502.3(b) and may be the same one that was filed with the petition.

(2) Contest. The statement may be contested as provided in Rule 502.3(d) within 7 days after the opposing party receives notice that the statement was filed.

(3) Appeal If Contest Sustained. If the contest is sustained, the appellant may appeal that decision by filing notice with the justice court within 7 days of that court's written order. The justice court must then forward all related documents to the county court for resolution. The county court must set the matter for hearing within 14 days and hear the contest de novo, as if there had been no previous hearing, and if the appeal is granted, must direct the justice court to transmit to the clerk of the county court the transcript, records, and papers of the case, as provided in these rules.

(4) If No Appeal or If Appeal Overruled. If the appellant does not appeal the ruling sustaining the contest, or if the county court denies the appeal, the appellant may, within five days, post an appeal bond or make a cash deposit in compliance with this rule.

(e) *Notice to Other Parties Required.* If a statement of inability to pay is filed, the court must provide notice to all other parties that the statement was filed no later than the next business day. Within 7 days of filing a bond or making a cash deposit, an appellant must serve written notice of the appeal on all other parties using a method approved under Rule 501.4.

(f) *No Default on Appeal Without Compliance With Rule.* The county court to which an appeal is taken must not render default judgment against any party without first determining that the appellant has fully complied with this rule.

(g) *No Dismissal of Appeal Without Opportunity for Correction.* An appeal must not be dismissed for defects or irregularities in procedure, either of form or substance, without allowing the appellant, after 7 days' notice from the court, the opportunity to correct such defect.

(h) *Appeal Perfected.* An appeal is perfected when a bond, cash deposit, or statement of inability to pay is filed in accordance with this rule.

(i) *Costs.* The appellant must pay the costs on appeal to a county court in accordance with Rule 143a.

Adopted by order of April 15, 2013, eff. Aug. 31, 2013.

Rule 506.2. Record on Appeal

When an appeal has been perfected from the justice court, the judge must immediately send to the clerk of the county court a certified copy of all docket entries, a certified copy of the bill of costs, and the original papers in the case.

Adopted by order of April 15, 2013, eff. Aug. 31, 2013.

Rule 506.3. Trial De Novo

The case must be tried de novo in the county court. A trial de novo is a new trial in which the entire case is presented as if there had been no previous trial.
Adopted by order of April 15, 2013, eff. Aug. 31, 2013.

Rule 506.4. Writ of Certiorari

(a) *Application.* Except in eviction cases, after final judgment in a case tried in justice court, a party may apply to the county court for a writ of certiorari.

(b) *Grounds.* An application must be granted only if it contains a sworn statement setting forth facts showing that either:

(1) the justice court did not have jurisdiction; or

(2) the final determination of the suit worked an injustice to the applicant that was not caused by the applicant's own inexcusable neglect.

(c) *Bond, Cash Deposit, or Sworn Statement of Indigency to Pay Required.* If the application is granted, a writ of certiorari must not issue until the applicant has filed a bond, made a cash deposit, or filed a sworn statement of indigency that complies with Rule 145.

(d) *Time for Filing.* An application for writ of certiorari must be filed within 90 days after the date the final judgment is signed.

(e) *Contents of Writ.* The writ of certiorari must command the justice court to immediately make and certify a copy of the entries in the case on the docket, and immediately transmit the transcript of the proceedings in the justice court, together with the original papers and a bill of costs, to the proper court.

(f) *Clerk to Issue Writ and Citation.* When the application is granted and the bond, cash deposit, or sworn statement of indigency have been filed, the clerk must issue a writ of certiorari to the justice court and citation to the adverse party.

(g) *Stay of Proceedings.* When the writ of certiorari is served on the justice court, the court must stay further proceedings on the judgment and comply with the writ.

(h) *Cause Docketed.* The action must be docketed in the name of the original plaintiff, as plaintiff, and of the original defendant, as defendant.

(i) *Motion to Dismiss.* Within 30 days after the service of citation on the writ of certiorari, the adverse party may move to dismiss the certiorari for want of sufficient cause appearing in the affidavit, or for want of sufficient bond. If the certiorari is dismissed, the judgment must direct the justice court to proceed with the execution of the judgment below.

(j) *Amendment of Bond or Oath.* The affidavit or bond may be amended at the discretion of the court in which it is filed.

(k) *Trial De Novo.* The case must be tried de novo in the county court and judgment must be rendered as in cases appealed from justice courts. A trial de novo is a new trial in which the entire case is presented as if there had been no previous trial.
Adopted by order of April 15, 2013, eff. Aug. 31, 2013.

Rule 507. Administrative Rules for Judges and Court Personnel

Rule 507.1. Plenary Power

A justice court loses plenary power over a case when an appeal is perfected or if no appeal is perfected, 21 days after the later of the date judgment is signed or the date a motion to set aside, motion to reinstate, or motion for new trial, if any, is denied.
Adopted by order of April 15, 2013, eff. Aug. 31, 2013.

Rule 507.2. Forms

The court may provide forms to enable a party to file documents that comply with these rules. No party may be forced to use the court's forms.
Adopted by order of April 15, 2013, eff. Aug. 31, 2013.

Rule 507.3. Docket and Other Records

(a) *Docket.* Each judge must keep a civil docket in a permanent record containing the following information:

(1) the title of all suits commenced before the court;

(2) the date when the first process was issued against the defendant, when returnable, and the nature of that process;

(3) the date when the parties, or either of them, appeared before the court, either with or without a citation;

(4) a description of the petition and any documents filed with the petition;

(5) every adjournment, stating at whose request and to what time;

(6) the date of the trial, stating whether the same was by a jury or by the judge;

(7) the verdict of the jury, if any;

(8) the judgment signed by the judge and the date the judgment was signed;

(9) all applications for setting aside judgments or granting new trials and the orders of the judge thereon, with the date;

(10) the date of issuing execution, to whom directed and delivered, and the amount of debt, damages and costs and, when any execution is returned, the date of the return and the manner in which it was executed; and

(11) all stays and appeals that may be taken, and the date when taken, the amount of the bond and the names of the sureties.

(b) *Other Records.* The judge must also keep copies of all documents filed; other dockets, books, and records as may be required by law or these rules; and a fee book in which all costs accruing in every suit commenced before the court are taxed.

(c) *Form of Records.* All records required to be kept under this rule may be maintained electronically.

Adopted by order of April 15, 2013, eff. Aug. 31, 2013.

Rule 507.4. Issuance of Writs

Every writ from the justice courts must be in writing and be issued and signed by the judge officially. The style thereof must be "The State of Texas." It must, except where otherwise specially provided by law or these rules, be directed to the person or party upon whom it is to be served, be made returnable to the court, and note the date of its issuance.

Adopted by order of April 15, 2013, eff. Aug. 31, 2013.

Rule 508. Debt Claim Cases

Rule 508.1. Application

Rule 508 applies to a claim for the recovery of a debt brought by an assignee of a claim, a financial institution, a debt collector or collection agency, or a person or entity primarily engaged in the business of lending money at interest.

Adopted by order of April 15, 2013, eff. Aug. 31, 2013.

Rule 508.2. Petition

(a) *Contents.* In addition to the information required by Rule 502.2, a petition filed in a lawsuit governed by this rule must contain the following information:

(1) Credit Accounts. In a claim based upon a credit card, revolving credit, or open account, the petition must state:

(A) the account name or credit card name;

(B) the account number (which may be masked);

(C) the date of issue or origination of the account, if known;

(D) the date of charge-off or breach of the account, if known;

(E) the amount owed as of a date certain; and

(F) whether the plaintiff seeks ongoing interest.

(2) Personal and Business Loans. In a claim based upon a promissory note or other promise to pay a specific amount as of a date certain, the petition must state:

(A) the date and amount of the original loan;

(B) whether the repayment of the debt was accelerated, if known;

(C) the date final payment was due;

(D) the amount due as of the final payment date;

(E) the amount owed as of a date certain; and

(F) whether plaintiff seeks ongoing interest.

(3) Ongoing Interest. If a plaintiff seeks ongoing interest, the petition must state:

(A) the effective interest rate claimed;

(B) whether the interest rate is based upon contract or statute; and

(C) the dollar amount of interest claimed as of a date certain.

(4) Assigned Debt. If the debt that is the subject of the claim has been assigned or transferred, the petition must state:

(A) that the debt claim has been transferred or assigned;

(B) the date of the transfer or assignment;

(C) the name of any prior holders of the debt; and

(D) the name or a description of the original creditor.

Adopted by order of April 15, 2013, eff. Aug. 31, 2013.

Rule 508.3. Default Judgment

(a) *Generally.* If the defendant does not file an answer to a claim by the answer date or otherwise appear in the case, the judge must promptly render a default judgment upon the plaintiff's proof of the amount of damages.

(b) *Proof of the Amount of Damages.*

(1) Evidence Must Be Served or Submitted. Evidence of plaintiff's damages must either be attached to the petition and served on the defendant or submitted to the court after defendant's failure to answer by the answer date.

(2) Form of Evidence. Evidence of plaintiff's damages may be offered in a sworn statement or in live testimony. The evidence offered may include documentary evidence.

(3) Establishment of the Amount of Damages. The amount of damages is established by evidence:

(A) that the account or loan was issued to the defendant and the defendant is obligated to pay it;

(B) that the account was closed or the defendant breached the terms of the account or loan agreement;

(C) of the amount due on the account or loan as of a date certain after all payment credits and offsets have been applied; and

(D) that the plaintiff owns the account or loan and, if applicable, how the plaintiff acquired the account or loan.

(4) Documentary Evidence Offered By Sworn Statement. Documentary evidence may be considered if it is attached to a sworn statement made by the plaintiff or its representative, a prior holder of the debt or its representative, or the original creditor or its representative, that attests to the following:

(A) the documents were kept in the regular course of business;

(B) it was the regular course of business for an employee or representative with knowledge of the act recorded to make the record or to transmit information to be included in such record;

(C) the documents were created at or near the time or reasonably soon thereafter; and

(D) the documents attached are the original or exact duplicates of the original.

(5) Consideration of Sworn Statement. A judge is not required to accept a sworn statement if the source of information or the method or circumstances of preparation indicate lack of trustworthiness. But a judge may not reject a sworn statement only because it is not made by the original creditor or because the documents attested to were created by a third party and subsequently incorporated into and relied upon by the business of the plaintiff.

(c) *Hearing.* The judge may enter a default judgment without a hearing if the plaintiff submits sufficient written evidence of its damages and should do so to avoid undue expense and delay. Otherwise, the plaintiff may request a default judgment hearing at which the plaintiff must appear, in person or by telephonic or electronic means, and prove its damages. If the plaintiff proves its damages, the judge must render judgment for the plaintiff in the amount proven. If the plaintiff is unable to prove its damages, the judge must render judgment in favor of the defendant.

(d) *Appearance.* If the defendant files an answer or otherwise appears in a case before a default judgment is signed by the judge, the judge must not render a default judgment and must set the case for trial.

(e) *Post–Answer Default.* If a defendant who has answered fails to appear for trial, the court may proceed to hear evidence on liability and damages and render judgment accordingly.

Adopted by order of April 15, 2013, eff. Aug. 31, 2013.

Rule 509. Repair and Remedy Cases

Rule 509.1. Applicability of Rule

Rule 509 applies to a lawsuit filed in a justice court by a residential tenant under Chapter 92, Subchapter B of the Texas Property Code to enforce the landlord's duty to repair or remedy a condition materially affecting the physical health or safety of an ordinary tenant.

Adopted by order of April 15, 2013, eff. Aug. 31, 2013.

Rule 509.2. Contents of Petition; Copies; Forms and Amendments

(a) *Contents of Petition.* The petition must be in writing and must include the following:

(1) the street address of the residential rental property;

(2) a statement indicating whether the tenant has received in writing the name and business street address of the landlord and landlord's management company;

(3) to the extent known and applicable, the name, business street address, and telephone number of the landlord and the landlord's management company, on-premises manager, and rent collector serving the residential rental property;

(4) for all notices the tenant gave to the landlord requesting that the condition be repaired or remedied:

(A) the date of the notice;

(B) the name of the person to whom the notice was given or the place where the notice was given;

(C) whether the tenant's lease is in writing and requires written notice;

(D) whether the notice was in writing or oral;

(E) whether any written notice was given by certified mail, return receipt requested, or by registered mail; and

(F) whether the rent was current or had been timely tendered at the time notice was given;

(5) a description of the property condition materially affecting the physical health or safety of an ordinary tenant that the tenant seeks to have repaired or remedied;

(6) a statement of the relief requested by the tenant, including an order to repair or remedy a condition, a reduction in rent, actual damages, civil penalties, attorney's fees, and court costs;

(7) if the petition includes a request to reduce the rent:

(A) the amount of rent paid by the tenant, the amount of rent paid by the government, if known, the rental period, and when the rent is due; and

(B) the amount of the requested rent reduction and the date it should begin;

(8) a statement that the total relief requested does not exceed $10,000, excluding interest and court costs but including attorney's fees; and

(9) the tenant's name, address, and telephone number.

(b) *Copies.* The tenant must provide the court with copies of the petition and any attachments to the petition for service on the landlord.

(c) *Forms and Amendments.* A petition substantially in the form promulgated by the Supreme Court is sufficient. A suit may not be dismissed for a defect in the petition unless the tenant is given an opportunity to correct the defect and does not promptly correct it.

Adopted by order of April 15, 2013, eff. Aug. 31, 2013.

Rule 509.3. Citation: Issuance; Appearance Date; Answer

(a) *Issuance.* When the tenant files a written petition with a justice court, the judge must immediately issue citation directed to the landlord, commanding the landlord to appear before such judge at the time and place named in the citation.

(b) *Appearance Date; Answer.* The appearance date on the citation must not be less than 10 days nor more than 21 days after the petition is filed. For purposes of this rule, the appearance date on the citation is the trial date. The landlord may, but is not required to, file a written answer on or before the appearance date.

Adopted by order of April 15, 2013, eff. Aug. 31, 2013.

Rule 509.4. Service and Return of Citation; Alternative Service of Citation

(a) *Service and Return of Citation.* The sheriff, constable, or other person authorized by Rule 501.2 who receives the citation must serve the citation by delivering a copy of it, along with a copy of the petition and any attachments, to the landlord at least 6 days before the appearance date. At least one day before the appearance date, the person serving the citation must file a return of service with the court that issued the citation. The citation must be issued, served, and returned in like manner as ordinary citations issued from a justice court.

(b) *Alternative Service of Citation.*

(1) If the petition does not include the landlord's name and business street address, or if, after making diligent efforts on at least two occasions, the officer or authorized person is unsuccessful in serving the citation on the landlord under (a), the officer or authorized person must serve the citation by delivering a copy of the citation, petition, and any attachments to:

(A) the landlord's management company if the tenant has received written notice of the name and business street address of the landlord's management company; or

(B) if (b)(1)(A) does not apply and the tenant has not received the landlord's name and business street address in writing, the landlord's authorized agent for service of process, which may be the landlord's management company, on-premise manager, or rent collector serving the residential rental property.

(2) If the officer or authorized person is unsuccessful in serving citation under (b)(1) after making diligent efforts on at least two occasions at either the business street address of the landlord's management company, if (b)(1)(A) applies, or at each available business street address of the landlord's authorized agent for service of process, if (b)(1)(B) applies, the officer or authorized person must execute and file in the justice court a sworn statement that the officer or authorized person made diligent efforts to serve the citation on at least two occasions at all available business street addresses of the landlord and, to the extent applicable, the landlord's management company, on-premises manager, and rent collector serving the residential rental property, providing the times, dates, and places of each attempted service. The judge may then authorize the officer or authorized person to serve citation by:

(A) delivering a copy of the citation, petition, and any attachments to someone over the age of 16 years, at any business street address listed in the petition, or, if nobody answers the door at a business street address, either placing the citation, petition, and any attachments through a door mail chute or slipping them under the front door, and if neither of these latter methods is practical, affixing the citation, petition, and any attachments to the front door or main entry to the business street address;

(B) within 24 hours of complying with (b)(2)(A), sending by first class mail a true copy of the citation, petition, and any attachments addressed to the landlord at the landlord's business street address provided in the petition; and

(C) noting on the return of the citation the date of delivery under (b)(2)(A) and the date of mailing under (b)(2)(B).

The delivery and mailing to the business street address under (b)(2)(A)–(B) must occur at least 6 days before the appearance date. At least one day before the appearance date, a return of service must be completed and filed in accordance with Rule 501.3 with the court that issued the citation. It is not necessary for the tenant to request the alternative service authorized by this rule.

Adopted by order of April 15, 2013, eff. Aug. 31, 2013.

Rule 509.5. Docketing and Trial; Failure to Appear

(a) *Docketing and Trial.* The case must be docketed and tried as other cases. The judge may develop the facts of the case in order to ensure justice.

(b) *Failure to Appear.*

(1) If the tenant appears at trial and the landlord has been duly served and fails to appear at trial, the judge may proceed to hear evidence. If the tenant establishes that the tenant is entitled to recover, the judge must render judgment against the landlord in accordance with the evidence.

(2) If the tenant fails to appear for trial, the judge may dismiss the lawsuit.

Adopted by order of April 15, 2013, eff. Aug. 31, 2013.

Rule 509.6. Judgment: Amount; Form and Content; Issuance and Service; Failure to Comply

(a) *Amount.* Judgment may be rendered against the landlord for failure to repair or remedy a condition at the residential rental property if the total judgment does not exceed $10,000, excluding interest and court costs but including attorney's fees. Any party who prevails in a lawsuit brought under these rules may recover the party's court costs and reasonable attorney's fees as allowed by law.

(b) *Form and Content.*

(1) The judgment must be in writing, signed, and dated and must include the names of the parties to the proceeding and the street address of the residential rental property where the condition is to be repaired or remedied.

(2) In the judgment, the judge may:

(A) order the landlord to take reasonable action to repair or remedy the condition;

(B) order a reduction in the tenant's rent, from the date of the first repair notice, in proportion to the reduced rental value resulting from the condition until the condition is repaired or remedied;

(C) award a civil penalty of one month's rent plus $500;

(D) award the tenant's actual damages; and

(E) award court costs and attorney's fees, excluding any attorney's fees for a claim for damages relating to a personal injury.

(3) If the judge orders the landlord to repair or remedy a condition, the judgment must include in reasonable detail the actions the landlord must take to repair or remedy the condition and the date when the repair or remedy must be completed.

(4) If the judge orders a reduction in the tenant's rent, the judgment must state:

(A) the amount of the rent the tenant must pay, if any;

(B) the frequency with which the tenant must pay the rent;

(C) the condition justifying the reduction of rent;

(D) the effective date of the order reducing rent;

(E) that the order reducing rent will terminate on the date the condition is repaired or remedied; and

(F) that on the day the condition is repaired or remedied, the landlord must give the tenant written notice, served in accordance with Rule 501.4, that the condition justifying the reduction of rent has been repaired or remedied and the rent will revert to the rent amount specified in the lease.

(c) *Issuance and Service.* The judge must issue the judgment. The judgment may be served on the landlord in open court or by any means provided in Rule 501.4 at an address listed in the citation, the address listed on any answer, or such other address the landlord furnishes to the court in writing. Unless the judge serves the landlord in open court or by other means provided in Rule 501.4, the sheriff, constable, or other authorized person who serves the landlord must promptly file a return of service in the justice court.

(d) *Failure to Comply.* If the landlord fails to comply with an order to repair or remedy a condition or reduce the tenant's rent, the failure is grounds for citing the landlord for contempt of court under Section 21.002 of the Texas Government Code.

Adopted by order of April 15, 2013, eff. Aug. 31, 2013.

Rule 509.7. Counterclaims

Counterclaims and the joinder of suits against third parties are not permitted in suits under these rules. Compulsory counterclaims may be brought in a separate suit. Any potential causes of action, including a compulsory counterclaim, that are not asserted because of this rule are not precluded.

Adopted by order of April 15, 2013, eff. Aug. 31, 2013.

Rule 509.8. Appeal: Time and Manner; Perfection; Effect; Costs; Trial on Appeal

(a) *Time and Manner.* Either party may appeal the decision of the justice court to a statutory county court or, if there is no statutory county court with jurisdiction, a county court or district court with jurisdiction by filing a written notice of appeal with the justice court within 21 days after the date the judge signs the judgment. If the judgment is amended in any respect, any party has the right to appeal within 21 days after the date the judge signs the new judgment, in the same manner set out in this rule.

(b) *Perfection.* The posting of an appeal bond is not required for an appeal under this rule, and the appeal is considered perfected with the filing of a notice of appeal. Otherwise, the appeal is in the manner provided by law for appeal from a justice court.

(c) *Effect.* The timely filing of a notice of appeal stays the enforcement of any order to repair or remedy a condition or reduce the tenant's rent, as well as any other actions.

(d) *Costs.* The appellant must pay the costs on appeal to a county court in accordance with Rule 143a.

(e) *Trial on Appeal.* On appeal, the parties are entitled to a trial de novo. A trial de novo is a new trial in which the entire case is presented as if there had been no previous trial. Either party is entitled to trial by jury on timely request and payment of a fee, if required. An appeal of a judgment of a justice court under these rules takes precedence in the county court and may be held at any time after the eighth day after the date the transcript is filed in the county court.

Adopted by order of April 15, 2013, eff. Aug. 31, 2013.

Rule 509.9. Effect of Writ of Possession

If a judgment for the landlord for possession of the residential rental property becomes final, any order to repair or remedy a condition is vacated and unenforceable.

Adopted by order of April 15, 2013, eff. Aug. 31, 2013.

Rule 510. Eviction Cases

Rule 510.1. Application

Rule 510 applies to a lawsuit to recover possession of real property under Chapter 24 of the Texas Property Code.

Adopted by order of April 15, 2013, eff. Aug. 31, 2013.

Rule 510.2. Computation of Time for Eviction Cases

Rule 500.5 applies to the computation of time in an eviction case. But if a document is filed by mail and not received by the court by the due date, the court may take any action authorized by these rules, including issuing a writ of possession requiring a tenant to leave the property.

Adopted by order of April 15, 2013, eff. Aug. 31, 2013.

Rule 510.3. Petition

(a) *Contents.* In addition to the requirements of Rule 502.2, a petition in an eviction case must be sworn to by the plaintiff and must contain:

(1) a description, including the address, if any, of the premises that the plaintiff seeks possession of;

(2) a description of the facts and the grounds for eviction;

(3) a description of when and how notice to vacate was delivered;

(4) the total amount of rent due and unpaid at the time of filing, if any; and

(5) a statement that attorney fees are being sought, if applicable.

(b) *Where Filed.* The petition must be filed in the precinct where the premises is located. If it is filed elsewhere, the judge must dismiss the case. The plaintiff will not be entitled to a refund of the filing fee, but will be refunded any service fees paid if the case is dismissed before service is attempted.

(c) *Defendants Named.* If the eviction is based on a written residential lease, the plaintiff must name as defendants all tenants obligated under the lease residing at the premises whom plaintiff seeks to evict. No judgment or writ of possession may issue or be executed against a tenant obligated under a lease and residing at the premises who is not named in the petition and served with citation.

(d) *Claim for Rent.* A claim for rent within the justice court's jurisdiction may be asserted in an eviction case.

(e) *Only Issue.* The court must adjudicate the right to actual possession and not title. Counterclaims and the joinder of suits against third parties are not permitted in eviction cases. A claim that is not asserted because of this rule can be brought in a separate suit in a court of proper jurisdiction.

Adopted by order of April 15, 2013, eff. Aug. 31, 2013.

Rule 510.4. Issuance, Service, and Return of Citation

(a) *Issuance of Citation; Contents.* When a petition is filed, the court must immediately issue citation directed to each defendant. The citation must:

(1) be styled "The State of Texas";

(2) be signed by the clerk under seal of court or by the judge;

(3) contain the name, location, and address of the court;

(4) state the date of filing of the petition;

(5) state the date of issuance of the citation;

(6) state the file number and names of parties;

(7) state the plaintiff's cause of action and relief sought;

(8) be directed to the defendant;

(9) state the name and address of attorney for plaintiff, or if the plaintiff does not have an attorney, the address of plaintiff;

(10) state the day the defendant must appear in person for trial at the court issuing citation, which must not be less than 10 days nor more than 21 days after the petition is filed;

(11) notify the defendant that if the defendant fails to appear in person for trial, judgment by default may be rendered for the relief demanded in the petition;

(12) inform the defendant that, upon timely request and payment of a jury fee no later than 3 days before the day set for trial, the case will be heard by a jury;

(13) contain all warnings required by Chapter 2 4 of the Texas Property Code; and

(14) include the following statement: "For further information, consult Part V of the Texas Rules of Civil Procedure, which is available online and also at the court listed on this citation."

(b) *Service and Return of Citation.*

(1) Who May Serve. Unless otherwise authorized by written court order, citation must be served by a sheriff or constable.

(2) Method of Service. The constable, sheriff, or other person authorized by written court order receiving the citation must execute it by delivering a copy with a copy of the petition attached to the defendant, or by leaving a copy with a copy of the petition attached with some person, other than the plaintiff, over the age of 16 years, at the defendant's usual place of residence, at least 6 days before the day set for trial.

(3) Return of Service. At least one day before the day set for trial, the constable, sheriff, or other person authorized by written court order must complete and file a return of service in accordance with Rule 501.3 with the court that issued the citation.

(c) *Alternative Service by Delivery to the Premises.*

(1) When Allowed. The citation may be served by delivery to the premises if:

(A) the constable, sheriff, or other person authorized by written court order is unsuccessful in serving the citation under (b);

(B) the petition lists all home and work addresses of the defendant that are known to the plaintiff and states that the plaintiff knows of no other home or work addresses of the defendant in the county where the premises are located; and

(C) the constable, sheriff, or other person authorized files a sworn statement that it has made diligent efforts to serve such citation on at least two occasions at all addresses of the defendant in the county where the premises are located, stating the times and places of attempted service.

(2) Authorization. The judge must promptly consider a sworn statement filed under (1)(C) and determine whether citation may be served by delivery to the premises. The plaintiff is not required to make a request or motion for alternative service.

(3) Method. If the judge authorizes service by delivery to the premises, the constable, sheriff, or other person authorized by written court order must, at least 6 days before the day set for trial:

(A) deliver a copy of the citation with a copy of the petition attached to the premises by placing it through a door mail chute or slipping it under the front door; if neither method is possible, the officer may securely affix the citation to the front door or main entry to the premises; and

(B) deposit in the mail a copy of the citation with a copy of the petition attached, addressed to defendant at the premises and sent by first class mail.

(4) Notation on Return. The constable, sheriff, or other person authorized by written court order must note on the return of service the date the

citation was delivered and the date it was deposited in the mail.

Adopted by order of April 15, 2013, eff. Aug. 31, 2013.

Rule 510.5. Request for Immediate Possession

(a) *Immediate Possession Bond.* The plaintiff may, at the time of filing the petition or at any time prior to final judgment, file a possession bond to be approved by the judge in the probable amount of costs of suit and damages that may result to defendant in the event that the suit has been improperly instituted, and conditioned that the plaintiff will pay defendant all such costs and damages that are adjudged against plaintiff.

(b) *Notice to Defendant.* The court must notify a defendant that the plaintiff has filed a possession bond. The notice must be served in the same manner as service of citation and must inform the defendant that if the defendant does not file an answer or appear for trial, and judgment for possession is granted by default, an officer will place the plaintiff in possession of the property on or after the 7th day after the date defendant is served with the notice.

(c) *Time for Issuance and Execution of Writ.* If judgment for possession is rendered by default and a possession bond has been filed, approved, and served under this rule, a writ of possession must issue immediately upon demand and payment of any required fees. The writ must not be executed before the 7th day after the date defendant is served with notice under (b).

(d) *Effect of Appearance.* If the defendant files an answer or appears at trial, no writ of possession may issue before the 6th day after the date a judgment for possession is signed or the day following the deadline for the defendant to appeal the judgment, whichever is later.

Adopted by order of April 15, 2013, eff. Aug. 31, 2013.

Rule 510.6. Trial Date; Answer; Default Judgment

(a) *Trial Date and Answer.* The defendant must appear for trial on the day set for trial in the citation. The defendant may, but is not required to, file a written answer with the court on or before the day set for trial in the citation.

(b) *Default Judgment.* If the defendant fails to appear at trial and fails to file an answer before the case is called for trial, and proof of service has been filed in accordance with Rule 510.4, the allegations of the complaint must be taken as admitted and judgment by default rendered accordingly. If a defendant who has answered fails to appear for trial, the court may proceed to hear evidence and render judgment accordingly.

(c) *Notice of Default.* When a default judgment is signed, the clerk must immediately mail written notice of the judgment by first class mail to the defendant at the address of the premises.

Adopted by order of April 15, 2013, eff. Aug. 31, 2013.

Rule 510.7. Trial

(a) *Trial.* An eviction case will be docketed and tried as other cases. No eviction trial may be held less than 6 days after service under Rule 510.4 has been obtained.

(b) *Jury Trial Demanded.* Any party may file a written demand for trial by jury by making a request to the court at least 3 days before the trial date. The demand must be accompanied by payment of a jury fee or by filing a sworn statement of inability to pay the jury fee. If a jury is demanded by either party, the jury will be impaneled and sworn as in other cases; and after hearing the evidence it will return its verdict in favor of the plaintiff or the defendant. If no jury is timely demanded by either party, the judge will try the case.

(c) *Limit on Postponement.* Trial in an eviction case must not be postponed for more than 7 days total unless both parties agree in writing.

Adopted by order of April 15, 2013, eff. Aug. 31, 2013.

Rule 510.8. Judgment; Writ; No New Trial

(a) *Judgment Upon Jury Verdict.* Where a jury has returned a verdict, the judge may render judgment on the verdict or, if the verdict is contrary to the law or the evidence, judgment notwithstanding the verdict.

(b) *Judgment for Plaintiff.* If the judgment is in favor of the plaintiff, the judge must render judgment for plaintiff for possession of the premises, costs, delinquent rent as of the date of entry of judgment, if any, and attorney fees if recoverable by law.

(c) *Judgment for Defendant.* If the judgment is in favor of the defendant, the judge must render judgment for defendant against the plaintiff for costs and attorney fees if recoverable by law.

(d) *Writ.* If the judgment or verdict is in favor of the plaintiff, the judge must award a writ of possession upon demand of the plaintiff and payment of any required fees.

(1) Time to Issue. Except as provided by Rule 510.5, no writ of possession may issue before the 6th day after the date a judgment for possession is signed or the day following the deadline for the defendant to appeal the judgment, whichever is later. A writ of possession may not issue more than 60 days after a judgment for possession is signed. For good cause, the court may extend the deadline for issuance to 90 days after a judgment for possession is signed.

(2) Time to Execute. A writ of possession may not be executed after the 90th day after a judgment for possession is signed.

(3) Effect of Appeal. A writ of possession must not issue if an appeal is perfected and, if applicable, rent is paid into the registry, as required by these rules.

(e) *No Motion For New Trial.* No motion for new trial may be filed.

Adopted by order of April 15, 2013, eff. Aug. 31, 2013.

Rule 510.9. Appeal

(a) *How Taken; Time.* A party may appeal a judgment in an eviction case by filing a bond, making a cash deposit, or filing a sworn statement of inability to pay with the justice court within 5 days after the judgment is signed.

(b) *Amount of Security; Terms.* The justice court judge will set the amount of the bond or cash deposit to include the items enumerated in Rule 510.11. The bond or cash deposit must be payable to the appellee and must be conditioned on the appellant's prosecution of its appeal to effect and payment of any judgment and all costs rendered against it on appeal.

(c) *Sworn Statement of Inability to Pay.*

(1) Filing. An appellant who cannot furnish a bond or pay a cash deposit in the amount required may instead file a sworn statement of inability to pay. The statement must meet the requirements of Rule 502.3(b).

(2) Contest. The statement may be contested as provided in Rule 502.3(d) within 5 days after the opposing party receives notice that the statement was filed.

(3) Appeal If Contest Sustained. If the contest is sustained, the appellant may appeal that decision by filing notice with the justice court within 5 days of that court's written order. The justice court must then forward all related documents to the county court for resolution. The county court must set the matter for hearing within 5 days and hear the contest de novo, as if there had been no previous hearing, and, if the appeal is granted, must direct the justice court to transmit to the clerk of the county court the transcript, records, and papers of the case, as provided in these rules.

(4) If No Appeal or If Appeal Overruled. If the appellant does not appeal the ruling sustaining the contest, or if the county court denies the appeal, the appellant may, within one business day, post an appeal bond or make a cash deposit in compliance with this rule.

(5) Payment of Rent in Nonpayment of Rent Appeals.

(A) Notice. If a defendant appeals an eviction for nonpayment of rent by filing a sworn statement of inability to pay, the justice court must provide to the defendant a written notice at the time the statement is filed that contains the following information in bold or conspicuous type:

(i) the amount of the initial deposit of rent, equal to one rental period's rent under the terms of the rental agreement, that the defendant must pay into the justice court registry;

(ii) whether the initial deposit must be paid in cash, cashier's check, or money order, and to whom the cashier's check or money order, if applicable, must be made payable;

(iii) the calendar date by which the initial deposit must be paid into the justice court registry, which must be within 5 days of the date the sworn statement of inability to pay is filed; and

(iv) a statement that failure to pay the required amount into the justice court registry by the required date may result in the court issuing a writ of possession without hearing.

(B) Defendant May Remain in Possession. A defendant who appeals an eviction for nonpayment of rent by filing a sworn statement of inability to pay is entitled to stay in possession of the premises during the pendency of the appeal by complying with the following procedure:

(i) Within 5 days of the date that the defendant files a sworn statement of inability to pay, it must pay into the justice court registry the amount set forth in the notice provided at the time the defendant filed the statement. If the defendant was provided with notice and fails to pay the designated amount into the justice court registry within 5 days, and the transcript has not been transmitted to the county clerk, the plaintiff is entitled, upon request and payment of the applicable fee, to a writ of possession, which the justice court must issue immediately and without hearing.

(ii) During the appeal process as rent becomes due under the rental agreement, the defendant must pay the designated amount into the county court registry within 5 days of the rental due date under the terms of the rental agreement.

(iii) If a government agency is responsible for all or a portion of the rent, the defendant must pay only that portion of the rent determined by the justice court to be paid during appeal. Either party may contest the portion of the rent that the justice court determines must be paid into the county court registry by filing a contest within 5 days after the judgment is signed. If a contest is filed, the justice court must notify the parties and hold a hearing on the contest within 5 days. If the defendant objects to the justice court's ruling at the hearing, the defendant is required to pay only the portion claimed to be owed by the defendant until the issue is tried in county court.

(iv) If the defendant fails to pay the designated amount into the court registry within the time limits prescribed by these rules, the plaintiff may file a sworn motion that the defendant is in default in county court. The plaintiff must notify the defendant of the motion and the hearing date. Upon a showing that the defendant is in default, the court must issue a writ of possession.

(v) The plaintiff may withdraw any or all rent in the county court registry upon sworn motion and hearing, prior to final determination of the case, showing just cause; dismissal of the appeal; or order of the court after final hearing.

(vi) All hearings and motions under this subparagraph are entitled to precedence in the county court.

(d) *Notice to Other Parties Required.* If a statement of inability to pay is filed, the court must provide notice to all other parties that the statement was filed no later than the next business day. Within 5 days of filing a bond or making a cash deposit, an appellant must serve written notice of the appeal on all other parties using a method approved under Rule 501.4.

(e) *No Default on Appeal Without Compliance With Rule.* No judgment maybe taken by default against the adverse party in the court to which the case has been appealed without first showing substantial compliance with this rule.

(f) *Appeal Perfected.* An appeal is perfected when a bond, cash deposit, or statement of inability to pay is filed in accordance with this rule.

Adopted by order of April 15, 2013, eff. Aug. 31, 2013.

Rule 510.10. Record on Appeal; Docketing; Trial De Novo

(a) *Preparation and Transmission of Record.* Unless otherwise provided by law or these rules, when an appeal has been perfected, the judge must stay all further proceedings on the judgment and must immediately send to the clerk of the county court a certified copy of all docket entries, a certified copy of the bill of costs, and the original papers in the case together with any money in the court registry, including sums tendered pursuant to Rule 510.9(c)(5)(B).

(b) *Docketing; Notice.* The county clerk must docket the case and must immediately notify the parties of the date of receipt of the transcript and the docket number of the case. The notice must advise the defendant that it must file a written answer in the county court within 8 days if one was not filed in the justice court.

(c) *Trial De Novo.* The case must be tried de novo in the county court. A trial de novo is a new trial in which the entire case is presented as if there had been no previous trial. The trial, as well as any hearings and motions, is entitled to precedence in the county court.

Adopted by order of April 15, 2013, eff. Aug. 31, 2013.

Rule 510.11. Damages on Appeal

On the trial of the case in the county court the appellant or appellee will be permitted to plead, prove and recover his damages, if any, suffered for withholding or defending possession of the premises during the pendency of the appeal. Damages may include but are not limited to loss of rentals during the pendency of the appeal and attorney fees in the justice and county courts provided, as to attorney fees, that the requirements of Section 24.006 of the Texas Property Code have been met. Only the party prevailing in the county court will be entitled to recover damages against the adverse party. The prevailing party will also be entitled to recover court costs and to recover against the sureties on the appeal bond in cases where the adverse party has executed an appeal bond.

Adopted by order of April 15, 2013, eff. Aug. 31, 2013.

Rule 510.12. Judgment by Default on Appeal

An eviction case appealed to county court will be subject to trial at any time after the expiration of 8 days after the date the transcript is filed in the county court. If the defendant has filed a written answer in the justice court, it must be taken to constitute his appearance and answer in the county court and may be amended as in other cases. If the defendant made no answer in writing in the justice court and fails to file a written answer within 8 days after the transcript is filed in the county court, the allegations of the complaint may be taken as admitted and judgment by default may be entered accordingly.

Adopted by order of April 15, 2013, eff. Aug. 31, 2013.

Rule 510.13. Writ of Possession on Appeal

The writ of possession, or execution, or both, will be issued by the clerk of the county court according to the judgment rendered, and the same will be executed by the sheriff or constable, as in other cases. The judgment of the county court may not be stayed unless within 10 days from the judgment the appellant files a supersedeas bond in an amount set by the county court pursuant to Section 24.007 of the Texas Property Code.

Adopted by order of April 15, 2013, eff. Aug. 31, 2013.

Rule 511 to 513. Repealed by Order of Dec. 5, 1983, eff. April 1, 1984

Historical Notes

The repealed rules were all adopted by order of October 29, 1940, effective September 1, 1941.

Former rule 511 provided for an execution for costs assessed by the Supreme Court and Court of Civil Appeals. For subject matter of former rule 511, see, now, rules 447 and 491.

Former rule 512 provided for the return of the execution for costs.

Former rule 513 related to the failure of the officer to return the execution.

Rule 514. Repealed by Order of April 10, 1986, eff. Sept. 1, 1986

Historical Notes

See, now, Rules App.Proc., Rule 12.5.

Rule 515. Repealed by Order of April 10, 1986, eff. Sept. 1, 1986

Historical Notes

See, now, Rules App.Proc., rule 9.5 and 64.1 et seq.

Rule 516, 517. Repealed by Order of Dec. 5, 1983, eff. April 1, 1984

Historical Notes

See, now, rule 515.

Rules 518 to 522. Repealed by Order of Oct. 10, 1945, eff. Feb. 1, 1946

Rules 523 to 567. Repealed by Order of April 15, 2013, eff. Aug. 31, 2013

Historical Notes

For subject matter of former rule 524, see, now, Rules Civ.Proc., rule 507.3.

For subject matter of former rule 525, see, now, Rules Civ.Proc., rule 502.1.

For subject matter of former rule 526, see, now, Rules Civ.Proc., rule 502.5.

For subject matter of former rules 527 to 533, see, now, Rules Civ.Proc., rule 502.4.

For subject matter of former rule 534, see, now, Rules Civ.Proc., rule 501.1.

For subject matter of former rule 535, see, now, Rules Civ.Proc., rule 502.5.

For subject matter of former rule 536, see, now, Rules Civ.Proc., rule 501.2.

For subject matter of former rule 536a, see, now, Rules Civ.Proc., rule 501.3.

For subject matter of former rule 538, see, now, Rules Civ.Proc., rule 503.6.

For subject matter of former rule 540, see, now, Rules Civ.Proc., rule 504.1.

For subject matter of former rule 541, see, now, Rules Civ.Proc., rule 503.3.

For subject matter of former rule 543, see, now, Rules Civ.Proc., rule 503.6.

For subject matter of former rule 544, see, now, Rules Civ.Proc., rule 504.1.

For subject matter of former rules 548 to 553, see, now, Rules Civ.Proc., rule 504.2.

For subject matter of former rule 554, see, now, Rules Civ.Proc., rule 504.3.

For subject matter of former rule 555, see, now, Rules Civ.Proc., rule 504.4.

For subject matter of former rule 556 to 560, see, now, Rules Civ.Proc., rule 505.1.

For subject matter of former rule 561, see, now, Rules Civ.Proc., rule 505.2.

For subject matter of former rule 562, see, now, Rules Civ.Proc., rule 501.3.

For subject matter of former rules 566 and 567, see, now, Rules Civ.Proc., rule 505.3.

Rule 568. Repealed by Order of July 15, 1987, eff. Jan. 1, 1988

Historical Notes

See, now, rule 567.

Source

Vernon's Ann.Civ.St. art. 2441.

Rules 569 to 591. Repealed by Order of April 15, 2013, eff. Aug. 31, 2013

Historical Notes

For subject matter of former rule 569 and 570, see, now, Rules Civ.Proc., rule 505.3.

For subject matter of former rules 571 to 573, see, now, Rules Civ.Proc., rule 506.1.

For subject matter of former rule 574, see, now, Rules Civ.Proc., rule 506.2.

For subject matter of former rule 574b, see, now, Rules Civ.Proc., rule 506.3.

For subject matter of former rules 575 to 591, see, now, Rules Civ.Proc., rule 506.4.

PART VI

RULES RELATING TO ANCILLARY PROCEEDINGS

SECTION 1. ATTACHMENT

Rule 592. Application for Writ of Attachment and Order

Either at the commencement of a suit or at any time during its progress the plaintiff may file an application for the issuance of a writ of attachment. Such application shall be supported by affidavits of the plaintiff, his agent, his attorney, or other persons having knowledge of relevant facts. The application shall comply with all statutory requirements and shall state the grounds for issuing the writ and the specific facts relied upon by the plaintiff to warrant the required findings by the court. The writ shall not be quashed because two or more grounds are stated conjunctively or disjunctively. The application and any affidavits shall be made on personal knowledge and shall set forth such facts as would be admissible in evidence; provided that facts may be stated based upon information and belief if the grounds of such belief are specifically stated.

No writ shall issue except upon written order of the court after a hearing, which may be ex parte. The court, in its order granting the application, shall make specific findings of facts to support the statutory grounds found to exist, and shall specify the maximum value of property that may be attached, and the amount of bond required of plaintiff, and, further shall command that the attached property be kept safe and preserved subject to further orders of the court. Such bond shall be in an amount which, in the opinion of the court, will adequately compensate the defendant in the event plaintiff fails to prosecute his suit to effect, and to pay all damages and costs which may be adjudged against him for wrongfully suing out the writ of attachment. The court shall further find in its order the amount of bond required of defendant to replevy, which, unless the defendant chooses to exercise his option as provided in Rule 599, shall be the amount of plaintiff's claim, one year's accrual of interest if allowed by law on the claim, and the estimated costs of court. The order may direct the issuance of several writs at the same time, or in succession, to be sent to different counties.

July 11, 1977, eff. Jan. 1, 1978.

Historical Notes

Source

This is a new rule, designed to meet the constitutional demands of due process in prejudgment remedies. For provisions of former Rule 592, see, now, rule 592b.

Rule 592a. Bond for Attachment

No writ of attachment shall issue until the party applying therefor has filed with the officer authorized to issue such writ a bond payable to the defendant in the amount fixed by the court's order, with sufficient surety or sureties as provided by statute to be approved by such officer, conditioned that the plaintiff will prosecute his suit to effect and pay to the extent of the penal amount of the bond all damages and costs as may be adjudged against him for wrongfully suing out such writ of attachment.

After notice to the opposite party, either before or after the issuance of the writ, the defendant or plaintiff may file a motion to increase or reduce the amount of such bond, or to question the sufficiency of the sureties thereon, in the court in which such suit is pending. Upon hearing, the court shall enter its order with respect to such bond and sufficiency of the sureties.

July 11, 1977, eff. Jan. 1, 1978.

Historical Notes

This is a new rule.

Rule 592b. Form of Attachment Bond

The following form of bond may be used:

"The State of Texas,

County of ________,

"We, the undersigned, ____________________ as principal, and ____________ and ____________ as sureties, acknowledge ourselves bound to pay to C.D. the sum of ________ dollars, conditioned that the above bound plaintiff in attachment against the said C.D., defendant, will prosecute his said suit to effect, and that he will pay all such damages and costs to the extent of the penal amount of this bond as shall be adjudged against him for wrongfully suing out such attachment. Witness our hands this ______ day of __________, 19___."

Renumbered from Rule 592 and amended by order of July 11, 1977, eff. Jan. 1, 1978.

Historical Notes

Source

Vernon's Ann.Civ.St. art. 280.

Rule 593. Requisites for Writ

A writ of attachment shall be directed to the sheriff or any constable within the State of Texas. It shall command him to attach and hold, unless replevied, subject to the further order of the court, so much of the property of the defendant, of a reasonable value in approximately the amount fixed by the court, as shall be found within his county.

Amended by order of July 11, 1977, eff. Jan. 1, 1978.

Historical Notes

Source

Vernon's Ann.Civ.St. art. 282.

Rule 594. Form of Writ

The following form of writ may be issued:

"The State of Texas.

To the Sheriff or any Constable of any County of the State of Texas, greeting:

"We command you that you attach forthwith so much of the property of C. D., if it be found in your county, repleviable on security, as shall be of value sufficient to make the sum of ________ dollars, and the probable costs of suit, to satisfy the demand of A. B., and that you keep and secure in your hands the property so attached, unless replevied, that the same may be liable to further proceedings thereon to be had before our court in ________, County of ________. You will true return make of this writ on or before 10 a. m. of Monday, the ________ day of ________, 19___, showing how you have executed the same."

Historical Notes

Source

Vernon's Ann.Civ.St. art. 284.

Rule 595. Several Writs

Several writs of attachment may, at the option of the plaintiff, be issued at the same time, or in succession, and sent to different counties, until sufficient property shall be attached to satisfy the writ.

Historical Notes

Source

Vernon's Ann.Civ.St. art. 283.

Rule 596. Delivery of Writ

The writ of attachment shall be dated and tested as other writs, and may be delivered to the sheriff or constable by the officer issuing it, or he may deliver it to the plaintiff, his agent or attorney, for that purpose.

Historical Notes

Source

Vernon's Ann.Civ.St. art. 285.

Rule 597. Duty of Officer

The sheriff or constable receiving the writ shall immediately proceed to execute the same by levying upon so much of the property of the defendant subject to the writ, and found within his county, as may be sufficient to satisfy the command of the writ.

Historical Notes

Source

Vernon's Ann.Civ.St. art. 286.

Rule 598. Levy, How Made

The writ of attachment shall be levied in the same manner as is, or may be, the writ of execution upon similar property.

Historical Notes

Source

Vernon's Ann.Civ.St. art. 289.

Rule 598a. Service of Writ on Defendant

The defendant shall be served in any manner prescribed for service of citation, or as provided in Rule 21a, with a copy of the writ of attachment, the application, accompanying affidavits, and orders of the court as soon as practicable following the levy of the writ. There shall be prominently displayed on the face of the copy of the writ served on the defendant, in ten-point type and in a manner calculated to advise a reasonably attentive person of its contents, the following:

"To ________________, Defendant:

You are hereby notified that certain properties alleged to be owned by you have been attached. If you claim any rights in such property, you are advised:

"YOU HAVE A RIGHT TO REGAIN POSSESSION OF THE PROPERTY BY FILING A REPLEVY BOND. YOU HAVE A RIGHT TO SEEK TO REGAIN POSSESSION OF THE PROPERTY BY FILING WITH THE COURT A MOTION TO DISSOLVE THIS WRIT."

July 11, 1977, eff. Jan. 1, 1978.

Historical Notes

Source

This is a new rule. It affords the defendant notice of the proceedings and informs him of some of his rights.

Rule 599. Defendant May Replevy

At any time before judgment, should the attached property not have been previously claimed or sold, the defendant may replevy the same, or any part thereof, or the proceeds from the sale of the property if it has been sold under order of the court, by giving bond with sufficient surety or sureties as provided by statute, to be approved by the officer who levied the writ, payable to plaintiff, in the amount fixed by the court's order, or, at the defendant's option, for the value of the property sought to be replevied (to be estimated by the officer), plus one year's interest thereon at the legal rate from the date of the bond, conditioned that the defendant shall satisfy, to the extent of the penal amount of the bond, any judgment which may be rendered against him in such action.

On reasonable notice to the opposing party (which may be less than three days) either party shall have the right to prompt judicial review of the amount of bond required, denial of bond, sufficiency of sureties, and estimated value of the property, by the court which authorized issuance of the writ. The court's determination may be made upon the basis of affidavits, if uncontroverted, setting forth such facts as would be admissible in evidence; otherwise, the parties shall submit evidence. The court shall forthwith enter its order either approving or modifying the requirements of the officer or of the court's prior order, and such order of the court shall supersede and control with respect to such matters.

On reasonable notice to the opposing party (which may be less than three days) the defendant shall have the right to move the court for a substitution of property, of equal value as that attached, for the property attached. Provided that there has been located sufficient property of the defendants to satisfy the order of attachment, the court may authorize substitution of one or more items of defendant's property for all or for part of the property attached. The court shall first make findings as to the value of the property to be substituted. If property is substituted, the property released from attachment shall be delivered to defendant, if such property is personal property, and all liens upon such property from the original order of attachment or modification thereof shall be terminated. Attachment of substituted property shall be deemed to have existed from the date of levy on the original property attached, and no property on which liens have become affixed since the date of levy on the original property may be substituted.

July 11, 1977, eff. Jan. 1, 1978.

Historical Notes

Source

Vernon's Ann.Civ.St. art. 292.

Rule 600. Sale of Perishable Property

Whenever personal property which has been attached shall not have been claimed or replevied, the judge, or justice of the peace, out of whose court the writ was issued, may, either in term time or in vacation, order the same to be sold, when it shall be made to appear that such property is in danger of serious and immediate waste or decay, or that the keeping of the same until the trial will necessarily be attended with such expense or deterioration in value as greatly to lessen the amount likely to be realized therefrom.

Historical Notes

Source

Vernon's Ann.Civ.St. art. 293.

Rule 601. To Protect Interests

In determining whether the property attached is perishable, and the necessity or advantage of ordering a sale thereof, the judge or justice of the peace may act upon affidavits in writing or oral testimony, and may by a preliminary order entered of record, with or without notice to the parties as the urgency of the case in his opinion requires, direct the sheriff or constable to sell such property at public auction for cash, and thereupon the officer shall sell it accordingly.

Historical Notes

Source

Vernon's Ann.Civ.St. art. 294.

Rule 602. Bond of Applicant for Sale

If the application for an order of sale be filed by any person or party other than the defendant from whose possession the property was taken by levy, the court shall not grant such order unless the applicant shall file with such court a bond payable to such defendant, with two or more good and sufficient sureties, to be approved by said court, conditioned that they will be responsible to the defendant for such damages as he may sustain in case such sale be illegally and unjustly applied for, or be illegally and unjustly made.

Historical Notes

Source

Vernon's Ann.Civ.St. art. 5233.

Rule 603. Procedure for Sale

Such sale of attached perishable personal property shall be conducted in the same manner as sales of personal property under execution; provided, however, that the time of the sale, and at the time of advertisement thereof, may be fixed by the judge or justice of the peace at a time earlier than ten days, according to the exigency of the case, and in such event notice thereof shall be given in such manner as directed by the order.

Historical Notes

Source

Vernon's Ann.Civ.St. art. 295.

Rule 604. Return of Sale

The officer making such sale of perishable property shall promptly pay the proceeds of such sale to the clerk of such court or justice of the peace, as the case may be, and shall make written return of the order of sale signed by him officially, stating the time and place of the sale, the name of the purchaser, and the amount of money received, with an itemized account of the expenses attending the sale. Such return shall be filed with the papers of the case.

Historical Notes

Source

Vernon's Ann.Civ.St. art. 296.

Rule 605. Judge May Make Necessary Orders

When the perishable personal property levied on under the attachment writ has not been claimed or replevied, the judge or justice of the peace may make such orders, either in term time or vacation, as may be necessary for its preservation or use.

Historical Notes

Source

Vernon's Ann.Civ.St. art. 297.

Rule 606. Return of Writ

The officer executing the writ of attachment shall return the writ, with his action endorsed thereon, or attached thereto, signed by him officially, to the court from which it issued, at or before 10 o'clock a. m. of the Monday next after the expiration of fifteen days from the date of issuance of the writ. Such return shall describe the property attached with sufficient certainty to identify it, and state when the same was attached, and whether any personal property attached remains still in his hands, and, if not, the disposition made of the same. When property has been replevied he shall deliver the replevy bond to the clerk or justice of the peace to be filed with the papers of the cause.

Historical Notes

Source

Vernon's Ann.Civ.St. art. 298.

Rule 607. Report of Disposition of Property

When the property levied on is claimed, replevied or sold, or otherwise disposed of after the writ has been returned, the officer having the custody of the same shall immediately make a report in writing, signed by him officially, to the clerk, or justice of the peace, as the case may be, showing such disposition of the property. Such report shall be filed among the papers of the cause.

Historical Notes

Source

Vernon's Ann.Civ.St. art. 299.

Rule 608. Dissolution or Modification of Writ of Attachment

A defendant whose property has been attached or any intervening party who claims an interest in such property, may by sworn written motion, seek to vacate, dissolve, or modify the writ, and the order directing its issuance, for any grounds or cause, extrinsic or intrinsic. Such motion shall admit or deny each finding of the order directing the issuance of the writ except where the movant is unable to admit or deny the finding, in which case movant shall set forth the reasons why he cannot admit or deny. Unless the parties agree to an extension of time, the motion shall be heard promptly, after reasonable notice to the plaintiff (which may be less than three days), and the issue shall be determined not later than ten days after the motion is filed. The filing of the motion shall stay any further proceedings under the writ, except for any orders concerning the care, preservation, or sale of perishable property, until a hearing is had and the issue is determined. The writ shall be dissolved unless at such hearing, the plaintiff shall prove the grounds relied upon for its issuance, but the court may modify its previous order granting the writ and the writ issued pursuant thereto. The movant shall, however, have the burden to prove that the reasonable value of the property attached exceeds the amount necessary to secure the debt, interest for one year, and probable costs. He shall also have the burden to prove the facts to justify substitution of property.

The court's determination may be made upon the basis of affidavits, if uncontroverted, setting forth such facts as would be admissible in evidence; otherwise, the parties shall submit evidence. The court may make all such orders, including orders concerning the care, preservation, or disposition of the property (or the proceeds therefrom if the same has been sold), as justice may require. If the movant has given a replevy bond, an order to vacate or dissolve the writ shall vacate the replevy bond and discharge the sureties thereon, and if the court modifies its order or the writ issued pursuant thereto, it shall make such further orders with respect to the bond as may be consistent with its modification.

July 11, 1977, eff. Jan. 1, 1978.

Historical Notes

Source

Vernon's Ann.Civ.St. art. 303.

Rule 609. Amendment

Clerical errors in the affidavit, bond, or writ of attachment, or the officer's return thereof, may upon application in writing to the judge or justice of the court in which the suit is filed, and after notice to the opponent, be amended in such manner and on such terms as the judge or justice shall authorize by an order entered in the minutes of the court or noted on the docket of the justice of the peace, provided the amendment does not change or add to the grounds of such attachment as stated in the affidavit, and provided such amendment appears to the judge or justice to be in furtherance of justice.

Historical Notes

Source

New rule.

SECTION 2. DISTRESS WARRANT

Rule 610. Application for Distress Warrant and Order

Either at the commencement of a suit or at any time during its progress the plaintiff may file an application for the issuance of a distress warrant with the justice of the peace. Such application may be supported by affidavits of the plaintiff, his agent, his attorney, or other persons having knowledge of relevant facts, but shall include a statement that the amount sued for is rent, or advances described by statute, or shall produce a writing signed by the tenant to that effect, and shall further swear that such warrant is not sued out for the purpose of vexing and harassing the defendant. The application shall comply with all statutory requirements and shall state the grounds for issuing the warrant and the specific facts relied upon by the plaintiff to warrant the required findings by the justice of the peace. The warrant shall not be quashed because two or more grounds are stated conjunctively or disjunctively. The application and any affidavits shall be made on personal knowledge and shall set forth such facts as would be admissible in evidence provided that facts may be stated based upon information and belief if the grounds of such belief are specifically stated.

No warrant shall issue before final judgment except on written order of the justice of the peace after a hearing, which may be ex parte. Such warrant shall be made returnable to a court having jurisdiction of the amount in controversy. The justice of the peace in his order granting the application shall make specific findings of fact to support the statutory grounds found to exist, and shall specify the maximum value of property that may be seized, and the amount of bond required of plaintiff, and, further shall command that property be kept safe and preserved subject to further orders of the court having jurisdiction. Such bond shall be in an amount which, in the opinion of the court, shall adequately compensate defendant in the event plaintiff fails to prosecute his suit to effect, and pay all damages and costs as shall be adjudged against him for wrongfully suing out the warrant. The justice of the peace shall further find in his order the amount of bond required to replevy, which, unless the defendant chooses to exercise his option as provided in Rule 614, shall be the amount of plaintiff's claim, one year's accrual of interest if allowed by law on the claim, and the estimated costs of court. The order may direct the issuance of several warrants at the same time, or in succession, to be sent to different counties.

June 10, 1980, eff. Jan. 1, 1981.

Historical Notes

Source

This new rule is written to conform with the due process requirements of Fuentes v. Shevin, 407 U.S. 67, 92 S.Ct. 1983, 32 L.Ed.2d 556 (1972); Mitchell v. W. T. Grant Co., 416 U.S. 600, 94 S.Ct. 1895, 40 L.Ed.2d 406 (1974); and North Georgia Finishing, Inc. v. Di-Chem, Inc., 419 U.S. 601, 95 S.Ct. 719, 42 L.Ed.2d 751 (1975).

Rule 611. Bond for Distress Warrant

No distress warrant shall issue before final judgment until the party applying therefor has filed with the justice of the peace authorized to issue such warrant a bond payable to the defendant in an amount approved by the justice of the peace, with sufficient surety or sureties as provided by statute, conditioned that the plaintiff will prosecute his suit to effect and pay all damages and costs as may be adjudged against him for wrongfully suing out such warrant.

After notice to the opposite party, either before or after the issuance of the warrant, the defendant or plaintiff may file a motion to increase or reduce the amount of such bond, or to question the sufficiency of the sureties thereon, in a court having jurisdiction of the subject matter. Upon hearing, the court shall enter its order with respect to such bond and sufficiency of the sureties.

June 10, 1980, eff. Jan. 1, 1981.

Historical Notes

Source

This new rule is written to conform with the due process requirements of Fuentes v. Shevin, 92 S.Ct. 1983, 407 U.S. 67, 32 L.Ed.2d 556 (1972); Mitchell v. W. T. Grant Co., 94 S.Ct. 1895, 416 U.S. 600, 40 L.Ed.2d 406 (1974); and North Georgia Finishing, Inc. v. Di-Chem, Inc., 95 S.Ct. 719, 419 U.S. 601, 42 L.Ed.2d 751 (1975).

Rule 612. Requisites for Warrant

A distress warrant shall be directed to the sheriff or any constable within the State of Texas. It shall command him to attach and hold, unless replevied, subject to the further orders of the court having jurisdiction, so much of the property of the defendant, not exempt by statute, of reasonable value in approximately the amount fixed by the justice of the peace, as shall be found within his county.

June 10, 1980, eff. Jan. 1, 1981.

Historical Notes

Source

This new rule is written to conform with the due process requirements of Fuentes v. Shevin, 92 S.Ct. 1983, 407 U.S. 67, 32 L.Ed.2d 556 (1972); Mitchell v. W. T. Grant Co., 94 S.Ct. 1895, 416 U.S. 600, 40 L.Ed.2d 406 (1974); and North Georgia Finishing, Inc. v. Di-Chem, Inc., 419 U.S. 601, 95 S.Ct. 719, 42 L.Ed.2d 751 (1975).

Rule 613. Service of Warrant on Defendant

The defendant shall be served in any manner prescribed for service of citation, or as provided in Rule 21a, with a copy of the distress warrant, the application, accompanying affidavits, and orders of the justice of the peace as soon as practicable following the levy of the warrant. There shall be prominently displayed on the face of the copy of the warrant served on the defendant, in 10-point type and in a manner calculated to advise a reasonably attentive person of its contents, the following:

> To ____________________, Defendant: You are hereby notified that certain properties alleged to be owned by you have been seized. If you claim any rights in such property, you are advised:
>
> "YOU HAVE A RIGHT TO REGAIN POSSESSION OF THE PROPERTY BY FILING A REPLEVY BOND. YOU HAVE A RIGHT TO SEEK TO REGAIN POSSESSION OF THE PROPERTY BY FILING WITH THE COURT A MOTION TO DISSOLVE THIS WARRANT."

June 10, 1980, eff. Jan. 1, 1981.

Historical Notes

Source

This new rule is written to conform with the due process requirements of Fuentes v. Shevin, 92 S.Ct. 1983, 407 U.S. 67, 32 L.Ed.2d 556 (1972); Mitchell v. W. T. Grant Co., 94 S.Ct. 1895, 416 U.S. 600, 40 L.Ed.2d 406 (1974); and North Georgia Finishing, Inc. v. Di-Chem, Inc., 95 S.Ct. 719, 416 U.S. 601, 42 L.Ed.2d 751 (1975).

Rule 614. Defendant May Replevy

At any time before judgment, should the seized property not have been previously claimed or sold, the defendant may replevy the same, or any part thereof, or the proceeds from the sale of the property if it has been sold under order of the court, by giving bond with sufficient surety or sureties as provided by statute, to be approved by a court having jurisdiction of the amount in controversy payable to plaintiff in double the amount of the plaintiff's debt, or, at the defendant's option for not less than the value of the property sought to be replevied, plus one year's interest thereon at the legal rate from the date of the bond, conditioned that the defendant shall satisfy to the extent of the penal amount of the bond any judgment which may be rendered against him in such action.

On reasonable notice to the opposing party (which may be less than three days) either party shall have the right to prompt judicial review of the amount of bond required, denial of bond, sufficiency of sureties, and estimated value of the property, by a court having jurisdiction of the amount in controversy. The court's determination may be made upon the basis of affidavits if uncontroverted setting forth such facts as would be admissible in evidence, otherwise the parties shall submit evidence. The court shall forthwith enter its order either approving or modifying the requirements of the order of the justice of the peace, and such order of the court shall supersede and control with respect to such matters.

On reasonable notice to the opposing party (which may be less than three days) the defendant shall have the right to move the court for a substitution of property, of equal value as that attached, for the property seized. Provided that there has been located sufficient property of the defendant's to satisfy the order of seizure, the court may authorize substitution of one or more items of defendant's property for all or part of the property seized. The court shall first make findings as to the value of the property to be substituted. If property is substituted, the property released from seizure shall be delivered to defendant, if such property is personal property, and all liens upon such property from the original order of seizure or modification thereof shall be terminated. Seizure of substituted property shall be deemed to have existed from the date of levy on the original property seized, and no property on which liens have become affixed since the date of levy on the original property may be substituted.

June 10, 1980, eff. Jan. 1, 1981.

Historical Notes

Source

This new rule is written to conform with the due process requirements of Fuentes v. Shevin, 92 S.Ct. 1983, 407 U.S. 67, 32 L.Ed.2d 556 (1972); Mitchell v. W. T. Grant Co., 94 S.Ct. 1895, 416 U.S. 600, 40 L.Ed.2d 406 (1974); and North Georgia Finishing, Inc. v. Di-Chem, Inc., 95 S.Ct. 719, 419 U.S. 601, 42 L.Ed.2d 751 (1975).

Rule 614a. Dissolution or Modification of Distress Warrant

A defendant whose property has been seized or any intervening claimant who claims an interest in such property, may by sworn written motion, seek to vacate, dissolve, or modify the seizure, and the order directing its issuance, for any grounds or cause, extrinsic or intrinsic. Such motion shall admit or deny each finding of the order directing the issuance of the warrant except where the movant is unable to admit or deny the finding, in which case movant shall set forth the reasons why he cannot admit or deny. Unless the parties agree to an extension of time, the motion shall be heard promptly, after reasonable notice to the plaintiff (which may be less than three days), and the issue shall be determined not later than 10 days after the motion is filed. The filing of the motion shall stay any further proceedings under the warrant, except for any orders concerning the care, preservation, or sale of any perishable property, until a hearing is had, and the issue is determined. The warrant shall be dissolved unless, at such hearing, the plaintiff shall prove the specific facts alleged and the grounds relied upon for its issuance, but the court may modify the order of the justice of the peace granting the warrant and the warrant issued pursuant thereto. The movant shall however have the burden to prove that the reasonable value of the property seized exceeds the amount necessary to secure the debt, interest for one year, and probable costs. He shall also have the burden to prove the facts to justify substitution of property.

The court's determination may be made upon the basis of affidavits setting forth such facts as would be admissible in evidence, but additional evidence, if tendered by either party shall be received and considered. The court may make all such orders, including orders concerning the care, preservation, or disposition of the property (or the proceeds therefrom if the same has been sold), as justice may require. If the movant has given a replevy bond, an order to vacate or dissolve the warrant shall vacate the replevy bond and discharge the sureties thereon, and if the court modifies the order of the justice of the peace or the warrant issued pursuant thereto, it shall make such further orders with respect to the bond as may be consistent with its modification.

June 10, 1980, eff. Jan. 1, 1981.

Historical Notes

Source

This new rule is written to conform with the due process requirements of Fuentes v. Shevin, 92 S.Ct. 1983, 407 U.S. 67, 32 L.Ed.2d 556 (1972); Mitchell v. W. T. Grant Co., 94 S.Ct. 1895, 416 U.S. 600, 40 L.Ed.2d 406 (1974); and North Georgia Finishing, Inc. v. Di-Chem, Inc., 95 S.Ct. 719, 419 U.S. 601, 42 L.Ed.2d 751 (1975).

Rule 615. Sale of Perishable Property

Whenever personal property which has been levied on under a distress warrant shall not have been claimed or replevied, the judge, or justice of the peace, to whose court such writ is made returnable may, either in term time or in vacation, order the same to be sold, when it shall be made to appear that such property is in danger of serious and immediate waste or decay, or that the keeping of the same until the trial will necessarily be attended with such expense or deterioration in value as greatly to lessen the amount likely to be realized therefrom.

Historical Notes

Source

Vernon's Ann.Civ.St. art. 5233.

Rule 616. To Protect Interests

In determining whether the property levied upon is perishable, and the necessity or advantage of ordering a sale thereof, the judge or justice of the peace may act upon affidavits in writing or oral testimony, and may by a preliminary order entered of record with or without notice to the parties as the urgency of the case in his opinion requires, direct the sheriff or constable to sell such property at public auction for cash, and thereupon the sheriff or constable shall sell it accordingly. If the application for an order of sale be filed by any person or party other than the defendant from whose possession the property was taken by levy, the court shall not grant such order, unless the applicant shall file with such court a bond payable to such defendant, with two or more good and sufficient sureties, to be approved by said court, conditioned that they will be responsible to the defendant for such damages as he may sustain in case such sale be illegally and unjustly applied for, or be illegally and unjustly made.

Historical Notes

Source

Vernon's Ann.Civ.St. arts. 294, 5233.

Rule 617. Procedure for Sale

Such sale of perishable personal property shall be conducted in the same manner as sales of personal property under execution; provided, however, that the time of the sale, and the time of advertisement thereof, may be fixed by the judge or justice of the peace at a time earlier than ten days, according to the exigency of the case, and in such event notice thereof shall be given in such manner as directed by the order.

Historical Notes

Source

Vernon's Ann.Civ.St. art. 295.

Rule 618. Return of Sale

The officer making such sale of perishable property shall promptly pay the proceeds of such sale to the clerk of such court or to the justice of the peace, as the case may be, and shall make written return of the order of sale, signed by him officially, stating the time and place of the sale, the name of the purchaser, and the amount of money received, with an itemized account of the expenses attending the sale. Such return shall be filed with the papers of the case.

Historical Notes

Source

Vernon's Ann.Civ.St. art. 296.

Rule 619. Citation for Defendant

The justice at the time he issues the warrant shall issue a citation to the defendant requiring him to answer before such justice at the first day of the next succeeding term of court, stating the time and place of holding the same, if he has jurisdiction to finally try the cause, and upon its being returned served, to proceed to judgment as in ordinary cases; and, if he has not such jurisdiction, the citation shall require the defendant to answer before the court to which the warrant was made returnable at or before ten o'clock a. m. of the Monday next after the expiration of twenty days from the date of service thereof, stating the place of holding the court, and shall be returned with the other papers to such court. If the defendant has removed from the county without service, the proper officer shall state this fact in his return on the citation; and the court shall proceed to try the case ex parte, and may enter judgment.

Historical Notes

Source

Vernon's Ann.Civ.St. art. 5234.

Rule 620. Petition

When the warrant is made returnable to the district or county court, the plaintiff shall file his petition within ten days from the date of the issuance of the writ.

Historical Notes

Source

Vernon's Ann.Civ.St. art. 5235.

SECTION 3. EXECUTIONS

Rule 621. Enforcement of Judgment

The judgments of the district, county, and justice courts shall be enforced by execution or other appropriate process. Such execution or other process shall be returnable in thirty, sixty, or ninety days as requested by the plaintiff, his agent or attorney.

Historical Notes

Source

Vernon's Ann.Civ.St. arts. 2445, 3784.

Rule 621a. Discovery and Enforcement of Judgment

At any time after rendition of judgment, and so long as said judgment has not been suspended by a supersedeas bond or by order of a proper court and has not become dormant as provided by Article 3773, V.A.T.S.,[1] the successful party may, for the purpose of obtaining information to aid in the enforcement of such judgment, initiate and maintain in the trial court in the same suit in which said judgment was rendered any discovery proceeding authorized by these rules for pre-trial matters. Also, at any time after rendition of judgment, either party may, for the purpose of obtaining information relevant to motions allowed by Texas Rules of Appellate Procedure 47 and 49[2] initiate and maintain in the trial court in the same suit in which said judgment was rendered any discovery proceeding authorized by these rules for pre-trial matters. The rules governing and related to such pretrial discovery proceedings shall apply in like manner to discovery proceedings after judgment. The rights herein granted to the parties shall inure to their successors or assignees, in whole or in part. Judicial supervision of such discovery proceedings after judgment shall be the same as that provided by law or these rules for pre-trial discovery and proceedings insofar as applicable.

July 1, 1970, eff. Jan. 1, 1971. Amended by order of July 15, 1987, eff. Jan. 1, 1988.

1 Repealed. See now V.T.C.A., Civil Practice & Remedies Code § 34.001.

[2] So in original. Probably should be Rule 24.

Historical Notes

1988 Amendment

In the rule heading substituted "and" for "in aid of"; divided the first sentence into the first and third sentences by substituting ". The" for ", and the"; inserted the second sentence; in the fourth sentence substituted "parties" for "successful party", substituted "their successors or assignees" for "a successor or assignee" and deleted ", of the successful party" following "or in part"; and inserted "and" in the last sentence.

Source

Added effective Jan. 1, 1971.

Rule 622. Execution

An execution is a process of the court from which it is issued. The clerk of the district or county court or the justice of the peace, as the case may be, shall tax the costs in every case in which a final judgment has been rendered and shall issue execution to enforce such judgment and collect such costs. The execution and subsequent executions shall not be addressed to a particular county, but shall be addressed to any sheriff or any constable within the State of Texas.

Sept. 20, 1941, eff. Dec. 31, 1941.

Historical Notes

Source

Vernon's Ann.Civ.St. arts. 2446, 2447, 3770, 3780-3782.

Rule 623. On Death of Executor

When an executor, administrator, guardian or trustee of an express trust dies, or ceases to be such executor, administrator, guardian or trustee after judgment, execution shall issue on such judgment in the name of his successor, upon an affidavit of such death or termination being filed with the clerk of the court or the justice of the peace, as the case may be, together with the certificate of the appointment of such successor under the hand and seal of the clerk of the court wherein the appointment was made.

Historical Notes

Source

Vernon's Ann.Civ.St. art. 3776.

Rule 624. On Death of Nominal Plaintiff

When a person in whose favor a judgment is rendered for the use of another dies after judgment, execution shall issue in the name of the party for whose use the suit was brought upon an affidavit of such death being filed with the clerk of the court or the justice of the peace.

Historical Notes

Source

Vernon's Ann.Civ.St. art. 3777.

Rule 625. On Money of Deceased

If a sole defendant dies after judgment for money against him, execution shall not issue thereon, but the judgment may be proved up and paid in due course of administration.

Historical Notes

Source

Vernon's Ann.Civ.St. art. 3778.

Rule 626. On Property of Deceased

In any case of judgment other than a money judgment, where the sole defendant, or one or more of several joint defendants, shall die after judgment, upon an affidavit of such death being filed with the clerk, together with the certificate of the appointment of a representative of such decedent under the hand and seal of the clerk of the court wherein such appointment was made, the proper process on such judgment shall issue against such representative.

Historical Notes

Source

Vernon's Ann.Civ.St. art. 3779.

Rule 627. Time for Issuance

If no supersedeas bond or notice of appeal, as required of agencies exempt from filing bonds, has been filed and approved, the clerk of the court or justice of the peace shall issue the execution upon such judgment upon application of the successful party or his attorney after the expiration of thirty days from the time a final judgment is signed. If a timely motion for new trial or in arrest of judgment is filed, the clerk shall issue the execution upon the judgment on application of the party or his attorney after the expiration of thirty days from the time the order overruling the motion is signed or from the time the motion is overruled by operation of law.

July 22, 1975, eff. Jan. 1, 1976. Amended by orders of June 20, 1980, eff. Jan. 1, 1980; Dec. 5, 1983, eff. April 1, 1984.

Historical Notes

Source

Vernon's Ann.Civ.St. arts. 2448, 3771.

Rule 628. Execution Within Thirty Days

Such execution may be issued at any time before the thirtieth day upon the filing of an affidavit by the plaintiff in the judgment or his agent or attorney that the defendant is about to remove his personal property subject to execution by law out of the county, or is about to transfer or secrete such personal property for the purpose of defrauding his creditors.

July 22, 1975, eff. Jan. 1, 1976.

Historical Notes

Source

Vernon's Ann.Civ.St. arts. 2449, 3774.

Rule 629. Requisites of Execution

The style of the execution shall be "The State of Texas." It shall be directed to any sheriff or any constable within the State of Texas. It shall be signed by the clerk or justice officially, and bear the seal of the court, if issued out of the district or county court, and shall require the officer to execute it according to its terms, and to make the costs which have been adjudged against the defendant in execution and the further costs of executing the writ. It shall describe the judgment, stating the court in which, and the time when, rendered, and the names of the parties in whose favor and against whom the judgment was rendered. A correct copy of the bill of costs taxed against the defendant in execution shall be attached to the writ. It shall require the officer to return it within thirty, sixty, or ninety days, as directed by the plaintiff or his attorney.

Sept. 20, 1941, eff. Dec. 20, 1941.

Historical Notes

Source

Vernon's Ann.Civ.St. arts. 2446, 3783, 3784.

Rule 630. Execution on Judgment for Money

When an execution is issued upon a judgment for a sum of money, or directing the payment simply of a sum of money, it must specify in the body thereof the sum recovered or directed to be paid and the sum actually due when it is issued and the rate of interest upon the sum due. It must require the officer to satisfy the judgment and costs out of the property of the judgment debtor subject to execution by law.

Historical Notes

Source

Vernon's Ann.Civ.St. art. 3783, subd. 2.

Rule 631. Execution for Sale of Particular Property

An execution issued upon a judgment for the sale of particular chattels or personal property or real estate, must particularly describe the property, and shall direct the officer to make the sale by previously giving the public notice of the time and place of sale required by law and these rules.

Historical Notes

Source

Vernon's Ann.Civ.St. art. 3783, subd. 3.

Rule 632. Execution for Delivery of Certain Property

An execution issued upon a judgment for the delivery of the possession of a chattel or personal property, or for the delivery of the possession of real property, shall particularly describe the property, and designate the party to whom the judgment awards the possession. The writ shall require the officer to deliver the possession of the property to the party entitled thereto.

Historical Notes

Source

Vernon's Ann.Civ.St. art. 3783, subd. 4.

Rule 633. Execution for Possession or Value of Personal Property

If the judgment be for the recovery of personal property or its value, the writ shall command the officer, in case a delivery thereof cannot be had, to levy and collect the value thereof for which the judgment was recovered, to be specified therein, out of any property of the party against whom judgment was rendered, liable to execution.

Historical Notes

Source

Vernon's Ann.Civ.St. art. 3783, subd. 5.

Rule 634. Execution Superseded

The clerk or justice of the peace shall immediately issue a writ of supersedeas suspending all further proceedings under any execution previously issued when a supersedeas bond is afterward filed and approved within the time prescribed by law or these rules.

Historical Notes

Source

Vernon's Ann.Civ.St. art. 3772.

Rule 635. Stay of Execution in Justice Court

At any time within ten days after the rendition of any judgment in a justice court, the justice may grant a stay of execution thereof for three months from the date of such judgment, if the person against whom such judgment was rendered shall, with one or more good and sufficient sureties, to be approved by the justice, appear before him and acknowledge themselves and each of them bound to the successful party in such judgment for the full amount thereof, with interest and costs, which acknowledgment shall be entered in writing on the docket, and signed by the persons binding themselves as sureties; provided, no such stay of execution shall be granted unless the party applying therefor shall first file an affidavit with the justice that he has not the money with which to pay such judgment, and that the enforcement of same by execution prior to three months would be a hardship upon him and would cause a sacrifice of his property which would not likely be caused should said execution be stayed. Such acknowledgment shall be entered by the justice on his docket and shall constitute a judgment against the defendant and such sureties, upon which execution shall issue in case the same is not paid on or before the expiration of such day.

Historical Notes

Source

Vernon's Ann.Civ.St. art. 2453.

Rule 636. Indorsements by Officer

The officer receiving the execution shall indorse thereon the exact hour and day when he received it. If he receives more than one on the same day against the same person he shall number them as received.

Historical Notes

Source

Vernon's Ann.Civ.St. art. 3785 (part).

Rule 637. Levy of Execution

When an execution is delivered to an officer he shall proceed without delay to levy the same upon the property of the defendant found within his county not exempt from execution, unless otherwise directed by the plaintiff, his agent or attorney. The officer shall first call upon the defendant, if he can be found, or, if absent, upon his agent within the county, if known, to point out property to be levied upon, and the levy shall first be made upon the property designated by the defendant, or his agent. If in the opinion of the officer the property so designated will not sell for enough to satisfy the execution and costs of sale, he shall require an additional designation by the defendant. If no property be thus designated by the defendant, the officer shall levy the execution upon any property of the defendant subject to execution.

Historical Notes

Source

Vernon's Ann.Civ.St. arts. 3788-3790.

Rule 638. Property Not to be Designated

A defendant in execution shall not point out property which he has sold, mortgaged or conveyed in trust, or property exempt from forced sale.

Historical Notes

Source

Vernon's Ann.Civ.St. art. 3791.

Rule 639. Levy

In order to make a levy on real estate, it shall not be necessary for the officer to go upon the ground but it shall be sufficient for him to indorse such levy on the writ. Levy upon personal property is made by taking possession thereof, when the defendant in execution is entitled to the possession. Where the defendant in execution has an interest in personal property, but is not entitled to the possession thereof, a levy is made thereon by giving notice thereof to the person who is entitled to the possession, or one of them where there are several.

Historical Notes

Source

Vernon's Ann.Civ.St. art. 3793.

Rule 640. Levy on Stock Running at Large

A levy upon livestock running at large in a range, and which cannot be herded and penned without great inconvenience and expense, may be made by designating by reasonable estimate the number of animals and describing them by their marks and brands, or either; such levy shall be made in the presence of two or more credible persons, and notice thereof shall be given in writing to the owner or his herder or agent, if residing within the county and known to the officer.

Historical Notes

Source

Vernon's Ann.Civ.St. art. 3794.

Rule 641. Levy on Shares of Stock

A levy upon shares of stock of any corporation or joint stock company for which a certificate is outstanding is made by the officer seizing and taking possession of such certificate. Provided, however, that nothing herein shall be construed as restricting any rights granted under Section 8.317 of the Texas Uniform Commercial Code.

Aug. 18, 1947, eff. Dec. 31, 1947. Amended by order of July 21, 1970, eff. Jan. 1, 1971.

Historical Notes

Source

Vernon's Ann.Civ.St. art. 3795.

Rule 642. Repealed July 22, 1975, effective Jan. 1, 1976

Rule 643. Levy on Goods Pledged or Mortgaged

Goods and chattels pledged, assigned or mortgaged as security for any debt or contract, may be levied upon and sold on execution against the person making the pledge, assignment or mortgage subject thereto; and the purchaser shall be entitled to the possession when it is held by the pledgee, assignee or mortgagee, on complying with the conditions of the pledge, assignment or mortgage.

Historical Notes

Source

Vernon's Ann.Civ.St. art. 3797.

Rule 644. May Give Delivery Bond

Any personal property taken in execution may be returned to the defendant by the officer upon the delivery by the defendant to him of a bond, payable to the plaintiff, with two or more good and sufficient sureties, to be approved by the officer, conditioned that the property shall be delivered to the officer at the time and place named in the bond, to be sold according to law, or for the payment to the officer of a fair value thereof, which shall be stated in the bond.

Historical Notes

Source

Vernon's Ann.Civ.St. art. 3801.

Rule 645. Property May be Sold by Defendant

Where property has been replevied, as provided in the preceding rule, the defendant may sell or dispose of the same, paying the officer the stipulated value thereof.

Historical Notes

Source

Vernon's Ann.Civ.St. art. 3802.

Rule 646. Forfeited Delivery Bond

In case of the non-delivery of the property according to the terms of the delivery bond, and non-payment of the value thereof, the officer shall forthwith indorse the bond "Forfeited" and return the same to the clerk of the court or the justice of the peace from which the execution issued; whereupon, if the judgment remain unsatisfied in whole or in part, the clerk or justice shall issue execution against the principal debtor and the sureties on the bond for the amount due, not exceeding the stipulated value of the property, upon which execution no delivery bond shall be taken, which instruction shall be indorsed by the clerk or justice on the execution.

Historical Notes

Source

Vernon's Ann.Civ.St. art. 3803.

Rule 646a. Sale of Real Property

Real property taken by virtue of any execution shall be sold at public auction, at the courthouse door of the county, unless the court orders that such sale be at the place where the real property is situated, on the first Tuesday of the month, between the hours of ten o'clock, a. m. and four o'clock, p. m.

July 26, 1960, eff. Jan. 1, 1961.

Historical Notes

Source

New rule, added eff. Jan. 1, 1961. Derived from Vernon's Ann.Civ.St. art. 3804, adding "unless the court orders that such sale be at the place where the real property is situated."

Rule 647. Notice of Sale of Real Estate

The time and place of sale of real estate under execution, order of sale, or venditioni exponas, shall be advertised by the officer by having the notice thereof published in the English language once a week for three consecutive weeks preceding such sale, in some newspaper published in said county. The first of said publications shall appear not less than twenty days immediately preceding the day of sale. Said notice shall contain a statement of the authority by virtue of which the sale is to be made, the time of levy, and the time and place of sale; it shall also contain a brief description of the property to be sold, and shall give the number of acres, original survey, locality in the county, and the name by which the land is most generally known, but it shall not be necessary for it to contain field notes. Publishers of newspapers shall charge the legal rate of Two (2) Cents per word for the first insertion of such publication and One (1) Cent per word for such subsequent insertions, or such newspapers shall be entitled to charge for such publication at a rate equal to but not in excess of the published word or line rate of that newspaper for such class of advertising. If there be no newspaper published in the county, or none which will publish the notice of sale for the compensation herein fixed, the officer shall then post such notice in writing in three public places in the county, one of which shall be at the courthouse door of such county, for at least twenty days successively next before the day of sale. The officer making the levy shall give the defendant, or his attorney, written notice of such sale, either in person or by mail, which notice shall substantially conform to the foregoing requirements.

Sept. 20, 1941, eff. Dec. 31, 1941.

Historical Notes

Source

Vernon's Ann.Civ.St. art. 3808.

Rule 648. "Courthouse Door" Defined

By the term "courthouse door" of a county is meant either of the principal entrances to the house provided by the proper authority for the holding of the district court. If from any cause there is no such house, the door of the house where the district court was last held in that county shall be deemed to be the courthouse door. Where the courthouse, or house used by the court, has been destroyed by fire or other cause, and another has not been designated by the proper authority, the place where such house stood shall be deemed to be the courthouse door.

Historical Notes

Source

Vernon's Ann.Civ.St. art. 3809.

Rule 649. Sale of Personal Property

Personal property levied on under execution shall be offered for sale on the premises where it is taken in execution, or at the courthouse door of the county, or at some other place if, owing to the nature of the property, it is more convenient to exhibit it to purchasers at such place. Personal property susceptible of being exhibited shall not be sold unless the same be present and subject to the view of those attending the sale, except shares of stock in joint stock or incorporated companies, and in cases where the defendant in execution has merely an interest without right to the exclusive possession in which case the interest of defendant may be sold and conveyed without the presence or delivery of the property. When a levy is made upon livestock running at large on the range, it is not necessary that such stock, or any part thereof, be present at the place of sale, and the purchaser at such sale is authorized to gather and pen such stock and select therefrom the number purchased by him.

Historical Notes

Source

Vernon's Ann.Civ.St. art. 3811, 3813, 3814.

Rule 650. Notice of Sale of Personal Property

Previous notice of the time and place of the sale of any personal property levied on under execution shall be given by posting notice thereof for ten days successively immediately prior to the day of sale at the courthouse door of any county and at the place where the sale is to be made.

Historical Notes

Source

Vernon's Ann.Civ.St. art. 3812, reducing number of places where notice must be posted from three to two.

Rule 651. When Execution Not Satisfied

When the property levied upon does not sell for enough to satisfy the execution, the officer shall proceed anew, as in the first instance, to make the residue.

Historical Notes

Source

Vernon's Ann.Civ.St. art. 3815.

Rule 652. Purchaser Failing to Comply

If any person shall bid off property at any sale made by virtue of an execution, and shall fail to comply with the terms of the sale, he shall be liable to pay the plaintiff in execution twenty per cent on the value of the property thus bid off, besides costs, to be recovered on motion, five days notice of such motion being given to such purchaser; and should the property on a second sale bring less than on the former, he shall be liable to pay to the defendant in execution all loss which he sustains thereby, to be recovered on motion as above provided.

Historical Notes

Source

Vernon's Ann.Civ.St. art. 3821.

Rule 653. Resale of Property

When the terms of the sale shall not be complied with by the bidder the levying officer shall proceed to sell the same property again on the same day, if there be sufficient time; but if not, he shall re-advertise and sell the same as in the first instance.

Historical Notes

Source

Vernon's Ann.Civ.St. art. 3822.

Rule 654. Return of Execution

The levying officer shall make due return of the execution, in writing and signed by him officially, stating concisely what such officer has done in pursuance of the requirements of the writ and of the law. The return shall be filed with the clerk of the court or the justice of the peace as the case may be. The execution shall be returned forthwith if satisfied by the collection of the money or if ordered by the plaintiff or his attorney indorsed thereon.

Historical Notes

Source

Vernon's Ann.Civ.St. art. 3828.

Rule 655. Return of Execution by Mail

When an execution is placed in the hands of an officer of a county other than the one in which the judgment is rendered, return may be made by mail; but money cannot be thus sent except by direction of the party entitled to receive the same or his attorney of record.

Historical Notes

Source

Vernon's Ann.Civ.St. art. 3823.

Rule 656. Execution Docket

The clerk of each court shall keep an execution docket in which he shall enter a statement of all executions as they are issued by him, specifying the names of the parties, the amount of the judgment, the amount due thereon, the rate of interest when it exceeds six per cent, the costs, the date of issuing the execution, to whom delivered, and the return of the officer thereon, with the date of such return. Such docket entries shall be taken and deemed to be a record. The clerk shall keep an index and cross-index to the execution docket. When execution is in favor or against several persons, it shall be indexed in the name of each person. Any clerk who shall fail to keep said execution docket and index thereto, or shall neglect to make the entries therein, shall be liable upon his official bond to any person injured for the amount of damages sustained by such neglect.

Historical Notes

Source

Vernon's Ann.Civ.St. art. 3831, reducing eight per cent to six per cent.

SECTION 4. GARNISHMENT

Rule 657. Judgment Final for Garnishment

In the case mentioned in subsection 3, section 63.001, Civil Practice and Remedies Code, the judgment whether based upon a liquidated demand or an unliquidated demand, shall be deemed final and subsisting for the purpose of garnishment from and after the date it is signed, unless a supersedeas bond shall have been approved and filed in accordance with Texas Rules of Appellate Procedure 47.[1]

June 10, 1980, eff. Jan. 1, 1981. Amended by order of July 15, 1987, eff. Jan. 1, 1988.

[1] So in original. Probably should read Rule 24.

Historical Notes

1988 Amendment

Substituted the Civil Practice and Remedies Code citation for a Revised Civil Statute citation and substituted the Rule citation.

Source

New rule.

Rule 658. Application for Writ of Garnishment and Order

Either at the commencement of a suit or at any time during its progress the plaintiff may file an application for a writ of garnishment. Such application shall be supported by affidavits of the plaintiff, his agent, his attorney, or other person having knowledge of relevant facts. The application shall comply with all statutory requirements and shall state the grounds for issuing the writ and the specific facts relied upon by the plaintiff to warrant the required findings by the court. The writ shall not be quashed because two or more grounds are stated conjunctively or disjunctively. The application and any affidavits shall be made on personal knowledge and shall set forth such facts as would be admissible in evidence; provided that facts may be stated based upon information and belief if the grounds of such belief are specifically stated.

No writ shall issue before final judgment except upon written order of the court after a hearing, which may be ex parte. The court in its order granting the application shall make specific findings of facts to support the statutory grounds found to exist, and shall specify the maximum value of property or indebtedness that may be garnished and the amount of bond required of plaintiff. Such bond shall be in an amount which, in the opinion of the court, shall adequately compensate defendant in the event plaintiff fails to prosecute his suit to effect, and pay all damages and costs as shall be adjudged against him for wrongfully suing out the writ of garnishment. The court shall further find in its order the amount of bond required of defendant to replevy, which, unless defendant exercises his option as provided under Rule 664, shall be the amount of plaintiff's claim, one year's accrual of interest if allowed by law on the claim, and the estimated costs of court. The order may direct the issuance of several writs at the same time, or in succession, to be sent to different counties.

Aug. 18, 1947, eff. Dec. 31, 1947. Amended by order of July 11, 1977, eff. Jan. 1, 1978.

Historical Notes

Source

Vernon's Ann.Civ.St. art. 4078.

Rule 658a. Bond for Garnishment

No writ of garnishment shall issue before final judgment until the party applying therefor has filed with the officer authorized to issue such writ a bond payable to the defendant in the amount fixed by the court's order, with sufficient surety or sureties as provided by statute, conditioned that the plaintiff will prosecute his suit to effect and pay to the extent of the penal amount of the bond all damages and costs as may be adjudged against him for wrongfully suing out such writ of garnishment.

After notice to the opposite party, either before or after the issuance of the writ, the defendant or plaintiff may file a motion to increase or reduce the amount of such bond, or to question the sufficiency of the sureties. Upon hearing, the court shall enter its order with respect to such bond and the sufficiency of the sureties.

Should it be determined from the garnishee's answer if such is not controverted that the garnishee is indebted to the defendant, or has in his hands effects belonging to the defendant, in an amount or value less than the amount of the debt claimed by the plaintiff, then after notice to the defendant the court in which such garnishment is pending upon hearing may reduce the required amount of such bond to double the sum of the garnishee's indebtedness to the defendant plus the value of the effects in his hands belonging to the defendant.

July 26, 1960, eff. Jan. 1, 1961. Amended by order of July 11, 1977, eff. Jan. 1, 1978.

Historical Notes

Source

New rule, added eff. Jan. 1, 1961. Derived from Vernon's Ann.Civ.St. art. 4077.

Rule 659. Case Docketed

When the foregoing requirements of these rules have been complied with, the judge, or clerk, or justice of the peace, as the case may be, shall docket the case in the name of the plaintiff as plaintiff and of the garnishee as defendant; and shall immediately issue a writ of garnishment directed to the garnishee, commanding him to appear before the court out of which the same is issued at or before 10 o'clock a.m. of the Monday next following the expiration of twenty days from the date the writ was served, if the writ is issued out of the district or county court; or the Monday next after the expiration of ten days from the date the writ was served, if the writ is issued out of the justice court. The writ shall command the garnishee to answer under oath upon such return date what, if anything, he is indebted to the defendant, and was when the writ was served, and what effects, if any, of the defendant he has in his possession, and had when such writ was served, and what other persons, if any, within his knowledge, are indebted to the defendant or have effects belonging to him in their possession.

Sept. 20, 1941, eff. Dec. 31, 1941. Amended by orders of Aug. 18, 1947, eff. Dec. 31, 1947; July 11, 1977, eff. Jan. 1, 1978.

Historical Notes

Source

Vernon's Ann.Civ.St. art. 4079.

Rule 660. Repealed by Order of Aug. 18, 1947, eff. Dec. 31, 1947

Rule 661. Form of Writ

The following form of writ may be used:

"The State of Texas.

To E.F., Garnishee, greeting:

Whereas, in the __________ Court of __________ County (if a justice court, state also the number of the precinct), in a certain cause wherein A.B. is plaintiff and C.D. is defendant, the plaintiff, claiming an indebtedness against the said C.D. of __________ dollars, besides interest and costs of suit, has applied for a writ of garnishment against you, E.F.; therefore you are hereby commanded to be and appear before said court at __________ in said county (if the writ is issued from the county or district court, here proceed: 'at 10 o'clock a.m. on the Monday next following the expiration of twenty days from the date of service hereof.' If the writ is issued from a justice of the peace court, here proceed: 'at or before 10 o'clock a.m. on the Monday next after the expiration of ten days from the date of service hereof.' In either event, proceed as follows:) then and there to answer upon oath what, if anything, you are indebted to the said C.D., and were when this writ was served upon you, and what effects, if any, of the said C.D. you have in your possession, and had when this writ was served, and what other persons, if any, within your knowledge, are indebted to the said C.D. or have effects belonging to him in their possession. You are further commanded NOT to pay to defendant any debt or to deliver to him any effects, pending further order of this court. Herein fail not, but make due answer as the law directs."

Sept. 20, 1941, eff. Dec. 31, 1941. Amended by orders of Aug. 18, 1947, eff. Dec. 31, 1947; July 11, 1977, eff. Jan. 1, 1978.

Historical Notes

Source

Vernon's Ann.Civ.St. art. 4081, modified by directing writ to garnishee instead of officer and by change in return date in district and county courts.

Rule 662. Delivery of Writ

The writ of garnishment shall be dated and tested as other writs, and may be delivered to the sheriff or constable by the officer who issued it, or he may deliver it to the plaintiff, his agent or attorney, for that purpose.

Historical Notes

Source

Vernon's Ann.Civ.St. art. 4082.

Rule 663. Execution and Return of Writ

The sheriff or constable receiving the writ of garnishment shall immediately proceed to execute the same by delivering a copy thereof to the garnishee, and shall make return thereof as of other citations.

Historical Notes

Source

Vernon's Ann.Civ.St. art. 4083.

Rule 663a. Service of Writ on Defendant

The defendant shall be served in any manner prescribed for service of citation or as provided in Rule 21a with a copy of the writ of garnishment, the application, accompanying affidavits and orders of the court as soon as practicable following the service of the writ. There shall be prominently displayed on the face of the copy of the writ served on the defendant, in ten-point type and in a manner calculated to advise a reasonably attentive person of its contents, the following:

"To ____________________, Defendant:

You are hereby notified that certain properties alleged to be owned by you have been garnished. If you claim any rights in such property, you are advised:

"YOU HAVE A RIGHT TO REGAIN POSSESSION OF THE PROPERTY BY FILING A REPLEVY BOND. YOU HAVE A RIGHT TO SEEK TO REGAIN POSSESSION OF THE PROPERTY BY FILING WITH THE COURT A MOTION TO DISSOLVE THIS WRIT."

July 11, 1977, eff. Jan. 1, 1978.

Historical Notes

Source

This is a new rule. It affords the defendant notice of the proceedings and informs him of some of his rights.

Rule 664. Defendant May Replevy

At any time before judgment, should the garnished property not have been previously claimed or sold, the defendant may replevy the same, or any part thereof, or the proceeds from the sale of the property if it has been sold under order of the court, by giving bond with sufficient surety or sureties as provided by statute, to be approved by the officer who levied the writ, payable to plaintiff, in the amount fixed by the court's order, or, at the defendant's option, for the value of the property or indebtedness sought to be replevied (to be estimated by the officer), plus one year's interest thereon at the legal rate from the date of the bond, conditioned that the defendant, garnishee, shall satisfy, to the extent of the penal amount of the bond, any judgment which may be rendered against him in such action.

On reasonable notice to the opposing party (which may be less than three days) either party shall have the right to prompt judicial review of the amount of bond required, denial of bond, sufficiency of sureties, and estimated value of the property, by the court which authorized issuance of the writ. The court's determination may be made upon the basis of affidavits, if uncontroverted, setting forth such facts as would be admissible in evidence; otherwise, the parties shall submit evidence. The court shall forthwith enter its order either approving or modifying the requirements of the officer or of the court's prior order, and such order of the court shall supersede and control with respect to such matters.

On reasonable notice to the opposing party (which may be less than three days) the defendant shall have the right to move the court for a substitution of property, of equal value as that garnished, for the property garnished. Provided that there has been located sufficient property of the defendant's to satisfy the order of garnishment, the court may authorize substitution of one or more items of defendant's property for all or for part of the property garnished. The court shall first make findings as to the value of the property to be substituted. If property is substituted, the property released from garnishment shall be delivered to defendant, if such property is personal property, and all liens upon such property from the original order of garnishment or modification thereof shall be terminated. Garnishment of substituted property shall be deemed to have existed from date of garnishment on the original property garnished, and no property on which liens have become affixed since the date of garnishment of the original property may be substituted.

July 11, 1977, eff. Jan. 1, 1978.

Historical Notes

Source

Vernon's Ann.Civ.St. art. 4084 (part).

Rule 664a. Dissolution or Modification of Writ of Garnishment

A defendant whose property or account has been garnished or any intervening party who claims an interest in such property or account, may by sworn written motion, seek to vacate, dissolve or modify the writ of garnishment, and the order directing its issuance, for any grounds or cause, extrinsic or intrinsic. Such motion shall admit or deny each finding of the order directing the issuance of the writ except where the movant is unable to admit or deny the finding, in which case movant shall set forth the reasons why he cannot admit or deny. Unless the parties agree to an extension of time, the motion shall be heard promptly, after reasonable notice to the plaintiff (which may be less than three days), and the issue shall be determined not later than ten days after the motion is filed. The filing of the motion shall stay any further proceedings under the writ, except for any orders concerning the care, preservation or sale of any perishable property, until a hearing is had, and the issue is determined. The writ shall be dissolved unless, at such hearing, the plaintiff shall prove the grounds relied upon for its issuance, but the court may modify its previous order granting the writ and the writ issued pursuant thereto. The movant shall, however, have the burden to prove that the reasonable value of the property garnished exceeds the amount necessary to secure the debt, interest for one year, and probable costs. He shall also have the burden to prove facts to justify substitution of property.

The court's determination may be made upon the basis of affidavits, if uncontroverted, setting forth such facts as would be admissible in evidence; otherwise, the parties shall submit evidence. The court may make all such orders including orders concerning the care, preservation or disposition of the property (or the proceeds therefrom if the same has been sold), as justice may require. If the movant has given a replevy bond, an order to vacate or dissolve the writ shall vacate the replevy bond and discharge the sureties thereon, and if the court modifies its order or the writ issued pursuant thereto, it shall make such further orders with respect to the bond as may be consistent with its modification.

July 11, 1977, eff. Jan. 1, 1978.

Historical Notes

Source

This is a new rule which affords a prompt hearing, provides for the procedures, burden of proof and the kind of proof.

Rule 665. Answer to Writ

The answer of the garnishee shall be under oath, in writing and signed by him, and shall make true answers to the several matters inquired of in the writ of garnishment.

Historical Notes

Source

Vernon's Ann.Civ.St. art. 4085.

Rule 666. Garnishee Discharged

If it appears from the answer of the garnishee that he is not indebted to the defendant, and was not so indebted when the writ of garnishment was served upon him, and that he has not in his possession any effects of the defendant and had not when the writ was served, and if he has either denied that any other persons within his knowledge are indebted to the defendant or have in their possession effects belonging to the defendant, or else has named such persons, should the answer of the garnishee not be controverted as hereinafter provided, the court shall enter judgment discharging the garnishee.

Aug. 18, 1947, eff. Dec. 31, 1947.

Historical Notes

Source

Vernon's Ann.Civ.St. art. 4086.

Rule 667. Judgment by Default

If the garnishee fails to file an answer to the writ of garnishment at or before the time directed in the writ, it shall be lawful for the court, at any time after judgment shall have been rendered against the defendant, and on or after appearance day, to render judgment by default, as in other civil cases, against such garnishee for the full amount of such judgment against the defendant together with all interest and costs that may have accrued in the main case and also in the garnishment proceedings. The answer of the garnishee may be filed as in any other civil case at any time before such default judgment is rendered.

Historical Notes

Source

Vernon's Ann.Civ.St. art. 4087.

Rule 668. Judgment When Garnishee Is Indebted

Should it appear from the answer of the garnishee or should it be otherwise made to appear and be found by the court that the garnishee is indebted to the defendant in any amount, or was so indebted when the writ of garnishment was served, the court shall render judgment for the plaintiff against the garnishee for the amount so admitted or found to be due to the defendant from the garnishee, unless such amount is in excess of the amount of the plaintiff's judgment against the defendant with interest and costs, in which case, judgment shall be rendered against the garnishee for the full amount of the judgment already rendered against the defendant, together with interest and costs of the suit in the original case and also in the garnishment proceedings. If the garnishee fail or refuse to pay such judgment rendered against him, execution shall issue thereon in the same manner and under the same conditions as is or may be provided for the issuance of execution in other cases.

Historical Notes

Source

Vernon's Ann.Civ.St. art. 4088.

Rule 669. Judgment for Effects

Should it appear from the garnishee's answer, or otherwise, that the garnishee has in his possession, or had when the writ was served, any effects of the defendant liable to execution, including any certificates of stock in any corporation or joint stock company, the court shall render a decree ordering sale of such effects under execution in satisfaction of plaintiff's judgment and directing the garnishee to deliver them, or so much thereof as shall be necessary to satisfy plaintiff's judgment, to the proper officer for that purpose.

Aug. 18, 1947, eff. Dec. 31, 1947.

Historical Notes

Source

Vernon's Ann.Civ.St. art. 4089.

Rule 670. Refusal to Deliver Effects

Should the garnishee adjudged to have effects of the defendant in his possession, as provided in the preceding rule, fail or refuse to deliver them to the sheriff or constable on such demand, the officer shall immediately make return of such failure or refusal, whereupon on motion of the plaintiff, the garnishee shall be cited to show cause upon a date to be fixed by the court why he should not be attached for contempt of court for such failure or refusal. If the garnishee fails to show some good and sufficient excuse for such failure or refusal, he shall be fined for such contempt and imprisoned until he shall deliver such effects.

Historical Notes

Source

Vernon's Ann.Civ.St. art. 4090.

Rule 671. Repealed by Order of Aug. 18, 1947, eff. Dec. 31, 1947

Rule 672. Sale of Effects

The sale so ordered shall be conducted in all respects as other sales of personal property under execution; and the officer making such sale shall execute a transfer of such effects or interest to the purchaser, with a brief recital of the judgment of the court under which the same was sold.

Aug. 18, 1947, eff. Dec. 31, 1947.

Historical Notes

Source

Vernon's Ann.Civ.St. art. 4092.

Rule 673. May Traverse Answer

If the plaintiff should not be satisfied with the answer of any garnishee, he may controvert the same by his affidavit stating that he has good reason to believe, and does believe, that the answer of the garnishee is incorrect, stating in what particular he believes the same to be incorrect. The defendant may also, in like manner, controvert the answer of the garnishee.

Historical Notes

Source

Vernon's Ann.Civ.St. art. 4094.

Rule 674. Trial of Issue

If the garnishee whose answer is controverted, is a resident of the county in which the proceeding is pending, an issue shall be formed under the direction of the court and tried as in other cases.

Historical Notes

Source

Vernon's Ann.Civ.St. art. 4095.

Rule 675. Docket and Notice

The clerk of the court or the justice of the peace, on receiving certified copies filed in the county of the garnishee's residence under the provisions of the statutes, shall docket the case in the name of the plaintiff as plaintiff, and of the garnishee as defendant, and issue a notice to the garnishee, stating that his answer has been so controverted, and that such issue will stand for trial on the docket of such court. Such notice shall be directed to the garnishee, be dated and tested as other process from such court, and served by delivering a copy thereof to the garnishee. It shall be returnable, if issued from the district or county court, at ten o'clock a. m. of the Monday next after the expiration of twenty days from the date of its service; and if issued from the justice court, to the next term of such court convening after the expiration of twenty days after the service of such notice.

Sept. 20, 1941, eff. Dec. 31, 1941.

Historical Notes

Source

Vernon's Ann.Civ.St. art. 4097.

Rule 676. Issue Tried as in Other Cases

Upon the return of such notice served, an issue shall be formed under the direction of the court and tried as in other cases.

Historical Notes

Source

Vernon's Ann.Civ.St. art. 4098.

Rule 677. Costs

Where the garnishee is discharged upon his answer, the costs of the proceeding, including a reasonable compensation to the garnishee, shall be taxed against the plaintiff; where the answer of the garnishee has not been controverted and the garnishee is held thereon, such costs shall be taxed against the defendant and included in the execution provided for in this section; where the answer is contested, the costs shall abide the issue of such contest.

Historical Notes

Source

Vernon's Ann.Civ.St. art. 4100.

Rule 678. Garnishee Discharged on Proof

It shall be a sufficient answer to any claim of the defendant against the garnishee founded on an indebtedness of such garnishee, or on the possession by him of any effects, for the garnishee to show that such indebtedness has been paid, or such effects, including any certificates of stock in any incorporated or joint stock company, have been delivered to any sheriff or constable as provided for in Rule 669.

Aug. 18, 1947, eff. Dec. 13, 1947.

Historical Notes

Source

Vernon's Ann.Civ.St. art. 4101.

Rule 679. Amendment

Clerical errors in the affidavit, bond, or writ of garnishment or the officer's return thereof, may upon application in writing to the judge or justice of the court in which the suit is filed, and after notice to the opponent, be amended in such manner and on such terms as the judge or justice shall authorize by an order entered in the minutes of the court (or noted on the docket of the justice of the peace), provided such amendment appears to the judge or justice to be in furtherance of justice.

Historical Notes

Source

New rule.

SECTION 5. INJUNCTIONS

Rule 680. Temporary Restraining Order

No temporary restraining order shall be granted without notice to the adverse party unless it clearly appears from specific facts shown by affidavit or by the verified complaint that immediate and irreparable injury, loss, or damage will result to the applicant before notice can be served and a hearing had thereon. Every temporary restraining order granted without notice shall be endorsed with the date and hour of issuance; shall be filed forthwith in the clerk's office and entered of record; shall define the injury and state why it is irreparable and why the order was granted without notice; and shall expire by its terms within such time after signing, not to exceed fourteen days, as the court fixes, unless within the time so fixed the order, for good cause shown, is extended for a like period or unless the party against whom the order is directed consents that it may be extended for a longer period. The reasons for the extension shall be entered of record. No more than one extension may be granted unless subsequent extensions are unopposed. In case a temporary restraining order is granted without notice, the application for a temporary injunction shall be set down for hearing at the earliest possible date and takes precedence of all matters except older matters of the same character; and when the application comes on for hearing the party who obtained the temporary restraining order shall proceed with the application for a temporary injunction and, if he does not do so, the court shall dissolve the temporary restraining order. On two days' notice to the party who obtained the temporary restraining order without notice or on such shorter notice to that party as the court may prescribe, the adverse party may appear and move its dissolution or modification and in that event the court shall proceed to hear and determine such motion as expeditiously as the ends of justice require.

Every restraining order shall include an order setting a certain date for hearing on the temporary or permanent injunction sought.

Dec. 5, 1983, eff. April 1, 1984. Amended by order of July 15, 1987, eff. Jan. 1, 1988.

Historical Notes

1988 Amendment

Increases the initial temporary restraining order from 10 days to 14 days.

Source

Federal Rule 65(b).

Rule 681. Temporary Injunctions: Notice

No temporary injunction shall be issued without notice to the adverse party.

Historical Notes

Source

Federal Rule 65(a).

Rule 682. Sworn Petition

No writ of injunction shall be granted unless the applicant therefor shall present his petition to the judge verified by his affidavit and containing a plain and intelligible statement of the grounds for such relief.

March 31, 1941, eff. Sept. 1, 1941.

Historical Notes

Source

Vernon's Ann.Civ.St. art. 4647.

Rule 683. Form and Scope of Injunction or Restraining Order

Every order granting an injunction and every restraining order shall set forth the reasons for its issuance; shall be specific in terms; shall describe in reasonable detail and not by reference to the complaint or other document, the act or acts sought to be restrained; and is binding only upon the parties to the action, their officers, agents, servants, employees, and attorneys, and upon those persons in active concert or participation with them who receive actual notice of the order by personal service or otherwise.

Every order granting a temporary injunction shall include an order setting the cause for trial on the merits with respect to the ultimate relief sought. The appeal of a temporary injunction shall constitute no cause for delay of the trial.[1]

Dec. 5, 1983, eff. April 1, 1984.

[1] See V.T.C.A., Civil Practice and Remedies Code § 51.014(b) added by Acts 1997, 75th Leg., ch. 1296, § 1, effective June 20, 1997.

Historical Notes

Source

Federal Rule 65(d).

Rule 684. Applicant's Bond

In the order granting any temporary restraining order or temporary injunction, the court shall fix the amount of security to be given by the applicant. Before the issuance of the temporary restraining order or temporary injunction the applicant shall execute and file with the clerk a bond to the adverse party, with two or more good and sufficient sureties, to be approved by the clerk, in the sum fixed by the judge, conditioned that the applicant will abide the decision which may be made in the cause, and that he will pay all sums of money and costs that may be adjudged against him if the restraining order or temporary injunction shall be dissolved in whole or in part.

Where the temporary restraining order or temporary injunction is against the State, a municipality, a State agency, or a subdivision of the State in its governmental capacity, and is such that the State, municipality, State agency, or subdivision of the State in its governmental capacity, has no pecuniary interest in the suit and no monetary damages can be shown, the bond shall be allowed in the sum fixed by the judge, and the liability of the applicant shall be for its face amount if the restraining order or temporary injunction shall be dissolved in whole or in part. The discretion of the trial court in fixing the amount of the bond shall be subject to review. Provided that under equitable circumstances and for good cause shown by affidavit or otherwise the court rendering judgment on the bond may allow recovery for less than its full face amount, the action of the court to be subject to review.

June 16, 1943, eff. Dec. 31, 1943. Amended by orders of Oct. 12, 1949, eff. March 1, 1950; June 10, 1980, eff. Jan. 1, 1981.

Historical Notes

Source

Vernon's Ann.Civ.St. art. 4649, modified to conform to Federal rule relating to injunction.

Rule 685. Filing and Docketing

Upon the grant of a temporary restraining order or an order fixing a time for hearing upon an application for a temporary injunction, the party to whom the same is granted shall file his petition therefor, together with the order of the judge, with the clerk of the proper court; and, if such orders do not pertain to a pending suit in said court, the cause shall be entered on the docket of the court in its regular order in the name of the party applying for the writ as plaintiff and of the opposite party as defendant.

Historical Notes

Source

Vernon's Ann.Civ.St. art. 4650. Minor textual change.

Rule 686. Citation

Upon the filing of such petition and order not pertaining to a suit pending in the court, the clerk of such court shall issue a citation to the defendant as in other civil cases, which shall be served and returned in like manner as ordinary citations issued from said court; provided, however, that when a temporary restraining order is issued and is accompanied with a true copy of plaintiff's petition, it shall not be necessary for the citation in the original suit to be accompanied with a copy of plaintiff's petition, nor contain a statement of the nature of plaintiff's demand, but it shall be sufficient for said citation to refer to plaintiff's claim as set forth in a true copy of plaintiff's petition which accompanies the temporary restraining order; and provided further that the court may have a hearing upon an application for a temporary restraining order or temporary injunction at such time and upon such reasonable notice given in such manner as the court may direct.

June 16, 1943, eff. Dec. 31, 1943. Amended by order of Aug. 18, 1947, eff. Dec. 31, 1947.

Historical Notes

Source

Vernon's Ann.Civ.St. art. 4655.

Rule 687. Requisites of Writ

The writ of injunction shall be sufficient if it contains substantially the following requisites:

(a) Its style shall be, "The State of Texas."

(b) It shall be directed to the person or persons enjoined.

(c) It must state the names of the parties to the proceedings, plaintiff and defendant, and the nature of the plaintiff's application, with the action of the judge thereon.

(d) It must command the person or persons to whom it is directed to desist and refrain from the commission or continuance of the act enjoined, or to obey and execute such order as the judge has seen proper to make.

(e) If it is a temporary restraining order, it shall state the day and time set for hearing, which shall not exceed fourteen days from the date of the court's order granting such temporary restraining order; but if it is a temporary injunction, issued after notice, it shall be made returnable at or before ten o'clock a.m. of the Monday next after the expiration of twenty days from the date of service thereof, as in the case of ordinary citations.

(f) It shall be dated and signed by the clerk officially and attested with the seal of his office and the date of its issuance must be indorsed thereon.

April 24, 1990, eff. Sept. 1, 1990.

Historical Notes

1990 Amendment

Substituted "fourteen" for "ten" in subd. (e).

Source

Vernon's Ann.Civ.St. art. 4651.

Rule 688. Clerk to Issue Writ

When the petition, order of the judge and bond have been filed, the clerk shall issue the temporary restraining order or temporary injunction, as the case may be, in conformity with the terms of the order, and deliver the same to the sheriff or any constable of the county of the residence of the person enjoined, or to the applicant, as the latter shall direct. If several persons are enjoined, residing in different counties, the clerk shall issue such additional copies of the writ as shall be requested by the applicant. The clerk must retain a copy of the temporary restraining order or temporary injunction in the court's file.

Amended by order of Dec. 12, 2011, eff. Jan. 1, 2012.

Historical Notes

2011 Amendment

The order dated December 12, 2011 added the last sentence.

Source

Vernon's Ann.Civ.St. art. 4652.

Rule 689. Service and Return

The officer receiving a writ of injunction shall indorse thereon the date of its receipt by him, and shall forthwith execute the same by delivering to the party enjoined a true copy thereof. The officer must complete and file a return in accordance with Rule 107.

Amended by order of Dec. 12, 2011, eff. Jan. 1, 2012.

Historical Notes

2011 Amendment

The order dated December 12, 2011 substituted "The officer must complete and file a return in accordance with Rule 107" for "The original shall be returned to the court from which it issued on or before the return day named therein with the action of the officer indorsed thereon or annexed thereto showing how and when he executed the same".

Source

Vernon's Ann.Civ.St. art. 4653.

Rule 690. The Answer

The defendant to an injunction proceeding may answer as in other civil actions; but no injunction shall be dissolved before final hearing because of the denial of the material allegations of the plaintiff's petition, unless the answer denying the same is verified by the oath of the defendant.

Historical Notes

Source

Vernon's Ann.Civ.St. art. 4657.

Rule 691. Bond on Dissolution

Upon the dissolution of an injunction restraining the collection of money, by an interlocutory order of the court or judge, made in term time or vacation, if the petition be continued over for trial, the court or judge shall require of the defendant in such injunction proceedings a bond, with two or more good and sufficient sureties, to be approved by the clerk of the court, payable to the complainant in double the amount of the sum enjoined, and conditioned to refund to the complainant the amount of money, interest and costs which may be collected of him in the suit or proceeding enjoined if such injunction is made perpetual on final hearing. If such injunction is so perpetuated, the court, on motion of the complainant, may enter judgment against the principal and sureties in such bond for such amount as may be shown to have been collected from such defendant.

Historical Notes

Source

Vernon's Ann.Civ.St. art. 4659.

Rule 692. Disobedience

Disobedience of an injunction may be punished by the court or judge, in term time or in vacation, as a contempt. In case of such disobedience, the complainant, his agent or attorney, may file in the court in which such injunction is pending or with the judge in vacation, his affidavit stating what person is guilty of such disobedience and describing the acts constituting the same; and thereupon the court or judge shall cause to be issued an attachment for such person, directed to the sheriff or any constable of any county, and requiring such officer to arrest the person therein named if found within his county and have him before the court or judge at the time and place named in such writ; or said court or judge may issue a show cause order, directing and requiring such person to appear on such date as may be designated and show cause why he should not be adjudged in contempt of court. On return of such attachment or show cause order, the judge shall proceed to hear proof; and if satisfied that such person has disobeyed the injunction, either directly or indirectly, may commit such person to jail without bail until he purges himself of such contempt, in such manner and form as the court or judge may direct.

June 16, 1943, eff. Dec. 31, 1943.

Historical Notes

Source

Vernon's Ann.Civ.St. art. 4661 (part).

Rule 693. Principles of Equity Applicable

The principles, practice and procedure governing courts of equity shall govern proceedings in injunctions when the same are not in conflict with these rules or the provisions of the statutes.

Historical Notes

Source

Vernon's Ann.Civ.St. art. 4663.

Rule 693a. Bond in Divorce Case

In a divorce case the court in its discretion may dispense with the necessity of a bond in connection with an ancillary injunction in behalf of one spouse against the other. Promulgated by order of June 16, 1943, effective December 31, 1943.

Historical Notes

Source

New rule, added eff. Dec. 31, 1943.

SECTION 6. MANDAMUS

Rule 694. No Mandamus Without Notice

No mandamus shall be granted by the district or county court on ex parte hearing, and any peremptory mandamus granted without notice shall be abated on motion.

Historical Notes

Source

Vernon's Ann.Civ.St. art. 2328.

SECTION 7. RECEIVERS

Rule 695. No Receiver of Immovable Property Appointed Without Notice

Except where otherwise provided by statute, no receiver shall be appointed without notice to take charge of property which is fixed and immovable. When an application for appointment of a receiver to take possession of property of this type is filed, the judge or court shall set the same down for hearing and notice of such hearing shall be given to the adverse party by serving notice thereof not less than three days prior to such hearing. If the order finds that the defendant is a non-resident or that his whereabouts is unknown, the notice may be served by affixing the same in a conspicuous manner and place upon the property or if that is impracticable it may be served in such other manner as the court or judge may require.

June 16, 1943, eff. Dec. 31, 1943.

Historical Notes

Source

New rule.

Rule 695a. Bond, and Bond in Divorce Case

No receiver shall be appointed with authority to take charge of property until the party applying therefor has filed with the clerk of the court a good and sufficient bond, to be approved by such clerk, payable to the defendant in the amount fixed by the court, conditioned for the payment of all damages and cost in such suit, in case it should be decided that such receiver was wrongfully appointed to take charge of such property. The amount of such bond shall be fixed at a sum sufficient to cover all such probable damages and costs. In a divorce case the court or judge, as a matter of discretion, may dispense with the necessity of a bond.

June 16, 1943, eff. Dec. 31, 1943.

Historical Notes

Source

New rule, eff. Dec. 31, 1943.

SECTION 8. SEQUESTRATION

Rule 696. Application for Writ of Sequestration and Order

Either at the commencement of a suit or at any time during its progress the plaintiff may file an application for a writ of sequestration. The application shall be supported by affidavits of the plaintiff, his agent, his attorney, or other persons having knowledge of relevant facts. The application shall comply with all statutory requirements and shall state the grounds for issuing the writ, including the description of the property to be sequestered with such certainty that it may be identified and distinguished from property of a like kind, giving the value of each article of the property and the county in which it is located, and the specific facts relied upon by the plaintiff to warrant the required findings by the court. The writ shall not be quashed because two or more grounds are stated conjunctively or disjunctively. The application and any affidavits shall be made on personal knowledge and shall set forth such facts as would be admissible in evidence; provided that facts may be stated based upon information and belief if the grounds of such belief are specifically stated.

No writ shall issue except upon written order of the court after a hearing, which may be ex parte. The court, in its order granting the application, shall make specific findings of facts to support the statutory grounds found to exist, and shall describe the property to be sequestered with such certainty that it may be identified and distinguished from property of a like kind, giving the value of each article of the property and the county in which it is located. Such order shall further specify the amount of bond required of plaintiff which shall be in an amount which, in the opinion of the court, shall adequately compensate defendant in the event plaintiff fails to prosecute his suit to effect and pay all damages and costs as shall be adjudged against him for wrongfully suing out the writ of sequestration including the elements of damages stated in Sections 62.044 and 62.045, Civil Practice and Remedies Code. The court shall further find in its order the amount of bond required of defendant to replevy, which shall be in an amount equivalent to the value of the property sequestered or to the amount of plaintiff's claim and one year's accrual of interest if allowed by law on the claim, whichever is the lesser amount, and the estimated costs of court. The order may direct the issuance of several writs at the same time, or in succession, to be sent to different counties.

July 11, 1977, eff. Jan. 1, 1978. Amended by order of July 15, 1987, eff. Jan. 1, 1988.

Historical Notes

1988 Amendment

Substituted a Civil Practice and Remedies Code citation for a Revised Civil Statute citation.

Source

Vernon's Ann.Civ.St. art. 6841. Last sentence added.

Rule 697. Petition

If the suit be in the district or county court, no writ of sequestration shall issue, unless a petition shall have been first filed therein, as in other suits in said courts.

Historical Notes

Source

Vernon's Ann.Civ.St. art. 6842.

Rule 698. Bond for Sequestration

No writ of sequestration shall issue until the party applying therefor has filed with the officer authorized to issue such writ a bond payable to the defendant in the amount fixed by the court's order, with sufficient surety or sureties as provided by statute to be approved by such officer, conditioned that the plaintiff will prosecute his suit to effect and pay to the extent of the penal amount of the bond all damages and costs as may be adjudged against him for wrongfully suing out such writ of sequestration, and plaintiff may further condition the bond pursuant to the provisions of Rule 708, in which case he shall not be required to give additional bond to replevy unless so ordered by the court.

After notice to the opposite party, either before or after the issuance of the writ, the defendant or plaintiff may file a motion to increase or reduce the amount of such bond, or to question the sufficiency of the sureties thereon, in the court in which such suit is pending. Upon hearing, the court shall enter its order with respect to such bond and sufficiency of the sureties as justice may require.

July 11, 1977, eff. Jan. 1, 1978.

Historical Notes

Source

Vernon's Ann.Civ.St. art. 6843.

Rule 699. Requisites of Writ

The writ of sequestration shall be directed "To the Sheriff or any Constable within the State of Texas" (not naming a specific county) and shall command him to take into his possession the property, describing the same as it is described in the application or affidavits, if to be found in his county, and to keep the same subject to further orders of the court, unless the same is replevied. There shall be prominently displayed on the face of the writ, in ten-point type and in a manner calculated to advise a reasonably attentive person of its contents, the following:

"YOU HAVE A RIGHT TO REGAIN POSSESSION OF THE PROPERTY BY FILING A REPLEVY BOND. YOU HAVE A RIGHT TO SEEK TO REGAIN POSSESSION OF THE PROPERTY BY FILING WITH THE COURT A MOTION TO DISSOLVE THIS WRIT."

July 11, 1977, eff. Jan. 1, 1978.

Historical Notes

Source

Vernon's Ann.Civ.St. art. 6845.

Rule 700. Amendment

Clerical errors in the affidavit, bond, or writ of sequestration or the officer's return thereof may upon application in writing to the judge of the court in which the suit is filed and after notice to the opponent, be amended in such manner and on such terms as the judge shall authorize by an order entered in the minutes of the court, provided the amendment does not change or add to the grounds of such sequestration as stated in the affidavit, and provided such amendment appears to the judge to be in furtherance of justice.

Historical Notes

Source

New rule.

Rule 700a. Service of Writ on Defendant

The defendant shall be served in any manner provided for service of citation or as provided in Rule 21a, with a copy of the writ of sequestration, the application, accompanying affidavits, and orders of the court as soon as practicable following the levy of the writ. There shall also be prominently displayed on the face of the copy of the writ served on defendant, in ten-point type and in a manner calculated to advise a reasonably attentive person of its contents, the following:

"To ____________________, Defendant:

You are hereby notified that certain properties alleged to be claimed by you have been sequestered. If you claim any rights in such property, you are advised:

"YOU HAVE A RIGHT TO REGAIN POSSESSION OF THE PROPERTY BY FILING A REPLEVY BOND. YOU HAVE A RIGHT TO SEEK TO REGAIN POSSESSION OF THE PROPERTY BY FILING WITH THE COURT A MOTION TO DISSOLVE THIS WRIT."

July 11, 1977, eff. Jan. 1, 1978.

Historical Notes

Source

This is a new rule. It affords the defendant notice of the proceedings and informs him of some of his rights.

Rule 701. Defendant May Replevy

At any time before judgment, should the sequestered property not have been previously claimed, replevied, or sold, the defendant may replevy the same, or any part thereof, or the proceeds from the sale of the property if it has been sold under order of the court, by giving bond, with sufficient surety or sureties as provided by statute, to be approved by the officer who levied the writ, payable to plaintiff in the amount fixed by the court's order, conditioned as provided in Rule 702 or Rule 703.

On reasonable notice to the opposing party (which may be less than three days) either party shall have the right to prompt judicial review of the amount of bond required, denial of bond, sufficiency of sureties, and estimated value of the property, by the court which authorized issuance of the writ. The court's determination may be made upon the basis of affidavits, if uncontroverted, setting forth such facts as would be admissible in evidence; otherwise, the parties shall submit evidence. The court shall forthwith enter its order either approving or modifying the requirements of the officer or of the court's prior order, and such order of the court shall supersede and control with respect to such matters.

July 11, 1977, eff. Jan. 1, 1978.

Historical Notes

Source

Vernon's Ann.Civ.St. art. 6849.

Rule 702. Bond for Personal Property

If the property to be replevied be personal property, the condition of the bond shall be that the defendant will not remove the same out of the county, or that he will not waste, ill-treat, injure, destroy, or dispose of the same, according to the plaintiff's affidavit, and that he will have such property, in the same condition as when it is replevied, together with the value of the fruits, hire or revenue thereof, forthcoming to abide the decision of the court, or that he will pay the value thereof, or the difference between its value at the time of replevy and the time of judgment and of the fruits, hire or revenue of the same in case he shall be condemned to do so.

Historical Notes

Source

Vernon's Ann.Civ.St. art. 6850.

Rule 703. Bond for Real Estate

If the property be real estate, the condition of such bond shall be that the defendant will not injure the property, and that he will pay the value of the rents of the same in case he shall be condemned so to do.

Historical Notes

Source

Vernon's Ann.Civ.St. art. 6851.

Rule 704. Return of Bond and Entry of Judgment

The bond provided for in the three preceding rules shall be returned with the writ to the court from whence the writ issued. In case the suit is decided against the defendant, final judgment shall be rendered against all the obligors in such bond, jointly and severally, for the value of the property replevied as of the date of the execution of the replevy bond, and the value of the fruits, hire, revenue, or rent thereof, as the case may be.

June 10, 1980, eff. Jan. 1, 1981.

Historical Notes

Source

Vernon's Ann.Civ.St. art. 6852.

Rule 705. Defendant May Return Sequestered Property

Within ten days after final judgment for personal property the defendant may deliver to the plaintiff, or to the officer who levied the sequestration or to his successor in office the personal property in question, and such officer shall deliver same to plaintiff upon his demand therefor; or such defendant shall deliver such property to the officer demanding same under execution issued therefor upon a judgment for the title or possession of the same; and such officer shall receipt the defendant for such property; provided, however, that such delivery to the plaintiff or to such officer shall be without prejudice to any rights of the plaintiff under the replevy bond given by the defendant. Where a mortgage or other lien of any kind is foreclosed upon personal property sequestered and replevied, the defendant shall deliver such property to the officer calling for same under order of sale issued upon a judgment foreclosing such mortgage or other lien, either in the county of defendant's residence or in the county where sequestered, as demanded by such officer; provided, however, that such delivery by the defendant shall be without prejudice to any rights of the plaintiff under the replevy bond given by the defendant.

Sept. 20, 1941, eff. Dec. 31, 1941.

Historical Notes

Source

Vernon's Ann.Civ.St. art. 6853.

Rule 706. Disposition of the Property by Officer

When the property is tendered back by the defendant to the officer who sequestered the same or to the officer calling for same under an order of sale, such officer shall receive said property and hold or dispose of the same as ordered by the court; provided, however, that such return to and receipt of same by the officer and any sale or disposition of said property by the officer under order or judgment of the court shall not affect or limit any rights of the plaintiff under the bond provided for in Rule 702.

Sept. 20, 1941, eff. Dec. 31, 1941.

Historical Notes

Source

Vernon's Ann.Civ.St. art. 6854.

Rule 707. Execution

If the property be not returned and received, as provided in the two preceding rules, execution shall issue upon said judgment for the amount due thereon, as in other cases.

Historical Notes

Source

Vernon's Ann.Civ.St. art. 6855.

Rule 708. Plaintiff May Replevy

When the defendant fails to replevy the property within ten days after the levy of the writ and service of notice on defendant, the officer having the property in possession shall at any time thereafter and before final judgment, deliver the same to the plaintiff upon his giving bond payable to defendant in a sum of money not less than the amount fixed by the court's order, with sufficient surety or sureties as provided by statute to be approved by such officer. If the property to be replevied be personal property, the condition of the bond shall be that he will have such property, in the same condition as when it is replevied, together with the value of the fruits, hire or revenue thereof, forthcoming to abide the decision of the court, or that he will pay the value thereof, or the difference between its value at the time of replevy and the time of judgment (regardless of the cause of such difference in value, and of the fruits, hire or revenue of the same in case he shall be condemned to do so). If the property be real estate, the condition of such bond shall be that the plaintiff will not injure the property, and that he will pay the value of the rents of the same in case he shall be condemned to do so.

On reasonable notice to the opposing party (which may be less than three days) either party shall have the right to prompt judicial review of the amount of bond required, denial of bond, sufficiency of sureties, and estimated value of the property, by the court which authorized issuance of the writ. The court's determination may be made upon the basis of affidavits, if uncontroverted, setting forth such facts as would be admissible in evidence; otherwise, the parties shall submit evidence. The court shall forthwith enter its order either approving or modifying the requirements of the officer or of the court's prior order, and such order of the court shall supersede and control with respect to such matters.

July 11, 1977, eff. Jan. 1, 1978. Amended by order of Dec. 5, 1983, eff. April 1, 1984.

Historical Notes

Source

Vernon's Ann.Civ.St. art. 6856.

Rule 709. When Bond Forfeited

The bond provided for in the preceding rule shall be returned by the officer to the court issuing the writ immediately after he has approved same, and in case the suit is decided against the plaintiff, final judgment shall be entered against all the obligors in such bond, jointly and severally for the value of the property replevied as of the date of the execution of the replevy bond, and the value of the fruits, hire, revenue or rent thereof as the case may be. The same rules which govern the discharge or enforcement of a judgment against the obligors in the defendant's replevy bond shall be applicable to and govern in case of a judgment against the obligors in the plaintiff's replevy bond.

Historical Notes

Source

Vernon's Ann.Civ.St. art. 6857.

Rule 710. Sale of Perishable Goods

If after the expiration of ten days from the levy of a writ of sequestration the defendant has failed to replevy the same, if the plaintiff or defendant shall make affidavit in writing that the property levied upon, or any portion thereof, is likely to be wasted or destroyed or greatly depreciated in value by keeping, and if the officer having possession of such property shall certify to the truth of such affidavit, it shall be the duty of the judge or justice of the peace to whose court the writ is returnable, upon the presentation of such affidavit and certificate, either in term time or vacation, to order the sale of said property or so much thereof as is likely to be so wasted, destroyed or depreciated in value by keeping, but either party may replevy the property at any time before such sale.

Historical Notes

Source

Vernon's Ann.Civ.St. art. 6859.

Rule 711. Order of Sale For

The judge or justice granting the order provided for in the preceding rule shall issue an order directed to the officer having such property in possession, commanding such officer to sell such property in the same manner as under execution.

Historical Notes

Source

Vernon's Ann.Civ.St. art. 6860.

Rule 712. Return of Order

The officer making such sale shall, within five days thereafter, return the order of sale to the court from whence the same issued, with his proceedings thereon, and shall, at the time of making such return, pay over to the clerk or justice of the peace the proceeds of such sale.

Historical Notes

Source

Vernon's Ann.Civ.St. art. 6861.

Rule 712a. Dissolution or Modification of Writ of Sequestration

A defendant whose property has been sequestered or any intervening party who claims an interest in such property, may by sworn written motion, seek to vacate, dissolve, or modify the writ and the order directing its issuance, for any grounds or cause, extrinsic or intrinsic, including a motion to reduce the amount of property sequestered when the total amount described and authorized by such order exceeds the amount necessary to secure the plaintiff's claim, one year's interest if allowed by law on the claim, and costs. Such motion shall admit or deny each finding of the order directing the issuance of the writ except where the movant is unable to admit or deny the finding, in which case movant shall set forth the reasons why he cannot admit or deny. Unless the parties agree to an extension of time, the motion shall be heard promptly, after reasonable notice to the plaintiff (which may be less than three days), and the issue shall be determined not later than ten days after the motion is filed. The filing of the motion shall stay any further proceedings under the writ, except for any orders concerning the care, preservation, or sale of any perishable property, until a hearing is had, and the issue is determined. The writ shall be dissolved unless, at such hearing, the plaintiff shall prove the grounds relied upon for its issuance, but the court may modify its previous order granting the writ and the writ issued pursuant thereto. The movant shall, however, have the burden to prove that the reasonable value of the property sequestered exceeds the amount necessary to secure the debt, interest for one year, and probable costs.

The court's determination may be made upon the basis of affidavits, if uncontroverted, setting forth such facts as would be admissible in evidence; otherwise, the parties shall submit evidence. The court may make all such orders, including orders concerning the care, preservation, or disposition of the property (or the proceeds therefrom if the same has been sold) as justice may require. If the movant has given a replevy bond, an order to vacate or dissolve the writ shall vacate the replevy bond and discharge the sureties thereon, and if the court modifies its order or the writ issued pursuant thereto, it shall make such further orders with respect to the bond as may be consistent with its modification.

July 11, 1977, eff. Jan. 1, 1978.

Historical Notes

Source

This is a new rule, which affords a prompt hearing, provides for the procedures, the burden of proof and the kind of proof.

Rule 713. Sale on Debt Not Due

If the suit in which the sequestration issued be for a debt or demand not yet due, and the property sequestered be likely to be wasted, destroyed or greatly depreciated in value by keeping, the judge or justice of the peace shall, under the regulations hereinbefore provided, order the same to be sold, giving credit on such sale until such debt or demand shall become due.

Historical Notes

Source

Vernon's Ann.Civ.St. art. 6862.

Rule 714. Purchaser's Bond

In the case of a sale as provided for in the preceding rule, the purchaser of the property shall execute his bond, with two or more good and sufficient sureties, to be approved by the officer making the sale, and payable to such officer, in a sum not less than double the amount of the purchase money, conditioned that such purchaser shall pay such purchase money at the expiration of the time given.

Historical Notes

Source

Vernon's Ann.Civ.St. art. 6863.

Rule 715. Return of Bond

The bond provided for in the preceding rule shall be returned by the officer taking the same to the clerk or justice of the peace from whose court the order of sale issued, with such order, and shall be filed among the papers in the cause.

Historical Notes

Source

Vernon's Ann.Civ.St. art. 6864 (part).

Rule 716. Recovery on Bond

In case the purchaser does not pay the purchase money at the expiration of the time given, judgment shall be rendered against all the obligors in such bond for the amount of such purchase money, interest thereon and all costs incurred in the enforcement and collection of the same; and execution shall issue thereon in the name of the plaintiff in the suit, as in other cases, and the money when collected shall be paid to the clerk or justice of the peace to abide the final decision of the cause.

Historical Notes

Source

Vernon's Ann.Civ.St. art. 6864 (part).

SECTION 9. TRIAL OF RIGHT OF PROPERTY

Rule 717. Claimant Must Make Affidavit

Whenever a distress warrant, writ of execution, sequestration, attachment, or other like writ is levied upon personal property, and such property, or any part thereof, shall be claimed by any claimant who is not a party to such writ, such claimant may make application that such claim is made in good faith, and file such application with the court in which such suit is pending. Such application may be supported by affidavits of the claimant, his agent, his attorney, or other persons having knowledge of relevant facts. The application shall comply with all statutory requirements and shall state the grounds for such claim and the specific facts relied upon by the claimant to warrant the required findings by the court.

The claim shall not be quashed because two or more grounds are stated conjunctively or disjunctively. The application and any affidavits shall be made on personal knowledge and shall set forth such facts as would be admissible in evidence; provided that facts may be stated based upon information and belief if the grounds of such belief are specifically stated.

No property shall be delivered to the claimant except on written order of the court after a hearing pursuant to Rule 718. The court in its order granting the application shall make specific findings of facts to support the statutory grounds found to exist and shall specify the amount of the bond required of the claimant.

June 10, 1980, eff. Jan. 1, 1981.

Rule 718. Property Delivered to Claimant

Any claimant who claims an interest in property on which a writ has been levied may, by sworn written motion, seek to obtain possession of such property. Such motion shall admit or deny each finding of the order directing the issuance of the writ except where the claimant is unable to admit or deny the finding, in which case claimant shall set forth the reasons why he cannot admit or deny. Such motion shall also contain the reasons why the claimant has superior right or title to the property claimed as against the plaintiff in the writ. Unless the parties agree to an extension of time, the motion shall be heard promptly, after reasonable notice to the plaintiff (which may be less than three days), and the issue shall be determined not later than 10 days after the motion is filed. The filing of the motion shall stay any further proceedings under the writ, except for any orders concerning the care, preservation, or sale of any perishable property, until a hearing is had, and the issue is determined. The claimant shall have the burden to show superior right or title to the property claimed as against the plaintiff and defendant in the writ.

The court's determination may be made upon the basis of affidavits, if uncontroverted, setting forth such facts as would be admissible in evidence, but additional evidence, if tendered by either party shall be received and considered. The court may make all such orders, including orders concerning the care, preservation, or disposition of the property, or the proceeds therefrom if the same has been sold, as justice may require, and if the court modifies its order or the writ issued pursuant thereto, it shall make such further orders with respect to the bond as may be consistent with its modification.

June 10, 1980, eff. Jan. 1, 1981.

Rule 719. Bond

No property shall be put in the custody of the claimant until the claimant has filed with the officer who made the levy, a bond in an amount fixed by the court's order equal to double the value of the property so claimed, payable to the plaintiff in the writ, with sufficient surety or sureties as provided by statute to be approved by such officer, conditioned that the claimant will return the same to the officer making the levy, or his successor, in as good condition as he received it, and shall also pay the reasonable value of the use, hire, increase and fruits thereof from the date of said bond, or, in case he fails so to return said property and pay for the use of the same, that he shall pay the plaintiff the value of said property, with legal interest thereon from the date of the bond, and shall also pay all damages and costs that may be awarded against him for wrongfully suing out such claim.

The plaintiff or claimant may file a motion to increase or reduce the amount of such bond, or to question the sufficiency of the sureties thereon, in the court in which such suit is pending. Upon hearing, the court shall enter its order with respect to such bond and sufficiency of the sureties.

June 10, 1980, eff. Jan. 1, 1981.

Rule 720. Return of Bond

Whenever any person shall claim property and shall duly make the application and give the bond, if the writ under which the levy was made was issued by a justice of the peace or a court of the county where such levy was made, the officer receiving such application and bond shall endorse on the writ that such claim has been made and application and bond given, and by whom; and shall also endorse on such bond the value of the property as assessed by himself, and shall forthwith return such bond with a copy of the writ to the proper court having jurisdiction to try such claim.

June 10, 1980, eff. Jan. 1, 1981.

Rule 721. Out-County Levy

Whenever any person shall claim property and shall make the application and give the bond as provided for herein, if the writ under which such levy was made was issued by a justice of the peace or a court of another county than that in which such levy was made, then the officer receiving such bond shall endorse on such bond the value of the property as assessed by himself, and shall forthwith return such bond with a copy of the writ, to the proper court having jurisdiction to try such claim.

June 10, 1980, eff. Jan. 1, 1981.

Rule 722. Return of Original Writ

The officer taking such bond shall also endorse on the original writ, if in his possession, that such claim has been made and application and bond given, stating by whom, the names of the surety or sureties, and to what justice or court the bond has been returned; and

he shall forthwith return such original writ to the tribunal from which it issued.
June 10, 1980, eff. Jan. 1, 1981.

Rule 723. Docketing Cause

Whenever any bond for the trial of the right of property shall be returned, the clerk of the court, or such justice of the peace, shall docket the same in the original writ proceeding in the name of the plaintiff in the writ as the plaintiff, and the claimant of the property as intervening claimant.
June 10, 1980, eff. Jan. 1, 1981.

Rule 724. Issue Made Up

After the claim proceedings have been docketed, and on the hearing day set by the court, then the court, or the justice of the peace, as the case may be, shall enter an order directing the making and joinder of issues by the parties. Such issues shall be in writing and signed by each party or his attorney. The plaintiff shall make a brief statement of the authority and right by which he seeks to subject the property levied on to the process, and it shall be sufficient for the claimant and other parties to make brief statements of the nature of their claims thereto.
June 10. 1980, eff. Jan. 1, 1981.

Rule 725. Judgment by Default

If the plaintiff appears and the claimant fails to appear or neglects or refuses to join issue under the direction of the court or justice within the time prescribed for pleading, the plaintiff shall have judgment by default.
June 10, 1980, eff. Jan. 1, 1981.

Rule 726. Judgment of Non-Suit

If the plaintiff does not appear, he shall be non-suited.
June 10, 1980, eff. Jan. 1, 1981.

Rule 727. Proceedings

The proceedings and practice on the trial shall be as nearly as may be the same as in other cases before such court or justice.
June 10, 1980, eff. Jan. 1, 1981.

Rule 728. Burden of Proof

If the property was taken from the possession of the claimant pursuant to the original writ, the burden of proof shall be on the plaintiff in the writ. If it was taken from the possession of the defendant in such writ, or any other person than the claimant, the burden of proof shall be on the claimant.
June 10, 1980, eff. Jan. 1, 1981.

Rule 729. Copy of Writ Evidence

In all trials of the right of property, under the provisions of this section in any county other than that in which the writ issued under which the levy was made, the copy of the writ herein required to be returned by the officer making the levy shall be received in evidence in like manner as the original could be.
June 10, 1980, eff. Jan. 1, 1981.

Rule 730. Failure to Establish Title

Where any claimant has obtained possession of property, and shall ultimately fail to establish his right thereto, judgment may be rendered against him and his sureties for the value of the property, with legal interest thereon from the date of such bond. Such judgment shall be rendered in favor of the plaintiff or defendant in the writ, or of the several plaintiffs or defendants, if more than one, and shall fix the amount of the claim of each.
June 10, 1980, eff. Jan. 1, 1981.

Rule 731. Execution Shall Issue

If such judgment should not be satisfied by a return of the property, then after the expiration of ten days from the date of the judgment, execution shall issue thereon in the name of the plaintiff or defendant for the amount of the claim, or of all the plaintiffs or defendants for the sum of their several claims, provided the amount of such judgment shall inure to the benefit of any person who shall show superior right or title to the property claimed as against the claimant; but if such judgment be for a less amount than the sum of the several plaintiffs' or defendants' claims, then the respective rights and priorities of the several plaintiffs or defendants shall be fixed and adjusted in the judgment.
June 10, 1980, eff. Jan. 1, 1981.

Rule 732. Return of Property by Claimant

If, within ten days from the rendition of said judgment, the claimant shall return such property in as good condition as he received it, and pay for the use of the same together with the damages and costs, such delivery and payment shall operate as a satisfaction of such judgment.
June 10, 1980, eff. Jan. 1, 1981.

Rule 733. Claim Is a Release of Damages

A claim made to the property, under the provisions of this section, shall operate as a release of all damages by the claimant against the officer who levied upon said property.

June 10, 1980, eff. Jan. 1, 1981.

Rule 734. Levy on Other Property

Proceedings for the trial of right of property under these rules shall in no case prevent the plaintiff in the writ from having a levy made upon any other property of the defendant.

June 10, 1980, eff. June 1, 1981.

PART VII

RULES RELATING TO SPECIAL PROCEEDINGS

SECTION 1. PROCEDURES RELATED TO FORECLOSURES OF CERTAIN LIENS

Rule 735. Foreclosures Requiring a Court Order

735.1. Liens Affected

Rule 736 provides the procedure for obtaining a court order, when required, to allow foreclosure of a lien containing a power of sale in the security instrument, dedicatory instrument, or declaration creating the lien, including a lien securing any of the following:

(a) a home equity loan, reverse mortgage, or home equity line of credit under article XVI, sections 50(a)(6), 50(k), and 50(t) of the Texas Constitution;

(b) a tax lien transfer or property tax loan under sections 32.06 and 32. 065 of the Tax Code; or

(c) a property owners' association assessment under section 209.0092 of the Property Code.

Adopted by order of Oct. 17, 2011, eff. Jan. 1, 2012. Amended by order of Dec. 12, 2011, and Dec. 30, 2011, eff. Jan. 1, 2012.

Comment—2011

See comment following Rule 735.3.

735.2. Other Statutory and Contractual Foreclosure

A Rule 736 order does not alter any foreclosure requirement or duty imposed under applicable law or the terms of the loan agreement, contract, or lien sought to be foreclosed. The only issue to be determined in a Rule 736 proceeding is whether a party may obtain an order under Rule 736 to proceed with foreclosure under applicable law and the terms of the loan agreement, contract, or lien sought to be foreclosed.

Adopted by order of Oct. 17, 2011, eff. Jan. 1, 2012. Amended by order of Dec. 12, 2011, and Dec. 30, 2011, eff. Jan. 1, 2012.

Comment—2011

See comment following Rule 735.3.

735.3. Judicial Foreclosure Unaffected

A Rule 736 order is not a substitute for a judgment for judicial foreclosure, but any loan agreement, contract, or lien that may be foreclosed using Rule 736 procedures may also be foreclosed by judgment in an action for judicial foreclosure.

Adopted by order of Oct. 17, 2011, eff. Jan. 1, 2012. Amended by order of Dec. 12, 2011, and Dec. 30, 2011, eff. Jan. 1, 2012.

Comment—2011

Rules 735 and 736 have been rewritten and expanded to cover property owners' associations' assessment liens, in accordance with amendments to chapter 209 of the Property Code. Rule 735.1 makes the expedited procedures of Rule 736 available only when the lienholder has a power of sale but a court order is nevertheless required by law to foreclose the lien. Rule 735.2 makes clear that Rule 736 is procedural only and does not affect other contractual or legal rights or duties. Any lien which can be foreclosed under Rule 736 may also be foreclosed in an action for judicial foreclosure, as Rule 735.3 states, but no lienholder is required to obtain both a Rule 736 order and a judgment for judicial foreclosure. The requirement of conspicuousness in Rule 736.1(d)(5) has reference to section 1.201(b)(10) of the Business and Commerce Code.

Rule 736. Expedited Order Proceeding

736.1. Application

(a) *Where Filed.* An application for an expedited order allowing the foreclosure of a lien listed in Rule 735 to proceed must be filed in a county where all or part of the real property encumbered by the loan agreement, contract, or lien sought to be foreclosed is located or in a probate court with jurisdiction over proceedings involving the property.

(b) *Style.* An application must be styled "In re: Order for Foreclosure Concerning [state: property's mailing address] under Tex. R. Civ. P. 736."

(c) *When Filed.* An application may not be filed until the opportunity to cure has expired under applicable law and the loan agreement, contract, or lien sought to be foreclosed.

(d) *Contents.* The application must:

(1) Identify by name and last known address each of the following parties:

(A) "Petitioner" — any person legally authorized to prosecute the foreclosure;

(B) "Respondent" — according to the records of the holder or servicer of the loan agreement, contract, or lien sought to be foreclosed:

(i) for a home equity loan, reverse mortgage, or home equity line of credit, each person obligated to pay the loan agreement, contract, or lien sought to be foreclosed and each mortgagor, if any, of the loan agreement, contract, or lien sought to be foreclosed;

(ii) for a tax lien transfer or property tax loan, each person obligated to pay the loan agreement, contract, or lien sought to be foreclosed, each mortgagor, if any, of the loan agreement, contract, or lien sought to be foreclosed, each owner of the property, and the holder of any recorded preexisting first lien secured by the property;

(iii) for a property owners' association assessment, each person obligated to pay the loan agreement, contract, or lien sought to be foreclosed who has a current ownership interest in the property.

(2) Identify the property encumbered by the loan agreement, contract, or lien sought to be foreclosed by its commonly known street address and legal description.

(3) Describe or state:

(A) the type of lien listed in Rule 735 sought to be foreclosed and its constitutional or statutory reference;

(B) the authority of the party seeking foreclosure, whether as the servicer, beneficiary, lender, investor, property owners' association, or other person with authority to prosecute the foreclosure;

(C) each person obligated to pay the loan agreement, contract, or lien sought to be foreclosed;

(D) each mortgagor, if any, of the loan agreement, contract, or lien sought to be foreclosed who is not a maker or assumer of the underlying debt;

(E) as of a date that is not more than sixty days prior to the date the application is filed:

(i) if the default is monetary, the number of unpaid scheduled payments,

(ii) if the default is monetary, the amount required to cure the default,

(iii) if the default is non-monetary, the facts creating the default, and

(iv) if applicable, the total amount required to pay off the loan agreement, contract, or lien;

(F) that the requisite notice or notices to cure the default has or have been mailed to each person as required under applicable law and the loan agreement, contract, or lien sought to be foreclosed and that the opportunity to cure has expired; and

(G) that before the application was filed, any other action required under applicable law and the loan agreement, contract, or lien sought to be foreclosed was performed.

(4) For a tax lien transfer or property tax loan, state all allegations required to be contained in the application in accordance with section 32.06(c–l)(1) of the Tax Code.

(5) Conspicuously state:

(A) that legal action is not being sought against the occupant of the property unless the occupant is also named as a respondent in the application; and

(B) that if the petitioner obtains a court order, the petitioner will proceed with a foreclosure of the property in accordance with applicable law and the terms of the loan agreement, contract, or lien sought to be foreclosed.

(6) Include an affidavit of material facts in accordance with Rule 166a(f) signed by the petitioner or the servicer describing the basis for foreclosure and, depending on the type of lien sought to be foreclosed, attach a legible copy of:

(A) the note, original recorded lien, or pertinent part of a property owners' association declaration or dedicatory instrument establishing the lien, and current assignment of the lien, if assigned;

(B) each notice required to be mailed to any person under applicable law and the loan agreement, contract, or lien sought to be foreclosed before the application was filed and proof of mailing of each notice; and

(C) for a tax lien transfer or property tax loan:

(i) the property owner's sworn document required under section 32.06(a–1) of the Tax Code; and

(ii) the taxing authority's certified statement attesting to the transfer of the lien, required under section 32.06(b) of the Tax Code.

Adopted by order of Oct. 17, 2011, eff. Jan. 1, 2012. Amended by order of Dec. 12, 2011, and Dec. 30, 2011, eff. Jan. 1, 2012.

Comment—2011

See comment following Rule 736.13.

736.2. Costs

All filing, citation, mailing, service, and other court costs and fees are costs of court and must be paid by petitioner at the time of filing an application with the clerk of the court.

Adopted by order of Oct. 17, 2011, eff. Jan. 1, 2012. Amended by order of Dec. 12, 2011, and Dec. 30, 2011, eff. Jan. 1, 2012

Comment—2011

See comment following Rule 736.13.

736.3. Citation

(a) *Issuance.*

(1) When the application is filed, the clerk must issue a separate citation for each respondent named in the application and one additional citation for the occupant of the property sought to be foreclosed.

(2) Each citation that is directed to a respondent must state that any response to the application is due the first Monday after the expiration of 38 days from the date the citation was placed in the custody of the U.S. Postal Service in accordance with the clerk's standard mailing procedures and state the date that the citation was placed in the custody of the U.S. Postal Service by the clerk.

(b) *Service and Return.*

(1) The clerk of the court must serve each citation, with a copy of the application attached, by both first class mail and certified mail. A citation directed to a respondent must be mailed to the respondent's last known address that is stated in the application. A citation directed to the occupant of the property sought to be foreclosed must be mailed to Occupant of [state: property's mailing address] at the address of the property sought to be foreclosed that is stated in the application.

(2) Concurrently with service, the clerk must complete a return of service in accordance with Rule 107, except that the return of service need not contain a return receipt. For a citation mailed by the clerk in accordance with (b)(1), the date of service is the date and time the citation was placed in the custody of the U.S. Postal Service in a properly addressed, postage prepaid envelope in accordance with the clerk's standard mailing procedures.

(3) The clerk must only charge one fee per respondent or occupant served under this rule.

Adopted by order of Oct. 17, 2011, eff. Jan. 1, 2012. Amended by order of Dec. 12, 2011, and Dec. 30, 2011, eff. Jan. 1, 2012.

Comment—2011

See comment following Rule 736.13.

736.4. Discovery

No discovery is permitted in a Rule 736 proceeding.

Adopted by order of Oct. 17, 2011, eff. Jan. 1, 2012. Amended by order of Dec. 12, 2011, and Dec. 30, 2011, eff. Jan. 1, 2012.

Comment—2011

See comment following Rule 736.13.

736.5. Response

(a) *Generally.* A respondent may file a response contesting the application.

(b) *Due Date.* Any response to the application is due the first Monday after the expiration of 38 days from the date the citation was placed in the custody of the U.S. Postal Service in accordance with the clerk's standard mailing procedures, as stated on the citation.

(c) *Form.* A response must be signed in accordance with Rule 57 and may be in the form of a general denial under Rule 92, except that a respondent must affirmatively plead:

(1) why the respondent believes a respondent did not sign a loan agreement document, if applicable, that is specifically identified by the respondent;

(2) why the respondent is not obligated for payment of the lien;

(3) why the number of months of alleged default or the reinstatement or pay off amounts are materially incorrect;

(4) why any document attached to the application is not a true and correct copy of the original; or

(5) proof of payment in accordance with Rule 95.

(d) *Other Claims.* A response may not state an independent claim for relief. The court must, without a hearing, strike and dismiss any counterclaim, cross claim, third party claim, intervention, or cause of action filed by any person in a Rule 736 proceeding.

Adopted by order of Oct. 17, 2011, eff. Jan. 1, 2012. Amended by order of Dec. 12, 2011, and Dec. 30, 2011, eff. Jan. 1, 2012.

Comment—2011

See comment following Rule 736.13.

736.6. Hearing Required When Response Filed

The court must not conduct a hearing under this rule unless a response is filed. If a response is filed, the court must hold a hearing after reasonable notice to the parties. The hearing on the application must not be held earlier than 20 days or later than 30 days after a request for a hearing is made by any party. At the hearing, the petitioner has the burden to prove by affidavits on file or evidence presented the grounds for granting the order sought in the application.

Adopted by order of Oct. 17, 2011, eff. Jan. 1, 2012. Amended by order of Dec. 12, 2011, and Dec. 30, 2011, eff. Jan. 1, 2012.

Comment—2011

See comment following Rule 736.13.

736.7. Default When No Response Filed

(a) If no response to the application is filed by the due date, the petitioner may file a motion and proposed order to obtain a default order. For the purposes of obtaining a default order, all facts alleged in the application and supported by the affidavit of material facts constitute prima facie evidence of the truth of the matters alleged.

(b) The court must grant the application by default order no later than 30 days after a motion is filed under (a) if the application complies with the requirements of Rule 736.1 and was properly served in accordance with Rule 736.3. The petitioner need not appear in court to obtain a default order.

(c) The return of service must be on file with the clerk of the court for at least 10 days before the court may grant the application by default.

Adopted by order of Oct. 17, 2011, eff. Jan. 1, 2012. Amended by order of Dec. 12, 2011, and Dec. 30, 2011, eff. Jan. 1, 2012.

Comment—2011

See comment following Rule 736.13.

736.8. Order

(a) The court must issue an order granting the application if the petitioner establishes the basis for the foreclosure. Otherwise, the court must deny the application.

(b) An order granting the application must describe:

(1) the material facts establishing the basis for foreclosure;

(2) the property to be foreclosed by commonly known mailing address and legal description;

(3) the name and last known address of each respondent subject to the order; and

(4) the recording or indexing information of each lien to be foreclosed.

(c) An order granting or denying the application is not subject to a motion for rehearing, new trial, bill of review, or appeal. Any challenge to a Rule 736 order must be made in a suit filed in a separate, independent, original proceeding in a court of competent jurisdiction.

Adopted by order of Oct. 17, 2011, eff. Jan. 1, 2012. Amended by order of Dec. 12, 2011, and Dec. 30, 2011, eff. Jan. 1, 2012.

Comment—2011

See comment following Rule 736.13.

736.9. Effect of the Order

An order is without prejudice and has no res judicata, collateral estoppel, estoppel by judgment, or other effect in any other judicial proceeding. After an order is obtained, a person may proceed with the foreclosure process under applicable law and the terms of the lien sought to be foreclosed.

Adopted by order of Oct. 17, 2011, eff. Jan. 1, 2012. Amended by order of Dec. 12, 2011, and Dec. 30, 2011, eff. Jan. 1, 2012.

Comment—2011

See comment following Rule 736.13.

736.10. Bankruptcy

If a respondent provides proof to the clerk of the court that respondent filed bankruptcy before an order is signed, the proceeding under this rule must be abated so long as the automatic stay is effective.

Adopted by order of Oct. 17, 2011, eff. Jan. 1, 2012. Amended by order of Dec. 12, 2011, and Dec. 30, 2011, eff. Jan. 1, 2012.

Comment—2011

See comment following Rule 736.13.

736.11. Automatic Stay and Dismissal if Independent Suit Filed

(a) A proceeding or order under this rule is automatically stayed if a respondent files a separate, original proceeding in a court of competent jurisdiction that puts in issue any matter related to the origination, servicing, or enforcement of the loan agreement, contract, or lien sought to be foreclosed prior to 5:00 p.m. on the Monday before the scheduled foreclosure sale.

(b) Respondent must give prompt notice of the filing of the suit to petitioner or petitioner's attorney and the foreclosure trustee or substitute trustee by any reasonable means necessary to stop the scheduled foreclosure sale.

(c) Within ten days of filing suit, the respondent must file a motion and proposed order to dismiss or vacate with the clerk of the court in which the application was filed giving notice that respondent has filed an original proceeding contesting the right to foreclose in a court of competent jurisdiction. If no order has been signed, the court must dismiss a pending proceeding. If an order has been signed, the court must vacate the Rule 736 order.

(d) If the automatic stay under this rule is in effect, any foreclosure sale of the property is void. Within 10 business days of notice that the foreclosure sale was void, the trustee or substitute trustee must return to the buyer of the foreclosed property the purchase price paid by the buyer.

(e) The court may enforce the Rule 736 process under chapters 9 and 10 of the Civil Practices and Remedies Code.

Adopted by order of Oct. 17, 2011, eff. Jan. 1, 2012. Amended by order of Dec. 12, 2011, and Dec. 30, 2011, eff. Jan. 1, 2012.

Comment—2011

See comment following Rule 736.13.

736.12. Attachment of Order to Trustee's Deed

A conformed copy of the order must be attached to the trustee or substitute trustee's foreclosure deed.

Adopted by order of Oct. 17, 2011, eff. Jan. 1, 2012. Amended by order of Dec. 12, 2011, and Dec. 30, 2011, eff. Jan. 1, 2012.

Comment—2011

See comment following Rule 736.13.

736.13. Promulgated Forms

The Supreme Court of Texas may promulgate forms that conform to this rule.

Adopted by order of Oct. 17, 2011, eff. Jan. 1, 2012. Amended by order of Dec. 12, 2011, and Dec. 30, 2011, eff. Jan. 1, 2012.

Comment—2011

Rules 735 and 736 have been rewritten and expanded to cover property owners' associations' assessment liens, in accordance with amendments to chapter 209 of the Property Code. Rule 735.1 makes the expedited procedures of Rule 736 available only when the lienholder has a power of sale but a court order is nevertheless required by law to foreclose the lien. Rule 735.2 makes clear that Rule 736 is procedural only and does not affect other contractual or legal rights or duties. Any lien which can be foreclosed under Rule 736 may also be foreclosed in an action for judicial foreclosure, as Rule 735.3 states, but no lienholder is required to obtain both a Rule 736 order and a judgment for judicial foreclosure. The requirement of conspicuousness in Rule 736.1(d)(5) has reference to section 1.201(b)(10) of the Business and Commerce Code.

SECTION 2. JUSTICE COURT PROCEEDINGS TO ENFORCE LANDLORD'S DUTY TO REPAIR OR REMEDY RESIDENTIAL RENTAL PROPERTY [Repealed by Order of April 15, 2013, effective August 31, 2013]

A former Section 2, Bill of Discovery, consisting of Rule 737, was repealed by the Order of Aug. 5, 1998, and Nov. 9, 1998, effective Jan. 1, 1999.

Rule 737. [Deleted]

Rules 737.1 to 737.13. Repealed by Order of April 15, 2013, eff. Aug. 31, 2013

Historical Notes

For subject matter of former rule 737.1, see, now, Rules Civ.Proc., rule 509.1.

For subject matter of former rule 737.2, see, now, Rules Civ.Proc., rule 509.2.

For subject matter of former rule 737.3, see, now, Rules Civ.Proc., rule 509.3.

For subject matter of former rule 737.4 to 533, see, now, Rules Civ.Proc., rule 509.4.

For subject matter of former rule 737.6, see, now, Rules Civ.Proc., rule 509.5.

For subject matter of former rule 737.8, see, now, Rules Civ.Proc., rule 509.6.

For subject matter of former rule 737.9, see, now, Rules Civ.Proc., rule 509.7.

For subject matter of former rule 737.12, see, now, Rules Civ.Proc., rule 509.8.

For subject matter of former rule 737.13, see, now, Rules Civ.Proc., rule 509.9.

SECTION 3. FORCIBLE ENTRY AND DETAINER [Repealed by Order of April 15, 2013, effective August 31, 2013]

Rules 738 to 755. Repealed by Order of April 15, 2013, eff. Aug. 31, 2013

Historical Notes

For subject matter of former rule 738, see, now, Rules Civ.Proc., rule 510.3.

For subject matter of former rule 739, see, now, Rules Civ.Proc., rule 510.4.

For subject matter of former rule 740, see, now, Rules Civ.Proc., rule 510.5.

For subject matter of former rule 741, see, now, Rules Civ.Proc., rule 510.3.

For subject matter of former rules 742 and 742a, see, now, Rules Civ.Proc., rule 510.4.

For subject matter of former rules 743 to 745, see, now, Rules Civ.Proc., rule 510.7.

For subject matter of former rule 747, see, now, Rules Civ.Proc., rule 510.7.

For subject matter of former rule 747a, see, now, Rules Civ.Proc., rule 500.4.

For subject matter of former rule 748, see, now, Rules Civ.Proc., rule 510.8.

For subject matter of former rules 749 to 750, see, now, Rules Civ.Proc., rule 510.9.

For subject matter of former rule 751, see, now, Rules Civ.Proc., rule 510.10.

For subject matter of former rule 752, see, now, Rules Civ.Proc., rule 510.11.

For subject matter of former rule 753, see, now, Rules Civ.Proc., rule 510.12.

For subject matter of former rule 755, see, now, Rules Civ.Proc., rule 510.13.

SECTION 4. PARTITION OF REAL ESTATE

Rule 756. Petition

The plaintiff's petition shall state:

(a) The names and residence, if known, of each of the other joint owners, or joint claimants, of such property.

(b) The share or interest which the plaintiff and the other joint owners, or joint claimants, of same own or claim so far as known to the plaintiff.

(c) The land sought to be partitioned shall be so described as that the same may be distinguished from any other and the estimated value thereof stated.

Historical Notes

Source

Vernon's Ann.Civ.St. art. 6083 (part).

Rule 757. Citation and Service

Upon the filing of a petition for partition, the clerk shall issue citation for each of the joint owners, or joint claimants, named therein, as in other cases, and such citations shall be served in the manner and for the time provided for the service of citations in other cases.

Historical Notes

Source

Vernon's Ann.Civ.St. art. 6084.

Rule 758. Where Defendant is Unknown or Residence is Unknown

If the plaintiff, his agent or attorney, at the commencement of any suit, or during the progress thereof, for the partition of land, shall make affidavit that an undivided portion of the land described in plaintiff's petition in said suit is owned by some person unknown to affiant, or that the place of residence of any known party owning an interest in land sought to be partitioned is unknown to affiant, the Clerk of the Court shall issue citation for publication, conforming to the requirements of Rules 114 and 115, and served in accordance with the directions of Rule 116. In case of unknown residence or party, the affidavit shall include a statement that after due diligence plaintiff and the affiant have been unable to ascertain the name or locate the residence of such party, as the case may be, and in such case it shall be the duty of the court trying the action to inquire into the sufficiency of the diligence so stated before granting any judgment.

July 20, 1954, eff. Jan. 1, 1955. Amended by order of Dec. 19, 1984, eff. April 1, 1985.

Historical Notes

1985 Amendment

In the second sentence deleted ", but the proviso of Rule 109, adapted to this situation, shall apply".

Source

Vernon's Ann.Civ.St. art. 6085.

Rule 759. Judgment Where Defendant Cited by Publication

When the defendant has been duly cited by publication in accordance with the preceding rule, and no appearance is entered within the time prescribed for pleadings, the court shall appoint an attorney to defend in behalf of such owner or owners, and proceed as in other causes where service is made by publication. It shall be the special duty of the court in all cases to see that its decree protects the rights of the unknown parties thereto. The judge of the court shall fix the fee of the attorney so appointed, which shall be entered and collected as costs against said unknown owner or owners.

Historical Notes

Source

Vernon's Ann.Civ.St. art. 6085 (part).

Rule 760. Court Shall Determine, What

Upon the hearing of the cause, the court shall determine the share or interest of each of the joint owners or claimants in the real estate sought to be divided, and all questions of law or equity affecting the title to such land which may arise.

Historical Notes

Source

Vernon's Ann.Civ.St. art. 6086.

Rule 761. Appointment of Commissioners

The court shall determine before entering the decree of partition whether the property, or any part thereof, is susceptible of partition; and, if the court determines that the whole, or any part of such property is susceptible of partition, then the court for that part of such property held to be susceptible of partition shall enter a decree directing the partition of such real estate, describing the same, to be made in accordance with the respective shares or interests of each of such parties entitled thereto, specify in such decree the share or interest of each party, and shall appoint three or more competent and disinterested persons as commissioners to make such partition in accordance with such decree and the law, a majority of which commissioners may act.

Historical Notes

Source

Vernon's Ann.Civ.St. art. 6087.

Rule 762. Writ of Partition

The clerk shall issue a writ of partition, directed to the sheriff or any constable of the county, commanding such sheriff or constable to notify each of the commissioners of their appointment as such, and shall accompany such writ with a certified copy of the decree of the court directing the partition.

Historical Notes

Source

Vernon's Ann.Civ.St. art. 6088.

Rule 763. Service of Writ of Partition

The writ of partition shall be served by reading the same to each of the persons named therein as commissioners, and by delivering to any one of them the accompanying certified copy of the decree of the court.

Historical Notes

Source

Vernon's Ann.Civ.St. art. 6089.

Rule 764. May Appoint Surveyor

The court may, should it be deemed necessary, appoint a surveyor to assist the commissioners in making the partition, in which case the writ of partition shall name such surveyor, and shall be served upon him by reading the same to him.

Historical Notes

Source

Vernon's Ann.Civ.St. art. 6090.

Rule 765. Return of Writ

A writ of partition, unless otherwise directed by the court, shall be made returnable twenty days from date of service on the commissioner last served; and the officer serving it shall endorse thereon the time and manner of such service.

Historical Notes

Source

Vernon's Ann.Civ.St. art. 6091.

Rule 766. Shall Proceed To Partition

The commissioners, or a majority of them, shall proceed to partition the real estate described in the decree of the court, in accordance with the directions contained in such decree and with the provisions of law and these rules.

Historical Notes

Source

Vernon's Ann.Civ.St. art. 6092.

Rule 767. May Cause Survey

If the commissioners deem it necessary, they may cause to be surveyed the real estate to be partitioned into several tracts or parcels.

Historical Notes

Source

Vernon's Ann.Civ.St. art. 6093.

Rule 768. Shall Divide Real Estate

The commissioners shall divide the real estate to be partitioned into as many shares as there are persons entitled thereto, as determined by the court, each share to contain one or more tracts or parcels, as the commissioners may think proper, having due regard in the division to the situation, quantity and advantages of each share, so that the shares may be equal in value, as nearly as may be, in proportion to the respective interests of the parties entitled. The commissioners shall then proceed by lot to set apart to each of the parties entitled one of said shares, as determined by the decrees of the court.

Historical Notes

Source

Vernon's Ann.Civ.St. art. 6094.

Rule 769. Report of Commissioners

When the commissioners have completed the partition, they shall report the same in writing and under oath to the court, which report shall show:

(a) The property divided, describing the same.

(b) The several tracts or parcels into which the same was divided by them, describing each particularly.

(c) The number of shares and the land which constitutes each share, and the estimated value of each share.

(d) The allotment of each share.

(e) The report shall be accompanied by such field notes and maps as may be necessary to make the same intelligible.

The clerk shall immediately mail written notice of the filing of the report to all parties.

April 24, 1990, eff. Sept. 1, 1990.

Comment—1990

Requirement added that clerk notify parties of the filing of the report.

Historical Notes

1990 Amendment

Added the last paragraph.

Source

Vernon's Ann.Civ.St. art. 6095.

Rule 770. Property Incapable of Division

Should the court be of the opinion that a fair and equitable division of the real estate, or any part thereof, cannot be made, it shall order a sale of so much as is incapable of partition, which sale shall be for cash, or upon such other terms as the court may direct, and shall be made as under execution or by private or public sale through a receiver, if the court so order, and the proceeds thereof shall be returned into court and be partitioned among the persons entitled thereto, according to their respective interests.

Oct. 12, 1949, eff. March 1, 1950.

Historical Notes

Source

Vernon's Ann.Civ.St. art. 6096.

Rule 771. Objections to Report

Either party to the suit may file objections to any report of the commissioners in partition within thirty days of the date the report is filed, and in such case a trial of the issues thereon shall be had as in other cases. If the report be found to be erroneous in any material respect, or unequal and unjust, the same shall be rejected, and other commissioners shall be appointed by the Court, and the same proceedings had as in the first instance.

April 24, 1990, eff. Sept. 1, 1990.

Comment—1990

To set a time within which objections to a commissioners report must be filed.

Historical Notes

1990 Amendment

Inserted "within thirty days of the date the report is filed".

Source

Vernon's Ann.Civ.St. art. 6097.

SECTION 5. PARTITION OF PERSONAL PROPERTY

Rule 772. Procedure

An action seeking partition of personal property as authorized by Section 23.001, Texas Property Code, shall be commenced in the same manner as other civil suits, and the several owners or claimants of such property shall be cited as in other cases.

July 15, 1987, eff. Jan. 1, 1988.

Historical Notes

Source

Vernon's Ann.Civ.St. art. 6102 (part).

Rule 773. Value Ascertained

The separate value of each article of such personal property, and the allotment in kind to which each owner is entitled, shall be ascertained by the court, with or without a jury.

Historical Notes

Source

Vernon's Ann.Civ.St. art. 6103, unchanged.

Rule 774. Decree of Court Executed

When partition in kind of personal property is ordered by the judgment of the court, a writ shall be issued in accordance with such judgment, commanding the sheriff or constable of the county where the property may be to put the parties forthwith in possession of the property allotted to each respectively.

Historical Notes

Source

Vernon's Ann.Civ.St. art. 6104, unchanged.

Rule 775. Property Sold

When personal property will not admit of a fair and equitable partition, the court shall ascertain the proportion to which each owner thereof is entitled, and order the property to be sold, and execution shall be issued to the sheriff or any constable of the county where the property may be describing such property and commanding such officer to sell the same as in other cases of execution, and pay over the proceeds of sale to the parties entitled thereto, in the proportion ascertained by the judgment of the court.

Historical Notes

Source

Vernon's Ann.Civ.St. art. 6105, unchanged.

SECTION 6. PARTITION: MISCELLANEOUS PROVISIONS

Rule 776. Construction

No provision of the statutes or rules relating to partition shall affect the mode of proceeding prescribed by law for the partition of estates of decedents among the heirs and legatees, nor preclude partition in any other manner authorized by the rules of equity, which rules shall govern in proceedings for partition in all respects not provided for by law or these rules.

Historical Notes

Source

Vernon's Ann.Civ.St. art. 6106.

Rule 777. Pleading and Practice

The same rules of pleading, practice and evidence which govern in other civil actions shall govern in suits for partition, when not in conflict with any provisions of the law or these rules relating to partition.

Historical Notes

Source

Vernon's Ann.Civ.St. art. 6107.

Rule 778. Costs

The court shall adjudge the costs in a partition suit to be paid by each party to whom a share has been allotted in proportion to the value of such share.

Historical Notes

Source

Vernon's Ann.Civ.St. art. 6109.

SECTION 7. QUO WARRANTO

Rule 779. Joinder of Parties

When it appears to the court or judge that the several rights of divers parties to the same office or franchise may properly be determined on one information, the court or judge may give leave to join all such persons in the same information in order to try their respective rights to such office or franchise.

Historical Notes

Source

Vernon's Ann.Civ.St. art. 6254, unchanged.

Rule 780. Citation to Issue

When such information is filed, the clerk shall issue citation as in civil actions, commanding the defendant to appear and answer the relator in an information in the nature of a quo warranto.

Historical Notes

Source

Vernon's Ann.Civ.St. art. 6255.

Rule 781. Proceedings as in Civil Cases

Every person or corporation who shall be cited as hereinbefore provided shall be entitled to all the rights in the trial and investigation of the matters alleged against him, as in cases of trial in civil cases in this State. Either party may prosecute an appeal or writ of error from any judgment rendered, as in other civil cases, subject, however, to the provisions of Rule 42, Texas Rules of Appellate Procedure,[1] and the appellate court shall give preference to such case, and hear and determine the same as early as practicable.

Aug. 18, 1947, eff. Dec. 31, 1947. Amended by order of April 24, 1990, eff. Sept. 1, 1990.

1 See, now, Vernon's Ann.Texas Rules App.Proc., rules 26.1, 28.1 to 28.3, 35.1, and 38.6.

Historical Notes

1990 Amendment

Substituted "Rule 42, Texas Rules of Appellate Procedure" for "Rule 384".

Source

Vernon's Ann.Civ.St. art. 6256, unchanged.

Rule 782. Remedy Cumulative

The remedy and mode of procedure hereby prescribed shall be construed to be cumulative of any now existing.

Historical Notes

Source

Vernon's Ann.Civ.St. art. 6258, unchanged.

SECTION 8. TRESPASS TO TRY TITLE

Rule 783. Requisites of Petition

The petition shall state:

(a) The real names of the plaintiff and defendant and their residences, if known.

(b) A description of the premises by metes and bounds, or with sufficient certainty to identify the same, so that from such description possession thereof may be delivered, and state the county or counties in which the same are situated.

(c) The interest which the plaintiff claims in the premises, whether it be a fee simple or other estate; and, if he claims an undivided interest, the petition shall state the same and the amount thereof.

(d) That the plaintiff was in possession of the premises or entitled to such possession.

(e) That the defendant afterward unlawfully entered upon and dispossessed him of such premises, stating the date, and withholds from him the possession thereof.

(f) If rents and profits or damages are claimed, such facts as show the plaintiff to be entitled thereto and the amount thereof.

(g) It shall conclude with a prayer for the relief sought.

Historical Notes

Source

Vernon's Ann.Civ.St. art. 7366.

Rule 784. The Possessor Shall Be Defendant

The defendant in the action shall be the person in possession if the premises are occupied, or some person claiming title thereto in case they are unoccupied.

Historical Notes

Source

Vernon's Ann.Civ.St. art. 7370, unchanged.

Rule 785. May Join As Defendants, When

The plaintiff may join as a defendant with the person in possession, any other person who, as landlord, remainderman, reversioner or otherwise, may claim title to the premises, or any part thereof, adversely to the plaintiff.

Historical Notes

Source

Vernon's Ann.Civ.St. art. 7371, unchanged.

Rule 786. Warrantor, etc., May Be Made a Party

When a party is sued for lands, the real owner or warrantor may make himself, or may be made, a party defendant in the suit, and shall be entitled to make such defense as if he had been the original defendant in the action.

Historical Notes

Source

Vernon's Ann.Civ.St. art. 7368, unchanged.

Rule 787. Landlord May Become Defendant

When such action shall be commenced against a tenant in possession, the landlord may enter himself as the defendant, or he may be made a party on motion of such tenant; and he shall be entitled to make the same defense as if the suit had been originally commenced against him.

Historical Notes

Source

Vernon's Ann.Civ.St. art. 7369, unchanged.

Rule 788. May File Plea of "Not Guilty" Only

The defendant in such action may file only the plea of "not guilty," which shall state in substance that he is not guilty of the injury complained of in the petition filed by the plaintiff against him, except that if he claims an allowance for improvements, he shall state the facts entitling him to the same.

Historical Notes

Source

Vernon's Ann.Civ.St. art. 7372, unchanged.

Rule 789. Proof Under Such Plea

Under such plea of "not guilty" the defendant may give in evidence any lawful defense to the action except the defense of limitations, which shall be specially pleaded.

Historical Notes

Source

Vernon's Ann.Civ.St. art. 7373, unchanged.

Rule 790. Answer Taken As Admitting Possession

Such plea or any other answer to the merits shall be an admission by the defendant, for the purpose of that action, that he was in possession of the premises sued for, or that he claimed title thereto at the time of commencing the action, unless he states distinctly in his answer the extent of his possession or claim, in which case it shall be an admission to such extent only.

Historical Notes

Source

Vernon's Ann.Civ.St. art. 7374, unchanged.

Rule 791. May Demand Abstract of Title

After answer filed, either party may, by notice in writing, duly served on the opposite party or his attorney of record, not less than ten days before the trial of the cause, demand an abstract in writing of the claim or title to the premises in question upon which he relies.

Historical Notes

Source

Vernon's Ann.Civ.St. art. 7376, unchanged.

Rule 792. Time to File Abstract

Such abstract of title shall be filed with the papers of the cause that within thirty days after the service of the notice, or within such further time that the court on good cause shown may grant; and in default thereof, the court may, after notice and hearing prior to the beginning of trial, order that no written instruments which are evidence of the claim or title of such opposite party by given on trial.

July 15, 1987, eff. Jan. 1, 1988. Amended by order of April 24, 1990, eff. Sept. 1, 1990.

Historical Notes

1990 Amendment

Inserted "written instruments which are" preceding "evidence of the".

Source

Vernon's Ann.Civ.St. art. 7377, unchanged.

Rule 793. Abstract Shall State, What

The abstract mentioned in the two preceding rules shall state:

(a) The nature of each document or written instrument intended to be used as evidence and its date; or

(b) If a contract or conveyance, its date, the parties thereto and the date of the proof of acknowledgment, and before what officer the same was made; and

(c) Where recorded, stating the book and page of the record.

(d) If not recorded in the county when the trial is had, copies of such instrument, with the names of the subscribing witnesses, shall be included. If such unrecorded instrument be lost or destroyed it shall be sufficient to state the nature of such instrument and its loss or destruction.

Historical Notes

Source

Vernon's Ann.Civ.St. art. 7378.

Rule 794. Amended Abstract

The court may allow either party to file an amended abstract of title, under the same rules, which authorize the amendment of pleadings so far as they are applicable; but in all cases the documentary evidence of title shall at the trial be confined to the matters contained in the abstract of title.

Historical Notes

Source

Vernon's Ann.Civ.St. art. 7379, unchanged.

Rule 795. Rules in Other Cases Observed

The trial shall be conducted according to the rules of pleading, practice and evidence in other cases in the district court and conformable to the principles of trial by ejectment, except as otherwise provided by these rules.

Historical Notes

Source

Vernon's Ann.Civ.St. art. 7365.

Rule 796. Surveyor Appointed, etc.

The judge of the court may, either in term time or in vacation, at his own discretion, or on motion of either party to the action appoint a surveyor, who shall survey the premises in controversy pursuant to the order of the court, and report his action under oath to such court. If said report be not rejected for good cause shown, the same shall be admitted as evidence on the trial.

Historical Notes

Source

Vernon's Ann.Civ.St. art. 7380.

Rule 797. Survey Unnecessary, When

Where there is no dispute as to the lines or boundaries of the land in controversy, or where the defendant admits that he is in possession of the lands or tenements included in the plaintiff's claim, or title, an order of survey shall be unnecessary.

Historical Notes

Source

Vernon's Ann.Civ.St. art. 7381, unchanged.

Rule 798. Common Source of Title

It shall not be necessary for the plaintiff to deraign title beyond a common source. Proof of a common source may be made by the plaintiff by certified copies of the deeds showing a chain of title to the defendant emanating from and under such common source. Before any such certified copies shall be read in evidence, they shall be filed with the papers of the suit three days before the trial, and the adverse party served with notice of such filing as in other cases. Such certified copies shall not be evidence of title in the defendant unless offered in evidence by him. The plaintiff may make any legal objection to such certified copies, or the originals thereof, when introduced by the defendant.

Historical Notes

Source

Vernon's Ann.Civ.St. art. 7382, unchanged.

Rule 799. Judgment by Default

If the defendant, who has been personally served with citation according to law or these rules fails to appear and answer by himself or attorney within the time prescribed by law or these rules for other actions in the district court, then judgment by default may be entered against him and in favor of the plaintiff for the title to the premises, or the possession thereof, or for both, according to the petition, and for all costs, without any proof of title by the plaintiff.

Historical Notes

Source

Vernon's Ann.Civ.St. art. 7383.

Rule 800. Proof Ex Parte

If the defendant has been cited only by publication, and fails to appear and answer by himself, or by attorney of his own selection, or if any defendant, having answered, fails to appear by himself or attorney when the case is called for trial on its merits, the plaintiff shall make such proof as will entitle him prima facie to recover, whereupon the proper judgment shall be entered.

Historical Notes

Source

Vernon's Ann.Civ.St. art. 7384.

Rule 801. When Defendant Claims Part Only

Where the defendant claims part of the premises only, the answer shall be equivalent to a disclaimer of the balance.

Historical Notes

Source

Vernon's Ann.Civ.St. art. 7385, unchanged.

Rule 802. When Plaintiff Proves Part

Where the defendant claims the whole premises, and the plaintiff shows himself entitled to recover part, the plaintiff shall recover such part and costs.

Historical Notes

Source

Vernon's Ann.Civ.St. art. 7386, unchanged.

Rule 803. May Recover a Part

When there are two or more plaintiffs or defendants any one or more of the plaintiffs may recover against one or more of the defendants the premises, or any part thereof, or any interest therein, or damages, according to the rights of the parties.

Historical Notes

Source

Vernon's Ann.Civ.St. art. 7387, unchanged.

Rule 804. The Judgment

Upon the finding of the jury, or of the court where the case is tried by the court, in favor of the plaintiff for the whole or any part of the premises in controversy, the judgment shall be that the plaintiff recover of the defendant the title or possession, or both, as the case may be, of such premises, describing them, and where he recovers the possession, that he have his writ of possession.

Historical Notes

Source

Vernon's Ann.Civ.St. art. 7388, unchanged.

Rule 805. Damages

Where it is alleged and proved that one of the parties is in possession of the premises, the court or jury, if they find for the adverse party, shall assess the damages for the use and occupation of the premises. If special injury to the property be alleged and proved, the damages for such injury shall also be assessed, and the proper judgment shall be entered therefor, on which execution may issue.

Historical Notes

Source

Vernon's Ann.Civ.St. art. 7389 (part).

Rule 806. Claim for Improvements

When the defendant or person in possession has claimed an allowance for improvements in accordance with Sections 22.021–22.024, Texas Property Code, the claim for use and occupation and damages mentioned in the preceding rule shall be considered and acted on in connection with such claim by the defendant or person in possession.

Dec. 5, 1983, eff. April 1, 1984. Amended by order of July 15, 1987, eff. Jan. 1, 1988.

Historical Notes

Source

Vernon's Ann.Civ.St. art. 7390.

Rule 807. Judgment When Claim for Improvements is Made

When a claim for improvements is successfully made under Sections 22.021–22.024, Texas Property Code, the judgment shall recite the estimated value of the premises without the improvements, and shall also include the conditions, stipulations and directions contained in Sections 22.021–22.024, Texas Property Code so far as applicable to the case before the court.

Dec. 5, 1983, eff. April 1, 1984. Amended by order of July 15, 1987, eff. Jan. 1, 1988.

Historical Notes

Source

Vernon's Ann.Civ.St. art. 7400.

Rule 808. These Rules Shall Not Govern, When

Nothing in Sections 22.001–22.045, Texas Property Code, shall be so construed as to alter, impair or take away the rights of parties, as arising under the laws in force before the introduction of the common law, but the same shall be decided by the principles of the law under which the same accrued, or by which the same were regulated or in any manner affected.

Dec. 5, 1983, eff. April 1, 1984. Amended by order of July 15, 1987, eff. Jan. 1, 1988.

Historical Notes

Source

Vernon's Ann.Civ.St. art. 7392.

Rule 809. These Rules Shall Not Govern, When

Nothing in these rules relating to trespass to try title shall be so construed as to alter, impair or take away the rights of parties, as arising under the laws in force before the introduction of the common law, but the same shall be decided by the principles of the law under which the same accrued, or by which the same were regulated or in any manner affected.

Historical Notes

Source

New rule.

SECTION 9. SUITS AGAINST NON-RESIDENTS

Rule 810. Requisites of Pleadings

The petition in actions authorized by Section 17.003, Civil Practice and Remedies Code, shall state the real names of the plaintiff and defendant, and shall describe the property involved with sufficient certainty to identify the same, the interest which the plaintiff claims, and such proceedings shall be had in such action as may be necessary to fully settle and determine the question of right or title in and to said property between the parties to said suit, and to decree the title or right of the party entitled thereto; and the court may issue the appropriate order to carry such decree, judgment or order into effect; and whenever such petition has been duly filed and citation thereon has been duly served by publication as required by Rules 114–116, the plaintiff may, at any time prior to entering the decree by leave of court first had and obtained, file amended and supplemental pleadings that do not subject additional property to said suit without the necessity of reciting the defendants so cited as aforesaid.

Dec. 5, 1983, eff. April 1, 1984. Amended by order of July 15, 1987, eff. Jan. 1, 1988.

Historical Notes

1988 Amendment

Substituted the Civil Practice and Remedies Code citation for the Revised Civil Statute citation.

Source

Vernon's Ann.Civ.St. art. 1977.

Rule 811. Service by Publication in Actions Under Section 17.003, Civil Practice and Remedies Code

In actions authorized by Section 17.003, Civil Practice and Remedies Code, service on the defendant or defendants may be made by publication as is provided by Rules 114–116 or by service of notice of the character and in the manner provided by Rule 108.

Dec. 5, 1983, eff. April 1, 1984. Amended by order of July 15, 1987, eff. Jan. 1, 1988.

Historical Notes

1988 Amendment

Substituted Civil Practice and Remedies Code citations for Revised Civil Statutes citations in both the rule heading and text.

Source

Vernon's Ann.Civ.St. art. 1976 (part).

Rule 812. No Judgment by Default

No judgment by default shall be taken in such case when service has been had by publication, but in such case the facts entitling the plaintiff to judgment shall be exhibited to the court on the trial; and a statement of facts shall be filed as provided by law and these rules in suits against nonresidents of this State served by publication, where no appearance has been made by them.

Oct. 12, 1949, eff. March 1, 1950.

Historical Notes

Source

Vernon's Ann.Civ.St. art. 1978, with minor textual change.

Rule 813. Suit to Extinguish Lien

If said suit shall be for the extinguishment of a lien or claim for money on said property that may be held by the defendant, the amount thereof, with interest, shall be ascertained by the court; and the same deposited in the registry of the court, subject to be drawn by the parties entitled thereto; but in such case no decree shall be entered until said sum is deposited; which fact shall be noted in said decree.

Historical Notes

Source

Vernon's Ann.Civ.St. Art. 1979, unchanged.

PART VIII

CLOSING RULES

Rule 814. Effective Date

These rules shall take effect on September 1st, 1941. They shall govern all proceedings in actions brought after they take effect, and also all further proceedings in actions then pending, except to the extent that in the opinion of the court their application in a particular action pending when the rules take effect would not be feasible or would work injustice, in which event the former procedure shall apply. All things properly done under any previously existing rule or statutes prior to the taking effect of these rules shall be treated as valid. Where citation or other process is issued and served in compliance with existing rules or laws prior to the taking effect of these rules, the party upon whom such citation or other process has been served shall have the time provided for under such previously existing rules or laws in which to comply therewith.

Historical Notes

Source

Federal Rule 86.

Rule 815. Substantive Rights Unaffected

These rules shall not be construed to enlarge or diminish any substantive rights or obligations of any parties to any civil action.

Historical Notes

Source

New rule.

Rule 816. Jurisdiction and Venue Unaffected

These rules shall not be construed to extend or limit the jurisdiction of the courts of the State of Texas nor the venue of actions therein.

Historical Notes

Source

Federal Rule 82.

Rule 817. Renumbered as Rule 3a by Order of Dec. 5, 1983, eff. April 1, 1984

Rule 818. Reference to Former Statutes

Wherever any statute or rule refers to any practice or procedure in any law, laws, statute or statutes, or to a title, chapter, section, or article of the statutes, or contains any reference of any such nature, and the matter referred to has been supplanted in whole or in part by these rules, every such reference shall be deemed to be to the pertinent part or parts of these rules.

Historical Notes

Source

New rule.

Rule 819. Procedure Continued

All procedure prescribed by statutes of the State of Texas not specifically listed in the accompanying enumeration of repealed articles shall, insofar as the same is not inconsistent with the provisions of these rules, continue in accordance with the provisions of such statutes as rules of court. In case of inconsistency between the provisions of these rules and any statutory procedure not specifically listed as repealed, these rules shall apply.

Historical Notes

Source

New rule.

Rule 820. Workers' Compensation Law

All portions of the Workers' Compensation Law, Articles 8306—8309-1, Revised Civil Statutes[1], and amendments thereto, which relate to matters of practice and procedure are hereby adopted and retained in force and effect as rules of court.

Amended by order of Dec. 5, 1983, eff. April 1, 1984.

1 Repealed, see, now, V.T.C.A., Labor Code § 401.001 et seq.

Historical Notes

Source

New rule.

Rule 821. Prior Court Rules Repealed

These rules shall supersede all Court Rules heretofore promulgated for any court; and all of said prior Court Rules are hereby repealed; provided, however, any rules of procedure heretofore adopted by a particular county or district court or by any Court of Appeals which were not of general application but were solely to regulate procedure in the particular court promulgating such rules are to remain in force and effect insofar as they are not inconsistent with these rules.

Dec. 5, 1983, eff. April 1, 1984.

Historical Notes

Source

New rule.

Rule 822. Title

These rules may be known and cited as the Texas Rules of Civil Procedure.

Historical Notes

Source

Federal Rule 85.

APPENDIX TO THE TEXAS RULES OF CIVIL PROCEDURE

APPENDIX A – Form for Rule 78a (Civil Case Information Sheet)

CAUSE NUMBER *(FOR CLERK USE ONLY)*: ______________________ COURT *(FOR CLERK USE ONLY)*: ______________

STYLED ____
(e.g., John Smith v. All American Insurance Co; In re Mary Ann Jones; In the Matter of the Estate of George Jackson)

A civil case information sheet must be completed and submitted when an original petition or application is filed to initiate a new civil, family law, probate, or mental health case or when a post-judgment petition for modification or motion for enforcement is filed in a family law case. The information should be the best available at the time of filing.

1. Contact information for person completing case information sheet:		Names of parties in case:	Person or entity completing sheet is:
Name:	Email:	Plaintiff(s)/Petitioner(s):	☐Attorney for Plaintiff/Petitioner ☐*Pro Se* Plaintiff/Petitioner ☐Title IV-D Agency ☐Other: ______
Address:	Telephone:		Additional Parties in Child Support Case:
City/State/Zip:	Fax:	Defendant(s)/Respondent(s):	Custodial Parent:
			Non-Custodial Parent:
Signature:	State Bar No:	[Attach additional page as necessary to list all parties]	Presumed Father:

2. Indicate case type, or identify the most important issue in the case *(select only 1)*:

Civil

Contract	Injury or Damage	Real Property	Related to Criminal Matters
Debt/Contract ☐Consumer/DTPA ☐Debt/Contract ☐Fraud/Misrepresentation ☐Other Debt/Contract: ______ *Foreclosure* ☐Home Equity—Expedited ☐Other Foreclosure ☐Franchise ☐Insurance ☐Landlord/Tenant ☐Non-Competition ☐Partnership ☐Other Contract: ______	☐Assault/Battery ☐Construction ☐Defamation *Malpractice* ☐Accounting ☐Legal ☐Medical ☐Other Professional Liability: ______ ☐Motor Vehicle Accident ☐Premises *Product Liability* ☐Asbestos/Silica ☐Other Product Liability List Product: ______ ☐Other Injury or Damage: ______	☐Eminent Domain/ Condemnation ☐Partition ☐Quiet Title ☐Trespass to Try Title ☐Other Property: ______	☐Expunction ☐Judgment Nisi ☐Non-Disclosure ☐Seizure/Forfeiture ☐Writ of Habeas Corpus—Pre-indictment ☐Other: ______

Employment	Other Civil	
☐Discrimination ☐Retaliation ☐Termination ☐Workers' Compensation ☐Other Employment: ______	☐Administrative Appeal ☐Antitrust/Unfair Competition ☐Code Violations ☐Foreign Judgment ☐Intellectual Property	☐Lawyer Discipline ☐Perpetuate Testimony ☐Securities/Stock ☐Tortious Interference ☐Other: ______

Family Law

Marriage Relationship	Post-judgment Actions (non-Title IV-D)	Title IV-D
☐Annulment ☐Declare Marriage Void *Divorce* ☐With Children ☐No Children	☐Enforcement ☐Modification—Custody ☐Modification—Other	☐Enforcement/Modification ☐Paternity ☐Reciprocals (UIFSA) ☐Support Order

Other Family Law	Parent-Child Relationship
☐Enforce Foreign Judgment ☐Habeas Corpus ☐Name Change ☐Protective Order ☐Removal of Disabilities of Minority ☐Other: ______	☐Adoption/Adoption with Termination ☐Child Protection ☐Child Support ☐Custody or Visitation ☐Gestational Parenting ☐Grandparent Access ☐Parentage/Paternity ☐Termination of Parental Rights ☐Other Parent-Child: ______

Tax	*Probate & Mental Health*	
☐Tax Appraisal ☐Tax Delinquency ☐Other Tax	*Probate/Wills/Intestate Administration* ☐Dependent Administration ☐Independent Administration ☐Other Estate Proceedings	☐Guardianship—Adult ☐Guardianship—Minor ☐Mental Health ☐Other: ______

3. Indicate procedure or remedy, if applicable *(may select more than 1)*:

☐Appeal from Municipal or Justice Court	☐Declaratory Judgment	☐Prejudgment Remedy
☐Arbitration-related	☐Garnishment	☐Protective Order
☐Attachment	☐Interpleader	☐Receiver
☐Bill of Review	☐License	☐Sequestration
☐Certiorari	☐Mandamus	☐Temporary Restraining Order/Injunction
☐Class Action	☐Post-judgment	☐Turnover

4. Indicate damages sought *(do not select if it is a family law case)*:

☐Less than $100,000, including damages of any kind, penalties, costs, expenses, pre-judgment interest, and attorney fees
☐Less than $100,000 and non-monetary relief
☐Over $100, 000 but not more than $200,000
☐Over $200,000 but not more than $1,000,000
☐Over $1,000,000

Adopted by order of Feb. 12, 2013, eff. March 1, 2013.

APPENDIX B – Form for Rule 502 (Justice Court Civil Case Information Sheet)

CAUSE NUMBER *(FOR CLERK USE ONLY)*: ______________________________

STYLED ____

(e.g., John Smith v. All American Insurance Co; In re Mary Ann Jones; In the Matter of the Estate of George Jackson)

A civil case information sheet must be completed and submitted when an original petition is filed to initiate a new suit. The information should be the best available at the time of filing. This sheet, required by Rule of Civil Procedure 502, is intended to collect information that will be used for statistical purposes only. It neither replaces nor supplements the filings or service of pleading or other documents as required by law or rule. The sheet does not constitute a discovery request, response, or supplementation, and it is not admissible at trial.

1. Contact information for person completing case information sheet:		2. Names of parties in case:
Name: ______________	Telephone: ______________	Plaintiff(s): ______________ ______________
Address: ______________	Fax: ______________	Defendant(s): ______________ ______________ ______________
City/State/Zip: ______________	State Bar No: ______________	[Attach additional page as necessary to list all parties]
Email: ______________		
Signature: ______________		

3. Indicate case type, or identify the most important issue in the case *(select only 1)*:	
☐ ***Debt Claim***: A debt claim case is a lawsuit brought to recover a debt by an assignee of a claim, a debt collector or collection agency, a financial institution, or a person or entity primarily engaged in the business of lending money at interest. The claim can be for no more than $10,000, excluding statutory interest and court costs but including attorney fees, if any.	☐ ***Eviction:*** An eviction case is a lawsuit brought to recover possession of real property, often by a landlord against a tenant. A claim for rent may be joined with an eviction case if the amount of rent due and unpaid is not more than $10,000, excluding statutory interest and court costs but including attorney fees, if any.
☐ ***Repair and Remedy***: A repair and remedy case is a lawsuit filed by a residential tenant under Chapter 92, Subchapter B of the Texas Property Code to enforce the landlord's duty to repair or remedy a condition materially affecting the physical health or safety of an ordinary tenant. The relief sought can be for no more than $10,000, excluding statutory interest and court costs but including attorney fees, if any.	☐ ***Small Claims:*** A small claims case is a lawsuit brought for the recovery of money damages, civil penalties, personal property, or other relief allowed by law. The claim can be for no more than $10,000, excluding statutory interest and court costs but including attorney fees, if any.

Adopted by order of April 15, 2013, eff. Aug. 31, 2013.

INDEX TO TEXAS RULES OF CIVIL PROCEDURE

TEXAS RULES OF EVIDENCE

Effective March 1, 1998

Including Amendments Received Through February 1, 2016

Research Note

See Vernon's Texas Rules Annotated, *Volume 7, for judicial constructions and other research aids.*

ARTICLE I. GENERAL PROVISIONS

Rule 101. Title, Scope, and Applicability of the Rules; Definitions

(a) Title. These rules may be cited as the Texas Rules of Evidence.

(b) Scope. These rules apply to proceedings in Texas courts except as otherwise provided in subdivisions (d)–(f).

(c) Rules on Privilege. The rules on privilege apply to all stages of a case or proceeding.

(d) Exception for Constitutional or Statutory Provisions or Other Rules. Despite these rules, a court must admit or exclude evidence if required to do so by the United States or Texas Constitution, a federal or Texas statute, or a rule prescribed by the United States or Texas Supreme Court or the Texas Court of Criminal Appeals. If possible, a court should resolve by reasonable construction any inconsistency between these rules and applicable constitutional or statutory provisions or other rules.

(e) Exceptions. These rules—except for those on privilege—do not apply to:

(1) the court's determination, under Rule 104(a), on a preliminary question of fact governing admissibility;

(2) grand jury proceedings; and

(3) the following miscellaneous proceedings:

(A) an application for habeas corpus in extradition, rendition, or interstate detainer proceedings;

(B) an inquiry by the court under Code of Criminal Procedure article 46B.004 to determine whether evidence exists that would support a finding that the defendant may be incompetent to stand trial;

(C) bail proceedings other than hearings to deny, revoke, or increase bail;

(D) hearings on justification for pretrial detention not involving bail;

(E) proceedings to issue a search or arrest warrant; and

(F) direct contempt determination proceedings.

(f) Exception for Justice Court Cases. These rules do not apply to justice court cases except as authorized by Texas Rule of Civil Procedure 500.3.

(g) Exception for Military Justice Hearings. The Texas Code of Military Justice, Tex. Gov't Code §§ 432.001–432.195, governs the admissibility of evidence in hearings held under that Code.

(h) Definitions. In these rules:

(1) "civil case" means a civil action or proceeding;

(2) "criminal case" means a criminal action or proceeding, including an examining trial;

(3) "public office" includes a public agency;

(4) "record" includes a memorandum, report, or data compilation;

(5) a "rule prescribed by the United States or Texas Supreme Court or the Texas Court of Criminal Appeals" means a rule adopted by any of those courts under statutory authority;

(6) "unsworn declaration" means an unsworn declaration made in accordance with Tex. Civ. Prac. & Rem. Code § 132.001; and

(7) a reference to any kind of written material or any other medium includes electronically stored information.

Eff. March 1, 1998. Amended by orders of Supreme Court March 10, 2015 and Court of Criminal Appeals March 12, 2015, eff. April 1, 2015.

Notes and Comments

Comment to 1998 change: "Criminal proceedings" rather than "criminal cases" is used since that was the terminology used in the prior Rules of Criminal Evidence. In subpart (b), the reference to "trials before magistrates" comes from prior Criminal Rule 1101(a). In the prior Criminal Rules, both Rule 101 and Rule 1101 dealt with the same thing—the applicability of the rules. Thus, Rules 101(c) and (d) have been written to incorporate the provisions of former Criminal Rule 1101 and that rule is omitted.

Comment to 2015 Restyling: The reference to "hierarchical governance" in former Rule 101(c) has been deleted as unnecessary. The textual limitation of former Rule 101(c) to criminal cases has been eliminated. Courts in civil cases must also admit or exclude evidence when required to do so by constitutional or statutory provisions or other rules that take precedence over these rules. Likewise, the title to former Rule 101(d) has been changed to more accurately indicate the purpose and scope of the subdivision

Rule 102. Purpose

These rules should be construed so as to administer every proceeding fairly, eliminate unjustifiable expense and delay, and promote the development of evidence law, to the end of ascertaining the truth and securing a just determination.

Eff. March 1, 1998. Amended by orders of Supreme Court March 10, 2015 and Court of Criminal Appeals March 12, 2015, eff. April 1, 2015.

Rule 103. Rulings on Evidence

(a) Preserving a Claim of Error. A party may claim error in a ruling to admit or exclude evidence only if the error affects a substantial right of the party and:

(1) if the ruling admits evidence, a party, on the record:

(A) timely objects or moves to strike; and

(B) states the specific ground, unless it was apparent from the context; or

(2) if the ruling excludes evidence, a party informs the court of its substance by an offer of proof, unless the substance was apparent from the context.

(b) Not Needing to Renew an Objection. When the court hears a party's objections outside the presence of the jury and rules that evidence is admissible, a party need not renew an objection to preserve a claim of error for appeal.

(c) Court's Statement About the Ruling; Directing an Offer of Proof. The court must allow a party to make an offer of proof outside the jury's presence as soon as practicable—and before the court reads its charge to the jury. The court may make any statement about the character or form of the evidence, the objection made, and the ruling. At a party's request, the court must direct that an offer of proof be made in question-and-answer form. Or the court may do so on its own.

(d) Preventing the Jury from Hearing Inadmissible Evidence. To the extent practicable, the court must conduct a jury trial so that inadmissible evidence is not suggested to the jury by any means.

(e) Taking Notice of Fundamental Error in Criminal Cases. In criminal cases, a court may take notice of a fundamental error affecting a substantial right, even if the claim of error was not properly preserved.

Eff. March 1, 1998. Amended by orders of Supreme Court March 10, 2015 and Court of Criminal Appeals March 12, 2015, eff. April 1, 2015.

Notes and Comments

Comment to 1998 change: The exception to the requirement of an offer of proof for matters that were apparent from the context within which questions were asked, found in paragraph (a)(2), is now applicable to civil as well as criminal cases.

Rule 104. Preliminary Questions

(a) In General. The court must decide any preliminary question about whether a witness is qualified, a privilege exists, or evidence is admissible. In so deciding, the court is not bound by evidence rules, except those on privilege.

(b) Relevance That Depends on a Fact. When the relevance of evidence depends on whether a fact exists, proof must be introduced sufficient to support a finding that the fact does exist. The court may admit the proposed evidence on the condition that the proof be introduced later.

(c) Conducting a Hearing So That the Jury Cannot Hear It. The court must conduct any hearing on a preliminary question so that the jury cannot hear it if:

(1) the hearing involves the admissibility of a confession in a criminal case;

(2) a defendant in a criminal case is a witness and so requests; or

(3) justice so requires.

(d) Cross–Examining a Defendant in a Criminal Case. By testifying outside the jury's hearing on a preliminary question, a defendant in a criminal case does not become subject to cross-examination on other issues in the case.

(e) Evidence Relevant to Weight and Credibility. This rule does not limit a party's right to introduce before the jury evidence that is relevant to the weight or credibility of other evidence.

Eff. March 1, 1998. Amended by orders of Supreme Court March 10, 2015 and Court of Criminal Appeals March 12, 2015, eff. April 1, 2015.

Rule 105. Evidence That Is Not Admissible Against Other Parties or for Other Purposes

(a) Limiting Admitted Evidence. If the court admits evidence that is admissible against a party or for a purpose—but not against another party or for another purpose—the court, on request, must restrict the evidence to its proper scope and instruct the jury accordingly.

(b) Preserving a Claim of Error.

(1) ***Court Admits the Evidence Without Restriction.*** A party may claim error in a ruling to admit evidence that is admissible against a party or for a purpose—but not against another party or for another purpose—only if the party requests the court to restrict the evidence to its proper scope and instruct the jury accordingly.

(2) ***Court Excludes the Evidence.*** A party may claim error in a ruling to exclude evidence that is admissible against a party or for a purpose—but not against another party or for another purpose—only if the party limits its offer to the party against whom or the purpose for which the evidence is admissible.

Eff. March 1, 1998. Amended by orders of Supreme Court March 10, 2015 and Court of Criminal Appeals March 12, 2015, eff. April 1, 2015.

Rule 106. Remainder of or Related Writings or Recorded Statements

If a party introduces all or part of a writing or recorded statement, an adverse party may introduce, at that time, any other part—or any other writing or recorded statement—that in fairness ought to be considered at the same time. "Writing or recorded statement" includes depositions.

Eff. March 1, 1998. Amended by orders of Supreme Court March 10, 2015 and Court of Criminal Appeals March 12, 2015, eff. April 1, 2015.

Rule 107. Rule of Optional Completeness

If a party introduces part of an act, declaration, conversation, writing, or recorded statement, an adverse party may inquire into any other part on the same subject. An adverse party may also introduce any other act, declaration, conversation, writing, or recorded statement that is necessary to explain or allow the trier of fact to fully understand the part offered by the opponent. "Writing or recorded statement" includes a deposition.

Eff. March 1, 1998. Amended by orders of Supreme Court March 10, 2015 and Court of Criminal Appeals March 12, 2015,, eff. April 1, 2015.

Notes and Comments

Comment to 1998 change: This rule is the former Criminal Rule 107 except that the example regarding "when a letter is read" has been relocated in the rule so as to more accurately indicate the provision it explains. While this rule appeared only in the prior criminal rules, it is made applicable to civil cases because it accurately reflects the common law rule of optional completeness in civil cases.

ARTICLE II. JUDICIAL NOTICE

Rule 201. Judicial Notice of Adjudicative Facts

(a) Scope. This rule governs judicial notice of an adjudicative fact only, not a legislative fact.

(b) Kinds of Facts That May Be Judicially Noticed. The court may judicially notice a fact that is not subject to reasonable dispute because it:

(1) is generally known within the trial court's territorial jurisdiction; or

(2) can be accurately and readily determined from sources whose accuracy cannot reasonably be questioned.

(c) Taking Notice. The court:

(1) may take judicial notice on its own; or

(2) must take judicial notice if a party requests it and the court is supplied with the necessary information.

(d) Timing. The court may take judicial notice at any stage of the proceeding.

(e) Opportunity to Be Heard. On timely request, a party is entitled to be heard on the propriety of taking judicial notice and the nature of the fact to be noticed. If the court takes judicial notice before notifying a party, the party, on request, is still entitled to be heard.

(f) Instructing the Jury. In a civil case, the court must instruct the jury to accept the noticed fact as conclusive. In a criminal case, the court must instruct the jury that it may or may not accept the noticed fact as conclusive.

Eff. March 1, 1998. Amended by orders of Supreme Court March 10, 2015 and Court of Criminal Appeals March 12, 2015, eff. April 1, 2015.

Rule 202. Judicial Notice of Other States' Law

(a) Scope. This rule governs judicial notice of another state's, territory's, or federal jurisdiction's:

- Constitution;
- public statutes;

- rules;
- regulations;
- ordinances;
- court decisions; and
- common law.

(b) Taking Notice. The court:

(1) may take judicial notice on its own; or

(2) must take judicial notice if a party requests it and the court is supplied with the necessary information.

(c) Notice and Opportunity to Be Heard.

(1) ***Notice.*** The court may require a party requesting judicial notice to notify all other parties of the request so they may respond to it.

(2) ***Opportunity to Be Heard.*** On timely request, a party is entitled to be heard on the propriety of taking judicial notice and the nature of the matter to be noticed. If the court takes judicial notice before a party has been notified, the party, on request, is still entitled to be heard.

(d) Timing. The court may take judicial notice at any stage of the proceeding.

(e) Determination and Review. The court—not the jury—must determine the law of another state, territory, or federal jurisdiction. The court's determination must be treated as a ruling on a question of law.

Eff. March 1, 1998. Amended by orders of Supreme Court March 10, 2015 and Court of Criminal Appeals March 12, 2015, eff. April 1, 2015.

Rule 203. Determining Foreign Law

(a) Raising a Foreign Law Issue. A party who intends to raise an issue about a foreign country's law must:

(1) give reasonable notice by a pleading or other writing; and

(2) at least 30 days before trial, supply all parties a copy of any written materials or sources the party intends to use to prove the foreign law.

(b) Translations. If the materials or sources were originally written in a language other than English, the party intending to rely on them must, at least 30 days before trial, supply all parties both a copy of the foreign language text and an English translation.

(c) Materials the Court May Consider; Notice. In determining foreign law, the court may consider any material or source, whether or not admissible. If the court considers any material or source not submitted by a party, it must give all parties notice and a reasonable opportunity to comment and submit additional materials.

(d) Determination and Review. The court—not the jury—must determine foreign law. The court's determination must be treated as a ruling on a question of law.

Eff. March 1, 1998. Amended by orders of Supreme Court March 10, 2015 and Court of Criminal Appeals March 12, 2015, eff. April 1, 2015.

Rule 204. Judicial Notice of Texas Municipal and County Ordinances, Texas Register Contents, and Published Agency Rules

(a) Scope. This rule governs judicial notice of Texas municipal and county ordinances, the contents of the Texas Register, and agency rules published in the Texas Administrative Code.

(b) Taking Notice. The court:

(1) may take judicial notice on its own; or

(2) must take judicial notice if a party requests it and the court is supplied with the necessary information.

(c) Notice and Opportunity to Be Heard.

(1) ***Notice.*** The court may require a party requesting judicial notice to notify all other parties of the request so they may respond to it.

(2) ***Opportunity to Be Heard.*** On timely request, a party is entitled to be heard on the propriety of taking judicial notice and the nature of the matter to be noticed. If the court takes judicial notice before a party has been notified, the party, on request, is still entitled to be heard.

(d) Determination and Review. The court—not the jury—must determine municipal and county ordinances, the contents of the Texas Register, and published agency rules. The court's determination must be treated as a ruling on a question of law.

Eff. March 1, 1998. Amended by orders of Supreme Court March 10, 2015 and Court of Criminal Appeals March 12, 2015, eff. April 1, 2015.

ARTICLE III. PRESUMPTIONS

[No rules adopted at this time.]

ARTICLE IV. RELEVANCE AND ITS LIMITS

Rule 401. Test for Relevant Evidence

Evidence is relevant if:

(a) it has any tendency to make a fact more or less probable than it would be without the evidence; and

(b) the fact is of consequence in determining the action.

Eff. March 1, 1998. Amended by orders of Supreme Court March 10, 2015 and Court of Criminal Appeals March 12, 2015, eff. April 1, 2015.

Rule 402. General Admissibility of Relevant Evidence

Relevant evidence is admissible unless any of the following provides otherwise:

- the United States or Texas Constitution;
- a statute;
- these rules; or
- other rules prescribed under statutory authority.

Irrelevant evidence is not admissible.

Eff. March 1, 1998. Amended by orders of Supreme Court March 10, 2015 and Court of Criminal Appeals March 12, 2015, eff. April 1, 2015.

Rule 403. Excluding Relevant Evidence for Prejudice, Confusion, or Other Reasons

The court may exclude relevant evidence if its probative value is substantially outweighed by a danger of one or more of the following: unfair prejudice, confusing the issues, misleading the jury, undue delay, or needlessly presenting cumulative evidence.

Eff. March 1, 1998. Amended by orders of Supreme Court March 10, 2015 and Court of Criminal Appeals March 12, 2015, eff. April 1, 2015.

Rule 404. Character Evidence; Crimes or Other Acts

(a) Character Evidence.

(1) ***Prohibited Uses.*** Evidence of a person's character or character trait is not admissible to prove that on a particular occasion the person acted in accordance with the character or trait.

(2) ***Exceptions for an Accused.***

(A) In a criminal case, a defendant may offer evidence of the defendant's pertinent trait, and if the evidence is admitted, the prosecutor may offer evidence to rebut it.

(B) In a civil case, a party accused of conduct involving moral turpitude may offer evidence of the party's pertinent trait, and if the evidence is admitted, the accusing party may offer evidence to rebut it.

(3) ***Exceptions for a Victim.***

(A) In a criminal case, subject to the limitations in Rule 412, a defendant may offer evidence of a victim's pertinent trait, and if the evidence is admitted, the prosecutor may offer evidence to rebut it.

(B) In a homicide case, the prosecutor may offer evidence of the victim's trait of peacefulness to rebut evidence that the victim was the first aggressor.

(C) In a civil case, a party accused of assaultive conduct may offer evidence of the victim's trait of violence to prove self-defense, and if the evidence is admitted, the accusing party may offer evidence of the victim's trait of peacefulness.

(4) ***Exceptions for a Witness.*** Evidence of a witness's character may be admitted under Rules 607, 608, and 609.

(5) ***Definition of "Victim."*** In this rule, "victim" includes an alleged victim.

(b) Crimes, Wrongs, or Other Acts.

(1) ***Prohibited Uses.*** Evidence of a crime, wrong, or other act is not admissible to prove a person's character in order to show that on a particular occasion the person acted in accordance with the character.

(2) ***Permitted Uses; Notice in Criminal Case.*** This evidence may be admissible for another purpose, such as proving motive, opportunity, intent, preparation, plan, knowledge, identity, absence of mistake, or lack of accident. On timely request by a defendant in a criminal case, the prosecutor must provide reasonable notice before trial that the prosecution intends to introduce such evidence—other than that arising in the same transaction—in its case-in-chief.

Eff. March 1, 1998. Amended by orders of Supreme Court March 10, 2015 and Court of Criminal Appeals March 12, 2015, eff. April 1, 2015.

Rule 405. Methods of Proving Character

(a) By Reputation or Opinion.

(1) ***In General.*** When evidence of a person's character or character trait is admissible, it may be proved by testimony about the person's reputation or by testimony in the form of an opinion. On cross-examination of the character witness, inquiry may be made into relevant specific instances of the person's conduct.

(2) ***Accused's Character in a Criminal Case.*** In the guilt stage of a criminal case, a witness may testify to the defendant's character or character trait only if, before the day of the offense, the witness was familiar with the defendant's reputation or the facts or information that form the basis of the witness's opinion.

(b) By Specific Instances of Conduct. When a person's character or character trait is an essential element of a charge, claim, or defense, the character or trait may also be proved by relevant specific instances of the person's conduct.

Eff. March 1, 1998. Amended by orders of Supreme Court March 10, 2015 and Court of Criminal Appeals March 12, 2015, eff. April 1, 2015.

Rule 406. Habit; Routine Practice

Evidence of a person's habit or an organization's routine practice may be admitted to prove that on a particular occasion the person or organization acted in accordance with the habit or routine practice. The court may admit this evidence regardless of whether it is corroborated or whether there was an eyewitness.

Eff. March 1, 1998. Amended by orders of Supreme Court March 10, 2015 and Court of Criminal Appeals March 12, 2015, eff. April 1, 2015.

Rule 407. Subsequent Remedial Measures; Notification of Defect

(a) Subsequent Remedial Measures. When measures are taken that would have made an earlier injury or harm less likely to occur, evidence of the subsequent measures is not admissible to prove:

- negligence;
- culpable conduct;
- a defect in a product or its design; or
- a need for a warning or instruction.

But the court may admit this evidence for another purpose, such as impeachment or—if disputed—proving ownership, control, or the feasibility of precautionary measures.

(b) Notification of Defect. A manufacturer's written notification to a purchaser of a defect in one of its products is admissible against the manufacturer to prove the defect.

Eff. March 1, 1998; amended by Supreme Court Aug. 29, 2003, eff. July 1, 2003. Amended by orders of Supreme Court March 10, 2015 and Court of Criminal Appeals March 12, 2015, eff. April 1, 2015.

Notes and Comments

Comment to 2015 Restyling: Rule 407 previously provided that evidence was not excluded if offered for a purpose not explicitly prohibited by the Rule. To improve the language of the Rule, it now provides that the court may admit evidence if offered for a permissible purpose. There is no intent to change the process for admitting evidence covered by the Rule. It remains the case that if offered for an impermissible purpose, it must be excluded, and if offered for a purpose not barred by the Rule, its admissibility remains governed by the general principles of Rules 402, 403, 801, etc.

Historical Notes

2003 Legislation

Section 5.03 of Acts 2003, 78th Leg., ch. 204 provides:

"As soon as practicable after the effective date [Sept. 1, 2003] of this Act, the supreme court shall amend Rule 407(a), Texas Rules of Evidence, to conform that rule to Rule 407, Federal Rules of Evidence."

2003 Amendment

The order dated August 29, 2003 provides that amendments are effective in all cases filed on or after July 1, 2003. The order rewrote subsec. (a), which prior thereto read:

"(a) Subsequent Remedial Measures. When, after an event, measures are taken which, if taken previously, would have made the event less likely to occur, evidence of the subsequent remedial measures is not admissible to prove negligence or culpable conduct in connection with the event. This rule does not require the exclusion of evidence of subsequent remedial measures when offered for another purpose, such as proving ownership, control or feasibility of precautionary measures, if controverted, or impeachment. Nothing in this rule shall preclude admissibility in products liability cases based on strict liability."

Rule 408. Compromise Offers and Negotiations

(a) Prohibited Uses. Evidence of the following is not admissible either to prove or disprove the validity or amount of a disputed claim:

(1) furnishing, promising, or offering—or accepting, promising to accept, or offering to accept—a valuable consideration in compromising or attempting to compromise the claim; and

(2) conduct or statements made during compromise negotiations about the claim.

(b) Permissible Uses. The court may admit this evidence for another purpose, such as proving a party's or witness's bias, prejudice, or interest, negating a contention of undue delay, or proving an effort to obstruct a criminal investigation or prosecution.

Eff. March 1, 1998. Amended by orders of Supreme Court March 10, 2015 and Court of Criminal Appeals March 12, 2015, eff. April 1, 2015.

Notes and Comments

Comment to 2015 Restyling: Rule 408 previously provided that evidence was not excluded if offered for a purpose not explicitly prohibited by the Rule. To improve the language of the Rule, it now provides that the court may admit evidence if offered for a permissible purpose. There is no intent to change the process for admitting evidence covered by the Rule. It remains the case that if offered for an impermissible purpose, it must be excluded, and if offered for a purpose not barred by the Rule, its admissibility remains governed by the general principles of Rules 402, 403, 801, etc.

The reference to "liability" has been deleted on the ground that the deletion makes the Rule flow better and easier to read, and because "liability" is covered by the broader term "validity." Courts have not made substantive decisions on the basis of any distinction between validity and liability. No change in current practice or in the coverage of the Rule is intended.

Finally, the sentence of the Rule referring to evidence "otherwise discoverable" has been deleted as superfluous. The intent of the sentence was to prevent a party from trying to immunize admissible information, such as a pre-existing document, through the pretense of disclosing it during compromise negotiations. But even without the sentence, the Rule cannot be read to protect pre-existing information simply because it was presented to the adversary in compromise negotiations.

Rule 409. Offers to Pay Medical and Similar Expenses

Evidence of furnishing, promising to pay, or offering to pay medical, hospital, or similar expenses resulting from an injury is not admissible to prove liability for the injury.

Eff. March 1, 1998. Amended by orders of Supreme Court March 10, 2015 and Court of Criminal Appeals March 12, 2015, eff. April 1, 2015.

Rule 410. Pleas, Plea Discussions, and Related Statements

(a) Prohibited Uses in Civil Cases. In a civil case, evidence of the following is not admissible against the defendant who made the plea or was a participant in the plea discussions:

(1) a guilty plea that was later withdrawn;

(2) a nolo contendere plea;

(3) a statement made during a proceeding on either of those pleas under Federal Rule of Criminal Procedure 11 or a comparable state procedure; or

(4) a statement made during plea discussions with an attorney for the prosecuting authority if the discussions did not result in a guilty plea or they resulted in a later-withdrawn guilty plea.

(b) Prohibited Uses in Criminal Cases. In a criminal case, evidence of the following is not admissible against the defendant who made the plea or was a participant in the plea discussions:

(1) a guilty plea that was later withdrawn;

(2) a nolo contendere plea that was later withdrawn;

(3) a statement made during a proceeding on either of those pleas under Federal Rule of Criminal Procedure 11 or a comparable state procedure; or

(4) a statement made during plea discussions with an attorney for the prosecuting authority if the discussions did not result in a guilty or nolo contendere plea or they resulted in a later-withdrawn guilty or nolo contendere plea.

(c) Exception. In a civil case, the court may admit a statement described in paragraph (a)(3) or (4) and in a criminal case, the court may admit a statement described in paragraph (b)(3) or (4), when another statement made during the same plea or plea discussions has been introduced and in fairness the statements ought to be considered together.

Eff. March 1, 1998. Amended by orders of Supreme Court March 10, 2015 and Court of Criminal Appeals March 12, 2015, eff. April 1, 2015.

Rule 411. Liability Insurance

Evidence that a person was or was not insured against liability is not admissible to prove whether the person acted negligently or otherwise wrongfully. But the court may admit this evidence for another purpose, such as proving a witness's bias or prejudice or, if disputed, proving agency, ownership, or control.

Eff. March 1, 1998. Amended by orders of Supreme Court March 10, 2015 and Court of Criminal Appeals March 12, 2015, eff. April 1, 2015.

Rule 412. Evidence of Previous Sexual Conduct in Criminal Cases

(a) In General. The following evidence is not admissible in a prosecution for sexual assault, aggravated sexual assault, or attempt to commit sexual assault or aggravated sexual assault:

(1) reputation or opinion evidence of a victim's past sexual behavior; or

(2) specific instances of a victim's past sexual behavior.

(b) Exceptions for Specific Instances. Evidence of specific instances of a victim's past sexual behavior is admissible if:

(1) the court admits the evidence in accordance with subdivisions (c) and (d);

(2) the evidence:

(A) is necessary to rebut or explain scientific or medical evidence offered by the prosecutor;

(B) concerns past sexual behavior with the defendant and is offered by the defendant to prove consent;

(C) relates to the victim's motive or bias;

(D) is admissible under Rule 609; or

(E) is constitutionally required to be admitted; and

(3) the probative value of the evidence outweighs the danger of unfair prejudice.

(c) Procedure for Offering Evidence. Before offering any evidence of the victim's past sexual behavior, the defendant must inform the court outside the jury's presence. The court must then conduct an in camera hearing, recorded by a court reporter, and determine whether the proposed evidence is admissible. The defendant may not refer to any evidence ruled inadmissible without first requesting and gaining the court's approval outside the jury's presence.

(d) Record Sealed. The court must preserve the record of the in camera hearing, under seal, as part of the record.

(e) Definition of "Victim." In this rule, "victim" includes an alleged victim.

Eff. March 1, 1998. Amended by Court of Criminal Appeals Dec. 13, 2006, eff. Jan. 1, 2007. Amended by orders of Supreme Court March 10, 2015 and Court of Criminal Appeals March 12, 2015, eff. April 1, 2015.

Historical Notes

Section 1.17 of Acts 1993, 73rd Leg., ch. 900, provides:

"Under the terms of Section 22.109(b), Government Code, Rule 412(e), Texas Rules of Criminal Evidence is disapproved."

2006 Amendment

The order dated December 13, 2006 provides that amendments are effective January 1, 2007. The order deleted subsection (e).

ARTICLE V. PRIVILEGES

Rule 501. Privileges in General

Unless a Constitution, a statute, or these or other rules prescribed under statutory authority provide otherwise, no person has a privilege to:

(a) refuse to be a witness;

(b) refuse to disclose any matter;

(c) refuse to produce any object or writing; or

(d) prevent another from being a witness, disclosing any matter, or producing any object or writing.

Eff. March 1, 1998. Amended by orders of Supreme Court March 10, 2015 and Court of Criminal Appeals March 12, 2015, eff. April 1, 2015.

Rule 502. Required Reports Privileged By Statute

(a) In General. If a law requiring a return or report to be made so provides:

(1) a person, corporation, association, or other organization or entity—whether public or private—that makes the required return or report has a privilege to refuse to disclose it and to prevent any other person from disclosing it; and

(2) a public officer or agency to whom the return or report must be made has a privilege to refuse to disclose it.

(b) Exceptions. This privilege does not apply in an action involving perjury, false statements, fraud in the return or report, or other failure to comply with the law in question.

Eff. March 1, 1998. Amended by orders of Supreme Court March 10, 2015 and Court of Criminal Appeals March 12, 2015, eff. April 1, 2015.

Rule 503. Lawyer–Client Privilege

(a) Definitions. In this rule:

(1) A "client" is a person, public officer, or corporation, association, or other organization or entity—whether public or private—that:

(A) is rendered professional legal services by a lawyer; or

(B) consults a lawyer with a view to obtaining professional legal services from the lawyer.

(2) A "client's representative" is:

(A) a person who has authority to obtain professional legal services for the client or to act for the client on the legal advice rendered; or

(B) any other person who, to facilitate the rendition of professional legal services to the client, makes or receives a confidential communication while acting in the scope of employment for the client.

(3) A "lawyer" is a person authorized, or who the client reasonably believes is authorized, to practice law in any state or nation.

(4) A "lawyer's representative" is:

(A) one employed by the lawyer to assist in the rendition of professional legal services; or

(B) an accountant who is reasonably necessary for the lawyer's rendition of professional legal services.

(5) A communication is "confidential" if not intended to be disclosed to third persons other than those:

(A) to whom disclosure is made to further the rendition of professional legal services to the client; or

(B) reasonably necessary to transmit the communication.

(b) Rules of Privilege.

(1) ***General Rule.*** A client has a privilege to refuse to disclose and to prevent any other person from disclosing confidential communications made to facilitate the rendition of professional legal services to the client:

(A) between the client or the client's representative and the client's lawyer or the lawyer's representative;

(B) between the client's lawyer and the lawyer's representative;

(C) by the client, the client's representative, the client's lawyer, or the lawyer's representative to a lawyer representing another party in a pending action or that lawyer's representative, if the communications concern a matter of common interest in the pending action;

(D) between the client's representatives or between the client and the client's representative; or

(E) among lawyers and their representatives representing the same client.

(2) ***Special Rule in a Criminal Case.*** In a criminal case, a client has a privilege to prevent a lawyer or lawyer's representative from disclosing any other fact that came to the knowledge of the lawyer or the lawyer's representative by reason of the attorney-client relationship.

(c) Who May Claim. The privilege may be claimed by:

(1) the client;

(2) the client's guardian or conservator;

(3) a deceased client's personal representative; or

(4) the successor, trustee, or similar representative of a corporation, association, or other organization or entity—whether or not in existence.

The person who was the client's lawyer or the lawyer's representative when the communication was made may claim the privilege on the client's behalf—and is presumed to have authority to do so.

(d) Exceptions. This privilege does not apply:

(1) ***Furtherance of Crime or Fraud.*** If the lawyer's services were sought or obtained to enable or aid anyone to commit or plan to commit what the client knew or reasonably should have known to be a crime or fraud.

(2) ***Claimants Through Same Deceased Client.*** If the communication is relevant to an issue between parties claiming through the same deceased client.

(3) ***Breach of Duty By a Lawyer or Client.*** If the communication is relevant to an issue of breach of duty by a lawyer to the client or by a client to the lawyer.

(4) ***Document Attested By a Lawyer.*** If the communication is relevant to an issue concerning an attested document to which the lawyer is an attesting witness.

(5) ***Joint Clients.*** If the communication:

(A) is offered in an action between clients who retained or consulted a lawyer in common;

(B) was made by any of the clients to the lawyer; and

(C) is relevant to a matter of common interest between the clients.

Eff. March 1, 1998. Amended by orders of Supreme Court March 10, 2015 and Court of Criminal Appeals March 12, 2015, eff. April 1, 2015.

Notes and Comments

Comment to 1998 change: The addition of subsection (a)(2)(B) adopts a subject matter test for the privilege of an entity, in place of the control group test previously used. See *National Tank Co. v. Brotherton*, 851 S.W.2d 193, 197-198 (Tex. 1993).

Rule 504. Spousal Privileges

(a) Confidential Communication Privilege.

(1) ***Definition.*** A communication is "confidential" if a person makes it privately to the person's spouse and does not intend its disclosure to any other person.

(2) ***General Rule.*** A person has a privilege to refuse to disclose and to prevent any other person from disclosing a confidential communication made to the person's spouse while they were married. This privilege survives termination of the marriage.

(3) ***Who May Claim.*** The privilege may be claimed by:

(A) the communicating spouse;

(B) the guardian of a communicating spouse who is incompetent; or

(C) the personal representative of a communicating spouse who is deceased.

The other spouse may claim the privilege on the communicating spouse's behalf—and is presumed to have authority to do so.

(4) ***Exceptions.*** This privilege does not apply:

(A) ***Furtherance of Crime or Fraud.*** If the communication is made—wholly or partially—to enable or aid anyone to commit or plan to commit a crime or fraud.

(B) ***Proceeding Between Spouse and Other Spouse or Claimant Through Deceased Spouse.*** In a civil proceeding:

(i) brought by or on behalf of one spouse against the other; or

(ii) between a surviving spouse and a person claiming through the deceased spouse.

(C) ***Crime Against Family, Spouse, Household Member, or Minor Child.*** In a:

(i) proceeding in which a party is accused of conduct that, if proved, is a crime against the person of the other spouse, any member of the household of either spouse, or any minor child; or

(ii) criminal proceeding involving a charge of bigamy under Section 25.01 of the Penal Code.

(D) ***Commitment or Similar Proceeding.*** In a proceeding to commit either spouse or otherwise to place the spouse or the spouse's property under another's control because of a mental or physical condition.

(E) ***Proceeding to Establish Competence.*** In a proceeding brought by or on behalf of either spouse to establish competence.

(b) Privilege Not to Testify in a Criminal Case.

(1) ***General Rule.*** In a criminal case, an accused's spouse has a privilege not to be called to testify for the state. But this rule neither prohibits a spouse from testifying voluntarily for the state nor gives a spouse a privilege to refuse to be called to testify for the accused.

(2) ***Failure to Call Spouse.*** If other evidence indicates that the accused's spouse could testify to relevant matters, an accused's failure to call the spouse to testify is a proper subject of comment by counsel.

(3) ***Who May Claim.*** The privilege not to testify may be claimed by the accused's spouse or the spouse's guardian or representative, but not by the accused.

(4) ***Exceptions.*** This privilege does not apply:

(A) ***Certain Criminal Proceedings.*** In a criminal proceeding in which a spouse is charged with:

(i) a crime against the other spouse, any member of the household of either spouse, or any minor child; or

(ii) bigamy under Section 25.01 of the Penal Code.

(B) ***Matters That Occurred Before the Marriage.*** If the spouse is called to testify about matters that occurred before the marriage.

Eff. March 1, 1998. Amended by Court of Criminal Appeals Dec. 13, 2006, eff. January 1, 2007. Amended by orders of Supreme Court March 10, 2015 and Court of Criminal Appeals March 12, 2015, eff. April 1, 2015.

Notes and Comments

Comment to 1998 change: The rule eliminates the spousal testimonial privilege for prosecutions in which the testifying spouse is the alleged victim of a crime by the accused. This is intended to be consistent with Code of Criminal Procedure article 38.10, effective September 1, 1995.

Comment to 2015 Restyling: Previously, Rule 504(b)(1) provided that, "A spouse who testifies on behalf of an accused is subject to cross-examination as provided in Rule 611(b)." That sentence was included in the original version of Rule 504 when the Texas Rules of Criminal Evidence were promulgated in 1986 and changed the rule to a testimonial privilege held by the witness spouse. Until then, a spouse was deemed incompetent to testify against his or her defendant spouse, and when a spouse testified on behalf of a defendant spouse, the state was limited to cross-examining the spouse about matters relating to the spouse's direct testimony. The quoted sentence from the original Criminal Rule 504(b) was designed to overturn this limitation and allow the state to cross-examine a testifying spouse in the same manner as any other witness. More than twenty-five years later, it is clear that a spouse who testifies either for or against a defendant spouse may be cross-examined in the same manner as any other witness. Therefore, the continued inclusion in the rule of a provision that refers only to the cross-examination of a spouse who testifies on behalf of the accused is more confusing than helpful. Its deletion is designed to clarify the rule and does not change existing law.

Historical Notes

2006 Amendment

The order dated December 13, 2006, effective January 1, 2007, in subsec. (a)(4)(c) added", or, in a criminal proceeding, when the offense changed is under" Section 25.01, Penal Code (Bigamy) and in subsec. (b)(4)(A) added ", or in an offense changed under Section 25.01, Penal Code (Bigamy)".

Rule 505. Privilege For Communications to a Clergy Member

(a) Definitions. In this rule:

(1) A "clergy member" is a minister, priest, rabbi, accredited Christian Science Practitioner, or other similar functionary of a religious organization or someone whom a communicant reasonably believes is a clergy member.

(2) A "communicant" is a person who consults a clergy member in the clergy member's professional capacity as a spiritual adviser.

(3) A communication is "confidential" if made privately and not intended for further disclosure except to other persons present to further the purpose of the communication.

(b) General Rule. A communicant has a privilege to refuse to disclose and to prevent any other person from disclosing a confidential communication by the communicant to a clergy member in the clergy member's professional capacity as spiritual adviser.

(c) Who May Claim. The privilege may be claimed by:

(1) the communicant;

(2) the communicant's guardian or conservator; or

(3) a deceased communicant's personal representative.

The clergy member to whom the communication was made may claim the privilege on the communicant's behalf—and is presumed to have authority to do so.

Eff. March 1, 1998. Amended by orders of Supreme Court March 10, 2015 and Court of Criminal Appeals March 12, 2015, eff. April 1, 2015.

Rule 506. Political Vote Privilege

A person has a privilege to refuse to disclose the person's vote at a political election conducted by secret ballot unless the vote was cast illegally.

Eff. March 1, 1998. Amended by orders of Supreme Court March 10, 2015 and Court of Criminal Appeals March 12, 2015, eff. April 1, 2015.

Rule 507. Trade Secrets Privilege

(a) General Rule. A person has a privilege to refuse to disclose and to prevent other persons from disclosing a trade secret owned by the person, unless the court finds that nondisclosure will tend to conceal fraud or otherwise work injustice.

(b) Who May Claim. The privilege may be claimed by the person who owns the trade secret or the person's agent or employee.

(c) Protective Measure. If a court orders a person to disclose a trade secret, it must take any protective measure required by the interests of the privilege holder and the parties and to further justice.

Eff. March 1, 1998. Amended by orders of Supreme Court March 10, 2015 and Court of Criminal Appeals March 12, 2015, eff. April 1, 2015.

Rule 508. Informer's Identity Privilege

(a) General Rule. The United States, a state, or a subdivision of either has a privilege to refuse to disclose a person's identity if:

(1) the person has furnished information to a law enforcement officer or a member of a legislative committee or its staff conducting an investigation of a possible violation of law; and

(2) the information relates to or assists in the investigation.

(b) Who May Claim. The privilege may be claimed by an appropriate representative of the public entity to which the informer furnished the information. The court in a criminal case must reject the privilege claim if the state objects.

(c) Exceptions.

(1) ***Voluntary Disclosure; Informer a Witness.*** This privilege does not apply if:

(A) the informer's identity or the informer's interest in the communication's subject matter has been disclosed—by a privilege holder or the informer's own action—to a person who would have cause to resent the communication; or

(B) the informer appears as a witness for the public entity.

(2) ***Testimony About the Merits.***

(A) ***Criminal Case.*** In a criminal case, this privilege does not apply if the court finds a reasonable probability exists that the informer can give testimony necessary to a fair determination of guilt or innocence. If the court so finds and the public entity elects not to disclose the informer's identity:

(i) on the defendant's motion, the court must dismiss the charges to which the testimony would relate; or

(ii) on its own motion, the court may dismiss the charges to which the testimony would relate.

(B) ***Certain Civil Cases.*** In a civil case in which the public entity is a party, this privilege does not apply if the court finds a reasonable probability exists that the informer can give testimony necessary to a fair determination of a material issue on the merits. If the court so finds and the public entity elects not to disclose the informer's identity, the court may make any order that justice requires.

(C) ***Procedures.***

(i) If it appears that an informer may be able to give the testimony required to invoke this exception and the public entity claims the privilege, the court must give the public entity an opportunity to show in camera facts relevant to determining whether this exception is met. The showing should ordinarily be made by affidavits, but the court may take testimony if it finds the matter cannot be satisfactorily resolved by affidavits.

(ii) No counsel or party may attend the in camera showing.

(iii) The court must seal and preserve for appeal evidence submitted under this subparagraph (2)(C). The evidence must not otherwise be revealed without the public entity's consent.

(3) ***Legality of Obtaining Evidence.***

(A) ***Court May Order Disclosure.*** The court may order the public entity to disclose an informer's identity if:

(i) information from an informer is relied on to establish the legality of the means by which evidence was obtained; and

(ii) the court is not satisfied that the information was received from an informer reasonably believed to be reliable or credible.

(B) ***Procedures.***

(i) On the public entity's request, the court must order the disclosure be made in camera.

(ii) No counsel or party may attend the in camera disclosure.

(iii) If the informer's identity is disclosed in camera, the court must seal and preserve for appeal the record of the in camera proceeding. The record of the in camera proceeding must not otherwise be revealed without the public entity's consent.

Eff. March 1, 1998. Amended by orders of Supreme Court March 10, 2015 and Court of Criminal Appeals March 12, 2015, eff. April 1, 2015.

Rule 509. Physician–Patient Privilege

(a) Definitions. In this rule:

(1) A "patient" is a person who consults or is seen by a physician for medical care.

(2) A "physician" is a person licensed, or who the patient reasonably believes is licensed, to practice medicine in any state or nation.

(3) A communication is "confidential" if not intended to be disclosed to third persons other than those:

(A) present to further the patient's interest in the consultation, examination, or interview;

(B) reasonably necessary to transmit the communication; or

(C) participating in the diagnosis and treatment under the physician's direction, including members of the patient's family.

(b) Limited Privilege in a Criminal Case. There is no physician-patient privilege in a criminal case. But a confidential communication is not admissible in a criminal case if made:

(1) to a person involved in the treatment of or examination for alcohol or drug abuse; and

(2) by a person being treated voluntarily or being examined for admission to treatment for alcohol or drug abuse.

(c) General Rule in a Civil Case. In a civil case, a patient has a privilege to refuse to disclose and to prevent any other person from disclosing:

(1) a confidential communication between a physician and the patient that relates to or was made in connection with any professional services the physician rendered the patient; and

(2) a record of the patient's identity, diagnosis, evaluation, or treatment created or maintained by a physician.

(d) Who May Claim in a Civil Case. The privilege may be claimed by:

(1) the patient; or

(2) the patient's representative on the patient's behalf.

The physician may claim the privilege on the patient's behalf—and is presumed to have authority to do so.

(e) Exceptions in a Civil Case. This privilege does not apply:

(1) ***Proceeding Against Physician.*** If the communication or record is relevant to a physician's claim or defense in:

(A) a proceeding the patient brings against a physician; or

(B) a license revocation proceeding in which the patient is a complaining witness.

(2) ***Consent.*** If the patient or a person authorized to act on the patient's behalf consents in writing to the release of any privileged information, as provided in subdivision (f).

(3) ***Action to Collect.*** In an action to collect a claim for medical services rendered to the patient.

(4) ***Party Relies on Patient's Condition.*** If any party relies on the patient's physical, mental, or emotional condition as a part of the party's claim or defense and the communication or record is relevant to that condition.

(5) ***Disciplinary Investigation or Proceeding.*** In a disciplinary investigation of or proceeding against a physician under the Medical Practice Act, Tex. Occ. Code § 164.001 et seq., or a registered nurse under Tex. Occ. Code § 301.451 et seq. But the board conducting the investigation or proceeding must protect the identity of any patient whose medical records are examined unless:

(A) the patient's records would be subject to disclosure under paragraph (e)(1); or

(B) the patient has consented in writing to the release of medical records, as provided in subdivision (f).

(6) ***Involuntary Civil Commitment or Similar Proceeding.*** In a proceeding for involuntary civil commitment or court-ordered treatment, or a probable cause hearing under Tex. Health & Safety Code:

(A) chapter 464 (Facilities Treating Alcoholics and Drug–Dependent Persons);

(B) title 7, subtitle C (Texas Mental Health Code); or

(C) title 7, subtitle D (Persons With Mental Retardation Act).

(7) ***Abuse or Neglect of "Institution" Resident.*** In a proceeding regarding the abuse or neglect, or the cause of any abuse or neglect, of a resident of an "institution" as defined in Tex. Health & Safety Code § 242.002.

(f) Consent For Release of Privileged Information.

(1) Consent for the release of privileged information must be in writing and signed by:

(A) the patient;

(B) a parent or legal guardian if the patient is a minor;

(C) a legal guardian if the patient has been adjudicated incompetent to manage personal affairs;

(D) an attorney appointed for the patient under Tex. Health & Safety Code title 7, subtitles C and D;

(E) an attorney ad litem appointed for the patient under Tex. Estates Code title 3, subtitle C;

(F) an attorney ad litem or guardian ad litem appointed for a minor under Tex. Fam. Code chapter 107, subchapter B; or

(G) a personal representative if the patient is deceased.

(2) The consent must specify:

(A) the information or medical records covered by the release;

(B) the reasons or purposes for the release; and

(C) the person to whom the information is to be released.

(3) The patient, or other person authorized to consent, may withdraw consent to the release of any information. But a withdrawal of consent does not affect any information disclosed before the patient or authorized person gave written notice of the withdrawal.

(4) Any person who receives information privileged under this rule may disclose the information only to the extent consistent with the purposes specified in the consent.

Eff. March 1, 1998. Amended by orders of Supreme Court March 10, 2015 and Court of Criminal Appeals March 12, 2015, eff. April 1, 2015.

Notes and Comments

Comment to 1998 change: This comment is intended to inform the construction and application of this rule. Prior Criminal Rules of Evidence 509 and 510 are now in subparagraph (b) of this Rule. This rule governs disclosures of patient-physician communications only in judicial or administrative proceedings. Whether a physician may or must disclose such communications in other circumstances is governed by Tex.Rev.Civ.Stat.Ann. art. 4495b, § 5.08. Former subparagraph (d)(6) of the Civil Evidence Rules, regarding disclosures in a suit affecting the parent-child relationship, is omitted, not because there should be no exception to the privilege in suits affecting the parent-child relationship, but because the exception in such suits is properly considered under subparagraph (e)(4) of the new rule (formerly subparagraph (d)(4)), as construed in *R.K. v. Ramirez*, 887 S.W.2d 836 (Tex. 1994). In determining the proper application of an exception in such suits, the trial court must ensure that the precise need for the information is not outweighed by legitimate privacy interests protected by the privilege. Subparagraph (e) of the new rule does not except from the privilege information relating to a nonparty patient who is or may be a consulting or testifying expert in the suit.

Comment to 2015 Restyling: The physician-patient privilege in a civil case was first enacted in Texas in 1981 as part of the Medical Practice Act, formerly codified in Tex. Rev. Civ. Stat. art. 4495b. That statute provided that the privilege applied even if a patient had received a physician's services before the statute's enactment. Because more than thirty years have now passed, it is no longer necessary to burden the text of the rule with a statement regarding the privilege's retroactive application. But deleting this statement from the rule's text is not intended as a substantive change in the law.

The former rule's reference to "confidentiality or" and "administrative proceedings" in subdivision (e) [Exceptions in a Civil Case] has been deleted. First, this rule is a privilege rule only. Tex. Occ. Code § 159.004 sets forth exceptions to a physician's duty to maintain confidentiality of patient information outside court and administrative proceedings. Second, by their own terms the rules of evidence govern only proceedings in Texas courts.

See Rule 101(b). To the extent the rules apply in administrative proceedings, it is because the Administrative Procedure Act mandates their applicability. Tex. Gov't Code § 2001.083 provides that "[i]n a contested case, a state agency shall give effect to the rules of privilege recognized by law." Section 2001.091 excludes privileged material from discovery in contested administrative cases.

Statutory references in the former rule that are no longer up-to-date have been revised. Finally, reconciling the provisions of Rule 509 with the parts of Tex. Occ. Code ch. 159 that address a physician-patient privilege applicable to court proceedings is beyond the scope of the restyling project.

Historical Notes

The Supreme Court and Court of Criminal Appeals Orders dated February 25, 1998, which finally approved amendments to Texas Rules of Evidence effective March 1, 1998, provide in part: "With the exception of the notes and comments to Rules 509 and 510, the notes and comments appended to these changes are incomplete, are included only for the convenience of the bench and bar, and are not a part of the rules. The notes and comments to Rules 509 and 510 are intended to inform the construction and application of those rules."

Rule 510. Mental Health Information Privilege in Civil Cases

(a) Definitions. In this rule:

(1) A "professional" is a person:

(A) authorized to practice medicine in any state or nation;

(B) licensed or certified by the State of Texas in the diagnosis, evaluation, or treatment of any mental or emotional disorder;

(C) involved in the treatment or examination of drug abusers; or

(D) who the patient reasonably believes to be a professional under this rule.

(2) A "patient" is a person who:

(A) consults or is interviewed by a professional for diagnosis, evaluation, or treatment of any mental or emotional condition or disorder, including alcoholism and drug addiction; or

(B) is being treated voluntarily or being examined for admission to voluntary treatment for drug abuse.

(3) A "patient's representative" is:

(A) any person who has the patient's written consent;

(B) the parent of a minor patient;

(C) the guardian of a patient who has been adjudicated incompetent to manage personal affairs; or

(D) the personal representative of a deceased patient.

(4) A communication is "confidential" if not intended to be disclosed to third persons other than those:

(A) present to further the patient's interest in the diagnosis, examination, evaluation, or treatment;

(B) reasonably necessary to transmit the communication; or

(C) participating in the diagnosis, examination, evaluation, or treatment under the professional's direction, including members of the patient's family.

(b) General Rule; Disclosure.

(1) In a civil case, a patient has a privilege to refuse to disclose and to prevent any other person from disclosing:

(A) a confidential communication between the patient and a professional; and

(B) a record of the patient's identity, diagnosis, evaluation, or treatment that is created or maintained by a professional.

(2) In a civil case, any person—other than a patient's representative acting on the patient's behalf—who receives information privileged under this rule may disclose the information only to the extent consistent with the purposes for which it was obtained.

(c) Who May Claim. The privilege may be claimed by:

(1) the patient; or

(2) the patient's representative on the patient's behalf.

The professional may claim the privilege on the patient's behalf—and is presumed to have authority to do so.

(d) Exceptions. This privilege does not apply:

(1) ***Proceeding Against Professional.*** If the communication or record is relevant to a professional's claim or defense in:

(A) a proceeding the patient brings against a professional; or

(B) a license revocation proceeding in which the patient is a complaining witness.

(2) ***Written Waiver.*** If the patient or a person authorized to act on the patient's behalf waives the privilege in writing.

(3) ***Action to Collect.*** In an action to collect a claim for mental or emotional health services rendered to the patient.

(4) ***Communication Made in Court–Ordered Examination.*** To a communication the patient made to a professional during a court-ordered examination relating to the patient's mental or emotional condition or disorder if:

(A) the patient made the communication after being informed that it would not be privileged;

(B) the communication is offered to prove an issue involving the patient's mental or emotional health; and

(C) the court imposes appropriate safeguards against unauthorized disclosure.

(5) ***Party Relies on Patient's Condition.*** If any party relies on the patient's physical, mental, or emotional condition as a part of the party's claim or defense and the communication or record is relevant to that condition.

(6) ***Abuse or Neglect of "Institution" Resident.*** In a proceeding regarding the abuse or neglect, or the cause of any abuse or neglect, of a resident of an "institution" as defined in Tex. Health & Safety Code § 242.002.

Eff. March 1, 1998. Amended by orders of Supreme Court March 10, 2015 and Court of Criminal Appeals March 12, 2015, eff. April 1, 2015.

Notes and Comments

Comment to 1998 change: This comment is intended to inform the construction and application of this rule. This rule governs disclosures of patient-professional communications only in judicial or administrative proceedings. Whether a professional may or must disclose such communications in other circumstances is governed by TEX. HEALTH & SAFETY CODE §§ 611.001-611.008. Former subparagraph (d)(6) of the Civil Evidence Rules, regarding disclosures in a suit affecting the parent-child relationship, is omitted, not because there should be no exception to the privilege in suits affecting the parent-child relationship, but because the exception in such suits is properly considered under subparagraph (d)(5), as construed in *R.K. v. Ramirez*, 887 S.W.2d 836 (Tex. 1994). In determining the proper application of an exception in such suits, the trial court must ensure that the precise need for the information is not outweighed by legitimate privacy interests protected by the privilege. Subparagraph (d) does not except from the privilege information relating to a nonparty patient who is or may be a consulting or testifying expert in the suit.

Comment to 2015 Restyling: The mental-health-information privilege in civil cases was enacted in Texas in 1979. Tex. Rev. Civ. Stat. art. 5561h (later codified at Tex. Health & Safety Code § 611.001 et seq.) provided that the privilege applied even if the patient had received the professional's services before the statute's enactment. Because more than thirty years have now passed, it is no longer necessary to burden the text of the rule with a statement regarding the privilege's retroactive application. But deleting this statement from the rule's text is not intended as a substantive change in the law.

Tex. Health & Safety Code ch. 611 addresses confidentiality rules for communications between a patient and a mental-health professional and for the professional's treatment records. Many of these provisions apply in contexts other than court proceedings. Reconciling the provisions of Rule 510 with the parts of chapter 611 that address a mental-health-information privilege applicable to court proceedings is beyond the scope of the restyling project

Historical Notes

The Supreme Court and Court of Criminal Appeals Orders dated February 25, 1998, which finally approved amendments to Texas Rules of Evidence effective March 1, 1998, provide in part: "With the exception of the notes and comments to Rules 509 and 510, the notes and comments appended to these changes are incomplete, are included only for the convenience of the bench and bar, and are not a part of the rules. The notes and comments to Rules 509 and 510 are intended to inform the construction and application of those rules."

Rule 511. Waiver by Voluntary Disclosure

(a) General Rule.

A person upon whom these rules confer a privilege against disclosure waives the privilege if:

(1) the person or a predecessor of the person while holder of the privilege voluntarily discloses or consents to disclosure of any significant part of the privileged matter unless such disclosure itself is privileged; or

(2) the person or a representative of the person calls a person to whom privileged communications have been made to testify as to the person's character or character trait insofar as such communications are relevant to such character or character trait.

(b) Lawyer–Client Privilege and Work Product; Limitations on Waiver.

Notwithstanding paragraph (a), the following provisions apply, in the circumstances set out, to disclosure of a communication or information covered by the lawyer-client privilege or work-product protection.

(1) ***Disclosure Made in a Federal or State Proceeding or to a Federal or State Office or Agency; Scope of a Waiver.*** When the disclosure is made in a federal proceeding or state proceeding of any state or to a federal office or agency or state office or agency of any state and waives the lawyer-client privilege or work-product protection, the waiver extends to an undisclosed communication or information only if:

(A) the waiver is intentional;

(B) the disclosed and undisclosed communications or information concern the same subject matter; and

(C) they ought in fairness to be considered together.

(2) ***Inadvertent Disclosure in State Civil Proceedings.*** When made in a Texas state proceeding, an inadvertent disclosure does not operate as a waiver if the holder followed the procedures of Rule of Civil Procedure 193.3(d).

(3) ***Controlling Effect of a Court Order.*** A disclosure made in litigation pending before a federal court or a state court of any state that has entered an order that the privilege or protection is not waived by disclosure connected with the litigation pending before that court is also not a waiver in a Texas state proceeding.

(4) ***Controlling Effect of a Party Agreement.*** An agreement on the effect of disclosure in a state proceeding of any state is binding only on the parties to the agreement, unless it is incorporated into a court order.

Eff. March 1, 1998. Amended by orders of Supreme Court March 10, 2015 and Court of Criminal Appeals March 12, 2015, eff. April 1, 2015.

Notes and Comments

Comment to 2015 Restyling: The amendments to Rule 511 are designed to align Texas law with federal law on waiver of privilege by voluntary disclosure. Subsection (a) sets forth the general rule. Subsection (b) incorporates the provisions of Federal Rule of Evidence 502. Like the federal rule, subsection (b) only addresses disclosure of communications or information covered by the lawyer-client privilege or work-product protection. These amendments do not affect the law governing waiver of other privileges or protections.

Rule 512. Privileged Matter Disclosed Under Compulsion or Without Opportunity to Claim Privilege

A privilege claim is not defeated by a disclosure that was:

(a) compelled erroneously; or

(b) made without opportunity to claim the privilege.

Eff. March 1, 1998. Amended by orders of Supreme Court March 10, 2015 and Court of Criminal Appeals March 12, 2015, eff. April 1, 2015.

Rule 513. Comment On or Inference From a Privilege Claim; Instruction

(a) Comment or Inference Not Permitted. Except as permitted in Rule 504(b)(2), neither the court nor counsel may comment on a privilege claim—whether made in the present proceeding or previously—and the factfinder may not draw an inference from the claim.

(b) Claiming Privilege Without the Jury's Knowledge. To the extent practicable, the court must conduct a jury trial so that the making of a privilege claim is not suggested to the jury by any means.

(c) Claim of Privilege Against Self–Incrimination in a Civil Case. Subdivisions (a) and (b) do not apply to a party's claim, in the present civil case, of the privilege against self-incrimination.

(d) Jury Instruction. When this rule forbids a jury from drawing an inference from a privilege claim, the court must, on request of a party against whom the jury might draw the inference, instruct the jury accordingly.

Eff. March 1, 1998. Amended by orders of Supreme Court March 10, 2015 and Court of Criminal Appeals March 12, 2015, eff. April 1, 2015.

Notes and Comments

Comment to 1998 change. Subdivision (d) regarding a party's entitlement to a jury instruction about a claim of privilege is made applicable to civil cases.

ARTICLE VI. WITNESSES

Rule 601. Competency to Testify in General; "Dead Man's Rule"

(a) In General. Every person is competent to be a witness unless these rules provide otherwise. The following witnesses are incompetent:

(1) ***Insane Persons.*** A person who is now insane or was insane at the time of the events about which the person is called to testify.

(2) ***Persons Lacking Sufficient Intellect.*** A child—or any other person—whom the court examines and finds lacks sufficient intellect to testify concerning the matters in issue.

(b) The "Dead Man's Rule."

(1) ***Applicability.*** The "Dead Man's Rule" applies only in a civil case:

(A) by or against a party in the party's capacity as an executor, administrator, or guardian; or

(B) by or against a decedent's heirs or legal representatives and based in whole or in part on the decedent's oral statement.

(2) ***General Rule.*** In cases described in subparagraph (b)(1)(A), a party may not testify against another party about an oral statement by the testator, intestate, or ward. In cases described in subparagraph (b)(1)(B), a party may not testify against

another party about an oral statement by the decedent.

(3) ***Exceptions.*** A party may testify against another party about an oral statement by the testator, intestate, ward, or decedent if:

(A) the party's testimony about the statement is corroborated; or

(B) the opposing party calls the party to testify at the trial about the statement.

(4) ***Instructions.*** If a court excludes evidence under paragraph (b)(2), the court must instruct the jury that the law prohibits a party from testifying about an oral statement by the testator, intestate, ward, or decedent unless the oral statement is corroborated or the opposing party calls the party to testify at the trial about the statement.

Eff. March 1, 1998. Amended by orders of Supreme Court March 10, 2015 and Court of Criminal Appeals March 12, 2015, eff. April 1, 2015.

Notes and Comments

Comment to 2015 Restyling: The text of the "Dead Man's Rule" has been streamlined to clarify its meaning without making any substantive changes. The text of former Rule 601(b) (as well as its statutory predecessor, Vernon's Ann. Civ. St. art. 3716) prohibits only a "party" from testifying about the dead man's statements. Despite this, the last sentence of former Rule 601(b) requires the court to instruct the jury when the rule "prohibits an interested party or witness" from testifying. Because the rule prohibits only a "party" from testifying, restyled Rule 601(b)(4) references only "a party," and not "an interested party or witness." To be sure, courts have indicated that the rule (or its statutory predecessor) may be applicable to a witness who is not nominally a party and inapplicable to a witness who is only nominally a party. *See, e.g., Chandler v. Welborn*, 156 Tex. 312, 294 S.W.2d 801, 809 (1956); *Ragsdale v. Ragsdale*, 142 Tex. 476, 179 S.W.2d 291, 295 (1944). But these decisions are based on an interpretation of the meaning of "party." Therefore, limiting the court's instruction under restyled Rule 601(b)(4) to "a party" does not change Texas practice. In addition, restyled Rule 601(b) deletes the sentence in former Rule 601(b) that states "[e]xcept for the foregoing, a witness is not precluded from giving evidence . . . because the witness is a party to the action . . ." This sentence is surplusage. Rule 601(b) is a rule of exclusion. If the testimony falls outside the rule of exclusion, its admissibility will be determined by other applicable rules of evidence.

Rule 602. Need for Personal Knowledge

A witness may testify to a matter only if evidence is introduced sufficient to support a finding that the witness has personal knowledge of the matter. Evidence to prove personal knowledge may consist of the witness's own testimony. This rule does not apply to a witness's expert testimony under Rule 703.

Eff. March 1, 1998. Amended by orders of Supreme Court March 10, 2015 and Court of Criminal Appeals March 12, 2015, eff. April 1, 2015.

Rule 603. Oath or Affirmation to Testify Truthfully

Before testifying, a witness must give an oath or affirmation to testify truthfully. It must be in a form designed to impress that duty on the witness's conscience.

Eff. March 1, 1998. Amended by orders of Supreme Court March 10, 2015 and Court of Criminal Appeals March 12, 2015, eff. April 1, 2015.

Rule 604. Interpreter

An interpreter must be qualified and must give an oath or affirmation to make a true translation.

Eff. March 1, 1998. Amended by orders of Supreme Court March 10, 2015 and Court of Criminal Appeals March 12, 2015, eff. April 1, 2015.

Rule 605. Judge's Competency as a Witness

The presiding judge may not testify as a witness at the trial. A party need not object to preserve the issue.

Eff. March 1, 1998. Amended by orders of Supreme Court March 10, 2015 and Court of Criminal Appeals March 12, 2015, eff. April 1, 2015.

Rule 606. Juror's Competency as a Witness

(a) At the Trial. A juror may not testify as a witness before the other jurors at the trial. If a juror is called to testify, the court must give a party an opportunity to object outside the jury's presence.

(b) During an Inquiry into the Validity of a Verdict or Indictment.

(1) ***Prohibited Testimony or Other Evidence.*** During an inquiry into the validity of a verdict or indictment, a juror may not testify about any statement made or incident that occurred during the jury's deliberations; the effect of anything on that juror's or another juror's vote; or any juror's mental processes concerning the verdict or indictment. The court may not receive a juror's affidavit or evidence of a juror's statement on these matters.

(2) ***Exceptions.*** A juror may testify:

(A) about whether an outside influence was improperly brought to bear on any juror; or

(B) to rebut a claim that the juror was not qualified to serve.

Eff. March 1, 1998. Amended by orders of Supreme Court March 10, 2015 and Court of Criminal Appeals March 12, 2015, eff. April 1, 2015.

Rule 607. Who May Impeach a Witness

Any party, including the party that called the witness, may attack the witness's credibility.

Eff. March 1, 1998. Amended by orders of Supreme Court March 10, 2015 and Court of Criminal Appeals March 12, 2015, eff. April 1, 2015.

Rule 608. A Witness's Character for Truthfulness or Untruthfulness

(a) Reputation or Opinion Evidence. A witness's credibility may be attacked or supported by testimony about the witness's reputation for having a character for truthfulness or untruthfulness, or by testimony in the form of an opinion about that character. But evidence of truthful character is admissible only after the witness's character for truthfulness has been attacked.

(b) Specific Instances of Conduct. Except for a criminal conviction under Rule 609, a party may not inquire into or offer extrinsic evidence to prove specific instances of the witness's conduct in order to attack or support the witness's character for truthfulness.

Eff. March 1, 1998. Amended by orders of Supreme Court March 10, 2015 and Court of Criminal Appeals March 12, 2015, eff. April 1, 2015.

Rule 609. Impeachment by Evidence of a Criminal Conviction

(a) In General. Evidence of a criminal conviction offered to attack a witness's character for truthfulness must be admitted if:

(1) the crime was a felony or involved moral turpitude, regardless of punishment;

(2) the probative value of the evidence outweighs its prejudicial effect to a party; and

(3) it is elicited from the witness or established by public record.

(b) Limit on Using the Evidence After 10 Years. This subdivision (b) applies if more than 10 years have passed since the witness's conviction or release from confinement for it, whichever is later. Evidence of the conviction is admissible only if its probative value, supported by specific facts and circumstances, substantially outweighs its prejudicial effect.

(c) Effect of a Pardon, Annulment, or Certificate of Rehabilitation. Evidence of a conviction is not admissible if:

(1) the conviction has been the subject of a pardon, annulment, certificate of rehabilitation, or other equivalent procedure based on a finding that the person has been rehabilitated, and the person has not been convicted of a later crime that was classified as a felony or involved moral turpitude, regardless of punishment;

(2) probation has been satisfactorily completed for the conviction, and the person has not been convicted of a later crime that was classified as a felony or involved moral turpitude, regardless of punishment; or

(3) the conviction has been the subject of a pardon, annulment, or other equivalent procedure based on a finding of innocence.

(d) Juvenile Adjudications. Evidence of a juvenile adjudication is admissible under this rule only if:

(1) the witness is a party in a proceeding conducted under title 3 of the Texas Family Code; or

(2) the United States or Texas Constitution requires that it be admitted.

(e) Pendency of an Appeal. A conviction for which an appeal is pending is not admissible under this rule.

(f) Notice. Evidence of a witness's conviction is not admissible under this rule if, after receiving from the adverse party a timely written request specifying the witness, the proponent of the conviction fails to provide sufficient written notice of intent to use the conviction. Notice is sufficient if it provides a fair opportunity to contest the use of such evidence.

Eff. March 1, 1998. Amended by orders of Supreme Court March 10, 2015 and Court of Criminal Appeals March 12, 2015, eff. April 1, 2015.

Rule 610. Religious Beliefs or Opinions

Evidence of a witness's religious beliefs or opinions is not admissible to attack or support the witness's credibility.

Eff. March 1, 1998. Amended by orders of Supreme Court March 10, 2015 and Court of Criminal Appeals March 12, 2015, eff. April 1, 2015.

Notes and Comments

Comment to 1998 change: This is prior Rule of Criminal Evidence 615.

Rule 611. Mode and Order of Examining Witnesses and Presenting Evidence

(a) Control by the Court; Purposes. The court should exercise reasonable control over the mode and order of examining witnesses and presenting evidence so as to:

(1) make those procedures effective for determining the truth;

(2) avoid wasting time; and

(3) protect witnesses from harassment or undue embarrassment.

(b) Scope of Cross–Examination. A witness may be cross-examined on any relevant matter, including credibility.

(c) Leading Questions. Leading questions should not be used on direct examination except as necessary to develop the witness's testimony. Ordinarily, the court should allow leading questions:

(1) on cross-examination; and

(2) when a party calls a hostile witness, an adverse party, or a witness identified with an adverse party.

Eff. March 1, 1998. Amended by orders of Supreme Court March 10, 2015 and Court of Criminal Appeals March 12, 2015, eff. April 1, 2015.

Rule 612. Writing Used to Refresh a Witness's Memory

(a) Scope. This rule gives an adverse party certain options when a witness uses a writing to refresh memory:

(1) while testifying;

(2) before testifying, in civil cases, if the court decides that justice requires the party to have those options; or

(3) before testifying, in criminal cases.

(b) Adverse Party's Options; Deleting Unrelated Matter. An adverse party is entitled to have the writing produced at the hearing, to inspect it, to cross-examine the witness about it, and to introduce in evidence any portion that relates to the witness's testimony. If the producing party claims that the writing includes unrelated matter, the court must examine the writing in camera, delete any unrelated portion, and order that the rest be delivered to the adverse party. Any portion deleted over objection must be preserved for the record.

(c) Failure to Produce or Deliver the Writing. If a writing is not produced or is not delivered as ordered, the court may issue any appropriate order. But if the prosecution does not comply in a criminal case, the court must strike the witness's testimony or—if justice so requires—declare a mistrial.

Eff. March 1, 1998. Amended by orders of Supreme Court March 10, 2015 and Court of Criminal Appeals March 12, 2015, eff. April 1, 2015.

Rule 613. Witness's Prior Statement and Bias or Interest

(a) Witness's Prior Inconsistent Statement.

(1) ***Foundation Requirement.*** When examining a witness about the witness's prior inconsistent statement—whether oral or written—a party must first tell the witness:

(A) the contents of the statement;

(B) the time and place of the statement; and

(C) the person to whom the witness made the statement.

(2) ***Need Not Show Written Statement.*** If the witness's prior inconsistent statement is written, a party need not show it to the witness before inquiring about it, but must, upon request, show it to opposing counsel.

(3) ***Opportunity to Explain or Deny.*** A witness must be given the opportunity to explain or deny the prior inconsistent statement.

(4) ***Extrinsic Evidence.*** Extrinsic evidence of a witness's prior inconsistent statement is not admissible unless the witness is first examined about the statement and fails to unequivocally admit making the statement.

(5) ***Opposing Party's Statement.*** This subdivision (a) does not apply to an opposing party's statement under Rule 801(e)(2).

(b) Witness's Bias or Interest.

(1) ***Foundation Requirement.*** When examining a witness about the witness's bias or interest, a party must first tell the witness the circumstances or statements that tend to show the witness's bias or interest. If examining a witness about a statement—whether oral or written—to prove the witness's bias or interest, a party must tell the witness:

(A) the contents of the statement;

(B) the time and place of the statement; and

(C) the person to whom the statement was made.

(2) ***Need Not Show Written Statement.*** If a party uses a written statement to prove the witness's bias or interest, a party need not show the statement to the witness before inquiring about it, but must, upon request, show it to opposing counsel.

(3) ***Opportunity to Explain or Deny.*** A witness must be given the opportunity to explain or deny the circumstances or statements that tend to show the witness's bias or interest. And the witness's proponent may present evidence to rebut the charge of bias or interest.

(4) ***Extrinsic Evidence.*** Extrinsic evidence of a witness's bias or interest is not admissible unless the witness is first examined about the bias or interest and fails to unequivocally admit it.

(c) Witness's Prior Consistent Statement. Unless Rule 801(e)(1)(B) provides otherwise, a witness's prior consistent statement is not admissible if offered solely to enhance the witness's credibility.

Eff. March 1, 1998. Amended by orders of Supreme Court March 10, 2015 and Court of Criminal Appeals March 12, 2015, eff. April 1, 2015.

Notes and Comments

Comment to 2015 Restyling: The amended rule retains the requirement that a witness be given an opportunity to explain or deny (a) a prior inconsistent statement or (b) the circumstances or a statement showing the witness's bias or interest, but this requirement is not imposed on the examining attorney. A witness may have to wait until redirect examination to explain a prior inconsistent statement or the circumstances or a statement that shows bias. But the impeaching attorney still is not permitted to introduce extrinsic evidence of the witness's prior inconsistent statement or bias unless the witness has first been examined about the statement or bias and has failed to unequivocally admit it. All other changes to the rule are intended to be stylistic only.

Rule 614. Excluding Witnesses

At a party's request, the court must order witnesses excluded so that they cannot hear other witnesses' testimony. Or the court may do so on its own. But this rule does not authorize excluding:

(a) a party who is a natural person and, in civil cases, that person's spouse;

(b) after being designated as the party's representative by its attorney:

(1) in a civil case, an officer or employee of a party that is not a natural person; or

(2) in a criminal case, a defendant that is not a natural person;

(c) a person whose presence a party shows to be essential to presenting the party's claim or defense; or

(d) the victim in a criminal case, unless the court determines that the victim's testimony would be materially affected by hearing other testimony at the trial.

Eff. March 1, 1998. Amended by orders of Supreme Court March 10, 2015 and Court of Criminal Appeals March 12, 2015, eff. April 1, 2015.

Rule 615. Producing a Witness's Statement in Criminal Cases

(a) Motion to Produce. After a witness other than the defendant testifies on direct examination, the court, on motion of a party who did not call the witness, must order an attorney for the state or the defendant and the defendant's attorney to produce, for the examination and use of the moving party, any statement of the witness that:

(1) is in their possession;

(2) relates to the subject matter of the witness's testimony; and

(3) has not previously been produced.

(b) Producing the Entire Statement. If the entire statement relates to the subject matter of the witness's testimony, the court must order that the statement be delivered to the moving party.

(c) Producing a Redacted Statement. If the party who called the witness claims that the statement contains information that does not relate to the subject matter of the witness's testimony, the court must inspect the statement in camera. After excising any unrelated portions, the court must order delivery of the redacted statement to the moving party. If a party objects to an excision, the court must preserve the entire statement with the excised portion indicated, under seal, as part of the record.

(d) Recess to Examine a Statement. If the court orders production of a witness's statement, the court, on request, must recess the proceedings to allow the moving party time to examine the statement and prepare for its use.

(e) Sanction for Failure to Produce or Deliver a Statement. If the party who called the witness disobeys an order to produce or deliver a statement, the court must strike the witness's testimony from the record. If an attorney for the state disobeys the order, the court must declare a mistrial if justice so requires.

(f) "Statement" Defined. As used in this rule, a witness's "statement" means:

(1) a written statement that the witness makes and signs, or otherwise adopts or approves;

(2) a substantially verbatim, contemporaneously recorded recital of the witness's oral statement that is contained in any recording or any transcription of a recording; or

(3) the witness's statement to a grand jury, however taken or recorded, or a transcription of such a statement.

Eff. March 1, 1998. Amended by orders of Supreme Court March 10, 2015 and Court of Criminal Appeals March 12, 2015, eff. April 1, 2015. Amended by orders of Supreme Court February 16, 2016, and Court of Criminal Appeals Dec. 7, 2015, and February 29, 2016, eff. Jan. 1, 2016.

Notes and Comments

Comment to 1998 change: This is prior Rule of Criminal Evidence 614.

Comment to 2015 Amendment: The Michael Morton Act, codified at Texas Code of Criminal Procedure art. 39.14, affords defendants substantial pre-trial discovery, requiring the state, upon request from the defendant, to produce and permit the defendant to inspect and copy various items, including witness statements. In many instances, therefore, art. 39.14 eliminates the need, after the witness testifies on direct examination, for a defendant to request, and the court to order, production of a witness's statement.

But art. 39.14 does not entirely eliminate the need for in-trial discovery of witness statements. Art. 39.14 does not extend equivalent discovery rights to the prosecution, and so prosecutors will still need to use Rule 615 to obtain witness statements of defense witnesses. Moreover, some defendants may fail to exercise their discovery rights under art. 39.14 and so may wish to obtain a witness statement under Rule 615. In addition, the Michael Morton Act applies only to the prosecution of offenses committed after December 31, 2013. Defendants on trial for offenses committed before then have no right to pre-trial discovery of the witness statements of prosecution witnesses.

Consequently, Rule 615(a) has been amended to account for the changed pre-trial discovery regime introduced by the Michael Morton Act. If a party's adversary has already produced a witness's statement—whether through formal discovery under art. 39.14 or through more informal means—Rule 615(a) no longer gives a party the right to obtain, after the witness testifies on direct examination, a court order for production of the witness's statement. But if a party's adversary has not already produced a witness's statement, the party may still use Rule 615(a) to request and obtain a court order requiring production of the witness's statement after the witness finishes testifying on direct examination.

ARTICLE VII. OPINIONS AND EXPERT TESTIMONY

Rule 701. Opinion Testimony by Lay Witnesses

If a witness is not testifying as an expert, testimony in the form of an opinion is limited to one that is:

(a) rationally based on the witness's perception; and

(b) helpful to clearly understanding the witness's testimony or to determining a fact in issue.

Eff. March 1, 1998. Amended by orders of Supreme Court March 10, 2015 and Court of Criminal Appeals March 12, 2015, eff. April 1, 2015.

Notes and Comments

Comment to 2015 Restyling: All references to an "inference" have been deleted because this makes the Rule flow better and easier to read, and because any "inference" is covered by the broader term "opinion." Courts have not made substantive decisions on the basis of any distinction between an opinion and an inference. No change in current practice is intended.

Rule 702. Testimony by Expert Witnesses

A witness who is qualified as an expert by knowledge, skill, experience, training, or education may testify in the form of an opinion or otherwise if the expert's scientific, technical, or other specialized knowledge will help the trier of fact to understand the evidence or to determine a fact in issue.

Eff. March 1, 1998. Amended by orders of Supreme Court March 10, 2015 and Court of Criminal Appeals March 12, 2015, eff. April 1, 2015.

Rule 703. Bases of an Expert's Opinion Testimony

An expert may base an opinion on facts or data in the case that the expert has been made aware of, reviewed, or personally observed. If experts in the particular field would reasonably rely on those kinds of facts or data in forming an opinion on the subject, they need not be admissible for the opinion to be admitted.

Eff. March 1, 1998. Amended by orders of Supreme Court March 10, 2015 and Court of Criminal Appeals March 12, 2015, eff. April 1, 2015.

Notes and Comments

Comment to 1998 change: The former Civil Rule referred to facts or data "perceived by or reviewed by" the expert. The former Criminal Rule referred to facts or data "perceived by or made known to" the expert. The terminology is now conformed, but no change in meaning is intended.

Comment to 2015 Restyling: All references to an "inference" have been deleted because this makes the Rule flow better and easier to read, and because any "inference" is covered by the broader term "opinion." Courts have not made substantive decisions on the basis of any distinction between an opinion and an inference. No change in current practice is intended.

Rule 704. Opinion on an Ultimate Issue

An opinion is not objectionable just because it embraces an ultimate issue.

Eff. March 1, 1998. Amended by orders of Supreme Court March 10, 2015 and Court of Criminal Appeals March 12, 2015, eff. April 1, 2015.

Rule 705. Disclosing the Underlying Facts or Data and Examining an Expert About Them

(a) Stating an Opinion Without Disclosing the Underlying Facts or Data. Unless the court orders otherwise, an expert may state an opinion—and give the reasons for it—without first testifying to the underlying facts or data. But the expert may be required to disclose those facts or data on cross-examination.

(b) Voir Dire Examination of an Expert About the Underlying Facts or Data. Before an expert states an opinion or discloses the underlying facts or data, an adverse party in a civil case may—or in a criminal case must—be permitted to examine the expert about the underlying facts or data. This examination must take place outside the jury's hearing.

(c) Admissibility of Opinion. An expert's opinion is inadmissible if the underlying facts or data do not provide a sufficient basis for the opinion.

(d) When Otherwise Inadmissible Underlying Facts or Data May Be Disclosed; Instructing the Jury. If the underlying facts or data would otherwise be inadmissible, the proponent of the opinion may not disclose them to the jury if their probative value in helping the jury evaluate the opinion is outweighed by their prejudicial effect. If the court allows the proponent to disclose those facts or data the court must, upon timely request, restrict the evidence to its proper scope and instruct the jury accordingly.

Eff. March 1, 1998. Amended by orders of Supreme Court March 10, 2015 and Court of Criminal Appeals March 12, 2015, eff. April 1, 2015.

Notes and Comments

Comment to 1998 change: Paragraphs (b), (c), and (d) are based on the former Criminal Rule and are made applicable to civil cases. This rule does not preclude a party in any case from conducting a *voir dire* examination into the qualifications of an expert.

Comment to 2015 Restyling: All references to an "inference" have been deleted because this makes the Rule flow better and easier to read, and because any "inference" is covered by the broader term "opinion." Courts have not made substantive decisions on the basis of any distinction between an opinion and an inference. No change in current practice is intended.

Rule 706. Audit in Civil Cases

Notwithstanding any other evidence rule, the court must admit an auditor's verified report prepared under Rule of Civil Procedure 172 and offered by a party. If a party files exceptions to the report, a party may offer evidence supporting the exceptions to contradict the report.

Eff. March 1, 1998. Amended by orders of Supreme Court March 10, 2015 and Court of Criminal Appeals March 12, 2015, eff. April 1, 2015.

ARTICLE VIII. HEARSAY

Rule 801. Definitions That Apply to This Article; Exclusions from Hearsay

(a) Statement. "Statement" means a person's oral or written verbal expression, or nonverbal conduct that a person intended as a substitute for verbal expression.

(b) Declarant. "Declarant" means the person who made the statement.

(c) Matter Asserted. "Matter asserted" means:

(1) any matter a declarant explicitly asserts; and

(2) any matter implied by a statement, if the probative value of the statement as offered flows from the declarant's belief about the matter.

(d) Hearsay. "Hearsay" means a statement that:

(1) the declarant does not make while testifying at the current trial or hearing; and

(2) a party offers in evidence to prove the truth of the matter asserted in the statement.

(e) Statements That Are Not Hearsay. A statement that meets the following conditions is not hearsay:

(1) ***A Declarant-Witness's Prior Statement.*** The declarant testifies and is subject to cross-examination about a prior statement, and the statement:

(A) is inconsistent with the declarant's testimony and:

(i) when offered in a civil case, was given under penalty of perjury at a trial, hearing, or other proceeding or in a deposition; or

(ii) when offered in a criminal case, was given under penalty of perjury at a trial, hearing, or other proceeding—except a grand jury proceeding—or in a deposition;

(B) is consistent with the declarant's testimony and is offered to rebut an express or implied charge that the declarant recently fabricated it or acted from a recent improper influence or motive in so testifying; or

(C) identifies a person as someone the declarant perceived earlier.

(2) ***An Opposing Party's Statement.*** The statement is offered against an opposing party and:

(A) was made by the party in an individual or representative capacity;

(B) is one the party manifested that it adopted or believed to be true;

(C) was made by a person whom the party authorized to make a statement on the subject;

(D) was made by the party's agent or employee on a matter within the scope of that relationship and while it existed; or

(E) was made by the party's coconspirator during and in furtherance of the conspiracy.

(3) ***A Deponent's Statement.*** In a civil case, the statement was made in a deposition taken in the same proceeding. "Same proceeding" is defined in

Rule of Civil Procedure 203.6(b). The deponent's unavailability as a witness is not a requirement for admissibility.

Adopted eff. March 1, 1998. Amended eff. Jan. 1, 1999. Amended by orders of Supreme Court March 10, 2015 and Court of Criminal Appeals March 12, 2015, eff. April 1, 2015.

Notes and Comments

Comment to 2015 Restyling: Statements falling under the hearsay exclusion provided by Rule 801(e)(2) are no longer referred to as "admissions" in the title to the subdivision. The term "admissions" is confusing because not all statements covered by the exclusion are admissions in the colloquial sense—a statement can be within the exclusion even if it "admitted" nothing and was not against the party's interest when made. The term "admissions" also raises confusion in comparison with the Rule 803(24) exception for declarations against interest. No change in application of the exclusion is intended.

The deletion of former Rule 801(e)(1)(D), which cross-references Code of Criminal Procedure art. 38.071, is not intended as a substantive change. Including this cross-reference made sense when the Texas Rules of Criminal Evidence were first promulgated, but with subsequent changes to the statutory provision, its inclusion is no longer appropriate. The version of article 38.071 that was initially cross-referenced in the Rules of Criminal Evidence required the declarant-victim to be available to testify at the trial. That requirement has since been deleted from the statute, and the statute no longer requires either the availability or testimony of the declarant-victim. Thus, cross-referencing the statute in Rule 801(e)(1), which applies only when the declarant testifies at trial about the prior statement, no longer makes sense. Moreover, article 38.071 is but one of a number of statutes that mandate the admission of certain hearsay statements in particular circumstances. *See, e.g.*, Code of Criminal Procedure art. 38.072; Family Code §§ 54.031, 104.002, 104.006. These statutory provisions take precedence over the general rule excluding hearsay, see Rules 101(c) and 802, and there is no apparent justification for cross-referencing article 38.071 and not all other such provisions.

Historical Notes

1998 Amendment

Supreme Court order dated December 31, 1998, effective January 1, 1999, in subsec. (e)(3) substituted "203.6" for "207".

Rule 802. The Rule Against Hearsay

Hearsay is not admissible unless any of the following provides otherwise:

- a statute;
- these rules; or
- other rules prescribed under statutory authority.

Inadmissible hearsay admitted without objection may not be denied probative value merely because it is hearsay.

Eff. March 1, 1998. Amended by orders of Supreme Court March 10, 2015 and Court of Criminal Appeals March 12, 2015, eff. April 1, 2015.

Rule 803. Exceptions to the Rule Against Hearsay—Regardless of Whether the Declarant Is Available as a Witness

The following are not excluded by the rule against hearsay, regardless of whether the declarant is available as a witness:

(1) ***Present Sense Impression.*** A statement describing or explaining an event or condition, made while or immediately after the declarant perceived it.

(2) ***Excited Utterance.*** A statement relating to a startling event or condition, made while the declarant was under the stress of excitement that it caused.

(3) ***Then-Existing Mental, Emotional, or Physical Condition.*** A statement of the declarant's then-existing state of mind (such as motive, intent, or plan) or emotional, sensory, or physical condition (such as mental feeling, pain, or bodily health), but not including a statement of memory or belief to prove the fact remembered or believed unless it relates to the validity or terms of the declarant's will.

(4) ***Statement Made for Medical Diagnosis or Treatment.*** A statement that:

(A) is made for—and is reasonably pertinent to—medical diagnosis or treatment; and

(B) describes medical history; past or present symptoms or sensations; their inception; or their general cause.

(5) ***Recorded Recollection.*** A record that:

(A) is on a matter the witness once knew about but now cannot recall well enough to testify fully and accurately;

(B) was made or adopted by the witness when the matter was fresh in the witness's memory; and

(C) accurately reflects the witness's knowledge, unless the circumstances of the record's preparation cast doubt on its trustworthiness.

If admitted, the record may be read into evidence but may be received as an exhibit only if offered by an adverse party.

(6) ***Records of a Regularly Conducted Activity.*** A record of an act, event, condition, opinion, or diagnosis if:

(A) the record was made at or near the time by—or from information transmitted by—someone with knowledge;

(B) the record was kept in the course of a regularly conducted business activity;

(C) making the record was a regular practice of that activity;

(D) all these conditions are shown by the testimony of the custodian or another qualified witness, or by an affidavit or unsworn declaration that complies with Rule 902(10); and

(E) the opponent fails to demonstrate that the source of information or the method or circumstances of preparation indicate a lack of trustworthiness. "Business" as used in this paragraph includes every kind of regular organized activity whether conducted for profit or not.

(7) ***Absence of a Record of a Regularly Conducted Activity.*** Evidence that a matter is not included in a record described in paragraph (6) if:

(A) the evidence is admitted to prove that the matter did not occur or exist;

(B) a record was regularly kept for a matter of that kind; and

(C) the opponent fails to show that the possible source of the information or other circumstances indicate a lack of trustworthiness.

(8) ***Public Records.*** A record or statement of a public office if:

(A) it sets out:

(i) the office's activities;

(ii) a matter observed while under a legal duty to report, but not including, in a criminal case, a matter observed by law-enforcement personnel; or

(iii) in a civil case or against the government in a criminal case, factual findings from a legally authorized investigation; and

(B) the opponent fails to demonstrate that the source of information or other circumstances indicate a lack of trustworthiness.

(9) ***Public Records of Vital Statistics.*** A record of a birth, death, or marriage, if reported to a public office in accordance with a legal duty.

(10) ***Absence of a Public Record.*** Testimony—or a certification under Rule 902—that a diligent search failed to disclose a public record or statement if the testimony or certification is admitted to prove that:

(A) the record or statement does not exist; or

(B) a matter did not occur or exist, if a public office regularly kept a record or statement for a matter of that kind.

(11) ***Records of Religious Organizations Concerning Personal or Family History.*** A statement of birth, legitimacy, ancestry, marriage, divorce, death, relationship by blood or marriage, or similar facts of personal or family history, contained in a regularly kept record of a religious organization.

(12) ***Certificates of Marriage, Baptism, and Similar Ceremonies.*** A statement of fact contained in a certificate:

(A) made by a person who is authorized by a religious organization or by law to perform the act certified;

(B) attesting that the person performed a marriage or similar ceremony or administered a sacrament; and

(C) purporting to have been issued at the time of the act or within a reasonable time after it.

(13) ***Family Records.*** A statement of fact about personal or family history contained in a family record, such as a Bible, genealogy, chart, engraving on a ring, inscription on a portrait, or engraving on an urn or burial marker.

(14) ***Records of Documents That Affect an Interest in Property.*** The record of a document that purports to establish or affect an interest in property if:

(A) the record is admitted to prove the content of the original recorded document, along with its signing and its delivery by each person who purports to have signed it;

(B) the record is kept in a public office; and

(C) a statute authorizes recording documents of that kind in that office.

(15) ***Statements in Documents That Affect an Interest in Property.*** A statement contained in a document that purports to establish or affect an interest in property if the matter stated was relevant to the document's purpose—unless later dealings with the property are inconsistent with the truth of the statement or the purport of the document.

(16) ***Statements in Ancient Documents.*** A statement in a document that is at least 20 years old and whose authenticity is established.

(17) ***Market Reports and Similar Commercial Publications.*** Market quotations, lists, directories, or other compilations that are generally relied on by the public or by persons in particular occupations.

(18) ***Statements in Learned Treatises, Periodicals, or Pamphlets.*** A statement contained in a treatise, periodical, or pamphlet if:

(A) the statement is called to the attention of an expert witness on cross-examination or relied on by the expert on direct examination; and

(B) the publication is established as a reliable authority by the expert's admission or testimony, by another expert's testimony, or by judicial notice.

If admitted, the statement may be read into evidence but not received as an exhibit.

(19) ***Reputation Concerning Personal or Family History.*** A reputation among a person's family by blood, adoption, or marriage—or among a person's associates or in the community—concerning the person's birth, adoption, legitimacy, ancestry, marriage, divorce, death, relationship by blood, adoption, or marriage, or similar facts of personal or family history.

(20) ***Reputation Concerning Boundaries or General History.*** A reputation in a community—arising before the controversy—concerning boundaries of land in the community or customs that affect the land, or concerning general historical events important to that community, state, or nation.

(21) ***Reputation Concerning Character.*** A reputation among a person's associates or in the community concerning the person's character.

(22) ***Judgment of a Previous Conviction.*** Evidence of a final judgment of conviction if:

(A) it is offered in a civil case and:

(i) the judgment was entered after a trial or guilty plea, but not a nolo contendere plea;

(ii) the conviction was for a felony;

(iii) the evidence is admitted to prove any fact essential to the judgment; and

(iv) an appeal of the conviction is not pending; or

(B) it is offered in a criminal case and:

(i) the judgment was entered after a trial or a guilty or nolo contendere plea;

(ii) the conviction was for a criminal offense;

(iii) the evidence is admitted to prove any fact essential to the judgment;

(iv) when offered by the prosecutor for a purpose other than impeachment, the judgment was against the defendant; and

(v) an appeal of the conviction is not pending.

(23) ***Judgments Involving Personal, Family, or General History or a Boundary.*** A judgment that is admitted to prove a matter of personal, family, or general history, or boundaries, if the matter:

(A) was essential to the judgment; and

(B) could be proved by evidence of reputation.

(24) ***Statement Against Interest.*** A statement that:

(A) a reasonable person in the declarant's position would have made only if the person believed it to be true because, when made, it was so contrary to the declarant's proprietary or pecuniary interest or had so great a tendency to invalidate the declarant's claim against someone else or to expose the declarant to civil or criminal liability or to make the declarant an object of hatred, ridicule, or disgrace; and

(B) is supported by corroborating circumstances that clearly indicate its trustworthiness, if it is offered in a criminal case as one that tends to expose the declarant to criminal liability.

Eff. March 1, 1998. Amended by orders of Supreme Court March 10, 2015 and Court of Criminal Appeals March 12, 2015, eff. April 1, 2015.

Rule 804. Exceptions to the Rule Against Hearsay—When the Declarant Is Unavailable as a Witness

(a) Criteria for Being Unavailable. A declarant is considered to be unavailable as a witness if the declarant:

(1) is exempted from testifying about the subject matter of the declarant's statement because the court rules that a privilege applies;

(2) refuses to testify about the subject matter despite a court order to do so;

(3) testifies to not remembering the subject matter;

(4) cannot be present or testify at the trial or hearing because of death or a then-existing infirmity, physical illness, or mental illness; or

(5) is absent from the trial or hearing and the statement's proponent has not been able, by process or other reasonable means, to procure the declarant's attendance or testimony.

But this subdivision (a) does not apply if the statement's proponent procured or wrongfully caused the declarant's unavailability as a witness in order to prevent the declarant from attending or testifying.

(b) The Exceptions. The following are not excluded by the rule against hearsay if the declarant is unavailable as a witness:

(1) ***Former Testimony.*** Testimony that:

(A) when offered in a civil case:

(i) was given as a witness at a trial or hearing of the current or a different proceeding or in a deposition in a different proceeding; and

(ii) is now offered against a party and the party—or a person with similar interest—had an opportunity and similar motive to develop the testimony by direct, cross-, or redirect examination.

(B) when offered in a criminal case:

(i) was given as a witness at a trial or hearing of the current or a different proceeding; and

(ii) is now offered against a party who had an opportunity and similar motive to develop it by direct, cross-, or redirect examination; or

(iii) was taken in a deposition under—and is now offered in accordance with—chapter 39 of the Code of Criminal Procedure.

(2) ***Statement Under the Belief of Imminent Death.*** A statement that the declarant, while believing the declarant's death to be imminent, made about its cause or circumstances.

(3) ***Statement of Personal or Family History.*** A statement about:

(A) the declarant's own birth, adoption, legitimacy, ancestry, marriage, divorce, relationship by blood, adoption or marriage, or similar facts of personal or family history, even though the declarant had no way of acquiring personal knowledge about that fact; or

(B) another person concerning any of these facts, as well as death, if the declarant was related to the person by blood, adoption, or marriage or was so intimately associated with the person's family that the declarant's information is likely to be accurate.

Eff. March 1, 1998. Amended by orders of Supreme Court March 10, 2015 and Court of Criminal Appeals March 12, 2015, eff. April 1, 2015.

Rule 805. Hearsay Within Hearsay

Hearsay within hearsay is not excluded by the rule against hearsay if each part of the combined statements conforms with an exception to the rule.

Eff. March 1, 1998. Amended by orders of Supreme Court March 10, 2015 and Court of Criminal Appeals March 12, 2015, eff. April 1, 2015.

Rule 806. Attacking and Supporting the Declarant's Credibility

When a hearsay statement—or a statement described in Rule 801(e)(2)(C), (D), or (E), or, in a civil case, a statement described in Rule 801(e)(3)—has been admitted in evidence, the declarant's credibility may be attacked, and then supported, by any evidence that would be admissible for those purposes if the declarant had testified as a witness. The court may admit evidence of the declarant's statement or conduct, offered to impeach the declarant, regardless of when it occurred or whether the declarant had an opportunity to explain or deny it. If the party against whom the statement was admitted calls the declarant as a witness, the party may examine the declarant on the statement as if on cross-examination.

Eff. March 1, 1998. Amended by orders of Supreme Court March 10, 2015 and Court of Criminal Appeals March 12, 2015, eff. April 1, 2015.

ARTICLE IX. AUTHENTICATION AND IDENTIFICATION

Rule 901. Authenticating or Identifying Evidence

(a) In General. To satisfy the requirement of authenticating or identifying an item of evidence, the proponent must produce evidence sufficient to support a finding that the item is what the proponent claims it is.

(b) Examples. The following are examples only—not a complete list—of evidence that satisfies the requirement:

(1) ***Testimony of a Witness with Knowledge.*** Testimony that an item is what it is claimed to be.

(2) ***Nonexpert Opinion About Handwriting.*** A nonexpert's opinion that handwriting is genuine, based on a familiarity with it that was not acquired for the current litigation.

(3) ***Comparison by an Expert Witness or the Trier of Fact.*** A comparison by an expert witness or the trier of fact with a specimen that the court has found is genuine.

(4) ***Distinctive Characteristics and the Like.*** The appearance, contents, substance, internal patterns, or other distinctive characteristics of the item, taken together with all the circumstances.

(5) ***Opinion About a Voice.*** An opinion identifying a person's voice—whether heard firsthand or through mechanical or electronic transmission or recording—based on hearing the voice at any time under circumstances that connect it with the alleged speaker.

(6) ***Evidence About a Telephone Conversation.*** For a telephone conversation, evidence that a call was made to the number assigned at the time to:

(A) a particular person, if circumstances, including self-identification, show that the person answering was the one called; or

(B) a particular business, if the call was made to a business and the call related to business reasonably transacted over the telephone.

(7) ***Evidence About Public Records.*** Evidence that:

(A) a document was recorded or filed in a public office as authorized by law; or

(B) a purported public record or statement is from the office where items of this kind are kept.

(8) ***Evidence About Ancient Documents or Data Compilations.*** For a document or data compilation, evidence that it:

(A) is in a condition that creates no suspicion about its authenticity;

(B) was in a place where, if authentic, it would likely be; and

(C) is at least 20 years old when offered.

(9) ***Evidence About a Process or System.*** Evidence describing a process or system and showing that it produces an accurate result.

(10) ***Methods Provided by a Statute or Rule.*** Any method of authentication or identification allowed by a statute or other rule prescribed under statutory authority.

Eff. March 1, 1998. Amended by orders of Supreme Court March 10, 2015 and Court of Criminal Appeals March 12, 2015, eff. April 1, 2015.

Rule 902. Evidence That Is Self–Authenticating

The following items of evidence are self-authenticating; they require no extrinsic evidence of authenticity in order to be admitted:

(1) ***Domestic Public Documents That Are Sealed and Signed.*** A document that bears:

(A) a seal purporting to be that of the United States; any state, district, commonwealth, territory, or insular possession of the United States; the former Panama Canal Zone; the Trust Territory of the Pacific Islands; a political subdivision of any of these entities; or a department, agency, or officer of any entity named above; and

(B) a signature purporting to be an execution or attestation.

(2) ***Domestic Public Documents That Are Not Sealed But Are Signed and Certified.*** A document that bears no seal if:

(A) it bears the signature of an officer or employee of an entity named in Rule 902(1)(A); and

(B) another public officer who has a seal and official duties within that same entity certifies under seal—or its equivalent—that the signer has the official capacity and that the signature is genuine.

(3) ***Foreign Public Documents.*** A document that purports to be signed or attested by a person who is authorized by a foreign country's law to do so.

(A) ***In General.*** The document must be accompanied by a final certification that certifies the genuineness of the signature and official position of the signer or attester—or of any foreign official whose certificate of genuineness relates to the signature or attestation or is in a chain of certificates of genuineness relating to the signature or attestation. The certification may be made by a secretary of a United States embassy or legation; by a consul general, vice consul, or consular agent of the United States; or by a diplomatic or consular official of the foreign country assigned or accredited to the United States.

(B) ***If Parties Have Reasonable Opportunity to Investigate.*** If all parties have been given a reasonable opportunity to investigate the document's authenticity and accuracy, the court may, for good cause, either:

(i) order that it be treated as presumptively authentic without final certification; or

(ii) allow it to be evidenced by an attested summary with or without final certification.

(C) ***If a Treaty Abolishes or Displaces the Final Certification Requirement.*** If the United States and the foreign country in which the official record is located are parties to a treaty or convention that abolishes or displaces the final certification requirement, the record and attestation must be certified under the terms of the treaty or convention.

(4) ***Certified Copies of Public Records.*** A copy of an official record—or a copy of a document that was recorded or filed in a public office as authorized by law—if the copy is certified as correct by:

(A) the custodian or another person authorized to make the certification; or

(B) a certificate that complies with Rule 902(1), (2), or (3), a statute, or a rule prescribed under statutory authority.

(5) ***Official Publications.*** A book, pamphlet, or other publication purporting to be issued by a public authority.

(6) ***Newspapers and Periodicals.*** Printed material purporting to be a newspaper or periodical.

(7) ***Trade Inscriptions and the Like.*** An inscription, sign, tag, or label purporting to have been affixed in the course of business and indicating origin, ownership, or control.

(8) ***Acknowledged Documents.*** A document accompanied by a certificate of acknowledgment that is

lawfully executed by a notary public or another officer who is authorized to take acknowledgments.

(9) ***Commercial Paper and Related Documents.*** Commercial paper, a signature on it, and related documents, to the extent allowed by general commercial law.

(10) ***Business Records Accompanied by Affidavit.*** The original or a copy of a record that meets the requirements of Rule 803(6) or (7), if the record is accompanied by an affidavit that complies with subparagraph (B) of this rule and any other requirements of law, and the record and affidavit are served in accordance with subparagraph (A). For good cause shown, the court may order that a business record be treated as presumptively authentic even if the proponent fails to comply with subparagraph (A).

(A) ***Service Requirement.*** The proponent of a record must serve the record and the accompanying affidavit on each other party to the case at least 14 days before trial. The record and affidavit may be served by any method permitted by Rule of Civil Procedure 21a.

(B) ***Form of Affidavit.*** An affidavit is sufficient if it includes the following language, but this form is not exclusive. The proponent may use an unsworn declaration made under penalty of perjury in place of an affidavit.

1. I am the custodian of records [*or* I am an employee or owner] of __________ and am familiar with the manner in which its records are created and maintained by virtue of my duties and responsibilities.

2. Attached are ___ pages of records. These are the original records or exact duplicates of the original records.

3. The records were made at or near the time of each act, event, condition, opinion, or diagnosis set forth. [*or* It is the regular practice of __________ to make this type of record at or near the time of each act, event, condition, opinion, or diagnosis set forth in the record.]

4. The records were made by, or from information transmitted by, persons with knowledge of the matters set forth. [*or* It is the regular practice of __________ for this type of record to be made by, or from information transmitted by, persons with knowledge of the matters set forth in them.]

5. The records were kept in the course of regularly conducted business activity. [*or* It is the regular practice of __________ to keep this type of record in the course of regularly conducted business activity.]

6. It is the regular practice of the business activity to make the records.

(11) ***Presumptions Under a Statute or Rule.*** A signature, document, or anything else that a statute or rule prescribed under statutory authority declares to be presumptively or prima facie genuine or authentic.

Eff. March 1, 1998. Amended by orders of Feb. 12, 2013, and March 26, 2013, eff. March 1, 2013. Amended by orders of Supreme Court and Court of Criminal Appeals April 14, 2014, and August 19, 2014, eff. Sept. 1, 2014. Amended by order of orders of Supreme Court March 10, 2015 and Court of Criminal Appeals March 12, 2015, eff. April 1, 2015.

Notes and Comments

Comment to 2013 change: Rule 902(10)(c) is added to provide a form affidavit for proof of medical expenses. The affidavit is intended to comport with Section 41.0105 of the Civil Practice and Remedies Code, which allows evidence of only those medical expenses that have been paid or will be paid, after any required credits or adjustments. *See Haygood v. Escabedo,* 356 S.W.3d 390 (Tex. 2011). The records attached to the affidavit must also meet the admissibility standard of *Haygood,* 356 S.W.3d at 399–400 ("[O]nly evidence of recoverable medical expenses is admissible at trial.").

Comment to 2014 change: At the direction of the Legislature, the requirement that records be filed with the court before trial has been removed. *See* Act of May 17, 2013, 83rd Leg., R.S., ch. 560, § 3, 2013 Tex. Gen. Laws 1509, 1510 (SB 679). The word "affidavit" in this rule includes an unsworn declaration made under penalty of perjury. Tex. Civ. Prac. & Rem. Code § 132.001. The reference to "any other requirements of law" incorporates the requirements of Sections 18.001 and 18.002 of the Civil Practice and Remedies Code for affidavits offered as prima facie proof of the cost or necessity of services or medical expenses. The form medical expenses affidavit that was added to this rule in 2013 has been removed as unnecessary. It can now be found in Section 18.002(b–1) of the Civil Practice and Remedies Code.

Rule 903. Subscribing Witness's Testimony

A subscribing witness's testimony is necessary to authenticate a writing only if required by the law of the jurisdiction that governs its validity.

Eff. March 1, 1998. Amended by orders of Supreme Court March 10, 2015 and Court of Criminal Appeals March 12, 2015, eff. April 1, 2015.

ARTICLE X. CONTENTS OF WRITINGS, RECORDINGS, AND PHOTOGRAPHS

Rule 1001. Definitions That Apply to This Article

In this article:

(a) A "writing" consists of letters, words, numbers, or their equivalent set down in any form.

(b) A "recording" consists of letters, words, numbers, or their equivalent recorded in any manner.

(c) A "photograph" means a photographic image or its equivalent stored in any form.

(d) An "original" of a writing or recording means the writing or recording itself or any counterpart intended to have the same effect by the person who executed or issued it. For electronically stored information, "original" means any printout—or other output readable by sight—if it accurately reflects the information. An "original" of a photograph includes the negative or a print from it.

(e) A "duplicate" means a counterpart produced by a mechanical, photographic, chemical, electronic, or other equivalent process or technique that accurately reproduces the original.

Eff. March 1, 1998. Amended by orders of Supreme Court March 10, 2015 and Court of Criminal Appeals March 12, 2015, eff. April 1, 2015.

Rule 1002. Requirement of the Original

An original writing, recording, or photograph is required in order to prove its content unless these rules or other law provides otherwise.

Eff. March 1, 1998. Amended by orders of Supreme Court March 10, 2015 and Court of Criminal Appeals March 12, 2015, eff. April 1, 2015.

Rule 1003. Admissibility of Duplicates

A duplicate is admissible to the same extent as the original unless a question is raised about the original's authenticity or the circumstances make it unfair to admit the duplicate.

Eff. March 1, 1998. Amended by orders of Supreme Court March 10, 2015 and Court of Criminal Appeals March 12, 2015, eff. April 1, 2015.

Rule 1004. Admissibility of Other Evidence of Content

An original is not required and other evidence of the content of a writing, recording, or photograph is admissible if:

(a) all the originals are lost or destroyed, unless the proponent lost or destroyed them in bad faith;

(b) an original cannot be obtained by any available judicial process;

(c) an original is not located in Texas;

(d) the party against whom the original would be offered had control of the original; was at that time put on notice, by pleadings or otherwise, that the original would be a subject of proof at the trial or hearing; and fails to produce it at the trial or hearing; or

(e) the writing, recording, or photograph is not closely related to a controlling issue.

Eff. March 1, 1998. Amended by orders of Supreme Court March 10, 2015 and Court of Criminal Appeals March 12, 2015, eff. April 1, 2015.

Rule 1005. Copies of Public Records to Prove Content

The proponent may use a copy to prove the content of an official record—or of a document that was recorded or filed in a public office as authorized by law—if these conditions are met: the record or document is otherwise admissible; and the copy is certified as correct in accordance with Rule 902(4) or is testified to be correct by a witness who has compared it with the original. If no such copy can be obtained by reasonable diligence, then the proponent may use other evidence to prove the content.

Eff. March 1, 1998. Amended by orders of Supreme Court March 10, 2015 and Court of Criminal Appeals March 12, 2015, eff. April 1, 2015.

Rule 1006. Summaries to Prove Content

The proponent may use a summary, chart, or calculation to prove the content of voluminous writings, recordings, or photographs that cannot be conveniently examined in court. The proponent must make the originals or duplicates available for examination or copying, or both, by other parties at a reasonable time and place. And the court may order the proponent to produce them in court.

Eff. March 1, 1998. Amended by orders of Supreme Court March 10, 2015 and Court of Criminal Appeals March 12, 2015, eff. April 1, 2015.

Rule 1007. Testimony or Statement of a Party to Prove Content

The proponent may prove the content of a writing, recording, or photograph by the testimony, deposition, or written statement of the party against whom the evidence is offered. The proponent need not account for the original.

Eff. March 1, 1998. Amended by orders of Supreme Court March 10, 2015 and Court of Criminal Appeals March 12, 2015, eff. April 1, 2015.

Rule 1008. Functions of the Court and Jury

Ordinarily, the court determines whether the proponent has fulfilled the factual conditions for admitting other evidence of the content of a writing, recording, or photograph under Rule 1004 or 1005. But in a jury trial, the jury determines—in accordance with Rule 104(b)—any issue about whether:

(a) an asserted writing, recording, or photograph ever existed;

(b) another one produced at the trial or hearing is the original; or

(c) other evidence of content accurately reflects the content.

Eff. March 1, 1998. Amended by orders of Supreme Court March 10, 2015 and Court of Criminal Appeals March 12, 2015, eff. April 1, 2015.

Rule 1009. Translating a Foreign Language Document

(a) Submitting a Translation. A translation of a foreign language document is admissible if, at least 45 days before trial, the proponent serves on all parties:

(1) the translation and the underlying foreign language document; and

(2) a qualified translator's affidavit or unsworn declaration that sets forth the translator's qualifications and certifies that the translation is accurate.

(b) Objection. When objecting to a translation's accuracy, a party should specifically indicate its inaccuracies and offer an accurate translation. A party must serve the objection on all parties at least 15 days before trial.

(c) Effect of Failing to Object or Submit a Conflicting Translation. If the underlying foreign language document is otherwise admissible, the court must admit—and may not allow a party to attack the accuracy of—a translation submitted under subdivision (a) unless the party has:

(1) submitted a conflicting translation under subdivision (a); or

(2) objected to the translation under subdivision (b).

(d) Effect of Objecting or Submitting a Conflicting Translation. If conflicting translations are submitted under subdivision (a) or an objection is made under subdivision (b), the court must determine whether there is a genuine issue about the accuracy of a material part of the translation. If so, the trier of fact must resolve the issue.

(e) Qualified Translator May Testify. Except for subdivision (c), this rule does not preclude a party from offering the testimony of a qualified translator to translate a foreign language document.

(f) Time Limits. On a party's motion and for good cause, the court may alter this rule's time limits.

(g) Court–Appointed Translator. If necessary, the court may appoint a qualified translator. The reasonable value of the translator's services must be taxed as court costs.

Eff. March 1, 1998. Amended by orders of Supreme Court March 10, 2015 and Court of Criminal Appeals March 12, 2015, eff. April 1, 2015.

Notes and Comments

Comment to 1998 change: This is a new rule.

INDEX TO TEXAS RULES OF EVIDENCE

TEXAS RULES OF APPELLATE PROCEDURE

As Amended by the Supreme Court and Court of Criminal Appeals of Texas

Effective September 1, 1997

Including Amendments Received Through February 1, 2016

Research Note

See Vernon's Texas Rules Annotated, *Volume 8, for judicial constructions and other research aids*

SECTION ONE. GENERAL PROVISIONS

Rule 1. Scope of Rules; Local Rules of Courts of Appeals

Notes and Comments

Comment to 1997 change: Subdivision 1.1 is simplified without substantive change. Subdivision 1.2 is amended to make clear that any person is entitled to a copy of local rules. Paragraph 1.2(c), restricting dismissal of a case for noncompliance with a local rule, is added.

1.1. Scope

These rules govern procedure in appellate courts and before appellate judges and post-trial procedure in trial courts in criminal cases.

Eff. Sept. 1, 1997.

1.2. Local Rules

(a) *Promulgation.* A court of appeals may promulgate rules governing its practice that are not inconsistent with these rules. Local rules governing civil cases must first be approved by the Supreme Court. Local rules governing criminal cases must first be approved by the Court of Criminal Appeals.

(b) *Copies.* The clerk must provide a copy of the court's local rules to anyone who requests it.

(c) *Party's Noncompliance.* A court must not dismiss an appeal for noncompliance with a local rule without giving the noncomplying party notice and a reasonable opportunity to cure the noncompliance.

Eff. Sept. 1, 1997.

Rule 2. Suspension of Rules

Rule 2. Suspension of Rules

On a party's motion or on its own initiative an appellate court may—to expedite a decision or for other good cause—suspend a rule's operation in a particular case and order a different procedure; but a court must not construe this rule to suspend any provision in the Code of Criminal Procedure or to alter the time for perfecting an appeal in a civil case.

Eff. Sept. 1, 1997.

Notes and Comments

Comment to 1997 change: Former subdivision (a) regarding appellate court jurisdiction is deleted. The power to suspend rules is extended to civil cases. Other nonsubstantive changes are made.

Rule 3. Definitions; Uniform Terminology

Notes and Comments

Comment to 1997 change: The definition of *court below* and the reference to "suing out a writ of error to the court of appeals," are deleted as those terms are no longer used in these rules. Other changes are made.

3.1. Definitions

(a) *Appellant* means a party taking an appeal to an appellate court.

(b) *Appellate court* means the courts of appeals, the Court of Criminal Appeals, and the Supreme Court.

(c) *Appellee* means a party adverse to an appellant.

(d) *Applicant* means a person seeking relief by a habeas corpus in a criminal case.

(e) *Petitioner* means a party petitioning the Supreme Court or the Court of Criminal Appeals for review.

(f) *Relator* means a person seeking relief in an original proceeding in an appellate court other than by habeas corpus in a criminal case.

(g) *Reporter* or *court reporter* means the court reporter or court recorder.

(h) *Respondent* means:

(1) a party adverse to a petitioner in the Supreme Court or the Court of Criminal Appeals; or

(2) a party against whom relief is sought in an original proceeding in an appellate court.

Eff. Sept. 1, 1997.

3.2. Uniform Terminology in Criminal Cases

In documents filed in criminal appeals, the parties are the *State* and the *appellant.* But if the State has appealed under Article 44.01 of the Code of Criminal Procedure, the defendant is the *appellee.* Otherwise, papers should use real names for parties, and such labels as *appellee, petitioner, respondent,* and *movant* should be avoided unless necessary for clarity. In habeas corpus proceedings, the person for whose relief the writ is requested is the *applicant;* Code of Criminal Procedure article 11.13.

Eff. Sept. 1, 1997.

Rule 4. Time and Notice Provisions

Notes and Comments

Comment to 1997 change: This is former Rule 5. Paragraph 4.1(b) is added. Former paragraph (b)(1) is omitted because it is covered by other provisions of the rules. Former paragraphs (b)(2) and (b)(3) are omitted because they are duplicative of provisions in the Rules of Civil Procedure, which prescribes the applicable procedure. The phrase "modified, corrected or reformed in any respect" in paragraph 4.3(a) is changed to "modified in any respect," but no change in substance is intended. Former subdivision (e) regarding notice of judgment by the court of appeals is moved to Rule 12.6. Subdivision 4.5 is revised and now makes clear that the court must grant the motion for additional time if the court finds that the party did not receive the notice or acquire actual knowledge in time. Other changes are made throughout the rule.

4.1. Computing Time

(a) *In General.* The day of an act, event, or default after which a designated period begins to run is not included when computing a period prescribed or allowed by these rules, by court order, or by statute. The last day of the period is included, but if that day is a Saturday, Sunday, or legal holiday, the period extends to the end of the next day that is not a Saturday, Sunday, or legal holiday.

(b) *Clerk's Office Closed or Inaccessible.* If the act to be done is filing a document, and if the clerk's office where the document is to be filed is closed or inaccessible during regular hours on the last day for filing the document, the period for filing the document extends to the end of the next day when the clerk's office is open and accessible. The closing or inaccessibility of the clerk's office may be proved by a certificate of the clerk or counsel, by a party's affidavit, or by other satisfactory proof, and may be controverted in the same manner.

Eff. Sept. 1, 1997.

4.2. No Notice of Trial Court's Judgment in Civil Case

(a) *Additional Time to File Documents.*

(1) In general. If a party affected by a judgment or other appealable order has not—within 20 days after the judgment or order was signed—either received the notice required by Texas Rule of Civil Procedure 306a.3 or acquired actual knowledge of the signing, then a period that, under these rules, runs from the signing will begin for that party on the earlier of the date when the party receives notice or acquires actual knowledge of the signing. But in no event may the period begin more than 90 days after the judgment or order was signed.

(2) Exception for restricted appeal. Subparagraph (1) does not extend the time for perfecting a restricted appeal.

(b) *Procedure to Gain Additional Time.* The procedure to gain additional time is governed by Texas Rule of Civil Procedure 306a.5.

(c) *The Court's Order.* After hearing the motion, the trial court must sign a written order that finds the date when the party or the party's attorney first either received notice or acquired actual knowledge that the judgment or order was signed.

Eff. Sept. 1, 1997.

4.3. Periods Affected by Modified Judgment in Civil Case

(a) *During Plenary-Power Period.* If a judgment is modified in any respect while the trial court retains plenary power, a period that, under these rules, runs from the date when the judgment is signed will run from the date when the modified judgment is signed.

(b) *After Plenary Power Expires.* If the trial court corrects or reforms the judgment under Texas Rule of Civil Procedure 316 after expiration of the trial court's plenary power, all periods provided in these rules that run from the date the judgment is signed run from the date the corrected judgment is signed for complaints that would not apply to the original judgment.

Eff. Sept. 1, 1997.

4.4. Periods Affected When Process Served by Publication

If process was served by publication and if a motion for new trial was filed under Texas Rule of Civil Procedure 329 more than 30 days after the judgment was signed, a period that, under these rules, runs from the date when the judgment is signed will be computed as if the judgment were signed on the date when the motion for new trial was filed.

Eff. Sept. 1, 1997.

4.5. No Notice of Judgment or Order of Appellate Court; Effect on Time to File Certain Documents

(a) *Additional Time to File Documents.* A party may move for additional time to file a motion for rehearing or en banc reconsideration in the court of appeals, a petition for review, or a petition for discretionary review, if the party did not—until after the time expired for filing the document—either receive notice of the judgment or order from the clerk or acquire actual knowledge of the rendition of the judgment or order.

(b) *Procedure to Gain Additional Time.* The motion must state the earliest date when the party or the party's attorney received notice or acquired actual knowledge that the judgment or order had been rendered. The motion must be filed within 15 days of that date but in no event more than 90 days after the date of the judgment or order.

(c) *Where to File.*

(1) A motion for additional time to file a motion for rehearing or en banc reconsideration in the court of appeals must be filed in and ruled on by the court of appeals in which the case is pending.

(2) A motion for additional time to file a petition for review must be filed in and ruled on by the Supreme Court.

(3) A motion for additional time to file a petition for discretionary review must be filed in and ruled on by the Court of Criminal Appeals.

(d) *Order of the Court.* If the court finds that the motion for additional time was timely filed and the party did not—within the time for filing the motion for rehearing or en banc reconsideration, petition for review, or petition for discretionary review, as the case may be—receive the notice or have actual knowledge of the judgment or order, the court must grant the motion. The time for filing the document will begin to run on the date when the court grants the motion.

Eff. Sept. 1, 1997. Amended by Supreme Court Dec. 23, 2002, eff. Jan. 1, 2003; Aug. 20, 2008, eff. Sept. 1, 2008. Approved by Court of Criminal Appeals, Sept. 30, 2008, eff. Sept. 30, 2008.

Notes and Comments

Comment to 2008 change: Subdivision 4.5 is changed, consistent with other changes in the rules, to specifically address a motion for en banc reconsideration and treat it as a motion for rehearing.

Comment to 2002 change: Subdivision 4.5 is amended to clarify that a party may obtain additional time to file documents when the party fails to receive notice not only of an appellate court judgment, but of an appellate court order—such as one denying a motion for rehearing—that triggers the appeal period.

Rule 5. Fees in Civil Cases

A party who is not excused by statute or these rules from paying costs must pay—at the time an item is presented for filing—whatever fees are required by statute or Supreme Court order. The appellate court may enforce this rule by any order that is just.

Eff. Sept. 1, 1997.

Notes and Comments

Comment to 1997 change: This is former Rule 13. The rule is simplified. The fees an appellate court may charge in a civil case are now specified by Supreme Court order.

Rule 6. Representation by Counsel

Notes and Comments

Comment to 1997 change: Former Rules 7 and 57 are merged and substantially revised. Former Rule 8 regarding agreements of counsel is included here as subdivision 6.6 and the requirement that an agreement be filed and included in the record is deleted.

6.1. Lead Counsel

(a) *For Appellant.* Unless another attorney is designated, lead counsel for an appellant is the attorney whose signature first appears on the notice of appeal.

(b) *For a Party Other Than Appellant.* Unless another attorney is designated, lead counsel for a party other than an appellant is the attorney whose signature first appears on the first document filed in the appellate court on that party's behalf.

(c) *How to Designate.* The original or a new lead counsel may be designated by filing a notice stating that attorney's name, mailing address, telephone number, fax number, if any, email address, and State Bar of Texas identification number. If a new lead counsel is being designated, both the new attorney and either the party or the former lead counsel must sign the notice.

Eff. Sept. 1, 1997. Amended by Supreme Court Dec. 11, 2013, eff. Jan. 1, 2014. Approved by Court of Criminal Appeals Dec. 11, 2013, eff. Jan. 1, 2014.

6.2. Appearance of Other Attorneys

An attorney other than lead counsel may file a notice stating that the attorney represents a specified party to the proceeding and giving that attorney's name, mailing address, telephone number, fax number, if any, email address, and State Bar of Texas identification number. The clerk will note on the docket the attorney's appearance. When a brief or motion is filed, the clerk will note on the docket the name of each attorney, if not already noted, who appears on the document.

Eff. Sept. 1, 1997. Amended by Supreme Court Dec. 11, 2013, eff. Jan. 1, 2014. Approved by Court of Criminal Appeals Dec. 11, 2013, eff. Jan. 1, 2014.

6.3. To Whom Communications Sent

Any notice, copies of documents filed in an appellate court, or other communications must be sent to:

(a) each party's lead counsel on appeal;

(b) a party's lead counsel in the trial court if:

(1) that party was represented by counsel in the trial court;

(2) lead counsel on appeal has not yet been designated for that party; and

(3) lead counsel in the trial court has not filed a nonrepresentation notice or been allowed to withdraw;

(c) a party if the party is not represented by counsel.

Eff. Sept. 1, 1997.

6.4. Nonrepresentation Notice

(a) *In General.* If, in accordance with paragraph 6.3(b), the lead counsel in the trial court is being sent notices, copies of documents, or other communications, that attorney may file a nonrepresentation notice in the appellate court. The notice must:

(1) state that the attorney is not representing the party on appeal;

(2) state that the court and other counsel should communicate directly with the party in the future;

(3) give the party's name and last known address and telephone number; and

(4) be signed by the party.

(b) *Appointed Counsel.* In a criminal case, an attorney appointed by the trial court to represent an indigent party cannot file a nonrepresentation notice.

Eff. Sept. 1, 1997.

6.5. Withdrawal

An appellate court may, on appropriate terms and conditions, permit an attorney to withdraw from representing a party in the appellate court.

(a) *Contents of Motion.* A motion for leave to withdraw must contain the following:

(1) a list of current deadlines and settings in the case;

(2) the party's name and last known address and telephone number;

(3) a statement that a copy of the motion was delivered to the party; and

(4) a statement that the party was notified in writing of the right to object to the motion.

(b) *Delivery to Party.* The motion must be delivered to the party in person or mailed—both by certified and by first-class mail—to the party at the party's last known address.

(c) *If Motion Granted.* If the court grants the motion, the withdrawing attorney must immediately notify the party, in writing, of any deadlines or settings that the attorney knows about at the time of withdrawal but that were not previously disclosed to the party. The withdrawing attorney must file a copy of that notice with the court clerk.

(d) *Exception for Substitution of Counsel.* If an attorney substitutes for a withdrawing attorney, the motion to withdraw need not comply with (a) but must state only the substitute attorney's name, mailing address, telephone number, fax number, if any, and State Bar of Texas identification number. The withdrawing attorney must comply with (b) but not (c).

Eff. Sept. 1, 1997.

6.6. Agreements of Parties or Counsel

To be enforceable, an agreement of parties or their counsel concerning an appellate court proceeding must be in writing and signed by the parties or their counsel. Such an agreement is subject to any appellate court order necessary to ensure that the case is properly presented.

Eff. Sept. 1, 1997.

Rule 7. Substituting Parties

Notes and Comments

Comment to 1997 change: This is former Rule 9. Former subdivision (a) regarding death of a party in a civil case is now subparagraph 7.1(a)(1). Former subdivision (b) regarding death of a party in a criminal case is now subparagraph 7.1(a)(2). Former subdivision (c) regarding separation of office by public officers is now subdivision 7.2. Former paragraph (c)(3) regarding a successor's liability for costs is omitted as unnecessary. Former subdivision (d) regarding substitution for other causes is now paragraph 7.1(b). Subdivision 7.2 is revised to make it applicable to all cases in which a public officer is a party, and to make substitution automatic if appropriate.

7.1. Parties Who Are Not Public Officers

(a) *Death of a Party.*

(1) Civil Cases. If a party to a civil case dies after the trial court renders judgment but before the case has been finally disposed of on appeal, the appeal may be perfected, and the appellate court will proceed to adjudicate the appeal as if all parties were alive. The appellate court's judgment will have the same force and effect as if rendered when all parties were living. The decedent party's name may be used on all papers.

(2) Criminal Cases. If the appellant in a criminal case dies after an appeal is perfected but before the appellate court issues the mandate, the appeal will be permanently abated.

(b) *Substitution for Other Reasons.* If substitution of a party in the appellate court is necessary for a reason other than death, the appellate court may order substitution on any party's motion at any time.

Eff. Sept. 1, 1997.

7.2. Public Officers

(a) *Automatic Substitution of Officer.* When a public officer is a party in an official capacity to an appeal or original proceeding, and if that person ceases to hold office before the appeal or original proceeding is finally disposed of, the public officer's successor is automatically substituted as a party if appropriate. Proceedings following substitution are to be in the name of the substituted party, but any misnomer that does not affect the substantial rights of the parties may be disregarded. Substitution may be ordered at any time, but failure to order substitution of the successor does not affect the substitution.

(b) *Abatement.* If the case is an original proceeding under Rule 52, the court must abate the proceeding to allow the successor to reconsider the original party's decision. In all other cases, the suit will not abate, and the successor will be bound by the appellate court's judgment or order as if the successor were the original party.

Eff. Sept. 1, 1997.

Rule 8. Bankruptcy in Civil Cases

Notes and Comments

Comment to 1997 change: This is a new rule.

8.1 Notice of Bankruptcy

Any party may file a notice that a party is in bankruptcy. The notice must contain:

(a) the bankrupt party's name;

(b) the court in which the bankruptcy proceeding is pending;

(c) the bankruptcy proceeding's style and case number; and

(d) the date when the bankruptcy petition was filed.

Eff. Sept. 1, 1997. Amended by Supreme Court March 10, 2008, and Aug. 20, 2008, eff. Sept. 1, 2008. Approved by Court of Criminal Appeals Sept. 30, 2008, eff. Sept. 30, 2008.

Notes and Comments

Comment to 2008 change: The requirement that the bankruptcy notice contain certain pages of the bankruptcy petition is eliminated, given that electronic filing is now prevalent in bankruptcy courts and bankruptcy petitions are available through the federal PACER system.

8.2. Effect of Bankruptcy

A bankruptcy suspends the appeal and all periods in these rules from the date when the bankruptcy petition is filed until the appellate court reinstates or severs the appeal in accordance with federal law. A period that began to run and had not expired at the time the proceeding was suspended begins anew when the proceeding is reinstated or severed under 8.3. A document filed by a party while the proceeding is suspended will be deemed filed on the same day, but after, the court reinstates or severs the appeal and will not be considered ineffective because it was filed while the proceeding was suspended.

Eff. Sept. 1, 1997.

8.3. Motion to Reinstate or Sever Appeal Suspended by Bankruptcy

(a) *Motion to Reinstate.* If a case has been suspended by a bankruptcy filing, a party may move that the appellate court reinstate the appeal if permitted by federal law or the bankruptcy court. If the bankruptcy court has lifted or terminated the stay, a certified copy of the order must be attached to the motion.

(b) *Motion to Sever.* A party may move to sever the appeal with respect to the bankrupt party and to reinstate the appeal with respect to the other parties. The motion must show that the case is severable and must comply with applicable federal law regarding severance of a bankrupt party. The court may proceed under this paragraph on its own initiative.

Eff. Sept. 1, 1997.

Rule 9. Documents Generally

Notes and Comments

Comment to 1997 change: This is former Rule 4. Subdivision 9.4, prescribing the form of documents filed in the appellate courts, is changed and the form to be used is stated in significantly more detail. Former subdivisions (f) and (g), regarding service of documents, are merged into subdivision 9.5. Former Rule 6 is included as subdivision 9.6, but no substantive change is made. Other changes are made throughout the rule. Electronic filing is authorized by §§ 51.801–.807 of the Government Code.

9.1. Signing

(a) *Represented Parties.* If a party is represented by counsel, a document filed on that party's behalf must be signed by at least one of the party's attorneys. For each attorney whose name appears on a document as representing that party, the document must contain that attorney's State Bar of Texas identification number, mailing address, telephone number, and fax number, if any, and email address.

(b) *Unrepresented Parties.* A party not represented by counsel must sign any document that the party files and give the party's mailing address, telephone number, fax number, if any, and email address.

(c) *Electronic Signatures.* A document that is electronically served, filed, or issued by a court or clerk is considered signed if the document includes:

(1) a "/s/" and name typed in the space where the signature would otherwise appear, unless the document is notarized or sworn; or

(2) an electronic image or scanned image of the signature.

Eff. Sept. 1, 1997. Amended by Supreme Court Dec. 11, 2013, eff. Jan. 1, 2014. Approved by Court of Criminal Appeals Dec. 11, 2013, eff. Jan. 1, 2014.

Notes and Comments

Comment to 2013 Change: Rule 9 is revised to incorporate rules for electronic filing, in accordance with the Supreme Court's order—Misc. Docket Nos. 12-9208 and 13-9164, amended by Misc. Docket No. 13-9092—mandating electronic filing in civil cases in appellate courts, effective January 1, 2014. In addition, Rule 9.9 is added to provide privacy protection for all documents, both paper and electronic, filed in civil cases in appellate courts.

9.2. Filing

(a) *With Whom.* A document is filed in an appellate court by delivering it to:

(1) the clerk of the court in which the document is to be filed; or

(2) a justice or judge of that court who is willing to accept delivery. A justice or judge who accepts delivery must note on the document the date and time of delivery, which will be considered the time of filing, and must promptly send it to the clerk.

(b) *Filing by Mail.*

(1) Timely Filing. A document received within ten days after the filing deadline is considered timely filed if:

(A) it was sent to the proper clerk by United States Postal Service or a commercial delivery service;

(B) it was placed in an envelope or wrapper properly addressed and stamped; and

(C) it was deposited in the mail or delivered to a commercial delivery service on or before the last day for filing.

(2) Proof of Mailing. Though it may consider other proof, the appellate court will accept the following as conclusive proof of the date of mailing:

(A) a legible postmark affixed by the United States Postal Service;

(B) a receipt for registered or certified mail if the receipt is endorsed by the United States Postal Service;

(C) a certificate of mailing by the United States Postal Service; or

(D) a receipt endorsed by the commercial delivery service.

(c) *Electronic Filing.*

(1) Requirement. Attorneys in civil cases must electronically file documents. Attorneys in criminal cases must electronically file documents except for good cause shown in a motion filed in the appellate court. Unrepresented parties in civil and criminal cases may electronically file documents, but it is not required.

(2) Mechanism. Electronic filing must be done through the electronic filing manager established by the Office of Court Administration and an electronic filing service provider certified by the Office of Court Administration.

(3) Exceptions. Documents filed under seal, subject to a pending motion to seal, or to which access is otherwise restricted by law or court order must not be electronically filed. For good cause, an appellate court may permit a party to file other documents in paper form in a particular case.

(4) Timely Filing. Unless a document must be filed by a certain time of day, a document is considered timely filed if it is electronically filed at any time before midnight (in the court's time zone) on the filing deadline. An electronically filed document is deemed filed when transmitted to the filing party's electronic filing service provider, except:

(A) if a document is transmitted on a Saturday, Sunday, or legal holiday, it is deemed filed on the next day that is not a Saturday, Sunday, or legal holiday; and

(B) if a document requires a motion and an order allowing its filing, the document is deemed filed on the date the motion is granted.

(5) Technical Failure. If a document is untimely due to a technical failure or a system outage, the filing party may seek appropriate relief from the court.

(6) Confirmation of Filing. The electronic filing manager will send a filing confirmation notice to the filing party.

(7) Electronic Notices From the Court. The clerk may send notices, orders, or other communications about the case to the party electronically. A court seal may be electronic.

Eff. Sept. 1, 1997. Amended by Supreme Court Feb. 28, 2011, eff. June 30, 2011. Approved by Court of Criminal Appeals Feb. 28, 2011, eff. June 30, 2011. Amended by Supreme Court June 27, 2011, eff. June 30, 2011. Amended by Supreme Court Dec. 11, 2013, eff. Jan. 1, 2014. Approved by Court of Criminal Appeals Dec. 11, 2013, eff. Jan. 1, 2014.

Notes and Comments

Comment to 2013 Change: Rule 9 is revised to incorporate rules for electronic filing, in accordance with the Supreme Court's order—Misc. Docket No. 12–9208, amended by Misc. Docket Nos. 13–9092 and 13–9164—mandating electronic filing in civil cases in appellate courts, effective January 1, 2014. In addition, Rule 9.9 is added to provide privacy protection for all documents, both paper and electronic, filed in civil cases in appellate courts.

9.3. Number of Copies

(a) *Courts of Appeals.*

(1) Document Filed in Paper Form. If a document is not electronically filed, a party must file the original and one unbound copy of the document unless otherwise required by local rule. The unbound copy of an appendix must contain a separate page before each document and must not include tabs that extend beyond the edge of the page.

(2) Electronically Filed Document. Unless required by local rule, a party need not file a paper copy of an electronically filed document.

(b) *Supreme Court and Court of Criminal Appeals.*

(1) Document Filed in Paper Form. If a document is not electronically filed, a party must file the original and 11 copies of any document addressed to either the Supreme Court or the Court of Criminal Appeals, except that in the Supreme Court only an original and one copy must be filed of any motion, response to the motion, and reply in support of the motion, and in the Court of Criminal Appeals, only the original must be filed of a motion for extension of time or a response to the motion, or a pleading under Code of Criminal Procedure article 11.07.

(2) Electronically Filed Document. Paper copies of each document that is electronically filed with the Supreme Court or the Court of Criminal Appeals must be mailed or hand-delivered to the Supreme Court or the Court of Criminal Appeals, as appropriate, within three business days after the document is electronically filed. The number of paper copies required shall be determined, respectively, by order of the Supreme Court or the Court of Criminal Appeals.

(c) *Exception for Record.* Only the original record need be filed in any proceeding.

Eff. Sept. 1, 1997. Amended by Supreme Court March 10, 2008, and Aug. 20, 2008, eff. Sept. 1, 2008. Approved by Court of Criminal Appeals Sept. 30, 2008, eff. Sept. 30, 2008. Amended by Supreme Court Feb. 28, 2011, eff. June 30, 2011. Approved by Court of Criminal Appeals Feb. 28, 2011, eff. June 30, 2011. Amended by Supreme Court June 27, 2011, eff. June 30, 2011. Amended by Supreme Court Dec. 11, 2013, eff. Jan. 1, 2014. Approved by Court of Criminal Appeals Dec. 11, 2013, eff. Jan. 1, 2014.

Notes and Comments

Comment to 2008 change: Subdivision 9.3 is amended to reduce the number of copies of a motion for extension of time or response filed in the Supreme Court. Subdivision 9.8 is new. To protect the privacy of minors in suits affecting the parent-child relationship (SAPCR), including suits to terminate parental rights, Section 109.002(d) of the Family Code authorizes appellate courts, in their opinions, to identify parties only by fictitious names or by initials. Similarly, Section 56.01(j) of the Family Code prohibits identification of a minor or a minor's family in an appellate opinion related to juvenile court proceedings. But as appellate briefing becomes more widely available through electronic media sources, appellate courts' efforts to protect minors' privacy by disguising their identities in appellate opinions may be defeated if the same children are fully identified in briefs and other court papers available to the public. The rule provides protection from such disclosures. Any fictitious name should not be pejorative or suggest the person's true identity. The rule does not limit an appellate court's authority to disguise parties' identities in appropriate circumstances in other cases. Although appellate courts are authorized to enforce the rule's provisions requiring redaction, parties and amici curiae are responsible for ensuring that briefs and other papers submitted to the court fully comply with the rule.

Comment to 2013 Change: Rule 9 is revised to incorporate rules for electronic filing, in accordance with the Supreme Court's order— Misc. Docket No. 12–9208, amended by Misc. Docket Nos. 13–9092 and 13–9164—mandating electronic filing in civil cases in appellate courts, effective January 1, 2014. In addition, Rule 9.9 is added to provide privacy protection for all documents, both paper and electronic, filed in civil cases in appellate courts.

9.4. Form

Except for the record, a document filed with an appellate court, including a paper copy of an electronically filed document, must—unless the court accepts another form in the interest of justice — be in the following form:

(a) *Printing.* A document may be produced by standard typographic printing or by any duplicating process that produces a distinct black image. Printing must be on one side of the paper.

(b) *Paper Type and Size.* The paper on which a document is produced must be 8 1/2 by 11 inches, white or nearly white, and opaque.

(c) *Margins.* Documents must have at least one-inch margins on both sides and at the top and bottom.

(d) *Spacing.* Text must be double-spaced, but footnotes, block quotations, short lists, and issues or points of error may be single-spaced.

(e) *Typeface.* A document produced on a computer must be printed in a conventional typeface no smaller than 14–point except for footnotes, which must be no smaller than 12–point. A typewritten document must be printed in standard 10–character–per–inch (cpi) monospaced typeface.

(f) *Binding and Covering.* A paper document must be bound so as to ensure that it will not lose its cover or fall apart in regular use. A paper document should be stapled once in the top left-hand corner or be bound so that it will lie flat when open. A paper petition or brief should have durable front and back covers which must not be plastic or be red, black, or dark blue.

(g) *Contents of Cover.* A document's front cover, if any, must contain the case style, the case number, the title of the document being filed, the name of the party filing the document, and the name, mailing address, telephone number, fax number, if any, email address, and State Bar of Texas identification number of the lead counsel for the filing party. If a party requests oral argument in the court of appeals, the request must appear on the front cover of that party's first brief.

(h) *Appendix and Original Proceeding Record.* A paper appendix may be bound either with the document to which it is related or separately. If separately bound, the appendix must comply with paragraph (f). A paper record in an original proceeding or a paper appendix must be tabbed and indexed. An electronically filed record in an original proceeding or an electronically filed appendix that includes more than one item must contain bookmarks to assist in locating each item.

(i) *Length.*

(1) Contents Included and Excluded. In calculating the length of a document, every word and every part of the document, including headings, footnotes, and quotations, must be counted except the following: caption, identity of parties and counsel, statement regarding oral argument, table of contents, index of authorities, statement of the case, statement of issues presented, statement of jurisdiction, statement of procedural history, signature, proof of service, certification, certificate of compliance, and appendix.

(2) Maximum Length. The documents listed below must not exceed the following limits:

(A) A brief and response in a direct appeal to the Court of Criminal Appeals in a case in which the death penalty has been assessed: 37,500 words if computer-generated, and 125 pages if not.

(B) A brief and response in an appellate court (other than a brief under subparagraph (A)) and a petition and response in an original proceeding in the court of appeals: 15,000 words if computer-generated, and 50 pages if not. In a civil case in the court of appeals, the aggregate of all briefs filed by a party must not exceed 27,000 words if computer-generated, and 90 pages if not.

(C) A reply brief in an appellate court and a reply to a response to a petition in an original proceeding in the court of appeals: 7,500 words if computer-generated, and 25 pages if not.

(D) A petition and response in an original proceeding in the Supreme Court, a petition for review and response in the Supreme Court, a petition for discretionary review in the Court of Criminal Appeals, and a motion for rehearing in an appellate court: 4,500 words if computer-generated, and 15 pages if not.

(E) A reply to a response to a petition for review in the Supreme Court, a reply to a response to a petition in an original proceeding in the Supreme Court, and a reply to a petition for discretionary review in the Court of Criminal Appeals: 2,400 words if computer-generated, and 8 pages if not.

(3) Certificate of Compliance. A computer-generated document that is subject to a word limit under this rule must include a certificate by counsel or an unrepresented party stating the number of words in the document. The person certifying may rely on the word count of the computer program used to prepare the document.

(4) Extensions. A court may, on motion, permit a document that exceeds the prescribed limit.

(j) *Electronically Filed Documents.* An electronically filed document must:

(1) be in text-searchable portable document format (PDF);

(2) be directly converted to PDF rather than scanned, if possible;

(3) not be locked;

(4) be combined with any appendix into one computer file, unless that file would exceed the size limit prescribed by the electronic filing manager; and

(5) otherwise comply with the Technology Standards set by the Judicial Committee on Information Technology and approved by the Supreme Court.

(k) *Nonconforming Documents.* If a document fails to conform with these rules, the court may strike the document or identify the error and permit the party to resubmit the document in a conforming format by a specified deadline.

Eff. Sept. 1, 1997. Amended by Supreme Court Nov. 13, 2012, eff. Dec. 1, 2012; March 4, 2013, eff. immediately. Amended by Supreme Court Dec. 11, 2013, eff. Jan. 1, 2014. Approved by Court of Criminal Appeals Dec. 11, 2013, eff. Jan. 1, 2014.

Notes and Comments

Comment to 2012 Change: Rule 9 is revised to consolidate all length limits and establish word limits for documents produced on a computer. All documents produced on a computer must comply with the word limits. Page limits are retained for documents that are typewritten or otherwise not produced on a computer.

Comment to 2013 Change: Rule 9 is revised to incorporate rules for electronic filing, in accordance with the Supreme Court's order—Misc. Docket No. 12–9208, amended by Misc. Docket Nos. 13–9092 and 13–9164—mandating electronic filing in civil cases in appellate courts, effective January 1, 2014. In addition, Rule 9.9 is added to provide privacy protection for all documents, both paper and electronic, filed in civil cases in appellate courts.

9.5. Service

(a) *Service of All Documents Required.* At or before the time of a document's filing, the filing party must serve a copy on all parties to the proceeding. Service on a party represented by counsel must be made on that party's lead counsel. Except in original proceedings, a party need not serve a copy of the record.

(b) *Manner of Service.*

(1) Documents Filed Electronically. A document filed electronically under Rule 9.2 must be served electronically through the electronic filing manager if the email address of the party or attorney to be served is on file with the electronic filing manager. If the email address of the party or attorney to be served is not on file with the electronic filing manager, the document may be served on that party or attorney under subparagraph (2).

(2) Documents Not Filed Electronically. A document that is not filed electronically may be served in person, by mail, by commercial delivery service, by fax, or by email. Personal service includes delivery to any responsible person at the office of the lead counsel for the party served.

(c) *When Complete.*

(1) Service by mail is complete on mailing.

(2) Service by commercial delivery service is complete when the document is placed in the control of the delivery service.

(3) Service by fax is complete on receipt.

(4) Electronic service is complete on transmission of the document to the serving party's electronic filing service provider. The electronic filing manager will send confirmation of service to the serving party.

(d) *Proof of Service.* A document presented for filing must contain a proof of service in the form of either an acknowledgment of service by the person served or a certificate of service. Proof of service may appear on or be affixed to the filed document. The clerk may permit a document to be filed without proof of service, but will require the proof to be filed promptly.

(e) *Certificate Requirements.* A certificate of service must be signed by the person who made the service and must state:

(1) the date and manner of service;

(2) the name and address of each person served; and

(3) if the person served is a party's attorney, the name of the party represented by that attorney.

Eff. Sept. 1, 1997. Amended by Supreme Court Dec. 23, 2002, eff. Jan. 1, 2003. Amended by Supreme Court Dec. 11, 2013, eff. Jan. 1, 2014. Approved by Court of Criminal Appeals Dec. 11, 2013, eff. Jan. 1, 2014.

Notes and Comments

Comment to 2002 change: The change clarifies that the filing party must serve a copy of the document filed on all other parties, not only in an appeal or review, but in original proceedings as well. The rule applies only to filing *parties*. Thus, when the clerk or court reporter is responsible for filing the record, as in cases on appeal, a copy need not be served on the parties. The rule for original civil proceedings, in which a party is responsible for filing the record, is stated in subdivision 52.7.

Comment to 2013 change: Rule 9 is revised to incorporate rules for electronic filing, in accordance with the Supreme Court's order—Misc. Docket No. 12–9208, amended by Misc. Docket Nos. 13–9092 and 13–9164—mandating electronic filing in civil cases in appellate courts, effective January 1, 2014. In addition, Rule 9.9 is added to provide privacy protection for all documents, both paper and electronic, filed in civil cases in appellate courts.

9.6. Communications With the Court

Parties and counsel may communicate with the appellate court about a case only through the clerk.

Eff. Sept. 1, 1997. Amended by order of Jan. 1, 2014, eff. Jan. 1, 2014.

9.7. Adoption by Reference

Any party may join in or adopt by reference all or any part of a brief, petition, response, motion, or other document filed in an appellate court by another party in the same case.

Added by Supreme Court Dec. 23, 2002, eff. Jan. 1, 2003. Amended by order of Jan. 1, 2014, eff. Jan. 1, 2014.

Notes and Comments

Comment to 2002 change: Subdivision 9.7 is added to provide express authorization for the practice of adopting by reference all or part of another party's filing.

9.8. Protection of Minor's Identity in Parental–Rights Termination Cases and Juvenile Court Cases

(a) *Alias Defined.* For purposes of this rule, an alias means one or more of a person's initials or a fictitious name, used to refer to the person.

(b) *Parental–Rights Termination Cases.* In an appeal or an original proceeding in an appellate court, arising out of a case in which the termination of parental rights was at issue:

(1) except for a docketing statement, in all papers submitted to the court, including all appendix items submitted with a brief, petition, or motion:

(A) a minor must be identified only by an alias unless the court orders otherwise;

(B) the court may order that a minor's parent or other family member be identified only by an alias if necessary to protect a minor's identity, and

(C) all documents must be redacted accordingly;

(2) the court must, in its opinion, use an alias to refer to a minor, and if necessary to protect the minor's identity, to the minor's parent or other family member.

(c) *Juvenile Court Cases.* In an appeal or an original proceeding in an appellate court, arising out of a case under Title 3 of the Family Code:

(1) except for a docketing statement, in all papers submitted to the court, including all appendix items submitted with a brief, petition, or motion:

(A) a minor must be identified only by an alias;

(B) a minor's parent or other family member must be identified only by an alias; and

(C) all documents must be redacted accordingly;

(2) the court must, in its opinion, use an alias to refer to a minor and to the minor's parent or other family member.

(d) *No Alteration of Appellate Record.* Nothing in this rule permits alteration of the original appellate record except as specifically authorized by court order.

Added by Supreme Court March 10, 2008, eff. Sept. 1, 2008. Amended by Supreme Court Aug. 20, 2008, eff. Sept. 1, 2008. Approved by Court of Criminal Appeals Sept. 30, 2008, eff. Sept. 30, 2008. Amended by order of Jan. 1, 2014, eff. Jan. 1, 2014.

Notes and Comments

Comment to 2008 change: Subdivision 9.3 is amended to reduce the number of copies of a motion for extension of time or response filed in the Supreme Court. Subdivision 9.8 is new. To protect the privacy of minors in suits affecting the parent-child relationship (SAPCR), including suits to terminate parental rights, Section 109.002(d) of the Family Code authorizes appellate courts, in their opinions, to identify parties only by fictitious names or by initials. Similarly, Section 56.01(j) of the Family Code prohibits identification of a minor or a minor's family in an appellate opinion related to juvenile court proceedings. But as appellate briefing becomes more widely available through electronic media sources, appellate courts' efforts to protect minors' privacy by disguising their identities in appellate opinions may be defeated if the same children are fully identified in briefs and other court papers available to the public. The rule provides protection from such disclosures. Any fictitious name should not be pejorative or suggest the person's true identity. The rule does not limit an appellate court's authority to disguise parties' identities in appropriate circumstances in other cases. Although appellate courts are authorized to enforce the rule's provisions requiring redaction, parties and amici curiae are responsible for ensuring that briefs and other papers submitted to the court fully comply with the rule.

9.9. Privacy Protection for Documents Filed in Civil Cases

(a) *Sensitive Data Defined.* Sensitive data consists of:

(1) a driver's license number, passport number, social security number, tax identification number or similar government-issued personal identification number;

(2) a bank account number, credit card number, or other financial account number; and

(3) a birth date, home address, and the name of any person who was a minor when the underlying suit was filed.

(b) *Filing of Documents Containing Sensitive Data Prohibited.* Unless the inclusion of sensitive data is specifically required by a statute, court rule, or administrative regulation, an electronic or paper document containing sensitive data may not be filed with a court unless the sensitive data is redacted, except for the record in an appeal under Section Two.

(c) *Redaction of Sensitive Data; Retention Requirement.* Sensitive data must be redacted by using the letter "X" in place of each omitted digit or character or by removing the sensitive data in a manner indicating that the data has been redacted. The filing party must retain an unredacted version of the filed document during the pendency of the appeal and any related proceedings filed within six months of the date the judgment is signed.

(d) *Notice to Clerk.* If a document must contain sensitive data, the filing party must notify the clerk by:

(1) designating the document as containing sensitive data when the document is electronically filed; or

(2) if the document is not electronically filed, by including, on the upper left-hand side of the first page, the phrase: "NOTICE: THIS DOCUMENT CONTAINS SENSITIVE DATA."

(e) *Restriction on Remote Access.* Documents that contain unredacted sensitive data in violation of this rule must not be posted on the Internet.

Adopted by Supreme Court Dec. 11, 2013, eff. Jan. 1, 2014. Approved by Court of Criminal Appeals Dec. 11, 2013, eff. Jan. 1, 2014.

Notes and Comments

Comment to 2013 Change: Rule 9 is revised to incorporate rules for electronic filing, in accordance with the Supreme Court's order—Misc. Docket No. 12–9206, amended by Misc. Docket Nos. 13–9092 and 13–9164—mandating electronic filing in civil cases in appellate courts, effective January 1, 2014. In addition, Rule 9.9 is added to provide privacy protection for all documents, both paper and electronic, filed in civil cases in appellate courts.

9.10. Privacy Protection for Documents Filed in Criminal Cases

(a) *Sensitive Data Defined.* Sensitive data consists of:

(1) a driver's license number, passport number, social security number, tax identification number or similar government-issued personal identification number;

(2) bank account number, credit card number, and other financial account number;

(3) a birth date, a home address, and the name of any person who was a minor at the time the offense was committed.

(b) *Redacted Filings.* Unless a court orders otherwise, an electronic or paper filing with the court, including the contents of any appendices, must not contain sensitive data.

(c) *Exemptions from the Redaction Requirement.* The redaction requirement does not apply to the following:

(1) A court filing that is related to a criminal matter or investigation and that is prepared before the filing of a criminal charge or is not filed as part of any docketed criminal case;

(2) An arrest or search warrant;

(3) A charging document and an affidavit filed in support of any charging document;

(4) A defendant's date of birth;

(5) A defendant's address; and

(6) Any government issued number intended to identify the defendant associated with a criminal filing, except for the defendant's social security number or driver's license number.

(d) *Redaction procedures.* Sensitive data must be redacted by using the letter "X" in place of each omitted digit or character or by removing the sensitive data in a manner indicating that the data has been redacted. The filer must retain an unredacted version of the filed document during the pendency of the appeal and any related proceedings filed within three years of the date the judgment is signed. If a district court clerk or appellate court clerk discovers unredacted sensitive data in the record, the clerk shall notify the parties and seek a ruling from the court.

(e) *Certification.* The filing of a document constitutes a certification by the filer that the document complies with paragraphs (a) and (b) of this rule.

(f) *Reference List.* If a filer believes any information described in paragraph (a) of this rule is essential to a document or that the document would be confusing without the information, the filer may submit the information to the court in a reference list that is in paper form and under seal. The reference list must specify an appropriate identifier that corresponds uniquely to each item listed. Any reference in the document to a listed identifier will be construed to refer to the corresponding item of information. If the filer provides a reference list pursuant to this rule, the front page of the document containing the redacted information must indicate that the reference list has been, or will be, provided. On its own initiative, the court may order a sealed reference list in any case.

(g) *Sealed materials.* Materials that are required by statute to be sealed, redacted, or kept confidential, such as the items set out in Articles 35.29 (Personal Information About Jurors), 38.45 (Evidence Depicting or Describing Abuse of or Sexual Conduct by Child or Minor), and 42.12, § 9(j), must be treated in accordance with the pertinent statutes and shall not be publicly available on the internet. A court may also order that a document be filed under seal in paper form or electronic form, without redaction. The court may later unseal the document or order the filer to provide a redacted version of the document for the public record. If a court orders material sealed, whether it be sensitive data or other materials, the court's sealing order must be affixed to the outside of the sealed container if the sealed material is filed in paper form, or be the first document that appears if filed in electronic form. Sealed portions of the clerk's and reporter's records should be clearly marked and separated from unsealed portions and tendered as separate records, whether in paper form or electronic form. Sealed material shall not be available either on the internet or in other form without court order.

(h) *Waiver of Protection of Identifiers.* A person waives the protection of this rule as to a person's own information by filing it without redaction and not under seal.

Adopted by Supreme Court Dec. 11, 2013, eff. Jan. 1, 2014. Approved by Court of Criminal Appeals Dec. 11, 2013, eff. Jan. 1, 2014. Amended by Court of Criminal Appeals Oct. 5, 2015, eff. Nov. 1, 2015.

Rule 10. Motions in the Appellate Courts

Notes and Comments

Comment to 1997 change: This is former Rule 19. Under subdivision 10.1, a response may be filed at any time before the court rules on the motion. The provision of former subdivision (b) regarding docketing motions is incorporated in Rule 12.2. The provision of former subdivision (b) for noting attorneys' names on the docket is incorporated in Rule 6.2. Former subdivision (c), requiring the clerk to send notices of the filing of motions is deleted as unnecessary because the parties must serve all motions under Rule 9.5. Subdivision 10.2 is amended to eliminate the requirement of an oath where the facts are within the personal knowledge of the attorney. Subdivision 10.5 is new and incorporates the provisions of other rules concerning motions, as follows: 10.5(a) from former Rule 71; 10.5(b) from former Rules 73, 130(d), and 160; and 10.5(c) from former Rule 70. Other changes are made.

10.1. Contents of Motions; Response

(a) *Motion.* Unless these rules prescribe another form, a party must apply by motion for an order or other relief. The motion must:

(1) contain or be accompanied by any matter specifically required by a rule governing such a motion;

(2) state with particularity the grounds on which it is based;

(3) set forth the order or relief sought;

(4) be served and filed with any brief, affidavit, or other paper filed in support of the motion; and

(5) in civil cases, except for motions for rehearing and en banc reconsideration, contain or be accompanied by a certificate stating that the filing party conferred, or made a reasonable attempt to confer, with all other parties about the merits of the motion and whether those parties oppose the motion.

(b) *Response.* A party may file a response to a motion at any time before the court rules on the motion or by any deadline set by the court. The court may determine a motion before a response is filed.

Eff. Sept. 1, 1997. Amended by Supreme Court March 10, 2008, and Aug. 20, 2008, eff. Sept. 1, 2008. Approved by Court of Criminal Appeals Sept. 30, 2008, eff. Sept. 30, 2008.

Notes and Comments

Comment to 2008 change: It happens so infrequently that a non-movant does not oppose a motion for rehearing or en banc reconsideration that such motions are excepted from the certificate-of-conference requirement in Subdivision 10.1(a)(5). Subdivision 10.2 is revised to clarify that facts supporting a motion need not be verified by the filer if supporting evidence is in the record, the facts are known to the court, or the filer has personal knowledge of them. Subdivision 10.5(b)(3)(D) is added.

10.2. Evidence on Motions

A motion need not be verified unless it depends on the following types of facts, in which case the motion must be supported by affidavit or other satisfactory evidence. The types of facts requiring proof are those that are:

(a) not in the record;

(b) not within the court's knowledge in its official capacity; and

(c) not within the personal knowledge of the attorney signing the motion.

Eff. Sept. 1, 1997. Amended by Supreme Court March 10, 2008, and Aug. 20, 2008, eff. Sept. 1, 2008. Approved by Court of Criminal Appeals Sept. 30, 2008, eff. Sept. 30, 2008.

Notes and Comments

Comment to 2008 change: It happens so infrequently that a non-movant does not oppose a motion for rehearing or en banc reconsideration that such motions are excepted from the certificate-of-conference requirement in Subdivision 10.1(a)(5). Subdivision 10.2 is revised to clarify that facts supporting a motion need not be verified by the filer if supporting evidence is in the record, the facts are known to the court, or the filer has personal knowledge of them. Subdivision 10.5(b)(3)(D) is added.

10.3. Determining Motions

(a) *Time for Determination.* A court should not hear or determine a motion until 10 days after the motion was filed, unless:

(1) the motion is to extend time to file a brief, a petition for review, or a petition for discretionary review;

(2) the motion states that the parties have conferred and that no party opposes the motion; or

(3) the motion is an emergency.

(b) *Reconsideration.* If a motion is determined prematurely, any party adversely affected may request the court to reconsider its order.

Eff. Sept. 1, 1997.

10.4. Power of Panel or Single Justice or Judge to Entertain Motions

(a) *Single Justice.* In addition to the authority expressly conferred by these rules or by law, a single justice or judge of an appellate court may grant or deny a request for relief that these rules allow to be sought by motion. But in a civil case, a single justice should not do the following:

(1) act on a petition for an extraordinary writ; or

(2) dismiss or otherwise determine an appeal or a motion for rehearing.

(b) *Panel.* An appellate court may provide, by order or rule, that a panel or the full court must act on any motion or class of motions.

Eff. Sept. 1, 1997.

10.5. Particular Motions

(a) *Motions Relating to Informalities in the Record.* A motion relating to informalities in the manner of bringing a case into court must be filed within 30 days after the record is filed in the court of appeals. The objection, if waivable, will otherwise be deemed waived.

(b) *Motions to Extend Time.*

(1) Contents of Motion in General. All motions to extend time, except a motion to extend time for filing a notice of appeal, must state:

(A) the deadline for filing the item in question;

(B) the length of the extension sought;

(C) the facts relied on to reasonably explain the need for an extension; and

(D) the number of previous extensions granted regarding the item in question.

(2) Contents of Motion to Extend Time to File Notice of Appeal. A motion to extend the time for filing a notice of appeal must:

(A) comply with (1)(A) and (C);

(B) identify the trial court;

(C) state the date of the trial court's judgment or appealable order; and

(D) state the case number and style of the case in the trial court.

(3) Contents of Motion to Extend Time to File Petition for Review or Petition for Discretionary Review. A motion to extend time to file a petition for review or petition for discretionary review must also specify:

(A) the court of appeals;

(B) the date of the court of appeals' judgment;

(C) the case number and style of the case in the court of appeals; and

(D) the date every motion for rehearing or en banc reconsideration was filed, and either the date and nature of the court of appeals' ruling on the motion, or that it remains pending.

(c) *Motions to Postpone Argument.* Unless all parties agree, or unless sufficient cause is apparent to the court, a motion to postpone argument of a case must be supported by sufficient cause.

Eff. Sept. 1, 1997. Amended by Supreme Court Aug. 20, 2008, eff. Sept. 1, 2008. Approved by Court of Criminal Appeals Sept. 30, 2008, eff. Sept. 30, 2008.

Notes and Comments

Comment to 2008 change: It happens so infrequently that a non-movant does not oppose a motion for rehearing or en banc reconsideration that such motions are excepted from the certificate-of-conference requirement in Subdivision 10.1(a)(5). Subdivision 10.2 is revised to clarify that facts supporting a motion need not be verified by the filer if supporting evidence is in the record, the facts are known to the court, or the filer has personal knowledge of them. Subdivision 10.5(b)(3)(D) is added.

Rule 11. Amicus Curiae Briefs

An appellate clerk may receive, but not file, an amicus curiae brief. But the court for good cause may refuse to consider the brief and order that it be returned. An amicus curiae brief must:

(a) comply with the briefing rules for parties;

(b) identify the person or entity on whose behalf the brief is tendered;

(c) disclose the source of any fee paid or to be paid for preparing the brief; and

(d) certify that copies have been served on all parties.

Eff. Sept. 1, 1997. Amended by Supreme Court Dec. 23, 2002, eff. Jan. 1, 2003.

Notes and Comments

Comment to 1997 change: This is former Rule 20. The rule is rewritten and now requires disclosure of the identity of the person or entity on whose behalf the brief is filed, and the source of any fee paid.

Comment to 2002 change: The change expressly recognizes that a court may refuse to consider an amicus curiae brief for good cause.

Rule 12. Duties of Appellate Clerk

Notes and Comments

Comment to 1997 change: This is former Rule 18. Former subdivision (b), regarding the preparation of the record, is moved to the order concerning the preparation of the appellate record. Former Rule 14, which is revised and simplified, is relocated here as subdivision 12.5. Subdivision 12.6, requiring the clerk to send a notice of any order or judgment of an appellate court, is added. Other changes are made.

12.1. Docketing the Case

On receiving a copy of the notice of appeal, the petition for review, the petition for discretionary review, the petition in an original proceeding, or a certified question, the appellate clerk must:

(a) endorse on the document the date of receipt;

(b) collect any filing fee;

(c) docket the case;

(d) notify all parties of the receipt of the document; and

(e) if the document filed is a petition for review filed in the Supreme Court, notify the court of appeals clerk of the filing of the petition.

12.2. Docket Numbers

The clerk must put the case's docket number on each item received in connection with the case and must put the docket number on the envelope in which the record is stored.

(a) *Numbering System.* Each case filed in a court of appeals must be assigned a docket number consisting of the following four parts, separated by hyphens:

(1) the number of the court of appeals district;

(2) the last two digits of the year in which the case is filed;

(3) the number assigned to the case; and

(4) the designation "CV" for a civil case or "CR" for a criminal case.

(b) *Numbering Order.* Each case must be docketed in the order of its filing.

(c) *Multiple Notices of Appeal.* All notices of appeal filed in the same case must be given the same docket number.

(d) *Appeals Not Yet Filed.* A motion relating to an appeal that has been perfected but not yet filed must be docketed and assigned a docket number that will also be assigned to the appeal when it is filed.

Eff. Sept. 1, 1997.

12.3. Custody of Papers

The clerk must safeguard the record and every other item filed in a case. If the record or any part of it or any other item is missing, the court will make an order for the replacement of the record or item that is just under the circumstances.

Eff. Sept. 1, 1997.

12.4. Withdrawing Papers

The clerk may permit the record or other filed item to be taken from the clerk's office at any time, on the following conditions:

(a) the clerk must have a receipt for the record or item;

(b) the clerk should make reasonable conditions to ensure that the withdrawn record or item is preserved and returned;

(c) the clerk may demand the return of the record or item at any time;

(d) after the case is submitted to the court and before the court's decision, the record cannot be withdrawn;

(e) after the court's decision, the losing party must be given priority in withdrawing the record;

(f) the clerk may not allow original documents filed under Rule 34.5(f) or original exhibits filed under Rule 34.6(g) to be taken from the clerk's office;

(g) if the court allows an original document or exhibit to be taken by a party and it is not returned, the court may accept the opposing party's statement concerning the document's or exhibit's nature and contents;

(h) withdrawn material must not be removed from the court's jurisdiction; and

(i) the court may, on the motion of any party or its own initiative, modify any of these conditions.

12.5. Clerk's Duty to Account

The clerk of an appellate court who receives money due another court must promptly pay the money to the court to whom it is due. This rule is enforceable by the Supreme Court.

Eff. Sept. 1, 1997.

12.6. Notices of Court's Judgments and Orders

In any proceeding, the clerk of an appellate court must promptly send a notice of any judgment, mandate, or other court order to all parties to the proceeding.

Eff. Sept. 1, 1997. Amended by Supreme Court Dec. 23, 2002, eff. Jan. 1, 2003.

Notes and Comments

Comment to 2002 change: Subdivision 12.6 is amended to require the clerk to notify the parties of all of the court's rulings, including the mandate.

Rule 13. Court Reporters and Court Recorders

Notes and Comments

Comment to 1997 change: Former Rules 11 and 12 are merged. Former Rules 11(a), (c) and (d) now appear as subdivisions 13.1, 13.5 and 13.6. Former Rule 11(b) is omitted as unnecessary. The provisions of former Rule 12(a) are moved to Rule 35.3. Former Rules 12(b) and (c) now appear as subdivisions 13.3 and 13.4. The rule is made to apply to court recorders as well as court reporters. Paragraph 13.1(a) merges paragraphs (a)(1) and (2) of former Rule 11, and now requires the reporter to make a record of voir dire and closing argument unless excused by agreement of the parties. Paragraph 13.1(b) is new, but codifies current practice. Subdivision 13.2 is new and specifies rules for electronic recording of proceedings. A provision requiring a deputy court reporter to file with the trial court clerk a document identifying the proceedings in which the reporter worked is included in paragraph 13.5. Other changes are made.

13.1. Duties of Court Reporters and Recorders

The official court reporter or court recorder must:

(a) unless excused by agreement of the parties, attend court sessions and make a full record of the proceedings;

(b) take all exhibits offered in evidence during a proceeding and ensure that they are marked;

(c) file all exhibits with the trial court clerk after a proceeding ends;

(d) perform the duties prescribed by Rules 34.6 and 35; and

(e) perform other acts relating to the reporter's or recorder's official duties, as the trial court directs.

Eff. Sept. 1, 1997. Amended by Supreme Court Dec. 23, 2002, eff. Jan. 1, 2003.

Notes and Comments

Comment to 2002 change: Subdivision 13.1(a) is amended merely for clarification.

13.2. Additional Duties of Court Recorder

The official court recorder must also:

(a) ensure that the recording system functions properly throughout the proceeding and that a complete, clear, and transcribable recording is made;

(b) make a detailed, legible log of all proceedings being recorded, showing:

(1) the number and style of the case before the court;

(2) the name of each person speaking;

(3) the event being recorded such as the voir dire, the opening statement, direct and cross-examinations, and bench conferences;

(4) each exhibit offered, admitted, or excluded;

(5) the time of day of each event; and

(6) the index number on the recording device showing where each event is recorded;

(c) after a proceeding ends, file with the clerk the original log;

(d) have the original recording stored to ensure that it is preserved and is accessible; and

(e) ensure that no one gains access to the original recording without the court's written order.

Eff. Sept. 1, 1997.

13.3. Priorities of Reporters

The trial court must help ensure that the court reporter's work is timely accomplished by setting work priorities. The reporter's duties relating to proceedings before the court take preference over other work.

Eff. Sept. 1, 1997.

13.4. Report of Reporters

To aid the trial court in setting priorities under 13.3, each court reporter must give the trial court a monthly written report showing the amount and nature of the business pending in the reporter's office. A copy of this report must be filed with the appellate clerk of each district in which the court sits.

Eff. Sept. 1, 1997.

13.5. Appointing Deputy Reporter

When the official court reporter is unable to perform the duties in 13.1 or 13.2 because of illness, press of official work, or unavoidable absence or disability, the trial court may designate a deputy reporter. If the court appoints a deputy reporter, that person must file with the trial court clerk a document stating:

(a) the date the deputy worked;

(b) the court in which the deputy worked; and

(c) the number and style of the case on which the deputy worked.

Eff. Sept. 1, 1997.

13.6. Filing of Notes in a Criminal Case

When a defendant is convicted and sentenced, or is granted deferred adjudication for a felony other than a state jail felony, and does not appeal, the court reporter must—within 20 days after the time to perfect the appeal has expired—file the untranscribed notes or the original recording of the proceeding with the trial court clerk. The trial court clerk need not retain the notes beyond 15 years of their filing date.

Eff. Sept. 1, 1997.

Rule 14. Recording and Broadcasting Court Proceedings

Notes and Comments

Comment to 1997 change: This is former Rule 21. The rule is rewritten and now allows recording and broadcasting of court proceedings at the discretion of the court and subject to the stated guidelines.

14.1. Recording and Broadcasting Permitted

An appellate court may permit courtroom proceedings to be broadcast, televised, recorded, or photographed in accordance with this rule.

Eff. Sept. 1, 1997.

14.2. Procedure

(a) *Request to Cover Court Proceeding.*

(1) A person wishing to broadcast, televise, record, or photograph a court proceeding must file with the court clerk a request to cover the proceeding. The request must state:

(A) the case style and number;

(B) the date and time when the proceeding is to begin;

(C) the name of the requesting person or organization;

(D) the type of coverage requested (for example, televising or photographing); and

(E) the type and extent of equipment to be used.

(2) A request to cover argument of a case must be filed no later than five days before the date the case is set for argument and must be served on all parties to the case. A request to cover any other proceeding must be filed no later than two days before the date when the proceeding is to begin.

(b) *Response.* Any party may file a response to the request. If the request is to cover argument, the response must be filed no later than two days before the date set for argument. If a party objects to coverage of the argument, the response should state the injury that will allegedly result from coverage.

(c) *Court May Shorten Time.* The court may, in the interest of justice, shorten the time for filing a document under this rule if no party or interested person would be unduly prejudiced.

(d) *Decision of Court.* In deciding whether to allow coverage, the court may consider information known *ex parte* to the court. The court may allow, deny, limit, or terminate coverage for any reason the court considers necessary or appropriate, such as protecting the parties' rights or the dignity of the court and ensuring the orderly conduct of the proceedings.

Eff. Sept. 1, 1997.

14.3. Equipment and Personnel

The court may, among other things:

(a) require that a person seeking to cover a proceeding demonstrate or display the equipment that will be used;

(b) prohibit equipment that produces distracting sound or light;

(c) prohibit signal lights or devices showing when equipment is operating, or require their concealment;

(d) prohibit moving lights, flash attachments, or sudden lighting changes;

(e) require the use of the courtroom's existing video, audio, and lighting systems, if any;

(f) specify the placement of personnel and equipment;

(g) determine the number of cameras to be allowed in the courtroom; and

(h) require pooling of equipment if more than one person wishes to cover a proceeding.

Eff. Sept. 1, 1997.

14.4. Enforcement

The court may sanction a violation of this rule by measures that include barring a person or organization from access to future coverage of proceedings in that court for a defined period.

Eff. Sept. 1, 1997.

Rule 15. Issuance of Writ or Process by Appellate Court

Notes and Comments

Comment to 1997 change: This is former Rule 17. Nonsubstantive changes are made.

15.1. In General

(a) *Signature Under Seal.* A writ or process issuing from an appellate court must bear the court's seal and be signed by the clerk.

(b) *To Whom Directed; by Whom Served.* Unless a rule or statute provides otherwise, the writ or process must be directed to the person or court to be served. The writ or process may be served by the sheriff, constable, or other peace officer whose jurisdiction includes the county in which the person or court to be served may be found.

(c) *Return; Lack of Execution; Simultaneous Writs.* The writ or process must be returned to the issuing court according to the writ's direction. If the writ or process is not executed, the clerk may issue another writ or process if requested by the party who requested the former writ or process. At a party's request, the clerk may issue two or more writs simultaneously.

Eff. Sept. 1, 1997.

15.2. Appearance Without Service; Actual Knowledge

A party who appears in person or by attorney in an appellate court proceeding—or who has actual knowledge of the court's opinion, judgment, or order related to a writ or process—is bound by the opinion, judgment, or order to the same extent as if personally served under 15.1.

Eff. Sept. 1, 1997.

Rule 16. Disqualification or Recusal of Appellate Judges

Notes and Comments

Comment to 1997 change: Former Rules 15 and 15a are merged. Former Rule 15a appears as subdivision 16.2. For grounds for disqualification, reference is made to the Constitution and statutes rather than the Rules of Civil Procedure. The procedure for disqualification is not specified. The nature of prior participation in a proceeding that requires recusal is clarified. Former subdivision (b) of Rule 15, requiring service of the motion, is omitted as unnecessary. The remaining subdivisions of former Rule 15 are contained in subdivision 16.3. Other changes are made.

16.1. Grounds for Disqualification

The grounds for disqualification of an appellate court justice or judge are determined by the Constitution and laws of Texas.

Eff. Sept. 1, 1997.

16.2. Grounds for Recusal

The grounds for recusal of an appellate court justice or judge are the same as those provided in the Rules of Civil Procedure. In addition, a justice or judge must recuse in a proceeding if it presents a material issue which the justice or judge participated in deciding while serving on another court in which the proceeding was pending.

Eff. Sept. 1, 1997.

16.3. Procedure for Recusal

(a) *Motion.* A party may file a motion to recuse a justice or judge before whom the case is pending. The motion must be filed promptly after the party has reason to believe that the justice or judge should not participate in deciding the case.

(b) *Decision.* Before any further proceeding in the case, the challenged justice or judge must either remove himself or herself from all participation in the case or certify the matter to the entire court, which will decide the motion by a majority of the remaining judges sitting en banc. The challenged justice or judge must not sit with the remainder of the court to consider the motion as to him or her.

(c) *Appeal.* An order of recusal is not reviewable, but the denial of a recusal motion is reviewable.

Eff. Sept. 1, 1997.

Rule 17. Court of Appeals Unable to Take Immediate Action

Notes and Comments

Comment to 1997 change: This is former Rule 16. The rule is rewritten and simplified.

17.1. Inability to Act

A court of appeals is unable to take immediate action if it cannot—within the time when action must be taken—assemble a panel because members of the court are ill, absent, or unavailable. A justice who is disqualified or recused is unavailable. A court of appeals' inability to act immediately may be established by certificate of the clerk, a member of the court, or a party's counsel, or by affidavit of a party.

Eff. Sept. 1, 1997.

17.2. Nearest Available Court of Appeals

If a court of appeals is unable to take immediate action, the nearest court of appeals that is able to take immediate action may do so with the same effect as the other court. The nearest court of appeals is the one whose courthouse is nearest—measured by a straight line—the courthouse of the trial court.

Eff. Sept. 1, 1997.

17.3. Further Proceedings

After acting or refusing to act, the nearest court of appeals must promptly send a copy of its order, and the original or a copy of any document presented to it, to the other court, which will conduct any further proceedings in the matter.

Eff. Sept. 1, 1997.

Rule 18. Mandate

Notes and Comments

Comment to 1997 change: This is a new rule that combines the provisions of former Rules 43(g), 86, 186, 231, and 232.

18.1. Issuance

The clerk of the appellate court that rendered the judgment must issue a mandate in accordance with the judgment and send it to the clerk of the court to which it is directed and to all parties to the proceeding when one of the following periods expires:

(a) *In the Court of Appeals.*

(1) Ten days after the time has expired for filing a motion to extend time to file a petition for review or a petition for discretionary review if:

(A) no timely petition for review or petition for discretionary review has been filed;

(B) no timely filed motion to extend time to file a petition for review or petition for discretionary review is pending; and

(C) in a criminal case, the Court of Criminal Appeals has not granted review on its own initiative.

(2) Ten days after the time has expired for filing a motion to extend time to file a motion for rehearing of a denial, refusal, or dismissal of a petition for review, or a refusal or dismissal of a petition for discretionary review, if no timely filed motion for rehearing or motion to extend time is pending.

(b) *In the Supreme Court and the Court of Criminal Appeals.* Ten days after the time has expired for filing a motion to extend time to file a motion for rehearing if no timely filed motion for rehearing or motion to extend time is pending.

(c) *Agreement to Issue.* The mandate may be issued earlier if the parties so agree, or for good cause on the motion of a party.

Eff. Sept. 1, 1997. Amended by Supreme Court Dec. 23, 2002, eff. Jan. 1, 2003.

Notes and Comments

Comment to 2002 change: Subdivision 18.1 is amended consistent with the change in subdivision 12.6.

18.2. Stay of Mandate

A party may move to stay issuance of the mandate pending the United States Supreme Court's disposition of a petition for writ of certiorari. The motion must state the grounds for the petition and the circumstances requiring the stay. The appellate court authorized to issue the mandate may grant a stay if it finds that the grounds are substantial and that the petitioner or others would incur serious hardship from the mandate's issuance if the United States Supreme Court were later to reverse the judgment. In a criminal case, the stay will last for no more than 90 days, to permit the timely filing of a petition for writ of certiorari. After that period and others mentioned in this rule expire, the mandate will issue.

Eff. Sept. 1, 1997.

18.3. Trial Court Case Number

The mandate must state the trial court case number.

Eff. Sept. 1, 1997.

18.4. Filing of Mandate

The clerk receiving the mandate will file it with the case's other papers and note it on the docket.

Eff. Sept. 1, 1997.

18.5. Costs

The mandate will be issued without waiting for costs to be paid. If the Supreme Court declines to grant review, Supreme Court costs must be included in the court of appeals' mandate.

Eff. Sept. 1, 1997.

18.6. Mandate in Accelerated Appeals

The appellate court's judgment on an appeal from an interlocutory order takes effect when the mandate is issued. The court may issue the mandate with its judgment or delay the mandate until the appeal is finally disposed of. If the mandate is issued, any further proceeding in the trial court must conform to the mandate.

Eff. Sept. 1, 1997.

18.7. Recall of Mandate

If an appellate court vacates or modifies its judgment or order after issuing its mandate, the appellate clerk must promptly notify the clerk of the court to which the mandate was directed and all parties. The mandate will have no effect and a new mandate may be issued.

Eff. Sept. 1, 1997.

Rule 19. Plenary Power of the Courts of Appeals and Expiration of Term

Notes and Comments

Comment to 1997 change: This is a new rule except the provisions of former Rule 234 are incorporated in subdivision 19.4.

19.1. Plenary Power of Courts of Appeals

A court of appeals' plenary power over its judgment expires:

(a) 60 days after judgment if no timely filed motion for rehearing or en banc reconsideration, or timely filed motion to extend time to file such a motion, is then pending; or

(b) 30 days after the court overrules all timely filed motions for rehearing or en banc reconsideration, and all timely filed motions to extend time to file such a motion.

Eff. Sept. 1, 1997. Amended by Supreme Court Dec. 23, 2002, eff. Jan. 1, 2003; March 10, 2008, and Aug. 20, 2008, eff. Sept. 1, 2008. Approved by Court of Criminal Appeals Sept. 30, 2008, eff. Sept. 30, 2008.

Notes and Comments

Comment to 2008 change: Subdivision 19.1 is changed, consistent with other changes in the rules, to specifically address a motion for en banc reconsideration and treat it as a motion for rehearing.

Comment to 2002 change: Subdivision 19.1 amended to clarify that a motion for en banc reconsideration extends the court of appeals' plenary power in the same manner as a motion for rehearing addressed to the panel of justices who rendered the judgment or under consideration.

19.2. Plenary Power Continues After Petition Filed

In a civil case, the court of appeals retains plenary power to vacate or modify its judgment during the periods prescribed in 19.1 even if a party has filed a petition for review in the Supreme Court.

Eff. Sept. 1, 1997.

19.3. Proceedings After Plenary Power Expires

After its plenary power expires, the court cannot vacate or modify its judgment. But the court may:

(a) correct a clerical error in its judgment or opinion;

(b) issue and recall its mandate as these rules provide;

(c) enforce or suspend enforcement of its judgment as these rules or applicable law provide;

(d) order or modify the amount and type of security required to suspend a judgment, and decide the sufficiency of the sureties, under Rule 24[1]; and

(e) order its opinion published in accordance with Rule 47.[2]

Eff. Sept. 1, 1997.

1 Vernon's Ann.Rules App.Proc., rule 24.1 et seq.

2 Vernon's Ann.Rules App.Proc., rule 47.1 et seq.

19.4. Expiration of Term

The expiration of the appellate court's term does not affect the court's plenary power or its jurisdiction over a case that is pending when the court's term expires.

Eff. Sept. 1, 1997.

Rule 20. When Party Is Indigent

Notes and Comments

Comment to 1997 change: The rule is new and combines the provisions of former Rules 13(k), 40(a)(3), and 53(j). The procedure for proceeding in civil cases in an appellate court without advance payment of costs, in both appeals and original proceedings, is stated. The information that must be given in the affidavit is prescribed. An extension of time to file the affidavit is now available. The indigent party is no longer required to serve the court reporter, but must file the affidavit with the appropriate clerk who is to notify the court reporter. A contest need not be under oath. Provision is made for later ability to pay the costs. Nonsubstantive changes are made to the rule for criminal cases.

Reference

See also Civil Practice and Remedies Code § 13.003.

20.1. Civil Cases

(a) *Establishing Indigence.*

(1) By Certificate. If the appellant proceeded in the trial court without advance payment of costs pursuant to a certificate under Texas Rule of Civil Procedure 145(c) confirming that the appellant was screened for eligibility to receive free legal services under income guidelines used by a program funded by Interest on Lawyers Trust Accounts or the Texas Access to Justice Foundation, an additional certificate may be filed in the appellate court confirming that the appellant was rescreened after rendition of the trial court's judgment and again found eligible under program guidelines. A party's affidavit of inability accompanied by the certificate may not be contested.

(2) By Affidavit. A party who cannot pay the costs in an appellate court may proceed without advance payment of costs if:

(A) the party files an affidavit of indigence in compliance with this rule;

(B) the claim of indigence is not contestable, is not contested, or, if contested, the contest is not sustained by written order; and

(C) the party timely files a notice of appeal.

(3) By Presumption of Indigence. In a suit filed by a governmental entity in which termination of the parent-child relationship or managing conservatorship is requested, a parent determined by the trial court to be indigent is presumed to remain indigent for the duration of the suit and any subsequent appeal, as provided by section 107.013 of the Family Code, and may proceed without advance payment of costs.

(b) *Contents of Affidavit.* The affidavit of indigence must identify the party filing the affidavit and must state what amount of costs, if any, the party can pay. The affidavit must also contain complete information about:

(1) the nature and amount of the party's current employment income, government-entitlement income, and other income;

(2) the income of the party's spouse and whether that income is available to the party;

(3) real and personal property the party owns;

(4) cash the party holds and amounts on deposit that the party may withdraw;

(5) the party's other assets;

(6) the number and relationship to the party of any dependents;

(7) the nature and amount of the party's debts;

(8) the nature and amount of the party's monthly expenses;

(9) the party's ability to obtain a loan for court costs;

(10) whether an attorney is providing free legal services to the party without a contingent fee;

(11) whether an attorney has agreed to pay or advance court costs; and

(12) if applicable, the party's lack of the skill and access to equipment necessary to prepare the appendix, as required by Rule 38.5(d).

(c) *When and Where Affidavit Filed.*

(1) Appeals. An appellant must file the affidavit of indigence in the trial court with or before the notice of appeal. The prior filing of an affidavit of indigence in the trial court pursuant to Texas Rule of Civil Procedure 145 does not meet the requirements of this rule, which requires a separate affidavit and proof of current indigence, except in cases in which a presumption of indigence has been established as provided by Rule 20.1(a)(3). An appellee who is required to pay part of the cost of preparation of the record under Rule 34.5(b)(3) or 34.6(c)(3) must file an affidavit of indigence in the trial court within 15 days after the date when the appellee becomes responsible for paying that cost.

(2) Other Proceedings. In any other appellate court proceeding, except in cases in which a presumption of indigence has been established as provided by Rule 20.1(a)(3), a petitioner must file the affidavit of indigence in the court in which the proceeding is filed, with or before the document seeking relief. A respondent who requests preparation of a record in connection with an appellate court proceeding must file an affidavit of indigence in the appellate court within 15 days after the date when the respondent requests preparation of the record, except in cases in which a presumption of indigence has been established as provided by Rule 20.1(a)(3).

(3) Extension of Time. The appellate court may extend the time to file an affidavit of indigence if, within 15 days after the deadline for filing the affidavit, the party files in the appellate court a motion complying with Rule 10.5(b). But the court may not dismiss the appeal or affirm the trial court's judgment on the ground that the appellant has failed to file an affidavit or a sufficient affidavit of indigence unless the court has first provided the appellant notice of the deficiency and a reasonable time to remedy it.

(d) *Duty of Clerk.*

(1) Trial Court Clerk. If the affidavit of indigence is filed with the trial court clerk under (c)(1), the clerk must promptly send a copy of the affidavit to the appropriate court reporter.

(2) Appellate Court Clerk. If the affidavit of indigence is filed with the appellate court clerk and if the filing party is requesting the preparation of a record, the appellate court clerk must:

(A) send a copy of the affidavit to the trial court clerk and the appropriate court reporter; and

(B) send to the trial court clerk, the court reporter, and all parties, a notice stating the deadline for filing a contest to the affidavit of indigence.

(e) *Contest to Indigence.*

(1) If Affidavit Filed. The clerk, the court reporter, the court recorder, or any party may challenge an affidavit that is not accompanied by a TAJF certificate by filing—in the court in which the affidavit was filed—a contest to the affidavit. The contest must be filed on or before the date set by the clerk if the affidavit was filed in the appellate court, or within 10 days after the date when the affidavit was filed if the affidavit was filed in the trial court. The contest need not be sworn.

(2) If Indigence Presumed. The clerk, the court reporter, the court recorder, or any party may challenge a presumption of indigence that has been established as provided by Rule 20.1(a)(3) by filing a contest in the trial court. The contest must be filed within three days after a notice of appeal is filed. The contest must state specific facts demonstrating a good faith belief that the parent is no longer indigent due to a material and substantial change in the parent's financial circumstances. The contest need not be sworn.

(f) *No Contest Filed.* Unless a contest is timely filed, no hearing will be conducted, the affidavit's allegations will be deemed true, and the party will be allowed to proceed without advance payment of costs.

(g) *Burden of Proof.*

(1) If Affidavit Filed. If a contest is filed, the party who filed the affidavit of indigence must prove the affidavit's allegations. If the indigent party is incarcerated at the time the hearing on a contest is held, the affidavit must be considered as evidence and is sufficient to meet the indigent party's burden to present evidence without the indigent party's attending the hearing.

(2) If Indigence Presumed. If a presumption of indigence has been established as provided by Rule 20.1(a)(3). the party filing the contest must prove that the parent is no longer indigent due to a material and substantial change in the parent's financial circumstances since the most recent determination of indigence.

(h) *Decision in Appellate Court.* If the affidavit of indigence is filed in an appellate court and a contest is filed, the court may:

(1) conduct a hearing and decide the contest;

(2) decide the contest based on the affidavit and any other timely filed documents;

(3) request the written submission of additional evidence and, without conducting a hearing, decide the contest based on the evidence; or

(4) refer the matter to the trial court with instructions to hear evidence and grant the appropriate relief.

(i) *Hearing and Decision in the Trial Court.*

(1) Notice Required. If the affidavit of indigence is filed in the trial court or a presumption of indigence has been established as provided by Rule 20.1(a)(3) and a contest is filed, or if the appellate court refers a contest to the trial court, the trial court must set a hearing and notify the parties and the appropriate court reporter of the setting.

(2) Time for Hearing. The trial court must either conduct a hearing or sign an order extending the time to conduct a hearing:

(A) within 10 days after the contest was filed, if initially filed in the trial court; or

(B) within 10 days after the trial court received a contest referred from the appellate court.

(3) Extension of Time for Hearing. The time for conducting a hearing on the contest must not be extended for more than 20 days from the date the order is signed.

(4) Time for Written Decision; Effect. Unless—within the period set for the hearing—the trial court signs an order sustaining the contest, the affidavit's allegations will be deemed true or the presumption of indigence will continue unabated, and the party will be allowed to proceed without advance payment of costs.

(j) *Review of Trial Court's Decision.*

(1) Motion. If the trial court sustains a contest, the party claiming indigence may seek review of the court's order by filing a motion challenging the order with the appellate court without advance payment of costs.

(2) Time for Filing; Extension. The motion must be filed within 10 days after the order sustaining the contest is signed, or within 10 days after the notice of appeal is filed, whichever is later. The appellate court may extend the time for filing on motion complying with Rule 10.5(b).

(3) Record. Within three days after a motion is filed, the trial court clerk and court reporter, respectively, must prepare, certify, and file the clerk's record and reporter's record of the indigence hearing, if any, and the hearing on the contest. The record must be provided without advance payment of costs.

(4) Ruling by Operation of Law. If the appellate court does not deny the motion within 10 days after it is filed, the motion is granted by operation of law

(5) No Review of Order Overruling Contest. An order overruling a contest is not subject to appellate review.

(k) *Record to be Prepared Without Prepayment.* If a party establishes indigence, the trial court clerk and the court reporter must prepare the appellate record without prepayment.

(*l*) *Partial Payment of Costs.* If the party can pay or give security for some of the costs, the court must order the party, in writing, to pay or give security, or both, to the extent of the party's ability. The court will allocate the payment among the officials to whom payment is due.

(m) *Later Ability to Pay.* If a party who has proceeded in the appellate court without having to pay all the costs is later able to pay some or all of the costs, the appellate court may order the party to pay costs to the extent of the party's ability.

(n) *Costs Defined.* As used in this rule, costs means:

(1) a filing fee relating to the case in which the affidavit of inability is filed; and

(2) the charges for preparing the appellate record in that case.

Eff. Sept. 1, 1997. Amended by Supreme Court March 10, 2008, and Aug. 20, 2008, eff. Sept. 1, 2008. Approved by the Court of Criminal Appeals Sept. 30, 2008, eff. Sept. 30, 2008. Amended by Supreme Court Aug. 31, 2011, eff. Sept. 1, 2011; Feb. 13, 2012, eff. March 1, 2012.

Notes and Comments

Comment to 2008 change: Subdivision 20.1(a) is added to provide, as in Texas Rule of Civil Procedure 145, that an affidavit of indigence accompanied by an IOLTA or other Texas Access to Justice Foundation certificate cannot be challenged. Subdivision 20.1(c)(1) is revised to clarify that an affidavit of indigence filed to proceed in the trial court without advance payment of costs is insufficient to establish indigence on appeal; a separate affidavit must be filed with or before the notice of appeal. Subdivision 20.1(c)(3) is revised to provide that an appellate court must give an appellant who fails to file a proper appellate indigence affidavit notice of the defect and an opportunity to cure it before dismissing the appeal or affirming the judgment on that basis. *See Higgins v. Randall County Sheriff's Office*, 193 S.W.3d 898 (Tex. 2006). The limiting phrase "under (c)(2)" in Subdivision 20.1(d)(2) is deleted to clarify that the appellate clerk's duty to forward copies of the affidavit to the trial court clerk and the court reporter, along with a notice setting a deadline to contest the affidavit, applies to affidavits on appeal erroneously filed in the appellate court, not only to affidavits in other appellate proceedings properly filed in the appellate court under subdivision 20.1(c)(2). Although Subdivision 3.1(g) defines "court reporter" to include court recorder, subdivision 20.1(e) is amended to make clear that a court recorder can contest an affidavit.

20.2. Criminal Cases

Within the time for perfecting the appeal, an appellant who is unable to pay for the appellate record may, by motion and affidavit, ask the trial court to have the appellate record furnished without charge. If after hearing the motion the court finds that the appellant cannot pay or give security for the appellate record, the court must order the reporter to transcribe the proceedings. When the court certifies that the appellate record has been furnished to the appellant, the reporter must be paid from the general funds of the county in which the offense was committed, in the amount set by the trial court.

Eff. Sept. 1, 1997.

SECTION TWO. APPEALS FROM TRIAL COURT JUDGMENTS AND ORDERS

Rule 21. New Trials in Criminal Cases

Notes and Comments

Comment to 1997 change: Former Rules 30, 31, and 32 are merged. Paragraph (b)(6) of former Rule 30 is deleted because the rule-making authority of the Court of Criminal Appeals was withdrawn. *See* Code of Criminal Procedure article 40.001. Other nonsubstantive changes are made.

21.1. Definitions

(a) *New trial* means the rehearing of a criminal action after the trial court has, on the defendant's motion, set aside a finding or verdict of guilt.

(b) *New trial on punishment* means a new hearing of the punishment stage of a criminal action after the trial court has, on the defendant's motion, set aside an assessment of punishment without setting aside a finding or verdict of guilt.

Eff. Sept. 1, 1997. Amended by Court of Criminal Appeals Dec. 13, 2006, eff. Jan. 1, 2007.

21.2. When Motion for New Trial Required

A motion for new trial is a prerequisite to presenting a point of error on appeal only when necessary to adduce facts not in the record.

Eff. Sept. 1, 1997.

21.3. Grounds

The defendant must be granted a new trial, or a new trial on punishment, for any of the following reasons:

(a) except in a misdemeanor case in which the maximum possible punishment is a fine, when the defendant has been unlawfully tried in absentia or has been denied counsel;

(b) when the court has misdirected the jury about the law or has committed some other material error likely to injure the defendant's rights;

(c) when the verdict has been decided by lot or in any manner other than a fair expression of the jurors' opinion;

(d) when a juror has been bribed to convict or has been guilty of any other corrupt conduct;

(e) when a material defense witness has been kept from court by force, threats, or fraud, or when evidence tending to establish the defendant's innocence has been intentionally destroyed or withheld, thus preventing its production at trial;

(f) when, after retiring to deliberate, the jury has received other evidence; when a juror has talked with anyone about the case; or when a juror became so intoxicated that his or her vote was probably influenced as a result;

(g) when the jury has engaged in such misconduct that the defendant did not receive a fair and impartial trial; or

(h) when the verdict is contrary to the law and the evidence.

Eff. Sept. 1, 1997. Amended by Court of Criminal Appeals Dec. 13, 2006, eff. Jan. 1, 2007.

21.4. Time to File and Amend Motion

(a) *To File.* The defendant may file a motion for new trial before, but no later than 30 days after, the date when the trial court imposes or suspends sentence in open court.

(b) *To Amend.* Within 30 days after the date when the trial court imposes or suspends sentence in open court but before the court overrules any preceding motion for new trial, a defendant may, without leave of court, file one or more amended motions for new trial.

Eff. Sept. 1, 1997.

21.5. State May Controvert; Effect

The State may oppose in writing any reason the defendant sets forth in the motion for new trial. The State's having opposed a motion for new trial does not affect a defendant's responsibilities under 21.6.

Eff. Sept. 1, 1997.

21.6. Time to Present

The defendant must present the motion for new trial to the trial court within 10 days of filing it, unless the trial court in its discretion permits it to be presented and heard within 75 days from the date when the court imposes or suspends sentence in open court.

Eff. Sept. 1, 1997.

21.7. Types of Evidence Allowed at Hearing

The court may receive evidence by affidavit or otherwise.

Eff. Sept. 1, 1997.

21.8. Court's Ruling

(a) *Time to Rule.* The court must rule on a motion for new trial within 75 days after imposing or suspending sentence in open court.

(b) *Ruling.* In ruling on a motion for new trial, the court may make oral or written findings of fact. The granting of a motion for new trial must be accomplished by written order. A docket entry does not constitute a written order.

(c) *Failure to Rule.* A motion not timely ruled on by written order will be deemed denied when the period prescribed in (a) expires.

Eff. Sept. 1, 1997. Amended by Court of Criminal Appeals Dec. 13, 2006, eff. Jan. 1, 2007.

21.9. Granting a New Trial

(a) A court must grant a new trial when it has found a meritorious ground for new trial, but a court must grant only a new trial on punishment when it has found a ground that affected only the assessment of punishment.

(b) Granting a new trial restores the case to its position before the former trial, including, at any party's option, arraignment or pretrial proceedings initiated by that party.

(c) Granting a new trial on punishment restores the case to its position after the defendant was found guilty. Unless the defendant, State, and trial court all agree to a change, punishment in a new trial shall be assessed in accordance with the defendant's original election under article 37.07, § 2(b) of the Code of Criminal Procedure.

(d) A finding or verdict of guilt in the former trial must not be regarded as a presumption of guilt, nor may it be alluded to in the presence of the jury that hears the case on retrial of guilt. A finding of fact or an assessment of punishment in the former trial may not be alluded to in the presence of the jury that hears the case on retrial of punishment.

Eff. Sept. 1, 1997. Amended by Court of Criminal Appeals Dec. 13, 2006, eff. Jan. 1, 2007.

Rule 22. Arrest of Judgment in Criminal Cases

Notes and Comments

Comment to 1997 change: Former Rules 33, 34, and 35 are merged without substantive change.

22.1. Definition

Motion in arrest of judgment means a defendant's oral or written suggestion that, for reasons stated in the motion, the judgment rendered against the defendant was contrary to law. Such a motion is made in the trial court.

Eff. Sept. 1, 1997.

22.2. Grounds

The motion may be based on any of the following grounds:

(a) that the indictment or information is subject to an exception on substantive grounds;

(b) that in relation to the indictment or information a verdict is substantively defective; or

(c) that the judgment is invalid for some other reason.

Eff. Sept. 1, 1997.

22.3. Time to File Motion

A defendant may file a motion in arrest of judgment before, but no later than 30 days after, the date when the trial court imposes or suspends sentence in open court.

Eff. Sept. 1, 1997.

22.4. Court's Ruling

(a) *Time to Rule; Form of Ruling.* The court must rule on a motion in arrest of judgment within 75 days after imposing or suspending sentence in open court. The ruling may be oral or in writing.

(b) *Failure to Rule.* A motion not timely ruled on will be deemed denied when the period prescribed in (a) expires.

Eff. Sept. 1, 1997.

22.5. Effect of Denying

For purposes of the defendant's giving notice of appeal, an order denying a motion in arrest of judgment will be considered an order denying a motion for new trial.

Eff. Sept. 1, 1997.

22.6. Effect of Granting

(a) *Defendant Restored.* If judgment is arrested, the defendant is restored to the position that he or she had before the indictment or information was presented.

(b) *Defendant Discharged or Remanded.* If the judgment is arrested, the defendant will be discharged. But the trial court may remand the defendant to custody or fix bail if the court determines, from the evidence adduced at trial, that the defendant may be convicted on a proper indictment or information, or on a proper verdict in relation to the indictment or information.

Eff. Sept 1, 1997.

Rule 23. Nunc Pro Tunc Proceedings in Criminal Cases

Notes and Comments

Comment to 1997 change: This is former Rule 36. The rule is amended without substantive change.

23.1. Judgment and Sentence

Unless the trial court has granted a new trial or arrested the judgment, or unless the defendant has appealed, a failure to render judgment and pronounce sentence may be corrected at any time by the court's doing so.

Eff. Sept. 1, 1997.

23.2. Credit on Sentence

When sentence is pronounced, the trial court must give the defendant credit on that sentence for:

(a) all time the defendant has been confined since the time when judgment and sentence should have been entered and pronounced; and

(b) all time between the defendant's arrest and confinement to the time when judgment and sentence should have been entered and pronounced.

Eff. Sept. 1, 1997.

Rule 24. Suspension of Enforcement of Judgment Pending Appeal in Civil Cases

Notes and Comments

Comment to 1997 change: Former Rules 47, 48, and 49 are merged. The rule is substantially revised. Paragraph 24.1(a) now provides for superseding the judgment by agreement. Paragraph 24.1(c) is taken from former Rule 48 and provides for a deposit in lieu of the bond, including specific provisions for the release of the deposit. Paragraph 24.1(d) provides the conditions for the surety to honor the bond and for the deposit to be paid to the judgment creditor. In subdivision 24.2, the provisions for determining the amount of the bond or deposit are simplified. All provisions regarding superseding a judgment for an interest in property are merged into subparagraph 24.2(a)(2). The procedure for allowing security in a lesser amount is moved to paragraph 24.2(b) and is made applicable to all judgments. Subdivision 24.4 is taken from former Rule 49. The procedure for appellate review is more precisely stated.

24.1. Suspension of Enforcement

(a) *Methods.* Unless the law or these rules provide otherwise, a judgment debtor may supersede the judgment by:

(1) filing with the trial court clerk a written agreement with the judgment creditor for suspending enforcement of the judgment;

(2) filing with the trial court clerk a good and sufficient bond;

(3) making a deposit with the trial court clerk in lieu of a bond; or

(4) providing alternate security ordered by the court.

(b) *Bonds.*

(1) A bond must be:

(A) in the amount required by 24.2;

(B) payable to the judgment creditor;

(C) signed by the judgment debtor or the debtor's agent;

(D) signed by a sufficient surety or sureties as obligors; and

(E) conditioned as required by (d).

(2) To be effective a bond must be approved by the trial court clerk. On motion of any party, the trial court will review the bond.

(c) *Deposit in Lieu of Bond.*

(1) Types of Deposits. Instead of filing a surety bond, a party may deposit with the trial court clerk:

(A) cash;

(B) a cashier's check payable to the clerk, drawn on any federally insured and federally or state-chartered bank or savings-and-loan association; or

(C) with leave of court, a negotiable obligation of the federal government or of any federally insured and federally or state-chartered bank or savings-and-loan association.

(2) Amount of Deposit. The deposit must be in the amount required by 24.2.

(3) Clerk's Duties; Interest. The clerk must promptly deposit any cash or a cashier's check in accordance with law. The clerk must hold the deposit until the conditions of liability in (d) are extinguished. The clerk must then release any remaining funds in the deposit to the judgment debtor.

(d) *Conditions of Liability.* The surety or sureties on a bond, any deposit in lieu of a bond, or any alternate security ordered by the court is subject to liability for all damages and costs that may be awarded against the debtor—up to the amount of the bond, deposit, or security—if:

(1) the debtor does not perfect an appeal or the debtor's appeal is dismissed, and the debtor does not perform the trial court's judgment;

(2) the debtor does not perform an adverse judgment final on appeal; or

(3) the judgment is for the recovery of an interest in real or personal property, and the debtor does not pay the creditor the value of the property interest's rent or revenue during the pendency of the appeal.

(e) *Orders of Trial Court.* The trial court may make any order necessary to adequately protect the judgment creditor against loss or damage that the appeal might cause.

(f) *Effect of Supersedeas.* Enforcement of a judgment must be suspended if the judgment is superseded. Enforcement begun before the judgment is superseded must cease when the judgment is superseded. If execution has been issued, the clerk will promptly issue a writ of supersedeas.

Eff. Sept. 1, 1997.

24.2. Amount of Bond, Deposit or Security

(a) *Type of Judgment.*

(1) For Recovery of Money. When the judgment is for money, the amount of the bond, deposit, or security must equal the sum of compensatory damages awarded in the judgment, interest for the estimated duration of the appeal, and costs awarded in the judgment. But the amount must not exceed the lesser of:

(A) 50 percent of the judgment debtor's current net worth; or

(B) 25 million dollars.

(2) For Recovery of Property. When the judgment is for the recovery of an interest in real or personal property, the trial court will determine the type of security that the judgment debtor must post. The amount of that security must be at least:

(A) the value of the property interest's rent or revenue, if the property interest is real; or

(B) the value of the property interest on the date when the court rendered judgment, if the property interest is personal.

(3) Other Judgment. When the judgment is for something other than money or an interest in property, the trial court must set the amount and type of security that the judgment debtor must post. The security must adequately protect the judgment creditor against loss or damage that the appeal might cause. But the trial court may decline to permit the judgment to be superseded if the judgment creditor posts security ordered by the trial court in an amount and type that will secure the judgment debtor against any loss or damage caused by the relief granted the judgment creditor if an appellate court determines, on final disposition, that that relief was improper.

(4) Conservatorship or Custody. When the judgment involves the conservatorship or custody of a minor or other person under legal disability, enforcement of the judgment will not be suspended, with or without security, unless ordered by the trial court. But upon a proper showing, the appellate court may suspend enforcement of the judgment with or without security.

(5) For a Governmental Entity. When a judgment in favor of a governmental entity in its governmental capacity is one in which the entity has no pecuniary interest, the trial court must determine whether to suspend enforcement, with or without

security, taking into account the harm that is likely to result to the judgment debtor if enforcement is not suspended, and the harm that is likely to result to others if enforcement is suspended. The appellate court may review the trial court's determination and suspend enforcement of the judgment, with or without security, or refuse to suspend the judgment. If security is required, recovery is limited to the governmental entity's actual damages resulting from suspension of the judgment.

(b) *Lesser Amount.* The trial court must lower the amount of security required by (a) to an amount that will not cause the judgment debtor substantial economic harm if, after notice to all parties and a hearing, the court finds that posting a bond, deposit, or security in the amount required by (a) is likely to cause the judgment debtor substantial economic harm.

(c) *Determination of Net Worth.*

(1) Judgment Debtor's Affidavit Required; Contents; Prima Facie Evidence. A judgment debtor who provides a bond, deposit, or security under (a)(1)(A) in an amount based on the debtor's net worth must simultaneously file with the trial court clerk an affidavit that states the debtor's net worth and states complete, detailed information concerning the debtor's assets and liabilities from which net worth can be ascertained. An affidavit that meets these requirements is prima facie evidence of the debtor's net worth for the purpose of establishing the amount of the bond, deposit, or security required to suspend enforcement of the judgment. A trial court clerk must receive and file a net-worth affidavit tendered for filing by a judgment debtor.

(2) Contest; Discovery. A judgment creditor may file a contest to the debtor's claimed net worth. The contest need not be sworn. The creditor may conduct reasonable discovery concerning the judgment debtor's net worth.

(3) Hearing; Burden of Proof; Findings; Additional Security. The trial court must hear a judgment creditor's contest of the judgment debtor's claimed net worth promptly after any discovery has been completed. The judgment debtor has the burden of proving net worth. The trial court must issue an order that states the debtor's net worth and states with particularity the factual basis for that determination. If the trial court orders additional or other security to supersede the judgment, the enforcement of the judgment will be suspended for twenty days after the trial court's order. If the judgment debtor does not comply with the order within that period, the judgment may be enforced against the judgment debtor.

(d) *Injunction.* The trial court may enjoin the judgment debtor from dissipating or transferring assets to avoid satisfaction of the judgment, but the trial court may not make any order that interferes with the judgment debtor's use, transfer, conveyance, or dissipation of assets in the normal course of business.

Eff. Sept. 1, 1997. Amended by Supreme Court Aug. 29, 2003 and Sept. 10, 2003, eff. Sept. 1, 2003; March 10, 2008, and Aug. 20, 2008, eff. Sept. 1, 2008. Approved by Court of Criminal Appeals Sept. 30, 2008, eff. Sept. 30, 2008.

Notes and Comments

Comment to 2008 change: Subdivision 24.2(c) is amended to clarify the procedure in determining net worth. A debtor's affidavit of net worth must be detailed, but the clerk must file what is tendered without determining whether it complies with the rule. If the trial court orders that additional or other security be given, the debtor is afforded time to comply. Subdivision 24.4(a) is revised to clarify that a party seeking relief from a supersedeas ruling should file a motion in the court of appeals that has or presumably will have jurisdiction of the appeal. After the court of appeals has ruled, a party may seek review by filing a petition for writ of mandamus in the Supreme Court. *See In re Smith / In re Main Place Custom Homes, Inc.*, 192 S.W.3d 564, 568 (Tex. 2006) (per curiam).

24.3. Continuing Trial Court Jurisdiction; Duties of Judgment Debtor

(a) *Continuing Jurisdiction.* Even after the trial court's plenary power expires, the trial court has continuing jurisdiction to do the following:

(1) order the amount and type of security and decide the sufficiency of sureties; and

(2) if circumstances change, modify the amount or type of security required to continue the suspension of a judgment's execution.

(b) *Duties of Judgment Debtor.* If, after jurisdiction attaches in an appellate court, the trial court orders or modifies the security or decides the sufficiency of sureties, the judgment debtor must notify the appellate court of the trial court's action.

Eff. Sept. 1, 1997.

24.4. Appellate Review

(a) *Motions; Review.* A party may seek review of the trial court's ruling by motion filed in the court of appeals with jurisdiction or potential jurisdiction over the appeal from the judgment in the case. A party may seek review of the court of appeals' ruling on the motion by petition for writ of mandamus in the Supreme Court. The appellate court may review:

(1) the sufficiency or excessiveness of the amount of security, but when the judgment is for money, the appellate court must not modify the amount of

security to exceed the limits imposed by Rule 24.2(a)(1);

(2) the sureties on any bond;

(3) the type of security;

(4) the determination whether to permit suspension of enforcement; and

(5) the trial court's exercise of discretion under Rule 24.3(a).

(b) *Grounds of Review.* Review may be based both on conditions as they existed at the time the trial court signed an order, and on changes in those conditions afterward.

(c) *Temporary Orders.* The appellate court may issue any temporary orders necessary to preserve the parties' rights.

(d) *Action by Appellate Court.* The motion must be heard at the earliest practicable time. The appellate court may require that the amount of a bond, deposit, or other security be increased or decreased, and that another bond, deposit, or security be provided and approved by the trial court clerk. The appellate court may require other changes in the trial court order. The appellate court may remand to the trial court for entry of findings of fact or for the taking of evidence.

(e) *Effect of Ruling.* If the appellate court orders additional or other security to supersede the judgment, enforcement will be suspended for 20 days after the appellate court's order. If the judgment debtor does not comply with the order within that period, the judgment may be enforced. When any additional bond, deposit, or security has been filed, the trial court clerk must notify the appellate court. The posting of additional security will not release the previously posted security or affect any alternative security arrangements that the judgment debtor previously made unless specifically ordered by the appellate court.

Eff. Sept. 1, 1997. Amended by Supreme Court Aug. 29, 2003, eff. Sept. 1, 2003; March 10, 2008, and Aug. 20, 2008, eff. Sept. 1, 2008. Approved by Court of Criminal Appeals Sept. 30, 2008, eff. Sept. 30, 2008.

Notes and Comments

Comment to 2008 change: Subdivision 24.2(c) is amended to clarify the procedure in determining net worth. A debtor's affidavit of net worth must be detailed, but the clerk must file what is tendered without determining whether it complies with the rule. If the trial court orders that additional or other security be given, the debtor is afforded time to comply. Subdivision 24.4(a) is revised to clarify that a party seeking relief from a supersedeas ruling should file a motion in the court of appeals that has or presumably will have jurisdiction of the appeal. After the court of appeals has ruled, a party may seek review by filing a petition for writ of mandamus in the Supreme Court. *See In re Smith / In re Main Place Custom Homes, Inc.*, 192 S.W.3d 564, 568 (Tex. 2006) (per curiam).

Rule 25. Perfecting Appeal

Notes and Comments

Comment on 1997 change: This is former Rule 40. In civil cases, the requirement of an appeal bond is repealed. Appeal is perfected by filing a notice of appeal. A notice must be filed by any party seeking to alter the trial court's judgment. The restricted appeal—formerly the appeal by writ of error—is perfected by filing a notice of appeal in the trial court as in other appeals. The contents of the notice of appeal is prescribed. The notice of limitation of appeal is repealed. In criminal cases, the rule is amended to apply to notices by the State, and to refer to additional statutory requirements for the State's notice. In felony cases in which the defendant waived trial by jury, pleaded guilty or nolo contendere, and received a punishment that did not exceed what the defendant agreed to in a plea bargain, the rule is amended to make clear that regardless of when the alleged error occurred, an appeal must be based on a jurisdictional defect or a written motion ruled on before trial, or be with the permission of the trial court.

25.1. Civil Cases

(a) *Notice of Appeal.* An appeal is perfected when a written notice of appeal is filed with the trial court clerk. If a notice of appeal is mistakenly filed with the appellate court, the notice is deemed to have been filed the same day with the trial court clerk, and the appellate clerk must immediately send the trial court clerk a copy of the notice.

(b) *Jurisdiction of Appellate Court.* The filing of a notice of appeal by any party invokes the appellate court's jurisdiction over all parties to the trial court's judgment or order appealed from. Any party's failure to take any other step required by these rules, including the failure of another party to perfect an appeal under (c), does not deprive the appellate court of jurisdiction but is ground only for the appellate court to act appropriately, including dismissing the appeal.

(c) *Who Must File Notice.* A party who seeks to alter the trial court's judgment or other appealable order must file a notice of appeal. Parties whose interests are aligned may file a joint notice of appeal. The appellate court may not grant a party who does not file a notice of appeal more favorable relief than did the trial court except for just cause.

(d) *Contents of Notice.* The notice of appeal must:

(1) identify the trial court and state the case's trial court number and style;

(2) state the date of the judgment or order appealed from;

(3) state that the party desires to appeal;

(4) state the court to which the appeal is taken unless the appeal is to either the First or Fourteenth Court of Appeals, in which case the notice must state that the appeal is to either of those courts;

(5) state the name of each party filing the notice;

(6) in an accelerated appeal, state that the appeal is accelerated and state whether it is a parental termination or child protection case, as defined in Rule 28.4;

(7) in a restricted appeal:

(A) state that the appellant is a party affected by the trial court's judgment but did not participate—either in person or through counsel—in the hearing that resulted in the judgment complained of;

(B) state that the appellant did not timely file either a postjudgment motion, request for findings of fact and conclusions of law, or notice of appeal; and

(C) be verified by the appellant if the appellant does not have counsel.

(8) state, if applicable, that the appellant is presumed indigent and may proceed without advance payment of costs as provided in Rule 20.1(a)(3).

(e) *Service of Notice.* The notice of appeal must be served on all parties to the trial court's final judgment or, in an interlocutory appeal, on all parties to the trial court proceeding.

(f) *Clerk's Duties.* The trial court clerk must immediately send a copy of the notice of appeal to the appellate court clerk and to the court reporter or court reporters responsible for preparing the reporter's record.

(g) *Amending the Notice.* An amended notice of appeal correcting a defect or omission in an earlier filed notice may be filed in the appellate court at any time before the appellant's brief is filed. The amended notice is subject to being struck for cause on the motion of any party affected by the amended notice. After the appellant's brief is filed, the notice may be amended only on leave of the appellate court and on such terms as the court may prescribe.

(h) *Enforcement of Judgment Not Suspended by Appeal.* The filing of a notice of appeal does not suspend enforcement of the judgment. Enforcement of the judgment may proceed unless:

(1) the judgment is superseded in accordance with Rule 24[1], or

(2) the appellant is entitled to supersede the judgment without security by filing a notice of appeal.

Eff. Sept. 1, 1997. Amended by Supreme Court Aug. 31, 2011, eff. Sept. 1, 2011; Feb. 13, 2012, eff. March 1, 2012.

1 Vernon's Ann.Rules App.Proc., rule 24.1 et seq.

25.2. Criminal Cases

(a) *Rights to Appeal.*

(1) Of the State. The State is entitled to appeal a court's order in a criminal case as provided by Code of Criminal Procedure article 44.01.

(2) Of the Defendant. A defendant in a criminal case has the right of appeal under Code of Criminal Procedure article 44.02 and these rules. The trial court shall enter a certification of the defendant's right of appeal each time it enters a judgment of guilt or other appealable order. In a plea bargain case—that is, a case in which a defendant's plea was guilty or nolo contendere and the punishment did not exceed the punishment recommended by the prosecutor and agreed to by the defendant—a defendant may appeal only:

(A) those matters that were raised by written motion filed and ruled on before trial, or

(B) after getting the trial court's permission to appeal.

(b) *Perfection of Appeal.* In a criminal case, appeal is perfected by timely filing a sufficient notice of appeal. In a death-penalty case it is unnecessary to file a notice of appeal, but, in every death-penalty case, the clerk of the trial court shall file a notice of conviction with the Court of Criminal Appeals within thirty days after the defendant is sentenced to death.

(c) *Form and Sufficiency of Notice.*

(1) Notice must be given in writing and filed with the trial court clerk. If the notice of appeal is received in the court of appeals, the clerk of that court shall immediately record on the notice the date that it was received and send the notice to the trial court clerk.

(2) Notice is sufficient if it shows the party's desire to appeal from the judgment or other appealable order, and, if the State is the appellant, the notice complies with Code of Criminal Procedure article 44.01.

(d) *Certification of Defendant's Rights of Appeal.* If the defendant is the appellant, the record must include the trial court's certification of the defendant's right of appeal under Rule 25.2(a)(2). The certification shall include a notice that the defendant has been informed of his rights concerning an appeal, as well as any right to file a *pro se* petition for discretionary review. This notification shall be signed by the defendant, with a copy given to him. The certification should be part of the record when notice is filed, but may be added by timely amendment or supplementation under this rule or Rule 34.5(c)(1) or Rule 37.1 or by order of the appellate court under Rule 34.5(c)(2). The appeal must be dismissed if a certification that shows the defendant has the right of appeal has not been made part of the record under these rules.

(e) *Clerk's Duties.* The trial court clerk must note on the copies of the notice of appeal and the trial court's certification of the defendant's right of appeal the case number and the date when each was filed. The clerk must then immediately send one copy of each to the clerk of the appropriate court of appeals and, if the defendant is the appellant, one copy of each to the State's attorney.

(f) *Amending the Notice or Certification.* An amended notice of appeal or trial court's certification of the defendant's right of appeal correcting a defect or omission in an earlier filed notice or certification, including a defect in the notification of the defendant's appellate rights, may be filed in the appellate court in accordance with Rule 37.1, or at any time before the appealing party's brief is filed if the court of appeals has not used Rule 37.1. The amended notice or certification is subject to being struck for cause on the motion of any party affected by the amended notice or certification. After the appealing party's brief is filed, the notice or certification may be amended only on leave of the appellate court and on such terms as the court may prescribe.

(g) *Effect of Appeal.* Once the record has been filed in the appellate court, all further proceedings in the trial court—except as provided otherwise by law or by these rules—will be suspended until the trial court receives the appellate-court mandate.

(h) *Advice of Right of Appeal.* When a court enters a judgment or other appealable order and the defendant has a right of appeal, the court (orally or in writing) shall advise the defendant of his right of appeal and of the requirements for timely filing a sufficient notice of appeal.

Eff. Sept. 1, 1997. Amended by Supreme Court Dec. 23, 2002, eff. Jan. 1, 2003; Aug. 20, 2008, eff. Sept. 1, 2008; Court of Criminal Appeals Dec. 13, 2006, eff. Jan. 1, 2007; May 2, 2007 and Aug. 20, 2007, eff. Sept. 1, 2007; June 30, 2008, eff. Sept. 1, 2008; Sept. 30, 2008, eff. Sept. 30, 2008.

Notes and Comments

Comment to 2002 change: Rule 25.2, for criminal cases, is amended. Subdivision 25.2(a) states the parties' rights of appeal that are established by Code of Criminal Procedure article 44.01 and by article 44.02, the proviso of which was repealed when rulemaking power was given to the Court of Criminal Appeals. Subdivision 25.2(b) is given the requirement that a notice of appeal be in "sufficient" form, which codifies the decisional law. The requirement in former subdivision 25.2(b)(3) that a plea-bargaining appellant's notice of appeal specify the right of appeal is replaced by a requirement in subdivision 25.2(d) that the trial court certify the defendant's right of appeal in every case in which a judgment or other appealable order is entered. The certificate should be signed at the time the judgment or other appealable order is pronounced. The form of certification of the defendant's right of appeal is provided in an appendix to these rules. If the record does not include the trial court's certification that the defendant has the right of appeal, the appeal must be dismissed. If a sufficient notice of appeal or certification is not filed after the appellate court deals with the defect (see Rules 34.5(c) and 37.1), preparation of an appellate record and representation by an appointed attorney may cease.

Rule 26. Time to Perfect Appeal

Notes and Comments

Comment to 1997 change: This is former Rule 41. All times for perfecting appeal in civil cases—including the time for perfecting a restricted appeal—are stated. An extension of time is available for all appeals. The provisions of former Rule 41(c) regarding prematurely filed documents are moved to Rule 27. Nonsubstantive changes are made in the rule for criminal cases.

26.1. Civil Cases

The notice of appeal must be filed within 30 days after the judgment is signed, except as follows:

(a) the notice of appeal must be filed within 90 days after the judgment is signed if any party timely files:

(1) a motion for new trial;

(2) a motion to modify the judgment;

(3) a motion to reinstate under Texas Rule of Civil Procedure 165a; or

(4) a request for findings of fact and conclusions of law if findings and conclusions either are required by the Rules of Civil Procedure or, if not required, could properly be considered by the appellate court;

(b) in an accelerated appeal, the notice of appeal must be filed within 20 days after the judgment or order is signed;

(c) in a restricted appeal, the notice of appeal must be filed within six months after the judgment or order is signed; and

(d) if any party timely files a notice of appeal, another party may file a notice of appeal within the applicable period stated above or 14 days after the first filed notice of appeal, whichever is later.

Eff. Sept. 1, 1997.

26.2. Criminal Cases

(a) *By the Defendant.* The notice of appeal must be filed:

(1) within 30 days after the day sentence is imposed or suspended in open court, or after the day the trial court enters an appealable order; or

(2) within 90 days after the day sentence is imposed or suspended in open court if the defendant timely files a motion for new trial.

(b) *By the State.* The notice of appeal must be filed within 20 days after the day the trial court enters the order, ruling, or sentence to be appealed.

Eff. Sept. 1, 1997. Amended by Court of Criminal Appeals March 4, 2008, and June 30, 2008, eff. Sept. 1, 2008 Sept. 30, 2008, eff. Sept. 30, 2008. Amended by Supreme Court March 10, 2008, and Aug. 20, 2008, eff. Sept. 1, 2008.

26.3. Extension of Time

The appellate court may extend the time to file the notice of appeal if, within 15 days after the deadline for filing the notice of appeal, the party:

(a) files in the trial court the notice of appeal; and

(b) files in the appellate court a motion complying with Rule 10.5(b).

Eff. Sept. 1, 1997.

Rule 27. Premature Filings

Notes and Comments

Comment to 1997 change: This rule is new and combines the provisions of former Rules 41(c) and 58.

27.1. Prematurely Filed Notice of Appeal

(a) *Civil Cases.* In a civil case, a prematurely filed notice of appeal is effective and deemed filed on the day of, but after, the event that begins the period for perfecting the appeal.

(b) *Criminal Cases.* In a criminal case, a prematurely filed notice of appeal is effective and deemed filed on the same day, but after, sentence is imposed or suspended in open court, or the appealable order is signed by the trial court. But a notice of appeal is not effective if filed before the trial court makes a finding of guilt or receives a jury verdict.

Eff. Sept. 1, 1997.

27.2. Other Premature Actions

The appellate court may treat actions taken before an appealable order is signed as relating to an appeal of that order and give them effect as if they had been taken after the order was signed. The appellate court may allow an appealed order that is not final to be modified so as to be made final and may allow the modified order and all proceedings relating to it to be included in a supplemental record.

Eff. Sept. 1, 1997.

27.3. If Appealed Order Modified or Vacated

After an order or judgment in a civil case has been appealed, if the trial court modifies the order or judgment, or if the trial court vacates the order or judgment and replaces it with another appealable order or judgment, the appellate court must treat the appeal as from the subsequent order or judgment and may treat actions relating to the appeal of the first order or judgment as relating to the appeal of the subsequent order or judgment. The subsequent order or judgment and actions relating to it may be included in the original or supplemental record. Any party may nonetheless appeal from the subsequent order or judgment.

Eff. Sept. 1, 1997.

Rule 28. Accelerated, Agreed, and Permissive Appeals in Civil Cases

Notes and Comments

Comment to 2011 Change: Section 51.014(d)–(f) of the Texas Civil Practice and Remedies Code, as amended in 2011, provides for appeals of orders not otherwise appealable when permitted by the trial court. The 2011 amendments, which explicitly apply only to cases commenced on or after September 1, 2011, eliminated the prior requirement that the parties agree to the appeal and reinstated a requirement that the court of appeals also permit the appeal. Act of May 25, 2011, 82nd Leg., R.S., ch. 203, §§ 3.01, 6.01 [HB 274], amending Act of May 27, 2005, 79th Leg. R.S., ch. 1051 [HB 1294], §§ 1–2, 2005 Tex. Gen. Laws 3512, 3512–3513 and Act of May 17, 2001, 77th Leg., R.S., ch. 1389 [HB 978], § 1, 2001 Tex. Gen. Laws 3575. The amendments necessitated the addition of Rule 28.3 and the adoption of Rule of Civil Procedure 168, which governs the procedure for obtaining permission to appeal from the trial court.

New Rule 28.3 applies only to appeals in cases that were filed in the trial court on or after September 1, 2011. Rule 28.2 applies only to appeals in cases that were filed in the trial court before September 1, 2011.

Rule of Civil Procedure 168 clarifies that the trial court's permission to appeal should be included in the order to be appealed rather than in a separate order. As stated in Rule 28.3(c), if a prior order containing the trial court's ruling is amended to include such permission, the time for appeal runs from the amended order. Rule 28.3(k) further clarifies that if the petition is granted, appeal is thereby perfected, and the appeal proceeds as an accelerated appeal, with all deadlines—including deadlines and obligations for preparing the record—running from the date the petition was granted. A separate notice of appeal need not be filed. The petition procedure in Rule 28.3 is intended to be similar to the Rule 53 procedure governing petitions for review in the Supreme Court.

Comment to 2008 change: Rule 28 is rewritten. Subdivision 28.1 more clearly defines accelerated appeals and provides a uniform appellate timetable. But many statutes that provide for accelerated or expedited appeals also set appellate timetables, and statutory deadlines govern over deadlines provided in the rule. Subdivision 28.2 provides procedures for an agreed appeal of an interlocutory order permitted by statute. Such appeals are now permitted under Section 51.014(d) of the Civil Practice and Remedies Code. The requirements for perfecting appeal are generally set out in Rule 25.1, and as provided there, only the notice of appeal is jurisdictional.

Comment to 1997 change: This is former Rule 42. A motion for new trial is now permitted in an appeal from an interlocutory order, but it does not extend the time to perfect appeal. The deadlines for filing items in an accelerated appeal are moved to other rules. *See* Rules 26.1, 35.1 and 38.6. Former Rule 42(b), regarding discretionary acceleration, is omitted as unnecessary. *See* Rule 40.1. The provision in former Rule 42(c) allowing the court to shorten the time to file briefs is omitted as unnecessary. *See* Rule 38.6.

28.1. Accelerated Appeal

(a) *Types of Accelerated Appeals.* Appeals from interlocutory orders (when allowed by statute), appeals in quo warranto proceedings, appeals required by statute to be accelerated or expedited, and appeals required by law to be filed or perfected within less than 30 days after the date of the order or judgment being appealed are accelerated appeals.

(b) *Perfection of Accelerated Appeal.* Unless otherwise provided by statute, an accelerated appeal is perfected by filing a notice of appeal in compliance with Rule 25.1 within the time allowed by Rule 26.1(b) or as extended by Rule 26.3. Filing a motion for new trial, any other post-trial motion, or a request for findings of fact will not extend the time to perfect an accelerated appeal.

(c) *Appeals of Interlocutory Orders.* The trial court need not file findings of fact and conclusions of law but may do so within 30 days after the order is signed.

(d) *Quo Warranto Appeals.* The trial court may grant a motion for new trial timely filed under Texas Rule of Civil Procedure 329b(a)–(b) until 50 days after the trial court's final judgment is signed. If not determined by signed written order within that period, the motion will be deemed overruled by operation of law on expiration of that period.

(e) *Record and Briefs.* In lieu of the clerk's record, the appellate court may hear an accelerated appeal on the original papers forwarded by the trial court or on sworn and uncontroverted copies of those papers. The appellate court may allow the case to be submitted without briefs. The deadlines and procedures for filing the record and briefs in an accelerated appeal are provided in Rules 35.1 and 38.6.

Eff. Sept. 1, 1997. Amended by Supreme Court March 10, 2008, Aug. 20, 2008, and Aug. 25, 2008, eff. Sept. 1, 2008. Approved by Court of Criminal Appeals Sept. 30, 2008, eff. Sept. 30, 2008. Amended by Supreme Court Sept. 9, 2011, eff. Sept. 9, 2011.

Notes and Comments

Comment to 2011 Change: Section 51.014(d)–(f) of the Texas Civil Practice and Remedies Code, as amended in 2011, provides for appeals of orders not otherwise appealable when permitted by the trial court. The 2011 amendments, which explicitly apply only to cases commenced on or after September 1, 2011, eliminated the prior requirement that the parties agree to the appeal and reinstated a requirement that the court of appeals also permit the appeal. Act of May 25, 2011, 82nd Leg., R.S., ch. 203, §§ 3.01, 6.01 [HB 274], amending Act of May 27, 2005, 79th Leg. R.S., ch. 1051 [HB 1294], §§ 1–2, 2005 Tex. Gen. Laws 3512, 3512–3513 and Act of May 17, 2001, 77th Leg., R.S., ch. 1389 [HB 978], § 1, 2001 Tex. Gen. Laws 3575. The amendments necessitated the addition of Rule 28.3 and the adoption of Rule of Civil Procedure 168, which governs the procedure for obtaining permission to appeal from the trial court.

New Rule 28.3 applies only to appeals in cases that were filed in the trial court on or after September 1, 2011. Rule 28.2 applies only to appeals in cases that were filed in the trial court before September 1, 2011.

Rule of Civil Procedure 168 clarifies that the trial court's permission to appeal should be included in the order to be appealed rather than in a separate order. As stated in Rule 28.3(c), if a prior order containing the trial court's ruling is amended to include such permission, the time for appeal runs from the amended order. Rule 28.3(k) further clarifies that if the petition is granted, appeal is thereby perfected, and the appeal proceeds as an accelerated appeal, with all deadlines—including deadlines and obligations for preparing the record—running from the date the petition was granted. A separate notice of appeal need not be filed. The petition procedure in Rule 28.3 is intended to be similar to the Rule 53 procedure governing petitions for review in the Supreme Court.

Comment to 2008 change: Rule 28 is rewritten. Subdivision 28.1 more clearly defines accelerated appeals and provides a uniform appellate timetable. But many statutes that provide for accelerated or expedited appeals also set appellate timetables, and statutory deadlines govern over deadlines provided in the rule. Subdivision 28.2 provides procedures for an agreed appeal of an interlocutory order permitted by statute. Such appeals are now permitted under Section 51.014(d) of the Civil Practice and Remedies Code. The requirements for perfecting appeal are generally set out in Rule

25.1, and as provided there, only the notice of appeal is jurisdictional.

28.2. Agreed Interlocutory Appeals in Civil Cases

(a) *Perfecting Appeal.* An agreed appeal of an interlocutory order permitted by statute must be perfected as provided in Rule 25.1. The notice of appeal must be filed no later than the 20th day after the date the trial court signs a written order granting permission to appeal, unless the court of appeals extends the time for filing pursuant to Rule 26.3.

(b) *Other Requirements.* In addition to perfecting appeal, the appellant must file with the clerk of the appellate court a docketing statement as provided in Rule 32.1 and pay to the clerk of the appellate court all required fees authorized to be collected by the clerk.

(c) *Contents of Notice.* The notice of accelerated appeal must contain, in addition to the items required by Rule 25.1(d), the following:

(1) a list of the names of all parties to the trial court proceeding and the names, addresses, and telefax numbers of all trial and appellate counsel;

(2) a copy of the trial court's order granting permission to appeal;

(3) a copy of the trial court order appealed from;

(4) a statement that all parties to the trial court proceeding agreed to the trial court's order granting permission to appeal;

(5) a statement that all parties to the trial court proceeding agreed that the order granting permission to appeal involves a controlling question of law as to which there is a substantial ground for difference of opinion;

(6) a brief statement of the issues or points presented; and

(7) a concise explanation of how an immediate appeal may materially advance the ultimate termination of the litigation.

(d) *Determination of Jurisdiction.* If the court of appeals determines that a notice of appeal filed under this rule does not demonstrate the court's jurisdiction, it may order the appellant to file an amended notice of appeal. On a party's motion or its own initiative, the court of appeals may also order the appellant or any other party to file briefing addressing whether the appeal meets the statutory requirements, and may direct the parties to file supporting evidence. If, after providing an opportunity to file an amended notice of appeal or briefing addressing potential jurisdictional defects, the court of appeals concludes that a jurisdictional defect exists, it may dismiss the appeal for want of jurisdiction at any stage of the appeal.

(e) *Record; Briefs.* The rules governing the filing of the appellate record and briefs in accelerated appeals apply. A party may address in its brief any issues related to the court of appeals' jurisdiction, including whether the appeal meets the statutory requirements.

(f) *No Automatic Stay of Proceedings in Trial Court.* An agreed appeal of an interlocutory order permitted by statute does not stay proceedings in the trial court except as agreed by the parties and ordered by the trial court or the court of appeals.

Eff. Sept. 1, 1997. Amended by Supreme Court March 10, 2008, and Aug. 20, 2008, eff. Sept. 1, 2008. Approved by Court of Criminal Appeals Sept. 30, 2008, eff. Sept. 30, 2008.

Notes and Comments

Comment to 2008 change: Rule 28 is rewritten. Subdivision 28.1 more clearly defines accelerated appeals and provides a uniform appellate timetable. But many statutes that provide for accelerated or expedited appeals also set appellate timetables, and statutory deadlines govern over deadlines provided in the rule. Subdivision 28.2 provides procedures for an agreed appeal of an interlocutory order permitted by statute. Such appeals are now permitted under Section 51.014(d) of the Civil Practice and Remedies Code. The requirements for perfecting appeal are generally set out in Rule 25.1, and as provided there, only the notice of appeal is jurisdictional.

28.3. Permissive Appeals in Civil Cases

(a) *Petition Required.* When a trial court has permitted an appeal from an interlocutory order that would not otherwise be appealable, a party seeking to appeal must petition the court of appeals for permission to appeal.

(b) *Where Filed.* The petition must be filed with the clerk of the court of appeals having appellate jurisdiction over the action in which the order to be appealed is issued. The First and Fourteenth Courts of Appeals must determine in which of those two courts a petition will be filed.

(c) *When Filed.* The petition must be filed within 15 days after the order to be appealed is signed. If the order is amended by the trial court, either on its own or in response to a party's motion, to include the court's permission to appeal, the time to petition the court of appeals runs from the date the amended order is signed.

(d) *Extension of Time to File Petition.* The court of appeals may extend the time to file the petition if the party:

(1) files the petition within 15 days after the deadline, and

(2) files a motion complying with Rule 10.5(b).

(e) *Contents.* The petition must:

(1) contain the information required by Rule 25.1(d) to be included in a notice of appeal:

(2) attach a copy of the order from which appeal is sought:

(3) contain a table of contents, index of authorities, issues presented, and a statement of facts; and

(4) argue clearly and concisely why the order to be appealed involves a controlling question of law as to which there is a substantial ground for difference of opinion and how an immediate appeal from the order may materially advance the ultimate termination of the litigation.

(f) *Response; Reply; Cross–Petition; Time for Filing.* If any party timely files a petition, any other party may file a response or a cross-petition within 10 days. A party may file a response to a cross-petition within 10 days of the date the cross-petition is filed. A petitioner or cross-petitioner may reply to any matter in a response within 7 days of the date the response is filed. The court of appeals may extend the time to file a response, reply, and cross-petition.

(g) *Length of Petition, Cross–Petition, Response, and Reply.* A petition, cross-petition, response, and reply must comply with the length limitations in Rule 9.4(i)(2)(D)–(E).

(h) *Service.* A petition, cross-petition, response, and reply must be served on all parties to the trial court proceeding.

(i) *Docketing Statement.* Upon filing the petition, the petitioner must file the docketing statement required by Rule 32.1.

(j) *Time for Determination.* Unless the court of appeals orders otherwise, a petition, and any cross-petition, response, and reply, will be determined without oral argument, no earlier than 10 days after the petition is filed.

(k) *When Petition Granted.* If the petition is granted, a notice of appeal is deemed to have been filed under Rule 26.1(b) on that date, and the appeal is governed by the rules for accelerated appeals. A separate notice of appeal need not be filed. A copy of the order granting the petition must be filed with the trial court clerk.

Adopted by Supreme Court Sept. 9, 2011, eff. Sept. 9, 2011. Amended by order of March 4, 2013, eff. immediately.

Notes and Comments

Comment to 2011 Change: Section 51.014(d)–(f) of the Texas Civil Practice and Remedies Code, as amended in 2011, provides for appeals of orders not otherwise appealable when permitted by the trial court. The 2011 amendments, which explicitly apply only to cases commenced on or after September 1, 2011, eliminated the prior requirement that the parties agree to the appeal and reinstated a requirement that the court of appeals also permit the appeal. Act of May 25, 2011, 82nd Leg., R.S., ch. 203, §§ 3.01, 6.01 [HB 274], amending Act of May 27, 2005, 79th Leg. R.S., ch. 1051 [HB 1294], §§ 1–2, 2005 Tex. Gen. Laws 3512, 3512–3513 and Act of May 17, 2001, 77th Leg., R.S., ch. 1389 [HB 978], § 1, 2001 Tex. Gen. Laws 3575. The amendments necessitated the addition of Rule 28.3 and the adoption of Rule of Civil Procedure 168, which governs the procedure for obtaining permission to appeal from the trial court.

New Rule 28.3 applies only to appeals in cases that were filed in the trial court on or after September 1, 2011. Rule 28.2 applies only to appeals in cases that were filed in the trial court before September 1, 2011.

Rule of Civil Procedure 168 clarifies that the trial court's permission to appeal should be included in the order to be appealed rather than in a separate order. As stated in Rule 28.3(c), if a prior order containing the trial court's ruling is amended to include such permission, the time for appeal runs from the amended order. Rule 28.3(k) further clarifies that if the petition is granted, appeal is thereby perfected, and the appeal proceeds as an accelerated appeal, with all deadlines—including deadlines and obligations for preparing the record—running from the date the petition was granted. A separate notice of appeal need not be filed. The petition procedure in Rule 28.3 is intended to be similar to the Rule 53 procedure governing petitions for review in the Supreme Court.

28.4. Accelerated Appeals in Parental Termination and Child Protection Cases

(a) *Application and Definitions.*

(1) Appeals in parental termination and child protection cases are governed by the rules of appellate procedure for accelerated appeals, except as otherwise provided in Rule 28.4.

(2) In Rule 28.4:

(A) a "parental termination case" means a suit in which termination of the parent-child relationship is at issue.

(B) a "child protection case" means a suit affecting the parent-child relationship filed by a governmental entity for managing conservatorship.

(b) *Appellate Record.*

(1) Responsibility for Preparation of Reporter's Record. In addition to the responsibility imposed on the trial court in Rule 35.3(c). when the reporter's responsibility to prepare, certify and timely file the reporter's record arises under Rule 35.3(b) the trial court must direct the official or deputy report-

er to immediately commence the preparation of the reporter's record. The trial court must arrange for a substitute reporter, if necessary.

(2) Extension of Time. The appellate court may grant an extension of time to file a record under Rule 35.3(c); however, the extension or extensions granted must not exceed 30 days cumulatively, absent extraordinary circumstances.

(3) Restriction on Preparation Inapplicable. Section 13.003 of the Civil Practice & Remedies Code does not apply to an appeal from a parental termination or child protection case.

(c) *Remand for New Trial.* If the judgment of the appellate court reverses and remands a parental termination or child protection case for a new trial, the judgment must instruct the trial court to commence the new trial no later than 180 days after the mandate is issued by the appellate court.

Adopted by order of Supreme Court Feb. 13, 2012, eff. March 1, 2012.

Rule 29. Orders Pending Interlocutory Appeal in Civil Cases

Notes and Comments

Comment to 1997 change: This is former Rule 43. The provision in the former rule that an appeal from an order certifying a class suspends the order is repealed. The provision in the former rule that an order denying interlocutory relief cannot be suspended is omitted as unnecessary because the rule provides for superseding only orders granting relief. No substantive change is intended. The provision in former Rule 43(d) prohibiting the trial court from making an order granting substantially the same relief as the order appealed is repealed as being too broad. The provisions of former Rule 43(g) regarding the mandate are moved to Rule 18.6 and 18.7. The provision of former Rule 43(h) regarding rehearings is moved to Rule 49.4.

29.1. Effect of Appeal

Perfecting an appeal from an order granting interlocutory relief does not suspend the order appealed from unless:

(a) the order is superseded in accordance with 29.2; or

(b) the appellant is entitled to supersede the order without security by filing a notice of appeal.

Eff. Sept. 1, 1997.

29.2. Security

The trial court may permit an order granting interlocutory relief to be superseded pending an appeal from the order, in which event the appellant may supersede the order in accordance with Rule 24.[1] If the trial court refuses to permit the appellant to supersede the order, the appellant may move the appellate court to review that decision for abuse of discretion.

Eff. Sept. 1, 1997.

[1] Vernon's Ann.Rules App.Proc., rule 24.1 et seq.

29.3. Temporary Orders of Appellate Court

When an appeal from an interlocutory order is perfected, the appellate court may make any temporary orders necessary to preserve the parties' rights until disposition of the appeal and may require appropriate security. But the appellate court must not suspend the trial court's order if the appellant's rights would be adequately protected by supersedeas or another order made under Rule 24.[1]

Eff. Sept. 1, 1997.

[1] Vernon's Ann.Rules App.Proc., rule 24.1 et seq.

29.4. Enforcement of Temporary Orders

While an appeal from an interlocutory order is pending, only the appellate court in which the appeal is pending may enforce the order. But the appellate court may refer any enforcement proceeding to the trial court with instructions to:

(a) hear evidence and grant appropriate relief; or

(b) make findings and recommendations and report them to the appellate court.

Eff. Sept. 1, 1997.

29.5. Further Proceedings in Trial Court

While an appeal from an interlocutory order is pending, the trial court retains jurisdiction of the case and unless prohibited by statute may make further orders, including one dissolving the order complained of on appeal. If permitted by law, the trial court may proceed with a trial on the merits. But the court must not make an order that:

(a) is inconsistent with any appellate court temporary order; or

(b) interferes with or impairs the jurisdiction of the appellate court or effectiveness of any relief sought or that may be granted on appeal.

Eff. Sept. 1, 1997. Amended by Supreme Court Dec. 23, 2002, eff. Jan. 1, 2003; March 10, 2008, and Aug. 20, 2008, eff. Sept. 1, 2008. Approved by Court of Criminal Appeals Sept. 30, 2008, eff. Sept. 30, 2008.

Notes and Comments

Comment to 2008 change: Rule 29.5 is amended to be consistent with Section 51.014(b) of the Civil Practice and Remedies Code, as amended in 2003, staying all proceedings in the trial court pending resolution of interlocutory appeals of class certification orders, denials of summary judgments based on assertions of immunity by governmental officers or employees, and orders granting or denying a governmental unit's plea to the jurisdiction.

Comment to 2002 change: Rule 29.5 is amended to acknowledge that a trial court may be prohibited by law from proceeding to trial during the pendency of an interlocutory appeal, as for example by section 51.014(b) of the Texas Civil Practice and Remedies Code.

29.6. Review of Further Orders

(a) *Motion to Review Further Orders.* While an appeal from an interlocutory order is pending, on a party's motion or on the appellate court's own initiative, the appellate court may review the following:

(1) a further appealable interlocutory order concerning the same subject matter; and

(2) any interlocutory order that interferes with or impairs the effectiveness of the relief sought or that may be granted on appeal.

(b) *Record.* The party filing the motion may rely on the original record or may file a supplemental record with the motion.

Eff. Sept. 1, 1997.

Rule 30. Restricted Appeal to Court of Appeals in Civil Cases

A party who did not participate—either in person or through counsel—in the hearing that resulted in the judgment complained of and who did not timely file a postjudgment motion or request for findings of fact and conclusions of law, or a notice of appeal within the time permitted by Rule 26.1(a), may file a notice of appeal within the time permitted by Rule 26.1(c). Restricted appeals replace writ of error appeals to the court of appeals. Statutes pertaining to writ of error appeals to the court of appeals apply equally to restricted appeals.

Eff. Sept. 1, 1997.

Notes and Comments

Comment to 1997 change: This is former Rule 45. The appeal by writ of error procedure is repealed. A procedure for an appeal filed within 6 months—called a restricted appeal—is substituted. This rule sets out who may take a restricted appeal. Rules 25.1 and 26.1 set out the method of perfection and the time for perfecting the appeal.

Rule 31. Appeals in Habeas Corpus, Bail, and Extradition Proceedings in Criminal Cases

Notes and Comments

Comment to 1997 change: This is former Rule 44. Since the purpose of the appeal is to do substantial justice, it is extended to both parties in recognition that both parties now have the right to appeal. Other nonsubstantive changes are made.

31.1. Filing the Record; Submission

When written notice of appeal from a judgment or order in a habeas corpus or bail proceeding is filed, the trial court clerk must prepare and certify the clerk's record and, if the appellant requests, the court reporter must prepare and certify a reporter's record. The clerk must send the clerk's record and the court reporter must send the reporter's record to the appellate court within 15 days after the notice of appeal is filed. On reasonable explanation, the appellate court may shorten or extend the time to file the record. When the appellate court receives the record, the court will—if it desires briefs—set the time for filing briefs, and will set the appeal for submission.

Eff. Sept. 1, 1997.

31.2. Hearing

An appeal in a habeas corpus or bail proceeding will be heard at the earliest practicable time. The applicant need not personally appear, and the appeal will be heard and determined upon the law and the facts shown by the record. The appellate court will not review any incidental question that might have arisen on the hearing of the application before the trial court. The sole purpose of the appeal is to do substantial justice to the parties.

Eff. Sept. 1, 1997.

31.3. Orders on Appeal

The appellate court will render whatever judgment and make whatever orders the law and the nature of the case require. The court may make an appropriate order relating to costs, whether allowing costs and fixing the amount, or allowing no costs.

Eff. Sept. 1, 1997.

31.4. Stay of Mandate

(a) *When Motion for Stay Required.* Despite Rule 18[1] or any other of these rules, in the following circumstances a party who in good faith intends to seek discretionary review must—within 15 days after the court of appeals renders judgment—file with the court of appeals clerk a motion for stay of mandate, to which is appended the party's petition for discretionary review showing reasons why the Court of Criminal Appeals should review the appellate court judgment:

(1) when a court of appeals affirms the judgment of the trial court in an extradition matter and thereby sanctions a defendant's extradition; or

(2) when a court of appeals reverses the trial court's judgment in a bail matter—including bail pending appeal under Code of Criminal Procedure article 44.04(g)—and thereby grants or reduces the amount of bail.

(b) *Determination of the Motion.* The clerk must promptly submit the motion and appendix to the court of appeals, or to one or more judges as the court deems appropriate, for immediate consideration and determination.

(1) If the motion for stay is granted, the clerk will immediately forward the petition for discretionary review to the clerk of the Court of Criminal Appeals.

(2) If the motion is denied, the clerk will issue a mandate in accordance with the court of appeals' judgment.

(c) *Denial of Stay.* If the motion for stay is denied under 31.4(b)(2), the losing party may then present the motion and appendix to the clerk of the Court of Criminal Appeals, who will promptly submit them to the Court, or to one or more judges as the Court deems appropriate, for immediate consideration and determination. The Court of Criminal Appeals may deny the motion or stay or recall the mandate. If the mandate is stayed or recalled, the clerk of the Court of Criminal Appeals will file the petition for discretionary review and process the case in accordance with Rule 68.7.

Eff. Sept. 1, 1997. Amended by Supreme Court Oct. 17, 2011, eff. Oct. 17, 2011.

[1] Vernon's Ann.Rules App.Proc., rule 18.1 et seq.

31.5. Judgment Conclusive

The court of appeals' judgment is final and conclusive if the Court of Criminal Appeals does not grant discretionary review. If the Court of Criminal Appeals grants discretionary review, that court's judgment is final and conclusive. In either case, no further application in the same case can be made for the writ unless the law provides otherwise.

Eff. Sept. 1, 1997.

31.6. Defendant Detained by Other Than Officer

If the defendant is held by a person other than an officer, the sheriff receiving the appellate court mandate so ordering must immediately cause the defendant to be discharged, for which discharge the mandate is sufficient authority.

Eff. Sept. 1, 1997.

31.7. Judgment to Be Certified

The appellate court clerk will certify the court's judgment to the officer holding the defendant in custody or, if the defendant is held by a person other than an officer, to the appropriate sheriff.

Eff. Sept. 1, 1997.

Rule 32. Docketing Statement

Notes and Comments

Comment to 1997 change: The rule is new.

32.1. Civil Cases

Promptly upon filing the notice of appeal in a civil case, the appellant must file in the appellate court a docketing statement that includes the following information:

(a)(1) if the appellant filing the statement has counsel, the name of that appellant and the name, address, telephone number, fax number, if any, and State Bar of Texas identification number of the appellant's lead counsel; or

(2) if the appellant filing the statement is not represented by an attorney, that party's name, address, telephone number, and fax number, if any;

(b) the date the notice of appeal was filed in the court and, if mailed to the trial court clerk, the date of mailing;

(c) the trial court's name and county, the name of the judge who tried the case, and the date the judgment or order appealed from was signed;

(d) the date of filing of any motion for new trial, motion to modify the judgment, request for findings of fact, motion to reinstate, or other filing that affects the time for perfecting the appeal;

(e) the names of all other parties to the trial court's judgment or the order appealed from, and:

(1) if represented by counsel, their lead counsel's names, addresses, telephone numbers, and fax numbers, if any; or

(2) if not represented by counsel, the name, address, and telephone number of the party, or a statement that the appellant diligently inquired but could not discover that information;

(f) the general nature of the case—for example, personal injury, breach of contract, or temporary injunction;

(g) whether the appeal's submission should be given priority, whether the appeal is an accelerated one under Rule 28 [1] or another rule or statute, and whether it is a parental termination or child protection case, as defined in Rule 28.4;

(h) whether the appellant has requested or will request a reporter's record, and whether the trial was electronically recorded;

(i) the name of the court reporter;

(j) whether the appellant intends to seek temporary or ancillary relief while the appeal is pending;

(k)(1) the date of filing of any affidavit of indigence;

(2) the date of filing of any contest;

(3) the date of any order on the contest; and

(4) whether the contest was sustained or overruled;

(*l*) whether the appellant has filed or will file a supersedeas bond; and

(m) any other information the appellate court requires.

Eff. Sept. 1, 1997. Amended by order of Supreme Court Feb. 13, 2012, eff. March 1, 2012.

1 Vernon's Ann.Rules App.Proc., rule 28.1 et seq.

32.2. Criminal Cases

Upon perfecting the appeal in a criminal case, the appellant must file in the appellate court a docketing statement that includes the following information:

(a)(1) if the appellant has counsel, the name of the appellant and the name, address, telephone number, fax number, if any, and State Bar of Texas identification number of the appellant's counsel, and whether the counsel is appointed or retained; or

(2) if the appellant is not represented by an attorney, that party's name, address, telephone number, and fax number, if any;

(b) the date the notice of appeal was filed in the trial court and, if mailed to the trial court clerk, the date of mailing;

(c) the trial court's name and county, and the name of the judge who tried the case;

(d) the date the trial court imposed or suspended sentence in open court, or the date the judgment or order appealed from was signed;

(e) the date of filing any motion for new trial, motion in arrest of judgment, or any other filing that affects the time for perfecting the appeal;

(f) the offense charged and the date of the offense;

(g) the defendant's plea;

(h) whether the trial was jury or nonjury;

(i) the punishment assessed;

(j) whether the appeal is from a pretrial order;

(k) whether the appeal involves the validity of a statute, ordinance, or rule;

(*l*) whether a reporter's record has been or will be requested, and whether the trial was electronically recorded;

(m) the name of the court reporter;

(n)(1) the dates of filing of any motion and affidavit of indigence;

(2) the date of any hearing;

(3) the date of any order; and

(4) whether the motion was granted or denied; and

(*o*) any other information the appellate court requires.

Eff. Sept. 1, 1997.

32.3. Supplemental Statements

Any party may file a statement supplementing or correcting the docketing statement.

Eff. Sept. 1, 1997.

32.4. Purpose of Statement

The docketing statement is for administrative purposes and does not affect the appellate court's jurisdiction.

Eff. Sept. 1, 1997.

Rule 33. Preservation of Appellate Complaints

Notes and Comments

Comment to 1997 change: This is former Rule 52. Subdivision 33.1 is rewritten. Former Rule 52(b), regarding offers of proof, is omitted as unnecessary. *See* TEX.R.CIV.EVID. 103; TEX. R.CRIM.EVID. 103. Subdivision 33.2 is also rewritten and the procedure is more definitely stated. Former Rule 52(d), regarding motions for new trial, is omitted as unnecessary. *See* TEX. R.CIV.P. 324(a) & (b).

33.1. Preservation; How Shown

(a) *In General.* As a prerequisite to presenting a complaint for appellate review, the record must show that:

(1) the complaint was made to the trial court by a timely request, objection, or motion that:

(A) stated the grounds for the ruling that the complaining party sought from the trial court with sufficient specificity to make the trial court aware of the complaint, unless the specific grounds were apparent from the context; and

(B) complied with the requirements of the Texas Rules of Civil or Criminal Evidence or the Texas Rules of Civil or Appellate Procedure; and

(2) the trial court:

(A) ruled on the request, objection, or motion, either expressly or implicitly; or

(B) refused to rule on the request, objection, or motion, and the complaining party objected to the refusal.

(b) *Ruling by Operation of Law.* In a civil case, the overruling by operation of law of a motion for new trial or a motion to modify the judgment preserves for appellate review a complaint properly made in the motion, unless taking evidence was necessary to properly present the complaint in the trial court.

(c) *Formal Exception and Separate Order Not Required.* Neither a formal exception to a trial court ruling or order nor a signed, separate order is required to preserve a complaint for appeal.

(d) *Sufficiency of Evidence Complaints in Nonjury Cases.* In a nonjury case, a complaint regarding the legal or factual insufficiency of the evidence—including a complaint that the damages found by the court are excessive or inadequate, as distinguished from a complaint that the trial court erred in refusing to amend a fact finding or to make an additional finding of fact—may be made for the first time on appeal in the complaining party's brief.

Eff. Sept. 1, 1997. Amended by Supreme Court Dec. 23, 2002, eff. Jan. 1, 2003.

Notes and Comments

Comment to 2002 change: The last sentence of former Rule 52(d) of the Rules of Appellate Procedure has been reinstated in substance.

33.2. Formal Bills of Exception

To complain on appeal about a matter that would not otherwise appear in the record, a party must file a formal bill of exception.

(a) *Form.* No particular form of words is required in a bill of exception. But the objection to the court's ruling or action, and the ruling complained of, must be stated with sufficient specificity to make the trial court aware of the complaint.

(b) *Evidence.* When the appellate record contains the evidence needed to explain a bill of exception, the bill itself need not repeat the evidence, and a party may attach and incorporate a transcription of the evidence certified by the court reporter.

(c) *Procedure.*

(1) The complaining party must first present a formal bill of exception to the trial court.

(2) If the parties agree on the contents of the bill of exception, the judge must sign the bill and file it with the trial court clerk. If the parties do not agree on the contents of the bill, the trial judge must—after notice and hearing—do one of the following things:

(A) sign the bill of exception and file it with the trial court clerk if the judge finds that it is correct;

(B) suggest to the complaining party those corrections to the bill that the judge believes are necessary to make it accurately reflect the proceedings in the trial court, and if the party agrees to the corrections, have the corrections made, sign the bill, and file it with the trial court clerk; or

(C) if the complaining party will not agree to the corrections suggested by the judge, return the bill to the complaining party with the judge's refusal written on it, and prepare, sign, and file with the trial court clerk such bill as will, in the judge's opinion, accurately reflect the proceedings in the trial court.

(3) If the complaining party is dissatisfied with the bill of exception filed by the judge under (2)(C), the party may file with the trial court clerk the bill that was rejected by the judge. That party must also file the affidavits of at least three people who observed the matter to which the bill of exception is addressed. The affidavits must attest to the correctness of the bill as presented by the party. The matters contained in that bill of exception may be controverted and maintained by additional affidavits filed by any party within ten days after the filing of that bill. The truth of the bill of exception will be determined by the appellate court.

(d) *Conflict.* If a formal bill of exception conflicts with the reporter's record, the bill controls.

(e) *Time to File.*

(1) Civil Cases. In a civil case, a formal bill of exception must be filed no later than 30 days after the filing party's notice of appeal is filed.

(2) Criminal Cases. In a criminal case, a formal bill of exception must be filed:

(A) no later than 60 days after the trial court pronounces or suspends sentence in open court; or

(B) if a motion for new trial has been timely filed, no later than 90 days after the trial court pronounces or suspends sentence in open court.

(3) Extension of Time. The appellate court may extend the time to file a formal bill of exception if, within 15 days after the deadline for filing the bill, the party files in the appellate court a motion complying with Rule 10.5(b).

(f) *Inclusion in Clerk's Record.* When filed, a formal bill of exception should be included in the appellate record.

Eff. Sept. 1, 1997.

Rule 34. Appellate Record

Notes and Comments

Comment to 1997 change: Former Rules 50, 51 and 53 are merged. *Clerk's record* is substituted for *transcript*, and *reporter's record* is substituted for *statement of facts* throughout the rules. In subdivision 34.2, the requisites of an agreed record are more clearly stated. Former Rule 50(d), regarding the burden to file a complete record, is repealed. Subdivision 34.4 is from former Rules 51(c) and 53(h). Former Rule 50(f), regarding a violation of the rules, is repealed. Subparagraph 34.5(b)(3) allows the appellate court to tax costs against a party for requiring unnecessary items to be included in the clerk's record. Paragraph 34.5(c) is new and provides for supplementation of the clerk's record. The provisions of paragraph 34.5(d) are from former Rule 55(b). The provisions of paragraph 34.5(e) are from former Rule 50(e). Paragraph 34.5(h) specifically allows the clerk to consult with the parties to determine the contents of the clerk's record. Paragraph 34.6(a), defining the reporter's record, is new. Former Rules 53(b) (Other Requests), (d) (Partial Statement), and (e) (Unnecessary Portions) are merged into paragraph 34.6(c). Paragraph 34.6(d) is new. Paragraph 34.6(e) is from former Rule 55. Paragraph 34.6(f) is from former Rule 50(d). The provisions of former Rules 53(f) (Certification by Court Reporter) and (h) (Form) are moved to the Order of the Supreme Court and the Court of Criminal Appeals on the preparation of the record. Former Rule 53(i) (Narrative Statement) is repealed. The provisions of former Rule 53(j) (Free Statement of Facts) are moved to Rule 20. Former Rule 53(k) (Duty of Appellant to File) is repealed; it is now the duty of the court reporter to file the reporter's record. Paragraph 34.6(g) is from former Rule 51(d). Former Rule 53(g) is now paragraph 34.6(i). Former Rule 53(*l*) is now paragraph 34.6(h). The need for two duplicate records in a death penalty case was created by the habeas corpus provision in Code of Criminal Procedure article 11.071.

34.1. Contents

The appellate record consists of the clerk's record and, if necessary to the appeal, the reporter's record. Even if more than one notice of appeal is filed, there should be only one appellate record in a case.

Eff. Sept. 1, 1997.

34.2. Agreed Record

By written stipulation filed with the trial court clerk, the parties may agree on the contents of the appellate record. An agreed record will be presumed to contain all evidence and filings relevant to the appeal. To request matter to be included in the agreed record, the parties must comply with the procedures in Rules 34.5 and 34.6.

Eff. Sept. 1, 1997.

34.3. Agreed Statement of the Case

In lieu of a reporter's record, the parties may agree on a brief statement of the case. The statement must be filed with the trial court clerk and included in the appellate record.

Eff. Sept. 1, 1997.

34.4. Form

The Supreme Court and Court of Criminal Appeals will prescribe the form of the appellate record.

Eff. Sept. 1, 1997.

34.5. Clerk's Record

(a) *Contents.* Unless the parties designate the filings in the appellate record by agreement under Rule 34.2, the record must include copies of the following:

(1) in civil cases, all pleadings on which the trial was held;

(2) in criminal cases, the indictment or information, any special plea or defense motion that was presented to the court and overruled, any written waiver, any written stipulation, and, in cases in which a plea of guilty or nolo contendere has been entered, any documents executed for the plea;

(3) the court's docket sheet;

(4) the court's charge and the jury's verdict, or the court's findings of fact and conclusions of law;

(5) the court's judgment or other order that is being appealed;

(6) any request for findings of fact and conclusions of law, any post-judgment motion, and the court's order on the motion;

(7) the notice of appeal;

(8) any formal bill of exception;

(9) any request for a reporter's record, including any statement of points or issues under Rule 34.6(c);

(10) any request for preparation of the clerk's record;

(11) in civil cases, a certified bill of costs including the cost of preparing the clerk's record, showing credits for payments made;

(12) in criminal cases the trial court's certification of the defendant's right of appeal under Rule 25.2; and

(13) subject to (b), any filing that a party designates to have included in the record.

(b) *Request for Additional Items.*

(1) Time for Request. At any time before the clerk's record is prepared, any party may file with the trial court clerk a written designation specifying items to be included in the record.

(2) Request Must Be Specific. A party requesting that an item be included in the clerk's record must specifically describe the item so that the clerk can readily identify it. The clerk will disregard a general designation, such as one for "all papers filed in the case."

(3) Requesting Unnecessary Items. In a civil case, if a party requests that more items than

necessary be included in the clerk's record or any supplement, the appellate court may—regardless of the appeal's outcome—require that party to pay the costs for the preparation of the unnecessary portion.

(4) Failure to Timely Request. An appellate court must not refuse to file the clerk's record or a supplemental clerk's record because of a failure to timely request items to be included in the clerk's record.

(c) *Supplementation.*

(1) If a relevant item has been omitted from the clerk's record, the trial court, the appellate court, or any party may by letter direct the trial court clerk to prepare, certify, and file in the appellate court a supplement containing the omitted item.

(2) If the appellate court in a criminal case orders the trial court to prepare and file findings of fact and conclusions of law as required by law, or certification of the defendant's right of appeal as required by these rules, the trial court clerk must prepare, certify, and file in the appellate court a supplemental clerk's record containing those findings and conclusions.

(3) Any supplemental clerk's record will be part of the appellate record.

(d) *Defects or Inaccuracies.* If the clerk's record is defective or inaccurate, the appellate clerk must inform the trial court clerk of the defect or inaccuracy and instruct the clerk to make the correction.

(e) *Clerk's Record Lost or Destroyed.* If a filing designated for inclusion in the clerk's record has been lost or destroyed, the parties may, by written stipulation, deliver a copy of that item to the trial court clerk for inclusion in the clerk's record or a supplement. If the parties cannot agree, the trial court must—on any party's motion or at the appellate court's request—determine what constitutes an accurate copy of the missing item and order it to be included in the clerk's record or a supplement.

(f) *Original Documents.* If the trial court determines that original documents filed with the trial court clerk should be inspected by the appellate court or sent to that court in lieu of copies, the trial court must make an order for the safekeeping, transportation, and return of those original documents. The order must list the original documents and briefly describe them. All the documents must be arranged in their listed sequence and bound firmly together. On any party's motion or its own initiative, the appellate court may direct the trial court clerk to send it any original document.

(g) *Additional Copies of Clerk's Record in Criminal Cases.* In a criminal case, the clerk's record must be made in duplicate, and in a case in which the death penalty was assessed, in triplicate. The trial court clerk must retain the copy or copies for the parties to use with the court's permission.

(h) *Clerk May Consult With Parties.* The clerk may consult with the parties concerning the contents of the clerk's record.

Eff. Sept. 1, 1997. Amended by Supreme Court Dec. 23, 2002, eff. Jan. 1, 2003.

Notes and Comments

Comment to 2002 change: Rule 34.5(a) is amended to require that the record in a criminal case include the certification of defendant's right of appeal; see Rule 25.2(d). Rule 34.5(c) is amended to make clear that an appellate court may order the trial court to make such a certification for inclusion in a supplemental clerk's record.

34.6. Reporter's Record

(a) *Contents.*

(1) Stenographic Recording. If the proceedings were stenographically recorded, the reporter's record consists of the court reporter's transcription of so much of the proceedings, and any of the exhibits, that the parties to the appeal designate.

(2) Electronic Recording. If the proceedings were electronically recorded, the reporter's record consists of certified copies of all tapes or other audio-storage devices on which the proceedings were recorded, any of the exhibits that the parties to the appeal designate, and certified copies of the logs prepared by the court recorder under Rule 13.2.

(b) *Request for Preparation.*

(1) Request to Court Reporter. At or before the time for perfecting the appeal, the appellant must request in writing that the official reporter prepare the reporter's record. The request must designate the exhibits to be included. A request to the court reporter—but not the court recorder—must also designate the portions of the proceedings to be included.

(2) Filing. The appellant must file a copy of the request with the trial court clerk.

(3) Failure to Timely Request. An appellate court must not refuse to file a reporter's record or a supplemental reporter's record because of a failure to timely request it.

(c) *Partial Reporter's Record.*

(1) Effect on Appellate Points or Issues. If the appellant requests a partial reporter's record, the appellant must include in the request a statement of

the points or issues to be presented on appeal and will then be limited to those points or issues.

(2) Other Parties May Designate Additions. Any other party may designate additional exhibits and portions of the testimony to be included in the reporter's record.

(3) Costs; Requesting Unnecessary Matter. Additions requested by another party must be included in the reporter's record at the appellant's cost. But if the trial court finds that all or part of the designated additions are unnecessary to the appeal, the trial court may order the other party to pay the costs for the preparation of the unnecessary additions. This paragraph does not affect the appellate court's power to tax costs differently.

(4) Presumptions. The appellate court must presume that the partial reporter's record designated by the parties constitutes the entire record for purposes of reviewing the stated points or issues. This presumption applies even if the statement includes a point or issue complaining of the legal or factual insufficiency of the evidence to support a specific factual finding identified in that point or issue.

(5) Criminal Cases. In a criminal case, if the statement contains a point complaining that the evidence is insufficient to support a finding of guilt, the record must include all the evidence admitted at the trial on the issue of guilt or innocence and punishment.

(d) *Supplementation.* If anything relevant is omitted from the reporter's record, the trial court, the appellate court, or any party may by letter direct the official court reporter to prepare, certify, and file in the appellate court a supplemental reporter's record containing the omitted items. Any supplemental reporter's record is part of the appellate record.

(e) *Inaccuracies in the Reporter's Record.*

(1) Correction of Inaccuracies by Agreement. The parties may agree to correct an inaccuracy in the reporter's record, including an exhibit, without the court reporter's recertification.

(2) Correction of Inaccuracies by Trial Court. If the parties cannot agree on whether or how to correct the reporter's record so that the text accurately discloses what occurred in the trial court and the exhibits are accurate, the trial court must—after notice and hearing—settle the dispute. If the court finds any inaccuracy, it must order the court reporter to conform the reporter's record (including text and any exhibits) to what occurred in the trial court, and to file certified corrections in the appellate court.

(3) Correction After Filing in Appellate Court. If the dispute arises after the reporter's record has been filed in the appellate court, that court may submit the dispute to the trial court for resolution. The trial court must then proceed as under subparagraph (e)(2).

(f) *Reporter's Record Lost or Destroyed.* An appellant is entitled to a new trial under the following circumstances:

(1) if the appellant has timely requested a reporter's record;

(2) if, without the appellant's fault, a significant exhibit or a significant portion of the court reporter's notes and records has been lost or destroyed or—if the proceedings were electronically recorded—a significant portion of the recording has been lost or destroyed or is inaudible;

(3) if the lost, destroyed, or inaudible portion of the reporter's record, or the lost or destroyed exhibit, is necessary to the appeal's resolution; and

(4) if the lost, destroyed or inaudible portion of the reporter's record cannot be replaced by agreement of the parties, or the lost or destroyed exhibit cannot be replaced either by agreement of the parties or with a copy determined by the trial court to accurately duplicate with reasonable certainty the original exhibit.

(g) *Original Exhibits.*

(1) Reporter May Use in Preparing Reporter's Record. At the court reporter's request, the trial court clerk must give all original exhibits to the reporter for use in preparing the reporter's record. Unless ordered to include original exhibits in the reporter's record, the court reporter must return the original exhibits to the clerk after copying them for inclusion in the reporter's record. If someone other than the trial court clerk possesses an original exhibit, either the trial court or the appellate court may order that person to deliver the exhibit to the trial court clerk.

(2) Use of Original Exhibits by Appellate Court. If the trial court determines that original exhibits should be inspected by the appellate court or sent to that court in lieu of copies, the trial court must make an order for the safekeeping, transportation, and return of those exhibits. The order must list the exhibits and briefly describe them. To the extent practicable, all the exhibits must be arranged in their listed order and bound firmly together before being sent to the appellate clerk. On any party's motion or its own initiative, the appellate court may direct the trial court clerk to send it any original exhibit.

(h) *Additional Copies of Reporter's Record in Criminal Cases.* In a criminal case in which a party requests a reporter's record, the court reporter must prepare a duplicate of the reporter's record and file it with the trial court clerk. In a case where the death penalty was assessed, the court reporter must prepare two duplicates of the reporter's record.

(i) *Supreme Court and Court of Criminal Appeals May Set Fee.* From time to time, the Supreme Court and the Court of Criminal Appeals may set the fee that the court reporters may charge for preparing the reporter's record.

Eff. Sept. 1, 1997. Amended by Supreme Court Dec. 23, 2002, eff. Jan. 1, 2003.

Notes and Comments

Comment to 2002 change: Subparagraphs 34.6(e) and (f) are amended to clarify the application to exhibits. The language is subparagraphs (e)(2) referring to the text of the record is simplified without substantive change. Subparagraph (e)(3) incorporates the procedures specified in (e)(2). The language in subparagraph (f) is clarified to require agreement only as to the portion of the text at issue, and to provide that the trial court may determine that a copy of an exhibit should be used even if the parties cannot agree.

Rule 35. Time to File Record; Responsibility for Filing Record

Notes and Comments

Comment to 1997 change: This is former Rule 54. In subdivision 35.1, the time to file the record in civil cases is based on the date the judgment is signed except in accelerated and restricted appeals, in which the time to file the record is based on the date the notice of appeal is filed. Subdivision 35.3 is new and makes it the responsibility of the trial court clerk and court reporter to file the record. Former Rule 54(c), providing for an extension of time to file the record, is repealed as unnecessary. The trial court clerk and court reporter should make arrangements with the court of appeals if additional time is required to file the record, as suggested in Rule 37.3.

35.1. Civil Cases

The appellate record must be filed in the appellate court within 60 days after the judgment is signed, except as follows:

(a) if Rule 26.1(a) applies, within 120 days after the judgment is signed;

(b) if Rule 26.1(b) applies, within 10 days after the notice of appeal is filed; or

(c) if Rule 26.1(c) applies, within 30 days after the notice of appeal is filed.

Eff. Sept. 1, 1997.

35.2. Criminal Cases

The appellate record must be filed in the appellate court:

(a) if a motion for new trial is not filed, within 60 days after the date the sentence is imposed or suspended in open court or the order appealed from is signed;

(b) if a timely motion for new trial is filed and denied, within 120 days after the date the sentence is imposed or suspended in open court; or

(c) if a motion for new trial is granted, within 60 days after the order granting the motion is signed.

Eff. Sept. 1, 1997.

35.3. Responsibility for Filing Record

(a) *Clerk's Record.* The trial court clerk is responsible for preparing, certifying, and timely filing the clerk's record if:

(1) a notice of appeal has been filed, and in criminal proceedings, the trial court has certified the defendant's right of appeal, as required by Rule 25.2(d); and

(2) the party responsible for paying for the preparation of the clerk's record has paid the clerk's fee, has made satisfactory arrangements with the clerk to pay the fee, or is entitled to appeal without paying the fee.

(b) *Reporter's Record.* The official or deputy reporter is responsible for preparing, certifying, and timely filing the reporter's record if:

(1) a notice of appeal has been filed;

(2) the appellant has requested that the reporter's record be prepared; and

(3) the party responsible for paying for the preparation of the reporter's record has paid the reporter's fee, or has made satisfactory arrangements with the reporter to pay the fee, or is entitled to appeal without paying the fee.

(c) *Courts to Ensure Record Timely Filed.* The trial and appellate courts are jointly responsible for ensuring that the appellate record is timely filed. The appellate court may extend the deadline to file the record if requested by the clerk or reporter. Each extension must not exceed 30 days in an ordinary or restricted appeal, or 10 days in an accelerated appeal. The appellate court must allow the record to be filed late when the delay is not the appellant's fault, and may do so when the delay is the appellant's fault.

The appellate court may enter any order necessary to ensure the timely filing of the appellate record.

Eff. Sept. 1, 1997. Amended by Court of Criminal Appeals Dec. 13, 2006, eff. Jan. 1, 2007. Amended by order of Supreme Court Feb. 13, 2012, eff. March 1, 2012.

Rule 36. Agency Record in Administrative Appeals

Notes and Comments

Comment to 1997 change: The rule is new.

36.1. Scope

This rule applies only to cases involving judicial review of state agency decisions in contested cases under the Administrative Procedure Act.

Eff. Sept. 1, 1997.

36.2. Inclusion in Appellate Record

The record of an agency proceeding filed in the trial court may be included in either the clerk's record or the reporter's record.

Eff. Sept. 1, 1997.

36.3. Correcting the Record.

(a) *Correction by Agreement.* At any stage of the proceeding, the parties may agree to correct an agency record filed under Section 2001.175(b) of the Government Code to ensure that the agency record accurately reflects the contested case proceedings before the agency. The court reporter need not recertify the agency record.

(b) *Correction by Trial Court.* If the parties cannot agree to a correction to the agency record, the appellate court must—on any party's motion or its own incentive—send the question to the trial court. After notice and hearing, the trial court must determine what constitutes an accurate copy of the agency record and order the agency to send an accurate copy to the clerk of the court in which the case is pending.

Eff. Sept. 1, 1997.

Rule 37. Duties of the Appellate Clerk on Receiving the Notice of Appeal and Record

Notes and Comments

Comment to 1997 change: Former Rules 56 and 57(a) are merged. Subdivisions 37.2 and 37.3 are new.

37.1. On Receiving the Notice of Appeal

If the appellate clerk determines that the notice of appeal or certification of defendant's right of appeal in a criminal case is defective, the clerk must notify the parties of the defect so that it can be remedied, if possible. If a proper notice of appeal or certification of a criminal defendant's right of appeal is not filed in the trial court within 30 days of the date of the clerk's notice, the clerk must refer the matter to the appellate court, which will make an appropriate order under this rule or Rule 34.5(c)(2).

Eff. Sept. 1, 1997. Amended by Supreme Court Dec. 23, 2002, eff. Jan. 1, 2003.

37.2. On Receiving the Record

On receiving the clerk's record or the reporter's record, the appellate clerk must determine whether each complies with the Supreme Court's and Court of Criminal Appeals' order on preparation of the record. If so, the clerk must endorse on each the date of receipt, file it, and notify the parties of the filing and the date. If not, the clerk must endorse on the clerk's record or reporter's record — whichever is defective — the date of receipt and return it to the official responsible for filing it. The appellate court clerk must specify the defects and instruct the official to correct the defects and return the record to the appellate court by a specified date. In a criminal case, the record must not be posted on the Internet.

Eff. Sept. 1, 1997. Amended by Court of Criminal Appeals Dec. 11, 2013, eff. Jan. 1, 2014.

37.3. If No Record Filed

(a) *Notice of Late Record.*

(1) Civil Cases. If the clerk's record or reporter's record has not been timely filed, the appellate clerk must send notice to the official responsible for filing it, stating that the record is late and requesting that the record be filed within 30 days if an ordinary or restricted appeal, or 10 days if an accelerated appeal. The appellate clerk must send a copy of this notice to the parties and the trial court. If the clerk does not receive the record within the stated period, the clerk must refer the matter to the appellate court. The court must make whatever order is appropriate to avoid further delay and to preserve the parties' rights.

(2) Criminal Cases. If the clerk's record or reporter's record has not been timely filed, the appellate court clerk must refer the matter to the appellate court. The court must make whatever order is appropriate to avoid further delay and to preserve the parties' rights.

(b) *If No Clerk's Record Filed Due to Appellant's Fault.* If the trial court clerk failed to file the clerk's record because the appellant failed to pay or make arrangements to pay the clerk's fee for preparing the clerk's record, the appellate court may—on a party's motion or its own initiative—dismiss the appeal for want of prosecution unless the appellant was entitled to proceed without payment of costs. The court must give the appellant a reasonable opportunity to cure before dismissal.

(c) *If No Reporter's Record Filed Due to Appellant's Fault.* Under the following circumstances, and if the clerk's record has been filed, the appellate court may—after first giving the appellant notice and a reasonable opportunity to cure—consider and decide those issues or points that do not require a reporter's record for a decision. The court may do this if no reporter's record has been filed because:

(1) the appellant failed to request a reporter's record; or

(2)(A) appellant failed to pay or make arrangements to pay the reporter's fee to prepare the reporter's record; and

(B) the appellant is not entitled to proceed without payment of costs.

Eff. Sept. 1, 1997.

Rule 38. Requisites of Briefs

Notes and Comments

Comment to 2008 change: A party may choose to include a statement in the brief regarding oral argument. The optional statement does not count toward the briefing page limit.

Comment to 1997 change: This is former Rule 74. The rule is substantially rewritten. Paragraph 38.1(e) now specifically allows a party to either present issues or points of error. Paragraphs 38.1(f) and (g) are new and require a brief to include a statement of facts and summary of the argument. Paragraph 38.2(b) is new and gives specific requirements for cross-points. *See also* TEX.R.CIV.P. 324(c). Subdivision 38.3 is new and provides for a reply brief. Subdivision 38.4 imposes a total brief limit of 90 pages on each party. Thus, if more than one party has filed a notice of appeal, there will be multiple appellant's, appellee's, and reply briefs, but each party is limited to a total of 90 pages. Subdivision 38.5 is new and provides for an appendix in cases recorded electronically in the trial court. Paragraph 38.6(b) now provides that the appellee has 30—rather than 25—days to file a brief. The provisions of former Rules 74(i) (Number of Copies), (j) (Briefs Typewritten or Printed), and (q) (Service of Briefs) are omitted as unnecessary. *See* Rule 9.

38.1. Appellant's Brief

The appellant's brief must, under appropriate headings and in the order here indicated, contain the following:

(a) *Identity of Parties and Counsel.* The brief must give a complete list of all parties to the trial court's judgment or order appealed from, and the names and addresses of all trial and appellate counsel, except as otherwise provided in Rule 9.8.

(b) *Table of Contents.* The brief must have a table of contents with references to the pages of the brief. The table of contents must indicate the subject matter of each issue or point, or group of issues or points.

(c) *Index of Authorities.* The brief must have an index of authorities arranged alphabetically and indicating the pages of the brief where the authorities are cited.

(d) *Statement of the Case.* The brief must state concisely the nature of the case (e.g., whether it is a suit for damages, on a note, or involving a murder prosecution), the course of proceedings, and the trial court's disposition of the case. The statement should be supported by record references, should seldom exceed one-half page, and should not discuss the facts.

(e) *Any Statement Regarding Oral Argument.* The brief may include a statement explaining why oral argument should or should not be permitted. Any such statement must not exceed one page and should address how the court's decisional process would, or would not, be aided by oral argument. As required by Rule 39.7, any party requesting oral argument must note that request on the front cover of the party's brief.

(f) *Issues Presented.* The brief must state concisely all issues or points presented for review. The statement of an issue or point will be treated as covering every subsidiary question that is fairly included.

(g) *Statement of Facts.* The brief must state concisely and without argument the facts pertinent to the issues or points presented. In a civil case, the court will accept as true the facts stated unless another party contradicts them. The statement must be supported by record references.

(h) *Summary of the Argument.* The brief must contain a succinct, clear, and accurate statement of the arguments made in the body of the brief. This summary must not merely repeat the issues or points presented for review.

(i) *Argument.* The brief must contain a clear and concise argument for the contentions made, with appropriate citations to authorities and to the record.

(j) *Prayer.* The brief must contain a short conclusion that clearly states the nature of the relief sought.

(k) *Appendix in Civil Cases.*

(1) Necessary Contents. Unless voluminous or impracticable, the appendix must contain a copy of:

(A) the trial court's judgment or other appealable order from which relief is sought;

(B) the jury charge and verdict, if any, or the trial court's findings of fact and conclusions of law, if any; and

(C) the text of any rule, regulation, ordinance, statute, constitutional provision, or other law (excluding case law) on which the argument is based, and the text of any contract or other document that is central to the argument.

(2) Optional Contents. The appendix may contain any other item pertinent to the issues or points presented for review, including copies or excerpts of relevant court opinions, laws, documents on which the suit was based, pleadings, excerpts from the reporter's record, and similar material. Items should not be included in the appendix to attempt to avoid the page limits for the brief.

Eff. Sept. 1, 1997. Amended by Supreme Court March 10, 2008, and Aug. 20, 2008, eff. Sept. 1, 2008. Approved by Court of Criminal Appeals Sept. 30, 2008, eff. Sept. 30, 2008.

38.2. Appellee's Brief

(a) *Form of Brief.*

(1) An appellee's brief must conform to the requirements of Rule 38.1, except that:

(A) the list of parties and counsel is not required unless necessary to supplement or correct the appellant's list;

(B) the appellee's brief need not include a statement of the case, a statement of the issues presented, or a statement of facts, unless the appellee is dissatisfied with that portion of the appellant's brief; and

(C) the appendix to the appellee's brief need not contain any item already contained in an appendix filed by the appellant.

(2) When practicable, the appellee's brief should respond to the appellant's issues or points in the order the appellant presented those issues or points.

(b) *Cross-Points.*

(1) Judgment Notwithstanding the Verdict. When the trial court renders judgment notwithstanding the verdict on one or more questions, the appellee must bring forward by cross-point any issue or point that would have vitiated the verdict or that would have prevented an affirmance of the judgment if the trial court had rendered judgment on the verdict. Failure to bring forward by cross-point an issue or point that would vitiate the verdict or prevent an affirmance of the judgment waives that complaint. Included in this requirement is a point that:

(A) the verdict or one or more jury findings have insufficient evidentiary support or are against the overwhelming preponderance of the evidence as a matter of fact; or

(B) the verdict should be set aside because of improper argument of counsel.

(2) When Evidentiary Hearing Needed. The appellate court must remand a case to the trial court to take evidence if:

(A) the appellate court has sustained a point raised by the appellant; and

(B) the appellee raised a cross-point that requires the taking of additional evidence.

Eff. Sept. 1, 1997. Amended by Supreme Court Dec. 23, 2002, eff. Jan. 1, 2003.

38.3. Reply Brief

The appellant may file a reply brief addressing any matter in the appellee's brief. However, the appellate court may consider and decide the case before a reply brief is filed.

Eff. Sept. 1, 1997.

38.4. Repealed by Order of Nov. 13, 2012, eff. Dec. 1, 2012

38.5. Appendix for Cases Recorded Electronically

In cases where the proceedings were electronically recorded, the following rules apply:

(a) *Appendix.*

(1) In General. At or before the time a party's brief is due, the party must file one copy of an appendix containing a transcription of all portions of the recording that the party considers relevant to the appellate issues or points. Unless another party objects, the transcription will be presumed accurate.

(2) Repetition Not Required. A party's appendix need not repeat evidence included in any previously filed appendix.

(3) Form. The form of the appendix and transcription must conform to any specifications of the Supreme Court and Court of Criminal Appeals concerning the form of the reporter's record except that it need not have the reporter's certificate.

(4) Notice. At the time the appendix is filed, the party must give written notice of the filing to all parties to the trial court's judgment or order. The notice must specify, by referring to the index numbers in the court recorder's logs, those parts of the recording that are included in the appendix. The filing party need not serve a copy of the appendix but must make a copy available to all parties for inspection and copying.

(b) *Presumptions.* The same presumptions that apply to a partial reporter's record under Rule 34.6(c)(4) apply to the parties' appendixes. The appellate court need not review any part of the electronic recording.

(c) *Supplemental Appendix.* The appellate court may direct or allow a party to file a supplemental appendix containing a transcription of additional portions of the recording.

(d) *Inability to Pay.* A party who cannot pay the cost of an appendix must file the affidavit provided for by Rule 20.[1] The party must also state in the affidavit or a supplemental affidavit that the party has neither the access to the equipment necessary nor the skill necessary to prepare the appendix. If a contest to the affidavit is not sustained by written order, the court recorder must transcribe or have transcribed those portions of the recording that the party designates and must file the transcription as that party's appendix, along with all exhibits.

(e) *Inaccuracies.*

(1) Correction by Agreement. The parties may agree to correct an inaccuracy in the transcription of the recording.

(2) Correction by Appellate or Trial Court. If the parties dispute whether an electronic recording or transcription accurately discloses what occurred in the trial court but cannot agree on corrections, the appellate court may:

(A) settle the dispute by reviewing the recording; or

(B) submit the dispute to the trial court, which must—after notice and hearing—settle the dispute and ensure that the recording or transcription is made to conform to what occurred in the trial court.

(f) *Costs.* The actual expense of preparing the appendixes or the amount prescribed for official reporters, whichever is less, is taxed as costs. The appellate court may disallow the cost of any portion of the appendixes that it considers surplusage or that does not conform to any specifications prescribed by the Supreme Court or Court of Criminal Appeals.

Eff. Sept. 1, 1997.

1 Vernon's Ann.Rules App.Proc., rule 20.1 et seq.

38.6. Time to File Briefs

(a) *Appellant's Filing Date.* Except in a habeas corpus or bail appeal, which is governed by Rule 31,[1] an appellant must file a brief within 30 days—20 days in an accelerated appeal—after the later of:

(1) the date the clerk's record was filed; or

(2) the date the reporter's record was filed.

(b) *Appellee's Filing Date.* The appellee's brief must be filed within 30 days—20 days in an accelerated appeal—after the date the appellant's brief was filed. In a civil case, if the appellant has not filed a brief as provided in this rule, an appellee may file a brief within 30 days—20 days in an accelerated appeal—after the date the appellant's brief was due.

(c) *Filing Date for Reply Brief.* A reply brief, if any, must be filed within 20 days after the date the appellee's brief was filed.

(d) *Modifications of Filing Time.* On motion complying with Rule 10.5(b), the appellate court may extend the time for filing a brief and may postpone submission of the case. A motion to extend the time to file a brief may be filed before or after the date the brief is due. The court may also, in the interests of justice, shorten the time for filing briefs and for submission of the case.

Eff. Sept. 1, 1997. Amended by Supreme Court Dec. 23, 2002, eff. Jan. 1, 2003.

1 Vernon's Ann.Rules App.Proc., rule 31.1 et seq.

Notes and Comments

Comment to 2002 change: Rule 38.6(d) is amended to clarify that an appellate court may postpone the filing of any brief, not just the appellant's brief.

38.7. Amendment or Supplementation

A brief may be amended or supplemented whenever justice requires, on whatever reasonable terms the court may prescribe.

Eff. Sept. 1, 1997.

38.8. Failure of Appellant to File Brief

(a) *Civil Cases.* If an appellant fails to timely file a brief, the appellate court may:

(1) dismiss the appeal for want of prosecution, unless the appellant reasonably explains the failure and the appellee is not significantly injured by the appellant's failure to timely file a brief;

(2) decline to dismiss the appeal and give further direction to the case as it considers proper; or

(3) if an appellee's brief is filed, the court may regard that brief as correctly presenting the case and may affirm the trial court's judgment upon that brief without examining the record.

(b) *Criminal Cases.*

(1) Effect. An appellant's failure to timely file a brief does not authorize either dismissal of the appeal or, except as provided in (4), consideration of the appeal without briefs.

(2) Notice. If the appellant's brief is not timely filed, the appellate clerk must notify counsel for the parties and the trial court of that fact. If the appellate court does not receive a satisfactory response within ten days, the court must order the trial court to immediately conduct a hearing to determine whether the appellant desires to prosecute his appeal, whether the appellant is indigent,

or, if not indigent, whether retained counsel has abandoned the appeal, and to make appropriate findings and recommendations.

(3) Hearing. In accordance with (2), the trial court must conduct any necessary hearings, make appropriate findings and recommendations, and have a record of the proceedings prepared, which record—including any order and findings—must be sent to the appellate court.

(4) Appellate Court Action. Based on the trial court's record, the appellate court may act appropriately to ensure that the appellant's rights are protected, including initiating contempt proceedings against appellant's counsel. If the trial court has found that the appellant no longer desires to prosecute the appeal, or that the appellant is not indigent but has not made the necessary arrangements for filing a brief, the appellate court may consider the appeal without briefs, as justice may require.

Eff. Sept. 1, 1997.

38.9. Briefing Rules to Be Construed Liberally

Because briefs are meant to acquaint the court with the issues in a case and to present argument that will enable the court to decide the case, substantial compliance with this rule is sufficient, subject to the following.

(a) *Formal Defects.* If the court determines that this rule has been flagrantly violated, it may require a brief to be amended, supplemented, or redrawn. If another brief that does not comply with this rule is filed, the court may strike the brief, prohibit the party from filing another, and proceed as if the party had failed to file a brief.

(b) *Substantive Defects.* If the court determines, either before or after submission, that the case has not been properly presented in the briefs, or that the law and authorities have not been properly cited in the briefs, the court may postpone submission, require additional briefing, and make any other order necessary for a satisfactory submission of the case.

Eff. Sept. 1, 1997.

Rule 39. Oral Argument; Decision Without Argument

Notes and Comments

Comment to 1997 change: This is former Rule 75. Technical and nonsubstantive changes are made.

39.1. Right to Oral Argument

A party who has filed a brief and who has timely requested oral argument may argue the case to the court unless the court, after examining the briefs, decides that oral argument is unnecessary for any of the following reasons:

(a) the appeal is frivolous;

(b) the dispositive issue or issues have been authoritatively decided;

(c) the facts and legal arguments are adequately presented in the briefs and record; or

(d) the decisional process would not be significantly aided by oral argument.

Eff. Sept. 1, 1997. Amended by Supreme Court March 10, 2008, and Aug. 20, 2008, eff. Sept. 1, 2008. Approved by Court of Criminal Appeals Sept. 30, 2008, eff. Sept. 30, 2008.

Notes and Comments

Comment to 2008 change: Subdivision 39.1 is amended to provide for oral argument unless the court determines it is unnecessary and to set out the reasons why argument may be unnecessary. The appellate court must evaluate these reasons in view of the traditional importance of oral argument. The court need not agree on, and generally should not announce, a specific reason or reasons for declining oral argument.

39.2. Purpose of Argument

Oral argument should emphasize and clarify the written arguments in the briefs. Counsel should not merely read from prepared text. Counsel should assume that all members of the court have read the briefs before oral argument and counsel should be prepared to respond to questions. A party should not refer to or comment on matters not involved in or pertaining to what is in the record.

Eff. Sept. 1, 1997.

39.3. Time Allowed

The court will set the time that will be allowed for argument. Counsel must complete argument in the time allotted and may continue after the expiration of the allotted time only with permission of the court. Counsel is not required to use all the allotted time. The appellant must be allowed to conclude the argument.

Eff. Sept. 1, 1997.

39.4. Number of Counsel

Generally, only one counsel should argue for each side. Except on leave of court, no more than two counsel on each side may argue. Only one counsel may argue in rebuttal.

Eff. Sept. 1, 1997.

39.5. Argument by Amicus

With leave of court obtained before the argument and with a party's consent, an amicus curiae may share allotted time with that party. Otherwise, counsel for amicus may not argue.

Eff. Sept. 1, 1997.

39.6. When Only One Party Files a Brief

If counsel for only one party has filed a brief, the court may allow that party to argue.

Eff. Sept. 1, 1997.

39.7. Request and Waiver

A party desiring oral argument must note that request on the front cover of the party's brief. A party's failure to request oral argument waives the party's right to argue. But even if a party has waived oral argument, the court may direct the party to appear and argue.

Eff. Sept. 1, 1997.

39.8. Clerk's Notice.

The clerk must send to the parties—at least 21 days before the date the case is set for argument or submission without argument—a notice telling the parties:

(a) whether the court will allow oral argument or will submit the case without argument;

(b) the date of argument or submission without argument;

(c) if argument is allowed, the time allotted for argument; and

(d) the names of the members of the panel to which the case will be argued or submitted, subject to change by the court.

A party's failure to receive the notice does not prevent a case's argument or submission on the scheduled date.

Eff. Sept. 1, 1997. Amended by Supreme Court March 10, 2008, and Aug. 20, 2008, eff. Sept. 1, 2008. Approved by Court of Criminal Appeals Sept. 30, 2008, eff. Sept. 30, 2008.

Notes and Comments

Comment to 2008 change: Subdivision 39.1 is amended to provide for oral argument unless the court determines it is unnecessary and to set out the reasons why argument may be unnecessary. The appellate court must evaluate these reasons in view of the traditional importance of oral argument. The court need not agree on, and generally should not announce, a specific reason or reasons for declining oral argument.

39.9. [Deleted]

Rule 40. Order of Decision

Notes and Comments

Comment on 1997 change: The provisions of former Rules 76, 77 and 78 are merged. Civil cases involving the Railroad Commission, the State, and "cases submitted on oral argument for all parties" are no longer given preference unless given preference by law.

40.1. Civil Cases

The court of appeals may determine the order in which civil cases will be decided. But the following types of cases have precedence over all others:

(a) a case given precedence by law;

(b) an accelerated appeal; and

(c) a case that the court determines should be given precedence in the interest of justice.

Eff. Sept. 1, 1997.

40.2. Criminal Cases

In cases not otherwise given precedence by law, the court of appeals must hear and determine a criminal appeal at the earliest possible time, having due regard for the parties' rights and for the proper administration of justice.

Eff. Sept. 1, 1997.

Rule 41. Panel and En Banc Decision

Notes and Comments

Comment to 1997 change: This is former Rule 79. The rule is reorganized. Paragraphs 41.1(b) and (c) are amended to make clear that a three judge panel must hear the case. Therefore, only if a member of a panel is lost after argument do the provisions for appointment of another justice to break a deadlock come into play. Paragraph 41.2(a) is amended to define an en banc court.

41.1. Decision by Panel

(a) *Constitution of Panel.* Unless a court of appeals with more than three justices votes to decide a case en banc, a case must be assigned for decision to a panel of the court consisting of three justices, although not every member of the panel must be present for argument. If the case is decided without argument, three justices must participate in the decision. A majority of the panel, which constitutes a quorum, must agree on the judgment. Except as otherwise provided in these rules, a panel's opinion constitutes the court's opinion, and the court must render a judgment in accordance with the panel opinion.

(b) *When Panel Cannot Agree on Judgment.* After argument, if for any reason a member of the panel cannot participate in deciding a case, the case may be decided by the two remaining justices. If they cannot agree on a judgment, the chief justice of the court of appeals must:

(1) designate another justice of the court to sit on the panel to consider the case;

(2) request the Chief Justice of the Supreme Court to temporarily assign an eligible justice or judge to sit on the panel to consider the case; or

(3) convene the court en banc to consider the case.

The reconstituted panel or the en banc court may order the case reargued.

(c) *When Court Cannot Agree on Judgment.* After argument, if for any reason a member of a court consisting of only three justices cannot participate in deciding a case, the case may be decided by the two remaining justices. If they cannot agree on a judgment, that fact must be certified to the Chief Justice of the Supreme Court. The Chief Justice may then temporarily assign an eligible justice or judge to sit with the court of appeals to consider the case. The reconstituted court may order the case reargued.

Eff. Sept. 1, 1997. Amended by Supreme Court March 10, 2008, and Aug. 20, 2008, eff. Sept. 1, 2008. Approved by Court of Criminal Appeals Sept. 30, 2008, eff. Sept. 30, 2008.

Notes and Comments

Comment to 2008 change: Subdivisions 41.1 and 41.2 are amended to acknowledge the full authority of the Chief Justice of the Supreme Court to temporarily assign a justice or judge to hear a matter pending in an appellate court. The statutory provisions governing the assignment of judges to appellate courts are located in Chapters 74 and 75 of the Government Code. Other minor changes are made for consistency. Subdivision 41.3 is added to require, in appellate cases transferred by the Supreme Court under Section 73.001 of the Government Code for docket equalization or other purposes, that the transferee court must generally resolve any conflict between the precedent of the transferor court and the precedent of the transferee court—or that of any other intermediate appellate court the transferee court otherwise would have followed—by following the precedent of the transferor court, unless it appears that the transferor court itself would not be bound by that precedent. The rule requires the transferee court to "stand in the shoes" of the transferor court so that an appellate transfer will not produce a different outcome, based on application of substantive law, than would have resulted had the case not been transferred. The transferee court is not expected to follow the transferor court's local rules or otherwise supplant its own local procedures with those of the transferor court.

41.2. Decision by En Banc Court

(a) *Constitution of En Banc Court.* An en banc court consists of all members of the court who are not disqualified or recused and—if the case was originally argued before or decided by a panel—any members of the panel who are not members of the court but remain eligible for assignment to the court. A majority of the en banc court constitutes a quorum. A majority of the en banc court must agree on a judgment.

(b) *When En Banc Court Cannot Agree on Judgment.* If a majority of an en banc court cannot agree on a judgment, that fact must be certified to the Chief Justice of the Supreme Court. The Chief Justice may then temporarily assign an eligible justice or judge to sit with the court of appeals to consider the case. The reconstituted court may order the case reargued.

(c) *En Banc Consideration Disfavored.* En banc consideration of a case is not favored and should not be ordered unless necessary to secure or maintain uniformity of the court's decisions or unless extraordinary circumstances require en banc consideration. A vote to determine whether a case will be heard or reheard en banc need not be taken unless a justice of the court requests a vote. If a vote is requested and a majority of the court's members vote to hear or rehear the case en banc, the en banc court will hear or rehear the case. Otherwise, a panel of the court will consider the case.

Eff. Sept. 1, 1997. Amended by Supreme Court March 10, 2008, and Aug. 20, 2008, eff. Sept. 1, 2008. Approved by Court of Criminal Appeals Sept. 30, 2008, eff. Sept. 30, 2008.

Notes and Comments

Comment to 2008 change: Subdivisions 41.1 and 41.2 are amended to acknowledge the full authority of the Chief Justice of the Supreme Court to temporarily assign a justice or judge to hear a matter pending in an appellate court. The statutory provisions governing the assignment of judges to appellate courts are located in Chapters 74 and 75 of the Government Code. Other minor changes are made for consistency. Subdivision 41.3 is added to require, in appellate cases transferred by the Supreme Court under Section 73.001 of the Government Code for docket equalization or other purposes, that the transferee court must generally resolve any conflict between the precedent of the transferor court and the precedent of the transferee court—or that of any other intermediate appellate court the transferee court otherwise would have followed—by following the precedent of the transferor court, unless it appears that the transferor court itself would not be bound by that precedent. The rule requires the transferee court to "stand in the shoes" of the transferor court so that an appellate transfer will not produce a different outcome, based on application of substantive law, than would have resulted had the case not been transferred. The transferee court is not expected to follow the transferor court's local rules or otherwise supplant its own local procedures with those of the transferor court.

41.3. Precedent in Transferred Cases.

In cases transferred by the Supreme Court from one court of appeals to another, the court of appeals to which the case is transferred must decide the case in accordance with the precedent of the transferor court under principles of stare decisis if the transferee court's decision otherwise would have been inconsistent with the precedent of the transferor court. The court's opinion may state whether the outcome would have been different had the transferee court not been required to decide the case in accordance with the transferor court's precedent.

Added by Supreme Court March 10, 2008, and Aug. 20, 2008, eff. Sept. 1, 2008. Approved by Court of Criminal Appeals Sept. 30, 2008, eff. Sept. 30, 2008.

Notes and Comments

Comment to 2008 change: Subdivisions 41.1 and 41.2 are amended to acknowledge the full authority of the Chief Justice of the Supreme Court to temporarily assign a justice or judge to hear a matter pending in an appellate court. The statutory provisions governing the assignment of judges to appellate courts are located in Chapters 74 and 75 of the Government Code. Other minor changes are made for consistency. Subdivision 41.3 is added to require, in appellate cases transferred by the Supreme Court under Section 73.001 of the Government Code for docket equalization or other purposes, that the transferee court must generally resolve any conflict between the precedent of the transferor court and the precedent of the transferee court—or that of any other intermediate appellate court the transferee court otherwise would have followed—by following the precedent of the transferor court, unless it appears that the transferor court itself would not be bound by that precedent. The rule requires the transferee court to "stand in the shoes" of the transferor court so that an appellate transfer will not produce a different outcome, based on application of substantive law, than would have resulted had the case not been transferred. The transferee court is not expected to follow the transferor court's local rules or otherwise supplant its own local procedures with those of the transferor court.

Rule 42. Dismissal

Notes and Comments

Comment to 1997 change: Former Rules 59 and 60 are merged. Paragraph 42.1(c), allowing a court of appeals to withdraw its opinion, is new. Provision is made in paragraph 42.3(c) for dismissal of an appeal for failure to comply with a notice from the clerk. Other changes are made.

42.1. Voluntary Dismissal in Civil Cases

(a) *On Motion or By Agreement.* The appellate court may dispose of an appeal as follows:

(1) On Motion of Appellant. In accordance with a motion of appellant, the court may dismiss the appeal or affirm the appealed judgment or order unless disposition would prevent a party from seeking relief to which it would otherwise be entitled.

(2) By Agreement. In accordance with an agreement signed by the parties or their attorneys and filed with the clerk, the court may:

(A) render judgment effectuating the parties' agreements;

(B) set aside the trial court's judgment without regard to the merits and remand the case to the trial court for rendition of judgment in accordance with the agreements; or

(C) abate the appeal and permit proceedings in the trial court to effectuate the agreement.

(b) *Partial Disposition.* A severable portion of the proceeding may be disposed of under (a) if it will not prejudice the remaining parties.

(c) *Effect on Court's Opinion.* In dismissing a proceeding, the appellate court will determine whether to withdraw any opinion it has already issued. An agreement or motion for dismissal cannot be conditioned on withdrawal of the opinion.

(d) *Costs.* Absent agreement of the parties, the court will tax costs against the appellant.

Eff. Sept. 1, 1997. Amended by Supreme Court Dec. 23, 2002, eff. Jan. 1, 2003.

Notes and Comments

Comment to 2002 change: Rule 42.1 is amended to clarify the procedures for implementing settlements on appeal and to expressly give courts flexibility in effectuating settlements. The rule is also clarified to expressly permit the dismissal of appeal without dismissal of the action itself. The rules does not permit an appellate court to order a new trial merely on the agreement of the parties absent reversible error, or to vacate a trial court's judgment absent reversible error or a settlement.

42.2. Voluntary Dismissal in Criminal Cases

(a) At any time before the appellate court's decision, the appellate court may dismiss the appeal upon the appellant's motion. The appellant and his or her attorney must sign the written motion to dismiss and file it in duplicate with the appellate clerk, who must immediately send the duplicate copy to the trial court clerk.

(b) After the court of appeals hands down its opinion, it may not grant an appellant's motion to dismiss the appeal unless the other parties consent. If the other parties consent and the court of appeals grants the appellant's motion to dismiss the appeal, the appellate opinion must be withdrawn and the appeal dismissed. The appellate clerk must send notice of the dismissal to the trial court clerk.

Eff. Sept. 1, 1997. Amended by Court of Criminal Appeals Aug. 10, 2000 and Oct. 16, 2000, eff. Jan. 1, 2001; Supreme Court Sept. 12, 2000, eff. Jan. 1, 2001; Court of Criminal Appeals Dec. 13, 2006, eff. Jan. 1, 2007.

Notes and Comments

Comment to 2000 change: In the first sentence of Rule 42.2(a) "appellant" is replaced by "party that appealed," to make it clear that the rule applies to the State when it is the appealing party. See State v. Miles, 994 S.W.2d 410 (Tex.App.—

Waco 1999). The requirement that the appellant's attorney must sign the withdrawal is deleted, and the last sentence is added, to remove any implication that the attorney may veto the appellant's decision to withdraw the notice of appeal. The word "personally" is added to emphasize that the appellant must participate in the withdrawal of his or her appeal. The provisions of Rule 9.1(a) do not restrict the appellant's ability to withdraw the notice of appeal.

42.3. Involuntary Dismissal in Civil Cases

Under the following circumstances, on any party's motion—or on its own initiative after giving ten days' notice to all parties—the appellate court may dismiss the appeal or affirm the appealed judgment or order. Dismissal or affirmance may occur if the appeal is subject to dismissal:

(a) for want of jurisdiction;

(b) for want of prosecution; or

(c) because the appellant has failed to comply with a requirement of these rules, a court order, or a notice from the clerk requiring a response or other action within a specified time.

Eff. Sept. 1, 1997.

42.4. Involuntary Dismissal in Criminal Cases

The appellate court must dismiss an appeal on the State's motion, supported by affidavit, showing that the appellant has escaped from custody pending the appeal and that to the affiant's knowledge, the appellant has not, within ten days after escaping, voluntarily returned to lawful custody within the state.

(a) *Timely Return to Custody; Reinstatement.* The appeal may not be dismissed—or, if dismissed, must be reinstated—if an affidavit of an officer or other credible person is filed showing that the appellant, within ten days after escaping, voluntarily returned to lawful custody within the state.

(b) *Life Sentence.* The appellate court may overrule the motion to dismiss—or, if the motion was granted, may reinstate the appeal—if:

(1) the appellant received a life sentence; and

(2) the appellant is recaptured or voluntarily surrenders within 30 days after escaping.

Eff. Sept. 1, 1997.

Historical Notes

The Court of Criminal Appeals order dated October 16, 2000, provides in part:

"2. These changes take effect January 1, 2001. Unless this order provides otherwise, they shall govern all proceedings in motions for new trial, appeals, petitions for discretionary review, and petitions or applications for extraordinary writs thereafter brought and in all such proceedings then pending, except to the extent that in the opinion of the court their application in a particular proceeding then pending would not be feasible or would work injustice, in which case the former procedure may be followed.

"3. The notes and comments appended to these changes are incomplete, are included only for the convenience of the bench and bar, and are not a part of the rules."

Rule 43. Judgment of the Court of Appeals

Notes and Comments

Comment to 1997 changes: Former Rules 80(a)–(c) and 82 are merged. Paragraph 43.2(e) allows the court of appeals to vacate the trial court's judgment and dismiss the case; paragraph 43.2(f) allows the court of appeals to dismiss the appeal. Both provisions are new but codify current practice. Paragraph 43.3(a) is moved here from former Rule 81(c). Paragraph 43.3(b), allowing a remand in the interest of justice, is new. Subdivisions 43.4 and 43.5 are from former Rule 82.

43.1. Time

The court of appeals should render its judgment promptly after submission of a case.

Eff. Sept. 1, 1997.

43.2. Types of Judgment

The court of appeals may:

(a) affirm the trial court's judgment in whole or in part;

(b) modify the trial court's judgment and affirm it as modified;

(c) reverse the trial court's judgment in whole or in part and render the judgment that the trial court should have rendered;

(d) reverse the trial court's judgment and remand the case for further proceedings;

(e) vacate the trial court's judgment and dismiss the case; or

(f) dismiss the appeal.

Eff. Sept. 1, 1997.

43.3. Rendition Appropriate Unless Remand Necessary

When reversing a trial court's judgment, the court must render the judgment that the trial court should have rendered, except when:

(a) a remand is necessary for further proceedings; or

(b) the interests of justice require a remand for another trial.

Eff. Sept. 1, 1997.

43.4. Judgment for Costs in Civil Cases

In a civil case, the court of appeal's judgment should award to the prevailing party the appellate costs—including preparation costs for the clerk's record and the reporter's record—that were incurred by that party. But the court of appeals may tax costs otherwise as required by law or for good cause.

Eff. Sept. 1, 1997.

43.5. Judgment Against Sureties in Civil Cases

When a court of appeals affirms the trial court judgment, or modifies that judgment and renders judgment against the appellant, the court of appeals must render judgment against the sureties on the appellant's supersedeas bond, if any, for the performance of the judgment and for any costs taxed against the appellant.

Eff. Sept. 1, 1997.

43.6. Other Orders

The court of appeals may make any other appropriate order that the law and the nature of the case require.

Eff. Sept. 1, 1997.

Rule 44. Reversible Error

Notes and Comments

Comment to 1997 change: Former Rules 80(d), 81 and 83 are merged. The reversible error standard in subdivision 44.1 is amended to omit the reference to an action "reasonably calculated to cause" an improper judgment, but no substantive change is intended. Paragraph 44.2(a) is amended to limit its standard of review to constitutional errors that are subject to harmless error review. Paragraph 44.2(b) is new and is taken from Federal Rule of Criminal Procedure 52(a) without substantive change. Paragraph 44.2(c) is former Rule 80(d) without substantive change. Subdivision 44.3 is amended to delete the reference to defects of "substance" and to delete the provisions regarding the late filing of the record.

44.1. Reversible Error in Civil Cases

(a) *Standard for Reversible Error.* No judgment may be reversed on appeal on the ground that the trial court made an error of law unless the court of appeals concludes that the error complained of:

(1) probably caused the rendition of an improper judgment; or

(2) probably prevented the appellant from properly presenting the case to the court of appeals.

(b) *Error Affecting Only Part of Case.* If the error affects part of, but not all, the matter in controversy and that part is separable without unfairness to the parties, the judgment must be reversed and a new trial ordered only as to the part affected by the error. The court may not order a separate trial solely on unliquidated damages if liability is contested.

Eff. Sept. 1, 1997.

44.2. Reversible Error in Criminal Cases

(a) *Constitutional Error.* If the appellate record in a criminal case reveals constitutional error that is subject to harmless error review, the court of appeals must reverse a judgment of conviction or punishment unless the court determines beyond a reasonable doubt that the error did not contribute to the conviction or punishment.

(b) *Other Errors.* Any other error, defect, irregularity, or variance that does not affect substantial rights must be disregarded.

(c) *Presumptions.* Unless the following matters were disputed in the trial court, or unless the record affirmatively shows the contrary, the court of appeals must presume:

(1) that venue was proved in the trial court;

(2) that the jury was properly impaneled and sworn;

(3) that the defendant was arraigned;

(4) that the defendant pleaded to the indictment or other charging instrument; and

(5) that the court's charge was certified by the trial court and filed by the clerk before it was read to the jury.

Eff. Sept. 1, 1997.

44.3. Defects in Procedure

A court of appeals must not affirm or reverse a judgment or dismiss an appeal for formal defects or irregularities in appellate procedure without allowing a reasonable time to correct or amend the defects or irregularities.

Eff. Sept. 1, 1997.

44.4. Remediable Error of the Trial Court

(a) *Generally.* A court of appeals must not affirm or reverse a judgment or dismiss an appeal if:

(1) the trial court's erroneous action or failure or refusal to act prevents the proper presentation of a case to the court of appeals; and

(2) the trial court can correct its action or failure to act.

(b) *Court of Appeals Direction if Error Remediable.* If the circumstances described in (a) exist, the court of appeals must direct the trial court to correct the error. The court of appeals will then proceed as if the erroneous action or failure to act had not occurred.

Eff. Sept. 1, 1997.

Rule 45. Damages for Frivolous Appeals in Civil Cases

If the court of appeals determines that an appeal is frivolous, it may—on motion of any party or on its own initiative, after notice and a reasonable opportunity for response—award each prevailing party just damages. In determining whether to award damages, the court must not consider any matter that does not appear in the record, briefs, or other papers filed in the court of appeals.

Eff. Sept. 1, 1997.

Notes and Comments

Comment to 1997 change: This is former Rule 84. The limit on the amount of the sanction that may be imposed is repealed. A requirement of notice and opportunity to respond is added.

Rule 46. Remittitur in Civil Cases

Notes and Comments

Comment to 1997 change: This is former Rule 85. The rule is revised without substantive change.

46.1. Remittitur After Appeal Perfected

If the trial court suggests a remittitur but the case is appealed before the remittitur is filed, the party who would make the remittitur may do so in the court of appeals in the same manner as in the trial court. The court of appeals must then render the judgment that the trial court should have rendered if the remittitur had been made in the trial court.

Eff. Sept. 1, 1997.

46.2. Appeal on Remittitur

If a party makes the remittitur at the trial judge's suggestion and the party benefitting from the remittitur appeals, the remitting party is not barred from contending in the court of appeals that all or part of the remittitur should not have been required, but the remitting party must perfect an appeal to raise that point. If the court of appeals sustains the remitting party's contention that remittitur should not have been required, the court must render the judgment that the trial court should have rendered.

Eff. Sept. 1, 1997.

46.3. Suggestion of Remittitur by Court of Appeals

The court of appeals may suggest a remittitur. If the remittitur is timely filed, the court must reform and affirm the trial court's judgment in accordance with the remittitur. If the remittitur is not timely filed, the court must reverse the trial court's judgment.

Eff. Sept. 1, 1997.

46.4. Refusal to Remit Must Not Be Mentioned in Later Trial

If the court of appeals suggests a remittitur, but no remittitur is filed, evidence of the court's determination regarding remittitur is inadmissible in a later trial of the case.

Eff. Sept. 1, 1997.

46.5. Voluntary Remittitur

If a court of appeals reverses the trial court's judgment because of a legal error that affects only part of the damages awarded by the judgment, the affected party may—within 15 days after the court of appeals' judgment—voluntarily remit the amount that the affected party believes will cure the reversible error. A party may include in a motion for rehearing—without waiving any complaint that the court of appeals erred—a conditional request that the court accept the remittitur and affirm the trial court's judgment as reduced. If the court of appeals determines that the voluntary remittitur is not sufficient to cure the reversible error, but that remittitur is appropriate, the court must suggest a remittitur in accordance with Rule 46.3. If the remittitur is timely filed and the court of appeals determines that the voluntary remittitur cures the reversible error, then the court must accept the remittitur and reform and affirm the trial court judgment in accordance with the remittitur.

Eff. Sept. 1, 1997. Amended by Supreme Court Dec. 23, 2002, eff. Jan. 1, 2003.

Notes and Comments

Comment to 2002 change: Subdivision 46.5 is amended to clarify the procedure for offering a voluntary remittitur. The offer many be made in a motion for rehearing without waiving any complaint that the court of appeals erred, thereby extending the deadlines for further appeal.

Rule 47. Opinions, Publication, and Citation

Notes and Comments

Comment to 1997 change: This is former Rule 90. Subdivision 47.1 makes clear that a memorandum opinion should not be any longer than necessary. Subdivision 47.5 is amended to make clear that only justices who participated in the decision may file an opinion in the case. Judges who are not on a panel may file an opinion only in respect to a hearing or rehearing en banc. Former Rule 90(h), regarding publication of opinions after the Supreme Court grants review, is repealed.

Comment to 2002 change: The rule is substantively changed to discontinue the use of the "do not publish" designation in civil cases, to require that all opinions of the court of appeals be made available to public reporting services, and to remove prospectively any prohibition against the citation of opinions as authority in civil cases. The rule favors the use "memorandum opinions" designated as such except in certain types of cases but does not change other requirements, such as those in *Pool v. Ford Motor Co.,* 715 S.W.2d 629, 635–636 (Tex. 1986). An opinion previously designated "do not publish" has not precedential value but may be cited. The citation must include the notation, "(not designated for publication)." Of course, whenever an opinion not readily available is cited, copies should be furnished to the court and opposing counsel.

47.1. Written Opinions

The court of appeals must hand down a written opinion that is as brief as practicable but that addresses every issue raised and necessary to final disposition of the appeal.

Eff. Sept. 1, 1997. Amended by Supreme Court Dec. 23, 2002, eff. Jan. 1, 2003.

47.2. Designation and Signing of Opinions; Participating Justices

(a) *Civil and Criminal Cases.* Each opinion of the court must be designated either an "Opinion" or a "Memorandum Opinion." A majority of the justices who participate in considering the case must determine whether the opinion will be signed by a justice or will be per curiam and whether it will be designated an opinion or memorandum opinion. The names of the participating justices must be noted on all written opinions or orders of the court or a panel of the court.

(b) *Criminal Cases.* In addition, each opinion and memorandum opinion in a criminal case must bear the notation "publish" or "do not publish" as determined—before the opinion is handed down—by a majority of the justices who participate in considering the case. Any party may move the appellate court to change the notation, but the court of appeals must not change the notation after the Court of Criminal Appeals has acted on any party's petition for discretionary review or other request for relief. The Court of Criminal Appeals may, at any time, order that a "do not publish" notation be changed to "publish."

(c) *Civil Cases.* Opinions and memorandum opinions in civil cases issued on or after January 1, 2003 shall not be designated "do not publish."

Eff. Sept. 1, 1997. Amended by Supreme Court Dec. 23, 2002, eff. Jan. 1, 2003; March 10, 2008, and Aug. 20, 2008, eff. Sept. 1, 2008. Approved by Court of Criminal Appeals Sept. 30, 2008, eff. Sept. 30, 2008.

Notes and Comments

Comment to 2008 change: Effective January 1, 2003, Rule 47 was amended to prospectively discontinue designating opinions in civil cases as either "published" or "unpublished." Subdivision 47.7 is revised to clarify that, with respect to civil cases, only opinions issued prior to the 2003 amendment and affirmatively designated "do not publish" should be considered "unpublished" cases lacking precedential value. All opinions and memorandum opinions in civil cases issued after the 2003 amendment have precedential value. The provisions governing citation of unpublished opinions in criminal cases are substantively unchanged. Subdivisions 47.2 and 47.7 are amended to clarify that memorandum opinions are subject to those rules.

47.3. Distribution of Opinions

All opinions of the courts of appeals are open to the public and must be made available to public reporting services, print or electronic.

Eff. Sept. 1, 1997. Amended by Supreme Court Dec. 23, 2002, eff. Jan. 1, 2003.

47.4. Memorandum Opinions

If the issues are settled, the court should write a brief memorandum opinion no longer than necessary to advise the parties of the court's decision and the basic reasons for it. An opinion may not be designated a memorandum opinion if the author of a concurrence or dissent opposes that designation. An opinion must be designated a memorandum opinion unless it does any of the following:

(a) establishes a new rule of law, alters or modifies an existing rule, or applies an existing rule to a novel fact situation likely to recur in future cases;

(b) involves issues of constitutional law or other legal issues important to the jurisprudence of Texas;

(c) criticizes existing law; or

(d) resolves an apparent conflict of authority.

Eff. Sept. 1, 1997. Amended by Supreme Court Dec. 23, 2002, eff. Jan. 1, 2003.

47.5. Concurring and Dissenting Opinions

Only a justice who participated in the decision of a case may file or join in an opinion concurring in or dissenting from the judgment of the court of appeals. Any justice on the court may file an opinion in connection with a denial of a hearing or rehearing en banc.

Eff. Sept. 1, 1997. Amended by Supreme Court Dec. 23, 2002, eff. Jan. 1, 2003.

47.6. Change in Designation by En Banc Court

A court en banc may change a panel's designation of an opinion.

Eff. Sept. 1, 1997. Amended by Supreme Court Dec. 23, 2002, eff. Jan. 1, 2003.

47.7. Citation of Unpublished Opinions

(a) *Criminal Cases.* Opinions and memorandum opinions not designated for publication by the court of appeals under these or prior rules have no precedential value but may be cited with the notation, "(not designated for publication)."

(b) *Civil Cases.* Opinions and memorandum opinions designated "do not publish" under these rules by the courts of appeals prior to January 1, 2003 have no precedential value but may be cited with the notation, "(not designated for publication)." If an opinion or memorandum opinion issued on or after that date is erroneously designated "do not publish," the erroneous designation will not affect the precedential value of the decision.

Eff. Sept. 1, 1997. Amended by Supreme Court Dec. 23, 2002, eff. Jan. 1, 2003; March 10, 2008, and Aug. 20, 2008, eff. Sept. 1, 2008. Approved by Court of Criminal Appeals Sept. 30, 2008, eff. Sept. 30, 2008.

Notes and Comments

Comment to 2008 change: Effective January 1, 2003, Rule 47 was amended to prospectively discontinue designating opinions in civil cases as either "published" or "unpublished." Subdivision 47.7 is revised to clarify that, with respect to civil cases, only opinions issued prior to the 2003 amendment and affirmatively designated "do not publish" should be considered "unpublished" cases lacking precedential value. All opinions and memorandum opinions in civil cases issued after the 2003 amendment have precedential value. The provisions governing citation of unpublished opinions in criminal cases are substantively unchanged. Subdivisions 47.2 and 47.7 are amended to clarify that memorandum opinions are subject to those rules.

Rule 48. Copy of Opinion and Judgment to Interested Parties and Other Courts

Notes and Comments

Comment to 1997 change: This is former Rule 91 with changes.

48.1. Recipients of Opinion and Judgment in All Cases

On the date when an appellate court's opinion is handed down, the appellate clerk must send or deliver copies of the opinion and judgment to the following persons:

(a) the trial judge;

(b) the trial court clerk;

(c) the regional administrative judge; and

(d) all parties to the appeal.

Eff. Sept. 1, 1997. Amended by Supreme Court Dec. 11, 2013, eff. Jan. 1, 2014. Approved by Court of Criminal Appeals Dec. 11, 2013, eff. Jan. 1, 2014.

48.2. Additional Recipients in Criminal Cases

In criminal cases, copies of the opinion and judgment will also be mailed or delivered to the State Prosecuting Attorney.

Eff. Sept. 1, 1997.

48.3. Filing Opinion and Judgment

The trial court clerk must file a copy of the opinion and judgment among the papers of the case in that court.

Eff. Sept. 1, 1997.

48.4. Opinion Sent to Criminal Defendant

In criminal cases, the attorney representing the defendant on appeal shall, within five days after the opinion is handed down, send his client a copy of the opinion and judgment, along with notification of the defendant's right to file a *pro se* petition for discretionary review under Rule 68. This notification shall be sent certified mail, return receipt requested, to the defendant at his last known address. The attorney shall also send the court of appeals a letter certifying his compliance with this rule and attaching a copy of the return receipt within the time for filing a motion for rehearing. The court of appeals shall file this letter in its record of the appeal.

Adopted by Court of Criminal Appeals May 2, 2007 and Aug. 20, 2007, eff. Sept. 1, 2007.

Rule 49. Motion for Rehearing and En Banc Reconsideration

Notes and Comments

Comment to 1997 change: This is former Rule 100. Subdivision 49.4 is moved here from former Rule 43(h). Subdivisions 49.9 and 49.10 are added.

49.1. Motion for Rehearing

A motion for rehearing may be filed within 15 days after the court of appeals' judgment or order is rendered. The motion must clearly state the points relied on for the rehearing.

Eff. Sept. 1, 1997.

49.2. Response

No response to a motion for rehearing need be filed unless the court so requests. A motion will not be granted unless a response has been filed or requested by the court.

Eff. Sept. 1, 1997.

49.3. Decision on Motion

A motion for rehearing may be granted by a majority of the justices who participated in the decision of the case. Otherwise, it must be denied. If rehearing is granted, the court or panel may dispose of the case with or without rebriefing and oral argument.

Eff. Sept. 1, 1997.

49.4. Accelerated Appeals

In an accelerated appeal, the appellate court may deny the right to file a motion for rehearing or shorten the time to file such a motion.

Eff. Sept. 1, 1997.

49.5 Further Motion for Rehearing.

After a motion for rehearing is decided, a further motion for rehearing may be filed within 15 days of the court's action if the court:

(a) modifies its judgment;

(b) vacates its judgment and renders a new judgment; or

(c) issues a different opinion.

Eff. Sept. 1, 1997. Amended by Supreme Court March 10, 2008, and Aug. 20, 2008, eff. Sept. 1, 2008. Approved by Court of Criminal Appeals Sept. 30, 2008, eff. Sept. 30, 2008.

Notes and Comments

Comment to 2008 change: Rule 49 is revised to treat a motion for en banc reconsideration as a motion for rehearing and to include procedures governing the filing of a motion for en banc reconsideration. Subdivision 49.5(c) is amended to clarify that a further motion for rehearing may be filed if the court issues a different opinion, irrespective of whether the opinion is issued in connection with the overruling of a prior motion for rehearing. Issuance of a new opinion that is not substantially different should not occasion a further motion for rehearing, but a motion's lack of merit does not affect appellate deadlines. The provisions of former Rule 53.7(b) that address motions for rehearing are moved to new subdivision 49.11 without change, leaving the provisions of Rule 53.7(b) that address petitions for review undisturbed. Subdivision 49.12 mirrors Rule 10.1(a)(5) in excepting motions for rehearing and motions for en banc reconsideration from the certificate-of-conference requirement.

49.6. Amendments

A motion for rehearing or en banc reconsideration may be amended as a matter of right anytime before the 15–day period allowed for filing the motion expires, and with leave of the court, anytime before the court of appeals decides the motion.

Eff. Sept. 1, 1997 Amended by Supreme Court March 10, 2008, and Aug. 20, 2008 eff. Sept. 1, 2008. Approved by Court of Criminal Appeals Sept. 30, 2008, eff. Sept. 30, 2008.

Notes and Comments

Comment to 2008 change: Rule 49 is revised to treat a motion for en banc reconsideration as a motion for rehearing and to include procedures governing the filing of a motion for en banc reconsideration. Subdivision 49.5(c) is amended to clarify that a further motion for rehearing may be filed if the court issues a different opinion, irrespective of whether the opinion is issued in connection with the overruling of a prior motion for rehearing. Issuance of a new opinion that is not substantially different should not occasion a further motion for rehearing, but a motion's lack of merit does not affect appellate deadlines. The provisions of former Rule 53.7(b) that address motions for rehearing are moved to new subdivision 49.11 without change, leaving the provisions of Rule 53.7(b) that address petitions for review undisturbed. Subdivision 49.12 mirrors Rule 10.1(a)(5) in excepting motions for rehearing and motions for en banc reconsideration from the certificate-of-conference requirement.

49.7. En Banc Reconsideration

A party may file a motion for en banc reconsideration as a separate motion, with or without filing a motion for rehearing. The motion must be filed within 15 days after the court of appeals' judgment or order, or when permitted, within 15 days after the court of appeals' denial of the party's last timely filed motion for rehearing or en banc reconsideration. While the court has plenary power, a majority of the en banc court may, with or without a motion, order en banc reconsideration of a panel's decision. If a majority orders reconsideration, the panel's judgment or order does not become final, and the case will be resubmitted to the court for en banc review and disposition.

Eff. Sept. 1, 1997. Amended by Supreme Court March 10, 2008, Aug. 20, 2008, and Aug. 25, 2008, eff. Sept. 1, 2008. Approved by Court of Criminal Appeals Sept. 30, 2008, eff. Sept. 30, 2008.

Notes and Comments

Comment to 2008 change: Rule 49 is revised to treat a motion for en banc reconsideration as a motion for rehearing and to include procedures governing the filing of a motion for en banc reconsideration. Subdivision 49.5(c) is amended to clarify that a further motion for rehearing may be filed if the court issues a different opinion, irrespective of whether the opinion is issued in connection with the overruling of a prior motion for rehearing. Issuance of a new opinion that is not substantially different should not occasion a further motion for rehearing, but a motion's lack of merit does not affect appellate deadlines. The provisions of former Rule 53.7(b) that address motions for rehearing are moved to new subdivision 49.11 without change, leaving the provisions of Rule 53.7(b) that address petitions for review undisturbed. Subdivision 49.12 mirrors Rule 10.1(a)(5) in excepting motions for rehearing and motions for en banc reconsideration from the certificate-of-conference requirement.

49.8. Extension of Time

A court of appeals may extend the time for filing a motion for rehearing or en banc reconsideration if a party files a motion complying with Rule 10.5(b) no later than 15 days after the last date for filing the motion.

Eff. Sept. 1, 1997. Amended by Supreme Court March 10, 2008, and Aug. 20, 2008, eff. Sept. 1, 2008. Approved by Court of Criminal Appeals Sept. 30, 2008, eff. Sept. 30, 2008.

Notes and Comments

Comment to 2008 change: Rule 49 is revised to treat a motion for en banc reconsideration as a motion for rehearing and to include procedures governing the filing of a motion for en banc reconsideration. Subdivision 49.5(c) is amended to clarify that a further motion for rehearing may be filed if the court issues a different opinion, irrespective of whether the opinion is issued in connection with the overruling of a prior motion for rehearing. Issuance of a new opinion that is not substantially different should not occasion a further motion for rehearing, but a motion's lack of merit does not affect appellate deadlines. The provisions of former Rule 53.7(b) that address motions for rehearing are moved to new subdivision 49.11 without change, leaving the provisions of Rule 53.7(b) that address petitions for review undisturbed. Subdivision 49.12 mirrors Rule 10.1(a)(5) in excepting motions for rehearing and motions for en banc reconsideration from the certificate-of-conference requirement.

49.9. Not Required for Review

A motion for rehearing is not a prerequisite to filing a petition for review in the Supreme Court or a petition for discretionary review in the Court of Criminal Appeals nor is it required to preserve error.

Eff. Sept. 1, 1997.

49.10. Repealed by Order of Nov. 13, 2012, eff. Dec. 1, 2012

49.11. Relationship to Petition for Review

A party may not file a motion for rehearing or en banc reconsideration in the court of appeals after that party has filed a petition for review in the Supreme Court unless the court of appeals modifies its opinion or judgment after the petition for review is filed. The filing of a petition for review does not preclude another party from filing a motion for rehearing or en banc reconsideration or preclude the court of appeals from ruling on the motion. If a motion for rehearing or en banc reconsideration is timely filed after a petition for review is filed, the petitioner must immediately notify the Supreme Court clerk of the filing of the motion, and must notify the clerk when the last timely filed motion is overruled by the court of appeals.

Eff. Sept. 1, 1997. Amended by Supreme Court March 10, 2008, and Aug. 20, 2008, eff. Sept. 1, 2008. Approved by Court of Criminal Appeals Sept. 30, 2008, eff. Sept. 30, 2008.

Notes and Comments

Comment to 2008 change: Rule 49 is revised to treat a motion for en banc reconsideration as a motion for rehearing and to include procedures governing the filing of a motion for en banc reconsideration. Subdivision 49.5(c) is amended to clarify that a further motion for rehearing may be filed if the court issues a different opinion, irrespective of whether the opinion is issued in connection with the overruling of a prior motion for rehearing. Issuance of a new opinion that is not substantially different should not occasion a further motion for rehearing, but a motion's lack of merit does not affect appellate deadlines. The provisions of former Rule 53.7(b) that address motions for rehearing are moved to new subdivision 49.11 without change, leaving the provisions of Rule 53.7(b) that address petitions for review undisturbed. Subdivision 49.12 mirrors Rule 10.1(a)(5) in excepting motions for rehearing and motions for en banc reconsideration from the certificate-of-conference requirement.

49.12. Certificate of Conference Not Required

A certificate of conference is not required for a motion for rehearing or en banc reconsideration of a panel's decision.

Added by Supreme Court March 10, 2008, and Aug. 20, 2008, eff. Sept. 1, 2008. Approved by Court of Criminal Appeals Sept. 30, 2008, eff. Sept. 30, 2008.

Notes and Comments

Comment to 2008 change: Rule 49 is revised to treat a motion for en banc reconsideration as a motion for rehearing and to include procedures governing the filing of a motion for en banc reconsideration. Subdivision 49.5(c) is amended to clarify that a further motion for rehearing may be filed if the court issues a different opinion, irrespective of whether the opinion is issued in connection with the overruling of a prior motion for rehearing. Issuance of a new opinion that is not substantially different should not occasion a further motion for rehearing, but a motion's lack of merit does not affect appellate deadlines. The provisions of former Rule 53.7(b) that address motions for rehearing are moved to new subdivision 49.11 without change, leaving the provisions of Rule 53.7(b) that address petitions for review undisturbed. Subdivision 49.12 mirrors Rule 10.1(a)(5) in excepting motions for rehearing and motions for en banc reconsideration from the certificate-of-conference requirement.

Rule 50. Abolished by Order of July 12, 2011, eff. Sept. 1, 2011

Notes and Comments

Comment to 2011 change: Rule 50 is abolished. Motions for rehearing serve the same purpose.

Comment to 1997 change: This is former Rule 101. The rule is amended to allow 30 days for the court of appeals to review the petition for discretionary review and to require the withdrawal of the prior opinion and judgment if the court of appeals renders a new judgment or hands down a new opinion.

Rule 51. Enforcement of Judgments After Mandate

Notes and Comments

Comment to 1997 change: Former Rules 87 and 88 are merged. The reference to costs in tax suits is deleted.

51.1. Civil Cases

(a) *Statement of Costs.* The appellate clerk must prepare, and send to the trial court clerk with the mandate, a statement of costs showing:

(1) the preparation costs for the appellate record, and any court of appeals filing fees, with a notation of those items that have been paid and those that are owing; and

(2) the party or parties against whom costs have been adjudged.

(b) *Enforcement of Judgment.* When the trial court clerk receives the mandate, the appellate court's judgment must be enforced. Appellate court costs must be included with the trial court costs in any process to enforce the judgment. If all or part of the costs are collected, the trial court clerk must immediately remit to the appellate court clerk any amount due to that clerk. The trial court need not make any further order in the case, and the appellate court's judgment may be enforced as in other cases, when the appellate judgment:

(1) affirms the trial court's judgment;

(2) modifies the trial court's judgment and, as so modified, affirms that judgment; or

(3) renders the judgment the trial court should have rendered.

Eff. Sept. 1, 1997.

51.2. Criminal Cases

When the trial court clerk receives the mandate, the appellate court's judgment must be enforced as follows:

(a) *Clerk's Duties.* The trial court clerk must:

(1) send an acknowledgment to the appellate clerk of the mandate's receipt; and

(2) immediately file the mandate.

(b) *Judgment of Affirmance; Defendant Not in Custody.*

(1) Capias to Be Issued. If the judgment contains a sentence of confinement or imprisonment that has not been suspended, the trial court must promptly issue a capias for the defendant's arrest so that the court's sentence can be executed.

(2) Contents of Capias. The capias may issue to any county of this state and must be executed and returned as in felony cases, except that no bail may be taken. The capias must:

(A) recite the fact of conviction;

(B) set forth the offense and the court's judgment and sentence;

(C) state that the judgment was appealed from and affirmed, and that the mandate has been filed; and

(D) command the sheriff to arrest and take the defendant into his custody, and to place and keep the defendant in custody until delivered to the proper authorities as directed by the sentence.

(3) Sheriff's Duties. The sheriff must promptly execute the capias as directed. The sheriff must notify the trial court clerk and the appellate clerk when the mandate has been carried out and executed.

(c) *Judgment of Reversal.*

(1) When New Trial Ordered. When the appellate court reverses the trial court's judgment and grants the defendant a new trial, the procedure is governed by Code of Criminal Procedure article 44.29. If the defendant is in custody and entitled to bail, the defendant must be released upon giving bail.

(2) When Case Dismissed. When the appellate court reverses the trial court's judgment and orders the case to be dismissed, the defendant—if in custody—must be discharged.

(d) *Judgment of Acquittal.* When the appellate court reverses a judgment and orders the defendant's acquittal, the defendant—if in custody—must be discharged, and no further order or judgment of the trial court is necessary.

Eff. Sept. 1, 1997.

SECTION THREE. ORIGINAL PROCEEDINGS IN THE SUPREME COURT AND THE COURTS OF APPEALS

Rule 52. Original Proceedings

Notes and Comments

Comment to 1997 change: Former Rules 120, 121, and 122 are merged into this rule. The requirement of a motion for leave in original proceedings is repealed. The form of the petition and response, contents of the appendix and record, page limits, and relief that may be granted are specifically stated. Specific provision is now made for a motion for rehearing. A provision for sanctions is added.

52.1. Commencement

An original appellate proceeding seeking extraordinary relief—such as a writ of habeas corpus, mandamus, prohibition, injunction, or quo warranto—is commenced by filing a petition with the clerk of the appropriate appellate court. The petition must be captioned "*In re* [name of relator]."

Eff. Sept. 1, 1997.

52.2. Designation of Parties

The party seeking the relief is the relator. In original proceedings other than habeas corpus, the person against whom relief is sought—whether a judge, court, tribunal, officer, or other person—is the respondent. A person whose interest would be directly affected by the relief sought is a real party in interest and a party to the case.

Eff. Sept. 1, 1997.

52.3. Form and Contents of Petition.

The petition must, under appropriate headings and in the order here indicated, contain the following:

(a) *Identity of Parties and Counsel.* The petition must give a complete list of all parties, and the names, and addresses of all counsel.

(b) *Table of Contents.* The petition must include a table of contents with references to the pages of the petition. The table of contents must indicate the subject matter of each issue or point, or group of issues or points.

(c) *Index of Authorities.* The petition must include an index of authorities arranged alphabetically and indicating the pages of the petition where the authorities are cited.

(d) *Statement of the Case.* The petition must contain a statement of the case that should seldom exceed one page and should not discuss the facts. The statement must contain the following:

(1) a concise description of the nature of any underlying proceeding (e.g., a suit for damages, a contempt proceeding for failure to pay child support, or the certification of a candidate for inclusion on an election ballot);

(2) if the respondent is a judge, the name of the judge, the designation of the court in which the judge was sitting, and the county in which the court is located; and if the respondent is an official other than a judge, the designation and location of the office held by the respondent;

(3) a concise description of the respondent's action from which the relator seeks relief;

(4) if the relator seeks a writ of habeas corpus, a statement describing how and where the relator is being deprived of liberty;

(5) if the petition is filed in the Supreme Court after a petition requesting the same relief was filed in the court of appeals:

(A) the date the petition was filed in the court of appeals;

(B) the district of the court of appeals and the names of the justices who participated in the decision;

(C) the author of any opinion for the court of appeals and the author of any separate opinion;

(D) the citation of the court's opinion;

(E) the disposition of the case by the court of appeals, and the date of the court of appeals' order.

(e) *Statement of Jurisdiction.* The petition must state, without argument, the basis of the court's jurisdiction. If the Supreme Court and the court of appeals have concurrent jurisdiction, the petition must be presented first to the court of appeals unless there is a compelling reason not to do so. If the petition is filed in the Supreme Court without first being presented to the court of appeals, the petition must state the compelling reason why the petition was not first presented to the court of appeals.

(f) *Issues Presented.* The petition must state concisely all issues or points presented for relief. The statement of an issue or point will be treated as covering every subsidiary question that is fairly included.

(g) *Statement of Facts.* The petition must state concisely and without argument the facts pertinent to the issues or points presented. Every statement of fact in the petition must be supported by citation to competent evidence included in the appendix or record.

(h) *Argument.* The petition must contain a clear and concise argument for the contentions made, with appropriate citations to authorities and to the appendix or record.

(i) *Prayer.* The petition must contain a short conclusion that clearly states the nature of the relief sought.

(j) *Certification.* The person filing the petition must certify that he or she has reviewed the petition and concluded that every factual statement in the petition is supported by competent evidence included in the appendix or record.

(k) *Appendix.*

(1) Necessary Contents. The appendix must contain:

(A) a certified or sworn copy of any order complained of, or any other document showing the matter complained of;

(B) any order or opinion of the court of appeals, if the petition is filed in the Supreme Court;

(C) unless voluminous or impracticable, the text of any rule, regulation, ordinance, statute, constitutional provision, or other law (excluding case law) on which the argument is based; and

(D) if a writ of habeas corpus is sought, proof that the relator is being restrained.

(2) Optional Contents. The appendix may contain any other item pertinent to the issues or points presented for review, including copies or excerpts of relevant court opinions, statutes, constitutional provisions, documents on which the suit was based, pleadings, and similar material. Items should not be included in the appendix to attempt to avoid the page limits for the petition. The appendix should not contain any evidence or other item that is not necessary for a decision.

Eff. Sept. 1, 1997. Amended by Supreme Court March 10, 2008, and Aug. 20, 2008, eff. Sept. 1, 2008. Approved by Court of Criminal Appeals Sept. 30, 2008, eff. Sept. 30, 2008.

Notes and Comments

Comment to 2008 change: The reference to "unpublished" opinions in Subdivision 52.3(d)(5)(D) is deleted. The filer should provide the best cite available for the court of appeals' opinion, which may be a LEXIS, Westlaw, or other citation to an electronic medium. Subdivision 52.3 is further amended to delete the requirement that all factual statements be verified by affidavit. Instead, the filer—in the usual case of a party with legal representation, the lead counsel—must include a statement certifying that all factual statements are supported by competent evidence in the appendix or record to which the petition has cited. The certification required by subdivision 52.3(j) does not count against the page limitations.

52.4. Response

Any party may file a response to the petition, but it is not mandatory. The court must not grant relief—other than temporary relief—before a response has been filed or requested by the court. The response must conform to the requirements of 52.3, except that:

(a) the list of parties and counsel is not required unless necessary to supplement or correct the list contained in the petition;

(b) the response need not include a statement of the case, a statement of the issues presented, or a statement of the facts unless the responding party is dissatisfied with that portion of the petition;

(c) a statement of jurisdiction should be omitted unless the petition fails to assert valid grounds for jurisdiction, in which case the reasons why the court lacks jurisdiction must be concisely stated;

(d) the argument must be confined to the issues or points presented in the petition; and

(e) the appendix to the response need not contain any item already contained in an appendix filed by the relator.

Eff. Sept. 1, 1997.

52.5. Relator's Reply to Response

The relator may file a reply addressing any matter in the response. However, the court may consider and decide the case before a reply brief is filed.

Eff. Sept. 1, 1997.

52.6. Repealed by Order of Nov. 13, 2012, eff. Dec. 1, 2012

52.7. Record

(a) *Filing by Relator Required.* Relator must file with the petition:

(1) a certified or sworn copy of every document that is material to the relator's claim for relief and that was filed in any underlying proceeding; and

(2) a properly authenticated transcript of any relevant testimony from any underlying proceeding, including any exhibits offered in evidence, or a statement that no testimony was adduced in connection with the matter complained.

(b) *Supplementation Permitted.* After the record is filed, relator or any other party to the proceeding may file additional materials for inclusion in the record.

(c) *Service of Record on All Parties.* Relator and any party who files materials for inclusion in the record must—at the same time—serve each party.

(1) those materials not previously served on that party as part of the record in another original appellate proceeding in the same or another court; and

(2) an index listing the materials filed and describing them in sufficient detail to identify them.

Eff. Sept. 1, 1997. Amended by Supreme Court Dec. 23, 2002, eff. Jan. 1, 2003.

Notes and Comments

Comment to 2002 change: Subdivision 52.7(c) added to specify how record materials in original proceedings are to be served. Ordinarily, a party must serve records materials and an index of those materials on all other parties. But when materials have already been served in related original proceedings, they need not be served again. Examples are when original proceedings, raising the same issues are brought in both the court of appeals and the Supreme Court, or when separate original proceedings are filed arising out of the same underlying lawsuit. The purpose of this procedure is to ensure that all parties have record materials readily available without requiring unnecessary duplication.

52.8. Action on Petition

(a) *Relief Denied.* If the court determines from the petition and any response and reply that the relator is not entitled to the relief sought, the court must deny the petition. If the relator in a habeas corpus proceeding has been released on bond, the court must remand the relator to custody and issue an order of commitment. If the relator is not returned to custody, the court may declare the bond to be forfeited and render judgment against the surety.

(b) *Interim Action.* If the court is of the tentative opinion that relator is entitled to the relief sought or that a serious question concerning the relief requires further consideration:

(1) the court must request a response if one has not been filed;

(2) the Supreme Court may request full briefing under Rule 55;

(3) in a habeas corpus proceeding, the court may order that relator be discharged on execution and filing of a bond in an amount set by the court; and

(4) the court may set the case for oral argument.

(c) *Relief Granted.* If the court determines that relator is entitled to relief, it must make an appropriate order. The court may grant relief without hearing oral argument.

(d) *Opinion.* When denying relief, the court may hand down an opinion but is not required to do so. When granting relief, the court must hand down an opinion as in any other case. Rule 47 is applicable to an order or opinion by a court of appeals except that the court of appeals may not order an unpublished opinion published after the Supreme Court or Court of Criminal Appeals has acted on any party's petition for extraordinary relief addressing the same issues.

Eff. Sept. 1, 1997.

52.9. Motion for Rehearing

Any party may file a motion for rehearing within 15 days after the final order is rendered. The motion must clearly state the points relied on for the rehearing. No response to a motion for rehearing need be filed unless the court so requests. The court will not grant a motion for rehearing unless a response has been filed or requested.

Eff. Sept. 1, 1997. Amended by order of March 4, 2013, eff. immediately.

52.10. Temporary Relief

(a) *Motion for Temporary Relief; Certificate of Compliance.* The relator may file a motion to stay any underlying proceedings or for any other temporary relief pending the court's action on the petition. The relator must notify or make a diligent effort to notify all parties by expedited means (such as by telephone or fax) that a motion for temporary relief has been or will be filed and must certify to the court that the relator has complied with this paragraph before temporary relief will be granted.

(b) *Grant of Temporary Relief.* The court—on motion of any party or on its own initiative—may without notice grant any just relief pending the court's action on the petition. As a condition of granting temporary relief, the court may require a bond to protect the parties who will be affected by the relief. Unless vacated or modified, an order granting temporary relief is effective until the case is finally decided.

(c) *Motion to Reconsider.* Any party may move the court at any time to reconsider a grant of temporary relief.

Eff. Sept. 1, 1997.

52.11. Groundless Petition or Misleading Statement or Record

On motion of any party or on its own initiative, the court may—after notice and a reasonable opportunity to respond—impose just sanctions on a party or attorney who is not acting in good faith as indicated by any of the following:

(a) filing a petition that is clearly groundless;

(b) bringing the petition solely for delay of an underlying proceeding;

(c) grossly misstating or omitting an obviously important and material fact in the petition or response; or

(d) filing an appendix or record that is clearly misleading because of the omission of obviously important and material evidence or documents.

Eff. Sept. 1, 1997.

SECTION FOUR. PROCEEDINGS IN THE SUPREME COURT

Rule 53. Petition for Review

Notes and Comments

Comment to 1997 change: Former Rules 130 and 131 are merged. The 50–page application for writ of error is replaced by a 15–page petition for review, which is filed in the Supreme Court and should concentrate on the reasons the Court should exercise jurisdiction to hear the case. The contents of the petition and response, the length of the documents, the time for filing are all specifically stated.

53.1. Method of Review

The Supreme Court may review a court of appeals' final judgment on a petition for review addressed to "The Supreme Court of Texas." A party who seeks to alter the court of appeals' judgment must file a petition for review. The petition for review procedure replaces the writ of error procedure. Statutes pertaining to the writ of error in the Supreme Court apply equally to the petition for review.

Eff. Sept. 1, 1997.

53.2. Contents of Petition

The petition for review must, under appropriate headings and in the order here indicated, contain the following items:

(a) *Identity of Parties and Counsel.* The petition must give a complete list of all parties to the trial court's final judgment, and the names and addresses of all trial and appellate counsel.

(b) *Table of Contents.* The petition must have a table of contents with references to the pages of the petition. The table of contents must indicate the subject matter of each issue or point, or group of issues or points.

(c) *Index of Authorities.* The petition must have an index of authorities arranged alphabetically and indicating the pages of the petition where the authorities are cited.

(d) *Statement of the Case.* The petition must contain a statement of the case that should seldom exceed one page and should not discuss the facts. The statement must contain the following:

(1) a concise description of the nature of the case (e.g., whether it is a suit for damages, on a note, or in trespass to try title);

(2) the name of the judge who signed the order or judgment appealed from;

(3) the designation of the trial court and the county in which it is located;

(4) the disposition of the case by the trial court;

(5) the parties in the court of appeals;

(6) the district of the court of appeals;

(7) the names of the justices who participated in the decision in the court of appeals, the author of the opinion for the court, and the author of any separate opinion;

(8) the citation for the court of appeals' opinion; and

(9) the disposition of the case by the court of appeals, including the disposition of any motions for rehearing or en banc reconsideration, and whether any motions for rehearing or en banc reconsideration are pending in the court of appeals at the time the petition for review is filed.

(e) *Statement of Jurisdiction.* The petition must state, without argument, the basis of the Court's jurisdiction.

(f) *Issues Presented.* The petition must state concisely all issues or points presented for review. The statement of an issue or point will be treated as covering every subsidiary question that is fairly included. If the matter complained of originated in the trial court, it should have been preserved for appellate review in the trial court and assigned as error in the court of appeals.

(g) *Statement of Facts.* The petition must affirm that the court of appeals correctly stated the nature of the case, except in any particulars pointed out. The petition must state concisely and without argument the facts and procedural background pertinent to the issues or points presented. The statement must be supported by record references.

(h) *Summary of the Argument.* The petition must contain a succinct, clear, and accurate statement of the arguments made in the body of the petition. This summary must not merely repeat the issues or points presented for review.

(i) *Argument.* The petition must contain a clear and concise argument for the contentions made, with appropriate citations to authorities and to the record. The argument need not address every issue or point included in the statement of issues or points. Any issue or point not addressed may be addressed in the brief on the merits if one is requested by the Court. The argument should state the reasons why the Supreme Court should exercise jurisdiction to hear the case with specific reference to the factors listed in Rule 56.1(a). The petition need not quote at length from a matter included in the appendix; a reference to the appendix is sufficient. The Court will consider the court of appeals' opinion along with the petition, so statements in that opinion need not be repeated.

(j) *Prayer.* The petition must contain a short conclusion that clearly states the nature of the relief sought.

(k) *Appendix.*

(1) Necessary Contents. Unless voluminous or impracticable, the appendix must contain a copy of:

(A) the judgment or other appealable order of the trial court from which relief in the court of appeals was sought;

(B) the jury charge and verdict, if any, or the trial court's findings of fact and conclusions of law, if any;

(C) the opinion and judgment of the court of appeals; and

(D) the text of any rule, regulation, ordinance, statute, constitutional provision, or other law on which the argument is based (excluding case law), and the text of any contract or other document that is central to the argument.

(2) Optional Contents. The appendix may contain any other item pertinent to the issues or points presented for review, including copies or excerpts of relevant court opinions, statutes, constitutional provisions, documents on which the suit was based, pleadings, and similar material. Items should not be included in the appendix to attempt to avoid the page limits for the petition.

Eff. Sept. 1, 1997. Amended by Supreme Court March 10, 2008, and Aug. 20, 2008, eff. Sept. 1, 2008. Approved by Court of Criminal Appeals Sept. 30, 2008, eff. Sept. 30, 2008.

Notes and Comments

Comment to 2008 change: Subdivision 53.7(a) is amended to clarify that the Supreme Court may shorten the time for filing a petition for review and that the timely filing of a motion for en banc reconsideration tolls the commencement of the 45–day period for filing a petition for review until the motion is overruled. Subdivision 53.2(d)(8) is amended to delete the reference to unpublished opinions in civil cases. Subdivision 53.2(d)(9) is amended to require a party that prematurely files a petition for review to notify the Supreme Court of any panel rehearing or en banc reconsideration motions still pending in the court of appeals. Subdivision 53.7(b) is revised to reference this new requirement and to relocate to new Rule 49.11 those provisions governing motions for rehearing.

53.3. Response to Petition for Review

Any other party to the appeal may file a response to the petition for review, but it is not mandatory. If no response is timely filed, or if a party files a waiver of response, the Court will consider the petition without a response. A petition will not be granted before a response has been filed or requested by the Court. The response must conform to the requirements of 53.2, except that:

(a) the list of parties and counsel is not required unless necessary to supplement or correct the list contained in the petition;

(b) a statement of the case and a statement of the facts need not be made unless the respondent is dissatisfied with that portion of the petition;

(c) a statement of the issues presented need not be made unless:

(1) the respondent is dissatisfied with the statement made in the petition;

(2) the respondent is asserting independent grounds for affirmance of the court of appeals' judgment; or

(3) the respondent is asserting grounds that establish the respondent's right to a judgment that is less favorable to the respondent than the judgment rendered by the court of appeals but more favorable to the respondent than the judgment that might be awarded to the petitioner (e.g., a remand for a new trial rather than a rendition of judgment in favor of the petitioner);

(d) a statement of jurisdiction should be omitted unless the petition fails to assert valid grounds for jurisdiction, in which case the reasons why the Supreme Court lacks jurisdiction must be concisely stated;

(e) the respondent's argument must be confined to the issues or points presented in the petition or asserted by the respondent in the respondent's statement of issues; and

(f) the appendix to the response need not contain any item already contained in an appendix filed by the petitioner.

Eff. Sept. 1, 1997.

53.4. Points Not Considered in Court of Appeals

To obtain a remand to the court of appeals for consideration of issues or points briefed in that court but not decided by that court, or to request that the Supreme Court consider such issues or points, a party may raise those issues or points in the petition, the response, the reply, any brief, or a motion for rehearing.

Eff. Sept. 1, 1997.

53.5. Petitioner's Reply to Response

The petitioner may file a reply addressing any matter in the response. However, the Court may consider and decide the case before a reply brief is filed.

Eff. Sept. 1, 1997.

53.6. Repealed by Order of Nov. 13, 2012, eff. Dec. 1, 2012

53.7 Time and Place of Filing

(a) *Petition.* Unless the Supreme Court orders an earlier filing deadline, the petition must be filed with the Supreme Court clerk within 45 days after the following:

(1) the date the court of appeals rendered judgment, if no motion for rehearing or en banc reconsideration is timely filed; or

(2) the date of the court of appeals' last ruling on all timely filed motions for rehearing or en banc reconsideration.

(b) *Premature Filing.* A petition filed before the last ruling on all timely filed motions for rehearing and en banc reconsideration is treated as having been filed on the date of, but after, the last ruling on any such motion. If a party files a petition for review while a motion for rehearing or en banc reconsideration is pending in the court of appeals, the party must include that information in its petition for review.

(c) *Petitions Filed by Other Parties.* If a party files a petition for review within the time specified in 53.7(a)—or within the time specified by the Supreme Court in an order granting an extension of time to file a petition—any other party required to file a petition may do so within 45 days after the last timely motion for rehearing is overruled or within 30 days after any preceding petition is filed, whichever date is later.

(d) *Response.* Any response must be filed with the Supreme Court clerk within 30 days after the petition is filed.

(e) *Reply.* Any reply must be filed with the Supreme Court clerk within 15 days after the response is filed.

(f) *Extension of Time.* The Supreme Court may extend the time to file a petition for review if a party files a motion complying with Rule 10.5(b) no later than 15 days after the last day for filing the petition. The Supreme Court may extend the time to file a response or reply if a party files a motion complying with Rule 10.5(b) either before or after the response or reply is due.

(g) *Petition Filed in Court of Appeals.* If a petition is mistakenly filed in the court of appeals, the petition is deemed to have been filed the same day with the Supreme Court clerk, and the court of appeals clerk must immediately send the petition to the Supreme Court clerk.

Eff. Sept. 1, 1997. Amended by Supreme Court March 10, 2008, and Aug. 20, 2008, eff. Sept. 1, 2008. Approved by Court of Criminal Appeals Sept. 30, 2008, eff. Sept. 30, 2008.

Notes and Comments

Comment to 2008 change: Subdivision 53.7(a) is amended to clarify that the Supreme Court may shorten the time for filing a petition for review and that the timely filing of a motion for en banc reconsideration tolls the commencement of the 45–day period for filing a petition for review until the motion is overruled. Subdivision 53.2(d)(8) is amended to delete the reference to unpublished opinions in civil cases. Subdivision 53.2(d)(9) is amended to require a party that prematurely files a petition for review to notify the Supreme Court of any panel rehearing or en banc reconsideration motions still pending in the court of appeals. Subdivision 53.7(b) is revised to reference this new requirement and to relocate to new Rule 49.11 those provisions governing motions for rehearing.

53.8. Amendment

On motion showing good cause, the Court may allow the petition, response, or reply to be amended on such reasonable terms as the Court may prescribe.

Eff. Sept. 1, 1997.

53.9. Court May Require Revision

If a petition, response, or reply does not conform with these rules, the Supreme Court may require the document to be revised or may return the document to the party who filed it and consider the case without allowing the document to be revised.

Eff. Sept. 1, 1997.

Rule 54. Filing the Record

Notes and Comments

Comment to 1997 change: This is former Rule 132. Subdivision 54.1 is new and provides for the Supreme Court to request the filing of the record. Other changes are made.

54.1. Request for Record

With or without granting the petition for review, the Supreme Court may request that the record from the court of appeals be filed with the clerk of the Supreme Court.

Eff. Sept. 1, 1997.

54.2. Duty of Court of Appeals Clerk

(a) *Request for Record.* The court of appeals clerk must not send the record to the Supreme Court unless it is requested. Upon receiving the Supreme Court clerk's request for the record, the court of appeals clerk must promptly send to the Supreme Court clerk all of the following:

(1) the original record;

(2) any motion filed in the court of appeals;

(3) copies of all orders of the court of appeals; and

(4) copies of all opinions and the judgment of the court of appeals.

(b) *Nondocumentary Exhibits.* The clerk should not send any nondocumentary exhibits unless the Supreme Court specifically requests.

Eff. Sept. 1, 1997.

54.3. Expenses

The petitioner must pay to the court of appeals clerk a sum sufficient to pay the cost of mailing or shipping the record to and from the Supreme Court clerk.

Eff. Sept. 1, 1997.

54.4. Duty of Supreme Court Clerk

Upon receiving the record, the Supreme Court clerk must file it and enter the filing on the docket. The clerk may refuse the record if the charges for mailing or shipping have not been paid.

Eff. Sept. 1, 1997.

Rule 55. Briefs on the Merits

Notes and Comments

Comment to 1997 change: The rule is new and provides for a 50 page brief on the merits if requested by the Supreme Court.

55.1. Request by Court

A brief on the merits must not be filed unless requested by the Court. With or without granting the petition for review, the Court may request the parties to file briefs on the merits. In appropriate cases, the Court may realign parties and direct that parties file consolidated briefs.

Eff. Sept. 1, 1997. Amended by Supreme Court Dec. 23, 2002, eff. Jan. 1, 2003.

Notes and Comments

Comment to 2002 change: Subdivision 55.1 is clarified to provide that the Court may realign parties require consolidated briefing for a clearer and more efficient presentation of the case.

55.2. Petitioner's Brief on the Merits

The petitioner's brief on the merits must be confined to the issues or points stated in the petition for review and must, under appropriate headings and in the order here indicated, contain the following items:

(a) *Identity of Parties and Counsel.* The brief must give a complete list of all parties to the trial court's final judgment, and the names and addresses of all trial and appellate counsel.

(b) *Table of Contents.* The brief must have a table of contents with references to the pages of the brief. The table of contents must indicate the subject matter of each issue or point, or group of issues or points.

(c) *Index of Authorities.* The brief must have an index of authorities arranged alphabetically and indicating the pages of the brief where the authorities are cited.

(d) *Statement of the Case.* The brief must contain a statement of the case that should seldom exceed one page and should not discuss the facts. The statement must contain the following:

(1) a concise description of the nature of the case (e.g., whether it is a suit for damages, on a note, or in trespass to try title);

(2) the name of the judge who signed the order or judgment appealed from;

(3) the designation of the trial court and the county in which it is located;

(4) the disposition of the case by the trial court;

(5) the parties in the court of appeals;

(6) the district of the court of appeals;

(7) the names of the justices who participated in the decision in the court of appeals, the author of the opinion for the court, and the author of any separate opinion;

(8) the citation for the court of appeals' opinion, if available, or a statement that the opinion was unpublished; and

(9) the disposition of the case by the court of appeals;

(e) *Statement of Jurisdiction.* The brief must state, without argument, the basis of the Court's jurisdiction.

(f) *Issues Presented.* The brief must state concisely all issues or points presented for review. The statement of an issue or point will be treated as covering every subsidiary question that is fairly included. The phrasing of the issues or points need not be identical to the statement of issues or points in the petition for review, but the brief may not raise additional issues or points or change the substance of the issues or points presented in the petition.

(g) *Statement of Facts.* The brief must affirm that the court of appeals correctly stated the nature of the case, except in any particulars pointed out. The brief must state concisely and without argument the facts and procedural background pertinent to the issues or points presented. The statement must be supported by record references.

(h) *Summary of the Argument.* The brief must contain a succinct, clear, and accurate statement of the arguments made in the body of the brief. This summary must not merely repeat the issues or points presented for review.

(i) *Argument.* The brief must contain a clear and concise argument for the contentions made, with appropriate citations to authorities and to the record.

(j) *Prayer.* The brief must contain a short conclusion that clearly states the nature of the relief sought.

Eff. Sept. 1, 1997. Amended by Supreme Court Dec. 23, 2002, eff. Jan. 1, 2003.

55.3. Respondent's Brief

If the petitioner files a brief on the merits, any other party to the appeal may file a brief in response, which must conform to 55.2, except that:

(a) the list of parties and counsel is not required unless necessary to supplement or correct the list contained in the petitioner's brief;

(b) a statement of the case and a statement of the facts need not be made unless the respondent is dissatisfied with that portion of the petitioner's brief; and

(c) a statement of the issues presented need not be made unless:

(1) the respondent is dissatisfied with the statement made in the petitioner's brief;

(2) the respondent is asserting independent grounds for affirmance of the court of appeals' judgment; or

(3) the respondent is asserting grounds that establish the respondent's right to a judgment that is less favorable to the respondent than the judgment rendered by the court of appeals but more favorable to the respondent than the judgment that might be awarded to the petitioner (e.g., a remand for a new trial rather than a rendition of judgment in favor of the petitioner);

(d) a statement of jurisdiction should be omitted unless the petition fails to assert valid grounds for jurisdiction; and

(e) the respondent's argument must be confined to the issues or points presented in the petitioner's brief or asserted by the respondent in the respondent's statement of issues.

Eff. Sept 1, 1997.

55.4. Petitioner's Brief in Reply

The petitioner may file a reply brief addressing any matter in the brief in response. However, the Court may consider and decide the case before a reply brief is filed.

Eff. Sept. 1, 1997.

55.5. Reliance on Prior Brief

As a brief on the merits or a brief in response, a party may file the brief that the party filed in the court of appeals.

Eff. Sept. 1, 1997.

55.6. Repealed by Order of Nov. 13, 2012, eff. Dec. 1, 2012

55.7. Time and Place of Filing; Extension of Time

Briefs must be filed with the Supreme Court clerk in accordance with the schedule stated in the clerk's notice that the Court has requested briefs on the merits. If no schedule is stated in the notice, petitioner must file a brief on the merits within 30 days after the date of the notice, respondent must file a brief in response within 20 days after receiving petitioner's brief, and petitioner must file any reply brief within 15 days after receiving respondent's brief. On motion complying with Rule 10.5(b) either before or after the brief is due, the Supreme Court may extend the time to file a brief.

Eff. Sept. 1, 1997.

55.8. Amendment

On motion showing good cause, the Court may allow a party to amend a brief on such reasonable terms as the Court may prescribe.

Eff. Sept. 1, 1997.

55.9. Court May Require Revision

If a brief does not conform with these rules, the Supreme Court may require the brief to be revised or may return it to the party who filed it and consider the case without further briefing by that party.

Eff. Sept. 1, 1997.

Rule 56. Orders on Petition for Review

Notes and Comments

Comment to 1997 change: The rule is from former Rule 133. Subdivision 56.3 regarding settled cases is added.

56.1. Orders on Petition for Review

(a) *Considerations in Granting Review.* Whether to grant review is a matter of judicial discretion. Among the factors the Supreme Court considers in deciding whether to grant a petition for review are the following:

(1) whether the justices of the court of appeals disagree on an important point of law;

(2) whether there is a conflict between the courts of appeals on an important point of law;

(3) whether a case involves the construction or validity of a statute;

(4) whether a case involves constitutional issues;

(5) whether the court of appeals appears to have committed an error of law of such importance to the state's jurisprudence that it should be corrected; and

(6) whether the court of appeals has decided an important question of state law that should be, but has not been, resolved by the Supreme Court.

(b) *Petition Denied or Dismissed.* When the petition has been on file in the Supreme Court for 30 days, the Court may deny or dismiss the petition—whether or not a response has been filed—with one of the following notations:

(1) "Denied." If the Supreme Court is not satisfied that the opinion of the court of appeals has correctly declared the law in all respects, but determines that the petition presents no error that requires reversal or that is of such importance to the jurisprudence of the state as to require correction, the Court will deny the petition with the notation "Denied."

(2) "Dismissed w.o.j." If the Supreme Court lacks jurisdiction, the Court will dismiss the petition with the notation "Dismissed for Want of Jurisdiction."

(c) *Petition Refused.* If the Supreme Court determines—after a response has been filed or requested—that the court of appeals' judgment is correct and that the legal principles announced in the opinion are likewise correct, the Court will refuse the petition with the notation "Refused." The court of appeals' opinion in the case has the same precedential value as an opinion of the Supreme Court.

(d) *Improvident Grant.* If the Court has granted review but later decides that review should not have been granted, the Court may, without opinion, set aside the order granting review and dismiss the petition or deny or refuse review as though review had never been granted.

Eff. Sept. 1, 1997.

56.2. Moot Cases

If a case is moot, the Supreme Court may, after notice to the parties, grant the petition and, without hearing argument, dismiss the case or the appealable portion of it without addressing the merits of the appeal.

Eff. Sept. 1, 1997.

56.3. Settled Cases

If a case is settled by agreement of the parties and all parties so move, the Supreme Court may grant the petition if it has not already been granted and, without hearing argument or considering the merits, render a judgment to effectuate the agreement. The Supreme Court's action may include setting aside the judgment of the court of appeals or the trial court without regard to the merits and remanding the case to the trial court for rendition of a judgment in accordance with the agreement. The Supreme Court may abate the case until the lower court's proceedings to effectuate the agreement are complete. A severable portion of the proceeding may be disposed of if it will not prejudice the remaining parties. In any event, the Supreme Court's order does not vacate the court of appeals' opinion unless the order specifically provides otherwise. An agreement or motion cannot be conditioned on vacating the court of appeals' opinion.

Eff. Sept. 1, 1997. Amended by Supreme Court Dec. 23, 2002, eff. Jan. 1, 2003.

Notes and Comments

Comment to 2002 change: Subdivision 56.3 is clarified to provide for partial settlements.

56.4. Notice to Parties

When the Supreme Court grants, denies, refuses, or dismisses a petition for review, the Supreme Court clerk must send a written notice of the disposition to the court of appeals, the trial court, and all parties to the appeal.

Eff. Sept. 1, 1997.

56.5. Return of Documents to Court of Appeals

When the Supreme Court denies, refuses, or dismisses a petition for review, the clerk will retain the petition, together with the record and accompanying papers, for 30 days after the order is rendered. If no motion for rehearing has been filed by the end of that period or when any motion for rehearing of the order has been overruled, the clerk must send a certified copy of its order to the court of appeals and return the record and all papers (except for documents filed in the Supreme Court) to the court of appeals clerk.

Eff. Sept. 1, 1997.

Rule 57. Direct Appeals to the Supreme Court

Notes and Comments

Comment to 1997 change: This is former Rule 140. The rule is amended without substantive change except subdivision 57.5 is amended to make clear that no party to the direct appeal may pursue the appeal in the court of appeals while the direct appeal is pending, but allowing 10 days to perfect a subsequent appeal.

57.1. Application

This rule governs direct appeals to the Supreme Court that are authorized by the Constitution and by statute. Except when inconsistent with a statute or this rule, the rules governing appeals to courts of appeals also apply to direct appeals to the Supreme Court.

Eff. Sept. 1, 1997.

57.2. Jurisdiction

The Supreme Court may not take jurisdiction over a direct appeal from the decision of any court other than a district court or county court, or over any question of fact. The Supreme Court may decline to exercise jurisdiction over a direct appeal of an interlocutory order if the record is not adequately developed, or if its decision would be advisory, or if the case is not of such importance to the jurisprudence of the state that a direct appeal should be allowed.

Eff. Sept. 1, 1997.

57.3. Statement of Jurisdiction

Appellant must file with the record a statement fully but plainly setting out the basis asserted for exercise of the Supreme Court's jurisdiction. Appellee may file a response to appellant's statement of jurisdiction within ten days after the statement is filed.

Eff. Sept. 1, 1997.

57.4. Preliminary Ruling on Jurisdiction

If the Supreme Court notes probable jurisdiction over a direct appeal, the parties must file briefs under Rule 38[1] as in any other case. If the Supreme Court does not note probable jurisdiction over a direct appeal, the appeal will be dismissed.

Eff. Sept. 1, 1997.

1 Vernon's Ann.Rules App.Proc., rule 38.1 et seq.

57.5. Direct Appeal Exclusive While Pending

If a direct appeal to the Supreme Court is filed, the parties to the appeal must not, while that appeal is pending, pursue an appeal to the court of appeals. But if the direct appeal is dismissed, any party may pursue any other appeal available at the time when the direct appeal was filed. The other appeal must be perfected within ten days after dismissal of the direct appeal.

Eff. Sept. 1, 1997.

Rule 58. Certification of Questions of Law by United States Courts

Notes and Comments

Comment to 1997 change: This is former Rule 114. The rule is substantially revised, but no substantive change in procedure is intended.

58.1. Certification

The Supreme Court of Texas may answer questions of law certified to it by any federal appellate court if the certifying court is presented with determinative questions of Texas law having no controlling Supreme Court precedent. The Supreme Court may decline to answer the questions certified to it.

Eff. Sept. 1, 1997.

58.2. Contents of the Certification Order

An order from the certifying court must set forth:

(a) the questions of law to be answered; and

(b) a stipulated statement of all facts relevant to the questions certified, showing fully the nature of the controversy in which the questions arose.

Eff. Sept. 1, 1997.

58.3. Transmission of Certification Order

The clerk of the certifying court must send to the clerk of the Supreme Court of Texas the following:

(a) the certification order under the certifying court's official seal;

(b) a list of the names of all parties to the pending case, giving the address and telephone number, if known, of any party not represented by counsel; and

(c) a list of the names, addresses, and telephone numbers of counsel for each party.

Eff. Sept. 1, 1997.

58.4. Transmission of Record

The certifying court should not send the Supreme Court of Texas the record in the pending case with the certification order. The Supreme Court may later require the original or copies of all or part of the record before the certifying court to be filed with the Supreme Court clerk.

Eff. Sept. 1, 1997.

58.5. Fees and Costs

Unless the certifying court orders otherwise in its certification order, the parties must bear equally the fees under Rule 5.

Eff. Sept. 1, 1997.

58.6. Notice

If the Supreme Court agrees to answer the questions certified to it, the Court will notify all parties and the certifying court. The Supreme Court clerk must also send a notice to the Attorney General of Texas if:

(a) the constitutionality of a Texas statute is the subject of a certified question that the Supreme Court has agreed to answer; and

(b) the State of Texas or an officer, agency, or employee of the state is not a party to the proceeding in the certifying court.

Eff. Sept. 1, 1997.

58.7. Briefs and Oral Argument

(a) *Briefs.* The appealing party in the certifying court must file a brief with the Supreme Court clerk within 30 days after the date of the notice. Opposing parties must file an answering brief within 20 days after receiving the opening brief. Briefs must comply with Rule 55[1] to the extent its provisions apply. On motion complying with Rule 10.5(b), either before or after the brief is due, the Supreme Court may extend the time to file a brief.

(b) *Oral Argument.* Oral argument may be granted either on a party's request or on the Court's own initiative. Argument is governed by Rule 59.[2]

Eff. Sept. 1, 1997.

[1] Vernon's Ann.Rules App.Proc., rule 55.1 et seq.

[2] Vernon's Ann.Rules App.Proc., rule 59.1 et seq.

58.8. Intervention by the State

If the constitutionality of a Texas statute is the subject of a certified question that the Supreme Court has agreed to answer the State of Texas may intervene at any reasonable time for briefing and oral argument (if argument is allowed), on the question of constitutionality.

Eff. Sept. 1, 1997.

58.9. Opinion on Certified Questions

If the Supreme Court has agreed to answer a certified question, it will hand down an opinion as in any other case.

Eff. Sept. 1, 1997.

58.10. Answering Certified Questions

After all motions for rehearing have been overruled, the Supreme Court clerk must send to the certifying court the written opinion on the certified questions. The opinion must be under the Supreme Court's seal.

Eff. Sept. 1, 1997.

Rule 59. Submission and Argument

Notes and Comments

Comment to 1997 change: Former Rules 170, 171, and 172 are merged. Subdivisions 59.2 and 59.3 are new. Other changes are made.

59.1. Submission Without Argument

If at least six members of the Court so vote, a petition may be granted and an opinion handed down without oral argument.

Eff. Sept. 1, 1997.

59.2. Submission With Argument

If the Supreme Court decides that oral argument would aid the Court, the Court will set the case for argument. The clerk will notify all parties of the submission date.

Eff. Sept. 1, 1997.

59.3. Purpose of Argument

Oral argument should emphasize and clarify the written arguments in the briefs. Counsel should not merely read from a prepared text. Counsel should assume that all Justices have read the briefs before oral argument and should be prepared to respond to the Justices' questions.

Eff. Sept. 1, 1997.

59.4. Time for Argument

Each side is allowed only as much time as the Court orders. Counsel is not required to use all the allotted time. On motion filed before the day of argument, the Court may extend the time for argument. The Court may also align the parties for purposes of presenting argument.

Eff. Sept. 1, 1997.

59.5. Number of Counsel

Generally, only one counsel should argue for each side. Except on leave of court, no more than two counsel on each side may argue. Only one counsel may argue in rebuttal.

59.6. Argument by Amicus Curiae

With leave of court obtained before the argument and with a party's consent, an amicus may share allotted time with that party. Otherwise, counsel for amicus curiae may not argue.

Eff. Sept. 1, 1997.

Rule 60. Judgments in the Supreme Court

Notes and Comments

Comment to 1997 change: Former Rules 180 and 182(a) are merged. Subdivision 60.1 is from former Rule 181. Paragraphs 60.2(b), (e), and (f) are new but codify current practice. Subdivision 60.6 is new. Other changes are made.

60.1. Announcement of Judgments

The Court's judgments will be announced by the clerk.

Eff. Sept. 1, 1997.

60.2. Types of Judgment

The Supreme Court may:

(a) affirm the lower court's judgment in whole or in part;

(b) modify the lower court's judgment and affirm it as modified;

(c) reverse the lower court's judgment in whole or in part and render the judgment that the lower court should have rendered;

(d) reverse the lower court's judgment and remand the case for further proceedings;

(e) vacate the judgments of the lower courts and dismiss the case; or

(f) vacate the lower court's judgment and remand the case for further proceedings in light of changes in the law.

Eff. Sept. 1, 1997.

60.3. Remand in the Interest of Justice

When reversing the court of appeals' judgment, the Supreme Court may, in the interest of justice, remand the case to the trial court even if a rendition of judgment is otherwise appropriate.

Eff. Sept. 1, 1997.

60.4. Judgment for Costs

The Supreme Court's judgment will award to the prevailing party the costs incurred by that party in the Supreme Court. If appropriate, the judgment may also award the prevailing party the costs—including preparation costs for the record—incurred by that party in the court of appeals and in the trial court. But the Court may tax costs otherwise as required by law or for good cause.

Eff. Sept. 1, 1997.

60.5. Judgment Against Sureties

When affirming, modifying, or rendering a judgment against the party who was the appellant in the court of appeals, the Supreme Court must render judgment against the sureties on that party's supersedeas bond, if any, for the performance of the judgment. If the Supreme Court taxes costs against the party who was the appellant in the court of appeals, the Court must render judgment for those costs against the sureties on that party's supersedeas bond, if any.

60.6. Other Orders

The Supreme Court may make any other appropriate order required by the law and the nature of the case.

Eff. Sept. 1, 1997.

Rule 61. Reversible Error

Notes and Comments

Comment to 1997 change: Former Rules 184 and 185 are merged. The reversible error standard is amended to omit the reference to an action "reasonably calculated to cause" an improper judgment, but no substantive change is intended. Subdivision 61.3 is amended to delete the reference to defects of "substance."

61.1. Standard for Reversible Error

No judgment may be reversed on appeal on the ground that the trial court made an error of law unless the Supreme Court concludes that the error complained of:

(a) probably caused the rendition of an improper judgment; or

(b) probably prevented the petitioner from properly presenting the case to the appellate courts.

Eff. Sept. 1, 1997.

61.2. Error Affecting Only Part of the Case

If the error affects a part, but not all, of the matter in controversy, and that part is separable without unfairness to the parties, the judgment must be reversed and a new trial ordered only as to the part affected by the error. The Court may not order a separate trial solely on unliquidated damages if liability is contested.

Eff. Sept. 1, 1997.

61.3. Defects in Procedure

The Supreme Court will not affirm or reverse a judgment or dismiss a petition for review for formal defects or irregularities in appellate procedure without allowing a reasonable time to correct or amend the defects or irregularities.

Eff. Sept. 1, 1997.

61.4. Remediable Error of the Trial Court or Court of Appeals

(a) *Generally.* The Supreme Court will not affirm or reverse a judgment or dismiss a petition for review if:

(1) the trial court's or court of appeals' erroneous action or failure or refusal to act prevents the proper presentation of a case to the Supreme Court; and

(2) the trial court or court of appeals can correct its action or failure to act.

(b) *Supreme Court Direction if Error Remediable.* If the circumstances described in (a) exist, the Supreme Court will direct the trial court or court of appeals to correct the error. The Supreme Court will then proceed as if the error had not occurred.

Eff. Sept. 1, 1997.

Rule 62. Damages for Frivolous Appeals

If the Supreme Court determines that a direct appeal or a petition for review is frivolous, it may—on motion of any party or on its own initiative, after notice and a reasonable opportunity for response—award to each prevailing party just damages. In determining whether to award damages, the Court must not consider any matter that does not appear in the record, briefs, or other papers filed in the court of appeals or the Supreme Court.

Eff. Sept. 1, 1997.

Notes and Comments

Comment to 1997 change: This is former Rule 182(b). The rule is changed from allowing a sanction when an appeal "filed for delay and without sufficient cause" to allowing a sanction when the appeal is "frivolous." A requirement for notice and an opportunity to respond is included.

Rule 63. Opinions; Copy of Opinion and Judgment to Interested Parties and Other Courts

The Supreme Court will hand down a written opinion in all cases in which it renders a judgment. The clerk will send a copy of the opinion and judgment to the court of appeals clerk, the trial court clerk, the regional administrative judge, and all parties to the appeal.

Eff. Sept. 1, 1997.

Notes and Comments

Comment to 1997 change: This is former Rule 181 with changes.

Rule 64. Motion for Rehearing

Notes and Comments

Comment to 1997 change: This is former Rule 190. The service and notice provisions of former subdivisions (b) and (c) are deleted. *See* Rule 9.5. Other changes are made.

64.1. Time for Filing

A motion for rehearing may be filed with the Supreme Court clerk within 15 days from the date when the Court renders judgment or makes an order disposing of a petition for review. In exceptional cases, if justice requires, the Court may shorten the time within which the motion may be filed or even deny the right to file it altogether.

Eff. Sept. 1, 1997.

64.2. Contents

The motion must specify the points relied on for the rehearing.

Eff. Sept. 1, 1997.

64.3. Response and Decision

No response to a motion for rehearing need be filed unless the Court so requests. A motion will not be granted unless a response has been filed or requested by the Court. But in exceptional cases, if justice so requires, the Court may deny the right to file a response and act on a motion any time after it is filed.

Eff. Sept. 1, 1997.

64.4. Second Motion

The Court will not consider a second motion for rehearing unless the Court modifies its judgment, vacates its judgment and renders a new judgment, or issues a different opinion.

Eff. Sept. 1, 1997. Amended by Supreme Court Aug. 20, 2008, eff. Sept. 1, 2008. Approved by Court of Criminal Appeals Sept. 30, 2008, eff. Sept. 30, 2008.

Notes and Comments

Comment to 2008 change: Subdivision 64.4 is amended to reflect the Court's practice of considering a second motion for rehearing after modifying its judgment or opinion in response to a prior motion for rehearing. When the Court modifies its opinion without modifying its judgment, the Court will ordinarily deny a second motion for rehearing unless the new opinion is substantially different from the original opinion.

64.5. Extensions of Time

The Court may extend the time to file a motion for rehearing in the Supreme Court, if a motion complying with Rule 10.5(b) is filed with the Court no later than 15 days after the last date for filing a motion for rehearing.

Eff. Sept. 1, 1997.

64.6. Repealed by Order of Nov. 13, 2012, eff. Dec. 1, 2012

Rule 65. Enforcement of Judgment after Mandate

Notes and Comments

Comment to 1997 change: Subdivision 65.1 is new. Subdivision 65.2 is from former Rule 183.

65.1. Statement of Costs

The Supreme Court clerk will prepare, and send to the clerk to whom the mandate is directed, a statement of costs showing:

(a) the costs that were incurred in the Supreme Court, with a notation of those items that have been paid and those that are owing; and

(b) the party or parties against whom costs have been adjudged.

Eff. Sept. 1, 1997.

65.2. Enforcement of Judgment

If the Supreme Court renders judgment, the trial court need not make any further order. Upon receiving the Supreme Court's mandate, the trial court clerk must proceed to enforce the judgment of the Supreme Court's as in any other case. Appellate court costs must be included with the trial court costs in any process to enforce the judgment. If all or part of the costs are collected, the trial court clerk must immediately remit to the appellate court clerk any amount due to that clerk.

Eff. Sept. 1, 1997.

SECTION FIVE. PROCEEDINGS IN THE COURT OF CRIMINAL APPEALS

Rule 66. Discretionary Review in General

Notes and Comments

Comment to 1997 change: This is former Rule 200. The former rule's reference to motions for rehearing now appears in Rule 49.9. The rule is otherwise amended without substantive change.

66.1. With or Without Petition

The Court of Criminal Appeals may review a court of appeals' decision in a criminal case on its own initiative under Rule 67[1] or on the petition of a party under Rule 68.[2]

Eff. Sept. 1, 1997.

1 Vernon's Ann.Rules App.Proc., rule 67.1 et seq.

2 Vernon's Ann.Rules App.Proc., rule 68.1 et seq.

66.2. Not a Matter of Right

Discretionary review by the Court of Criminal Appeals is not a matter of right, but of the Court's discretion.

Eff. Sept. 1, 1997.

66.3. Reasons for Granting Review

While neither controlling nor fully measuring the Court of Criminal Appeals' discretion, the following will be considered by the Court in deciding whether to grant discretionary review:

(a) whether a court of appeals' decision conflicts with another court of appeals' decision on the same issue;

(b) whether a court of appeals has decided an important question of state or federal law that has not been, but should be, settled by the Court of Criminal Appeals;

(c) whether a court of appeals has decided an important question of state or federal law in a way that conflicts with the applicable decisions of the Court of Criminal Appeals or the Supreme Court of the United States;

(d) whether a court of appeals has declared a statute, rule, regulation, or ordinance unconstitutional, or appears to have misconstrued a statute, rule, regulation, or ordinance;

(e) whether the justices of a court of appeals have disagreed on a material question of law necessary to the court's decision; and

(f) whether a court of appeals has so far departed from the accepted and usual course of judicial proceedings, or so far sanctioned such a departure by a lower court, as to call for an exercise of the Court of Criminal Appeals' power of supervision.

Eff. Sept. 1, 1997.

66.4. Documents to Aid Decision

(a) *Acquiring Documents.* The Court of Criminal Appeals—or any judge of the Court—may order the court of appeals clerk to promptly send the following items to the Court in order to aid it in deciding whether to grant discretionary review:

(1) the appellate record;

(2) a copy of the opinions of the court of appeals;

(3) a copy of the motions filed in the court of appeals; and

(4) certified copies of any judgment or order of the court of appeals.

(b) *Return of Documents.* If discretionary review is not granted, the clerk of the Court of Criminal Appeals will return the appellate record to the court of appeals clerk.

Eff. Sept. 1, 1997.

Rule 67. Discretionary Review Without Petition

Notes and Comments

Comment to 1997 change: This is former Rule 201. The rule is amended without substantive change.

67.1. Four Judges Vote

By a vote of at least four judges, the Court of Criminal Appeals may grant review of a court of appeals' decision in a criminal case at any time before the mandate of the court of appeals issues. An order granting review will be filed with the clerk of the Court of Criminal Appeals, who must send a copy to the court of appeals clerk.

Eff. Sept. 1, 1997. Amended by Court of Criminal Appeals Aug. 10, 2000 and Oct. 16, 2000, eff. Jan. 1, 2001; Supreme Court Sept. 12, 2000, eff. Jan. 1, 2001.

Notes and Comments

Comment to 2000 change: Language which was in the catchline of former Rule 201 has been deleted from Rule 67.1, to restore the substance of the rule, and to remove any implication that the court may not grant review on its own motion when a petition for discretionary review has been filed.

The Court of Criminal Appeals order dated October 16, 2000, provides in part:

"2. These changes take effect January 1, 2001. Unless this order provides otherwise, they shall govern all proceedings in motions for new trial, appeals, petitions for discretionary review, and petitions or applications for extraordinary writs thereafter brought and in all such proceedings then pending, except to the extent that in the opinion of the court their application in a particular proceeding then pending would not be feasible or would work injustice, in which case the former procedure may be followed.

"3. The notes and comments appended to these changes are incomplete, are included only for the convenience of the bench and bar, and are not a part of the rules."

67.2. Order Staying Mandate

To provide enough time for the Court of Criminal Appeals to decide whether to grant discretionary review under 67.1, the Court—or any judge of the Court—may file with the clerk of the court of appeals an order staying the court of appeals' mandate. The order must be signed by a judge of the Court of Criminal Appeals. The clerk of the Court of Criminal Appeals must immediately send a copy of the order to the court of appeals clerk.

Eff. Sept. 1, 1997.

67.3. Time to Issue Mandate Extended

Unless otherwise limited in the order itself, an order staying the court of appeals' mandate under 67.2 will extend for an additional 45 days the time before issuance of the court of appeals' mandate. An order granting review prevents the issuance of the court of appeals' mandate pending the further order of the Court of Criminal Appeals. If four judges do not agree to grant review within that time the court of appeals clerk must issue the mandate.

Eff. Sept. 1, 1997.

Rule 68. Discretionary Review With Petition

Notes and Comments

Comment to 1997 change: This is former Rule 202. Subdivisions (k) and (*l*) of the former rule have been relocated to Rule 69. The new rule limits the length of a petition and reply. The time for amendment of a petition or reply is increased to conform with the amendment in Rule 50. The rule is otherwise amended without substantive change.

68.1. Generally

On petition by any party, the Court of Criminal Appeals may review a court of appeals' decision in a criminal case.

Eff. Sept. 1, 1997.

68.2. Time to File Petition

(a) *First Petition.* The petition must be filed within 30 days after either the day the court of appeals' judgment was rendered or the day the last timely motion for rehearing or timely motion for en banc reconsideration was overruled by the court of appeals.

(b) *Subsequent Petition.* Even if the time specified in (a) has expired, a party who otherwise may file a petition may do so within 10 days after the timely filing of another party's petition.

(c) *Extension of Time.* The Court of Criminal Appeals may extend the time to file a petition for discretionary review if a party files a motion complying with Rule 10.5(b) no later than 15 days after the last day for filing the petition. The Court of Criminal Appeals may extend the time to file a response or reply if a party files a motion complying with Rule 10.5(b) either before or after the response or reply is due.

Eff. Sept. 1, 1997. Amended by Court of Criminal Appeals July 12, 2011, eff. Sept. 1, 2011.

Notes and Comments

Comment to 2011 change: The amendment to Rule 68.2(a) resolves timely tiling questions concerning motions for en banc reconsideration by including those motions in calculating time to file.

68.3. Where to File Petition

(a) The petition and all copies of the petition must be filed with the clerk of the Court of Criminal Appeals.

(b) *Petition filed in Court of Appeals.* If a petition is mistakenly filed in the court of appeals, the petition is deemed to have been filed the same day with the clerk of the Court of Criminal Appeals, and the court of appeals clerk must immediately send the petition to the clerk of the Court of Criminal Appeals.

Eff. Sept. 1, 1997. Amended by Court of Criminal Appeals July 12, 2011, eff. Sept. 1, 2011.

Notes and Comments

Comment to 2011 change: Rule 68.3 is changed to require petitions for discretionary review to be filed in the Court of Criminal Appeals rather than in the court of appeals. With the deletion of Rule 50, there is no reason to file petitions in the court of appeals, Rule 68.3(b) is added to address and prevent the untimely filing of petitions for discretionary review that are incorrectly filed in the court of appeals rather than in the Court of Criminal Appeals.

68.4. Contents of Petition

A petition for discretionary review must be as brief as possible. It must be addressed to the "Court of Criminal Appeals of Texas" and must state the name of the party or parties applying for review. The petition must contain the following items:

(a) *Identity of Judge, Parties, and Counsel.* The petition must list the trial court judge, all parties to the judgment or order appealed from, and the names and addresses of all trial and appellate counsel.

(b) *Table of Contents.* The petition must include a table of contents with references to the pages of the petition. The table of contents must indicate the subject matter of each ground or question presented for review.

(c) *Index of Authorities.* The petition must include an index of authorities arranged alphabetically and indicating the pages of the petition where the authorities are cited.

(d) *Statement Regarding Oral Argument.* The petition must include a short statement of why oral argument would be helpful, or a statement that oral argument is waived. If a reply or cross-petition is filed, it likewise must include a statement of why oral argument should or should not be heard.

(e) *Statement of the Case.* The petition must state briefly the nature of the case. This statement should seldom exceed half a page. The details of the case should be reserved and stated with the pertinent grounds or questions.

(f) *Statement of Procedural History.* The petition must state:

(1) the date any opinion of the court of appeals was handed down, or the date of any order of the court of appeals disposing of the case without an opinion;

(2) the date any motion for rehearing was filed (or a statement that none was filed); and

(3) the date the motion for rehearing was overruled or otherwise disposed of.

(g) *Grounds for Review.* The petition must state briefly, without argument, the grounds on which the petition is based. The grounds must be separately numbered. If the petitioner has access to the record, the petitioner must (after each ground) refer to the page of the record where the matter complained of is found. Instead of listing grounds for review, the petition may contain the questions presented for review, expressed in the terms and circumstances of the case but without unnecessary detail. The statement of questions should be short and concise, not argumentative or repetitious.

(h) *Argument.* The petition must contain a direct and concise argument, with supporting authorities, amplifying the reasons for granting review. See Rule 66.3. The court of appeals' opinions will be considered with the petition, and statements in those opinions need not be repeated if counsel accepts them as correct.

(i) *Prayer for Relief.* The petition must state clearly the nature of the relief sought.

(j) *Appendix.* The petition must contain a copy of any opinion of the court of appeals.

Eff. Sept. 1, 1997. Amended by Supreme Court order of Dec. 23, 2002, eff. Jan. 1, 2003; Court of Criminal Appeals order of Dec. 11, 2013, eff. Jan. 1, 2014.

Notes and Comments

Comment to 2002 change: The original catchline of subdivision 68.4(g) was "Reasons for Review," which caused confusion because of its similarity to the catch line in subdivision 66.3 ("Reasons for Granting Review"). It is changed to "Argument."

68.5. Repealed by Order of Nov. 13, 2012, eff. Dec. 1, 2012

68.6. Nonconforming Petition

The Court may strike, order redrawn, or summarily refuse a petition for discretionary review that is unnecessarily lengthy or that does not conform to these rules.

Eff. Sept. 1, 1997.

68.7. Court of Appeals Clerk's Duties

Within 15 days of receiving notice of the filing of a petition for discretionary review from the clerk of the Court of Criminal Appeals, the clerk of the court of appeals must send to the clerk of the Court of Criminal Appeals the record, any motions filed in the case, and copies of any judgments, opinions, and orders of the court of appeals. The clerk need not forward any nondocumentary exhibits unless ordered to do so by the Court of Criminal Appeals.

Eff. Sept. 1, 1997. Amended by Court of Criminal Appeals March 4, 2008, and June 30, 2008, eff. Sept. 1, 2008; Sept. 30, 2008, eff. Sept. 30, 2008; Supreme Court March 10, 2008, and Aug. 20, 2008, eff. Sept. 1, 2008. Amended by Court of Criminal Appeals July 12, 2011, eff. September 1, 2011.

Notes and Comments

Comment to 2011 change: Rule 68.7(a) and (b) are deleted and (c) is amended to reflect changes consistent with filing the petition and reply in the Court of Criminal Appeals rather than in the court of appeals, and to order the record to be sent to the Court of Criminal Appeals. Additionally, Rule 68.7(c) is amended to delete reference to Rule 50, which is abolished.

68.8. Court of Criminal Appeals Clerk's Duties

Upon receipt of the record from the court of appeals, the clerk of the Court of Criminal Appeals will file the record and enter the filing on the docket.

Eff. Sept. 1, 1997. Amended by Court of Criminal Appeals July 12, 2011, eff. Sept. 1, 2011.

Notes and Comments

Comment to 2011 change: Rule 68.8 is amended to reflect changes consistent with filing the petition in the Court of Criminal Appeals.

68.9. Reply

The opposing party has 15 days after the timely filing of the petition in the Court of Criminal Appeals to file a reply petition with the clerk of the Court of Criminal Appeals.
Added eff. Sept. 1, 2011.

Notes and Comments

Comment to 2011 change: This Rule is added so that any reply will be filed in the Court of Criminal Appeals since the petition is also filed in the Court of Criminal Appeals.

68.10. Amendment

Upon motion the petition or a reply may be amended or supplemented at any time justice requires.
Eff. Sept. 1, 1997. Amended by Court of Criminal Appeals July 12, 2011, eff. Sept. 1, 2011.

Notes and Comments

Comment to 2011 change: This Rule is changed to reflect the filing of the petition and any reply in the Court of Criminal Appeals. Thus, the rule is also changed to require a motion and to delete a time frame because the petition will be filed in the Court of Criminal Appeals.

68.11. Service on State Prosecuting Attorney

In addition to the service required by Rule 9.5, service of the petition, the reply, and any amendment or supplementation of a petition or reply must be made on the State Prosecuting Attorney.
Eff. Sept. 1, 1997. Amended by Court of Criminal Appeals July 12, 2011, eff. September 1, 2011.

Notes and Comments

Comment to 2011 change: The address for the State Prosecuting Attorney is deleted because it is has changed and may change again.

Rule 69. Action of Court on Petition for Discretionary Review and After Granting Review

Notes and Comments

Comment to 1997 change: This is former subdivisions (k) and (*l*) of Rule 202. Internal procedures of the Court are deleted. Provisions are added in 69.4(a) and (b) for the clerk to send notice of the granting, refusal, or dismissal of a petition for discretionary review. Other nonsubstantive changes are made.

69.1. Granting or Refusal

If four judges do not vote to grant a petition for discretionary review, the Court will enter a docket notation that the petition is *refused.* If four judges vote to grant a petition, the Court will enter a docket notation that discretionary review is *granted.*
Eff. Sept. 1, 1997.

69.2. Setting Case for Submission

If discretionary review is granted, either on the petition of a party or by the Court on its own initiative, the case will be set for submission.
Eff. Sept. 1, 1997.

69.3. Improvident Grant of Review

If, after granting discretionary review, five judges are of the opinion that discretionary review should not have been granted, the case will be dismissed.
Eff. Sept. 1, 1997.

69.4. Clerk's Duties

(a) *On Refusal or Dismissal.* When the Court refuses or dismisses a petition, the clerk will send to the parties and the State Prosecuting Attorney a notice informing them that the petition was refused or dismissed. The clerk will retain the petition and all other items filed in the case for at least 15 days from the date of the refusal or dismissal. At the end of that time, if no motion for rehearing has been timely filed, or upon the overruling or dismissal of such a motion, the clerk will send to the court of appeals clerk a certified copy of the order refusing or dismissing the petition (as well as any order overruling a motion for rehearing). The clerk of the Court of Criminal Appeals will return the appellate record to the court of appeals clerk but will retain the petition, and other documents filed in the Court of Criminal Appeals.

(b) *On Granting Review.* If the Court grants discretionary review, the clerk will send to the parties and the State Prosecuting Attorney a notice informing them that discretionary review was granted.
Eff. Sept. 1, 1997.

Rule 70. Brief on the Merits

Notes and Comments

Comment to 1997 change: This is former Rule 203. The rule is amended without substantive change.

70.1. Initial Brief

If review is granted, the petitioner—or, if there was no petition, the party who lost in the court of appeals—must file a brief within 30 days after review is granted.
Eff. Sept. 1, 1997.

70.2. Respondent's Brief

The opposing party must file a brief within 30 days after the petitioner's brief is filed.

Eff. Sept. 1, 1997. Amended by Court of Criminal Appeals Dec. 11, 2013, eff. Jan. 1, 2014.

70.3. Brief Contents and Form

Briefs must comply with the requirements of Rules 9 and 38, except that they need not contain the appendix (Rule 38.1(k)). Copies must be served as required by Rule 68.11.

Eff. Sept. 1, 1997. Amended by Supreme Court March 10, 2008, and Aug. 20, 2008, eff. Sept. 1, 2008. Approved by Court of Criminal Appeals Sept. 30, 2008, eff. Sept. 30, 2008. Amended by Supreme Court Nov. 13, 2012, eff. Dec. 1, 2012.

70.4. Other Briefs

The Court of Criminal Appeals may direct that a party file a brief, or an additional brief, in a particular case. Additionally, upon motion by a party the Court may permit the filing of additional briefs.

Eff. Sept. 1, 1997. Amended by Court of Criminal Appeals Dec. 11, 2013, eff. Jan. 1, 2014.

Rule 71. Direct Appeals

Notes and Comments

Comment to 1997 change: This is former Rule 210. The rule is extended to all direct appeals. A page limit is added for death penalty cases. Other nonsubstantive changes are made.

71.1. Direct Appeal

Cases in which the death penalty has been assessed under Code of Criminal Procedure article 37.071, and cases in which bail has been denied in non-capital cases under Article I, Section 11a of the Constitution, are appealed directly to the Court of Criminal Appeals.

Eff. Sept. 1, 1997.

71.2. Record

The appellate record should be prepared and filed in accordance with Rules 31, 32, 34, 35 and 37,[1] except that the record must be filed in the Court of Criminal Appeals. After disposition of the appeal, the Court may discard copies of juror information cards or other portions of the clerk's record that are not relevant to an issue on appeal.

Eff. Sept. 1, 1997. Amended by Supreme Court Dec. 23, 2002, eff. Jan. 1, 2003.

[1] Vernon's Ann.Rules App.Proc., rules 31.1 et seq., 32.1 et seq., 34.1 et seq., 35.1 et seq., 37.1 et seq.

71.3. Briefs

Briefs in a direct appeal should be prepared and filed in accordance with Rules 9 and 38, except that the brief need not contain an appendix (Rule 38.1(k)). All briefs must be filed in the Court of Criminal Appeals. The brief must include a short statement of why oral argument would be helpful, or a statement that oral argument is waived.

Eff. Sept. 1, 1997. Amended by Supreme Court March 10, 2008, and Aug. 20, 2008, eff. Sept. 1, 2008. Approved by Court of Criminal Appeals Sept. 30, 2008, eff. Sept. 30, 2008. Amended by Supreme Court Nov. 13, 2012, eff. Dec. 1, 2012.

Notes and Comments

Comment to 2002 change: A requirement that briefs include a statement regarding oral argument is added.

71.4. Additional Briefs

Upon motion by a party the Court may permit the filing of additional briefs other than those provided for in Rule 38.

Adopted by Court of Criminal Appeals Dec. 11, 2013, eff. Jan. 1, 2014.

Rule 72. Extraordinary Matters

Notes and Comments

Comment to 1997 change: This is former Rule 211. The rule is amended to include all the Court's jurisdiction of extraordinary matters. Internal procedures of the Court are deleted. Other nonsubstantive changes are made.

72.1. Leave to File

A motion for leave to file must accompany an original petition for writ of habeas corpus, mandamus, procedendo, prohibition, certiorari, or other extraordinary writ, or any other motion not otherwise provided for in these rules.

Eff. Sept. 1, 1997.

72.2. Disposition

If five judges tentatively believe that the case should be filed and set for submission, the motion for leave will be granted and the case will then be handled and disposed of in accordance with Rule 52.7. If the motion for leave is denied, no motions for rehearing or reconsideration will be entertained. But the Court may, on its own initiative, reconsider a denial of a motion for leave.

Eff. Sept. 1, 1997.

Rule 73. Postconviction Applications for Writs of Habeas Corpus

Notes and Comments

Comment to 2000 change: Rules 73.1 and 73.2 are added, and a form is added in an appendix.

The Court of Criminal Appeals order dated October 16, 2000, provides in part:

"2. These changes take effect January 1, 2001. Unless this order provides otherwise, they shall govern all proceedings in motions for new trial, appeals, petitions for discretionary review, and petitions or applications for extraordinary writs thereafter brought and in all such proceedings then pending, except to the extent that in the opinion of the court their application in a particular proceeding then pending would not be feasible or would work injustice, in which case the former procedure may be followed.

"3. The notes and comments appended to these changes are incomplete, are included only for the convenience of the bench and bar, and are not a part of the rules."

Comment to 1997 change: This is former Rule 4 of the Appendix for Criminal Cases. The rule is amended without substantive change.

73.1. Form for Application Filed Under Article 11.07 of the Code of Criminal Procedure

(a) *Prescribed Form.* An application filed under Article 11.07 must be on the form prescribed by the Court of Criminal Appeals.

(b) *Availability of Form.* The district clerk of the county of conviction shall make the form available to applicants on request, without charge.

(c) *Contents.* The applicant or petitioner must provide all information required by the form. The form must include all grounds for relief and set forth in summary fashion the facts supporting each ground. Any ground not raised on the form will not be considered. Legal citations and arguments may be made in a separate memorandum. The form must be computer-generated, typewritten, or legibly handwritten.

(d) *Length.* Each ground for relief and supporting facts raised on the form shall not exceed the two pages provided for each ground in the form. The applicant or petitioner may file a separate memorandum. This memorandum shall comply with these rules and shall not exceed 15,000 words if computer-generated or 50 pages if not. If the total number of pages, including those in the original and any additional memoranda, exceed the word or page limits, an application may be dismissed unless the convicting court for good cause shown grants leave to exceed the prescribed limits. The prescribed limits do not include appendices, exhibits, cover page, table of contents, table of authorities, and certificate of compliance.

(e) *Typeface.* A computer-generated memorandum must be printed in a conventional typeface no smaller than 14–point except for footnotes, which must be no smaller than 12–point. A typewritten document must be printed in standard 10–character–per–inch (cpi) monospaced typeface.

(f) *Certificate of compliance.* A computer-generated memorandum, including any additional memoranda, must include a certificate by the applicant or petitioner stating the number of words in the document. The person certifying may rely on the word count of the computer program used to prepare the document.

(g) *Verification.* The application must be verified by either:

(1) oath made before a notary public or other officer authorized to administer oaths; or

(2) if the person making the application is an inmate in the Institutional Division of the Department of Criminal Justice or in a county jail, an unsworn declaration in substantially the form required in Civil Practices and Remedies Code chapter 132.

Adopted by Court of Criminal Appeals Aug. 10, 2000 and Oct. 16, 2000, eff. Jan. 1, 2001; adopted by Supreme Court Sept. 12, 2000, eff. Jan. 1, 2001. Amended by Court of Criminal Appeals Dec. 11, 2013, eff. Jan. 1, 2014.

73.2. Non–Compliant Applications

The Court of Criminal Appeals may dismiss an application that does not comply with these rules.

Adopted by Court of Criminal Appeals Aug. 10, 2000 and Oct. 16, 2000, eff. Jan. 1, 2001; adopted by Supreme Court Sept. 12, 2000, eff. Jan. 1, 2001. Amended by Court of Criminal Appeals Dec. 11, 2013, eff. Jan. 1, 2014.

73.3. State's Response

Any response by the State must comply with length, typeface, and certificate of compliance requirements set out in rule 73.1 (d),(e) and (f).

Adopted by Court of Criminal Appeals Dec. 11, 2013, eff. Jan. 1, 2014.

73.4. Filing and Transmission of Habeas Record

(a) The district clerk of the county of conviction shall accept and file all Code of Criminal Procedure article 11.07 applications.

(b) In addition to the duties set out in Article 11.07, the clerk shall do the following:

(1) If the convicting court enters an order designating issues, the clerk shall immediately transmit to the Court of Criminal Appeals a copy of that order and proof of the date the district attorney received the habeas application.

(2) When any pleadings, objections, motions, affidavits, exhibits, proposed or entered findings of fact and conclusions of law, or other orders are filed or made a part of the record, the district clerk shall immediately send a copy to all parties in the case. A party has ten days from the date he receives the trial court's findings of facts and conclusions of law to file objections, but the trial court may, neverthe-

less, order the district clerk to transmit the record to the Court of Criminal Appeals before the expiration of the ten days.

(3) When a district clerk transmits the record in a postconviction application for a writ of habeas corpus under Code of Criminal Procedure articles 11.07 or 11.071, the district clerk must prepare and transmit a summary sheet that includes the following information:

(A) the convicting court's name and county, and the name of the judge who tried the case;

(B) the applicant's name, the offense, the plea, the cause number, the sentence, and the date of sentence, as shown in the judgment of conviction;

(C) the cause number of any appeal from the conviction and the citation to any published report;

(D) whether a hearing was held on the application, whether findings of fact were made, any recommendation of the convicting court, and the name of the judge who presided over the application;

(E) the name of counsel if applicant is represented.

The Court of Criminal Appeals may by order adopt a form of summary sheet that the district clerks must use.

(4) The district clerk shall also include in the record transmitted to the Court of Criminal Appeals, among any other pertinent papers or supplements, the indictment or information, any plea papers, the court's docket sheet, the court's charge and the jury's verdict, any proposed findings of fact and conclusions of law, the court's findings of fact and conclusions of law, any objections to the court's findings of fact and conclusions of law filed by either party, and the transcript of any hearings held.

(5) On the 181st day from the date of receipt of the application by the State of a postconviction application for writ of habeas corpus under Article 11.07, the district clerk shall forward the writ record to this Court unless the district court has received an extension of time from the Court of Criminal Appeals pursuant to Rule 73.5.

Former Rule 73.1 adopted eff. Sept. 1, 1997. Renumbered as Rule 73.3 by Court of Criminal Appeals Nov. 8, 2000, eff. Jan. 1, 2001. Renumbered as Rule 73.4 and amended by Court of Criminal Appeals Dec. 11, 2013, eff. Jan. 1, 2014. Amended by orders of Supreme Court February 16, 2016, and Court of Criminal Appeals Dec. 7, 2015, and February 29, 2016, eff. Jan. 1, 2016.

73.5. Time Frame for Resolution of Claims Raised in Application

Within 180 days from the date of receipt of the application by the State, the convicting court shall resolve any issues that the court has timely designated for resolution. Any motion for extension of time must be filed in the Court of Criminal Appeals before the expiration of the 180–day period.

Adopted by Court of Criminal Appeals Dec. 11, 2013, eff. Jan. 1, 2014.

73.6. Action on Application

The Court may deny relief based upon its own review of the application or may issue such other instructions or orders as may be appropriate.

Former Rule 73.2 adopted eff. Sept. 1, 1997. Renumbered as Rule 73.4 by Court of Criminal Appeals Nov. 8, 2000, eff. Jan. 1, 2001. Renumbered as Rule 73.6 by Court of Criminal Appeals Dec. 11, 2013, eff. Jan. 1, 2014.

Rule 74. Review of Certified State Criminal-Law Questions

Notes and Comments

Comment to 1997 change: This is former Rule 214. The rule is amended without substantive change.

74.1. Certification

The Court of Criminal Appeals may answer questions of Texas criminal law certified to it by any federal appellate court if the certifying court is presented with determinative questions of Texas criminal law having no controlling Court of Criminal Appeals precedent. The Court may decline to answer the questions certified to it.

Eff. Sept. 1, 1997.

74.2. Contents of the Certification Order

An order from the certifying court must set forth:

(a) the questions of law to be answered; and

(b) a stipulated statement of all facts relevant to the questions certified, showing fully the nature of the controversy in which the questions arose.

Eff. Sept. 1, 1997.

74.3. Transmission of Certification Order

The clerk of the certifying court must send to the clerk of the Court of Criminal Appeals the following:

(a) the certification order under the certifying court's official seal;

(b) a list of the names of each party to the pending case, giving the address and telephone number, if known, of any party not represented by counsel; and

(c) a list of the names and addresses of counsel for each party.

Eff. Sept. 1, 1997.

74.4. Transmission of Record

The certifying court should not send to the Court of Criminal Appeals the record in the pending case with the certification order. The Court of Criminal Appeals may later require the original or copies of all or part of the record before the certifying court to be filed with the Court of Criminal Appeals clerk.

Eff. Sept. 1, 1997.

74.5. Notice

If the Court of Criminal Appeals agrees to answer the questions certified to it, the Court will notify all parties and the certifying court. The Court of Criminal Appeals clerk must also send a notice to the Attorney General of Texas if:

(a) the constitutionality of a Texas statute is the subject of a certified question that the Court of Criminal Appeals has agreed to answer; and

(b) the State of Texas or an officer, agency, or employee of the State is not a party to the proceeding in the certifying court.

Eff. Sept. 1, 1997.

74.6. Briefs and Oral Argument

(a) *Briefs.* The appealing party in the certifying court must file a brief with the clerk of the Court of Criminal Appeals within 30 days after the date of the notice. Opposing parties must file an answering brief within 15 days of receiving the opening brief. Briefs must comply with Rule 38[1] to the extent that its provisions apply.

(b) *Oral Argument.* Oral argument may be granted either on a party's request or on the Court's own initiative. Argument is governed by Rule 39.[2]

Eff. Sept. 1, 1997.

1 Vernon's Ann.Rules App.Proc., rule 38.1 et seq.

2 Vernon's Ann.Rules App.Proc., rule 39.1 et seq.

74.7. Intervention by the State

If the constitutionality of a Texas statute is the subject of a certified question that the Court of Criminal Appeals has agreed to answer, the State of Texas may intervene at any reasonable time for briefing and oral argument (if argument is allowed) on the question of constitutionality.

Eff. Sept. 1, 1997.

74.8. Opinion on Certified Question

If the Court of Criminal Appeals has agreed to answer a certified question, it will hand down an opinion as in any other case.

Eff. Sept. 1, 1997.

74.9. Motion for Rehearing

Any party may file a motion for rehearing within 15 days after the opinion is handed down. The motion must clearly state the points relied on for the rehearing. No reply to a motion for rehearing need be filed unless the Court so requests. The Court will not grant a motion for rehearing unless a response has been filed or requested.

Eff. Sept. 1, 1997.

74.10. Answering Certified Questions

After all motions for rehearing have been overruled, the clerk of the Court of Criminal Appeals must send to the certifying court the written opinion on the certified questions. The opinion must be under the Court of Criminal Appeals' seal.

Eff. Sept. 1, 1997.

Rule 75. Notification; Oral Argument

Notes and Comments

Comment to 1997 change: This is former Rule 220. The rule is amended without substantive change.

75.1. Notification of Argument or Submission

Oral argument will be permitted only in cases designated by the Court of Criminal Appeals. If the Court permits argument in a case, the clerk will notify the parties of the date set for argument. If a case will be submitted without argument, the clerk will notify the parties of the date of submission. The clerk must use all reasonable diligence to notify counsel of settings, but counsel's failure to receive notice will not necessarily prevent argument or submission of the case on the day it is set.

Eff. Sept. 1, 1997.

75.2. Request for Argument

If a case is not designated for oral argument but counsel desires oral argument, counsel may—within 30 days of the date of the clerk's notice—petition the Court to allow oral argument. This petition must contain specific reasons why oral argument is desired.

75.3. Oral Argument

Unless extended in a special case, the total maximum time for oral argument is 20 minutes per side. Counsel for the appellant or petitioner is entitled to open and conclude the argument. Counsel should not read at length from the briefs, records, or authorities. Counsel may orally correct a brief, but multiple additional citations should not be given orally; instead, these citations should be filed in writing with the clerk.

Eff. Sept. 1, 1997.

Rule 76. Submissions En Banc

The Court will sit en banc to consider the following types of cases:

(a) direct appeals;

(b) cases of discretionary review;

(c) cases in which leave to file was granted under Rule 72[1];

(d) cases that were docketed under Code of Criminal Procedure articles 11.07 or 11.071;

(e) certified questions; and

(f) rehearings under Rule 79.[2]

Eff. Sept. 1, 1997.

[1] Vernon's Ann.Rules App.Proc., rule 72.1 et seq.

[2] Vernon's Ann.Rules App.Proc., rule 79.1 et seq.

Notes and Comments

Comment to 1997 change: This is former Rule 222. The rule is expanded to include other kinds of cases. Internal procedures of the Court are deleted. Other nonsubstantive changes are made.

Rule 77. Opinions

Notes and Comments

Comment to 1997 change: This is former Rule 223. The rule is amended without substantive change.

77.1. Generally

In each case that is argued or submitted without argument to the Court of Criminal Appeals, the Court will hand down a written opinion setting forth the reasons for its decision and any germane precedent. Any judge may file an opinion dissenting from or concurring in the Court's judgment.

Eff. Sept. 1, 1997.

77.2. Signing; Publication

A majority of the judges will determine whether an opinion will be signed by a judge or issued per curiam, and whether the opinion (or a portion of the opinion) will be published.

Eff. Sept. 1, 1997.

77.3. Unpublished Opinions

Unpublished opinions have no precedential value and must not be cited as authority by counsel or by a court.

Eff. Sept. 1, 1997.

77.4. Copies

On the date when an opinion is handed down or an order rendered, the clerk of the Court of Criminal Appeals must mail copies of the opinion or order to:

(a) the parties;

(b) the State Prosecuting Attorney;

(c) the trial court clerk; and

(d) if the case is of discretionary review, the court of appeals clerk.

Eff. Sept. 1, 1997.

Rule 78. Judgments in the Court of Criminal Appeals

Notes and Comments

Comment to 1997 change: The rule is new.

78.1. Types of Judgment

The Court of Criminal Appeals may:

(a) affirm the lower court's judgment in whole or in part;

(b) modify the lower court's judgment and affirm it as modified;

(c) reverse the court's judgment in whole or in part and render the judgment that the lower court should have rendered;

(d) reverse the lower court's judgment and remand the case for further proceedings;

(e) vacate the judgments of the lower courts and dismiss the case;

(f) vacate the lower court's judgment and remand the case for further proceedings in light of changes in the law; or

(g) dismiss the appeal.

Eff. Sept. 1, 1997.

78.2. Remand in the Interests of Justice

When reversing the court of appeals' judgment, the Court of Criminal Appeals may, in the interests of justice, remand the case to the trial court even if a rendition of judgment is otherwise appropriate.

Eff. Sept. 1, 1997.

78.3. Other Orders

The Court of Criminal Appeals may make any other appropriate order required by the law and the nature of the case.

Eff. Sept. 1, 1997.

Rule 79. Rehearings

Notes and Comments

Comment to 1997 change: This is former Rule 230, and the portion of former Rule 213 that prohibited motions for rehearing. The Court may now permit oral argument after granting rehearing, although it is disfavored. A further motion for rehearing may now be filed by any party, rather than only the losing party. Other nonsubstantive changes are made.

79.1. Motion for Rehearing

A motion for rehearing may be filed with the Court of Criminal Appeals clerk within 15 days from the date of the judgment or order. In exceptional cases, if justice requires, the Court may shorten the time within which the motion may be filed or even deny the right to file it altogether.

Eff. Sept. 1, 1997.

79.2. Contents

(a) The motion must briefly and distinctly state the grounds and arguments relied on for rehearing.

(b) A motion for rehearing an order that grants discretionary review may not be filed.

(c) A motion for rehearing an order that refuses a petition for discretionary review may be grounded only on substantial intervening circumstances or on other significant circumstances which are specified in the motion. Counsel must certify that the motion is so grounded and that the motion is made in good faith and not for delay.

(d) A motion for rehearing an order that denies habeas corpus relief or dismisses a habeas corpus application under Code of Criminal Procedure, articles 11.07 or 11.071, may not be filed. The Court may on its own initiative reconsider the case.

Eff. Sept. 1, 1997. Amended by Court of Criminal Appeals July 12, 2011, eff. September 1, 2011. Amended by orders of Supreme Court February 16, 2016, and Court of Criminal Appeals December 7, 2015, and February 29, 2016, eff. January 1, 2016.

Notes and Comments

Comment to 2011 change: Rule 79.2(c) is amended so that it applies only to petitions for discretionary review that are refused. Additionally, the certification requirement is changed to encompass a broader basis for rehearing.

79.3. Amendments

A motion for rehearing may be amended anytime before the period allowed for filing the motion expires, and with leave of the court, anytime before the Court decides the motion.

Eff. Sept. 1, 1997.

79.4. Decision

If the Court grants rehearing, the case will be set for submission. Oral argument may, but normally will not, be permitted.

Eff. Sept. 1, 1997.

79.5. Further Motion for Rehearing

The Court will not consider a second motion for rehearing after rehearing is denied. If rehearing is granted and the Court delivers an opinion on rehearing, a party may file a further motion for rehearing.

Eff. Sept. 1, 1997.

79.6. Extension of Time

The Court may extend the time for filing a motion or a further motion for rehearing if a party files a motion complying with Rule 10.5(b) within the time for filing a motion or further motion for rehearing.

Eff. Sept. 1, 1997.

79.7. Service

The requirements of Rule 68.11 apply.

Eff. Sept. 1, 1997.

STANDARDS FOR APPELLATE CONDUCT

Lawyers are an indispensable part of the pursuit of justice. They are officers of courts charged with safeguarding, interpreting, and applying the law through which justice is achieved. Appellate courts rely on counsel to present opposing views of how the law should be applied to facts established in other proceedings. The appellate lawyer's role is to present the law controlling the disposition of a case in a manner that clearly reveals the legal issues raised by the record while persuading the court that an interpretation or application favored by the lawyer's clients is in the best interest of the administration of equal justice under law.

The duties lawyers owe to the justice system, other officers of the court, and lawyers' clients are generally well-defined and understood by the appellate bar. Problems that arise when duties conflict can be resolved through understanding the nature and extent of a lawyer's respective duties, avoiding the tendency to emphasize a particular duty at the expense of others, and detached common sense. To that end, the following standards of conduct for appellate lawyers are set forth by reference to the duties owed by every appellate practitioner.

Use of these standards for appellate conduct as a basis for motions for sanctions, civil liability or litigation would be contrary to their intended purpose and shall not be permitted. Nothing in these standards alters existing standards of conduct under the Texas Disciplinary Rules of Professional Conduct, the Texas Rules of Disciplinary Procedure or the Code of Judicial Conduct.

LAWYERS' DUTIES TO CLIENTS

A lawyer owes to a client allegiance, learning, skill, and industry. A lawyer shall employ all appropriate means to protect and advance the client's legitimate rights, claims, and objectives. A lawyer shall not be deterred by a real or imagined fear of judicial disfavor or public unpopularity, nor be influenced by mere self-interest. The lawyer's duty to a client does not militate against the concurrent obligation to treat with consideration all persons involved in the legal process and to avoid the infliction of harm on the appellate process, the courts, and the law itself.

1. Counsel will advise their clients of the contents of these Standards of Conduct when undertaking representation.

2. Counsel will explain the fee agreement and cost expectation to their clients. Counsel will then endeavor to achieve the client's lawful appellate objectives as quickly, efficiently, and economically as possible.

3. Counsel will maintain sympathetic detachment, recognizing that lawyers should not become so closely associated with clients that the lawyer's objective judgment is impaired.

4. Counsel will be faithful to their clients' lawful objectives, while mindful of their concurrent duties to the legal system and the public good.

5. Counsel will explain the appellate process to their clients. Counsel will advise clients of the range of potential outcomes, likely costs, timetables, effect of the judgment pending appeal, and the availability of alternative dispute resolution.

6. Counsel will not foster clients' unrealistic expectations.

7. Negative opinions of the court or opposing counsel shall not be expressed unless relevant to a client's decision process.

8. Counsel will keep clients informed and involved in decisions and will promptly respond to inquiries.

9. Counsel will advise their clients of proper behavior, including that civility and courtesy are expected.

10. Counsel will advise their clients that counsel reserves the right to grant accommodations to opposing counsel in matters that do not adversely affect the client's lawful objectives. A client has no right to instruct a lawyer to refuse reasonable requests made by other counsel.

11. A client has no right to demand that counsel abuse anyone or engage in any offensive conduct.

12. Counsel will advise clients that an appeal should only be pursued in a good faith belief that the trial court has committed error or that there is a reasonable basis for the extension, modification, or reversal of existing law, or that an appeal is otherwise warranted.

13. Counsel will advise clients that they will not take frivolous positions in an appellate court, explaining the penalties associated therewith. Appointed appellate counsel in criminal cases shall be deemed to have complied with this standard of conduct if they comply with the requirements imposed on appointed counsel by courts and statutes.

LAWYERS' DUTIES TO THE COURT

As professionals and advocates, counsel assist the Court in the administration of justice at the appellate level. Through briefs and oral submissions, counsel provide a fair and accurate understanding of the facts and law applicable to their case. Counsel also serve the Court by respecting and maintaining the dignity and integrity of the appellate process.

1. An appellate remedy should not be pursued unless counsel believes in good faith that error has been committed, that there is a reasonable basis for the extension, modification, or reversal of existing law, or that an appeal is otherwise warranted.

2. An appellate remedy should not be pursued primarily for purposes of delay or harassment.

3. Counsel should not misrepresent, mischaracterize, misquote, or miscite the factual record or legal authorities.

4. Counsel will advise the Court of controlling legal authorities, including those adverse to their position, and should not cite authority that has been reversed, overruled, or restricted without informing the court of those limitations.

5. Counsel will present the Court with a thoughtful, organized, and clearly written brief.

6. Counsel will not submit reply briefs on issues previously briefed in order to obtain the last word.

7. Counsel will conduct themselves before the Court in a professional manner, respecting the decorum and integrity of the judicial process.

8. Counsel will be civil and respectful in all communications with the judges and staff.

9. Counsel will be prepared and punctual for all Court appearances, and will be prepared to assist the Court in understanding the record, controlling authority, and the effect of the court's decision.

10. Counsel will not permit a client's or their own ill feelings toward the opposing party, opposing counsel, trial judges or members of the appellate court to influence their conduct or demeanor in dealings with the judges, staff, other counsel, and parties.

LAWYERS' DUTIES TO LAWYERS

Lawyers bear a responsibility to conduct themselves with dignity towards and respect for each other, for the sake of maintaining the effectiveness and credibility of the system they serve. The duty that lawyers owe their clients and the system can be most effectively carried out when lawyers treat each other honorably.

1. Counsel will treat each other and all parties with respect.

2. Counsel will not unreasonably withhold consent to a reasonable request for cooperation or scheduling accommodation by opposing counsel.

3. Counsel will not request an extension of time solely for the purpose of unjustified delay.

4. Counsel will be punctual in communications with opposing counsel.

5. Counsel will not make personal attacks on opposing counsel or parties.

6. Counsel will not attribute bad motives or improper conduct to other counsel without good cause, or make unfounded accusations of impropriety.

7. Counsel will not lightly seek court sanctions.

8. Counsel will adhere to oral or written promises and agreements with other counsel.

9. Counsel will neither ascribe to another counsel or party a position that counsel or the party has not taken, nor seek to create an unjustified inference based on counsel's statements or conduct.

10. Counsel will not attempt to obtain an improper advantage by manipulation of margins and type size in a manner to avoid court rules regarding page limits.

11. Counsel will not serve briefs or other communications in a manner or at a time that unfairly limits another party's opportunity to respond.

THE COURT'S RELATIONSHIP WITH COUNSEL

Unprofessionalism can exist only to the extent it is tolerated by the court. Because courts grant the right to practice law, they control the manner in which the practice is conducted. The right to practice requires counsel to conduct themselves in a manner compatible with the role of the appellate courts in administering justice. Likewise, no one more surely sets the tone and the pattern for the conduct of appellate lawyers than appellate judges. Judges must practice civility in order to foster professionalism in those appearing before them.

1. Inappropriate conduct will not be rewarded, while exemplary conduct will be appreciated.

2. The court will take special care not to reward departures from the record.

3. The court will be courteous, respectful, and civil to counsel.

4. The court will not disparage the professionalism or integrity of counsel based upon the conduct or reputation of counsel's client or co-counsel.

5. The court will endeavor to avoid the injustice that can result from delay after submission of a case.

6. The court will abide by the same standards of professionalism that it expects of counsel in its treatment of the facts, the law, and the arguments.

7. Members of the court will demonstrate respect for other judges and courts.

APPENDIX TO THE TEXAS RULES OF APPELLATE PROCEDURE

APPENDIX A

APPENDIX TO THE TEXAS RULES OF APPELLATE PROCEDURE

APPENDIX A

IN THE SUPREME COURT OF TEXAS

ORDER REGARDING FEES CHARGED IN CIVIL CASES IN THE SUPREME COURT AND THE COURTS OF APPEALS AND BEFORE THE JUDICIAL PANEL ON MULTIDISTRICT LITIGATION

A. In the Supreme Court:

1. The following fees have been set by statute (TEX. GOV'T CODE §§51.005, 51.0051, and 51.941) and will be collected by the clerk except from parties who are exempt by statute:

(a)	petition for review	$155
(b)	additional fee if petition for review is granted	$75
(c)	original proceeding	$155
(d)	additional fee if original proceeding is granted	$75
(e)	certified question from a federal court of appeals	$180
(f)	direct appeals to the Supreme Court	$205
(g)	any other proceeding filed in the Supreme Court	$180
(h)	administering an oath with sealed certificate of oath	$5
(i)	certified copies of any papers of record in offices, including certificate and seal	$.50 per page $5 minimum

2. The following fees have been set consistent with (TEX. GOV'T CODE §§552.262 and 1 TEX. ADMIN. CODE §70.3 (2007) (Tex. Atty. Gen.. Charges for Providing Copies of Public Information):

(a)	standard paper copy of document without certificate or seal (single-sided)	$0.10 per page or part of page
(b)	standard paper copy of document without certificate or seal (double-sided)	$0.10 per page or part of side of page
(c)	personnel, overhead, and document retrieval charges	as provided by 1 TEX. ADMIN. CODE §70.3
(d)	audio tape of oral argument	$1 per tape
(e)	digital video disc of oral argument	$3 per DVD

Note: the fees listed above for audio tapes, DVDs, and paper copies do not include any personnel, overhead, or document retrieval charges; those charges may be added to the fees listed above if appropriate, as determined by the Court.

3. Pursuant to TEX. GOV'T CODE § 51.005, the following additional fees are set:

(a) comparing and certifying copies of documents .... $1.00 per page, $5 minimum

(b) motions for rehearing $15

(c) motions not otherwise listed $10

(d) exhibits tendered for oral argument $25

B. In the courts of appeals:

1. The following fees have been set by statute (TEX. GOV'T CODE §§51.207, 51.208, and 51.941) and will be collected by the clerk except from parties who are exempt by statute.

(a) appeals to the court of appeals from the district and county courts $205

(b) original proceeding $155

(c) administering an oath with sealed certificate of oath $5

(d) certified copies of any papers of record in offices, including certificate and seal certification .... $1.00 per page, $5 minimum

(e) comparing and certifying copies of documents .... $1.00 per page, $5 minimum

2. The following fees have been set consistent with TEX. GOV'T CODE §552.262 and 1 TEX. ADMIN. CODE §70.3 (2007) (Tex. Att'y Gen., Charges for Providing Copies of Public Information):

(a) standard paper copy of document without certificate or seal (single-sided) .... $0.10 per page or part of page

(b) standard paper copy of document without certification or seal (double-sided) .... $0.10 per side of page or part of side of page

(c) personnel, overhead, and document retrieval charges .... as provided by 1 TEX. ADMIN. CODE §70.3

(d) audio tape or oral argument (if available) .... $1 per tape

(e) VHS video tape of oral argument (if available) .... $2.50 per tape

(f) digital video disc of oral argument (if available) .... $3 per DVD

Note: the fees listed above for audio tapes, videotapes, DVDs, and paper copies do not include any personnel, overhead, or document retrieval charges; those charges may be added to the fees listed above if appropriate, as determined by the court charging the fee.

3. Pursuant to § 51.207(c)(4), TEX. GOV'T CODE, the following additional fees are set:

(a) motions not otherwise listed $10

(b) motion for rehearing or for en banc reconsideration $15

(c) exhibits tendered for oral argument $25

C. Before the Judicial Panel on Multi-District Litigation:

1. Pursuant to TEX. GOV'T CODE §51.005(c)(3) and §51.0051, and Rule of Judicial Administration 13.3(g), the following fees are set:

(a) motion to transfer to pretrial court under Rule of Judicial Administration 13.3(a) or appeal of an order of a pretrial court by motion for rehearing under Rule 13.5(e) $275

(b) any other motion or document filed under Rules of Judicial Administration 13 .... $50

D. Nothing in this order shall be construed as prohibiting a clerk from contracting with an entity or organization to provide copies of documents, audio and video tapes, and other organizational services at a reasonable rate which may exceed the fees provided herein.

Adopted by order of August 15, 1997, eff. Sept. 1, 1997. Amended by orders of July 21, 1998, eff. Sept. 1, 1998; Sept. 10, 2003, eff. Sept. 10, 2003; Aug. 28, 2007, eff. Sept. 1, 2007; Aug. 16, 2013, eff. Sept. 1, 2013; Aug. 28, 2015, eff. Sept. 1, 2015.

Adopted Aug. 15, 1997, eff. Sept. 1, 1997. Amended July 21, 1998, eff. Sept. 1, 1998; Sept. 10, 2003, eff. Sept. 10, 2003; Aug. 28, 2007, eff. Sept. 1, 2007; Aug. 16, 2013, eff. Sept. 1, 2013; Aug. 28, 2015, eff. Sept. 1, 2015.

APPENDIX B

IN THE SUPREME COURT OF TEXAS

ORDER REGARDING DISPOSITION OF COURT PAPERS IN CIVIL CASES

ORDERED that:

A. Definitions.

1. *Court records* or *records* means:

(a) the clerk's record;

(b) the reporter's record; and

(c) any other documents or items filed, or presented for filing and received in an appellate court in a particular case.

2. *Appellate record* means the clerk's record and the reporter's record and any supplements.

B. In the Courts of Appeals. The following paragraphs govern disposing of court records by the courts of appeals:

1. *Determination of permanent preservation.* Before any court records are destroyed, the court of appeals must—under Section 51.205 of the Government Code and State Archives guidelines—determine whether the records should be permanently preserved.

2. *Initial determination.* Immediately after final disposition of an appeal or other proceeding, the panel that decided the case must determine whether the case's records should be permanently preserved and must file with the records a statement declaring that the records should or should not be permanently preserved.

3. *Later determination.* After its initial determination, but before any court records are destroyed, the court of appeals may reexamine its initial determination under 2. and may change its designation.

4. *Original papers and exhibits in appeals.* Whatever the court determines concerning permanent preservation of a case's records, any original documents or exhibits must, within 30 days after final disposition of an appeal or other proceeding, be returned to the trial court in accordance with any trial court order entered under Rules 34.5(f) and 34.6(g). The court of appeals may, but need not, copy those documents and exhibits before returning them to the trial court. The court of appeals may dispose of copies of nondocumentary exhibits after the case is final on appeal.

5. *All other papers and exhibits.* Subject to paragraph 4., the court of appeals must keep and preserve all records of a case (except duplicates) until they are ultimately disposed of under this rule.

6. *Ultimate disposition.* After the period prescribed by Section 51.204 of the Government Code or other applicable statute has expired, the court of appeals must:

(a) destroy those records the court has determined need not be permanently preserved; and

(b) turn over to the State Archives or other repository allowed by law those records the court has determined should be permanently preserved.

C. In the Supreme Court. The following paragraphs govern disposing of court records by the Supreme Court:

1. *If case reversed and remanded to court of appeals.* If the Supreme Court grants review and remands the case to the court of appeals, the Supreme Court will return the appellate record to the court of appeals. The court of appeals will then dispose of the court records in accordance with subdivision B. The Supreme Court will keep and preserve all remaining items (except duplicates) until they are turned over to the State Archives as provided by law.

2. *If case affirmed or reversed and remanded to trial court.* If the Supreme Court grants review and either affirms the court of appeals or reverses and remands to the trial court, the Supreme Court will not return the appellate record but will keep and preserve all records of the case (except duplicates) until those records are turned over to the State Archives as provided by law.

3. *In all other cases.* In all other cases, the Supreme court will return the appellate record to the court of appeals and keep and preserve all remaining records of the case (except duplicates) until they are turned over to the State Archives as provided by law.

APPENDIX C

IN THE SUPREME COURT OF TEXAS
IN THE COURT OF CRIMINAL APPEALS
ORDER DIRECTING
THE FORM OF THE APPELLATE RECORD

RULE 1 CLERK'S RECORD

1.1. Preparation of Electronic or Paper Clerk's Record.

The trial court clerk must prepare and file the clerk's record in accordance with Rules of Appellate Procedure 34.5 and 35. Even if more than one notice of appeal or request for inclusion of items is filed, the clerk should prepare only one consolidated record in a case. To prepare the clerk's record, the trial court clerk must:

(a) gather the documents required by Rule of Appellate Procedure 34.5(a) and those requested by a party under Rule of Appellate Procedure 34.5(b);

(b) start each document on a new page;

(c) include the date of filing on each document;

(d) arrange the documents in ascending chronological order, by date of filing or occurrence;

(e) start the page numbering on the front cover of the first volume of the clerk's record and continue to number all pages consecutively—including the front and back covers, tables of contents, certification page, and separator pages, if any—until the final page of the clerk's record, without regard for the number of volumes in the clerk's record, and place each page number at the bottom of each page;

(f) prepare, label, and certify the clerk's record as required by this rule;

(g) as far as practicable, include the date of signing by the judge on each order and judgment;

(h) include on the front cover of the first volume, and any subsequent volumes, of the clerk's record, whether filed in paper or electronic form, the following information, in substantially the following form:

CLERK'S RECORD

VOLUME ___ of ______________________________

Trial Court Cause No. ______________________________

In the ________ (District or County) Court of ________ County, Texas,

Honorable ________, Judge Presiding

________, Plaintiff(s)

vs.

________, Defendant(s)

Appealed to the
(Supreme Court of Texas at Austin, Texas,
or Court of Criminal Appeals of Texas at Austin, Texas,
or Court of Appeals for the ________ District of Texas, at ________, Texas).

Attorney for Appellant(s):
Name ______________________________
Address
____

Telephone no.: ______________________________

Fax no.: ______________________________

E–mail address: ______________________________

SBOT no.: ______________________________

Attorney for: __________, Appellant(s)

____

Name of clerk preparing the clerk's record: ______________________________

(i) prepare and include after the front cover of the clerk's record a detailed table of contents identifying each document in the entire record (including sealed documents), the date each document was filed, and, except for sealed documents, the page on which each document begins. The table of contents must be double-spaced and conform to the order in which documents appear in the clerk's record, rather than in alphabetical order. If the clerk's record consists of multiple volumes, the table of contents must indicate the page on which each volume begins. If the clerk's record is filed in electronic form, the clerk must use bookmarks to link each document description in the table of contents, except descriptions of sealed documents, to the page on which each document begins; and

(j) conclude the clerk's record with a certificate in substantially the following form:

The State of Texas)
County of __________)

I, __________, Clerk of the __________ Court of __________ County, Texas do hereby certify that the documents contained in this record to which this certification is attached are all of the documents specified by Texas Rule of Appellate Procedure 34.5(a) and all other documents timely requested by a party to this proceeding under Texas Rule of Appellate Procedure 34.5(b).

GIVEN UNDER MY HAND AND SEAL at my office in __________, County, Texas this ___ day of __________.
signature of clerk ______________________________
name of clerk ______________________________
title ______________________________

If the clerk's record is filed in electronic form, the trial court clerk must include either a scanned image of the clerk's signature or "/s/" and the clerk's name typed in the space where the signature would otherwise appear.

1.2. Filing an Electronic Clerk's Record.

Unless the clerk receives permission from the appellate court to file the record in paper form, the clerk must file the record electronically. When filing a clerk's record in electronic form, the trial court clerk must:

(a) file each computer file in text-searchable Portable Document Format (PDF);

(b) create electronic bookmarks to mark the first page of each document in the clerk's record;

(c) limit the size of each computer file to 100 MB or less, if possible;

(d) directly convert, rather than scan, the record to PDF, if possible;

(e) comply with the Technology Standards set by the Judicial Committee on Information Technology;

(f) include the following elements in the computer file name, exemplified as CR (01 of 02).pdf:

(1) "CR";

(2) the volume number, using at least two digits, with leading zeroes if needed; "of"; and the total number of volumes;

(3) a period; and

(4) "pdf";

(g) file each sealed document separately from the remainder of the clerk's record and include the word "sealed" in the computer file name;

(h) if filing a supplement to the clerk's record, include the number of the supplement and "Supp";

(i) submit each computer file to the Texas Appeals Management and E–filing System (TAMES) web portal using the instructions provided on the appellate court's website; and

(j) not lock any document that is part of the record.

1.3. Filing a Paper Clerk's Record.

When filing a paper record with the appellate court, the trial court clerk must:

(a) bind the documents together in one or more volumes with a top bound, two-inch capacity, two-and-three-quarter-inch, center-to-center removable fastener and no other binding materials, like wax, ribbon, glue, staples, tape, etc.;

(b) include no more than 500 pages in each volume, or limit the thickness of each volume to a maximum of two inches;

(c) include only one-sided copies in the clerk's record;

(d) number the first volume "1" and each succeeding volume sequentially;

(e) if practicable, make a legible copy of the documents on opaque, white, 8 1/2 × 11 inch paper; and

(f) place each sealed document in a securely sealed, manila envelope that is not bound with the other documents in the clerk's record.

1.4. Non–Conforming Records and Supplements.

In the event of a material violation of this rule in the preparation or filing of the clerk's record, on motion of a party or on its own initiative, the appellate court may require the trial court clerk to amend the clerk's record or to prepare a new clerk's record in proper form—and provide it to any party who has previously made a copy of the original, defective clerk's record—at the trial clerk's expense. A supplement to a clerk's record must also be prepared in conformity with this rule.

RULE 2. ELECTRONIC REPORTER'S RECORD.

(a) The court reporter or court recorder must prepare and file the reporter's record in accordance with Rules of Appellate Procedure 34.6 and 35 and the Uniform Format Manual for Texas Reporters' Records [1], and the court's local rules. Even if more than one notice of appeal or request for preparation of the record is filed, the court reporter or court recorder should prepare only one consolidated record in the case.

(b) If proceedings were recorded stenographically, the court reporter or recorder must file the reporter's record in an electronic format via the Texas Appeals Management and E–filing System (TAMES) web portal and in accordance with Section 8 of the Uniform Format Manual for Texas Reporters' Records, the court's local rules, and any guidelines posted on the appellate court's website.

(c) If the record is filed in electronic format, the court reporter or recorder must include either a scanned image of any required signature or "/s/" and name typed in the space where the signature would otherwise appear.

(d) A court reporter or recorder must not lock any document that is part of the record.

(e) In exhibit volumes, the court reporter or recorder must create bookmarks to mark the first page of each exhibit document.

Court of Criminal Appeals Dec. 11, 2013, eff. Jan. 1, 2014.

(f) In the event of a material violation of this rule in the preparation of a reporter's record, on motion of a party or on the court's own initiative, the appellate court may require the court reporter or court recorder to amend the reporter's record or to prepare a new reporter's record in proper form—and provide it to any party who has previously made a copy of the original, defective reporter's record—at the reporter's or recorder's expense. A court reporter who fails to comply with the requirements of the Uniform Format Manual for Texas Reporters' Records is also subject to discipline by the Court Reporters Certification Board.

Amended April 8, 1999, effective May 1, 1999. Amended by Supreme Court Dec. 11, 2013, eff. Jan. 1, 2014. Approved by

1 Publisher's Note: The text of the Manual is not included in this publication

APPENDIX D

Appendix: Certification of Defendant's Right of Appeal

No. ________

The State of Texas   In the ________ Court

v.   of

________________________   ________ County, Texas

Defendant

TRIAL COURT'S CERTIFICATION OF DEFENDANT'S RIGHT OF APPEAL *

I, judge of the trial court, certify this criminal case:

[] is not a plea-bargain case, and the defendant has the right of appeal, [*or*]

[] is a plea-bargain case, but matters were raised by written motion filed and ruled on before trial and not withdrawn or waived, and the defendant has the right of appeal. [*or*]

[] is a plea-bargain case, but the trial court has given permission to appeal, and the defendant has the right of appeal. [*or*]

[] is a plea-bargain case, and the defendant has NO right of appeal. [*or*]

[] the defendant has waived the right of appeal.

________________________   ________________________

Judge   Date Signed

I have received a copy of this certification. I have also been informed of my rights concerning any appeal of this criminal case, including any right to file a *pro se* petition for discretionary review pursuant to Rule 68 of the Texas Rules of Appellate Procedure. I have been admonished that my attorney must mail a copy of the court of appeals's judgment and opinion to my last known address and that I have only 30 days in which to file a *pro se* petition for discretionary review in the Court of Criminal Appeals. Tex. R. App. P. 68.2. I acknowledge that, if I wish to appeal this case and if I am entitled to do so. it is my duty to inform my appellate attorney, by written communication, of any change in the address at which I am currently living or any change in my current prison unit. I understand that, because of appellate deadlines, if I fail to timely inform my appellate attorney of any change in my address, I may lose the opportunity to file a *pro se* petition for discretionary review.

________________________   ________________________

Defendant	Defendant's Counsel
Mailing address:	State Bar of Texas ID number
Telephone number:	Mailing address:
Fax number (if any):	Telephone number:
	Fax number (if any):

Amended May 2, 2007 and Aug. 20, 2007, eff. Sept. 1, 2007; Sept. 30, 2011, eff. Sept. 30, 2011; Oct. 17, 2011, eff. Oct. 17, 2011.

* "A defendant in a criminal case has the right of appeal under these rules. The trial court shall enter a certification of the defendant's right to appeal in every case in which it enters a judgment of guilt or other appealable order. In a plea bargain case—that is, a case in which a defendant's plea was guilty or nolo contendere and the punishment did not exceed the punishment recommended by the prosecutor and agreed to by the defendant—a defendant may appeal only: (A) those matters that were raised by written motion filed and ruled on before trial, or (B) after getting the trial court's permission to appeal." Texas Rule Of Appellate Procedure 25.2(a)(2)

APPENDIX E

COURT OF CRIMINAL APPEALS OF TEXAS
APPLICATION FOR A WRIT OF HABEAS CORPUS
SEEKING RELIEF FROM FINAL FELONY CONVICTION
UNDER CODE OF CRIMINAL PROCEDURE, ARTICLE 11.07

INSTRUCTIONS

1. You must use the complete form, which begins on the following page, to file an application for a writ of habeas corpus seeking relief from a final felony conviction under Article 11.07 of the Code of Criminal Procedure. (This form is not for death-penalty cases, probated sentences which have not been revoked, or misdemeanors.)

2. The district clerk of the county in which you were convicted will make this form available to you on request, without charge.

3. You must file the entire writ application form, including those sections that do not apply to you. If any pages are missing from the form, or if the questions have been renumbered or omitted, your entire application may be dismissed as non-compliant.

4. You must make a separate application on a separate form for each judgment of conviction you seek relief from. Even if the judgments were entered in the same court on the same day, you must make a separate application for each one.

5. Answer every item that applies to you on the form. Do not attach any additional pages for any item.

6. You must include all grounds for relief on the application form as provided by the instructions under item 17. You must also briefly summarize the facts of your claim on the application form as provided by the instructions under item 17. Each ground shall begin on a new page, and the recitation of the facts supporting the ground shall be no longer than the two pages provided for the claim in the form.

7. Legal citations and arguments may be made in a separate memorandum that complies with Texas Rule of Appellate Procedure 73 and does not exceed 15,000 words if computer-generated or 50 pages if not.

8. You must verify the application by signing either the Oath Before Notary Public or the Inmate's Declaration, which are at the end of this form on pages 11 and 12. You may be prosecuted and convicted for aggravated perjury if you make any false statement of a material fact in this application.

9. When the application is fully completed, mail the original to the district clerk of the county of conviction. Keep a copy of the application for your records.

10. You must notify the district clerk of the county of conviction of any change in address after you have filed your application.

Case No. ________

(The Clerk of the convicting court will fill this line in.)

IN THE COURT OF CRIMINAL APPEALS OF TEXAS

APPLICATION FOR A WRIT OF HABEAS CORPUS
SEEKING RELIEF FROM FINAL FELONY CONVICTION
UNDER CODE OF CRIMINAL PROCEDURE, ARTICLE 11.07

NAME: ______________________________

DATE OF BIRTH: ______________________________

PLACE OF CONFINEMENT: ______________________________

TDCJ–CID NUMBER: ________ **SID NUMBER:** ______________________________

(1) This application concerns (check all that apply):

____

☐ a conviction ☐ parole

☐ a sentence ☐ mandatory supervision

☐ time credit ☐ out–of–time appeal or petition for discretionary review

(2) What district court entered the judgment of the conviction you want relief from? (Include the court number and county.)

____

(3) What was the case number in the trial court?

____

(4) What was the name of the trial judge?

(5) Were you represented by counsel? If yes, provide the attorney's name:

____

(6) What was the date that the judgment was entered?

____

(7) For what offense were you convicted and what was the sentence?

____

(8) If you were sentenced on more than one count of an indictment in the same court at the same time, what counts were you convicted of and what was the sentence in each count?

____

____

(9) What was the plea you entered? (Check one.)

☐ guilty–open plea ☐ guilty–plea bargain
☐ not guilty ☐ *nolo contendere*/no contest

If you entered different pleas to counts in a multi-count indictment, please explain:

____

____

(10) What kind of trial did you have?

☐ no jury ☐ jury for guilt and punishment

☐ jury for guilt, judge for punishment

(11) Did you testify at trial? If yes, at what phase of the trial did you testify?

____

(12) Did you appeal from the judgment of conviction?

☐ yes ☐ no

If you did appeal, answer the following questions:

(A) What court of appeals did you appeal to? ______________________

(B) What was the case number? ______________________

(C) Were you represented by counsel on appeal? If yes, provide the attorney's name:

____

(D) What was the decision and the date of the decision? ______________________

(13) Did you file a petition for discretionary review in the Court of Criminal Appeals?

☐ **yes** ☐ **no**

If you did file a petition for discretionary review, answer the following questions:

(A) What was the case number? ______________________

(B) What was the decision and the date of the decision? ______________________

(14) Have you previously filed an application for a writ of habeas corpus under Article 11.07 of the Texas Code of Criminal Procedure challenging *this conviction?*

☐ **yes** ☐ **no**

If you answered yes, answer the following questions:

(A) What was the Court of Criminal Appeals' writ number?

(B) What was the decision and the date of the decision? ______________________

(C) Please identify the reason that the current claims were not presented and could not have been presented on your previous application.

____

____

____

____

(15) Do you currently have any petition or appeal pending in any other state or federal court?

☐ **yes** ☐ **no**

If you answered yes, please provide the name of the court and the case number:

____

(16) If you are presenting a claim for time credit, have you exhausted your administrative remedies by presenting your claim to the time credit resolution system of the Texas Department of Criminal Justice? (This requirement applies to any final felony conviction, including state jail felonies)

☐ **yes** ☐ **no**

If you answered yes, answer the following questions:

(A) What date did you present the claim? ______________________

(B) Did you receive a decision and, if yes, what was the date of the decision?

____

If you answered no, please explain why you have not submitted your claim:

____

____

____

(17) Beginning on page 6, state *concisely* every legal ground for your claim that you are being unlawfully restrained, and then briefly summarize the facts supporting each ground. You must present each ground on the form application and a brief summary of the facts. *If your grounds and brief summary of the facts have not been presented on the form application, the Court will not consider your grounds.*

If you have more than four grounds, use pages 14 and 15 of the form, which you may copy as many times as needed to give you a separate page for each ground, with each ground numbered in sequence. The recitation of the facts supporting each ground must be no longer than the two pages provided for the ground in the form.

You may include with the form a memorandum of law if you want to present legal authorities, but the Court will *not* consider grounds for relief set out in a memorandum of law that were not raised on the form. The citations and argument must be in a memorandum that complies with Texas Rule of Appellate Procedure 73 and does not exceed 15,000 words if computer-generated or 50 pages if not. If you are challenging the validity of your conviction, please include a summary of the facts pertaining to your offense and trial in your memorandum.

GROUND ONE:

FACTS SUPPORTING GROUND ONE:

GROUND TWO:

FACTS SUPPORTING GROUND TWO:

GROUND THREE:

FACTS SUPPORTING GROUND THREE:

GROUND FOUR:

FACTS SUPPORTING GROUND FOUR:

GROUND:

FACTS SUPPORTING GROUND:

WHEREFORE, APPLICANT PRAYS THAT THE COURT GRANT APPLICANT RELIEF TO WHICH HE MAY BE ENTITLED IN THIS PROCEEDING.

VERIFICATION

This application must be verified or it will be dismissed for non-compliance. For verification purposes, an applicant is a person filing the application on his or her own behalf. A petitioner is a person filing the application on behalf of an applicant, for example, an applicant's attorney. An inmate is a person who is in custody.

The inmate applicant must sign either the "Oath Before a Notary Public" before a notary public or the "Inmate's Declaration" without a notary public. If the inmate is represented by a licensed attorney, the attorney may sign the "Oath Before a Notary Public" as petitioner and then complete "Petitioner's Information." A non-inmate applicant must sign the "Oath Before a Notary Public" before a notary public unless he is represented by a licensed attorney, in which case the attorney may sign the verification as petitioner.

A non-inmate non-attorney petitioner must sign the "Oath Before a Notary Public" before a notary public and must also complete "Petitioner's Information." An inmate petitioner must sign either the "Oath Before a Notary Public" before a notary public or the "Inmate's Declaration" without a notary public and must also complete the appropriate "Petitioner's Information."

OATH BEFORE A NOTARY PUBLIC

STATE OF TEXAS

COUNTY OF ________________________________

__________, being duly sworn, under oath says: "I am the applicant / petitioner (circle one) in this action and know the contents of the above application for a writ of habeas corpus and, according to my belief, the facts stated in the application are true."

____

Signature of Applicant / Petitioner (circle one)

SUBSCRIBED AND SWORN TO BEFORE ME THIS ___ DAY OF _________, 20 ___.

____

Signature of Notary Public

PETITIONER'S INFORMATION

Petitioner's printed name: ________________________________

State bar number, if applicable: ________________________________

Address: ________________________________

____

____

Telephone: ________________________________

Fax: ________________________________

INMATE'S DECLARATION

I, __________, am the applicant / petitioner (circle one) and being presently incarcerated in __________, declare under penalty of perjury that, according to my belief, the facts stated in the above application are true and correct.

Signed on __________, 20 ___.

____

Signature of Applicant / Petitioner (circle one)

PETITIONER'S INFORMATION

Petitioner's printed name: ______________________________

Address: ______________________________

____

____

Telephone: ______________________________

Fax: ______________________________

Signed on __________, 20 ___.

____

Signature of Petitioner

Former Appendix F amended March 5, 2007, eff. March 5, 2007; July 12, 2011, eff. Sept. 1, 2011. Renumbered as Appendix E and amended Dec. 11, 2013, eff. Jan. 1, 2014.

APPENDIX F

IN THE COURT OF CRIMINAL APPEALS OF TEXAS

ORDER ADOPTING SUMMARY SHEET FOR POSTCONVICTION APPLICATIONS FOR WRIT OF HABEAS CORPUS

Application for Writ of Habeas Corpus
Ex Parte ____________________ from ____________________ County
(Name of Applicant) ____________________ Court

TRIAL COURT WRIT NO. ____________________

CLERK'S SUMMARY SHEET

APPLICANT'S NAME: ____________________
(As reflected in judgment)
OFFENSE: ____________________
(As reflected in judgment)
CAUSE NO: ____________________
(As reflected in judgment)
PLEA: __________ GUILTY __________ NOT GUILTY
SENTENCE: __________ DATE: ____________________
(Terms of years reflected in judgment)
TRIAL DATE: ____________________
JUDGE'S NAME: ____________________
(Judge presiding at trial)
APPEAL NO: ____________________
(If applicable)
CITATION TO OPINION: __________ S.W.3d ____________________
(If applicable)
HEARING HELD: __________ YES __________ NO
(Pertaining to the application for writ of habeas corpus)
FINDINGS & CONCLUSIONS FILED: __________ YES __________ NO
(Pertaining to the application for writ of habeas corpus)
RECOMMENDATION: __________ GRANT __________ DENY __________ NONE
(Trial court's recommendation regarding application for writ of habeas corpus)
JUDGE'S NAME:
(Judge presiding over habeas corpus proceeding)
NAME OF COUNSEL IF APPLICANT IS REPRESENTED: ____________________

Former Appendix G renumbered as Appendix F and amended by Court of Criminal Appeals Dec. 11, 2013, eff. Jan. 1, 2014.

APPENDIX G [Renumbered as Appendix F by Order of Dec. 11, 2013, eff. Jan. 1, 2014]

APPENDIX H [Repealed by Order of Dec. 11, 2013, eff. Jan. 1, 2014]

INDEX TO TEXAS RULES OF APPELLATE PROCEDURE

RULES GOVERNING THE PROCEDURE FOR MAKING A RECORD OF COURT PROCEEDINGS BY ELECTRONIC RECORDING

Including Amendments Received Through February 1, 2016

INTRODUCTION

The Texas Supreme Court has authorized courts in Bexar, Brazos, Dallas, Harris, Kleberg, Liberty and Montgomery Counties, and the 39th District Court in Haskell, Throckmorton, Stonewall and Kent Counties, to make a record in civil proceedings by electronic tape recording. Rules for such proceedings, both in the trial court and on appeal, have been adopted in separate orders, each applicable to a specific court or county, as follows:

Bexar County: Misc. Docket No. 90–0017, signed Nov. 9, 1990.

Brazos County: Misc. Docket No. 90–0016, signed Nov. 9, 1990.

Dallas County: Misc. Docket No. 91–0059, signed Aug. 7, 1991 (replacing prior rules and eff. Jan. 1, 1991).

Harris County: Misc. Docket No. 91–0017, signed Feb. 27, 1991.

Kleberg County: Misc. Docket No. 92–0072, signed March 30, 1992.

Liberty County: Misc. Docket No. 91–0058, signed July 30, 1991.

Montgomery County: Misc. Docket No. 90–0015, signed Nov. 9, 1990.

39th District Court in Haskell, Throckmorton, Stonewall and Kent Counties: Misc. Docket No. 93–0154, signed Sept. 1, 1993.

The provisions of the rules are identical, except that paragraph 1 specifies the county or court to which the rules apply.

1. Application. The following rules govern the procedures * in proceedings in civil matters in which a record is made by electronic tape recording, and appeals from such proceedings.

2. Duties of Court Recorders. No stenographic record shall be required of any civil proceedings electronically tape recorded. The court shall designate one or more persons as court recorders, whose duties shall be:

a. Assuring that the recording system is functioning and that a complete, distinct, clear and transcribable recording is made;

b. Making a detailed, legible log of all proceedings while recording, indexed by time of day, showing the number and style of the proceeding before the court, the correct name of each person speaking, the nature of the proceeding (e.g., voir dire, opening, examination of witnesses, cross-examination, argument, bench conferences, whether in the presence of the jury, etc.), and the offer, admission or exclusion of all exhibits;

c. Filing with the clerk the original log and a typewritten log prepared from the original;

d. Filing all exhibits with the clerk;

e. Storing or providing for storing of the original recording to assure its preservation as required by law;

f. Prohibiting or providing for prohibition of access by any person to the original recording without written order of the presiding judge of the court;

g. Preparing or obtaining a certified cassette copy of the original recording of any proceeding, upon full payment of any charge imposed therefor, at the request of any person entitled to such recording, or at the direction of the presiding judge of the court, or at the direction of any appellate judge who is presiding over any matter involving the same proceeding, subject to the laws of this state, rules of procedure, and the instructions of the presiding judge of the court;

h. Performing such other duties as may be directed by the judge presiding.

3. Statement of Facts. The statement of facts on appeal from any proceeding of which an electronic tape recording has been made shall be:

a. A standard cassette recording, labeled to reflect clearly the contents of the cassette, and numbered if more than one cassette is required, certified by the court recorder to be a clear and accurate copy of the original recording of the entire proceeding;

b. A copy of the typewritten and original logs filed in the case certified by the court recorder; and

c. All exhibits, arranged in numerical order and firmly bound together so far as practicable, with a list in numerical order and a brief identifying description of each.

4. Time for Filing. The court recorder shall file the statement of facts with the court of appeals within fifteen days of the perfection of an appeal or writ of error. No other filing deadlines as set out in the Texas Rules of Appellate Procedure are changed.

5. Appendix. Each party shall file with his brief an appendix containing a written transcription of all portions of the recorded statement of facts and a copy of all exhibits relevant to the error asserted. Transcriptions shall be presumed to be accurate unless objection is made. The form of the appendix and transcription shall conform to any specifications of the Supreme Court.

6. Presumption. The appellate court shall presume that nothing omitted from the transcriptions in the appendices is relevant to any point raised or to the disposition of the appeal. The appellate court shall have no duty to review any part of an electronic recording.

7. Supplemental Appendix. The appellate court may direct a party to file a supplemental appendix containing a written transcription of additional portions of the recorded statement of facts.

8. Paupers. Texas Rule of Appellate Procedure 53(j)(1) ** shall be interpreted to require the court recorder to transcribe or have transcribed the recorded statement of facts and file it as appellant's appendix.

9. Accuracy. Any inaccuracies in transcriptions of the recorded statement of facts may be corrected by agreement of the parties. Should any dispute arise after the statement of facts or appendices are filed as to whether an electronic tape recording or any transcription of it accurately discloses what occurred in the trial court, the appellate court may resolve the dispute by reviewing the recording, or submit the matter to the trial court, which shall, after notice to the parties and hearing, settle the dispute and make the statement of facts or transcription conform to what occurred in the trial court.

10. Costs. The expense of appendices shall be taxed as costs at the rate prescribed by law. The appellate court may disallow the cost of portions of appendices that it considers surplusage or that do not conform to any specifications prescribed by the Supreme Court.

11. Other Provisions. Except to the extent inconsistent with these rules, all other statutes and rules governing the procedures in civil actions shall continue to apply to those proceedings of which a record is made by electronic tape recording.

Rules applicable to Bexar County by Order signed Nov. 9, 1990; to Brazos County by Order signed Nov. 9, 1990; to Montgomery County by Order signed Nov. 9, 1990; to Harris County by Order signed Feb. 27, 1991; to Liberty County by Order signed July 20, 1991; to Dallas County by Order signed Aug. 7, 1991 [replacing prior rules and eff. Jan. 1, 1991]; to Kleberg County by Order signed Mar. 30, 1992; to 39th District Count in Haskell, Throckmorton, Stonewall, and Kent Counties by Order signed Sept. 1, 1993.

* The respective orders provide: "in the courts of Bexar County"; "in the courts of Brazos County"; "in the courts of Dallas County"; "in the courts of Harris County"; "in the courts of Kleberg County"; "in the courts of Liberty County"; "in the courts of Montgomery County"; "in the 39th District Court of Haskell, Throckmorton, Stonewall and Kent Counties".

** Reference to Texas Rule of Appellate Procedure 40(j)(1), rather than 53(j)(1), in several of the orders is apparently a typographical error.

COURT OF CRIMINAL APPEALS MISCELLANEOUS RULES AND PROCEDURES

Including Amendments Received Through February 1, 2016

Hazardous Papers or Items Sent to the Court of Criminal Appeals

(a) Persons shall not send or deliver to this Court (including the Clerk of the Court, any judge, or any member of the staff of the Court) papers or items that constitute a health hazard as defined in Section (b).

(b) The Clerk of the Court is authorized to routinely and immediately dispose of, without seeking a judge's permission, any papers or items sent or delivered to this Court that are smeared with or contain corrosive or dangerous chemicals, blood, food, feces, urine, or other bodily fluids. Such items constitute a health hazard to Court employees and shall be disposed of by the Clerk for that reason.

(c) The Clerk of the Court shall maintain a written log of items that have been disposed of under this rule. The log shall contain all available information concerning the name, address, and identification numbers of the person who sent the offending material, and a brief description of the item disposed of.

(d) The Clerk of the Court shall also notify the sender and, if applicable, the appropriate supervising official of any prison or jail in which a sender-prisoner is held, that the item was destroyed and that sanctions may be imposed if the prisoner continues to send or deliver papers or items in violation of Section (b) of this Rule.

Adopted by order of Dec. 17, 2007, eff. Dec. 17, 2007.

Court of Criminal Appeals Emergency E–mail Filing Seeking Relief in Death–Penalty Execution Cases or Other Extraordinary Emergency Matters

In the event that an emergency e-mail filing is necessary, you must follow the steps listed below:

1. You must first phone the Clerk's Office of the Court of Criminal Appeals between 8:00 a.m. and 5:00 p.m. at (512) 463–1551, to inform the Clerk that you will be sending an emergency e-mail pleading. Pleadings sent by e-mail may not exceed 5MB.

2. You will e-mail your emergency pleading by clicking this e-mail link: CCA Emergency E–Mail[1] and attaching the pleading. In your e-mail, you must include your name, address, telephone number, and Texas State Bar Card number. You must also e-mail the pleading to all those who must be served under TEX. R. APP. P. 6.3 or any other applicable rule.

3. You must confirm by phone that the e-mail filing was received by the Clerk of the Court of Criminal Appeals or the Clerk's designated agent. A representative of the Court will then send a reply e-mail verifying that your filing has been received by the duty judge who will then decide whether to accept delivery of the pleading on an emergency basis pursuant to TEX. R. APP. P. 9.2(a)(2).

4. You must file your pleading in standard paper format, with the required number of copies, in the Court of Criminal Appeals Clerk's office by 9:30 a.m. Central Time the next business day.

[1] CCAEmergencyE–Mail@cca.courts.state.tx.us

Procedures in Death Penalty Cases Involving Requests for Stay of Execution and Related Filings in Texas State Trial Courts and the Court of Criminal Appeals

1. *Time Requirements for Habeas Petitions or Other Motions.* Inmates sentenced to death who seek a stay of execution or who wish to file a subsequent writ application or other motion seeking any affirmative relief from, or relating to, a death sentence must exercise reasonable diligence in timely filing such requests. A motion for stay of execution, or any other pleading relating to a death sentence, must be filed in the proper court at least seven days before the date of the scheduled execution date (exclusive of the scheduled execution date). A pleading shall be deemed untimely if it is filed in the proper court fewer than seven days before the scheduled execution date. For example, a request for a stay of execution filed at 8:00 a.m. on a Wednesday morning when the execution is

scheduled for the following Wednesday at 6:00 p.m. is untimely.

2. *Special Requirements for Untimely Petitions or Other Motions.* Counsel who seek to file an untimely motion for a stay of execution or who wish to file any other untimely pleading requesting affirmative relief in an impending execution case, must attach to the proposed filing a detailed explanation stating under oath, subject to the penalties of perjury, the reason for the delay and why counsel found it physically, legally, or factually impossible to file a timely request, motion, or other pleading. Counsel is required to show good cause for the untimely filing.

3. *Sanctions.* Counsel who fails to attach a sworn detailed explanation to an untimely filing or who fails to adequately justify the necessity for an untimely filing shall be sanctioned. Such sanctions include, but are not limited to (1) referral to the Chief Disciplinary Counsel of the State Bar of Texas; (2) contempt of court; (3) removal from the list of Tex. Code Crim. Proc. Art. 11.071 list of attorneys; (4) restitution of costs incurred by the opposing party; and (5) any other sanction allowed by law (see, *e.g.*, Tex. R. Civ. P. 215.2).

IN THE COURT OF CRIMINAL APPEALS OF TEXAS

To ensure that all appropriate state and federal courts, officials, and parties shall have an adequate opportunity to review and resolve legal and factual issues concerning an impending execution, the Court of Criminal Appeals has adopted Miscellaneous Rule 11–003, effective immediately. This rule is modeled upon an analogous rule adopted by the Fifth Circuit Court of Appeals.

Adopted by order of June 23, 2008. Amended by order of June 30, 2011, eff. June 30, 2011.

CHECKLIST FOR COURT OF CRIMINAL APPEALS
(Updated 9/1/2011)

PETITIONS FOR DISCRETIONARY REVIEW	**RULE 68**
Time to file (Rule 68.2)	30 days after court of appeals judgment or 30 days after rehearing overruled.
Extension of time (Rule 68.2(c))	File with Court of Criminal Appeals Original only
Where to file (Rule 68.3)	Court of Criminal Appeals (effective 9-1-11)
Contents of Petition (Rule 68.4)	
Length of Petition (Rule 68.5)	15 pages
Number of copies (Rule 9.3(b))	Original + eleven copies
Amend/Supplement (Rule 68.10)	
Reply to Petition (Rule 68.9)	File with Court of Criminal Appeals (effective 9-1-11)

BRIEFS ON THE MERIT (PDR)	**RULE 70**
All briefs should comply with (Rule 38)	(See Rule 70.3)
All briefs should conform to (Rule 9.4)	
Binding and covers (Rule 9.4(f))	
Covers should not be dark blue, red, black or plastic (Rule 9.4(f))	

Granted Petitions for Discretionary Review

Number of copies (Rule 9.3(b))	Original + eleven copies
Time to file (Rule 70.1)	Due within 30 days
Page limit (Rule 38.4)	50 page limit

Reply Briefs

Number of copies (Rule 9.3(b))	Original + eleven copies
Time to file (Rule 70.2)	30 days after filing of brief
Page limit (Rule 38.3 & 38.4)	25 page limit

AMICUS BRIEFS	**RULE 11**
Comply with briefing rules	

Received not filed
No extensions of time to file

MOTION FOR REHEARING	**RULE 79**
Due date (Rule 79.1)	15 days after judgment or order of Court of Criminal Appeals
Extension of Time (Rule 79.6)	File with Court of Criminal Appeals Original only
Contents (Rule 79.2)	
Contents (Rule 79.2(c))	For Refused PDRs only
Amendments (Rule 79.3)	

EXTRAORDINARY MATTERS	**RULE 72**
Number of copies (Rule 9.3(b))	Original + eleven copies
Must be accompanied by motion for leave to file	

POSTCONVICTION APPLICATIONS FOR WRITS OF HABEAS CORPUS (11.07)	**RULE 73**

Must be filed in convicting court
on prescribed form (Art. 11.07, Sec. 2; Rule 73.1(a))

DEATH PENALTY CASES DIRECT APPEALS	**RULE 71**
Death Penalty Briefs Appellant's Brief (Rule 38.6(a), Rule 71.3)	Appellant's brief is due 30 days after the reporter's record is filed in this court.
State's Brief (Rule 38.6(b), Rule 71.3)	State's brief is due 30 days after the appellant's brief is filed in this court.
Number of copies (Rule 9.3(b))	Original + eleven copies
Page limit (Rule 38 & Rule 71.3)	125 page limit
Where to file (Rule 71.3)	Court of Criminal Appeals
Statement re: Oral Argt (Rule 71.3)	

CLERK'S RECORD	**RULE 34.5**
Contents (Rule 34.5(a)(2))	

Due Date (Rule 35.2(a))	The clerk's record is due 60 days from the date sentence is imposed if no motion for new trial is filed
Due Date (Rule 35.2(b))	or 120 days if motion for new trial is filed
REPORTER'S RECORD	**RULE 34.6**
Contents (Rule 34 (a)(1)(2))	
Due Date (Rule 35.2(a))	The reporter's record is due 60 days from the date sentence is imposed if no motion for new trial is filed
Due Date (Rule 35.2(b))	or 120 days if a motion for new trial is filed.

(SEE ALSO UNIFORM FORMAT MANUAL FOR COURT REPORTERS)

APPEALS FROM TRIAL COURT ORDERS ON DNA CASES	**See C.C.P. Chapter 64, Art. 64.01**

Texas Court of Criminal Appeals' Amended Rules for the Appointment of Attorneys as Counsel Under Article 11.071 Sec. 2(d), Texas Code of Criminal Procedure [Repealed]

Publisher's Note

Acts 2009, 81st Leg., ch. 781, § 11, repealed Texas Code of Criminal Procedure § 11.071(d), relating to the Court of Criminal Appeals' amended rules for the appointment of attorneys as counsel.

Adopted by order of Dec. 11, 2006, eff. Dec. 15, 2006. Amended effective Sept. 1, 2011.

Court of Criminal Appeals

State of Texas
Supreme Court Building
201 W. 14th Street, Room 106
Austin, TX 78701
(512) 463-1551

In 2004, the Appellate Section of the State Bar of Texas and the Court of Criminal Appeals worked together to identify key information needed by appellate attorneys and pro se litigants to practice effectively before the court. To assist the court in this effort, the Appellate Section collected and formatted the relevant information and published it in the Appellate Advocate in February 2005. The Appellate Section and the court updated the information in March 2007. Hereafter, the court intends to keep the information updated for the use of persons with matters before the court.

Internal Operating Procedures – Court of Criminal Appeals
(September 1, 2011)

The Basics

1. Address: Court of Criminal Appeals, P.O. Box 12308, Austin, TX 78711 or Supreme Court Bldg, 201 W. 14th St., Austin, TX 78701
2. Telephone numbers: Phone: (512) 463-1551; Fax: (512) 463-7061
3. Website address: http://www.cca.courts.state.tx.us
4. Judges: Presiding Judge Sharon Keller, Serving Judges Lawrence E. Meyers, Tom Price, Paul Womack, Cheryl Johnson, Michael Keasler, Barbara Hervey, Cathy Cochran, and Elsa Alcala
5. Clerk of the Court: Abel Acosta
6. Local Rules: None

The Ins and Outs

PROCEDURE	WHAT AND HOW TO FILE	HOW HANDLED	COURT'S PARTICULAR PRACTICES	SPECIAL NOTES
Motions	Original only of motions for extension of time; Original plus 11 copies of all other motions	First motions for extension of time are routinely granted. Motions for extension of time must comply with TRAP 10.5(b) and 68.2(c).		
Briefs	Original plus 11 copies		Briefs must comply with TRAP 38 and 71.3 Amendment and supplementation is allowed only with leave of Court.	

PROCEDURE	WHAT AND HOW TO FILE	HOW HANDLED	COURT'S PARTICULAR PRACTICES	SPECIAL NOTES
Oral Argument	n/a	The Court will designate whether a case requires oral argument. Notification of such designation shall be sent to counsel along with notification of submission. If counsel desires oral argument and the Court has not so designated the case, counsel may petition the Court within 30 days of the submission notification.	The total maximum time for oral argument is 20 minutes per side. If a motion for rehearing is granted and the cause re-submitted, oral argument is limited to 15 minutes per side	Multiple additional citations should not be made orally during argument, but should be reduced to writing and filed with the Clerk.
Opinions			Orders are released Wednesday mornings at 9:00 a.m.	
Motions for Rehearing	Original plus 11 copies			

Technology

1. Westlaw anc Lexis are both available to the Court.
2. The Court does not accept fax filings.
3. The Court does not accept electronic filings.
4. The Court posts its orders on its website at this URL: http://www.cca.courts.state.tx.us/opinions/docketsearch.asp .
5. The Court makes audio recordings of oral arguments available on CD-Rom for $5.

LOCAL RULES OF THE COURTS OF APPEALS

Including Amendments Received Through February 1, 2016

Court of Appeals	
First	(Houston)
Second	(Fort Worth)
Third	(Austin)
Fourth	(San Antonio)
Fifth	(Dallas)
Eighth	(El Paso)
Tenth	(Waco)
Fourteenth	(Houston)

FIRST COURT OF APPEALS LOCAL RULES (Houston)

Rule

Rule 1. Assignment of Related Cases to and Transfers of Related Cases between the First and Fourteenth Courts of Appeals

Rule 1.1. Definitions.

(a) "Underlying case" means a trial court case number that is filed in one of the counties that comprise the jurisdiction of the First and Fourteenth Courts of Appeals and is subsequently the subject of either an appeal or original proceeding in the First or Fourteenth Court of Appeals.

(b) "Related" means arising from the same underlying case or a case that has been remanded by either the First or Fourteenth Court of Appeals and includes cases severed from the main case.

(c) "Previously filed" means that a case has been opened at either the First or Fourteenth Court of Appeals and that an appellate case number has been assigned to the underlying case.

Rule 1.2. Assignment of Original Proceedings to either the First or Fourteenth Court of Appeals.

(a) Except as noted below, assignment of original proceedings must be alternated between the First and Fourteenth Courts of Appeals.

(b) During the first six months of a calendar year, relators must first present any original proceeding to the clerk of the First Court of Appeals. During the last six months of a calendar year, relators must first present any original proceeding to the clerk of the Fourteenth Court of Appeals. Hereinafter, the "intake clerk" means the clerk receiving the original proceeding.

(c) The intake clerk must log in each original proceeding sequentially, assigning original proceedings between the First and Fourteenth Courts of Appeals on an alternating basis.

(d) If a related appeal or original proceeding has been previously filed in one of the courts, the intake clerk must assign the original proceeding in the manner provided for in Rule 1.3(a)–(b) below.

Rule 1.3. Notice of and Assignment of Related Cases in Original Proceedings.

(a) At the time an original proceeding is filed in either the First or Fourteenth Court of Appeals, the relator must file a notice indicating whether any related appeal or original proceeding has been previously filed in either the First or Fourteenth Court of Appeals. The notice must include the caption, trial court case number, and appellate court case number of the related appeal or original proceeding.

(b) If any related appeal or original proceeding has been previously filed in or assigned to either the First or Fourteenth Court of Appeals, the clerk of the appellate court receiving the original proceeding must assign it to the court of appeals in which the related appeal or original proceeding was previously filed.

(c) If related appeals or original proceedings have been filed in both the First and Fourteenth Courts of Appeals, the clerk of the appellate court receiving the original proceeding must assign it to the court of appeals in which the most recent related appeal or original proceeding was previously filed or assigned.

Rule 1.4. Notice of and Assignment of Related Cases in Appeals.

(a) At the time the notice of appeal is filed in the trial court, the notice of appeal must contain a statement indicating whether a related appeal or original proceeding has been previously filed in either the First or Fourteenth Court of Appeals and must include the caption, trial court case number, and appellate court case number of the related appeal or original proceeding.

(b) If a related appeal or original proceeding has been previously filed in or assigned to either the First or Fourteenth Court of Appeals, the trial court clerk must assign the appeal to the court of appeals in which the related appeal or original proceeding was previously filed, pursuant to TEX. GOV'T CODE ANN.

§ 22.202(h) (Vernon 2004), which provides for companion cases to be assigned to the same court of appeals.

(c) If related appeals or original proceedings have been previously filed in both the First and Fourteenth Courts of Appeals, the trial court clerk must assign the appeal to the court of appeals in which the most recent related appeal or original proceeding was previously filed or assigned, pursuant to TEX. GOV'T CODE ANN. § 22.202(h) (Vernon 2004), which provides for companion cases to be assigned to the same court of appeals.

Rule 1.5. Transfers of Related Cases Between the First and Fourteenth Courts of Appeals.

(a) The First or Fourteenth Court of Appeals may, either sua sponte or on motion of a party, transfer an appeal or an original proceeding to the other Houston court of appeals when a related appeal or original proceeding has been previously filed.

(b) The transferring court must forward the case file, together with a transfer order, to the clerk of the transferee court. The clerk of the transferee court must docket the transferred appeal or original proceeding and must assign it a new appellate case number pursuant to TEX. R. APP. P. 12.1 and 12.2.

Rule 1.6. Assignment of Permissive Appeals to either the First or Fourteenth Court of Appeals.

(a) Except as noted below, assignment of permissive appeals must be alternated between the First and Fourteenth Courts of Appeals.

(b) During the first six months of a calendar year applicants must first present any petition for permission to appeal to the clerk of the First Court of Appeals. During the last six months of a calendar year, applicants must first present any petition for permission to appeal to the clerk of the Fourteenth Court of Appeals. Hereinafter, the "intake clerk" means the clerk receiving the petition for permission to appeal.

(c) The intake clerk must log in each petition for permission to appeal sequentially, assigning petitions between the First and Fourteenth Courts of Appeals on an alternating basis.

(d) At any time a petition for permission to appeal is filed, it must contain a statement indicating whether a related appeal or original proceeding has been previously filed in or assigned to either the First or Fourteenth Court of Appeals. If a related appeal or original proceeding has been previously filed in one of the courts, the intake clerk must assign the petition for permission to the court of appeals in which the related appeal or original proceeding was previously filed.

Approved by the Supreme Court Dec. 7, 2006, eff. Dec. 7, 2006. Amended by Supreme Court Sept. 28, 2010, eff. Nov. 1, 2010. Amended by Supreme Court March 11, 2011, eff. March 14, 2011. Amended with permission of the Supreme Court and the Court of Criminal Appeals Dec. 12, 2011, eff. Dec. 1, 2011. Amended by Supreme Court Jan. 24, 2012, eff. Jan. 24, 2012.

SECOND COURT OF APPEALS LOCAL RULES (Fort Worth)

Rule 1. Briefs

All briefs, in both civil and criminal cases, must conform to Rules 9 and 38 of the Texas Rules of Appellate Procedure. All briefs must also meet the following requirements, unless the court, upon motion, permits an exception to the rules:

A. Cover. The front cover of the brief must (1) be addressed to the Court of Appeals for the Second District of Texas and (2) identify the presiding judge and the trial court from which the appeal is taken, for example, "Appeal from the [number] District Court, [name] County, Texas, the Hon. [name] presiding."

B. Number of Copies. If a brief is not electronically filed, the original and four copies of every brief and any separately-bound appendix must be filed with the clerk.

C. Motions for Leave to File Briefs. The appellant's opening brief, the appellee's opening brief, and the appellant's reply brief may be filed without leave of court, if timely. After the appellant's reply brief has been timely filed, any later brief merely replying to the last brief filed will be filed without a motion, if tendered at least seven days prior to the date of the scheduled oral argument or submission date. All other briefs, including amended briefs, supplemental briefs, post-submission briefs, and letter briefs must be accompanied by a motion for leave to file, unless the brief is requested by the court.

D. Letter Briefs. Letter briefs must be addressed to the clerk and refer to the style and number of the case. They must be double-spaced, except for the address to the clerk.

E. Filing Dates. The court will set filing dates for appellant's and appellee's opening briefs when the record is filed and notify the parties of the filing dates. Motions to extend the filing dates for briefs will not be granted except upon a reasonable explanation of the need for an extension.

F. Recording or Exhibit. Whenever a party raises an issue in a brief that requires the court to view a video or audio recording or physical exhibit, the party must file in this court a motion to supplement the appellate record with the recording or exhibit when the party files its brief if the party did not designate the exhibit to be included in the reporter's record.

Approved by Court of Appeals Aug. 28, 1997, approved by Supreme Court Nov. 12, 1997, approved by Court of Criminal Appeals April 21, 1998. Amended by Supreme Court June 8, 2009, eff. June 8, 2009, amended by Court of Criminal Appeals June 15, 2009, eff. June 15, 2009. Amended by the Court of Criminal Appeals, with approval of the Supreme Court May 14, 2012, eff. June 1, 2012. Amended by the Court of Criminal Appeals, with approval of the Supreme Court April 28, 2014, eff. April 28, 2014.

[1] Vernon's Ann.Rules App.Proc., rules 9.1 et seq., 38.1 et seq.

Rule 2. Original Proceedings

Original proceedings are governed by Rule 52 of the Texas Rules of Appellate Procedure and this rule.

A. Number of Copies. If a petition is not electronically filed, the original and four copies of every petition and any separately bound record or appendix must be filed with the clerk.

B. Notice. If the court is of the tentative opinion that relator is entitled to relief or that a serious question concerning the relief requires further consideration, the clerk will send the parties notice stating (1) the date the real party in interest's response must be filed, if one has not been filed, (2) the date the relator's reply to the response must be filed, if permitted by the court, (3) whether the court will allow argument or will submit the case without oral argument, (4) if oral argument is permitted, the date and the time allotted for argument, and (5) the names of the members of the panel to which the case will be argued or submitted, subject to change by the court.

Approved by Court of Appeals Aug. 28, 1997, approved by Supreme Court Nov. 12, 1997, approved by Court of Criminal Appeals April 21, 1998. Amended by the Court of Criminal Appeals, with approval of the Supreme Court May 14, 2012, eff. June 1, 2012. Amended by the Court of Criminal Appeals, with approval of the Supreme Court April 28, 2014, eff. April 28, 2014.

Rule 3. Motions

All motions must comply with Rules 9 and 10 of the Texas Rules of Appellate Procedure and this rule.

A. Number of Copies. If a motion is not electronically filed, the original and one copy of every motion must be filed with the clerk.

B. Signatures and Certificates. In both civil and criminal cases, all motions must contain an original signature, a certificate of service, and, except motions for rehearing, a certificate of conference stating substantially one of the following:

(1) A conference was held on [date] with the opposing party on the merits of this motion, and the opposing party [does] [does not] oppose the motion.

(2) A conference was not held with the opposing party because [explanation].

C. Motions for Extension of Time in Criminal Cases. In addition to complying with Rule 10 of the Texas Rules of Appellate Procedure, all motions for extension of time in criminal cases must state whether the defendant is incarcerated.

D. Motions for Rehearing and En Banc Reconsideration. A motion for rehearing and a motion for en banc reconsideration must include a copy of the opinion and judgment of the court of appeals.

Approved by Court of Appeals Aug. 28, 1997, approved by Supreme Court Nov. 12, 1997, approved by Court of Criminal Appeals April 21, 1998. Amended by the Court of Criminal Appeals, with approval of the Supreme Court April 28, 2014, eff. April 28, 2014.

Rule 4. Oral Argument

Oral argument is governed by Rule 39 of the Texas Rules of Appellate Procedure and this rule.

A. Request. Oral argument should not be requested unless the party requesting argument intends to appear on the date set for submission. Conditional requests for argument (e.g., "Appellant requests oral argument only if oral argument is requested by appellee.") are acceptable.

B. Time Allowed. Unless additional time is granted by the presiding justice of the panel to which the case is assigned, oral argument will be limited to fifteen (15) minutes for the appellant's opening argument, fifteen (15) minutes for the appellee's argument, and five (5) minutes for the appellant's rebuttal. Requests for additional time must be made by motion filed at least ten (10) days prior to the scheduled submission date.

C. Continuance. After a case has been set for argument, oral argument may be continued only by an order of the court for good cause. It may not be continued by agreement of the parties.

D. Waiver. A party who desires to waive an oral argument that has been previously requested or scheduled must notify the clerk and all opposing parties at least seven days prior to the scheduled submission date.

Approved by Court of Appeals Aug. 28, 1997, approved by Supreme Court Nov. 12, 1997, approved by Court of Criminal Appeals April 21, 1998. Amended by the Court of Criminal Appeals, with approval of the Supreme Court May 14, 2012, eff. June 1, 2012. Amended by the Court of Criminal Appeals, with approval of the Supreme Court April 28, 2014, eff. April 28, 2014.

Rule 5. Fax Filing of Documents

A. By the Court. Except as specifically required by the Texas Rules of Appellate Procedure, any notices issued by the clerk of the court or any orders issued by the court may be made by fax, at the discretion of the court. Fax notification will be made to the fax number provided by the attorney of record for each party to the appeal.

B. By the Parties.

(1) **Permissible Fax Filings.** A party may fax file a document only if the party is not required to electronically file the document. The clerk will accept for fax filing any document that is a total of ten transmitted pages or less, excluding the cover sheet. Documents may be faxed to the court (fax number: 817–884–1932) both during and after normal working hours, but documents received after 4:45 p.m. will be considered filed the next day the court is open to the public.

(2) **Cover Sheet.** A cover sheet must accompany all documents transmitted by fax and must clearly identify: 1) the name, address, telephone number, fax number, and email address, if any, of the sender; 2) the name of the party the sender represents; 3) the document being transmitted; 4) the cause number; 5) the number of pages being transmitted; 6) and the name of the clerk or deputy clerk, if any, to whose attention the document is directed.

(3) **Receipt of Transmission.** The quality of the original must be clear and dark enough to be transmitted legibly by fax. The clerk will be responsible for events that disrupt, impair, or render impossible the receipt of documents transmitted by fax. The sender is obligated to ensure that documents transmitted by fax have been received legibly and completely by the clerk. Although the clerk's office will verify by telephone that a document has been received legibly and completely, it will not initiate the telephone call. If a document transmitted by fax is not complete or is otherwise illegible, the clerk will nonetheless file it and bring it to the attention of the court. However, the incompleteness or illegibil-

ity of a document may be grounds for striking or denying a motion.

(4) **Service on Parties.** The party transmitting a document by fax must serve a copy of the document on all parties to the appeal by fax or other expedited means.

(5) **Fees.** The sender must deposit any applicable fees in the U.S. mail on the day the fax is transmitted. Failure of the clerk to receive the fees within seven days after the day the fax is filed may result in the striking of the filing transmitted by fax.

(6) **Signature on Original.** The sender must maintain the original of any document transmitted by fax, with the original signature affixed, as required by section 51.806 of the Texas Government Code

Added by Court of Appeals, May 27, 2004, approved by the Supreme Court Oct. 20, 2004, approved by the Court of Criminal Appeals Nov. 17, 2004. Amended by the Court of Criminal Appeals, with approval of the Supreme Court May 14, 2012, eff. June 1, 2012. Amended by the Court of Criminal Appeals, with approval of the Supreme Court April 28, 2014, eff. April 28, 2014.

Rule 6. Withdrawal of Record on Appeal

In addition to the conditions in Rule 12.4 of the Texas Rules of Appellate Procedure, the clerk may permit a paper-filed record or other paper-filed item to be taken from the clerk's office on the following conditions:

A. Civil Cases. In civil cases, attorneys may check out a paper-filed record from the clerk at any time up to three days before the date on which the case is scheduled to be submitted to the court. After that time, attorneys may not check out the court of appeals's record except on the leave of the court. An attorney who checks out the record must return it promptly to the clerk on demand. Pro se parties may inspect a paper-filed record only on the premises of this court. Parties may request one CD copy of an electronically filed record at any time.

B. Criminal Cases. In criminal cases, the court will not allow the record to be checked out. Records must be checked out through the district clerk's office or county clerk's office in the county from which the appeal arose.

Approved by Court of Appeals Aug. 28, 1997, approved by Supreme Court Nov. 12, 1997, approved by Court of Criminal Appeals April 21, 1998; amendment approved by Court of Appeals Jan. 5, 2001, approved by Supreme Court, Aug. 17, 2004, approved by Court of Criminal Appeals Sept. 29, 2004; renumbered from former rule 5 by Court of Appeals May 27, 2004, approved by Supreme Court Oct. 20, 2004, approved by Court of Criminal Appeals Nov. 17, 2004. Amended by the Court of Criminal Appeals, with approval of the Supreme Court May 14, 2012, eff. June 1, 2012. Amended by the Court of Criminal Appeals, with approval of the Supreme Court April 28, 2014, eff. April 28, 2014.

Rule 7. Protection of Parties' Identities in Filed Documents

In parental termination and child protection cases, as defined in Rule 28. 4(a) of the Texas Rules of Appellate Procedure, and juvenile court cases, in all documents submitted to the court other than a docketing statement—including all appendix items submitted with a brief, petition, or motion—a party must use an alias, as defined in Rule 9.8(a) of the Texas Rules of Appellate Procedure, to identify not only a minor, but also a minor's parent, family member, foster parent, and any other person necessary to protect a minor's identity and must redact all such documents accordingly. Additionally, in other appeals or original proceedings in which the court determines that a child's or other person's identify should be protected, the Clerk's office may request that the parties use aliases in their documents filed with the court.

Added by Court of Appeals Jan. 5, 2001, approved by Supreme Court, Aug. 17, 2004, approved by Court of Criminal Appeals Sept. 29, 2004; renumbered from former rule 6 by Court of Appeals May 27, 2004, approved by Supreme Court Oct. 20, 2004, approved by Court of Criminal Appeals Nov. 17, 2004. Amended by the Court of Criminal Appeals, with approval of the Supreme Court May 14, 2012, eff. June 1, 2012. Amended by the Court of Criminal Appeals, with approval of the Supreme Court April 28, 2014, eff. April 28, 2014.

THIRD COURT OF APPEALS LOCAL RULES (Austin)

Introduction

The procedures prescribed by this local rule apply in addition to those prescribed by the Texas Rules of Appellate Procedure. The Rules of Appellate Procedure continue to apply with full force and effect.

Local Rule 1. Frivolous Appeals in Criminal Cases

(a) **Pre-withdrawal Compliance.** An appointed attorney who believes that an appeal in a criminal case is frivolous must comply with all legal requirements before filing an *Anders* brief. The Third Court requires counsel to demonstrate compliance with these pre-withdrawal requirements by filing, contemporaneously with counsel's motion to withdraw and *Anders* brief, a completed *Certificate of Counsel.* The form for this certificate is attached hereto and is available on the Court's website. It provides written verification to the Court that counsel has provided copies of the motion and brief to appellant, advised appellant of his rights, explained to appellant the procedures to be followed in a frivolous appeal, and informed appellant of the applicable deadlines.

(b) **Notice to Appellant.** A sample cover letter for appointed counsel to send to appellant in a frivolous criminal appeal is attached hereto and is available on the Court's website. Though not required to be used by counsel, the Court strongly encourages counsel to use this letter to assist in fulfilling counsel's obligations pursuant to *Anders.*

(c) **Content of *Anders* Brief.** The Third Court does not require counsel to expressly address any particular area in the *Anders* brief. However, counsel must demonstrate a diligent review of the record and the applicable law. Accordingly, the Court recommends examining the following areas of the record and the law to ensure compliance with *Anders*:

(1) the charging instrument;
(2) jurisdiction;
(3) pre-trial matters and motions;
(4) any required admonishments (for example, in before a guilty plea);
(5) jury selection;
(6) expert testimony;
(7) jury argument;
(8) the court's jury charge;
(9) sufficiency of the evidence;
(10) assistance of counsel;
(11) assessment of court costs or attorney's fees;
(12) the judgment

This list is not exhaustive and depends, of course, on the nature of the case being appealed. However, discussion of these areas is helpful to the Court in making its determination of whether the appeal is frivolous. Counsel is also encouraged to discuss in the brief any other potential errors present in the record considered by counsel.

NO. 03–1X–00XXX–CR

[APPELLANT]	§	IN THE COURT OF APPEALS
	§	
v.	§	THIRD JUDICIAL DISTRICT
	§	
THE STATE OF TEXAS	§	SITTING AT AUSTIN, TEXAS

CERTIFICATE OF COUNSEL

In compliance with the requirements of *Anders v. California*, 386 U.S. 378 (1967), I, [**Name of Attorney**], court-appointed counsel for appellant, [**Name of Appellant**], in the above-referenced appeal, do hereby verify, in writing, to the Court that I have:

1. notified appellant that I filed a motion to withdraw as counsel with an accompanying *Anders* brief, and provided a copy of each to appellant;

2. informed appellant of his right to file a pro se response identifying what he believes to be meritorious grounds to be raised in his appeal, should he so desire;

3. advised appellant of his right to review the appellate record, should he wish to do so, preparatory to filing that response;

4. explained the process for obtaining the appellate record, provided a *Motion for Pro Se Access to the Appellate Record* lacking only appellant's signature and the date, and provided the mailing address for this Court; and

5. informed appellant of his right to seek discretionary review pro se should this Court declare his appeal frivolous.

Respectfully submitted,

____
Attorney for Appellant

Dear [**Appellant**]:

Enclosed please find a copy of the motion to withdraw as counsel and brief pursuant to *Anders v. California* that I have prepared and filed in your case. After a diligent search of both the clerk's record and reporter's record in your case and a review of the applicable law, it is my opinion that no reversible error occurred at your **[trial / plea proceeding / sentencing proceeding / revocation proceeding / adjudication proceeding]**.

Whenever appellate counsel files a motion such as this, the law provides the appellant the right to review the record and file a response identifying to the appellate court any grounds he thinks are non-frivolous issues to be raised on his behalf that the appellate court should consider in deciding whether the case presents any meritorious grounds for appeal. Because I have filed this motion and brief, you now have the right to review the record and file a response or brief if you so choose. To assist you in obtaining the record if you wish to review it, I have enclosed a *Motion for Pro Se Access to the Appellate Record* for you to file. In order to obtain the appellate record, you must sign and date the motion and mail it to the Third Court of Appeals within ten days of the date of this letter at the following address:

Jeffrey D. Kyle, Clerk
Third Court of Appeals
Post Office Box 12547
Austin, Texas 78711

The Court of Appeals will then direct the clerk of the trial court to provide you with a copy of the appellate record. Your response will be due to be filed in the Third Court of Appeals within 30 days of the date the clerk provides the record to you.

Whether or not you file a response, the law requires the Court of Appeals to review the record to determine if the Court agrees with my assessment that no meritorious grounds for appeal exist, i.e., that no reversible error exists. If the Court does not agree, but instead believes there are non-frivolous issues to be raised on your behalf, the Court must abate the appeal to have another attorney appointed to review the record on your behalf.

Should the Court of Appeals ultimately determine that there are no meritorious grounds to be raised and that your appeal is frivolous, the Court will affirm your **[conviction and sentence / revocation / adjudication]**. You may then file a pro se petition for discretionary review with the Texas Court of Criminal Appeals. Such petition must be filed within 30 days of the date the Court of Appeals renders its judgment.

Feel free to write me if you have any questions about the procedure utilized in your appeal. I will do my best to answer any questions you may have.

Sincerely,
[Appellant's Attorney]

FOURTH COURT OF APPEALS LOCAL RULES
(San Antonio)

ORDER ADOPTING LOCAL RULES

IT IS ORDERED that, effective October 1, 1998, these rules are adopted as local rules for the Fourth Court of Appeals with the permission of the Texas Supreme Court and Texas Court of Criminal Appeals. The notes and comments appended to the local rules are not part of the rules and do not have the same force and effect as the rules. All local rules promulgated before October 1, 1998 are rescinded, but this shall not affect any proper action taken pursuant to such rescinded rules prior to the effective date of the rules adopted herein. Done September 23, 1998, effective October 1, 1998.

IT IS ORDERED that, effective June 1, 2011, an amendment to Local Rule 7 has been adopted to add five additional subsections to the local rules for the Fourth Court of Appeals subject to the approval of the Texas Supreme Court and the Texas Court of Criminal Appeals. Done April 19, 2011, effective June 1, 2011.

IT IS ORDERED that, effective September 27, 2011, an amendment to the local rules for the Fourth Court of Appeals was adopted to amend Local Rule 7.4(f) and to add Local Rules 10 and 11. Done September 6, 2011, effective September 27, 2011.

IT IS ORDERED that, effective January 1, 2014, an amendment to the local rules for the Fourth Court of Appeals was adopted, amending Local Rule 7 to delete subsections 7.4, 7.5, 7.6, and 7.7, and deleting Local Rules 10 and 11. Done October 16, 2013, effective January 1, 2014.

Rule 1. Scope of Local Rules

(TEX.R.APP.P. 1.2)

1.1 Relationship to TEX.R.APP.P. These rules supplement the procedures in the Texas Rules of Appellate Procedure and, unless otherwise specified, apply to both civil and criminal cases. If the Texas Rules of Appellate Procedure conflict with these local rules, the Texas Rules of Appellate Procedure govern.

1.2 Relationship to Jurisdiction. These rules do not extend or limit the jurisdiction of this Court, but failure to comply with these rules may result in the dismissal of an appeal after the Court gives the noncomplying party notice and a reasonable opportunity to cure.

Adopted by Court of Appeals Sept. 23, 1998 with permission of the Supreme Court and the Court of Criminal Appeals to be eff. Oct. 1, 1998.

Notes and Comments

The notes and comments appended to the local rules are not part of the rules. Instead, they reflect the Court's general procedures and preferences and are provided for the convenience of the public.

Rule 2. Alternative Dispute Resolution (ADR)

On a party's motion, or on the court's own initiative after reviewing the docketing statement, the Court may refer a civil case to alternative dispute resolution.

Adopted by Court of Appeals Sept. 23, 1998 with permission of the Supreme Court and the Court of Criminal Appeals to be eff. Oct. 1, 1998.

Rule 3. Papers Generally

(TEX.R.APP.P. 9)

3.1 Papers Filed Before the Docketing Statement. If a document is filed in this Court before the appellant's docketing statement is filed, the certificate of service must include the names, addresses, and telephone numbers of each person served.

3.2 Filing by Fax. Documents of ten pages or less may be filed in this Court by fax. Documents may be faxed to the Court both during and after normal working hours. The Court is not responsible for events that disrupt, impair, or render impossible the receipt of documents transmitted by fax.

Adopted by Court of Appeals Sept. 23, 1998 with permission of the Supreme Court and the Court of Criminal Appeals to be eff. Oct. 1, 1998.

Notes and Comments

The Clerk will mail a file-marked copy of a document to any party who tenders an extra copy of the document and a postage-paid self-addressed envelope. The Court encourages parties to use the same method of service of a document on a party as is used in filing the document with the Court.

Rule 4. Bankruptcy and Other Stays in Civil Cases

(TEX.R.APP.P. 8)

Any party may file a notice of bankruptcy or otherwise claim an automatic stay of the appeal as provided by federal or state law. The notice must be accompanied by an appropriate form of proof. The appeal will be abated and, for administrative purposes, treated as a closed case. However, the appeal may be reinstated on prompt motion of any party showing the stay has been lifted and specifying what further action, if any, is required from this Court.

Adopted by Court of Appeals Sept. 23, 1998 with permission of the Supreme Court and the Court of Criminal Appeals to be eff. Oct. 1, 1998.

Rule 5. Docketing Statements

(TEX.R.APP.P. 32)

5.1 Forms. Each appellant must file a docketing statement and attach a signed copy of the judgment or order being appealed.

5.2 Time to File. The docketing statement must be filed in the Fourth Court of Appeals when the notice of appeal is filed.

Adopted by Court of Appeals Sept. 23, 1998 with permission of the Supreme Court and the Court of Criminal Appeals to be eff. Oct. 1, 1998.

Notes and Comments

To assist the efficient handling of cases, the Court encourages appellants to accurately complete the docketing statements adopted by the Court. See Appendix A (civil appeals), Appendix B (ADR), and Appendix C (criminal appeals).

Rule 6. Motions

(TEX.R.APP.P. 10, 26.3, 38.6(d) & 49.8(c))

6.1 Number of Copies. A party need only file an original and one copy of each motion.

6.2 Motions for Rehearing. A motion for rehearing en banc must be filed separately from a motion for rehearing.

Adopted by Court of Appeals Sept. 23, 1998 with permission of the Supreme Court and the Court of Criminal Appeals to be eff. Oct. 1, 1998.

Notes and Comments

Motions for extension of time are no longer required to file the appellate record, but they may be used for filing briefs, including appellee's opening brief. The titles of motions should be descriptive and indicate whether agreed or opposed and whether emergency relief is requested. Proposed orders should not be submitted. Parties should not wait for the Court's ruling on a motion for extension of time but should meet all deadlines at the earliest possible date. Any objection to a visiting judge should be filed within ten days of the date the Clerk sends the parties notice that a visiting judge has been assigned to the appeal.

Rule 7. Appellate Record

(TEX.R.APP.P. 12.4, 34 & 35)

7.1 Notice of Late Record. If an official requires additional time to file a record, the official must request additional time from the Court using the form adopted by the Court. See Appendix D ("Official's Notice of Late Record"). Failure to file the record by the due date or according to the Court's directives will result in appropriate court action.

7.2 Withdrawal of the Record.

(a) Attorneys of Record. At any time before an appeal is set for submission, attorneys of record may withdraw all or part of a record without a motion for a period of 14 days. After the Clerk sends the parties notice setting the appeal for submission, attorneys may review a record in the Court's offices only.

(b) Pro Se Parties. Parties who are representing themselves and are not licensed attorneys may inspect a record only in designated areas within the Court's offices. However, the Court may grant a motion requesting permission to review the record on other terms.

(c) Protection of the Record. The record must not be disassembled.

7.3 Preparation of Clerk's Record. The trial court clerk must prepare and file the clerk's record in accordance with Rules 34.5 and 35. Even if more than one notice of appeal or request for inclusion of items is filed, the clerk should prepare only one record in a case. To prepare the clerk's record, the trial court clerk must:

(a) gather the documents required by Rule 34.5(a) and those requested by a party under Rule 34.5(b);

(b) start each document on a new page;

(c) include the date of filing on each document;

(d) arrange the documents in ascending chronological order, by date of filing or occurrence;

(e) start the page numbering on the front cover of the first volume of the clerk's record and continue to number all pages consecutively-including the front and back covers, tables of contents, certification page, and separator pages, if any-until the final page of the clerk's record, without regard for the number of volumes in the clerk's record, and place each page number at the bottom of each page;

(f) prepare, label, and certify the clerk's record as required by this rule;

(g) as far as practicable, include the date of signing by the judge on each order and judgment;

(h) include on the front cover of the first volume of the clerk's record, whether filed in paper or electronic form, the following information, in substantially the following form:

CLERK'S RECORD
VOLUME ________ of ____________
Trial Court Cause No. ____________
In the ________ (District or County) Court of
________ County, Texas,
Honorable ________, Judge Presiding
________, Plaintiffs)
vs.
________, Defendant(s)
Appealed to the
(Supreme Court of Texas at Austin, Texas, or Court of Criminal Appeals of Texas at Austin, Texas, or Court of Appeals for the ________ District of Texas, at ________, Texas).

Attorney for Appellant(s):

Name: ____________
Address: ____________
Telephone no.: ____________
Fax no.: ____________
E-mail address: ____________
SBOT no.: ____________

Attorney for:

____________, Appellant(s)
Name of clerk preparing the clerk's record: ________

(i) prepare and include after the front cover of the clerk's record a detailed table of contents identifying each document in the entire record (including sealed documents), the date each document was filed, and, except for sealed documents, the page on which each document begins. The table of contents must be double-spaced and conform to the order in which documents appear in the clerk's record, rather than in alphabetical order. If the clerk's record consists of multiple volumes, the table of contents must indicate the page on which each volume begins. If the clerk's record is filed in electronic form, the clerk must use bookmarks to link each document description in the table of contents, except descriptions of sealed documents, to the page on which each document begins; and

(j) conclude the clerk's record with a certificate in substantially the following form:

The State of Texas)
County of ____________)

I, ________, Clerk of the ________ Court of ________ County, Texas do hereby certify that the documents contained in this record to which this certification is attached are all of the documents specified by Texas Rule of Appellate Procedure 34.5(a) and all other documents timely requested by a party to this proceeding under Texas Rule of Appellate Procedure 34.5(b).

GIVEN UNDER MY HAND AND SEAL at my office in ________, County, Texas ________ this day of ________. signature of clerk ________ name of clerk ________ title ________

If the clerk's record is filed in electronic form, the trial court clerk's login and password serves as the clerk's signature on the certification page. The clerk also must include either a scanned image of the clerk's signature or "/s/" and the clerk's name typed in the space where the signature would otherwise appear.

Adopted by Court of Appeals Sept. 23, 1998 with permission of the Supreme Court and the Court of Criminal Appeals to be eff. Oct. 1, 1998; amended effective June 1, 2011; amended by the Court of Appeals Sept. 26, 2011, with approval of the Supreme Court and the Court of Criminal Appeals, eff. Sept. 26, 2011. Amended Jan. 1, 2014.

Notes and Comments

In addition to the hardbound copy of the record, the court reporter should provide a computer disk of the proceedings in ASCII format. The Court generally permits additional time to file a record, up to 60 days from the original due date. Any additional time may be permitted at the Court's discretion. Counsel is reminded that filing a supplemental record does not alter the briefing schedule. Counsel and trial court clerks are also reminded that documents sealed by order of the trial court or otherwise described by statute as confidential (such as juror information sheets) should be filed separately from unsealed portions of the record and should be accompanied by the sealing order, if any. This Court may also seal records if requested. If a record is damaged by a party or attorney, the Court may order the record recertified and invoke any available remedy, including those provided by the Texas Penal Code. In criminal cases, the parties may use the copy of the appellate record filed with the trial court clerk in addition to the copy filed with this Court.

Rule 8. Briefs

(TEX.R.APP.P. 9, 31.1 & 38)

8.1 Number of Copies. The number of copies of a brief that must be filed is governed by Rule 9.3 of the Texas Rules of Appellate Procedure.

8.2 Time for Filing Briefs in Appeals in Habeas Corpus & Bail Proceedings.

(a) *Appellant's Brief.* The appellant's brief must be filed no later than 20 days after the date the clerk's record or the reporter's record is filed, whichever is later.

(b) *State's Brief.* The State's brief must be filed no later than 20 days after the date the appellant's brief is filed.

8.3 Additional Citations. A party may file a letter containing additional citations with succinct comment, at any time without leave of court.

8.4 Amendment or Supplementation. If a party wishes to amend or supplement the party's brief other than in the manner permitted by Local Rule 8.3, the party must obtain the Court's permission.

8.5 Post–Submission Briefs.

(a) *Requested by the Court.* If the Court requests a post-submission brief, the brief must be filed at the time indicated by the Court; or, if no time is specified, within ten days after the Court's request. An opposing party's reply to a post-submission brief requested by the Court must be filed no later than ten days after the date of the brief requested by the Court. If an additional post-submission brief is requested by the Court, the aggregate page limits contained in the Texas Rules of Appellate Procedure do not apply.

(b) *Not Requested by the Court.* If a party wishes to file a post-submission brief that has not been requested by the Court, the party must obtain the Court's permission.

Adopted by Court of Appeals Sept. 23, 1998 with permission of the Supreme Court and the Court of Criminal Appeals to be eff. Oct. 1, 1998. Rule 8.1 amended by the Court of Appeals Aug. 29, 2005 with approval of the Supreme Court and the Court of Criminal Appeals to be effective Aug. 29, 2005.

Notes and Comments

Citations should use jump cites or pinpoint cites and should conform to the most recent editions of HARVARD L. REV., A UNIFORM SYSTEM OF CITATION (the Bluebook), and TEX. L. REV., TEXAS RULES OF FORM (the Greenbook). The Court encourages the use of appendices, especially for federal authorities not found in its own library. The reporter's record may be referred to as "RR" and the clerk's record as "CR." As a general rule, the Court will not give permission to file a brief containing additional issues or points of error after a case has been submitted to the Court for decision. The Court interprets the term "amended brief" to mean a brief that completely replaces the original brief. Pursuant to administrative order of the Court, the Clerk of the Court is authorized to attest to per curiam orders granting extensions of time to file briefs. The Court generally grants a requested extension of time to file a brief, up to 60 days from the original due date. Additional time may be granted at the Court's discretion. An appellant who is also in the position of appellee may request permission to file a combination brief.

Rule 9. Oral Argument

(TEX.R.APP.P. 39)

9.1 Time Allowed. Oral argument will be limited to 20 minutes for the appellant's opening argument, 20 minutes for the appellee's argument, and ten minutes for the appellant's rebuttal.

9.2 Waiver. Any party who requests oral argument and later decides to waive argument must notify the Court and the other parties in writing before the date set for submission.

9.3 Failure to Appear. Any attorney or party who wishes to present argument must register in the Clerk's office 30 minutes before the time scheduled for argument and must also orally announce their appearance in the courtroom at the time scheduled for argument. If an attorney or party fails to comply with this rule, the Court will deem oral argument waived and may take any other appropriate action.

9.4 Audio Recordings. The Court makes audio recordings of oral argument for its own use. However, a party may purchase a copy of the recording from the Clerk. The Court does not guarantee the recording will be clear or audible, and the Court will generally not grant a rehearing because the recording is not clear or audible.

Adopted by Court of Appeals Sept. 23, 1998 with permission of the Supreme Court and the Court of Criminal Appeals to be eff. Oct. 1, 1998.

Notes and Comments

If oral argument is waived, a case may receive expedited consideration. If an issue or point of error raised in a brief is not discussed at argument, the Court will nonetheless consider the issue or point of error preserved for appellate review. If an attorney or party intends to cite a case that is not contained in the briefs, the attorney or party should provide a copy of the case to the Clerk and opposing counsel before argument. The Court monitors the time during oral argument.

Rules 10 and 11. Repealed eff. January 1, 2014

FIFTH COURT OF APPEALS LOCAL RULES
(Dallas)

(Cite these rules as 5th Tex.App. (Dallas) Loc.R.)

Rule 1. Scope of Local Rules

(Tex. R. App. P. 1.2)

These rules govern procedure for appeals, original proceedings, and other matters before the Court of Appeals for the Fifth District of Texas at Dallas. In the event of a conflict between these local rules and the Texas Rules of Appellate Procedure or any other state statute or rule, the Texas Rules of Appellate Procedure, statute, or rule shall control.

Rule 2. Change of Address or Other Information

(Tex. R. App. P. 9.1)

Counsel or a party proceeding pro se shall file a notice of change of address, telephone number, or facsimile number within ten (10) days of the date of the change. The notice shall include the style and cause number of each case the notifying party has pending before the Court.

Rule 3. Oral Argument

(Tex. R. App. P. 39)

1. In civil cases, oral arguments in each appeal are heard at the time designated by the sitting panel. As a general rule, one case will be set for oral argument each hour, beginning at 9:00 a.m. or 1:00 p.m.

2. In criminal cases, all counsel who have requested oral argument are expected to be present at 9:00 a.m. or 1:00 p.m. as instructed by written notice. At that time, the presiding justice will call the docket and determine which attorneys will argue. Oral argument will be heard, insofar as practicable, in the order the cases appear on the submission docket for that date.

3. If there is more than one appellant or appellee, counsel shall be expected to announce to the Court, at docket call, how the time is to be divided among the parties.

4. In both civil and criminal cases, each side is allowed twenty (20) minutes, and the appellant or appellants are allowed five (5) minutes for rebuttal. Requests for additional time must be made by written motion filed at least ten (10) days prior to the scheduled submission date.

Amended April 26, 2011, eff. May 1, 2011; June 13, 2012, eff. July 1, 2012; June 9, 2014.

Rule 4. Settlement

(Tex. R. App. P. 42.1)

In the event a civil case settles before submission, the parties shall notify the Clerk by filing an appropriate motion. The motion shall specify (1) the manner of disposition, and (2) the parties' agreement on the allocation of costs of appeal.

Amended eff. Aug. 17, 2004; June 13, 2012, eff. July 1, 2012; June 9, 2014.

Rules 5 to 12. Repealed eff. June 9, 2014.

EIGHTH COURT OF APPEALS LOCAL RULES (El Paso)

Rule 1. Briefs in Cross–appeals

(a) In a civil appeal in which a cross-appeal has been timely filed, the briefs to be filed by the parties are:

(1) the appellant's brief;

(2) a combined appellee's and cross-appellant's brief;

(3) a combined appellant's reply and cross-appellee's brief; and

(4) the cross-appellant's reply brief.

(b) The aggregate number of pages for all briefs filed by any party may not exceed 37,500 words if computer-generated or 125 pages if not. The calculation of length will be made as specified by Texas Rule of Appellate Procedure 9.4(i). The limitations on length are those set forth in Rule 9.4(i)(2), except as provided for herein for the combined appellee/cross–appellant's and appellant's reply/cross–appellee's briefs. The combined appellee/cross–appellant's brief may be 30,000 words if computer-generated or 100 pages if not, 15,000 words (50 pages) for the appellee's portion and 15,000 words (50 pages) for the cross-appellant's portion. The combined appellant's reply/cross–appellee's brief may be 22,500 words if computer-generated or 75 pages if not, 7,500 words (25 pages) for the reply brief and 15,000 words (50 pages) for the cross-appellee's brief.

(c) The deadlines for filing the briefs are:

(1) The appellant's brief is due no later than thirty days after the date the record is filed with the court.

(2) The appellee/cross–appellant's brief is due no later than thirty days after the date the appellant's brief is filed.

(3) The appellant's reply/cross–appellee's brief is due no later than thirty days after the date the appellee/cross–appellant's brief is filed.

(4) The cross-appellant's reply brief is due twenty days after the date the cross-appellee's brief is filed.

(d) If appellant or cross-appellant's appeal is dismissed and the appeal remains pending on the undismissed notice of appeal, the briefing schedule and page limitations will be as provided for in the rules of appellate procedure.

(e) The court may change the requirements of this rule on its own motion or motion of any party to the appeal.

Adopted eff. Oct. 1, 1999, approved by Supreme Court Sept. 21, 1999, approved by Court of Criminal Appeals May 10, 1999. Amended eff. Sept. 1, 2013, approved by the Supreme Court May 13, 2013, approved by Court of Criminal Appeals April 8, 2013. Amended eff. Oct. 6, 2014, approved by the Supreme Court Sept. 30, 2014, approved by Court of Criminal Appeals Sept. 30, 2014.

Rule 2. Request for Temporary or Emergency Relief in Original Proceedings

If temporary relief is requested in an original proceeding, a separate motion must be filed. The motion must comply with the requirements of Rule 52.10 of the Texas Rules of Appellate Procedure.

Adopted eff. Oct. 1, 1999, approved by Supreme Court Sept. 21, 1999, approved by Court of Criminal Appeals May 10, 1999. Amended eff. Sept. 1, 2013, approved by the Supreme Court May 13, 2013, approved by Court of Criminal Appeals April 8, 2013. Amended eff. Oct. 6, 2014, approved by the Supreme Court Sept. 30, 2014, approved by Court of Criminal Appeals Sept. 30, 2014.

Rule 3. Identity of Parties, Attorneys, and Trial Judges

In addition to the requirement of Rules 38.1(a) and 52.3 of the Texas Rules of Appellate Procedure that the brief give a complete list of all parties and the names and addresses of counsel, the appellant's brief and the relator's petition should include the identity of all trial judges, including visiting judges, presiding in the case below.

Adopted eff. Sept. 1, 2013, approved by the Supreme Court May 13, 2013, approved by Court of Criminal Appeals April 8, 2013. Amended eff. Oct. 6, 2014, approved by the Supreme Court Sept. 30, 2014, approved by Court of Criminal Appeals Sept. 30, 2014.

TENTH COURT OF APPEALS LOCAL RULES (Waco)

Rule 1. Scope of Local Rules

(a) These rules have been approved by the Supreme Court of Texas and the Court of Criminal Appeals and apply to all cases in the Tenth Court of Appeals (the Court).

(b) These rules supplement the procedures in the Texas Rules of Appellate Procedure and, unless otherwise specified, apply to both civil and criminal cases. If a local rule conflicts with the Rules of Appellate Procedure, the Rules of Appellate Procedure control.

(c) These rules do not extend or limit the jurisdiction of the Court.

(d) The Court may require any document not prepared in conformity with these rules to be rewritten. If another non-conforming document is filed, the Court may strike the document.

(e) Subject to the limitations of Rule of Appellate Procedure 2, the Court may, to expedite a decision or for other good cause, suspend the operation of a local rule in a particular case and order a different procedure.

Adopted by the Court of Appeals Nov. 22, 2005, approved by the Supreme Court Dec. 7, 2005, approved by the Court of Criminal Appeals Dec. 12, 2005, eff. Dec. 12, 2005.

Rule 2. Appearance

(a) Only attorneys of record will be allowed to practice before the Court. A party may appear *pro se* unless an attorney of record is designated.

(b) If an out-of-state attorney wishes to practice before the Court, a motion to appear *pro hac vice* shall be filed.

Adopted by the Court of Appeals Nov. 22, 2005, approved by the Supreme Court Dec. 7, 2005, approved by the Court of Criminal Appeals Dec. 12, 2005, eff. Dec. 12, 2005.

Rule 3. Ex Parte Communications

Under Rule of Appellate Procedure 9.6, parties and counsel may communicate with the Court about a case only through the Clerk. Members of the legal staff of the Court are subject to the same rules regarding *ex parte* communications as the justices. Therefore, parties and counsel may not communicate about a case with a justice or any member of the legal staff in person or by letter, phone, fax, or electronic mail.

Adopted by the Court of Appeals Nov. 22, 2005, approved by the Supreme Court Dec. 7, 2005, approved by the Court of Criminal Appeals Dec. 12, 2005, eff. Dec. 12, 2005.

Rule 4. Location and Business Hours

(a) The Court is located at 501 Washington Avenue, Room 415, McLennan County Courthouse, Waco, Texas 76701–1327. The Courthouse is closed on some dates that this Court is open. Access to the Court on these dates may be arranged by calling the Clerk (254–757–5200).

(b) Normal business hours of the Court are Monday through Friday (other than legal holidays as that term is defined by section 662.021 of the Texas Government Code) from 8:00 a.m. to 5:00 p.m. Parties are responsible for determining if there are any changes in normal business hours.

Adopted by the Court of Appeals Nov. 22, 2005, approved by the Supreme Court Dec. 7, 2005, approved by the Court of Criminal Appeals Dec. 12, 2005, eff. Dec. 12, 2005.

Rule 5. Filing Fees in Civil Cases

(a) The filing fee for an appeal is due contemporaneously with the filing of the notice of appeal. The filing fee for an original proceeding is due when the petition is filed.

(b) The filing fee for a motion is due when the document is filed.

(c) The Court may enforce this rule by any order that is just.

Adopted by the Court of Appeals Nov. 22, 2005, approved by the Supreme Court Dec. 7, 2005, approved by the Court of Criminal Appeals Dec. 12, 2005, eff. Dec. 12, 2005.

Rule 6. Docketing Statement

Within 10 days after perfecting appeal, a "Tenth Court of Appeals Docketing Statement—Civil" or a "Tenth Court of Appeals Docketing Statement—Criminal" must be completed and returned to the Clerk. Such form will be provided by the Clerk's Office at the time the appeal is filed and also may be downloaded from the Court's website.

Adopted by the Court of Appeals Nov. 22, 2005, approved by the Supreme Court Dec. 7, 2005, approved by the Court of Criminal Appeals Dec. 12, 2005, eff. Dec. 12, 2005.

Rule 7. Motions

(a) All motions must comply with and will be determined as provided in Rules of Appellate Procedure 9 and 10. A request for a more expeditious decision and grounds supporting same must be stated in the motion.

(b) A motion for extension of time to file an appellant's brief must state: the date the clerk's record and reporter's record were filed; the name of the party or parties requesting the extension; the length of the extension requested, up to and including a date certain; and a reasonable explanation as to why the brief cannot be tendered on time.

(c) A motion for extension of time to file an appellee's brief must state: the date the appellant's brief was filed; the name of the party or parties requesting the extension; the length of the extension requested, up to and including a date certain; and a reasonable explanation as to why the brief cannot be tendered on time.

(d) A motion requesting an extension of more than 60 days to file a brief and successive motions for extensions of time to file a brief are disfavored and will rarely be granted.

Adopted by the Court of Appeals Nov. 22, 2005, approved by the Supreme Court Dec. 7, 2005, approved by the Court of Criminal Appeals Dec. 12, 2005, eff. Dec. 12, 2005.

Rule 8. Fax Filing of Documents

(a) Pursuant to Rule of Appellate Procedure 9.2(c), the Clerk will accept for filing the following documents transmitted by fax: (1) motions to extend the time to file a notice of appeal, (2) motions to extend the time to file a brief, (3) notices changing the designation of lead counsel, (4) motions to extend the time to file a motion for rehearing, and (5) upon prior approval of the Clerk, any other document.

(b) A cover sheet must accompany every document transmitted by fax and must clearly identify (1) the name, address, telephone number, and fax number of the sender; (2) the document being transmitted; (3) the number of pages; and (4) the name of the Clerk or Deputy Clerk, if any, to whose attention the document is directed.

(c) The quality of the original must be clear and sufficiently dark to be transmitted legibly. The Clerk will not be responsible for events that disrupt, impair, or render impossible the receipt of documents transmitted by fax. The sender is obligated to ensure that documents transmitted by fax have been received legibly and completely by the Clerk. Although the Clerk's office will verify by phone that a document has been received legibly and completely, it will not initiate the phone call. If a document electronically transmitted is not complete or is otherwise illegible, the Clerk will nonetheless file it and bring it to the attention of the Court. However, incompleteness or illegibility may be grounds for striking the document.

(d) The sender must forward the original of any document transmitted by fax, the appropriate number of copies, and filing fees to the Clerk on the same day the document is transmitted by fax. If the Clerk does not receive the original, copies, or the fee within five business days after receipt of the fax, the document will be stricken. (See the Fee Schedule attached as Appendix A).[1]

(e) The date of successful transmission by fax will be the filing date; provided, however, that any transmission started after 5:00 p.m. shall be deemed filed on the next day the Court is open to the public.

Adopted by the Court of Appeals Nov. 22, 2005, approved by the Supreme Court Dec. 7, 2005, approved by the Court of Criminal Appeals Dec. 12, 2005, eff. Dec. 12, 2005.

[1] Appendix A, which is not included in this publication, is available from the Court of Appeals.

Rule 9. Alternative Dispute Resolution

The Court may, under section 154.021 of the Texas Civil Practice and Remedies Code, on a party's motion or on its own initiative, refer a civil case for alternative dispute resolution.

Adopted by the Court of Appeals Nov. 22, 2005, approved by the Supreme Court Dec. 7, 2005, approved by the Court of Criminal Appeals Dec. 12, 2005, eff. Dec. 12, 2005.

Rule 10. Record on Appeal

(a) If the clerk's record or reporter's record is not timely filed, the Court may compel completion of the appellate record or impose sanctions on the official responsible for filing the record for failure to complete the record.

(b) Each clerk's and reporter's record in a civil case must comply with the Supreme Court's "Order Directing the Form of the Appellate Record in Civil Cases." Each clerk's and reporter's record in a criminal case must comply with the Court of Criminal Appeals' "Order Directing the Form of the Appellate Record in Criminal Cases." Each reporter's record must also comply with the Uniform Format Manual for Texas Court Reporters.

(c) In addition to the foregoing requirements, each volume of the clerk's record must contain no more than 200 pages and include at the front a detailed index of all documents included in the entire clerk's record. The index must show the date of filing of each document and the volume number and page where it first appears in the record. A clerk's record that does not comply with these requirements may be returned for revision before filing.

(d) In addition to the foregoing requirements, each volume of the reporter's record must be no more than two inches thick. Each exhibit volume must contain an exhibit index at the front that provides a complete description of each exhibit and the volume and page at which the exhibit was, if applicable, identified, offered and admitted into evidence. A reporter's record which does not comply with these requirements may be returned for revision before filing.

(e) Pending adoption of a rule by the Supreme Court of Texas and/or the Court of Criminal Appeals, at the option of the trial court clerk and reporter, respectively, a CD–ROM may be submitted *in addition to* the printed clerk's record or reporter's record, containing the same information as in the printed record, in *searchable* Portable Document Format (PDF).

Adopted by the Court of Appeals Nov. 22, 2005, approved by the Supreme Court Dec. 7, 2005, approved by the Court of Criminal Appeals Dec. 12, 2005, eff. Dec. 12, 2005.

Rule 11. Withdrawal of Record on Appeal

(a) Before submission in civil cases, attorneys of record may check out the record from the Clerk by completing a receipt and providing a billing account number for shipping services. The Court will not incur shipping expenses. After submission, attorneys may not check out the record except at the discretion and on the order of one of the justices of the Court. An attorney who checks out the record must return it promptly to the Clerk on demand.

(b) In criminal cases, the record cannot be checked out from this Court but may be obtained from the county or district clerk's office.

(c) A party who has checked out the record in a civil case shall not break the binding of the record or disassemble the record for copying, inspection, or any other purpose.

Adopted by the Court of Appeals Nov. 22, 2005, approved by the Supreme Court Dec. 7, 2005, approved by the Court of Criminal Appeals Dec. 12, 2005, eff. Dec. 12, 2005.

Rule 12. Briefs

(a) An original and five copies of each brief shall be filed with the Clerk. The Court prefers that the cover of the brief of the appellant be light blue; that of the appellee (and the State as appellee in criminal cases), white or off-white; that of a reply brief, gray; and that of an intervenor or amicus curiae, green.

(b) In addition to complying with Rules of Appellate Procedure 9 and 38, proper citation form should be observed and subsequent history should be provided. In citing cases, specific page citations should be given to the pages where the relevant holdings or quotations may be found. The Court encourages citations to pertinent decisions of this Court.

(c) In addition to complying with Rules of Appellate Procedure 38.1(h) and 38.2(a), parenthetical references to the clerk's record and the reporter's record should be made to the volume and page where any referenced material is found, *e.g.,* (I C.R. at 20), (II R.R. at 150).

(d) To comply with Rule of Appellate Procedure 39.7, a request for oral argument must be noted on the front cover of the brief, *e.g.,* ORAL ARGUMENT REQUESTED. A party's failure to properly request argument shall be deemed a waiver of that party's right to argue, even if another party has requested argument.

(e) If oral argument is requested, the brief should provide a short statement about why oral argument would assist the Court.

(f) Before submission, supplemental briefs may be filed without leave of the Court if no new issues are raised. If new issues are raised, leave of the Court must be obtained before such a brief will be filed. After submission, supplemental briefs may be filed only with leave of the Court.

Adopted by the Court of Appeals Nov. 22, 2005, approved by the Supreme Court Dec. 7, 2005, approved by the Court of Criminal Appeals Dec. 12, 2005, eff. Dec. 12, 2005. Amended by order of May 28, 2014, eff. May 28, 2014.

Rule 13. Appendices

Any appendix required by Rule of Appellate Procedure 38.1(j) and which contains "necessary contents" as defined by such rule must be bound with the party's brief, if practicable. Any appendix which contains "optional contents" must be bound separately and an original and five copies filed with the Clerk. Every "necessary" and "optional" appendix must have an index and each appended document must be preceded by a numbered or lettered tab.

Adopted by the Court of Appeals Nov. 22, 2005, approved by the Supreme Court Dec. 7, 2005, approved by the Court of Criminal Appeals Dec. 12, 2005, eff. Dec. 12, 2005.

Rule 14. Appeals in Habeas Corpus, Bail, and Extradition Proceedings in Criminal Cases

In appeals governed by Rule of Appellate Procedure 31.1 the appellant's brief must be filed within 20 days after the filing of the clerk's record or reporter's record, whichever is later. The State's brief must be filed within 20 days after the date the appellant's brief is filed.

Adopted by the Court of Appeals Nov. 22, 2005, approved by the Supreme Court Dec. 7, 2005, approved by the Court of Criminal Appeals Dec. 12, 2005, eff. Dec. 12, 2005.

Rule 15. Oral Argument

(a) Oral arguments in cases routinely set will be heard at 9:00 o'clock a.m. on Wednesday at the McLennan County Courthouse in Waco unless the notice specifies another day, time, or place. The Court occasionally sits in other counties in the district as authorized by section 22.211(a) of the Government Code.

(b) The docket is called at the day, time, and location specified for arguments in the notice. A representative for each party scheduled for oral argument who is authorized to argue the case must be present at docket call and announce whether the party is ready to proceed with argument. The failure to make an announcement at docket call constitutes a waiver of oral argument by that party.

(c) A party who desires to waive oral argument previously requested must promptly notify the Clerk and all opposing parties.

(d) The standard times alloted[1] for oral argument are twenty minutes for each side and five minutes for rebuttal. The Court may restrict the time allotted, grant additional time, or reallocate the time among the parties on its own motion.

(e) A motion to reschedule an argument or requesting additional time for oral argument should be filed at least 7 days before the case will be argued. Motions filed thereafter will be considered only in exceptional circumstances.

(f) All cases to be argued have been discussed by the Court and its legal staff in a pre-submission conference. The Court is generally familiar with the facts, and Counsel should not dwell unnecessarily on them.

(g) Authorities cited during oral argument that are not contained in the party's briefs shall be submitted to the Clerk and all opposing parties by letter-brief not later than the Friday following oral argument. The opposing party may respond to the new authority in a letter-brief filed by the following Friday.

(h) A copy of each demonstrative aid or exhibit to be used during oral argument must be provided to opposing counsel prior to docket call. If any demonstrative aid or exhibit is not conducive to reproduction then a written description of such must be provided to opposing counsel. The Court will hear an objection to a demonstrative aid, and any response thereto, immediately prior to the commencement of the argument in that case.

(i) The broadcasting, televising, recording, or photographing of any proceeding of the Court without the Court's permission is prohibited. All cellular phones, beepers, and other electronic devices must be turned off before docket call. A person who violates this rule is subject to sanctions as the Court deems appropriate.

Adopted by the Court of Appeals Nov. 22, 2005, approved by the Supreme Court Dec. 7, 2005, approved by the Court of Criminal Appeals Dec. 12, 2005, eff. Dec. 12, 2005. Amended by order of Supreme Court May 14, 2008, effective May 14, 2008.

1 So in original order.

Rule 16. Original Proceedings

(a) The relator must file an original and five copies of the petition and, unless otherwise directed by the Court, an original and five copies of the appendix required by Rule 52.3(j).

(b) An original proceeding is submitted for decision on the date it is filed. Original proceedings may be set for argument or decided without argument. Counsel should notify the Clerk of circumstances requiring an expeditious hearing in an original proceeding.

Adopted by the Court of Appeals Nov. 22, 2005, approved by the Supreme Court Dec. 7, 2005, approved by the Court of Criminal Appeals Dec. 12, 2005, eff. Dec. 12, 2005.

Rule 17. Bankruptcy Stays in Civil Cases

The party claiming the benefits of a bankruptcy stay must file with the Clerk, every 180 days, a letter informing the Court of the status of the bankruptcy proceeding.

Adopted by the Court of Appeals Nov. 22, 2005, approved by the Supreme Court Dec. 7, 2005, approved by the Court of Criminal Appeals Dec. 12, 2005, eff. Dec. 12, 2005.

Rule 18. Captions of Special Types of Cases

(a) An appeal from an order granting or denying a petition for expunction filed under Chapter 55 of the Texas Code of Criminal Procedure will be captioned "Ex parte [initials of party seeking expunction]."

(b) An appeal from an order or decree under Title 1, Subtitle C, of the Texas Family Code (Dissolution of Marriage) will be captioned "In the Matter of the Marriage of __________ and __________."

(c) An appeal from an order or decree rendered under Title 5 of the Texas Family Code (Suits Affecting the Parent–Child Relationship), other than an order granting the adoption of an adult, will be captioned "In the Interest of [initials of child(ren)], (a) Child(ren)."

(d) An appeal from an order or decree under Title 3 of the Texas Family Code (the Juvenile Justice Code) will be captioned "In the Matter of [initials of child]."

Adopted by the Court of Appeals Nov. 22, 2005, approved by the Supreme Court Dec. 7, 2005, approved by the Court of Criminal Appeals Dec. 12, 2005, eff. Dec. 12, 2005.

Rule 19. Cases on Remand

After a case is remanded from the Supreme Court or the Court of Criminal Appeals, the parties are encouraged to file supplemental briefs reflecting any recent changes in the law. Briefs are due in this Court within 30 days after the date the case is remanded for further consideration.

Adopted by the Court of Appeals Nov. 22, 2005, approved by the Supreme Court Dec. 7, 2005, approved by the Court of Criminal Appeals Dec. 12, 2005, eff. Dec. 12, 2005.

FOURTEENTH COURT OF APPEALS LOCAL RULES (Houston)

Rule

Rule 1. Assignment of Related Cases to and Transfers of Related Cases between the First and Fourteenth Courts of Appeals

Rule 1.1. Definitions.

(a) "Underlying case" means a trial court case number that is filed in one of the counties that comprise the jurisdiction of the First and Fourteenth Courts of Appeals and is subsequently the subject of either an appeal or original proceeding in the First or Fourteenth Court of Appeals.

(b) "Related" means arising from the same underlying case or a case that has been remanded by either the First or Fourteenth Court of Appeals and includes cases severed from the main case.

(c) "Previously filed" means that a case has been opened at either the First or Fourteenth Court of Appeals and that an appellate case number has been assigned to the underlying case.

Rule 1.2. Assignment of Original Proceedings to either the First or Fourteenth Court of Appeals.

(a) Except as noted below, assignment of original proceedings must be alternated between the First and Fourteenth Courts of Appeals.

(b) During the first six months of a calendar year, relators must first present any original proceeding to the clerk of the First Court of Appeals. During the last six months of a calendar year, relators must first present any original proceeding to the clerk of the Fourteenth Court of Appeals. Hereinafter, the "intake clerk" means the clerk receiving the original proceeding.

(c) The intake clerk must log in each original proceeding sequentially, assigning original proceedings between the First and Fourteenth Courts of Appeals on an alternating basis.

(d) If a related appeal or original proceeding has been previously filed in one of the courts, the intake clerk must assign the original proceeding in the manner provided for in Rule 1.3(a)–(b) below.

Rule 1.3. Notice of and Assignment of Related Cases in Original Proceedings.

(a) At the time an original proceeding is filed in either the First or Fourteenth Court of Appeals, the relator must file a notice indicating whether any related appeal or original proceeding has been previously filed in either the First or Fourteenth Court of Appeals. The notice must include the caption, trial court case number, and appellate court case number of the related appeal or original proceeding.

(b) If any related appeal or original proceeding has been previously filed in or assigned to either the First or Fourteenth Court of Appeals, the clerk of the appellate court receiving the original proceeding must assign it to the court of appeals in which the related appeal or original proceeding was previously filed.

(c) If related appeals or original proceedings have been filed in both the First and Fourteenth Courts of Appeals, the clerk of the appellate court receiving the original proceeding must assign it to the court of appeals in which the most recent related appeal or original proceeding was previously filed or assigned.

Rule 1.4. Notice of and Assignment of Related Cases in Appeals.

(a) At the time the notice of appeal is filed in the trial court, the notice of appeal must contain a statement indicating whether a related appeal or original proceeding has been previously filed in either the First or Fourteenth Court of Appeals and must include the caption, trial court case number, and appellate court case number of the related appeal or original proceeding.

(b) If a related appeal or original proceeding has been previously filed in or assigned to either the First or Fourteenth Court of Appeals, the trial court clerk must assign the appeal to the court of appeals in which the related appeal or original proceeding was previously filed, pursuant to TEX. GOV'T CODE ANN.

§ 22.202(h) (Vernon 2004), which provides for companion cases to be assigned to the same court of appeals.

(c) If related appeals or original proceedings have been previously filed in both the First and Fourteenth Courts of Appeals, the trial court clerk must assign the appeal to the court of appeals in which the most recent related appeal or original proceeding was previously filed or assigned, pursuant to Tex. Gov't Code Ann. § 22.202(h) (Vernon 2004), which provides for companion cases to be assigned to the same court of appeals.

Rule 1.5. Transfers of Related Cases Between the First and Fourteenth Courts of Appeals.

(a) The First or Fourteenth Court of Appeals may, either sua sponte or on motion of a party, transfer an appeal or an original proceeding to the other Houston court of appeals when a related appeal or original proceeding has been previously filed.

(b) The transferring court must forward the case file, together with a transfer order, to the clerk of the transferee court. The clerk of the transferee court must docket the transferred appeal or original proceeding and must assign it a new appellate case number pursuant to Tex. R. App. P. 12.1 and 12.2.

Rule 1.6. Assignment of Permissive Appeals to either the First or Fourteenth Court of Appeals.

(a) Except as noted below, assignment of permissive appeals must be alternated between the First and Fourteenth Courts of Appeals.

(b) During the first six months of a calendar year appellants must first present any petition for permission to appeal to the clerk of the First Court of Appeals. During the last six months of a calendar year, appellants must first present any petition for permission to appeal to the clerk of the Fourteenth Court of Appeals. Hereinafter, the "intake clerk" means the clerk receiving the petition for permission to appeal.

(c) The intake clerk must log in each petition for permission to appeal sequentially, assigning petitions between the First and Fourteenth Courts of Appeals on an alternating basis.

(d) At the time a petition for permission to appeal is filed, it must contain a statement indicating whether a related appeal or original proceeding has been previously filed in or assigned to either the First or Fourteenth Court of Appeals. If a related appeal or original proceeding has been previously filed in one of the courts, the intake clerk must assign the petition for permission to the court of appeals in which the related appeal or original proceeding was previously filed.

Adopted eff. Sept. 1, 2004, approved by Supreme Court May 25, 2004. Amended by Supreme Court Sept. 28, 2010, eff. Nov. 1, 2010; March 11, 2011, eff. March 14, 2011; Dec. 12, 2011, eff. Nov. 14, 2011.

RULES GOVERNING ELECTRONIC FILING IN CRIMINAL CASES

Including Amendments Received Through February 1, 2016

PART 1. GENERAL PROVISIONS

Rule 1.1. Scope

These rules govern the electronic filing of documents with the clerk in criminal cases in district courts, statutory county courts, constitutional county courts, justice courts, and municipal courts in those counties in which criminal case electronic filing has been implemented pursuant to Rule 1.2 of these rules.

Adopted by orders of Supreme Court June 9, 2015, and Oct. 1, 2015, and Court of Criminal Appeals June 9, 2015, and Oct. 5, 2015, eff. Sept. 1, 2015 for Hidalgo County and Nov. 1, 2015 for all other counties.

Comment to Part 1

These rules apply to electronic filers who would otherwise have been filing manually with clerks. These rules do not affect court reporters, exhibits filed in a hearing or trial, or documents filed directly with a judge. Further, permitting electronic filing should not be construed as authority to mandate electronic filing. These rules also do not affect whether electronically filed documents may be posted on the internet.

Rule 1.2. Electronic Filing Permitted

A clerk may implement criminal case electronic filing in that clerk's office when he or she has the written consent of a majority of the judges in the county who have jurisdiction in criminal cases and who are served by that clerk. Where criminal case electronic filing has been implemented in a clerk's office, a filer may file and serve documents in a case either through the electronic filing system or by paper.

Adopted by orders of Supreme Court June 9, 2015, and Oct. 1, 2015, and Court of Criminal Appeals June 9, 2015, and Oct. 5, 2015, eff. Sept. 1, 2015 for Hidalgo County and Nov. 1, 2015 for all other counties.

Comment to Part 1

These rules apply to electronic filers who would otherwise have been filing manually with clerks. These rules do not affect court reporters, exhibits filed in a hearing or trial, or documents filed directly with a judge. Further, permitting electronic filing should not be construed as authority to mandate electronic filing. These rules also do not affect whether electronically filed documents may be posted on the internet.

Rule 1.3. Documents That May Be Electronically Filed

Any document that can be filed with a court in paper form may be electronically filed with the following exceptions:

(1) charging instruments;

(2) documents filed under seal or presented to the court in camera; and

(3) documents to which access is otherwise restricted by these rules, law, or court order.

Adopted by orders of Supreme Court Oct. 1, 2015, and Court of Criminal Appeals Oct. 5, 2015, eff. Nov. 1, 2015.

Comment to Part 1

These rules apply to electronic filers who would otherwise have been filing manually with clerks. These rules do not affect court reporters, exhibits filed in a hearing or trial, or documents filed directly with a judge. Further, permitting electronic filing should not be construed as authority to mandate electronic filing. These rules also do not affect whether electronically filed documents may be posted on the internet.

Rule 1.4. Documents Containing Signatures

(a) A document that is electronically served, filed, or issued by a court or clerk is considered signed if the document includes:

(1) a "/s/" and name typed in the space where the signature would otherwise appear, unless the document is notarized or sworn; or

(2) an electronic image or scanned image of the signature.

(b) If a paper document must be notarized, sworn to, or made under oath, the filer may electronically file the paper document as a scanned image containing the necessary signature(s).

(c) If a paper document requires the signature of an opposing party, the filer may electronically file the paper document as a scanned image containing the opposing party's signature.

Adopted by orders of Supreme Court Oct. 1, 2015, and Court of Criminal Appeals Oct. 5, 2015, eff. Nov. 1, 2015.

Comment to Part 1

These rules apply to electronic filers who would otherwise have been filing manually with clerks. These rules do not affect court reporters, exhibits filed in a hearing or trial, or documents filed directly with a judge. Further, permitting electronic filing should not be construed as authority to mandate electronic filing. These rules also do not affect whether electronically filed documents may be posted on the internet.

PART 2. FILING MECHANISM

Rule 2.1. Office of Court Administration established Electronic Filing Manager

Electronic filing must be done through the electronic filing manager established by the Office of Court Administration and an electronic filing service provider certified by the Office of Court Administration.

Adopted by orders of Supreme Court June 9, 2015, and Oct. 1, 2015, and Court of Criminal Appeals June 9, 2015, and Oct. 5, 2015, eff. Sept. 1, 2015 for Hidalgo County and Nov. 1, 2015 for all other counties.

Rule 2.2. Format

An electronically filed document must:

(1) be in text-searchable portable document format (PDF);

(2) be directly converted to PDF rather than scanned, if possible;

(3) not be locked; and

(4) otherwise comply with the Technology Standards set by the Judicial Committee on Information Technology and approved by the Supreme Court and the Court of Criminal Appeals.

Adopted by orders of Supreme Court Oct. 1, 2015, and Court of Criminal Appeals Oct. 5, 2015, eff. Nov. 1, 2015.

Rule 2.3. Timely Filing

(a) Unless a statute, rule, or court order requires that a document be filed by a certain time of day, a document is considered timely filed if it is electronically filed at any time before midnight (in the court's time zone) on the day of the filing deadline. An electronically filed document is deemed filed when transmitted to the filing party's electronic filing service provider, except:

(1) if a document is transmitted on a Saturday, Sunday, or legal holiday, it is deemed filed on the next day that is not a Saturday, Sunday, or legal holiday; and

(2) if a document requires a motion and an order allowing its filing, the document is deemed filed on the date the motion is granted.

(b) If a document is untimely filed due to a technical failure or a system outage, the filing party may seek appropriate relief from the court.

Adopted by orders of Supreme Court Oct. 1, 2015, and Court of Criminal Appeals Oct. 5, 2015, eff. Nov. 1, 2015.

Comment

This rule addresses when a document is timely filed for purposes of meeting a legal deadline imposed by a statute or a court. A clerk's acceptance of a document on a weekend or legal holiday does not impact whether a document is timely filed under this rule.

Rule 2.4. Official Record

The clerk may designate an electronically filed document or a scanned paper document as the official court record. The clerk is not required to keep both paper and electronic versions of the same document.

Adopted by orders of Supreme Court Oct. 1, 2015, and Court of Criminal Appeals Oct. 5, 2015, eff. Nov. 1, 2015.

Rule 2.5. E-Mail Address Required

The email address of any person who electronically files a document must be included on the document.

Adopted by orders of Supreme Court Oct. 1, 2015, and Court of Criminal Appeals Oct. 5, 2015, eff. Nov. 1, 2015.

Rule 2.6. Paper Copies

At the time of filing, a filer need not provide paper copies of an electronically filed document. A filer should provide paper copies of electronically filed documents upon request by a court.

Adopted by orders of Supreme Court Oct. 1, 2015, and Court of Criminal Appeals Oct. 5, 2015, eff. Nov. 1, 2015.

Rule 2.7. Electronic Notices From the Court

The clerk may send notices, orders, or other communications about the case to the party electronically. A court seal may be electronic.

Adopted by orders of Supreme Court Oct. 1, 2015, and Court of Criminal Appeals Oct. 5, 2015, eff. Nov. 1, 2015.

Rule 2.8. Non-Conforming Documents

The clerk may not refuse a document that fails to conform to these rules. But the clerk may identify the error to be corrected and state a deadline for the party to resubmit the document in a conforming format.

Adopted by orders of Supreme Court Oct. 1, 2015, and Court of Criminal Appeals Oct. 5, 2015, eff. Nov. 1, 2015.

Comment

The intent of this rule is to establish that a clerk *may not* refuse a document for any perceived violation of these rules. However, the rule permits a clerk the limited authority to identify errors the clerk perceives with whether a filing complies with the Judicial Committee on Information Technology Standards currently in effect. When a clerk notifies a filer of an error, it is inconsequential to a judicial determination regarding whether the document submitted actually violates these rules, and it does not constitute an extension of time to file the document. The purpose of the deadline is to allow for a non-conforming document to be conformed to these rules. The deadline for correction established by the clerk should permit only a reasonable amount of time to allow for the filing to be conformed to the requirements of these rules, and, in general, the deadline should not exceed 72 hours.

PART 3. SERVICE OF DOCUMENTS

Rule 3.1. Electronic Service of Documents Permissible

Every notice required by these rules, and every pleading, plea, motion, or other form of request required to be served, except as otherwise expressly provided in these rules, may be served by delivering a copy to the party to be served, or the party's duly authorized agent or attorney of record.

Documents Filed Electronically. A document filed electronically under these rules must be served electronically through the electronic filing manager if the email address of the party or attorney to be served is on file with the electronic filing manager. If the email address of the party or attorney to be served is not on file with the electronic filing manager, the document may be served on that party or attorney as permitted by law.

Adopted by orders of Supreme Court June 9, 2015, and Oct. 1, 2015, and Court of Criminal Appeals June 9, 2015, and Oct. 5, 2015, eff. Sept. 1, 2015 for Hidalgo County and Nov. 1, 2015 for all other counties.

Rule 3.2. Electronic Service Complete

Electronic service is complete on transmission of the document to the serving party's electronic filing service provider. The electronic filing manager will send confirmation of service to the serving party.

Adopted by orders of Supreme Court June 9, 2015, and Oct. 1, 2015, and Court of Criminal Appeals June 9, 2015, and Oct. 5, 2015, eff. Sept. 1, 2015 for Hidalgo County and Nov. 1, 2015 for all other counties.

Rule 3.3. Proof of Service

The party or attorney of record shall certify to the court compliance with this rule in writing above the signature on the filed instrument. A certificate by a party or an attorney of record, or the return of the officer, or the affidavit of any other person showing service of a notice shall be prima facie evidence of the fact of service. Nothing herein shall preclude any party from offering proof that the document, notice, or instrument was not received, and upon so finding, the court may extend the time for taking the action required of such party or grant such other relief as it deems just.

Adopted by orders of Supreme Court June 9, 2015, and Oct. 1, 2015, and Court of Criminal Appeals June 9, 2015, and Oct. 5, 2015, eff. Sept. 1, 2015 for Hidalgo County and Nov. 1, 2015 for all other counties.

PART 4. ELECTRONIC ORDERS AND VIEWING OF ELECTRONICALLY-FILED DOCUMENTS

Rule 4.1. Courts Authorized to Make Electronic Orders

A judge may electronically sign an order by applying his or her electronic signature to the order. Judges are not required to electronically sign orders.

Adopted by orders of Supreme Court June 9, 2015, and Oct. 1, 2015, and Court of Criminal Appeals June 9, 2015, and Oct. 5, 2015, eff. Sept. 1, 2015 for Hidalgo County and Nov. 1, 2015 for all other counties.

PART 5. PRIVACY PROTECTION FOR FILED DOCUMENTS

Rule 5.1. Sensitive Data Defined

Sensitive data consists of:

(1) a driver's license number, passport number, social security number, tax identification number, or similar government-issued personal identification number;

(2) a bank account number, credit card number, or other financial account number; and

(3) a birth date, home address, and the name of any person who was a minor when the underlying suit was filed.

Adopted by orders of Supreme Court June 9, 2015, and Oct. 1, 2015, and Court of Criminal Appeals June 9, 2015, and Oct. 5, 2015, eff. Sept. 1, 2015 for Hidalgo County and Nov. 1, 2015 for all other counties.

Rule 5.2. Filing of Documents Containing Sensitive Data Prohibited

An electronic or paper document containing sensitive data may not be filed with a court unless the sensitive data is redacted. Documents containing sensitive data may be filed with a court when the data's inclusion is specifically required by a statute, court rule, or administrative regulation, or when the data is exempt from redaction under Texas Rules of Appellate Procedure rule 9.10.

Adopted by orders of Supreme Court June 9, 2015, and Oct. 1, 2015, and Court of Criminal Appeals June 9, 2015, and Oct. 5, 2015, eff. Sept. 1, 2015 for Hidalgo County and Nov. 1, 2015 for all other counties.

Rule 5.3. Redaction of Sensitive Data; Retention Requirement

Sensitive data must be redacted by using the letter "X" in place of each omitted digit or character or by removing the sensitive data in a manner indicating that the data has been redacted. The filing party must retain an unredacted version of the filed document during the pendency of the case and any related appellate proceedings filed within three years of the date the judgment is signed.

Adopted by orders of Supreme Court June 9, 2015, and Oct. 1, 2015, and Court of Criminal Appeals June 9, 2015, and Oct. 5, 2015, eff. Sept. 1, 2015 for Hidalgo County and Nov. 1, 2015 for all other counties.

Rule 5.4. Notice to Clerk

If an electronic or paper document must contain sensitive data, the filing party must state on the upper left-hand side of the first page, "NOTICE: THIS DOCUMENT CONTAINS SENSITIVE DATA." This notice is not required if the only sensitive data contained in the document is exempt from redaction under Texas Rule of Appellate Procedure 9.10.

Adopted by orders of Supreme Court Oct. 1, 2015, and Court of Criminal Appeals Oct. 5, 2015, eff. Nov. 1, 2015.

Rule 5.5. Non-Conforming Documents

The clerk may not refuse a document that contains sensitive data in violation of these rules or any other statute, rule, or court order. But the clerk may identify the error to be corrected and state a deadline for the party to resubmit a redacted, substitute document.

Adopted by orders of Supreme Court Oct. 1, 2015, and Court of Criminal Appeals Oct. 5, 2015, eff. Nov. 1, 2015.

Comment

The intent of this rule is to establish that a clerk *may not* refuse a document for any perceived violation of these rules. However, the rule permits a clerk the limited authority to identify information the clerk perceives to be sensitive data. When a clerk identifies such information to a filer, it does not constitute an extension of time to file the document. The purpose of the deadline is to allow for a non-conforming document to be conformed to these rules. The deadline for correction established by the clerk should permit only a reasonable amount of time to allow for the filing to be conformed to the requirements of these rules, and, in general, the deadline should not exceed 72 hours.

Rule 5.6. Restriction on Remote Access

Documents that contain sensitive data in violation of these rules must not be posted on the internet.

Adopted by orders of Supreme Court Oct. 1, 2015, and Court of Criminal Appeals Oct. 5, 2015, eff. Nov. 1, 2015.

STATE BAR RULES

Including Amendments Received Through February 1, 2016

Research Note

See Vernon's Texas Codes Annotated, Government Code, *Volume 3A, for judicial constructions and other research aids.*

Preamble

These Rules are adopted in aid of the Court's inherent power to regulate the practice of law and nothing shall be construed as a modification or limitation thereof.

Adopted by order of March 14, 1983. Amended by order of Feb. 2, 1988.

ARTICLE I—DEFINITIONS

The following words shall have the meaning set out below, unless a different meaning is apparent from the context:

1. "State Bar" means the State Bar of Texas.

2. "Clerk" means the clerk of the Supreme Court of Texas.

3. "Board" means the State Bar board of directors.

4. "Act" means the State Bar Act, Chapter 510, Acts of the 66th Legislature of Texas, Regular Session, 1979, being also Senate Bill No. 287 as passed by the 66th Legislature of Texas, Regular Session, 1979, and signed by the Governor on June 11, 1979, currently codified at Title 2, Subtitle G. Chapter 81 of the Texas Government Code and as it may be amended.

5. "Metropolitan County" includes any of the counties of Bexar, Dallas, Harris, Tarrant and Travis of the State of Texas, as well as any other county hereafter so designated by the board.

6. "Member in Good Standing" is a member of the State Bar who is not in default in payment of dues and who is not under suspension from practice.

7. "Registered Address" is the address of a member as shown on the membership rolls maintained by the State Bar on behalf of the clerk of the Supreme Court. A member's registered address will be used for receiving official notices from the State Bar including membership compliance information, member benefits, and disciplinary matters.

8. "Good Cause" for failure to attend a meeting exists if such failure was for a good reason or if there is justification or excuse for such failure.

9. "Court" is the Supreme Court of Texas.

10. "Properly Addressed" when used in reference to any mailing to a member of the State Bar, means addressed to the member at the last known address of such member as shown on the rolls of the State Bar at the time of such mailing.

11. "He" includes "she". The masculine gender includes the feminine gender.

12. "Ex Officio" means by virtue or because of an office. Unless otherwise provided, one serving as an ex officio member of a body shall be entitled to vote.

13. "Rules" means the State Bar Rules.

14. "Member" means a member of the State Bar of Texas.

Adopted by order of March 14, 1983. Amended by orders of Feb. 2, 1988; Feb. 7, 2005; Dec. 18, 2006, eff. March 31, 2007; May 14, 2008, and Aug. 20, 2008, eff. Sept. 1, 2008.

Notes:

The 1991 Legislature adopted amendments to the State Bar Act: See Chapter 795, Acts of the 72nd Legislature of Texas, Regular Session, as passed by the 72nd Legislature of Texas, Regular Session, 1991, and being also Section 81.001, et seq., of the Texas Government Code.

The State Bar Act as amended by the 72nd Legislature, 1991, includes the following:

"81.002(5)* 'Commission' means the Commission for Lawyer discipline described by Section 81.076 and as provided in the Texas Rules of Disciplinary Procedure adopted by the Supreme Court of Texas."

"81.002(7)** 'Minority member' means a member of the state bar who is female, African-American, Hispanic-American, Native-American, or Asian-American."

*Publisher's Note: See V.T.C.A., Government Code § 81.002(5).

**Publisher's Note: See V.T.C.A., Government Code § 81.002(7).

Historical Notes

Supreme Court order of February 7, 2005 revised the definition of "Metropolitan County" to delete the county of El Paso. The Court took this action after the State Bar Board of Directors voted to adopt the change at a regularly called and posted meeting on June 23, 2004, at which a quorum was present.

ARTICLE II—GENERAL PROVISIONS

Section 1. Official Name

The official name of the State Bar is "State Bar of Texas."

Adopted by order of March 14, 1983.

Section 2. Purposes of the Organization

The purposes of the State Bar are those as set out in the Act.

Adopted by order of March 14, 1983.

Section 3. Purposes of These Rules

These Rules are adopted for the operation, maintenance and conduct of the State Bar and for the disciplining of its members.

Adopted by order of March 14. 1983.

Section 4. Seal

The State Bar shall have a seal in the form of a five-pointed star, around the upper portion of which shall be written in capital letters, "STATE BAR OF TEXAS" and around the lower portion of which shall be written in capital letters, "CREATED IN 1939." The seal may be used only for official business of the State Bar, its sections and committees.

Adopted by order of March 14, 1983.

Section 5. Principal Office of the State Bar

The principal office of the State Bar shall be maintained in Austin, Travis County, Texas.

Adopted by order of March 14, 1983.

Section 6. Service of Process

Service of citation or other process may be had upon the State Bar by serving either the executive director or the general counsel.

Adopted by order of March 14, 1983.

Section 7. Fiscal Year

The fiscal year of the State Bar shall be as determined by the board.

Adopted by order of March 14, 1983.

Section 8. Organizational Year

The organizational year of the State Bar shall be from time of adjournment of the annual meeting of the State Bar one year to the time of adjournment of the annual meeting of the State Bar of the next year.

Adopted by order of March 14, 1983.

Section 9. Oath of Office

Officers and directors of the State Bar, before entering upon the duties of office, shall take the official oath or affirmation set out in Art. 16, Sec. I of the Constitution of the State of Texas.

Adopted by order of March 14, 1983.

Section 10. Elections and Balloting

Except as may otherwise be provided, elections shall be conducted under the supervision of the executive director.

Adopted by order of March 14, 1983.

Section 11. Officers and Directors Holding Over

Each officer and director shall continue to serve and perform the duties of his office until his successor has qualified.

Adopted by order of March 14, 1983.

Section 12. Publication of New Rules and Amendments to Rules

These Rules and any amendments thereto shall be published in a manner directed by the board.

Adopted by order of March 14, 1983.

Section 13. Spokesman for the Bar

The president of the State Bar or, in the absence of the president, the president-elect, shall be the public representative of the State Bar and shall enunciate the policies of the State Bar as promulgated by the board, except that the Board or the president may delegate such authority under such conditions as the board may prescribe. The board may authorize sections and committees, and those properly authorized by such sections and committees, to publicly represent the views of a section or committee.

Adopted by order of March 14, 1983.

Section 14. Procedures for Meetings

A. All proceedings at meetings of the State Bar, of the board, of the executive committee and of all other committees and sections shall be governed by the most recent edition of Robert's Rules of Order Newly Revised.

B. Voting by those entitled to vote at all such meetings shall be in person. Voting by proxy shall not be allowed.

C. The presence of a majority of those persons entitled to vote at all such meetings shall constitute a quorum, except that:

(1) at any meeting of the State Bar, one hundred (100) members shall constitute a quorum for the transaction of business; and

(2) at any meeting of a State Bar section or committee, a quorum may be less than a majority if the board has determined. Action shall be taken only upon a majority vote of those entitled to vote, a quorum being present.

Adopted by order of March 14, 1983. Amended by order of Dec. 18, 2006, eff. March 31, 2007.

ARTICLE III—MEMBERSHIP

Section 1. Members

The members of the State Bar are those persons designated in the Act.

Adopted by order of March 14, 1983.

Section 2. Enrollment in the State Bar

A. Each person who is licensed to practice law in Texas shall, in accordance with the applicable Supreme Court rules governing admission to the bar, and no later than ten (10) days following the date of admission, (i) file with the clerk an enrollment form stating his or her name, preferred physical address or post office box, telephone number, facsimile number, e-mail address, and such other information as may be required by the clerk and (ii) pay all fees and assessments then required. This filing and payment shall constitute enrollment in the State Bar. The preferred physical address or post office box shall constitute the member's registered address and will be used for receiving official notices from the State Bar, including membership compliance information, member benefits, and disciplinary matters. A member is mandated to notify the State Bar of any change in the information required above within thirty (30) days of such change.

B. Associate members, as authorized by the Act, may be enrolled under rules prescribed by the Court.

Adopted by order of March 14, 1983. Amended by order of Oct. 6, 2008, eff. Oct. 6, 2008.

Notes:

Section 552.1176 of the Government Code prescribes the confidentiality of certain information maintained by the State Bar, including the home address, home telephone number, e-mail address, social security number, and date of birth of a person licensed to practice law in Texas.

Section 3. Membership Fees

All membership fees shall be payable at the time of enrollment as a member of the State Bar and annually thereafter on the first day of the State Bar's fiscal year.

Adopted by order of March 14, 1983.

Section 4. Membership Rolls and Membership Cards

Upon enrollment, the clerk shall enter that person's name on the membership rolls and issue an appropriate membership card which shall be evidence of membership.

Adopted by order of March 14, 1983.

Section 5. Default in Payment of Fees or Assessments

If a member is in default of payment of membership fees or any assessment levied by the Court on the thirtieth day after the due date, the clerk shall forthwith notify the member of default. If the fees and assessments are not paid on or before sixty (60) days after the mailing of the notice of default, the defaulting member shall automatically be suspended from the practice of law. Any practice of law during such suspension shall constitute professional misconduct and subject the member to discipline.

Adopted by order of March 14, 1983.

Section 6. Resignation from Membership Other Than in Face of Pending Disciplinary Action

The Court may accept a member's voluntary resignation provided that the tender is in writing, addressed to the Court and is accompanied by:

A. The member's affidavit that his purpose in resigning is not to avoid disciplinary action and that he has no knowledge of any unresolved allegation of professional misconduct against him.

B. A certificate by the general counsel that there are no disciplinary actions pending against such mem-

ber and that such member is not at such time the subject of an investigation for professional misconduct.
Adopted by order of March 14, 1983.

Section 7. Return to Former Status

A. When a member, who has been suspended for nonpayment of fees or assessments, removes such default by payment of fees or assessments then owing, plus an additional amount equivalent to one-half the delinquency, the suspension shall automatically be lifted and the member restored to former status. Return to former status shall be retroactive to inception of suspension, but shall not affect any proceeding for discipline of the member for professional misconduct.

B. A person who has voluntarily resigned from membership shall be required to apply to the Board of Law Examiners and to comply with the rules of the Court pertaining to admission to the practice of law before resuming the practice of law.

C. An inactive member may return to active status upon written application to the clerk and payment of fees for the current year.
Adopted by order of March 14, 1983.

Section 8. Administration of Attorney Occupation Tax

An occupation tax of $200.00 per year is imposed on each attorney pursuant to [§ 191.142 of] [1] the Texas Tax Code.

(a) Every member of the State Bar of Texas is subject to the tax except those members who are:

(1) 70 years of age of older;

(2) on inactive status under the State Bar Act;

(3) out of state attorneys who are not practicing law in Texas;

(4) judges;

(5) federal or state government employees;

(6) attorneys employed by city, county, and District attorneys' who do not have a private practice that accounts for more than 50% of their time;

(7) employees of an Internal Revenue Code § 501(c)(3) or § 501(c)(6) non-profit corporation that is prohibited from private practice; or

(8) associate members under the State Bar Act;

(b) Except as provided by Subsection (c), each attorney shall pay the tax for each tax year on or before June 1 of the tax year.

(c) If a person is licensed to practice law after the beginning of the tax year or resumes active status to practice law after the beginning of the tax year, the person being licensed or resuming active status shall pay the tax imposed by this section in proportion to the number of months for which the person will be licensed during that tax year. If a person is licensed after the beginning of a calendar month, the month in which the person is licensed shall count as a month for purposes of payment of taxes under this subsection.

(d) A penalty of 5 percent of the tax due shall be imposed on a person who fails to pay the tax imposed by this section when due, and, if the person fails to pay the tax within 30 days after the day on which the tax or report is due, an additional 5 percent shall be imposed.

(e) The yearly interest rate on delinquent tax imposed by this section is 12 percent. Delinquent taxes draw interest beginning 60 days from the due date.

(f) The State Bar shall suspend from the practice of law a member who does not pay, within 90 days after the date it is due, the tax imposed or a penalty relating to that tax.

(g) An attorney who is suspended under Subsection (f) shall be reinstated on payment of the tax and any interest and penalties.
Adopted by order of July 1, 1998.

[1] So in original.

ARTICLE IV—ADMINISTRATION

Section 1. Board of Directors; Duties

A. The State Bar shall be governed by a board which shall enforce the Act and these Rules.

B. The term of office for each elected, public, and minority director shall be three (3) years. The terms of elected and public directors shall be staggered with one-third (1/3) of such directors elected or appointed each year. The terms of minority directors shall be staggered with as near to one-third (1/3) as possible appointed each year.

C. The regular term of office of an elected public, or minority director shall commence on adjournment of the annual meeting of the State Bar next following election or appointment and continue until the adjournment of the third annual meeting next following election or appointment.

D. The board shall take such action and adopt such regulations and policies, consistent with the Act or these Rules, as shall be necessary and proper for the administration and management of the affairs of

the State Bar, for the protection of the property of the State Bar and for the preservation of good order.
Adopted by order of March 14, 1983. Amended by order of Dec. 18, 2006, eff. March 31, 2007.

Section 2. Meetings of the Board

The board shall meet regularly at least four (4) times annually, and may meet specially, at such times and places as the board shall determine. All meetings, however, shall be held within the State of Texas.
Adopted by order of March 14, 1983.

Section 3. Composition of the Board

The board shall be composed of the officers of the State Bar, the president, president-elect, and immediate past president of the Texas Young Lawyers Association, not more than thirty (30) members of the State Bar elected by the membership from their district as may be determined by the board, six (6) persons who are not licensed attorneys, known as public directors, who do not have, other than as consumers, a financial interest in the practice of law, and four (4) minority directors appointed by the president and confirmed by the Board The Board may, in its discretion, also include other members who shall be non-voting board members.
Adopted by order of March 14, 1983. Amended by order of Dec. 18, 2006, eff. March 31, 2007.

Notes:

The State Bar Act as amended by the 72nd Legislature, 1991, includes the following:

"81.020(b) (5)* Four minority member directors appointed by the president as provided by Subsection (d)."

"81.020(d)** The president of the state bar appoints the minority member directors, subject to confirmation by the board of directors. In making appointments under this subsection, the president shall attempt to appoint members of the different minority groups listed in Section 81.002(7). Minority member directors serve three-year terms. To be eligible for appointment as minority member director, a person must: (1) be a minority member of the bar; (2) not be serving as an elected director as the time of appointment; and (3) not be serving as a minority member director at the time of appointment."

*Publisher's Note: See V.T.C.A., Government Code § 81.020(b)(5).

**Publisher's Note: See V.T.C.A., Government Code § 81.020(d).

Section 4. Chairperson of Board

The board shall elect annually from its membership, under such procedures as it shall prescribe, a chairperson to serve for the next succeeding organizational year. Such person shall be elected from the class of directors then serving the second year of their terms.
Adopted by order of March 14, 1983.

Section 5. Qualification of Officers and Directors

A. No person may serve as an officer or director who,

1. ... has not taken the official oath by the second regular board meeting next following the commencement of the term for which he was elected or appointed,

2. ... as to an elected or ex officio director or an officer, is not an active member in good standing,

3. ... as to an elected or ex officio director or an officer, has ever been suspended or disbarred from the practice of law,

4. ... as to an elected director, does not maintain in the district from which elected, his principal place of practice,

5. ... as to an elected director, has his principal place of practice in the same county as the last preceding director from that district, except for an elected director in a Metropolitan County or in El Paso County, and except as necessary to achieve a rebalancing of the sizes of the Board classes in accordance with the provisions of Art. IV, § 8(C).

6. ... as to an elected director, has previously served at east one and a half (1½) years of the immediately preceding director term,

7. ... is, or becomes, incapacitated from performing the duties of such office for all or a substantial portion of such term,

8. ... as to a director, is absent from more than half of the regularly scheduled board meetings that the director is eligible to attend during a calendar year without an excuse approved by a majority vote of the board.

9. ... as to a public director, has failed confirmation by the senate of the State of Texas,

10. ... is an elected official paid by the State of Texas, except that such prohibition shall not apply to public directors.

11. ... as to a director or a director's spouse, is an officer, employee, or paid consultant of a Texas trade association in the field of board interest as defined in State Bar Act § 81.028.

B. The board shall be the judge of the qualifications of officers and directors.

C. The board shall provide a training program for board members that meets the requirements of § 81.0201 of the State Bar Act. No person who is elected or appointed to and qualifies for office as a member of the board of directors may vote, deliberate, or be counted as a member in attendance at a meeting of the board until the person completes a training program that complies with the requirements of § 81.0201 of the State Bar Act.

Adopted by order of March 14, 1983. Amended by order of Dec. 18, 2006, eff. March 31, 2007.

Section 6. How Directors Shall Be Elected

Elected directors shall be elected by a majority of the active and emeritus members of the State Bar voting who have their principal place of practice in the same Bar district as that of the candidate. If no candidate receives a majority, a run off shall be held at such time as the board shall prescribe between the two candidates receiving the greatest number of votes.

Adopted by order of March 14, 1983.

Section 7. Nominees for Office of Elected Director

A. An active member's name may be placed in nomination for the office of elected director by a written petition in form prescribed by the board and signed by the lesser of five percent (5%) of the active members whose principal place of practice is within the district to be represented by the nominee if elected, or one hundred (100) of such members, which petition must be received in the office of the executive director on or before March 1 of the year of election. The executive director shall promptly review the petition to verify the eligibility of the nominee. If from the petition it appears the nominee is eligible, that person's name shall be listed upon the ballot. If from the petition the executive director finds the nominee to be ineligible, that fact shall immediately be communicated to the nominee. Any nominee desiring to appeal the findings of the executive director shall forthwith notify the executive director, who shall forthwith convene the executive committee to hear and determine the matter. The executive committee shall have final authority to determine questions of eligibility of the nominee and the validity of the nominating petition and shall do so within ten (10) days of the notice to the executive director.

B. The petitions may be in counterparts, and it shall be sufficient that the signatures on all the counterparts aggregate the required number of signatures.

C. If no valid petition nominating an eligible person shall have been received by the executive director by March 1 in respect to a district in the year in which such district is to elect a director, or if all persons who have been nominated in the foregoing manner shall have died or become disqualified from serving at any time prior to the printing of the ballot in such election, then the president of the State Bar with the advice of the person then serving as elected director from that district shall name a qualified person to stand for election as director from that district.

D. If an elected director fails to qualify, such position shall be deemed vacant.

Adopted by order of March 14, 1983. Amended by order of Feb. 7, 2005.

Historical Notes

In a Supreme Court order dated February 7, 2005, references to March 15 were substituted with references to March 1 to accommodate electronic voting in the State Bar members' elections of its President-elect and District Directors by allowing more time for the voting to take place. The State Bar Board of Directors voted to adopt these changes at a regularly called and posted meeting on June 23, 2004, at which a quorum was present.

Section 8. Director Vacancies and How Filled

A. Death of a board member, judgment of incompetency, a board member's resignation or any failure to qualify shall create a vacancy. In case of a vacancy as to an elected director, the president, shall appoint a member whose principal place of practice is within the district within which the vacancy has occurred. Vacancies in ex officio directorships shall be filled by the person who succeeds to the office in the State Bar or in the Texas Young Lawyers Association to which such directorship is incident, except that the directorship incident to the office of immediate past president of the State Bar or Texas Young Lawyers Association or immediate past chairperson of the board of the State Bar shall be filled by the most recent holder of such offices respectively who is willing to serve. Vacancies in public and minority directorships shall be filled in the same manner and by the same authority designated by statute to fill such positions.

B. Persons filling such vacancies shall meet the same requirements and shall qualify in the same manner as those assuming the office of director for the full term.

C. The board may adopt appropriate procedures for the purpose of equalizing the size of the classes of the board of directors. Once such equalization is accomplished, then those appointed to fill a vacancy shall serve the balance of the term of the particular position vacated.

D. The board of directors may remove a director from the board at any regular meeting by resolution declaring the director's position vacant, pursuant to

§ 81.027(a) of the State Bar Act or Article IV, § 5 of these Rules.

Adopted by order of March 14, 1983. Amended by order of Dec. 18, 2006, eff. March 31, 2007.

Notes:

The State Bar Act as amended by the 72nd Legislature 1991 includes the following:

"81.027* Removal of Director. (a) The board of directors may remove a director from the board at any regular meeting by resolution declaring the director's position vacant if: (1) the director, in the board's determination, has become incapacitated and cannot perform his duties as a director; (2) the director has been absent, without cause considered adequate by the board, from any two consecutive regular meetings of the board or from a total of four meetings; (3) the director violates a prohibition established by Section 81.028; or (4) the director has violated the terms or provisions of Section 81.031. (b) The validity of an action of the board of directors is not affected by the fact that it is taken when a ground for removal of a director exists. (c) If the executive director has knowledge that a potential ground for removal of a director exists, the executive director shall notify the president of the state bar and the director of the ground."

* Publisher's Note: See V.T.C.A., Government Code § 81.027.

Section 9. Executive Committee

A. The executive committee of the board shall consist of the president, president-elect, the chair of the board, the immediate past president of the State Bar, president of the Texas Young Lawyers Association and such other persons as the president may appoint. The president shall be chair, and the board chair shall be the vice-chair of the executive committee and shall preside in the chair's absence.

B. The general purpose of the executive committee shall be to perform between meetings of the board such functions, consistent with the Act or these Rules, as the Board may assign to it from time to time.

C. The general counsel and the executive director of the State Bar shall be ex officio, non-voting members of the executive committee.

Adopted by order of March 14, 1983. Amended by order of Dec. 18, 2006, eff. March 31, 2007.

Section 10. Officers

A. The officers of the State Bar shall be the president, the president-elect and the immediate past president.

B. The president shall preside at all meetings of the State Bar, be the official representative and spokesperson for the State Bar in all public matters and have general responsibility for carrying out the policy of the State Bar.

C. The president-elect shall preside at meetings of the State Bar in the absence of the president and otherwise assist the president, as the president shall request, in carrying out the responsibilities of the office of president.

Adopted by order of March 14, 1983.

Section 11. President-Elect, Nominations and Elections

(A) At its regular meeting next following the first day of each calendar year, the board of directors shall nominate two (2) or more members of the State Bar of Texas to stand for election to the office of president-elect for the ensuing bar year. Such nomination shall be by majority vote of the board.

(B) Any other member of the State Bar of Texas shall also be privileged to stand for election to the office of president-elect when a written petition in form prescribed by the board of directors, signed by no fewer than five percent (5%) of the active members of the State Bar of Texas in good standing, is filed with the executive director or on before March 1 next preceding the election to be held for the office of president-elect for the ensuing year.

(C) The names of all nominees for the office of president-elect shall be published in the *Texas Bar Journal* and otherwise publicized by such other practical means as the board shall determine.

(D) In making nominations to the office of president-elect, both the board of directors and those persons who may be nominated by petition pursuant to Section 11(B) herein, shall be bound by the following geographical rotation:

(1) nominees from metropolitan counties in the first year of rotation;

(2) nominees from other than metropolitan counties in the second year of rotation;

(3) nominees from any county during the third year of rotation.

Any person nominated by either the board or by petition who does not meet the requirements of this rotation shall be ineligible to stand for election in the year nominated. For purposes of this rule, the first year of rotation shall be the election for president-elect for 1988.

(E) The ballot shall be distributed to each member of the State Bar of Texas entitled to vote at the same time as ballots for the election of elected directors are distributed. A combined ballot for the office of president-elect and for the office of director may be used in those bar districts in which an election for director is to be conducted.

(F) If no candidate for president-elect receives a majority of the votes, a run-off election shall be held at such time as the board shall prescribe between the two candidates receiving the greatest number of votes. The person receiving a majority of the votes in either the general election or the run-off election shall be declared to be elected to the office of president-elect.

(G) The office of president shall be filled by the succession of the president-elect to such office at the expiration of the term for which such person was elected to serve as president-elect.

Adopted by order of March 14, 1983. Amended by order of Dec. 8, 1986; Feb. 7, 2005.

Historical Notes

The February 7, 2005 order substituted "March 1" for "March 15" in subsec. (B) and substituted "distributed" for "mailed" twice in subsec. (E). The State Bar Board of Directors voted to adopt these changes at a regularly called and posted meeting on June 23, 2004, at which a quorum was present.

Section 12. Term of Office of Officers

The regular term of office for officers of the State Bar shall be from adjournment of the annual meeting for the year preceding the year of service and shall end with such adjournment the following year.

Adopted by order of March 14, 1983.

Section 13. Vacancy in an Office

A. Death of an officer, judgment of incompetency, an officer's resignation or failure to qualify shall create a vacancy in the office.

B. If a vacancy occurs in the office of president, it shall be filled by the succession of the president-elect to the office of president, in which case a special election shall be called by the board to fill the office of president-elect at such times and under such procedures as are prescribed by the board.

C. If the vacancy occurs in the office of president-elect, a special election shall be held for the office of president-elect. In such event the procedures for a regular election shall be followed subject to such necessary changes as shall be required in order to meet the exigencies of the situation.

D. Should the president-elect succeed to the office of president and have less than six (6) months to serve in the unexpired term, he shall in such event, serve the next full term to which he would have normally succeeded.

E. In the event a simultaneous vacancy exists in the office of the president and president-elect, a special election shall be held for each office and in the meanwhile the chairperson of the board shall serve as interim president.

Adopted by order of March 14, 1983.

Section 14. Other Executive Positions

The executive director and general counsel shall be elected by the board and shall perform such duties as the board may prescribe.

Adopted by order of March 14, 1983.

ARTICLE V—FISCAL

Section 1. Budget Committee

There shall be a budget committee, comprised of the president of the State Bar, the president-elect, the chairperson of the board, and two (2) or more members of the board of directors appointed by the president. The president or his designee shall be chairperson of this committee.

Adopted by order of March 14, 1983.

Section 2. Public Hearing on Budget

A public hearing shall be held each year to consider the State Bar's proposed budget in accordance with the Act.

Adopted by order of March 14, 1983.

Section 3. Annual Budget

A. The budget committee shall consult with the executive director and the general counsel with respect to the annual budget for the State Bar for the fiscal year next after the committee's appointment. The proposed budget shall be prepared and submitted to the board at its first quarterly meeting each calendar year, and shall be acted on by the board at such meeting. After adoption by the board, the budget shall be submitted to the Court for approval.

B. The budget may be amended by majority vote of the board at any regular or special meeting in order to meet any unforeseen contingency, subject to the Court's approval.

Adopted by order of March 14, 1983.

Section 4. Expenses

The board may provide for the payment of necessary expenses incurred by the officers, directors, committee members, and employees of the State Bar in the discharge of their duties.

Adopted by order of March 14, 1983.

ARTICLE VI—ADOPTING AND AMENDING THE STATE BAR RULES

New rules for the governance of the State Bar, and amendments to these Rules shall be adopted and promulgated by the Court as provided in the Act.
Adopted by order of March 14, 1983.

ARTICLE VII—MEETINGS OF THE STATE BAR OF TEXAS

Section 1. Annual Meeting

The annual meeting of the State Bar shall be held during the month of June or July of each year at a time and place to be determined by the board.
Adopted by order of March 14, 1983.

Section 2. Special Meetings

A. Special meetings of the State Bar shall be called by the president upon two-thirds (⅔) vote of the directors, or upon written petition of at least five hundred (500) members of the State Bar.

B. The time and place of such meeting shall be in accordance with the call.

C. Prior to any special meeting, the executive director shall mail to each member in good standing a notice of the time and place of the meeting and purposes for which the meeting is to be held. The notices shall be mailed sufficiently in advance of such meeting date so as to afford reasonable notice of the meeting.
Adopted by order of March 14, 1983.

Section 3. Procedure as to Proposed Resolutions

The board shall adopt a procedure by which resolutions may be proposed for adoption by the State Bar and for their review as to form in advance of presentation to the general assembly at the annual meeting. A brief resume of this procedure shall be published in the *Texas Bar Journal* prior to the annual meeting.
Adopted by order of March 14, 1983.

Notes:

The State Bar Act as amended by the 72nd Legislature 1991 includes the following:

"81.021* Open Meetings; Public Participation. (a) Meetings of the board of directors of the state bar are subject to the open meetings law, Chap. 271, Acts of the 60th Legislature Regular Session, 1967 (Article 6252–17, Vernon's Texas Civil Statutes)...".

* Publisher's Note: See V.T.C.A., Government Code § 81.021.

ARTICLE VIII—COMMITTEES, SECTIONS AND DIVISIONS

Section 1. Creation, Membership, Officers; Vacancies

A. The board may create or dissolve from time to time such State Bar and board committees, sections and divisions as it may deem advisable. Their organizational structure, purpose and bylaws shall be subject to approval of the board. Membership of committees shall be comprised of presidential appointees. Membership of sections shall be comprised of members of the State Bar who pay the section dues and are otherwise qualified under the bylaws of the section. Membership of divisions shall be determined by their respective bylaws.

B. As soon as practicable after assuming office, and not later than the April board meeting of the calendar year in which he will assume the presidency, the president-elect shall prepare and present to the Board for its advice and consent, a proposed roster of State Bar committees, committee chairpersons and committee members for his presidential year. The board at the April meeting shall approve the list of State Bar committees and the president-elect shall promptly notify the proposed chairpersons and members of their selection and obtain their consent to serve. Any necessary changes or additions in committee organization and personnel shall be reported by the president-elect to the retiring board at its June meeting and shall be finally approved by the incoming board at its first meeting of the new organizational year. Subsequent creation of special committees by the president and the appointment of the personnel thereof, shall be subject to approval by the executive committee or by the board at the earliest opportunity.

C. Officers of sections and divisions for the ensuing year shall be elected according to the respective bylaws at their annual meeting coinciding with the annual meeting of the Bar.

D. Vacancies occurring in membership of State Bar committees shall be filled by the president for the unexpired term and vacancies occurring in section committees shall be filled by the chairperson of the section, except that if a vacancy occurs in the position of chairperson and there is no vice-chairperson to assume the position of chairperson, it shall be filled by a majority vote of the section council. Vacancies in division committees shall be filled in accordance with the bylaws of the division.

Adopted by order of March 14, 1983.

Section 2. Reports

The sections and divisions and State Bar committees shall deliver to the president and executive director at least sixty (60) days before the annual meeting of the State Bar, annual reports and recommendations. Such reports and recommendations may be printed and sent to members of the State Bar before the annual meeting, but any section, division or committee may present at the annual meeting any additional report or recommendation. The president, president-elect, immediate past president and the board may also present reports and recommendations in the same manner.

Adopted by order of March 14, 1983.

ARTICLE IX—*TEXAS BAR JOURNAL*

A publication, under the name *Texas Bar Journal*, and devoted to legal matters and the affairs of the State Bar and its members may be published and circulated under the direction of the board.

Adopted by order of March 14, 1983.

ARTICLE X—DISCIPLINE AND SUSPENSION OF MEMBERS

Sections 1 to 8. Repealed by order of Feb. 26, 1991, eff. May 1, 1992

Historical Notes

The repealed sections, relating to procedures for discipline of members, and adopted by order of Feb. 29, 1984, were repealed except to the extent that they applied to disciplinary matters pending on the effective date [March 1, 1992] of the repealing order.

Section 9. Texas Disciplinary Rules of Professional Conduct

Effective January 1, 1990

Preamble: A Lawyer's Responsibilities

1. A lawyer is a representative of clients, an officer of the legal system and a public citizen having special responsibility for the quality of justice. Lawyers, as guardians of the law, play a vital role in the preservation of society. The fulfillment of this role requires an understanding by lawyers of their relationship with and function in our legal system. A consequent obligation of lawyers is to maintain the highest standards of ethical conduct.

2. As a representative of clients, a lawyer performs various functions. As advisor, a lawyer provides a client with an informed understanding of the client's legal rights and obligations and explains their practical implications. As advocate, a lawyer zealously asserts the client's position under the rules of the adversary system. As negotiator, a lawyer seeks a result advantageous to the client but consistent with requirements of honest dealing with others. As intermediary between clients, a lawyer seeks to reconcile their divergent interests as an advisor and, to a limited extent, as a spokesperson for each client. A lawyer acts as evaluator by examining a client's affairs and reporting about them to the client or to others.

3. In all professional functions, a lawyer should zealously pursue clients' interests within the bounds of the law. In doing so, a lawyer should be competent, prompt and diligent. A lawyer should maintain communication with a client concerning the representation. A lawyer should keep in confidence information relating to representation of a client except so far as disclosure is required or permitted by the Texas Disciplinary Rules of Professional Conduct or other law.

4. A lawyer's conduct should conform to the requirements of the law, both in professional service to clients and in the lawyer's business and personal affairs. A lawyer should use the law's procedures only for legitimate purposes and not to harass or intimidate others. A lawyer should demonstrate respect for the legal system and for those who serve it, including judges, other lawyers and public officials. While it is a lawyer's duty, when necessary, to challenge the rectitude of official action, it is also a lawyer's duty to uphold legal process.

5. As a public citizen, a lawyer should seek improvement of the law, the administration of justice and the quality of service rendered by the legal profession. As a member of a learned profession, a lawyer should cultivate knowledge of the law beyond its use for clients, employ that knowledge in reform of the law and work to strengthen legal education. A lawyer should be mindful of deficiencies in the administration of justice and of the fact that the poor, and sometimes persons who are not poor, cannot afford adequate legal assistance, and should therefore devote professional time and civic influence in their behalf. A lawyer should aid the legal profession in pursuing these objectives and should help the bar regulate itself in the public interest.

6. A lawyer should render public interest legal service. The basic responsibility for providing legal services for those unable to pay ultimately rests upon the individual lawyer, and personal involvement in the problems of the disadvantaged can be one of the most rewarding experiences in the life of a lawyer. Every lawyer, regardless of professional prominence or professional workload, should find time to participate in or otherwise support the provision of legal services to the disadvantaged. The provision of free legal services to those unable to pay reasonable fees is a moral obligation of each lawyer as well as the profession generally. A lawyer may discharge this basic responsibility by providing public interest legal services without fee, or at a substantially reduced fee, in one or more of the following areas: poverty law, civil rights law, public rights law, charitable organization representation, the administration of justice, and by financial support for organizations that provide legal services to persons of limited means.

7. In the nature of law practice, conflicting responsibilities are encountered. Virtually all difficult ethical problems arise from apparent conflict between a lawyer's responsibilities to clients, to the legal system and to the lawyer's own interests. The Texas Disciplinary Rules of Professional Conduct prescribe terms for resolving such tensions. They do so by stating minimum standards of conduct below which no lawyer can fall without being subject to disciplinary action. Within the framework of these Rules many difficult issues of professional discretion can arise. The Rules and their Comments constitute a body of principles upon which the lawyer can rely for guidance in resolving such issues through the exercise of sensitive professional and moral judgment. In applying these rules, lawyers may find interpretive guidance in the principles developed in the Comments.

8. The legal profession has a responsibility to assure that its regulation is undertaken in the public interest rather than in furtherance of parochial or self-interested concerns of the bar, and to insist that every lawyer both comply with its minimum disciplinary standards and aid in securing their observance by

other lawyers. Neglect of these responsibilities compromises the independence of the profession and the public interest which it serves.

9. Each lawyer's own conscience is the touchstone against which to test the extent to which his actions may rise above the disciplinary standards prescribed by these rules. The desire for the respect and confidence of the members of the profession and of the society which it serves provides the lawyer the incentive to attain the highest possible degree of ethical conduct. The possible loss of that respect and confidence is the ultimate sanction. So long as its practitioners are guided by these principles, the law will continue to be a noble profession. This is its greatness and its strength, which permit of no compromise.

Adopted by order of Oct. 17, 1989, eff. Jan. 1, 1990.

Preamble: Scope

10. The Texas Disciplinary Rules of Professional Conduct are rules of reason. The Texas Rules of Professional Conduct define proper conduct for purposes of professional discipline. They are imperatives, cast in the terms "shall" or "shall not." The Comments are cast often in the terms of "may" or "should" and are permissive, defining areas in which the lawyer has professional discretion. When a lawyer exercises such discretion, whether by acting or not acting, no disciplinary action may be taken. The Comments also frequently illustrate or explain applications of the rules, in order to provide guidance for interpreting the rules and for practicing in compliance with the spirit of the rules. The Comments do not, however, add obligations to the rules and no disciplinary action may be taken for failure to conform to the Comments.

11. The rules presuppose a larger legal context shaping the lawyer's role. That context includes court rules and statutes relating to matters of licensure, laws defining specific obligations of lawyers and substantive and procedural law in general. Compliance with the rules, as with all law in an open society, depends primarily upon understanding and voluntary compliance, secondarily upon reinforcement by peer and public opinion and finally, when necessary, upon enforcement through disciplinary proceedings. The rules and Comments do not, however, exhaust the moral and ethical considerations that should guide a lawyer, for no worthwhile human activity can be completely defined by legal rules.

12. Most of the duties flowing from the client-lawyer relationship attach only after the client has requested the lawyer to render legal services and the lawyer has agreed to do so. For purposes of determining the lawyer's authority and responsibility, individual circumstances and principles of substantive law external to these rules determine whether a client-lawyer relationship may be found to exist. But there are some duties, such as of that of confidentiality, that may attach before a client-lawyer relationship has been established.

13. The responsibilities of government lawyers, under various legal provisions, including constitutional, statutory and common law, may include authority concerning legal matters that ordinarily reposes in the client in private client-lawyer relationships. For example, a lawyer for a government agency may have authority on behalf of the government to decide upon settlement or whether to appeal from an adverse judgment. Such authority in various respects is generally vested in the attorney general and the state's attorney in state government, and their federal counterparts, and the same may be true of other government law officers. Also, lawyers under the supervision of these officers may be authorized to represent several government agencies in intragovernmental legal controversies in circumstances where a private lawyer could not represent multiple private clients. They also may have authority to represent the "public interest" in circumstances where a private lawyer would not be authorized to do so. These rules do not abrogate any such authority.

14. These rules make no attempt to prescribe either disciplinary procedures or penalties for violation of a rule.

15. These rules do not undertake to define standards of civil liability of lawyers for professional conduct. Violation of a rule does not give rise to a private cause of action nor does it create any presumption that a legal duty to a client has been breached. Likewise, these rules are not designed to be standards for procedural decisions. Furthermore, the purpose of these rules can be abused when they are invoked by opposing parties as procedural weapons. The fact that a rule is a just basis for a lawyer's self-assessment, or for sanctioning a lawyer under the administration of a disciplinary authority, does not imply that an antagonist in a collateral proceeding or transaction has standing to seek enforcement of the rule. Accordingly, nothing in the rules should be deemed to augment any substantive legal duty of lawyers or the extra-disciplinary consequences of violating such a duty.

16. Moreover, these rules are not intended to govern or affect judicial application of either the attorney-client or work product privilege. The fact that in exceptional situations the lawyer under the Rules has a limited discretion to disclose a client confidence does

not vitiate the proposition that, as a general matter, the client has a reasonable expectation that information relating to the client will not be voluntarily disclosed and that disclosure of such information may be judicially compelled only in accordance with recognized exceptions to the attorney-client and work product privileges.

Adopted by order of Oct. 17, 1989, eff. Jan. 1, 1990. Amended Oct. 23, 1991.

Terminology

"Adjudicatory Official" denotes a person who serves on a Tribunal.

"Adjudicatory Proceeding" denotes the consideration of a matter by a Tribunal.

"Belief" or "Believes" denotes that the person involved actually supposed the fact in question to be true. A person's belief may be inferred from circumstances.

"Competent" or "Competence" denotes possession or the ability to timely acquire the legal knowledge, skill, and training reasonably necessary for the representation of the client.

"Consult" or "Consultation" denotes communication of information and advice reasonably sufficient to permit the client to appreciate the significance of the matter in question.

"Firm" or "Law firm" denotes a lawyer or lawyers in a private firm; or a lawyer or lawyers employed in the legal department of a corporation, legal services organization, or other organization, or in a unit of government.

"Fitness" denotes those qualities of physical, mental and psychological health that enable a person to discharge a lawyer's responsibilities to clients in conformity with the Texas Disciplinary Rules of Professional Conduct. Normally a lack of fitness is indicated most clearly by a persistent inability to discharge, or unreliability in carrying out, significant obligations.

"Fraud" or "Fraudulent" denotes conduct having a purpose to deceive and not merely negligent misrepresentation or failure to apprise another of relevant information.

"Knowingly," "Known," or "Knows" denotes actual knowledge of the fact in question. A person's knowledge may be inferred from circumstances.

"Law firm": see "Firm."

"Partner" denotes an individual or corporate member of a partnership or a shareholder in a law firm organized as a professional corporation.

"Person" includes a legal entity as well as an individual.

"Reasonable" or "Reasonably" when used in relation to conduct by a lawyer denotes the conduct of a reasonably prudent and competent lawyer.

"Reasonable belief" or "Reasonably believes" when used in reference to a lawyer denotes that the lawyer believes the matter in question and that the circumstances are such that the belief is reasonable.

"Should know" when used in reference to a lawyer denotes that a reasonable lawyer under the same or similar circumstances would know the matter in question.

"Substantial" when used in reference to degree or extent denotes a matter of meaningful significance or involvement.

"Tribunal" denotes any governmental body or official or any other person engaged in a process of resolving a particular dispute or controversy. "Tribunal" includes such institutions as courts and administrative agencies when engaging in adjudicatory or licensing activities as defined by applicable law or rules of practice or procedure, as well as judges, magistrates, special masters, referees, arbitrators, mediators, hearing officers and comparable persons empowered to resolve or to recommend a resolution of a particular matter; but it does not include jurors, prospective jurors, legislative bodies or their committees, members or staffs, nor does it include other governmental bodies when acting in a legislative or rule-making capacity.

Adopted by order of Oct. 17, 1989, eff. Jan. 1, 1990.

I. Client-Lawyer Relationship

Rule 1.01. Competent and Diligent Representation

(a) A lawyer shall not accept or continue employment in a legal matter which the lawyer knows or should know is beyond the lawyer's competence, unless:

(1) another lawyer who is competent to handle the matter is, with the prior informed consent of the client, associated in the matter; or

(2) the advice or assistance of the lawyer is reasonably required in an emergency and the lawyer limits the advice and assistance to that which is reasonably necessary in the circumstances.

(b) In representing a client, a lawyer shall not:

(1) neglect a legal matter entrusted to the lawyer; or

(2) frequently fail to carry out completely the obligations that the lawyer owes to a client or clients.

(c) As used in this Rule, "neglect" signifies inattentiveness involving a conscious disregard for the responsibilities owed to a client or clients.

Adopted by order of Oct. 17, 1989, eff. Jan. 1, 1990.

Comment:

Accepting Employment

1. A lawyer generally should not accept or continue employment in any area of the law in which the lawyer is not and will not be prepared to render competent legal services. "Competence" is defined in Terminology as possession of the legal knowledge, skill, and training reasonably necessary for the representation. Competent representation contemplates appropriate application by the lawyer of that legal knowledge, skill and training, reasonable thoroughness in the study and analysis of the law and facts, and reasonable attentiveness to the responsibilities owed to the client.

2. In determining whether a matter is beyond a lawyer's competence, relevant factors include the relative complexity and specialized nature of the matter, the lawyer's general experience in the field in question, the preparation and study the lawyer will be able to give the matter, and whether it is feasible either to refer the matter to or associate a lawyer of established competence in the field in question. The required attention and preparation are determined in part by what is at stake; major litigation and complex transactions ordinarily require more elaborate treatment than matters of lesser consequences.

3. A lawyer may not need to have special training or prior experience to accept employment to handle legal problems of a type with which the lawyer is unfamiliar. Although expertise in a particular field of law may be useful in some circumstances, the appropriate proficiency in many instances is that of a general practitioner. A newly admitted lawyer can be as competent in some matters as a practitioner with long experience. Some important legal skills, such as the analysis of precedent, the evaluation of evidence and legal drafting, are required in all legal problems. Perhaps the most fundamental legal skill consists of determining what kind of legal problems a situation may involve, a skill that necessarily transcends any particular specialized knowledge.

4. A lawyer possessing the normal skill and training reasonably necessary for the representation of a client in an area of law is not subject to discipline for accepting employment in a matter in which, in order to represent the client properly, the lawyer must become more competent in regard to relevant legal knowledge by additional study and investigation. If the additional study and preparation will result in unusual delay or expense to the client, the lawyer should not accept employment except with the informed consent of the client.

5. A lawyer offered employment or employed in a matter beyond the lawyer's competence generally must decline or withdraw from the employment or, with the prior informed consent of the client, associate a lawyer who is competent in the matter. Paragraph (a)(2) permits a lawyer, however, to give advice or assistance in an emergency in a matter even though the lawyer does not have the skill ordinarily required if referral to or consultation with another lawyer would be impractical and if the assistance is limited to that which is reasonably necessary in the circumstances.

Competent and Diligent Representation

6. Having accepted employment, a lawyer should act with competence, commitment and dedication to the interest of the client and with zeal in advocacy upon the client's behalf. A lawyer should feel a moral or professional obligation to pursue a matter on behalf of a client with reasonable diligence and promptness despite opposition, obstruction or personal inconvenience to the lawyer. A lawyer's workload should be controlled so that each matter can be handled with diligence and competence. As provided in paragraph (a), an incompetent lawyer is subject to discipline.

Neglect

7. Perhaps no professional shortcoming is more widely resented than procrastination. A client's interests often can be adversely affected by the passage of time or the change of conditions; in extreme instances, as when a lawyer overlooks a statute of limitations, the client's legal position may be destroyed. Under paragraph (b), a lawyer is subject to professional discipline for neglecting a particular legal matter as well as for frequent failures to carry out fully the obligations owed to one or more clients. A lawyer who acts in good faith is not subject to discipline, under those provisions for an isolated inadvertent or unskilled act or omission, tactical error, or error of judgment. Because delay can cause a client needless anxiety and undermine confidence in the lawyer's trustworthiness, there is a duty to communicate reasonably with clients; see Rule 1.03.

Maintaining Competence

8. Because of the vital role of lawyers in the legal process, each lawyer should strive to become and remain proficient and competent in the practice of law. To maintain the requisite knowledge and skill of a competent practitioner, a lawyer should engage in continuing study and education. If a system of peer review has been established, the lawyer should consider making use of it in appropriate circumstances. Isolated instances of faulty conduct or decision should be identified for purposes of additional study or instruction.

Rule 1.02. Scope and Objectives of Representation

(a) Subject to paragraphs (b), (c), (d), and (e), (f), and (g), a lawyer shall abide by a client's decisions:

(1) concerning the objectives and general methods of representation;

(2) whether to accept an offer of settlement of a matter, except as otherwise authorized by law;

(3) In a criminal case, after consultation with the lawyer, as to a plea to be entered, whether to waive jury trial, and whether the client will testify.

(b) A lawyer may limit the scope, objectives and general methods of the representation if the client consents after consultation.

(c) A lawyer shall not assist or counsel a client to engage in conduct that the lawyer knows is criminal or fraudulent. A lawyer may discuss the legal consequences of any proposed course of conduct with a client and may counsel and represent a client in connection with the making of a good faith effort to determine the validity, scope, meaning or application of the law.

(d) When a lawyer has confidential information clearly establishing that a client is likely to commit a criminal or fraudulent act that is likely to result in substantial injury to the financial interests or property of another, the lawyer shall promptly make reasonable efforts under the circumstances to dissuade the client from committing the crime or fraud.

(e) When a lawyer has confidential information clearly establishing that the lawyer's client has committed a criminal or fraudulent act in the commission of which the lawyer's services have been used, the lawyer shall make reasonable efforts under the circumstances to persuade the client to take corrective action.

(f) When a lawyer knows that a client expects representation not permitted by the rules of professional conduct or other law, the lawyer shall consult with the client regarding the relevant limitations on the lawyer's conduct.

(g) A lawyer shall take reasonable action to secure the appointment of a guardian or other legal representative for, or seek other protective orders with respect to, a client whenever the lawyer reasonably believes that the client lacks legal competence and that such action should be taken to protect the client.

Adopted by order of Oct. 17, 1989, eff. Jan. 1, 1990.

Comment:

Scope of Representation

1. Both lawyer and client have authority and responsibility in the objectives and means of representation. The client has ultimate authority to determine the objectives to be served by legal representation, within the limits imposed by law, the lawyer's professional obligations, and the agreed scope of representation. Within those limits, a client also has a right to consult with the lawyer about the general methods to be used in pursuing those objectives. The lawyer should assume responsibility for the means by which the client's objectives are best achieved. Thus, a lawyer has very broad discretion to determine technical and legal tactics, subject to the client's wishes regarding such matters as the expense to be incurred and concern for third persons who might be adversely affected.

2. Except where prior communications have made it clear that a particular proposal would be unacceptable to the client, a lawyer is obligated to communicate any settlement offer to the client in a civil case; and a lawyer has a comparable responsibility with respect to a proposed plea bargain in a criminal case.

3. A lawyer should consult with the client concerning any such proposal, and generally it is for the client to decide whether or not to accept it. This principle is subject to several exceptions or qualifications. First, in class actions a lawyer may recommend a settlement of the matter to the court over the objections of named plaintiffs in the case. Second, in insurance defense cases a lawyer's ability to implement an insured client's wishes with respect to settlement may be qualified by the contractual rights of the insurer under its policy. Finally, a lawyer's normal deference to a client's wishes concerning settlement may be abrogated if the client has validly relinquished to a third party any rights to pass upon settlement offers. Whether any such waiver is enforceable is a question largely beyond the scope of these rules. But see comment 5 below. A lawyer reasonably relying on any of these exceptions in not implementing a client's desires concerning settlement is, however, not subject to discipline under this Rule.

Limited Scope of Representation

4. The scope of representation provided by a lawyer may be limited by agreement with the client or by the terms under which the lawyer's services are made available to the client. For example, a retainer may be for a specifically defined objective. Likewise, representation provided through a legal aid agency may be subject to limitations on the types of cases the agency handles. Similarly, when a lawyer has been retained by an insurer to represent an insured, the representation may be limited to matters related to the insurance coverage. The scope within which the representation is undertaken also may exclude specific objectives or means, such as those that the lawyer or client regards as repugnant or imprudent.

5. An agreement concerning the scope of representation must accord with the Disciplinary Rules of Professional Conduct and other law. Thus, the client may not be asked to agree to representation so limited in scope as to violate Rule 1.01, or to surrender the right to terminate the lawyer's services or the right to settle or continue litigation that the lawyer might wish to handle differently.

6. Unless the representation is terminated as provided in Rule 1.15, a lawyer should carry through to conclusion all matters undertaken for a client. If a lawyer's representation is limited to a specific matter or matters, the relationship terminates when the matter has been resolved. If a lawyer has represented a client over a substantial period in a variety of matters, the client may sometimes assume that the lawyer will continue to serve on a continuing basis unless the lawyer gives notice to the contrary. Doubt about whether a client-lawyer relationship still exists should be clarified by the lawyer, preferably in writing, so that the client will not mistakenly suppose the lawyer is looking after the client's affairs when the lawyer has ceased to do so. For example, if a lawyer has handled a judicial or administrative proceeding that produced a result adverse to the client but has not been specifically instructed concerning pursuit of an appeal, the lawyer should advise the client of the possibility of appeal before relinquishing responsibility for the matter.

Criminal, Fraudulent and Prohibited Transactions

7. A lawyer is required to give an honest opinion about the actual consequences that appear likely to result from a client's conduct. The fact that a client uses advice in a course of action that is criminal or fraudulent does not, of itself, make a lawyer a party to the course of action. However, a lawyer may not knowingly assist a client in criminal or fraudulent conduct. There is a critical distinction between presenting an analysis of legal aspects of questionable conduct and recommending the means by which a crime or fraud might be committed with impunity.

Comment:

1. A lawyer in good conscience should not charge or collect more than a reasonable fee, although he may charge less or no fee at all. The determination of the reasonableness of a fee, or of the range of reasonableness, can be a difficult question, and a standard of "reasonableness" is too vague and uncertain to be an appropriate standard in a disciplinary action. For this reason, paragraph (a) adopts, for disciplinary purposes only, a clearer standard: the lawyer is subject to discipline for an illegal fee or an unconscionable fee. Paragraph (a) defines an unconscionable fee in terms of the reasonableness of the fee but in a way to eliminate factual disputes as to the fee's reasonableness. The Rule's "unconscionable" standard, however, does not preclude use of the "reasonableness" standard of paragraph (b) in other settings.

Basis or Rate of Fee

2. When the lawyer has regularly represented a client, they ordinarily will have evolved an understanding concerning the basis or rate of the fee. If, however, the basis or rate of fee being charged to a regularly represented client differs from the understanding that has evolved, the lawyer should so advise the client. In a new client-lawyer relationship, an understanding as to the fee should be promptly established. It is not necessary to recite all the factors that underlie the basis of the fee, but only those that are directly involved in its computation. It is sufficient, for example, to state that the basic rate is an hourly charge or a fixed amount or an estimated amount, in order to identity the factors that may be taken into account in finally fixing the fee. When developments occur during the representation that render an earlier estimate substantially inaccurate, a revised estimate should be provided to the client. A written statement concerning the fee reduces the possibility of misunderstanding, and when the lawyer has not regularly represented the client it is preferable for the basis or rate of the fee to be communicated to the client in writing. Furnishing the client with a simple memorandum or a copy of the lawyer's customary fee schedule is sufficient if the basis or rate of the fee is set forth. In the case of a contingent fee, a written agreement is mandatory.

Types of Fees

3. Historically lawyers have determined what fees to charge by a variety of methods. Commonly employed are percentage fees and contingent fees (which may vary in accordance with the amount at stake or recovered), hourly rates, and flat fee arrangements, or combinations thereof.

4. The determination of a proper fee requires consideration of the interests of both client and lawyer. The determination of reasonableness requires consideration of all relevant circumstances, including those stated in paragraph (b). Obviously, in a particular situation not all of the factors listed in paragraph (b) may be relevant and factors not listed could be relevant. The fees of a lawyer will vary according to many factors, including the time required, the lawyer's experience, ability and reputation, the nature of the employment, the responsibility involved, and the results obtained.

5. When there is a doubt whether a particular fee arrangement is consistent with the client's best interest, the lawyer should discuss with the client alternative bases for the fee and explain their implications.

6. Once a fee arrangement is agreed to, a lawyer should not handle the matter so as to further the lawyer's financial interests to the detriment of the client. For example, a lawyer should not abuse a fee arrangement based primarily on hourly charges by using wasteful procedures.

Unconscionable Fees

7. Two principal circumstances combine to make it difficult to determine whether a particular fee is unconscionable within the disciplinary test provided by paragraph (a) of this Rule. The first is the subjectivity of a number of the factors relied on to determine the reasonableness of fees under paragraph (b). Because those factors do not permit more than an approximation of a range of fees that might be found reasonable in any given case, there is a corresponding degree of uncertainty in determining whether a given fee is unconscionable. Secondly, fee arrangements normally are made at the outset of representation, a time when many uncertainties and contingencies exist, while claims of unconscionability are made in hindsight when the contingencies have been resolved. The "unconscionability" standard adopts that difference in perspective and requires that a lawyer be given the benefit of any such uncertainties for disciplinary purposes only. Except in very unusual situations, therefore, the circumstances at the time a fee arrangement is made should control in determining a question of unconscionability.

8. Two factors in otherwise borderline cases might indicate a fee may be unconscionable. The first is overreaching by a lawyer, particularly of a client who was unusually susceptible to such overreaching. The second is a failure of the lawyer to give at the outset a clear and accurate explanation of how a fee was to be calculated. For example, a fee arrangement negotiated at arm's length with an experienced business client would rarely be subject to question. On the other hand, a fee arrangement with an uneducated or unsophisticated individual having no prior experience in such matters should be more carefully scrutinized for overreaching. While the fact that a client was at a marked disadvantage in bargaining with a lawyer over fees will not make a fee unconscionable, application of the disciplinary test may require some consideration of the personal circumstances of the individuals involved.

Fees in Family Law Matters

9. Contingent and percentage fees in family law matters may tend to promote divorce and may be inconsistent with a lawyer's obligation to encourage reconciliation. Such fee arrangements also may tend to create a conflict of interest between lawyer and client regarding the appraisal of assets obtained for client. See also Rule 1.08(h). In certain family law matters, such as child custody and adoption, no res is created to fund a fee. Because of the human relationships involved and the unique character of the proceedings, contingent fee arrangements in domestic relations cases are rarely justified.

Division of Fees

10. A division of fees is a single billing to a client covering the fee of two or more lawyers who are not in the same firm. A division of fees facilitates association of more than one lawyer in a matter in which neither alone could serve the client as well, and most often is used when the fee is contingent and the division is between a referring or associating lawyer initially retained by the client and a trial specialist, but it applies in all cases in which two or more lawyers are representing a single client in the same matter, and without regard to whether litigation is involved. Paragraph (f) permits the lawyers to divide a fee either on the basis of the proportion of services they render or if each lawyer assumes joint responsibility for the representation.

11. Contingent fee agreements must be in a writing signed by the client and must otherwise comply with paragraph (d) of this Rule.

12. A division of a fee based on the proportion of services rendered by two or more lawyers contemplates that each lawyer is performing substantial legal services on behalf of the client with respect to the matter. In particular, it requires that each lawyer who participates in the fee have performed services beyond those involved in initially seeking to acquire and being engaged by the client. There must be a reasonable correlation between the amount or value of services rendered and responsibility assumed, and the share of the fee to be received. However, if each participating lawyer performs substantial legal services on behalf of the client, the agreed division should control even though the division is not directly proportional to actual work performed. If a division of fee is to be based on the proportion of services rendered, the arrangement may provide that the allocation not be made until the end of the representation. When the allocation is deferred until the end of the representation, the terms of the arrangement must include the basis by which the division will be made.

13. Joint responsibility for the representation entails ethical and perhaps financial responsibility for the representation. The ethical responsibility assumed requires that a referring or associating lawyer make reasonable efforts to assure adequacy of representation and to provide adequate client communication. Adequacy of representation requires that the referring or associating lawyer conduct a reasonable investigation of the client's legal matter and refer the matter to a lawyer whom the referring or associating lawyer reasonably believes is competent to handle it. See Rule 1.01. Adequate attorney-client communication requires that a referring or associating lawyer monitor the matter throughout the representation and ensure that the client is informed of those matters that come to that lawyer's attention and that a reasonable lawyer would believe the client should be aware. See Rule 1.03. Attending all depositions and hearings or requiring that copies of all pleadings and correspondence be provided a referring or associating lawyer is not necessary in order to meet the monitoring requirement proposed by this rule. These types of activities may increase the transactional costs, which ultimately the client will bear and unless some benefit will be derived by the client, they should be avoided. The monitoring requirement is only that the referring lawyer be reasonably informed of the matter, respond to client questions, and assist the handling lawyer when necessary. Any referral or association of other counsel should be made based solely on the client's best interest.

14. In the aggregate, the minimum activities that must be undertaken by referring or associating lawyers pursuant to an arrangement for a division of fees are substantially greater than those assumed by a lawyer who forwarded a matter to other counsel, undertook no ongoing obligations with respect to it, and yet received a portion of the handling lawyer's fee once the matter was concluded, as was permitted under the prior version of this rule. Whether such activities, or any additional activities that a lawyer might agree to undertake, suffice to make one lawyer participating in such an arrangement responsible for the professional misconduct of another lawyer who is participating in it and, if so, to what extent, are intended to be resolved by Texas Civil Practice and Remedies Code, ch. 33, or other applicable law.

15. A client must consent in writing to the terms of the arrangement prior to the time of the association or referral proposed. For this consent to be effective, the client must have been advised of at least the key features of that arrangement. Those essential terms, which are specified in subparagraph (f)(2), are 1) the identity of all lawyers or law firms who will participate in the fee-sharing agreement, 2) whether fees will be divided based on the proportion of services performed or by lawyers agreeing to assume joint responsibility for the representation, and 3) the share of the fee that each lawyer or law firm will receive or the basis on which the division will be made if the division is based on proportion of service performed. Consent by a client or prospective client to the referral to or association of other counsel, made prior to any actual such referral or association, but without knowledge of the information specified in subparagraph (f)(2) does not constitute sufficient client confirmation within the meaning of this rule. The referring or associating lawyer or any other lawyer who employs another lawyer to assist in the representation has the primary duty to ensure full disclosure and compliance with this rule.

16. Paragraph (g) facilitates the enforcement of the requirements of paragraph (f). It does so by providing that agreements that authorize an attorney either to refer a person's case to another lawyer, or to associate other counsel in the handling of a client's case, and that actually result in such a referral or association with counsel in a different law firm from the one entering into the agreement, must be confirmed by an arrangement between the person and the lawyers involved that conforms to paragraph (f). As noted there, that arrangement must be presented to and agreed to by the person before the referral or association between the lawyers involved occurs. See subparagraph (f)(2). Because paragraph (g) refers to the party whose matter is involved as a "person" rather than as a "client," it is not possible to evade its requirements by having a referring lawyer not formally enter into an attorney-client relationship with the person involved before referring that person's matter to other counsel. Paragraph (g) does provide, however, for recovery in quantum meruit in instances where its requirements are not met. See subparagraphs (g)(1) and (g)(2).P

17. What should be done with any otherwise agreed-to fee that is forfeited in whole or in part due to a lawyer's failure to comply with paragraph (g) is not resolved by these rules.

18. Subparagraph (f)(3) requires that the aggregate fee charged to clients in connection with a given matter by all of the lawyers involved meet the standards of paragraph (a)—that is, not be unconscionable.

Fee Disputes and Determinations

19. If a procedure has been established for resolution of fee disputes, such as an arbitration or mediation procedure established by a bar association, the lawyer should conscientiously consider submitting to it. Law may prescribe a procedure for determining a lawyer's fee, for example, in representation of an executor or administrator, or when a class or a person is entitled to recover a reasonable attorney's fee as part of the measure of damages. All involved lawyers should comply with any prescribed procedures.

(Comment amended by Supreme Court Jan. 28, 2005, eff. March 1, 2005.)

Rule 1.05. Confidentiality of Information

(a) "Confidential information" includes both "privileged information" and "unprivileged client information." "Privileged information" refers to the information of a client protected by the lawyer-client privilege of Rule 503 of the Texas Rules of Evidence or of Rule 503 of the Texas Rules of Criminal Evidence or by the principles of attorney-client privilege governed by Rule 501 of the Federal Rules of Evidence for United States Courts and Magistrates. "Unprivileged client information" means all information relating to a client or furnished by the client, other than privileged information, acquired by the lawyer during the course of or by reason of the representation of the client.

(b) Except as permitted by paragraphs (c) and (d), or as required by paragraphs (e) and (f), a lawyer shall not knowingly:

(1) Reveal confidential information of a client or a former client to:

(i) a person that the client has instructed is not to receive the information; or

(ii) anyone else, other than the client, the client's representatives, or the members, associates, or employees of the lawyer's law firm.

(2) Use confidential information of a client to the disadvantage of the client unless the client consents after consultation.

(3) Use confidential information of a former client to the disadvantage of the former client after the representation is concluded unless the former client consents after consultation or the confidential information has become generally known.

(4) Use privileged information of a client for the advantage of the lawyer or of a third person, unless the client consents after consultation.

(c) A lawyer may reveal confidential information:

(1) When the lawyer has been expressly authorized to do so in order to carry out the representation.

(2) When the client consents after consultation.

(3) To the client, the client's representatives, or the members, associates, and employees of the lawyer's firm, except when otherwise instructed by the client.

(4) When the lawyer has reason to believe it is necessary to do so in order to comply with a court order, a Texas Disciplinary Rules of Professional Conduct, or other law.

(5) To the extent reasonably necessary to enforce a claim or establish a defense on behalf of the lawyer in a controversy between the lawyer and the client.

(6) To establish a defense to a criminal charge, civil claim or disciplinary complaint against the lawyer or the lawyer's associates based upon conduct involving the client or the representation of the client.

(7) When the lawyer has reason to believe it is necessary to do so in order to prevent the client from committing a criminal or fraudulent act.

(8) To the extent revelation reasonably appears necessary to rectify the consequences of a client's criminal or fraudulent act in the commission of which the lawyer's services had been used.

(d) A lawyer also may reveal unprivileged client information:

(1) When impliedly authorized to do so in order to carry out the representation.

(2) When the lawyer has reason to believe it is necessary to do so in order to:

(i) carry out the representation effectively;

(ii) defend the lawyer or the lawyer's employees or associates against a claim of wrongful conduct;

(iii) respond to allegations in any proceeding concerning the lawyer's representation of the client; or

(iv) prove the services rendered to a client, or the reasonable value thereof, or both, in an action against another person or organization responsible for the payment of the fee for services rendered to the client.

(e) When a lawyer has confidential information clearly establishing that a client is likely to commit a criminal or fraudulent act that is likely to result in death or substantial bodily harm to a person, the lawyer shall reveal confidential information to the extent revelation reasonably appears necessary to prevent the client from committing the criminal or fraudulent act.

(f) A lawyer shall reveal confidential information when required to do so by Rule 3.03(a)(2), 3.03(b), or by Rule 4.01(b).

Adopted by order of Oct. 17, 1989, eff. Jan. 1, 1990. Amended by order of Oct. 23, 1991.

Comment:

Confidentiality Generally

1. Both the fiduciary relationship existing between lawyer and client and the proper functioning of the legal system require the preservation by the lawyer of confidential information of one who has employed or sought to employ the lawyer. Free discussion should prevail between lawyer and client in order for the lawyer to be fully informed and for the client to obtain the full benefit of the legal system. The ethical obligation of the lawyer to protect the confidential information of the client not only facilitates the proper representation of the client but also encourages potential clients to seek early legal assistance.

2. Subject to the mandatory disclosure requirements of paragraphs (e) and (f) the lawyer generally should be required to maintain confidentiality of information acquired by the lawyer during the course of or by reason of the represen-

tation of the client. This principle involves an ethical obligation not to use the information to the detriment of the client or for the benefit of the lawyer or a third person. In regard to an evaluation of a matter affecting a client for use by a third person, see Rule 2.02.

3. The principle of confidentiality is given effect not only in the Texas Disciplinary Rules of Professional Conduct but also in the law of evidence regarding the attorney-client privilege and in the law of agency. The attorney-client privilege, developed through many decades, provides the client a right to prevent certain confidential communications from being revealed by compulsion of law. Several sound exceptions to confidentiality have been developed in the evidence law of privilege. Exceptions exist in evidence law where the services of the lawyer were sought or used by a client in planning or committing a crime or fraud as well as where issues have arisen as to breach of duty by the lawyer or by the client to the other.

4. Rule 1.05 reinforces the principles of evidence law relating to the attorney-client privilege. Rule 1.05 also furnishes considerable protection to other information falling outside the scope of the privilege. Rule 1.05 extends ethical protection generally to unprivileged information relating to the client or furnished by the client during the course of or by reason of the representation of the client. In this respect Rule 1.05 accords with general fiduciary principles of agency.

5. The requirement of confidentiality applies to government lawyers who may disagree with the policy goals that their representation is designed to advance.

Disclosure for Benefit of Client

6. A lawyer may be expressly authorized to make disclosures to carry out the representation and generally is recognized as having implied-in-fact authority to make disclosures about a client when appropriate in carrying out the representation to the extent that the client's instructions do not limit that authority. In litigation, for example, a lawyer may disclose information by admitting a fact that cannot properly be disputed, or in negotiation by making a disclosure that facilitates a satisfactory conclusion. The effect of Rule 1.05 is to require the lawyer to invoke, for the client, the attorney-client privilege when applicable; but if the court improperly denies the privilege, under paragraph (c)(4) the lawyer may testify as ordered by the court or may test the ruling as permitted by Rule 3.04(d).

7. In the course of a firm's practice, lawyers may disclose to each other and to appropriate employees information relating to a client, unless the client has instructed that particular information be confined to specified lawyers. Subparagraphs (b)(1) and (c)(3) continue these practices concerning disclosure of confidential information within the firm.

Use of Information

8. Following sound principles of agency law, subparagraphs (b)(2) and (4) subject a lawyer to discipline for using information relating to the representation in a manner disadvantageous to the client or beneficial to the lawyer or a third person, absent the informed consent of the client. The duty not to misuse client information continues after the client-lawyer relationship has terminated. Therefore, the lawyer is forbidden by subparagraph (b)(3) to use, in absence of the client's informed consent, confidential information of the former client to the client's disadvantage, unless the information is generally known.

Discretionary Disclosure Adverse to Client

9. In becoming privy to information about a client, a lawyer may foresee that the client intends serious and perhaps irreparable harm. To the extent a lawyer is prohibited from making disclosure, the interests of the potential victim are sacrificed in favor of preserving the client's information—usually unprivileged information—even though the client's purpose is wrongful. On the other hand, a client who knows or believes that a lawyer is required or permitted to disclose a client's wrongful purposes may be inhibited from revealing facts which would enable the lawyer to counsel effectively against wrongful action. Rule 1.05 thus involves balancing the interests of one group of potential victims against those of another. The criteria provided by the Rule are discussed below.

10. Rule 503(d)(1), Texas Rules of Civil Evidence (Tex. R.Civ.Evid.), and Rule 503(d)(1), Texas Rules of Criminal Evidence (Tex.R.Crim.Evid.), indicate the underlying public policy of furnishing no protection to client information where the client seeks or uses the services of the lawyer to aid in the commission of a crime or fraud. That public policy governs the dictates of Rule 1.05. Where the client is planning or engaging in criminal or fraudulent conduct or where the culpability of the lawyer's conduct is involved, full protection of client information is not justified.

11. Several other situations must be distinguished. First, the lawyer may not counsel or assist a client in conduct that is criminal or fraudulent. See Rule 1.02(c). As noted in the Comment to that Rule, there can be situations where the lawyer may have to reveal information relating to the representation in order to avoid assisting a client's criminal or fraudulent conduct, and sub-paragraph (c)(4) permits doing so. A lawyer's duty under Rule 3.03(a) not to use false or fabricated evidence is a special instance of the duty prescribed in Rule 1.02(c) to avoid assisting a client in criminal or fraudulent conduct, and sub-paragraph (c)(4) permits revealing information necessary to comply with Rule 3.03(a) or (b). The same is true of compliance with Rule 4.01. See also paragraph (f).

12. Second, the lawyer may have been innocently involved in past conduct by the client that was criminal or fraudulent. In such a situation the lawyer has not violated Rule 1.02(c), because to "counsel or assist" criminal or fraudulent conduct requires knowing that the conduct is of that character. Since the lawyer's services were made an instrument of the client's crime or fraud, the lawyer has a legitimate interest both in rectifying the consequences of such conduct and in avoiding charges that the lawyer's participation was culpable. Sub-paragraph (c)(6) and (8) give the lawyer professional discretion to reveal both unprivileged and privileged information in order to serve those interests. See paragraph (g). In view of Tex.R.Civ.Evid. Rule 503(d)(1), and Tex.R.Crim.Evid. 503(d)(1), however, rarely will such information be privileged.

13. Third, the lawyer may learn that a client intends prospective conduct that is criminal or fraudulent. The lawyer's knowledge of the client's purpose may enable the lawyer to prevent commission of the prospective crime or fraud. When the threatened injury is grave, the lawyer's interest in preventing the harm may be more compelling than the interest in preserving confidentiality of information. As stated in sub-paragraph (c)(7), the lawyer has professional discretion, based on reasonable appearances, to reveal both privileged and unprivileged information in order to prevent the client's commission of any criminal or fraudulent act. In

some situations of this sort, disclosure is mandatory. See paragraph (e) and Comments 18–20.

14. The lawyer's exercise of discretion under paragraphs (c) and (d) involves consideration of such factors as the magnitude, proximity, and likelihood of the contemplated wrong, the nature of the lawyer's relationship with the client and with those who might be injured by the client, the lawyer's own involvement in the transaction, and factors that may extenuate the client's conduct in question. In any case, a disclosure adverse to the client's interest should be no greater than the lawyer believes necessary to the purpose. Although preventive action is permitted by paragraphs (c) and (d), failure to take preventive action does not violate those paragraphs. But see paragraphs (e) and (f). Because these rules do not define standards of civil liability of lawyers for professional conduct, paragraphs (c) and (d) do not create a duty on the lawyer to make any disclosure and no civil liability is intended to arise from the failure to make such disclosure.

15. A lawyer entitled to a fee necessarily must be permitted to prove the services rendered in an action to collect it, and this necessity is recognized by sub-paragraphs (c)(5) and (d)(2)(iv). This aspect of the rule, in regard to privileged information, expresses the principle that the beneficiary of a fiduciary relationship may not exploit the relationship to the detriment of the fiduciary. Any disclosure by the lawyer, however, should be as protective of the client's interests as possible.

16. If the client is an organization, a lawyer also should refer to Rule 1.12 in order to determine the appropriate conduct in connection with this Rule.

Client Under a Disability

17. In some situations, Rule 1.02(g) requires a lawyer representing a client under a disability to seek the appointment of a legal representative for the client or to seek other orders for the protection of the client. The client may or may not, in a particular matter, effectively consent to the lawyer's revealing to the court confidential information and facts reasonably necessary to secure the desired appointment or order. Nevertheless, the lawyer is authorized by paragraph (c)(4) to reveal such information in order to comply with Rule 1.02(g). See also paragraph 5, Comment to Rule 1.03.

Mandatory Disclosure Adverse to Client

18. Rule 1.05(e) and (f) place upon a lawyer professional obligations in certain situations to make disclosure in order to prevent certain serious crimes by a client or to prevent involvement by the lawyer in a client's crimes or frauds. Except when death or serious bodily harm is likely to result, a lawyer's initial obligation is to attempt to dissuade the client from committing the crime or fraud or to persuade the client to take corrective action; see Rule 1.02(d) and (e).

19. Because it is very difficult for a lawyer to know when a client's criminal or fraudulent purpose actually will be carried out, the lawyer is required by paragraph (e) to act only if the lawyer has information "clearly establishing" the likelihood of such acts and consequences. If the information shows clearly that the client's contemplated crime or fraud is likely to result in death or serious injury, the lawyer must seek to avoid those lamentable results by revealing information necessary to prevent the criminal or fraudulent act. When the threatened crime or fraud is likely to have the less serious result of substantial injury to the financial interests or property of another, the lawyer is not required to reveal preventive information but may do so in conformity to paragraph (c)(7). See also paragraph (f); Rule 1.02(d) and (e); and Rule 3.03(b) and (c).

20. Although a violation of paragraph (e) will subject a lawyer to disciplinary action, the lawyer's decisions whether or how to act should not constitute grounds for discipline unless the lawyer's conduct in the light of those decisions was unreasonable under all existing circumstances as they reasonably appeared to the lawyer. This construction necessarily follows from the fact that paragraph (e) bases the lawyer's affirmative duty to act on how the situation "reasonably appears" to the lawyer, while that imposed by paragraph (f) arises only when a lawyer "knows" that the lawyer's services have been misused by the client. See also Rule 3.03(b).

Withdrawal

21. If the lawyer's services will be used by the client in materially furthering a course of criminal or fraudulent conduct, the lawyer must withdraw, as stated in Rule 1.15(a)(1). After withdrawal, a lawyer's conduct continues to be governed by Rule 1.05. The lawyer's duties of mandatory disclosure under paragraph (e) are not affected by termination of the relationship. If disclosure during the relationship was permissive, disclosure thereafter remains permissive under paragraphs (6), (7), and (8) if the further requirements of such paragraph are met. Neither this Rule nor Rule 1.15 prevents the lawyer from giving notice of the fact of withdrawal, and no rule forbids the lawyer to withdraw or disaffirm any opinion, document, affirmation, or the like.

Other Rules

22. Various other Texas Disciplinary Rules of Professional Conduct permit or require a lawyer to disclose information relating to the representation. See Rules 1.07, 1.12, 2.02, 3.03 and 4.01. In addition to these provisions, a lawyer may be obligated by other provisions of statutes or other law to give information about a client. Whether another provision of law supersedes Rule 1.05 is a matter of interpretation beyond the scope of these Rules, but sub-paragraph (c)(4) protects the lawyer from discipline who acts on reasonable belief as to the effect of such laws.

(Comment amended by Supreme Court Oct. 23, 1991; by State Bar Board of Directors Sept. 16, 1994.)

Rule 1.06. Conflict of Interest: General Rule

(a) A lawyer shall not represent opposing parties to the same litigation.

(b) In other situations and except to the extent permitted by paragraph (c), a lawyer shall not represent a person if the representation of that person:

(1) involves a substantially related matter in which that person's interests are materially and directly adverse to the interests of another client of the lawyer or the lawyer's firm; or

(2) reasonably appears to be or become adversely limited by the lawyer's or law firm's responsibilities to another client or to a third person or by the lawyer's or law firm's own interests.

(c) A lawyer may represent a client in the circumstances described in (b) if:

(1) the lawyer reasonably believes the representation of each client will not be materially affected; and

(2) each affected or potentially affected client consents to such representation after full disclosure of the existence, nature, implications, and possible adverse consequences of the common representation and the advantages involved, if any.

(d) A lawyer who has represented multiple parties in a matter shall not thereafter represent any of such parties in a dispute among the parties arising out of the matter, unless prior consent is obtained from all such parties to the dispute.

(e) If a lawyer has accepted representation in violation of this Rule, or if multiple representation properly accepted becomes improper under this Rule, the lawyer shall promptly withdraw from one or more representations to the extent necessary for any remaining representation not to be in violation of these Rules.

(f) If a lawyer would be prohibited by this Rule from engaging in particular conduct, no other lawyer while a member or associated with that lawyer's firm may engage in that conduct.

Adopted by order of Oct. 17, 1989, eff. Jan. 1, 1990.

Comment:

Loyalty to a Client

1. Loyalty is an essential element in the lawyer's relationship to a client. An impermissible conflict of interest may exist before representation is undertaken, in which event the representation should be declined. If such a conflict arises after representation has been undertaken, the lawyer must take effective action to eliminate the conflict, including withdrawal if necessary to rectify the situation. See also Rule 1.16. When more than one client is involved and the lawyer withdraws because a conflict arises after representation, whether the lawyer may continue to represent any of the clients is determined by this Rule and Rules 1.05 and 1.09. See also Rule 1.07(c). Under this Rule, any conflict that prevents a particular lawyer from undertaking or continuing a representation of a client also prevents any other lawyer who is or becomes a member of or an associate with that lawyer's firm from doing so. See paragraph (f).

2. A fundamental principle recognized by paragraph (a) is that a lawyer may not represent opposing parties in litigation. The term "opposing parties" as used in this Rule contemplates a situation where a judgment favorable to one of the parties will directly impact unfavorably upon the other party. Moreover, as a general proposition loyalty to a client prohibits undertaking representation directly adverse to the representation of that client in a substantially related matter unless that client's fully informed consent is obtained and unless the lawyer reasonably believes that the lawyer's representation will be reasonably protective of that client's interests. Paragraphs (b) and (c) express that general concept.

Conflicts in Litigation

3. Paragraph (a) prohibits representation of opposing parties in litigation. Simultaneous representation of parties whose interests in litigation are not actually directly adverse but where the potential for conflict exists, such as co-plaintiffs or co-defendants, is governed by paragraph (b). An impermissible conflict may exist or develop by reason of substantial discrepancy in the parties' testimony, incompatibility in positions in relation to an opposing party or the fact that there are substantially different possibilities of settlement of the claims or liabilities in question. Such conflicts can arise in criminal cases as well as civil. The potential for conflict of interest in representing multiple defendants in a criminal case is so grave that ordinarily a lawyer should decline to represent more than one co-defendant. On the other hand, common representation of persons having similar interests is proper if the risk of adverse effect is minimal and the requirements of paragraph (b) are met. Compare Rule 1.07 involving intermediation between clients.

Conflict with Lawyer's Own Interests

4. Loyalty to a client is impaired not only by the representation of opposing parties in situations within paragraphs (a) and (b)(1) but also in any situation when a lawyer may not be able to consider, recommend or carry out an appropriate course of action for one client because of the lawyer's own interests or responsibilities to others. The conflict in effect forecloses alternatives that would otherwise be available to the client. Paragraph (b)(2) addresses such situations. A potential possible conflict does not itself necessarily preclude the representation. The critical questions are the likelihood that a conflict exists or will eventuate and, if it does, whether it will materially and adversely affect the lawyer's independent professional judgment in considering alternatives or foreclose courses of action that reasonably should be pursued on behalf of the client. It is for the client to decide whether the client wishes to accommodate the other interest involved. However, the client's consent to the representation by the lawyer of another whose interests are directly adverse is insufficient unless the lawyer also believes that there will be no materially adverse effect upon the interests of either client. See paragraph (c).

5. The lawyer's own interests should not be permitted to have adverse effect on representation of a client, even where paragraph (b)(2) is not violated. For example, a lawyer's need for income should not lead the lawyer to undertake matters that cannot be handled competently and at a reasonable fee. See Rules 1.01 and 1.04. If the probity of a lawyer's own conduct in a transaction is in question, it may be difficult for the lawyer to give a client detached advice. A lawyer should not allow related business interests to affect representation, for example, by referring clients to an enterprise in which the lawyer has an undisclosed interest.

Meaning of Directly Adverse

6. Within the meaning of Rule 1.06(b), the representation of one client is "directly adverse" to the representation of another client if the lawyer's independent judgment on behalf of a client or the lawyer's ability or willingness to consider, recommend or carry out a course of action will be or is reasonably likely to be adversely affected by the lawyer's representation of, or responsibilities to, the other client. The dual representation also is directly adverse if the lawyer reasonably appears to be called upon to espouse adverse positions in the same matter or a related matter. On the other hand, simultaneous representation in unrelated matters of clients whose interests are only generally adverse, such as

competing economic enterprises, does not constitute the representation of directly adverse interests. Even when neither paragraph (a) nor (b) is applicable, a lawyer should realize that a business rivalry or personal differences between two clients or potential clients may be so important to one or both that one or the other would consider it contrary to its interests to have the same lawyer as its rival even in unrelated matters; and in those situations a wise lawyer would forego the dual representation.

Full Disclosure and Informed Consent

7. A client under some circumstances may consent to representation notwithstanding a conflict or potential conflict. However, as indicated in paragraph (c)(1), when a disinterested lawyer would conclude that the client should not agree to the representation under the circumstances, the lawyer involved should not ask for such agreement or provide representation on the basis of the client's consent. When more than one client is involved, the question of conflict must be resolved as to each client. Moreover, there may be circumstances where it is impossible to make the full disclosure necessary to obtain informed consent. For example, when the lawyer represents different clients in related matters and one of the clients refuses to consent to the disclosure necessary to permit the other client to make an informed decision, the lawyer cannot properly ask the latter to consent.

8. Disclosure and consent are not formalities. Disclosure sufficient for sophisticated clients may not be sufficient to permit less sophisticated clients to provide fully informed consent. While it is not required that the disclosure and consent be in writing, it would be prudent for the lawyer to provide potential dual clients with at least a written summary of the considerations disclosed.

9. In certain situations, such as in the preparation of loan papers or the preparation of a partnership agreement, a lawyer might have properly undertaken multiple representation and be confronted subsequently by a dispute among those clients in regard to that matter. Paragraph (d) forbids the representation of any of those parties in regard to that dispute unless informed consent is obtained from all of the parties to the dispute who had been represented by the lawyer in that matter.

10. A lawyer may represent parties having antagonistic positions on a legal question that has arisen in different cases, unless representation of either client would be adversely affected. Thus, it is ordinarily not improper to assert such positions in cases pending in different trial courts, but it may be improper to do so in cases pending at the same time in an appellate court.

11. Ordinarily, it is not advisable for a lawyer to act as advocate against a client the lawyer represents in some other matter, even if the other matter is wholly unrelated and even if paragraphs (a), (b), and (d) are not applicable. However, there are circumstances in which a lawyer may act as advocate against a client, for a lawyer is free to do so unless this Rule or another rule of the Texas Disciplinary Rules of Professional Conduct would be violated. For example, a lawyer representing an enterprise with diverse operations may accept employment as an advocate against the enterprise in a matter unrelated to any matter being handled for the enterprise if the representation of one client is not directly adverse to the representation of the other client. The propriety of concurrent representation can depend on the nature of the litigation. For example, a suit charging fraud entails conflict to a degree not involved in a suit for declaratory judgment concerning statutory interpretation.

Interest of Person Paying for a Lawyer's Service

12. A lawyer may be paid from a source other than the client, if the client is informed of that fact and consents and the arrangement does not compromise the lawyer's duty of loyalty to the client. See Rule 1.08(e). For example, when an insurer and its insured have conflicting interests in a matter arising from a liability insurance agreement, and the insurer is required to provide special counsel for the insured, the arrangement should assure the special counsel's professional independence. So also, when a corporation and its directors or employees are involved in a controversy in which they have conflicting interests, the corporation may provide funds for separate legal representation of the directors or employees, if the clients consent after consultation and the arrangement ensures the lawyer's professional independence.

Non-litigation Conflict Situations

13. Conflicts of interest in contexts other than litigation sometimes may be difficult to assess. Relevant factors in determining whether there is potential for adverse effect include the duration and intimacy of the lawyer's relationship with the client or clients involved, the functions being performed by the lawyer, the likelihood that actual conflict will arise and the likely prejudice to the client from the conflict if it does arise. The question is often one of proximity and degree.

14. For example, a lawyer may not represent multiple parties to a negotiation whose interests are fundamentally antagonistic to each other, but common representation may be permissible where the clients are generally aligned in interest even though there is some difference of interest among them.

15. Conflict questions may also arise in estate planning and estate administration. A lawyer may be called upon to prepare wills for several family members, such as husband and wife, and, depending upon the circumstances, a conflict of interest may arise. In estate administration it may be unclear whether the client is the fiduciary or is the estate or trust, including its beneficiaries. The lawyer should make clear the relationship to the parties involved.

16. A lawyer for a corporation or other organization who is also a member of its board of directors should determine whether the responsibilities of the two roles may conflict. The lawyer may be called on to advise the corporation in matters involving actions of the directors. Consideration should be given to the frequency with which such situations may arise, the potential intensity of the conflict, the effect of the lawyer's resignation from the board and the possibility of the corporation's obtaining legal advice from another lawyer in such situations. If there is material risk that the dual role will compromise the lawyer's independence of professional judgment, the lawyer should not serve as a director.

Conflict Charged by an Opposing Party

17. Raising questions of conflict of interest is primarily the responsibility of the lawyer undertaking the representation. In litigation, a court may raise the question when there is reason to infer that the lawyer has neglected the responsibility. In a criminal case, inquiry by the court is generally required when a lawyer represents multiple defendants. Where the conflict is such as clearly to call in question the fair or efficient administration of justice, opposing counsel may properly raise the question. Such an objection should

be viewed with great caution, however, for it can be misused as a technique of harassment. See Preamble: Scope.

18. Except when the absolute prohibition of this rule applies or in litigation when a court passes upon issues of conflicting interests in determining a question of disqualification of counsel, resolving questions of conflict of interests may require decisions by all affected clients as well as by the lawyer.

(Comment amended by Supreme Court Oct. 23, 1991.)

Rule 1.07. Conflict of Interest: Intermediary

(a) A lawyer shall not act as intermediary between clients unless:

(1) the lawyer consults with each client concerning the implications of the common representation, including the advantages and risks involved, and the effect on the attorney-client privileges, and obtains each client's written consent to the common representation;

(2) the lawyer reasonably believes that the matter can be resolved without the necessity of contested litigation on terms compatible with the clients' best interests, that each client will be able to make adequately informed decisions in the matter and that there is little risk of material prejudice to the interests of any of the clients if the contemplated resolution is unsuccessful; and

(3) the lawyer reasonably believes that the common representation can be undertaken impartially and without improper effect on other responsibilities the lawyer has to any of the clients.

(b) While acting as intermediary, the lawyer shall consult with each client concerning the decision to be made and the considerations relevant in making them, so that each client can make adequately informed decisions.

(c) A lawyer shall withdraw as intermediary if any of the clients so requests, or if any of the conditions stated in paragraph (a) is no longer satisfied. Upon withdrawal, the lawyer shall not continue to represent any of the clients in the matter that was the subject of the intermediation.

(d) Within the meaning of this Rule, a lawyer acts as intermediary if the lawyer represents two or more parties with potentially conflicting interests.

(e) If a lawyer would be prohibited by this Rule from engaging in particular conduct, no other lawyer while a member of or associated with that lawyer's firm may engage in that conduct.

Adopted by order of Oct. 17, 1989, eff. Jan. 1, 1990.

Comment:

1. A lawyer acting as intermediary may seek to establish or adjust a relationship between clients on an amicable and mutually advantageous basis. For example, the lawyer may assist in organizing a business in which two or more clients are entrepreneurs, in working out the financial reorganization of an enterprise in which two or more clients have an interest, in arranging a property distribution in settlement of an estate or in mediating a dispute between clients. The lawyer seeks to resolve potentially conflicting interests by developing the parties' mutual interests. The alternative can be that each party may have to obtain separate representation, with the possibility in some situations of incurring additional cost, complication or even litigation. Given these and other relevant factors, all the clients may prefer that the lawyer act as intermediary.

2. Because confusion can arise as to the lawyer's role where each party is not separately represented, it is important that the lawyer make clear the relationship; hence, the requirement of written consent. Moreover, a lawyer should not permit his personal interests to influence his advice relative to a suggestion by his client that additional counsel be employed. See also Rule 1.06(b).

3. The Rule does not apply to a lawyer acting as arbitrator or mediator between or among parties who are not clients of the lawyer, even where the lawyer has been appointed with the concurrence of the parties. In performing such a role the lawyer may be subject to applicable codes of ethics, such as the Code of Ethics for Arbitration in Commercial Disputes prepared by a joint Committee of the American Bar Association and the American Arbitration Association.

4. In considering whether to act as intermediary between clients, a lawyer should be mindful that if the intermediation fails the result can be additional cost, embarrassment and recrimination. In some situations, the risk of failure is so great that intermediation is plainly impossible. Moreover, a lawyer cannot undertake common representation of clients between whom contested litigation is reasonably expected or who contemplate contentious negotiations. More generally, if the relationship between the parties has already assumed definite antagonism, the possibility that the clients' interests can be adjusted by intermediation ordinarily is not very good.

5. The appropriateness of intermediation can depend on its form. Forms of intermediation range from informal arbitration, where each client's case is presented by the respective client and the lawyer decides the outcome, to mediation, to common representation where the clients' interests are substantially though not entirely compatible. One form may be appropriate in circumstances where another would not. Other relevant factors are whether the lawyer subsequently will represent both parties on a continuing basis and whether the situation involves creating a relationship between the parties or terminating one.

Confidentiality and Privilege

6. A particularly important factor in determining the appropriateness of intermediation is the effect on client-lawyer confidentiality and the attorney-client privilege. In a common representation, the lawyer is still required both to keep each client adequately informed and to maintain confidentiality of information relating to the representation, except as to such clients. See Rules 1.03 and 1.05. Complying with both requirements while acting as intermediary requires a delicate balance. If the balance cannot be maintained, the common representation is improper. With regard to the attorney-client privilege, the general rule is that as between commonly represented clients the privilege does not attach. Hence, it must be assumed that if litigation eventuates between the clients, the privilege will not protect any such communications, and the clients should be so advised.

7. Since the lawyer is required to be impartial between commonly represented clients, intermediation is improper when that impartiality cannot be maintained. For example, a lawyer who has represented one of the clients for a long period and in a variety of matters might have difficulty being impartial between that client and one to whom the lawyer has only recently been introduced.

Consultation

8. In acting as intermediary between clients, the lawyer should consult with the clients on the implications of doing so, and proceed only upon informed consent based on such a consultation. The consultation should make clear that the lawyer's role is not that of partisanship normally expected in other circumstances.

9. Paragraph (b) is an application of the principle expressed in Rule 1.03. Where the lawyer is intermediary, the clients ordinarily must assume greater responsibility for decisions than when each client is independently represented.

10. Under this Rule, any condition or circumstance that prevents a particular lawyer either from acting as intermediary between clients, or from representing those clients individually in connection with a matter after an unsuccessful intermediation, also prevents any other lawyer who is or becomes a member of or associates with that lawyer's firm from doing so. See paragraphs (c) and (e).

Withdrawal

11. In the event of withdrawal by one or more parties from the enterprise, the lawyer may continue to act for the remaining parties and the enterprise. See also Rule 1.06(c)(2) which authorizes continuation of the representation with consent.

Rule 1.08. Conflict of Interest: Prohibited Transactions

(a) A lawyer shall not enter into a business transaction with a client unless:

(1) the transaction and terms on which the lawyer acquires the interest are fair and reasonable to the client and are fully disclosed in a manner which can be reasonably understood by the client;

(2) the client is given a reasonable opportunity to seek the advice of independent counsel in the transaction; and

(3) the client consents in writing thereto.

(b) A lawyer shall not prepare an instrument giving the lawyer or a person related to the lawyer as a parent, child, sibling, or spouse any substantial gift from a client, including a testamentary gift, except where the client is related to the donee.

(c) Prior to the conclusion of all aspects of the matter giving rise to the lawyer's employment, a lawyer shall not make or negotiate an agreement with a client, prospective client, or former client giving the lawyer literary or media rights to a portrayal or account based in substantial part on information relating to the representation.

(d) A lawyer shall not provide financial assistance to a client in connection with pending or contemplated litigation or administrative proceedings, except that:

(1) a lawyer may advance or guarantee court costs, expenses of litigation or administrative proceedings, and reasonably necessary medical and living expenses, the repayment of which may be contingent on the outcome of the matter; and

(2) a lawyer representing an indigent client may pay court costs and expenses of litigation on behalf of the client.

(e) A lawyer shall not accept compensation for representing a client from one other than the client unless:

(1) the client consents;

(2) there is no interference with the lawyer's independence of professional judgment or with the client-lawyer relationship; and

(3) information relating to representation of a client is protected as required by Rule 1.05.

(f) A lawyer who represents two or more clients shall not participate in making an aggregate settlement of the claims of or against the clients, or in a criminal case an aggregated agreement to guilty or nolo contendere pleas, unless each client has consented after consultation, including disclosure of the existence and nature of all the claims or pleas involved and of the nature and extent of the participation of each person in the settlement.

(g) A lawyer shall not make an agreement prospectively limiting the lawyer's liability to a client for malpractice unless permitted by law and the client is independently represented in making the agreement, or settle a claim for such liability with an unrepresented client or former client with out first advising that person in writing that independent representation is appropriate in connection therewith.

(h) A lawyer shall not acquire a proprietary interest in the cause of action or subject matter of litigation the lawyer is conducting for a client, except that the lawyer may:

(1) acquire a lien granted by law to secure the lawyer's fee or expenses; and

(2) contract in a civil case with a client for a contingent fee that is permissible under Rule 1.04.

(i) If a lawyer would be prohibited by this Rule from engaging in particular conduct, no other lawyer while a member of or associated with that lawyer's firm may engage in that conduct.

(j) As used in this Rule, "business transactions" does not include standard commercial transactions between the lawyer and the client for products or services that the client generally markets to others.

Adopted by order of Oct. 17, 1989, eff. Jan. 1, 1990. Amended by order of Oct. 23, 1991.

Comment:

Transactions between Client and Lawyer

1. This rule deals with certain transactions that per se involve unacceptable conflicts of interests.

2. As a general principle, all transactions between client and lawyer should be fair and reasonable to the client. In such transactions a review by independent counsel on behalf of the client is often advisable. Paragraph (a) does not, however, apply to standard commercial transactions between the lawyer and the client for products or services that the client generally markets to others such as banking or brokerage services, medical services, products manufactured or distributed by the client, and utilities services. In such transactions, the lawyer has no advantage in dealing with the client, and the restrictions in paragraph (a) are unnecessary and impracticable.

3. A lawyer may accept a gift from a client, if the transaction meets general standards of fairness. For example, a simple gift such as a present given at a holiday or as a token of appreciation is permitted. If effectuation of a substantial gift requires preparing a legal instrument such as a will or conveyance, however, the client should have the detached advice that another lawyer can provide. Paragraph (b) recognizes an exception where the client is a relative of the donee or the gift is not substantial.

Literary Rights

4. An agreement by which a lawyer acquires literary or media rights concerning the conduct of representation creates a conflict between the interests of the client and the personal interests of the lawyer. Measures suitable in the representation of the client may detract from the publication value of an account of the representation. Paragraph (c) does not prohibit a lawyer representing a client in a transaction concerning literary property from agreeing that the lawyer's fee shall consist of a share in ownership in the property, if the arrangement conforms to Rule 1.04 and to paragraph (h) of this Rule.

Person Paying for Lawyer's Services

5. Paragraph (e) requires disclosure to the client of the fact that the lawyer's services are being paid for by a third party. Such an arrangement must also conform to the requirements of Rule 1.05 concerning confidentiality and Rule 1.06 concerning conflict of interest. Where the client is a class, consent may be obtained on behalf of the class by court-supervised procedure. Where an insurance company pays the lawyer's fee for representing an insured, normally the insured has consented to the arrangement by the terms of the insurance contract.

Prospectively Limiting Liability

6. Paragraph (g) is not intended to apply to customary qualification and limitations in legal opinions and memoranda.

Acquisition of Interest in Litigation

7. This Rule embodies the traditional general precept that lawyers are prohibited from acquiring a proprietary interest in the subject matter of litigation. This general precept, which has its basis in common law champerty and maintenance, is subject to specific exceptions developed in decisional law and continued in these Rules, such as the exception for contingent fees set forth in Rule 1.04 and the exception for certain advances of the costs of litigation set forth in paragraph (d). A special instance arises when a lawyer proposes to incur litigation or other expenses with an entity in which the lawyer has a pecuniary interest. A lawyer should not incur such expenses unless the client has entered into a written agreement complying with paragraph (a) that contains a full disclosure of the nature and amount of the possible expenses and the relationship between the lawyer and the other entity involved.

Imputed Disqualifications

8. The prohibitions imposed on an individual lawyer by this Rule are imposed by paragraph (i) upon all other lawyers while practicing with that lawyer's firm.

Rule 1.09. Conflict of Interest: Former Client

(a) Without prior consent, a lawyer who personally has formerly represented a client in a matter shall not thereafter represent another person in a matter adverse to the former client:

(1) in which such other person questions the validity of the lawyer's services or work product for the former client;

(2) if the representation in reasonable probability will involve a violation of Rule 1.05; or

(3) if it is the same or a substantially related matter.

(b) Except to the extent authorized by Rule 1.10, when lawyers are or have become members of or associated with a firm, none of them shall knowingly represent a client if any one of them practicing alone would be prohibited from doing so by paragraph (a).

(c) When the association of a lawyer with a firm has terminated, the lawyers who were then associated with that lawyer shall not knowingly represent a client if the lawyer whose association with that firm has terminated would be prohibited from doing so by paragraph (a)(1) or if the representation in reasonable probability will involve a violation of Rule 1.05.

Adopted by order of Oct. 17, 1989, eff. Jan. 1, 1990. Amended by order of Oct. 23, 1991.

Comment:

1. Rule 1.09 addresses the circumstances in which a lawyer in private practice, and other lawyers who were, are or become members of or associated with a firm in which that lawyer practiced or practices, may represent a client against a former client of that lawyer or the lawyer's former firm. Whether a lawyer, or that lawyer's present or former firm, is prohibited from representing a client in a matter by reason of the lawyer's successive government and private employment is governed by Rule 1.10 rather than by this Rule.

2. Paragraph (a) concerns the situation where a lawyer once personally represented a client and now wishes to represent a second client against that former client. Whether such a personal attorney-client relationship existed involves questions of both fact and law that are beyond the

scope of these Rules. See Preamble: Scope. Among the relevant factors, however, would be how the former representation actually was conducted within the firm; the nature and scope of the former client's contacts with the firm (including any restrictions the client may have placed on the dissemination of confidential information within the firm); and the size of the firm.

3. Although paragraph (a) does not absolutely prohibit a lawyer from representing a client against a former client, it does provide that the latter representation is improper if any of three circumstances exists, except with prior consent. The first circumstance is that the lawyer may not represent a client who questions the validity of the lawyer's services or work product for the former client. Thus, for example, a lawyer who drew a will leaving a substantial portion of the testator's property to a designated beneficiary would violate paragraph (a) by representing the testator's heirs at law in an action seeking to overturn the will.

4. Paragraph (a)'s second limitation on undertaking a representation against a former client is that it may not be done if there is a "reasonable probability" that the representation would cause the lawyer to violate the obligations owed the former client under Rule 1.05. Thus, for example, if there were a reasonable probability that the subsequent representation would involve either an unauthorized disclosure of confidential information under Rule 1.05(b)(1) or an improper use of such information to the disadvantage of the former client under Rule 1.05(b)(3), that representation would be improper under paragraph (a). Whether such a reasonable probability exists in any given case will be a question of fact.

4A. The third situation where representation adverse to a former client is prohibited is where the representation involved the same or a substantially related matter. The "same" matter aspect of this prohibition prevents a lawyer from switching sides and representing a party whose interests are adverse to a person who disclosed confidences to the lawyer while seeking in good faith to retain the lawyer. The prohibition applies when an actual attorney-client relationship was established even if the lawyer withdrew from the representation before the client had disclosed any confidential information. This aspect of the prohibition includes, but is somewhat broader than, that contained in paragraph (a)(1) of this Rule.

4B. The "substantially related" aspect, on the other hand, has a different focus. Although that term is not defined in the Rule, it primarily involves situations where a lawyer could have acquired confidential information concerning a prior client that could be used either to that prior client's disadvantage or for the advantage of the lawyer's current client or some other person. It thus largely overlaps the prohibition contained in paragraph (a)(2) of this Rule.

5. Paragraph (b) extends paragraph (a)'s limitations on an individual lawyer's freedom to undertake a representation against that lawyer's former client to all other lawyers who are or become members of or associated with the firm in which that lawyer is practicing. Thus, for example, if a client severs the attorney-client relationship with a lawyer who remains in a firm, the entitlement of that individual lawyer to undertake a representation against that former client is governed by paragraph (a); and all other lawyers who are or become members of or associated with that lawyer's firm are treated in the same manner by paragraph (b). Similarly, if a lawyer severs his or her association with a firm and that firm retains as a client a person whom the lawyer personally represented while with the firm, that lawyer's ability thereafter to undertake a representation against that client is governed by paragraph (a); and all other lawyers who are or become members of or associates with that lawyer's new firm are treated in the same manner by paragraph (b).

6. Paragraph (c) addresses the situation of former partners or associates of a lawyer who once had represented a client when the relationship between the former partners or associates and the lawyer has been terminated. In that situation, the former partners or associates are prohibited from questioning the validity of such lawyer's work product and from undertaking representation which in reasonable probability will involve a violation of Rule 1.05. Such a violation could occur, for example, when the former partners or associates retained materials in their files from the earlier representation of the client that, if disclosed or used in connection with the subsequent representation, would violate Rule 1.05(b)(1) or (b)(3).

7. Thus, the effect of paragraphs (b) is to extend any inability of a particular lawyer under paragraph (a) to undertake a representation against a former client to all other lawyers who are or become members of or associated with any firm in which that lawyer is practicing. If, on the other hand, a lawyer disqualified by paragraph (a) should leave a firm, paragraph (c) prohibits lawyers remaining in that firm from undertaking a representation that would be forbidden to the departed lawyer only if that representation would violate subparagraphs (a)(1) or (a)(2). Finally, should those other lawyers cease to be members of the same firm as the lawyer affected by paragraph (a) without personally coming within its restrictions, they thereafter may undertake the representation against the lawyer's former client unless prevented from doing so by some other of these Rules.

8. Although not required to do so by Rule 1.05 or this Rule, some courts, as a procedural decision, disqualify a lawyer for representing a present client against a former client when the subject matter of the present representation is so closely related to the subject matter of the prior representation that confidences obtained from the former client might be useful in the representation of the present client. See Comment 17 to Rule 1.06. This so-called "substantial relationship" test is defended by asserting that to require a showing that confidences of the first client were in fact used for the benefit of the subsequent client as a condition to procedural disqualification would cause disclosure of the confidences that the court seeks to protect. A lawyer is not subject to discipline under Rule 1.05(b)(1), (3), or (4), however, unless the protected information is actually used. Likewise, a lawyer is not subject to discipline under this Rule unless the new representation by the lawyer in reasonable probability would result in a violation of those provisions.

9. Whether the "substantial relationship" test will continue to be employed as a standard for procedural disqualification is a matter beyond the scope of these Rules. See Preamble: Scope. The possibility that such a disqualification might be sought by the former client or granted by a court, however, is a matter that could be of substantial importance to the present client in deciding whether or not to retain or continue to employ a particular lawyer or law firm as its counsel. Consequently, a lawyer should disclose those possibilities, as well as their potential consequences for the representation, to the present client as soon as the lawyer becomes aware of them; and the client then should be

allowed to decide whether or not to obtain new counsel. See Rules 1.03(b) and 1.06(b).

10. This Rule is primarily for the protection of clients and its protections can be waived by them. A waiver is effective only if there is consent after disclosure of the relevant circumstances, including the lawyer's past or intended role on behalf of each client, as appropriate. See Comments 7 and 8 to Rule 1.06.

(Comment amended by Supreme Court Oct. 23, 1991; by the State Bar Board of Directors as published in the January 1995 issue of the *Texas Bar Journal.*)

Rule 1.10. Successive Government and Private Employment

(a) Except as law may otherwise expressly permit, a lawyer shall not represent a private client in connection with a matter in which the lawyer participated personally and substantially as a public officer or employee, unless the appropriate government agency consents after consultation.

(b) No lawyer in a firm with which a lawyer subject to paragraph (a) is associated may knowingly undertake or continue representation in such a matter unless:

(1) The lawyer subject to paragraph (a) is screened from any participation in the matter and is apportioned no part of the fee therefrom; and

(2) written notice is given with reasonable promptness to the appropriate government agency.

(c) Except as law may otherwise expressly permit, a lawyer having information that the lawyer knows or should know is confidential government information about a person or other legal entity acquired when the lawyer was a public officer or employee may not represent a private client whose interests are adverse to that person or legal entity.

(d) After learning that a lawyer in the firm is subject to paragraph (c) with respect to a particular matter, a firm may undertake or continue representation in that matter only if that disqualified lawyer is screened from any participation in the matter and is apportioned no part of the fee therefrom.

(e) Except as law may otherwise expressly permit, a lawyer serving as a public officer or employee shall not:

(1) Participate in a matter involving a private client when the lawyer had represented that client in the same matter while in private practice or nongovernmental employment, unless under applicable law no one is, or by lawful delegation may be, authorized to act in the lawyer's stead in the matter; or

(2) Negotiate for private employment with any person who is involved as a party or as attorney for a party in a matter in which the lawyer is participating personally and substantially.

(f) As used in this rule, the term "matter" does not include regulation-making or rule-making proceedings or assignments, but includes:

(1) Any adjudicatory proceeding, application, request for a ruling or other determination, contract, claim, controversy, investigation, charge accusation, arrest or other similar, particular transaction involving a specific party or parties; and

(2) any other action or transaction covered by the conflict of interest rules of the appropriate government agency.

(g) As used in this rule, the term "confidential government information" means information which has been obtained under governmental authority and which, at the time this rule is applied, the government is prohibited by law from disclosing to the public or has a legal privilege not to disclose, and which is not otherwise available to the public.

(h) As used in this Rule, "Private Client" includes not only a private party but also a governmental agency if the lawyer is not a public officer or employee of that agency.

(i) A lawyer who serves as a public officer or employee of one body politic after having served as a public officer of another body politic shall comply with paragraphs (a) and (c) as if the second body politic were a private client and with paragraph (e) as if the first body politic were a private client.

Adopted by order of Oct. 17, 1989, eff. Jan. 1, 1990.

Comment:

1. This Rule prevents a lawyer from exploiting public office for the advantage of a private client.

2. A lawyer licensed or specially admitted in Texas and representing a government agency is subject to the Texas Disciplinary Rules of Professional Conduct, including the prohibition against representing adverse interests stated in Rule 1.06 and the protections afforded former clients in Rule 1.09. In addition, such a lawyer is subject to this Rule and to statutes and government regulations regarding conflict of interest. Such statutes and regulations may circumscribe the extent to which the government agency may give consent under paragraph (a) of this Rule.

3. Where a public agency and a private client are represented in succession by a lawyer, the risk exists that power or discretion vested in public authority might be used for the special benefit of the private client. A lawyer should not be in a position where benefit to a private client might affect performance of the lawyer's professional functions on behalf of public authority. Also, unfair advantage could accrue to the private client by reason of access to confidential government information about the client's adversary obtainable only through the lawyer's government service. However, the rules governing lawyers presently or formerly employed by a government agency should not be so restrictive as to inhibit transfer of employment to and from the government. The

government has a legitimate need to attract qualified lawyers as well as to maintain high ethical standards. The provisions for screening and waiver are necessary to avoid imposing too severe a deterrent against entering public service. Although "screening" is not defined, the screening provisions contemplate that the screened lawyer has not furnished and will not furnish other lawyers with information relating to the matter, will not have access to the files pertaining to the matter, and will not participate in any way as a lawyer or adviser in the matter.

4. When the client of a lawyer in private practice is an agency of one government, that agency is a private client for purposes of this Rule. See paragraph (h). If the lawyer thereafter becomes an officer or employee of an agency of another government, as when a lawyer represents a city and subsequently is employed by a federal agency, the lawyer is subject to paragraph (e). A lawyer who has been a public officer or employee of one body politic and who becomes a public officer or employee of another body politic is subject to paragraphs (a), (c) and (e). See paragraph (i). Thus, paragraph (i) protects a governmental agency without regard to whether the lawyer was or becomes a private practitioner or a public officer or employee.

5. Paragraphs (b)(1) and (d)(1) do not prohibit a lawyer from receiving a salary or partnership share established by prior independent agreement. They prohibit directly relating the attorney's compensation to the fee in the matter in which the lawyer is disqualified.

6. Paragraph (b)(2) does not require that a lawyer give notice to the governmental agency at a time when premature disclosure would injure the client; a requirement for premature disclosure might preclude engagement of the lawyer. such notice is, however, required to be given as soon as practicable in order that the government agency or affected person will have a reasonable opportunity to ascertain compliance with Rule 1.10 and to take appropriate action if necessary.

7. Paragraph (c) operates only when the lawyer in question has actual as opposed to imputed knowledge of the confidential government information.

8. Paragraphs (a) and (e) do not prohibit a lawyer from jointly representing a private party and a government agency when doing so is permitted by Rule 1.06 and is not otherwise prohibited by law.

9. Paragraph (e)(1) does not disqualify other lawyers in the agency with which the lawyer in question has become associated. Although the rule does not require that the lawyer in question be screened from participation in the matter, the sound practice would be to screen the lawyer to the extent feasible. In any event, the lawyer in question must comply with Rule 1.05.

10. As used in paragraph (i), "one body politic" refers to one unit or level of government such as the federal government, a state government, a county, a city or a precinct. The term does not refer to different agencies within the same body politic or unit of government.

(Comment amended by Supreme Court Oct. 23, 1991.)

Rule 1.11. Adjudicatory Official or Law Clerk

(a) A lawyer shall not represent anyone in connection with a matter in which the lawyer has passed upon the merits or otherwise participated personally and substantially as an adjudicatory official or law clerk to an adjudicatory official, unless all parties to the proceeding consent after disclosure.

(b) A lawyer who is an adjudicatory official shall not negotiate for employment with any person who is involved as a party or as attorney for a party in a pending matter in which that official is participating personally and substantially. A lawyer serving as a law clerk to an adjudicatory official may negotiate for employment with a party or attorney involved in a matter in which the clerk is participating personally and substantially, but only after the clerk has notified the adjudicatory official.

(c) If paragraph (a) is applicable to a lawyer, no other lawyer in a firm with which that lawyer is associated may knowingly undertake or continue representation in the matter unless:

(1) the lawyer who is subject to paragraph (a) is screened from participation in the matter and is apportioned no part of the fee therefrom; and

(2) written notice is promptly given to the other parties to the proceeding.

Adopted by order of Oct. 17, 1989, eff. Jan. 1, 1990.

Comment:

1. This Rule generally parallels Rule 1.10. The term "personally and substantially" signifies that a judge who was a member of a multi-member court and thereafter left judicial office to practice law is not prohibited from representing a client in a matter pending in the court but in which the former judge did not participate. So also the fact that a former judge exercised administrative responsibility in a court does not prevent the former judge from acting as a lawyer in matters where the judge had previously exercised remote or incidental administrative responsibility that did not affect the merits. Compare the Comments to Rule 1.10.

2. The term "Adjudicatory Official" includes not only judges but also comparable officials serving on tribunals, such as judges pro tempore, referees, special masters, hearing officers and other parajudicial officers, as well as lawyers who serve as part-time judges. Compliance provisions B(2) and C of the Texas Code of Judicial Conduct provide that a part-time judge or judge pro tempore may not "act as a lawyer in a proceeding in which he has served as a judge or in any other proceeding related thereto." Although phrased differently from this rule, those provisions correspond in meaning.

3. Some law clerks have not been licensed as lawyers at the time they commence service as law clerks. Obviously, paragraph (b) cannot apply to a law clerk until the clerk has been licensed as a lawyer. Paragraph (a) applies, however, to a lawyer without regard to whether the lawyer had been licensed at the time of the service as a law clerk, and once that law clerk is licensed as a lawyer and joins a firm, paragraph (c) applies to the firm.

4. Paragraph (c) does not prohibit a lawyer from receiving a salary or partnership share established by prior independent agreement. It prohibits directly relating the lawyer's compensation to the fee in the matter in which the lawyer is disqualified.

Rule 1.12. Organization as a Client

(a) A lawyer employed or retained by an organization represents the entity. While the lawyer in the ordinary course of working relationships may report to, and accept direction from, an entity's duly authorized constituents, in the situations described in paragraph (b) the lawyer shall proceed as reasonably necessary in the best interest of the organization without involving unreasonable risks of disrupting the organization and of revealing information relating to the representation to persons outside the organization.

(b) A lawyer representing an organization must take reasonable remedial actions whenever the lawyer learns or knows that:

(1) an officer, employee, or other person associated with the organization has committed or intends to commit a violation of a legal obligation to the organization or a violation of law which reasonably might be imputed to the organization;

(2) the violation is likely to result in substantial injury to the organization; and

(3) the violation is related to a matter within the scope of the lawyer's representation of the organization.

(c) Except where prior disclosure to persons outside the organization is required by law or other Rules, a lawyer shall first attempt to resolve a violation by taking measures within the organization. In determining the internal procedures, actions or measures that are reasonably necessary in order to comply with paragraphs (a) and (b), a lawyer shall give due consideration to the seriousness of the violation and its consequences, the scope and nature of the lawyer's representation, the responsibility in the organization and the apparent motivation of the person involved, the policies of the organization concerning such matters, and any other relevant considerations. Such procedures, actions and measures may include, but are not limited to, the following:

(1) asking reconsideration of the matter;

(2) advising that a separate legal opinion on the matter be sought for presentation to appropriate authority in the organization; and

(3) referring the matter to higher authority in the organization, including, if warranted by the seriousness of the matter, referral to the highest authority that can act in behalf of the organization as determined by applicable law.

(d) Upon a lawyer's resignation or termination of the relationship in compliance with Rule 1.15, a lawyer is excused from further proceeding as required by paragraphs (a), (b) and (c), and any further obligations of the lawyer are determined by Rule 1.05.

(e) In dealing with an organization's directors, officers, employees, members, shareholders or other constituents, a lawyer shall explain the identity of the client when it is apparent that the organization's interests are adverse to those of the constituents with whom the lawyer is dealing or when explanation appears reasonably necessary to avoid misunderstanding on their part.

Adopted by order of Oct. 17, 1989, eff. Jan. 1, 1990.

Comment:

The Entity as the Client

1. A lawyer employed or retained to represent an organization represents the organization as distinct from its directors, officers, employees, members, shareholders or other constituents. Unlike individual clients who can speak and decide finally and authoritatively for themselves, an organization can speak and decide only through its agents or constituents such as its officers or employees. In effect, the lawyer-client relationship must be maintained through a constituent who acts as an intermediary between the organizational client and the lawyer. This fact requires the lawyer under certain conditions to be concerned whether the intermediary legitimately represents the organizational client.

2. As used in this Rule, the constituents of an organizational client, whether incorporated or an unincorporated association, include its directors, officers, employees, shareholders, members, and others serving in capacities similar to those positions or capacities. This Rule applies not only to lawyers representing corporations but to those representing an organization, such as an unincorporated association, union, or other entity.

3. When one of the constituents of an organizational client communicates with the organization's lawyer in that person's organizational capacity, the communication is protected by Rule 1.05. Thus, by way of example, if an officer of an organizational client requests its lawyers to investigate allegations of wrongdoing, interviews made in the course of that investigation between the lawyer and the client's employees or other constituents are covered by Rule 1.05. The lawyer may not disclose to such constituents information relating to the representation except for disclosures permitted by Rule 1.05.

Clarifying the Lawyer's Role

4. There are times when the organization's interest may be or become adverse to those of one or more of its constituents. In such circumstances the lawyers should advise any constituent, whose interest the lawyer finds adverse to that of the organization of the conflict or potential conflict of interest, that the lawyer cannot represent such constituent, and that such person may wish to obtain independent representation. Care should be taken to assure that the individual understands that, when there is such adversity of interest, the lawyer for the organization cannot provide legal representation for that constituent individual, and that discussions between the lawyer for the organization and the individual may not be privileged insofar as that individual is concerned. Whether such a warming should be given by the lawyer for the organization to any constituent individual may turn on the facts of each case.

5. A lawyer representing an organization may, of course, also represent any of its directors, officers, employees, members, shareholders, or other constituents, subject to the

provisions of Rule 1.06. If the organization's consent to the dual representation is required by Rule 1.06, the consent of the organization should be given by the appropriate official or officials of the organization other than the individual who is to be represented, or by the shareholders.

Decisions by Constituents

6. When constituents of the organization make decisions for it, the decisions ordinarily must be accepted by the lawyer even if their utility or prudence is doubtful. Decisions concerning policy and operations, including ones entailing serious risk, are not as such in the lawyer's province. However, different considerations arise when the lawyer knows, in regard to a matter within the scope of the lawyer's responsibility, that the organization is likely to be substantially injured by the action of a constituent that is in violation of law or in violation of a legal obligation to the organization. In such circumstances, the lawyer must take reasonable remedial measure. See paragraph (b). It may be reasonably necessary, for example, for the lawyer to ask the constituent to reconsider the matter. If that fails, or if the matter is of sufficient seriousness and importance to the organization, it may be reasonably necessary for the lawyer to take steps to have the matter reviewed by a higher authority in the organization. The stated policy of the organization may define circumstances and prescribe channels for such review, and a lawyer should encourage the formulation of such a policy. Even in the absence of organization policy, however, the lawyer may have an obligation to refer a matter to higher authority, depending on the seriousness of the matter and whether the constituent in question has apparent motives to act at variance with the organization's interest. At some point it may be useful or essential to obtain an independent legal opinion.

7. In some cases, it may be reasonably necessary for the lawyer to refer the matter to the organization's highest responsible authority. See paragraph (c)(3). Ordinarily, that is the board of directors or similar governing body. However, applicable law may prescribe that under certain conditions highest authority reposes elsewhere, such as in the independent directors of a corporation. Even that step may be unsuccessful. The ultimate and difficult ethical question is whether the lawyer should circumvent the organization's highest authority when it persists in a course of action that is clearly violative of law or of a legal obligation to the organization and is likely to result in substantial injury to the organization. These situations are governed by Rule 1.05; see paragraph (d) of this Rule. If the lawyer does not violate a provision of Rule 1.02 or Rule 1.05 by doing so, the lawyer's further remedial action, after exhausting remedies within the organization, may include revealing information relating to the representation to persons outside the organization. If the conduct of the constituent of the organization is likely to result in death or serious bodily injury to another, the lawyer may have a duty of revelation under Rule 1.05(e). The lawyer may resign, of course, in accordance with Rule 1.15, in which event the lawyer is excused from further proceeding as required by paragraphs (a), (b), and (c), and any further obligations are determined by Rule 1.05.

Relation to Other Rules

8. The authority and responsibility provided in this Rule are concurrent with the authority and responsibility provided in other Rules. In particular, this Rule is consistent with the lawyer's responsibility under Rules 1.05, 1.08, 1.15, 3.03, and 4.01. If the lawyer's services are being used by an organization to further a crime or fraud by the organization, Rule 1.02(c) can be applicable.

Government Agency

9. The duty defined in this Rule applies to governmental organizations. However, when the client is a governmental organization, a different balance may be appropriate between maintaining confidentiality and assuring that the wrongful official act is prevented or rectified, for public business is involved. In addition, duties of lawyers employed by the government or lawyers in military service may be defined by statutes and regulations. Therefore, defining precisely the identity of the client and prescribing the resulting obligations of such lawyers may be more difficult in the government context. Although in some circumstances the client may be a specific agency, it is generally the government as a whole. For example, if the action or failure to act involves the head of a bureau, either the department of which the bureau is a part or the government as a whole may be the client for purpose of this Rule. Moreover, in a matter involving the conduct of government officials, a government lawyer may have authority to question such conduct more extensively than that of a lawyer for a private organization in similar circumstances. This Rule does not limit that authority. See Preamble: Scope.

Derivative Actions

10. Under generally prevailing law, the shareholders or members of a corporation may bring suit to compel the directors to perform their legal obligations in the supervision of the organization. Members of unincorporated associations have essentially the same right. Such an action may be brought nominally by the organization, but usually is, in fact, a legal controversy over management of the organization.

11. The question can arise whether counsel for the organization may defend such an action. The proposition that the organization is the lawyer's client does not alone resolve the issue. Most derivative actions are a normal incident of an organization's affairs, to be defended by the organization's lawyer like any other suit. However, if the claim involves serious charges of wrongdoing by those in control of the organization, a conflict may arise between the lawyer's duty to the organization and the lawyer's relationship with those managing or controlling its affairs.

Rule 1.13. Conflicts: Public Interests Activities

A lawyer serving as a director, officer or member of a legal services, civic, charitable or law reform organization, apart from the law firm in which the lawyer practices, shall not knowingly participate in a decision or action of the organization:

(a) if participating in the decision would violate the lawyer's obligations to a client under Rule 1.06; or

(b) where the decision could have a material adverse effect on the representation of any client of the organization whose interests are adverse to a client of the lawyer.

Adopted by order of Oct. 17, 1989, eff. Jan. 1, 1990.

Comment:

1. Lawyers are encouraged to serve as directors, officers or members of legal services, civic, charitable or law reform organizations, and, with two exceptions, they may do so

notwithstanding that the organization either itself has interests adverse to a client of the lawyer or else serves persons having such adverse interests.

2. When the lawyer is a director, officer or member of a legal services organization, further problems can arise when a client served by the organization has interests adverse to those of a client served by the lawyer. A lawyer-client relationship with persons served by the organization does not result solely from the lawyer's service in those capacities. Nonetheless, if the lawyer were to participate in an action or decision of the organization concerning that representation, a real danger of having this quality of the organizational client's representation being dictated by its adversary would be presented. To avoid that possibility, paragraph (b) prohibits a lawyer's participation in actions or decisions of the organization that could have a material adverse effect on the representation of any client of the organization, if that client's interests are adverse to those of a client of the lawyer.

3. Law reform organizations (like civic and charitable organizations) generally do not have clients, in which event paragraph (b) does not apply. For reasons of public policy, it is not generally considered a conflict of interest for a lawyer to engage in law reform activities even though such activities are adverse to the interests of the lawyer's private clients. A lawyer's representation of a client does not constitute an endorsement of the client's political, economic, social or moral views, nor does he forego his own. When the lawyer knows that the interests of a client may be materially benefitted by a law reform decision in which the lawyer participates, the lawyer should disclose that fact but need not identify the client.

Rule 1.14. Safekeeping Property

(a) A lawyer shall hold funds and other property belonging in whole or in part to clients or third persons that are in a lawyer's possession in connection with a representation separate from the lawyer's own property. Such funds shall be kept in a separate account, designated as a "trust" or "escrow" account, maintained in the state where the lawyer's office is situated, or elsewhere with the consent of the client or third person. Other client property shall be identified as such and appropriately safeguarded. Complete records of such account funds and other property shall be kept by the lawyer and shall be preserved for a period of five years after termination of the representation.

(b) Upon receiving funds or other property in which a client or third person has an interest, a lawyer shall promptly notify the client or third person. Except as stated in this rule or otherwise permitted by law or by agreement with the client, a lawyer shall promptly deliver to the client or third person any funds or other property that the client or third person is entitled to receive and, upon request by the client or third person, shall promptly render a full accounting regarding such property.

(c) When in the course of representation a lawyer is in possession of funds or other property in which both the lawyer and other person claim interests, the property shall be kept separate by the lawyer until there is an accounting and severance of their interest. All funds in a trust or escrow account shall be disbursed only to those persons entitled to receive them by virtue of the representation or by law. If a dispute arises concerning their respective interests, the portion in dispute shall be kept separated by the lawyer until the dispute is resolved, and the undisputed portion shall be distributed appropriately.

Adopted by order of Oct. 17, 1989, eff. Jan. 1, 1990.

Comment:

1. A lawyer should hold property of others with the care required of a professional fiduciary. Securities should be kept in a safe deposit box, except when some other form of safekeeping is warranted by special circumstances. All property which is the property of clients or third persons should be kept separate form the lawyer's business and personal property and, if monies, in one or more trust accounts. Separate trust accounts may be warranted when administering estate monies or acting in similar fiduciary capacities. Paragraph (a) requires that complete records of the funds and other property be maintained.

2. Lawyers often receive funds from third parties from which the lawyer's fee will be paid. These funds should be deposited into a lawyer's trust account. If there is risk that the client may divert the funds without paying the fee, the lawyer is not required to remit the portion from which the fee is to be paid. However, a lawyer may not hold funds to coerce a client into accepting the lawyer's contention. The disputed portion of the funds should be kept in trust and the lawyer should suggest means for prompt resolution of the dispute, such as arbitration. The undisputed portion of the funds should be promptly distributed to those entitled to receive them by virtue of the representation. A lawyer should not use even that portion of trust account funds due to the lawyer to make direct payment to general creditors of the lawyer of the lawyer's firm, because such a course of dealing increases the risk that all the assets of that account will be viewed as the lawyer's property rather than that of clients, and thus as available to satisfy the claims of such creditors. When a lawyer receives from a client monies that constitute a prepayment of a fee and that belongs to the client until the services are rendered, the lawyer should handle the fund in accordance with paragraph (c). After advising the client that the service has been rendered and the fee earned, and in the absence of a dispute, the lawyer may withdraw the fund from the separate account. Paragraph (c) does not prohibit participation in an IOLTA or similar program.

3. Third parties, such as client's creditors, may have just claims against funds or other property in a lawyer's custody. A lawyer may have a duty under applicable law to protect such third-party claims against wrongful interference by the client, and accordingly may refuse to surrender the property to the client. However, a lawyer should not unilaterally assume to arbitrate a dispute between the client and the third party.

4. The obligations of a lawyer under this Rule are independent of those arising from activity other than rendering legal service. For example, a lawyer who serves as an escrow agent is governed by the applicable law relating to

fiduciaries even though the lawyer does not render legal services in the transaction.

5. The "client's security fund" in Texas provides a means through the collective efforts of the bar to reimburse persons who have lost money or property as a result of dishonest conduct of a lawyer.

Rule 1.15. Declining or Terminating Representation

(a) A lawyer shall decline to represent a client or, where representation has commenced, shall withdraw, except as stated in paragraph (c), from the representation of a client, if:

(1) the representation will result in violation of Rule 3.08, other applicable rules of professional conduct or other law;

(2) the lawyer's physical, mental or psychological condition materially impairs the lawyer's fitness to represent the client; or

(3) the lawyer is discharged, with or without good cause.

(b) Except as required by paragraph (a), a lawyer shall not withdraw from representing a client unless:

(1) withdrawal can be accomplished without material adverse effect on the interests of the client;

(2) the client persists in a course of action involving the lawyer's services that the lawyer reasonably believes may be criminal or fraudulent;

(3) the client has used the lawyer's services to perpetrate a crime or fraud;

(4) a client insists upon pursuing an objective that the lawyer considers repugnant or imprudent or with which the lawyer has fundamental disagreement;

(5) the client fails substantially to fulfill an obligation to the lawyer regarding the lawyer's services, including an obligation to pay the lawyer's fee as agreed, and has been given reasonable warning that the lawyer will withdraw unless the obligation is fulfilled;

(6) the representation will result in an unreasonable financial burden on the lawyer or has been rendered unreasonably difficult by the client; or

(7) other good cause for withdrawal exists.

(c) When ordered to do so by a tribunal, a lawyer shall continue representation notwithstanding good cause for terminating the representation.

(d) Upon termination of representation, a lawyer shall take steps to the extent reasonably practicable to protect a client's interests, such as giving reasonable notice to the client, allowing time for employment of other counsel, surrendering papers and property to which the client is entitled and refunding any advance payments of fee that has not been earned. The lawyer may retain papers relating to the client to the extent permitted by other law only if such retention will not prejudice the client in the subject matter of the representation.

Adopted by order of Oct. 17, 1989, eff. Jan. 1, 1990.

Comment:

1. A lawyer should not accept representation in a matter unless it can be performed competently, promptly, and without improper conflict of interest. See generally Rules 1.01, 1.06, 1.07, 1.08, and 1.09. Having accepted the representation, a lawyer normally should endeavor to handle the matter to completion. Nevertheless, in certain situations the lawyer must terminate the representation and in certain other situations the lawyer is permitted to withdraw.

Mandatory Withdrawal

2. A lawyer ordinarily must decline employment if the employment will cause the lawyer to engage in conduct that the lawyer knows is illegal or that violates the Texas Disciplinary Rules of Professional Conduct. Rule 1.15(a)(1); cf. Rules 1.02(c), 3.01, 3.02, 3.03, 3.04, 3.08, 4.01, and 8.04. Similarly, paragraph (a)(1) of this Rule requires a lawyer to withdraw from employment when the lawyer knows that the employment will result in a violation of a rule of professional conduct or other law. The lawyer is not obliged to decline or withdraw simply because the client suggests such a course of conduct; a client may have made such a suggestion in the ill-founded hope that a lawyer will not be constrained by a professional obligation. Cf. Rule 1.02(c) and (d).

3. When a lawyer has been appointed to represent a client and in certain other instances in litigation, withdrawal ordinarily requires approval of the appointing authority or presiding judge. See also Rule 6.01. Difficulty may be encountered if withdrawal is based on the client's demand that the lawyer engage in unprofessional conduct. The tribunal may wish an explanation for the withdrawal, while the lawyer may be bound to keep confidential the facts that would constitute such an explanation. The lawyer's statement that professional considerations require termination of the representation ordinarily should be accepted as sufficient. See also Rule 1.06(e).

Discharge

4. A client has the power to discharge a lawyer at any time, with or without cause, subject to liability for payment for the lawyer's services, and paragraph (a) of this Rule requires that the discharged lawyer withdraw. Where future dispute about the withdrawal may be anticipated, it may be advisable to prepare a written statement reciting the circumstances.

5. Whether a client can discharge an appointed counsel depends on the applicable law. A client seeking to do so should be given full explanation of the consequences. In some instances the consequences may include a decision by the appointing authority or presiding judge that appointment of successor counsel is unjustified, thus requiring the client to represent himself.

Mentally Incompetent Client

6. If the client is mentally incompetent, the client may lack the legal capacity to discharge the lawyer (see paragraphs 11 and 12 of Comment to Rule 1.02), and in any event the discharge may be seriously adverse to the client's interests. The lawyer should make special effort to help the incompetent client consider the consequences (see paragraph 5 of Comment to Rule 1.03) and in some situations may

initiate proceedings for a conservatorship or similar protection of the client. See Rule 1.02(e).

Optional Withdrawal

7. Paragraph (b) supplements paragraph (a) by permitting a lawyer to withdraw from representation in some certain additional circumstances. The lawyer has the option to withdraw if it can be accomplished without material adverse effect on the client's interests. Withdrawal is also justified if the client persists in a course of action that the lawyer reasonably believes is criminal or fraudulent, for a lawyer is not required to be associated with such conduct even if the lawyer does not further it. A lawyer is not required to discontinue the representation until the lawyer knows the conduct will be illegal or in violation of these rules, at which point the lawyer's withdrawal is mandated by paragraph (a)(1). Withdrawal is also permitted if the lawyer's services were misused in the past. The lawyer also may withdraw where the client insists on pursuing a repugnant or imprudent objective or one with which the lawyer has fundamental disagreement. A lawyer may withdraw if the client refuses, after being duly warned, to abide by the terms of an agreement relating to the representation, such as an agreement concerning fees or court costs or an agreement limiting the objectives of the representation.

8. Withdrawal permitted by paragraph (b)(2) through (7) is optional with the lawyer even though the withdrawal may have a material adverse effect upon the interests of the client.

Assisting the Client Upon Withdrawal

9. In every instance of withdrawal and even if the lawyer has been unfairly discharged by the client, a lawyer must take all reasonable steps to mitigate the consequences to the client. See paragraph (d). The lawyer may retain papers as security for a fee only to the extent permitted by law.

10. Other rules, in addition to Rule 1.15, require or suggest withdrawal in certain situations. See Rules 1.01, 1.05 Comment 22, 1.06(e) and 1.07(c), 1.11(c), 1.12(d), and 3.08(a).

(Comment amended by Supreme Court Oct. 23, 1991.)

II. Counselor

Rule 2.01. Advisor

In advising or otherwise representing a client, a lawyer shall exercise independent professional judgment and render candid advice.

Adopted by order of Oct. 17, 1989, eff. Jan. 1, 1990.

Comment:

Scope of Advice

1. A client is entitled to straightforward advice expressing the lawyer's honest assessment. Legal advice often involves unpleasant facts and alternatives that a client may be disinclined to confront. In presenting advice, a lawyer endeavors to sustain the client's morale and may put advice in as acceptable a form as honesty permits. However, a lawyer should not be deterred from giving candid advice by the prospect that the advice will be unpalatable to the client.

2. Advice couched in narrow legal terms may be of little value to a client, especially where practical considerations, such as costs or effects on other people, are predominant. Purely technical legal advice, therefore, can sometimes be inadequate. It is proper for a lawyer to refer to relevant moral and ethical considerations in giving advice. Although a lawyer is not a moral advisor as such, moral and ethical considerations impinge upon most legal questions and may decisively influence how the law will be applied.

3. A client may expressly or impliedly ask the lawyer for purely technical advice. When such a request is made by a client experienced in legal matters, the lawyer may accept it at face value. When such a request is made by a client inexperienced in legal matters, however, the lawyer's responsibility as advisor may include indicating that more may be involved than strictly legal considerations.

4. Matters that go beyond strictly legal questions may also be in the domain of another profession. Family matters can involve problems within the professional competence of psychiatry, clinical psychology or social work; business matters can involve problems within the competence of the accounting profession or of financial specialists. Where consultation with a professional in another field is itself something a competent lawyer would recommend, the lawyer should make such a recommendation. At the same time, a lawyer's advice at its best often consists of recommending a course of action in the face of conflicting recommendations of experts.

Offering Advice

5. In general, a lawyer is not expected to give advice until asked by the client. However, when a lawyer knows that a client proposes a course of action that is likely to result in substantial adverse legal consequences to the client, duty to the client may require that the lawyer act if the client's course of action is related to the representation. A lawyer ordinarily has no duty to initiate investigation of a client's affairs or to give advice that the client has indicated is unwanted, but a lawyer may initiate advice to a client when doing so appears to be in the client's interest.

Intermediary

6. In regard to a lawyer serving as intermediary for clients with conflicting interests, see Rule 1.07.

Rule 2.02. Evaluation for Use by Third Persons

A lawyer shall not undertake an evaluation of a matter affecting a client for the use of someone other than the client unless:

(a) the lawyer reasonably believes that making the evaluation is compatible with other aspects of the lawyer's relationship with the client; and

(b) the client consents after consultation.

Adopted by order of Oct. 17, 1989, eff. Jan. 1, 1990.

Comment:

Definition

1. An evaluation may be performed at the client's direction but for the primary purpose of establishing information for the benefit of third parties; for example, an opinion concerning the title of property rendered at the behest of a vendor for the information of a prospective purchaser, or at the behest of a borrower for the information of a prospective lender. In some situations, the evaluation may be required

by a government agency; for example, an opinion concerning the legality of the securities registered for sale under the securities laws. In other instances, the evaluation may be required by a third person, such as a purchaser of a business.

2. Lawyers for the government may be called upon to serve as advisors or as evaluators. A lawyer for the government serves as advisor when the lawyer is an advocate for a government agency or is a counselor for a government agency. When serving as an advisor the rule of confidentiality of information applies. See Rules 1.05 and 2.01.

3. A lawyer for the government serves as evaluator when the lawyer's official responsibility is to render opinions establishing the limits on authorized government activity. In that situation this Rule applies.

4. In addition to serving as advisors or as evaluators, lawyers may be called upon to serve as investigators. When serving as investigator, the identity of the client is critical, because only the client has a confidential relationship with the lawyer. See Rule 1.05. Thus, a lawyer who makes an investigative contact with a non-client in circumstances which might cause the non-client to believe that the lawyer is representing him in the matter should make that non-client aware that rules concerning client loyalty and confidentiality are not applicable. See Rule 1.05. See also Rule 1.12(e).

Third Persons

5. When the evaluation is intended for the information or use of a third person, the evaluation involves a departure from the normal client-lawyer relationship. The lawyer must be satisfied as a matter of professional judgment that making the evaluation is compatible with other functions undertaken in behalf of the client. For example, if the lawyer is acting as advocate in defending the client against charges of fraud, it would normally be incompatible with that responsibility for the lawyer to perform an evaluation for others concerning the same or a related transaction. Assuming no such impediment is apparent, however, the lawyer should advise the client of the implications of the evaluation, particularly the lawyer's responsibilities to third persons and the duty to disseminate the findings.

Access to and Disclosure of Information

6. The quality of an evaluation depends on the freedom and extent of the investigation upon which it is based. Ordinarily a lawyer should have whatever latitude of investigation seems necessary as a matter of professional judgment. Under some circumstances, however, the terms of the evaluation may be limited. See Rule 1.02. For example, certain issues or sources may be categorically excluded, or the scope of search may be limited by time constraints or the noncooperation of persons having relevant information. Any such limitations which are material to the evaluation should be described in the report. If after a lawyer has commenced an evaluation, the client refused to comply with the terms upon which it was understood the evaluation was to have been made, the lawyer's obligations are determined by law, having reference to the terms of the client's agreement and the surrounding circumstances.

Financial Auditors' Requests for Information

7. When a question concerning the legal situation of a client arises at the instance of the client's financial auditor and the question is referred to the lawyer, any response by the lawyer should be made in accordance with procedures recognized in the legal profession.

III. Advocate

Rule 3.01. Meritorious Claims and Contentions

A lawyer shall not bring or defend a proceeding, or assert or controvert an issue therein, unless the lawyer reasonably believes that there is a basis for doing so that is not frivolous.

Adopted by order of Oct. 17, 1989, eff. Jan. 1, 1990.

Comment:

1. The advocate has a duty to use legal procedure for the fullest benefit of the client's cause, but also a duty not to abuse legal procedure. The law, both procedural and substantive, affects the limits within which an advocate may proceed. Likewise, these Rules impose limitations on the types of actions that a lawyer may take on behalf of his client. See Rules 3.02–3.06, 4.01–4.04, and 8.04. However, the law is not always clear and never is static. Accordingly, in determining the proper scope of advocacy, account must be taken of the law's ambiguities and potential for change.

2. All judicial systems prohibit, at a minimum, the filing of frivolous or knowingly false pleadings, motions or other papers with the court or the assertion in an adjudicatory proceeding of a knowingly false claim or defense. A filing or assertion is frivolous if it is made primarily for the purpose of harassing or maliciously injuring a person. It also is frivolous if the lawyer is unable either to make a good faith argument that the action taken is consistent with existing law or that it may be supported by a good faith argument for an extension, modification or reversal of existing law.

3. A filing or contention is frivolous if it contains knowingly false statements of fact. It is not frivolous, however, merely because the facts have not been first substantiated fully or because the lawyer expects to develop vital evidence only by discovery. Neither is it frivolous even though the lawyer believes that the client's position ultimately may not prevail. In addition, this Rule does not prohibit the use of a general denial or other pleading to the extent authorized by applicable rules of practice or procedure. Likewise, a lawyer for a defendant in any criminal proceeding or for the respondent in a proceeding that could result in commitment may so defend the proceeding as to require that every element of the case be established.

4. A lawyer should conform not only to this Rule's prohibition of frivolous filings or assertions but also to any more stringent applicable rule of practice or procedure. For example, the duties imposed on a lawyer by Rule 11 of the Federal Rules of Civil Procedure exceed those set out in this Rule. A lawyer must prepare all filings subject to Rule 11 in accordance with its requirements. See Rule 3.04(c)(1).

Rule 3.02. Minimizing the Burdens and Delays of Litigation

In the course of litigation, a lawyer shall not take a position that unreasonably increases the costs or other burdens of the case or that unreasonably delays resolution of the matter.

Adopted by order of Oct. 17, 1989, eff. Jan. 1, 1990.

Comment:

1. This Rule addresses those situations where a lawyer or the lawyer's client perceive the client's interests as served by conduct that delays resolution of the matter or that increases the costs or other burdens of a case. Because such tactics are frequently an appropriate way of achieving the legitimate interests of the client that are at stake in the litigation, only those instances that are "unreasonable" are prohibited. As to situations where such tactics are inconsistent with the client's interests, see Rule 1.01. As to those where the lawyer's conduct is motivated primarily by his desire to receive a larger fee, see Rule 1.04 and Comment, paragraph 6 thereto.

2. A lawyer's obligations under this Rule are substantially fulfilled by complying with Rules 3.01, 3.03, and 3.04 as supplemented by applicable rules of practice or procedure. See paragraph 4 to the Comment to Rule 3.01.

Unreasonable Delay

3. Dilatory practices indulged in merely for the convenience of lawyers bring the administration of justice into disrepute and normally will be "unreasonable" within the meaning of this Rule. See also Rule 1.01(b) and (c) and paragraphs 6 and 7 of the Comment thereto. This Rule, however, does not require a lawyer to eliminate all conflicts between the demands placed on the lawyer's time by different clients and proceedings. Consequently, it is not professional misconduct either to seek (or as a matter of professional courtesy, to grant) reasonable delays in some matters in order to permit the competent discharge of a lawyer's multiple obligations.

4. Frequently, a lawyer seeks a delay in some aspect of a proceeding in order to serve the legitimate interests of the client rather than merely the lawyer's own interests. Seeking such delays is justifiable. For example, in order to represent the legitimate interests of the client effectively, a diligent lawyer representing a party named as a defendant in a complex civil or criminal action may need more time to prepare a proper response than allowed by applicable rules of practice or procedure. Similar considerations may pertain in preparing responses to extensive discovery requests. Seeking reasonable delays in such circumstances is both the right and the duty of a lawyer.

5. On the other hand, a client may seek to have a lawyer delay a proceeding primarily for the purpose of harassing or maliciously injuring another. Under this Rule, a lawyer is obliged not to take such an action. See also Rule 3.01. It is not a justification that similar conduct is often tolerated by the bench and the bar. The question is whether a competent lawyer acting in good faith would regard the course of action as having some substantial purpose other than delay undertaken for the purpose of harassing or malicious injuring. The fact that a client realizes a financial or other benefit from such otherwise unreasonable delay does not make that delay reasonable.

Unreasonable Costs and Other Burdens of Litigation

6. Like delay, increases in the costs or other burdens of litigation may be viewed as serving a wide range of interests of the client. Many of these interests are entirely legitimate and merit the most stringent protection. Litigation by its very nature often is costly and burdensome. This Rule does not subject a lawyer to discipline for taking any actions not otherwise prohibited by these Rules in order to fully and effectively protect the legitimate interests of a client that are at stake in litigation.

7. Not all conduct that increases the costs or other burdens of litigation, however, can be justified in this manner. One example of such impermissible conduct is a lawyer who counsels or assists a client in seeking a multiplication of the costs or other burdens of litigation as the primary purpose, because the client perceives himself as more readily able to bear those burdens than is the opponent, and so hopes to gain an advantage in resolving the matter unrelated to the merits of the client's position.

Rule 3.03. Candor Toward the Tribunal

(a) A lawyer shall not knowingly:

(1) make a false statement of material fact or law to a tribunal;

(2) fail to disclose a fact to a tribunal when disclosure is necessary to avoid assisting a criminal or fraudulent act;

(3) in an ex parte proceeding, fail to disclose to the tribunal an unprivileged fact which the lawyer reasonably believes should be known by that entity for it to make an informed decision;

(4) fail to disclose to the tribunal authority in the controlling jurisdiction known to the lawyer to be directly adverse to the position of the client and not disclosed by opposing counsel; or

(5) offer or use evidence that the lawyer knows to be false.

(b) If a lawyer has offered material evidence and comes to know of its falsity, the lawyer shall make a good faith effort to persuade the client to authorize the lawyer to correct or withdraw the false evidence. If such efforts are unsuccessful, the lawyer shall take reasonable remedial measures, including disclosure of the true facts.

(c) The duties stated in paragraphs (a) and (b) continue until remedial legal measures are no longer reasonably possible.

Adopted by order of Oct. 17, 1989, eff. Jan. 1, 1990.

Comment:

1. The advocate's task is to present the client's case with persuasive force. Performance of that duty while maintaining confidences of the client is qualified by the advocate's duty of candor to the tribunal.

Factual Representations by a Lawyer

2. An advocate is responsible for pleadings and other documents prepared for litigation, but is usually not required to have personal knowledge of matters asserted therein, for litigation documents ordinarily present assertions by the client, or by someone on the client's behalf, and not assertions by the lawyer. Compare Rule 3.01. However, an assertion purporting to be on the lawyer's own knowledge, as in an affidavit by the lawyer or a representation of fact in open court, may properly be made only when the lawyer knows the assertion is true or believes it to be true on the basis of a reasonably diligent inquiry. There are circumstances where failure to make a disclosure is the equivalent of an affirmative misrepresentation. The obligation prescribed in Rule 1.02(c) not to counsel a client to commit or

assist the client in committing a fraud applies in litigation. See the Comments to Rules 1.02(c) and 8.04(a).

Misleading Legal Argument

3. Legal argument based on a knowingly false representation of law constitutes dishonesty toward the tribunal. A lawyer is not required to make a disinterested exposition of the law, but should recognize the existence of pertinent legal authorities. Furthermore, as stated in paragraph (a)(4), an advocate has a duty to disclose directly adverse authority in the controlling jurisdiction which has not been disclosed by the opposing party. The underlying concept is that legal argument is a discussion seeking to determine the legal premises properly applicable to the case.

Ex Parte Proceedings

4. Ordinarily, an advocate has the limited responsibility of presenting one side of the matters that a tribunal should consider in reaching a decision; the conflicting position is expected to be presented by the opposing party. However, in an ex parte proceeding, such as an application for a temporary restraining order, there is no balance of presentation by opposing advocates. The object of an ex parte proceeding is nevertheless to yield a substantially just result. The judge has an affirmative responsibility to accord the absent party just consideration. The lawyer for the represented party has the correlative duty to make disclosures of unprivileged material facts known to the lawyer if the lawyer reasonably believes the tribunal will not reach a just decision unless informed of those facts.

Anticipated False Evidence

5. On occasion a lawyer may be asked to place into evidence testimony or other material that the lawyer knows to be false. Initially in such situations, a lawyer should urge the client or other person involved to not offer false or fabricated evidence. However, whether such evidence is provided by the client or by another person, the lawyer must refuse to offer it, regardless of the client's wishes. As to a lawyer's right to refuse to offer testimony or other evidence that the lawyer believes is false, see paragraph 15 of this Comment.

6. If the request to place false testimony or other material into evidence came from the lawyer's client, the lawyer also would be justified in seeking to withdraw from the case. See Rules 1.15(a)(1) and (b)(2), (4). If withdrawal is allowed by the tribunal, the lawyer may be authorized under Rule 1.05(c)(7) to reveal the reasons for that withdrawal to any other lawyer subsequently retained by the client in the matter; but normally that rule would not allow the lawyer to reveal that information to another person or to the tribunal. If the lawyer either chooses not to withdraw or is not allowed to do so by the tribunal, the lawyer should again urge the client not to offer false testimony or other evidence and advise the client of the steps the lawyer will take if such false evidence is offered. Even though the lawyer does not receive satisfactory assurances that the client or other witness will testify truthfully as to a particular matter, the lawyer may use that person as a witness as to other matters that the lawyer believes will not result in perjured testimony.

Past False Evidence

7. It is possible, however, that a lawyer will place testimony or other material into evidence and only later learn of its falsity. When such testimony or other evidence is offered by the client, problems arise between the lawyer's duty to keep the client's revelations confidential and the lawyer's duty of candor to the tribunal. Under this Rule, upon ascertaining that material testimony or other evidence is false, the lawyer must first seek to persuade the client to correct the false testimony or to withdraw the false evidence. If the persuasion is ineffective, the lawyer must take additional remedial measures.

8. When a lawyer learns that the lawyer's services have been improperly utilized in a civil case to place false testimony or other material into evidence, the rule generally recognized is that the lawyer must disclose the existence of the deception to the court or to the other party, if necessary rectify the deception. See paragraph (b) and Rule 1.05(h). See also Rule 1.05(g). Such a disclosure can result in grave consequences to the client, including not only a sense of betrayal by the lawyer but also loss of the case and perhaps a prosecution for perjury. But the alternative is that the lawyer would be aiding in the deception of the tribunal or jury, thereby subverting the truth-finding process which the adversary system is designed to implement. See Rule 1.02(c). Furthermore, unless it is clearly understood that the lawyer will act upon the duty to disclose the existence of false evidence, the client can simply reject the lawyer's advice to reveal the false evidence and insist that the lawyer keep silent. Thus the client could in effect coerce the lawyer into being a party to fraud on the court.

Perjury by a Criminal Defendant

9. Whether an advocate for a criminally accused has the same duty of disclosure has been intensely debated. While it is agreed that in such cases, as in others, the lawyer should seek to persuade the client to refrain from suborning or offering perjurious testimony or other false evidence, there has been dispute concerning the lawyer's duty when that persuasion fails. If the confrontation with the client occurs before trial, the lawyer ordinarily can withdraw. Withdrawal before trial may not be possible, however, either because trial is imminent, or because the confrontation with the client does not take place until the trial itself, or because no other counsel is available.

10. The proper resolution of the lawyer's dilemma in criminal cases is complicated by two considerations. The first is the substantial penalties that a criminal accused will face upon conviction, and the lawyer's resulting reluctance to impair any defenses the accused wishes to offer on his own behalf having any possible basis in fact. The second is the right of a defendant to take the stand should he so desire, even over the objections of the lawyer. Consequently, in any criminal case where the accused either insists on testifying when the lawyer knows that the testimony is perjurious or else surprises the lawyer with such testimony at trial, the lawyer's effort to rectify the situation can increase the likelihood of the client's being convicted as well as opening the possibility of a prosecution for perjury. On the other hand, if the lawyer does not exercise control over the proof, the lawyer participates, although in a merely passive way, in deception of the court.

11. Three resolutions of this dilemma have been proposed. One is to permit the accused to testify by a narrative without guidance through the lawyer's questioning. This compromises both contending principles; it exempts the lawyer from the duty to disclose false evidence but subjects the client to an implicit disclosure of information imparted to counsel. Another suggested resolution is that the advocate be entirely excused from the duty to reveal perjury if the perjury is that of the client. This solution, however, makes the advocate a knowing instrument of perjury.

12. The other resolution of the dilemma, and the one this Rule adopts, is that the lawyer must take reasonable remedial measure which may include revealing the client's perjury. A criminal accused has a right to the assistance of an advocate, a right to testify and a right of confidential communication with counsel. However, an accused should not have a right to assistance of counsel in committing perjury. Furthermore, an advocate has an obligation, not only in professional ethics but under the law as well, to avoid implication in the commission of perjury or other falsification of evidence.

False Evidence Not Introduced by the Lawyer

13. A lawyer may have introduced the testimony of a client or other witness who testified truthfully under direct examination but who offered false testimony or other evidence during examination by another party. Although the lawyer should urge that the false evidence be corrected or withdrawn, the full range of obligation imposed by paragraphs (a)(5) and (b) of this Rule do not apply to such situations. A subsequent use of that false testimony or other evidence by the lawyer in support of the client's case, however, would violate paragraph (a)(5).

Duration of Obligation

14. The time limit on the obligation to rectify the presentation of false testimony or other evidence varies from case to case but continues as long as there is a reasonable possibility of taking corrective legal actions before a tribunal.

Refusing to Offer Proof Believed to be False

15. A lawyer may refuse to offer evidence that the lawyer reasonably believes is untrustworthy, even if the lawyer does not know that the evidence is false. That discretion should be exercised cautiously, however, in order not to impair the legitimate interests of the client. Where a client wishes to have such suspect evidence introduced, generally the lawyer should do so and allow the finder of fact to assess its probative value. A lawyer's obligations under paragraphs (a)(2), (a)(5) and (b) of this Rule are not triggered by the introduction of testimony or other evidence that is believed by the lawyer to be false, but not known to be so.

Rule 3.04. Fairness in Adjudicatory Proceedings

A lawyer shall not:

(a) unlawfully obstruct another party's access to evidence; in anticipation of a dispute unlawfully alter, destroy or conceal a document or other material that a competent lawyer would believe has potential or actual evidentiary value; or counsel or assist another person to do any such act.

(b) falsify evidence, counsel or assist a witness to testify falsely, or pay, offer to pay, or acquiesce in the offer or payment of compensation to a witness or other entity contingent upon the content of the testimony of the witness or the outcome of the case. But a lawyer may advance, guarantee, or acquiesce in the payment of:

(1) expenses reasonably incurred by a witness in attending or testifying;

(2) reasonable compensation to a witness for his loss of time in attending or testifying;

(3) a reasonable fee for the professional services of an expert witness.

(c) except as stated in paragraph (d), in representing a client before a tribunal:

(1) habitually violate an established rule of procedure or of evidence;

(2) state or allude to any matter that the lawyer does not reasonably believe is relevant to such proceeding or that will not be supported by admissible evidence, or assert personal knowledge of facts in issue except when testifying as a witness;

(3) state a personal opinion as to the justness of a cause, the credibility of a witness, the culpability of a civil litigant or the guilt or innocence of an accused, except that a lawyer may argue on his analysis of the evidence and other permissible considerations for any position or conclusion with respect to the matters stated herein;

(4) ask any question intended to degrade a witness or other person except where the lawyer reasonably believes that the question will lead to relevant and admissible evidence; or

(5) engage in conduct intended to disrupt the proceedings.

(d) knowingly disobey, or advise the client to disobey, an obligation under the standing rules of or a ruling by a tribunal except for an open refusal based either on an assertion that no valid obligation exists or on the client's willingness to accept any sanctions arising from such disobedience.

(e) request a person other than a client to refrain from voluntarily giving relevant information to another party unless:

(1) the person is a relative or an employee or other agent of a client; and

(2) the lawyer reasonably believes that the person's interests will not be adversely affected by refraining from giving such information.

Adopted by order of Oct. 17, 1989, eff. Jan. 1, 1990.

Comment:

1. The procedure of the adversary system contemplates that the evidence in a case is to be marshalled competitively by the contending parties. Fair competition in the adversary system is secured by prohibitions against destruction or concealment of evidence, improperly influencing witnesses, obstructive tactics in discovery procedures, and the like.

2. Documents and other evidence are often essential to establish a claim or defense. The right of a party, including the government, to obtain evidence through discovery or subpoena is an important procedural right. The exercise of that right can be frustrated if relevant material is altered, concealed or destroyed. Applicable law in many jurisdictions, including Texas, makes it an offense to destroy material for the purpose of impairing its availability in a pending

proceeding or one whose commencement can be foreseen. See Texas Penal Code, §§ 37.09(a)(1), 37.10(a)(3). See also 18 U.S.C. §§ 1501–1515. Falsifying evidence is also generally a criminal offense. *Id.* §§ 37.09(a)(2), 37.10(a)(1), (2). Paragraph (a) of this Rule applies to evidentiary material generally, including computerized information.

3. Paragraph (c)(1) subjects a lawyer to discipline only for habitual abuses of procedural or evidentiary rules, including those relating to the discovery process. That position was adopted in order to employ the superior ability of the presiding tribunal to assess the merits of such disputes and to avoid inappropriate resort to disciplinary proceedings as a means of furthering tactical litigation objectives. A lawyer in good conscience should not engage in even a single intentional violation of those rules, however, and a lawyer may be subject to judicial sanctions for doing so.

4. Paragraph (c) restates the traditional Texas position regarding the proper role of argument and comment in litigation. The obligations imposed by that paragraph to avoid seeking to influence the outcome of a matter by introducing irrelevant or improper considerations into the deliberative process are important aspects of a lawyer's duty to maintain the fairness and impartiality of adjudicatory proceedings.

5. By the same token, the advocate's function is to present evidence and argument so that the cause may be decided according to law. Refraining from abusive or disruptive conduct is a corollary of the advocate's right to speak on behalf of litigants. A lawyer may stand firm against abuse by a tribunal but should avoid reciprocation.

6. Paragraph (d) prohibits the practice of a lawyer not disclosing a client's actual or intended noncompliance with a standing rule or particular ruling of an adjudicatory body or official to other concerned entities. It provides instead that a lawyer must openly acknowledge the client's noncompliance.

7. Paragraph (d) also prohibits a lawyer from disobeying, or advising a client to disobey, any such obligations unless either of two circumstances exists. The first is the lawyer's open refusal based on an assertion that no valid obligation exists. In order to assure due regard for formal rulings and standing rules of practice or procedure, the lawyer's assertion in this regard should be based on a reasonable belief. The second circumstance is that a lawyer may acquiesce in a client's position that the sanctions arising from noncompliance are preferable to the costs of compliance. This situation can arise in criminal cases, for example, where the court orders disclosure of the identity of an informant to the defendant and the government decides that it would prefer to allow the case to be dismissed rather than to make that disclosure. A lawyer should consult with a client about the likely consequences of any such act of disobedience should the client appear to be inclined to pursue that course; but the final decision in that regard rests with the client.

Rule 3.05. Maintaining Impartiality of Tribunal

A lawyer shall not:

(a) seek to influence a tribunal concerning a pending matter by means prohibited by law or applicable rules of practice or procedure;

(b) except as otherwise permitted by law and not prohibited by applicable rules of practice or procedure, communicate or cause another to communicate ex parte with a tribunal for the purpose of influencing that entity or person concerning a pending matter other than:

(1) in the course of official proceedings in the cause;

(2) in writing if he promptly delivers a copy of the writing to opposing counsel or the adverse party if he is not represented by a lawyer;

(3) orally upon adequate notice to opposing counsel or to the adverse party if he is not represented by a lawyer.

(c) For purposes of this rule:

(1) "Matter" has the meanings ascribed by it in Rule 1.10(f) of these Rules;

(2) A matter is "pending" before a particular tribunal either when that entity has been selected to determine the matter or when it is reasonably foreseeable that that entity will be so selected.

Adopted by order of Oct. 17, 1989, eff. Jan. 1, 1990.

Comment:

Undue Influence

1. Many forms of improper influence upon tribunals are proscribed by criminal law or by applicable rules of practice or procedure. Others are specified in the Texas Code of Judicial Conduct. A lawyer is required to be familiar with, and to avoid contributing to a violation of, all such provisions. See also Rule 3.06.

2. In recent years, however, there has been an increase in alternative methods of dispute resolution, such as arbitration, for which the standards governing a lawyer's conduct are not as well developed. In such situations, as in more traditional settings, a lawyer should avoid any conduct that is or could reasonably be construed as being intended to corrupt or to unfairly influence the decision-maker.

Ex Parte Contacts

3. Historically, ex parte contacts between a lawyer and a tribunal have been subjected to stringent control because of the potential for abuse such contacts present. For example, Canon 3A(4) of the Texas Code of Judicial Conduct prohibits many ex parte contacts with judicial officials. A lawyer in turn violates Rule 8.04(a)(6) by communicating with such an official in a manner that causes that official to violate Canon 3A(4). This rule maintains that traditional posture towards ex parte communications and extends it to the new settings discussed in paragraph 2 of this Comment.

4. There are certain types of adjudicatory proceedings, however, which have permitted pending issues to be discussed ex parte with a tribunal. Certain classes of zoning questions, for example, are frequently handled in that way. As long as such contacts are not prohibited by law or applicable rules of practice and procedure, and as long as paragraph (a) of this Rule is adhered to, such ex parte contacts will not serve as a basis for discipline.

5. For limitations on the circumstances and the manner in which lawyers may communicate or cause another to communicate with veniremen or jurors, see Rule 3.06.

Rule 3.06. Maintaining Integrity of Jury System

(a) A lawyer shall not:

(1) conduct or cause another, by financial support or otherwise, to conduct a vexatious or harassing investigation of a venireman or juror; or

(2) seek to influence a venireman or juror concerning the merits of a pending matter by means prohibited by law or applicable rules of practice or procedure.

(b) Prior to discharge of the jury from further consideration of a matter, a lawyer connected therewith shall not communicate with or cause another to communicate with anyone he knows to be a member of the venire from which the jury will be selected or any juror or alternate juror, except in the course of official proceedings.

(c) During the trial of a case, a lawyer not connected therewith shall not communicate with or cause another to communicate with a juror or alternate juror concerning the matter.

(d) After discharge of the jury from further consideration of a matter with which the lawyer was connected, the lawyer shall not ask questions of or make comments to a member of that jury that are calculated merely to harass or embarrass the juror or to influence his actions in future jury service.

(e) All restrictions imposed by this Rule upon a lawyer also apply to communications with or investigations of members of a family of a venireman or a juror.

(f) A lawyer shall reveal promptly to the court improper conduct by a venireman or a juror, or by another toward a venireman or a juror or a member of his family, of which the lawyer has knowledge.

(g) As used in this Rule, the terms "matter" and "pending" have the meanings specified in Rule 3.05(c).

Adopted by order of Oct. 17, 1989, eff. Jan. 1, 1990.

Comment:

1. To safeguard the impartiality that is essential to the judicial process, veniremen and jurors should be protected against extraneous influences. When impartiality is present, public confidence in the judicial system is enhanced. There should be no extrajudicial communication with veniremen prior to trial or with jurors during trial or on behalf of a lawyer connected with the case. Furthermore, a lawyer who is not connected with the case should not communicate with or cause another to communicate with a venireman or a juror about the case. After the trial, communication by a lawyer with jurors is not prohibited by this Rule so long as he refrains from asking questions or making comments that tend to harass or embarrass the juror or to influence actions of the juror in future cases. Contacts with discharged jurors, however, are governed by procedural rules the violation of which could subject a lawyer to discipline under Rule 3.04. When an extrajudicial communication by a lawyer with a juror is permitted by law, it should be made considerately and with deference to the personal feelings of the juror.

2. Vexatious or harassing investigations of jurors seriously impair the effectiveness of our jury system. For this reason, a lawyer or anyone on his behalf who conducts an investigation of veniremen or jurors should act with circumspection and restraint.

3. Communications with or investigations of members of families of veniremen or jurors by a lawyer or by anyone on his behalf are subject to the restrictions imposed upon the lawyer with respect to his communications with or investigations of veniremen and jurors.

4. Because of the extremely serious nature of any actions that threaten the integrity of the jury system, a lawyer who learns of improper conduct by or towards a venireman, a juror, or a member of the family of either should make a prompt report to the court regarding such conduct. If such improper actions were taken by or on behalf of a lawyer, either the reporting lawyer or the court normally should initiate appropriate disciplinary proceedings. See Rules 1.05, 8.03, 8.04.

Rule 3.07. Trial Publicity

(a) In the course of representing a client, a lawyer shall not make an extrajudicial statement that a reasonable person would expect to be disseminated by means of public communication if the lawyer knows or reasonably should know that it will have a substantial likelihood of materially prejudicing an adjudicatory proceeding. A lawyer shall not counsel or assist another person to make such a statement.

(b) A lawyer ordinarily will violate paragraph (a), and the likelihood of a violation increases if the adjudication is ongoing or imminent, by making an extrajudicial statement of the type referred to in that paragraph when the statement refers to:

(1) the character, credibility, reputation or criminal record of a party, suspect in a criminal investigation or witness; or the expected testimony of a party or witness;

(2) in a criminal case or proceeding that could result in incarceration, the possibility of a plea of guilty to the offense; the existence or contents of any confession, admission, or statement given by a defendant or suspect; or that person's refusal or failure to make a statement;

(3) the performance, refusal to perform, or results of any examination or test; the refusal or failure of a person to allow or submit to an examination or test; or the identity or nature of physical evidence expected to be presented;

(4) any opinion as to the guilt or innocence of a defendant or suspect in a criminal case or proceeding that could result in incarceration; or

(5) information the lawyer knows or reasonably should know is likely to be inadmissible as evidence

in a trial and would if disclosed create a substantial risk of prejudicing an impartial trial.

(c) A lawyer ordinarily will not violate paragraph (a) by making an extrajudicial statement of the type referred to in that paragraph when the lawyer merely states:

(1) the general nature of the claim or defense;

(2) the information contained in a public record;

(3) that an investigation of the matter is in progress, including the general scope of the investigation, the offense, claim or defense involved;

(4) except when prohibited by law, the identity of the persons involved in the matter;

(5) the scheduling or result of any step in litigation;

(6) a request for assistance in obtaining evidence, and information necessary thereto;

(7) a warning of danger concerning the behavior of a person involved, when there is a reason to believe that there exists the likelihood of substantial harm to an individual or to the public interest; and

(8) if a criminal case:

(i) the identity, residence, occupation and family status of the accused;

(ii) if the accused has not been apprehended, information necessary to aid in apprehension of that person;

(iii) the fact, time and place of arrest; and

(iv) the identity of investigating and arresting officers or agencies and the length of the investigation.

Adopted by order of Oct. 17, 1989, eff. Jan. 1, 1990. Amended by order of June 15, 1994, eff. Oct. 1, 1994.

Comment:

1. Paragraph (a) is premised on the idea that preserving the right to a fair trial necessarily entails some curtailment of the information that may be disseminated about a party prior to trial. This is particularly so where trial by jury or lay judge is involved. If there were no such limits, the results would be the practical nullification of the protective effect of the rules of forensic decorum and the exclusionary rules of evidence. Thus, paragraph (a) provides that in the course of representing a client, a lawyer's right to free speech is subordinate to the constitutional requirements of a fair trial. On the other hand, there are vital social interests served by the free dissemination of information about events having legal consequences and about legal proceedings themselves. The public has a right to know about threats to its safety and measures aimed at assuring its security. It also has a legitimate interest in the conduct of judicial proceedings, particularly in matters of general public concern. Furthermore, the subject matter of legal proceedings is often of direct significance in debate and deliberation over questions of public policy.

2. Because no body of rules can simultaneously satisfy all interests of fair trial and all those of free expression, some balancing of those interests is required. It is difficult to strike that balance. The formula embodied in this Rule, prohibiting those extrajudicial statements that the lawyer knows or reasonably should know have a reasonable likelihood of materially prejudicing an adjudicatory proceeding, is intended to incorporate the degree of concern for the first amendment rights of lawyers, listeners, and the media necessary to pass constitutional muster. The obligations imposed upon a lawyer by this Rule are subordinate to those rights. If a particular statement would be inappropriate for a lawyer to make, however, the lawyer is as readily subject to discipline for counseling or assisting another person to make it as he or she would be for doing so directly. See paragraph (a).

3. The existence of "material prejudice" normally depends on the circumstances in which a particular statement is made. For example, an otherwise objectionable statement may be excusable if reasonably calculated to counter the unfair prejudicial effect of another public statement. Applicable constitutional principles require that the disciplinary standard in this area retain the flexibility needed to take such unique considerations into account.

4. Although they are not standards of discipline, paragraphs (b) and (c) seek to give some guidance concerning what types of statements are or are not apt to violate paragraph (a). Paragraph (b) sets forth conditions under which statements of the types listed in subparagraphs (b)(1) through (5) would likely violate paragraph (a) in the absence of exceptional extenuating circumstances. Paragraph (c), on the other hand, describes statements that are unlikely to violate paragraph (a) in the absence of exceptional aggravating circumstances. Neither paragraph (b) nor paragraph (c) is an exhaustive listing.

5. Special rules of confidentiality may validly govern proceedings in juvenile, domestic relations and mental disability proceedings, and perhaps other types of litigation. Rule 3.04(c)(1) and (d) govern a lawyer's duty with respect to such Rules. Frequently, a lawyer's obligations to the client under Rule 1.05 also will prevent the disclosure of confidential information.

Rule 3.08. Lawyer as Witness

(a) A lawyer shall not accept or continue employment as an advocate before a tribunal in a contemplated or pending adjudicatory proceeding if the lawyer knows or believes that the lawyer is or may be a witness necessary to establish an essential fact on behalf of the lawyer's client, unless:

(1) the testimony relates to an uncontested issue;

(2) the testimony will relate solely to a matter of formality and there is no reason to believe that substantial evidence will be offered in opposition to the testimony;

(3) the testimony relates to the nature and value of legal services rendered in the case;

(4) the lawyer is a party to the action and is appearing pro se; or

(5) the lawyer has promptly notified opposing counsel that the lawyer expects to testify in the matter and disqualification of the lawyer would work substantial hardship on the client.

(b) A lawyer shall not continue as an advocate in a pending adjudicatory proceeding if the lawyer believes that the lawyer will be compelled to furnish testimony that will be substantially adverse to the lawyer's client, unless the client consents after full disclosure.

(c) Without the client's informed consent, a lawyer may not act as advocate in an adjudicatory proceeding in which another lawyer in the lawyer's firm is prohibited by paragraphs (a) or (b) from serving as advocate. If the lawyer to be called as a witness could not also serve as an advocate under this Rule, that lawyer shall not take an active role before the tribunal in the presentation of the matter.

Adopted by order of Oct. 17, 1989, eff. Jan. 1, 1990. Amended by order of June 15, 1994, eff. Oct. 1, 1994.

Comment:

1. A lawyer who is considering accepting or continuing employment in a contemplated or pending adjudicatory proceeding in which that lawyer knows or believes that he or she may be a necessary witness is obligated by this Rule to consider the possible consequences of those dual roles for both the lawyer's own client and for opposing parties.

2. One important variable in this context is the anticipated tenor of the lawyer's testimony. If that testimony will be substantially adverse to the client, paragraphs (b) and (c) provide the governing standard. In other situations, paragraphs (a) and (c) control.

3. A lawyer who is considering both representing a client in an adjudicatory proceeding and serving as a witness in that proceeding may possess information pertinent to the representation that would be substantially adverse to the client were it to be disclosed. A lawyer who believes that he or she will be compelled to furnish testimony concerning such matters should not continue to act as an advocate for his or her client except with the client's informed consent, because of the substantial likelihood that such adverse testimony would damage the lawyer's ability to represent the client effectively.

4. In all other circumstances, the principal concern over allowing a lawyer to serve as both an advocate and witness for a client is the possible confusion that those dual roles could create for the finder of fact. Normally those dual roles are unlikely to create exceptional difficulties when the lawyer's testimony is limited to the areas set out in sub-paragraphs (a)(1)–(4) of this Rule. If, however, the lawyer's testimony concerns a controversial or contested matter, combining the roles of advocate and witness can unfairly prejudice the opposing party. A witness is required to testify on the basis of personal knowledge, while an advocate is expected to explain and comment on evidence given by others. It may not be clear whether a statement by an advocate-witness should be taken as proof or as an analysis of the proof.

5. Paragraph (a)(1) recognizes that if the testimony will be uncontested, the ambiguities in the dual role are purely theoretical. Paragraph (a)(2) recognizes that similar considerations apply if a lawyer's testimony relates solely to a matter of formality and there is no reason to believe that substantial opposing evidence will be offered. In each of those situations requiring the involvement of another lawyer would be a costly procedure that would serve no significant countervailing purpose.

6. Sub-paragraph (a)(3) recognizes that where the testimony concerns the extent and value of legal services rendered in the action in which the testimony is offered, permitting the lawyers to testify avoids the need for a second trial with new counsel to resolve that issue. Moreover, in such a situation the judge has firsthand knowledge of the matter in issue; hence, there is less dependence on the adversary process to test the credibility of the testimony. Sub-paragraph (a)(4) makes it clear that this Rule is not intended to affect a lawyer's right to self representation.

7. Apart from these four exceptions, sub-paragraph (a)(5) recognizes an additional exception based upon a balancing of the interests of the client and those of the opposing party. In implementing this exception, it is relevant that one or both parties could reasonably foresee that the lawyer would probably be a witness. For example, sub-paragraph (a)(5) requires that a lawyer relying on that sub-paragraph as a basis for serving as both an advocate and a witness for a party give timely notification of that fact to opposing counsel. That requirement serves two purposes. First, it prevents the testifying lawyer from creating a "substantial hardship," where none once existed, by virtue of a lengthy representation of the client in the matter at hand. Second, it puts opposing parties on notice of the situation, thus enabling them to make any desired response at the earliest opportunity.

8. This rule does not prohibit the lawyer who may or will be a witness from participating in the preparation of a matter for presentation to a tribunal. To minimize the possibility of unfair prejudice to an opposing party, however, the Rule prohibits any testifying lawyer who could not serve as an advocate from taking an active role before the tribunal in the presentation of the matter. See paragraph (c). Even in those situations, however, another lawyer in the testifying lawyer's firm may act as an advocate, provided the client's informed consent is obtained.

9. Rule 3.08 sets out a disciplinary standard and is not well suited to use as a standard for procedural disqualification. As a disciplinary rule it serves two principal purposes. The first is to insure that a client's case is not compromised by being represented by a lawyer who could be a more effective witness for the client by not also serving as an advocate. See paragraph (a). The second is to insure that a client is not burdened by counsel who may have to offer testimony that is substantially adverse to the client's cause. See paragraph (b).

10. This Rule may furnish some guidance in those procedural disqualification disputes where the party seeking disqualification can demonstrate actual prejudice to itself resulting from the opposing lawyer's service in the dual roles. However, it should not be used as a tactical weapon to deprive the opposing party of the right to be represented by the lawyer of his or her choice. For example, a lawyer should not seek to disqualify an opposing lawyer under this Rule merely because the opposing lawyer's dual roles may involve an improper conflict of interest with respect to the opposing lawyer's client, for that is a matter to be resolved between lawyer and client or in a subsequent disciplinary proceeding. Likewise, a lawyer should not seek to disqualify an opposing lawyer by unnecessarily calling that lawyer as a witness. Such unintended applications of this Rule, if allowed, would subvert its true purpose by converting it into a mere tactical weapon in litigation.

Rule 3.09. Special Responsibilities of a Prosecutor

The prosecutor in a criminal case shall:

(a) refrain from prosecuting or threatening to prosecute a charge that the prosecutor knows is not supported by probable cause;

(b) refrain from conducting or assisting in a custodial interrogation of an accused unless the prosecutor has made reasonable efforts to be assured that the accused has been advised of any right to, and the procedure for obtaining, counsel and has been given reasonable opportunity to obtain counsel;

(c) not initiate or encourage efforts to obtain from an unrepresented accused a waiver of important pretrial, trial or post-trial rights;

(d) make timely disclosure to the defense of all evidence or information known to the prosecutor that tends to negate the guilt of the accused or mitigates the offense, and, in connection with sentencing, disclose to the defense and to the tribunal all unprivileged mitigating information known to the prosecutor, except when the prosecutor is relieved of this responsibility by a protective order of the tribunal; and

(e) exercise reasonable care to prevent persons employed or controlled by the prosecutor in a criminal case from making an extrajudicial statement that the prosecutor would be prohibited from making under Rule 3.07.

Adopted by order of Oct. 17, 1989, eff. Jan. 1, 1990.

Comment:

Source and Scope of Obligations

1. A prosecutor has the responsibility to see that justice is done, and not simply to be an advocate. This responsibility carries with it a number of specific obligations. Among these is to see that no person is threatened with or subjected to the rigors of a criminal prosecution without good cause. See paragraph (a). In addition a prosecutor should not initiate or exploit any violation of a suspect's right to counsel, nor should he initiate or encourage efforts to obtain waivers of important pretrial, trial or post-trial rights from unrepresented persons. See paragraphs (b) and (c). In addition, a prosecutor is obliged to see that the defendant is accorded procedural justice, that the defendant's guilt is decided upon the basis of sufficient evidence, and that any sentence imposed is based on all unprivileged information known to the prosecutor. See paragraph (d). Finally, a prosecutor is obliged by this rule to take reasonable measures to see that persons employed or controlled by him refrain from making extrajudicial statements that are prejudicial to the accused. See paragraph (e) and Rule 3.07. See also Rule 3.03(a)(3), governing ex parte proceedings, among which grand jury proceedings are included. Applicable law may require other measures by the prosecutor and knowing disregard of those obligations or a systematic abuse of prosecutorial discretion could constitute a violation of Rule 8.04.

2. Paragraph (a) does not apply to situations where the prosecutor is using a grand jury to determine whether any crime has been committed, nor does it prevent a prosecutor from presenting a matter to a grand jury even though he has some doubt as to what charge, if any, the grand jury may decide is appropriate, as long as he believes that the grand jury could reasonably conclude that some charge is proper. A prosecutor's obligations under that paragraph are satisfied by the return of a true bill by a grand jury, unless the prosecutor believes that material inculpatory information presented to the grand jury was false.

3. Paragraph (b) does not forbid the lawful questioning of any person who has knowingly, intelligently and voluntarily waived the rights to counsel and to silence, nor does it forbid such questioning of any unrepresented person who has not stated that he wishes to retain a lawyer and who is not entitled to appointed counsel. See also Rule 4.03.

4. Paragraph (c) does not apply to any person who has knowingly, intelligently and voluntarily waived the rights referred to therein in open court, nor does it apply to any person appearing pro se with the approval of the tribunal. Finally, that paragraph does not forbid a prosecutor from advising an unrepresented accused who has not stated he wishes to retain a lawyer and who is not entitled to appointed counsel and who has indicated in open court that he wishes to plead guilty to charges against him of his pre-trial, trial and post-trial rights, provided that the advice given is accurate; that it is undertaken with the knowledge and approval of the court; and that such a practice is not otherwise prohibited by law or applicable rules of practice or procedure.

5. The exception in paragraph (d) recognizes that a prosecutor may seek an appropriate protective order from the tribunal if disclosure of information to the defense could result in substantial harm to an individual or to the public interest.

6. Subparagraph (e) does not subject a prosecutor to discipline for failing to take measures to prevent investigators, law enforcement personnel or other persons assisting or associated with the prosecutor, but not in his employ or under his control, from making extrajudicial statements that the prosecutor would be prohibited from making under Rule 3.07. To the extent feasible, however, the prosecutor should make reasonable efforts to discourage such persons from making statements of that kind.

Rule 3.10. Advocate in Nonadjudicative Proceedings

A lawyer representing a client before a legislative or administrative body in a nonadjudicative proceeding shall disclose that the appearance is in a representative capacity and shall conform to the provisions of Rules 3.04(a) through (d), 3.05(a), and 4.01.

Adopted by order of Oct. 17, 1989, eff. Jan. 1, 1990.

Comment:

1. In appearing before bodies such as legislatures, municipal councils, and executive and administrative agencies acting in a rule-making or policy-making capacity, lawyers present facts, formulate issues and advance argument in the matters under consideration. The decision-making body, like a court, should be able to rely on the integrity of the submissions made to it. A lawyer appearing before such a body should deal with the tribunal honestly and in conformity with applicable rules of procedure. A lawyer is required to disclose whether a particular appearance is in a representative capacity. Although not required to do so by Rule 3.10, a

lawyer should reveal the identities of the lawyer's clients, unless privileged or otherwise protected, so that the decision-making body can weigh the lawyer's presentation more accurately. See Rule 4.01, Comment 1.

2. Lawyers have no exclusive right to appear before nonadjudicative bodies, as they do before a court. The requirements of this Rule therefore may subject lawyers to regulations inapplicable to advocates who are not lawyers.

3. As to the representation of a client in a negotiation or other bilateral transaction with a governmental agency, see Rules 4.01 through 4.04.

IV. Non-Client Relationships

Rule 4.01. Truthfulness in Statements to Others

In the course of representing a client a lawyer shall not knowingly:

(a) make a false statement of material fact or law to a third person; or

(b) fail to disclose a material fact to a third person when disclosure is necessary to avoid making the lawyer a party to a criminal act or knowingly assisting a fraudulent act perpetrated by a client.

Adopted by order of Oct. 17, 1989, eff. Jan. 1, 1990.

Comment:

False Statements of Fact

1. Paragraph (a) of this Rule refers to statements of *material* fact. Whether a particular statement should be regarded as one of *material* fact can depend on the circumstances. For example, certain types of statements ordinarily are not taken as statements of material fact because they are viewed as matters of opinion or conjecture. Estimates of price or value placed on the subject of a transaction are in this category. Similarly, under generally accepted conventions in negotiation, a party's supposed intentions as to an acceptable settlement of a claim may be viewed merely as negotiating positions rather than as accurate representation of material fact. Likewise, according to commercial conventions, the fact that a particular transaction is being undertaken on behalf of an undisclosed principal need not be disclosed except where non-disclosure of the principal would constitute fraud.

2. A lawyer violates paragraph (a) of this Rule either by making a false statement of law or material fact or by incorporating or affirming such a statement made by another person. Such statements will violate this Rule, however, only if the lawyer knows they are false and intends thereby to mislead. As to a lawyer's duty to decline or terminate representation in such situations, see Rule 1.15.

Failure to Disclose a Material Fact

3. Paragraph (b) of this Rule also relates only to failures to disclose *material* facts. Generally, in the course of representing a client a lawyer has no duty to inform a third person of relevant or material facts, except as required by law or by applicable rules of practice or procedure, such as formal discovery. However, a lawyer must not allow fidelity to a client to become a vehicle for a criminal act or a fraud being perpetrated by that client. Consequently a lawyer must disclose a material fact to a third party if the lawyer knows that the client is perpetrating a crime or a fraud and the lawyer knows that disclosure is necessary to prevent the lawyer from becoming a party to that crime or fraud. Failure to disclose under such circumstances is misconduct only if the lawyer intends thereby to mislead.

4. When a lawyer discovers that a client has committed a criminal or fraudulent act in the course of which the lawyer's services have been used, or that the client is committing or intends to commit any criminal or fraudulent act, other of these Rules require the lawyer to urge the client to take appropriate action. See Rules 1.02(d), (e), (f); 3.03(b). Since the disclosures called for by paragraph (b) of this Rule will be "necessary" only if the lawyer's attempts to counsel his client not to commit the crime or fraud are unsuccessful, a lawyer is not authorized to make them without having first undertaken those other remedial actions. See also Rule 1.05.

Fraud by a Client

5. A lawyer should never knowingly assist a client in the commission of a criminal act or a fraudulent act. See Rule 1.02(c).

6. This rule governs a lawyer's conduct during "the course of representing a client." If the lawyer has terminated representation prior to learning of a client's intention to commit a criminal or fraudulent act, paragraph (b) of this Rule does not apply. See "Fraud" under TERMINOLOGY.

Rule 4.02. Communication with One Represented by Counsel

(a) In representing a client, a lawyer shall not communicate or cause or encourage another to communicate about the subject of the representation with a person, organization or entity of government the lawyer knows to be represented by another lawyer regarding that subject, unless the lawyer has the consent of the other lawyer or is authorized by law to do so.

(b) In representing a client a lawyer shall not communicate or cause another to communicate about the subject of representation with a person or organization a lawyer knows to be employed or retained for the purpose of conferring with or advising another lawyer about the subject of the representation, unless the lawyer has the consent of the other lawyer or is authorized by law to do so.

(c) For the purpose of this rule, "organization or entity of government" includes: (1) those persons presently having a managerial responsibility with an organization or entity of government that relates to the subject of the representation, or (2) those persons presently employed by such organization or entity and whose act or omission in connection with the subject of representation may make the organization or entity of government vicariously liable for such act or omission.

(d) When a person, organization, or entity of government that is represented by a lawyer in a matter seeks advice regarding that matter from another lawyer, the second lawyer is not prohibited by paragraph (a) from giving such advice without notifying or seeking consent of the first lawyer.

Adopted by order of Oct. 17, 1989, eff. Jan. 1, 1990.

Comment:

1. Paragraph (a) of this Rule is directed at efforts to circumvent the lawyer-client relationship existing between other persons, organizations or entities of government and their respective counsel. It prohibits communications that in form are between a lawyer's client and another person, organization or entity of government represented by counsel where, because of the lawyer's involvement in devising and controlling their content, such communication in substance are between the lawyer and the represented person, organization or entity of government.

2. Paragraph (a) does not, however, prohibit communication between a lawyer's client and persons, organizations, or entities of government represented by counsel, as long as the lawyer does not cause or encourage the communication without the consent of the lawyer for the other party. Consent may be implied as well as express, as, for example, where the communication occurs in the form of a private placement memorandum or similar document that obviously is intended for multiple recipients and that normally is furnished directly to persons, even if known to be represented by counsel. Similarly, that paragraph does not impose a duty on a lawyer to affirmatively discourage communication between the lawyer's client and other represented persons, organizations or entities of government. Furthermore, it does not prohibit client communications concerning matters outside the subject of the representation with any such person, organization, or entity of government. Finally, it does not prohibit a lawyer from furnishing a "second opinion" in a matter to one requesting such opinion, nor from discussing employment in the matter if requested to do so. But see Rule 7.02.

3. Paragraph (b) of this Rule provides that unless authorized by law, experts employed or retained by a lawyer for a particular matter should not be contacted by opposing counsel regarding that matter without the consent of the lawyer who retained them. However, certain governmental agents or employees such as police may be contacted due to their obligations to the public at large.

4. In the case of an organization or entity of government, this Rule prohibits communications by a lawyer for one party concerning the subject of the representation with persons having a managerial responsibility on behalf of the organization that relates to the subject of the representation and with those persons presently employed by such organization or entity whose act or omission may make the organization or entity vicariously liable for the matter at issue, without the consent of the lawyer for the organization or entity of government involved. This Rule is based on the presumption that such persons are so closely identified with the interests of the organization or entity of government that its lawyers will represent them as well. If, however, such an agent or employee is represented in the matter by his or her own counsel that presumption is inapplicable. In such cases, the consent by that counsel to communicate will be sufficient for purposes of this Rule. Compare Rule 3.04(f). Moreover, this Rule does not prohibit a lawyer from contacting a former employee of a represented organization or entity of a government, nor from contacting a person presently employed by such an organization or entity whose conduct is not a matter at issue but who might possess knowledge concerning the matter at issue.

Rule 4.03. Dealing With Unrepresented Person

In dealing on behalf of a client with a person who is not represented by counsel, a lawyer shall not state or imply that the lawyer is disinterested. When the lawyer knows or reasonably should know that the unrepresented person misunderstands the lawyer's role in the matter, the lawyer shall make reasonable efforts to correct the misunderstanding.

Adopted by order of Oct. 17, 1989, eff. Jan. 1, 1990.

Comment:

An unrepresented person, particularly one not experienced in dealing with legal matters, might assume that a lawyer is disinterested in loyalties or is a disinterested authority on the law even when the lawyer represents a client. During the course of a lawyer's representation of a client, the lawyer should not give advice to an unrepresented person other than the advice to obtain counsel. With regard to the special responsibilities of a prosecutor, see Rule 3.09.

Rule 4.04. Respect for Rights of Third Persons

(a) In representing a client, a lawyer shall not use means that have no substantial purpose other than to embarrass, delay, or burden a third person, or use methods of obtaining evidence that violate the legal rights of such a person.

(b) A lawyer shall not present, participate in presenting, or threaten to present:

(1) criminal or disciplinary charges solely to gain an advantage in a civil matter; or

(2) civil, criminal or disciplinary charges against a complainant, a witness, or a potential witness in a bar disciplinary proceeding solely to prevent participation by the complainant, witness or potential witness therein.

Adopted by order of Oct. 17, 1989, eff. Jan. 1, 1990.

Comment:

1. Although in most cases a lawyer's responsibility to the interest of his client is paramount to the interest of other persons, a lawyer should avoid the infliction of needless harm.

2. Using or threatening to use the criminal process solely to coerce a party in a private matter improperly suggests that the criminal process can be manipulated by private interests for personal gain. However, giving any notice required by law or applicable rules of practice or procedure as a prerequisite to instituting criminal charges does not violate this Rule, unless the underlying criminal charges were made without probable cause.

3. Using or threatening to use the civil, criminal, or disciplinary processes to coerce a complainant, a witness, or a

potential witness in a bar disciplinary proceeding is an implication that lawyers can manipulate the legal system to their personal advantage. Creating such false impressions is an abuse of the legal system that diminishes public confidence in the legal profession and in the fairness of the legal system as a whole.

V. Law Firms and Associations

Rule 5.01. Responsibilities of a Partner or Supervisory Lawyer

A lawyer shall be subject to discipline because of another lawyer's violation of these rules of professional conduct if:

(a) The lawyer is a partner or supervising lawyer and orders, encourages, or knowingly permits the conduct involved; or

(b) The lawyer is a partner in the law firm in which the other lawyer practices, is the general counsel of a government agency's legal department in which the other lawyer is employed, or has direct supervisory authority over the other lawyer, and with knowledge of the other lawyer's violation of these rules knowingly fails to take reasonable remedial action to avoid or mitigate the consequences of the other lawyer's violation.

Adopted by order of Oct. 17, 1989, eff. Jan. 1, 1990.

Comment:

1. Rule 5.01 conforms to the general principle that a lawyer is not vicariously subjected to discipline for the misconduct of another person. under Rule 8.04, a lawyer is subject to discipline if the lawyer knowingly assists or induces another to violate these rules. Rule 5.01(a) additionally provides that a partner or supervising lawyer is subject to discipline for ordering or encouraging another lawyer's violation of these rules. Moreover, a partner or supervising lawyer is in a position of authority over the work of other lawyers and the partner or supervising lawyer may be disciplined for permitting another lawyer to violate these rules.

2. Rule 5.01(b) likewise is concerned with the lawyer who is in a position of authority over another lawyer and who knows that the other lawyer has committed a violation of a rule of professional conduct. A partner in a law firm, the general counsel of a government agency's legal department, or a lawyer having direct supervisory authority over specific legal work by another lawyer, occupies the position of authority contemplated by Rule 5.01(b).

3. Whether a lawyer has "direct supervisory authority over the other lawyer" in particular circumstances is a question of fact. In some instances, a senior associate may be a supervising attorney.

4. The duty imposed upon the partner or other authoritative lawyer by Rule 5.01(b) is to take reasonable remedial action to avoid or mitigate the consequences of the other lawyer's known violation. Appropriate remedial action by a partner or other supervisory lawyer would depend on may factors, such as the immediacy of the partner's or supervisory lawyer's knowledge and involvement, the nature of the action that can reasonably be expected to avoid or mitigate injurious consequences, and the seriousness of the anticipated consequences. In some circumstances, it may be sufficient for a junior partner to refer the ethical problem directly to a designated senior partner or a management committee. A lawyer supervising a specific legal matter may be required to intervene more directly. For example if a supervising lawyer knows that a supervised lawyer misrepresented a matter to an opposing party in negotiation, the supervisor as well as the other lawyer may be required by Rule 5.01(b) to correct the resulting misapprehension.

5. Thus, neither Rule 5.01(a) nor Rule 5.01(b) visits vicarious disciplinary liability upon the lawyer in a position of authority. Rather, the lawyer in such authoritative position is exposed to discipline only for his or her own knowing actions or failures to act. Whether a lawyer may be liable civilly or criminally for another lawyer's conduct is a question of law beyond the scope of these rules.

6. Wholly aside from the dictates of these rules for discipline, a lawyer in a position of authority in a firm or government agency or over another lawyer should feel a moral compunction to make reasonable efforts to ensure that the office, firm, or agency has in effect appropriate procedural measures giving reasonable assurance that all lawyers in the office conform to these rules. This moral obligation, although not required by these rules, should fall also upon lawyers who have intermediate managerial responsibilities in the law department of an organization or government agency.

7. The measures that should be undertaken to give such reasonable assurance may depend on the structure of the firm or organization and upon the nature of the legal work performed. In a small firm, informal supervision and an occasional admonition ordinarily will suffice. In a large firm, or in practice situations where intensely difficult ethical problems frequently arise, more elaborate procedures may be called for in order to give such assurance. Obviously, the ethical atmosphere of a firm influences the conduct of all of its lawyers. Lawyers may rely also on continuing legal education in professional ethics to guard against unintentional misconduct by members of their firm or organization.

Rule 5.02. Responsibilities of a Supervised Lawyer

A lawyer is bound by these rules notwithstanding that the lawyer acted under the supervision of another person, except that a supervised lawyer does not violate these rules if that lawyer acts in accordance with a supervisory lawyer's reasonable resolution of an arguable question of professional conduct.

Adopted by order of Oct. 17, 1989, eff. Jan. 1, 1990.

Comment:

1. Rule 5.02 embodies the fundamental concept that every lawyer is a trained, mature, licensed professional who has sworn to uphold ethical standards and who is responsible for the lawyer's own conduct. Accordingly, a lawyer is not relieved from compliance with these rules because the lawyer acted under the supervision of an employer or other person. In some situations, the fact that a lawyer acted at the direction or order of another person may be relevant in determining whether the lawyer had the knowledge required

to render the conduct a violation of these rules. The fact of supervision may also, of course, be a circumstance to be considered by a grievance committee or court in mitigation of the penalty to be imposed for violation of a rule.

2. In many law firms and organizations, the relatively inexperienced lawyer works as an assistant to a more experienced lawyer or is directed, supervised or given guidance by an experienced lawyer in the firm. In the normal course of practice the senior lawyer has the responsibility for making the decisions involving professional judgment as to procedures to be taken, the status of the law, and the propriety of actions to be taken by the lawyers. Otherwise a consistent course of action could not be taken on behalf of clients. The junior lawyer reasonably can be expected to acquiesce in the decisions made by the senior lawyer unless the decision is clearly wrong.

3. Rule 5.02 take a realistic attitude toward those prevailing modes of practice by lawyers not engaged in solo practice. Accordingly, Rule 5.02 provides the supervised lawyer with a special defense in a disciplinary proceeding in which the lawyer is charged with having violated a rule of professional conduct. The supervised lawyer is entitled to this defense only if it appears that an arguable question of professional conduct was resolved by a supervising lawyer and that a resolution made by the supervising lawyer was a reasonable resolution. The resolution is a reasonable one, even if it is ultimately found to be officially unacceptable, provided it would have appeared reasonable to a disinterested, competent lawyer based on the information reasonably available to the supervising lawyer at the time the resolution was made. "Supervisory lawyer" as used in Rule 5.02 should be construed in conformity with prevailing modes of practice in firms and other groups and, therefore, should include a senior lawyer who undertakes to resolve the question of professional propriety as well as a lawyer who more directly supervises the supervised lawyer.

4. By providing such a defense to the supervised lawyer, Rule 5.02 recognizes that the inexperienced lawyer working under the direction or supervision of an employer or senior attorney is not in a favorable position to disagree with reasonable decisions made by the experienced lawyer. Often, the only choices available to the supervised lawyer would be to accept the decision made by the senior lawyer or to resign or otherwise lose the employment. This provision of Rule 5.02 also recognizes that it is not necessarily improper for the inexperienced lawyer to rely, reasonably and in good faith, upon decisions made in unclear matters by senior lawyers in the organization.

5. The defense provided by this Rule is available without regard to whether the conduct in question was originally proposed by the supervised lawyer or another person. Nevertheless, the supervised lawyer is not permitted to accept an unreasonable decision as to the propriety of professional conduct. The Rule obviously provides no defense to the supervised lawyer who participates in clearly wrongful conduct. Reliance can be placed only upon a reasonable resolution made by the supervisory lawyer.

6. The protection afforded by Rule 5.02 to a supervised lawyer relates only to professional disciplinary proceedings. Whether a similar defense may exist in actions in tort or for breach of contract is a question beyond the scope of the Texas Rules of Professional Conduct.

Rule 5.03. Responsibilities Regarding Nonlawyer Assistants

With respect to a nonlawyer employed or retained by or associated with a lawyer:

(a) a lawyer having direct supervisory authority over the nonlawyer shall make reasonable efforts to ensure that the person's conduct is compatible with the professional obligations of the lawyer; and

(b) a lawyer shall be subject to discipline for the conduct of such a person that would be a violation of these rules if engaged in by a lawyer if:

(1) the lawyer orders, encourages, or permits the conduct involved; or

(2) the lawyer:

(i) is a partner in the law firm in which the person is employed, retained by, or associated with; or is the general counsel of a government agency's legal department in which the person is employed, retained by or associated with; or has direct supervisory authority over such person; and

(ii) with knowledge of such misconduct by the nonlawyer knowingly fails to take reasonable remedial action to avoid or mitigate the consequences of that person's misconduct.

Adopted by order of Oct. 17, 1989, eff. Jan. 1, 1990.

Comment:

1. Lawyers generally employ assistants in their practice, including secretaries, investigators, law student interns, and paraprofessionals. Such assistants act for the lawyer in rendition of the lawyer's professional services. A lawyer should give such assistants appropriate instruction and supervision concerning the ethical aspects of their employment, particularly regarding the obligation not to disclose information relating to representation of the client, and should be responsible for their work product. The measures employed in supervising non-lawyers should take account of the fact that they do not have legal training and are not subject to professional discipline.

2. Each lawyer in a position of authority in a law firm or in a government agency should make reasonable efforts to ensure that the organization has in effect measures giving reasonable assurance that the conduct of nonlawyers employed or retained by or associated with the firm or legal department is compatible with the professional obligations of the lawyer. This ethical obligation includes lawyers having supervisory authority or intermediate managerial responsibilities in the law department of any enterprise or government agency.

Rule 5.04. Professional Independence of a Lawyer

(a) A lawyer or law firm shall not share or promise to share legal fees with a non-lawyer, except that:

(1) an agreement by a lawyer with the lawyer's firm, partner, or associate, or a lawful court order,

may provide for the payment of money, over a reasonable period of time, to the lawyer's estate to or for the benefit of the lawyer's heirs or personal representatives, beneficiaries, or former spouse, after the lawyer's death or as otherwise provided by law or court order.

(2) a lawyer who undertakes to complete unfinished legal business of a deceased lawyer may pay to the estate of the deceased lawyer that proportion of the total compensation which fairly represents the services rendered by the deceased lawyer; and

(3) a lawyer or law firm may include non-lawyer employees in a retirement plan, even though the plan is based in whole or in part on a profit-sharing arrangement.

(b) A lawyer shall not form a partnership with a non-lawyer if any of the activities of the partnership consist of the practice of law.

(c) A lawyer shall not permit a person who recommends, employs, or pays the lawyer to render legal services for another to direct or regulate the lawyer's professional judgment in rendering such legal services.

(d) A lawyer shall not practice with or in the form of a professional corporation or association authorized to practice law for a profit, if:

(1) a nonlawyer owns any interest therein, except that a fiduciary representative of the estate of a lawyer may hold the stock or interest of the lawyer for a reasonable time during administration;

(2) a nonlawyer is a corporate director or officer thereof; or

(3) a nonlawyer has the right to direct or control the professional judgment of a lawyer.

Adopted by order of Oct. 17, 1989, eff. Jan. 1, 1990.

Comment:

1. The provisions of Rule 5.04(a) express traditional limitations on sharing legal fees with nonlawyers. The principal reasons for these limitations are to prevent solicitation by lay persons of clients for lawyers and to avoid encouraging or assisting nonlawyers in the practice of law. See Rules 5.04(d), 5.05 and 7.03. The same reasons support Rule 5.04(b).

2. The exceptions stated in Rule 5.04(a) involve situations where the sharing of legal fees with a nonlawyer is not likely to encourage improper solicitation or unauthorized practice of law. For example, it is appropriate for a law firm agreement to provide for the payment of money after the death of a lawyer, or after the establishment of a guardianship for an incapacitated lawyer, to the estate of or to a trust created by the lawyer. A court order, such as a divorce decree, may provide, when appropriate, for the division of legal fees with a nonlawyer. Likewise, the inclusion of a secretary or nonlawyer office administrator in a retirement plan to which the law firm contributes a portion of its profits or legal fees is proper because this division of legal fees is unlikely to encourage improper solicitation or unauthorized practice of law.

3. Rule 5.04(a) forbids only the sharing of legal fees with a nonlawyer and does not necessarily mandate that employees by paid only on the basis of a fixed salary. Thus, the payment of an annual or other bonus does not constitute the sharing of legal fees if the bonus is neither based on a percentage of the law firm's profits or on a percentage of particular legal fees nor is given as a reward for conduct forbidden to lawyers. Similarly, the division between lawyer and client of the proceeds of a settlement judgment or other award in which both damages and attorney fees have been included does not constitute an improper sharing of legal fees with a nonlawyer. Reimbursement by a lawyer made to a bona fide or pro bono legal services entity for its reasonable expenses in connection with the matter referred to or being handled by the lawyer does not constitute a division of legal fees within the meaning of Rule 5.04.

4. Because the lawyer-client relationship is a personal relationship in which the client generally must trust the lawyer to exercise appropriate professional judgment on the client's behalf, Rule 5.04(c) provides that a lawyer shall not permit improper interference with the exercise of the lawyer's professional judgment solely on behalf of the client. The lawyer's professional judgment should be exercised only for the benefit of the client, free of compromising influences and loyalties. Therefore, under Rule 5.04(c) a person who recommends, employs, or pays the lawyer to render legal services for another cannot be permitted to interfere with the lawyer's professional relationship with that client. Similarly, neither the lawyer's personal interests, the interests of other clients, nor the desires of third persons should be permitted to dilute the lawyer's loyalty to the client.

5. Because a lawyer must always be free to exercise professional judgment without regard to the interests or motives of a third person, the lawyer who is employed or paid by one to represent another should guard constantly against erosion of the lawyer's professional judgment. The lawyer should recognize that a person or organization that pays or furnishes lawyers to represent others possesses a potential power to exert strong pressures against the independent judgment of the lawyer. The lawyer should be watchful that such persons or organizations are not seeking to further their own economic, political, or social goals without regard to the lawyer's responsibility to the client. Moreover, a lawyer employed by an organization is required by Rule 5.04(c) to decline to accept direction of the lawyer's professional judgment from any nonlawyer in the organization.

6. Rule 5.04(d) forbids a lawyer to practice with or in the form of a professional corporation or association in certain specific situations where erosion of the lawyer's professional independence may be threatened. The danger of erosion of the lawyer's professional independence sometimes may exist when a lawyer practices with associations or organizations not covered by Rule 5.04(d). For example, various types of legal aid offices are administered by boards of directors composed of lawyers and nonlawyers, and a lawyer should not accept or continue employment with such an organization unless the board sets only broad policies and does not interfere in the relationship of the lawyer and the individual client that the lawyer serves. See Rule 1.13. Whenever a lawyer is employed by an organization, a written agreement that defines the relationship between the lawyer and the

organization and that provides for the lawyer's professional independence is desirable since it may serve to prevent misunderstanding as to their respective roles.

Rule 5.05. Unauthorized Practice of Law

A lawyer shall not:

(a) practice law in a jurisdiction where doing so violates the regulation of the legal profession in that jurisdiction; or

(b) assist a person who is not a member of the bar in the performance of activity that constitutes the unauthorized practice of law.

Adopted by order of Oct. 17, 1989, eff. Jan. 1, 1990. Amended by order of June 15, 1994, eff. Oct. 1, 1994.

Comment:

1. Courts generally have prohibited the unauthorized practice of law because of a perceived need to protect individuals and the public from the mistakes of the untrained and the schemes of the unscrupulous, who are not subject to the judicially imposed disciplinary standards of competence, responsibility and accountability.

2. Neither statutory nor judicial definitions offer clear guidelines as to what constitutes the practice of law or the unauthorized practice of law. All too frequently, the definitions are so broad as to be meaningless and amount to little more than the statement that "the practice of law" is merely whatever lawyers do or are traditionally understood to do. The definition of the practice of law is established by law and varies from one jurisdiction to another. Whatever the definition, limiting the practice of law to members of the bar protects the public against rendition of legal services by unqualified persons.

3. Rule 5.05 does not attempt to define what constitutes the "unauthorized practice of law" but leaves the definition to judicial development. Judicial development of the concept of "law practice" should emphasize that the concept is broad enough—but only broad enough—to cover all situations where there is rendition of services for others that call for the professional judgment of a lawyer and where the one receiving the services generally will be unable to judge whether adequate services are being rendered and is, therefore, in need of the protection afforded by the regulation of the legal profession.

Competent professional judgment is the product of a trained familiarity with law and legal processes, a disciplined, analytical approach to legal problems, and a firm ethical commitment; and the essence of the professional judgment of the lawyer is the lawyer's educated ability to relate the general body and philosophy of law to a specific legal problem of a client.

4. Paragraph (b) of Rule 5.05 does not prohibit a lawyer from employing the services of paraprofessionals and delegating functions to them. So long as the lawyer supervises the delegated work, and retains responsibility for the work, and maintains a direct relationship with the client, the paraprofessional cannot reasonably be said to have engaged in activity that constitutes the unauthorized practice of law. See Rule 5.03. Likewise, paragraph (b) does not prohibit lawyers from providing professional advice and instructions to nonlawyers whose employment requires knowledge of law. For example, claims adjusters, employees of financial institutions, social workers, abstracters, police officers, accountants, and persons employed in government agencies are engaged in occupations requiring knowledge of law; and a lawyer who assists them to carry out their proper functions is not assisting the unauthorized practice of law. In addition, a lawyer may counsel nonlawyers who wish to proceed pro se, since a nonlawyer who represents himself or herself is not engaged in the unauthorized practice of law.

5. Authority to engage in the practice of law conferred in any jurisdiction is not necessarily a grant of the right to practice elsewhere, and it is improper for a lawyer to engage in practice where doing so violates the regulation of the practice of law in that jurisdiction. However, the demands of business and the mobility of our society pose distinct problems in the regulation of the practice of law by individual states. In furtherance of the public interest, lawyers should discourage regulations that unreasonably impose territorial limitations upon the right of a lawyer to handle the legal affairs of a client or upon the opportunity of a client to obtain the services of a lawyer of his or her choice.

Rule 5.06. Restrictions on Right to Practice

A lawyer shall not participate in offering or making:

(a) a partnership or employment agreement that restricts the rights of a lawyer to practice after termination of the relationship, except an agreement concerning benefits upon retirement; or

(b) an agreement in which a restriction on the lawyer's right to practice is part of the settlement of a suit or controversy, except that as part of the settlement of a disciplinary proceedings against a lawyer an agreement may be made placing restrictions on the right of that lawyer to practice.

Adopted by order of Oct. 17, 1989, eff. Jan. 1, 1990.

Comment:

1. An agreement restricting the rights of partners or associates to practice after leaving a firm not only limits their professional autonomy but also limits the freedom of clients to choose a lawyer. Paragraph (a) prohibits such agreements except for restrictions incident to provisions concerning retirement benefits for service with the firm.

2. Paragraph (b) prohibits a lawyer from agreeing not to represent other persons in connection with settling a claim on behalf of a client.

Rule 5.07. [Blank]

Rule 5.08. Prohibited Discriminatory Activities

(a) A lawyer shall not willfully, in connection with an adjudicatory proceeding, except as provided in paragraph (b), manifest, by words or conduct, bias or prejudice based on race, color, national origin, religion, disability, age, sex, or sexual orientation towards any person involved in that proceeding in any capacity.

(b) Paragraph (a) does not apply to a lawyer's decision whether to represent a particular person in connection with an adjudicatory proceeding, nor to the process of jury selection, nor to communications protected as "confidential information" under these Rules. See Rule 1.05(a), (b). It also does not preclude advocacy in connection with an adjudicatory proceeding involving any of the factors set out in paragraph (a) if that advocacy:

(i) is necessary in order to address any substantive or procedural issues raised by the proceeding; and

(ii) is conducted in conformity with applicable rulings and orders of a tribunal and applicable rules of practice and procedure.

Adopted by order of June 15, 1994, eff. Oct. 1, 1994.

Comment:

1. Subject to certain exemptions, paragraph (a) of this Rule prohibits willful expressions of bias or prejudice in connection with adjudicatory proceedings that are directed towards any persons involved with those proceedings in any capacity. Because the prohibited conduct only must occur "in connection with" an adjudicatory proceeding, it applies to misconduct transpiring outside of as well as in the presence of the tribunal's presiding adjudicatory official. Moreover, the broad definition given to the term "adjudicatory proceeding" under these Rules means that paragraph (a)'s prohibition applies to many settings besides conventional litigation in federal or state courts. See Preamble: Terminology (definitions of "Adjudicatory Proceeding" and "Tribunal").

2. The Rule, however, contains several important limitations and exemptions. The first, found in paragraph (a), is that a lawyer's allegedly improper words or conduct must be shown to have been "willful" before the lawyer may be subjected to discipline.

3. In addition, paragraph (b) sets out four exemptions from the prohibition of paragraph (a). The first is a lawyer's decision whether to represent a client. The second is any communication made by the lawyer that is "confidential" under Rule 1.05(a) and (b). The third is a lawyer's communication that is necessary to represent a client properly and that complies with applicable rulings and orders of the tribunal as well as with applicable rules of practice or procedure.

4. The fourth exemption in paragraph (b) relates to the lawyer's words or conduct in selecting a jury. This exemption ensures that a lawyer will be free to thoroughly probe the venire in an effort to identify potential jurors having a bias or prejudice towards the lawyer's client, or in favor of the client's opponent, based on, among other things, the factors enumerated in paragraph (a). A lawyer, should remember, however, that the use of peremptory challenges to remove persons from juries based solely on some of the factors listed in paragraph (a) raises separate constitutional issues.

(Comment adopted by State Bar Board of Directors Sept. 16, 1994.)

VI. Public Service

Rule 6.01. Accepting Appointments by a Tribunal

A lawyer shall not seek to avoid appointment by a tribunal to represent a person except for good cause, such as:

(a) representing the client is likely to result in violation of law or rules of professional conduct;

(b) representing the client is likely to result in an unreasonable financial burden on the lawyer; or

(c) the client or the cause is so repugnant to the lawyer as to be likely to impair the client-lawyer relationship or the lawyer's ability to represent the client.

Adopted by order of Oct. 17, 1989, eff. Jan. 1, 1990. Amended by order of June 15, 1994, eff. Oct. 1, 1994.

Comment:

Appointment

1. A lawyer may be subject to appointment by a court to serve unpopular clients or persons unable to afford legal services. For good cause a lawyer may seek to decline an appointment to represent a person who cannot afford to retain counsel or whose cause is unpopular. Good cause exists if the lawyer could not handle the matter competently, see Rule 1.01, or if undertaking the representation would result in an improper conflict of interest, for example, when the client or the cause is so repugnant to the lawyer as to be likely to impair the client-lawyer relationship or the lawyer's ability to represent the client. Compare Rules 1.06(b), 1.15(a)(2), 1.15(b)(4). A lawyer may also seek to decline an appointment if acceptance would be unreasonably burdensome, for example, when it would impose a financial sacrifice so great as to be unjust. Compare Rule 1.15(b)(6). However, a lawyer should not seek to decline an appointment because of such factors as a distaste for the subject matter or the proceeding, the identity or position of a person involved in the case, the lawyer's belief that a defendant in a criminal proceeding is guilty, or the lawyer's belief regarding the merits of a civil case.

2. An appointed lawyer has the same obligations to the client as retained counsel, including the obligations of loyalty and confidentiality, and is subject to the same limitations on the client-lawyer relationship, such as the obligation to refrain from assisting the client in violation of the Rules.

Public Interest Service

3. The rights and responsibilities of individuals and organizations in Texas and throughout the United States are increasingly defined in legal terms. As a consequence, legal assistance in coping with the web of statutes, rules and regulations is imperative for all persons. Consequently, each lawyer engaged in the practice of law should render public interest legal service. Personal involvement in the problems of the disadvantaged can be one of the most rewarding experiences in the life of a lawyer.

Unpopular Causes

4. A lawyer ordinarily is not obliged to accept a client whose character or cause the lawyer regards as repugnant. Frequently, however, the needs of such a client for a lawyer's services are particularly pressing and, in some cases, the client may have a right to legal representation. At the same time, either financial considerations or the same qualities of the client or the client's cause that make a lawyer reluctant

to accept employment may severely limit the client's ability to obtain counsel. As a consequence, the lawyer's freedom to reject clients is morally qualified. Legal representation should not be denied to people who are unable to afford legal services, or whose cause is controversial or the subject of popular disapproval. By the same token, a lawyer's representation of a client, including representation by appointment, does not constitute an endorsement of the client's political, economic, social or moral views or activities.

5. An individual lawyer may fulfill the ethical responsibility to provide public interest legal service by accepting a fair share of unpopular matters or indigent or unpopular clients. History is replete with instances of distinguished and sacrificial services by lawyers who have represented unpopular clients and causes. Regardless of his personal feelings, a lawyer should not decline representation because a client or a cause is unpopular or community reaction is adverse. Likewise, a lawyer should not reject tendered employment because of the personal preference of a lawyer to avoid adversary alignment against judges, other lawyers, public officials, or influential members of the community.

VII. Information About Legal Services

Rule 7.01. Firm Names and Letterhead

(a) A lawyer in private practice shall not practice under a trade name, a name that is misleading as to the identity of the lawyer or lawyers practicing under such name, or a firm name containing names other than those of one or more of the lawyers in the firm, except that the names of a professional corporation, professional association, limited liability partnership, or professional limited liability company may contain "P.C.," "L.L.P.," "P.L.L.C.," or similar symbols indicating the nature of the organization, and if otherwise lawful a firm may use as, or continue to include in, its name the name or names of one or more deceased or retired members of the firm or of a predecessor firm in a continuing line of succession. Nothing herein shall prohibit a married woman from practicing under her maiden name.

(b) A firm with offices in more than one jurisdiction may use the same name in each jurisdiction, but identification of the lawyers in an office of the firm shall indicate the jurisdictional limitations on those not licensed to practice in the jurisdiction where the office is located.

(c) The name of a lawyer occupying a judicial, legislative, or public executive or administrative position shall not be used in the name of a firm, or in communications on its behalf, during any substantial period in which the lawyer is not actively and regularly practicing with the firm.

(d) A lawyer shall not hold himself or herself out as being a partner, shareholder, or associate with one or more other lawyers unless they are in fact partners, shareholders, or associates.

(e) A lawyer shall not advertise in the public media or seek professional employment by any communication under a trade or fictitious name, except that a lawyer who practices under a firm name as authorized by paragraph (a) of this Rule may use that name in such advertisement or communication but only if that name is the firm name that appears on the lawyer's letterhead, business cards, office sign, fee contracts, and with the lawyer's signature on pleadings and other legal documents.

(f) A lawyer shall not use a firm name, letterhead, or other professional designation that violates Rule 7.02(a).

Adopted by order of Oct. 17, 1989, eff. Jan. 1, 1990. Renumbered from Rule 7.04 and amended by order of Nov. 15, 1994. Amended by order of March 31, 1995; Feb. 7, 2005, eff. June 1, 2005.

Comment:

1. A lawyer or law firm may not practice law using a name that is misleading as to the identity of the lawyers practicing under such name, but the continued use of the name of a deceased or retired member of the firm or of a predecessor firm is not considered to be misleading. Trade names are generally considered inherently misleading. Other types of firm names can be misleading as well, such as a firm name that creates the appearance that lawyers are partners or employees of a single law firm when in fact they are merely associated for the purpose of sharing expenses. In such cases, the lawyers involved may not denominate themselves in any manner suggesting such an ongoing professional relationship as, for example, "Smith and Jones" or "Smith and Jones Associates" or "Smith and Associates." Such titles create the false impression that the lawyers named have assumed a joint professional responsibility for clients' legal affairs. See paragraph (d).

2. The practice of law firms having offices in more than one state is commonplace. Although it is not necessary that the name of an interstate firm include Texas lawyers, a letterhead including the name of any lawyer not licensed in Texas must indicate the lawyer is not licensed in Texas.

3. Paragraph (c) is designed to prevent the exploitation of a lawyer's public position for the benefit of the lawyer's firm. Likewise, because it may be misleading under paragraph (a), a lawyer who occupies a judicial, legislative, or public executive or administrative position should not indicate that fact on a letterhead which identifies that person as an attorney in the private practice of law. However, a firm name any include the name of a public official who is actively and regularly practicing law with the firm. But see Rule 7.02(a)(5).

4. With certain limited exceptions, paragraph (a) forbids a lawyer from using a trade name or fictitious name. Paragraph (e) sets out this same prohibition with respect to advertising in public media or communications seeking professional employment and contains additional restrictions on the use of trade names or fictitious names in those contexts. In a largely overlapping measure, paragraph (f) forbids the

use of any such name or designation if it would amount to a "false or misleading communication" under Rule 7.02(a).

(Comment amended by the State Bar Board of Directors April 8, 2005, eff. June 1, 2005.)

The order of Nov. 15, 1994 amended all of Part VII.

By Supreme Court order 95–9074, dated March 31, 1995, the Supreme Court modified its order of Nov. 15, 1994, to provide that those rules upheld be made effective 120 days after the date of judgment of the United States district Court for the Eastern District of Texas in the lawsuit styled Texans Against Censorship, et al versus State Bar of Texas, et al. [Judgment was entered in *Texans Against Censorship, Inc. v. State Bar of Texas*, E.D.Tex.1995, 888 F.Supp. 1328, On March 31, 1995.]

The order of Feb. 7, 2005, in par. (a), deleted " 'P.A.,' " following "company may contain 'P.C.,' " , and in par. (e) deleted "written" preceding "communication" twice and substituted a reference to "firm name" for "trade name".

Rule 7.02. Communications Concerning a Lawyer's Services

(a) A lawyer shall not make or sponsor a false or misleading communication about the qualifications or the services of any lawyer or firm. A communication is false or misleading if it:

(1) contains a material misrepresentation of fact or law, or omits a fact necessary to make the statement considered as a whole not materially misleading;

(2) contains any reference in a public media advertisement to past successes or results obtained unless

(i) the communicating lawyer or member of the law firm served as lead counsel in the matter giving rise to the recovery, or was primarily responsible for the settlement or verdict.

(ii) the amount involved was actually received by the client,

(iii) the reference is accompanied by adequate information regarding the nature of the case or matter, and the damages or injuries sustained by the client, and

(iv) if the gross amount received is stated, the attorney's fees and litigation expenses withheld from the amount are stated as well;

(3) is likely to create an unjustified expectation about results the lawyer can achieve, or states or implies that the lawyer can achieve results by means that violate these rules or other law;

(4) compares the lawyer's services with other lawyers' services, unless the comparison can be substantiated by reference to verifiable, objective data;

(5) states or implies that the lawyer is able to influence improperly or upon irrelevant grounds any tribunal, legislative body, or public official;

(6) designates one or more specific areas of practice in an advertisement in the public media or in a solicitation communication unless the advertising or soliciting lawyer is competent to handle legal matters in each such area of practice; or

(7) uses an actor or model to portray a client of the lawyer or law firm.

(b) Rule 7.02(a)(6) does not require that a lawyer be certified by the Texas Board of Legal Specialization at the time of advertising in a specific area of practice, but such certification shall conclusively establish that such lawyer satisfies the requirements of Rule 7.02(a)(6) with respect to the area(s) of practice in which such lawyer is certified.

(c) A lawyer shall not advertise in the public media or state in a solicitation communication that the lawyer is a specialist except as permitted under Rule 7.04.

(d) Any statement or disclaimer required by these rules shall be made in each language used in the advertisement or solicitation communication with respect to which such required statement or disclaimer relates; provided however, the mere statement that a particular language is spoken or understood shall not alone result in the need for a statement or disclaimer in that language.

Adopted by order of Oct. 17, 1989, eff. Jan. 1, 1990. Redesignated from Rule 7.01(a) and amended by order of Nov. 15, 1994. Amended by order of March 31, 1995; Feb. 7, 2005, eff. June 1, 2005.

Comment:

1. The Rules within Part VII are intended to regulate communications made for the purpose of obtaining professional employment. They are not intended to affect other forms of speech by lawyers, such as political advertisements or political commentary, except insofar as a lawyer's effort to obtain employment is linked to a matter of current public debate.

2. This Rule governs all communications about a lawyer's services, including advertisements regulated by Rule 7.04 and solicitation communications regulated by Rules 7.03 and 7.05. Whatever means are used to make known a lawyer's services, statements about them must be truthful and nondeceptive.

3. Sub-paragraph (a)(1) recognizes that statements can be misleading both by what they contain and what they leave out. Statements that are false or misleading for either reason are prohibited. A truthful statement is misleading if it omits a fact necessary to make the lawyer's communication considered as a whole not materially misleading. A truthful statement is also misleading if there is a substantial likelihood that it will lead a reasonable person to formulate a specific conclusion about the lawyer or the lawyer's services for which there is no reasonable factual foundation.

4. Sub-paragraphs (a)(2) and (3) recognize that truthful statements may create "unjustified expectations." For example, an advertisement that truthfully reports that a lawyer obtained a jury verdict of a certain amount on behalf of a client would nonetheless be misleading if it were to turn out that the verdict was overturned on appeal or later com-

promised for a substantially reduced amount, and the advertisement did not disclose such facts as well. Even an advertisement that fully and accurately reports a lawyer's achievements on behalf of clients or former clients may be misleading if presented so as to lead a reasonable person to form an unjustified expectation that the same results could be obtained for other clients in similar matters without reference to the specific factual and legal circumstances of each client's case. Those unique circumstances would ordinarily preclude advertisements in the public media and solicitation communications that discuss the results obtained on behalf of a client, such as the amount of a damage award, the lawyer's record in obtaining favorable settlements or verdicts, as well as those that contain client endorsements.

5. Sub-paragraph (a)(4) recognizes that comparisons of lawyer's services may also be misleading unless those comparisons "can be substantiated by reference to verifiable objective data." Similarly, an unsubstantiated comparison of the lawyer's services or fees with the services or fees of other lawyers may be misleading if presented with such specificity as would lead a reasonable person to conclude that the comparison can be substantiated. Statements comparing a lawyer's services with those of another where the comparisons are not susceptible of precise measurement or verification, such as "we are the toughest lawyers in town", "we will get money for you when other lawyers can't", or "we are the best law firm in Texas if you want a large recovery," can deceive or mislead prospective clients.

6. The inclusion of a disclaimer or qualifying language may preclude a finding that a statement is likely to create unjustified expectations or otherwise mislead a prospective client, but it will not necessarily do so. Unless any such qualifications and disclaimers are both sufficient and displayed with equal prominence to the information to which they pertain, that information can still readily mislead prospective clients into believing that similar results can be obtained for them without reference to their specific factual and legal circumstances. Consequently, in order not to be false, misleading, or deceptive, other of these Rules require that appropriate disclaimers or qualifying language must be presented in the same manner as the communication and with equal prominence. See Rules 7.04 (q) and 7.05(a)(2).

7. On the other hand, a simple statement of a lawyer's own qualifications devoid of comparisons to other lawyers does not pose the same risk of being misleading and so does not violate sub-paragraph (a)(4). Similarly, a lawyer making a referral to another lawyer may express a good faith subjective opinion regarding that other lawyer.

8. Thus, this Rule does not prohibit communication of information concerning a lawyer's name or firm name, address, and telephone numbers; the basis on which the lawyer's fees are determined, including prices for specific services and payment and credit arrangements; names of references and with their consent, names of clients regularly represented; and other truthful information that might invite the attention of those seeking legal assistance. When a communication permitted by Rule 7.02 is made in the public media, the lawyer should consult Rule 7.04 for further guidance and restrictions. When a communication permitted by Rule 7.02 is made by a lawyer through a solicitation communication, the lawyer should consult Rules 7.03 and 7.05 for further guidance and restrictions.

9. Sub-paragraph (a)(5) prohibits a lawyer from stating or implying that the lawyer has an ability to influence a tribunal, legislative body, or other public official through improper conduct or upon irrelevant grounds. Such conduct brings the profession into disrepute, even though the improper or irrelevant activities referred to are never carried out, and so are prohibited without regard to the lawyer's actual intent to engage in such activities.

Communication of Fields of Practice

10. Paragraphs (a)(6), (b) and (c) of Rule 7.02 regulate communications concerning a lawyer's fields of practice and should be construed together with Rule 7.04 or 7.05, as applicable. If a lawyer in a public media advertisement or in a solicitation communication designates one or more specific areas of practice, that designation is at least an implicit representation that the lawyer is qualified in the areas designated. Accordingly, Rule 7.02(a)(6) prohibits the designation of a field of practice unless the communicating lawyer is in fact competent in the area.

11. Typically, one would expect competency to be measured by special education, training, or experience in the particular area of law designated. Because certification by the Texas Board of Legal Specialization involves special education, training, and experience, certification by the Texas Board of Legal Specialization conclusively establishes that a lawyer meets the requirements of Rule 7.02(a)(6) in any area in which the Board has certified the lawyer. However, competency may be established by means other than certification by the Texas Board of Legal Specialization. See Rule 7.04(b).

12. Lawyers who wish to advertise in the public media that they specialize should refer to Rule 7.04. Lawyers who wish to assert a specialty in a solicitation communication should refer to Rule 7.05.

Actor Portrayal Of Clients

13. Sub-paragraph (a)(7) further protects prospective clients from false, misleading, or deceptive advertisements and solicitations by prohibiting the use of actors to portray clients of a lawyer or law firm. Other rules prohibit the use of actors to portray lawyers in the advertising or soliciting lawyer's firm. See Rules 7.04(g), 7.05(a). The truthfulness of such portrayals is extremely difficult to monitor, and almost inevitably they involve actors whose apparent physical and mental attributes differ in a number of material respects from those of the actual clients portrayed.

Communication in a Second Language

14. The ability of lawyers to communicate in a second language can facilitate the delivery and receipt of legal services. Accordingly, it is in the best interest of the public that potential clients be made aware of a lawyer's language ability. A lawyer may state an ability to communicate in a second language without any further elaboration. However, if a lawyer chooses to communicate with potential clients in a second language, all statements or disclaimers required by the Texas Disciplinary Rules of Professional Conduct must also be made in that language. See paragraph (d). Communicating some information in one language while communicating the rest in another is potentially misleading if the recipient understands only one of the languages.

(Comment amended by the State Bar Board of Directors Jan. 20, 1995; April 8, 2005, eff. June 1, 2005.)

The order of Feb. 7, 2005, rewrote the rule which prior thereto read:

"(a) A lawyer shall not make a false or misleading communication about the qualifications or the services of any lawyer or firm. A communication is false or misleading if it:

"(1) contains a material misrepresentation of fact or law, or omits a fact necessary to make the statement considered as a whole not materially misleading;

"(2) is likely to create an unjustified expectation about results the lawyer can achieve, or states or implies that the lawyer can achieve results by means that violate these rules or other law;

"(3) compares the lawyer's services with other lawyers' services, unless the comparison can be substantiated by reference to verifiable, objective data;

"(4) states or implies that the lawyer is able to influence improperly or upon irrelevant grounds any tribunal, legislative body, or public official; or

"(5) designates one or more specific areas of practice in an advertisement in the public media or in a written solicitation unless the advertising lawyer is competent to handle legal matters in each such area of practice.

"(b) Rule 7.02(a)(5) does not require that a lawyer be certified by the Texas Board of Legal Specialization at the time of advertising in a specific area of practice, but such certification shall conclusively establish that such lawyer satisfies the requirements of Rule 7.02(a)(5) with respect to the area(s) of practice in which such lawyer is certified.

"(c) A lawyer shall not advertise in the public media that the lawyer is a specialist except as permitted under Rule 7.04.

"(d) Any statement or disclaimer required by these rules shall be made in each language used in the advertisement or writing with respect to which such required statement or disclaimer relates; provided however, the mere statement that a particular language is spoken or understood shall not alone result in the need for a statement or disclaimer in that language."

Rule 7.03. Prohibited Solicitations and Payments

(a) A lawyer shall not by in-person contact, or by regulated telephone or other electronic contact as defined in paragraph (f) seek professional employment concerning a matter arising out of a particular occurrence or event, or series of occurrences or events, from a prospective client or nonclient who has not sought the lawyer's advice regarding employment or with whom the lawyer has no family or past or present attorney-client relationship when a significant motive for the lawyer's doing so is the lawyer's pecuniary gain. Notwithstanding the provisions of this paragraph, a lawyer for a qualified nonprofit organization may communicate with the organization's members for the purpose of educating the members to understand the law, to recognize legal problems, to make intelligent selection of counsel, or to use legal services. In those situations where in-person or telephone or other electronic contact is permitted by this paragraph, a lawyer shall not have such a contact with a prospective client if:

(1) the communication involves coercion, duress, fraud, overreaching, intimidation, undue influence, or harassment;

(2) the communication contains information prohibited by Rule 7.02(a); or

(3) the communication contains a false, fraudulent, misleading, deceptive, or unfair statement or claim.

(b) A lawyer shall not pay, give, or offer to pay or give anything of value to a person not licensed to practice law for soliciting prospective clients for, or referring clients or prospective clients to, any lawyer or firm, except that a lawyer may pay reasonable fees for advertising and public relations services rendered in accordance with this Rule and may pay the usual charges of a lawyer referral service that meets the requirements of Occupational Code Title 5, Subtitle B, Chapter 952.

(c) A lawyer, in order to solicit professional employment, shall not pay, give, advance, or offer to pay, give, or advance anything of value, other than actual litigation expenses and other financial assistance as permitted by Rule 1.08(d), to a prospective client or any other person; provided however, this provision does not prohibit the payment of legitimate referral fees as permitted by Rule 1.04(f) or by paragraph (b) of this Rule.

(d) A lawyer shall not enter into an agreement for, charge for, or collect a fee for professional employment obtained in violation of Rule 7.03(a), (b), or (c).

(e) A lawyer shall not participate with or accept referrals from a lawyer referral service unless the lawyer knows or reasonably believes that the lawyer referral service meets the requirements of Occupational Code Title 5, Subtitle B, Chapter 952.

(f) As used in paragraph (a), "regulated telephone or other electronic contact" means any electronic communication initiated by a lawyer or by any person acting on behalf of a lawyer or law firm that will result in the person contacted communicating in a live, interactive manner with any other person by telephone or other electronic means. For purposes of this Rule a website for a lawyer or law firm is not considered a communication initiated by or on behalf of that lawyer or firm.

Adopted by order of Oct. 17, 1989, eff. Jan. 1, 1990. Redesignated from Rules 7.01(i) and 7.02 and amended by order of Nov. 15, 1994. Amended by order of Feb. 23, 1995; March 31, 1995; Feb. 7, 2005, eff. June 1, 2005.

Comment:

1. In many situations, in-person, telephone, or other prohibited electronic solicitations by lawyers involve well-known opportunities for abuse of prospective clients. Traditionally, the principal concerns presented by such contacts are that they can overbear the prospective client's will, lead to hasty and ill advised decisions concerning choice of counsel, and be very difficult to police. The approach taken by this Rule

may be found in paragraph (f), which prohibits such communications if they are initiated by or in behalf of a lawyer or law firm and will result in the person contacted communicating with any person by telephone or other electronic means. Thus, forms of electronic communications are prohibited that pose comparable dangers to face-to-face solicitations, such as soliciting business and "chat rooms" or transmitting an unsolicited, interactive communication to a prospective client that, when accessed, puts the recipient in direct contact with another person. Those that do not present such opportunities for abuse, such as pre-recorded telephone messages requiring a separate return call to speak to or retain an attorney or websites that must be accessed by an interested person and that provide relevant and truthful information concerning a lawyer or law firm, are permitted.

2. Nonetheless, paragraph (a) and (f) unconditionally prohibit those activities only when profit for the lawyer is a significant motive and the solicitation concerns matters arising out of a particular occurrence, event, or series of occurrences or events. The reason this outright ban is so limited is that there are circumstances where the dangers of such contacts can be reduced by less restrictive means. As long as the conditions of sub-paragraphs (a)(1) through (a)(3) are not violated by a given contact, a lawyer may engage in in-person, telephone, or other electronic solicitations when the solicitation is unrelated to a specific occurrence, event, or series of occurrences or events. Similarly, subject to the same restrictions, in-person, telephone, or other electronic solicitations are permitted where the prospective client either has a family or past or present attorney-client relationship with the lawyer or where the potential client had previously contacted the lawyer about possible employment in the matter.

3. In addition, Rule 7.03(a) does not prohibit a lawyer for a qualified non-profit organization from in-person, telephone, or other electronic solicitation of prospective clients for purposes related to that organization. Historically and by law, nonprofit legal aid agencies, unions, and other qualified nonprofit organizations and their lawyers have been permitted to solicit clients in-person or by telephone, and more modern electronic means of communication pose no additional threats to consumers justifying a more restrictive treatment. Consequently, Rule 7.03(a) is not in derogation of those organizations' constitutional rights to employ such methods. Attorneys for such nonprofit organizations, however, remain subject to this Rule's general prohibitions against undue influence, intimidation, overreaching, and the like.

Paying for Solicitation

4. Rule 7.03(b) does not prohibit a lawyer from paying standard commercial fees for advertising or public relations services rendered in accordance with these Rules. In addition, a lawyer may pay the fees required by a lawyer referral service that meet the requirements of Occupational Code Title 5, Subtitle B, Chapter 952. However, paying, giving, or offering to pay or give anything of value to persons not licensed to practice law who solicit prospective clients for lawyers has always been considered to be against the best interest of both the public and the legal profession. Such actions circumvent these Rules by having a non-lawyer do what a lawyer is ethically proscribed from doing. Accordingly, the practice is forbidden by Rule 7.03(b). As to payments or gifts of value to licensed lawyers for soliciting prospective clients, see Rule 1.04(f).

5. Rule 7.03(c) prohibits a lawyer from paying or giving value directly to a prospective client or any other person as consideration for employment by that client except as permitted by Rule 1.08(d).

6. Paragraph (d) prohibits a lawyer from agreeing to or charging for professional employment obtained in violation of Rule 7.03. Paragraph (e) further requires a lawyer to decline business generated by a lawyer referral service unless the lawyer knows or reasonably believes that service is operated in conformity with statutory requirements.

7. References to "a lawyer" in this and other Rules include lawyers who practice in law firms. A lawyer associated with a firm cannot circumvent these Rules by soliciting or advertising in the name of that firm in a way that violates these Rules. See Rule 7.04(e).

(Comment amended by the State Bar Board of Directors Jan. 20, 1995; April 8, 2005, eff. June 1, 2005.)

The order of Nov. 15, 1994 amended all of Part VII.

By Supreme Court order 95–9074, dated March 31, 1995, the Supreme Court modified its order of Nov. 15, 1994, to provide that those rules upheld be made effective 120 days after the date of judgment of the United States District Court for the Eastern District of Texas in the lawsuit styled Texans Against Censorship, et al versus State Bar of Texas, et al. [Judgment was entered in *Texans Against Censorship, Inc. v. State Bar of Texas*, E.D.Tex.1995, 888 F.Supp. 1328, on March 31, 1995.]

The order of Feb. 23, 1995 made technical corrections.

The order of Feb. 7, 2005 inserted references to other electronic contact in par. (a); made citation changes in pars. (b) and (e); and added par. (f).

Rule 7.04. Advertisements in the Public Media

(a) A lawyer shall not advertise in the public media by stating that the lawyer is a specialist, except as permitted under Rule 7.04(b) or as follows:

(1) A lawyer admitted to practice before the United States Patent Office may use the designation "Patents," "Patent Attorney," or "Patent Lawyer," or any combination of those terms. A lawyer engaged in the trademark practice may use the designation "Trademark," "Trademark Attorney," or "Trademark Lawyer," or any combination of those terms. A lawyer engaged in patent and trademark practice may hold himself or herself out as specializing in "Intellectual Property Law," "Patent, Trademark, Copyright Law and Unfair Competition," or any of those terms.

(2) A lawyer may permit his or her name to be listed in lawyer referral service offices that meet the requirements of Occupational Code Title 5, Subtitle B, Chapter 952, according to the areas of law in which the lawyer will accept referrals.

(3) A lawyer available to practice in a particular area of law or legal service may distribute to other lawyers and publish in legal directories and legal newspapers (whether written or electronic) a listing or an announcement of such availability. The listing shall not contain a false or misleading represen-

tation of special competence or experience, but may contain the kind of information that traditionally has been included in such publications.

(b) A lawyer who advertises in the public media:

(1) shall publish or broadcast the name of at least one lawyer who is responsible for the content of such advertisement; and

(2) shall not include a statement that the lawyer has been certified or designated by an organization as possessing special competence or a statement that the lawyer is a member of an organization the name of which implies that its members possess special competence, except that:

(i) a lawyer who has been awarded a Certificate of Special Competence by the Texas Board of Legal Specialization in the area so advertised, may state with respect to each such area, "Board Certified, area of specialization — Texas Board of Legal Specialization;" and

(ii) a lawyer who is a member of an organization the name of which implies that its members possess special competence, or who has been certified or designated by an organization as possessing special competence, may include a factually accurate statement of such membership or may include a factually accurate statement, "Certified area of specialization name of certifying organization," but such statements may be made only if that organization has been accredited by the Texas Board of Legal Specialization as a bona fide organization that admits to membership or grants certification only on the basis of objective, exacting, publicly available standards (including high standards of individual character, conduct, and reputation) that are reasonably relevant to the special training or special competence that is implied and that are in excess of the level of training and competence generally required for admission to the Bar; and

(3) shall, in the case of infomercial or comparable presentation, state that the presentation is an advertisement;

(i) both verbally and in writing at its outset, after any commercial interruption, and at its conclusion; and

(ii) in writing during any portion of the presentation that explains how to contact a lawyer or law firm.

(c) Separate and apart from any other statements, the statements referred to in paragraph (b) shall be displayed conspicuously, and in language easily understood by an ordinary consumer.

(d) Subject to the requirements of Rules 7.02 and 7.03 and of paragraphs (a), (b), and (c) of this Rule, a lawyer may, either directly or through a public relations or advertising representative, advertise services in the public media, such as (but not limited to) a telephone directory, legal directory, newspaper or other periodical, outdoor display, radio, television, the Internet, or electronic, or digital media.

(e) All advertisements in the public media for a lawyer or firm must be reviewed and approved in writing by the lawyer or a lawyer in the firm.

(f) A copy or recording of each advertisement in the public media and relevant approval referred to in paragraph (e), and a record of when and where the advertisement was used, shall be kept by the lawyer or firm for four years after its last dissemination.

(g) In advertisements in the public media, any person who portrays a lawyer whose services or whose firm's services are being advertised, or who narrates an advertisement as if he or she were such a lawyer, shall be one or more of the lawyers whose services are being advertised.

(h) If an advertisement in the public media by a lawyer or firm discloses the willingness or potential willingness of the lawyer or firm to render services on a contingent fee basis, the advertisement must state whether the client will be obligated to pay all or any portion of the court costs and, if a client may be liable for other expenses, this fact must be disclosed. If specific percentage fees or fee ranges of contingent fee work are disclosed in such advertisement, it must also disclose whether the percentage is computed before or after expenses are deducted from the recovery.

(i) A lawyer who advertises in the public media a specific fee or range of fees for a particular service shall conform to the advertised fee or range of fees for the period during which the advertisement is reasonably expected to be in circulation or otherwise expected to be effective in attracting clients, unless the advertisement specifies a shorter period; but in no instance is the lawyer bound to conform to the advertised fee or range of fees for a period of more than one year after the date of publication.

(j) A lawyer or firm who advertises in the public media must disclose the geographic location, by city or town, of the lawyer's or firm's principal office. A lawyer or firm shall not advertise the existence of any office other than the principal office unless:

(1) that other office is staffed by a lawyer at least three days a week; or

(2) the advertisement states:

(i) the days and times during which a lawyer will be present at that office, or

(ii) that meetings with lawyers will be by appointment only.

(k) A lawyer may not, directly or indirectly, pay all or a part of the cost of an advertisement in the public media for a lawyer not in the same firm unless such advertisement discloses the name and address of the financing lawyer, the relationship between the advertising lawyer and the financing lawyer, and whether the advertising lawyer is likely to refer cases received through the advertisement to the financing lawyer.

(*l*) If an advertising lawyer knows or should know at the time of an advertisement in the public media that a case or matter will likely be referred to another lawyer or firm, a statement of such fact shall be conspicuously included in such advertisement.

(m) No motto, slogan or jingle that is false or misleading may be used in any advertisement in the public media.

(n) A lawyer shall not include in any advertisement in the public media the lawyer's association with a lawyer referral service unless the lawyer knows or reasonably believes that the lawyer referral service meets the requirements of Occupational Code Title 5, Subtitle B, Chapter 952.

(*o*) A lawyer may not advertise in the public media as part of an advertising cooperative or venture of two or more lawyers not in the same firm unless each such advertisement:

(1) states that the advertisement is paid for by the cooperating lawyers;

(2) names each of the cooperating lawyers;

(3) sets forth conspicuously the special competency requirements required by Rule 7.04(b) of lawyers who advertise in the public media;

(4) does not state or imply that the lawyers participating in the advertising cooperative or venture possess professional superiority, are able to perform services in a superior manner, or possess special competence in any area of law advertised, except that the advertisement may contain the information permitted by Rule 7.04(b)(2); and

(5) does not otherwise violate the Texas Disciplinary Rules of Professional Conduct.

(p) Each lawyer who advertises in the public media as part of an advertising cooperative or venture shall be individually responsible for:

(1) ensuring that each advertisement does not violate this Rule; and

(2) complying with the filing requirements of Rule 7.07.

(q) If these rules require that specific qualifications, disclaimers or disclosures of information accompany communications concerning a lawyer's services, the required qualifications, disclaimers or disclosures must be presented in the same manner as the communication and with equal prominence.

(r) A lawyer who advertises on the Internet must display the statements and disclosures required by Rule 7.04.

Adopted by order of Oct. 17, 1989, eff. Jan. 1, 1990. Redesignated from Rule 7.01(b) to (e), (g), (h) and amended by order of Nov. 15, 1994. Amended by order of Feb. 23, 1995; March 31, 1995; July 1, 1998; Feb. 7, 2005, eff. June 1, 2005.

Comment:

1. Neither Rule 7.04 nor Rule 7.05 prohibits communications authorized by law, such as notice to members of a class in class action litigation.

Advertising Areas of Practice and Special Competence

2. Paragraphs (a) and (b) permit a lawyer, under the restrictions set forth, to indicate areas of practice in advertisements about the lawyer's services. See also paragraph (d). The restrictions are designed primarily to require that accurate information be conveyed. These restrictions recognize that a lawyer has a right protected by the United States Constitution to advertise publicly, but that the right may be regulated by reasonable restrictions designed to protect the public from false or misleading information. The restrictions contained in Rule 7.04 are based on the experience of the legal profession in the State of Texas and are designed to curtail what experience has shown to be misleading and deceptive advertising. To ensure accountability, sub-paragraph (b)(1) requires identification of at least one lawyer responsible for the content of the advertisement.

3. Because of long-standing tradition a lawyer admitted to practice before the United States Patent Office may use the designation "patents," "patent attorney," or "patent lawyer" or any combination of those terms. As recognized by paragraph (a)(1), a lawyer engaged in patent and trademark practice may hold himself out as concentrating in "intellectual property law," "patents, or trademarks and related matters," or "patent, trademark, copyright law and unfair competition" or any combination of those terms.

4. Paragraph (a)(2) recognizes the propriety of listing a lawyer's name in legal directories according to the areas of law in which the lawyer will accept new matters. The same right is given with respect to lawyer referral service offices, but only if those services comply with statutory guidelines. The restriction in paragraph (a)(2) does not prevent a legal aid agency or prepaid legal services plan from advertising legal services provided under its auspices.

5. Paragraph (a)(3) continues the historical exception that permits advertisements by lawyers to other lawyers in legal directories and legal newspapers (whether written or electronic), subject to the same requirements of truthfulness that apply to all other forms of lawyer advertising. Such advertisements traditionally contain information about the name, location, telephone numbers, and general availability of a lawyer to work on particular legal matters. Other information may be included so long as it is not false or misleading. Because advertisements in these publications are not available to the general public, lawyers who list various areas of practice are not required to comply with paragraph (b).

6. Some advertisements, sometimes known as tombstone advertisements, mention only such matters as the name of the lawyer or law firm, a listing of lawyers associated with the firm, office addresses and telephone numbers, office and telephone service hours, dates of admission to bars, the acceptance of credit cards, and fees. The content of such advertisements is not the kind of information intended to be regulated by Rule 7.04 (b). However, if the advertisement in the public media mentions any area of the law in which the lawyer practices, then, because of the likelihood of misleading material, the lawyer must comply with paragraph (b).

7. Sometimes lawyers choose to advertise in the public media the fact that they have been certified or designated by a particular organization or that they are members of a particular organization. Such statements naturally lead the public to believe that the lawyer possesses special competence in the area of law mentioned. Consequently, in order to ensure that the public will not be misled by such statements, sub-paragraph (b)(2) and paragraph (c) place limited but necessary restrictions upon a lawyer's basic right to advertise those affiliations.

8. Rule 7.04(b)(2) gives lawyers who possess certificates of specialization from the Texas Board of Legal Specialization or other meritorious credentials from organizations approved by the Board the option of stating that fact, provided that the restrictions set forth in subparagraphs (b)(2)(i) and (b)(2)(ii) are followed.

9. Paragraph (c) is intended to ensure against misleading or material variations from the statements required by paragraph (b).

10. Paragraphs (e) and (f) provide the advertising lawyer, the Bar, and the public with requisite records should questions arise regarding the propriety of a public media advertisement. Paragraph (e), like paragraph (b)(1), ensures that a particular attorney accepts responsibility for the advertisement. It is in the public interest and in the interest of the legal profession that the records of those advertisements and approvals be maintained.

Examples of Prohibited Advertising

11. Paragraphs (g) through (*o*) regulate conduct that has been found to mislead or be likely to mislead the public. Each paragraph is designed to protect the public and to guard the legal profession against these documented misleading practices while at the same time respecting the constitutional rights of any lawyer to advertise.

12. Paragraph (g) prohibits lawyers from misleading the public into believing a non-lawyer portrayor or narrator in the advertisement is one of the lawyers prepared to perform services for the public. It does not prohibit the narration of an advertisement in the third person by an actor, as long as it is clear to those hearing or seeing the advertisement that the actor is not a lawyer prepared to perform services for the public.

13. Contingent fee contracts present unusual opportunities for deception by lawyers or for misunderstanding by the public. By requiring certain disclosures, paragraph (h) safeguards the public from misleading or potentially misleading advertisements that involve representation on a contingent fee basis. The affirmative requirements of paragraph (h) are not triggered solely by the expression of "contingent fee" or "percentage fee" in the advertisement. To the contrary, they encompass advertisements in the public media where the lawyer or firm expresses a mere willingness or potential willingness to render services for a contingent fee. Therefore, statements in an advertisement such as "no fee if no recovery" or "fees in the event of recovery only" are clearly included as a form of advertisement subject to the disclosure requirements of paragraph (h).

14. Paragraphs (i), (j), (k) and (*l*) jointly address the problem of advertising that experience has shown misleads the public concerning the fees that will be charged, the location where services will be provided, or the attorney who will be performing these services. Together they prohibit the same sort of "bait and switch" advertising tactics by lawyers that are universally condemned.

15. Paragraph (i) requires a lawyer who advertises a specific fee or range of fees in the public media to honor those commitments for the period during which the advertisement is reasonably expected to be in circulation or otherwise expected to be effective in attracting clients, unless the advertisement itself specifies a shorter period. In no event, however, is a lawyer required to honor an advertised fee or range of fees for more than one year after publication.

16. Paragraph (j) prohibits advertising the availability of a satellite office unless the requirements of subparagraphs (1) or (2) are satisfied. Paragraph (j) does not require, however, that a lawyer or firm specify which of several properly advertised offices is its "principal" one, as long as the principal office is among those advertised and the advertisement discloses the city or town in which that office is located. Experience has shown that, in the absence of such regulation, members of the public have been misled into employing a lawyer in a distant city who advertises that there is a nearby satellite office, only to learn later that the lawyer is rarely available to the client because the nearby office is seldom open or is staffed only by lay personnel. Paragraph (j) is not intended to restrict the ability of legal services programs to advertise satellite offices in remote parts of the program's service area even if those satellite offices are staffed irregularly by attorneys. Otherwise low-income individuals in and near such communities might be denied access to the only legal services truly available to them.

17. When a lawyer or firm advertises, the public has a right to expect that lawyer or firm will perform the legal services. Experience has shown that attorneys not in the same firm may create a relationship wherein one will finance advertising for the other in return for referrals. Nondisclosure of such a referral relationship is misleading to the public. Accordingly, paragraph (k) prohibits such a relationship between an advertising lawyer and a lawyer who finances the advertising unless the advertisement discloses the nature of the financial relationship between the two lawyers. Paragraph (*l*) addresses the same problem from a different perspective, requiring a lawyer who advertises the availability of legal services and who know or should know at the time that the advertisement is placed in the media that business will likely be referred to another lawyer or firm, to include a conspicuous statement of that fact in any such advertising. This requirement applies whether or not the lawyer to whom the business is referred is financing the advertisements of the referring lawyer. It does not, however, require disclosure of all possible scenarios under which a referral could occur, such as an unforeseen need to associate with a specialist in accordance with Rule 1.01(a) or the possibility of a referral if a prospective client turns out to have a conflict of interest precluding representation by the advertising lawyer. Lawyers participating in any type of arrangement to refer cases must comply with Rule 1.04(f).

18. Paragraph (m) protects the public by forbidding mottos, slogans, and jingles that are false or misleading. There are, however, mottos, slogans, and jingles that are informative rather than false or misleading. Accordingly, paragraph (m) recognizes an advertising lawyer's constitutional right to include appropriate mottos, slogans, and jingles in advertising.

19. Some lawyers choose to band together in a cooperative or joint venture to advertise. Although those arrangements are lawful, the fact that several independent lawyers have joined together in a single advertisement increases the risk of misrepresentation or other forms of inappropriate expression. Special care must be taken to ensure that cooperative advertisements identify each cooperating lawyer, state that each cooperating lawyer is paying for the advertisement, and accurately describe the professional qualifications of each cooperating lawyer. See paragraph *(o)*. Furthermore, each cooperating lawyer must comply with the filing requirements of Rule 7.07. See paragraph (p).

20. The use of disclosures, disclaimers and qualifying information is necessary to inform the public about various aspects of a lawyer or firm's practice in public media advertising and solicitation communications. In order to ensure that disclaimers required by these rules are conspicuously displayed, paragraph (q) requires that such statements be presented in the same manner as the communication and with prominence equal to that of the matter to which it refers. For example, in a television advertisement that necessitates the use of a disclaimer, if a statement or claim is made verbally, the disclaimer should also be included verbally in the commercial. When a statement or claim appears in print, the accompanying disclaimer must also appear in print with equal prominence and legibility.

(Comment amended by the State Bar Board of Directors Jan. 20, 1995; April 8, 2005, eff. June 1, 2005.)

The order of Nov. 15, 1994 amended all of Part VII.

By Supreme Court order 95–9074, dated March 31, 1995, the Supreme Court modified its order of Nov. 15, 1994, to provide that those rules upheld be made effective 120 days after the date of judgment of the United States District Court for the Eastern District of Texas in the lawsuit styled Texans Against Censorship, et al versus State Bar of Texas, et al. [Judgment was entered in *Texans Against Censorship, Inc. v. State Bar of Texas,* E.D.Tex.1995, 888 F.Supp. 1328, on March 31, 1995.]

The order of Feb. 23, 1995 made technical corrections.

Rule 7.05. Prohibited Written, Electronic, Or Digital Solicitations

(a) A lawyer shall not send, deliver, or transmit or knowingly permit or knowingly cause another person to send, deliver, or transmit a written. audio, audio-visual, digital media, recorded telephone message, or other electronic communication to a prospective client for the purpose of obtaining professional employment on behalf of any lawyer or law firm if:

(1) the communication involves coercion, duress, fraud, overreaching, intimidation, undue influence, or harassment;

(2) the communication contains information prohibited by Rule 7.02 or fails to satisfy each of the requirements of Rule 7.04(a) through (c), and (g) through (q) that would be applicable to the communication if it were an advertisement in the public media; or

(3) the communication contains a false, fraudulent, misleading, deceptive, or unfair statement or claim.

(b) Except as provided in paragraph (f) of this Rule, a written, electronic, or digital solicitation communication to prospective clients for the purpose of obtaining professional employment:

(1) shall, in the case of a non-electronically transmitted written communication, be plainly marked "ADVERTISEMENT" on its first page, and on the face of the envelope or other packaging used to transmit the communication. If the written communication is in the form of a self-mailing brochure or pamphlet, the word "ADVERTISEMENT" shall be:

(i) in a color that contrasts sharply with the background color; and

(ii) in a size of at least 3/8″ vertically or three times the vertical height of the letters used in the body of such communication, whichever is larger

(2) shall, in the case of an electronic mail message, be plainly marked "ADVERTISEMENT" in the subject portion of the electronic mail and at the beginning of the message's text;

(3) shall not be made to resemble legal pleadings or other legal documents;

(4) shall not reveal on the envelope or other packaging or electronic mail subject line used to transmit the communication, or on the outside of a self-mailing brochure or pamphlet, the nature of the legal problem of the prospective client or non-client; and

(5) shall disclose how the lawyer obtained the information prompting the communication to solicit professional employment if such contact was prompted by a specific occurrence involving the recipient of the communication, or a family member of such person(s).

(c) Except as provided in paragraph (f) of this Rule, an audio, audio-visual, digital media, recorded telephone message, or other electronic communication sent to prospective clients for the purpose of obtaining professional employment:

(1) shall, in the case of any such communication delivered to the recipient by non-electronic means, plainly and conspicuously state in writing on the outside of any envelope or other packaging used to transmit the communication, that it is an "ADVERTISEMENT."

(2) shall not reveal on any such envelope or other packaging the nature of the legal problem of the prospective client or non-client;

(3) shall disclose, either in the communication itself or in accompanying transmittal message, how the lawyer obtained the information prompting such audio, audio-visual, digital media, recorded telephone message, or other electronic communication to solicit professional employment, if such contact was prompted by a specific occurrence involving the recipient of the communication or a family member of such person(s);

(4) shall, in the case of a recorded audio presentation or a recorded telephone message, plainly state that it is an advertisement prior to any other words being spoken and again at the presentation's or message's conclusion; and

(5) shall, in the case of an audio-visual or digital media presentation, plainly state that the presentation is an advertisement;

(i) both verbally and in writing at the outset of the presentation and again at its conclusion; and

(ii) in writing during any portion of the presentation that explains how to contact a lawyer or law firm.

(d) All written, audio, audio-visual, digital media, recorded telephone message, or other electronic communications made to a prospective client for the purpose of obtaining professional employment of a lawyer or law firm must be reviewed and either signed by or approved in writing by the lawyer or a lawyer in the firm.

(e) A copy of each written, audio, audio-visual, digital media, recorded telephone message, or other electronic solicitation communication, the relevant approval thereof, and a record of the date of each such communication; the name, address,. telephone number, or electronic address to which each such communication was sent; and the means by which each such communication was sent shall be kept by the lawyer or firm for four years after its dissemination.

(f) The provisions of paragraphs (b) and (c) of this Rule do not apply to a written, audio, audiovisual, digital media, recorded telephone message, or other form, of electronic solicitation communication:

(1) directed to a family member or a person with whom the lawyer had or has an attorney client relationship;

(2) that is not motivated by or concerned with a particular past occurrence or event or a particular series of past occurrences or events, and also is not motivated by or concerned with the prospective client's specific existing legal problem of which the lawyer is aware;

(3) if the lawyer's use of the communication to secure professional employment was not significantly motivated by a desire for, or by the possibility of obtaining, pecuniary gain; or

(4) that is requested by the prospective client.

Adopted by order of Oct. 17, 1989, eff. Jan. 1, 1990. Redesignated from Rule 7.01(f), (g) and amended by order of Nov. 15, 1994. Amended by order of Feb. 23, 1995; March 31, 1995; July 1, 1998; Feb. 7, 2005, eff. June 1, 2005.

Comment:

1. Rule 7.03 deals with in-person, telephone, and other prohibited electronic contact between a lawyer and a prospective client wherein the lawyer seeks professional employment. Rule 7.04 deals with advertisements in the public media by a lawyer seeking professional employment. This Rule deals with solicitations between a lawyer and a prospective client. Typical examples are letters or other forms of correspondence (including those sent, delivered, or transmitted electronically), recorded telephone messages, audiotapes, videotapes, digital media, and the like, addressed to a prospective client.

2. Written, audio, audio-visual, and other forms of electronic solicitations raise more concerns than do comparable advertisements. Being private, they are more difficult to monitor, and for that reason paragraph (e) requires retention for four years of certain information regarding all such solicitations. See also Rule 7.07(a). Paragraph (a) addresses such concerns as well as problems stemming from exceptionally outrageous communications such as solicitations involving fraud, intimidation, or deceptive and misleading claims. Because receipt of multiple solicitations appears to be most pronounced and vexatious in situations involving accident victims, paragraphs (b)(1), (b)(2), (c)(1), (c)(4) and (c)(5) require that the envelope or other packaging used to transmit the communication, as well as the communication itself, plainly disclose that the communication is an advertisement, while paragraphs (b)(5) and (c)(3) require disclosure of the source of information if the solicitation was prompted by a specific occurrence.

3. Because experience has shown that many written, audio, audio-visual, electronic mail, and other forms of electronic solicitations have been intrusive or misleading by reason of being personalized or being disguised as some form of official communication, special prohibitions against such practices are necessary. The requirements of paragraph (b) and (c) greatly lessen those dangers of deception and harassment.

4. Newsletters or other works published by a lawyer that are not circulated for the purpose of obtaining professional employment are not within the ambit of paragraph (b) or (c).

5. This Rule also regulates audio, audio-visual, or other forms of electronic communications being used to solicit business. It includes such formats as recorded telephone messages, movies, audio or audio-visual recordings or tapes, digital media, the Internet, and other comparable forms of electronic communications. It requires that such communications comply with all of the substantive requirements applicable to written solicitations that are compatible with the different forms of media involved, as well as with all requirements related to approval of the communications and

retention of records concerning them. See paragraphs (c), (d), and (e).

6. In addition to addressing these special problems posed by solicitations, Rule 7.05 regulates the content of those communications. It does so by incorporating the standards of Rule 7.02 and those of Rule 7.04 that would apply to the solicitation were it instead a comparable form of advertisement in the public media. See paragraphs (a)(2) and (3). In brief, this approach means that, except as provided in paragraph (f), a lawyer may not include or omit anything from a solicitation unless the lawyer could do so were the communication a comparable form of advertisement in the public media.

7. Paragraph (f) provides that the restrictions in paragraph (b) and (c) do not apply in certain situations because the dangers of deception, harassment, vexation and overreaching are quite low. For example, a written solicitation may be directed to a family member or a present or a former client, or in response to a request by a prospective client without stating that it is an advertisement. Similarly, a written solicitation may be used in seeking general employment in commercial matters from a bank or other corporation, when there is neither concern with specific existing legal problems nor concern with a particular past event or series of events. All such communications, however, remain subject to Rule 7.02 and paragraphs (h) through (*o*) of Rule 7.04. See sub-paragraph (a)(2).

8. In addition, paragraph (f) allows such communications in situations not involving the lawyer's pecuniary gain. For purposes of these rules, it is presumed that communications made on behalf of a nonprofit legal aid agency, union, or other qualified nonprofit organization are not motivated by a desire for, or by the possibility of obtaining, pecuniary gain, but that presumption may be rebutted.

(Comment amended by the State Bar Board of Directors Jan. 20, 1995; April 8, 2005, eff. June 1, 2005.)

The order of Nov. 15, 1994 amended all of Part VII.

By Supreme Court order 95–9074, dated March 31, 1995, the Supreme Court modified its order of Nov. 15, 1994, to provide that those rules upheld be made effective 120 days after the date of judgment of the United States District Court for the Eastern District of Texas in the lawsuit styled Texans Against Censorship, et al. versus State Bar of Texas, et al. [Judgment was entered in *Texans Against Censorship, Inc. v. State Bar of Texas*, E.D.Tex.1995, 888 F.Supp. 1328, on March 31, 1995.]

The order of Feb. 23, 1995 made technical corrections.

The order of Feb. 7, 2005 rewrote the rule which prior thereto read:

"Prohibited Written Solicitations

"(a) A lawyer shall not send or deliver, or knowingly permit or cause another person to send or deliver on the lawyer's behalf, a written communication to a prospective client for the purpose of obtaining professional employment if:

"(1) the communication involves coercion, duress, fraud, overreaching, intimidation, undue influence, or harassment;

"(2) the communication contains information prohibited by Rule 7.02 or fails to satisfy each of the requirements of Rule 7.04(a) through (c), and (h) through (*o*) that would be applicable to the communication if it were an advertisement in the public media; or

"(3) the communication contains a false, fraudulent, misleading, deceptive, or unfair statement or claim.

"(b) Except as provided in paragraph (e) of this Rule, a written solicitation communication to prospective clients for the purpose of obtaining professional employment:

"(1) shall conform to the provisions of Rule 7.04(a) through (c);

"(2) shall be plainly marked "ADVERTISEMENT" on the first page of the written communication, and the face of the envelope also shall be plainly marked "ADVERTISEMENT," however, if the written communication is in the form of a self-mailing brochure or pamphlet, the word "ADVERTISEMENT" shall be: (i) in a color that contrasts sharply with the background color; and (ii) in a size of at least ⅜" vertically or three times the vertical height of the letters used in the body of such communication, whichever is larger.

"(3) shall not be made to resemble legal pleadings or other legal documents;

"(4), (5) [Deleted by the Supreme Court of Texas July 1, 1998]

"(6) shall not reveal on the envelope used for the communication, or on the outside of a self-mailing brochure or pamphlet, the nature of the legal problem of the prospective client or nonclient; and

"(7) shall disclose how the lawyer obtained the information prompting such written communication to solicit professional employment if such contact was prompted by a specific occurrence involving the recipient of the communication or a family member of such person(s).

"(c) All written communications to a prospective client for the purpose of obtaining professional employment must be reviewed and either signed by or approved in writing by the lawyer or a lawyer in the firm.

"(d) A copy of each written solicitation communication, the relevant approval thereof, and a record of the date of each such communication; the name and address to which each such communication was sent; and the means by which each such communication was sent shall be kept by the lawyer or firm for four years after its dissemination.

"(e) The provisions of paragraph (b) of this Rule do not apply to a written solicitation communication:

"(1) directed to a family member or a person with whom the lawyer had or has an attorney-client relationship;

"(2) that is not motivated by or concerned with a particular past occurrence or event or a particular series of past occurrences or events, and also is not motivated by or concerned with the prospective client's specific existing legal problem of which the lawyer is aware;

"(3) if the lawyer's use of the communication to secure professional employment was not significantly motivated by a desire for, or by the possibility of obtaining, pecuniary gain; or

"(4) that is requested by the prospective client."

Rule 7.06. Prohibited Employment

(a) A lawyer shall not accept or continue employment in a matter when that employment was procured by conduct prohibited by any of Rules 7.01 through 7.05, 8.04(a)(2), or 8.04(a)(9), engaged in by that lawyer personally or by any other person whom the lawyer ordered, encouraged, or knowingly permitted to engage in such conduct.

(b) A lawyer shall not accept or continue employment in a matter when the lawyer knows or reasonably should know that employment was procured by conduct prohibited by any of Rules 7.01 through 7.05, 8.04(a)(2), or 8.04(a)(9), engaged in by any other person or entity that is a shareholder, partner, or member of, an associate in, or of counsel to that lawyer's firm; or by any other person whom any of the foregoing persons or entities ordered, encouraged, or knowingly permitted to engage in such conduct.

(c) A lawyer who has not violated paragraph (a) or (b) in accepting employment in a matter shall not continue employment in that matter once the lawyer knows or reasonably should know that the person procuring the lawyer's employment in the matter engaged in, or ordered, encouraged, or knowingly permitted another to engage in, conduct prohibited by any of Rules 7.01 through 7.05, 8.04(a)(2), or 8.04(a)(9) in connection with the matter unless nothing of value is given thereafter in return for that employment.

Adopted by order of Oct. 17, 1989, eff. Jan. 1, 1990. Renumbered from Rule 7.03 and amended by order of Nov. 15, 1994. Amended by order of March 31, 1995; Feb. 7, 2005, eff. June 1, 2005.

Comment:

Selection of a lawyer by a client often is a result of the advice and recommendation of third parties—relatives, friends, acquaintances, business associates, and other lawyers. Although that method of referral is perfectly legitimate, the client is best served if the recommendation is disinterested and informed. All lawyers must guard against creating situations where referral from others is the consequence of some form of prohibited compensation or from some form of false or misleading communication, or by virtue of some other violation of any of Rules 7.01 through 7.05, 8.04(a)(2), or 8.04(a)(9). Paragraph (a) forbids a lawyer who violated these rules in procuring employment in a matter from accepting or continuing employment in that matter. This prohibition also applies if the lawyer ordered, encouraged, or knowingly permitted another to violate these rules. Paragraph (b) also forbids a lawyer from accepting or continuing employment in a matter if the lawyer knows or reasonably should know that a member or employee of his or her firm or any other person has procured employment in a matter as a result of conduct that violates these rules. Paragraph (c) addresses the situation where the lawyer becomes aware that the matter was procured in violation of these rules by an attorney or individual, but had no culpability. In such circumstances, the lawyer may continue employment and collect a fee in the matter as long as nothing of value is given to the attorney or individual involved in the violation of the rule(s). See also Rule 7.03(d), forbidding a lawyer to charge or collect a fee where the misconduct involves violations of Rule 7.03(a), (b), or (c).

(Comment amended by the State Bar Board of Directors Jan. 20, 1995; April 8, 2005, eff. June 1, 2005.)

The order of Nov. 15, 1994 amended all of Part VII.

By Supreme Court order 95–9074, dated March 31, 1995, the Supreme Court modified its order of Nov. 15, 1994, to provide that those rules upheld be made effective 120 days after the date of judgment of the United States District Court for the Eastern District of Texas in the lawsuit styled Texans Against Censorship, et al versus State Bar of Texas, et al. [Judgment was entered in *Texans Against Censorship, Inc. v. State Bar of Texas*, E.D.Tex.1995, 888 F.Supp. 1328, on March 31, 1995.]

The order of Feb. 7, 2005 rewrote the rule which prior thereto read:

"A lawyer shall not accept or continue employment when the lawyer knows or reasonably should know that the person who seeks the lawyer's services does so as a result of conduct prohibited by these rules."

Rule 7.07. Filing Requirements for Public Advertisements and Written, Recorded, Electronic, or Other Digital Solicitations

(a) Except as provided in paragraphs (c) and (e) of this Rule, a lawyer shall file with the Advertising Review Committee of the State Bar of Texas, no later than the mailing or sending by any means, including electronic, of a written, audio, audio-visual, digital or other electronic solicitation communication:

(1) a copy of the written, audio, audio-visual, digital, or other electronic solicitation communication being sent or to be sent to one or more prospective clients for the purpose of obtaining professional employment, together with a representative sample of the envelopes or other packaging in which the communications are enclosed;

(2) a completed lawyer advertising and solicitation communication application form; and

(3) a check or money order payable to the State Bar of Texas for the fee set by the Board of Directors. Such fee shall be for the sole purpose of defraying the expense of enforcing the rules related to such solicitations.

(b) Except as provided in paragraph (e) of this Rule, a lawyer shall file with the Advertising Review Committee of the State Bar of Texas, no later than the first dissemination of an advertisement in the public media, a copy of each of the lawyer's advertisements in the public media. The filing shall include:

(1) a copy of the advertisement in the form in which it appears or will appear upon dissemination, such as a videotape, audiotape, DVD, CD, a print copy, or a photograph of outdoor advertising;

(2) a production script of the advertisement setting forth all words used and describing in detail the actions, events, scenes, and background sounds used in such advertisement together with a listing of the names and addresses of persons portrayed or heard to speak, if the advertisement is in or will be

in a form in which the advertised message is not fully revealed by a print copy or photograph;

(3) a statement of when and where the advertisement has been, is, or will be used;

(4) a completed lawyer advertising and solicitation communication application form; and

(5) a check or money order payable to the State Bar of Texas for the fee set by the Board of Directors. Such fee shall be for the sole purpose of defraying the expense of enforcing the rules related to such advertisements.

(c) Except as provided in paragraph (e) of this Rule, a lawyer shall file with the Advertising Review Committee of the State Bar of Texas no later than its first posting on the internet or other comparable network of computers information concerning the lawyer's or lawyer's firm's website. As used in this Rule, a "website" means a single or multiple page file, posted on a computer server, which describes a lawyer or law firm's practice or qualifications, to which public access is provided through publication of a uniform resource locator (URL). The filing shall include:

(1) the intended initial access page of a website.

(2) a completed lawyer advertising and solicitation communication application form; and

(3) a check or money order payable to the State Bar of Texas for the fee set by the Board of Directors. Such fee shall be set for the sole purpose of defraying the expense of enforcing the rules related to such websites,

(d) A lawyer who desires to secure an advance advisory opinion, referred to as a request for pre-approval, concerning compliance of a contemplated solicitation communication or advertisement may submit to the Advertising Review Committee, not less than thirty (30) days prior to the date of first dissemination, the material specified in paragraph (a) or (b), or the intended initial access page submitted pursuant to paragraph (c), including the application form and required fee; provided however, it shall not be necessary to submit a videotape or DVD if the videotape or DVD has not then been prepared and the production script submitted reflects in detail and accurately the actions, events, scenes, and background sounds that will be depicted or contained on such videotapes or DVDs, when prepared, as well as the narrative transcript of the verbal and printed portions of such advertisement. If a lawyer submits an advertisement or solicitation communication for pre-approval, a finding of noncompliance by the Advertising Review Committee is not binding in a disciplinary proceeding or disciplinary action but a finding of compliance is binding in favor of the submitting lawyer as to all materials actually submitted for pre-approval if the representations, statements, materials, facts and written assurances received in connection therewith are true and are not misleading. The finding of compliance constitutes admissible evidence if offered by a party.

(e) The filing requirements of paragraphs (a), (b), and (c) do not extend to any of the following materials, provided those materials comply with Rule 7.02(a) through (c) and, where applicable. Rule 7.04(a) through (c):

(1) an advertisement in the public media that contains only part or all of the following information:

(i) the name of the lawyer or firm and lawyers associated with the firm, with office addresses, electronic addresses, telephone numbers, office and telephone service hours, telecopier numbers, and a designation of the profession such as "attorney", "lawyer", "law office", or "firm;"

(ii) the particular areas of law in which the lawyer or firm specializes or possesses special competence;

(iii) the particular areas of law in which the lawyer or firm practices or concentrates or to which it limits its practice;

(iv) the date of admission of the lawyer or lawyers to the State Bar of Texas, to particular federal courts, and to the bars of other jurisdictions;

(v) technical and professional licenses granted by this state and other recognized licensing authorities;

(vi) foreign language ability;

(vii) fields of law in which one or more lawyers are certified or designated, provided the statement of this information is in compliance with Rule 7.02(a) through (c).

(viii) identification of prepaid or group legal service plans in which the lawyer participates;

(ix) the acceptance or nonacceptance of credit cards;

(x) any fee for initial consultation and fee schedule;

(xi) other publicly available information concerning legal issues, not prepared or paid for by the firm or any of its lawyers, such as news articles, legal articles, editorial opinions, or other legal developments or events, such as proposed or enacted rules, regulations, or legislation;

(xii) in the case of a website, links to other websites;

(xiii) that the lawyer or firm is a sponsor of a charitable, civic, or community program or event, or is a sponsor of a public service announcement;

(xiv) any disclosure or statement required by these rules; and

(xv) any other information specified from time to time in orders promulgated by the Supreme Court of Texas;

(2) an advertisement in the public media that:

(i) identifies one or more lawyers or a firm as a contributor to a specified charity or as a sponsor of a specified charitable, community, or public interest program, activity, or event; and

(ii) contains no information about the lawyers or firm other than names of the lawyers or firm or both, location of the law offices, and the fact of the sponsorship or contribution;

(3) a listing or entry in a regularly published law list;

(4) an announcement card stating new or changed associations, new offices, or similar changes relating to a lawyer or firm, or a tombstone professional card;

(5) in the case of communications sent, delivered, or transmitted to, rather than accessed by, intended recipients, a newsletter, whether written, digital, or electronic, provided that it is sent, delivered, or transmitted only to:

(i) existing or former clients;

(ii) other lawyers or professionals; or

(iii) members of a nonprofit organization that meets the following conditions: the primary purposes of the organization do not include the rendition of legal services; the recommending, furnishing, paying for, or educating persons regarding legal services is incidental and reasonably related to the primary purposes of the organization; the organization does not derive a financial benefit from the rendition of legal services by a lawyer; and the person for whom the legal services are rendered, and not the organization, is recognized as the client of the lawyer who is recommended, furnished, or paid by the organization;

(6) a solicitation communication that is not motivated by or concerned with a particular past occurrence or event or a particular series of past occurrences or events, and also is not motivated by or concerned with the prospective client's specific existing legal problem of which the lawyer is aware;

(7) a solicitation communication if the lawyer's use of the communication to secure professional employment was not significantly motivated by a desire for, or by the possibility of obtaining, pecuniary gain; or

(8) a solicitation communication that is requested by the prospective client.

(f) if requested by the Advertising Review Committee, a lawyer shall promptly submit information to substantiate statements or representations made or implied in any advertisement in the public media or solicitation communication by which the lawyer seeks paid professional employment.

Adopted by order of Nov. 15, 1994. Amended by order of Feb. 23, 1995; March 31, 1995; Feb. 7, 2005, eff. June 1, 2005.

Comment:

1. Rule 7.07 covers the filing requirements for public media advertisements (see Rule 7.04) and written, recorded, or other electronic solicitations (see Rule 7.05). Rule 7.07(a) deals with solicitation communication sent by a lawyer to one or more specified prospective clients. Rule 7.07(b) deals with advertisements in the public media. Rules 7.07(c) deals with websites. Although websites are a form of advertisement in the public media, they require different treatment in some respects and so are dealt with separately. Each provision allows the Bar to charge a fee for reviewing submitted materials, but requires that fee be set solely to defray the expenses of enforcing those provisions.

2. Copies of non-exempt solicitations communication or advertisements in public media (including websites) must be provided to the Advertising Review Committee of the State Bar of Texas either in advance or concurrently with dissemination, together with the fee required by the State Bar of Texas Board of Directors. Presumably, the Advertising Review Committee will report to the appropriate grievance committee any lawyer whom it finds from the reviewed products has disseminated an advertisement in the public media or solicitation communication that violates Rules 7.02, 7.03, 7.04, or 7.05, or, at a minimum, any lawyer whose violation raises a substantial question as to that lawyer's honesty, trustworthiness, or fitness as a lawyer in other respects. See Rule 8.03(a).

3. Paragraph (a) does not require that a lawyer submit a copy of each and every written solicitation letter a lawyer sends. If the same form letter is sent to several people, only a representative sample of each form letter, along with a representative sample of the envelopes used to mail the letters, need be filed.

4. A lawyer wishing to do so may secure an advisory opinion from the Advertising Review Committee concerning any proposed advertisement in the public media (including a website) or any solicitation communication in advance of its first use or dissemination by complying with Rule 7.07(d). This procedure is intended as a service to those lawyers who want to resolve any possible doubts about their proposed advertisements' or solicitations' compliance with these Rules before utilizing them. Its use is purely optional. No lawyer is required to obtain advance clearance of any advertisement in the public media (including a website) or any solicitation communication from the State Bar. Although a finding of noncompliance by the Advertising Review Committee is not binding in a disciplinary proceeding, a finding of compliance is binding in favor of the submitting lawyer as to all materials actually submitted for review, as long as the lawyer's

presentation to the Advertising Review Committee in connection with that advisory opinion is true and not misleading.

5. Under its Internal Rules and Operating Procedures, the Advertising Review Committee is to complete its evaluations no later than 25 days after the date of receipt of a filing. The only way that the Committee can extend that review period is to: (1) determine that there is reasonable doubt whether the advertisement or solicitation communication complies with these Rules; (2) conclude that further examination is warranted but cannot be completed within the 25–day period; and (3) advise the lawyer of those determinations in writing within that 25 day period. The Committee's Internal Rules and Operating Procedures also provide that a failure to send such a communication to the lawyer within the 25–day period constitutes approval of the advertisement or solicitation communication. Consequently, if an attorney submits an advertisement in the public media (including a website) or a solicitation communication to the Committee for advance approval not less than 30 days prior to the date of first dissemination as required by these Rules, the attorney will receive an assessment of that advertisement or communication before the date of its first intended use.

6. Consistent with the effort to protect the first amendment rights of lawyers while ensuring the right of the public to be free from misleading advertising and the right of the Texas legal profession to maintain its integrity, paragraph (e) exempts certain types of advertisements and solicitation communications prepared for the purpose of seeking paid professional employment from the filing requirements of paragraphs (a), (b), and (c). Those types of communications need not be filed at all if they were not prepared to secure paid professional employment.

7. For the most part, the types of exempted advertising listed in sub-paragraphs (e)(1) to (e)(5) are objective and less likely to result in false, misleading or fraudulent content. Similarly the types of exempted solicitation communications listed in sub-paragraphs (e)(6) to (e)(8) are those found least likely to result in harm to the public. See Rule 7.05(f), and comment 7 to Rule 7.05. The fact that a particular advertisement or solicitation made by a lawyer is exempted from the filing requirements of this Rule does not exempt a lawyer from the other applicable obligations of these Rules. See generally Rules 7.01 through 7.06.

8. Paragraph (f) does not empower the Advertising Review Committee to seek information from a lawyer to substantiate statements or representations made or implied in advertisements or written communications that do not seek to obtain paid professional employment for that lawyer.

(Comment amended by the State Bar Board of Directors Jan. 20, 1995; April 8, 2005, eff. June 1, 2005.)

The order of Nov. 15, 1994 amended all of Part VII.

By Supreme Court order 95–9074, dated March 31, 1995, the Supreme Court modified its order of Nov. 15, 1994, to provide that those rules upheld be made effective 120 days after the date of judgment of the United States District Court for the Eastern District of Texas in the lawsuit styled Texans Against Censorship, et al versus State Bar of Texas, et al. [Judgment was entered in *Texans Against Censorship, Inc. v. State Bar of Texas*, E.D.Tex.1995, 888 F.Supp. 1328, on March 31, 1995.]

The order of Feb. 23, 1995 made technical corrections.

The order of Feb. 7, 2005 rewrote the rule which prior thereto read:

"(a) Except as provided in paragraph (d) of this Rule, a lawyer shall file with the Lawyer Advertisement and Solicitation Review Committee of the State Bar of Texas, either before or concurrently with the mailing or sending of a written solicitation communication:

"(1) a copy of the written solicitation communication being sent or to be sent to one or more prospective clients for the purpose of obtaining professional employment, together with a representative sample of the envelopes in which the communications are enclosed; and

"(2) a check or money order payable to the State Bar of Texas for the fee set by the Board of Directors. Such fee shall be for the sole purpose of defraying the expense of enforcing the rules related to such solicitations.

"(b) Except as provided in paragraph (d) of this Rule, a lawyer shall file with the Lawyer Advertisement and Solicitation Review Committee of the State Bar of Texas, either before or concurrently with the first dissemination of an advertisement in the public media, a copy of that advertisement. The filing shall include:

"(1) a copy of the advertisement in the form in which it appears or is or will be disseminated, such as a videotape, an audiotape, a print copy, or a photograph of outdoor advertising;

"(2) a production script of the advertisement setting forth all words used and describing in detail the actions, events, scenes, and background sounds used in such advertisement together with a listing of the names and addresses of persons portrayed or heard to speak, if the advertisement is in or will be in a form in which the advertised message is not fully revealed by a print copy or photograph;

"(3) a statement of when and where the advertisement has been, is, or will be used; and

"(4) a check or money order payable to the State Bar of Texas for the fee set by the Board of Directors. Such fee shall be for the sole purpose of defraying the expense of enforcing the rules related to such advertisements.

"(c) A lawyer who desires to secure an advance advisory opinion concerning compliance of a contemplated written solicitation communication or advertisement may submit to the Lawyer Advertisement and Solicitation Review Committee, not less than thirty (30) days prior to the date of first dissemination, the material specified in paragraph (a) or (b) of this Rule, including the required fee; provided however, it shall not be necessary to submit a videotape it the videotape has not then been prepared and the production script submitted reflects in detail and accurately the actions, events, scenes, and background sounds that will be depicted or contained on such videotapes, when prepared, as well as the narrative transcript of the verbal and printed portions of such advertisement. An advisory opinion of the Lawyer Advertisement and Solicitation Review Committee of noncompliance is not binding in a disciplinary proceeding or disciplinary action but a finding of compliance is binding in favor of the submitting lawyer if the representations, statements, materials, facts and written assurances received in connection therewith are true and are not misleading. The finding constitutes admissible evidence if offered by a party.

"(d) The filing requirements of paragraphs (a) and (b) do not extend to any of the following materials:

"(1) an advertisement in the public media that contains only part or all of the following information, provided the information is not false or misleading:

"(i) the name of a lawyer or firm and lawyers associated with the firm, with office addresses, telephone numbers, office and telephone service hours, telecopier numbers, and a designation of the profession such as 'attorney,' 'lawyer,' 'law office,' or 'firm';

"(ii) the fields of law in which the lawyer or firm advertises specialization and the statements required by Rule 7.04(a) through (c);

"(iii) the date of admission of the lawyer or lawyers to the State Bar of Texas, to particular federal courts, and to the bars of other jurisdictions;

"(iv) technical and professional licenses granted by this state and other recognized licensing authorities;

"(v) foreign language ability;

"(vi) fields of law in which one or more lawyers are certified or designated, provided the statement of this information is in compliance with Rule 7.02(a) through (c);

"(vii) identification of prepaid or group legal service plans in which the lawyer participates;

"(viii) the acceptance or nonacceptance of credit cards;

"(ix) any fee for initial consultation and fee schedule;

"(x) that the lawyer or firm is a sponsor of a charitable, civic, or community program or event, or is a sponsor of a public service announcement;

"(xi) any disclosure or statement required by these rules; and

"(xii) any other information specified from time to time in orders promulgated by the Supreme Court of Texas:

"(2) an advertisement in the public media that:

"(i) identifies one or more lawyers or a firm as a contributor to a specified charity or as a sponsor of a specified charitable, community, or public interest program, activity, or event; and

"(ii) contains no information about the lawyers or firm other than name of the lawyers or firm or both, location of the law offices, and the fact of the sponsorship or contribution;

"(3) a listing or entry in a regularly published law list;

"(4) an announcement card stating new or changed associations, new offices, or similar changes relating to a lawyer or firm, or a tombstone professional card;

"(5) a newsletter mailed only to:

"(i) existing or former clients;

"(ii) other lawyers or professionals; and

"(iii) members of a nonprofit organization that meets the following conditions: the primary purposes of the organization do not include the rendition of legal services; the recommending, furnishing, paying for, or educating persons regarding legal services is incidental and reasonably related to the primary purposes of the organization; the organization does not derive a financial benefit from the rendition of legal services by a lawyer; and the person for whom the legal services are rendered, and not the organization, is recognized as the client of the lawyer who is recommended, furnished, or paid by the organization;

"(6) a written solicitation communication that is not motivated by or concerned with a particular past occurrence or event or a particular series of past occurrences or events, and also is not motivated by or concerned with the prospective client's specific existing legal problem of which the lawyer is award;

"(7) a written solicitation communication if the lawyer's use of the communication to secure professional employment was not significantly motivated by a desire for, or by the possibility of obtaining, pecuniary gain; or

"(8) a written solicitation communication that is requested by the prospective client.

"(e) If requested by the Lawyer Advertisement and Solicitation Review Committee, a lawyer shall promptly submit information to substantiate statements or representations made or implied in any advertisement in the public media and/or written solicitation."

VIII. Maintaining the Integrity of the Profession

Rule 8.01. Bar Admission, Reinstatement, and Disciplinary Matters

An applicant for admission to the bar, a petitioner for reinstatement to the bar, or a lawyer in connection with a bar admission application, a petition for reinstatement, or a disciplinary matter, shall not:

(a) knowingly make a false statement of material fact; or

(b) fail to correct a misapprehension known by the person to have arisen in the matter, or knowingly fail to respond to a lawful demand for information from an admission, reinstatement, or disciplinary authority, except that this rule does not require disclosure of information otherwise protected by Rule 1.05.

Adopted by order of Oct. 17, 1989, eff. Jan. 1, 1990.

Comment:

1. The duty imposed by this Rule extends to persons seeking admission or reinstatement to the bar as well as to lawyers. Hence, if a person makes a material false statement in connection with an application for admission or a petition for reinstatement, it may be the basis for subsequent disciplinary action if the person is admitted or reinstated, and in any event may be relevant in any subsequent application for admission or petition for reinstatement. The duty imposed by this Rule applies to a lawyer's own admission, reinstatement or discipline as well as that of others. Thus, for example, it is a separate professional offense for a lawyer to knowingly make a material misrepresentation or omission in connection with a disciplinary investigation of the lawyer's own conduct. Likewise, it is a separate professional offense for a lawyer to fail to respond to a lawful demand for information of a disciplinary authority inquiring into that lawyer's professional activities or conduct. Cf. State Bar Rules, art. X, sec. 7(4). This Rule also requires affirmative clarification of any misunderstanding on the part of the admissions, reinstatement or disciplinary authority of which the person involved becomes aware.

2. This Rule is subject to the provisions of the Fifth Amendment of the United States Constitution and corresponding provisions of Article 1, Section 10 of the Texas

Constitution. A person relying on such a provision in response to a specific question or more general demand for information, however, should do so openly and not use the right of nondisclosure as an unasserted justification for failure to comply with this Rule. Cf. State Bar Rules, art. X, sec. 7(4).

3. A lawyer representing an applicant for admission or petitioner for reinstatement to the bar, or representing a lawyer who is the subject of a disciplinary inquiry or proceeding, is governed by the rules applicable to the client-lawyer relationship, including those concerning the confidentiality of attorney-client communications. If such communications are protected under Rule 1.05, the lawyer need not and should not disclose them under this Rule. See also Rule 8.03(c).

Rule 8.02. Judicial and Legal Officials

(a) A lawyer shall not make a statement that the lawyer knows to be false or with reckless disregard as to its truth or falsity concerning the qualifications or integrity of a judge, adjudicatory official or public legal officer, or of a candidate for election or appointment to judicial or legal office.

(b) A lawyer who is a candidate for judicial office shall comply with the applicable provisions of the Texas Code of Judicial Conduct.

(c) A lawyer who is a candidate for an elective public office shall comply with the applicable provisions of the Texas Election Code.

Adopted by order of Oct. 17, 1989, eff. Jan. 1, 1990.

Comment:

1. Assessments by lawyers are relied on in evaluating the professional or personal fitness of persons being considered for election or appointment to judicial office and to public legal offices, such as attorney general, prosecuting attorney and public defender. Expressing honest and candid opinions on such matters contributes to improving the administration of justice. Conversely, false statements by a lawyer can unfairly undermine public confidence in the administration of justice.

2. When a lawyer seeks judicial or other elective public office, the lawyer should be bound by applicable limitations on political activity.

3. To maintain the fair and independent administration of justice, lawyers are encouraged to continue traditional efforts to defend judges and courts unjustly criticized.

Rule 8.03. Reporting Professional Misconduct

(a) Except as permitted in paragraphs (c) or (d), a lawyer having knowledge that another lawyer has committed a violation of applicable rules of professional conduct that raises a substantial question as to that lawyer's honesty, trustworthiness or fitness as a lawyer in other respects, shall inform the appropriate disciplinary authority.

(b) Except as permitted in paragraphs (c) or (d), a lawyer having knowledge that a judge has committed a violation of applicable rules of judicial conduct that raises a substantial question as to the judge's fitness for office shall inform the appropriate authority.

(c) A lawyer having knowledge or suspecting that another lawyer or judge whose conduct the lawyer is required to report pursuant to paragraphs (a) or (b) of this Rule is impaired by chemical dependency on alcohol or drugs or by mental illness may report that person to an approved peer assistance program rather than to an appropriate disciplinary authority. If a lawyer elects that option, the lawyer's report to the approved peer assistance program shall disclose any disciplinary violations that the reporting lawyer would otherwise have to disclose to the authorities referred to in paragraphs (a) and (b).

(d) This rule does not require disclosure of knowledge or information otherwise protected as confidential information:

(1) by Rule 1.05 or

(2) by any statutory or regulatory provisions applicable to the counseling activities of the approved peer assistance program.

Adopted by order of Oct. 17, 1989, eff. Jan. 1, 1990. Amended by order of June 15, 1994, eff. Oct. 1, 1994.

Comment:

1. Self-regulation of the legal profession requires that members of the profession initiate disciplinary investigations when they have knowledge not protected by Rule 1.05 that a violation of these rules has occurred. Lawyers have a similar obligation with respect to judicial misconduct. Frequently, the existence of a violation cannot be established with certainty until a disciplinary investigation has been undertaken. Similarly, an apparently isolated violation may indicate a pattern of misconduct that only a disciplinary investigation can uncover. Consequently, a lawyer should not fail to report an apparent disciplinary violation merely because he cannot determine its existence or scope with absolute certainty. Reporting a violation is especially important where the victim is unlikely to discover the offense.

2. It should be noted that this Rule describes only those disciplinary violations that must be revealed by the disclosing lawyer in order to avoid violating these rules himself. It is not intended to, nor does it, limit those actual or suspected violations that a lawyer may report. However, if a lawyer were obliged to report every violation of these rules, the failure to report any violation would itself be a professional offense. Such a requirement existed in many jurisdictions but proved to be unenforceable. This Rule limits the reporting obligation to those offenses that a self-regulating profession must vigorously endeavor to prevent. A measure of judgment is, therefore, required in complying with the provisions of this Rule. Similar considerations apply to the reporting of judicial misconduct. The term "substantial" refers to the seriousness of the possible offense and not the quantum of evidence of which the lawyer is aware. The term "fitness" has the meanings ascribed to it in the Terminology provisions of these Rules.

3. A report of professional misconduct by a lawyer should be made and processed in accordance with Article X of the State Bar Rules. A lawyer need not report misconduct

where the report would involve a violation of Rule 1.05. However, a lawyer should encourage a client to consent to disclosure where prosecution of the violation would not substantially prejudice the client's interests. Likewise, the duty to report professional misconduct does not apply to a lawyer retained to represent a lawyer whose past professional conduct is in question. Such a situation is governed by the rules applicable to the client-lawyer relationship.

Rule 8.04. Misconduct

(a) A lawyer shall not:

(1) violate these rules, knowingly assist or induce another to do so, or do so through the acts of another, whether or not such violation occurred in the course of a client-lawyer relationship;

(2) commit a serious crime or commit any other criminal act that reflects adversely on the lawyer's honesty, trustworthiness or fitness as a lawyer in other respects;

(3) engage in conduct involving dishonesty, fraud, deceit or misrepresentation;

(4) engage in conduct constituting obstruction of justice;

(5) state or imply an ability to influence improperly a government agency or official;

(6) knowingly assist a judge or judicial officer in conduct that is a violation of applicable rules of judicial conduct or other law;

(7) violate any disciplinary or disability order or judgment;

(8) fail to timely furnish to the Chief Disciplinary Counsel's office or a district grievance committee a response or other information as required by the Texas Rules of Disciplinary Procedure, unless he or she in good faith timely asserts a privilege or other legal ground for failure to do so;

(9) engage in conduct that constitutes barratry as defined by the law of this state;

(10) fail to comply with section 13.01 of the Texas Rules of Disciplinary Procedure relating to notification of an attorney's cessation of practice;

(11) engage in the practice of law when the lawyer is on inactive status or when the lawyer's right to practice has been suspended or terminated including but not limited to situations where a lawyer's right to practice has been administratively suspended for failure to timely pay required fees or assessments or for failure to comply with Article XII of the State Bar Rules relating to Mandatory Continuing Legal Education; or

(12) violate any other laws of this state relating to the professional conduct of lawyers and to the practice of law.

(b) As used in subsection (a)(2) of this Rule, "serious crime" means barratry; any felony involving moral turpitude; any misdemeanor involving theft, embezzlement, or fraudulent or reckless misappropriation of money or other property; or any attempt, conspiracy, or solicitation of another to commit any of the foregoing crimes.

Adopted by order of Oct. 17, 1989, eff. Jan. 1, 1990. Amended by order of June 15, 1994, eff. Oct. 1, 1994.

Comment:

1. There are three principal sources of professional obligations for lawyers in Texas: these rules, the State Bar Act, and the State Bar Rules. Article X, section 7 of the State Bar Rules contains a listing of the grounds for discipline under those Rules.

2. Rule 8.04 provides a comprehensive restatement of all forms of conduct that will subject a lawyer to discipline under either these Rules, the State Bar Act or the State Bar Rules. In that regard, Rule 8.04(a)(1) is intended to correspond to article X, section 7(1) of the State Bar Rules; Rules 8.04(a)(2) and 8.04(b) are intended to correspond to the provisions of article X, sections 7(8) and 26 of those Rules; and Rules 8.04(a)(7)-(10) are intended to correspond to article X, sections 7(3), 7(5), 7(6) and 7(7), respectively, of the State Bar Rules. Rule 8.04(a)(11) of these Rules corresponds to a prohibition contained in the last (unnumbered) paragraph of article X, section 7.

3. The only two provisions of article X, section 7 not specifically referred to in Rule 8.04 are addressed by other Rules. In particular, article X, section 7(2)'s provision for imposing discipline on an attorney here for conduct resulting in that lawyer's discipline in another jurisdiction is provided for by Rule 8.05 of these Rules. Similarly, article X, section 7(4)'s provision prohibiting a lawyer from failing either to provide information to a grievance or review committee, or to assert grounds for failure to do so, is made a subject of discipline by Rule 8.01 of these Rules. Violations of either of those Rules, in turn, subjects a lawyer to discipline pursuant to Rule 8.04(a)(1).

4. Many kinds of illegal conduct reflect adversely on fitness to practice law. However, some kinds of offenses carry no such implication. Traditionally in this state, the distinction has been drawn in terms of "serious crimes" and other offenses. See article X, sections 7(8) and 26 of the State Bar Rules. These Rules continue that distinction by making only those criminal offenses either amounting to "serious crimes" or having the salient characteristics of such crimes the subject of discipline. See Rules 8.04(a)(2), 8.04(b).

5. Although a lawyer is personally answerable to the entire criminal law, a lawyer should be professionally answerable only for offenses that indicate lack of those characteristics relevant to his fitness for the practice of law, as "fitness" is defined in these Rules. A pattern of repeated offenses, even ones of minor significance when considered separately, can indicate indifference to legal obligations that legitimately could call a lawyer's overall fitness to practice into question.

6. A lawyer may refuse to comply with an obligation imposed by law upon a good faith belief, openly asserted, that no valid obligation exists. The provisions of Rule 1.02(d) concerning a good faith challenge to the validity, scope, meaning or application of the law apply to challenges to legal regulation of the practice of law.

7. Lawyers holding public office assume legal responsibilities going beyond those of other citizens. A lawyer's abuse

of public office can suggest an inability to fulfill the professional role of attorney. The same is true of abuse of positions of private trust.

Rule 8.05. Jurisdiction

(a) A lawyer is subject to the disciplinary authority of this state, if admitted to practice in this state or if specially admitted by a court of this state for a particular proceeding. In addition to being answerable for his or her conduct occurring in this state, any such lawyer also may be disciplined here for conduct occurring in another jurisdiction or resulting in lawyer discipline in another jurisdiction, if it is professional misconduct under Rule 8.04.

(b) A lawyer admitted to practice in this state is also subject to the disciplinary authority for:

(1) an advertisement in the public media that does not comply with these rules and that is broadcast or disseminated in another jurisdiction, even if the advertisement complies with the rules governing lawyer advertisements in that jurisdiction, if the broadcast or dissemination of the advertisement is intended to be received by prospective clients in this state and is intended to secure employment to be performed in this state; and

(2) a written solicitation communication that does not comply with these rules and that is mailed in another jurisdiction, even if the communication complies with the rules governing written solicitation communications by lawyers in that jurisdiction, if the communication is mailed to an addressee in this state or is intended to secure employment to be performed in this state.

Adopted by order of Oct. 17, 1989, eff. Jan. 1, 1990. Amended by order of Nov. 15, 1994; March 31, 1995.

Comment:

1. This Rule describes those lawyers who are subject to the disciplinary authority of this state. It includes all lawyers licensed to practice here, as well as lawyers admitted specially for a particular proceeding. This Rule is not intended to have any effect on the powers of a court to punish lawyers for contempt or for other breaches of applicable rules of practice or procedure.

2. In modern practice lawyers licensed in Texas frequently act outside the territorial limits or judicial system of this state. In doing so, they remain subject to the governing authority of this state. If their activity in another jurisdiction is substantial and continuous, it may constitute the practice of law in that jurisdiction. See Rule 5.05.

3. If the rules of professional conduct of this state and that other jurisdiction differ, principles of conflict of laws may apply. Similar problems can arise when a lawyer is licensed to practice in more than one jurisdiction and these jurisdictions impose conflicting obligations. A related problem arises with respect to practice before a federal tribunal, where the general authority of the state to regulate the practice of law must be reconciled with such authority as federal tribunals may have to regulate practice before them. In such cases, this state will not impose discipline for conduct arising in connection with the practice of law in another jurisdiction or resulting in lawyer discipline in another jurisdiction unless that conduct constitutes professional misconduct under Rule 8.04.

4. Normally, discipline will not be imposed in this state for conduct occurring solely in another jurisdiction or judicial system and authorized by the rules of professional conduct applicable thereto, even if that conduct would violate these Rules.

(Comment amended by State Bar Board of Directors Jan. 20, 1995.)

IX. Severability of Rules

Rule 9.01. Severability

If any provision of these rules or any application of these rules to any person or circumstances if held invalid, such invalidity shall not affect any other provision or application of these rules that can be given effect without the invalid provision or application and, to this end, the provisions of these rules are severable.

Adopted by order of Nov. 15, 1994. Amended by order of March 31, 1995.

Comment:

The history of the regulation of American lawyers is replete with challenges to various rules on grounds of unconstitutionality. Because many of these Rules, particularly those in Article VII, are interrelated to an extent, the voiding of a particular rule or of a single provision in a rule could raise questions as to whether other provisions should survive. Rule 9.01 makes it clear that these Rules should be construed so as to minimize the effect of a determination that a particular application or provision of them is unconstitutional. The process of amending the Texas Disciplinary Rules of Professional Conduct is unusually difficult and time consuming and a decision invalidating one provision or application of a rule should not be expanded unnecessarily so as to invalidate other provisions or applications. These Disciplinary Rules have the specificity found in statutes, and it is appropriate for Rule 9.01 to contain a provision, frequently found in legislation, that reasonably limits the effect of the invalidity of one provision or one application of a rule.

(Comment amended by State Bar Board of Directors Jan. 20, 1995.)

By Supreme Court order 95–9074, dated March 31, 1995, the Supreme Court modified its order of Nov. 15, 1994, to provide that those rules upheld be made effective 120 days after the date of judgment of the United States District Court for the Eastern District of Texas in the lawsuit styled Texans Against Censorship, et al versus State Bar of Texas, et al. [Judgment was entered in *Texans Against Censorship, Inc. v. State Bar of Texas*, E.D.Tex.1995, 888 F.Supp. 1328, on March 31, 1995.]

Sections 10 to 38. Repealed by order of Feb. 26, 1991, eff. May 1, 1992

ARTICLE XI—INTEREST EARNED ON CLIENT FUNDS HELD BY ATTORNEYS

Section 1. Short Title

This Article may be referred to as the Texas Equal Access to Justice Program.

Adopted by order of May 9, 1984.

Section 2. Findings; Purpose

The Supreme Court of Texas finds that:

(A) On certain client funds held by attorneys, interest income cannot reasonably be earned to benefit individual clients for whom the funds are held;

(B) Income can be earned on those client funds pursuant to the program provided for in this Article and that income should be used to provide additional legal services to the indigent in civil matters;

(C) This Court is the proper and appropriate body, through the adoption of rules as set forth in this Article, to create and administer, or cause to be created and administered, a program to carry out the purposes of this Article; and

(D) This Article is adopted in furtherance of the inherent powers of this Court to regulate the practice of law in the State of Texas.

Adopted by order of May 9, 1984.

Section 3. Rules

This Court shall hereafter promulgate rules, consistent with the provisions of this Article, that are necessary and appropriate to carry out the purposes of this Article and conform the program created as provided by this Article to applicable statutes, regulations, and rulings. The rules, which may be amended or revoked by this Court from time to time as it deems necessary to carry out this Article, shall provide for:

(A) The formation of a corporation, incorporated without members under the Texas Non-Profit Corporation Act (TEX.REV.CIV.STAT.ANN. art. 1396–1.01 *et seq.*), to be the recipient of and disbursing agent for interest earned on client funds as provided by this Article;

(B) The operation of the nonprofit corporation and the program created as provided by this Article, including the provisions to be contained in the articles of incorporation and bylaws of the corporation;

(C) The designation of persons to serve as directors of the corporation and their terms of office;

(D) Definitions of the client funds subject to Section 5 of this Article;

(E) Exemptions from Section 5 of this Article when deemed by the Court to be appropriate;

(F) Provisions specifying the types of financial institutions eligible for the deposit of the funds, the types of organizations and programs eligible to receive funds from the nonprofit corporation, and the persons and types of matters and cases eligible to receive legal services funded by grants from the nonprofit corporation; and

(G) Provisions relating to recordkeeping, reporting, and audits of the nonprofit corporation and the organizations and programs receiving funds from the nonprofit corporation.

Adopted by order of May 9, 1984.

Section 4. Provisions Relating to the Nonprofit Corporation

(A) The nonprofit corporation provided for in this Article shall be organized in such a manner as to be exempt from federal income taxation under the Internal Revenue Code of 1954 [1] or any subsequent United States internal revenue law.

(B) The exclusive purpose of the nonprofit corporation provided for in this Article shall be to grant funds received by it, as provided in this Article, to organizations that will use the funds exclusively to provide legal services to the indigent in civil matters.

(C) The nonprofit corporation provided for in this Article shall be governed by a board of directors consisting of a chairman and twelve members. The chairman and six directors shall be persons appointed by this Court and the other six directors shall be persons appointed by the president of the State Bar of Texas, with the approval of the board of directors of the State Bar of Texas. At least two of each group of appointees to the board of directors, other than the chairman, shall not be attorneys, and shall not have, other than as consumers, a financial interest in the practice of law.

(D) Funds granted by the nonprofit corporation provided for in this Article to organizations to provide legal services to the indigent in civil matters may not be used for any case or matter that, if undertaken on behalf of an indigent person by an attorney in private practice, might reasonably be expected to result in payment of a fee for legal services from an award to a client, from public funds, or from the opposing party. This subsection does not apply if it is determined, pursuant to rules adopted by this Court, that adequate legal services would otherwise be unavailable to the indigent person in the case or matter.

(E) Neither the nonprofit corporation provided for in this Article nor any organization or program to which it grants funds may take an action or require an attorney to take an action in violation of the Code of Professional Responsibility (Article X, Section 9, State Bar Rules) or in violation of any other code of professional responsibility adopted by this state for attorneys.

(F) No funds shall be granted by the nonprofit corporation to directly or indirectly fund class action suits, lawsuits against governmental entities, or lobbying for or against any candidate or issue. Provided, however, that funds may be granted to finance suits against governmental entities on behalf of individuals in order to secure entitlement to benefits such as, but not limited to, Social Security, Aid to Families with Dependent Children, and the like.

(G) The nonprofit corporation provided for in this Article shall require, as a condition to the granting of funds to any organization or program, that adequate provision be made, in accordance with rules adopted by this Court, for reports as to the actual use of funds and for audit of the reports. The violation of any prohibition contained in Subsection 4(F) of this Article shall render the offending organization or program ineligible to receive funds from the nonprofit corporation.

(H) The records of the nonprofit corporation provided for in this Article, including applications for funds, whether or not granted, shall be open for public inspection, in accordance with rules this Court may promulgate.

(I) The nonprofit corporation provided for in this Article may expend funds for administrative costs of the program, including any costs incurred after the adoption of this Article, and may provide a reasonable reserve for administrative costs.

Adopted by order of May 9, 1984.

1 26 U.S.C.A. § 1 et seq.

Section 5. Deposit of Certain Client Funds

(A) An attorney, law firm, or professional corporation engaged in the practice of law, receiving in the course of the practice of law in this state, client funds that are nominal in amount or are reasonably anticipated to be held for a short period of time, shall establish and maintain a separate interest-bearing demand account at a financial institution and shall deposit in the account all those client funds. All the client funds may be deposited in a single unsegregated account. The interest earned on the account shall be paid in accordance with and used for the purposes set forth in this Article and the rules adopted by this Court. Funds to be deposited under this article do not include those funds evidenced by a financial institution instrument, such as a draft, until the instrument is fully credited to the financial institution in which the account is maintained.

(B) This Article does not prohibit an attorney, law firm, or professional corporation engaged in the practice of law from establishing one or more interest-bearing accounts or other investments permitted by the Texas Code of Professional Responsibility (Article X, Section 9, State Bar Rules) with the interest or dividends earned on the accounts or investments payable as directed by clients for whom funds are not deposited in accordance with Subsection (A) of this section.

(C) An attorney, law firm, or professional corporation engaged in the practice of law which maintains accounts provided for in this Section 5 must so advise the nonprofit corporation in writing within thirty (30) days of the establishment of such account or accounts.

Adopted by order of May 9, 1984. Amended by order of Dec. 13, 1988, eff. July 1, 1989.

Section 6. Depositories

(A) The interest-bearing demand account required by Section 5 of this Article shall be established with any financial institution meeting the requirements set forth in the rules adopted by this Court.

(B) The attorney, law firm, or professional corporation establishing the interest-bearing demand account shall attempt in good faith to obtain a rate of interest payable on the account not less than the rate paid by the depository institution to other depositors with accounts of similar size. A higher rate offered by the institution on deposits meeting certain time requirements or minimum amounts, such as those offered in the form of certificates of deposit, may be obtained if there is no impairment of the right to withdraw or transfer principal immediately, other than the statutory notification requirements generally applicable to those accounts, even though interest may be lost because of the withdrawal or transfer.

(C) The depository institution shall be directed by the attorney, law firm, or professional corporation establishing the account:

(1) To remit, at least quarterly, interest earned on the average daily balance in the account, less reasonable service charges, to the nonprofit corporation provided for in this Article;

(2) To transmit to the nonprofit corporation provided for in this Article with each remittance a statement showing the name of the attorney, law firm, or professional corporation with respect to which the remittance is sent, the rate or rates of interest applied, and the amount of service charges deducted, if any; and

(3) To transmit to the depositing attorney, law firm, or professional corporation at the same time a report is sent to the nonprofit corporation provided for in this Article, a report showing the amount paid to the nonprofit corporation for that period, the rate or rates of interest applied, the amount of service charges deducted, if any, and the average daily account balance for each month of the period for which the report is made.

Adopted by order of May 9, 1984.

Section 7. Attorney Liability

Nothing in this Article affects the obligations of attorneys, law firms, or professional corporations engaged in the practice of law with respect to client funds other than client funds reasonably determined to be "nominal in amount" or reasonably anticipated to be held for a "short period of time," as those terms are defined by the rules adopted by this Court. An attorney, law firm, or professional corporation is not liable in determining which funds are nominal in amount or on deposit for a short period of time if the determination is made in good faith in accordance with the rules.

Adopted by order of May 9, 1984.

Section 8. Liability of Nonprofit Corporation

If client funds that are neither nominal in amount nor on deposit for a short period of time are deposited under Section 5(A) of this Article, the liability of the nonprofit corporation provided in this Article may not exceed the amount of interest attributable to client funds actually paid by the depository to the nonprofit corporation.

Adopted by order of May 9, 1984.

Section 9. Initial Distribution of Funds

The initial distribution of funds under this Article shall be made at a time when, in the determination of the board of directors of the nonprofit corporation provided for in this Article, there are sufficient funds to provide an adequate distribution.

Adopted by order of May 9, 1984.

ARTICLE XII—MINIMUM CONTINUING LEGAL EDUCATION

Section 1. Purpose

The purpose of minimum continuing legal education requirements is to ensure that every active member of the State Bar of Texas pursues a plan of continuing legal education throughout his or her career in order to remain current on the law in our rapidly changing society.

Adopted by order of Dec. 19, 1985. Amended by order of Nov. 24, 1987.

Section 2. Definitions

(A) "MCLE" means Minimum Continuing Legal Education.

(B) "Committee" means the Committee on Minimum Continuing Legal Education.

(C) "Committee member" is a member of the Committee on Minimum Continuing Legal Education.

(D) "MCLE Department" means the departmental staff of the State Bar of Texas with the responsibility of administering all aspects of the MCLE program as determined by this Article and any regulations established pursuant hereto.

(E) "The Director" means the Director of the MCLE Department of the State Bar of Texas.

(F) "Continuing legal education activity" means any organized legal educational activity accredited by the Committee.

(G) "CLE Credit Hours" means the actual amount of instruction time for an accredited continuing legal education activity expressed in terms of hours rounded to the nearest one-quarter hour. The number of CLE credit hours shall be based on sixty (60) minutes of instruction per hour, unless otherwise specified herein.

(H) "Self-study" includes individual viewing or listening to audio, video, or digital media, reading written material, or attending organized in-office educational programs, or such other activities as may be approved by the Committee.

(I) "Accredited sponsor" means any provider who receives presumptive approval of the Committee to conduct continuing legal education activities that satisfy the requirements of this Article.

(J) "Accredited CLE Activity" means any CLE activity that receives MCLE accreditation under the MCLE Rules, Regulations, and accreditation criteria adopted by the MCLE Committee.

(K) "MCLE compliance record" means the official record of a member's CLE credit hours earned during any MCLE compliance year that shall be maintained by the MCLE Department and used to verify a member's compliance with the MCLE requirements. It shall be the responsibility of each member to ensure that his/her MCLE compliance record is accurate and complete.

(L) "MCLE compliance year" means the twelve (12) month period that begins each year on the first day of an attorney's birth month and ends on the last day of the month that immediately precedes the attorney's birth month in the following year.

(M) "MCLE reporting month" means the birth month during which the attorney is required to show completion of CLE requirements. If an extension has been granted in accordance with the Article (Section 9), the reporting month shall mean the month immediately following the last date of the extension and shall replace the birth month for that current compliance year.

(N) "MCLE Annual Verification Report" means the written report containing a listing of all CLE credit hours recorded in a member's MCLE compliance record for an MCLE compliance year. This report shall be furnished to each member annually by the MCLE Department.

(O) "Preferred Address" means the member's physical address, post office box, E-mail address or other address, that is on file with the State Bar of Texas Membership department and that is designated as the member's preferred address for receiving written notifications.

(P) "Secondary Address" means any or all of the member's physical addresses, post office boxes, E-mail addresses, or other addresses on file with the State Bar of Texas Membership department and that are not designated as the member's preferred address for receiving written notifications.

Adopted by order of Dec. 19, 1985. Amended by order of Nov. 24, 1987; June 15, 1994, eff. Oct. 1, 1994; Aug. 28, 2001, eff. Sept. 1, 2001; Jan. 27, 2005, eff. Jan. 1, 2005.

The 2005 amendment rewrote this section, which prior thereto read:

"(A) 'Committee' means the Committee on Minimum Continuing Legal Education.

"(B) 'MCLE' means Minimum Continuing Legal Education.

"(C) 'Continuing legal education activity' means any organized legal, judicial or other educational activity accredited by the Committee.

"(D) 'Self-study' includes viewing videotapes, listening to audiotapes, reading written material, or attending organized in-office educational programs, or such other activities as may be approved by the Committee.

"(E) 'Committee member' means a member of the Committee on Minimum Continuing Legal Education.

"(F) 'Accredited sponsor' means any provider who receives approval of the Committee to conduct continuing legal education activities that satisfy the requirements of this Article.

"(G) 'CLE Credit Hours' means the actual amount of instruction time for an accredited continuing legal education activity expressed in terms of hours rounded to the nearest one-quarter hour. The number of CLE credit hours shall be based on sixty (60) minutes of instruction per hour, unless otherwise specified herein.

"(H) 'The Director' means the Director of the MCLE Department of the State Bar of Texas.

"(I) 'MCLE Annual Verification Report' means the written report containing a listing of all CLE credit hours recorded in a member's MCLE compliance record for an MCLE compliance year. This report shall be furnished to each member annually by the MCLE Department.

"(J) 'MCLE Department' means the departmental staff of the State Bar of Texas with the responsibility of administering all aspects of the MCLE program as determined by this Article and any regulations established pursuant hereto.

"(K) 'CLE compliance record' means the official record of a member's CLE credit hours earned during any MCLE compliance year that shall be maintained by the MCLE Department and used to verify a member's compliance with the MCLE requirements. It shall be the responsibility of each member to ensure that his/her MCLE compliance record is accurate and complete.

"(L) 'MCLE compliance year' means the twelve (12) month period that begins each year on the first day of an attorney's birth month and ends on the last day of the month that immediately precedes the attorney's birth month in the following year."

Section 3. Committee on Minimum Continuing Legal Education

(A) There is hereby established the Committee which shall be composed of twelve (12) members. Nine (9) of the members shall be residents of this State who are active members of the State Bar, at least two (2) of whom shall be under the age of thirty–six (36) years as of June 1 of the year being appointed. Of the nine (9) attorney members, not more than two (2) shall be judges. The remaining three (3) members of the Committee shall be residents of this State who are not attorneys. The President–Elect, with the approval of the Board, shall appoint any Committee members whose terms will begin at the beginning of the bar year during which he or she will be President. Should a vacancy on the Committee occur during the bar year, the President, with the approval of the Board, shall appoint a successor to fill the unexpired term. Each member of the Committee shall continue to serve until his or her successor is appointed and qualified. The President–Elect shall designate one (1) of the attorney members of the Committee to serve as chairperson during his or her term as President. The

Board may remove a member of the Committee for good cause. No Committee member shall be appointed for more than two (2) terms. Committee members shall serve without compensation, but shall be reimbursed for reasonable and necessary expenses incurred in the performance of their official duties.

(B) The State Bar shall employ such staff as may be necessary to perform the record keeping, auditing, reporting, accreditation, and other functions required by these rules.

(C) The Committee, subject to these rules and such regulations as it may propose and may be adopted by the Board, shall administer the program of minimum continuing legal education established by this Article. It may propose regulations and prepare forms not inconsistent with this Article pertaining to its function and modify or amend the same from time to time. All such regulations, forms, modifications or amendments shall be submitted to the Board for approval, and upon such approval, shall be published in the *Texas Bar Journal.*

Adopted by order of Dec. 19, 1985. Amended by order of Nov. 24, 1987; Aug. 28, 2001, eff. Sept. 1, 2001; Jan. 27, 2005, eff. Jan. 1, 2005.

The 2005 amendment made a nonsubstantive change.

Section 4. Accreditation

(A) The Committee shall develop criteria for the accreditation of continuing legal education activities and shall designate the number of hours to be earned by participation in such activities, as approved by the Committee. In order for an activity to be accredited, the subject matter must directly relate to legal subjects and the legal profession, including professional responsibility, legal ethics, or law practice management. The Committee may, in appropriate cases, extend accreditation to qualified activities that have already occurred. The Committee shall not extend credit to activities completed in the ordinary course of the practice of law, in the performance of regular employment, as a volunteer service to clients or the general public, as a volunteer service to government entities, or in a member's regular duties on a committee, section or division of any bar related organization. The Committee may extend accredited status, subject to periodic review, to a qualified sponsor for its overall continuing legal education curriculum. No examinations shall be required.

(B) Self–study credit may be given for individual viewing or listening to audio, video, or digital media; reading written material; attending organized in-office educational programs; or other activities approved by the Committee. No more than three hours of credit may be given during a compliance year for self-study activities. Time spent viewing or listening to audio, video, or digital media as part of an organized CLE activity approved by the Committee counts as conventional continuing legal education and is not subject to the self-study limitation.

(C) Credit may be earned through teaching or participating in an accredited CLE activity. Credit shall be granted for preparation time and presentation time, including preparation credit for repeated presentations.

(D) Credit may be earned through legal research-based writing upon application to the Committee provided the activity (1) produced material published or to be published in the form of an article, chapter, or book written, in whole or in part, by the applicant; (2) contributed substantially to the continuing legal education of the applicant and other attorneys; and (3) is not done in the ordinary course of the practice of law, the performance of regular employment, or as a service to clients.

(E) The Committee may, in appropriate cases, charge a reasonable fee to the sponsor for accrediting CLE activities.

(F) A member who holds a full-time faculty position in any law school which is approved by the American Bar Association may be credited as fulfilling the requirements of this article, except as to the minimum requirements for CLE in legal ethics and professional responsibility. A member who holds a part-time faculty position in any such law school may claim participatory credit for the actual hours of class instruction time not to exceed 12 hours per compliance year, except as to the minimum requirements for CLE in legal ethics and professional responsibility.

(G) Credit to meet the minimum educational requirement shall be extended to attorneys who are members of the Senate and House of Representatives of present and future United States and Texas Legislatures for each regular session in which the attorney member shall serve.

(H) No credit shall be given for activities directed primarily to persons preparing for admission to practice law.

(I) Credit, not to exceed 30 hours in any compliance year, may be earned for attending a law school class after admission to practice in Texas provided (1) that the member officially registered for the class with the law school; and (2) that the member completed the course as required by the terms of registration. Credit for approved attendance at law school classes shall be for the actual number of hours of class instruction time the member is in attendance at the law school course.

Adopted by order of Dec. 19, 1985. Amended by order of Nov. 24, 1987; Aug. 28, 2001, eff. Sept. 1, 2001; Jan. 27, 2005, eff. Jan. 1, 2005; Dec. 16, 2014, eff. immediately; April 28, 2015 and Aug. 28, 2015, eff. June 1, 2016

Historical Notes

The order dated December 16, 2014 in subd. (B) substituted "or other activities approved" for "or such other activities as may be approved", substituted "three hours of credit" for "five (5) hours of credit", substituted "during a compliance year" for "during any compliance year", and before "an organized CLE" inserted "part of"; and made other nonsubstantive changes.

The order dated August 28, 2015, deleted former par. (G), which had read "The Committee shall grant exemption from this Article to any emeritus member of the State Bar of Texas. (Emeritus as defined by the State Bar Act, Section 81.052(e)).", and renumbered former pars. (H) to (J) as pars. (G) to (I), respectively.

The order dated August 28, 2015, also stated: "For compliance years that begin on or after June 1, 2016, an emeritus member must fulfill the MCLE requirements applicable to all members of the State Bar, unless the member is eligible for another exemption. Accredited continuing legal education and self-study completed within the 12 months immediately preceding the first compliance year for an emeritus member that begins on or after June 1, 2016, may be used to meet the MCLE requirements for that initial compliance year."

The 2005 amendment rewrote subsecs. (A) and (B); in subsec. (C) inserted "preparation" following "presentation time, including"; in subsec. (D) added ", or as a service to clients" to the end; in subsec. (G) added the parenthetical regarding how Emeritus is defined; in subsec. (H) extended credit to attorneys who are members of the United States Legislature; in subsec. (J) substituted "compliance year" for "reporting year"; and made nonsubstantive changes. Prior thereto subsecs. (A) and (B) read:

"(A) The Committee shall develop criteria for the accreditation of continuing legal education activities and shall designate the number of hours to be earned by participation in such activities, as approved by the Committee. In order for an activity to be accredited, the subject matter must directly relate to legal subjects and the legal profession, including professional responsibility, legal ethics, or law office management. The Committee may, in appropriate cases, extend accreditation to qualified activities which have already occurred. The Committee may extend accredited status, subject to periodic review, to a qualified sponsor for its overall continuing legal education curriculum. No examinations shall be required.

"(B) Self study credit may be given for viewing videotapes, listening to audiotapes, reading written material, attending organized in-office educational programs or such other activities as may be approved by the Committee. No more than five (5) hours of credit may be given during any reporting period for self-study activities. Time spent viewing videotapes as an organized CLE activity approved by the Committee counts as conventional continuing legal education and is not subject to the self-study limitation."

The order dated December 16, 2014 in subd. (B) substituted "or other activities approved" for "or such other activities as may be approved", substituted "three hours of credit" for "five (5) hours of credit", substituted "during a compliance year" for "during any compliance year", and before "an organized CLE" inserted "part of"; and made other nonsubstantive changes.

The order dated August 28, 2015, deleted former par. (G), which had read "The Committee shall grant exemption from this Article to any emeritus member of the State Bar of Texas. (Emeritus as defined by the State Bar Act, Section 81.052(e)).", and renumbered former pars. (H) to (J) as pars. (G) to (I), respectively.

The order dated August 28, 2015, also stated: "For compliance years that begin on or after June 1, 2016, an emeritus member must fulfill the MCLE requirements applicable to all members of the State Bar, unless the member is eligible for another exemption. Accredited continuing legal education and self-study completed within the 12 months immediately preceding the first compliance year for an emeritus member that begins on or after June 1, 2016, may be used to meet the MCLE requirements for that initial compliance year."

Section 5. Compliance Year

(A) Each member's compliance year shall begin on the first day of the month in which his or her birthday occurs.

(B) The initial compliance year for each member shall be the 24-month period that begins on the first birth month following the date of admission.

Adopted by order of Dec. 19, 1985. Amended by order of Nov. 24, 1987; Jan. 27, 2005, eff. Jan. 1, 2005.

Section 6. Minimum Educational Requirements

(A) Every member must complete 15 hours of continuing legal education during each compliance year as provided by this article. No more than three credit hours may be given for completion of self-study activities during any compliance year.

(B) At least three of the 15 hours must be devoted to legal ethics/professional responsibility subjects. One of the three legal ethics/professional responsibility hours may be completed through self-study.

(C) All persons admitted, and any person who has been suspended, disbarred, or who has resigned pursuant to Article X of the State Bar Rules, or who has resigned pursuant to Article III of the State Bar Rules, or who has been suspended pursuant to Section 8 of this Article, or who has taken inactive status pursuant to Section 81.052, Texas Government Code, and who desires to return to active status shall be required, in addition to such other requirements as the State Bar Rules may contain, to comply with the requirements of Section 6(A) and 6(B) hereof.

(D) Accredited continuing legal education and self-study completed within a 12–month period immediately preceding a member's initial compliance year may be used to meet the educational requirement for the initial compliance year. Exception: Credit for the educational activity entitled "The Guide to the Basics of Law Practice," sponsored by the Texas Center for Legal Ethics and Professionalism, completed anytime during the third year of law school or during the initial compliance year, may be used toward meeting the educational requirements for the initial compliance year.

(E) Accredited continuing legal education and self-study completed during any compliance year in excess of the minimum 15 hour requirement for such period will be applied to the following compliance year's requirement. This carryover provision applies to one year only.

Adopted by order of Dec. 19, 1985. Amended by order of Nov. 24, 1987; May 22, 1988; Aug. 28, 2001, eff. Sept. 1, 2001; Jan. 27, 2005, eff. Jan. 1, 2005; Dec. 16, 2014, eff. immediately.

The 2005 amendment rewrote this section, which prior thereto read:

"(A) Every member shall complete fifteen (15) hours of continuing legal education during each reporting period as provided by this Article. No more than five (5) credit hours may be given for self-study activities during any reporting period.

"(B) At least three (3) hours of the fifteen (15) hours shall be devoted to legal ethics/professional responsibility subjects.

"(C) After the effective date of this Article, all persons admitted, and any person who has been suspended, disbarred, or who has resigned pursuant to Article X of the State Bar Rules, or who has resigned pursuant to Article III of the State Bar Rules, or who has been suspended pursuant to Section 8 of this Article, or who has taken inactive status pursuant to Section 81.052, Texas Government Code, and who desires to return to active status shall be required, in addition to such other requirements as the State Bar Rules may contain, to comply with the requirements of Sections 6(A) and 6(B) hereof.

"(D) Accredited continuing legal education and self-study completed within a one (1) year period immediately preceding a member's initial reporting period may be used to meet the educational requirement for the initial period.

"(E) Accredited continuing legal education and self-study completed during any reporting period in excess of the minimum fifteen (15) hour requirement for such period may be applied to the following period's requirement. This carryover provision applies to one (1) year only."

The order dated December 16, 2014 in subd. (A) substituted "must complete 15 hours" for "shall complete fifteen (15) hours", and substituted "three credit hours" for "five (5) credit hours"; in subd. (B) "three of the 15 hours must" for "three (3) hours of the fifteen (15) hours shall"; and made other nonsubstantive changes.

Section 7. Credit Computation

(A) Credit for attending accredited continuing legal education activities shall be based on net actual instruction time, which may include organized lecture, panel discussion, audio, video, and digital media presentations and organized question-and-answer periods. Sponsors are encouraged to calculate the number of hours of credit that should be given for any activity offered, using the above guide, and indicate the number on the activity brochure. Fractional hours should be stated as decimals.

(B) Credit for viewing or listening to audio, video, or digital media shall be based on the running time of the recording.

(C) Credit for reading approved material or attending in-office educational programs shall be based on actual time spent.

(D), (E) Deleted.

Adopted by order of Dec. 19, 1985. Amended by order of Nov. 24, 1987; Aug. 28, 2001, eff. Sept. 1, 2001; Jan. 27, 2005, eff. Jan. 1, 2005.

The 2005 amendment inserted references to digital media and made nonsubstantive changes.

Section 8. Compliance

(A) Two months before the end of a member's MCLE compliance year, the Director must send the member an MCLE Annual Verification Report. The Director may send the report by email to a member who has an email address on file with the State Bar. Members must review the report for accuracy. If the report is accurate and shows that the member has completed all MCLE requirements for the MCLE compliance year or that the member is exempt from MCLE, then no additional action is required by the member. If the report is inaccurate, the member must correct his or her MCLE compliance record by following the instructions on the report. To avoid a fine or suspension, all CLE credit hours must be completed, and all corrections to a member's MCLE compliance record must be received by the Director, before the end of the member's MCLE compliance year.

(B) On or about the first day of the birth month, the Director shall make available to the member, a report of amendments that have been made to the MCLE record for the compliance year that ended immediately prior to said birth month. The Director shall also notify any member who has not completed MCLE requirements for the compliance year that ended immediately prior to said birth month. A member, who has not completed his or her CLE requirements by the first day of the birth month, will receive an automatic grace period through the last day of the birth month to complete and report any remaining CLE credits. Members shall not be fined or penalized for completing and reporting CLE credits by the last day of the birth month (grace period).

(C) On or about the 12th day of the month immediately following a member's birth month, the Director shall notify all members who are in non-compliance for the MCLE compliance year just ended to advise such members of their non-compliance status. Such notice shall be in the form of a written notice, and sent to each member at the Preferred Address and via one Secondary Address (if any) that is then on file with the Membership Department of the State Bar.

(D) On or about the first day of the third month immediately following a member's birth month, the Director shall send final notice to any member who has not cured their noncompliance status. Such notice shall be in the form of a written notice, and sent to each member at the Preferred Address and via one Secondary Address (if any) that is then on file with the Membership Department of the State Bar.

(E) If by the last business day of the fourth month following the birth month (or reporting month if the member has been granted an extension in accordance with this article for completion of CLE requirements) the member has still not cured his or her noncompliance, the member shall be automatically suspended from the practice of law in Texas as directed by Order of the Supreme Court dated December 23, 2002.

(F) Upon the execution of suspension, the Director shall cause to be sent a written notification to each member who is suspended from practice by the order. Said notification shall be sent to each member at his or her Preferred Address and via one Secondary Address (if any) that is then on file with the Membership Department of the State Bar.

Adopted by order of Dec. 19, 1985. Amended by order of Nov. 24, 1987; June 15, 1994, eff. Oct. 1, 1994; Aug. 28, 2001, eff. Sept. 1, 2001; Jan. 27, 2005, eff. Jan. 1, 2005; Dec. 16, 2014, eff. immediately.

The 2005 amendment rewrote this section, which prior thereto read:

"(A) On or about the beginning of month ten (10) of each MCLE compliance year, the Director shall cause to be mailed a preliminary MCLE Annual Verification Report to each member for whom said MCLE compliance year applies, who is not in one of the exempt or special case categories specified in Section 9 above, and whose MCLE compliance record shows that the minimum CLE credits for said MCLE compliance year have not yet been obtained. If the Report does not accurately and completely reflect a member's CLE credits, then it should be annotated in accordance with the instructions on the Report and returned to the MCLE Department. However, a member is not subject to fine or suspension for failure to file or correct this report.

"(B) The Director shall cause to be mailed an MCLE Annual Verification Report to each member on or about the first day of the month in which such member's birthday occurs. Such MCLE Annual Verification Report shall be for the MCLE compliance year that ended immediately prior to said birth month.

"(C) Upon receipt of the MCLE Annual Verification Report, each member shall review the report for accuracy and completeness. If the report accurately reflects the member's MCLE compliance record for the MCLE compliance year just ended, and if it shows that the minimum CLE credit hours requirements have been met, then no additional action is required by the member. The Report should NOT be returned to the MCLE Department unless the Report does not accurately and completely reflect a member's MCLE compliance record, in which event it should be annotated in accordance with the instructions on the Report and returned to the MCLE Department. After the additions or modifications are made to the member's MCLE compliance record, the MCLE Department shall mail a revised MCLE Annual Verification Report to the member.

"(D) On or about the fifteenth (15th) day of the month immediately following a member's birth month, the Director shall cause to be mailed a written notice to all members who are in non-compliance for the MCLE compliance year just ended to advise such members of their non-compliance status. Such notice shall be mailed to each member at his or her preferred and alternate (if any) mailing addresses that are then on file with the Membership Department of the State Bar.

"(E) Any member who has not cured their non-compliance status by the last day of the third month following their birth month shall be included in a petition to the Supreme Court to suspend the member's license to practice law. The Supreme Court shall thereupon execute an order suspending the license to practice law in Texas of each such attorney.

"(F) Upon the execution of such suspension order, the Director shall cause to be mailed a true and correct copy of said order to each member who is suspended from practice by the order. Said order shall be mailed to each member at their preferred and alternate (if any) mailing addresses that are then on file with the Membership Department of the State Bar."

The order dated December 16, 2014 rewrote subd. (A), which prior thereto had read, "Two months prior to the end of the MCLE compliance year, the Director shall send a preliminary MCLE Annual Verification Report to each member's Preferred Address for who said MCLE compliance year applies. Upon receipt of the MCLE Annual Verification Report, the member shall review the report for accuracy and completeness. If the report accurately reflects the member's MCLE compliance record for the current MCLE compliance year, and it shows that the minimum CLE credit hours requirements have been met, then no additional action is required by the member. If the Report does not accurately and completely reflect a member's CLE credits, then the member shall correct his or her record according to the instructions on the Report. To avoid fines and/or suspension, all CLE credit hours corrections and additions to the MCLE record shall be completed, filed and received by the MCLE Director on or before the end of the compliance year."; and made other nonsubstantive changes.

Section 9. Review and Appeal

(A) A member may file a written request for exemption from compliance with any of the requirements of this Article, an extension of time for compliance, an extension of time to comply with a deficiency notice, or an extension of time to file an annual activity report. Such request for excuse or for extension shall be reviewed and determined by the Committee or by such of its members as the chairperson may, from time to time, designate. The member shall be promptly notified of the Committee's decision.

(B) "Good cause" shall exist when a member is unable to comply with this Article because of illness, medical disability, or other extraordinary hardship or extenuating circumstances that were not willful on the part of the member and were beyond his or her control.

(C) Should the decision of the Committee be adverse to the member, the member may request the Board of Directors of the State Bar to review the decision by making such request in writing to the Executive Director of the State Bar within thirty days of notification of the decision of the Committee. The Chairman of the Board may appoint a committee of the Board to review the decision of the Committee and make a recommendation to the Board. The decision shall be made by the Board.

(D) Should the decision of the Board be adverse to the member, the member may appeal such decision by filing suit within thirty (30) days of notification of the Board's action, failing which the decision of the Board shall be final. Such suit shall be brought against the State Bar, and shall be filed in a district court in Travis County, Texas. Trial shall be de novo, but (1) the burden of proof shall be on the member appealing; (2) the burden shall be by a preponderance of the evidence; and (3) the member shall prove the existence of "good cause" as defined herein. The trial court shall proceed to hear and determine the issue without a jury. Either party shall have a right to appeal.

(E) Any suspension of a member under this Article shall be vacated during the administrative review process and while any suit filed is pending.

Adopted by order of Dec. 19, 1985. Amended by order of Nov. 24, 1987; Aug. 28, 2001, eff. Sept. 1, 2001; Jan. 27, 2005, eff. Jan. 1, 2005.

The 2005 amendment made nonsubstantive changes.

Section 10. Return to Former Status

Any member whose license to practice law has been suspended under the terms of this Article who after the date of suspension files an activity report with the MCLE Director showing compliance and who has paid all applicable fees associated with non-compliance and suspension, shall be entitled to have such suspension promptly terminated and be returned to former status. Return to former status shall be retroactive to the inception of suspension, but shall not affect any proceeding for discipline of the member for professional misconduct. The MCLE Director shall promptly notify the Clerk that a member formerly suspended under this Article has now complied with this Article.

Adopted by order of Dec. 19, 1985. Amended by order of Nov. 24, 1987, Jan. 27, 2005, eff. Jan. 1, 2005.

Section 11. Exemption of Certain Judges

Judges subject to Supreme Court Order for Judicial Education dated August 21, 1985, Supreme Court Order for Judicial Education for Retired or Former District Judges dated July 2, 1986, and federal judicial officers, shall be exempt from these requirements.

Adopted by order of Dec. 19, 1985. Amended by order of Nov. 24, 1987.

Section 12. Confidentiality

A member who reports attendance credits individually to the MCLE Director, without the sponsoring organization's knowledge, automatically consents to release of his or her name to the sponsoring organization for the sole purpose of reconciling attendance records. Otherwise, the files, records and proceedings of the Committee, as they relate to the compliance or noncompliance of any member with the requirements of this Article, shall be confidential and shall not be disclosed except upon consent of the member affected or as directed in the course of judicial proceeding by a court of competent jurisdiction.

Adopted by order of Dec. 19, 1985. Amended by order of Nov. 24, 1987, Jan. 27, 2005, eff. Jan. 1, 2005.

Section 13. Repealed by order of Dec. 16, 2014, eff. immediately

Historical Notes

The repealed section, relating to the effective date of amendments, was adopted by order of Dec. 19, 1985.

ARTICLE XIII—EMERITUS ATTORNEYS PRO BONO PARTICIPATION PROGRAM

Section 1. Purpose

Individuals admitted to the practice of law in Texas have a responsibility to provide competent legal services for all persons, including those unable to pay for such services. As one means of meeting these legal needs, the following Article establishing the emeritus Attorneys Pro Bono Participation Program is adopted.

Adopted by order of March 14, 1988, eff. May 15, 1988. Amended by order of Jan. 3, 1996.

Section 2. Definitions

(A) "The active practice of law" means that an attorney has been engaged in the practice of law, which includes, but is not limited to, private practice, house counsel, public employment or academic employment.

(B) An "emeritus attorney" is any person, retired from the active practice of law, who is or was admitted to practice law before the highest court of Texas or any other state or territory of the United States of America or the District of Columbia, and

(1) Has been engaged in the active practice of law for a minimum of five out of the ten years immediately preceding the application to participate in the emeritus program; and

(2) Has been a member in good standing of the State Bar of Texas or the entity governing the practice of law of any other state, territory, or the District of Columbia and has not been disciplined for professional misconduct by the bar or courts of any jurisdiction within the past fifteen years; and

(3) If not a retired member of the State Bar of Texas has graduated from a law school accredited by the American Bar Association and has not failed the Texas bar examination three or more times; and

(4) Agrees to abide by the Texas Code of Professional Responsibility and submit to the jurisdiction of the Supreme Court of Texas and State Bar of Texas for disciplinary purposes; and

(5) Neither asks for nor receives compensation of any kind for the legal services to be rendered hereunder; and

(6) Is certified under Section 5 hereof.

(C) An "approved legal assistance organization" for the purposes of this article is a not-for-profit legal assistance organization which is approved by the Supreme Court of Texas as set forth herein. A legal assistance organization seeking approval from the Supreme Court of Texas for the purposes of this article shall file a petition with the clerk of the Supreme Court of Texas certifying that it is a not-for-profit organization and reciting with specificity:

(1) The structure of the organization and whether it accepts funds from its clients;

(2) The major sources of funds used by the organization;

(3) The criteria used to determine potential clients' eligibility for legal services performed by the organization;

(4) The types of legal and nonlegal service performed by the organization;

(5) The names of all members of the State Bar of Texas who are employed by the organization or who regularly perform legal work for the organization; and

(6) The existence and extent of malpractice insurance which will cover the emeritus attorney.

(D) A "supervising attorney" as used herein as an active member of the State Bar of Texas who directs and supervises an emeritus attorney engaged in activities permitted by this Article. The supervising attorney must:

(1) Be employed or be a participating volunteer for an approved legal assistance organization, and

(2) Assume personal professional responsibility for supervising the conduct of the litigation, administrative proceeding or other legal services in which the emeritus attorney participates.

(3) Assist the emeritus attorney in his preparation to the extent that the supervisory attorney considers it necessary.

Adopted by order of March 14, 1988, eff. May 15, 1988. Amended by order of Jan. 3, 1996.

Section 3. Activities

(A) An emeritus attorney, in association with an approved legal assistance organization and under the supervision of a supervising attorney, may perform the following activities:

(1) The emeritus attorney may appear in any court or before any administrative tribunal or arbitrator in this state on behalf of a client of an approved legal assistance organization if the person on whose behalf the emeritus attorney is appearing has consented in writing to that appearance and a supervising attorney has given written approval for that appearance. The written consent and approval shall be filed in the record of each case and shall be brought to the attention of a judge of the court, the presiding officer of the administrative tribunal or the arbitrator.

(2) The emeritus attorney may prepare pleadings and other documents to be filed in any court or before any administrative tribunal or arbitrator in this state in any matter in which the emeritus attorney is involved. Such pleadings also shall be signed by the supervising attorney.

(3) The emeritus attorney may render legal advice and perform other appropriate legal services but only after prior consultation with, and upon the express consent of, the supervising lawyer.

(4) The emeritus attorney may engage in such other preparatory activities as are necessary for any matter in which he or she is involved.

(B) The presiding judge, hearing officer or arbitrator may, in her or his discretion, determine the extent of the emeritus attorney's participation in any proceeding.

Adopted by order of March 14, 1988, eff. May 15, 1988. Amended by order of Jan. 3, 1996.

Section 4. Supervision and Limitations

(A) An emeritus attorney must perform all activities authorized by this Article under the direct supervision of a supervising attorney.

(B) Emeritus attorneys permitted to perform services under this Article are not, and shall not represent themselves to be, active members of the State Bar of Texas licensed to practice law in this state.

(C) The prohibition against compensation for the emeritus attorney contained in Section 2(A)(5) shall not prevent the approved legal assistance organization from reimbursing the emeritus attorney for actual expenses incurred while rendering services hereunder nor shall it prevent the approved legal assistance organization from making such charges for its services as it may otherwise properly charge. The approved legal assistance organization shall be entitled to receive all court-awarded attorneys' fees for any representation rendered by the emeritus attorney.

Adopted by order of March 14, 1988, eff. May 15, 1988. Amended by order of Jan. 3, 1996.

Section 5. Certification

Permission for an emeritus attorney to perform services under this Article shall become effective upon filing with and approval by the clerk of the Supreme Court of Texas of:

(A) A certification by an approved legal assistance organization stating that the emeritus attorney is currently associated with that legal assistance organization and that an attorney employed by or participating as a volunteer with that organization will assume the duties of the supervising attorney required hereunder;

(B) A certificate from the highest court or agency in the state, territory, or district in which the emeritus attorney previously has been licensed to practice law, certifying that the emeritus attorney has fulfilled the requirements of active bar membership and has a clear disciplinary record as required by Section 2(B) hereof; and

(C) A sworn statement by the emeritus attorney that he or she:

(1) Has read and is familiar with the Texas Code of Professional Responsibility as adopted by the Supreme Court of Texas and will abide by the provisions thereof; and

(2) Submits to the jurisdiction of the Supreme Court of Texas and State Bar of Texas for disciplinary purposes, as defined by Article 10 of the Rules; and

(3) Will neither ask for nor receive compensation of any kind for the legal services authorized hereunder.

Adopted by order of March 14, 1988, eff. May 15, 1988. Amended by order of Jan. 3, 1996.

Section 6. Withdrawal of Certification

(A) Permission to perform services under this article shall cease immediately upon the filing with the clerk of the Supreme Court of Texas of a notice either:

(1) By the approved legal assistance organization stating that:

(a) The emeritus attorney has ceased to be associated with the organization, which notice must be filed within five days after such association has ceased; or

(b) That certification of such attorney is withdrawn. An approved legal assistance organization may withdraw certification at any time and it is not necessary that the notice state the cause for such withdrawal. A copy of the notice filed with the clerk of the Supreme Court of Texas shall be mailed by the organization to the emeritus attorney concerned.

(2) By the Supreme Court of Texas, in its discretion, at any time, stating that permission to perform services under this article may be revoked. A copy of such notice shall be mailed by the clerk of the Supreme Court of Texas to the emeritus attorney involved and to the approved legal assistance organization to which he or she had been certified.

(B) If an emeritus attorneys' certification is withdrawn, for any reason, the supervising attorney shall immediately file a notice of such action in the official file of each matter pending before any court or tribunal in which the emeritus attorney was involved.

Adopted by order of March 14, 1988, eff. May 15, 1988. Amended by order of Jan. 3, 1996.

Section 7. Discipline

In addition to any appropriate proceedings and discipline which may be imposed by the Supreme Court of Texas or State Bar of Texas, the emeritus attorney shall be subject to the following disciplinary measures:

(A) The presiding judge or hearing officer for any matter in which the emeritus attorney has participated may hold the emeritus attorney in civil contempt for any failure to abide by such tribunal's orders; and

(B) The Supreme Court of Texas or the approved legal assistance organization may, at any time, with or without cause, withdraw certification hereunder.

Adopted by order of March 14, 1988, eff. May 15, 1988. Amended by order of Jan. 3, 1996.

RULES OF DISCIPLINARY PROCEDURE

Effective May 1, 1992

Including Amendments Received Through February 1, 2016

Research Note

See Vernon's Texas Codes Annotated, Government Code, *Volume 3A, for judicial constructions and other research aids.*

Preamble

The Supreme Court of Texas has the constitutional and statutory responsibility within the State for the lawyer discipline and disability system, and has inherent power to maintain appropriate standards of professional conduct and to dispose of individual cases of lawyer discipline and disability in a manner that does not discriminate by race, creed, color, sex, or national origin. To carry out this responsibility, the Court promulgates the following rules for lawyer discipline and disability proceedings. Subject to the inherent power of the Supreme Court of Texas, the responsibility for administering and supervising lawyer discipline and disability is delegated to the Board of Directors of the State Bar of Texas. Authority to adopt rules of procedure and administration not inconsistent with these rules is vested in the Board. This delegation is specifically limited to the rights, powers, and authority herein expressly delegated.

PART I. GENERAL RULES

1.01. Citation

These rules are to be called the Texas Rules of Disciplinary Procedure and shall be cited as such.
Adopted by orders of Feb. 26, 1991, and Oct. 9, 1991, eff. May 1, 1992.

1.02. Objective of the Rules

These rules establish the procedures to be used in the professional disciplinary and disability system for attorneys in the State of Texas.
Adopted by orders of Feb. 26, 1991, and Oct. 9, 1991, eff. May 1, 1992.

1.03. Construction of the Rules

These rules are to be broadly construed to ensure the operation, effectiveness, integrity, and continuation of the professional disciplinary and disability system. The following rules apply in the construction of these rules:

A. If any portion of these rules is held unconstitutional by any court, that determination does not affect the validity of the remaining rules.

B. The use of the singular includes the plural, and vice versa.

C. In computing any period of time prescribed or allowed by these rules, the day of the act or event after which the designated period of time begins to run is not to be included. The last day of the period so computed is to be included, unless it is a Saturday, Sunday, or legal holiday, in which event the period runs until the end of the next day that is not a Saturday, Sunday, or legal holiday.

Adopted by orders of Feb. 26, 1991, and Oct. 9, 1991, eff. May 1, 1992.

1.04. Integration and Concurrent Application of the Rules

These rules apply prospectively to all attorney professional disciplinary and disability proceedings commenced on and after the effective date as set forth in the Supreme Court's Order of promulgation. All disciplinary and disability proceedings commenced prior to the effective date of these rules as amended are governed by the Texas Rules of Disciplinary Procedure in effect as of the date of commencement of said disciplinary and disability proceedings.

Adopted by orders of Feb. 26, 1991, and Oct. 9, 1991, eff. May 1, 1992. Amended by order of Dec. 29, 2003, eff. Jan. 1, 2004.

1.05. Texas Disciplinary Rules of Professional Conduct

Nothing in these rules is to be be construed, explicitly or implicitly, to amend or repeal in any way the Texas Disciplinary Rules of Professional Conduct.

Adopted by orders of Feb. 26, 1991, and Oct. 9, 1991, eff. May 1, 1992.

1.06. Definitions

A. "Address" means the registered address provided by the attorney who is the subject of the Grievance, as that address is shown on the membership rolls maintained by the State Bar on behalf of the Clerk of the Supreme Court at the time of receipt of the Grievance by the Chief Disciplinary Counsel.

B. "Board" means the Board of Directors of the State Bar of Texas.

C. "Chief Disciplinary Counsel" means the person serving as Chief Disciplinary Counsel and any and all of his or her assistants.

D. "Commission" means the Commission for Lawyer Discipline, a permanent committee of the State Bar of Texas.

E. "Committee" means any of the grievance committees within a single District.

F. "Complainant" means the person, firm, corporation, or other entity, including the Chief Disciplinary Counsel, initiating a Complaint or Inquiry.

G. "Complaint" means those written matters received by the Office of the Chief Disciplinary Counsel that, either on the face thereof or upon screening or preliminary investigation, allege Professional Misconduct or attorney Disability, or both, cognizable under these rules or the Texas Disciplinary Rules of Professional Conduct.

H. "Director" means a member of the Board of Directors of the State Bar of Texas.

I. "Disability" means any physical, mental, or emotional condition that, with or without a substantive rule violation, results in the attorney's inability to practice law, provide client services, complete contracts of employment, or otherwise carry out his or her professional responsibilities to clients, courts, the profession, or the public.

J. "Disciplinary Action" means a proceeding brought by or against an attorney in a district court or any judicial proceeding covered by these rules other than an Evidentiary Hearing.

K. "Disciplinary Petition" means a pleading that satisfies the requirements of Rule 3.01.

L. "Disciplinary Proceedings" includes the processing of a Grievance, the investigation and processing of an Inquiry or Complaint, presentation of a Complaint before a Summary Disposition Panel, and the proceeding before an Evidentiary Panel.

M. "District" means disciplinary district.

N. "Evidentiary Hearing" means an adjudicatory proceeding before a panel of a grievance committee.

O. "Evidentiary Panel" means a panel of the District Grievance Committee performing an adjudicatory function other than that of a Summary Disposition Panel with regard to a Disciplinary Proceeding pending before the District Grievance Committee of which the Evidentiary Panel is a subcommittee.

P. "Evidentiary Petition" means a pleading that satisfies the requirements of Rule 2.17.

Q. "General Counsel" means the General Counsel of the State Bar of Texas and any and all of his or her assistants.

R. "Grievance" means a written statement, from whatever source, apparently intended to allege Professional Misconduct by a lawyer, or lawyer Disability, or both, received by the Office of the Chief Disciplinary Counsel.

S. "Inquiry" means any written matter concerning attorney conduct received by the Office of the Chief Disciplinary Counsel that, even if true, does not allege Professional Misconduct or Disability.

T. "Intentional Crime" means (1) any Serious Crime that requires proof of knowledge or intent as an essential element or (2) any crime involving misapplication of money or other property held as a fiduciary.

U. "Just Cause" means such cause as is found to exist upon a reasonable inquiry that would induce a reasonably intelligent and prudent person to believe that an attorney either has committed an act or acts of Professional Misconduct requiring that a Sanction be imposed, or suffers from a Disability that requires either suspension as an attorney licensed to practice law in the State of Texas or probation.

V. "Penal Institution" has the meaning assigned by Article 62.001, Code of Criminal Procedure.

W. "Professional Misconduct" includes:

1. Acts or omissions by an attorney, individually or in concert with another person or persons, that violate one or more of the Texas Disciplinary Rules of Professional Conduct.

2. Attorney conduct that occurs in another state or in the District of Columbia and results in the disciplining of an attorney in that other jurisdiction, if the conduct is Professional Misconduct under the Texas Disciplinary Rules of Professional Conduct.

3. Violation of any disciplinary or disability order or judgment.

4. Engaging in conduct that constitutes barratry as defined by the law of this state.

5. Failure to comply with Rule 13.01 of these rules relating to notification of an attorney's cessation of practice.

6. Engaging in the practice of law either during a period of suspension or when on inactive status.

7. Conviction of a Serious Crime, or being placed on probation for a Serious Crime with or without an adjudication of guilt.

8. Conviction of an Intentional Crime, or being placed on probation for an Intentional Crime with or without an adjudication of guilt.

X. "Reasonable Attorneys' Fees," for purposes of these rules only, means a reasonable fee for a competent private attorney, under the circumstances. Relevant factors that may be considered in determining the reasonableness of a fee include but are not limited to the following:

1. The time and labor required, the novelty and difficulty of the questions involved, and the skill requisite to perform the legal service properly;

2. The fee customarily charged in the locality for similar legal services;

3. The amount involved and the results obtained;

4. The time limitations imposed by the circumstances; and

5. The experience, reputation, and ability of the lawyer or lawyers performing the services.

Y. "Respondent" means any attorney who is the subject of a Grievance, Complaint, Disciplinary Proceeding, or Disciplinary Action.

Z. "Sanction" means any of the following:

1. Disbarment.
2. Resignation in lieu of discipline.
3. Indefinite Disability Suspension.
4. Suspension for a term certain.
5. Probation of suspension, which probation may be concurrent with the period of suspension, upon such reasonable terms as are appropriate under the circumstances.
6. Interim suspension.
7. Public reprimand.
8. Private reprimand.

The term "Sanction" may include the following additional ancillary requirements.

a. Restitution (which may include repayment to the Client Security Fund of the State Bar of any payments made by reason of Respondent's Professional Misconduct); and

b. Payment of Reasonable Attorneys' Fees and all direct expenses associated with the proceedings.

AA. "Serious Crime" means barratry; and felony involving moral turpitude; any misdemeanor involving theft, embezzlement, or fraudulent or reckless misappropriation of money or other property; or any attempt, conspiracy, or solicitation of another to commit any of the foregoing crimes.

BB. "State Bar" means the State Bar of Texas.

CC. "Summary Disposition Panel" means a panel of the Committee that determines whether a Complaint should proceed or should be dismissed based upon the absence of evidence to support a finding of Just Cause after a reasonable investigation by the Chief Disciplinary Counsel of the allegations in the Grievance.

DD. "Wrongfully Imprisoned Person" has the meaning assigned by Section 501.101, Government Code.

Adopted by orders of Feb. 26, 1991, and Oct. 9, 1991, eff. May 1, 1992. Amended by orders of Dec. 29, 2003, eff. Jan. 1, 2004; May 14, 2008, Aug. 20, 2008, eff. Sept. 1, 2008; Oct. 14, 2013, eff. Nov. 1, 2013.

PART II. THE DISTRICT GRIEVANCE COMMITTEES

2.01. Disciplinary Districts and Grievance Committee Subdistricts

The State of Texas is geographically divided into disciplinary districts that are coextensive with the districts of elected Directors of the State Bar. One or more Committee subdistricts shall be delineated by the Board within each such District. From time to time, if the Commission deems it useful for the efficient operation of the disciplinary system, it shall recommend to the Board that a redelineation be made of one or more subdistricts within a District. All Committees within a single disciplinary district have concurrent authority within the District but once a matter has been assigned to a Committee, that Committee has dominant jurisdiction, absent a transfer.

Adopted by orders of Feb. 26, 1991, and Oct. 9, 1991, eff. May 1, 1992.

2.02. Composition of Members

Each elected Director of the State Bar shall nominate, and the President of the State Bar shall appoint, the members of the Committees within the District that coincides with the Director's district, according to rules and policies adopted from time to time by the Board. Each Committee must consist of no fewer than nine members, two-thirds of whom must be attorneys licensed to practice law in the State of Texas and in good standing, and one-third of whom must be public members All Committee panels must be composed of two- thirds attorneys and one-third public members. Each member of the Committee shall reside within or maintain his or her principal place of employment or practice within the District for which appointed. Public members may not have, other than as consumers, any financial interest, direct or indirect, in the practice of law. There may be no ex officio members of any Committee.

Adopted by orders of Feb. 26, 1991, and Oct. 9, 1991, eff. May 1, 1992. Amended by order of Dec. 29, 2003, eff. Jan. 1, 2004.

2.03. Time for Appointment and Terms

All persons serving on a Committee at the time these rules become effective shall continue to serve for their then unexpired terms, subject to resignation or removal as herein provided. Nominations to Committees shall be made annually at the spring meeting of the Board; all appointments shall be made by the President no later than June 1 of each year, provided, however, that if a vacancy on a Committee arises after June 1, the Director(s) shall nominate and the President shall appoint an eligible person to serve for the remaining period of the unexpired term. If any Director fails or refuses to make nominations in a timely manner, or the President fails or refuses to make appointments in a timely manner, the existing members of the Committees shall continue to hold office until the nominations and appointments are made and the successor member is qualified. One–third of each new Committee will be appointed for initial terms of one year, one-third for an initial term of two years, and one-third for an initial term of three years. Thereafter, all terms will be for a period of three years, except for appointments to fill unexpired terms, which will be for the remaining period of the unexpired term. Any member of a Committee who has served two consecutive terms, whether full or partial terms, is not eligible for reappointment until at least three years have passed since his or her last prior service. No member may serve as chair for more than two consecutive terms of one year each. All members are eligible for election to the position of chair.

Adopted by orders of Feb. 26, 1991 and Oct. 9, 1991, eff. May 1, 1992. Amended by order of Dec. 18, 2006, eff. March 31, 2007.

2.04. Organizational Meeting of Grievance Committees

The last duly elected chair of a Committee shall call an organizational meeting of the Committee no later than July 15 of each year; shall administer the oath of office to each new member; and shall preside until the Committee has elected, by a majority vote, its new chair. Members may vote for themselves for the position of chair.

Adopted by orders of Feb. 26, 1991, and Oct. 9, 1991, eff. May 1, 1992.

2.05. Oath of Committee Members

As soon as possible after appointment, each newly appointed member of a Committee shall take the following oath to be administered by any person authorized by law to administer oaths:

"I do solemnly swear (or affirm) that I will faithfully execute my duties as a member of the District grievance committee, as required by the Texas Rules of Disciplinary Procedure, and will, to the best of my ability, preserve, protect, and defend the Constitution and laws of the United States and of the State of Texas. I further solemnly swear (or affirm) that I will keep secret all such matters and things as shall come to my knowledge as a member of the grievance committee arising from or in connection with each Disciplinary Action and Disciplinary Proceeding, unless permitted to disclose the same in accordance with the Rules of Disciplinary Procedure, or unless ordered to do so in the course of a judicial proceeding or a proceeding before the Board of Disciplinary Appeals. I further solemnly swear (or affirm) that I have neither directly nor indirectly paid, offered, or promised to pay, contributed any money or valuable thing, or promised any public or private office to secure my appointment. So help me God."

Adopted by orders of Feb. 26, 1991, and Oct. 9, 1991, eff. May 1, 1992.

2.06. Assignment of Committee Members

Each member of a Committee shall act through panels assigned by the chair of the Committee for summary disposition dockets and evidentiary hearings. Promptly after assignment, notice must be provided to the Respondent by United States certified mail, return receipt requested, of the names and addresses of the panel members assigned to each Complaint. A member is disqualified or is subject to recusal as a panel member for an evidentiary hearing if a district judge would, under similar circumstances, be disqualified or recused. If a member is disqualified or recused, another member shall be appointed by the Committee chair. No peremptory challenges of a Committee member are allowed. Any alleged grounds for disqualification or recusal of a panel member are conclusively waived if not brought to the attention of the panel within ten days after receipt of notification of the names and addresses of members of the panel; however, grounds for disqualification or recusal not reasonably discoverable within the ten day period may be asserted within ten days after they were discovered or in the exercise of reasonable diligence should have been discovered.

Adopted by orders of Feb. 26, 1991, and Oct. 9, 1991, eff. May 1, 1992. Amended by order of Dec. 29, 2003, eff. Jan. 1, 2004.

2.07. Duties of Committees

Committees shall act through panels, as assigned by the Committee chairs, to conduct summary disposition dockets and evidentiary hearings. No panel may consist of more than one-half of all members of the Committee or fewer than three members. If a member of a panel is disqualified, recused or otherwise unable to serve, the chair shall appoint a replacement. Panels must be composed of two attorney members for each public member. A quorum must include at least one public member for every two attorney members present and consists of a majority of the membership of the panel, and business shall be conducted upon majority vote of those members present, a quorum being had. In matters in which evidence is taken, no member may vote unless that member has heard or reviewed all the evidence. It shall be conclusively presumed, however, not subject to discovery or challenge in any subsequent proceeding, that every member casting a vote has heard or reviewed all the evidence. No member, attorney or public, may be appointed by the chair for both the Summary Disposition docket and the Evidentiary Panel pertaining to the same disciplinary matter. Any tie vote is a vote in favor of the position of the Respondent.

Adopted by orders of Feb. 26, 1991, and Oct. 9, 1991, eff. May 1, 1992. Amended by order of Dec. 29, 2003, eff. Jan. 1, 2004.

2.08. Expenses

Members of Committees serve without compensation but are entitled to reimbursement by the State Bar for their reasonable, actual, and necessary expenses.

Adopted by orders of Feb. 26, 1991, and Oct. 9, 1991, eff. May 1, 1992.

2.09. Notice to Parties

A. Every notice required by this Part to be served upon the Respondent may be served by U. S. certified mail, return receipt requested, or by any other means of service permitted by the Texas Rules of Civil Procedure to the Respondent at the Respondent's Address or to the Respondent's counsel.

B. Every notice required by this Part to be served upon the Commission may be served by U. S. certified mail, return receipt requested, or by any other means of service permitted by the Texas Rules of Civil Procedure, to the address of the Commission's counsel of record or, if none, to the address designated by the Commission.

C. Whenever a party has the right or is required to do some act or take some proceedings within a prescribed period after the service of a notice or other paper upon the party and the notice or paper is served upon the party by mail or telephonic document transfer, three days shall be added to the prescribed period.

Adopted by order of Dec. 29, 2003, eff. Jan. 1, 2004.

2.10. Classification of Inquiries and Complaints

The Chief Disciplinary Counsel shall within thirty days examine each Grievance received to determine whether it constitutes an Inquiry or a Complaint. If the Grievance is determined to constitute an Inquiry, the Chief Disciplinary Counsel shall notify the Complaint and Respondent of the dismissal. The Complainant may, within thirty days from notification of the dismissal, appeal the determination to the Board of Disciplinary Appeals. If the Board of Disciplinary Appeals affirms the classification as an Inquiry, the Complainant will be so notified and may within twenty days amend the Grievance one time only by providing new or additional evidence. The Complainant may appeal a decision by the Chief Disciplinary Counsel to dismiss the amended Complaint as an Inquiry to the Board of Disciplinary Appeals. No further amendments or appeals will be accepted. In all instances where a Grievance is dismissed as an Inquiry other than where the attorney is deceased or is not licensed to practice law in the State of Texas, the Chief Disciplinary Counsel shall refer the Inquiry to a voluntary mediation and dispute resolution procedure. If the Grievance is determined to constitute a Complaint, the Respondent shall be provided a copy of the Complaint with notice to respond, in writing, to the allegations of the Complaint. The notice shall advise the Respondent that the Chief Disciplinary Counsel may provide appropriate information, including the Respondent's response, to law enforcement agencies as permitted by Rule 6.08. The Respondent shall deliver the response to both the Office of the Chief Disciplinary Counsel and the Complainant within thirty days after receipt of the notice.

Adopted by orders of Feb. 26, 1991, and Oct. 9, 1991, eff. May 1, 1992. Amended by order of June 15, 1994, eff. Oct. 1, 1994. Renumbered from Rule 2.09 and amended by order of Dec. 29, 2003, eff. Jan. 1, 2004.

2.11. Venue

Venue of District Grievance Committee proceedings shall be in accordance with the following:

A. *Summary Disposition Panel Proceedings.* Proceedings of a Summary Disposition Panel shall be conducted by a Panel for the county where the alleged Professional Misconduct occurred, in whole or in part. If the acts or omissions complained of occurred wholly outside the State of Texas, proceedings shall be conducted by a Panel for the county of Respondent's residence and, if Respondent has no residence in Texas, by a Panel for Travis County, Texas.

B. *Evidentiary Panel Proceedings.* In an Evidentiary Panel proceeding, venue shall be in the county of Respondent's principal place of practice; or if the Respondent does not maintain a place of practice within the State of Texas, in the county of Respondent's residence; or if the Respondent maintains neither a residence nor a place of practice within the State of Texas, then in the county where the alleged Professional Misconduct occurred, in whole or in part. In all other instances, venue is in Travis County, Texas.

Adopted by orders of Feb. 26, 1991, and Oct. 9, 1991, eff. May 1, 1992. Amended by order of June 15, 1994, eff. Oct. 1, 1994. Renumbered from Rule 2.10 and amended by order of Dec. 29, 2003, eff. Jan. 1, 2004.

2.12. Investigation and Determination of Just Cause

No more than sixty days after the date by which the Respondent must file a written response to the Complaint as set forth in Rule 2.10, the Chief Disciplinary Counsel shall investigate the Complaint and determine whether there is Just Cause.

Adopted by orders of Feb. 26, 1991, and Oct. 9, 1991, eff. May 1, 1992. Amended by order of June 15, 1994, eff. Oct. 1, 1994. Renumbered from Rule 2.11 and amended by order of Dec. 29, 2003, eff. Jan. 1, 2004.

2.13. Summary Disposition Setting

Upon investigation, if the Chief Disciplinary Counsel determines that Just Cause does not exist to proceed on the Complaint, the Chief Disciplinary Counsel shall place the Complaint on a Summary Disposition Panel docket. At the Summary Disposition Panel docket, the Chief Disciplinary Counsel will present the Complaint together with any information, documents, evidence, and argument deemed necessary and appropriate by the Chief Disciplinary Counsel, without the presence of the Complainant or Respondent. The Summary Disposition Panel shall determine whether the Complaint should be dismissed or should proceed. If the Summary Disposition Panel dismisses the Complaint, both the Complainant and Respondent will be so notified. There is no appeal from a determination by the Summary Disposition Panel that the Complaint should be dismissed or should proceed. All Complaints presented to the Summary Disposition Panel and not dismissed shall be placed on the Hearing Docket. The fact that a Complaint was placed on the Summary Disposition Panel Docket and not dismissed is wholly inadmissible for any purpose in the instant or any subsequent Disciplinary Proceeding or Disciplinary Action. Files of dismissed Disciplinary Proceedings will be retained for one hundred eighty days, after which time the files may be destroyed. No permanent record will be kept of Complaints dismissed except to the extent necessary for statistical reporting purposes. In all instances where a Complaint is dismissed by a Summary Disposition Panel other than where the attorney is deceased or is not licensed to practice law in the State of Texas, the Chief Disciplinary Counsel shall refer the Inquiry to a voluntary mediation and dispute resolution procedure.

Adopted by orders of Feb. 26, 1991, and Oct. 9, 1991, eff. May 1, 1992. Renumbered from Rule 2.12 and amended by order of Dec. 29, 2003, eff. Jan. 1, 2004.

2.14. Proceeding Upon a Determination of Just Cause

All rights characteristically reposed in a client by the common law of this State as to every Complaint not dismissed by the Summary Disposition Panel are vested in the Commission.

A. *Client of Chief Disciplinary Counsel*: The Commission is the client of the Chief Disciplinary Counsel for every Complaint not dismissed by the Summary Disposition Panel.

B. *Interim Suspension*: In any instance in which the Chief Disciplinary Counsel reasonably believes based upon investigation of the Complaint that the Respondent poses a substantial threat of irreparable harm to clients or prospective clients, the Chief Disciplinary Counsel may seek and obtain authority from the Commission to pursue interim suspension of the Respondent's license in accordance with Part XIV of these rules.

C. *Disability*: In any instance in which the Chief Disciplinary Counsel reasonably believes based upon investigation of the Complaint that the Respondent is suffering from a Disability to such an extent that either (a) the Respondent's continued practice of law poses a substantial threat of irreparable harm to client or prospective clients; or (b) the Respondent is so impaired as to be unable to meaningfully participate in the preparation of a defense, the Chief Disciplinary Counsel shall seek and obtain client authority to refer the Complaint to the Board of Disciplinary Appeals pursuant to Part XII of these rules.

D. *Notification of Complaint*: For each Complaint not dismissed by a Summary Disposition Panel, the Chief Disciplinary Counsel shall give the Respondent written notice of the acts and/or omissions engaged in by the Respondent and of the Texas Disciplinary Rules of Professional Conduct that the Chief Disciplinary Counsel contends are violated by the alleged acts and/or omissions. Such notice shall be given by certified mail, return receipt requested, sent to the Respondent at the Address.

Adopted by orders of Feb. 26, 1991, and Oct. 9, 1991, eff. May 1, 1992. Amended by order of Dec. 23, 1992. Renumbered from Rule 2.13 and amended by order of Dec. 29, 2003, eff. Jan. 1, 2004.

2.15. Election

A Respondent given written notice of the allegations and rule violations complained of, in accordance with Rule 2.14, shall notify the Chief Disciplinary Counsel whether the Respondent seeks to have the Complaint heard in a district court of proper venue, with or without a jury, or by an Evidentiary Panel of the Committee. The election must be in writing and served upon the Chief Disciplinary Counsel no later than twenty days after the Respondent's receipt of written notification pursuant to Rule 2.14. If the Respondent timely elects to have the Complaint heard in a district court, the matter will proceed in accordance with Part III hereof. If the Respondent timely elects to have the Complaint heard by an Evidentiary Panel, the matter will proceed in accordance with Rules 2.17 and 2.18. A Respondent's failure to timely file an election shall conclusively be deemed as an affirmative election to proceed in accordance with Rules 2.17 and 2.18.

Adopted by orders of Feb. 26, 1991, and Oct. 9, 1991, eff. May 1, 1992. Renumbered from Rule 2.14 and amended by order of Dec. 29, 2003, eff. Jan. 1, 2004.

2.16. Confidentiality

A. All members and staff of the Office of Chief Disciplinary Counsel, Board of Disciplinary Appeals. Committees, and Commission shall maintain as confidential all Disciplinary Proceedings and associated records, except that:

1. the pendency, subject matter, status of an investigation, and final disposition, if any, may be disclosed by the Office of Chief Disciplinary Counsel or Board of Disciplinary Appeals if the Respondent has waived confidentiality, the Disciplinary Proceeding is based on conviction of a serious crime, or disclosure is ordered by a court of competent jurisdiction;

2. if the Evidentiary Panel finds that professional misconduct occurred and imposes any sanction other than a private reprimand.

a. the Evidentiary Panel's final judgment is a public record from the date the judgment is signed; and

b. once all appeals, if any, have been exhausted and the judgment is final, the Office of Chief Disciplinary Counsel shall, upon request, disclose all documents, statements, and other information relating to the Disciplinary Proceeding that came to the attention of the Evidentiary Panel during the Disciplinary Proceeding;

3. the record in any appeal to the Board of Disciplinary Appeals from an Evidentiary Panel's final judgment, other than an appeal from a judgment of private reprimand, is a public record; and

4. facts and evidence that are discoverable elsewhere are not made confidential merely because they are discussed or introduced in the course of a Disciplinary Proceeding.

B. The deliberations and voting of an Evidentiary Panel are strictly confidential and not subject to discovery. No person is competent to testify as to such deliberations and voting.

C. Rule 6.08 governs the provision of confidential information to authorized agencies investigating qualifications for admission to practice, attorney discipline enforcement agencies, law enforcement agencies, the State Bar's Client Security Fund, the State Bar's Lawyer Assistance Program, the Supreme Court's Unauthorized Practice of Law Committee and its subcommittees, and the Commission on Judicial Conduct.

Adopted by orders of Feb. 26, 1991, and Oct. 9, 1991, eff. May 1, 1992. Renumbered from Rule 2.15 and amended by orders of Dec. 29, 2003, eff. Jan. 1, 2004. Amended by order of Dec. 7, 2009, eff. Jan. 1, 2010.

2.17. Evidentiary Hearings

Within fifteen days of the earlier of the date of Chief Disciplinary Counsel's receipt of Respondent's election or the day following the expiration of Respondent's right to elect, the chair of a Committee having proper venue shall appoint an Evidentiary Panel to hear the Complaint. The Evidentiary Panel may not include any person who served on a Summary Disposition Docket panel that heard the Complaint and must have at least three members but must have no more than one-half as many members as on the Committee. Each Evidentiary Panel must have a ratio of two attorney members for every public member. Proceedings before an Evidentiary Panel of the Committee include:

A. *Evidentiary Petition and Service*: Not more than sixty days from the earlier of receipt of Respondent's election or Respondent's deadline to elect to proceed before an Evidentiary Panel, the Chief Disciplinary Counsel shall file with the Evidentiary Panel an Evidentiary Petition in the name of the Commission. The Evidentiary Petition shall be served upon the Respondent in accordance with Rule 2.09 and must contain:

1. Notice that the action is brought by the Commission for Lawyer Discipline, a committee of the State Bar.

2. The name of the Respondent and the fact that he or she is an attorney licensed to practice law in the State of Texas.

3. Allegations necessary to establish proper venue.

4. A description of the acts and conduct that gave rise to the alleged Professional Misconduct in detail sufficient to give fair notice to the Respondent of the claims made, which factual allegations may be grouped in one or more counts based upon one or more Complaints.

5. A listing of the specific rules of the Texas Disciplinary Rules of Professional Conduct allegedly violated by the acts or conduct, or other grounds for seeking Sanctions.

6. A demand for judgment that the Respondent be disciplined as warranted by the facts and for any other appropriate relief.

7. Any other matter that is required or may be permitted by law or by these rules.

B. *Answer*: A responsive pleading either admitting or denying each specific allegation of Professional Misconduct must be filed by or on behalf of the Respondent no later than 5:00 p.m. on the first Monday following the expiration of twenty days after service of the Evidentiary Petition.

C. *Default*: A failure to file an answer within the time permitted constitutes a default, and all facts alleged in the Evidentiary Petition shall be taken as true for the purposes of the Disciplinary Proceeding. Upon a showing of default, the Evidentiary Panel shall enter an order of default with a finding of Professional Misconduct and shall conduct a hearing to determine the Sanctions to be imposed.

D. *Request for Disclosure*: The Commission or Respondent may obtain disclosure from the other party of the information or material listed below by serving the other party, no later than thirty days before the first setting of the hearing. The responding party must serve a written response on the requesting party within thirty days after service of the request, except that a Respondent served with a request before the answer is due need not respond until fifty days after service of the request. A party who fails to make, amend, or supplement a disclosure in a timely manner may not introduce in evidence the material or information that was not timely disclosed, or offer the testimony of a witness (other than a named party) who was not timely identified, unless the panel finds that there was good cause for the failure to timely make, amend, or supplement the disclosure response; or the failure to timely make, amend, or supplement the discovery response will not unfairly surprise or unfairly prejudice the other party. No objection or assertion of work product is permitted to a request under this Rule. A party may request disclosure of any or all of the following:

1. The correct names of the parties to the Disciplinary Proceeding.
2. In general, the factual bases of the responding party's claims or defenses (the responding party need not marshal all evidence that may be offered at trial).
3. The name, address, and telephone number of persons having knowledge of relevant facts, and a brief statement of each identified person's connection with the disciplinary matter.
4. For any testifying expert, the expert's name, address, and telephone number; the subject matter on which the expert will testify, and the general substance of the expert's mental impressions and opinions and a brief summary of the basis for them.
5. Any witness statements.

E. *Limited Discovery*: In addition to the Request for Disclosure, the Commission and the Respondent may conduct further discovery with the following limitations:

1. All discovery must be conducted during the discovery period, which begins when the Evidentiary Petition is filed and continues until thirty days before the date set for hearing.
2. Each party may have no more than six hours in total to examine and cross-examine all witnesses in oral depositions.
3. Any party may serve on the other party no more than twenty-five written interrogatories, excluding interrogatories asking a party only to identify or authenticate specific documents. Each discrete subpart of an interrogatory is considered a separate interrogatory.
4. Any party may serve on the other party requests for production and inspection of documents and tangible things.
5. Any party may serve on the other party requests for admission.

F. *Modification of Discovery Limitations*: Upon a showing of reasonable need, the Evidentiary Panel chair may modify the discovery limitations set forth in Rule 2.17E. The parties may by agreement modify the discovery limitations set forth in Rule 2.17E.

G. *Discovery Dispute Resolution*: Except where modified by these rules, all discovery disputes shall be ruled upon by the Evidentiary Panel chair generally in accord with the Texas Rules of Civil Procedure; provided, however, that no ruling upon a discovery dispute shall be a basis for reversal solely because it fails to strictly comply with the Texas Rules of Civil Procedure.

H. *Subpoena Power*: Commission or Respondent may compel the attendance of witnesses, including the Respondent, and the production of books, documents, papers, banking records, and other things by subpoena. The subpoena must notify the witness of the time, date, and place of appearance and must contain a description of the materials to be produced. Subpoenas must be in writing and signed and issued by the Evidentiary Panel chair. The party seeking the subpoena shall submit it in a proper form and is responsible for securing service. Any contest between the Commission and the Respondent about the materiality of the testimony or production sought by a subpoena shall be determined by the Evidentiary Panel chair, and is subject to review. Subpoenas must be served on witnesses personally or in accordance with Rule 21a of the Texas Rules of Civil Procedure. Proof of service shall be by certification of the server or by the return receipt. The subpoena is enforceable by the district court of the county in which the attendance or production is required. Witnesses shall be paid witness fees and mileage the same as for a district court.

I. *Enforcement of Subpoenas and Examination Before a District Judge*: If any witness, including the Respondent, fails or refuses to appear or to produce the things named in the subpoena, or refuses to be sworn or to affirm or to testify, the witness may be compelled to appear and produce tangible evidence and to testify at a hearing before a district judge of the county in which the subpoena was served. The application for such a hearing is to be styled "In re: Hearing Before The District ________ Grievance Committee." The court shall order a time, date, and place for the hearing and shall notify the Commission, the Respondent, and the witness. Unless the Respondent requests a public hearing, the proceedings before the court shall be closed and all records relating to the hearing shall be sealed and made available only to the Commission, the Respondent, or the witness. If the witness fails or refuses to appear, testify, or produce such tangible evidence, he or she shall be punished for civil contempt.

J. *Right to Counsel*: The Respondent and the Complainant may, if they so choose, have counsel present during any evidentiary hearing.

K. *Alternative Dispute Resolution*: Upon motion made or otherwise, the Evidentiary Panel Chair may order the Commission and the Respondent to participate in mandatory alternative dispute resolution as provided by Chapter 154 of the Civil Practice and Remedies Code or as otherwise provided by law when deemed appropriate.

L. *Evidence*: The Respondent, individually or through his or her counsel if represented, and the Commission, through the Chief Disciplinary Counsel, may, if they so choose, offer evidence, examine witnesses and present argument [1] Witness examination may be conducted only by the Commission, the Respondent, and the panel members. The inability or failure to exercise this opportunity does not abate or preclude further proceedings. The Evidentiary Panel chair shall admit all such probative and relevant evidence as he or she deems necessary for a fair and complete hearing, generally in accord with the Texas Rules of Evidence; provided, however, that admission or exclusion of evidence shall be in the discretion of the Evidentiary Panel chair and no ruling upon the evidence shall be a basis for reversal solely because it fails to strictly comply with the Texas Rules of Evidence.

M. *Burden of Proof*: The burden of proof is upon the Commission for Lawyer Discipline to prove the material allegations of the Evidentiary Petition by a preponderance of the evidence.

N. *Record of the Hearing*: A verbatim record of the proceedings will be made by a certified shorthand reporter in a manner prescribed by the Board of Disciplinary Appeals. In the event of an appeal from the Evidentiary Panel to the Board of Disciplinary Appeals, the party initiating the appeal shall pay the costs of preparation of the transcript. Such costs shall be taxed at the conclusion of the appeal by the Board of Disciplinary Appeals.

O. *Setting*: Evidentiary Panel proceedings must be set for hearing with a minimum of forty-five days' notice to all parties unless waived by all parties. Evidentiary Panel proceedings shall be set for hearing on the merits on a date not later than 180 days after the date the answer is filed, except for good cause shown. If the Respondent fails to answer, a hearing for default may be set at any time not less than ten days after the answer date without further notice to the Respondent. No continuance may be granted unless required by the interests of justice.

P. *Decision*: After conducting the Evidentiary Hearing, the Evidentiary Panel shall issue a judgment within thirty days. In any Evidentiary Panel proceeding where Professional Misconduct is found to have occurred, such judgment shall include findings of fact, conclusions of law and the Sanctions to be imposed. The Evidentiary Panel may:

1. dismiss the Disciplinary Proceeding and refer it to the voluntary mediation and dispute resolution procedure;
2. find that the Respondent suffers from a disability and forward that finding to the Board of Disciplinary Appeals for referral to a district disability committee pursuant to Part XII; or
3. find that Professional Misconduct occurred and impose Sanctions.

Adopted by orders of Feb. 26, 1991, and Oct. 9, 1991, eff. May 1, 1992. Amended by order of June 15, 1994, eff. Oct. 1, 1994. Renumbered from Rule 2.16 and amended by order of Dec. 29, 2003, eff. Jan. 1, 2004.

[1] So in order.

2.18. Imposition of Sanctions

The Evidentiary Panel may, in its discretion, conduct a separate hearing and receive evidence as to the appropriate Sanctions to be imposed. Indefinite Disability sanction is not an available Sanction in a hearing before an Evidentiary Panel. In determining the appropriate Sanctions, the Evidentiary Panel shall consider:

A. The nature and degree of the Professional Misconduct for which the Respondent is being sanctioned;

B. The seriousness of and circumstances surrounding the Professional Misconduct;

C. The loss or damage to clients;

D. The damage to the profession;

E. The assurance that those who seek legal services in the future will be insulated from the type of Professional Misconduct found;

F. The profit to the attorney;

G. The avoidance of repetition;

H. The deterrent effect on others;

I. The maintenance of respect for the legal profession;

J. The conduct of the Respondent during the course of the Disciplinary Proceeding;

In addition, the Respondent's disciplinary record, including any private reprimands, is admissible on the appropriate Sanction to be imposed. Respondent's Disability may not be considered in mitigation, unless

Respondent demonstrates that he or she is successfully pursuing in good faith a program of recovery or appropriate course of treatment.

Adopted by orders of Feb. 26, 1991, and Oct. 9, 1991, eff. May 1, 1992. Renumbered from Rule 2.17 and amended by order of Dec. 29, 2003, eff. Jan. 1, 2004.

2.19. Terms of Judgment

In any judgment of disbarment or suspension that is not stayed, the Evidentiary Panel shall order the Respondent to surrender his or her law license and permanent State Bar card to Chief Disciplinary Counsel for transmittal to the Clerk of the Supreme Court. In all judgments imposing disbarment or suspension, the Evidentiary Panel shall enjoin the Respondent from practicing law or from holding himself or herself out as an attorney eligible to practice law during the period of disbarment or suspension. In all judgments of disbarment, suspension, or reprimand, the Evidentiary Panel shall make all other orders as it finds appropriate, including probation of all or any portion of suspension.

Adopted by order of Dec. 29, 2003, eff. Jan. 1, 2004.

2.20. Restitution

In all cases in which the proof establishes that the Respondent's misconduct involved the misappropriation of funds and the Respondent is disbarred or suspended, the panel's judgment must require the Respondent to make restitution during the period of suspension, or before any consideration of reinstatement from disbarment, and must further provide that its judgment of suspension shall remain in effect until evidence of satisfactory restitution is made by Respondent and verified by Chief Disciplinary Counsel.

Adopted by orders of Feb. 26, 1991, and Oct. 9, 1991, eff. May 1, 1992. Renumbered from Rule 2.18 and amended by order of Dec. 29, 2003, eff. Jan. 1, 2004.

2.21. Notice of Decision

The Complainant, the Respondent, and the Commission must be notified in writing of the judgment of the Evidentiary Panel. The notice sent to the Respondent and the Commission must clearly state that any appeal of the judgment must be filed with the Board of Disciplinary Appeals within thirty days of the date of the notice. If the Evidentiary Panel finds that the Respondent committed professional misconduct, a copy of the Evidentiary Petition and the judgment shall be transmitted by the Office of the Chief Disciplinary Counsel to the Clerk of the Supreme Court. The Clerk of the Supreme Court shall make an appropriate notation on the Respondent's permanent record.

Adopted by orders of Feb. 26, 1991, and Oct. 9, 1991, eff. May 1, 1992. Amended by order of June 15, 1994, eff. Oct. 1, 1994. Renumbered from Rule 2.19 and amended by order of Dec. 29, 2003, eff. Jan. 1, 2004.

2.22. Post Judgment Motions

Any motion for new hearing or motion to modify the judgment must comport with the provisions of the applicable Texas Rules of Civil Procedure pertaining to motions for new trial or to motions to modify judgments.

Adopted by order of Dec. 29, 2003, eff. Jan. 1, 2004.

2.23. Probated Suspension—Revocation Procedure

If all or any part of a suspension from the practice of law is probated under this Part II, the Board of Disciplinary Appeals is hereby granted jurisdiction for the full term of suspension, including any probationary period, to hear a motion to revoke probation. If the Chief Disciplinary Counsel files a motion to revoke probation, it shall be set for hearing within thirty days of service of the motion upon the Respondent. Service upon the Respondent shall be sufficient if made in accordance with Rule 21a of the Texas Rules of Civil Procedure. Upon proof, by a preponderance of the evidence, of a violation of probation, the same shall be revoked and the attorney suspended from the practice of law for the full term of suspension without credit for any probationary time served. The Board of Disciplinary Appeals' Order revoking a probated suspension cannot be superseded or stayed.

Adopted by orders of Feb. 26, 1991, and Oct. 9, 1991, eff. May 1, 1992. Amended by order of June 15, 1994, eff. Oct. 1, 1994. Renumbered from Rule 2.20 and amended by order of Dec. 29, 2003, eff. Jan. 1, 2004.

2.24. Appeals by Respondent or Commission:

The Respondent or Commission may appeal the judgment to the Board of Disciplinary Appeals. Such appeals must be on the record, determined under the standard of substantial evidence. Briefs may be filed as a matter of right. The time deadlines for such briefs shall be promulgated by the Board of Disciplinary Appeals. An appeal, if taken, is perfected when a written notice of appeal is filed with the Board of Disciplinary Appeals. The notice of appeal must reflect the intention of the Respondent or the Commission to appeal and identify the decision from which appeal is perfected. The notice of appeal must be filed within thirty days after the date of judgment, except that the notice of appeal must be filed within ninety days after the date of judgment if any party timely files a motion for new trial or a motion to modify the judgment.

Adopted by orders of Feb. 26, 1991, and Oct. 9, 1991, eff. May 1, 1992. Renumbered in part from Rule 2.21 and amended by order of Dec. 29, 2003, eff. Jan. 1, 2004.

2.25. No Supersedeas

An Evidentiary Panel's order of disbarment cannot be superseded or stayed. The Respondent may within thirty days from entry of judgment petition the Evidentiary Panel to stay a judgment of suspension. The Respondent carries the burden of proof by preponderance of the evidence to establish by competent evidence that the Respondent's continued practice of law does not pose a continuing threat to the welfare of Respondent's clients or to the public. An order of suspension must be stayed during the pendency of any appeals therefrom if the Evidentiary Panel finds that the Respondent has met that burden of proof. An Evidentiary Panel may condition its stay upon reasonable terms, which may include, but are not limited to, the cessation of any practice found to constitute Professional Misconduct, or it may impose a requirement of an affirmative act such as an audit of a Respondent's client trust account.

Adopted by orders of Feb. 26, 1991, and Oct. 9, 1991, eff. May 1, 1992. Renumbered in part from Rule 2.21 and amended by order of Dec. 29, 2003, eff. Jan. 1, 2004.

2.26. Disposition on Appeal

The Board of Disciplinary Appeals may, in any appeal of the judgment of an Evidentiary Panel within its jurisdiction:

A. Affirm the decision of the Evidentiary Panel, in whole or in part;

B. Modify the Evidentiary Panel's judgment and affirm it as modified;

C. Reverse the decision of the Evidentiary Panel, in whole or in part, and render the judgment that the Evidentiary Panel should have rendered;

D. Reverse the Evidentiary Panel's judgment and remand the Disciplinary Proceeding for further proceeding by either the Evidentiary Panel or a statewide grievance committee panel composed of members selected from state bar districts other than the district from which the appeal was taken;

E. Vacate the Evidentiary Panel's judgment and dismiss the case; or

F. Dismiss the appeal.

Adopted by order of Dec. 29, 2003, eff. Jan. 1, 2004.

2.27. Remand to Statewide Grievance Committee Panel

In determining whether a remand is heard by a statewide grievance committee panel, the Board of Disciplinary Appeals must find that good cause was shown in the record on appeal. The Board of Disciplinary Appeals shall randomly select the members of the statewide grievance committee panel from grievance committees other than the district from which the appeal was taken. Six such members shall be selected, four of whom are attorneys and two of whom are public members. The statewide grievance committee panel, once selected, shall have all duties and responsibilities of the Evidentiary Panel for purposes of the remand.

Adopted by order of Dec. 29, 2003, eff. Jan. 1, 2004.

2.28. Appeal to Supreme Court of Texas

An appeal from the decision of the Board of Disciplinary Appeals on an Evidentiary Proceeding is to the Supreme Court of Texas in accordance with Rule 7.11.

Adopted by order of Dec. 29, 2003, eff. Jan. 1, 2004.

PART III. TRIAL IN DISTRICT COURT

3.01. Disciplinary Petition

If the Respondent timely elects to have the Complaint heard by a district court, with or without a jury, in accordance with Rule 2.15, the Chief Disciplinary Counsel shall, not more than sixty days after receipt of Respondent's election to proceed in district court, notify the Supreme Court of Texas of the Respondent's election by transmitting a copy of the Disciplinary Petition in the name of the Commission to the Clerk of the Supreme Court of Texas. The petition must contain:

A. Notice that the action is brought by the Commission for Lawyer Discipline, a committee of the State Bar.

B. The name of the Respondent and the fact that he or she is an attorney licensed to practice law in the State of Texas.

C. Allegations necessary to establish proper venue.

D. A description of the acts and conduct that gave rise to the alleged Professional Misconduct in detail sufficient to give fair notice to Respondent of the claims made, which factual allegations may be grouped in one or more counts based upon one or more Complaints.

E. A listing of the specific rules of the Texas Disciplinary Rules of Professional Conduct allegedly violated by the acts or conduct, or other grounds for seeking Sanctions.

F. A demand for judgment that the Respondent be disciplined as warranted by the acts and for any other appropriate relief.

G. Any other matter that is required or may be permitted by law or by these rules.

Adopted by orders of Feb. 26, 1991, and Oct. 9, 1991, eff. May 1, 1992. Amended by order of Dec. 29, 2003, eff. Jan. 1, 2004; Sept. 19, 2012, eff. Oct. 1, 2012.

3.02. Assignment of Judge

Upon receipt of a Disciplinary Petition, the Clerk of the Supreme Court of Texas shall promptly bring the Petition to the attention of the Supreme Court. The Supreme Court shall promptly appoint an active district judge who does not reside in the Administrative Judicial District in which the Respondent resides to preside in the case and the Clerk of the Supreme Court shall transmit a copy of the Supreme Court's appointing order to the Chief Disciplinary Counsel. Should the judge so appointed be unable to fulfill the appointment, he or she shall immediately notify the Clerk of the Supreme Court, and the Supreme Court shall appoint a replacement judge. The judge appointed shall be subject to objection, recusal or disqualification as provided by law. The objection, motion seeking recusal or motion to disqualify must be filed by either party not later than sixty days from the date the Respondent is served with the Supreme Court's order appointing the judge. In the event of objection, recusal or disqualification, the Supreme Court shall appoint a replacement judge within thirty days.

Adopted by orders of Feb. 26, 1991, and Oct. 9, 1991, eff. May 1, 1992. Amended by order of June 15, 1994, eff. Oct. 1, 1994; Dec. 29, 2003, eff. Jan. 1, 2004; Sept. 19, 2012, eff. Oct. 1, 2012.

3.03. Filing, Service and Venue

After the trial judge has been appointed, the Chief Disciplinary Counsel shall promptly file the Disciplinary Petition and a copy of the Supreme Court's appointing Order with the district clerk of the county of alleged venue. The Respondent shall then be served as in civil cases generally with a copy of the Disciplinary Petition and a copy of the Supreme Court's appointing Order. In a Disciplinary Action, venue shall be in the county of Respondent's principal place of practice; or if the Respondent does not maintain a place of practice within the State of Texas, in the county of Respondent's residence; or if the Respondent maintains neither a residence nor a place of practice within the State of Texas, then in the county where the alleged Professional Misconduct occurred, in whole or in part. In all other instances, venue is in Travis County, Texas.

Adopted by orders of Feb. 26, 1991, and Oct. 9, 1991, eff. May 1, 1992. Amended by order of June 15, 1994, eff. Oct. 1, 1994; Dec. 29, 2003, eff. Jan. 1, 2004; Sept. 19, 2012, eff. Oct. 1, 2012.

3.04. Answer of the Respondent

The answer of the Respondent must follow the form of answers in civil cases generally and must be filed no later than 10:00 a.m. on the first Monday following the expiration of twenty days after service upon the Respondent.

Adopted by orders of Feb. 26, 1991, and Oct. 9, 1991, eff. May 1, 1992.

3.05. Discovery

Discovery is to be conducted as in civil cases generally, except that the following matters are not discoverable:

A. The discussions, thought processes, and individual votes of the members of a Summary Disposition Panel.

B. The thought processes of the Chief Disciplinary Counsel.

C. Any communication to or from the Chief Disciplinary Counsel that would be privileged in the case of a private attorney representing a private litigant.

Adopted by orders of Feb. 26, 1991, and Oct. 9, 1991, eff. May 1, 1992. Amended by order of Dec. 29, 2003, eff. Jan. 1, 2004.

3.06. Trial by Jury

In a Disciplinary Action, either the Respondent or the Commission shall have the right to a jury trial upon timely payment of the required fee and compliance with the provisions of Rule 216, Texas Rules of Civil Procedure. The Complainant has no right to demand a jury trial.

Adopted by orders of Feb. 26, 1991, and Oct. 9, 1991, eff. May 1, 1992.

3.07. Trial Setting

Disciplinary Actions shall be set for trial on a date not later than 180 days after the date the answer is filed, except for good cause shown. If the Respondent fails to answer, a default may be taken at any time appropriate under the Texas Rules of Civil Procedure. No motion for continuance, resetting, or agreed pass may be granted unless required by the interests of justice.

Adopted by orders of Feb. 26, 1991, and Oct. 9, 1991, eff. May 1, 1992. Amended by order of June 15, 1994, eff. Oct. 1, 1994; Dec. 29, 2003, eff. Jan. 1, 2004.

3.08. Additional Rules of Procedure in the Trial of Disciplinary Actions

In all Disciplinary Actions brought under this part, the following additional rules apply:

A. Disciplinary Actions are civil in nature.

B. Except as varied by these rules, the Texas Rules of Civil Procedure apply.

C. Disciplinary Actions must be proved by a preponderance of the evidence.

D. The burden of proof in a Disciplinary Action seeking Sanction is on the Commission. The burden of proof in reinstatement cases is upon the applicant.

E. The parties to a Disciplinary Action may not seek abatement or delay of trial because of substantial similarity to the material allegations in any other pending civil or criminal case.

F. The unwillingness or neglect of a Complainant to assist in the prosecution of a Disciplinary Action, or a compromise and settlement between the Complainant and the Respondent, does not alone justify the abatement or dismissal of the action.

G. It shall be the policy of the Commission to participate in alternative dispute resolution procedures where feasible; provided, however, that Disciplinary Actions shall be exempt from any requirements of mandatory alternative dispute resolution procedures as provided by Chapter 154 of the Civil Practice and Remedies Code or as otherwise provided by law.

Adopted by orders of Feb. 26, 1991, and Oct. 9, 1991, eff. May 1, 1992. Amended by order of June 15, 1994, eff. Oct. 1, 1994; Dec. 20, 2003, eff. Jan. 1, 2004.

3.09. Judgment

If the trial court fails to find from the evidence in a case tried without a jury, or from the verdict in a jury trial, that the Respondent's conduct constitutes Professional Misconduct, the court shall render judgment accordingly. If the court finds that the Respondent's conduct does constitute Professional Misconduct, the court shall determine the appropriate Sanction or Sanctions to be imposed. If the court finds that the Respondent committed an act or acts of Professional Misconduct, the court shall direct transmittal of certified copies of the judgment and all trial pleadings to the Clerk of the Supreme Court. The Clerk of the Supreme Court shall make an appropriate notation on the Respondent's permanent record. The trial court shall promptly enter judgment after the close of evidence (in the case of a nonjury trial) or after the return of the jury's verdict. Mandamus lies in the Supreme Court of Texas to enforce this provision, upon the petition of either the Respondent or the Chief Disciplinary Counsel.

Adopted by orders of Feb. 26, 1991, and Oct. 9, 1991, eff. May 1, 1992.

3.10. Imposition of Sanctions

The trial court may, in its discretion, conduct a separate hearing and receive evidence as to the appropriate Sanctions to be imposed. Private reprimand is not an available Sanction. Indefinite Disability suspension is not an available Sanction. In determining the appropriate Sanctions, the court shall consider:

A. The nature and degree of the Professional Misconduct for which the Respondent is being sanctioned;

B. The seriousness of and circumstances surrounding the Professional Misconduct;

C. The loss or damage to clients;

D. The damage to the profession;

E. The assurance that those who seek legal services in the future will be insulated from the type of Professional Misconduct found;

F. The profit to the attorney;

G. The avoidance of repetition;

H. The deterrent effect on others;

I. The maintenance of respect for the legal profession;

J. The conduct of the Respondent during the course of the Committee action;

K. The trial of the case; and

L. Other relevant evidence concerning the Respondent's personal and professional background.

In addition, the Respondent's disciplinary record, including any private reprimands, is admissible on the appropriate Sanction to be imposed. Respondent's Disability may not be considered in mitigation, unless Respondent demonstrates that he or she is successfully pursuing in good faith a program of recovery or appropriate course of treatment.

Adopted by orders of Feb. 26, 1991, and Oct. 9, 1991, eff. May 1, 1992. Amended by order of Dec. 29, 2003, eff. Jan. 1, 2004.

3.11. Terms of Judgment

In any judgment of disbarment or suspension that is not stayed, the court shall order the Respondent to surrender his or her law license and permanent State

Bar card to Chief Disciplinary Counsel for transmittal to the Clerk of the Supreme Court. In all judgments imposing disbarment or suspension, the court shall enjoin the Respondent from practicing law or from holding himself or herself out as an attorney eligible to practice law during the period of disbarment or suspension. In all judgments of disbarment, suspension, or reprimand, the court shall make all other orders as it finds appropriate, including probation of all or any portion of suspension. The continuing jurisdiction of the trial court to enforce a judgment does not give a trial court authority to terminate or reduce a period of active or probated suspension previously ordered.

Adopted by orders of Feb. 26, 1991, and Oct. 9, 1991, eff. May 1, 1992. Amended by order of June 15, 1994, eff. Oct. 1, 1994; Dec. 29, 2003, eff. Jan. 1, 2004.

3.12. Restitution

In all cases in which the proof establishes that the Respondent's conduct involved misapplication of funds and the judgment is one disbarring or suspending the Respondent, the judgment must require the Respondent to make restitution during the period of suspension, or before any consideration of reinstatement from disbarment, and shall further provide that a judgment of suspension shall remain in effect until proof is made of complete restitution.

Adopted by orders of Feb. 26, 1991, and Oct. 9, 1991, eff. May 1, 1992.

3.13. Probation Suspension—Revocation Procedure

If all or any part of a suspension from the practice of law is probated under this Part III, the court retains jurisdiction during the full term of suspension, including any probationary period, to hear a motion to revoke probation. If the Chief Disciplinary Counsel files a motion to revoke probation, it shall be set for hearing before the court without the aid of a jury within thirty days of service of the motion upon the Respondent. Service upon the Respondent shall be sufficient if made in accordance with Rule 21a of the Texas Rules of Civil Procedure. Upon proof by a preponderance of the evidence of a violation of probation, the same shall be revoked and the attorney suspended from the practice of law for the full term of suspension without credit for any probationary time served.

Adopted by orders of Feb. 26, 1991, and Oct. 9, 1991, eff. May 1, 1992. Amended by order of June 15, 1994, eff. Oct. 1, 1994.

3.14. No Supersedeas

A district court judgment of disbarment or an order revoking probation of a suspension from the practice of law cannot be superseded or stayed. The Respondent may within thirty days from entry of judgment petition the court to stay a judgment of suspension. The Respondent carries the burden of proof by preponderance of the evidence to establish by competent evidence that the Respondent's continued practice of law does not pose a continuing threat to the welfare of Respondent's clients or to the public. A judgment of suspension shall be stayed during the pendency of any appeals therefrom if the district court finds that the Respondent has met that burden of proof. The district court may condition its stay upon reasonable terms, which may include, but are not limited to, the cessation of any practice found to constitute Professional Misconduct, or it may impose a requirement of an affirmative act such as an audit of a Respondent's client trust account. There is no interlocutory appeal from a court's stay of a suspension, with or without conditions.

Adopted by orders of Feb. 26, 1991, and Oct. 9, 1991, eff. May 1, 1992. Amended by order of Dec. 29, 2003, eff. Jan. 1, 2004.

3.15. Exemption from Cost and Appeal Bond

No cost or appeal bond is required of the Chief Disciplinary Counsel or the Commission. In lieu thereof, when a cost or appeal bond would be otherwise required, a memorandum setting forth the exemption under this rule, when filed, suffices as a cost or appeal bond.

Adopted by orders of Feb. 26, 1991, and Oct. 9, 1991, eff. May 1, 1992.

3.16. Appeals

A final judgment of the district court and any order revoking or refusing to revoke probation of a suspension from the practice of law may be appealed as in civil cases generally.

Adopted by orders of Feb. 26, 1991, and Oct. 9, 1991, eff. May 1, 1992.

PART IV. THE COMMISSION FOR LAWYER DISCIPLINE

4.01 Composition and Membership

The Commission for Lawyer Discipline is hereby created as a permanent committee of the State Bar and is not subject to dissolution by the Board under Article VIII of the State Bar Rules. The Commission must be composed of twelve members. Six members shall be attorneys licensed to practice law in the State of Texas and in good standing as members of the

State Bar. Six members shall be public members who have, other than as consumers, no interest, direct or indirect, in the practice of law or the profession of law. No person may serve as a member of the Commission while he or she is a member of a Committee, an officer or Director of the State Bar, an employee of the State Bar, or an officer or director of the Texas Young Lawyers Association; provided, however, the Chairman of the Board of the State Bar shall appoint a Director of the State Bar as an adviser to the Commission and a Director of the State Bar as an alternate adviser to the Commission, and the President of the Texas Young Lawyers Association shall appoint a Director of the Texas Young Lawyers Association as an adviser to the Commission. Members of the Commission and its advisers will be compensated for their reasonable, actual, and necessary expenses, and members, but not advisers, will be compensated for their work as determined by the Board to be appropriate.

Adopted by orders of Feb. 26, 1991, and Oct. 9, 1991, eff. May 1, 1992. Amended by order of Dec. 29, 2003, eff. Jan. 1, 2004.

4.02. Appointment and Terms

Except for initial appointments as set forth in Rule 4.03 hereof, Commission members will serve three-year terms unless sooner terminated through disqualification, resignation, or other cause. Terms begin on September 1 of the year and expire on August 31 of the third year thereafter. The lawyer members of the Commission are appointed by the President of the State Bar, subject to the Board's concurrence, no later than June 1 of the year. The public members are appointed by the Supreme Court of Texas no later than June 1 of the year. Members may be removed by the Supreme Court, but only for good cause. Vacancies are to be filled in the same manner as term appointments but are only for the unexpired term of the position vacated. Members of the Commission are not eligible for reappointment to more than one additional three-year term.

Adopted by orders of Feb. 26, 1991, and Oct. 9, 1991, eff. May 1, 1992. Amended by order of Dec. 29, 2003, eff. Jan. 1, 2004.

4.03. Initial Appointments

Two lawyers shall initially be appointed for a term to expire on August 31 after at least twelve months of service; two lawyers shall initially be appointed for a term to expire on August 31 after twenty-four months of service; and two lawyers shall initially be appointed for a term to expire on August 31 after thirty-six months of service. One public member shall initially be appointed for a term to expire on August 31 after at least twelve months of service; one public member shall initially be appointed for a term to expire on August 31 after twenty-four months of service; and one public member shall initially be appointed for a term to expire on August 31 after thirty-six months of service. After the terms provided above, all terms shall be as provided in Rule 4.02.

Adopted by orders of Feb. 26, 1991, and Oct. 9, 1991, eff. May 1, 1992. Amended by order of Dec. 29, 2003, eff. Jan. 1, 2004.

4.04. Oath of Committee Members

As soon as possible after appointment, each newly appointed member of the Commission for Lawyer Discipline shall take the following oath to be administered by any person authorized by law to administer oaths:

"I do solemnly swear (or affirm) that I will faithfully execute my duties as a member of the Commission for Lawyer Discipline, as required by the Texas Rules of Disciplinary Procedure, and will, to the best of my ability, preserve, protect, and defend the Constitution and laws of the United States and of the State of Texas. I further solemnly swear (or affirm) that I will keep secret all such matters and things as shall come to my knowledge as a member of the Commission for Lawyer Discipline arising from or in connection with each Disciplinary Action and Disciplinary Proceeding unless permitted to disclose the same in accordance with the Rules of Disciplinary Procedure or unless ordered to do so in the course of a judicial proceeding or a proceeding before the Board of Disciplinary Appeals. I further solemnly swear (or affirm) that I have neither directly nor indirectly paid, offered, or promised to pay, contributed any money or valuable thing, or promised any public or private office to secure my appointment. So help me God."

Adopted by orders of Feb. 26, 1991, and Oct. 9, 1991, eff. May 1, 1992.

4.05. Chair

The President of the State Bar, subject to the concurrence of the Board, shall annually designate a lawyer member to chair the Commission and another member to serve as vice-chair, each for a one-year term.

Adopted by orders of Feb. 26, 1991, and Oct. 9, 1991, eff. May 1, 1992.

4.06. Duties and Authority of the Commission

The Commission has the following duties and responsibilities:

A. To exercise, in lawyer disciplinary and disability proceedings only, all rights characteristically reposed in a client by the common law of this State for all Complaints not dismissed by a Summary Disposition Panel.

B. To monitor and, from time to time as appropriate, to evaluate and report to the Board on the performance of the Chief Disciplinary Counsel.

C. To retain special counsel or local counsel when necessary.

D. To recommend to the Board such educational programs on legal ethics and lawyer discipline as it may consider advisable.

E. To recommend to the Board an annual budget for the operation of the attorney professional disciplinary and disability system.

F. To meet monthly or at such other times, in such places, and for such periods of time as the business of the Commission requires.

G. To draft and recommend for adoption to the Board the Commission's internal operating rules and procedures, which rules and procedures, as adopted by the Board, will then be submitted to the Supreme Court for approval and, after approval, be published in the Texas Bar Journal.

H To recommend to the Board the removal, for cause, of members of Committees.

I. To refer to an appropriate disability screening committee information coming to its attention indicating that an attorney is disabled physically, mentally, or emotionally, or by the use or abuse of alcohol or other drugs.

J. To report to the Board, at each regular meeting, and to the Grievance Oversight Committee, at least annually, on the state of the attorney professional disciplinary and disability system and to make recommendations and proposals to the Board on the refinement and improvement of the system.

K. To formulate and recommend to the Board for adoption a system for monitoring disabled lawyers.

L. To notify each jurisdiction in which an attorney is admitted to practice law of any Sanction imposed in this State, other than a private reprimand (which may include restitution and payment of Attorneys' Fees), and any disability suspension, resignation, and reinstatement.

M. To provide statistics and reports on lawyer discipline to the National Discipline Data Bank maintained by the American Bar Association.

N. To maintain, subject to the limitations elsewhere herein provided, permanent records of disciplinary and disability matters; and to transmit notice of all public discipline imposed against an attorney, suspensions due to Disability, and reinstatements to the National Discipline Data Bank maintained by the American Bar Association.

O. To make recommendations to the Board on the establishment and maintenance of regional offices as required for the expeditious handling of Inquiries, Complaints, and other disciplinary matters.

Adopted by orders of Feb. 26, 1991, and Oct. 9, 1991, eff. May 1, 1992. Amended by order of Dec. 29, 2003, eff. Jan. 1, 2004.

4.07. Meetings

A. Seven members shall constitute a quorum of the Commission, except that a panel of three members may consider such matters as may be specifically delegated by the Chair, or, in the absence of the Chair, the Vice–Chair, of the Commission. The Commission and each of its panels may act only with the concurrence of a majority of those members present and voting.

B. In any event in which the Commission shall conduct business in a panel of three members, at least one of the members assigned to each such panel shall be a public member of the Commission.

C. The Commission may, at the instance of the Chair, or, in the absence of the Chair, at the instance of the Vice–Chair of the Commission, conduct its business by conference telephone calls. Any action taken in a telephone conference must be reduced to writing and signed by each participant certifying the accuracy of the written record of action taken.

Adopted by orders of Feb. 26, 1991, and Oct. 9, 1991, eff. May 1, 1992. Amended by order of Dec. 29, 2003, eff. Jan. 1, 2004.

4.08. Funding

The State Bar shall allocate sufficient funds to pay all reasonable and necessary expenses incurred in the discharge of the duties of the Commission; of the Chief Disciplinary Counsel; of the Board of Disciplinary Appeals; of Committees and there individual members; and of witnesses. Further, the State Bar shall allocate funds to pay all other reasonable and necessary expenses to administer the disciplinary and disability system effectively and efficiently.

Adopted by orders of Feb. 26, 1991, and Oct. 9, 1991, eff. May 1, 1992.

4.09. Open Meetings and Open Records

The Commission is not a "governmental body" as that term is defined in Section 551.001(3) of V.T.C.A., Government Code, and is not subject to either the provisions of the Open Meetings Act or the Open Records Act.

Adopted by order of Dec. 29, 2003, eff. Jan. 1, 2004.

PART V. CHIEF DISCIPLINARY COUNSEL

5.01. Selection

The General Counsel of the State Bar shall, subject to the provisions of this Rule, serve as the Chief Disciplinary Counsel under these rules. If the Commission determines that the General Counsel of the State Bar should no longer function as the Chief Disciplinary Counsel, then the Commission shall notify the Board of such decision and, in the next succeeding fiscal year of the State Bar, funds shall be provided to the Commission sufficient for it to select and hire a lawyer as Chief Disciplinary Counsel and sufficient deputies and assistants as may be required to operate the disciplinary and disability system effectively and efficiently. The Commission's determination must be made, if at all, and the notification herein provided must be given, if at all, during the months of January or February 1993, or during the same months of any odd numbered year thereafter. In such event, the Commission shall alone possess the right of selection, but nothing herein precludes its employment of the General Counsel or a member of the General Counsel's staff for such positions.

Adopted by orders of Feb. 26, 1991, and Oct. 9, 1991, eff. May 1, 1992. Amended by order of Dec. 29, 2003, eff. Jan. 1, 2003.

5.02. Duties

In addition to the other disciplinary duties set forth in these rules, the Chief Disciplinary Counsel shall:

A. Review and screen all information coming to his or her attention or to the attention of the Commission relating to lawyer misconduct. Such review may encompass whatever active investigation is deemed necessary by the Chief Disciplinary Counsel independent of the filing of a writing.

B. Reject all matters and Inquiries not constituting a Complaint and so advise the Complainant.

C. Investigate Complaints to ascertain whether Just Cause exists.

D. Recommend dismissal of a Complaint, if appropriate, to a Summary Disposition Panel of appropriate venue.

E. Move the Board of Disciplinary Appeals to transfer a pending Disciplinary Proceeding from one Committee to another within the same District if the Committee fails or refuses to hear the Disciplinary Proceeding.

F. Move the Board of Disciplinary Appeals to transfer matters from one Committee to another, whether or not within the same District, when the requirements of fairness to the Complainant or the Respondent require.

G. Represent the Commission in all Complaints, Disciplinary Proceedings and Disciplinary Actions in which the Commission is the client.

H. When information regarding a Complaint becomes eligible for public disclosure under these rules, refer a Complaint and information related thereto to any other professional organizations or bodies that he or she deems appropriate for consultation on the nature of the Complaint, the events giving rise to the Complaint, and the proper manner of resolution of the Complaint. The Chief Disciplinary Counsel shall provide the Respondent written notice of the referral at the time it is made. Neither the Chief Disciplinary Counsel nor any person or body acting under these rules is bound by any recommendation of another professional organization to which the Complaint or related information is referred under this Rule.

I. Present cases to Evidentiary Panels of Committees, or in a district court if such has been elected by the Respondent, as provided in these rules, unless disqualified from doing so under the Texas Disciplinary Rules of Professional Conduct.

J. Represent the Commission, if the need arises, before all courts and administrative bodies.

K. Notify the Respondent and the Complainant promptly of the disposition of each Complaint.

L. Upon receiving information of a violation of any term or condition of probation by an attorney suspended from the practice of law where all or any part of the suspension has been probated, file on behalf of the Commission a motion to revoke probation. The motion must state the terms or conditions of the probation and the conduct alleged to violate the same. The Chief Disciplinary Counsel shall cause a copy of the motion to be served on the attorney involved.

M. Perform such other duties relating to disciplinary and disability matters as may be assigned by the Commission.

Adopted by orders of Feb. 26, 1991, and Oct. 9, 1991, eff. May 1, 1992. Amended by order of June 15, 1994, eff. Oct. 1, 1994; Dec. 29, 2003, eff. Jan. 1, 2004.

5.03. Accountability

On disciplinary and disability matters, the Chief Disciplinary Counsel is accountable only to the Commission.

Adopted by orders of Feb. 26, 1991, and Oct. 9, 1991, eff. May 1, 1992. Amended by order of Dec. 29, 2003, eff. Jan. 1, 2004.

PART VI. PUBLIC INFORMATION AND ACCESS

6.01. Availability of Materials

The Commission shall ensure that sufficient copies of these rules, the Texas Disciplinary Rules of Professional Conduct, and forms for the filing of disciplinary Grievances are made available to the public. In addition, the Commission shall make available to the public a brochure, summarizing in plain language the disciplinary and disability system for attorneys in the State of Texas. Such brochure shall be made available in English and in Spanish.

Adopted by orders of Feb. 26, 1991, and Oct. 9, 1991, eff. May 1, 1992. Amended by order of Dec. 29, 2003, eff. Jan. 1, 2004.

6.02. Public and Media Inquiries

The Commission shall respond, as appropriate, to all public and media inquiries concerning the operation of the attorney professional disciplinary and disability system, but in so doing may not disclose information that is confidential or privileged. The Commission shall disclose, upon proper request, information in its custody or control that is neither confidential nor privileged. Any attorney may waive confidentiality and privilege as to his or her disciplinary record by filing an appropriate waiver on a form to be prescribed by the Commission. The Commission shall maintain complete records and files of all disciplinary and disability matters and compile reports and statistics to aid in the administration of the system.

Adopted by orders of Feb. 26, 1991, and Oct. 9, 1991, eff. May 1, 1992.

6.03. Telephone Inquiries

The Commission shall maintain a toll-free telephone number. The toll-free number shall be publicized to ensure that all Texas residents have access to it. Telephone inquiries about specific attorney conduct will not be taken, but the Commission will send a Grievance form to any person or entity inquiring by telephone.

Adopted by orders of Feb. 26, 1991, and Oct. 9, 1991, eff. May 1, 1992. Amended by order of Dec. 29, 2003, eff. Jan. 1, 2004.

6.04. Abstracts of Appeals

Any Disciplinary Proceeding appealed to the Board of Disciplinary Appeals shall be abstracted by the Board of Disciplinary Appeals. A copy of the abstract shall be made available to any person or other entity upon proper request and shall be published in the Texas Bar Journal. No information that is otherwise confidential may be disclosed in an abstract under these provisions.

Adopted by orders of Feb. 26, 1991, and Oct. 9, 1991, eff. May 1, 1992. Amended by order of Dec. 29, 2003, eff. Jan. 1, 2004.

6.05. Report to the Clerk of the Supreme Court

The final disposition of any Disciplinary Proceeding or Disciplinary Action resulting in the imposition of a Sanction other than a private reprimand (which may include restitution and payment of attorneys' fees) shall be reported by the Commission to the Clerk of the Supreme Court of Texas.

Adopted by orders of Feb. 26, 1991, and Oct. 9, 1991, eff. May 1, 1992. Amended by order of Dec. 29, 2003, eff. Jan. 1, 2004.

6.06. Court and Board of Disciplinary Appeals Opinions

A. Court Opinions: In any case arising out of a Complaint, an opinion of a court of appeals issued on or after May 1, 1992 has precedential value regardless of its designation.

B. *Board of Disciplinary Appeals Opinions*: Board of Disciplinary Appeals opinions are open to the public and must be made available to public reporting services, print or electronic, for publishing. These opinions are persuasive, not precedential, in disciplinary proceedings tried in district court.

Comment to 2009 change: Rule 6.06 is divided into two subdivisions. The language in subdivision A is amended to remove an outdated reference to the official reporter system and to be consistent with Texas Rule of Appellate Procedure (TRAP) 47 amendments intended to prospectively discontinue designating opinions as either "published" or "unpublished." The erroneously designated opinions addressed in subdivision A have precedential value from May 1, 1992 on because that is the effective date of the prior version of the rule, which mandated publication of "[a]ll cases involving the Professional Misconduct or Disability of an attorney appealed to the Courts of Appeal [sic] or to the Supreme Court of Texas." New subdivision B addresses Board of Disciplinary Appeals (BODA) opinions and includes a distribution provision similar to TRAP 47.3. This change provides for the publication of BODA opinions issued in any type of case, whether pursuant to BODA's original or appellate jurisdiction.

Adopted by orders of Feb. 26, 1991, and Oct. 9, 1991, eff. May 1, 1992. Amended by order of Dec. 29, 2003, eff. Jan. 1, 2004; Feb. 24, 2009, and June 8, 2009, eff. July 1, 2009.

6.07. Publication of Disciplinary Results

The final disposition of all Disciplinary Proceedings and Disciplinary Actions shall be reported in the Texas Bar Journal, and shall be sent for publication to a newspaper of general circulation in the county of the disciplined attorney's residence or office. Private reprimands (which may include restitution and payment of attorneys' fees) shall be published in the Texas Bar Journal with the name of the attorney deleted. The Commission shall report all public discipline imposed against an attorney, suspensions due to Disability, and reinstatements to the National Discipline Data Bank of the American Bar Association.

Adopted by orders of Feb. 26, 1991, and Oct. 9, 1991, eff. May 1, 1992. Amended by order of Dec. 29, 2003, eff Jan. 1, 2004.

6.08. Access to Confidential Information

No officer or Director of the State Bar or any appointed adviser to the Commission shall have access to any confidential information relating to any Disciplinary Proceeding, Disciplinary Action, or Disability suspension. The Office of Chief Disciplinary Counsel may provide this information to authorized agencies investigating qualifications for admission to practice, attorney discipline enforcement agencies, law enforcement agencies, the State Bar's Client Security Fund, the State Bar's Lawyer Assistance Program, the Supreme Court's Unauthorized Practice of Law Committee and its subcommittees and the Commission on Judicial Conduct.

Adopted by orders of Feb. 26, 1991, and Oct. 9, 1991, eff. May 1, 1992. Amended by orders of June 15, 1994, eff. Oct. 1, 1994; Dec. 29, 2003, eff. Jan. 1, 2004; Dec. 7, 2009, eff. Jan. 1, 2010.

PART VII. BOARD OF DISCIPLINARY APPEALS

7.01. Membership

The Board of Disciplinary Appeals is hereby established. Its members shall be appointed by the Supreme Court of Texas. The Board of Disciplinary Appeals shall consist of twelve lawyer members with not more than eight of such members being residents of Harris, Dallas, Tarrant, Travis, or Bexar Counties, Texas, and with no more than two members from any one county. The term of office of all members of the Board of Disciplinary Appeals shall be for three years. Members are eligible for appointment to one additional three-year term. Members appointed to fill an unexpired term shall be eligible for reappointment for two subsequent terms. Vacancies shall be filled by appointment of the Supreme Court of Texas. Each member shall continue to perform the duties of office until his or her successor is duly qualified. No person may simultaneously be a member of the Board of Disciplinary Appeals and either the Commission, the Board, or a Committee.

Adopted by orders of Feb. 26, 1991, and Oct. 9, 1991, eff. May 1, 1992. Amended by order of June 15, 1994, eff. Oct. 1, 1994; Oct. 15, 1996; Jan. 9, 2004.

7.02. Initial Appointments

Three lawyers shall initially be appointed for a term to expire on August 31 after at least twelve months of service; three lawyers shall initially be appointed for a term to expire on August 31 after twenty-four months of service; and three lawyers shall initially be appointed for a term to expire on August 31 after thirty-six months of service. After the terms provided above, all terms shall be as provided in Rule 7.01.

Adopted by orders of Feb. 26, 1991, and Oct. 9, 1991, eff. May 1, 1992. Amended by order of Dec. 29, 2003, eff. Jan. 1, 2004.

7.03. Election of Officers

The Board of Disciplinary Appeals shall annually elect members as chair and vice-chair. The chair, or in his or her absence the vice-chair, shall perform the duties normally associated with that office and shall preside over all en banc meetings of the Board of Disciplinary Appeals.

Adopted by orders of Feb. 26, 1991, and Oct. 9, 1991, eff. May 1, 1992.

7.04. Oath of Committee Members

As soon as possible after appointment, each newly appointed member of the Board of Disciplinary Appeals shall take the following oath to be administered by any person authorized by law to administer oaths:

"I do solemnly swear (or affirm) that I will faithfully execute my duties as a member of the Board of Disciplinary Appeals, as required by the Texas Rules of Disciplinary Procedure, and will, to the best of my ability, preserve, protect, and defend the Constitution and laws of the United States and of the State of Texas. I further solemnly swear (or affirm) that I will keep secret all such matters and things as shall come to my knowledge as a member of the Board of Disciplinary Appeals arising from or in connection with each Disciplinary Action and Disciplinary Proceeding unless permitted to disclose the same in accordance with the Rules of Disciplinary Procedure or unless ordered to do so in the course of a judicial proceeding or a proceeding before the Board of Disciplinary Appeals. I further solemnly swear (or affirm) that I have neither directly nor indirectly paid, offered, or promised to pay, contributed any money or valuable thing, or promised any public or private office to secure my appointment. So help me God."

Adopted by orders of Feb. 26, 1991, and Oct. 9, 1991, eff. May 1, 1992. Amended by order of Dec. 29, 2003, eff. Jan. 1, 2004.

7.05. Quorum

Six members constitute a quorum of the Board of Disciplinary Appeals, except that a panel of three members may hear appeals and such other matters as may be specifically delegated to it by the Chair. The Board of Disciplinary Appeals and each of its panels may act only with the concurrence of a majority of those members present and voting.

Adopted by orders of Feb. 26, 1991, and Oct. 9, 1991, eff. May 1, 1992. Amended by order of June 23, 1992; order of June 15, 1994, eff. Oct. 1, 1994.

7.06. Compensation and Expenses

Members of the Board of Disciplinary Appeals are entitled to reasonable compensation for their services and reimbursement for travel and other expenses incident to the performance of their duties.

Adopted by orders of Feb. 26, 1991, and Oct. 9, 1991, eff. May 1, 1992.

7.07. Recusal and Disqualification of Members

Board of Disciplinary Appeals members shall refrain from taking part in any matter before the Board of Disciplinary Appeals in which recusal or disqualification would be required of a judge similarly situated.

Adopted by orders of Feb. 26, 1991, and Oct. 9, 1991, eff. May 1, 1992. Amended by order of June 23, 1992.

7.08. Powers and Duties

The Board of Disciplinary Appeals shall exercise the following powers and duties:

A. Propose rules of procedure and administration for its own operation to the Supreme Court of Texas for promulgation.

B. Review the operation of the Board of Disciplinary Appeals and periodically report to the Supreme Court and to the Board.

C. Affirm or reverse a determination by the Chief Disciplinary Counsel that a statement constitutes an Inquiry as opposed to a Complaint.

D. Hear and determine appeals by the Respondent or the Commission on the record from the judgment of an Evidentiary Panel. The appellate determination must be made in writing and signed by the chair or vice-chair of the Board of Disciplinary Appeals, or other person presiding.

E. Transfer any pending Disciplinary Proceeding from one Committee to another within the same District if the one Committee fails or refuses to hear the Disciplinary Proceeding.

F. Transfer matters from one Committee to another, whether or not within the same District, when the requirements of fairness to the Complainant or the Respondent require.

G. Hear and determine actions for compulsory discipline under Part VIII.

H. Hear and determine actions for reciprocal discipline under Part IX.

I. Hear and determine actions for disability suspension under Part XII.

J. Exercise all other powers and duties provided in these rules.

Adopted by orders of Feb. 26, 1991, and Oct. 9, 1991, eff. May 1, 1992. Amended by order of Dec. 29, 2003, eff. Jan. 1, 2004.

7.09. Meetings

The Board of Disciplinary Appeals shall meet en banc at least once each year at the call of its chair. Its members may meet more often en banc at the call of the chair or upon the written request to the chair of at least three of the members of the Board of Disciplinary Appeals.

Adopted by orders of Feb. 26, 1991, and Oct. 9, 1991, eff. May 1, 1992.

7.10. Conference Calls

The Board of Disciplinary Appeals may, at the instance of the chair, conduct its business by conference telephone calls. Any action taken in a telephone conference must be reduced to writing and signed by each participant certifying the accuracy of the written record of action taken.

Adopted by orders of Feb. 26, 1991, and Oct. 9, 1991, eff. May 1, 1992. Amended by order of June 15, 1994, eff. Oct. 1, 1994.

7.11. Judicial Review

An appeal from a determination of the Board of Disciplinary Appeals shall be to the Supreme Court. Within fourteen days after receipt of notice of a final determination by the Board of Disciplinary Appeals, the party appealing must file a notice of appeal directly with the Clerk of the Supreme Court. The record must be filed within sixty days after the Board of Disciplinary Appeals' determination. The appealing party's brief is due thirty days after the record is filed, and the responding party's brief must be filed within thirty days thereafter. Except as herein expressly provided, the appeal must be made pursuant to the then applicable Texas Rules of Appellate Procedure. Oral argument may be granted on motion. The case shall be reviewed under the substantial evidence rule. The Court may affirm a decision on the Board of Disciplinary Appeals by order without written opinion. Determinations by the Board of Disciplinary Appeals that a statement constitutes an Inquiry or transferring cases are conclusive, and may not be appealed to the Supreme Court.

Adopted by orders of Feb. 26, 1991, and Oct. 9, 1991, eff. May 1, 1992. Amended by order of June 15, 1994, eff. Oct. 1, 1994; Dec. 29, 2003, eff. Jan. 1, 2004.

7.12. Open Meetings and Open Records

The Board of Disciplinary Appeals is not a "governmental body" as that term is defined in Section 551.001 or Section 552.003 of V.T.C.A., Government Code, and is not subject to either the provisions of the Open Meetings Act [1] or the Open Records Act.[2]

Adopted by order of June 15, 1994, eff. Oct. 1, 1994.

[1] V.T.C.A., Government Code § 551.001 et seq.

[2] V.T.C.A., Government Code § 552.001 et seq.

PART VIII. COMPULSORY DISCIPLINE

8.01. Generally

When an attorney licensed to practice law in Texas has been convicted of an Intentional Crime or has been placed on probation for an Intentional Crime with or without an adjudication of guilt, the Chief Disciplinary Counsel shall initiate a Disciplinary Action seeking compulsory discipline pursuant to this part. The completion or termination of any term of incarceration, probation, parole, or any similar court ordered supervised period does not bar action under Part VIII of these rules as hereinafter provided. Proceedings under this part are not exclusive in that an attorney may be disciplined as a result of the underlying facts as well as being disciplined upon the conviction or probation through deferred adjudication.

Adopted by orders of Feb. 26, 1991, and Oct. 9, 1991, eff. May 1, 1992. Amended by order of June 15, 1994, eff. Oct. 1, 1994.

8.02. Conclusive Evidence

In any Disciplinary Action brought under this part, the record of conviction or order of deferred adjudication is conclusive evidence of the attorney's guilt.

Adopted by orders of Feb. 26, 1991, and Oct. 9, 1991, eff. May 1, 1992.

8.03. Commencement of Suit

A Disciplinary Action under this part must be initiated by the filing of a petition with the Board of Disciplinary Appeals. The petition must allege the adjudication of guilt (or probation without an adjudication of guilt) of an Intentional Crime; allege that the Respondent is the same person as the party adjudicated guilty or who received probation with or without an adjudication of guilt for such Intentional Crime; and seek the appropriate discipline.

Adopted by orders of Feb. 26, 1991, and Oct. 9, 1991, eff. May 1, 1992.

8.04. Procedure

The Board of Disciplinary Appeals shall hear and determine all questions of law and fact. When an attorney has been convicted of an Intentional Crime or has been placed on probation for an Intentional Crime without an adjudication of guilt, he or she shall be suspended as an attorney licensed to practice law in Texas during the appeal of the conviction or the order of deferred adjudication. Upon introduction into evidence of a certified copy of the judgment of conviction or order of deferred adjudication and a certificate of the Clerk of the Supreme Court that the attorney is licensed to practice law in Texas, the Board of Disciplinary Appeals shall immediately determine whether the attorney has been convicted of an Intentional Crime or granted probation without an adjudication of guilt for an Intentional Crime. Uncontroverted affidavits that the attorney is the same person as the person convicted or granted probation without an adjudication of guilt are competent and sufficient evidence of those facts. Nothing in these rules prohibits proof of the necessary elements in such Disciplinary Action by competent evidence in any other manner permitted by law. The Board of Disciplinary Appeals shall sit, hear, and determine whether the attorney should be disciplined and enter judgment accordingly within forty-five days of the answer day; however, any failure to do so within the time limit will not affect its jurisdiction to act. Any suspension ordered during the appeal of a criminal conviction or probation without an adjudication of guilt is interlocutory and immediately terminates if the conviction or probation is set aside or reversed.

Adopted by orders of Feb. 26, 1991, and Oct. 9, 1991, eff. May 1, 1992.

8.05. Disbarment

When an attorney has been convicted of an Intentional Crime, and that conviction has become final, or the attorney has accepted probation with or without an adjudication of guilt for an Intentional Crime, the attorney shall be disbarred unless the Board of Disciplinary Appeals, under Rule 8.06, suspends his or her license to practice law. If the attorney' s license to practice law has been suspended during the appeal of the criminal conviction, the Chief Disciplinary Counsel shall file a motion for final judgment of disbarment with the Board of Disciplinary Appeals. If the motion is supported by affidavits or certified copies of court documents showing that the conviction has become final, the motion shall be granted without hearing, unless within ten days following the service of the motion pursuant to Rule 21a of the Texas Rules of Civil Procedure, upon the attorney so convicted or his or her attorney of record, the attorney so convicted files a verified denial contesting the finality of the judgment, in which event the Board of Disciplinary Appeals will immediately conduct a hearing to determine the issue. If no Disciplinary Action is pending at the time the conviction becomes final, disbarment shall be initiated by filing a Disciplinary Action.

Adopted by orders of Feb. 26, 1991, and Oct. 9, 1991, eff. May 1, 1992. Amended by order of Dec. 29, 2003, eff. Jan. 1, 2004.

8.06. Suspension

If an attorney's sentence upon conviction of an Serious Crime is fully probated, or if an attorney receives probation through deferred adjudication in connection with a Serious Crime, the attorney's license to practice law shall be suspended during the term of probation. If an attorney is suspended during the term of probation, the suspension shall be conditioned upon the attorney's satisfactorily completing the terms of probation. If probation is revoked, the attorney shall be disbarred. An early termination of probation does not result in reinstatement until the entire probationary period, as originally assessed, has expired.

Adopted by orders of Feb. 26, 1991, and Oct. 9, 1991, eff. May 1, 1992.

8.07. Early Termination

An early termination of criminal probation shall have no effect on any judgment entered pursuant to Part VIII.

Adopted by order of June 15, 1994, eff. Oct. 1, 1994.

8.08. No Supersedeas

In compulsory discipline cases, either party shall have the right to appeal to the Supreme Court of Texas but no Respondent suspended or disbarred by the board of Disciplinary Appeals shall be entitled to practice law in any form while the appeal is pending and shall have no right to supersede the judgment by bond or otherwise.

Adopted by order of June 15, 1994, eff. Oct. 1, 1994.

PART IX. RECIPROCAL DISCIPLINE

9.01. Orders From Other Jurisdictions

Upon receipt of information indicating that an attorney licensed to practice law in Texas has been disciplined in another jurisdiction, the Chief Disciplinary Counsel shall diligently seek to obtain a certified copy of the order or judgment of discipline from the other jurisdiction, and file it with the Board of Disciplinary Appeals along with a petition requesting that the attorney be disciplined in Texas. A certified copy of the order or judgment is prima facie evidence of the matters contained therein, and a final adjudication in another jurisdiction that an attorney licensed to practice law in Texas has committed Professional Misconduct is conclusive for the purposes of a Disciplinary Action under this Part, subject to the defenses set forth in Rule 9.04 below.

Adopted by orders of Feb. 26, 1991, and Oct. 9, 1991, eff. May 1, 1992. Amended by order of Dec. 29, 2003, eff. Jan. 1, 2004.

9.02. Notice to the Respondent

Upon the filing of the petition, the Board of Disciplinary Appeals shall issue a notice to the attorney, containing a copy of the petition, a copy of the order or judgment from the other jurisdiction, and an order directing the attorney to show cause within thirty days from the date of the mailing of the notice why the imposition of the identical discipline in this state would be unwarranted.

Adopted by orders of Feb. 26, 1991, and Oct. 9, 1991, eff. May 1, 1992.

9.03. Discipline to be Imposed

If the attorney fails to file his or her answer with the Board of Disciplinary Appeals within the thirty-day period provided by Rule 9.02, the Board of Disciplinary Appeals shall enter a judgment imposing discipline identical, to the extent practicable, with that imposed in the other jurisdiction. If the attorney files an answer, the Board of Disciplinary Appeals shall proceed to determine the case upon the pleadings, the evidence, and the briefs, if any.

Adopted by orders of Feb. 26, 1991, and Oct. 9, 1991, eff. May 1, 1992. Amended by order of Dec. 29, 2003, eff. Jan. 1, 2004.

9.04. Defenses

If the Respondent files an answer, he or she shall allege, and thereafter be required to prove, by clear and convincing evidence, to the Board of Disciplinary Appeals one or more of the following defenses to avoid the imposition of discipline identical, to the extent practicable, with that directed by the judgment of the other jurisdiction:

A. That the procedure followed in the other jurisdiction on the disciplinary matter was so lacking in notice or opportunity to be heard as to constitute a deprivation of due process.

B. That there was such an infirmity of proof establishing the misconduct in the other jurisdiction as to give rise to the clear conviction that the Board of Disciplinary Appeals, consistent with its duty, should not accept as final the conclusion on the evidence reached in the other jurisdiction.

C. That the imposition by the Board of Disciplinary Appeals of discipline identical, to the extent practicable, with that imposed by the other jurisdiction would result in grave injustice.

D. That the misconduct established in the other jurisdiction warrants substantially different discipline in this state.

E. That the misconduct for which the attorney was disciplined in the other jurisdiction does not constitute Professional Misconduct in this state.

If the Board of Disciplinary Appeals determines that one or more of the foregoing defenses have been established, it shall enter such orders as it deems necessary and appropriate.

Adopted by orders of Feb. 26, 1991, and Oct. 9, 1991, eff. May 1, 1992.

PART X. RESIGNATION IN LIEU OF DISCIPLINE

10.01. Disciplinary Resignation

Any person licensed to practice law in the State of Texas shall be permitted to file a motion for resignation in lieu of discipline, in a form promulgated by the Commission, in the Supreme Court of Texas, attaching thereto his or her Texas law license and permanent State Bar membership card.

Adopted by orders of Feb. 26, 1991, and Oct. 9, 1991, eff. May 1, 1992. Amended by order of Dec. 29, 2003, eff. Jan. 1, 2004.

10.02. Response of Chief Disciplinary Counsel

The Chief Disciplinary Counsel shall, within twenty days after service upon him or her of a motion for resignation in lieu of discipline, file a response on behalf of the State Bar (acting through the Commission) stating whether the acceptance of the resignation is in the best interest of the public and the profession and setting forth a detailed statement of the Professional Misconduct with which the movant is charged. The movant may, within ten days after service of such response, withdraw the motion. If a motion to withdraw is not timely filed, the detailed statement of Professional Misconduct shall be deemed to have been conclusively established for all purposes.

Adopted by orders of Feb. 26, 1991, and Oct. 9, 1991, eff. May 1, 1992. Amended by order of Dec. 29, 2003, eff. Jan. 1, 2004.

10.03. Effect of Filing

The filing of a motion for resignation in lieu of discipline does not, without the consent of Chief Disciplinary Counsel, serve to delay or abate any then pending Grievance, Complaint, Disciplinary Proceeding, Disciplinary Action or disciplinary investigation.

Adopted by orders of Feb. 26, 1991, and Oct. 9, 1991, eff. May 1, 1992. Amended by order of Dec. 29, 2003, eff. Jan. 1, 2004.

10.04. Acceptance of Resignation and Notification

Any motion to resign in lieu of discipline under this part must be filed in the Supreme Court and is ineffective until and unless accepted by written order of the Supreme Court. The movant; the Evidentiary Panel Chair, if any; the Commission; and the Complainant, if any, shall be notified by the Chief Disciplinary Counsel of the Court's disposition of such motion.

Adopted by orders of Feb. 26, 1991, and Oct. 9, 1991, eff. May 1, 1992. Amended by order of Dec. 29, 2003, eff. Jan. 1, 2004.

10.05. Effect of Resignation

Any resignation under this part shall be treated as a disbarment for all purposes, including client notification, discontinuation of practice, and reinstatement.

Adopted by orders of Feb. 26, 1991, and Oct. 9, 1991, eff. May 1, 1992.

PART XI. REINSTATEMENT AFTER DISBARMENT OR RESIGNATION

11.01. Eligibility and Venue

A disbarred person or a person who has resigned in lieu of discipline may, at any time after the expiration of five years from the date of final judgment of disbarment or the date of Supreme Court order accepting resignation in lieu of discipline, petition the district court of the county of his or her residence for reinstatement; provided, however, that no person who has been disbarred or resigned in lieu of discipline by reason of conviction of or having been placed on probation without an adjudication of guilt for an Intentional Crime or a Serious Crime, is eligible to apply for reinstatement until five years following the date of completion of sentence, including any period of probation and/or parole. If, at the time the petition for reinstatement is filed, the disbarred person or person who has resigned in lieu of discipline is a nonresident of the State of Texas, then the petition shall be filed in Travis County, Texas.

Adopted by orders of Feb. 26, 1991, and Oct. 9, 1991, eff. May 1, 1992. Amended by order of June 15, 1994, eff. Oct. 1, 1994; Dec. 29, 2003, eff. Jan. 1, 2004.

11.02. Petition for Reinstatement

A petition for reinstatement shall be verified and shall set forth all the following information:

A. The name, age, and residential address of the petitioner.

B. The offenses, misconduct, or convictions upon which the disbarment or resignation was based.

C. The name of the body or entity where the Disciplinary Proceeding or Disciplinary Action was adjudicated and the identity of the Committee before whom the Just Cause hearing was held, if any.

D. A statement that the petitioner has made restitution to all persons, if any, naming them and their current addresses, who may have suffered financial loss by reason of the offenses, misconduct, or Serious Crimes for which the petitioner was disbarred or resigned, and that the petitioner has paid all costs and fines assessed in connection with the Disciplinary Proceeding or Disciplinary Action that resulted in his or her disbarment or resignation.

E. A statement that at the time of the filing of the petition the petitioner is of good moral character, possesses the mental and emotional fitness to practice law, and during the five years immediately preceding the filing of the petition, has been living a life of exemplary conduct.

F. A statement that the petitioner has recently read and understands the Texas Disciplinary Rules of Professional Conduct; that he or she has recently read and understands the Texas Lawyer's Creed — A Mandate For Professionalism; that he or she has a current knowledge of the law; and that the public and profession will be served by the petitioner's reinstatement.

G. A listing of the petitioner's occupations from the date of disbarment or resignation, including the names and current addresses of all partners, associates, and employers, if any, and the dates and duration of all such relationships and employment.

H. A statement listing all residences maintained from the date of disbarment or resignation, and the current names and addresses of all landlords.

I. A statement of the dates, cause numbers, courts, and the general nature of all civil actions in which the petitioner was a party or in which he or she claimed an interest, and that were pending at any time from the date of disbarment or resignation.

J. A statement of the dates, cause numbers, courts, the general nature and disposition of all matters pending at any time from the date of disbarment or resignation and involving the prosecution of the petitioner for any crime, felony, or misdemeanor, together with the names and current addresses of all complaining persons in each such matter.

K. A statement whether any application for a license requiring proof of good moral character for its procurement was filed at any time after the disbarment or resignation and, for each application, the name and address of the licensing authority and the disposition of the application.

L. A statement explaining any proceeding after the date of disbarment or resignation concerning the petitioner's standing as a member of any profession or organization or holder of any license or office that involved censure, removal, suspension of license, revocation of any license, or discipline of the petitioner and the disposition thereof, and the name and address of each authority in possession of the records.

M. A statement whether any allegations or charges, formal or informal, of fraud were made or claimed against the petitioner at any time after the disbarment or resignation and the names and current addresses of the persons or entities making such allegations or charges.

The petitioner has a duty to amend and keep current all information in the petition until the petition has been heard and determined by the trial court.

Adopted by orders of Feb. 26, 1991, and Oct. 9, 1991, eff. May 1, 1992. Amended by order of Dec. 29, 2003, eff. Jan. 1, 2004.

11.03. Burden of Proof

The petitioner has the burden of establishing by a preponderance of the evidence that the best interests of the public and the profession, as well as the ends of justice, would be served by his or her reinstatement. The court shall deny the petition for reinstatement if it contains any false statement of a material fact or if the petitioner fails to meet the burden of proof.

Adopted by orders of Feb. 26, 1991, and Oct. 9, 1991, eff. May 1, 1992.

11.04. Notice and Procedure

The petitioner shall serve notice of a petition for reinstatement by U.S. certified mail, return receipt requested, on the Chief Disciplinary Counsel and shall publish the notice as a paid classified announcement in the *Texas Bar Journal*. After the filing of the petition and service, the Texas Rules of Civil Procedure shall apply except when in conflict with these rules. All questions of fact and law shall be determined by the trial court without the aid of a jury.

Adopted by orders of Feb. 26, 1991, and Oct. 9, 1991, eff. May 1, 1992.

11.05. Relevant Factors to be Considered

In determining the petitioner's fitness for reinstatement, in addition to any other relevant matters, the trial court may consider:

A. Evidence concerning the nature and degree of Professional Misconduct for which the petitioner was disbarred or resigned and the circumstances attending the offenses.

B. The petitioner's understanding of the serious nature of the acts for which he or she was disbarred or resigned.

C. The petitioner's conduct during the Disciplinary Proceeding and Disciplinary Action.

D. The profit to the petitioner and the hardship to others.

E. The petitioner's attitude toward the administration of justice and the practice of law.

F. The petitioner's good works and other accomplishments.

G. Any other evidence relevant to the issues of the petitioner's fitness to practice law and the likelihood that the petitioner will not engage in further misconduct.

Adopted by orders of Feb. 26, 1991, and Oct. 9, 1991, eff. May 1, 1992. Amended by order of Dec. 29, 2003, eff. Jan. 1, 2004.

11.06. Judgment and Conditions

If the court is satisfied after hearing all the evidence, both in support and in opposition to the petition, that the material allegations of the petition are true and that the best interests of the public and the profession, as well as the ends of justice, will be served, the court may render judgment authorizing the petitioner to be reinstated upon his or her compliance within eighteen months from the date of the judgment with Rule II of the Rules Governing Admission to the Bar of Texas in effect as of the date upon which judgment authorizing reinstatement is entered. The judgment shall direct the Board of Law Examiners to admit the petitioner to a regularly scheduled bar examination in accordance with that board's rules and procedures relating to the examination of persons who have not previously been licensed as lawyers in Texas or in any other state. No judgment of reinstatement may be rendered by default. If after hearing all the evidence the court determines that the petitioner is not eligible for reinstatement, the court may, in its discretion, either enter a judgment denying the petition or direct that the petition be held in abeyance for a reasonable period of time until the petitioner provides additional proof that he or she has satisfied the requirements of these rules. The court's judgment may include such other orders as protecting the public and the petitioner's potential clients may require.

Adopted by orders of Feb. 26, 1991, and Oct. 9, 1991, eff. May 1, 1992. Amended by order of June 15, 1994, eff. Oct. 1, 1994.

11.07. Appeal and Readmission

When a judgment has been signed in any proceeding under this part, the petitioner and the Commission shall each have a right of appeal. If the petition is granted and an appeal is perfected, the trial court's judgment shall be stayed pending resolution of the appeal. After the petitioner has complied with the terms of the judgment of reinstatement and with this part, he or she shall furnish the Commission with a certified copy of the judgment and evidence of compliance and shall pay all membership fees, license fees and assessments then owed and the costs of the reinstatement proceeding. Upon receipt of a certified copy of the judgment, evidence of compliance and proof of payment of all membership fees, license fees and assessments then owed, the Commission shall direct the Chief Disciplinary Counsel to issue a declaration of the petitioner's eligibility for licensure to the Clerk of the Supreme Court. Upon receipt of such declaration, the Clerk of the Supreme Court shall enter the name of the petitioner on the membership rolls of the Supreme Court and shall issue a new Bar card and law license in the name of the petitioner reflecting as the date of licensure the date of the declaration of eligibility. Once the petitioner has taken the attorney's oath, the new Bar card and law license shall be delivered by the Clerk of the Supreme Court to the petitioner.

Adopted by orders of Feb. 26, 1991, and Oct. 9, 1991, eff. May 1, 1992. Amended by order of June 15, 1994, eff. Oct. 1, 1994.

11.08. Repetitioning

If a petition for reinstatement is denied after a hearing on the merits, the petitioner is not eligible to file another petition until after the expiration of three

years from the date of final judgment denying the last preceding petition.
Adopted by orders of Feb. 26, 1991, and Oct. 9, 1991, eff. May 1, 1992.

PART XII. DISABILITY SUSPENSION

12.01. Grounds for Suspension

Any person licensed to practice law in the State of Texas shall be suspended for an indefinite period upon a finding that the attorney is suffering from a Disability.
Adopted by orders of Feb. 26, 1991, and Oct. 9, 1991, eff. May 1, 1992.

12.02. Procedure

Should the Chief Disciplinary Counsel reasonably believe based upon investigation of the Complaint that an attorney is suffering from a Disability and be authorized or directed to do so by the Commission, the Chief Disciplinary Counsel shall forward the Complaint and any other documents or statements which support a finding that the attorney is suffering from a Disability immediately to the Board of Disciplinary Appeals. Upon receipt of the Complaint and documents, the Board of Disciplinary Appeals shall forward it to a District Disability Committee to be composed of one attorney; one doctor of medicine or mental health care provider holding a doctorate degree, trained in the area of Disability; and one public member who does not have any interest, directly or indirectly, in the practice of the law other than as a consumer. The members of the District Disability Committee shall be appointed ad hoc by the chair of the Board of Disciplinary Appeals. The Board of Disciplinary Appeals may appoint any attorney to represent the interests of the disabled attorney.
Adopted by orders of Feb. 26, 1991, and Oct. 9, 1991, eff. May 1, 1992. Amended by order of June 15, 1994, eff. Oct. 1, 1994; Dec. 29, 2003, eff. Jan. 1, 2004.

12.03. District Disability Committee

The same rules regarding immunity, expenses, and confidentiality as apply to members of a Committee shall apply to the members appointed to a District Disability Committee. The District Disability Committee shall proceed in a de novo proceeding to receive evidence and determine whether the attorney is suffering from a Disability. In all cases where the referral has been made by the Chief Disciplinary Counsel, the Commission shall carry the burden of establishing by a preponderance of the evidence that the attorney suffers from a Disability. In all cases where the referral is made by an Evidentiary Panel, the party asserting that the attorney is suffering from a Disability shall carry the burden of establishing by a preponderance of the evidence that the attorney suffers from a Disability. The Respondent shall be given reasonable notice and shall be afforded an opportunity to appear before, and present evidence to, the District Disability Committee. If there is no finding of Disability by the District Disability Committee, the entire record and the finding of the District Disability Committee will be returned to the Chief Disciplinary Counsel and the matter shall continue in the disciplinary process from the point where it was referred to the Board of Disciplinary Appeals for the determination of Disability. If, however, there is a finding of Disability, the District Disability Committee shall certify the finding to the Board of Disciplinary Appeals.
Adopted by orders of Feb. 26, 1991, and Oct. 9, 1991, eff. May 1, 1992. Amended by order of Dec. 29, 2003, eff. Jan. 1, 2004.

12.04. Board of Disciplinary Appeals' Responsibilities

Upon receiving a finding of Disability from the District Disability Committee, the Board of Disciplinary Appeals shall immediately enter its order suspending the attorney indefinitely. The record of all proceedings on disability must be sealed and must remain confidential, except as to the Respondent; only the order of indefinite suspension is to be made public.
Adopted by orders of Feb. 26, 1991, and Oct. 9, 1991, eff. May 1, 1992.

12.05. Effect on Limitations

Any statute of limitations applying to a disciplinary matter is tolled during the period of any Disability suspension.
Adopted by orders of Feb. 26, 1991, and Oct. 9, 1991, eff. May 1, 1992.

12.06. Reinstatement After Disability Suspension

A. *Venue*: An attorney who has been indefinitely suspended under this part may have the suspension terminated by filing a verified petition with the Board of Disciplinary Appeals or a district court. Venue of a district court action is:

1. In the county, immediately prior to suspension, of the Respondent's principal place of practice.
2. If the Respondent did not maintain a place of practice immediately before suspension within

the State of Texas, in the county of the Respondent's residence.

3. If neither A. nor B. applies, then in Travis County, Texas.

B. *Petition and Service*: The petition must set out the attorney's name, address, the date, and the docket number of the suspension, a detailed description of his or her activities since the suspension, including employment, the details of any hospitalization or medical treatment, and any other matters the attorney believes entitles him or her to termination of the suspension. A copy of the petition shall be served by U.S. certified mail, return receipt requested, upon the Chief Disciplinary Counsel and the matter shall promptly thereafter be set for hearing. The petition must have the following documents attached: a certified copy of any court order pertaining to the petitioner's competence; an affidavit from a mental health care provider as to the petitioner's current condition; and a report from a physician as to the petitioner's current condition if the suspension was based in whole or in part on the abuse or use of alcohol or other drugs. Such attachments shall not constitute evidence, per se, but the attachment of the same is a requirement of pleading. In an action for reinstatement under this part, either the petitioner or the Commission shall have the right to a jury trial upon timely payment of the required fee.

C. *Burden of Proof*: The petitioner has the burden to come forward and prove, by a preponderance of the evidence, that the reasons for suspension no longer exist and that termination of the suspension would be without danger to the public and the profession. The Board of Disciplinary Appeals or the district court, as the case may be, may order the petitioner to be examined by one or more health care providers trained in the area for which the attorney was suspended.

D. *Time for Filing Subsequent Petitions*: A first petition for termination of suspension may be filed at any time after the petitioner's license has been suspended under this part. If the first petition is denied after a hearing, subsequent petitions may not be filed until the expiration of one year from the date of the denial of the last preceding petition.

E. *Judgment*: If the attorney meets the burden of proof, the Board of Disciplinary Appeals or the district court shall order a termination of the period of suspension, provided that whenever an attorney has been suspended for a period of two or more consecutive years, he or she may be required by the Board of Disciplinary Appeals or the district court, as the case may be, to obtain a passing grade on the multistate Professional Responsibility portion of the State Bar examination administered by the Board of Law Examiners, or take a prescribed course of study through a law school or through continuing legal education courses, or do both.

F. *Disability Probation*: The Board of Disciplinary Appeals or the district court, as the case may be, may order that an attorney be placed on probation if the attorney has demonstrated each of the following:

1. The ability to perform legal services and that the attorney's continued practice of law will not cause the courts or profession to fall into disrepute.

2. The unlikelihood of any harm to the public during the period of rehabilitation and the adequate supervision of necessary conditions of probation.

3. A Disability that can be successfully arrested and treated while the attorney is engaged in the practice of law.

Probation shall be ordered for a specified period of time or until further order of the Board of Disciplinary Appeals or the district court, as the case may be, whenever a suspension is probated in whole or in part.

G. *Conditions*: The order placing an attorney on Disability probation must state the conditions of probation. The conditions must take into consideration the nature and circumstances of the Professional Misconduct and the history, character, and condition of the attorney. Any or all of the following conditions, and such others as the Board of Disciplinary Appeals or the district court deems appropriate, may be imposed:

1. Periodic reports to the Chief Disciplinary Counsel.

2. Supervision over client trust accounts as the Board of Disciplinary Appeals or the district court may direct.

3. Satisfactory completion of a course of study.

4. Successful completion of the multistate Professional Responsibility Examination.

5. Restitution.

6. Compliance with income tax laws and verification of such to Chief Disciplinary Counsel.

7. Limitations on practice.

8. Psychological evaluation, counseling, and treatment.

9. The abstinence from alcohol or drugs.

10. Payment of costs (including Reasonable Attorneys' Fees and all direct expenses) associated with the proceedings.

11. Substance abuse evaluation, counseling, and treatment.

12. Participation in an Impaired Attorney Recovery and Supervision Program if such a program has been adopted by the Board of Directors of the State Board of Texas.

H. *Administration*: The Chief Disciplinary Counsel is responsible for the supervision of attorneys placed on Disability probation. Where appropriate, he or she may recommend to the Board of Disciplinary Appeals or to the district court, as the case may be, the modification of the conditions and shall report any failure of the probationer to comply with the conditions of probation. Upon a showing of failure to comply with the conditions of probation, the Board of Disciplinary Appeals or the district court, as the case may be, may revoke the probation or impose such other conditions deemed necessary for the protection of the public and the rehabilitation of the attorney.

Adopted by orders of Feb. 26, 1991, and Oct. 9, 1991, eff. May 1, 1992. Renumbered in part from Rules 12.07 through 12.12 and amended by order of Dec. 29, 2003, eff. Jan. 1, 2004.

12.07. Appeals

A final judgment of the Board of Disciplinary Appeals denying a petition for reinstatement may be appealed to the Supreme Court. If such an appeal is taken, it must be filed with the Clerk of the Supreme Court within fourteen days after the receipt by the appealing party of the determination of the Board of Disciplinary Appeals. Except as herein expressly provided, an appeal must be made pursuant to the then applicable Texas Rules of Appellate Procedure. Oral argument may be granted on motion. The case shall be reviewed under the substantial-evidence rule. The Court may affirm a decision of the Board of Disciplinary Appeals by order without written opinion. A final judgment of a district court denying a petition for reinstatement may be appealed as in civil cases generally.

Adopted by orders of Feb. 26, 1991, and Oct. 9, 1991, eff. May 1, 1992. Renumbered from Rule 12.13 by order of Dec. 29, 2003, eff. Jan. 1, 2004.

12.08 to 12.12. Renumbered as Rule 12.06, pars. C to H and amended by order of Dec. 29, 2003, eff. Jan. 1, 2004

12.13. Renumbered as Rule 12.07 by order of Dec. 29, 2003, eff. Jan. 1, 2004

PART XIII. CESSATION OF PRACTICE

13.01. Notice of Attorney's Cessation of Practice

When an attorney licensed to practice law in Texas dies, resigns, becomes inactive, is disbarred, or is suspended, leaving an active client matter for which no other attorney licensed to practice in Texas, with the consent of the client, has agreed to assume responsibility, written notice of such cessation of practice shall be mailed to those clients, opposing counsel, courts, agencies with which the attorney has matters pending, malpractice insurers, and any other person or entity having reason to be informed of the cessation of practice. If the attorney has died, the notice may be given by the personal representative of the estate of the attorney or by any person having lawful custody of the files and records of the attorney, including those persons who have been employed by the deceased attorney. In all other cases, notice shall be given by the attorney, a person authorized by the attorney, a person having lawful custody of the files of the attorney, or by Chief Disciplinary Counsel. If the client has consented to the assumption of responsibility for the matter by another attorney licensed to practice law in Texas, then the above notification requirements are not necessary and no further action is required.

Adopted by orders of Feb. 26, 1991, and Oct. 9, 1991, eff. May 1, 1992. Amended by order Dec. 18, 2006, eff. March 31, 2007.

13.02. Assumption of Jurisdiction

A client of the attorney, Chief Disciplinary Counsel, or any other interested person may petition a district court in the county of the attorney's residence to assume jurisdiction over the attorney's law practice. If the attorney has died, such petition may be filed in a statutory probate court. The petition must be verified and must state the facts necessary to show cause to believe that notice of cessation is required under this part. It must state the following:

A. That an attorney licensed to practice law in Texas has died, disappeared, resigned, become inactive, been disbarred or suspended, or become physically, mentally or emotionally disabled and cannot provide legal services necessary to protect the interests of clients.

B. That cause exists to believe that court supervision is necessary because the attorney has left client matters for which no other attorney licensed to practice law in Texas has, with the consent of the client, agreed to assume responsibility.

C. That there is cause to believe that the interests of one or more clients of the attorney or one or more interested persons or entities will be prejudiced if these proceedings are not maintained.

Adopted by orders of Feb. 26, 1991, and Oct. 9, 1991, eff. May 1, 1992. Amended by order of Dec. 18, 2006, eff. March 31, 2007.

13.03. Hearing and Order on Application to Assume Jurisdiction

The court shall set the petition for hearing and may issue an order to show cause, directing the attorney or his or her personal representative, or if none exists, the person having custody of the attorney's files, to show cause why the court should not assume jurisdiction of the attorney's law practice. If the court finds that one or more of the events stated in Rule 13.02 has occurred and that the supervision of the court is required, the court shall assume jurisdiction and appoint one or more attorneys licensed to practice law in Texas to take such action as set out in the written order of the court including, but not limited to, one or more of the following:

A. Examine the client matters, including files and records of the attorney's practice, and obtain information about any matters that may require attention.

B. Notify persons and entities that appear to be clients of the attorney of the assumption of the law practice, and suggest that they obtain other legal counsel.

C. Apply for extension of time before any court or any administrative body pending the client's employment of other legal counsel.

D. With the prior consent of the client, file such motions and pleadings on behalf of the client as are required to prevent prejudice to the client's rights.

E. Give appropriate notice to persons or entities that may be affected other than the client.

F. Arrange for surrender or delivery to the client of the client's papers, files, or other property.

The custodian shall observe the attorney-client relationship and privilege as if the custodians were the attorney of the client and may make only such disclosures as are necessary to carry out the purposes of this part. Except for intentional misconduct or gross negligence, no person acting under this part may incur any liability by reason of the institution or maintenance of a proceeding under this Part XIII. No bond or other security is required.

Adopted by orders of Feb. 26, 1991, and Oct. 9, 1991, eff. May 1, 1992. Amended by order of Dec. 29, 2003, eff. Jan. 1, 2004; Dec. 18, 2006, eff. March 31, 2007.

PART XIV. INTERIM SUSPENSION

14.01. Irreparable Harm to Clients

Should the Chief Disciplinary Counsel reasonably believe based upon investigation of a Complaint that an attorney poses a substantial threat of irreparable harm to clients or prospective clients and be authorized or directed to do so by the Commission, the Chief Disciplinary Counsel shall seek the immediate interim suspension of the attorney. The Commission shall file a petition with a district court of proper venue alleging substantial threat of irreparable harm, and the district court shall, if the petition alleges facts that meet the evidentiary standard in Rule 14.02, set a hearing within ten days. If the Commission, at the hearing, meets the evidentiary standard and burden of proof as established in Rule 14.02, the court shall enter an order without requiring bond, immediately suspending the attorney pending the final disposition of the Disciplinary Proceedings or the Disciplinary Action based on the conduct causing the harm. The matter shall thereafter proceed in the district court as in matters involving temporary injunctions under the Texas Rules of Civil Procedure. If a temporary injunction is entered, the court may appoint a custodian under Part XIII. If, at the conclusion of all Disciplinary Proceedings and Disciplinary Actions, the Respondent is not found to have committed Professional Misconduct, the immediate interim suspension may not be deemed a "Sanction" for purposes of insurance applications or any other purpose.

Adopted by orders of Feb. 26, 1991, and Oct. 9, 1991, eff. May 1, 1992. Amended by order of Dec. 29, 2003, eff. Jan. 1, 2004.

14.02. Burden of Proof and Evidentiary Standard

The Commission has the burden to prove the case for an interim suspension by a preponderance of the evidence. If proved by a preponderance of the evidence, any one of the following elements establishes conclusively that the attorney poses a substantial threat of irreparable harm to clients or prospective clients:

A. Conduct by an attorney that includes all of the elements of a Serious Crime as defined in these rules.

B. Three or more acts of Professional Misconduct, as defined in subsections (a) (2) (3) (4) (6) (7) (8) or (10) of Rule 8.04 of the Texas Disciplinary Rules of Professional Conduct, whether or not actual harm or threatened harm is demonstrated.

C. Any other conduct by an attorney that, if continued, will probably cause harm to clients or prospective clients.

Adopted by orders of Feb. 26, 1991, and Oct. 9, 1991, eff. May 1, 1992. Amended by order of Dec. 29, 2003, eff. Jan. 1, 2004.

PART XV. MISCELLANEOUS PROVISIONS

15.01. Enforcement of Judgments

The following judgments have the force of a final judgment of a district court: final judgments of an Evidentiary Panel and judgments entered by the Board of Disciplinary Appeals. To enforce a judgment, the Commission may apply to a district court in the county of the residence of the Respondent. In enforcing the judgment, the court has available to it all writs and processes, as well as the power of contempt, to enforce the judgment as if the judgment had been the court's own.

Adopted by orders of Feb. 26, 1991, and Oct. 9, 1991, eff. May 1, 1992. Renumbered from Rule 15.03 and amended by order of Dec. 29, 2003, eff. Jan. 1, 2004.

15.02. Effect of Related Litigation

The processing of a Grievance, Complaint, Disciplinary Proceeding, or Disciplinary Action is not, except for good cause, to be delayed or abated because of substantial similarity to the material allegations in pending civil or criminal litigation.

Adopted by orders of Feb. 26, 1991, and Oct. 9, 1991, eff. May 1, 1992. Renumbered from Rule 15.04 and amended by order of Dec. 29, 2003, eff. Jan. 1, 2004.

15.03. Effect on Related Litigation

Neither the Complainant nor the Respondent is affected by the doctrines of res judicata or estoppel by judgment from any Disciplinary Action.

Adopted by orders of Feb. 26, 1991, and Oct. 9, 1991, eff. May 1, 1992. Renumbered from Rule 15.05 by order of Dec. 29, 2003, eff. Jan. 1, 2004.

15.04. Effect of Delay or Settlement by Complainant

None of the following alone justifies the discontinuance or abatement of a Grievance or Complaint being processed through the disciplinary system: (1) the unwillingness or the neglect of a Complainant to cooperate; (2) the settlement or compromise of matters between the Complainant and the Respondent; (3) the payment of monies by the Respondent to the Complainant.

Adopted by orders of Feb. 26, 1991, and Oct. 9, 1991, eff. May 1, 1992. Renumbered from Rule 15.06 and amended by order of Dec. 29, 2003, eff. Jan. 1, 2004.

15.05. Effect of Time Limitations

The time periods provided in Rules 2.10, 2.12, 2.15, 2.17C, 2.17E, 2.17P, 2.25, 3.02, 3.04, - 7.11,[1] 9.02, 9.03, 10.02, 11.01, 11.08, and 12.06(d) are mandatory. All other time periods herein provided are directory only and the failure to comply with them does not result in the invalidation of an act or event by reason of the noncompliance with those time limits.

Adopted by orders of Feb. 26, 1991, and Oct. 9, 1991, eff. May 1, 1992. Amended by order of Dec. 23, 1992. Renumbered from Rule 15.07 and amended by order of Dec. 29, 2003, eff. Jan. 1, 2004.

[1] So in order.

15.06. Limitations; General Rule and Exceptions

A. *General Rule*: No attorney may be disciplined for Professional Misconduct that occurred more than four years before the date on which a Grievance alleging the Professional Misconduct is received by the Chief Disciplinary Counsel.

B. *Exception: Compulsory Discipline*: The general rule does not apply to a Disciplinary Action seeking compulsory discipline under Part VIII.

C. *Exception: Alleged Violation of the Disclosure Rule*: A prosecutor may be disciplined for a violation of Rule 3.09(d), Texas Disciplinary Rules of Professional Conduct, that occurred in a prosecution that resulted in the wrongful imprisonment of a person if a Grievance alleging the violation is received by the Chief Disciplinary Counsel within four years after the date on which the Wrongfully Imprisoned Person was released from a Penal Institution.

D. *Effect of Fraud or Concealment*: Where fraud or concealment is involved, the time periods stated in this rule do not begin to run until the Complainant discovered, or in the exercise of reasonable diligence should have discovered, the Professional Misconduct.

Adopted by orders of Feb. 26, 1991, and Oct. 9, 1991, eff. May 1, 1992. Renumbered from Rule 15.08 by order of Dec. 29, 2003, eff. Jan. 1, 2004. Amended by orders of Oct. 14, 2013, eff. Nov. 1, 2013; Jan. 15, 2014, eff. immediately.

15.07. Residence

For purposes of these rules, a person licensed to practice law in Texas is considered a resident of the county in Texas of his or her principal residence. A person licensed to practice law in Texas but not residing in Texas is deemed to be a resident of Travis County, Texas, for all purposes.

Adopted by orders of Feb. 26, 1991, and Oct. 9, 1991, eff. May 1, 1992. Renumbered from Rule 15.09 by order of Dec. 29, 2003, eff. Jan. 1, 2004.

15.08. Privilege

All privileges of the attorney-client relationship shall apply to all communications, written and oral, and all other materials and statements between the Chief Disciplinary Counsel and the Commission subject to the provisions of Rule 6.08.

Adopted by orders of Feb. 26, 1991, and Oct. 9, 1991, eff. May 1, 1992. Renumbered from Rule 15.10 and amended by order of Dec. 29, 2003, eff. Jan. 1, 2004.

15.09. Immunity

No lawsuit may be instituted against any Complainant or witness predicated upon the filing of a Grievance or participation in the attorney disciplinary and disability system. All members of the Commission, the Chief Disciplinary Counsel (including Special Assistant Disciplinary Counsel appointed by the Commission and attorneys employed on a contract basis by the Chief Disciplinary Counsel), all members of Committees, all members of the Board of Disciplinary Appeals, all members of the District Disability Committees, all officers and Directors of the State Bar, and the staff members of the aforementioned entities are immune from suit for any conduct in the course of their official duties. The immunity is absolute and unqualified and extends to all actions at law or in equity.

Adopted by orders of Feb. 26, 1991, and Oct. 9, 1991, eff. May 1, 1992. Amended by order of June 15, 1994, as corrected by order of Sept. 12, 1994, eff. Oct. 1, 1994. Renumbered from Rule 15.11 and amended by order of Dec. 29, 2003, eff. Jan. 1, 2004.

15.10. Maintenance of Funds or Other Property Held for Clients and Others

Every attorney licensed to practice law in Texas who maintains, or is required to maintain, a separate client trust account or accounts, designated as such, into which funds of clients or other fiduciary funds must be deposited, shall further maintain and preserve for a period of five years after final disposition of the underlying matter, the records of such accounts, including checkbooks, canceled checks, check stubs, check registers, bank statements, vouchers, deposit slips, ledgers, journals, closing statements, accountings, and other statements of receipts and disbursements rendered to clients or other parties with regard to client trust funds or other similar records clearly reflecting the date, amount, source, and explanation for all receipts, withdrawals, deliveries, and disbursements of the funds or other property of a client.

Adopted by orders of Feb. 26, 1991, and Oct. 9, 1991, eff. May 1, 1992. Renumbered from 15.12 by order of Dec. 29, 2003, eff. Jan. 1, 2004.

15.11. Restrictions on Imposition of Certain Sanctions

A. Public reprimands shall not be utilized if:

1. A public reprimand has been imposed upon the Respondent within the preceding five (5) year period for a violation of the same disciplinary rule; or

2. The Respondent has previously received two or more public reprimands whether or not for violations of the same disciplinary rule within the preceding five year period.

B. Fully probated suspensions shall not be utilized if:

1. A public reprimand or fully probated suspension has been imposed upon the Respondent within the preceding five year period for a violation of the same disciplinary rule; or

2. The Respondent has previously received two or more fully probated suspensions whether or not for violations of the same disciplinary rule within the preceding five year period; or

3. The Respondent has previously received two or more sanctions of public reprimand or greater imposed for conflict of interest, theft, misapplication of fiduciary property, or the failure to return, after demand, a clearly unearned fee.

C. In the event that a fully probated suspension is not available under this rule, any sanction imposed shall be for no less than thirty days of active suspension.

Adopted by orders of June 15, 1994, and Sept. 12, 1994, eff. Oct. 1, 1994. Renumbered from Rule 15.13 and amended by order of Dec. 29, 2003, eff. Jan. 1, 2004.

15.12, 15.13. Renumbered as Rules 15.10, 15.11 and amended by order of Dec. 29, 2003, eff. Jan. 1, 2004

INTERNAL PROCEDURAL RULES OF THE BOARD OF DISCIPLINARY APPEALS

Including Amendments Received Through February 1, 2016

SECTION 1. GENERAL PROVISIONS

Rule 1.01. Definitions

(a) "BODA" is the Board of Disciplinary Appeals.

(b) "Chair" is the member elected by BODA to serve as chair or, in the Chair's absence, the member elected by BODA to serve as vice-chair.

(c) "Classification" is the determination by the CDC under TRDP 2.10 or by BODA under TRDP 7.08(C) whether a grievance constitutes a "complaint" or an "inquiry."

(d) "BODA Clerk" is the executive director of BODA or other person appointed by BODA to assume all duties normally performed by the clerk of a court.

(e) "CDC" is the Chief Disciplinary Counsel for the State Bar of Texas and his or her assistants.

(f) "Commission" is the Commission for Lawyer Discipline, a permanent committee of the State Bar of Texas.

(g) "Executive Director" is the executive director of BODA.

(h) "Panel" is any three-member grouping of BODA under TRDP 7.05.

(i) "Party" is a Complainant, a Respondent, or the Commission.

(j) "TDRPC" is the Texas Disciplinary Rules of Professional Conduct.

(k) "TRAP" is the Texas Rules of Appellate Procedure.

(*l*) "TRCP" is the Texas Rules of Civil Procedure.

(m) "TRDP" is the Texas Rules of Disciplinary Procedure.

(n) "TRE" is the Texas Rules of Evidence.

Eff. Oct. 15, 1996. Amended by order of April 21, 2004, eff. April 21, 2004; Feb. 19, 2015, eff. Feb. 19, 2015.

Rule 1.02. General Powers

Under TRDP 7.08, BODA has and may exercise all the powers of either a trial court or an appellate court, as the case may be, in hearing and determining disciplinary proceedings. But TRDP 15.01 applies to the enforcement of a judgment of BODA.

Eff. Oct. 15, 1996. Amended by order of April 21, 2004, eff. April 21, 2004; Feb. 19, 2015, eff. Feb. 19, 2015.

Rule 1.03. Additional Rules in Disciplinary Matters

Except as varied by these rules and to the extent applicable, the TRCP, TRAP, and TRE apply to all disciplinary matters before BODA, except for appeals from classification decisions, which are governed by TRDP 2.10 and by Section 3 of these rules.

Eff. Oct. 15, 1996. Amended by order of April 21, 2004, eff. April 21, 2004; Feb. 19, 2015, eff. Feb. 19, 2015.

Rule 1.04. Appointment of Panels

(a) BODA may consider any matter or motion by panel, except as specified in (b). The Chair may delegate to the Executive Director the duty to appoint a panel for any BODA action. Decisions are made by a majority vote of the panel; however, any panel member may refer a matter for consideration by BODA sitting en banc. Nothing in these rules gives a party the right to be heard by BODA sitting en banc.

(b) Any disciplinary matter naming a BODA member as Respondent must be considered by BODA sitting en banc. A disciplinary matter naming a BODA staff member as Respondent need not be heard en banc.

Eff. Oct. 15, 1996. Amended by order of April 21, 2004, eff. April 21, 2004; Feb. 19, 2015, eff. Feb. 19, 2015.

Rule 1.05. Filing of Pleadings, Motions, and Other Papers

(a) **Electronic Filing.** All documents must be filed electronically. Unrepresented persons or those without the means to file electronically may electronically file documents, but it is not required.

(1) **Email Address.** The email address of an attorney or an unrepresented party who electronically files a document must be included on the document.

(2) **Timely Filing.** Documents are filed electronically by emailing the document to the BODA Clerk at the email address designated by BODA for that purpose. A document filed by email will be considered filed the day that the email is sent. The date sent is the date shown for the message in the inbox of the email account designated for receiving filings. If a document is sent after 5:00 p.m. or on a weekend or holiday officially observed by the State of Texas, it is considered filed the next business day.

(3) It is the responsibility of the party filing a document by email to obtain the correct email address for BODA and to confirm that the document was received by BODA in legible form. Any document that is illegible or that cannot be opened as part of an email attachment will not be considered filed. If a document is untimely due to a technical failure or a system outage, the filing party may seek appropriate relief from BODA.

(4) **Exceptions.**

(i) An appeal to BODA of a decision by the CDC to classify a grievance as an inquiry is not required to be filed electronically.

(ii) The following documents must not be filed electronically:

a) documents that are filed under seal or subject to a pending motion to seal; and

b) documents to which access is otherwise restricted by court order.

(iii) For good cause, BODA may permit a party to file other documents in paper form in a particular case.

(5) **Format.** An electronically filed document must:

(i) be in text-searchable portable document format (PDF);

(ii) be directly converted to PDF rather than scanned, if possible; and

(iii) not be locked.

(b) A paper will not be deemed filed if it is sent to an individual BODA member or to another address other than the address designated by BODA under Rule 1.05(a)(2).

(c) **Signing.** Each brief, motion, or other paper filed must be signed by at least one attorney for the party or by the party pro se and must give the State Bar of Texas card number, mailing address, telephone number, email address, and fax number, if any, of each attorney whose name is signed or of the party (if applicable). A document is considered signed if the document includes:

(1) an "/s/" and name typed in the space where the signature would otherwise appear, unless the document is notarized or sworn; or

(2) an electronic image or scanned image of the signature.

(d) **Paper Copies.** Unless required by BODA, a party need not file a paper copy of an electronically filed document.

(e) **Service.** Copies of all documents filed by any party other than the record filed by the evidentiary panel clerk or the court reporter must, at or before the time of filing, be served on all other parties as required and authorized by the TRAP.

Adopted by order of Feb. 19, 2015, eff. Feb. 19, 2015.

Rule 1.06. Service of Petition

In any disciplinary proceeding before BODA initiated by service of a petition on the Respondent, the petition may be served by personal service; by certified mail with return receipt requested; or, if permitted by BODA, in any other manner that is authorized by the TRCP and reasonably calculated under all the circumstances to apprise the Respondent of the proceeding and to give him or her reasonable time to appear and answer. To establish service by certified mail, the return receipt must contain the Respondent's signature.

Former Rule 1.07 adopted eff. Oct. 15 1996. Amended by order of April 21, 2004, eff. April 21, 2004. Renumbered as Rule 1.06 and amended by order of Feb. 19, 2015, eff. Feb. 19, 2015.

Rule 1.07. Hearing Setting and Notice

(a) **Original Petitions.** In any kind of case initiated by the CDC's filing a petition or motion with BODA, the CDC may contact the BODA Clerk for the next regularly available hearing date before filing the original petition. If a hearing is set before the petition is filed, the petition must state the date, time, and place of the hearing. Except in the case of a petition to revoke probation under TRDP 2.23, the hearing date must be at least 30 days from the date that the petition is served on the Respondent.

(b) **Expedited Settings.** If a party desires a hearing on a matter on a date earlier than the next regularly available BODA hearing date, the party may request an expedited setting in a written motion setting out the reasons for the request. Unless the parties agree otherwise, and except in the case of a petition to revoke probation under TRDP 2.23, the expedited hearing setting must be at least 30 days from the date of service of the petition, motion, or other pleading. BODA has the sole discretion to grant or deny a request for an expedited hearing date.

(c) **Setting Notices.** BODA must notify the parties of any hearing date that is not noticed in an original petition or motion.

(d) **Announcement Docket.** Attorneys and parties appearing before BODA must confirm their presence and present any questions regarding procedure to the BODA Clerk in the courtroom immediately prior to the time docket call is scheduled to begin. Each party with a matter on the docket must appear at the docket call to give an announcement of readiness, to give a time estimate for the hearing, and to present any preliminary motions or matters. Immediately following the docket call, the Chair will set and announce the order of cases to be heard.

Former Rule 1.11 added by order of April 21, 2004, eff. April 21, 2004. Renumbered as Rule 1.07 and amended by order of Feb. 19, 2015, eff. Feb. 19, 2015.

Rule 1.08. Time to Answer

The Respondent may file an answer at any time, except where expressly provided otherwise by these rules or the TRDP, or when an answer date has been set by prior order of BODA. BODA may, but is not required to, consider an answer filed the day of the hearing.

Former Rule 1.12 added by order of April 21, 2004, eff. April 21, 2004. Renumbered as Rule 1.08 and amended by order of Feb. 19, 2015, eff. Feb. 19, 2015.

Rule 1.09. Pretrial Procedure

(a) Motions.

(1) **Generally.** To request an order or other relief, a party must file a motion supported by sufficient cause with proof of service on all other parties. The motion must state with particularity the grounds on which it is based and set forth the relief sought. All supporting briefs, affidavits, or other documents must be served and filed with the motion. A party may file a response to a motion at any time before BODA rules on the motion or by any deadline set by BODA. Unless otherwise required by these rules or the TRDP, the form of a motion must comply with the TRCP or the TRAP.

(2) **For Extension of Time.** All motions for extension of time in any matter before BODA must be in writing, comply with (a)(1), and specify the following:

(i) if applicable, the date of notice of decision of the evidentiary panel, together with the number and style of the case;

(ii) if an appeal has been perfected, the date when the appeal was perfected;

(iii) the original deadline for filing the item in question;

(iv) the length of time requested for the extension;

(v) the number of extensions of time that have been granted previously regarding the item in question; and

(vi) the facts relied on to reasonably explain the need for an extension.

(b) **Pretrial Scheduling Conference.** Any party may request a pretrial scheduling conference, or BODA on its own motion may require a pretrial scheduling conference.

(c) **Trial Briefs.** In any disciplinary proceeding before BODA, except with leave, all trial briefs and memoranda must be filed with the BODA Clerk no later than ten days before the day of the hearing.

(d) **Hearing Exhibits, Witness Lists, and Exhibits Tendered for Argument.** A party may file a witness list, exhibit, or any other document to be used at a hearing or oral argument before the hearing or argument. A party must bring to the hearing an original and 12 copies of any document that was not filed at least one business day before the hearing. The original and copies must be:

(1) marked;

(2) indexed with the title or description of the item offered as an exhibit; and

(3) if voluminous, bound to lie flat when open and tabbed in accordance with the index.

All documents must be marked and provided to the opposing party before the hearing or argument begins.

Eff. Oct. 15, 1996. Amended by order of April 21, 2004, eff. April 21, 2004; Feb. 19, 2015, eff. Feb. 19, 2015.

Rule 1.10. Decisions

(a) **Notice of Decisions.** The BODA Clerk must give notice of all decisions and opinions to the parties or their attorneys of record.

(b) **Publication of Decisions.** BODA must report judgments or orders of public discipline:

(1) as required by the TRDP; and

(2) on its website for a period of at least ten years following the date of the disciplinary judgment or order.

(c) **Abstracts of Classification Appeals.** BODA may, in its discretion, prepare an abstract of a classification appeal for a public reporting service.

Added by order of Sept. 1, 2003, eff. Sept. 1, 2003. Amended by order of April 21, 2004, eff. April 21, 2004; Feb. 19, 2015, eff. Feb. 19, 2015.

Rule 1.11. Board of Disciplinary Appeals Opinions

(a) BODA may render judgment in any disciplinary matter with or without written opinion. In accordance with TRDP 6.06, all written opinions of BODA are open to the public and must be made available to the public reporting services, print or electronic, for publishing. A majority of the members who participate in considering the disciplinary matter must determine if an opinion will be written. The names of the participating members must be noted on all written opinions of BODA.

(b) Only a BODA member who participated in the decision of a disciplinary matter may file or join in a written opinion concurring in or dissenting from the judgment of BODA. For purposes of this rule, in hearings in which evidence is taken, no member may participate in the decision unless that member was present at the hearing. In all other proceedings, no member may participate unless that member has reviewed the record. Any member of BODA may file a written opinion in connection with the denial of a hearing or rehearing en banc.

(c) A BODA determination in an appeal from a grievance classification decision under TRDP 2.10 is not a judgment for purposes of this rule and may be issued without a written opinion.

Former Rule 1.16 added by order of Feb. 24, 2009, and June 8, 2009, eff. July 1, 2009. Renumbered as Rule 1.11 and amended by order of Feb. 19, 2015, eff. Feb. 19, 2015.

Rule 1.12. BODA Work Product and Drafts

A document or record of any nature—regardless of its form, characteristics, or means of transmission—that is created or produced in connection with or related to BODA's adjudicative decision-making process is not subject to disclosure or discovery. This includes documents prepared by any BODA member, BODA staff, or any other person acting on behalf of or at the direction of BODA.

Former Rule 1.15 added by order of April 21, 2004, eff. April 21, 2004. Renumbered as Rule 1.12 and amended by order of Feb. 19, 2015, eff. Feb. 19, 2015.

Rule 1.13. Record Retention

Records of appeals from classification decisions must be retained by the BODA Clerk for a period of at least three years from the date of disposition. Records of other disciplinary matters must be retained for a period of at least five years from the date of final judgment, or for at least one year after the date a suspension or disbarment ends, whichever is later. For purposes of this rule, a record is any document, paper, letter, map, book, tape, photograph, film, recording, or other material filed with BODA, regardless of its form, characteristics, or means of transmission.

Former Rule 1.05 added eff. Oct. 15, 1996. Renumbered as Rule 1.13 and amended by order of Feb. 19, 2015, eff. Feb. 19, 2015.

Rule 1.14. Costs of Reproduction of Records

The BODA Clerk may charge a reasonable amount for the reproduction of nonconfidential records filed with BODA. The fee must be paid in advance to the BODA Clerk.

Added by order of April 21, 2004, eff. April 21, 2004. Amended by order of Feb. 19, 2015, eff. Feb. 19, 2015.

Rule 1.15. Publication of These Rules

These rules will be published as part of the TDRPC and TRDP.

Former Rule 1.08 eff. Oct. 15, 1996. Amended by order of April 21, 2004, eff. April 21, 2004. Renumbered as Rule 1.15 and amended by order of Feb. 19, 2015, eff. Feb. 19, 2015.

SECTION 2. ETHICAL CONSIDERATIONS

Rule 2.01. Representing or Counseling Parties in Disciplinary Matters and Legal Malpractice Cases

(a) A current member of BODA must not represent a party or testify voluntarily in a disciplinary action or proceeding. Any BODA member who is subpoenaed or otherwise compelled to appear at a disciplinary action or proceeding, including at a deposition, must promptly notify the BODA Chair.

(b) A current BODA member must not serve as an expert witness on the TDRPC.

(c) A BODA member may represent a party in a legal malpractice case, provided that he or she is later recused in accordance with these rules from any proceeding before BODA arising out of the same facts.

Eff. Oct. 15, 1996. Amended by order of April 21, 2004, eff. April 21, 2004; Feb. 19, 2015, eff. Feb. 19, 2015.

Rule 2.02. Confidentiality

(a) BODA deliberations are confidential, must not be disclosed by BODA members or staff, and are not subject to disclosure or discovery.

(b) Classification appeals, appeals from evidentiary judgments of private reprimand, appeals from an evidentiary judgment dismissing a case, interlocutory appeals or any interim proceedings from an ongoing evidentiary case, and disability cases are confidential under the TRDP. BODA must maintain all records associated with these cases as confidential, subject to disclosure only as provided in the TRDP and these rules.

(c) If a member of BODA is subpoenaed or otherwise compelled by law to testify in any proceeding, the member must not disclose a matter that was discussed in conference in connection with a disciplinary case unless the member is required to do so by a court of competent jurisdiction.

Eff. Oct. 15, 1996. Amended by order of Feb. 19, 2015, eff. Feb. 19, 2015.

Rule 2.03. Disqualification and Recusal of BODA Members

(a) BODA members are subject to disqualification and recusal as provided in TRCP 18b.

(b) BODA members may, in addition to recusals under (a), voluntarily recuse themselves from any discussion and voting for any reason. The reasons that a BODA member is recused from a case are not subject to discovery.

(c) These rules do not disqualify a lawyer who is a member of, or associated with, the law firm of a BODA member from serving on a grievance committee or representing a party in a disciplinary proceeding or legal malpractice case. But a BODA member must recuse himor herself from any matter in which a lawyer who is a member of, or associated with, the BODA member's firm is a party or represents a party.

Eff. Oct. 15, 1996. Amended by order of April 21, 2004, eff. April 21, 2004; Feb. 19, 2015, eff. Feb. 19, 2015.

SECTION 3. CLASSIFICATION APPEALS

Rule 3.01. Notice of Right to Appeal

(a) If a grievance filed by the Complainant under TRDP 2.10 is classified as an inquiry, the CDC must notify the Complainant of his or her right to appeal as set out in TRDP 2.10 or another applicable rule.

(b) To facilitate the potential filing of an appeal of a grievance classified as an inquiry, the CDC must send the Complainant an appeal notice form, approved by BODA, with the classification disposition. The form must include the docket number of the matter; the deadline for appealing; and information for mailing, faxing, or emailing the appeal notice form to BODA. The appeal notice form must be available in English and Spanish.

Eff. Oct. 15, 1996. Amended by order of April 21, 2004, eff. April 21, 2004; Feb. 19, 2015, eff. Feb. 19, 2015.

Rule 3.02. Record on Appeal

BODA must only consider documents that were filed with the CDC prior to the classification decision. When a notice of appeal from a classification decision has been filed, the CDC must forward to BODA a copy of the grievance and all supporting documentation. If the appeal challenges the classification of an amended grievance, the CDC must also send BODA a copy of the initial grievance, unless it has been destroyed.

Eff. Oct. 15, 1996. Amended by order of April 21, 2004, eff. April 21, 2004; Feb. 19, 2015, eff. Feb. 19, 2015.

SECTION 4. APPEALS FROM EVIDENTIARY PANEL HEARINGS

Rule 4.01. Perfecting Appeal

(a) **Appellate Timetable.** The date that the evidentiary judgment is signed starts the appellate timetable under this section. To make TRDP 2.21 consistent with this requirement, the date that the judgment is signed is the "date of notice" under Rule 2.21.

(b) **Notification of the Evidentiary Judgment.** The clerk of the evidentiary panel must notify the parties of the judgment as set out in TRDP 2.21.

(1) The evidentiary panel clerk must notify the Commission and the Respondent in writing of the judgment. The notice must contain a clear statement that any appeal of the judgment must be filed with BODA within 30 days of the date that the judgment was signed. The notice must include a copy of the judgment rendered.

(2) The evidentiary panel clerk must notify the Complainant that a judgment has been rendered and provide a copy of the judgment, unless the evidentiary panel dismissed the case or imposed a private reprimand. In the case of a dismissal or private reprimand, the evidentiary panel clerk must notify the Complainant of the decision and that the contents of the judgment are confidential. Under TRDP 2.16, no additional information regarding the contents of a judgment of dismissal or private reprimand may be disclosed to the Complainant.

(c) **Filing Notice of Appeal.** An appeal is perfected when a written notice of appeal is filed with BODA. If a notice of appeal and any other accompanying documents are mistakenly filed with the evidentiary panel clerk, the notice is deemed to have been filed the same day with BODA, and the evidentiary panel clerk must immediately send the BODA Clerk a copy of the notice and any accompanying documents.

(d) **Time to File.** In accordance with TRDP 2.24, the notice of appeal must be filed within 30 days after the date the judgment is signed. In the event a motion for new trial or motion to modify the judgment is timely filed with the evidentiary panel, the notice of appeal must be filed with BODA within 90 days from the date the judgment is signed.

(e) **Extension of Time.** A motion for an extension of time to file the notice of appeal must be filed no later than 15 days after the last day allowed for filing the notice of appeal. The motion must comply with Rule 1.09.

Eff. Oct. 15, 1996. Amended by order of April 21, 2004, eff. April 21, 2004; Feb. 19, 2015, eff. Feb. 19, 2015.

Rule 4.02. Record on Appeal

(a) **Contents.** The record on appeal consists of the evidentiary panel clerk's record and, where necessary to the appeal, a reporter's record of the evidentiary panel hearing.

(b) **Stipulation as to Record.** The parties may designate parts of the clerk's record and the reporter's record to be included in the record on appeal by written stipulation filed with the clerk of the evidentiary panel.

(c) **Responsibility for Filing Record.**

(1) Clerk's Record.

(i) After receiving notice that an appeal has been filed, the clerk of the evidentiary panel is responsible for preparing, certifying, and timely filing the clerk's record.

(ii) Unless the parties stipulate otherwise, the clerk's record on appeal must contain the items listed in TRAP 34.5(a) and any other paper on file with the evidentiary panel, including the election letter, all pleadings on which the hearing was held, the docket sheet, the evidentiary panel's charge, any findings of fact and conclusions of law, all other pleadings, the judgment or other orders appealed from, the notice of decision sent to each party, any postsubmission pleadings and briefs, and the notice of appeal.

(iii) If the clerk of the evidentiary panel is unable for any reason to prepare and transmit the clerk's record by the due date, he or she must promptly notify BODA and the parties, explain why the clerk's record cannot be timely filed, and give the date by which he or she expects the clerk's record to be filed.

(2) Reporter's Record.

(i) The court reporter for the evidentiary panel is responsible for timely filing the reporter's record if:

a) a notice of appeal has been filed;

b) a party has requested that all or part of the reporter's record be prepared; and

c) the party requesting all or part of the reporter's record has paid the reporter's fee or has made satisfactory arrangements with the reporter.

(ii) If the court reporter is unable for any reason to prepare and transmit the reporter's record by the due date, he or she must promptly notify BODA and the parties, explain the reasons why the reporter's record cannot be timely filed, and give the date by which he or she expects the reporter's record to be filed.

(d) Preparation of Clerk's Record.

(1) To prepare the clerk's record, the evidentiary panel clerk must:

(i) gather the documents designated by the parties' written stipulation or, if no stipulation was filed, the documents required under (c)(1)(ii);

(ii) start each document on a new page;

(iii) include the date of filing on each document;

(iv) arrange the documents in chronological order, either by the date of filing or the date of occurrence;

(v) number the pages of the clerk's record in the manner required by (d)(2);

(vi) prepare and include, after the front cover of the clerk's record, a detailed table of contents that complies with (d)(3); and

(vii) certify the clerk's record.

(2) The clerk must start the page numbering on the front cover of the first volume of the clerk's record and continue to number all pages consecutively—including the front and back covers, tables of contents, certification page, and separator pages, if any—until the final page of the clerk's record, without regard for the number of volumes in the clerk's record, and place each page number at the bottom of each page.

(3) The table of contents must:

(i) identify each document in the entire record (including sealed documents); the date each document was filed; and, except for sealed documents, the page on which each document begins;

(ii) be double-spaced;

(iii) conform to the order in which documents appear in the clerk's record, rather than in alphabetical order;

(iv) contain bookmarks linking each description in the table of contents (except for descriptions of sealed documents) to the page on which the document begins; and

(v) if the record consists of multiple volumes, indicate the page on which each volume begins.

(e) **Electronic Filing of the Clerk's Record.** The evidentiary panel clerk must file the record electronically. When filing a clerk's record in electronic form, the evidentiary panel clerk must:

(1) file each computer file in text-searchable Portable Document Format (PDF);

(2) create electronic bookmarks to mark the first page of each document in the clerk's record;

(3) limit the size of each computer file to 100 MB or less, if possible; and

(4) directly convert, rather than scan, the record to PDF, if possible.

(f) **Preparation of the Reporter's Record.**

(1) The appellant, at or before the time prescribed for perfecting the appeal, must make a written request for the reporter's record to the court reporter for the evidentiary panel. The request must designate the portion of the evidence and other proceedings to be included. A copy of the request must be filed with the evidentiary panel and BODA and must be served on the appellee. The reporter's record must be certified by the court reporter for the evidentiary panel.

(2) The court reporter or recorder must prepare and file the reporter's record in accordance with TRAP 34.6 and 35 and the Uniform Format Manual for Texas Reporters' Records.

(3) The court reporter or recorder must file the reporter's record in an electronic format by emailing the document to the email address designated by BODA for that purpose.

(4) The court reporter or recorder must include either a scanned image of any required signature or "/s/" and name typed in the space where the signature would otherwise

(6[1]) In exhibit volumes, the court reporter or recorder must create bookmarks to mark the first page of each exhibit document.

(g) **Other Requests.** At any time before the clerk's record is prepared, or within ten days after service of a copy of appellant's request for the reporter's record, any party may file a written designation requesting that additional exhibits and portions of testimony be included in the record. The request must be filed with the evidentiary panel and BODA and must be served on the other party.

(h) **Inaccuracies or Defects.** If the clerk's record is found to be defective or inaccurate, the BODA Clerk must inform the clerk of the evidentiary panel of the defect or inaccuracy and instruct the clerk to make the correction. Any inaccuracies in the reporter's record may be corrected by agreement of the parties without the court reporter's recertification. Any dispute regarding the reporter's record that the parties are unable to resolve by agreement must be resolved by the evidentiary panel.

(i) **Appeal from Private Reprimand.** Under TRDP 2.16, in an appeal from a judgment of private reprimand, BODA must mark the record as confidential, remove the attorney's name from the case style, and take any other steps necessary to preserve the confidentiality of the private reprimand.

Former Rule 4.03 eff. Oct. 15, 1996. Amended by order of April 21, 2004, eff. April 21, 2004. Renumbered as Rule 4.02 and amended by order of Feb. 19, 2015, eff. Feb. 19, 2015.

[1] So in original.

Rule 4.03. Time to File Record

(a) **Timetable.** The clerk's record and reporter's record must be filed within 60 days after the date the judgment is signed. If a motion for new trial or motion to modify the judgment is filed with the evidentiary panel, the clerk's record and the reporter's record must be filed within 120 days from the date the original judgment is signed, unless a modified judgment is signed, in which case the clerk's record and the reporter's record must be filed within 60 days of the signing of the modified judgment. Failure to file either the clerk's record or the reporter's record on time does not affect BODA's jurisdiction, but may result in BODA's exercising its discretion to dismiss the appeal, affirm the judgment appealed from, disregard materials filed late, or apply presumptions against the appellant.

(b) **If No Record Filed.**

(1) If the clerk's record or reporter's record has not been timely filed, the BODA Clerk must send notice to the party responsible for filing it, stating that the record is late and requesting that the record be filed within 30 days. The BODA Clerk must send a copy of this notice to all the parties and the clerk of the evidentiary panel.

(2) If no reporter's record is filed due to appellant's fault, and if the clerk's record has been filed, BODA may, after first giving the appellant notice and a reasonable opportunity to cure, consider and decide those issues or points that do not require a reporter's record for a decision. BODA may do this if no reporter's record has been filed because:

(i) the appellant failed to request a reporter's record; or

(ii) the appellant failed to pay or make arrangements to pay the reporter's fee to prepare the reporter's record, and the appellant is not entitled to proceed without payment of costs.

(c) **Extension of Time to File the Reporter's Record.** When an extension of time is requested for filing the reporter's record, the facts relied on to reasonably explain the need for an extension must be supported by an affidavit of the court reporter. The affidavit must include the court reporter's estimate of the earliest date when the reporter's record will be available for filing.

(d) **Supplemental Record.** If anything material to either party is omitted from the clerk's record or reporter's record, BODA may, on written motion of a party or on its own motion, direct a supplemental record to be certified and transmitted by the clerk for the evidentiary panel or the court reporter for the evidentiary panel.

Former Rule 4.04 eff. Oct. 15, 1996. Amended by order of April 21, 2004, eff. April 21, 2004. Renumbered as Rule 4.03 and amended by order of Feb. 19, 2015, eff. Feb. 19, 2015.

Rule 4.04. Copies of the Record

The record may not be withdrawn from the custody of the BODA Clerk. Any party may obtain a copy of the record or any designated part thereof by making a written request to the BODA Clerk and paying any charges for reproduction in advance.

Former Rule 4.05 eff. Oct. 15, 1996. Amended by order of April 21, 2004, eff. April 21, 2004. Renumbered as Rule 4.04 and amended by order of Feb. 19, 2015, eff. Feb. 19, 2015.

Rule 4.05. Requisites of Briefs

(a) **Appellant's Filing Date.** Appellant's brief must be filed within 30 days after the clerk's record or the reporter's record is filed, whichever is later.

(b) **Appellee's Filing Date.** Appellee's brief must be filed within 30 days after the appellant's brief is filed.

(c) **Contents.** Briefs must contain:

(1) a complete list of the names and addresses of all parties to the final decision and their counsel;

(2) a table of contents indicating the subject matter of each issue or point, or group of issues or points, with page references where the discussion of each point relied on may be found;

(3) an index of authorities arranged alphabetically and indicating the pages where the authorities are cited;

(4) a statement of the case containing a brief general statement of the nature of the cause or offense and the result;

(5) a statement, without argument, of the basis of BODA's jurisdiction;

(6) a statement of the issues presented for review or points of error on which the appeal is predicated;

(7) a statement of facts that is without argument, is supported by record references, and details the facts relating to the issues or points relied on in the appeal;

(8) the argument and authorities;

(9) conclusion and prayer for relief;

(10) a certificate of service; and

(11) an appendix of record excerpts pertinent to the issues presented for review.

(d) **Length of Briefs; Contents Included and Excluded.** In calculating the length of a document, every word and every part of the document, including headings, footnotes, and quotations, must be counted except the following: caption, identity of the parties and counsel, statement regarding oral argument, table of contents, index of authorities, statement of the case, statement of issues presented, statement of the jurisdiction, signature, proof of service, certificate of compliance, and appendix. Briefs must not exceed 15,000 words if computer-generated, and 50 pages if not, except on leave of BODA. A reply brief must not exceed 7,500 words if computer-generated, and 25 pages if not, except on leave of BODA. A computer-generated document must include a certificate by counsel or the unrepresented party stating the number of words in the document. The person who signs the certification may rely on the word count of the computer program used to prepare the document.

(e) **Amendment or Supplementation.** BODA has discretion to grant leave to amend or supplement briefs.

(f) **Failure of the Appellant to File a Brief.** If the appellant fails to timely file a brief, BODA may:

(1) dismiss the appeal for want of prosecution, unless the appellant reasonably explains the failure, and the appellee is not significantly injured by the appellant's failure to timely file a brief;

(2) decline to dismiss the appeal and make further orders within its discretion as it considers proper; or

(3) if an appellee's brief is filed, regard that brief as correctly presenting the case and affirm the evidentiary panel's judgment on that brief without examining the record.

Former Rule 4.06 eff. Oct. 15, 1996. Amended by order of April 21, 2004, eff. April 21, 2004. Renumbered as Rule 4.05 and amended by order of Feb. 19, 2015, eff. Feb. 19, 2015.

Rule 4.06. Oral Argument

(a) **Request.** A party desiring oral argument must note the request on the front cover of the party's brief. A party's failure to timely request oral argument waives the party's right to argue. A party who has requested argument may later withdraw the request. But even if a party has waived oral argument, BODA may direct the party to appear and argue. If oral argument is granted, the clerk will notify the parties of the time and place for submission.

(b) **Right to Oral Argument.** A party who has filed a brief and who has timely requested oral argument may argue the case to BODA unless BODA, after examining the briefs, decides that oral argument is unnecessary for any of the following reasons:

(1) the appeal is frivolous;

(2) the dispositive issue or issues have been authoritatively decided;

(3) the facts and legal arguments are adequately presented in the briefs and record; or

(4) the decisional process would not be significantly aided by oral argument.

(c) **Time Allowed.** Each party will have 20 minutes to argue. BODA may, on the request of a party or on its own, extend or shorten the time allowed for oral argument. The appellant may reserve a portion of his or her allotted time for rebuttal.

Former Rule 4.07 eff. Oct. 15, 1996. Amended by order of April 21, 2004, eff. April 21, 2004. Renumbered as Rule 4.06 and amended by order of Feb. 19, 2015, eff. Feb. 19, 2015.

Rule 4.07. Decision and Judgment

(a) **Decision.** BODA may do any of the following:

(1) affirm in whole or in part the decision of the evidentiary panel;

(2) modify the panel's findings and affirm the findings as modified;

(3) reverse in whole or in part the panel's findings and render the decision that the panel should have rendered; or

(4) reverse the panel's findings and remand the cause for further proceedings to be conducted by:

(i) the panel that entered the findings; or

(ii) a statewide grievance committee panel appointed by BODA and composed of members selected from the state bar districts other than the district from which the appeal was taken.

(b) Mandate. In every appeal, the BODA Clerk must issue a mandate in accordance with BODA's judgment and send it to the evidentiary panel and to all the parties.

Former Rule 4.10 eff. Oct. 15, 1996. Amended by order of April 21, 2004, eff. April 21, 2004; Feb. 24, 2009, and June 8, 2009, eff. July 1, 2009. Renumbered as Rule 4.07 and amended by order of Feb. 19, 2015, eff. Feb. 19, 2015.

Rule 4.08. Appointment of Statewide Grievance Committee

If BODA remands a cause for further proceedings before a statewide grievance committee, the BODA Chair will appoint the statewide grievance committee in accordance with TRDP 2.27. The committee must consist of six members: four attorney members and two public members randomly selected from the current pool of grievance committee members. Two alternates, consisting of one attorney and one public member, must also be selected. BODA will appoint the initial chair who will serve until the members of the statewide grievance committee elect a chair of the committee at the first meeting. The BODA Clerk will notify the Respondent and the CDC that a committee has been appointed.

Eff. Oct. 15, 1996. Amended by order of April 21, 2004, eff. April 21, 2004; Feb. 19, 2015, eff. Feb. 19, 2015.

Rule 4.09. Involuntary Dismissal

Under the following circumstances and on any party's motion or on its own initiative after giving at least ten days' notice to all parties, BODA may dismiss the appeal or affirm the appealed judgment or order. Dismissal or affirmance may occur if the appeal is subject to dismissal:

(a) for want of jurisdiction;

(b) for want of prosecution; or

(c) because the appellant has failed to comply with a requirement of these rules, a court order, or a notice from the clerk requiring a response or other action within a specified time.

Former Rule 4.11 added by order of April 21, 2004, eff. April 21, 2004. Renumbered as Rule 4.09 by order of Feb. 19, 2015, eff. Feb. 19, 2015.

SECTION 5. PETITIONS TO REVOKE PROBATION

Rule 5.01. Initiation and Service

(a) Before filing a motion to revoke the probation of an attorney who has been sanctioned, the CDC must contact the BODA Clerk to confirm whether the next regularly available hearing date will comply with the 30–day requirement of TRDP. The Chair may designate a three-member panel to hear the motion, if necessary, to meet the 30–day requirement of TRDP 2.23.

(b) Upon filing the motion, the CDC must serve the Respondent with the motion and any supporting documents in accordance with TRDP 2.23, the TRCP, and these rules. The CDC must notify BODA of the date that service is obtained on the Respondent.

Eff. Oct. 15, 1996. Amended by order of April 21, 2004, eff. April 21, 2004; Feb. 19, 2015, eff. Feb. 19, 2015.

Rule 5.02. Hearing

Within 30 days of service of the motion on the Respondent, BODA must docket and set the matter for a hearing and notify the parties of the time and place of the hearing. On a showing of good cause by a party or on its own motion, BODA may continue the case to a future hearing date as circumstances require.

Eff. Oct. 15, 1996. Amended by order of April 21, 2004, eff. April 21, 2004; Feb. 19, 2015, eff. Feb. 19, 2015.

SECTION 6. COMPULSORY DISCIPLINE

Rule 6.01. Initiation of Proceeding

Under TRDP 8.03, the CDC must file a petition for compulsory discipline with BODA and serve the Respondent in accordance with the TRDP and Rule 1.06 of these rules.

Eff. Oct. 15, 1996. Amended by order of April 21, 2004, eff. April 21, 2004; Feb. 19, 2015, eff. Feb. 19, 2015.

Rule 6.02. Interlocutory Suspension

(a) **Interlocutory Suspension.** In any compulsory proceeding under TRDP Part VIII in which BODA determines that the Respondent has been convicted of an Intentional Crime and that the criminal conviction is on direct appeal, BODA may suspend the Respondent's license to practice law by interlocutory order. In any compulsory case in which BODA has imposed an interlocutory order of suspension, BODA retains jurisdiction to render final judgment after the direct appeal of the criminal conviction is final. For purposes of rendering final judgment in a compulsory discipline case, the direct appeal of the criminal conviction is final when the appellate court issues its mandate.

(b) **Criminal Conviction Affirmed.** If the criminal conviction made the basis of a compulsory interlocutory suspension is affirmed and becomes final, the CDC must file a motion for final judgment that complies with TRDP 8.05.

(1) If the criminal sentence is fully probated or is an order of deferred adjudication, the motion for final judgment must contain notice of a hearing date. The motion will be set on BODA's next available hearing date.

(2) If the criminal sentence is not fully probated:

(i) BODA may proceed to decide the motion without a hearing if the attorney does not file a verified denial within ten days of service of the motion; or

(ii) BODA may set the motion for a hearing on the next available hearing date if the attorney timely files a verified denial.

(c) Criminal Conviction Reversed. If an appellate court issues a mandate reversing the criminal conviction while a Respondent is subject to an interlocutory suspension, the Respondent may file a motion to terminate the interlocutory suspension. The motion to terminate the interlocutory suspension must have certified copies of the decision and mandate of the reversing court attached. If the CDC does not file an opposition to the termination within ten days of being served with the motion, BODA may proceed to decide the motion without a hearing or set the matter for a hearing on its own motion. If the CDC timely opposes the motion, BODA must set the motion for a hearing on its next available hearing date. An order terminating an interlocutory order of suspension does not automatically reinstate a Respondent's license.

Eff. Oct. 15, 1996. Amended by order of April 21, 2004, eff. April 21, 2004; Feb. 19, 2015, eff. Feb. 19, 2015.

SECTION 7. RECIPROCAL DISCIPLINE

Rule 7.01. Initiation of Proceeding

The Commission for Lawyer Discipline may initiate an action for reciprocal discipline by filing a petition with BODA under TRDP Part IX and these rules. The petition must request that the Respondent be disciplined in Texas and have attached to it any information concerning the disciplinary matter from the other jurisdiction, including a certified copy of the order or judgment rendered against the Respondent.

Eff. Oct. 15, 1996. Amended by order of April 21, 2004, eff. April 21, 2004; Feb. 19, 2015, eff. Feb. 19, 2015.

Rule 7.02. Order to Show Cause

When a petition is filed, the Chair immediately issues a show cause order and a hearing notice and forwards them to the CDC, who must serve the order and notice on the Respondent. The CDC must notify BODA of the date that service is obtained.

Eff. Oct. 15, 1996. Amended by order of April 21, 2004, eff. April 21, 2004; Feb. 19, 2015, eff. Feb. 19, 2015.

Rule 7.03. Attorney's Response

If the Respondent does not file an answer within 30 days of being served with the order and notice but thereafter appears at the hearing, BODA may, at the discretion of the Chair, receive testimony from the Respondent relating to the merits of the petition.

Eff. Oct. 15, 1996. Amended by order of April 21, 2004, eff. April 21, 2004; Feb. 19, 2015, eff. Feb. 19, 2015.

SECTION 8. DISTRICT DISABILITY COMMITTEE HEARINGS

Rule 8.01. Appointment of District Disability Committee

(a) If the evidentiary panel of the grievance committee finds under TRDP 2.17(P)(2), or the CDC reasonably believes under TRDP 2.14(C), that a Respondent is suffering from a disability, the rules in this section will apply to the de novo proceeding before the District Disability Committee held under TRDP Part XII.

(b) Upon receiving an evidentiary panel's finding or the CDC's referral that an attorney is believed to be suffering from a disability, the BODA Chair must appoint a District Disability Committee in compliance with TRDP 12.02 and designate a chair. BODA will reimburse District Disability Committee members for reasonable expenses directly related to service on the District Disability Committee. The BODA Clerk must notify the CDC and the Respondent that a committee has been appointed and notify the Respondent where to locate the procedural rules governing disability proceedings.

(c) A Respondent who has been notified that a disability referral will be or has been made to BODA may, at any time, waive in writing the appointment of the District Disability Committee or the hearing before the District Disability Committee and enter into an agreed judgment of indefinite disability suspension, provided that the Respondent is competent to waive the hearing. If the Respondent is not represented, the waiver must include a statement affirming that the Respondent has been advised of the right to appointed counsel and waives that right as well.

(d) All pleadings, motions, briefs, or other matters to be filed with the District Disability Committee must be filed with the BODA Clerk.

(e) Should any member of the District Disability Committee become unable to serve, the BODA Chair may appoint a substitute member.

Eff. Oct. 15, 1996. Amended by order of April 21, 2004, eff. April 21, 2004; Feb. 19, 2015, eff. Feb. 19, 2015.

Rule 8.02. Petition and Answer

(a) **Petition.** Upon being notified that the District Disability Committee has been appointed by BODA, the CDC must, within 20 days, file with the BODA Clerk and serve on the Respondent a copy of a petition for indefinite disability suspension. Service may be made in person or by certified mail, return receipt requested. If service is by certified mail, the return receipt with the Respondent's signature must be filed with the BODA Clerk.

(b) **Answer.** The Respondent must, within 30 days after service of the petition for indefinite disability suspension, file an answer with the BODA Clerk and serve a copy of the answer on the CDC.

(c) **Hearing Setting.** The BODA Clerk must set the final hearing as instructed by the chair of the District Disability Committee and send notice of the hearing to the parties.

Eff. Oct. 15, 1996. Amended by order of April 21, 2004, eff. April 21, 2004; Feb. 19, 2015, eff. Feb. 19, 2015.

Rule 8.03. Discovery

(a) **Limited Discovery.** The District Disability Committee may permit limited discovery. The party seeking discovery must file with the BODA Clerk a written request that makes a clear showing of good cause and substantial need and a proposed order. If the District Disability Committee authorizes discovery in a case, it must issue a written order. The order may impose limitations or deadlines on the discovery.

(b) **Physical or Mental Examinations.** On written motion by the Commission or on its own motion, the District Disability Committee may order the Respondent to submit to a physical or mental examination by a qualified healthcare or mental healthcare professional. Nothing in this rule limits the Respondent's right to an examination by a professional of his or her choice in addition to any exam ordered by the District Disability Committee.

(1) **Motion.** The Respondent must be given reasonable notice of the examination by written order specifying the name, address, and telephone number of the person conducting the examination.

(2) **Report.** The examining professional must file with the BODA Clerk a detailed, written report that includes the results of all tests performed and the professional's findings, diagnoses, and conclusions. The professional must send a copy of the report to the CDC and the Respondent.

(c) **Objections.** A party must make any objection to a request for discovery within 15 days of receiving the motion by filing a written objection with the BODA Clerk. BODA may decide any objection or contest to a discovery motion.

Eff. Oct. 15, 1996. Amended by order of April 21, 2004, eff. April 21, 2004; Feb. 19, 2015, eff. Feb. 19, 2015.

Rule 8.04. Ability to Compel Attendance

The Respondent and the CDC may confront and cross-examine witnesses at the hearing. Compulsory process to compel the attendance of witnesses by subpoena, enforceable by an order of a district court of proper jurisdiction, is available to the Respondent and the CDC as provided in TRCP 176.

Eff. Oct. 15, 1996. Amended by order of April 21, 2004, eff. April 21, 2004; Feb. 19, 2015, eff. Feb. 19, 2015.

Rule 8.05. Respondent's Right to Counsel

(a) The notice to the Respondent that a District Disability Committee has been appointed and the petition for indefinite disability suspension must state that the Respondent may request appointment of counsel by BODA to represent him or her at the disability hearing. BODA will reimburse appointed counsel for reasonable expenses directly related to representation of the Respondent.

(b) To receive appointed counsel under TRDP 12.02, the Respondent must file a written request with the BODA Clerk within 30 days of the date that Respondent is served with the petition for indefinite disability suspension. A late request must demonstrate good cause for the Respondent's failure to file a timely request.

Eff. Oct. 15, 1996. Amended by order of April 21, 2004, eff. April 21, 2004; Feb. 19, 2015, eff. Feb. 19, 2015.

Rule 8.06. Hearing

The party seeking to establish the disability must prove by a preponderance of the evidence that the Respondent is suffering from a disability as defined in the TRDP. The chair of the District Disability Committee must admit all relevant evidence that is necessary for a fair and complete hearing. The TRE are advisory but not binding on the chair.

Former Rule 8.07 eff. Oct. 15, 1996. Amended by order of April 21, 2004, eff. April 21, 2004. Renumbered as Rule 8.06 and amended by order of Feb. 19, 2015, eff. Feb. 19, 2015.

Rule 8.07. Notice of Decision

The District Disability Committee must certify its finding regarding disability to BODA, which will issue the final judgment in the matter.

Former Rule 8.08 eff. Oct. 15, 1996. Amended by order of April 21, 2004, eff. April 21, 2004. Renumbered as Rule 8.07 and amended by order of Feb. 19, 2015, eff. Feb. 19, 2015.

Rule 8.08. Confidentiality

All proceedings before the District Disability Committee and BODA, if necessary, are closed to the public. All matters before the District Disability Committee are confidential and are not subject to disclosure or discovery, except as allowed by the TRDP or as may be required in the event of an appeal to the Supreme Court of Texas.

Former Rule 8.09 eff. Oct. 15, 1996. Renumbered as Rule 8.08 and amended by order of Feb. 19, 2015, eff. Feb. 19, 2015.

SECTION 9. DISABILITY REINSTATEMENTS

Rule 9.01. Petition for Reinstatement

(a) An attorney under an indefinite disability suspension may, at any time after he or she has been suspended, file a verified petition with BODA to have the suspension terminated and to be reinstated to the practice of law. The petitioner must serve a copy of the petition on the CDC in the manner required by TRDP 12.06. The TRCP apply to a reinstatement proceeding unless they conflict with these rules.

(b) The petition must include the information required by TRDP 12.06. If the judgment of disability suspension contained terms or conditions relating to misconduct by the petitioner prior to the suspension, the petition must affirmatively demonstrate that those terms have been complied with or explain why they have not been satisfied. The petitioner has a duty to amend and keep current all information in the petition until the final hearing on the merits. Failure to do so may result in dismissal without notice.

(c) Disability reinstatement proceedings before BODA are not confidential; however, BODA may make all or any part of the record of the proceeding confidential.

Eff. Oct. 15, 1996. Amended by order of April 21, 2004, eff. April 21, 2004; Feb. 19, 2015, eff. Feb. 19, 2015.

Rule 9.02. Discovery

The discovery period is 60 days from the date that the petition for reinstatement is filed. The BODA Clerk will set the petition for a hearing on the first date available after the close of the discovery period and must notify the parties of the time and place of the hearing. BODA may continue the hearing for good cause shown.

Eff. Oct. 15, 1996. Amended by order of Feb. 19, 2015, eff. Feb. 19, 2015.

Rule 9.03. Physical or Mental Examinations

(a) On written motion by the Commission or on its own, BODA may order the petitioner seeking reinstatement to submit to a physical or mental examination by a qualified healthcare or mental healthcare professional. The petitioner must be served with a copy of the motion and given at least seven days to respond. BODA may hold a hearing before ruling on the motion but is not required to do so.

(b) The petitioner must be given reasonable notice of the examination by written order specifying the name, address, and telephone number of the person conducting the examination.

(c) The examining professional must file a detailed, written report that includes the results of all tests performed and the professional's findings, diagnoses, and conclusions. The professional must send a copy of the report to the parties.

(d) If the petitioner fails to submit to an examination as ordered, BODA may dismiss the petition without notice.

(e) Nothing in this rule limits the petitioner's right to an examination by a professional of his or her choice in addition to any exam ordered by BODA.

Eff. Oct. 15, 1996. Amended by order of April 21, 2004, eff. April 21, 2004; Feb. 19, 2015, eff. Feb. 19, 2015.

Rule 9.04. Judgment

If, after hearing all the evidence, BODA determines that the petitioner is not eligible for reinstatement, BODA may, in its discretion, either enter an order denying the petition or direct that the petition be held in abeyance for a reasonable period of time until the petitioner provides additional proof as directed by BODA. The judgment may include other orders necessary to protect the public and the petitioner's potential clients.

Former Rule 9.05 eff. Oct. 15, 1996. Renumbered as Rule 9.04 and amended by order of April 21, 2004, eff. April 21, 2004. Amended by order of Feb. 19, 2015, eff. Feb. 19, 2015.

SECTION 10. APPEALS FROM BODA TO THE SUPREME COURT OF TEXAS

Rule 10.01. Appeals to the Supreme Court

(a) A final decision by BODA, except a determination that a statement constitutes an inquiry or a complaint under TRDP 2.10, may be appealed to the Supreme Court of Texas. The clerk of the Supreme Court of Texas must docket an appeal from a decision by BODA in the same manner as a petition for review without fee.

(b) The appealing party must file the notice of appeal directly with the clerk of the Supreme Court of Texas within 14 days of receiving notice of a final determination by BODA. The record must be filed within 60 days after BODA's determination. The appealing party's brief is due 30 days after the record is filed, and the responding party's brief is due 30 days thereafter. The BODA Clerk must send the parties a notice of BODA's final decision that includes the information in this paragraph.

(c) An appeal to the Supreme Court is governed by TRDP 7.11 and the TRAP.

Eff. Oct. 15, 1996. Amended by order of April 21, 2004, eff. April 21, 2004; Feb. 19, 2015, eff. Feb. 19, 2015.

RULES GOVERNING THE OPERATION OF THE TEXAS ACCESS TO JUSTICE FOUNDATION

Including Amendments Received Through February 1, 2016

Rule 1. Establishment of the Texas Access to Justice Foundation

The Texas Access to Justice Program ("the Program"), Article XI of the State Bar Rules Adopted and promulgated by the Supreme Court of Texas by Order dated April 30, 1984, shall be administered by the Texas Access to Justice Foundation (the "Foundation"), a Texas Non–Profit Corporation.

Amended Dec. 18, 2006, eff. March 1, 2007, Jan. 13, 2009, eff. Jan. 13, 2009.

Rule 2. Articles of Incorporation and Bylaws

The Articles of Incorporation and Bylaws of the Foundation shall be as set forth in Attachments 1 and 2, respectively, hereto.*

* Pub. Note: Copies of the Articles of Incorporation and Bylaws of the Foundation are available from the State Bar.

Amended Jan. 13, 2009, eff. Jan. 13, 2009.

Rule 3. Directors of the Foundation

Directors of the Foundation shall be appointed and their terms of office fixed as set forth in Attachment 2. The initial directors of the Foundation are named in Attachment 1.

Amended Jan. 13, 2009, eff. Jan. 13, 2009.

Rule 4. Deposit of Certain Client Funds

An attorney licensed by the Supreme Court of Texas, receiving in the course of the practice of law in this state, client funds that are nominal in amount or are reasonably anticipated to be held for a short period of time, must establish and maintain a separate interest or dividend-bearing insured depository trust account at an eligible institution and deposit such funds in the account. "Interest or dividend-bearing insured depository trust account" means a federally insured checking account or investment product, including a daily financial institution repurchase agreement or a money market fund at an eligible institution as defined in Rule (7). A daily financial institution repurchase agreement must be fully collateralized by, and an open-end money market fund must consist solely of United States Government Securities. A daily financial institution repurchase agreement may be established only with an eligible institution that is deemed to be "well capitalized" or "adequately capitalized" as defined by applicable federal statutes and regulations. An open-end money market fund must hold itself out as a money market fund as defined by applicable federal statutes and regulations under the Investment Company Act of 1940 and have total assets of at least $250,000,000.

The funds covered by this rule shall be subject to withdrawal upon request and without delay. All IOLTA-eligible client funds may be deposited in a single unsegregated account. Attorneys who practice in a law firm or for a professional corporation may utilize the interest-bearing trust account of such firm or corporation to comply with Rule 4. No funds belonging to the attorney or law firm, except funds reasonably sufficient to pay for fees or obtain a waiver of fees or to keep the account open, may be deposited in such an account. The interest earned on the account shall be paid in accordance with and used for the purposes set forth in these Rules. The Foundation shall hold the entire beneficial interest in the interest earned. Funds to be deposited under these Rules shall not include those funds evidenced by a financial institution instrument, such as a draft, until the instrument is fully credited to the financial institution in which the account is maintained. The term "draft" as herein used is defined in Section 3.104 (b) (1) of the Texas Business and Commerce Code. A draft or similar instrument need not be treated as a collected item unless it is the type of instrument which the financial institution generally treats as a collected item. Nothing in this or any other of these Rules prohibits the deposit of client funds into a general account or changes the legal relationship between depositor and financial institution from that established by contract or by applicable state and federal law.

Amended Dec. 13, 1988, eff. July 1, 1989; May 22, 1991, eff. Jan. 1, 1992; Nov. 22, 2004, eff. Nov. 30, 2004; Dec. 18, 2006, eff. March 1, 2007; Jan. 13, 2009, eff. Jan. 13, 2009.

Rule 4A. Attorneys Who Do Not Handle Client Trust Funds

Licensed attorneys who do not handle client trust funds are not required to establish an IOLTA account. Such attorneys must nevertheless advise the Foundation during the annual IOLTA compliance process that they do not handle client trust funds.

Adopted May 22, 1991, eff. Jan. 1, 1992; amended Jan. 13, 2009, eff. Jan. 13, 2009.

Rule 4B. Accounts Unable to Generate Net Interest

Licensed attorneys who maintain client trust funds that are nominal in amount or are reasonably anticipated to be held for a short period of time must attempt in good faith to locate an interest bearing account that would generate interest greater than service charges. If such an account cannot be located, the attorney must notify the Foundation during the annual IOLTA compliance process. Such attorney is required to maintain a non-interest bearing client trust account for such funds.

Adopted May 22, 1991, eff. Jan. 1, 1992; amended Jan. 13, 2009, eff. Jan. 13, 2009.

Rule 5. Annual Notice to Foundation

Licensed attorneys must advise the Foundation annually either electronically or in writing as to their IOLTA status as provided in Rule 23.

Amended Dec. 13, 1988, eff. July 1, 1989; May 22, 1991, eff. Jan. 1, 1992; Nov. 22, 2004, eff. Nov. 30, 2004; Jan. 13, 2009, eff. Jan. 13, 2009.

Rule 5A. Notice to Foundation of Change in Status

Licensed attorneys must notify the Foundation either electronically or in writing within thirty (30) days of any change in IOLTA status.

Adopted Dec. 13, 1988, eff. July 1, 1989; amended May 22, 1991, eff. Jan. 1, 1992; Dec. 18, 2006, eff. March 1, 2007; Jan. 13, 2009, eff. Jan. 13, 2009.

Rule 5B. Notice to Foundation of Closed Account

An attorney, law firm, or professional corporation engaged in the practice of law and maintaining accounts provided for in these Rules must notify the Foundation either electronically or in writing within thirty (30) days of the closing of such account(s).

Adopted Dec. 13, 1988, eff. July 1, 1989; amended Dec. 18, 2006, eff. March 1, 2007; Jan. 13, 2009, eff. Jan. 13, 2009.

Rule 5C. Deleted May 1, 1991, eff. Jan. 1, 1992

Rule 6. Funds Eligible for the Program

The funds of a particular client are nominal in amount or held for a short period of time, and thus eligible for use in the Program, if such funds could not reasonably be expected to earn interest for the client or if the interest which might be earned on such funds is not likely to be sufficient to offset the cost of establishing and maintaining the account, service charges, accounting costs and tax reporting costs which would be incurred in attempting to obtain interest on such funds for the client. Also to be considered are the nature of the proceeding or transaction involved and the likelihood of delay in the need for such funds in such proceeding or transaction. The attorney, law firm, or professional corporation should exercise good faith judgment in determining initially whether client funds should be included in the Program and should review at reasonable intervals whether changed circumstances require further action with respect to such funds.

Amended Jan. 13, 2009, eff. Jan. 13, 2009.

Rule 7. Accounts to be Maintained at Eligible Institutions

An Account established at an eligible institution pursuant to Rule 4 shall be a trust account from which withdrawals or transfers may be made on demand (subject only to any notice period which the financial institution is required to reserve by law or regulation) established in any bank, savings bank, credit union, savings and loan association authorized by federal or state law to engage in business in Texas, which is insured by the Federal Deposit Insurance Corporation or the National Credit Union Share Insurance Fund, or an investment company which is registered with the Securities & Exchange Commission and the State Securities Commission (as may be required). The determination of whether or not an institution is an eligible institution and whether it is meeting the requirements of this rule shall be made by the Texas Access to Justice Foundation, which must maintain a current list of eligible institutions on its website. Participation by banks, savings and loans associations, credit unions, and investment companies in the IOLTA Program is voluntary. Effective, March 1, 2007, attorneys may not maintain an IOLTA trust account at a financial institution which does not meet the requirements of this rule and is therefore not an eligible institution. An eligible institution that elects to offer and maintain IOLTA accounts is one that meets the requirements of this rule, including the following:

(a) The eligible institution shall pay no less on its IOLTA accounts than the highest interest rate or dividend generally available from the institution to its non-IOLTA customers when the IOLTA account meets or exceeds the same minimum balance or other eligibility qualifications on its non-IOLTA accounts, if any. In determining the highest interest rate or dividend generally available from the institution to its non-IOLTA customers, an eligible institution may consider, in addition to the balance in the IOLTA account, factors customarily considered by the institution when setting interest rates or dividends for its non-IOLTA customers; provided, however, that such factors shall not discriminate between IOLTA accounts and non-IOLTA accounts, nor shall such factors include or consider the fact that the account is an IOLTA account. An eligible institution will satisfy these requirements if it pays a qualifying rate on IOLTA accounts or a qualifying account product:

(1) The eligible institution may establish the IOLTA account as a qualifying higher rate product, including tiered interest rate checking accounts and a checking account with an automated, sweep account that provides a mechanism for the overnight investment of balances in the IOLTA account in an interest-bearing or dividend-bearing account that is a daily financial institution repurchase agreement or a money-market fund.

(2) An eligible institution may choose to pay the higher interest or dividend rate on an IOLTA checking account in lieu of establishing it as a qualifying higher rate product.

(3) An eligible institution may choose to pay a rate equal to the greater of 0.65% or 65% (the "index") of the federal funds target rate (the "benchmark") as of the first business day of the IOLTA remitting period, which rate is deemed to be net of allowable reasonable fees, on an IOLTA checking account. The index and benchmark are determined periodically, but not more frequently than every six months, by the Foundation to reflect an overall comparable rate for the Texas IOLTA Program. When applicable, the Foundation will express its benchmark in relation to the Federal Funds Target Rate.

(4) A yield specified by the Foundation, if the Foundation so chooses, which is agreed to by the financial institution. The qualifying yield would be in effect for and remain unchanged during a period of no more than twelve months from the inception of the agreement between the financial institution and the Foundation.

(b) Nothing in this rule shall preclude an eligible institution from paying a higher interest rate or dividend than described above or electing to waive any fees and service charges on an IOLTA account.

(c) Interest and dividends shall be calculated in accordance with the eligible institution's standard practices for non-IOLTA customers.

(d) Allowable reasonable fees are the only fees and service charges that may be deducted by an eligible institution from interest earned on an IOLTA account. Allowable reasonable fees may be deducted from interest or dividends on an IOLTA account only at the rates and in accordance with the customary practices of the eligible institution for non-IOLTA customers. No fees or service charges other than allowable reasonable fees may be assessed against the accrued interest or dividends on an IOLTA account. Any fees and service charges other than allowable reasonable fees shall be the sole responsibility of, and may only be charged to, the attorney or law firm maintaining the IOLTA

Amended May 22, 1991, eff. Jan. 1, 1992; Nov. 22, 2004, eff. Nov. 30, 2004; Dec. 18, 2006, eff. March 1, 2007; Jan. 13, 2009, eff. Jan. 13, 2009.

Rule 8. Directions to the Eligible Institution

The eligible institution shall be directed by the attorney, law firm or professional corporation establishing the account:

(a) To remit, at least quarterly, interest earned on the average daily balance in the account net of allowable reasonable fees, if any, to the Foundation. "Allowable reasonable fees" for IOLTA accounts are per check charges, per deposit charges, a fee in lieu of a minimum balance, federal deposit insurance fees, sweep fees, and a reasonable IOLTA account administrative or maintenance fee. All other fees are the responsibility of, and may be charged to, the lawyer maintaining the IOLTA account. Fees or charges in excess of the interest or dividends earned on the account for any month or quarter shall not be deducted from interest or dividends earned on other IOLTA accounts or from the principal of the account.

(b) To transmit to the Foundation with each remittance a statement showing the name of the attorney, law firm or professional corporation with respect to which the remittance is sent, the rate or rates of interest attributable to each IOLTA account, the amount and type of fees and service charges deducted, if any, and the average account balance for the account during the period for which the report is made and such other information as is reasonably required by the Texas Access to Justice Foundation.

(c) To transmit to the depositing attorney, law firm or professional corporation at the same time a report is sent to the Foundation, a report in accordance with normal procedures for reporting to depositors.

Amended Nov. 22, 2004, eff. Nov. 30, 2004; renumbered from Rule 9 and amended Dec. 18, 2006, eff. March 1, 2007; amended Jan. 13, 2009, eff. Jan. 13, 2009.

Rule 9. Organizations Eligible for Grants

The Foundation shall make grants to organizations, not individuals. Prior to making its first grant of funds, the Board of Directors of the Foundation shall promulgate a policy, consistent with these Rules, which shall state the criteria to be met by an organization to qualify for a grant. Such criteria shall provide, among other criteria to be specified by the Board of Directors, that the organization must be exempt from taxation under Section 501 (c) (3) of the United States Internal Revenue Code, as amended, or corresponding provisions of any subsequent United States Internal Revenue law or laws, have as a primary purpose the delivery of legal services to low-income persons pursuant to income and type of case criteria acceptable to the Board of Directors, be current in all filings required to be made by it with any governmental authority, maintain open records and conduct open meetings (subject to reasonable limitations for an organization of its type), be an equal employment opportunity employer, and be able to demonstrate that it can utilize any funds granted to it in a manner consistent with these Rules and policies adopted by the Board of Directors of the Foundation. Nothing herein shall be deemed to impair any attorney-client relationship.

Renumbered from Rule 10 Dec. 18, 2006, eff. March 1, 2007; amended Jan. 13, 2009, eff. Jan. 13, 2009.

Rule 10. Persons Eligible to Benefit from Grants

Organizations receiving grants of funds from the Foundation shall use such funds to provide legal services to individual indigent persons or client groups, associations, and nonprofit organizations. Prior to the making of its first grant, and at least annually thereafter, the Board of Directors of the Foundation shall adopt criteria relating to income, assets and liabilities defining the indigent persons eligible to benefit from Foundation grants. In representing a client group, association, or nonprofit organization, the grantee must comply with all of the other provisions of these Rules and is subject to all of the prohibitions contained herein. A client group, association, or nonprofit organization is eligible if it is (1) primarily composed of individual indigent persons; or (2) the organization's primary purpose is in furtherance of the interests of indigent persons and is seeking legal assistance on a matter relating to such purpose.

Renumbered from Rule 11 and amended Dec. 18, 2006, eff. March 1, 2007; amended Jan. 13, 2009, eff. Jan. 13, 2009.

Rule 11. Criteria for Grants

Prior to making its first grant of funds, the Board of Directors of the Foundation shall promulgate a policy, consistent with these Rules, which shall state the criteria to be made for a grant from the Foundation. Such criteria shall provide, among other criteria to be specified by the Board of Directors, that the funds granted by the Foundation may not be used to duplicate a service already funded by another entity or in place of other funds available for the same purpose.

Amended May 22, 1991, eff. Jan. 1, 1992; renumbered from Rule 12 Dec. 18, 2006, eff. Mar. 1, 2007; amended Jan. 13, 2009, eff. Jan. 13, 2009.

Rule 12. Use of Funds Limited to Cases Which Cannot Generate Fees

Funds granted by the Foundation to organizations to provide legal services to the indigent in civil matters may not be used for any case or matter that, if undertaken on behalf of an indigent person by an attorney in private practice, might reasonably be expected to result in payment of a fee for legal services from an award to a client from public funds, or from the opposing party.

Renumbered from Rule 13 Dec. 18, 2006, eff. March 1, 2007; amended Jan. 13, 2009, eff. Jan. 13, 2009.

Rule 13. Exception to Rule 12

The provisions of Rule 12 shall not be applicable in any case where the organization receiving funds granted by the Foundation determines in good faith that the indigent person seeking legal assistance has made reasonable efforts to obtain the services of an attorney in private practice for the particular matter (including contacting attorneys in private practice in the county of residence of the indigent person who normally accept cases of a similar nature), and has been unable to obtain such services because the potential fee is inadequate, is likely to be uncollectible, would substantially consume any recovery by the client, or because of any other reason which the organization, acting in good faith, believes prevents the client from obtaining the services of a private attorney.

Renumbered from Rule 14 and amended Dec. 18, 2006, eff. March 1, 2007; amended Jan. 13, 2009, eff. Jan. 13, 2009.

Rule 14. Funding of Certain Suits and Activities Not Permitted

No funds shall be granted by the Foundation to directly fund class action suits, lawsuits against governmental entities, or lobbying for or against any candidate or issue. Provided, however, that funds may be granted to finance suits against governmental entities on behalf of individuals in order to secure entitlement to benefits such as, but not limited to, social security, aid to families with dependent children, food stamps, special education for the handicapped, Medicare, Medicaid, subsidized or public housing, or other economic, shelter or medical benefits provided directly to indigent individuals.

Renumbered from Rule 15 and amended Dec. 18, 2006, eff. March 1, 2007; amended Jan. 13, 2009, eff. Jan. 13, 2009.

Rule 15. Records and Reports of Grantees

The Foundation shall require, as a condition to the granting of funds to any organization or program, that adequate provision be made for reports to the Foundation as to the actual use of the funds so granted and for audit of such reports. Each such organization or program receiving funds from the Foundation shall keep its financial records in accordance with generally accepted accounting principles for organizations of its type and shall furnish reports to the Foundation in such form and containing such information as shall be reasonably requested pursuant to policies adopted by the Board of Directors of the Foundation.

Renumbered from Rule 16 Dec. 18, 2006, eff. March 1, 2007; amended Jan. 13, 2009, eff. Jan. 13, 2009.

Rule 16. Cessation of Funding

The Foundation may cease funding an organization which fails to act in accordance with the requirements of the Order of the Supreme Court of Texas creating the Program, these Rules or the policies adopted by the Board of Directors of the Foundation as provided in these Rules. The Board of Directors of the Foundation shall adopt appropriate procedures to be followed when it has been determined to cease funding an organization, including reasonable notice to the organization involved, an opportunity to correct any deficiency (if reasonably possible to do so) and a hearing before the Board of Directors.

Renumbered from Rule 17 Dec. 18, 2006, eff. March 1, 2007; amended Jan. 13, 2009, eff. Jan. 13, 2009.

Rule 17. Administrative Costs of Foundation

The foundation may expend funds for administrative costs of the Program, including any costs incurred after April 30, 1984, and may provide a reasonable reserve for administrative costs.

Renumbered from Rule 18 Dec. 18, 2006, eff. March 1, 2007; amended Jan. 13, 2009, eff. Jan. 13, 2009.

Rule 18. Records of the Foundation

The records of the Foundation, including applications for funds, whether or not granted, shall be open for public inspection at reasonable times and subject to reasonable restrictions dictated by the operational needs of the Foundation. The Foundation shall maintain its books of account in accordance with generally accepted accounting principles for organizations of its type and shall maintain written minutes of meetings of its Board of Directors and committees. It shall also maintain such other records as are within reasonable policies established by its Board of Directors.

Renumbered from Rule 19 Dec. 19, 2006, eff. March 1, 2007; amended Jan. 13, 2009, eff. Jan. 13, 2009.

Rule 19. Initial Distribution of Funds by the Foundation

The initial distribution of funds under the Program shall be made at a time when, in the determination of the Board of Directors of the Foundation, there are sufficient funds to provide an adequate distribution.

Renumbered from Rule 20 Dec. 18, 2006, eff. March 1, 2007; amended Jan. 13, 2009, eff. Jan. 13, 2009.

Rule 20. Other Interest–Bearing Accounts

Participating in the Program does not prohibit an attorney, law firm or professional corporation engaged in the practice of law from establishing one or more interest-bearing accounts or other investments permitted by the Texas Code of Professional Responsibility (Article X, Section 9, State Bar Rules) with the interest or dividends earned on the accounts or investments payable as directed by clients for whom funds are not deposited in accordance with these Rules.

Renumbered from Rule 21 Dec. 18, 2006, eff. March 1, 2007; amended Jan. 13, 2009, eff. Jan. 13, 2009.

Rule 21. Compliance With Code of Professional Responsibility

Neither the Foundation nor any organization or program to which it grants funds may take an action or require an attorney to take an action in violation of the Code of Professional Responsibility (Article X, Section 9, State Bar Rules) or in violation of any other code of professional responsibility adopted by the state for attorneys.

Renumbered from Rule 22 Dec. 18, 2006, eff. March 1, 2007; amended Jan. 13, 2009, eff. Jan. 13, 2009.

Rule 22. Attorney Liability

Nothing in these Rules affects the obligations of attorneys, law firms or professional corporations engaged in the practice of law with respect to client funds other than client funds reasonably determined to be "nominal in amount" or reasonably anticipated to be held for a "short period of time," as those terms are defined by these Rules. An attorney, law firm or professional corporation is not liable in determining which funds are nominal in amount or on deposit for a short period of time if the determination is made in good faith in accordance with these Rules.

Renumbered from Rule 23 Dec. 18, 2006, eff. March 1, 2007; amended Jan. 13, 2009, eff. Jan. 13, 2009.

Rule 23. Compliance

(a) On or after March 1 of each year, all attorneys licensed by the Supreme Court of Texas shall report IOLTA compliance in a manner to be prescribed by the Texas Equal Access to Justice Foundation and the State Bar of Texas. Such compliance statements may require such information as is deemed reasonably necessary by the Foundation and the State Bar of Texas.

(b) An annual compliance statement must be completed and returned to the Foundation by the date stated on the compliance statement. If the compliance statement is timely filed, indicating compliance, there will be no acknowledgement. The presumption of compliance after timely filing shall obtain, absent some evidence to the contrary.

(c) Should a compliance statement filed by an attorney fail to evidence compliance, the Foundation shall contact the attorney and attempt to resolve administratively the non-compliance.

(d) The Foundation shall furnish annually to the State Bar of Texas a list of all attorneys licensed by the Supreme Court of Texas (i) who have not timely filed a compliance statement or (ii) as to whom the Foundation has been unable administratively to resolve any impediment to the proper filing of a compliance statement. The State Bar of Texas shall send to each person so reported, by certified mail, return receipt requested, a non-compliance notice. Should the attorney fail or refuse to file the compliance statement within thirty (30) days of such notice, the State Bar of Texas shall so notify the Clerk of The Supreme Court of Texas, and the attorney shall be immediately suspended as an attorney licensed to practice law in the State of Texas until a compliance statement is filed.

Adopted Dec. 13, 1988, eff. July 1, 1989; amended May 22, 1991, eff. Jan. 1, 1992; Nov. 22, 2004, eff. Nov. 30, 2004; renumbered from Rule 24 and amended Dec. 18, 2006, eff. Mar. 1, 2007; amended Jan. 13, 2009, eff. Jan. 13, 2009.

Rule 24. Review and Appeal

(a) An attorney may file a written request based upon good cause for exemption from compliance with any of the requirements of these Rules, an extension of time for compliance, an extension of time to comply with a deficiency notice, or an extension of time to file an annual compliance statement. Such request shall be reviewed and determined by a Committee established by the State Bar or by such committee as the chairperson may, from time to time, designate. The attorney shall be promptly notified of the decision by the Committee.

(b) "Good cause" shall exist when an attorney is unable to comply with this Article because of extraordinary hardship or extenuating circumstances which were not willful on the part of the attorney and were beyond his or her control.

(c) Should the decision of the Committee be adverse to the attorney, the attorney may request the Board of Directors of the State Bar to review the decision by making such request in writing to the Executive Director of the State Bar within thirty days of notification of the decision of the Committee. The Chairman of the Board may appoint a committee of the Board to review the decision of the Committee and make a recommendation to the Board. The decision shall be made by the Board.

(d) Should the decision of the Board be adverse to the attorney, the attorney may appeal such decision by filing suit within thirty days of notification of the Board's action, failing which the decision of the Board shall be final. Such suit shall be brought against the State Bar, and shall be filed in a district court in Travis County, Texas. Trial shall be de novo, but the burden of proof shall be on the attorney appealing, the burden shall be by a preponderance of the evidence, and the attorney shall prove the existence of "good cause" as defined herein. The trial court shall proceed to hear and determine the issue without a jury. Either party shall have a right to appeal.

(e) Any suspension of an attorney shall be vacated during the administrative review process and while any suit filed is pending.

Adopted Dec. 13, 1988, eff. July 1, 1989; amended May 22, 1991, eff. Jan. 1, 1992; renumbered from Rule 25 and amended Dec. 18, 2006, eff. Mar. 1, 2007; amended Jan. 13, 2009, eff. Jan. 13, 2009.

Rule 25. Return to Former Status

Any attorney whose license to practice law has been suspended under the terms of these Rules who after the date of suspension files a report with the Foundation showing compliance shall be entitled to have such suspension promptly terminated and be returned to former status. Return to former status shall be retroactive to the inception of suspension, but shall not affect any proceeding for discipline of the member for professional misconduct. The State Bar shall promptly notify the Clerk that an attorney formerly suspended under these Rules has now complied with these Rules.

Adopted Dec. 13, 1988, eff. July 1, 1989; amended May 22, 1991, eff. Jan. 1, 1992; renumbered from Rule 26 and amended Dec. 18, 2006, eff. March 1, 2007; amended Jan. 13, 2009, eff. Jan. 13, 2009.

Rule 26. Confidentiality

The files, records, proceedings, as they relate to the compliance or noncompliance of any attorney with the requirements of these Rules, shall be confidential and shall not be disclosed except upon consent of the attorney affected or as directed in the course of judicial proceeding by a court of competent jurisdiction.

Adopted Dec. 13, 1988, eff. July 1, 1989; amended May 22, 1991, eff. Jan. 1, 1992; Renumbered from Rule 27 Dec. 18, 2006, eff. March 1, 2007; amended Jan. 13, 2009, eff. Jan. 13, 2009.

RULES GOVERNING ADMISSION TO THE BAR OF TEXAS

Effective June 30, 1992

Including Amendments Received Through February 1, 2016

Rule I. Definitions and General Provisions

(a) Frequently used terms are defined as follows:

(1) "Accredited" means that a law school is recognized as being qualified by the competent accrediting agency of a state or foreign jurisdiction, by a political subdivision of a state or foreign jurisdiction, or by another authorized body of a state or foreign jurisdiction.

(2) "Applicant" means a person who files with the Board any Application or Re-application to take the Texas Bar Examination, to be admitted without examination, or for Certification as a Foreign Legal Consultant.

(3) "Application" means an Application or Re-application to take the Texas Bar Examination, to be admitted without examination to the Texas Bar, or for Certification as a Foreign Legal Consultant.

(4) "Approved law school" means a law school approved by the American Bar Association.

(5) "Authorized to practice law" means that the Applicant has achieved the ability to engage in activities that would be recognized in the United States as the practice of law.

(6) "Board" means the Board of Law Examiners.

(7) "Chemical dependency" means substance abuse or dependency as defined by the American Psychiatric Association in the Diagnostic and Statistical Manual DSM–IV–TR and any subsequent revisions thereof.

(8) "Controlled substance" has the meaning assigned by Section 462.001, Health and Safety Code.

(9) "Declarant" means a person who files with the Board a Declaration of Intention to Study Law.

(10) "Declaration" means a Declaration of Intention to Study Law.

(11) "Practice of law" includes:

(A) private practice as a sole practitioner or for a law firm, legal services office, legal clinic, public agency, or similar entity;

(B) practice as an attorney for an individual or for a corporation, partnership, trust, or other entity with the primary duties of furnishing legal counsel and advice; drafting and interpreting legal documents and pleadings; interpreting and giving advice regarding the law; or preparing, trying, or presenting cases before courts, departments of government, or administrative agencies;

(C) practice as an attorney for a local government or the state or federal government, with the same primary duties described in the preceding subsection;

(D) employment as a judge, magistrate, referee, or similar official for a local government or the state or federal government, provided that the employment is open only to licensed attorneys;

(E) employment as a full-time teacher of law at an approved law school;

(F) any combination of the preceding categories.

(12) "State" means any state or territory of the United States, as well as the District of Columbia.

(13) "Supreme Court" means the Supreme Court of Texas.

(14) "Texas Bar Examination" means the full bar examination.

(15) "Treatment" has the meaning assigned by Section 462.001, Texas Health and Safety Code.

(16) "Treatment facility" has the meaning assigned by Section 462.001, Texas Health and Safety Code.

(b) The terms "admitted," "admitted to the Bar," "admitted to the Texas Bar," "licensed," and "licensed to practice law in Texas" are used interchangeably in these Rules.

(c) A document is considered filed when:

(1) the document and any required fee are submitted electronically through the Board's website; or

(2) the document and any required fee are received by the Board in accordance with the Board's written policies and instructions.

(d) A document submitted electronically is considered signed if the document includes:

(1) a name typed in the space where the signature would otherwise appear;

(2) an electronic or scanned image of the signature;

(3) a digital signature; or

(4) any other form of signature allowed by the Board's written policies and instructions.

(e) The Board must not disclose to any third party any information obtained with respect to the character or fitness of any Applicant, Declarant, or probationary licensee, except:

(1) upon written authority of the Applicant, Declarant, or probationary licensee;

(2) in response to a valid subpoena from a court of competent jurisdiction; or

(3) to the Office of the Chief Disciplinary Counsel of the State Bar of Texas or to the Texas Unauthorized Practice of Law Committee.

Adopted eff. June 30, 1992. Amended eff. June 3, 1998; July 8, 2003; Jan. 30, 2004; June 9, 2014, and Sept. 15, 2014, eff. Oct. 1, 2014; June 23, 2015.

Rule II. General Eligibility Requirements for Admission to the Texas Bar

(a) To be eligible for admission or reinstatement as a licensed attorney in Texas, an Applicant must:

(1) comply with all applicable requirements of these Rules;

(2) be at least 18 years of age;

(3) be of present good moral character and fitness;

(4) have completed the law study required under these Rules, unless specifically exempted under Rule XIII;

(5) qualify under one of the following categories:

(A) be a United States citizen;

(B) be a United States national;

(C) be an alien lawfully admitted for permanent residence;

(D) be otherwise authorized to work lawfully in the United States, including in a period of Optional Practical Training; or

(E) be an Applicant who does not reside in the United States when the Application is submitted;

(6) have satisfactorily completed the Texas Bar Examination, unless exempted from the Bar Examination under Rule XIII (but in no event shall an Applicant for reinstatement be so exempted);

(7) have satisfactorily completed the Multistate Professional Responsibility Examination;

(8) be willing to take the oath required of attorneys in Texas;

(9) pay the appropriate licensing fee to the Clerk of the Supreme Court of Texas; and

(10) enroll in the State Bar of Texas by filing an enrollment form and paying the appropriate fees and assessments due within the time specified in Article III, Sec. 2(A) of the State Bar Rules.

(b) If an Applicant has not satisfied all requirements for admission to the Texas Bar within two years from the date that the Applicant is notified that the Applicant has passed all parts of the Texas Bar Examination, the Applicant's examination scores shall be void; provided, however, that the Board may waive this provision for good cause shown.

Adopted eff. June 30, 1992. Amended eff. Feb. 1, 1994; Dec. 3, 1997; June 9, 2014, and Sept. 15, 2014, eff. Oct. 1, 2014.

Rule III. Law Study Requirement

(a) The law study requirement for eligibility of an Applicant to take the Texas Bar Examination, unless otherwise provided by these Rules, is met by:

(1) graduation with a J.D. degree or its equivalent from an approved law school;

(2) satisfaction of all requirements for graduation from an approved law school with a J.D. degree or its equivalent; or

(3) study of law in an approved law school or schools by satisfying all requirements for graduation with a J.D. degree or its equivalent, except for not more than four semester hours or its equivalent in quarter hours; provided, however, that no person shall be licensed to practice law until graduation or satisfaction of all requirements for graduation, unless specifically exempted hereunder. If an Applicant under this subsection has not graduated with a J.D. degree or satisfied all the requirements for graduation within two years from the date that all parts of the bar examination are satisfactorily completed, the Applicant's examination scores shall be void.

(b) If a law school was an approved law school when the Applicant enrolled, the law school is deemed to be an approved law school as to that Applicant for four years thereafter, regardless of its status when the Applicant graduated. If a law school was an approved law school when the Applicant graduated, the Applicant is deemed to be a graduate of an approved law school, regardless of the status of the school when the Applicant enrolled.

(c) If an Applicant graduated from a law school that was not an approved law school when the Applicant enrolled and was not an approved law school when the Applicant graduated, the Applicant is not a graduate of an approved law school even if the law school later became or becomes an approved law school.

Adopted eff. June 30, 1992. Amended eff. July 8, 2003; June 9, 2014, and Sept. 15, 2014, eff. Oct. 1, 2014

Rule IV. Good Moral Character and Fitness Requirement

(a) No one shall be eligible for admission to the Texas Bar or for certification as a Foreign Legal Consultant until the investigation of such person's moral character and fitness has been completed, and it has been determined by the Board that such individual possesses good moral character and fitness.

(b) Good moral character is a functional assessment of character and fitness of a prospective lawyer. The purpose of requiring an Applicant to possess present good moral character is to exclude from the practice of law those persons possessing character traits that are likely to result in injury to future clients, in the obstruction of the administration of justice, or in a violation of the Texas Disciplinary Rules of Professional Conduct. These character traits usually involve either dishonesty or lack of trustworthiness in carrying out responsibilities. There may be other character traits that are relevant in the admission process, but such traits must have a rational connection with the Applicant's present fitness or capacity to practice law and accordingly must relate to the legitimate interests of Texas in protecting prospective clients and in safeguarding the system of justice within Texas.

(c) Fitness, as used in these Rules, is the assessment of mental and emotional health as it affects the competence of a prospective lawyer. The purpose of requiring an Applicant to possess this fitness is to exclude from the practice of law any person having a mental or emotional illness or condition which would be likely to prevent the person from carrying out duties to clients, courts or the profession. A person may be of good moral character, but may be incapacitated from proper discharge of his or her duties as a lawyer by such illness or condition. The fitness required is a present fitness, and prior mental or emotional illness or conditions are relevant only so far as they indicate the existence of a present lack of fitness.

(d) The following provisions shall govern the determination of present good moral character and fitness of a Declarant or an Applicant who has been convicted of a felony in Texas or placed on probation for a felony with or without an adjudication of guilt in Texas, or who has been convicted or placed on probation with or without an adjudication of guilt in another jurisdiction for a crime which would be a felony in Texas. A Declarant or Applicant may be found lacking in present good moral character and fitness under this rule based on the underlying facts of a felony conviction or deferred adjudication, as well as based on the conviction or probation through deferred adjudication itself.

(1) The record of conviction or order of deferred adjudication is conclusive evidence of guilt.

(2) An individual guilty of a felony under this rule is conclusively deemed not to have present good moral character and fitness and shall not be permitted to file a Declaration of Intention to Study Law or an Application for a period of five years after the completion of the sentence and/or period of probation.

(3) Upon a credible showing that a felony conviction or felony probation, either with or without an adjudication of guilt, has been reversed on review by an appellate court, or that an executive pardon has been granted, the Declarant or Applicant shall be permitted to file a Declaration of Intention to Study Law or an Application.

(e) The following provisions shall govern the determination of present good moral character and fitness of a Declarant or Applicant who has been licensed to practice law in any jurisdiction and has been disciplined, or allowed to resign in lieu of discipline, in that jurisdiction.

(1) A certified copy of the order or judgment of discipline from the jurisdiction is prima facie evidence of the matters contained in such order or judgment, and a final adjudication in the other jurisdiction that the individual in question has committed professional misconduct is conclusive of the professional misconduct alleged in such order or judgment.

(2) An individual disciplined for professional misconduct in the course of practicing law in any jurisdiction or an individual who resigned in lieu of disciplinary action ("disciplined individual") is deemed not to have present good moral character and fitness and is therefore ineligible to file an Application for Admission to the Texas Bar during the period of such discipline imposed by such jurisdiction, and in the case of disbarment or resignation in lieu of disciplinary action, until the disciplined individual has properly filed an application for re–licensure in the disciplining jurisdiction, in accordance with the procedures established for re–licensure in that jurisdiction, and has obtained a final determination on that application.

Notwithstanding the foregoing provision of this subsection (e)(2) and except as provided in Rule IV(d)(2), if the period of discipline imposed by another jurisdiction exceeds five years, the disciplined individual may file an Application after the expiration of five years from the date of imposition of such discipline, provided that (s)he has obtained a final determination on his/her application for re–licensure in the disciplining jurisdiction.

(3) The only defenses available to an Applicant or Declarant under section (e) are outlined below and must be proved by clear and convincing evidence:

(A) The procedure followed in the disciplining jurisdiction was so lacking in notice or opportunity to be heard as to constitute a deprivation of due process.

(B) There was such an infirmity of proof establishing the misconduct in the other jurisdiction as to give rise to the clear conviction that the Board, consistent with its duty, should not accept as final the conclusion on the evidence reached in the disciplining jurisdiction.

(C) The deeming of lack of present good moral character and fitness by the Board during the period required under the provisions of section (e) would result in grave injustice.

(D) The misconduct for which the individual was disciplined does not constitute professional misconduct in Texas.

(4) If the Board determines that one or more of the foregoing defenses has been established, it shall render such orders as it deems necessary and appropriate.

(f) An individual who applies for admission to practice law in Texas or who files a petition for redetermination of present moral character and fitness after the expiration of the five-year period required under subsection (d)(2) above or after the completion of the disciplinary period assessed or ineligibility period imposed by any jurisdiction under subsection (e) above shall be required to prove, by a preponderance of the evidence:

(1) that the best interest of the public and the profession, as well as the ends of justice, would be served by his or her admission to practice law;

(2) that (s)he is of present good moral character and fitness; and

(3) that during the five years immediately preceding the present action, (s)he has been living a life of exemplary conduct.

(g) An individual who files a petition for redetermination of present moral character and fitness after a negative determination based on a felony conviction, felony probation with or without adjudication of guilt, or professional misconduct or resignation in lieu of disciplinary action and whose petition is denied after a hearing, is not eligible to file another petition for redetermination until after the expiration of three years from the date of the Board's order denying the preceding petition for redetermination.

Adopted eff. June 30, 1992. Amended eff. Feb. 1, 1994; Dec. 8, 1995; June 30, 2000; Sept. 9, 2002.

Rule V. Professional Responsibility Examination Requirement

No Applicant for admission to the Texas Bar shall be issued a license to practice law in Texas until such person has furnished to the Board evidence that (s)he has passed the Multistate Professional Responsibility Examination (MPRE) with a scaled score of 85.

Adopted eff. June 30, 1992. Amended eff. Feb. 1, 1994; Feb. 1, 2000; July 8, 2003.

Rule VI. Declaration of Intention to Study Law; General Provisions

(a) Every person who is beginning law study in an approved law school in Texas for the first time (an "entrant") and intends to apply for admission to the

Bar of Texas shall, unless prohibited from filing by these Rules, file with the Board a Declaration of Intention to Study Law, on a form promulgated by the Board.

(1) The Declaration shall show:

(A) the history, experience, and educational qualifications of the Declarant;

(B) the approved law school in which the Declarant is or was enrolled;

(C) the Declarant's criminal history;

(D) the Declarant's history of mental illness;

(E) the Declarant's history with regard to charges of fraud in any legal proceeding;

(F) the Declarant's involvement in any civil litigation or bankruptcy proceedings;

(G) the Declarant's willingness to take the oath required of attorneys in Texas;

(H) the Declarant's history as to compliance with court orders regarding child support and spousal support;

(I) the Declarant's history regarding re-payment of federally guaranteed student loans;

(J) the Declarant's history regarding the filing of required federal income tax returns and the payment of federal income tax liability;

(K) the Declarant's history regarding payment to the IRS of payroll taxes (s)he collected as an employer of others; and

(L) such other information regarding the Declarant as the Board deems reasonably related to its investigation of the Declarant's moral character and fitness.

(2) The Board may require the Declarant to provide, in addition, such supporting documents relating to the Declarant as the Board deems reasonable.

(3) The Board may also require the Declarant to execute a consent form supplied by the Board, authorizing all persons, firms, officers, corporations, associations, organizations, and institutions to furnish to the Board or any of its authorized representatives, all relevant documents, records, or other information pertaining to the Declarant.

(b) The timely filing deadline for such Declaration, for which no late fees shall be charged, shall be as follows:

Fall entrants, October 1;

Regular Spring entrants, May 1;

Spring entrants at quarter-hour law schools, June 1;

Summer entrants, September 15.

(c) Declarations filed with the Board after the timely filing deadline will be accepted with the payment of the applicable late fees as set forth in Rule XVIII, so long as they are filed by the absolute deadline set out in Rule IX(a)(3). However, regardless of the date a Declaration is filed, the Board shall have 270 days from the date the Declaration is filed to conduct its character and fitness investigation and notify the Declarant of the Board's determination, as provided in Rule VIII(a).

(d) Upon receipt of a Declaration, the Board shall note the filing date in its records. Absent a Declarant's written request to retain a Declaration, all Declarations will be destroyed five years after the date of filing if the Declarant has not activated his or her file by applying to take the Texas Bar Examination during that five year period.

(e) The Board shall conduct a complete investigation of the moral character and fitness of the Declarant.

Adopted eff. June 30, 1992. Amended eff. Feb. 1, 1994; Dec. 8, 1995; May 15, 1997; Oct. 15, 2003.

Rule VII. Repealed by Order of July 8, 2003, eff. Sept. 1, 2003

Rule VIII. Determination of Declarant Character and Fitness

(a) After completing its own investigation, the Board shall thereupon determine whether, on all the documentation before it at this stage, the Board is satisfied that the Declarant possesses the good moral character and fitness necessary for admission to the Texas Bar and shall advise the Declarant accordingly, no later than the 270th day after the date the Declaration and fees were filed with the Board. If the determination is that the Declarant does not have the requisite good character and fitness, such notice shall include:

(1) a detailed analysis of the results of the investigation; and

(2) an objective list of actions, if any, which the Declarant may take to correct the deficiencies and become qualified for admission to the bar after passing the Texas Bar Examination.

(b) A hearing may be set on any such preliminary negative determination, in accordance with the provisions of Rule XV.

(c) If the Board determines that a Declarant may suffer from chemical dependency, the Board shall direct the Declarant to meet with representatives of the Lawyers Assistance Program of the State Bar of

Texas or a similar program of the State Bar, and may require that the Declarant submit to a treatment facility for evaluation.

(d) If the Board determines that a Declarant does suffer from chemical dependency, the Board shall assist the Declarant in working with the Lawyers Assistance Program of the State Bar of Texas or a similar program of the State Bar in order to address the dependency.

(e) Any preliminary determination that the Declarant possesses the good moral character and fitness necessary for admission to the Texas Bar is issued on the condition that the Declarant has faithfully complied with these Rules. If at any time before the Declarant is certified to the Supreme Court for licensure it appears that the Declarant obtained such preliminary determination via fraud, concealment, deception, material omission, or by failure to comply with these Rules, the Board may suspend such preliminary determination and continue its investigation for an additional 90 days from the date the Board discovers the apparent fraud, concealment, deception, material omission, or failure to comply with these Rules.

Adopted eff. June 30, 1992. Amended eff. July 8, 2003; March 24, 2009.

Rule IX. Application to Take the Texas Bar Examination

(a) Every Applicant to take the Texas Bar Examination, whether or not such Applicant was required under Rule VI to file a Declaration, shall, unless prohibited from filing by these Rules, file an Application therefor with the Board as follows:

(1) For the February Examination, an Application shall be timely filed if the Board receives the required forms and fees between June 30 and August 30 of the year preceding the examination.

(2) For the July Examination, an Application shall be timely filed if the Board receives the required forms and fees between the preceding November 30 and January 30.

(3) Upon a showing of good cause or to prevent hardship, the Board may permit the Application to be filed later, upon the payment of applicable late fees as set forth in Rule XVIII. Other than as provided in subsection (f) of this Rule or Texas Government Code, Section 82.027, no Applicant shall be eligible to take an examination until such Application has been on file with the Board by the preceding October 30, for the February examination, or by March 30, for the July examination.

(b) The Application shall be made on a form furnished by the Board and calling for information reasonably related to a thorough inquiry into the Applicant's good moral character, fitness, legal education and other qualifications required in these Rules. Applicants who have filed a Declaration required under these Rules shall be required to complete the Application with information relating only to the period since the filing of the Declaration.

(c) The Board may require the filing of a Supplemental Investigation Form in situations deemed appropriate by the Board.

(d) The Applicant shall furnish proof satisfactory to the Board of compliance with the law study requirements of Rule III, and no Applicant shall be admitted to the examination until the Board has determined that these requirements have been met.

(e) Upon the filing of an Application, the Board shall note the filing date and shall initiate an investigation of the Applicant. For Applicants who filed a Declaration required under these Rules, the investigation shall cover only the period of time subsequent to the filing of the Declaration, unless other matters relevant to moral character or fitness not previously revealed in such Declaration shall have come to the attention of the Board.

(f) The filing deadlines and applicability of the late fees set out in subsection (a) of this rule shall not apply to Re–Applicants who failed the immediately preceding Texas Bar Examination and therefore could not have met the subsection (a) deadlines. Any such Re–applicant may take the next examination given upon filing a Re–application and paying the required fees by:

November 30, for the February Examination; or

May 30, for the July Examination.

Adopted eff. June 30, 1992. Amended eff. Feb. 1, 1994; Dec. 8, 1995; Feb. 26, 1998; June 30, 1999.

Rule X. Determination of Applicant Moral Character and Fitness

(a) After completing its investigation on the Application, the Board shall determine whether, on all the documentation before it, the Board is satisfied that the Applicant possesses the requisite present good moral character and fitness and shall advise the Applicant accordingly, no later than the 150th day after the date the Application or Re-Application and fees were filed with the Board. If the determination is that the Applicant does not have the requisite present good moral character and fitness, such notice shall include:

(1) a detailed analysis of the results of the investigation; and

(2) an objective list of actions, if any, which the Declarant[1] may take to correct the deficiencies and become qualified for admission to the bar after passing the bar examination.

(b) If, after investigation, the Board determines:

(1) that an Applicant may suffer from chemical dependency, the Board shall require the Applicant to submit to a treatment facility for evaluation;

(2) that an Applicant suffers from chemical dependency, the Board shall assist the Applicant in working with the Lawyers Assistance Program of the State Bar of Texas or a similar program of the State Bar.

(c) A hearing may be set on any such preliminary negative determination, in accordance with the provisions of Rule XV.

(d) Any preliminary determination that the Applicant possesses the requisite present good moral character and fitness is issued on the condition that the Applicant has faithfully complied with these Rules. If at any time before the Applicant is certified to the Supreme Court for licensure it appears that the Applicant obtained such preliminary determination via fraud, concealment, deception, material omission, or by failure to comply with these Rules, the Board may suspend such preliminary determination and continue its investigation for an additional 90 days from the date the Board discovers the apparent fraud, concealment, deception, material omission, or failure to comply with these Rules.

(e) The Applicant has a continuing duty to ensure the accuracy and completeness of the Applicant's responses on the Application and to update those responses until the Applicant is certified to the Supreme Court for licensure. The Applicant shall notify the Board, in writing, as soon as practicable, but no later than 30 days after the Applicant knew or should have known of any information necessary to ensure the accuracy and completeness of the Applicant's responses. The Applicant shall promptly furnish any additional documentation requested by the Board in connection therewith. The Board is authorized to reopen its investigation for up to 90 days following receipt of any addition, change, or update to information previously provided to the Board.

Adopted eff. June 30, 1992. Amended eff. Feb. 1, 1994; March 24, 2009.

[1] Probably should read "Applicant".

Rule XI. Texas Bar Examination

(a) The Supreme Court, by separate order, has established a list of the subjects for the Texas Bar Examination which shall be open to public inspection at all reasonable times.[1]

(b) The Texas Bar Examination shall be given at such places as the Board may direct.

(c) The Texas Bar Examination shall be given two times each year, beginning on the Tuesday before the last Wednesday of the months of February and July, unless the Board otherwise directs.

(d) The approved Applicants for an examination are required to be in attendance at the time and place designated by the Board.

(e) The Texas Bar Examination shall last two and one-half days and shall consist of the Multistate Performance Test (MPT), given on Tuesday morning; the Procedure and Evidence Questions (P&E), given on Tuesday morning; the Multistate Bar Examination (MBE), given on Wednesday; and the Texas Essay Questions (Essays), given on Thursday. After grading the answers to the MPT, the P&E, and the Essays, the resulting raw scores on each of these portions will be scaled to the Multistate Bar Examination, using the standard deviation method. Scores on the various portions of the examination will be weighted as follows: MPT, 10%; P&E, 10%; MBE, 40%; and Essays, 40%. Applicants who earn a combined scaled score of 675 (out of a possible 1000 points) shall pass the examination. A partial score on any portion of a failed examination shall not be applied to any subsequent examination.

(f) An Applicant may take no more than five (5) examinations. However, for good cause shown, the Board at its discretion may waive this limitation upon such conditions as the Board may prescribe.

(g) Any Applicant who has failed at least two Texas Bar Examinations may submit a written request, within two weeks of the release of the examination results, for a Formal Review of the Applicant's performance on the immediately preceding examination (excluding the multistate portion). Such Formal Review shall take place in Austin, Texas, at a time selected by the Board and shall consist of an individual oral review of such examination papers by the examining members of the Board. Regardless of the number of examinations taken, an Applicant may receive only one Formal Review under the provisions of this paragraph, provided, however, that no Applicant may obtain both a Formal Review and Informal Review of the same examination.

(h) Any Applicant who has failed the examination may submit a written request, within two weeks of the release of the examination results, for an Informal Review of the Applicant's performance on his/her failed parts of the immediately preceding examination (excluding the MBE multistate portion). The form of such Informal Review shall be either oral or written, at the discretion of the examining members of the Board. An Applicant may request an Informal Review each time (s)he fails an examination.

(i) The Board shall keep, for one year from the date of every examination, all failing examinations. The Board shall not be required to keep any part of passing examinations.

Adopted eff. June 30, 1992. Amended eff. Feb. 1, 1994; Dec. 8, 1995; Aug. 2, 1997; Dec. 21, 1998; Sept. 8, 1999; July 8, 2003, eff. July, 8, 2003; July 29, 2005, eff. July 29, 2005; Dec. 12, 2006, eff. Dec. 12, 2006; July 25, 2007, eff. Jan. 1, 2008.

1 A list of such subjects, established by the Supreme Court as of the time of publication, is included in Appendix A to these Rules. In the event the Court changes such list, the Board will provide a copy of the revised list upon request.

Rule XII. Examinees with Disabilities

(a) The Texas Bar Examination shall be administered to all eligible Applicants in a reasonable manner, while maintaining the integrity of the examination. In each city in which an examination is administered, the Board shall provide facilities that are reasonably accessible and which enable persons having disabilities to take the examination.

(b) Any Applicant who desires special testing accommodations based upon a disability shall submit a written request to the Board on forms designated by the Board, such request to be submitted at the same time as the Application is submitted.

(c) A request for special testing accommodations must be accompanied by written proof evidencing the existence of the disability. Statements from licensed physicians or a professional specialist that specifically set forth the physical, mental or emotional handicap or disability and the relationship between the disability and the inability to take the examination under standard conditions shall be required. The Board may require additional information or evidence from the Applicant and may, at its option, seek professional evaluation of such data. The Applicant will be responsible for the cost of obtaining documented medical evidence and other required information.

(d) After considering the written request of the Applicant and the evidence submitted, the Board shall determine what reasonable special testing accommodations will be granted.

(e) Board deliberations and determinations regarding the request of an applicant for testing accommodations on the Texas Bar Examination shall be closed to the public and associated records are confidential. However, this does not limit the Board's option under (c) above to seek professional evaluation of any confidential information supplied by applicants.

Adopted eff. June 30, 1992. Amended eff. Feb. 1, 1994; July 8, 2003.

Rule XIII. Applicants From Other Jurisdictions

§ 1 Exemption from the Bar Examination for Applicants Who Are Authorized to Practice Law in Another State

An Applicant who is authorized to practice law in another state must meet the requirements imposed on any other Applicant under these Rules, except that the Applicant is exempt from the requirement of successfully completing the Texas Bar Examination if the Applicant:

(a) has been actively and substantially engaged in the lawful practice of law as the Applicant's principal business or occupation for at least five of the last seven years immediately preceding the filing of the Application;

(b) has a J.D. degree from an approved law school; and

(c) has not failed the Texas Bar Examination.

§ 2 Exemption from the Law Study Requirement for Applicants Who Are Authorized to Practice Law in Another State

An Applicant who is authorized to practice law in another state is exempt from the law study requirement prescribed by Rule III if the Applicant:

(a) has been actively and substantially engaged in the lawful practice of law as the Applicant's principal business or occupation for at least three of the last five years immediately preceding the filing of the most recent Application; and

(b) either:

(1) holds a J.D. degree from an unapproved law school that is accredited in the state where it is located; or

(2) holds the equivalent of a J.D. degree from a law school that is accredited in the state where it is located and that requires a course of study that is substantially equivalent in duration and substance to the legal education provided by an approved law school.

§ 3 Exemption from the Law Study Requirement for Foreign Applicants With a Common–Law Legal Education or Who Are Authorized to Practice Law in a Common–Law Country

An Applicant is exempt from the law study requirement prescribed by Rule III if the Applicant satisfies the requirements of subsection (a), (b), or (c) below:

(a) the Applicant:

(1) has completed a course of study at a foreign law school that is accredited in the jurisdiction where it is located, and the course of study is:

(A) based on the principles of English common law; and

(B) substantially equivalent in duration to the legal education provided by an approved U.S. law school;

(2) is authorized to practice law in a foreign jurisdiction or another state; and

(3) has been actively and substantially engaged in the lawful practice of law for at least three of the last five years immediately preceding the Applicant's most recent Application;

(b) the Applicant:

(1) has completed a course of study at a foreign law school that is accredited in the jurisdiction where it is located, and the course of study is:

(A) based on the principles of English common law; and

(B) at least two years in duration; and

(2) has completed an LL.M. degree that meets the curricular requirements of Section 8 at an approved U.S. law school; or

(c) the Applicant:

(1) is authorized to practice law in a foreign jurisdiction, the jurisprudence of which is based on the principles of English common law; and

(2) has completed an LL.M. degree that meets the curricular requirements of Section 8 at an approved U.S. law school.

§ 4 Exemption from Law Study Requirement for Foreign Applicants Without a Common–Law Legal Education

An Applicant is exempt from the law study requirement prescribed by Rule III if the Applicant satisfies the requirements of subsections (a)–(c) below:

(a) the Applicant has completed a course of study at a foreign law school that is accredited in the jurisdiction where it is located, and the course of study is:

(1) not based on the principles of English common law; and

(2) substantially equivalent in duration to the legal education provided by an approved U.S. law school;

(b) the Applicant has completed an LL.M. degree that meets the curricular requirements of Section 8 at an approved U.S. law school; and

(c) the Applicant is authorized to practice law in a foreign jurisdiction or in another state.

§ 5 No Degree By Correspondence

A J.D. degree or an equivalent degree completed at a foreign law school that is earned primarily through online courses or other distance-learning mediums does not satisfy the requirements of this Rule.

§ 6 Transfer of Foreign Law School

An Applicant may be exempt from the law study requirement under Sections 3 or 4 even if the Applicant completed his or her course of study at a different foreign law school than the school at which the Applicant began, provided that all coursework and credit hours that count towards the applicable durational requirement are based on the same type of legal system—English common law or other—and are earned at a school accredited in the jurisdiction where it is located.

§ 7 Accreditation of Foreign Law Schools

(a) If a law school was accredited when the Applicant enrolled, the law school is deemed to be an accredited law school as to that Applicant for four years thereafter, regardless of its status at the date of the Applicant's graduation. If a law school was accredited when the Applicant graduated, the Applicant is deemed to be a graduate of an accredited law school, regardless of the status of the school when the Applicant enrolled.

(b) If an Applicant graduated from a law school that was not accredited when the Applicant enrolled and was not accredited when the Applicant graduated, the Applicant is not a graduate of an accredited law school even if the law school later became or becomes an accredited law school.

(c) Notwithstanding Sections 3 and 4, an Applicant is excused from demonstrating that a foreign law school is accredited if the Applicant demonstrates that no entity accredits or approves law schools in the jurisdiction in which the school is located.

§ 8 LL.M. Curricular Criteria

(a) Unless subsection (b) or (c) applies, for an LL.M. degree to satisfy the requirements of this Rule, the course of study for which the degree is awarded must meet each of the following requirements:

(1) the program must consist of a minimum of 24 semester hours of credit—or the equivalent, if the law school is on an academic schedule other than a conventional semester system—which must consist of courses in substantive and procedural law or professional skills;

(2) the program must require at least 700 minutes of instruction time, exclusive of examination time, for the granting of one semester of credit;

(3) the program must include a period of instruction consisting of no fewer than two semesters of at least 13 calendar weeks each, or the equivalent thereof, exclusive of reading periods, examinations, and breaks;

(4) the program must not be completed exclusively during summer semesters, but a maximum of four semester hours of credit may be earned in courses completed during summer semesters;

(5) the program must be completed within 24 months of matriculation;

(6) all coursework for the program must be completed at the campus of an approved law school in the United States, except as otherwise permitted by paragraph 8 or subsection (b);

(7) the program must include:

(A) at least two semester hours of credit in professional responsibility;

(B) at least two semester hours of credit in legal research, writing, and analysis, which may not be satisfied by a research-and-writing requirement in a substantive law course;

(C) at least two semester hours of credit in a course designed to introduce students to distinctive aspects and fundamental principles of United States law, which may be satisfied by an introductory course in the American legal system or a course in United States constitutional law, civil procedure, or contract law—additional credit hours earned in a course that meets the requirements of this subparagraph may be applied towards the requirements of subparagraph (D); and

(D) at least six semester hours of credit in subjects tested on the Texas Bar Examination;

(8) the program may also include, towards satisfaction of the 24 semester hours of credit required by this Rule:

(A) up to four semester hours of credit in clinical coursework, if:

(i) the coursework includes a classroom instructional component that incorporates discussion, review, and evaluation of the clinical experience;

(ii) the clinical work is performed under the direct supervision of a member of the law school faculty or instructional staff; and

(iii) the time and effort required and the anticipated educational benefit are commensurate with the credit awarded; and

(B) up to six semester hours of credit in other coursework related to the law or legal training taught in conjunction with a joint degree program by a member of the law school faculty, a faculty member of the university or college with which the law school is affiliated, or a faculty member of a university or college with which the law school offers a joint degree program—provided that the coursework is completed at the U.S. campus of the law school, university, or college; and

(9) courses completed online or by other distance-learning mediums must not count towards the required minimum 24 semester hours of credit.

(b) A law school may petition the Board for an exception to the requirements of subsection (a)(6). The law school must demonstrate to the satisfaction of the Board that the quality of education provided at the school's campus abroad is substantially equivalent to the quality of education provided at the school's U.S. campus.

(c) An Applicant who completed an LL.M. degree prior to, or within two years after, the effective date of this Rule is exempt from demonstrating that the degree meets the curricular requirements of subsection (a).

§ 9 Proof of Active and Substantial Engagement in the Practice of Law and Authorization to Practice Law in a Foreign Jurisdiction

(a) An Applicant who seeks exemption from the Texas Bar Examination or the law study requirement under a section of this Rule that requires a period of active and substantial engagement in the practice of law preceding the Application must furnish to the Board proof of active and substantial engagement in the practice of law. But this requirement may not be satisfied by proof of practice *pro hac vice* under Rule XIX.

(b) Unless subsection (c) or (d) applies, an Applicant who seeks exemption from the Texas Bar Examination or the law study requirement under a section of this Rule that requires that the Applicant be authorized to practice law in a foreign jurisdiction or another state must submit written proof of the authorization from the entity with final jurisdiction over professional discipline in the foreign jurisdiction or state where the

Applicant is authorized to practice. The document must certify:

(1) that the Applicant is authorized to practice law in the jurisdiction or state;

(2) the date that the Applicant became authorized to practice law in the jurisdiction or state; and

(3) that the Applicant remains in good standing as an attorney or counselor at law in the jurisdiction or state.

(c) The Board may waive the requirements of subsection (b) if an Applicant demonstrates good cause for failing to obtain the certificate required by that subsection.

(d) Proof of authorization to practice law may be satisfied by proof that the Applicant is lawfully engaged in the practice of law as an in-house counsel in a foreign jurisdiction that requires a person to surrender the person's law license in order to practice in-house.

Adopted eff. June 30, 1992. Amended eff. Feb. 1, 1994; Aug. 26, 1998; June 30, 1999, eff. Sept. 1, 1999; Sept. 7, 1999, eff. Dec. 31, 2000; April 24, 2002, eff. April 24, 2002; July 8, 2003, eff. July 8, 2005; Nov. 22, 2005, eff. Dec. 1, 2005; June 9, 2014, and Sept. 15, 2014, eff. Oct. 1, 2014.

Rule XIV. Foreign Legal Consultants

§ 1 General Requirements as to Certification

In its discretion, the Supreme Court may certify to practice in Texas as a legal consultant (a "Foreign Legal Consultant"), without examination, an Applicant who satisfies the requirements of subsection (a) or (b):

(a) the Applicant:

(1) for at least three of the five years immediately preceding the Application, has been a member in good standing of a recognized legal profession in a foreign country, the members of which are authorized to practice as attorneys or counselors at law or the equivalent and are subject to effective regulation and discipline by a duly constituted professional body or a public authority;

(2) possesses the good moral character and general fitness requisite for a member of the Texas Bar;

(3) is at least 26 years of age; and

(4) intends to practice as a Foreign Legal Consultant in Texas and to maintain an office in Texas for that purpose; or

(b) the Applicant:

(1) for at least three of the five years immediately preceding the Application:

(A) has been authorized to practice law in a foreign jurisdiction;

(B) has been a member in good standing of the bar of another state; or

(C) has been actively and substantially engaged in the lawful practice of law in a foreign country or another United States jurisdiction;

(2) possesses the good moral character and general fitness requisite for a member of the Texas Bar;

(3) is at least 26 years of age; and

(4) intends to practice as a Foreign Legal Consultant in Texas only as an in-house counsel on behalf of an individual, corporation, limited liability company, partnership, association, nonprofit entity, or governmental agency whose primary business is not the provision of legal services to the public.

§ 2 Application for Certification

An Applicant under this Rule must submit to the Board:

(a) an Application, on the form designated by the Board, that is signed by both the Applicant and a sponsoring member of the Texas Bar who is in good standing and has been a member of the Texas Bar for at least five years;

(b) the fee required by Rule XVIII(a);

(c) either:

(1) a certificate or other document from the entity with final jurisdiction over professional discipline in the foreign jurisdiction or state where the Applicant is authorized to practice that certifies:

(A) that the Applicant is authorized to practice law in the jurisdiction or state;

(B) the date that the Applicant was authorized to practice law in the jurisdiction or state; and

(C) that the Applicant remains in good standing as an attorney or counselor at law in the jurisdiction or state; or

(2) if the Applicant seeks certification under Section 1(b)(1)(C) of this Rule, but the Applicant is not authorized to practice in a foreign jurisdiction or another state, proof that the Applicant has been actively and substantially engaged in the lawful practice of law in a foreign jurisdiction or another state for at least three of the five years immediately preceding the Application;

(d) a duly authenticated English translation of every document required by this Rule, if the original is not in English; and

(e) any other evidence demonstrating that the Applicant satisfies the requirements of Section 1 of this Rule that the Board may require.

Upon completion of the Board's review of the information submitted by the Applicant and its investigation of the Applicant's qualifications, moral character, and fitness, if the Board determines that Applicant has satisfied the requirements of Sections 1 and 2 of this Rule, the Board must recommend to the Court the certification of the Applicant to practice in Texas as a Foreign Legal Consultant.

§ 3 Scope of Practice

A person certified to practice as a Foreign Legal Consultant under this Rule may render legal services in Texas in the manner and to the extent permitted by the jurisdiction in which the person is authorized to practice or, in the case of a person who satisfies the requirements of Section 1(b)(1)(C) of this rule, to the extent permitted by the jurisdiction in which the person has been actively and substantially engaged in the lawful practice of law. But the Foreign Legal Consultant must not:

(a) appear for a person other than himself or herself as an attorney in any court, or before any magistrate or other judicial officer, in Texas;

(b) prepare any instrument effecting the transfer or registration of title to real estate located in the United States of America;

(c) prepare:

(1) any will or trust instrument effecting the disposition on death of any property located in the United States of America and owned by a resident thereof; or

(2) any instrument relating to the administration of a decedent's estate in the United States of America;

(d) prepare any instrument in respect of the marital or parental relations, rights, or duties of a resident of the United States of America, or the custody or care of the children of such a resident;

(e) render professional legal advice on the law of Texas or of the United States (unless the person is licensed in another state), except:

(1) on the basis of advice from a person, whom the Foreign Legal Consultant has identified to the client, who:

(A) is authorized to practice law in Texas or in the United States; and

(B) either:

(i) serves as co-counsel with the Foreign Legal Consultant on a matter for the client; or

(ii) is affiliated with the Foreign Legal Consultant through employment, partnership, or membership in the same law firm, company, or governmental agency; or

(2) as an in-house counsel advising the Foreign Legal Consultant's employer in the scope of his or her employment;

(f) in any way hold himself or herself out as a member of the Bar of Texas; or

(g) carry on his or her practice under, or utilize in connection with such practice, any name, title, or designation other than one or more of the following:

(1) his or her own name;

(2) the name of the law firm with which he or she is affiliated;

(3) his or her authorized title in the foreign country in which he or she is authorized to practice, which may be used in conjunction with the name of such country; and

(4) the title "Foreign Legal Consultant," which may be used in conjunction with the words "authorized to the practice of law in [name of the foreign country in which he or she is authorized to practice]."

§ 4 Rights and Obligations

Subject to the limitations set forth in Section 3 of this Rule, a person certified as a Foreign Legal Consultant under this Rule is considered to be a lawyer affiliated with the Bar of Texas and is entitled and subject to:

(a) the rights and obligations of a member of the Texas Bar that are set forth in the State Bar Act, the State Bar Rules, and the Texas Disciplinary Rules of Professional Conduct or that arise from the other conditions and requirements that apply to a member of the Bar of Texas under the Texas Disciplinary Rules of Professional Conduct; and

(b) the rights and obligations of a member of the Bar of Texas with respect to:

(1) affiliation in the same law firm with one or more members of the Bar of Texas, including by:

(A) employing one or more members of the Bar of Texas;

(B) being employed by one or more members of the Bar of Texas or by any partnership or professional corporation that includes members of the Bar of Texas or that maintains an office in Texas; and

(C) being a partner in any partnership or a shareholder in any professional corporation that includes members of the Bar of Texas or that maintains an office in Texas; and

(2) attorney–client privilege, work-product privilege, and similar professional privileges.

A person certified as a Foreign Legal Consultant under this Rule is not a "nonlawyer" as that term is used in Rule 5.03 or Rule 5.04 of the Texas Disciplinary Rules of Professional Conduct.

A person who receives legal advice from a Foreign Legal Consultant is entitled to all privileges arising from the attorney-client relationship.

§ 5 Disciplinary Provisions

(a) Every person certified to practice as a Foreign Legal Consultant under this Rule is subject to censure, suspension, removal, or revocation of his or her certification to practice by the Supreme Court.

(b) Every Foreign Legal Consultant must execute and file with the Board, in such form and manner as the Board may prescribe:

(1) a written commitment

(A) to observe the State Bar Act, the State Bar Rules, and the Texas Disciplinary Rules of Professional Conduct, to the extent that the Act and the Rules are applicable to the legal services authorized under Section 3 of this Rule; and

(B) to notify the Board of any change in the person's good standing as a member of a foreign legal profession and of any final disciplinary action of the professional body or public authority that regulates attorneys in the foreign jurisdiction in which the Foreign Legal Consultant is authorized to practice law; and

(2) a notarized document that sets forth the person's address in Texas and designates the Executive Director of the Board as the person's agent for service of process in any action or proceeding brought against the person that arises from legal services rendered or offered to be rendered by the person within or to residents of Texas, whenever after due diligence service cannot be made on the person at the address on file with the Board.

(c) Service of process on the Executive Director of the Board under subsection (b)(2) must be made by personally delivering to, and leaving with, the Executive Director, or another person at the office of the Board who is authorized to receive service, two copies of the citation and petition and a fee of $10. The Board must promptly send one copy to the Foreign Legal Consultant by certified mail, return receipt requested, at the address designated by the Foreign Legal Consultant under subsection (b)(2).

§ 6 Renewal of Certification

(a) Unless revoked by the Board under Section 7 of this Rule, a certification to practice as a Foreign Legal Consultant is valid for one year.

(b) A Foreign Legal Consultant may renew his or her certification by submitting to the Board at least 60 days before the certification expires:

(1) a written request for renewal of the certification;

(2) the renewal fee required by Rule XVIII(a);

(3) proof that the Applicant completed three hours of minimum continuing legal education in ethics courses accredited by the State Bar of Texas; and

(4) a written statement, signed by the Applicant under oath, that the Applicant complied with the terms of the certificate and this Rule during the certification period.

(c) The Board must grant the Applicant's request unless it determines that the Applicant is not entitled to renew his or her certification under this Rule.

(d) If the renewal application is timely submitted, the Board must notify the Applicant of the Board's decision before the Applicant's certification expires. If the renewal application is not timely submitted, the Applicant, upon a showing of good cause, may submit a renewal application up to 180 days after the Applicant's certification expires. After the 180–day grace period has passed, an Applicant must reapply for certification under Section 2 of this Rule.

§ 7 Revocation of Certification

If the Board determines that a person certified as a Foreign Legal Consultant under this Rule no longer meets the requirements for certification set forth in Section 1, the Board must recommend to the Court that the person's certification be revoked, unless the Board waives under Rule XX(e) the requirements that are lacking.

§ 8 Admission to Bar

If a person certified as a Foreign Legal Consultant under this Rule is subsequently admitted to the Texas Bar under other provisions of these Rules, the certification to practice as a Foreign Legal Consultant is superseded by the license to practice law as a person admitted to the Texas Bar.

Adopted eff. June 30, 1992. Amended eff. Feb. 1, 1994; Nov. 22, 2005, eff. Dec. 1, 2005; June 9, 2014, and Sept. 15, 2014, eff. Oct. 1, 2014.

Rule XV. Hearings

(a) The Board shall set a time and place for a hearing on the question of the requisite moral character and fitness of an Applicant or Declarant, under the following circumstances:

(1) When any Applicant or Declarant who is the subject of a preliminary negative character and fitness determination files a written request for such a hearing within thirty (30) days of his or her receipt of the Board's letter containing the notice of such determination; or

(2) When the Board determines that, in the interest of fairness, such a hearing is necessary regardless of whether the Applicant or Declarant files a timely request for hearing.

(b) If there are pending proceedings involving the Applicant or Declarant, the resolution of which could impact the determination of his/her character and fitness, the Board may exercise its discretion to defer the hearing until such time as the pending proceeding is resolved.

(c) Board hearings, deliberations, and determinations relating to the moral character and fitness of an Applicant or Declarant shall be closed to the public and records relating to these subjects are confidential. On written request of an Applicant or Declarant, however, the Applicant or Declarant is entitled to have the hearing open to persons designated by the Applicant or Declarant.

(d) The Applicant or Declarant shall be given reasonable notice, by registered or certified mail, return receipt requested, of the time and place of the hearing.

(e) An Applicant or Declarant, either before or after receiving notice of a hearing, may agree to waive the hearing, stipulate to the facts regarding good moral character and fitness, and allow the Board to proceed with making a final determination as to the Applicant's moral character and fitness under these Rules. An Applicant may additionally agree to a Probationary License and to any conditions imposed by the Board to protect the public.

(f) At the hearing:

(1) The Board or any opponent of approval of the moral character and fitness of the Applicant or Declarant, shall have the burden of proof and be required to present evidence that the Applicant or Declarant does not have the requisite good moral character or fitness. Upon the admission of such evidence, the burden of proof shall shift to the Applicant or Declarant to show that the Applicant possesses good moral character and fitness as defined in these Rules. However, in a redetermination hearing on a Probationary License, the burden of proof shall be on the Probationary Licensee to demonstrate that (s)he has complied with the conditions of the Probationary License.

(2) The Applicant or Declarant shall be given the opportunity to be present in person and by attorney, to present evidence, to confront and to cross-examine adverse witnesses, and to present argument to the Board on the issues of law and fact; provided, however, that evidence otherwise inadmissible may be admitted if the evidence is of a type on which a reasonably prudent person commonly relies in the conduct of the person's affairs.

(3) Evidence and argument for or against the Applicant or Declarant may be presented by the Board or any other interested party.

(g) In connection with hearings conducted under this Rule, the Board shall have the authority to administer oaths, issue subpoenas, take depositions, and employ court reporters.

(h) After the hearing, in closed deliberations, the Board may:

(1) determine that an Applicant or Declarant has the requisite present good moral character and fitness and, in the case of an Applicant, should be recommended for admission to the Texas Bar;

(2) determine that a Declarant should be granted conditional approval of his or her present good moral character and fitness and be required to meet such conditions as the Board deems appropriate;

(3) determine that an Applicant should be granted conditional approval of his or her present good moral character and fitness and be recommended for a Probationary License subject to the terms of Rule XVI, after meeting all other requirements of these Rules;

(4) determine that an Applicant or Declarant does not possess the requisite present good moral character and fitness required for admission to the Texas Bar;

(5) defer a decision until such time as the Board has the opportunity to consider further information, evaluations, or documentation as deemed necessary by the Board;

(6) in the case of either a temporary or probationary license, recommend to the Supreme Court that the license should be renewed in its present form, renewed with additional or amended conditions, or revoked and no regular license be issued.

(i) Within a reasonable period of time after the decision is made, the Board shall furnish to the Applicant or Declarant a written order setting forth the decision of the Board. If the decision is adverse, such order shall specify the bases of the Board's determination and shall include an objective list of actions, if any, the Applicant or Declarant may take to become qualified for a license to practice law in Texas. Any such order containing a determination that the Applicant or Declarant suffers from chemical dependency shall include provisions setting out the rights under Section 82.038, Texas Government Code.

(j) An individual who has been the subject of a Board order containing a negative character and fitness determination may petition the Board in writing for a redetermination hearing subject to the provisions of Rule XV herein on the issue of character and fitness, as follows:

(1) No petition for redetermination may be filed earlier than the date specified in the Board's order (or if none, then no earlier than twelve months from the date of the hearing), nor more often than once every twelve months.

(2) Such individual shall have the burden of proof as to rehabilitation and the possession of present good moral character and fitness.

(3) Such individual shall complete and file with the Board a Supplemental Investigation Form and pay the requisite fees therefor within thirty (30) days of the filing of the redetermination petition.

(4) This subsection (j) shall not apply to character and fitness redeterminations in Probationary License cases, which are governed under the provisions of Rule XVI.

(k) The following provisions shall govern judicial review of the Board's decisions:

(1) The affected Applicant or Declarant shall institute, in the district courts of Travis County, Texas proceedings for review of such decision within sixty (60) days after the date the written decision is mailed to the Applicant.

(2) The petition for review shall name the Board as defendant and shall be served on the Executive Director of the Board.

(3) After service of such petition, and within the time permitted for filing an answer, the Board shall file with the district court a certified copy of the record of the Board's proceedings.

(4) The review of the Board's decision shall be tried by the court without a jury.

(5) The court shall determine from the certified record on file whether or not the Board's decision is reasonably supported by substantial evidence. The reviewing court may affirm the action complained of or remand the matter to the Board for further proceedings.

(6) Appeals from any final judgment of the court may be taken by either party in the manner provided for in civil actions generally, but no appeal bond shall be required of the Board.

(l) The Board shall have the authority to adopt such other rules of procedure for hearings, not inconsistent with these Rules, as the Board deems necessary or appropriate to implement these Rules.

(m) The Board may assess costs against any Applicant or Declarant who has been sent reasonable notice of a hearing before the Board and who does not appear.

Adopted eff. June 30, 1992. Amended eff. Feb. 1, 1994; June 14, 1995; Dec. 8, 1995; July 8, 2003.

Rule XVI. Probationary Licenses

(a) The Board shall have the authority to grant conditional approval of the present good moral character and fitness of an Applicant and to recommend the granting of a Probationary License, after the Applicant meets all other requirements under these Rules, in the following circumstances:

(1) when the Board determines that the Applicant suffers from chemical dependency or has been convicted of, or is on probation for, a first offense of driving while intoxicated under Article 67011–1, V.T.C.A.; *or

(2) in other circumstances in which, on the record before it, the Board determines that the protection of the public requires the temporary monitoring of the Applicant in question.

(b) The Board shall not have the authority to refuse to recommend the granting of a Probationary License to an Applicant who has passed the applicable bar examination solely because the Applicant suffers from chemical dependency or has been convicted for a first offense for driving while intoxicated under Article 67011–1, V.T.C.A.

(c) In any order recommending the issuance of a Probationary License to practice law, the Board shall specify the conditions of the license, which may include, but are not limited to, the following:

(1) prohibiting the use of alcohol or controlled substances;

(2) requiring treatment for chemical dependency;

(3) requiring the individual to practice law under the supervision of an attorney admitted to the Texas Bar;

(4) requiring submission to periodic, random drug testing;

(5) requiring the individual to report periodically to the Board;

(6) requiring suspension, for any portion of the probationary period, of an activity for which a license to practice law is required;

(7) requiring the individual to reside continuously in Texas during the period of the Probationary License, unless for good cause shown, the Board waives such requirement; or

(8) requiring the individual to take specific actions designed to cure or end any deficiencies in his or her moral character and fitness, as determined by the Board.

(d) Probationary Licenses shall expire as follows:

(1) A Probationary License issued solely because of the Board's determination that the individual suffers from chemical dependency shall expire on the second anniversary of the date on which it is issued, unless temporarily extended hereunder.

(2) Any other Probationary License shall expire on the date specified by the Board in the Order recommending issuance of the Probationary License, unless temporarily extended hereunder.

(3) The term of a Probationary License may be temporarily extended, upon the request of the Probationary Licensee, in the event that the normal expiration date falls before the Board has had the opportunity to make a redetermination as provided hereunder.

(e) A Probationary Licensee may apply for a renewal of the Probationary License or for a regular license to practice law, by filing a written request and a Supplemental Investigation Form and the requisite fees, at least sixty (60) days prior to the expiration date of the Probationary License.

(f) The Board shall require any Probationary Licensee issued a Probationary License because of a determination of chemical dependency, prior to the redetermination hearing, to submit to an evaluation, at the sole cost of the Probationary Licensee, by a treatment facility approved by the Board.

(g) After a hearing held subject to the provisions of Rule XV herein on the redetermination of the character and fitness of a Probationary Licensee, the Board may:

(1) recommend, upon a finding of the requisite good moral character and fitness, the issuance of a regular license to practice law in Texas; provided, however, that in any case in which a Probationary License was issued on the basis of chemical dependency, the Board shall not recommend the Probationary Licensee for regular admission until the Board finds that the Probationary Licensee has successfully completed treatment and has been free from chemical dependency for the preceding two years;

(2) recommend, upon a finding that a condition of the Probationary License has been violated:

(A) extension of the Probationary License, or

(B) termination or immediate revocation of the Probationary License.

(h) The Board shall initiate and maintain a working relationship with the Lawyers' Assistance Program or similar program of the State Bar of Texas in order to provide for the evaluation and referral to treatment for those persons issued a Probationary License hereunder. The treatment and professional evaluation shall be at the sole expense of the Probationary Licensee.

(i) The Board shall initiate and maintain a working relationship with the State Bar of Texas to coordinate disclosure of information concerning an individual's status as a Probationary Licensee. On request, the Board, in coordination with the State Bar of Texas, shall inform a member of the public whether a particular individual is a Probationary Licensee. This disclosure may occur via the official website of the State Bar of Texas or other means reasonably available to members of the public. Any information that forms the basis for the issuance of the Probationary License is confidential, as required by statute.

(j) A person whose Probationary License has been terminated or revoked upon recommendation by the Board must begin the licensure process anew in accordance with the Board order recommending such termination or revocation if the person wishes to attempt re-licensure.

Adopted eff. June 30, 1992. Amended eff. June 30, 1999; Feb. 7, 2003; Dec. 12, 2011, , eff. Jan. 1, 2012.

*

Publisher's Note: Vernon's Ann.Civ.St. art. 6701*l*–1 has been repealed.

Rule XVII. Issuance of License Certificates and Cancellation of License Unlawfully Obtained

(a) Upon an Applicant's becoming entitled to a license under these Rules, the Board must certify the Applicant to the Supreme Court, whose Clerk will issue the corresponding license in the form of a written certificate. The license may be issued only in the name shown on a valid, government-issued identification card, except that a given name may be omitted or represented by an initial if the Applicant so requests in writing. No license may be issued using an alias, assumed name, nickname, or abbreviation of a name.

(b) All law licenses are issued on the condition that the Applicant has faithfully complied with these Rules. If at any time it appears that an Applicant has obtained a license fraudulently or by willful failure to comply with these Rules, after notice and a hearing, the Board may recommend to the Supreme Court that the license be withdrawn and canceled, and the name of the license holder stricken from the roll of attorneys.

(c) No license issued under this Rule is valid unless the license holder has paid the required fees and has enrolled in the State Bar of Texas in compliance with the State Bar Rules.

(d) The license certificate belongs to the Supreme Court of Texas and must be surrendered to the Court upon proper demand.

Adopted eff. June 30, 1992. Amended eff. Feb. 1, 1994; June 9, 2014, and Sept. 15, 2014, eff. Oct. 1, 2014.

Rule XVIII. Fees

(a) The following provisions shall govern the fees charged by the Board:

FEES RELATING TO DECLARATIONS

Declaration Investigation Fee	$150
Fingerprint Card Processing Fee	40
	$190
Late Filing Fee	$150
Fee for Check Returned for Insufficient Funds	$ 25

FEES RELATING TO ELIGIBILITY & EXAMINATIONS

Texas Law Student:

$ 150	Application Fee
95	Examination Fee
75	Investigation Fee
$ 320	

Out-of-State Law Student:

$ 150	Application Fee
40	Fingerprint Card Processing Fee
95	Examination Fee
150	Investigation Fee
$ 435	

Attorneys Licensed in Another State:

$ 700	Application Fee
40	Fingerprint Card Processing Fee
150	Examination Fee
150	Investigation Fee
$ 1,040	

Attorneys Qualified for Admission Without Examination Under Rule XIII:

$ 700	Application Fee
40	Fingerprint Card Processing Fee
150	Investigation Fee
$ 890	

Foreign Nation Attorney—Texas Bar Exam Application Only:

$ 700	Application Fee
40	Fingerprint Card Processing Fee
150	Examination Fee
150	Investigation Fee
100	Foreign Nation Inquiry Fee
$ 1,140	

Foreign Nation Attorney—Concurrent Texas Bar Exam and Foreign Legal Consultant Applications:

$ 700	Application Fee
150	Foreign Legal Consultant Supplemental Investigation Fee
40	Fingerprint Card Processing Fee
150	Examination Fee
150	Investigation Fee
100	Foreign Nation Inquiry Fee
$ 1,290	

Re-application for Examination

$ 150	Re-application Fee
95	Examination Fee
75	Investigation Fee on Re–Application
$ 320	

Foreign Legal Consultant Application Only:

$ 700	Application Fee
40	Fingerprint Card Processing Fee
150	Investigation Fee
100	Foreign Nation Inquiry Fee
$ 990	

Foreign Legal Consultant Re–Application Fee:

$ 150	Re–Application Fee
150	Supplemental Investigation Fee (every second renewal year only)
$ 300	($ 150 in alternate years)

Supplemental Investigation (S.I.) Fee (as required under Rule IX)	$ 150
Fingerprint Card Processing Fee	$ 40
	$ 190
Military Attorney Application Fee (as required under Rule XXII)	$ 25
Military Attorney Renewal Application Fee	$ 25

(as required under Rule XXII)

MISCELLANEOUS FEES

Late Filing Fee	$150
Fee for Check Returned for Insufficient Funds	$ 25
MBE Transfer Fee	$ 25
Application Deposit Fee [1]	$ 30
Incompleteness Fee [2]	$ 75
Laptop Examination Fee	$ 50

(b) No refund or transfer of fees will be made in the event of the withdrawal of any Declaration or Application, nor in the event a determination is made by the Board that the Applicant or Declarant does not meet the requirements imposed under these Rules.

(c) Any fee required under these Rules may be waived or lowered by the Board upon written request and proof of indigence.

Adopted eff. June 30, 1992. Amended eff. Aug. 26, 1998; June 30, 1999, eff. Sept. 1, 1999; July 8, 2003; Oct. 13, 2010, eff. Oct. 15, 2010; Dec. 12, 2011, eff. Dec. 12, 2011.

1 One deposit fee shall be credited toward the filing fee if the application is filed within 1 year of date the deposit is received.

2 This fee shall be imposed when a document (declaration, application, S.I., etc.) is received, for the second and subsequent times, which is determined to be incomplete (e.g., unanswered questions, not signed, not notarized, incorrect fees, etc.).

Rule XIX. Requirements for Participation in Texas Proceedings by a Non–Resident Attorney

(a) A reputable attorney, licensed in another state or in a foreign jurisdiction but not in Texas, who resides outside of Texas may seek permission to participate in the proceedings of any particular cause in a Texas court by complying with the requirements of Texas Government Code Section 82.0361 concerning payment of a non-resident attorney fee to the Board of Law Examiners as a mandatory initial requirement. Upon completion of this requirement and receipt of an acknowledgment issued by the Board of Law Examiners, the non-resident attorney shall file with the applicable Texas court a written, sworn motion requesting permission to participate in a particular cause. The motion shall contain:

(1) the office address, telephone number, fax number, and email address of the non-resident attorney movant;

(2) the name and State Bar card number of an attorney licensed in Texas with whom the non-resident attorney will be associated in the Texas proceedings and that attorney's office address, telephone number, fax number, and email address;

(3) a list of all cases and causes, including cause number and caption, in Texas courts in which the non-resident attorney has appeared or sought leave to appear or participate within the past two years;

(4) a list of jurisdictions in which the non-resident attorney is licensed, including federal courts, and a statement that the non-resident attorney is or is not an active member in good standing in each of those jurisdictions;

(5) a statement that the non-resident attorney has or has not been the subject of disciplinary action by the Bar or courts of any jurisdiction in which the attorney is licensed within the preceding five years, and a description of any such disciplinary actions;

(6) a statement that the non-resident attorney has or has not been denied admission to the courts of any State or to any federal court during the preceding five years;

(7) a statement that the non-resident attorney is familiar with the State Bar Act, the State Bar Rules, and the Texas Disciplinary Rules of Professional Conduct governing the conduct of members of the State Bar of Texas, and will at all times abide by and comply with the same so long as such Texas proceeding is pending and said Applicant has not withdrawn as counsel therein.

(b) The motion of the non-resident attorney seeking permission to participate in Texas proceedings must be accompanied by motion of the resident practicing Texas attorney with whom the non-resident attorney will be associated in the proceeding of a particular cause. The motion must contain a statement that the resident attorney finds the Applicant to be a reputable attorney and recommends that the Applicant be granted permission to participate in the particular proceeding before the court.

(c) The motion of the non-resident attorney must also be accompanied by the proof of payment or proof of indigency acknowledgment issued by the Board of Law Examiners.

(d) The court may examine the non-resident attorney to determine that the non-resident attorney is aware of and will observe the ethical standards required of attorneys licensed in Texas and to determine whether the non-resident attorney is appearing in courts in Texas on a frequent basis. If the court determines that the non-resident attorney is not a reputable attorney who will observe the ethical standards required of Texas attorneys, that the non-resident attorney has been appearing in courts in Texas on a frequent basis, that the non-resident attorney has been engaging in the unauthorized practice of law in the state of Texas, or that other good cause exists, the court or hearing officer may deny the motion.

(e) If, after being granted permission to participate in the proceedings of any particular cause in Texas, the non-resident attorney engages in professional misconduct as that term is defined by the State Bar Act, the State Bar Rules, or the Texas Disciplinary Rules of Professional Conduct, the court may revoke the non-resident attorney's permission to participate in the Texas proceedings and may cite the non-resident attorney for contempt. In addition, the court may refer the matter to the Grievance Committee of the Bar District in which the court is located.

(f) The filing of a motion under this Rule constitutes submission to the jurisdiction of the Grievance Committee for the District in which the court is located. The county in which the court is located is considered the county of residence of the non-resident attorney for purposes of determining venue in any disciplinary action involving the attorney.

Adopted eff. June 30, 1992. Amended eff. Oct. 15, 2003; June 9, 2014, and Sept. 15, 2014, eff. Oct. 1, 2014.

Rule XX. Organizational and Miscellaneous Powers of the Board

(a) Upon completion of the tabulation of grades given on an examination and approval of such tabulation by the Chairman, the grades shall be mailed to the examinees at the addresses given on their Applications. The Deans of the Law Schools in the State of Texas shall be furnished a list of the candidates passing the Bar examination after release of results to the individual candidates. Prior to mailing grades to examinees, no grades shall be given by the Board by telephone to any person nor shall any Board member or employee of the Board give grades in person to an examinee or anyone inquiring on behalf of an examinee.

(b) Unless the Court designates the member of the Board who shall serve as Chairman, the Board shall have authority to select a Chairman. The Board shall select other officers from its own membership, assign their respective duties, may delegate power and authority to one or more of its members, and shall have authority to formulate the procedure of the Board.

(c) The Board shall keep and maintain its files on Declarants and Applicants until such time as their destruction is authorized, as follows:

(1) Files in which a regular license has been issued shall be destroyed five (5) years from the date the license was issued.

(2) Files in which a Probationary License has been issued but no Regular License has been issued shall be destroyed ten (10) years from the date of the last formal activity on the file (i.e., petition for redetermination, hearing, order, expiration of last term of Probationary License, issuance of regular license following redetermination hearing, etc.).

(3) Files in which a Declaration, but not an Application, has been filed shall be destroyed five (5) years from the date the Declaration was filed.

(4) Files in which an Application has been filed, but no Regular or Probationary License issued, shall be destroyed five (5) years from the date of the last formal activity on the file (i.e., Re-Application, examination, hearing, petition for redetermination, etc.), after inputting into the Board's computer data base pertinent and necessary data contained therein.

(d) Insofar as may be consistent with these Rules, the Board is authorized to make all reasonable regulations, including written interpretations of general Application with respect to these Rules or provisions of general Application for relevant subjects not covered by these Rules. The Board may also prescribe forms and certificates to be executed by Applicants for admission to the Texas Bar, whether for a first license to practice law or as a practicing attorney of another jurisdiction, or certificates or other forms to be executed by or on behalf of the Board itself.

(e) The Board is given discretion in the interpretation and Application of these Rules. For good cause shown to the satisfaction of the Board, upon written request, waivers of specific requirements described in these Rules may be granted, unless it appears therefrom that no exceptions are contemplated by the Supreme Court.

(f) The Board may, in conjunction with its investigation of moral character and fitness or the administration of the bar examination, require Declarants and Applicants to furnish a complete set of fingerprints.

(g) The Board may delegate its duties to a panel of the Board or to the staff, as necessary and where not prohibited by law; provided, however, that the Board shall not delegate to staff its authority to make final determinations that an Applicant or Declarant lacks the requisite good moral character and fitness.

(h) The Supreme Court hereby creates the Board of Law Examiners Fund which shall be comprised of all fees and monies received and interest earned by the Board and shall be used by the Board to administer the functions of the Supreme Court and the Board relating to the licensing of lawyers as directed by the Court. The Fund shall be maintained in one or more financial institutions in Texas, as designated by the Board.

(i) The Board shall have full power to contract for the performance of all of its functions, and any person dealing or contracting with the Board shall be conclusively entitled to rely upon the Board's written determination that the expense thus incurred or contracted is for a proper function of the Board.

(j) The disbursement of funds shall be according to such rules, regulations and budgets as the Board may adopt. The Board shall keep a full record of such receipts and disbursements.

Adopted eff. June 30, 1992. Amended eff. Feb. 1, 1994.

Rule XXI. Civil Immunity

Without limiting, restricting, or waiving any privilege or immunity otherwise available under state or federal law:

(a) The Board and its members, employees, and agents are immune from all civil liability for damages for conduct and communications occurring in the performance of and within the scope of their official duties relating to the character and fitness qualification, eligibility, examination, monitoring, and licensing of Declarants, Applicants, and Probationary Licensees.

(b) Records, statements of opinion, and other information regarding a Declarant, Applicant, or Probationary Licensee communicated without malice to the Board or to its members, employees, or agents by any person, entity, firm, or institution are privileged, and civil suits for damages predicated thereon are barred.

Adopted eff. Aug. 26, 1998.

Rule XXII. Registration Program for Military Attorneys on Military Assignment in Texas but not Licensed in Texas

§ 1 General Requirements for Registration and Limited Permission to Practice Law

Upon the Board's approval, a military attorney who is admitted to practice law in a state other than Texas or in a territory of the United States or the District of Columbia., and who is a full-time, active-duty military officer serving in the office of a Staff Judge Advocate of the United States Air Force, Army, Navy, Marines, or Coast Guard, a Naval Legal Service Office, or a Trial Service Office, located in Texas, may appear as an attorney and practice law before the courts and other tribunals of Texas in any civil proceeding, subject to the conditions and limitations in this rule and applicable law. This rule does not preclude a nonresident military attorney's request under Rule XIX to participate in the proceedings of a particular cause in a Texas court.

§ 2 Specific Requirements

The military attorney must be of good moral character and apply for registration annually by:

(a) filing an application and paying fees in the form and manner that the Board prescribes;

(b) presenting satisfactory proof of admission to practice law and current good standing as a member of the bar in any state or territory of the United States or the District of Columbia:

(c) complying with the training requirements in this rule; and

(d) furnishing any additional information or proof that the Board requires in the course of processing the application.

§ 3 Training

Permission to practice law under this rule requires that the military attorney complete at least 15 credit hours of Accredited Continuing Legal Education (CLE) Activity, including a minimum of three hours of legal ethics or professional responsibility, within the first year of registration. The minimum of three hours of legal ethics or professional responsibility must also be completed within each subsequent year of registration. As used in this rule, the term Accredited CLE Activity has the meaning ascribed to it in Article XII of the State Bar Rules.

§ 4 No State Bar of Texas Membership or Texas Law License Granted

Military attorneys permitted to practice law under this rule are not, and shall not represent themselves to be, members of the State Bar of Texas or licensed to practice law in the State of Texas.

§ 5 Termination

The military attorney's privilege to practice law under this rule may be terminated by the Board at any time, with or without cause. In addition, the military attorney's privileges under this rule shall be terminated when the military attorney ends full-time, active-duty military service as described in section 1 of this rule. The military attorney registered under this rule or the military attorney's supervisory Staff Judge Advocate or other supervisory military attorney shall:

(a) advise the Board as soon as practicable of any change in the military attorney's status that may affect the military attorney's right to practice law under this rule;

(b) immediately notify each court or tribunal in which the military attorney is involved in a pending civil proceeding when the military attorney is unable to continue to serve as counsel under this rule; and

(c) immediately obtain substitution of counsel when the military attorney involved in any pending civil proceeding is unable to continue to serve as counsel under this rule.

§ 6 Subject Matter Jurisdiction, Authorized Clients, and Pleading Requirements

A military attorney granted limited permission to practice law under this rule may, with approval of the military attorney's supervisory Staff Judge Advocate or other supervisory military attorney, represent:

(a) enlisted military personnel in grades E–1 through E–4; and

(b) immediate family members who qualify under armed services regulations as dependents of enlisted military personnel in grades E–1 through E–4 if the military attorney's supervisory Staff Judge Advocate or other supervisory military attorney determines that retaining civilian legal counsel for the matter in controversy would present a substantial financial hardship for the family member involved.

A military attorney granted limited permission to practice law under this rule may represent other military personnel, as well as their immediate family members who qualify under armed services regulations as their dependents, only if the military attorney receives written approval from the Judge Advocate General of the Army, Navy, Coast Guard, or Air Force, or the Staff Judge Advocate to the Commandant of the Marine Corps, as appropriate. The written authorization must include a determination that retaining civilian legal counsel for the matter in controversy would present a substantial financial hardship for the service member or family member involved.

A military attorney granted limited permission to practice law under this rule may not demand or receive any compensation, beyond the military attorney's regular pay and allowances, for the legal services provided under this rule.

The practice of a military attorney under this rule shall be subject to the limitations and restrictions of 10 U.S.C. § 1044 and the regulations of that attorney's military service and shall be further limited to:

(a) cases arising under all Titles, except Title 3, of the Family Code:

(b) guardianships;

(c) landlord-tenant disputes on behalf of tenants;

(d) consumer-law cases on behalf of consumers:

(e) garnishment defenses:

(f) estate planning and probate matters:

(g) enforcement of rights under the Servicemembers Civil Relief Act:

(h) enforcement of rights under the Uniformed Services Employment and Reemployment Rights Act; and

(i) other cases within the discretion of the court or tribunal before which the civil proceeding is pending, provided that written permission of the court or tribunal is obtained in advance of the appearance.

All pleadings filed in a civil proceeding by a military attorney under this rule shall state that limited permission to practice in Texas has been obtained under this rule; include the name, complete address, and telephone number of the military legal office of the military attorney representing the client and of the military attorney's supervisory Staff Judge Advocate or other supervisory military attorney: and include the name, grade, and armed service of the military attorney who is registered under this rule and providing representation. Upon making an appearance in a civil proceeding, the military attorney shall file a document with the court or other tribunal in which the civil proceeding is pending, designating each individual authorized to accept service of process on the military attorney's behalf and providing the name and complete address of each authorized individual. If the military attorney does not file this document, the military attorney's agent for service of process shall be the supervisory Staff Judge Advocate or supervisory military attorney whose name appears on the military attorney's most recent application filed pursuant to this rule, or the successor to that office.

§ 7 Discipline

A military attorney granted limited permission to practice law in Texas under this rule is subject to the Rules Governing Admission to the Bar of Texas, the Texas Disciplinary Rules of Professional Conduct, the Texas Rules of Disciplinary Procedure, and any other rules and laws governing the discipline of attorneys admitted to the State Bar of Texas. The State Bar of Texas, Supreme Court of Texas, and other Texas courts have jurisdiction over the discipline of the military attorney, regardless of whether the military attorney retains the right to practice in the state, for the military attorney's professional conduct while practicing in this state. This jurisdiction includes, but is not limited to, the authority — concurrent with the Board's authority under section 5 of this rule — to terminate the military attorney's privilege to practice law in Texas under this rule.

Adopted by order of Oct. 15, 2010, eff. Oct. 15, 2010.

Appendix

TEXAS BAR EXAMINATION SUBJECTS

MULTISTATE SUBJECTS

- Constitutional Law
- Contracts
- Criminal Law
- Evidence
- Real Property
- Torts

MULTISTATE PERFORMANCE TEST

The Texas Bar Examination includes the Multistate Performance Test (MPT), a skills test designed to assess the examinee's ability to use fundamental lawyering skills in a realistic situation. ,During the test, each examinee will receive a "file" of source documents and a "library" of cases, statutes, and rules. Using these materials, the examinee will be required to perform an assigned lawyering task, such as writing a memorandum to a supervising attorney, a letter to a client, a contract provision, a proposal for settlement, or a closing argument. Contact the National Conference of Bar Examiners for sample MPT exams. The NCBE website is www.ncbex.org or reach the agency by telephone at 608-280-8550.

TEXAS ESSAY SUBJECTS

- Business associations, including agency, corporations, partnerships, limited liability companies and professional associations
- Trusts and guardianships
- Wills and administration
- Family law
- Uniform Commercial Code
- Consumer rights, including DTPA and insurance
- Real property, including oil and gas

CROSS–OVER TOPICS

- Income, estate, and gift taxes issues, to be included where appropriate, as an element of questions in other subjects, such as family law, oil and gas, wills, etc.
- Bankruptcy, to be included where appropriate, as an element of questions in other subjects, such as family law, wills and estates, real property, etc.

PROCEDURE AND EVIDENCE SUBJECTS

- Texas civil procedure and evidence, including jurisdiction
- Federal and Texas criminal procedure and evidence

Adopted eff. June 30, 1992; Amended eff. Feb. 1, 1994; Oct. 12, 1995, eff. with the July 1999 examination.

RULES AND REGULATIONS GOVERNING THE PARTICIPATION OF QUALIFIED LAW STUDENTS AND QUALIFIED UNLICENSED LAW SCHOOL GRADUATES IN THE TRIAL OF CASES IN TEXAS

Approved December 11, 1978

Including Amendments Received Through February 1, 2016

Rule I. Purpose

These rules are promulgated pursuant to House Bill 424 of the 64th Legislature (Acts 1975, 64th Leg., Ch. 56, p. 120) amending Acts 1971, 62nd Leg., Ch. 706, p. 2336, for the purpose of governing the participation of qualified law students and qualified unlicensed law school graduates in the trial of cases in Texas. These rules are promulgated in response by the Bench and Bar of the State of Texas to the responsibility to provide competent legal services for all persons, and to furnish practical training to qualified law students and to qualified unlicensed law school graduates.

Approved Dec. 11, 1978.

Rule II. Qualified Law Students and Qualified Unlicensed Law School Graduates

A. In order to perform those activities outlined in Paragraph IV, below, a person:

(1) shall be a qualified law student enrolled in a law school approved by the Supreme Court of Texas, except that he is not required to be enrolled during a summer term or when his school is not in session, or;

(2) shall be a qualified unlicensed law school graduate as hereinafter defined;

B. A qualified law student must be certified by the dean of his law school as having satisfactorily completed:

(1) not less than two-thirds (⅔) of the required curriculum for graduation as computed on an hourly basis and not be on scholastic probation, or;

(2) not less than one-half (½) of the required curriculum for graduation computed on an hourly basis if the student is enrolled in a clinical legal education course for which course credit is awarded, and not be on scholastic probation.

C. A qualified unlicensed law school graduate must be certified by the dean of his law school to be a graduate of an approved law school. He may begin or continue supervised student practice as herein provided during the interim between graduation and the first offering of the state bar examination after graduation from law school and during that period after he has taken the state bar examination for the first time, but has not received the results of that examination.

D. The qualified law student or the qualified unlicensed law school graduate shall:

(1) Be certified by the dean of his law school that the dean has no knowledge of any fact or facts which preclude the student from meeting the qualifications to take the state bar examination;

(2) Certify in writing:

(a) That he has read and is familiar with the Texas Code of Professional Responsibility, and

(b) That he will abide by the Texas Code of Professional Responsibility in activities permitted by these rules, and

(c) That he subjects himself to the grievance procedures of the State Bar of Texas.

Approved Dec. 11, 1978.

Rule III. Certification

The dean of each law school shall maintain on file a record of the certification of each participating qualified law student and qualified unlicensed law school graduate, and shall file their names with the General Counsel of the State Bar of Texas. The dean shall terminate certification when conditions of Section II are not maintained. In addition, the dean may terminate certification at any time without prior notice or hearing and without any showing of cause. The dean shall notify the qualified law student or the qualified unlicensed law school graduate, the supervising lawyer, and the General Counsel of the State Bar in writing of any such termination of certification.

Approved Dec. 11, 1978.

Rule IV. Activities

A. Subject to the approval of the presiding judge or presiding administrative officer, as the case may be, a qualified law student, or a qualified unlicensed law school graduate may appear in any court or before any administrative tribunal in this state on behalf of the State of Texas or any other party consenting thereto, subject to the following conditions:

(1) The qualified law student or the qualified unlicensed law school graduate must be accompanied at his appearance in the following matters by a supervising attorney, qualified under Section V herein, who is duly licensed to practice law in the State of Texas:

(a) Appearance for the purposes of trial of civil or criminal matters;

(b) The arguing of motions;

(c) The taking of depositions;

(d) The conduct of any hearing or trial before any administrative tribunal or in any court.

(2) The qualified law student or the qualified unlicensed law school graduate need not be accompanied by the supervising lawyer in any other matters assigned to him by the supervising attorney. Nothing herein shall be construed as regulating or attempting to regulate the use of law clerks by attorneys in any and all matters generally considered to be the office practice of law.

(3) All pleadings filed in any matter in which the qualified law student or the qualified unlicensed law school graduate is working shall be signed by the supervising attorney.

B. [Pub. Note: There is no paragraph B.]

Approved Dec. 11, 1978.

Rule V. Supervision

A. Except as otherwise provided herein, a lawyer who is supervising a qualified law student or qualified unlicensed law school graduate shall:

(1) Be a lawyer licensed by the Supreme Court of Texas for a minimum of three (3) years;

(2) Be registered in accordance with the provisions of Section VI hereof;

(3) Assume personal professional responsibility for the direct and immediate supervision for the professional work of the qualified law student or qualified unlicensed law school graduate;

(4) Maintain professional malpractice and errors and omissions insurance covering the supervised qualified law student and/or qualified unlicensed law school graduate, unless the lawyer is supervising the student or the graduate in the lawyer's official capacity as a public prosecutor or assistant public prosecutor or is a lawyer otherwise protected by governmental immunity.

(5) Supervise not more than four (4) persons qualified herein simultaneously;

(6) Demonstrate to the satisfaction of the General Counsel of the State Bar of Texas, by his personal affidavit or upon the certification of local bar officials, that he is skilled in the preparation and trial of cases.

B. A lawyer supervising a qualified law student in connection with a clinical legal education program for which the student earns law school course credit, or, a qualified unlicensed law school graduate in connection with matters commenced while the graduate was enrolled in a clinical legal education program for which he earned law school course credit, shall:

(1) Be a lawyer licensed by the Supreme Court of Texas;

(2) Be registered in accordance with the provisions of Section VI hereof;

(3) Assume personal professional responsibility for the direct and immediate supervision for the professional work of the qualified law student or qualified unlicensed law school graduate.

(4) Maintain professional malpractice and errors and omissions insurance covering the supervised qualified law student and/or qualified unlicensed law school graduate, unless the lawyer is supervising the student or the graduate in the lawyer's official capaci-

ty as a public prosecutor or is a lawyer otherwise protected by governmental immunity.

(5) Be approved in writing by the dean of the law school sponsoring the clinical program as a clinical supervisor under whose supervision qualified law students are allowed to receive credit for satisfactory completion of the established course and clinical practice requirements.

Approved Dec. 11, 1978.

Rule VI. Registration

A. The General Counsel of the State Bar of Texas shall register lawyers who meet the requirements of these rules and are certified by local bar officials as qualified ethically, morally, professionally, and financially to direct and supervise qualified law students and qualified unlicensed law school graduates and give practical training in the trial of cases.

B. Nothing herein shall be construed to effectively require any applicant supervising attorney to become a member of any local bar without his consent.

C. The General Counsel of the State Bar of Texas shall immediately revoke the registration of any supervising lawyer against whom any disciplinary action is pending before any grievance committee or court, or who has ceased to meet the requirements of Section VI.A. herein.

Approved Dec. 11, 1978.

Rule VII. Grievance

In the event a grievance is filed in a case in which a qualified law student or a qualified unlicensed law school graduate has participated under these rules, the chairman of the grievance committee with whom such grievance is filed shall immediately report the same to the dean of the student's law school, the supervising attorney, and the General Counsel of the State Bar of Texas.

Approved Dec. 11, 1978.

Rule VIII. Compensation

A qualified law student or a qualified unlicensed law school graduate shall not charge a client for his services or claim or receive a percentage fee, contingency fee, or origination fee; however, nothing in these rules is intended to prevent the qualified law student or qualified unlicensed law school graduate from being paid for his services by his supervising lawyer, or to prevent a supervising lawyer from charging a fee for the services rendered under his supervision.

Approved Dec. 11, 1978.

Rule IX. Miscellaneous

A. Nothing contained in these rules affects the right of any person who is not admitted to practice law to do anything that he might lawfully do prior to the adoption of these rules.

B. The rules of law and evidence relating to privileged communications between attorney and client shall govern communications made or received by qualified law students or by qualified unlicensed law school graduates certified under the provisions of these rules.

Approved Dec. 11, 1978.

CODE OF JUDICIAL CONDUCT

Revised Effective March 1, 1994

Including Amendments Received Through February 1, 2016

Preamble

Our legal system is based on the principle that an independent, fair and competent judiciary will interpret and apply the laws that govern us. The role of the judiciary is central to American concepts of justice and the rule of law. Intrinsic to all sections of this Code of Judicial Conduct are the precepts that judges, individually and collectively, must respect and honor the judicial office as a public trust and strive to enhance and maintain confidence in our legal system. The judge is an arbiter of facts and law for the resolution of disputes and a highly visible symbol of government under the rule of law.

The Code of Judicial Conduct is not intended as an exhaustive guide for the conduct of judges. They should also be governed in their judicial and personal conduct by general ethical standards. The Code is intended, however, to state basic standards which should govern the conduct of all judges and to provide guidance to assist judges in establishing and maintaining high standards of judicial and personal conduct.

Added by orders of June 30, 1993, and Nov. 4, 1993, eff. March 1, 1994.

Canon 1. Upholding the Integrity and Independence of the Judiciary

An independent and honorable judiciary is indispensable to justice in our society. A judge should participate in establishing, maintaining, and enforcing high standards of conduct, and should personally observe those standards so that the integrity and independence of the judiciary is preserved. The provisions of this Code are to be construed and applied to further that objective.

Amended by orders of June 30, 1993, and Nov. 4, 1993, eff. March 1, 1994.

Canon 2. Avoiding Impropriety and the Appearance of Impropriety in All of the Judge's Activities

A. A judge shall comply with the law and should act at all times in a manner that promotes public confidence in the integrity and impartiality of the judiciary.

B. A judge shall not allow any relationship to influence judicial conduct or judgment. A judge shall not lend the prestige of judicial office to advance the private interests of the judge or others; nor shall a judge convey or permit others to convey the impression that they are in a special position to influence the judge. A judge shall not testify voluntarily as a character witness.

C. A judge shall not knowingly hold membership in any organization that practices discrimination prohibited by law.

Amended by orders of June 30, 1993, and Nov. 4, 1993, eff. March 1, 1994; order of March 1, 1996.

Canon 3. Performing the Duties of Judicial Office Impartially and Diligently

A. Judicial Duties in General.

The judicial duties of a judge take precedence over all the judge's other activities. Judicial duties include all the duties of the judge's office prescribed by law. In the performance of these duties, the following standards apply.

B. Adjudicative Responsibilities.

(1) A judge shall hear and decide matters assigned to the judge except those in which disqualification is required or recusal is appropriate.

(2) A judge should be faithful to the law and shall maintain professional competence in it. A judge shall not be swayed by partisan interests, public clamor, or fear of criticism.

(3) A judge shall require order and decorum in proceedings before the judge.

(4) A judge shall be patient, dignified and courteous to litigants, jurors, witnesses, lawyers and others with whom the judge deals in an official capacity, and should require similar conduct of lawyers, and of staff, court officials and others subject to the judge's direction and control.

(5) A judge shall perform judicial duties without bias or prejudice.

(6) A judge shall not, in the performance of judicial duties, by words or conduct manifest bias or prejudice, including but not limited to bias or prejudice based upon race, sex, religion, national origin, disability, age, sexual orientation or socioeconomic status, and shall not knowingly permit staff, court officials and others subject to the judge's direction and control to do so.

(7) A judge shall require lawyers in proceedings before the court to refrain from manifesting, by words or conduct, bias or prejudice based on race, sex, religion, national origin, disability, age, sexual orientation or socioeconomic status against parties, witnesses, counsel or others. This requirement does not preclude legitimate advocacy when any of these factors is an issue in the proceeding.

(8) A judge shall accord to every person who has a legal interest in a proceeding, or that person's lawyer, the right to be heard according to law. A judge shall not initiate, permit, or consider *ex parte* communications or other communications made to the judge outside the presence of the parties between the judge and a party, an attorney, a guardian or attorney ad litem, an alternative dispute resolution neutral, or any other court appointee concerning the merits of a pending or impending judicial proceeding. A judge shall require compliance with this subsection by court personnel subject to the judge's direction and control. This subsection does not prohibit:

(a) communications concerning uncontested administrative or uncontested procedural matters;

(b) conferring separately with the parties and/or their lawyers in an effort to mediate or settle matters, provided, however, that the judge shall first give notice to all parties and not thereafter hear any contested matters between the parties except with the consent of all parties;

(c) obtaining the advice of a disinterested expert on the law applicable to a proceeding before the judge if the judge gives notice to the parties of the person consulted and the substance of the advice, and affords the parties reasonable opportunity to respond;

(d) consulting with other judges or with court personnel;

(e) considering an *ex parte* communication expressly authorized by law.

(9) A judge should dispose of all judicial matters promptly, efficiently and fairly.

(10) A judge shall abstain from public comment about a pending or impending proceeding which may come before the judge's court in a manner which suggests to a reasonable person the judge's probable decision on any particular case. This prohibition applies to any candidate for judicial office, with respect to judicial proceedings pending or impending in the court on which the candidate would serve if elected. A judge shall require similar abstention on the part of court personnel subject to the judge's direction and control. This section does not prohibit judges from making public statements in the course of their official duties or from explaining for public information the procedures of the court. This section does not apply to proceedings in which the judge or judicial candidate is a litigant in a personal capacity.

(11) A judge shall not disclose or use, for any purpose unrelated to judicial duties, nonpublic information acquired in a judicial capacity. The discussions, votes, positions taken, and writings of appellate judges and court personnel about causes are confidences of the court and shall be revealed only through a court's judgment, a written opinion or in accordance with Supreme Court guidelines for a court approved history project.

C. Administrative Responsibilities.

(1) A judge should diligently and promptly discharge the judge's administrative responsibilities without bias or prejudice and maintain professional competence in judicial administration, and should cooperate with other judges and court officials in the administration of court business.

(2) A judge should require staff, court officials and others subject to the judge's direction and control to observe the standards of fidelity and diligence that apply to the judge and to refrain from manifesting bias or prejudice in the performance of their official duties.

(3) A judge with supervisory authority for the judicial performance of other judges should take reason-

able measures to assure the prompt disposition of matters before them and the proper performance of their other judicial responsibilities.

(4) A judge shall not make unnecessary appointments. A judge shall exercise the power of appointment impartially and on the basis of merit. A judge shall avoid nepotism and favoritism. A judge shall not approve compensation of appointees beyond the fair value of services rendered.

(5) A judge shall not fail to comply with Rule 12 of the Rules of Judicial Administration, knowing that the failure to comply is in violation of the rule.

D. Disciplinary Responsibilities.

(1) A judge who receives information clearly establishing that another judge has committed a violation of this Code should take appropriate action. A judge having knowledge that another judge has committed a violation of this Code that raises a substantial question as to the other judge's fitness for office shall inform the State Commission on Judicial Conduct or take other appropriate action.

(2) A judge who receives information clearly establishing that a lawyer has committed a violation of the Texas Disciplinary Rules of Professional Conduct should take appropriate action. A judge having knowledge that a lawyer has committed a violation of the Texas Disciplinary Rules of Professional Conduct that raises a substantial question as to the lawyer's honesty, trustworthiness or fitness as a lawyer in other respects shall inform the Office of the General Counsel of the State Bar of Texas or take other appropriate action.

Amended by orders of June 30, 1993, and Nov. 4, 1993, eff. March 1, 1994; order of March 24, 1999, eff. April 1, 1999; order of August 22, 2002.

Canon 4. Conducting the Judge's Extra-Judicial Activities to Minimize the Risk of Conflict With Judicial Obligations

A. Extra-Judicial Activities in General.

A judge shall conduct all of the judge's extra-judicial activities so that they do not:

(1) cast reasonable doubt on the judge's capacity to act impartially as a judge; or

(2) interfere with the proper performance of judicial duties.

B. Activities to Improve the Law.

A judge may:

(1) speak, write, lecture, teach and participate in extra-judicial activities concerning the law, the legal system, the administration of justice and non-legal subjects, subject to the requirements of this Code; and

(2) serve as a member, officer, or director of an organization or governmental agency devoted to the improvement of the law, the legal system, or the administration of justice. A judge may assist such an organization in raising funds and may participate in their management and investment, but should not personally participate in public fund raising activities. He or she may make recommendations to public and private fund-granting agencies on projects and programs concerning the law, the legal system, and the administration of justice.

C. Civic or Charitable Activities.

A judge may participate in civic and charitable activities that do not reflect adversely upon the judge's impartiality or interfere with the performance of judicial duties. A judge may serve as an officer, director, trustee, or non-legal advisor of an educational, religious, charitable, fraternal, or civic organization not conducted for the profit of its members, subject to the following limitations:

(1) A judge should not serve if it is likely that the organization will be engaged in proceedings that would ordinarily come before the judge or will be regularly or frequently engaged in adversary proceedings in any court.

(2) A judge shall not solicit funds for any educational, religious, charitable, fraternal or civic organization, but may be listed as an officer, director, delegate, or trustee of such an organization, and may be a speaker or a guest of honor at an organization's fund raising events.

(3) A judge should not give investment advice to such an organization, but may serve on its board of directors or trustees even though it has the responsibility for approving investment decisions.

D. Financial Activities.

(1) A judge shall refrain from financial and business dealings that tend to reflect adversely on the judge's impartiality, interfere with the proper performance of the judicial duties, exploit his or her judicial position, or involve the judge in frequent transactions with lawyers or persons likely to come before the court on which the judge serves. This limitation does not prohibit either a judge or candidate from soliciting funds for appropriate campaign or officeholder expenses as permitted by state law.

(2) Subject to the requirements of subsection (1), a judge may hold and manage investments, including real estate, and engage in other remunerative activity

including the operation of a business. A judge shall not be an officer, director or manager of a publicly owned business. For purposes of this Canon, a "publicly owned business" is a business having more than ten owners who are not related to the judge by consanguinity or affinity within the third degree of relationship.

(3) A judge should manage any investments and other economic interests to minimize the number of cases in which the judge is disqualified. As soon as the judge can do so without serious financial detriment, the judge should divest himself or herself of investments and other economic interests that might require frequent disqualification. A judge shall be informed about the judge's personal and fiduciary economic interests, and make a reasonable effort to be informed about the personal economic interests of any family member residing in the judge's household.

(4) Neither a judge nor a family member residing in the judge's household shall accept a gift, bequest, favor, or loan from anyone except as follows:

(a) a judge may accept a gift incident to a public testimonial to the judge; books and other resource materials supplied by publishers on a complimentary basis for official use; or an invitation to the judge and spouse to attend a bar-related function or activity devoted to the improvement of the law, the legal system, or the administration of justice;

(b) a judge or a family member residing in the judge's household may accept ordinary social hospitality; a gift, bequest, favor, or loan from a relative; a gift from a friend for a special occasion such as a wedding, engagement, anniversary, or birthday, if the gift is fairly commensurate with the occasion and the relationship; a loan from a lending institution in its regular course of business on the same terms generally available to persons who are not judges; or a scholarship or fellowship awarded on the same terms applied to other applicants;

(c) a judge or a family member residing in the judge's household may accept any other gift, bequest, favor, or loan only if the donor is not a party or person whose interests have come or are likely to come before the judge;

(d) a gift, award or benefit incident to the business, profession or other separate activity of a spouse or other family member residing in the judge's household, including gifts, awards and benefits for the use of both the spouse or other family member and the judge (as spouse or family member), provided the gift, award or benefit could not reasonably be perceived as intended to influence the judge in the performance of judicial duties.

E. Fiduciary Activities.

(1) A judge shall not serve as executor, administrator or other personal representative, trustee, guardian, attorney in fact or other fiduciary, except for the estate, trust or person of a member of the judge's family, and then only if such service will not interfere with the proper performance of judicial duties.

(2) A judge shall not serve as a fiduciary if it is likely that the judge as a fiduciary will be engaged in proceedings that would ordinarily come before the judge, or if the estate, trust, or ward becomes involved in adversary proceedings in the court on which the judge serves or one under its appellate jurisdiction.

(3) The same restrictions on financial activities that apply to a judge personally also apply to the judge while acting in a fiduciary capacity.

F. Service as Arbitrator or Mediator.

An active full-time judge shall not act as an arbitrator or mediator for compensation outside the judicial system, but a judge may encourage settlement in the performance of official duties.

G. Practice of Law.

A judge shall not practice law except as permitted by statute or this Code. Notwithstanding this prohibition, a judge may act pro se and may, without compensation, give legal advice to and draft or review documents for a member of the judge's family.

H. Extra–Judicial Appointments.

Except as otherwise provided by constitution and statute, a judge should not accept appointment to a governmental committee, commission, or other position that is concerned with issues of fact or policy on matters other than the improvement of the law, the legal system, or the administration of justice. A judge, however, may represent his or her country, state, or locality on ceremonial occasions or in connection with historical, educational, and cultural activities.

I. Compensation, Reimbursement and Reporting.

(1) *Compensation and Reimbursement.* A judge may receive compensation and reimbursement of expenses for the extra-judicial activities permitted by this Code, if the source of such payments does not give the appearance of influencing the judge's performance of judicial duties or otherwise give the appearance of impropriety.

(a) Compensation shall not exceed a reasonable amount nor shall it exceed what a person who is not a judge would receive for the same activity.

(b) Expense reimbursement shall be limited to the actual cost of travel, food, and lodging reasonably incurred by the judge and, where appropriate to the occasion, by the judge's family. Any payment in excess of such an amount is compensation.

(2) *Public Reports.* A judge shall file financial and other reports as required by law.

Amended by orders of June 30, 1993, and Nov. 4, 1993, eff. March 1, 1994; order of Oct. 30, 1997, eff. Jan. 1, 1998; order of March 7, 2000, eff. March 7, 2000.

Canon 5. Refraining From Inappropriate Political Activity

(1) A judge or judicial candidate shall not:

(i) make pledges or promises of conduct in office regarding pending or impending cases, specific classes of cases, specific classes of litigants, or specific propositions of law that would suggest to a reasonable person that the judge is predisposed to a probable decision in cases within the scope of the pledge;

(ii) knowingly or recklessly misrepresent the identity, qualifications, present position, or other fact concerning the candidate or an opponent; or

(iii) make a statement that would violate Canon 3B(10).

(2) A judge or judicial candidate shall not authorize the public use of his or her name endorsing another candidate for any public office, except that either may indicate support for a political party. A judge or judicial candidate may attend political events and express his or her views on political matters in accord with this Canon and Canon 3B(10).

(3) A judge shall resign from judicial office upon becoming a candidate in a contested election for a non-judicial office either in a primary or in a general or in a special election. A judge may continue to hold judicial office while being a candidate for election to or serving as a delegate in a state constitutional convention or while being a candidate for election to any judicial office.

(4) A judge or judicial candidate subject to the Judicial Campaign Fairness Act, Tex. Elec. Code § 253.151, *et. seq.* (the "Act"), shall not knowingly commit an act for which he or she knows the Act imposes a penalty. Contributions returned in accordance with Sections 253.155(e), 253.157(b) or 253.160(b) of the Act are not a violation of this paragraph.

Amended by orders of June 30, 1993, and Nov. 4, 1993, eff. March 1, 1994; order of Sept. 21, 1994, eff. Jan. 1, 1995; order of March 1, 1996; order of Oct. 30, 1997, eff. Jan. 1, 1999; order of June 21, 1999, eff. July 1, 1999; order of Aug. 22, 2002.

Canon 6. Compliance With the Code of Judicial Conduct

A. The following persons shall comply with all provisions of this Code:

(1) An active, full-time justice or judge of one of the following courts:

(a) the Supreme Court,

(b) the Court of Criminal Appeals,

(c) courts of appeals,

(d) district courts,

(e) criminal district courts, and

(f) statutory county courts.

(2) A full-time commissioner, master, magistrate, or referee of a court listed in (1) above.

B. A County Judge who performs judicial functions shall comply with all provisions of this Code except the judge is not required to comply:

(1) when engaged in duties which relate to the judge's role in the administration of the county;

(2) with Canons 4D(2), 4D(3), or 4H;

(3) with Canon 4G, except practicing law in the court on which he or she serves or in any court subject to the appellate jurisdiction of the county court, or acting as a lawyer in a proceeding in which he or she has served as a judge or in any proceeding related thereto.

(4) with Canon (5)(3).

C. Justices of the Peace and Municipal Court Judges.

(1) A justice of the peace or municipal court judge shall comply with all provisions of this Code, except the judge is not required to comply:

(a) with Canon 3B(8) pertaining to *ex parte* communications; in lieu thereof a justice of the peace or municipal court judge shall comply with Canon 6C(2) below;

(b) with Canons 4D(2), 4D(3), 4E, or 4H;

(c) with Canon 4F, unless the court on which the judge serves may have jurisdiction of the matter or parties involved in the arbitration or mediation; or

(d) if an attorney, with Canon 4G, except practicing law in the court on which he or she serves, or acting as a lawyer in a proceeding in which he or she has served as a judge or in any proceeding related thereto.

(e) with Canon 5(3).

(2) A justice of the peace or a municipal court judge, except as authorized by law, shall not directly or indirectly initiate, permit, nor consider *ex parte* or

other communications concerning the merits of a pending judicial proceeding. This subsection does not prohibit communications concerning:

(a) uncontested administrative matters,

(b) uncontested procedural matters,

(c) magistrate duties and functions,

(d) determining where jurisdiction of an impending claim or dispute may lie,

(e) determining whether a claim or dispute might more appropriately be resolved in some other judicial or non-judicial forum,

(f) mitigating circumstances following a plea of nolo contendere or guilty for a fine-only offense, or

(g) any other matters where *ex parte* communications are contemplated or authorized by law.

D. A Part-time commissioner, master, magistrate, or referee of a court listed in Canon 6A(1) above:

(1) shall comply with all provisions of this Code, except he or she is not required to comply with Canons 4D(2), 4E, 4F, 4G or 4H, and

(2) should not practice law in the court which he or she serves or in any court subject to the appellate jurisdiction of the court which he or she serves, or act as a lawyer in a proceeding in which he or she has served as a commissioner, master, magistrate, or referee, or in any other proceeding related thereto.

E. A Judge Pro Tempore, while acting as such:

(1) shall comply with all provisions of this Code applicable to the court on which he or she is serving, except he or she is not required to comply with Canons 4D(2), 4D(3), 4E, 4F, 4G or 4H, and

(2) after serving as a judge pro tempore, should not act as a lawyer in a proceeding in which he or she has served as a judge or in any other proceeding related thereto.

F. A Senior Judge, or a former appellate or district judge, or a retired or former statutory county court judge who has consented to be subject to assignment as a judicial officer:

(1) shall comply with all the provisions of this Code except he or she is not required to comply with Canon 4D(2), 4E, 4F, 4G, or 4H, but

(2) should refrain from judicial service during the period of an extra-judicial appointment not permitted by Canon 4H.

G. Candidates for Judicial Office.

(1) Any person seeking elective judicial office listed in Canon 6A(1) shall be subject to the same standards of Canon 5 that are required of members of the judiciary.

(2) Any judge who violates this Code shall be subject to sanctions by the State Commission on Judicial Conduct.

(3) Any lawyer who is a candidate seeking judicial office who violates Canon 5 or other relevant provisions of this Code is subject to disciplinary action by the State Bar of Texas.

(4) The conduct of any other candidate for elective judicial office, not subject to paragraphs (2) and (3) of this section, who violates Canon 5 or other relevant provisions of the Code is subject to review by the Secretary of State, the Attorney General, or the local District Attorney for appropriate action.

H. Attorneys.

Any lawyer who contributes to the violation of Canons 3B(7), 3B(10), 4D(4), 5, or 6C(2), or other relevant provisions of this Code, is subject to disciplinary action by the State Bar of Texas.

Amended by orders of June 30, 1993, and Nov. 4, 1993, eff. March 1, 1994; order of Sept. 21, 1994, eff. Jan. 1, 1995; order of Oct. 30, 1997, eff. Jan. 1, 1999; order of June 21, 1999; order of Sept. 11, 2000, eff. Sept. 11, 2000; order of Aug. 22, 2002.

Canon 7. Effective Date of Compliance

A person to whom this Code becomes applicable should arrange his or her affairs as soon as reasonably possible to comply with it.

Amended by orders of June 30, 1993, and Nov. 4, 1993, eff. March 1, 1994.

Canon 8. Construction and Terminology of the Code

A. Construction. The Code of Judicial Conduct is intended to establish basic standards for ethical conduct of judges. It consists of specific rules set forth in Sections under broad captions called Canons.

The Sections are rules of reason, which should be applied consistent with constitutional requirements, statutes, other court rules and decisional law and in the context of all relevant circumstances. The Code is to be construed so as not to impinge on the essential independence of judges in making judicial decisions.

The Code is designed to provide guidance to judges and candidates for judicial office and to provide a structure for regulating conduct through the State Commission on Judicial Conduct. It is not designed or intended as a basis for civil liability or criminal prosecution. Furthermore, the purpose of the Code would be subverted if the Code were invoked by lawyers for mere tactical advantage in a proceeding.

It is not intended, however, that every transgression will result in disciplinary action. Whether disciplinary action is appropriate, and the degree of discipline to be imposed, should be determined through a reasonable and reasoned application of the text and should depend on such factors as the seriousness of the transgression, whether there is a pattern of improper activity and the effect of the improper activity on others or on the judicial system.

B. Terminology.

1. "Shall" or "shall not" denotes binding obligations the violation of which can result in disciplinary action.

2. "Should" or "should not" relates to aspirational goals and as a statement of what is or is not appropriate conduct but not as a binding rule under which a judge may be disciplined.

3. "May" denotes permissible discretion or, depending on the context, refers to action that is not covered by specific proscriptions.

4. "De minimis" denotes an insignificant interest that could not raise reasonable question as to a judge's impartiality.

5. "Economic interest" denotes ownership of a more than de minimis legal or equitable interest, or a relationship as officer, director, advisor or other active participant in the affairs of a party, except that:

(i) ownership of an interest in a mutual or common investment fund that holds securities is not an economic interest in such securities unless the judge participates in the management of the fund or a proceeding pending or impending before the judge could substantially affect the value of the interest;

(ii) service by a judge as an officer, director, advisor or other active participant, in an educational, religious, charitable, fraternal, or civic organization or service by a judge's spouse, parent or child as an officer, director, advisor or other active participant in any organization does not create an economic interest in securities held by that organization;

(iii) a deposit in a financial institution, the proprietary interest of a policy holder in a mutual insurance company, of a depositor in a mutual savings association or of a member in a credit union, or a similar proprietary interest, is not an economic interest in the organization unless a proceeding pending or impending before the judge could substantially affect the value of the interest; and

(iv) ownership of government securities is not an economic interest in the issuer unless a proceeding pending or impending before the judge could substantially affect the value of the securities.

6. "Fiduciary" includes such relationships as executor, administrator, trustee, and guardian.

7. "Knowingly," "knowledge," "known" or "knows" denotes actual knowledge of the fact in question. A person's knowledge may be inferred from circumstances.

8. "Law" denotes court rules as well as statutes, constitutional provisions and decisional law.

9. "Member of the judge's (or the candidate's) family" denotes a spouse, child, grandchild, parent, grandparent or other relative or person with whom the candidate maintains a close familial relationship.

10. "Family member residing in the judge's household" means any relative of a judge by blood or marriage, or a person treated by a judge as a member of the judge's family, who resides at the judge's household.

11. "Require." The rules prescribing that a judge "require" certain conduct of others are, like all of the rules in this Code, rules of reason. The use of the term "require" in that context means a judge is to exercise reasonable direction and control over the conduct of those persons subject to the judge's direction and control.

12. "Third degree of relationship." The following persons are relatives within the third degree of relationship: great-grandparent, grandparent, parent, uncle, aunt, brother, sister, child, grandchild, great-grandchild, nephew or niece.

13. "Retired Judge" means a person who receives from the Texas Judicial Retirement System, Plan One or Plan Two, an annuity based on service that was credited to the system. (Secs. 831.001 and 836.001, V.T.C.A. Government Code [Ch. 179, Sec. 1, 71st Legislature (1989)])

14. "Senior Judge" means a retired appellate or district judge who has consented to be subject to assignment pursuant to Section 75.001, Government Code. [Ch. 359, 69th Legislature, Reg. Session (1985)]

15. "Statutory County Court Judge" means the judge of a county court created by the legislature under Article V, Section 1, of the Texas Constitution, including county courts at law, statutory probate courts, county criminal courts, county criminal courts of appeals, and county civil courts at law. (Sec. 21.009, V.T.C.A. Government Code [Ch. 2, Sec. 16.01(18), 71st Legislature (1989)])

16. "County Judge" means the judge of the county court created in each county by Article V, Section 15, of the Texas Constitution. (Sec. 21.009, V.T.C.A. Gov-

ernment Code [Ch. 2, Sec. 16.01(18), 71st Legislature (1989)])

17. "Part-time" means service on a continuing or periodic basis, but with permission by law to devote time to some other profession or occupation and for which the compensation for that reason is less than that for full-time service.

18. "Judge Pro Tempore" means a person who is appointed to act temporarily as a judge.

Amended by orders of June 30, 1993, and Nov. 4, 1993, eff. March 1, 1994; order of March 1, 1996.

RULES FOR REMOVAL OR RETIREMENT OF JUDGES

Adopted May 21, 1992

Including Amendments Received Through February 1, 2016

Rule 1. Definitions

In these rules, unless the context or subject matter otherwise requires:

(a) "Commission" means the State Commission on Judicial Conduct.

(b) "Judge" means any Justice or Judge of the Appellate Courts and District and Criminal District Courts; any County Judge; any Judge of a County Court-at-Law, a Probate Court, or a Municipal Court; any Justice of the Peace; any Judge or presiding officer of any special court created by the Legislature; any retired judge or former judge who continues as a judicial officer subject to assignment to sit on any court of the state; and, any Master or Magistrate appointed to serve a trial court of this state.

(c) "Chairperson" includes the acting Chairperson of the Commission.

(d) "Special Master" means an individual appointed by the Supreme Court upon request of the Commission pursuant to Article V, Section 1–a, Paragraph (8) of the Texas Constitution.

(e) "Sanction" means any admonition, warning, reprimand, or requirement that the person obtain additional training or education, issued publicly or privately, by the Commission pursuant to the provisions of Article V, Section 1–a, Paragraph (8) of the Texas Constitution. A sanction is remedial in nature. It is issued prior to the institution of formal proceedings to deter similar misconduct by a judge or judges in the future, to promote proper administration of justice, and to reassure the public that the judicial system of this state neither permits nor condones misconduct.

(f) "Censure" means an order issued by the Commission pursuant to the provisions of Article V, Section 1–a, Paragraph (8) of the Texas Constitution or an order issued by a Review Tribunal pursuant to the provisions of Article V, Section 1–a, Paragraph (9) of the Texas Constitution. An order of censure is tantamount to denunciation of the offending conduct, and is more severe than the remedial sanctions issued prior to a formal hearing.

(g) "Special Court of Review" means a panel of three court of appeals justices selected by lot by the Chief Justice of the Supreme Court on petition, to review a censure or sanction issued by the Commission.

(h) "Review Tribunal" means a panel of seven court of appeals justices selected by lot by the Chief Justice of the Supreme Court to review the Commission's recommendation for the removal or retirement of a judge as provided in Article V, Section 1–a, Paragraph (9) of the Texas Constitution.

(i) "Formal Proceeding" means the proceedings ordered by the Commission concerning the possibility of public censure, removal, or retirement of a judge.

(j) "Examiner" means the person, including appropriate Commission staff or Special Counsel, appointed by the Commission to gather and present evidence before a special master, or the Commission, a Special Court of Review or a Review Tribunal.

(k) "Shall" is mandatory and "may" is permissive.

(*l*) "Mail" means First Class United States Mail.

(m) The masculine gender includes the feminine gender.

Adopted May 21, 1992. Amended eff. March 26, 2012.

Rule 2. Mailing of Notices and of Other Matter

Whenever these rules provide for giving notice or sending any matter to a judge, the same shall, unless otherwise expressly provided by the rules or requested in writing by the judge, be sent to him by mail at his office or last known place of residence; provided, that when the judge has a guardian or guardian ad litem, the notice or matter shall be sent to the guardian or guardian ad litem by mail at his office or last known place of residence.

Adopted May 21, 1992.

Rule 3. Preliminary Investigation

(a) The commission may, upon receipt of a verified statement, upon its own motion, or otherwise, make such preliminary investigation as is appropriate to the circumstances relating to an allegation or appearance of misconduct or disability of any judge to determine that such allegation or appearance is neither unfounded nor frivolous.

(b) If the preliminary investigation discloses that the allegation or appearance is unfounded or frivolous, the commission shall terminate further proceedings.

Adopted May 21, 1992.

Rule 4. Full Investigation

(a) If the preliminary investigation discloses that the allegations or appearances are neither unfounded nor frivolous, or if sufficient cause exists to warrant full inquiry into the facts and circumstances indicating that a judge may be guilty of willful or persistent conduct which is clearly inconsistent with the proper performance of his duties or casts public discredit upon the judiciary or the administration of justice, or that he has a disability seriously interfering with the performance of his duties, which is, or is likely to become, permanent in nature, the commission shall conduct a full investigation into the matter.

(b) The commission shall inform the judge in writing that an investigation has commenced and of the nature of the matters being investigated.

(c) The commission may request the judge's response in writing to the matters being investigated.

Adopted May 21, 1992.

Rule 5. Issuance, Service, and Return of Subpoenas

(a) In conducting an investigation, formal proceedings, or proceedings before a Special Court of Review, the Chairperson or any member of the Commission, or a special master when a hearing is being conducted before a special master, or member of a Special Court of Review, may, on his own motion, or on request of appropriate Commission staff, the examiner, or the judge, issue a subpoena for attendance of any witness or witnesses who may be represented to reside within the State of Texas.

(b) The style of the subpoena shall be "The State of Texas". It shall state the style of the proceeding, that the proceeding is pending before the Commission, the time and place at which the witness is required to appear, and the person or official body at whose instance the witness is summoned. It shall be signed by the Chairperson or some other member of the Commission, or by the special master when a hearing is before the special master, and the date of its issuance shall be noted thereon. It shall be addressed to any peace officer of the State of Texas or to a person designated by the Chairperson to make service thereof.

(c) A subpoena may also command the person to whom it is directed to produce the books, papers, documents or tangible things designated therein.

(d) Subpoenas may be executed and returned at any time, and shall be served by delivering a copy of such subpoena to the witness; the person serving the subpoena shall make due return thereof, showing the time and manner of service, or service thereof may be accepted by any witness by a written memorandum, signed by such witness, attached to the subpoena.

Adopted May 21, 1992. Amended eff. March 26, 2012.

Rule 6. Informal Appearance

(a) Before terminating an investigation, the commission may offer a judge an opportunity to appear informally before the commission.

(b) An informal appearance is confidential except that the judge may elect to have the appearance open to the public or to any person or persons designated by the judge. The right to an open appearance does not preclude placing of witnesses under the rule as provided by Rule 267 of the Texas Rules of Civil Procedure.

(c) No oral testimony other than the judge's shall be received during an informal appearance, although documentary evidence may be received. Testimony of the judge shall be under oath, and a recording of such testimony taken. A copy of such recording shall be furnished to the judge upon request.

(d) The judge may be represented by counsel at the informal appearance.

(e) Notice of the opportunity to appear informally before the commission shall be given by mail at least ten (10) days prior to the date of the scheduled appearance.

Adopted May 21, 1992.

Rule 7. Commission Voting

(a)[1] A quorum shall consist of seven (7) members. Proceedings shall be by majority vote of those present, except that recommendations for retirement, censure, suspension or removal of any Judge shall be by affirmative vote of at least seven (7) members.

Adopted eff. March 26, 2012.

1 No subd. (b) in original.

Rule 8. [Reserved for Future Promulgation]

Rule 9. Review of Commission Decision

(a) A judge who has received from the Commission a sanction in connection with a complaint filed subsequent to September 1, 1987, may file with the Chief Justice of the Supreme Court a written request for appointment of a Special Court of Review, not later than the 30th day after the date on which the Commission issued its sanction.

(b) Within 15 days after appointment of the Special Court of Review, the Commission shall furnish the petitioner and each justice on the Special Court of Review a charging document which shall include a copy of the sanction issued as well as any additional charges to be considered in the de novo proceeding and the papers, documents, records, and evidence upon which the Commission based its decision. The sanction and other records filed with the Special Court of Review are public information upon filing with the Special Court of Review.

(c) Within 30 days after the date upon which the Commission files the charging document and related materials with the Special Court of Review, the Special Court of Review shall conduct a hearing. The Special Court of Review may, if good cause is shown, grant one or more continuances not to exceed a total of 60 days. The procedure for the hearing shall be governed by the rules of law, evidence, and procedure that apply to civil actions, except the judge is not entitled to trial by jury, and the Special Court of Review's decision shall not be appealable. The hearing shall be held at a location determined by the Special Court of Review, and shall be public.

(d) Decision by the Special Court of Review may include dismissal, affirmation of the Commission's decision, imposition of a lesser or greater sanction, or order to the Commission to file formal proceedings.

(e) The opinion by the Special Court of Review shall be published if, in the judgment of a majority of the justices participating in the decision, it is one that (1) establishes a new rule of ethics or law, alters or modifies an existing rule, or applies an existing rule to a novel fact situation likely to recur in future cases; (2) involves a legal or ethical issue of continuing public interest; (3) criticizes existing legal or ethical principles; or (4) resolves an apparent conflict of authority. A concurring or dissenting opinion may be published if, in the judgment of its author, it meets one of the above indicated criteria, but in such event the majority opinion shall be published as well.

Adopted May 21, 1992. Amended eff. March 26, 2012.

Rule 10. Formal Proceedings

(a) NOTICE

(1) If after the investigation has been completed the Commission concludes that formal proceedings should be instituted, the matter shall be entered in a docket to be kept for that purpose and written notice of the institution of formal proceedings shall be issued to the judge without delay. Such proceedings shall be entitled:

"Before the State Commission on Judicial Conduct Inquiry Concerning a Judge, No. __"

(2) The notice shall specify in ordinary and concise language the charges against the judge, and the alleged facts upon which such charges are based and the specific standards contended to have been violated, and shall advise the judge of his right to file a written answer to the charges against him within 15 days after service of the notice upon him.

(3) The notice shall be served by personal service of a copy thereof upon the judge by a member of the Commission or by some person designated by the Chairperson, and the person serving the notice shall promptly notify the Commission in writing of the date on which the same was served. If it appears to the Chairperson upon affidavit that, after reasonable effort during a period of 10 days, personal service could not be had, service may be made by mailing, by registered or certified mail, copies of the notice addressed to the judge at his chambers and at his last known residence, and the date of mailing shall be entered in the docket.

(b) ANSWER

Within 15 days after service of the notice of formal proceedings, the judge may file with the Commission an original answer, which shall be verified, and twelve legible copies thereof.

(c) SETTING DATE FOR HEARING AND REQUEST FOR APPOINTMENT OF A SPECIAL MASTER

(1) Upon the filing of an answer or upon expiration of the time for its filing, the Commission shall set a time and place for hearing before itself or before a special master and shall give notice of such hearing by mail to the judge at least 20 days prior to the date set.

(2) If the Commission directs that the hearing be before a special master, the Commission shall, when it sets a time and place for the hearing, transmit a written request to the Supreme Court to appoint a special master for such hearing, and the Supreme Court shall, within 10 days from receipt of such request, appoint an active or retired District Judge, a Judge of a Court of Civil Appeals, either active or retired, or a retired Justice of the Court of Criminal Appeals or Supreme Court to hear and take evidence in such matters.

(d) HEARING

(1) At the time and place set for hearing, the Commission, or the special master when the hearing is before a special master, shall proceed with the hearing as nearly as may be according to the rules of procedure governing the trial of civil causes in this State, subject to the provisions of Rule 5, whether or not the judge has filed an answer or appears at the hearing. The examiner or other authorized officer shall present the case in support of the charges in the notice of formal proceedings.

(2) The failure of the judge to answer or to appear at the hearing shall not, standing alone, be taken as evidence of the truth of the facts alleged to constitute grounds for removal or retirement. The failure of the judge to testify in his own behalf or his failure to submit to a medical examination requested by the Commission or the master may be considered, unless it appears that such failure was due to circumstances unrelated to the facts in issue at the hearing.

(3) The proceedings at the hearing shall be reported by a phonographic reporter or by some qualified person appointed by the Commission and taking the oath of an official court reporter.

(4) When the hearing is before the Commission, not less than seven members shall be present while the hearing is in active progress. The Chairperson, when present, the Vice Chairperson in the absence of the Chairperson, or the member designated by the Chairperson in the absence of both, shall preside. Procedural and other interlocutory rulings shall be made by the person presiding and shall be taken as consented to by the other members unless one or more calls for a vote, in which latter event such rulings shall be made by a majority vote of those present.

(e) EVIDENCE

At a hearing before the Commission or a special master, legal evidence only shall be received as in the trial of civil cases, except upon consent evidenced by absence of objection, and oral evidence shall be taken only on oath or affirmation.

(f) AMENDMENTS TO NOTICE OR ANSWER

The special master, at any time prior to the conclusion of the hearing, or the Commission, at any time prior to its determination, may allow or require amendments to the notice of formal proceedings and may allow amendments to the answer. The notice may be amended to conform to proof or to set forth additional facts, whether occurring before or after the commencement of the hearing. In case such an amendment is made, the judge shall be given reasonable time both to answer the amendment and to prepare and present his defense against the matters charged thereby.

(g) PROCEDURAL RIGHTS OF JUDGES

(1) In the proceedings for his removal or retirement a judge shall have the right to be confronted by his accusers, the right and reasonable opportunity to defend against the charges by the introduction of evidence, to be represented by counsel, and to examine and cross-examine witnesses. He shall also have the right to the issuance of subpoenas for attendance of witnesses to testify or produce books, papers and other evidentiary matter.

(2) When a transcript of the testimony has been prepared at the expense of the Commission, a copy thereof shall, upon request, be available for use by the judge and his counsel in connection with the proceedings, or the judge may arrange to procure a copy at his expense. The judge shall have the right, without any order or approval, to have all or any portion of the testimony in the proceedings transcribed at his expense.

(3) If the judge is adjudged insane or incompetent, or if it appears to the Commission at any time during the proceedings that he is not competent to act for himself, the Commission shall appoint a guardian ad litem unless the judge has a guardian

who will represent him. In the appointment of a guardian ad litem, preference shall be given, so far as practicable, to members of the judge's immediate family. The guardian or guardian ad litem may claim and exercise any right and privilege and make any defense for the judge with the same force and effect as if claimed, exercised, or made by the judge, if competent.

(h) REPORT OF SPECIAL MASTER

(1) After the conclusion of the hearing before a special master, he shall promptly prepare and transmit to the Commission a report which shall contain a brief statement of the proceedings had and his findings of fact based on a preponderance of the evidence with respect to the issues presented by the notice of formal proceedings and the answer thereto, or if there be no answer, his findings of fact with respect to the allegations in the notice of formal proceedings. The report shall be accompanied by an original and two copies of a transcript of the proceedings before the special master.

(2) Upon receiving the report of the special master, the Commission shall promptly send a copy to the judge, and one copy of the transcript shall be retained for the judge's use.

(i) OBJECTIONS TO REPORT OF SPECIAL MASTER

Within 15 days after mailing of the copy of the special master's report to the judge, the examiner or the judge may file with the Commission an original and twelve legible copies of a statement of objections to the report of the special master, setting forth all objections to the report and all reasons in opposition to the findings as sufficient grounds for removal or retirement. A copy of any such statement filed by the examiner shall be sent to the judge.

(j) APPEARANCE BEFORE COMMISSION

If no statement of objections to the report of the special master is filed within the time provided, the findings of the special master may be deemed as agreed to, and the Commission may adopt them without a hearing. If a statement of objections is filed, or if the Commission in the absence of such statement proposes to modify or reject the findings of the special master, the Commission shall give the judge and the examiner an opportunity to be heard orally before the Commission, and written notice of the time and place of such hearing shall be sent to the judge at least ten days prior thereto.

(k) EXTENSION OF TIME

The Chairperson of the Commission may extend for periods not to exceed 30 days in the aggregate the time for filing an answer, for the commencement of a hearing before the Commission, and for filing a statement of objections to the report of a special master, and a special master may similarly extend the time for the commencement of a hearing before him.

(*l*) HEARING ADDITIONAL EVIDENCE

(1) The Commission may order a hearing for the taking of additional evidence at any time while the matter is pending before it. The order shall set the time and place of hearing and shall indicate the matters on which the evidence is to be taken. A copy of such order shall be sent to the judge at least ten days prior to the date of the hearing.

(2) The hearing of additional evidence may be before the Commission itself or before the special master, as the Commission shall direct; and if before a special master, the proceedings shall be in conformance with the provisions of Rule 10(d) to 10(g) inclusive.

(m) COMMISSION RECOMMENDATION

If, after hearing, upon considering the record and report of the special master, the Commission finds good cause therefore, it shall recommend to the Review Tribunal the removal, or retirement, as the case may be; or in the alternative, the Commission may dismiss the case or publicly order a censure, reprimand, warning, or admonition.

Adopted May 21, 1992. Amended eff. March 26, 2012.

Rule 11. Request by Commission for Appointment of Review Tribunal

Upon making a determination to recommend the removal or retirement of a judge, the commission shall promptly file a copy of a request for appointment of a review tribunal with the clerk of the supreme court, and shall immediately send the judge notice of such filing.

Adopted May 21, 1992.

Rule 12. Review of Formal Proceedings

(a) A recommendation of the Commission for the removal or retirement, of a judge shall be determined by a Review Tribunal of seven Justices selected from the Courts of Appeals. Members of the Review Tribunal shall be selected by lot by the Chief Justice of the Supreme Court from all Appeals Justices sitting at the time of selection. Each Court of Appeals shall designate one of its members for inclusion in the list from which the selection is made, except that no Justice who is a member of the Commission shall serve on the Review Tribunal. The Justice whose name is drawn first shall be chairperson of the Review

Tribunal. The clerk of the Supreme Court will serve as the Review Tribunal's staff, and will notify the Commission when selection of the Review Tribunal is complete.

(b) After receipt of notice that the Review Tribunal has been constituted, the Commission shall promptly file a copy of its recommendation certified by the Chairperson or Secretary of the Commission, together with the transcript and the findings and conclusions, with the clerk of the Supreme Court. The Commission shall immediately send the judge notice of such filing and a copy of the recommendation, findings and conclusions.

(c) A petition to reject the recommendation of the Commission for removal or retirement of a judge or justice may be filed with the clerk of the Supreme Court within thirty days after the filing with the clerk of the Supreme Court of a certified copy of the Commission's recommendation. The petition shall be verified, shall be based on the record, shall specify the grounds relied on and shall be accompanied by seven copies of petitioner's brief and proof of service of one copy of the petition and of the brief on the Chairperson of the Commission. Within twenty days after the filing of the petition and supporting brief, the Commission shall file seven copies of the Commission's brief, and shall serve a copy thereof on the judge.

(d) Failure to file a petition within the time provided may be deemed a consent to a determination on the merits based upon the record filed by the Commission.

(e) Rules 4[1] and 74,[2] Texas Rules of Appellate Procedure, shall govern the form and contents of briefs except where express provision is made to the contrary or where the application of a particular rule would be clearly impracticable, inappropriate, or inconsistent.

(f) The Review Tribunal, may, in its discretion and for good cause shown, permit the introduction of additional evidence, and may direct that the same be introduced before the special master or the Commission and be filed as a part of the record in the Court.

(g) Oral argument on a petition of a judge to reject a recommendation of the Commission shall, upon receipt of the petition, be set on a date not less than thirty days nor more than forty days from the date of receipt thereof. The order and length of time of argument shall, if not otherwise ordered or permitted by the Review Tribunal, be governed by Rule 172,[3] Texas Rules of Appellate Procedure.

(h) Within 90 days after the date on which the record is filed with the Review Tribunal, it shall order public censure, retirement, or removal, as it finds just and proper, or wholly reject the recommendation. The Review Tribunal, in an order for involuntary retirement for disability or an order for removal, may also prohibit such person from holding judicial office in the future.

(i) The opinion by the Review Tribunal shall be published if, in the judgment of a majority of the justices participating in the decision, it is one that (1) establishes a new rule of ethics or law, alters or modifies an existing rule, or applies an existing rule to a novel fact situation likely to recur in future cases; (2) involves a legal or ethical issue of continuing public interest; (3) criticizes existing legal or ethical principles; or (4) resolves an apparent conflict of authority. A concurring or dissenting opinion may be published if, in the judgment of its author, it meets one of the above indicated criteria, but in such event the majority opinion shall be published as well.

1 See, now, Vernon's Ann.Rules App.Proc., rule 9.1 et seq.

2 See, now, Vernon's Ann.Rules App.Proc., rules 9.3 to 9.5 and 38.1 et seq.

3 See, now, Vernon's Ann.Rules App.Proc., rules 59.4 to 59.6.

Adopted May 21, 1992. Amended eff. March 26, 2012.

Rule 13. Appeal to Supreme Court

A judge may appeal a decision of the review tribunal to the supreme court under the substantial evidence rule.

Adopted May 21, 1992.

Rule 14. Motion for Rehearing

A motion for rehearing may not be filed as a matter of right. In entering its judgment the Supreme Court or Review Tribunal may direct that no motion for rehearing will be entertained, in which event the judgment will be final on the day and date of its entry. If the Supreme Court or Review Tribunal does not so direct and the judge wishes to file a motion for rehearing, he shall present the motion together with a motion for leave to file the same to the clerk of the Supreme Court or Review Tribunal within fifteen days of the date of the judgment, and the clerk of the Supreme Court shall transmit it to the Supreme Court or Review Tribunal for such action as the appropriate body deems proper.

Adopted May 21, 1992. Amended eff. March 26, 2012.

Rule 15. Suspension of a Judge

(a) Any judge may be suspended from office with or without pay by the Commission immediately upon being indicted by a state or federal grand jury for a felony offense or charged with a misdemeanor involving official misconduct. However, the suspended judge has the right to a post-suspension hearing to demonstrate that continued service would not jeopardize the interests of parties involved in court proceedings over which the judge would preside nor impair public confidence in the judiciary. A written request for a post-suspension hearing must be filed with the Commission within 30 days from receipt of the Order of Suspension. Within 30 days from the receipt of a request, a hearing will be scheduled before one or more members or the executive director of the Commission as designated by the Chairperson of the Commission. The person or persons designated will report findings and make recommendations, and within 60 days from the close of the hearing, the Commission shall notify the judge whether the suspension will be continued, terminated, or modified.

(b) Upon the filing with the Commission of a sworn complaint charging a person holding such office with willful or persistent violation of rules promulgated by the Supreme Court of Texas, incompetence in performing the duties of office, willful violation of the Code of Judicial Conduct, or willful and persistent conduct that is clearly inconsistent with the proper performance of his duties or casts public discredit upon the judiciary or the administration of justice, the Commission, after giving the person notice and an opportunity to appear and be heard before the Commission (under Rule 6), may recommend to the Supreme Court the suspension of such person from office.

(c) When the Commission or the Supreme Court orders the suspension of a judge or justice, with or without pay, the appropriate city, county, and/or state officials shall be notified of such suspension by certified copy of such order.

Adopted May 21, 1992. Amended eff. March 26, 2012.

Rule 16. Record of Commission Proceedings

The commission shall keep a record of all informal appearances and formal proceedings concerning a judge. In all proceedings resulting in a recommendation to the review tribunal for removal or retirement, the commission shall prepare a transcript of the evidence and of all proceedings therein and shall make written findings of fact and conclusions of law with respect to the issues of fact and law in the proceeding.

Adopted May 21, 1992.

Rule 17. Confidentiality and Privilege of Proceedings

All papers filed with and proceedings before the Commission shall be confidential, and the filing of papers with, and the giving of testimony before the Commission shall be privileged; provided that:

(a) The formal hearing, and all papers, records, documents, and other evidence introduced during the formal hearing shall be public.

(b) If the Commission issues a public sanction, all papers, documents, evidence, and records considered by the Commission or forwarded to the Commission by its staff and related to the sanction shall be public.

(c) The judge may elect to open the informal appearance hearing pursuant to Rule 6(b).

(d) Any hearings of the Special Court of Review shall be public and held at the location determined by the Special Court of Review. Any evidence introduced during a hearing, including papers, records, documents, and pleadings filed in the proceedings, is public.

Adopted May 21, 1992. Amended eff. March 26, 2012.

Rule 18. Ex Parte Contacts by Members of the Commission

A Commissioner, except as authorized by law, shall not directly or indirectly initiate, permit, nor consider ex parte contacts with any judge who is the subject of an investigation being conducted by the Commission or involved in a proceeding before the Commission.

Adopted Jan. 20, 1994.

RULES OF JUDICIAL ADMINISTRATION

Effective February 4, 1987

Including Amendments Received Through February 1, 2016

Research Note

See Vernon's Texas Codes Annotated, Government Code, *Volume 3, for judicial constructions and other research aids.*

Rule 1. Authority

These rules are promulgated pursuant to Section 74.024 of the Texas Government Code.

Adopted by order of Feb. 4, 1987. Amended by order of Dec. 6, 1988.

Rule 2. Definitions

In these rules:

a. "Chief Justice" means the Chief Justice of the Supreme Court.

b. "Presiding Judge" means the presiding judge of an administrative region.

c. "Administrative region" means an administrative judicial region created by Section 74.042 of the Texas Government Code.

d. "Statutory county court" means a court created by the legislature under Article V, Section 1, of the Texas Constitution, including county courts at law, county criminal courts, county criminal courts of appeals, and county civil courts at law, but not including statutory probate courts as defined by Section 3(ii) of the Texas Probate Code.

Adopted by order of Feb. 4, 1987. Amended by order of Dec. 6, 1988.

Rule 3. Council of Presiding Judges

a. There is hereby created the Council of Presiding Judges, composed of the Chief Justice as chairman and the nine presiding judges of the administrative regions.

b. The Chief Justice shall call and preside over an annual meeting of the Council on a date and at a time and place in the State designated by the Chief Justice.

c. The Chief Justice may call and convene additional meetings of the Council that he considers necessary for the promotion of the orderly and efficient administration of justice.

d. At the will of the Chief Justice, the Council may choose one of its members to serve as chairman, who will serve for a period of two years.

e. At the meetings, the Council shall:

(1) study the condition of the dockets of the courts of the State to determine the existence of:

(a) a significant increase in the number of new cases filed;

(b) a disposition rate below the state average;

(c) fewer cases disposed of than new cases filed;

(d) an excessive number of cases pending on the docket for a lengthy period of time;

(e) a large number of inactive tax cases, nonarrest criminal cases, cases held pending action in other courts or other cases which are not ready for disposition;

(f) cases tried and awaiting the entry of judgment;

(g) the need for technical assistance in caseflow or case management; and

(h) the need for the assignment of visiting judges to any court;

(2) compare the regional and local rules of court to achieve the uniformity of rules that is practicable and consistent with local conditions;

(3) consider uniformity in the administration of Chapter 74 of the Texas Government Code in the various administrative regions; and

(4) promote more effective administration of justice through the use of Chapter 74 of the Texas Government Code.

f. The Office of Court Administration shall provide the necessary staff support for the operation of the Council and at the direction of the Chief Justice shall provide the Council with information concerning the operation of the courts of this State.

Adopted by order of Feb. 4, 1987. Amended by order of Dec. 6, 1988.

Rule 4. Council of Judges

a. There is hereby created in each of the administrative regions a Council of Judges, composed of the Presiding Judge as Chairman, judges of the district courts and statutory county courts within the region, senior judges, and former district and statutory county court judges residing in the region who have qualified to serve as judicial officers under the provisions of Section 74.055 of the Texas Government Code.

b. The Presiding Judge shall call at least one meeting each year of the Council of Judges of the administrative region, at a time and place designated by the Presiding Judge, for consultation and counseling on the state of the dockets and the civil and criminal business in the district and statutory county courts of the administrative region and arranging for the disposition of cases and other business pending on the court dockets. At the meeting, the Council shall study and act upon the matters listed in Rule 3.e and such other matters as may be presented to the meeting by the judges in attendance.

c. The Council of Judges shall adopt rules for the administration of the affairs of the district and statutory county courts within the administrative region, including, but not limited to, rules for:

(1) management of the business, administrative and nonjudicial affairs of the courts;

(2) docket management systems to provide the most efficient use of available court resources;

(3) the reporting of docket status information to reflect not only the numbers of cases on the dockets but also the types of cases relevant to the time needed to dispose of them;

(4) meaningful procedures for achieving the time standards for the disposition of cases provided by Rule 6;

(5) such other matters necessary to the administrative operations of the courts; and

(6) judicial budget matters.

d. The expenses of judges attending meetings of the Council of Judges may be paid from funds provided by law.

Adopted by order of Feb. 4, 1987. Amended by order of Dec. 6, 1988; order of Oct. 16, 1991.

Rule 5. Duties of the Presiding Judge

In addition to the duties placed on Presiding Judges by law and these rules, each Presiding Judge should oversee the general docket management, the prompt disposition of all cases filed in each district and statutory county court within the region, and the proper administration of the affairs of the courts within the administrative region. The Presiding Judge shall:

a. ensure the adoption of uniform local rules;

b. hold periodic meetings with the judges in counties with more than one court;

c. consult with each trial judge of the administrative region to implement more efficient methods of docket management;

d. study in detail the condition of the dockets in each county;

e. discover and encourage the implementation of systems to reduce delay in local dockets;

f. provide for the orientation and training of new judges in the administrative regions;

g. ensure adherence to the time standards provided by Rule 6 in the courts of the administrative region;

h. direct the district and county clerks within the regions to submit such statistical reports as may be requested by either the local administrative judge or the presiding judge; and

i. perform such other duties as may be assigned by the Chief Justice.

Adopted by order of Feb. 4, 1987.

Rule 6. Time Standards for the Disposition of Cases

Rule 6.1 District and Statutory County Courts.

District and statutory county court judges of the county in which cases are filed should, so far as reasonably possible, ensure that all cases are brought to trial or final disposition in conformity with the following time standards:

(a) Criminal Cases. As provided by Article 32A.02, Code of Criminal Procedure.

(b) Civil Cases Other Than Family Law.

(1) *Civil Jury Cases.* Within 18 months from appearance date.

(2) *Civil Nonjury Cases.* Within 12 months from appearance date.

(c) Family Law Cases.

(1) *Contested Family Law Cases.* Within 6 months from appearance date or within 6 months from the expiration of the waiting period provided by the Family Code where such is required, whichever is later.

(2) *Uncontested Family Law Cases.* Within 3 months from appearance date or within 3 months from the expiration of the waiting period provided by the Family Code where such is required, whichever is later.

(d) Juvenile Cases. In addition to the requirements of Title 3, Texas Family Code:[1]

(1) *Detention Hearings.* On the next business day following admission to any detention facility.

(2) *Adjudicatory or Transfer (Waiver) Hearings.*

(a) Concerning a juvenile in a detention facility: Not later than 10 days following admission to such a facility, except for good cause shown of record.

(b) Concerning a juvenile not in a detention facility: Not later than 30 days following the filing of the petition, except for good cause shown of record.

(3) *Disposition Hearing.* Not later than 15 days following the adjudicatory hearing. The court may grant additional time in exceptional cases that require more complex evaluation.

(4) Nothing herein shall prevent a judge from recessing a juvenile hearing at any stage of the proceeding where the parties are agreeable or when in the opinion of the judge presiding in the case the best interests of the child and of society shall be served.

(e) Complex Cases. It is recognized that in especially complex cases or special circumstances it may not be possible to adhere to these standards.

Rule 6.2 Appeals in Certain Cases Involving the Parent–Child Relationship.

In an appeal of a suit for termination of the parent-child relationship or a suit affecting the parent-child relationship filed by a governmental entity for managing conservatorship, appellate courts should, so far as reasonably possible, ensure that the appeal is brought to final disposition in conformity with the following time standards:

(a) Courts of Appeals. Within 180 days of the date the notice of appeal is filed.

(b) Supreme Court. Within 180 days of the date the petition for review is filed.

Adopted by order of Feb. 4, 1987. Amended by order of Dec. 6, 1988; order of Mar. 1, 2012, eff. May 1, 2012.

1 V.T.C.A., Family Code § 51.01 et seq.

Rule 7. Administrative Responsibilities

a.[1] A district or statutory county court judge shall:

(1) diligently discharge the administrative responsibilities of the office;

(2) rule on a case within three months after the case is taken under advisement;

(3) if an election contest or a suit for the removal of a local official is filed in his court, request the presiding judge to assign another judge who is not a resident of the county to dispose of the suit;

(4) on motion by either party in a disciplinary action against an attorney, request the presiding judge to assign another judge who is not a resident of the administrative region where the action is pending to dispose of the case;

(5) request the presiding judge to assign another judge of the administrative region to hear a motion relating to the recusal or disqualification of the judge from a case pending in his court; and

(6) to the extent consistent with safeguarding the rights of litigants to the just processing of their causes, utilize methods to expedite the disposition of cases on the docket of the court, including

(a) adherence to firm trial dates with strict continuance policies;

(b) the use of telephone or mail in lieu of personal appearance by attorneys for motion hearings, pretrial conferences, scheduling and the setting of trial dates;

(c) pretrial conferences to encourage settlements and to narrow trial issues;

(d) taxation of costs and imposition of other sanctions authorized by the Rules of Civil Procedure against attorneys or parties filing frivolous motions or pleadings or abusing discovery procedures; and

(e) local rules, consistently applied, to regulate docketing procedures and timely pleadings, discovery and motions.

Adopted by order of Feb. 4, 1987. Amended by order of Dec. 6, 1988.

[1] So in Supreme Court Order. There is no b.

Rule 8. Assignment of Judges

a. Judges may be assigned in the manner provided by Chapter 74 of the Texas Government Code to hold court when:

(1) the regular judge of the court is absent or is disabled, recuses himself, or is recused under the provisions of Rule 18a, T.R.C.P., or is disqualified for any cause;

(2) the regular judge of the court is present and is trying cases as authorized by the constitution and laws of this State; or

(3) the office of the judge is vacant because of death, resignation, or other cause.

b. A Presiding Judge from time to time shall assign the judges of the administrative region, including qualified retired appellate judges, to hold special or regular terms of court in any county of the administrative region to try cases and dispose of accumulated business.

c. The Presiding Judge of one administrative region may request the Presiding Judge of another administrative region to furnish judges to aid in the disposition of litigation pending in a court in the administrative region of the Presiding Judge who makes the request.

d. In addition to the assignment of judges by the Presiding Judges as authorized by Chapter 74 of the Texas Government Code, the Chief Justice may assign judges of one or more administrative regions for service in other administrative regions when he considers the assignment necessary to the prompt and efficient administration of justice. A judge assigned by the Chief Justice shall perform the same duties and functions that the judge would perform if he were assigned by the Presiding Judge.

Adopted by order of Feb. 4, 1987. Amended by order of July 13, 1988; order of Dec. 6, 1988.

Rule 9. Local Administrative Judges

a. In any county in which there are two or more district courts, the judges of those courts shall elect one of the district judges as the local administrative district judge. In any county in which there are two or more statutory county courts, the judges of those courts shall elect one of the statutory county court judges as the local administrative statutory county court judge. If a local administrative district judge or a local administrative statutory county court judge is not so chosen, the Presiding Judge of the administrative region shall designate one of the qualified judges of the county as the local administrative district judge or the local administrative statutory county court judge. The local administrative judges shall be responsible to the Presiding Judge of the administrative region for the expeditious dispatch of business in the district and statutory county courts of the county.

b. Under the direction of the local administrative judge, the district and statutory county court judges of the county shall adopt rules to provide for the orderly administration of the affairs of the district and statutory county courts of the county. The rules shall employ a uniform and consistent numbering system approved by the Supreme Court and the Council of Presiding Judges. These rules shall provide, among other matters, for the orderly discharge of the local judicial responsibilities for matters relating to:

(1) docket management of the local courts;

(2) regular meetings to address the matters set forth in Rule 3.e.;

(3) judicial budget matters;

(4) adult and juvenile probation matters;

(5) County Auditor matters;

(6) county purchasing matters;

(7) relationship with other governmental bodies, the public, and the news media;

(8) such other matters necessary to provide for the orderly, prompt, efficient, and effective administration of justice in the county;

(9) court reporters and timely preparation of records; and

(10) dismissals for want of prosecution so as to achieve and maintain compliance with the time standards of Rule 6.

Adopted by order of Feb. 4, 1987. Amended by order of Dec. 6, 1988; order of April 6, 1992.

Rule 10. Local Rules

The local rules adopted by the courts of each county shall conform to all provisions of state and administrative region rules. If approved by the Supreme Court pursuant to Rule 3a, T.R.C.P., the local rules shall be published and available to the Bar and public, and shall include the following:

a. In multi-court counties having two or more court divisions, each division must adopt a single set of local rules which shall govern all courts in the division.

b. Provisions for fair distribution of the caseload among the judges in the county.

c. Provisions to ensure uniformity of forms to be used by the courts under Rules 165a and 166, T.R.C.P.

d. Designation of the responsibility for emergency and special matters.

e. Plans for judicial vacation, sick leave, attendance at educational programs, and similar matters.

Adopted by order of Feb. 4, 1987.

Rule 11. Pretrial Proceedings in Certain Cases

11.1 Applicability. This rule applies to any case filed before September 1, 2003, that involves material questions of fact and law in common with another case pending in another court in another county on or after October 1, 1997.

11.2 Definitions.

(a) *Presiding judge* means the presiding judge of an administrative judicial region in which a case is pending;

(b) *Regular judge* means the regular judge of a court in which a case is pending.

(c) *Pretrial judge* means a judge assigned under this rule.

(d) *Related* means that cases involve common material issues of fact and law.

11.3 Assignment of Pretrial Judge.

(a) *By presiding judge.* On motion or request under 11.4, a presiding judge may assign an active district judge, including himself or herself, to a case to conduct all pretrial proceedings and decide all pretrial matters.

(b) *Authority of pretrial judge.* The pretrial judge will preside over all pretrial proceedings in the case in place of the regular judge. The pretrial judge will decide all pretrial motions, including motions to transfer venue and motions for summary judgment. The pretrial judge and the regular judge must consult on setting a trial date.

(c) *Different judges assigned.* The same pretrial judge need not be assigned in all related cases. If more than one pretrial judge is assigned in related cases, either in the same region or in different regions, the pretrial judges must consult with each other in conducting pretrial proceedings and deciding pretrial matters.

(d) *Assignment outside region.* The Chief Justice of the Supreme Court may assign an active district judge to other administrative regions to allow the judge to be assigned as a pretrial judge under this rule.

(e) *No objections to pretrial judge.* An assignment under this rule is not made pursuant to section 74.054 of the Government Code, and therefore a pretrial judge is not subject to an objection under section 74.053 of the Government Code.

(f) *Termination of assignment.* An assignment under this rule terminates when:

(i) all pretrial proceedings in a case have been completed;

(ii) the pretrial judge ceases to be an active district judge; or

(iii) the presiding judge in the exercise of discretion terminates the assignment.

11.4 Procedure for Obtaining Assignment of a Pretrial Judge.

(a) *Motion or request required; who may file.* A pretrial judge may be assigned only on the motion of a party to a case or at the request of the regular judge.

(b) *Contents of motion or request.* The motion or request must state:

(1) the number and style of the case;

(2) the number and style of the related case, and the court and county in which it is pending;

(3) the material questions of fact and law common to the cases;

(4) the reasons why the assignment would promote the just and efficient conduct of the action; and

(5) whether all parties agree to the motion.

(c) *Where filed.* The motion or request must be filed in all cases identified under (b)(1) and (b)(2).

(d) *Response.* A response may be filed by:

(1) any other party to the case;

(2) the regular judge of the court in which the case is pending;

(3) the regular judge of the court in which the related case is pending, if no pretrial judge has already been assigned in that case;

(4) the pretrial judge assigned to the related case, if a pretrial judge has already been assigned; and

(5) any party to the related case.

(e) *Briefs.* A motion, request, or response may be accompanied by a brief. The presiding judge may request briefs.

(f) *Hearing.* Unless all parties in the case agree to a motion or request, the presiding judge may not grant the motion without conducting an oral hearing.

The hearing may be held in any county within the region or in Travis County. The presiding judge must give notice of the time and place for the hearing to all parties and the regular or pretrial judges in the cases identified in (b)(1) and (b)(2).

(g) *Evidence.* In ruling on the motion or request, the presiding judge may consider all documents filed in the case or the related case, all discovery conducted in the case or the related case, any stipulations filed by the parties in the case or the related case, affidavits filed in connection with the motion, request, or response, and oral testimony.

(h) *Decision.* The presiding judge must grant the motion or request if the judge determines that:

(1) the case involves material questions of fact and law common to a case in another court and county; and

(2) assignment of a pretrial judge would promote the just and efficient conduct of the cases.

Otherwise, the presiding judge must deny the motion or request.

(i) *Order.* The presiding judge must issue an order deciding the motion or request. The order must be filed in the case in which assignment of a pretrial judge was sought.

(j) *Service and notice.* A party must serve any paper filed under this rule on all parties to the cases identified under (b)(1) and (b)(2) and on the presiding judge or judges for those cases. If a judge files any paper under this rule, the clerk of the court in which the paper is filed must send a copy to all parties to the cases identified under (b)(1) and (b)(2) and to the presiding judge or judges for those cases. The clerk of the court where a case is pending in which assignment of a pretrial judge is sought shall serve as the clerk for the presiding judge under this rule.

11.5 Review. A presiding judge's order granting or denying a motion or request for appointment of a pretrial judge may be reviewed only by the Supreme Court in an original mandamus proceeding.

11.6 Expenses of Pretrial Judge. If a pretrial judge travels outside the judge's county of residence to conduct proceedings, the county in which the proceedings are conducted must pay—on certification by the presiding judge of the administrative judicial region in which the other county is located—the pretrial judge's actual travel expenses and actual living expenses incurred for conducting the proceedings.

11.7 Relationship to Rule 13.

(a) *Generally.* This rule is to be construed and applied so as to facilitate the implementation of Rule 13 to the greatest extent possible.

(b) *Application of Rule 13 by Agreement of the Parties.* Parties may agree to the application of Rule 13. Such an agreement must be in writing and must be joined by all parties to the case. An agreement is effective and irrevocable when it is filed with the trial court if:

(1) no pretrial judge has been appointed in the case, or

(2) a pretrial judge has been appointed in the case, and the parties in all related cases to which the same pretrial judge has been assigned have likewise agreed to the application of Rule 13.

(c) *Assignments of Pretrial Judges After September 1, 2003.* An assignment of a pretrial judge to any case after September 1, 2003, must be made in consultation with the Chair of the Multidistrict Litigation Panel.

(d) *Consultation of Pretrial Judges.* In conducting pretrial proceedings and deciding pretrial matters, a pretrial judge assigned under this rule must consult with the judge of a pretrial court to which related cases have been transferred under Rule 13.

Adopted by Supreme Court Order eff. Oct. 1, 1997. Amended by Supreme Court Order eff. Nov. 12, 1997; Order of Aug. 29, 2003, eff. Aug. 31, 2003.

Rule 12. Public Access to Judicial Records

12.1 Policy. The purpose of this rule is to provide public access to information in the judiciary consistent with the mandates of the Texas Constitution that the public interests are best served by open courts and by an independent judiciary. The rule should be liberally construed to achieve its purpose.

12.2 Definitions. In this rule:

(a) Judge means a regularly appointed or elected judge or justice.

(b) Judicial agency means an office, board, commission, or other similar entity that is in the Judicial Department and that serves an administrative function for a court. A task force or committee created by a court or judge is a "judicial agency".

(c) Judicial officer means a judge, former or retired visiting judge, referee, commissioner, special master, court-appointed arbitrator, or other person exercising adjudicatory powers in the judiciary. A mediator or other provider of non-binding dispute resolution services is not a "judicial officer".

(d) Judicial record means a record made or maintained by or for a court or judicial agency in its regular course of business but not pertaining to its adjudicative function, regardless of whether that function relates to a specific case. A record of any nature created, produced, or filed in connection with any matter that is or has been before a court is not a judicial record. A record is a document, paper, letter, map, book, tape, photograph, film, recording, or other material, regardless of electronic or physical form, characteristics, or means of transmission.

(e) Records custodian means the person with custody of a judicial record determined as follows:

(1) The judicial records of a court with only one judge, such as any trial court, are in the custody of that judge. Judicial records pertaining to the joint administration of a number of those courts, such as the district courts in a particular county or region, are in the custody of the judge who presides over the joint administration, such as the local or regional administrative judge.

(2) The judicial records of a court with more than one judge, such as any appellate court, are in the custody of the chief justice or presiding judge, who must act under this rule in accordance with the vote of a majority of the judges of the court. But the judicial records relating specifically to the service of one such judge or that judge's own staff are in the custody of that judge.

(3) The judicial records of a judicial officer not covered by subparagraphs (1) and (2) are in the custody of that officer.

(4) The judicial records of a judicial agency are in the custody of its presiding officer, who must act under this rule in accordance with agency policy or the vote of a majority of the members of the agency.

12.3 Applicability. This rule does not apply to:

(a) records or information to which access is controlled by:

(1) a state or federal court rule, including:

(A) a rule of civil or criminal procedure, including Rule 76a, Texas Rules of Civil Procedure;

(B) a rule of appellate procedure;

(C) a rule of evidence;

(D) a rule of administration;

(2) a state or federal court order not issued merely to thwart the purpose of this rule;

(3) the Code of Judicial Conduct;

(4) Chapter 552, Government Code, or another statute or provision of law;

(b) records or information to which Chapter 552, Government Code, is made inapplicable by statute, rule, or other provision of law, other than Section 552.003(1)(B);

(c) records or information relating to an arrest or search warrant or a supporting affidavit, access to which is controlled by:

(1) a state or federal court rule, including a rule of civil or criminal procedure, appellate procedure, or evidence; or

(2) common law, court order, judicial decision, or another provision of law

(d) elected officials other than judges.

12.4 Access to Judicial Records.

(a) *Generally.* Judicial records other than those covered by Rules 12.3 and 12.5 are open to the general public for inspection and copying during regular business hours. But this rule does not require a court, judicial agency, or records custodian to:

(1) create a record, other than to print information stored in a computer;

(2) retain a judicial record for a specific period of time;

(3) allow the inspection of or provide a copy of information in a book or publication commercially available to the public; or

(4) respond to or comply with a request for a judicial record from or on behalf of an individual who is imprisoned or confined in a correctional facility as defined in Section 1.07(a), Penal Code, or in any other such facility in any state, federal, or foreign jurisdiction.

(b) *Voluntary Disclosure.* A records custodian may voluntarily make part or all of the information in a judicial record available to the public, subject to Rules 12.2(e)(2) and 12.2(e)(4), unless the disclosure is expressly prohibited by law or exempt under this rule, or the information is confidential under law. Information voluntarily disclosed must be made available to any person who requests it.

12.5 Exemptions from Disclosure. The following records are exempt from disclosure under this rule:

(a) *Judicial Work Product and Drafts.* Any record that relates to a judicial officer's adjudicative decision-making process prepared by that judicial officer, by another judicial officer, or by court staff, an intern, or any other person acting on behalf of or at the direction of the judicial officer.

(b) *Security Plans.* Any record, including a security plan or code, the release of which would jeopardize the security of an individual against physical injury or jeopardize information or property against theft, tampering, improper use, illegal disclosure, trespass, unauthorized access, or physical injury.

(c) *Personnel Information.* Any personnel record that, if disclosed, would constitute a clearly unwarranted invasion of personal privacy.

(d) *Home Address and Family Information.* Any record reflecting any person's home address, home or personal telephone number, social security number, or family members.

(e) *Applicants for Employment or Volunteer Services.* Any records relating to an applicant for employment or volunteer services.

(f) *Internal Deliberations on Court or Judicial Administration Matters.* Any record relating to internal deliberations of a court or judicial agency, or among judicial officers or members of a judicial agency, on matters of court or judicial administration.

(g) *Court Law Library Information.* Any record in a law library that links a patron's name with the materials requested or borrowed by that patron.

(h) *Judicial Calendar Information.* Any record that reflects a judicial officer's appointments or engagements that are in the future or that constitute an invasion of personal privacy.

(i) *Information Confidential Under Other Law.* Any record that is confidential or exempt from disclosure under a state or federal constitutional provision, statute or common law, including information that relates to:

(1) a complaint alleging misconduct against a judicial officer, if the complaint is exempt from disclosure under Chapter 33, Government Code, or other law;

(2) a complaint alleging misconduct against a person who is licensed or regulated by the courts, if the information is confidential under applicable law; or

(3) a trade secret or commercial or financial information made privileged or confidential by statute or judicial decision.

(j) *Litigation or Settlement Negotiations.* Any judicial record relating to civil or criminal litigation or settlement negotiations:

(1) in which a court or judicial agency is or may be a party; or

(2) in which a judicial officer or member of a judicial agency is or may be a party as a consequence of the person's office or employment.

(k) *Investigations of Character or Conduct.* Any record relating to an investigation of any person's character or conduct, unless:

(1) the record is requested by the person being investigated; and

(2) release of the record, in the judgment of the records custodian, would not impair the investigation.

(*l*) *Examinations.* Any record relating to an examination administered to any person, unless requested by the person after the examination is concluded.

12.6 Procedures for Obtaining Access to Judicial Records.

(a) *Request.* A request to inspect or copy a judicial record must be in writing and must include sufficient information to reasonably identify the record requested. The request must be sent to the records custodian and not to a court clerk or other agent for the records custodian. A requestor need not have detailed knowledge of the records custodian's filing system or procedures in order to obtain the information.

(b) *Time for Inspection and Delivery of Copies.* As soon as practicable—and not more than 14 days—after actual receipt of a request to inspect or copy a judicial record, if the record is available, the records custodian must either:

(1) allow the requestor to inspect the record and provide a copy if one is requested; or

(2) send written notice to the requestor stating that the record cannot within the prescribed period be produced or a copy provided, as applicable, and setting a reasonable date and time when the document will be produced or a copy provided, as applicable.

(c) *Place for Inspection.* A records custodian must produce a requested judicial record at a convenient, public area.

(d) *Part of Record Subject to Disclosure.* If part of a requested record is subject to disclosure under this rule and part is not, the records custodian must redact the portion of the record that is not subject to disclosure, permit the remainder of the record to be inspected, and provide a copy if requested.

(e) *Copying; Mailing.* The records custodian may deliver the record to a court clerk for copying. The records custodian may mail the copy to a requestor who has prepaid the postage.

(f) *Recipient of Request not Custodian of Record.* A judicial officer or a presiding officer of a judicial agency who receives a request for a judicial record not in his or her custody as defined by this rule must promptly attempt to ascertain who the custodian of the record is. If the recipient of the request can ascertain who the custodian of the requested record is, the recipient must promptly refer the request to that person and notify the requestor in writing of the referral. The time for response prescribed in Rule 12.6(b) does not begin to run until the referral is actually received by the records custodian. If the recipient cannot ascertain who the custodian of the requested record is, the recipient must promptly notify the requestor in writing that the recipient is not the custodian of the record and cannot ascertain who the custodian of the record is.

(g) *Inquiry to Requestor.* A person requesting a judicial record may not be asked to disclose the purpose of the request as a condition of obtaining the judicial record. But a records custodian may make inquiry to establish the proper identification of the requestor or to clarify the nature or scope of a request.

(h) *Uniform Treatment of Requests.* A records custodian must treat all requests for information uniformly without regard to the position or occupation of the requestor or the person on whose behalf a request is made, including whether the requestor or such person is a member of the media.

12.7 Costs for Copies of Judicial Records; Appeal of Assessment.

(a) *Cost.* The cost for a copy of a judicial record is either:

(1) the cost prescribed by statute, or

(2) if no statute prescribes the cost, the cost the Office of the Attorney General prescribes by rule in the Texas Administrative Code.

(b) *Waiver or Reduction of Cost Assessment by Records Custodian.* A records custodian may reduce or waive the charge for a copy of a judicial record if:

(1) doing so is in the public interest because providing the copy of the record primarily benefits the general public, or

(2) the cost of processing collection of a charge will exceed the amount of the charge.

(c) *Appeal of Cost Assessment.* A person who believes that a charge for a copy of a judicial record is excessive may appeal the overcharge in the manner prescribed by Rule 12.9 for the appeal of the denial of access to a judicial record.

(d) *Records Custodian not Personally Responsible for Cost.* A records custodian is not required to incur personal expense in furnishing a copy of a judicial record.

12.8 Denial of Access to a Judicial Record.

(a) *When Request May be Denied.* A records custodian may deny a request for a judicial record under this rule only if the records custodian:

(1) reasonably determines that the requested judicial record is exempt from required disclosure under this rule; or

(2) makes specific, non-conclusory findings that compliance with the request would substantially and unreasonably impede the routine operation of the court or judicial agency.

(b) *Time to Deny.* A records custodian who denies access to a judicial record must notify the person requesting the record of the denial within a reasonable time—not to exceed 14 days—after receipt of the request, or before the deadline for responding to the request extended under Rule 12.6 (b)(2).

(c) *Contents of Notice of Denial.* A notice of denial must be in writing and must:

(1) state the reason for the denial;

(2) inform the person of the right of appeal provided by Rule 12.9; and

(3) include the name and address of the Administrative Director of the Office of Court Administration.

12.9 Relief from Denial of Access to Judicial Records.

(a) *Appeal.* A person who is denied access to a judicial record may appeal the denial by filing a petition for review with the Administrative Director of the Office of Court Administration.

(b) *Contents of Petition for Review.* The petition for review:

(1) must include a copy of the request to the record custodian and the records custodian's notice of denial;

(2) may include any supporting facts, arguments, and authorities that the petitioner believes to be relevant; and

(3) may contain a request for expedited review, the grounds for which must be stated.

(c) *Time for Filing.* The petition must be filed not later than 30 days after the date that the petitioner receives notice of a denial of access to the judicial record.

(d) *Notification of Records Custodian and Presiding Judges.* Upon receipt of the petition for review, the Administrative Director must promptly notify the records custodian who denied access to the judicial record and the presiding judge of each administrative judicial region of the filing of the petition.

(e) *Response.* A records custodian who denies access to a judicial record and against whom relief is sought under this section may—within 14 days of receipt of notice from the Administrative Director—submit a written response to the petition for review and include supporting facts and authorities in the response. The records custodian must mail a copy of the response to the petitioner. The records custodian may also submit for in camera inspection any record, or a sample of records, to which access has been denied.

(f) *Formation of Special Committee.* Upon receiving notice under Rule 12.9(d), the presiding judges must refer the petition to a special committee of not less than five of the presiding judges for review. The presiding judges must notify the Administrative Director, the petitioner, and the records custodian of the names of the judges selected to serve on the committee.

(g) *Procedure for Review.* The special committee must review the petition and the records custodian's response and determine whether the requested judicial record should be made available under this rule to the petitioner. The special committee may request the records custodian to submit for in camera inspection a record, or a sample of records, to which access has been denied. The records custodian may respond to the request in whole or in part but it not required to do so.

(h) *Considerations.* When determining whether the requested judicial record should be made available under this rule to petition, the special committee must consider:

(1) the text and policy of this Rule;

(2) any supporting and controverting facts, arguments, and authorities in the petition and the response; and

(3) prior applications of this Rule by other special committees or by courts.

(i) *Expedited Review.* On request of the petitioner, and for good cause shown, the special committee may schedule an expedited review of the petition.

(j) *Decision.* The special committee's determination must be supported by a written decision that must:

(1) issue within 60 days of the date that the Administrative Director received the petition for review;

(2) either grant the petition in whole or in part or sustain the denial of access to the requested judicial record;

(3) state the reasons for the decision, including appropriate citations to this rule; and

(4) identify the record or portions of the record to which access is ordered or denied, but only if the description does not disclose confidential information.

(k) *Notice of Decision.* The special committee must send the decision to the Administrative Director. On receipt of the decision from the special committee, the Administrative Director must:

(1) immediately notify the petitioner and the records custodian of the decision and include a copy of the decision with the notice; and

(2) maintain a copy of the special committee's decision in the Administrative Director's office for public inspection.

(*l*) *Publication of Decisions.* The Administrative Director must publish periodically to the judiciary and the general public the special committees' decisions.

(m) *Final Decision.* A decision of a special committee under this rule is not appealable but is subject to review by mandamus.

(n) *Appeal to Special Committee Not Exclusive Remedy.* The right of review provided under this subdivision is not exclusive and does not preclude relief by mandamus.

12.10 Sanctions. A records custodian who fails to comply with this rule, knowing that the failure to comply is in violation of the rule, is subject to sanctions under the Code of Judicial Conduct.

Adopted by order of Oct. 9, 1998, and amended by order of March 24, 1999, eff. April 1, 1999; Nov. 27, 2008 and Feb. 10, 2009, eff. March 31, 2009.

Comment to 2008 change:

The Attorney General's rule, adopted in accordance with Section 552.262 of the Government Code, is in Section 70.3 of Title 1 of the Texas Administrative Code.

Comments

1. Although the definition of "judicial agency" in Rule 12.2(b) is comprehensive, applicability of the rule is restricted by Rule 12.3. The rule does not apply to judicial agencies whose records are expressly made subject to disclosure by statute, rule, or law. An example is the State Bar ("an administrative agency of the judicial department", Tex. Gov't Code § 81.011(a)), which is subject to the Public Information Act. Tex. Gov't Code § 81.033. Thus, no judicial agency must comply with both the Act and this rule; at most one can apply. Nor does the rule apply to judicial agencies expressly excepted from the Act by statute (other than by the general judiciary exception in section 552.003(b) of the Act), rule, or law. Examples are the Board of Legal Specialization, Tex. Gov't Code § 81.033, and the Board of Disciplinary Appeals,

Tex. R. Disciplinary App. 7.12. Because these boards are expressly excepted from the Act, their records are not subject to disclosure under this rule, even though no law affirmatively makes their records confidential. The Board of Law Examiners is partly subject to the Act and partly exempt, Tex. Gov't Code § 82.003, and therefore this rule is inapplicable to it. An example of a judicial agency subject to the rule is the Supreme Court Advisory Committee, which is neither subject to nor expressly excepted from the Act, and whose records are not made confidential by any law.

2. As stated in Rule 12.4, this rule does not require the creation or retention of records, but neither does it permit the destruction of records that are required to be maintained by statute or other law, such as Tex. Gov't Code §§ 441.158-.167, .180-.203; Tex. Local Gov't Code ch. 203; and 13 Tex. Admin. Code § 7.122.

3. Rule 12.8 allows a records custodian to deny a record request that would substantially and unreasonably impede the routine operation of the court or judicial agency. As an illustration, and not by way of limitation, a request for "all judicial records" that is submitted every day or even every few days by the same person or persons acting in concert could substantially and unreasonably impede the operations of a court or judicial agency that lacked the staff to respond to such repeated requests.

Rule 13. Multidistrict Litigation

13.1 Authority and Applicability.

(a) *Authority.* This rule is promulgated under sections 74.161–.164 of the Texas Government Code and chapter 90 of the Texas Civil Practices[1] and Remedies Code.

(b) *Applicability.* This rule applies to:

(1) civil actions that involve one or more common questions of fact and that were filed in a constitutional county court, county court at law, probate court, or district court on or after September 1, 2003;

(2) civil actions filed before September 1, 2003, that involve claims for asbestos- or silica-related injuries, to the extent permitted by chapter 90 of the Texas Civil Practice and Remedies Code.

(c) *Other Cases.* Cases to which this rule does not apply are governed by Rule 11 of these rules.

13.2 Definitions. As used in this rule:

(a) *MDL Panel* means the judicial panel on multidistrict litigation designated pursuant to section 74.161 of the Texas Government Code, including any temporary members designated by the Chief Justice of the Supreme Court of Texas in his or her discretion when regular members are unable to sit for any reason.

(b) *Chair* means the chair of the MDL Panel, who is designated by the Chief Justice of the Supreme Court of Texas.

(c) *MDL Panel Clerk* means the Clerk of the Supreme Court of Texas.

(d) *Trial court* means the court in which a case is filed.

(e) *Pretrial court* means the district court to which related cases are transferred for consolidated or coordinated pretrial proceedings under this rule.

(f) *Related* means that cases involve one or more common questions of fact.

(g) *Tag–along case* means a case related to cases in an MDL transfer order but not itself the subject of an initial MDL motion or order.

13.3 Procedure for Requesting Transfer.

(a) *Motion for Transfer; Who May File; Contents.* A party in a case may move for transfer of the case and related cases to a pretrial court. The motion must be in writing and must:

(1) state the common question or questions of fact involved in the cases;

(2) contain a clear and concise explanation of the reasons that transfer would be for the convenience of the parties and witnesses and would promote the just and efficient conduct of the cases;

(3) state whether all parties in those cases for which transfer is sought agree to the motion; and

(4) contain an appendix that lists:

(A) the cause number, style, and trial court of the related cases for which transfer is sought; and

(B) all parties in those cases and the names, addresses, telephone numbers, fax numbers, and email addresses of all counsel.

(b) *Request for Transfer by Judges.* A trial court or a presiding judge of an administrative judicial region may request a transfer of related cases to a pretrial court. The request must be in writing and must list the cases to be transferred.

(c) *Transfer on the MDL Panel's Own Initiative.* The MDL Panel may, on its own initiative, issue an order to show cause why related cases should not be transferred to a pretrial court.

(d) *Response; Reply; Who May File; When to File.* Any party in a related case may file:

(1) a response to a motion or request for transfer within twenty days after service of such motion or request;

(2) a response to an order to show cause issued under subparagraph (c) within the time provided in the order; and

(3) a reply to a response within ten days after service of such response.

(e) *Form of Motion, Response, Reply, and Other Documents.* A motion for transfer, response, reply, or other document addressed to the MDL Panel must conform to the requirements of Rule 9.4 of the Texas Rules of Appellate Procedure. Without leave of the MDL Panel, the following must not exceed 20 pages: the portions of a motion to transfer required by subparagraphs (a)(1)–(2); a response; and a reply. The MDL Panel may request additional briefing from any party.

(f) *Filing.* A motion, request, response, reply, or other document addressed to the MDL Panel must be filed with the MDL Panel Clerk. The MDL Panel Clerk may require that all documents also be transmitted to the clerk electronically. In addition, a party must send a copy of the motion, response, reply, or other document to each member of the MDL Panel.

(g) *Filing Fees.* The MDL Panel Clerk may set reasonable fees approved by the Supreme Court of Texas for filing and other services provided by the clerk.

(h) *Service.* A party must serve a motion, response, reply, or other document on all parties in related cases in which transfer is sought. The MDL Panel Clerk may designate a party or parties to serve a request for transfer on all other parties. Service is governed by Rule 9.5 of the Texas Rules of Appellate Procedure.

(i) *Notice to Trial Court.* A party must file in the trial court a notice — in the form prescribed by the MDL Panel — that a motion for transfer has been filed. The MDL Panel Clerk must cause such notice to be filed when a request for transfer by a judge has been filed.

(j) *Evidence.* The MDL Panel will accept as true facts stated in a motion, response, or reply unless another party contradicts them. A party may file evidence with the MDL Panel Clerk only with leave of the MDL Panel. The MDL Panel may order parties to submit evidence by affidavit or deposition and to file documents, discovery, or stipulations from related cases.

(k) *Hearing.* The MDL Panel may decide any matter on written submission or after an oral hearing before one or more of its members at a time and place of its choosing. Notice of the date of submission or the time and place of oral hearing must be given to all parties in all related cases.

(*l*) *Decision.* The MDL Panel may order transfer if three members concur in a written order finding that related cases involve one or more common questions of fact, and that transfer to a specified district court will be for the convenience of the parties and witnesses and will promote the just and efficient conduct of the related cases.

(m) *Orders Signed by Chair or Clerk; Members Identified.* Every order of the MDL Panel must be signed by either the chair or by the MDL Panel Clerk, and must identify the members of the MDL Panel who concurred in the ruling.

(n) *Notice of Actions by MDL Panel.* The MDL Panel Clerk must give notice to all parties in all related cases of all actions of the MDL Panel, including orders to show cause, settings of submissions and oral arguments, and decisions. The MDL Panel Clerk may direct a party or parties to give such notice. The clerk may determine the manner in which notice is to be given, including that notice should be given only by email or fax.

(o) *Retransfer.* On its own initiative, on a party's motion, or at the request of the pretrial court, the MDL Panel may order cases transferred from one pretrial court to another pretrial court when the pretrial judge has died, resigned, been replaced at an election, requested retransfer, recused, or been disqualified, or in other circumstances when retransfer will promote the just and efficient conduct of the cases.

13.4 Effect on the Trial Court of the Filing of a Motion for Transfer.

(a) *No Automatic Stay.* The filing of a motion under this rule does not limit the jurisdiction of the trial court or suspend proceedings or orders in that court.

(b) *Stay of Proceedings.* The trial court or the MDL Panel may stay all or part of any trial court proceedings until a ruling by the MDL Panel.

13.5 Transfer to a Pretrial Court.

(a) *Transfer Effective upon Notice.* A case is deemed transferred from the trial court to the pretrial court when a notice of transfer is filed with the trial court and the pretrial court. The notice must:

(1) list all parties who have appeared and remain in the case, and the names, addresses, phone numbers, and bar numbers of their attorneys or, if a party is pro se, the party's name, address, and phone number;

(2) list those parties who have not yet appeared in the case; and

(3) attach a copy of the MDL transfer order.

(b) *No Further Action in Trial Court.* After notice of transfer is filed in the trial court, the trial court must take no further action in the case except for good cause stated in the order in which such action is taken and after conferring with the pretrial court. But service of any process already issued by the trial court may be completed and the return filed in the pretrial court.

(c) *Transfer of Files; Master File and New Files in the Pretrial Court.* If the trial court and pretrial court are in the same county, the trial court must transfer the case file to the pretrial court in accordance with local rules governing the courts of that county. If the trial court and pretrial court are not in the same county, the trial court clerk must transmit the case file to the pretrial court clerk. The pretrial court clerk, after consultation with the judge of the pretrial court, must establish a master file and open new files for each case transferred using the information provided in the notice of transfer. The pretrial court may direct the manner in which pretrial documents are filed, including electronic filing.

(d) *Filing Fees and Costs.* Unless the MDL Panel assesses costs otherwise, the party moving for transfer must pay the cost of refiling the transferred cases in the pretrial court, including filing fees and other reasonable costs.

(e) *Transfer of Tag-along Cases.* A tag-along case is deemed transferred to the pretrial court when a notice of transfer — in the form described in Rule 13.5(a) — is filed in both the trial court and the pretrial court. Within 30 days after service of the notice, a party to the case or to any of the related cases already transferred to the pretrial court may move the pretrial court to remand the case to the trial court on the ground that it is not a tag-along case. If the motion to remand is granted, the case must be returned to the trial court, and costs including attorney fees may be assessed by the pretrial court in its remand order. The order of the pretrial court may be appealed to the MDL Panel by a motion for rehearing filed with the MDL Panel Clerk.

13.6 Proceedings in Pretrial Court.

(a) *Judges Who May Preside.* The MDL Panel may assign as judge of the pretrial court any active district judge, or any former or retired district or appellate judge who is approved by the Chief Justice of the Supreme Court of Texas. An assignment under this rule is not subject to objection under chapter 74 of the Government Code. The judge assigned as judge of the pretrial court has exclusive jurisdiction over each related case transferred pursuant to this rule unless a case is retransferred by the MDL Panel or is finally resolved or remanded to the trial court for trial.

(b) *Authority of Pretrial Court.* The pretrial court has the authority to decide, in place of the trial court, all pretrial matters in all related cases transferred to the court Those matters include, for example, jurisdiction, joinder, venue, discovery, trial preparation (such as motions to strike expert witnesses, preadmission of exhibits, and motions in limine), mediation, and disposition by means other than conventional trial on the merits (such as default judgment, summary judgment, and settlement). The pretrial court may set aside or modify any pretrial ruling made by the trial court before transfer over which the trial court's plenary power would not have expired had the case not been transferred.

(c) *Case Management.* The pretrial court should apply sound judicial management methods early, continuously, and actively, based on its knowledge of each individual case and the entire litigation, in order to set fair and firm time limits tailored to ensure the expeditious resolution of each case and the just and efficient conduct of the litigation as a whole. After a case is transferred, the pretrial court should, at the earliest practical date, conduct a hearing and enter a case management order. The pretrial court should consider at the hearing, and its order should address, all matters pertinent to the conduct of the litigation, including:

(1) settling the pleadings;

(2) determining whether severance, consolidation, or coordination with other actions is desirable and whether identification of separable triable portions of the case is desirable;

(3) scheduling preliminary motions;

(4) scheduling discovery proceedings and setting appropriate limitations on discovery, including the establishment and timing of discovery procedures;

(5) issuing protective orders;

(6) scheduling alternative dispute resolution conferences;

(7) appointing organizing or liaison counsel;

(8) scheduling dispositive motions;

(9) providing for an exchange of documents, including adopting a uniform numbering system for documents, establishing a document depository, and determining whether electronic service of discovery materials and pleadings is warranted;

(10) determining if the use of technology, videoconferencing, or teleconferencing is appropriate;

(11) considering such other matters the court or the parties deem appropriate for the just and efficient resolution of the cases; and

(12) scheduling further conferences as necessary.

(d) *Trial Settings.* The pretrial court, in conjunction with the trial court, may set a transferred case for trial at such a time and on such a date as will promote the convenience of the parties and witnesses and the just and efficient disposition of all related proceedings. The pretrial court must confer, or order the parties to confer, with the trial court regarding potential trial settings or other matters regarding remand. The trial court must cooperate reasonably with the pretrial court, and the pretrial court must defer appropriately to the trial court's docket. The trial court must not continue or postpone a trial setting without the concurrence of the pretrial court.

13.7 Remand to Trial Court.

(a) *No Remand If Final Disposition by Pretrial Court.* A case in which the pretrial court has rendered a final and appealable judgment will not be remanded to the trial court.

(b) *Remand.* The pretrial court may order remand of one or more cases, or separable triable portions of cases, when pretrial proceedings have been completed to such a degree that the purposes of the transfer have been fulfilled or no longer apply.

(c) *Transfer of Files.* When a case is remanded to the trial court, the clerk of the pretrial court will send the case file to the trial court without retaining a copy unless otherwise ordered. The parties may file in the remanded case copies of any pleadings or orders from the pretrial court's master file. The clerk of the trial court will reopen the trial court file under the cause number of the trial court, without a new filing fee.

13.8 Pretrial court orders binding in the trial court after remand.

(a) *Generally.* The trial court should recognize that to alter a pretrial court order without a compelling justification would frustrate the purpose of consolidated and coordinated pretrial proceedings. The pretrial court should recognize that its rulings should not unwisely restrict a trial court from responding to circumstances that arise following remand.

(b) *Concurrence of the Pretrial Court Required to Change Its Orders.* Without the written concurrence of the pretrial court, the trial court cannot, over objection, vacate, set aside, or modify pretrial court orders, including orders related to summary judgment, jurisdiction, venue, joinder, special exceptions, discovery, sanctions related to pretrial proceedings, privileges, the admissibility of expert testimony, and scheduling.

(c) *Exceptions.* The trial court need not obtain the written concurrence of the pretrial court to vacate, set aside, or modify pretrial court orders regarding the admissibility of evidence at trial (other than expert evidence) when necessary because of changed circumstances, to correct an error of law, or to prevent manifest injustice. But the trial court must support its action with specific findings and conclusions in a written order or stated on the record.

(d) *Unavailability of Pretrial Court.* If the pretrial court is unavailable to rule, for whatever reason, the concurrence of the MDL Panel Chair must be obtained.

13.9 Review.

(a) *MDL Panel Decision.* An order of the MDL Panel, including one granting or denying a motion for transfer, may be reviewed only by the Supreme Court in an original proceeding.

(b) *Orders by the Trial Court and Pretrial Court.* An order or judgment of the trial court or pretrial court may be reviewed by the appellate court that regularly reviews orders of the court in which the case is pending at the time review is sought, irrespective of whether that court issued the order or judgment to be reviewed. A case involving such review may not be transferred for purposes of docket equalization among appellate courts.

(c) *Review Expedited.* An appellate court must expedite review of an order or judgment in a case pending in a pretrial court.

13.10 MDL Panel Rules.

The MDL Panel will operate at the direction of its Chair in accordance with rules prescribed by the panel and approved by the Supreme Court of Texas.

13.11 Civil Actions Filed Before September 1, 2003, Involving Claims for Asbestos– and Silica–Related Injuries.

(a) *Applicability.* To the extent permitted by chapter 90 of the Texas Civil Practice and Remedies Code, Rule 13.11 applies to civil actions filed before September 1, 2003, that involve claims for asbestos- or silica-related injuries.

(b) *Statutory References; Definitions.* Statutory references in Rule 13.11 are to chapter 90 of the Texas Civil Practice and Remedies Code. "Claimant" has the meaning assigned in section 90.001(6). "Report" has the meaning assigned in section 90.001(24).

(c) *Notice of Transfer Under Section 90.010(b).* A notice of transfer under section 90.010(b) must be filed in the trial court and the pretrial court and must:

(1) be titled "Notice of Transfer Under Section 90.010(b)";

(2) list all parties who have appeared and remain in the case, and the names, addresses, phone numbers, and bar numbers of their attorneys or, if a party is pro se, the party's name, address and phone number;

(3) state the name of each claimant transferred;

(4) attach to the notice filed in the pretrial court a copy of the claimant's live petition; and

(5) if filed by a defendant, contain a certificate stating that the filing party conferred, or at least made a reasonable attempt to confer, with opposing counsel about whether the notice of transfer is appropriate as to each individual claimant transferred.

(d) *Effect on Pending Motion for Severance.* If, when a notice of transfer is filed in the trial court, a motion for severance has been filed but the trial court has not ruled, the trial court must rule on the motion within 14 days of the date the notice of transfer is filed, or the motion is deemed granted by operation of law.

(e) *When Transfer Effective.* A case is deemed transferred from the trial court to the pretrial court when a notice of transfer is filed with the trial court unless a motion for severance is pending. If a motion for severance is pending when a notice of transfer is filed with the trial court, a case is deemed transferred when the trial court rules on the motion or the motion is deemed granted by operation of law.

(f) *Further Action in Trial Court Limited.* After a notice of transfer is filed, the trial court must take no further action in the case except:

(1) to rule on a motion for severance pending when the notice of transfer was filed, or

(2) for good cause stated in the order in which such action is taken and after conferring with the pretrial court.

But service of any process already issued by the trial court may be completed and the return filed in the pretrial court.

(g) *Severed Case File.* If a claim is severed from a case that includes one or more claimants covered by section 90.010(a), the file for the severed claims in the trial court should be numerically linked to the original case file and should contain only the live petition containing the severed claim. The severed case file is deemed to include all papers in the original case file. The pretrial court may require a different procedure in the interests of justice and efficiency.

(h) *Transfer of Files.* The pretrial court may order the trial court clerk to transfer a case file to the pretrial court. A case file must not be transferred to the pretrial court except as ordered by that court.

(i) *Filing Fees and Costs.* A defendant who files a notice of transfer must pay the cost of filing the case in the pretrial court, including filing fees and other reasonable costs. If the pretrial court remands the case to the trial court, the pretrial court may order that costs be allocated between the parties in a way that encourages just and efficient compliance with this rule, and may award appropriate and reasonable attorney fees.

Adopted by order of Aug. 29, 2003, eff. Sept. 1, 2003; rule 13.9 amended by order of Jan. 27, 2005, eff. March 1, 2005; rule 13.1 amended and rule 13.11 adopted by order of Nov. 29, 2005, eff. Nov. 29, 2005.

1 So in original order.

Comment—2005

Subsections [13.1](a) and (b) are amended and subsection (c) is added to provide procedures for cases covered by chapter 90 of the Texas Civil Practices and Remedies Code, enacted effective September 1, 2005.

Comment—2005

Subsection [13.9](b) is amended and subsection (c) is added to clarify the handling of appeals by appellate courts. Subsection (b) forbids transfer for docket equalization but not for other purposes that might arise. Subsection (c) does not require that an appeal from an order or judgment of a case pending in a pretrial court be treated as an accelerated appeal under the Texas Rules of Appellate Procedure if it would otherwise not be accelerated. Rather, subsection (c) requires expedited consideration by the appellate court regardless of whether review is sought by an appeal that is or is not accelerated, or by mandamus.

Comment—2005

1. Rule 13.11 is added to provide procedures for cases covered by chapter 90 of the Texas Civil Practice and Remedies Code, enacted effective September 1, 2005.

2. The rule does not require a statement in the notice of transfer that no report has been served under chapter 90, or that a report has been served but does not comply with the provisions of that statute. The omission of such a requirement in the notice of transfer is not intended to limit the pretrial court's authority under Rule 166 of the Texas Rules of Civil Procedure to employ appropriate procedures to ascertain a party's position on the issue.

3. It is anticipated that the party filing a notice of transfer will usually be a defendant, and that the party filing a motion for severance will usually be a claimant. Ordinarily, a party filing the notice of transfer is responsible for filing fees and costs in the pretrial court, although there may be exceptions. See Rule 13.5(d). Also, a party who successfully moves to sever a claim into a separate proceeding in the trial court is customarily responsible for filing fees and costs, although severance is "on such terms as are just", Tex. R. Civ. P. 41, and again, there may be exceptions. The intent of this rule is that severance and transfer procedures minimize costs and burdens on parties and the courts.

4. A pretrial court has discretion under Rule 13.11(g)–(i) to order the maintenance and transfer of physical case files and to allocate costs and fees so as to minimize costs and burdens on parties and the courts.

Historical Notes

2005 Amendment

The Nov. 29, 2005 order provided:

"These amendments may be changed in response to comments received before April 1, 2006."

Rule 14. Repealed by order of the Supreme Court, dated Aug. 19, 2014, eff. Sept. 1, 2014

Rule 15. Appeals from Trial Courts in Counties Assigned to Multiple Appellate Districts

15.1 Applicability.

This rule applies to appeals from an order or judgment issued by a trial court in a county assigned by law to more than one court of appeals district unless assignment of such appeals is governed by statute. This rule does not apply to appeals to the Courts of Appeals for the First and Fourteenth Districts from trial courts in counties in those districts, as assignment of such appeals is governed by statute.

15.2 When Consolidation Required.

If notices of appeal filed by two or more parties from a single judgment or order designate different courts of appeals that have jurisdiction of the appeal because the county in which the trial court sits is assigned to more than one appellate district, the appeals must be consolidated in one of the courts of appeals.

15.3 Consolidation by Agreement; Notice to Courts of Appeals.

(a) *Appealing Parties to Confer Regarding Consolidation.* When any appealing party learns that two or more parties have properly designated different courts of appeals, that party must promptly confer with lead counsel for all other appealing parties (if represented, otherwise counsel must confer with the pro se party) and determine if all appealing parties will agree to consolidate the appeals in one of the courts of appeals.

(b) *Time to Provide Notice.* No later than 30 days—20 days in an accelerated appeal—after the filing date of the first-filed notice of appeal described in paragraph (a), the parties must submit to the clerks of both courts of appeals written notice either of the appealing parties' agreement to consolidate the appeals or of the appealing parties' inability to reach agreement regarding consolidation.

(c) *Contents of Notice.* The notice must identify each appealing party and the party's counsel (if represented, or state that the party is pro se), and must either identify the court of appeals designated by agreement or state that the appealing parties were unable to agree to consolidate all appeals in a particular court. The notice must also contain a certificate stating that the filing parties conferred, or made a reasonable attempt to confer, with all other appealing parties regarding consolidation of the appeals. If the notice states that all appealing parties have agreed to consolidation, it must identify every party or party's attorney who agreed to the consolidation.

(d) *Consolidation by Agreement of All Appealing Parties.* If the clerks of both courts of appeals receive notice that all appealing parties have agreed to consolidation, the chief justices of both courts will request the Chief Justice of the Supreme Court to transfer all pending appeals in the case to the court of appeals designated by the parties' agreement.

15.4 Consolidation When Appealing Parties Unable to Agree.

(a) *Clerks of Courts of Appeals to Jointly Notify Trial Court Clerk.*

(1) If both courts of appeals receive notice of the appealing parties' inability to reach agreement regarding consolidation, the clerks of both appellate courts must jointly notify the clerk of the trial court in writing of that fact.

(2) If the period described in Rule 15.3(b) has passed and the clerks of the two courts of appeals have not received any notice from the appealing parties regarding consolidation, the chief justices of the two courts of appeals shall confer and instruct the clerks of their respective courts to jointly notify the clerk of the trial court in writing that the appealing parties failed to timely submit notice of agreement regarding consolidation, and instruct the clerk to perform the selection process in Rule 15.4(b).

(b) *Consolidation by Trial Court Clerk.* After the trial court clerk receives notice from the clerks of the courts of appeals regarding either the appealing parties' inability to reach agreement as to consolidation or their failure to timely submit notice of agreement, the clerk shall write the numbers of the two courts of appeals on identical slips of paper and place the slips in a container folded in half or otherwise arranged so that the numbers are completely hidden from view. The trial court clerk shall draw a number from the container at random, in a public place, and shall assign the case to the court of appeals for the corresponding number drawn.

15.5 All Appeals From Same Judgment or Order to be Consolidated Together.

When appeals to multiple courts of appeals have been consolidated pursuant to this rule, other parties' appeals from the same judgment or order underlying the consolidated appeals must be assigned to the same court of appeals in which the previous appeals were consolidated.

Adopted by orders of March 10, 2008, and Aug. 20, 2008, eff. Sept. 1, 2008.

Comment

Assignments to the Courts of Appeals for the First and Fourteenth Districts are governed by Tex. Gov't Code § 22.202(h).

Rule 16. Additional Resources for Certain Cases

16.1 Authority and Applicability.

(a) *Authority.* This rule is promulgated under Sections 74.251–74.257 of the Government Code.

(b) *Applicability.* This rule applies to civil actions pending on or after May 1, 2012, in a constitutional county court, county court at law, probate court, or district court and that may require additional judicial resources.

(c) *Other Cases.* This rule does not apply to:

(1) criminal matters;

(2) grants for local court improvement under Section 72.029 of the Government Code;

(3) cases in which judicial review is sought under Chapter 2001, Subchapter G, of the Government Code;[1] or

(4) cases that have been transferred by the judicial panel on multidistrict litigation to a district court for consolidated or coordinated pretrial proceedings under Chapter 74, Subchapter H,[2] of the Government Code.

16.2 Definitions.

As used in this rule:

(a) *Judicial Committee for Additional Resources (JCAR)* means the judicial committee designated pursuant to Section 74.254 of the Government Code, including the chief justice of the Supreme Court of Texas and the presiding judges of the administrative judicial regions.

(b) *JCAR Clerk means* the Administrative Director of the Office of Court Administration (OCA).

(c) *Presiding Officer* means the Chief Justice of the Supreme Court of Texas.

(d) *Trial court* means the judge of the court in which a case is filed or assigned.

16.3 Duties of the Office of Court Administration.

(a) OCA will assist the JCAR in carrying out its duties under this rule by:

(1) providing support staff, meeting facilities, or technology to the JCAR;

(2) requesting appropriations for additional judicial resources from the legislature; and

(3) providing additional resources approved by the JCAR to the trial court.

(b) The JCAR Clerk must file any requests for additional resources, and any written determination by a presiding judge or the JCAR of such a request, made pursuant to this rule.

(c) At the conclusion of any case where additional resources were made available under this rule, OCA must prepare and file with the JCAR Clerk a report stating the additional resources provided and their estimated costs.

16.4 Considerations for Determining Whether a Case Requires Additional Resources.

In determining whether a case requires additional judicial resources, the trial court, presiding judge of the administrative judicial region in which the case is filed, and JCAR may consider whether a case involves or is likely to involve:

(a) a large number of parties who are separately represented by counsel;

(b) coordination with related actions pending in one or more courts in other counties of this state or in one or more United States district courts;

(c) numerous pre-trial motions that present difficult or novel legal issues that will be time consuming to resolve;

(d) a large number of witnesses or substantial documentary evidence;

(e) substantial post-judgment supervision;

(f) a trial that will last more than four weeks; or

(g) a substantial additional burden on the trial court's docket and the resources available to the trial court to hear the case.

16.5 Additional Resources.

One or more of the following resources may be made available under this rule:

(a) the assignment of an active or retired judge, subject to the consent of the trial court;

(b) additional legal, administrative, or clerical personnel;

(c) information and communication technology, including case management software, video teleconferencing, and specially designed courtroom presentation hardware or software to facilitate presentation of the evidence to the trier of fact;

(d) specialized continuing legal education;

(e) an associate judge;

(f) special accommodations or furnishings for the parties;

(g) other services or items determined necessary to try the case; and

(h) any other appropriate resources.

16.6 Procedure for Requesting Additional Resources.

(a) *Motion for Additional Resources.* A party in a case may move for the case to be designated as a case requiring additional resources. The motion must be in writing and must state:

(1) how the case involves or is likely to involve considerations that justify additional judicial resources;

(2) what additional judicial resources will promote the just and efficient conduct of the case;

(3) the time by which the additional resources are needed; and

(4) whether all parties in the case agree to the motion.

(b) *Determination by Trial Court.* The trial court, upon motion complying with subparagraph (a), or on its own initiative, must determine whether a case will require additional resources.

(c) *Request for Additional Judicial Resources.* If the trial court determines that a case requires additional resources under this rule it must:

(1) prepare a written request that states the nature of the case, the requested resources, and why the resources are needed;

(2) submit the request to the presiding judge of the administrative region in which the case is filed; and

(3) forward a copy of the request to the JCAR Clerk at the mailing address or email address listed on the "Contact Information" page of OCA's website.

(d) *Notice of Request for Additional Resources.* Upon receiving a request for additional resources, the JCAR clerk must send a copy of the request to the JCAR. Within 15 days of receiving the request, the presiding judge of the affected administrative judicial region or the JCAR Clerk must provide notice to the trial court of any action on the request, even if to report the inability to take action.

16.7 Review of Request for Additional Resources.

(a) *Review by Presiding Judge of Administrative Judicial Region.* Upon receipt, the presiding judge of the administrative judicial region in which the case is filed must review the trial court's request for additional resources. If the presiding judge agrees with the trial court's determination that the case requires additional resources, the presiding judge must:

(1) use resources previously allotted to the presiding judge, if the resources are permitted to be used for the purpose requested; or

(2) submit a request for additional resources to the JCAR.

(b) *Review by the JCAR.* If the presiding judge of the administrative judicial region in which the case is filed submits a request for additional resources to the JCAR under subparagraph (a)(2), the JCAR must determine whether the case requires additional resources. If the JCAR determines additional resources are required, the JCAR may make available any resources the JCAR considers necessary or appropriate.

(c) *Notice of Determination of Request.* The presiding judge of the administrative judicial region in which the case is filed or, if a request is submitted to the JCAR under subparagraph (a)(2), the JCAR must notify the JCAR Clerk in writing upon approval or denial of a request for additional resources. On receipt of such notice, the JCAR Clerk must transmit a copy to the affected trial court.

16.8 Implementation of Additional Resources.

If the JCAR determines that a case requires additional resources, the presiding judge of the administrative judicial region in which the case is filed and the Office of Court Administration must cooperate with the trial court or its designee in providing the approved additional resources.

16.9 Effect of Motion for Additional Resources.

(a) *Jurisdiction.* The filing of a motion under this rule does not deprive the trial court of jurisdiction or suspend proceedings or orders in that court.

(b) *No Stay or Continuance of Proceedings.* The filing of a motion under this rule is not grounds for a stay or continuance of the proceedings during the period the motion or request is being considered.

16.10 Review of Determinations by the Trial Court, Presiding Judge or JCAR.

A determination by the trial court, the presiding judge of the administrative region, or the JCAR of a request or motion for additional resources is not appealable or subject to review by mandamus.

16.11 Provisions for Additional Resources.

(a) *Costs for Additional Resources.* The costs for additional resources provided under this rule must be paid by the state and must not be taxed against any party in the case for which the resources are provided or against the county in which the case is pending.

(b) *Appropriations for Additional Resources.* Additional resources are subject to the availability of appropriations made by the legislature or as provided through budget execution authority or other budget adjustment method, or from funds made available by grants or donations.

Adopted by Supreme Court Order of Mar. 1, 2012, eff. May 1, 2012.

[1] V.T.C.A., Government Code § 2001.171 et seq.

[2] V.T.C.A., Government Code § 74.161 et seq.

Comment

Rule 16 is added to provide procedures for cases that require additional resources, as mandated by sections 74.252–74.257 of the Government Code, enacted effective January 1, 2012. The procedures in Rule 16 are not exclusive; judges may still be assigned as provided for in sections 74.052–74.062 of the Government Code.

MANDATORY REPORTS OF JUDICIAL APPOINTMENTS AND FEES

Effective April 1, 1994

Including Amendments Received Through February 1, 2016

SUPREME COURT ORDER

Section 1. Every appointment made in a civil case, probate case, or proceeding governed by Titles 1, 2, or 4 of the Family Code, by a regular or assigned judge of any district court, constitutional county court, statutory county court, statutory probate court, court master or court referee of a person to a position for which any type of fee may be paid shall be made by written order.

Section 2. Every application or request for the payment of a fee by such an appointee shall be approved by the court of the judge making the appointment. This approval shall be accomplished by a separate written order.

Section 3. Orders regarding appointments made and fees paid may not be sealed or otherwise withheld from public disclosure for any reason, regardless of whether any other information in the case is protected from disclosure.

Section 4. This order does not apply to appointments where compensation is solely by government salary rather than by fee, or where the right to select the person appointed is reserved by law to a party, as with independent executors and executrixes, or to appointments of private process servers pursuant to TEX. R. CIV. P. 103. This order does not apply to criminal cases and to proceedings governed by Title 3 of the Family Code (Delinquent Children and Children in Need of Supervision).

Section 5. At the end of each month, each district and county clerk shall prepare a report to include each fee approved during that month for payment in the amount of $500 or more. The report shall indicate:

(1) the name of each person appointed by the judge of each district court, county court, statutory county court, and statutory probate court in the county to a position for which a fee of $500 or more has been approved during the month to be paid from any source;

(2) the name of the judge approving the payment of the fees;

(3) the case number and style of the case in which the fee was approved to be paid;

(4) the date of the order approving the payment of the fee;

(5) the position to which the person was appointed;

(6) whether the appointee is an attorney, a private professional guardian, associated with a public guardianship program, or a friend or family member of the ward or the deceased; and

(7) the amount of the fee approved for payment, and the source of such payment.

Section 6. The clerk shall make a copy of this report available for public inspection in the clerk's office, and shall, before the twentieth day of the month following the month reported, transmit a copy of the report to the Supreme Court through the State Office of Court Administration in Austin.

Section 7. The clerk shall retain each report for at least two years following the date it is made available for public inspection.

Section 8. The clerk may charge the normal reasonable fee charged by the clerk for similar reproductions for reproducing the report for a person requesting a copy of a report.

Section 9. The orders signed pursuant to Sections 1 and 2 above shall be sufficiently specific to enable the clerk to prepare the report required by Section 5 above.

Section 10. This order is effective immediately, and applies to all fees of $500 or more approved for payment on or after November 1, 2007 and required to be reported before the twentieth day of the following month.

Section 11. A copy of this order shall be transmitted by the Clerk of the Supreme Court to each district and county-level judge and to each district and county clerk.

Section 12. This order amends and supersedes Miscellaneous Order No. 94–9143 (September 21, 1994) of this Court.

Adopted by order of Jan. 18, 1994, April 1, 1994. Amended by orders of Sept. 21, 1994, eff. Sept. 21, 1994; Oct. 30, 2007, eff. Oct. 30, 2007.

RULES GOVERNING COURT REPORTER CERTIFICATION AND COURT REPORTING FIRM REGISTRATION [REPEALED]

Repealed by Order of the Supreme Court, dated August 19, 2014, effective September 1, 2014

Rules I to XIV. Repealed by Order of the Supreme Court, dated Aug. 19, 2014, eff. Sept. 1, 2014

Historical Notes

For subject matter of former rules, see, now, Rules and Fees of the Judicial Branch Certification Commission.

CODE OF PROFESSIONAL CONDUCT FOR CERTIFIED SHORTHAND REPORTERS AND COURT REPORTING FIRMS

As Approved by the Supreme Court of Texas in Chambers on December 30, 2003 effective January 1, 2004

Including Amendments Received Through February 1, 2016

1. APPLICABILITY AND DEFINITIONS

The rules of professional conduct, where applicable, shall apply to and be observed by all Certified Shorthand Reporters and Court Reporting Firms engaged in the practice of court reporting or offering the services of a Certified Shorthand Reporter, unless otherwise provided by law.

The term Texas Court Reporters Certification Board will be hereinafter referred to as the CRCB or the Board.

The term Certified Shorthand Reporter will be hereinafter referred to as CSR.

The term Court Reporting Firm will be hereinafter referred to as CRF.

The term CRF includes officers, directors, managerial employees, and agents of the CRF or affiliate offices.

The term Code of Professional Conduct will be hereinafter referred to as the Code.

The term transcript shall include the reduction into writing of an oral deposition or any legal proceeding identified in 2(a) and 2(b).

2. LICENSE AND REGISTRATION REQUIREMENTS

An individual shall not provide court reporting services for use in litigation in the courts of this State, grand jury, arbitration, county or city proceedings unless the individual has a license issued by the CRCB, unless otherwise authorized by rule or statute. The license shall be in good standing.

A CRF shall not provide court reporting services for use in litigation in the courts of this State, grand jury, arbitration, county or city proceedings unless the firm has a current registration issued by the CRCB. The registration shall be in good standing at all times that court reporting services are provided by the CRF.

For purposes of this section, good standing is defined as a CSR whose license is eligible for renewal and a CRF with a current registration with the CRCB.

A CSR whose license has been suspended or revoked by another state or federal authority is subject to review and/or disciplinary action by the Board.

3. PROFESSIONAL JUDGMENT

A CSR or CRF shall not take any action or attempt to influence, directly or indirectly, the sound professional judgment of a CSR or to cause a CSR or CRF to violate the Code.

A CSR shall not allow a non-certified person or non-registered entity to interfere or intervene with the CSR's practice of court reporting; nor shall the CSR submit to such interference or intervention by a non-certified person or non-registered entity.

A CSR shall avoid all relationships, which could result in interference or intervention in the CSR's practice by a non-certified person or non-registered entity.

A CSR shall be responsible for his or her actions and is directly responsible to the parties and/or the Court in carrying out his or her duties in accordance with the Code.

A CRF shall be responsible for the actions of the firm and is directly responsible to the parties and/or the Court in carrying out the duties of the firm in accordance with the Code.

4. HONESTY, INTEGRITY AND FAIR DEALING

CSRs and CRFs shall conduct business with honesty, integrity, and fair dealing to all parties in a timely manner, in services rendered, and in the amount charged.

Honesty, integrity, and fair dealing include but are not limited to the following:

A CSR shall deliver a transcript or reporter's record to a client, court, or CRF in a timely manner as determined by statute, court order, or agreement.

A CRF shall deliver a transcript or reporter's record to a client or court in a timely manner as determined by statute, court order, or agreement.

A CSR shall not produce a partial transcript or partial reporter's record except upon order of a court, agreement of the parties, or request of a party.

A CSR or CRF shall notify all parties or their attorneys of a request for a transcript or reporter's record, or any part thereof, in sufficient time for copies to be prepared and delivered simultaneously with the original.

A CSR shall not go "off the record" during a deposition when not agreed to by all parties or their attorneys unless otherwise ordered by the Court.

A CSR shall go "on the record" during a deposition at the request of any party or the party's attorney.

A CSR or CRF shall not engage in a pattern of receiving, or benefiting from, or being employed as a result of, or giving, directly or indirectly, any incentive, reward or anything of value to attorneys, clients, witnesses, insurance companies, or any other persons or entities associated with the litigation, or to the representatives or agents of any of the foregoing, except for nominal items that do not exceed $100 in the aggregate per recipient per year.

Nothing in the above section shall be construed to define providing value-added business services, including long-term volume discounts, such as the pricing of products and services, as prohibited gifts, incentives, or rewards.

5. BEHAVIOR

The CSR or CRF shall treat lawyers and members of the judiciary with respect.

The CSR shall conduct herself/himself in a legal proceeding in a professional manner and demonstrate respect for the Court and the law.

The CSR shall not engage in any conduct that offends the dignity and decorum of any legal proceeding.

The CSR shall preserve the shorthand notes in accordance with statute or court order, or for a period of three years for oral depositions in civil cases. The required retention period stated by statute or court order shall prevail over this rule. Preservation shall be through storage of the original paper notes or an electronic copy of either the shorthand notes or the English transcript of the notes on computer disks, cassettes, backup tape systems, optical or laser disk systems, or any other reliable storage media.

6. COMPETENCY

A CSR shall produce an accurate transcript or reporter's record.

A CSR shall engage in the practice of shorthand reporting using only the method for which the reporter was certified.

A CSR shall prepare all records in accordance with the Uniform Format Manual for Texas Court Reporters.

A CSR shall not undertake any engagement for the performance of professional services that is beyond the reporter's competence.

A CSR shall meet promised delivery dates whenever possible, make timely delivery of transcripts when no date is specified, and provide immediate notification of delays.

7. DUTY TO NOTIFY

A CSR shall have the immediate duty to notify the parties, attorneys, and/or the Court in any case where the court reporting duties requested are beyond the CSR's capabilities. A CSR's decision on whether to accept or continue a job, which may require expertise beyond the CSR's capabilities, shall be based on the exercise of professional judgment by the CSR.

The duty to notify includes situations in which the CSR is not able to meet court-imposed or reasonable client deadlines for delivery of transcripts. The CSR is responsible for recognizing situations in which the CSR is required to notify the parties, attorneys, and/or the Court where the court reporting duties are beyond the CSR's capabilities.

8. OBSERVANCE OF CONFIDENTIALITY

A CSR or CRF shall preserve the confidentiality and ensure the security of information, oral or written, entrusted to CSR or CRF by any of the parties in a proceeding.

9. MISCONDUCT

A CSR or CRF shall not violate this Code, knowingly assist or induce another to do so, or violate this Code through the acts of another.

A CSR shall not engage in fraud or deceit in obtaining a certificate as a CSR.

A CSR shall not use or represent that he or she possesses any certificate, college degree, or title to which he or she is not entitled.

A CRF shall not engage in fraud or misrepresentation in obtaining registration as a CRF.

A CSR or CRF shall not commit any criminal act that reflects adversely on the CSR's honesty, trustworthiness, or fitness as a CSR.

A CSR or CRF shall not engage in conduct involving dishonesty, fraud, deceit, or misrepresentation.

A CSR or CRF shall not engage in conduct constituting obstruction of justice.

A CSR or CRF who has been held in contempt by a state or federal court is subject to review and/or disciplinary action by the Board.

With regard to a complaint or disciplinary proceeding, a CSR or CRF shall furnish to the CRCB a response or other information within the time frame requested unless the CSR or CRF in good faith timely asserts a privilege or other legal ground for failure to do so.

A CSR or CRF shall not engage in the practice of court reporting when the CSR or CRF is on inactive status or when the right to practice has been suspended or terminated, including but not limited to situations where a CSR's or CRF's right to practice has been administratively suspended for failure to timely pay required fees or assessments or, in the case of a CSR, for failure to comply with the continuing education requirements as stated in the Continuing Education Rules for Court Reporters as promulgated by the Supreme Court of Texas.

A CRF shall not engage the services of a CSR when the CSR is on inactive status or when the CSR's right to practice has been suspended or terminated.

A CSR shall not work for a CRF that has been placed on inactive status or when the CRF's registration has been suspended or terminated.

A CSR or CRF shall be considered to have engaged in misconduct upon violation of a Board order or negotiated settlement issued as a result of a complaint against the CSR or CRF, unless the Board order or negotiated settlement has been lawfully stayed.

A CSR or CRF shall not violate any other laws of the State of Texas, other states, or of the United

States, relating to the professional conduct of CSRs or CRFs or to the practice of court reporting.

A CSR or CRF shall not violate any Rule promulgated by the Supreme Court of Texas.

A CSR or CRF shall be considered to have engaged in misconduct upon a final conviction of a felony, or imposition of community supervision in connection with a criminal prosecution of a felony, under the laws of any state or the United States.

A CSR or CRF shall be considered to have engaged in misconduct upon a final conviction of any crime, or imposition of community supervision in connection with a criminal prosecution, an element of which is dishonesty or fraud, or involving a crime of moral turpitude, under the laws of any state or the United States.

A CSR or CRF may be considered to have engaged in misconduct upon the imposition of deferred adjudication in connection with a felony, any crime of moral turpitude, or any crime an element of which is dishonesty or fraud.

A CSR or CRF shall not fail to comply with a final order of any state or federal court unless said order has been lawfully stayed.

A CSR or CRF shall respond to a party's inquiry within a reasonable time. Repeated failure to respond without good cause shall be misconduct.

A CSR or CRF shall not misrepresent facts, qualifications, or make misleading or deceitful statements to parties.

A CSR or CRF shall not falsely swear or commit perjury in any communication to the Board or any other federal or state regulatory or licensing authority or court.

A CSR or CRF shall not threaten or commit assault or retaliation against parties, make libelous or slanderous statements, or make public allegations of a lack of mental capacity regarding parties, which cannot be supported in fact.

A CSR shall not cause or be party to, directly or indirectly, a breach in the security of the CSR examination or any court proceeding.

A CSR or CRF shall not enter into or provide services under a prohibited contract described by Section 52.034 of the Texas Government Code.

10. AVOID CONFLICTS OF INTEREST

A CSR or CRF who fails to disclose as soon as practical to the parties or their attorneys existing or past financial, business, professional, family or social relationships, including contracts for court reporting services which might reasonably create an appearance of partiality, may be subject to disciplinary action by the Board.

Reasonable disclosure shall be within five days of when the deposition or other reporting assignment is booked but no later than three days before such deposition or other reporting assignment is held. If such engagement is made less than three days before such deposition or other reporting assignment, the disclosure should be made immediately.

A CSR who reports any proceeding and is a relative of a party or their attorney within the second degree by affinity or consanguinity may be subject to disciplinary action by the Board, unless, as soon as practicable, the reporter discloses the relation in writing to all parties and the Court; and either no party or the Court objects to the use of the reporter on the grounds of the relation, or the Court enters an order finding that, under the circumstances, the relation does not reasonably create an appearance of partiality and that good cause exists to permit use of the reporter. If a party or the Court objects to the use of the reporter on the grounds of the relation, then the objection must be made as soon as practicable after the relation is disclosed.

A CSR who reports any proceeding in which the reporter is financially interested in the action or who is associated with a firm or entity who is financially interested in the action may be subject to disciplinary action by the Board.

A CSR or CRF shall be fair and impartial toward each participant in a legal proceeding.

A CSR working in the position as an official reporter shall refrain from freelance reporting activities that interfere with official duties and obligations.

11. EXPOSE CORRUPT OR DISHONEST CONDUCT OF ANOTHER LICENSEE

A CSR or CRF shall report to the CRCB any violation of this Code, which can be supported in fact.

A CSR or CRF shall not, without good cause, attribute bad motives or unethical conduct of another reporter nor bring the profession into disrepute by unfounded accusations of impropriety.

A CSR or CRF shall not file a frivolous complaint with the Board.

12. REPORTABLE EVENTS

A CSR or CRF shall report in writing to the Board the occurrence of any of the following events within thirty (30) days of the date the CSR or CRF has knowledge of these events:

1. Conviction or imposition of community supervision or deferred adjudication of the CSR or CRF of any of the following:

   a. a felony or any crime of which fraud or dishonesty is an element; or

   b. any crime involving moral turpitude; or

   c. any crime related to the qualifications, functions or duties of a CSR or CRF.

2. Any disciplinary action, including but not limited to revocation or suspension of a license, registration, or other authority to practice.

3. Refusal by another authority to renew a license, registration, or other authority to practice court reporting or provide court reporting services in another jurisdiction.

4. Finding of contempt by a state or federal court.

As used in this Section, a conviction includes the initial plea, verdict, or finding of guilt, plea of no contest, or pronouncement of sentence by a trial court even though that conviction may not be final or sentence may not be actually imposed until all appeals are exhausted.

13. SUPERVISORY RESPONSIBILITIES

A CSR who employs and/or supervises an unlicensed person to assist in the preparation of a transcript or reporter's record shall be responsible for any acts of the unlicensed person.

A CRF shall be subject to disciplinary action by the Board if the CRF has direct supervisory authority over a person and knows or should have known the person violated the Code and the CRF knowingly fails to take reasonable remedial action to avoid or mitigate the consequences of the person's actions.

A CRF shall be subject to disciplinary action by the Board if the CRF has engaged the services of an independent contractor and knows or should have known the person violated the Code and the CRF knowingly fails to take reasonable remedial action to avoid or mitigate the consequences of the person's actions.

14. CONTACT INFORMATION

Each CSR and CRF shall, at all times, keep the CRCB informed of the current mailing address of the CSR or CRF. Such mailing address shall be included on each license application and each license renewal form. In the absence of the submission of a specific written request to change that mailing address, which shall be separate from any other submission, the CSR's or CRF's current mailing address is presumed to be the address on the most recent license renewal or license application form, whichever is latest. Any request for a change of address shall be sent to the CRCB within 30 days after the change of address becomes effective.

Additionally, each CRF shall provide to the CRCB at the time of registration and renewal the name, mailing address, phone number, fax number and e-mail address of an individual designated to receive any request for information or other correspondence from the CRCB. This individual shall include any officer, director, or managerial employee of the CRF. Any change in this information is subject to the terms of this section.

15. DISPLAY OF LICENSE; COMPLAINT INFORMATION AND NOTICE TO CLIENTS

A CRF shall display the certificate received from the Board showing current registration as a CRF at each place of business in the area most frequented by the public, such as a waiting room or lobby. The current registration shall be in good standing.

A CSR may display his or her certificate only if the license is current and in good standing. A CSR shall provide proof of his or her current certification upon request by the Court or parties to an action or assignment.

A CSR shall provide upon request the necessary information to file complaints with the Board about his or her services. The contact information shall include the current address, phone number, and Internet address of the CRCB.

A CRF shall prominently display the contact information in order to file complaints with the Board about its services that is easily read and understood at each registered firm's place of business in the area most frequented by the public, such as a waiting room or lobby. The contact information shall contain the current address, phone number, and Internet address of the CRCB.

16. ADVERTISING

A CSR or CRF shall not use or participate in the use of any written, oral, or electronic communication having reference to the CSR's or CRF's professional services that contains a false, fraudulent, misleading or deceptive statement or claim.

A CSR or CRF shall not advertise or represent falsely the qualifications of a CSR or CRF, including professional designations or membership in professional organizations, or that an unlicensed individual is a CSR.

17. FEES

A CSR or CRF shall not provide court reporting services on a contingent fee basis under any circumstances.

A CSR or CRF shall charge all parties to an action the same price for an original transcript or reporter's record.

A CSR or CRF shall charge all parties to an action the same price for a copy of a transcript or reporter's record or for like services performed in an action.

A CSR or CRF shall disclose in writing to all parties or their attorneys upon request at any time an itemization of all rates and charges to all parties or their attorneys.

A CSR or CRF shall not charge for a copy at a rate more than one-third the per page cost of the original and first copy.

18. CONTINUING EDUCATION

A CSR shall comply with the continuing education requirements as set out in the Continuing Education Rules for Court Reporters as promulgated by the Supreme Court of Texas.

The use, submission, or filing of any document which is all or in part false or deceptive for the purpose of complying with the continuing education statutes and/or requirements by the Supreme Court may be subject to disciplinary action by the Board.

Obtaining or accepting any certificate of completion or certificate of attendance from a continuing education provider when the licensee has not met the minimum completion requirements may be subject to disciplinary action by the Board.

Cheating or using unauthorized materials or receiving unauthorized assistance during an exam to complete continuing education requirements may be subject to disciplinary action by the Board.

19. PROHIBITED DISCRIMINATORY ACTIVITIES

A CSR or CRF shall not willfully manifest, by words or conduct, bias or prejudice based on race, color, national origin, religion, disability, age, sex, or sexual orientation towards any person involved in an action or proceeding in any capacity or in hiring practices or in accepting business.

RULES AND FORMS FOR A JUDICIAL BYPASS OF PARENTAL NOTICE AND CONSENT UNDER CHAPTER 33 OF THE FAMILY CODE

Adopted December 22, 1999, effective January 1, 2000

Including Amendments Received Through February 1, 2016

EXPLANATORY STATEMENT

Text of rule effective until January 1, 2016. See, also, text of rule, subject to public comments received [comments period ends April 1, 2016], effective January 1, 2016.

Chapter 33 of the Texas Family Code, adopted by Act of May 25, 1999, 76th Leg., R.S., ch. 395, 1999 Tex. Gen. Laws 2466 (S.B. 30), provides for judicial authorization of an unemancipated minor to consent to an abortion in Texas without notice to her parents, managing conservator, or guardian. Section 2 of the Act states: "The Supreme Court of Texas shall issue promptly such rules as may be necessary in order that the process established by Sections 33.003 and 33.004, Family Code, as added by this Act, may be conducted in a manner that will ensure confidentiality and sufficient precedence over all other pending matters to ensure promptness of disposition." *See also* Tex. Fam. Code §§ 33.003(*l*), 33.004(c). Section 6 of the Act adds: "The clerk of the Supreme Court of Texas shall adopt the application form and notice of appeal form to be used under Sections 33.003 and 33.004, Family Code, as added by this Act, not later than December 15, 1999." *See also* Tex. Fam. Code §§ 33.003(m), 33.004(d).

The following rules and forms are promulgated as directed by the Act without any determination that the Act or any part of it comports with the United

States Constitution or the Texas Constitution. During the public hearings and debates on the rules and forms, questions were raised concerning the constitutionality of Chapter 33, among which were whether the statute can make court rulings secret, and whether the statute can require courts to act within the specified, short deadlines it imposes. Because such issues should not be resolved outside an adversarial proceeding with full briefing and argument, the rules and forms merely track statutory requirements of the Legislature. Adoption of these rules does not, of course, imply that abortion is or is not permitted in any specific situation. *See, e.g., Roe v. Wade*, 410 U.S. 113 (1973); Tex. Rev. Civ. Stat. Ann. art. 4495b, § 4.011 (restrictions on third trimester abortions of viable fetuses).

In 2005, the Legislature amended the Texas Occupations Code to prohibit a physician from performing an abortion on an unemancipated minor

> without the written consent of the child's parent, managing conservator, or legal guardian or without a court order, as provided by Section 33.003 or 33.004, Family Code, authorizing the minor to consent to the abortion, unless the physician concludes that on the basis of the physician's good faith clinical judgment, a condition exists that complicates the medical condition of the pregnant minor and necessitates the immediate abortion of her pregnancy to avert her death or to avoid a serious risk of substantial impairment of a major bodily function and that there is insufficient time to obtain the consent of the child's parent, managing conservator, or legal guardian.

Act of May 27, 2005, 79th Leg., R.S., ch. 269, § 1.42, 2005 Tex. Gen. Laws 734 (S.B. 419) (codified at Tex. Occ. Code § 164.052(a)(19)). The parental consent law does not direct the Supreme Court to provide procedural rules implementing its provisions but instead expressly references the judicial bypass provisions in the parental notification law as providing an exception to the parental consent requirement. The procedures governing application for a judicial bypass to the parental notification requirement are set forth in the existing Parental Notification Rules. In addition, the parental consent law requires the Texas Medical Board to adopt the forms necessary for physicians to obtain the consent required by law to perform an abortion upon an unemancipated minor. *See id.* (codified at Tex. Occ. Code § 164.052(c)). Those forms are published at 22 Tex. Admin. Code § 165.6(f) and are available on the Texas Medical Board's website, at www.tmb.state.tx.us/rules/docs/Current%20Rules%20–%20%201–4–07.doc.

The notes and comments appended to the rules are intended to inform their construction and application by courts and practitioners.

Amended by order of February 27, 2007, eff. March 5, 2007.

EXPLANATORY STATEMENT

Text of rule, subject to public comments received [comments period ends April 1, 2016], effective January 1, 2016. See, also, text of rule effective until January 1, 2016.

Chapter 33 of the Texas Family Code provides for judicial authorization of an unemancipated minor to consent to an abortion in Texas without notice to, or the consent of, a parent, managing conservator, or guardian. Sections 33.003 and 33.004, which govern proceedings in the trial and appellate courts, authorize the Court to make rules to ensure that judicial bypass applications are decided confidentially and promptly. *See* TEX. FAM. CODE §§ 33.003(*l*), 33.004(c). The statute also directs the Court to make forms for use in judicial bypass proceedings. *Id.* §§ 33.003(m), 33.004(d).

The Court approved the first set of rules and forms in 1999, following the enactment of Chapter 33. *See* Misc. Docket No. 99–9247 (Dec. 22, 1999); Act of May 25, 1999, 76th Leg., R.S., ch. 395, 1999 Tex. Gen. Laws 2466 (S.B. 30) (codified at TEX. FAM. CODE § 33.001 *et seq.*). The rules and forms have been amended to reflect the 2015 amendments to Chapter 33. *See* Act of June 1, 2015, 84th Leg., R.S., ch. 436 (H.B. 3994). The rules and forms track the statutory requirements. They do not reflect any judgment by the Court that Chapter 33, or any part of it, is constitutional. Constitutional questions should be resolved in an adversarial proceeding with full briefing and argument. Nor do the rules imply that abortion is—or is not—permitted in any specific situation. *See, e.g., Roe v. Wade*, 410 U.S. 113 (1973); TEX. HEALTH & SAFETY CODE § 170.002 (restrictions on third trimester abortions of viable fetuses).

The notes and comments appended to the rules are intended to inform their construction and application by courts and practitioners.

Amended by order of February 27, 2007, eff. March 5, 2007; December 29, 2015, eff. January 1, 2016.

Rule 1. General Provisions

Text of rule effective until January 1, 2016. See, also, text of rule, subject to public comments received [comments period ends April 1, 2016], effective January 1, 2016.

1.1 Applicability of These Rules. These rules govern proceedings for obtaining a court order authorizing a minor to consent to an abortion without notice to either of her parents or a managing conservator or guardian under Chapter 33, Family Code (or as amended). All references in these rules to "minor" refer to the minor applicant. Other Texas court rules — including the Rules of Civil Procedure, Rules of Evidence, Rules of Appellate Procedure, Rules of Judicial Administration, and local rules approved by the Supreme Court — also apply, but when the application of another rule would be inconsistent with the general framework or policy of Chapter 33, Family Code, or these rules, these rules control.

1.2 Expedition Required.

(a) *Proceedings.* A court must give proceedings under these rules precedence over all other pending matters to the extent necessary to assure that applications and appeals are adjudicated as soon as possible and within the time required by Rules 2.4(a), 2.5(d), and 3.3(c).

(b) *Prompt Actual Notice Required.* Without compromising the confidentiality and anonymity required by statute and these rules, courts and clerks must serve orders, decisions, findings, and notices required under these rules in a manner designed to give prompt actual notice in order that the deadlines imposed by Chapter 33, Family Code, can be met.

(c) *Instanter.* "Instanter" means immediately, without delay. An action required by these rules to be taken instanter should be done at the first possible time and with the most expeditious means available.

1.3 Anonymity of Minor Protected.

(a) *Generally.* Proceedings under these rules must be conducted in a way that protects the anonymity of the minor.

(b) *No Reference to Minor's Identity in Proceeding.* With the exception of the verification page required under Rule 2.1(c)(2) and the communications required under Rule 2.2(e), no reference may be made in any order, decision, finding, or notice, or on the record, to the name of the minor, her address, or other information by which she might be identified by persons not participating in the proceedings. Instead, the minor must be referred to as "Jane Doe" in a numbered cause.

(c) *Notice.* With the exception of orders and rulings released under Rule 1.4(b), all service and communications from the court to the minor must be directed to the minor's attorney with a copy to the guardian ad litem. A minor's attorney must serve on the guardian ad litem instanter a copy of any document filed with the court. A guardian ad litem must serve on a minor's attorney instanter a copy of any document filed with the court. These requirements take effect when an attorney appears for the minor, or when the clerk has notified the minor of the appointment of an attorney or guardian ad litem.

1.4 Confidentiality of Proceedings Required; Exceptions.

(a) *Generally.* All officials and court personnel involved in the proceedings must ensure that the minor's contact with the clerk and court is confidential and expeditious. Except as permitted by law, no officials or court personnel involved in the proceedings may ever disclose to anyone outside the proceedings — including the minor's parent, managing conservator, or legal guardian — that the minor is or has ever been pregnant, or that she wants or has ever wanted an abortion.

(b) *Documents and information pertaining to the proceeding.* As required by Chapter 33, Family Code, the application and all other court documents and information pertaining to the proceedings are confidential and privileged and are not subject to disclosure under Chapter 552, Government Code, or to discovery, subpoena, or other legal process. But documents and information may be disclosed when expressly authorized by these rules, and an order, ruling, opinion, or clerk's certificate may be released to:

(1) the minor;

(2) the minor's guardian ad litem;

(3) the minor's attorney;

(4) a person designated in writing by the minor to receive the order, ruling, opinion, or certificate;

(5) a governmental agency or governmental attorney, in connection with a criminal or administrative action seeking to assert or protect the minor's interests; or

(6) another court, judge, or clerk in the same or related proceedings.

(c) *Filing of Court Reporter's Notes Permitted.* To assure confidentiality, court reporter notes, in whatever form, may be filed with other court documents in the proceeding.

(d) *Duty to Report Possible Sexual Abuse.* A court, guardian ad litem, or attorney ad litem who reasonably believes, based on information obtained in the proceeding, that a violation of Section 22.011, 22.021, or 25.02, Penal Code, has occurred must report the information to the appropriate officials or agencies as required by Section 33.009, Family Code.

(e) ***Department of Protective and Regulatory Services to Disclose Certain Information in Proceeding.*** The Department of Protective and Regulatory Services may disclose to the court, the attorney ad litem, and the guardian ad litem any information obtained under Section 33.008, Family Code, without being ordered to do so. The trial court may order the Department to disclose such information to such persons, and the Department must comply.

1.5 Electronic Transmission of Documents; Hearings Conducted By Remote Electronic Means; Electronic Record Allowed When Necessary.

(a) ***Electronic Filing.*** Documents may be filed by facsimile or other electronic data transmission. If the sender communicates directly with the clerk the time at which the transmission will occur, the clerk must take all reasonable steps to assure that the confidentiality of the received transmission will be maintained.

(b) ***Electronic Transmission by Court and Clerk.*** The court and clerk may transmit orders, rulings, notices, and other documents by facsimile or other electronic data transmission. But before the transmission is initiated, the sender must take all reasonable steps to assure that the confidentiality of the received transmission will be maintained. The time and date of a transmission by the court is the time and date when it was initiated.

(c) ***Hearings by Electronic Means.*** Consistent with the anonymity and confidentiality requirements of these rules, with the court's permission, the attorney ad litem, the guardian ad litem, and any witnesses may participate in hearings under these rules by video conferencing, telephone, or other remote electronic means. The minor must appear before the court in person unless the court determines that the minor's appearance by video conferencing will allow the court to view the minor during the hearing sufficiently well to assess her credibility and demeanor.

(d) ***Record of Hearing Made by Electronic Means if Necessary.*** If the court determines that a court reporter is unavailable for a hearing, the court may have a record of the hearing made by audio recording or other electronic means. If a notice of appeal is filed, the court must have the recording transcribed if possible. The person transcribing the recording must certify to the accuracy of the transcription. The court must transmit both the recording and the transcription to the court of appeals.

1.6 Disqualification, Recusal, or Objection to a Judge.

(a) ***Time for filing and ruling.*** An objection to a trial judge, or a motion to recuse or disqualify a trial judge, must be filed before 10:00 a.m. of the first business day after an application is filed or promptly after the assignment of a judge to hear the case is made known to the minor or her attorney, whichever is later. An objection to an appellate judge, or a motion to recuse or disqualify an appellate judge must be filed before 10 a.m. of the first business day after a notice of appeal is filed. A judge who chooses to recuse voluntarily must do so instanter. An objection to a judge or a motion to disqualify or recuse does not extend the deadline for ruling on the minor's application.

(b) ***Voluntary Disqualification or Recusal, or Objection.*** A judge to whom objection is made under Chapter 74, Government Code, or a judge or justice who voluntarily does not sit, must notify instanter the appropriate authority for assigning another judge by local rules or by statute. That authority must instanter assign a judge or justice to the proceeding.

(c) ***Involuntary Disqualification or Recusal.*** A judge or justice who refuses to remove himself or herself voluntarily from a proceeding in response to a motion must instanter refer the motion to the appropriate judge or justice, pursuant to local rule, rule, or statute, for determination. The judge or justice to whom the motion is referred must rule on it as soon as possible and may do so with or without a hearing. If the motion is granted, the judge or justice to whom the motion was referred must instanter assign a judge or justice to the proceeding.

(d) ***Only One Objection or Motion to Recuse Permitted.*** A minor who objects to a judge assigned to the proceeding may not thereafter file a motion to recuse or disqualify, and a minor who files a motion to recuse or disqualify a judge may not thereafter object to a judge assigned to the proceeding.

(e) ***Issues on Appeal.*** Any error in the denial of a motion to recuse or disqualify, or any error in the disallowance of an objection, or any challenge to a judge that a minor is precluded from making by subsections (a) or (d), may be raised only on appeal from the court's denial of the application.

1.7 Rules and Forms to be Made Available. A copy of these rules, and a copy of the attached forms in English and Spanish, must be made available to any person without charge in the clerk's offices of all courts in which applications or appeals may be filed under these rules, on the Texas Judiciary Internet site at www.courts.state.tx.us, and by the Office of Court Administration upon request. A copy of a court's local rules relating to proceedings under Chapter 33, Family Code, must be made available to any person without charge in the office of the clerk for that court where applications may be filed. Rules and forms may be copied.

1.8 Duties of Attorneys Ad Litem. An attorney ad litem must represent the minor in the trial court in the proceeding in which the attorney is assigned, and in any appeal under these rules to the court of appeals or the Supreme Court. But an attorney ad litem is not required to represent the minor in any other court or any other proceeding.

1.9 Fees and Costs.

(a) ***No fees or costs charged to minor.*** No filing fee or court cost may be assessed against a minor for any proceeding in a trial or appellate court.

(b) ***State ordered to pay fees and costs.****

(1) Fees and costs that may be paid. The State may be ordered to pay the reasonable and necessary fees and expenses of the attorney ad litem, the reasonable and necessary fees and expenses of the guardian ad litem, the court reporter's fee as certified by the court reporter, and trial court filing fees and costs as certified by the clerk. Court costs include the expenses of an interpreter (Form 2H) but do not include the fees or expenses of a witness. Court costs do not include fees which must be remitted to the state treasury.

(2) To whom order directed and sent. The order must be directed to the Comptroller of Public Accounts but should be sent by the clerk to the Director, Fiscal Division, of the Texas Department of Health.

(3) Form and contents of the order. The order must state the amounts to be awarded the attorney ad litem and the guardian ad litem. The order must be separate from any other order in the proceeding and must not address any subject other than the assessment of costs. A trial court may use Forms 2F and 2G, but it is not required to do so.

(4) Time for signing and sending order. To be valid, the order must be signed by the judge and sent by the clerk to the Department of Health not later than the ninetieth day after the date of the final ruling in a proceeding, whether the application is granted, deemed granted, or denied, or the proceeding is dismissed or nonsuited.

(c) ***Motion to reconsider; time for filing.*** Within thirty days of actual receipt of the order, the Comptroller or any other person adversely affected by the order may file a motion in the trial court to reconsider the assessment of costs. The trial court retains jurisdiction of the case to hear and determine any timely filed motion to reconsider.

(d) ***Appeal.*** The Comptroller or any other person adversely affected by the order may appeal from the trial court's ruling on the motion to reconsider as from any other final judgment of the court.

(e) ***Report to the Office of Court Administration.*** The Department of Health must transmit to the Office of Court Administration a copy of every order assessing costs in a proceeding under Chapter 33, Family Code. Such orders are not subject to the Amended Order of the Supreme Court of Texas, dated September 21, 1994, in Misc. Docket No. 94–9143, regarding mandatory reports of judicial appointments and fees.

(f) ***Confidentiality.*** When transmitting an order awarding costs to the Department of Health, the clerk must take reasonable steps to preserve its confidentially. The confidentiality of an order awarding costs—as prescribed by Chapter 33, Family Code—is not affected by its transmission to the Comptroller, Texas Department of Health, or the Office of Court Administration, nor is the order subject to public disclosure in response to a request under any statute, rule or other law. But these rules do not preclude the Comptroller, Texas Department of Health, and the Office of Court Administration from disclosing summary information from orders assessing costs for statistical or other such purposes.

1.10. Amicus Briefs. Amicus briefs may be submitted and received by a court—but not filed—under either of the following procedures.

(a) ***Confidential, Case-Specific Briefs.*** A nonparty who is authorized to attend or participate in a particular proceeding under Chapter 33, Family Code may submit an amicus brief addressing matters, including confidential matters, specific to the proceeding. The brief and the manner in which it is submitted must comply with Rules 1.3 and 1.4 and be directed to the court in which the proceeding is pending. The person must submit the original brief and the same number of copies required for other submissions to the court, and must serve a copy of the brief on the minor's attorney and guardian ad litem. The court to which the brief is submitted must maintain the brief as part of the confidential case file in accordance with Rule 1.4.

(b) ***Public or General Briefs.*** Any person may submit a brief addressing any matter relating to proceedings under Chapter 33, Family Code. Such a brief must not contain any information in violation of Rules 1.3 and 1.4. The person must submit the original brief and the same number of copies required for other submissions to the court. If the brief is submitted to a court of appeals, the original and eleven copies of the brief, plus a computer disk containing an electronic copy of the brief, must also be submitted to the Supreme Court of Texas. When an appeal of a proceeding is filed, the clerk of the court of appeals or the Supreme Court must notify the minor's attorney and guardian ad litem of the existence of any brief submitted under this subsection and must make the brief available for inspection and copying. Upon receipt of an electronic copy of an amicus brief submitted under this subsection, the Clerk of the Supreme Court must, as soon as practicable, have the brief posted on the Texas Judiciary Internet site and make it available to the public for inspection and copying.

Adopted Dec. 22, 1999, eff. Jan. 1, 2000. Amended Nov. 8, 2000, eff. March 1, 2001; Nov. 14, 2006, eff. March 1, 2007; Feb. 27, 2007 eff. March 1, 2007.

* Pub. Note: The Supreme Court order of November 8, 2000 provides in part: "In a proceeding under Chapter 33 of the Family Code in which the final ruling in the proceeding occurred on or before February 28, 2001, an order for the State to pay fees and costs under Rule 1.9, Texas Parental Notification Rules, is valid only if the order is signed by the judge and sent to the Texas Department of Health not later than May 30, 2001."

Notes and Comments

1. Rule 1.1 contemplates that other court rules of procedure and administration remain as a "default" governing matters not addressed in these rules. Thus, for example, these rules do not state a deadline for filing notices of appeal, so the ordinary 30–day deadline controls, *see* Tex. R. App. P. 26.1, but these rules control over inconsistent provisions in the appellate rules governing the docketing statement, the record, and briefing.

2. Rule 1.1 also contemplates that individual jurisdictions may enact local rules pursuant to Tex. R. Civ. P. 3a, Tex. R. App. P. 1.2, or Tex. R. Jud. Admin. 10, to the extent consistent with Chapter 33, Family Code, and with these rules, to tailor the implementation of the statute and these rules to local needs and preferences. Local rules may address, for example, the specific location or office where applications are to be filed, how applications are to be assigned for hearing, and whether an appellate court will permit or require briefing or oral argument. *See also* Rule 2, Comment 1.

3. Any judge involved in a proceeding, whether as the judge assigned to hear and decide the application, the judge assigned to hear and decide any disqualification, recusal or objection, a judge authorized to transfer the application or assign another judge to it, or an appellate judge, may have access to all information (including the verification page) in the proceeding or any related proceeding, such as a prior filing by the minor. Similarly, a minor's attorney and guardian ad litem must, of course, have access to the case file to the extent necessary to perform their respective duties.

4. Section 33.008, Family Code, requires a physician who suspects that a minor has been physically or sexually abused by a person responsible for the minor's care to report the matter to the Texas Department of Protective and Regulatory Services. That section also requires the Department to investigate and to assist the minor in making an application, if appropriate. Section 33.010 makes confidential — "[n]otwithstanding any other law" — all information obtained by the Department under Section 33.008 except to the extent necessary to prove certain criminal conduct. Rule 1.4(e) construes Section 33.010 in harmony with Section 33.008. If Section 33.010 precluded the Department from disclosing information obtained under Section 33.008 to the court, the attorney ad litem, and the guardian ad litem in proceedings under section 33.003, the Department's statutorily mandated role in such proceedings would be seriously impaired. The Department could be required by Section 33.008 to assist a minor in filing an application but prohibited by Section 33.010 from providing the court with information supporting the application. The disclosure permitted and required by Rule 1.4(e) avoids this result.

5. Rule 1.5(a) constitutes the approval required by Section 51.803, Government Code, for electronic filing of documents in proceedings under these rules. To facilitate expedition of proceedings, restrictions imposed on electronic filing in other cases are not imposed here. However, electronic filing is only permitted, not required, and Rule 1.5(a) does not necessitate the provision of means for electronic filing. A person filing by electronic means cannot, of course, expect that the document will be treated confidentiality upon receipt unless the recipient has been told the time the transmission will occur.

6. Rule 1.6 controls to the extent that it conflicts with other provisions regarding the disqualification or recusal of judges, such as Tex. R. Civ. P. 18a, Tex. R. App. P. 16, and Tex. Gov't Code 25.00255. But the rule incorporates the referral and reassignment processes otherwise applicable by local rule, rule, or statute.

7. The archival requirements relating to proceedings under Chapter 33, Family Code, and these rules is governed by Sections 441.158 and 441.185, Government Code, and the schedules promulgated by the Texas State Library and Archives Commission pursuant to those authorities.

8. Because orders awarding costs contain information made confidential by Chapter 33, Family Code, that confidentiality should not be affected by the transmission to the Texas Department of Health and the Comptroller, which is necessary to effectuate payment, or to the Office of Court Administration, which is necessary to oversee the costs associated with the proceedings. Rule 1.9(f) does not preclude either the Comptroller, Texas Department of Health, or the Office of Court Administration from disclosing total amounts paid for all proceedings, or average amount per proceeding, or other such statistical summaries or analyses which do not impair the confidentiality of the proceedings.

9. Rule 1.10 adds a procedure for filing amicus curiae briefs uniquely designed for the expedited

and confidential nature of parental notification cases.

Rule 1. General Provisions

Text of rule, subject to public comments received [comments period ends April 1, 2016], effective January 1, 2016. See, also, text of rule effective until January 1, 2016.

1.1 Applicability of These Rules. These rules govern proceedings for obtaining a court order authorizing a minor to consent to an abortion without notice to, or the consent of, a parent, managing conservator, or guardian under Chapter 33, Family Code. All references in these rules to "minor" refer to the minor applicant. Other Texas court rules—including the Rules of Civil Procedure, Rules of Evidence, Rules of Appellate Procedure, Rules of Judicial Administration, and local rules approved by the Supreme Court—also apply, but when the application of another rule would be inconsistent with the general framework or policy of Chapter 33, Family Code, or these rules, these rules control.

1.2 Expedition Required.

(a) *Proceedings.* A court must give proceedings under these rules precedence over all other pending matters to the extent necessary to ensure that applications and appeals are adjudicated as soon as possible and within the time required by Chapter 33, Family Code, and these rules.

(b) *Prompt actual notice required.* Without compromising the confidentiality required by statute and these rules, courts and clerks must serve orders, decisions, findings, and notices required under these rules in a manner designed to give prompt actual notice in order that the deadlines imposed by Chapter 33, Family Code, can be met.

1.3 Identity of Minor Protected.

(a) *Generally.* Proceedings under these rules must be conducted in a way that protects the confidentiality of the identity of the minor.

(b) *No reference to minor's identity in proceeding.* With the exception of the verification page required under Rule 2.1(c)(2) and the communications required under Rule 2.2(e), no reference may be made in any order, decision, finding, or notice, or on the record, to the name of the minor, her address, or other information by which she might be identified by persons not participating in the proceedings. Instead, the minor must be referred to as "Jane Doe" in a numbered cause.

(c) *Notice.* With the exception of orders and rulings released under Rule 1.4(b), all notices and communications from the court to the minor must be directed to the minor's attorney with a copy to the guardian ad litem. The minor's attorney must immediately serve on the guardian ad litem a copy of any document filed with the court. These requirements take effect when an attorney appears for the minor or when the clerk has notified the minor of the appointment of an attorney or a guardian ad litem.

1.4 Confidentiality of Proceedings Required; Exceptions.

(a) *Generally.* All officials and court personnel involved in the proceedings must ensure that the minor's contact with the clerk and the court is confidential and expeditious. Except as permitted by law, officials and court personnel must never disclose to anyone outside the proceeding—including the minor's parent, managing conservator, or legal guardian—that the minor is or has ever been pregnant, or that she wants or has ever wanted an abortion.

(b) *Documents and information pertaining to the proceeding.*

(1) *General rule; disclosure prohibited.* As required by Chapter 33, Family Code, the application and all other court documents and information pertaining to the proceedings are confidential and privileged and are not subject to disclosure under Chapter 552, Government Code, or to discovery, subpoena, or other legal process.

(2) *Exception; disclosure to minor permitted.* The application and any other document in the court file may be disclosed to the minor.

(3) *Exception; disclosure of order to certain persons.* An order, ruling, opinion, or clerk's certificate may be released to:

- the minor;
- the minor's guardian ad litem;
- the minor's attorney;
- the physician who is to perform the abortion;
- a person designated in writing by the minor to receive the order, ruling, opinion, or certificate;
- a governmental agency or governmental attorney, in connection with a criminal or administrative action seeking to assert or protect the minor's interests; or
- another court, judge, or clerk in the same or related proceedings.

(c) *Filing of court reporter's notes required.* To ensure confidentiality, the court reporter's notes, in whatever form, must be filed with other court documents in the proceeding.

(d) *Duty to report possible abuse.*

(1) *Duty of the court.* A judge or justice who, as a result of a court proceeding governed by these rules, has reason to believe that a minor has been or may be physically or sexually abused must report the suspected abuse in accordance with Sections 33.0085 and 33.009, Family Code, and other law.

(2) *Duty of an attorney or guardian ad litem.* An attorney or a guardian ad litem who, as a result of a court proceeding governed by these rules, has reason to believe that a minor has been or may be physically or sexually abused must report the suspected abuse in accordance with Section 33.009, Family Code, and other law.

(e) *Department of Family and Protective Services or local law enforcement agency to disclose certain information in proceeding.* The Department of Family and Protective Services or a local law enforcement agency may disclose to the court, the minor's attorney, and the guardian ad litem any information obtained under Sections 33.008, 33.0085, and 33.009, Family Code, without being ordered to do so. The court may order the Department or a local law enforcement agency to disclose the information to the court, the minor's attorney, and the guardian ad litem, and the Department or agency must comply.

1.5 Methods of Transmitting Documents; Hearings Conducted By Remote Electronic Means; Electronic Record Allowed When Necessary.

(a) *Electronic filing through statewide portal prohibited.* Documents must not be filed through the electronic filing manager established by the Office of Court Administration.

(b) *Paper, fax, or email filing permitted.* Documents may be filed in paper form, by fax, or by email. The clerk of a court must designate an email address or a fax number for the filing of documents in proceedings governed by these rules and must take all reasonable steps to maintain the confidentiality of the filings. An attorney must notify the clerk by telephone before filing a document by email or fax.

(c) *Fax and email transmission by court and clerk.* The court and clerk may transmit orders, rulings, notices, and other documents by fax or email. But before the transmission is initiated, the sender must take all reasonable steps to maintain the confidentiality of the transmission. The time and date of a transmission by the court is the time and date when it was initiated.

(d) *Participation in hearings by electronic means.* Consistent with the confidentiality requirements of these rules, with the court's permission, a witness may participate in a hearing under these rules by video conferencing, telephone, or other remote electronic means. But the minor must appear before the court in person.

(e) *Record of hearing made by electronic means if necessary.* If the court determines that a court reporter is unavailable for a hearing, the court may have a record of the hearing made by audio recording or other electronic means. If a notice of appeal is filed, the court must have the recording transcribed if possible. The person transcribing the recording must certify to the accuracy of the transcription. The court must transmit both the recording and the transcription to the court of appeals.

1.6 Disqualification, Recusal, or Objection to a Judge.

(a) *Time for filing and ruling.* A motion to recuse or disqualify a trial judge or an objection to a trial judge under Section 74.053, Government Code, must be filed before 10 a.m. of the first business day after an application is filed or promptly after the assignment of a judge to hear the case is made known to the minor's attorney, whichever is later. A motion to recuse or disqualify an appellate judge or an objection to an appellate judge under Section 75.551, Government Code, must be filed before 10 a.m. of the first business day after a notice of appeal is filed or promptly after the assignment of a judge is made known to the minor's attorney, whichever is later. A judge who chooses to withdraw voluntarily must do so immediately. A motion to disqualify or recuse or an objection to an assigned judge does not extend the deadline for ruling on the minor's application.

(b) *Voluntary disqualification or recusal; objection.* A judge who removes himself or herself voluntarily—whether in response to a motion or on the judge's own initiative—or to whom objection is made under Sections 74.053 or 75.551, Government Code, must immediately notify the appropriate authority under rule or statute for assigning another judge. That authority must immediately assign a judge or justice to the proceeding.

(c) *Involuntary disqualification or recusal.* A judge who refuses to remove himself or herself voluntarily from a proceeding in response to a motion must immediately refer the motion to the appropriate judge under rule or statute for determination. The judge to whom the motion is referred must rule on it as soon as possible and may do so with or without a hearing. If the motion is granted, the judge to whom the motion was referred must immediately assign another judge to the proceeding.

(d) *Restrictions on the number of motions and objections.* A minor who objects under Section 74.053 or Section 75.551, Government Code, to a judge assigned to the proceeding may not thereafter file a motion to recuse the judge assigned to replace the judge to whom the objection was made. A minor who files a motion to recuse or disqualify a judge may not thereafter object under Section 74.053 or Section 75.551, Government Code, to another judge assigned to the proceeding.

(e) *Issues on appeal.* Any error in the denial of a motion to recuse or disqualify, any error in the disallowance of an objection, or any challenge to a judge that a minor is precluded from making by subsections (a) or (d), may be raised only on appeal from the court's denial of the application.

1.7 Rules and Forms to be Made Available.

(a) *Online.* A complete set of these rules and forms must be posted on the Texas Judiciary website at www.txcourts.gov. Forms 1A, 2A, and 2B must be translated into Spanish.

(b) *In clerks' offices.* The clerk of a court in which an application or appeal may be filed must make the rules and forms—including the Spanish version of Form 1A, 2A, and 2B—and any applicable local rules available to a minor without charge.

1.8 Duties of Attorneys Ad Litem. An attorney ad litem must represent the minor in the trial court in the proceeding in which the attorney is assigned and in any appeal under these rules to the court of appeals or the Supreme Court. But an attorney ad litem is not required to represent the minor in any other court or any other proceeding.

1.9 Fees and Costs.

(a) *No fees or costs charged to minor.* No filing fee or court cost may be assessed against a minor for any proceeding in a trial or appellate court.

(b) *State ordered to pay fees and costs.*

(1) *Fees and costs that may be paid.* The State may be ordered to pay the reasonable and necessary fees and expenses of the attorney ad litem, the reasonable and necessary fees and expenses of the guardian ad litem, the court reporter's fee as certified by the court reporter, and trial court filing fees and costs as certified by the clerk. Court costs include the expenses of an interpreter (Form 2H) and an evaluation by a licensed mental health counselor but do not include the fees or expenses of a witness. Court costs do not include fees that must be remitted to the state treasury.

(2) *To whom order directed and sent.* The order must be directed to the Comptroller of Public Accounts and sent to the Director, Fiscal Division, of the Texas Department of Health.

(3) *Form and contents of the order.* The order must state the amounts to be awarded the attorney ad litem and the guardian ad litem. The order must be separate from any other order in the proceeding and must not address any subject other than the assessment of fees, expenses, and costs. A trial court may use Forms 2F and 2G, but it is not required to do so.

(4) *Time for signing and sending order.* The order must be signed by the judge and sent by the clerk to the Department of Health not later than the ninetieth day after the date of the final ruling in a proceeding.

(c) *Motion to reconsider; time for filing.* Within thirty days of actual receipt of the order, the Comptroller or any other person adversely affected by the order may file a motion in the trial court to reconsider the assessment of fees, expenses, or costs. The trial court retains jurisdiction of the case to hear and determine any timely filed motion to reconsider.

(d) *Appeal.* The Comptroller or any other person adversely affected by the order may appeal from the trial court's ruling on the motion to reconsider as from any other final judgment of the court.

(e) *Report to the Office of Court Administration.* The Department of Health must transmit to the Office of Court Administration a copy of every order assessing fees, expenses, or costs in a proceeding under Chapter 33, Family Code. Orders assessing fees, expenses, or costs are not subject to any order of the Supreme Court of Texas requiring mandatory reports of judicial appointments and fees or to the reporting requirements of Chapter 36, Government Code.

(f) *Confidentiality.* When transmitting an order awarding costs to the Department of Health, the clerk must take reasonable steps to preserve its confidentiality. The confidentiality of an order awarding costs—as prescribed by Chapter 33, Family Code—is not affected by its transmission to the Comptroller, Texas Department of Health, or the Office of Court Administration, nor is the order subject to public disclosure in response to a request under any statute, rule, or other law. But these rules do not preclude the Comptroller, the Texas Department of Health, or the Office of Court Administration from disclosing summary information from orders assessing costs for statistical or other such purposes.

1.10 Amicus Briefs. Amicus briefs may be submitted and received by a court—but not filed—under either of the following procedures.

(a) ***Confidential, case-specific briefs.*** A nonparty who is authorized to attend or participate in a particular proceeding under Chapter 33, Family Code, may submit an amicus brief addressing matters, including confidential matters, specific to the proceeding. The brief and the manner in which it is submitted must comply with Rules 1.3 and 1.4 and be directed to the court in which the proceeding is pending. If the brief is filed in paper form, the person must submit the original brief and the same number of copies required for other paper submissions to the court. The person must serve a copy of the brief on the minor's attorney and guardian ad litem. The court to which the brief is submitted must maintain the brief as part of the confidential case file in accordance with Rule 1.4.

(b) ***Public or general briefs.*** Any person may submit a brief addressing any matter relating to proceedings under Chapter 33, Family Code. The brief must not contain any information in violation of Rules 1.3 and 1.4. If the brief is filed in paper form, the person must submit the original brief and the same number of copies required for other paper submissions to the court. If the brief is submitted to a court of appeals, one copy of the brief must also be submitted to the Supreme Court of Texas. Upon receipt of an amicus brief submitted under this subsection, the Clerk of the Supreme Court must, as soon as practicable, have the brief posted on the Texas Judiciary website.

Adopted Dec. 22, 1999, eff. Jan. 1, 2000. Amended Nov. 8, 2000, eff. March 1, 2001; Nov. 14, 2006, eff. March 1, 2007; Feb. 27, 2007 eff. March 1, 2007; Dec. 29, 2015, eff. Jan. 1, 2016.

Notes and Comments

1. Rule 1.1 contemplates that other court rules of procedure and administration remain as a "default" governing matters not addressed in these rules. Thus, for example, these rules do not state a deadline for filing notices of appeal, so the ordinary 30–day deadline controls, *see* Tex. R. App. P. 26.1, but these rules control over inconsistent provisions in the appellate rules governing the docketing statement, the record, and briefing.

2. Rule 1.1 also contemplates that individual jurisdictions may enact local rules pursuant to Tex. R. Civ. P. 3a, Tex. R. App. P. 1.2, or Tex. R. Jud. Admin. 10, to the extent consistent with Chapter 33, Family Code, and with these rules, to tailor the implementation of the statute and these rules to local needs and preferences. Local rules may address, for example, the specific location or office where applications are to be filed, how applications are to be assigned for hearing, and whether an appellate court will permit or require briefing or oral argument. *See also* Rule 2, Comment 1.

3. Any judge involved in a proceeding—whether as the judge assigned to hear and decide the application; the judge assigned to hear and decide any disqualification, recusal, or objection; a judge authorized to transfer the application or assign another judge to it; or an appellate judge—may have access to all information (including the verification page) in the proceeding or any related proceeding, such as a prior filing by the minor. Similarly, a minor's attorney and guardian ad litem must, of course, have access to the case file to the extent necessary to perform their respective duties.

4. Sections 33.008, 33.0085, and 33.009, Family Code, require physicians, judges, attorneys, and guardians ad litem to report suspected physical or sexual abuse to the Texas Department of Family and Protective Services and to a local law enforcement agency. Section 33.010 makes confidential—"[n]otwithstanding any other law"—all information obtained by the Department or a law enforcement agency under Sections 33.008, 33.0085, and 33.009 except to the extent necessary to prove certain criminal conduct. Rule 1.4(e) construes Section 33.010 in harmony with Section 33.003(i–2), which makes past or potential future abuse relevant to a claim that notifying or attempting to obtain the consent of a parent, managing conservator, or guardian would not be in the minor's best interest.

5. Rule 1.6 controls to the extent that it conflicts with other provisions regarding the disqualification or recusal of judges, such as Tex. R. Civ. P. 18a, Tex. R. App. P. 16, and Tex. Gov't Code 25.00255.

6. The archival requirements relating to proceedings under Chapter 33, Family Code, and these rules is governed by Sections 441.158 and 441.185, Government Code, and the schedules promulgated by the Texas State Library and Archives Commission pursuant to those authorities.

7. Orders awarding fees, expenses, and costs contain information that is made confidential by Chapter 33, Family Code. The confidentiality of the information should not be affected by the transmission of the order to the Texas Department of Health and to the Comptroller, which is necessary to effectuate payment, or to the Office of Court Administration, which is necessary to oversee the costs associated with the proceedings. Rule 1.9(f) does not preclude either the Comptroller, the Texas Department of Health, or the Office of Court Administration from disclosing total amounts paid for all proceedings, the average amount awarded per proceeding, or other statistical summaries or analyses that do not impair the confidentiality of the proceedings.

8. Rule 1.10 adds a procedure for filing amicus curiae briefs uniquely designed for the expedited and confidential nature of judicial bypass cases.

dentially until an att ney is app nted to represent her; and

(D) that all info the cover page and the contained in the application, includ true.

g. An application is filed when it verificaed by the district or county clerk.

(d) s Duties.

is stance in Filing. The clerk must give assistance — in a manner designed to protect inor's confidentiality and anonymity — to pers seeking to file an application. If requested, the lerk must administer the oath required for the verification page or provide a person authorized to do so. The clerk should also redact from the cover page any information identifying the minor. The clerk should ensure that both the cover page and the separate verification page are completed in full.

(b) ***Filing Procedure.*** The clerk must assign the application a cause number and affix it to both the cover page and the verification page. The clerk must then provide a certified copy of the verification page to the person filing the application. The clerk must file the verification page under seal in a secure place where access is limited to essential court personnel.

(c) ***Distribution.*** When an application is filed, the clerk must distribute the cover page and verification page, or a copy of them, to the appropriate court instanter. If appointment of a specific person as guardian ad litem has been requested, the clerk must also communicate the information to the appropriate court instanter.

(d) ***If Judge of Assigned Court Not Present in County.*** The clerk must determine instanter whether the judge of the court to which the application is assigned is present in the county. If that judge is not present in the county, the clerk must instanter notify the local administrative judge or judges and the presiding judge of the administrative judicial region and must send them any information requested, including the cover page and verification page.

(e) ***Notice of Hearing and Appointments.*** When the clerk is advised by the court of a time for hearing or an appointment of a guardian ad litem or attorney ad litem, the clerk must instanter give notice — as directed in the verification page and to each appointee — of the hearing time or appointment. A court coordinator or other court personnel may give notice instead of the clerk.

(f) ***Orders.*** The clerk must provide the minor's attorney and the guardian ad litem with copies of all court orders, including findings of fact and conclusions of law.

(g) ***Certificate of Court's Failure to Rule Within Time Prescribed by Statute.*** If the court fails to rule on an application within the time required by Section 33.002(g) and (h), Family Code, upon the minor's request, the clerk must instanter issue a certificate to that effect, stating that the application is deemed by statute to be granted. The clerk may use Form 2E but is not required to do so.

2.3. Court's Duties. Upon receipt of an application from the clerk, the court must promptly:

(a) appoint a qualified person to serve as guardian ad litem for the minor applicant;

(b) appoint an attorney for the minor, who may be the same person appointed guardian ad litem if that person is an attorney admitted to practice law in Texas and there is no conflict of interest in the same person serving as attorney ad litem and guardian ad litem;

(c) set a hearing on the application in accordance with Rule 2.4(a); and

(d) advise the clerk of the appointment or appointments and the hearing time.

2.4 Hearing.

(a) ***Time.*** The court must conduct a hearing in time to rule on the application as required by Rule 2.5(d). But the minor may postpone the hearing by written request to the clerk when the application is filed or thereafter. The request may be submitted on Form 2C, but use of the form is not required. The request must either specify a date on which the minor will be ready for the hearing, or state that the minor will later provide a date on which she will be ready for the hearing. Once the minor determines when she will be ready for the hearing, she must notify the clerk of that time in writing. The postponed hearing must be conducted in time for the court to rule on the application as required by Rule 2.5(d).

(b) ***Place.*** The hearing should be held in a location, such as a judge's chambers, that will assure confidentiality. The hearing may be held away from the courthouse.

(c) ***Persons Attending.*** Hearings must be closed to the public. Only the judge, the court reporter and any other essential court personnel, the minor, her attorney, her guardian ad litem, and witnesses on the minor's behalf may be present.

(d) ***Record.*** The court, the minor's attorney, or the guardian ad litem may request that the record — the

Rule 2. Proceedings in the Trial Court

Text of rule effective until January 1, 2016. See, also, text of rule, subject to public comments received [comments period ends April 1, 2016], effective January 1, 2016.

2.1 Where to File an Application; Court Assignment and Transfer; Application Form.

(a) *Counties in Which an Application May Be Filed.* An application for an order under Section 33.003, Family Code, may be filed in any county, regardless of the minor's residence or where the abortion sought is to be performed.

(b) *Courts in Which an Application May Be Filed; Assignment and Transfer.*

(1) *Courts with Jurisdiction.* An application may be filed in a district court (including a family district court), a county court–at–law, or a court having probate jurisdiction.

(2) *Application Filed With District or County Clerk.* An application must be filed with either the district clerk or the county clerk, who will assign the application to a court as provided by local rule or these rules. The clerk to whom the application is tendered cannot refuse to accept it because of any local rule or other rule or law that provides for filing and assignment of such applications but must accept the application and transfer it instanter to the proper clerk, advising the person tendering the application where it is being transferred.

(3) *Court Assignment and Transfer by Local Rule.* The courts in a county that have jurisdiction to hear applications may determine by local rule how applications will be assigned between or among them. A local rule must be approved by the Supreme Court under Rule 3a, Texas Rules of Civil Procedure.

(4) *Initial Court Assignment if No Local Rule.* Absent a local rule, the clerk that files an application — whether the district clerk or the county clerk — must assign it as follows:

(i) to a district court, if the active judge of the court, or a judge assigned to it, is then present in the county;

(ii) if the application cannot be assigned under (i), then to a statutory county or probate court, if the active judge of the court, or a judge assigned to it, is then present in the county;

(iii) if the application cannot be assigned under (i) or (ii), then to the constitutional county court, if it has probate jurisdiction, and if the active judge of the court, or a judge assigned to it, is then present in the county;

(iv) if the application cannot be assigned under (i), (ii), or (iii), then to the district court.

(5) *Judges Who May Hear and Determine Applications.* An application may be heard and determined (i) by the active judge of the court to which the application is assigned, or (ii) by any judge authorized to sit for the active judge, or (iii) by any judge who may be assigned to the court in which the application is pending. An application may not be heard or determined, or any proceedings under these rules conducted, by a master or magistrate.

(c) *Application Form.* An application consists of two pages: a cover page and a separate verification page.

(1) *Cover Page.* The cover page may be submitted on Form 2A, but use of the form is not required. The cover page must be styled "In re Jane Doe" and must not disclose the name of the minor or any information from which the minor's identity could be derived. The cover page must state:

(A) that the minor is pregnant;

(B) that the minor is unmarried, is under 18 years of age, and has not had her disabilities removed under Chapter 31, Family Code;

(C) that the minor wishes to have an abortion without notifying either of her parents or a managing conservator or guardian, and the statutory ground or grounds on which she relies;

(D) whether the minor has retained an attorney, and if so, the attorney's name, address, and telephone number;

(E) whether the minor requests the court to appoint a particular person as her guardian ad litem; and

(F) whether, concerning her current pregnancy, the minor has previously filed an application that was denied, and if so, where the application was filed.

(2) *Verification Page.* The verification page may be submitted on Form 2B, but use of the form is not required. The verification page must be separate from the cover page, must be signed under oath by the person completing the application, and must state:

(A) the minor's full name and date of birth;

(B) the name, address, telephone number, and relationship to the minor of any person the minor requests the court to appoint as her guardian ad litem;

(C) a telephone or pager number — whether that of the minor or someone else (such as a physician, friend, or relative) — at which the minor may be contacted immediately and confidentially until an attorney is appointed to represent her; and

(D) that all information contained in the application, including both the cover page and the verification page, is true.

(d) ***Time of Filing.*** An application is filed when it is actually received by the district or county clerk.

2.2 Clerk's Duties.

(a) ***Assistance in Filing.*** The clerk must give prompt assistance — in a manner designed to protect the minor's confidentiality and anonymity — to persons seeking to file an application. If requested, the clerk must administer the oath required for the verification page or provide a person authorized to do so. The clerk should also redact from the cover page any information identifying the minor. The clerk should ensure that both the cover page and the separate verification page are completed in full.

(b) ***Filing Procedure.*** The clerk must assign the application a cause number and affix it to both the cover page and the verification page. The clerk must then provide a certified copy of the verification page to the person filing the application. The clerk must file the verification page under seal in a secure place where access is limited to essential court personnel.

(c) ***Distribution.*** When an application is filed, the clerk must distribute the cover page and verification page, or a copy of them, to the appropriate court instanter. If appointment of a specific person as guardian ad litem has been requested, the clerk must also communicate the information to the appropriate court instanter.

(d) ***If Judge of Assigned Court Not Present in County.*** The clerk must determine instanter whether the judge of the court to which the application is assigned is present in the county. If that judge is not present in the county, the clerk must instanter notify the local administrative judge or judges and the presiding judge of the administrative judicial region and must send them any information requested, including the cover page and verification page.

(e) ***Notice of Hearing and Appointments.*** When the clerk is advised by the court of a time for hearing or an appointment of a guardian ad litem or attorney ad litem, the clerk must instanter give notice — as directed in the verification page and to each appointee — of the hearing time or appointment. A court coordinator or other court personnel may give notice instead of the clerk.

(f) ***Orders.*** The clerk must provide the minor's attorney and the guardian ad litem with copies of all court orders, including findings of fact and conclusions of law.

(g) ***Certificate of Court's Failure to Rule Within Time Prescribed by Statute.*** If the court fails to rule on an application within the time required by Section 33.002(g) and (h), Family Code, upon the minor's request, the clerk must instanter issue a certificate to that effect, stating that the application is deemed by statute to be granted. The clerk may use Form 2E but is not required to do so.

2.3. Court's Duties. Upon receipt of an application from the clerk, the court must promptly:

(a) appoint a qualified person to serve as guardian ad litem for the minor applicant;

(b) appoint an attorney for the minor, who may be the same person appointed guardian ad litem if that person is an attorney admitted to practice law in Texas and there is no conflict of interest in the same person serving as attorney ad litem and guardian ad litem;

(c) set a hearing on the application in accordance with Rule 2.4(a); and

(d) advise the clerk of the appointment or appointments and the hearing time.

2.4 Hearing.

(a) ***Time.*** The court must conduct a hearing in time to rule on the application as required by Rule 2.5(d). But the minor may postpone the hearing by written request to the clerk when the application is filed or thereafter. The request may be submitted on Form 2C, but use of the form is not required. The request must either specify a date on which the minor will be ready for the hearing, or state that the minor will later provide a date on which she will be ready for the hearing. Once the minor determines when she will be ready for the hearing, she must notify the clerk of that time in writing. The postponed hearing must be conducted in time for the court to rule on the application as required by Rule 2.5(d).

(b) ***Place.*** The hearing should be held in a location, such as a judge's chambers, that will assure confidentiality. The hearing may be held away from the courthouse.

(c) ***Persons Attending.*** Hearings must be closed to the public. Only the judge, the court reporter and any other essential court personnel, the minor, her attorney, her guardian ad litem, and witnesses on the minor's behalf may be present.

(d) ***Record.*** The court, the minor's attorney, or the guardian ad litem may request that the record — the clerk's record and reporter's record — be prepared. A request by the minor's attorney or guardian ad litem must be in writing and may be, but is not required to be, on Form 2I (if an appeal will be taken) or 2J (if an appeal will not be taken). The court reporter must provide an original and two copies of the reporter's record to the clerk. When the record has been prepared, the clerk must contact the minor's attorney and the guardian ad litem at the telephone numbers shown on Form 2I or 2J and make it available to them. The record must be prepared and made available instanter if it has been requested for appeal or if a belief that there is evidence of past or potential abuse of the minor is stated on the record or submitted to the court in writing. When a notice of appeal is filed, the clerk must forward the record to the court of appeals in accordance with Rule 3.2(b).

(e) ***Hearing to Be Informal.*** The court should attempt to rule on the application without regard to technical defects in the application or the evidence. Affidavits of persons other than applicants are admissible. Statements in the application cannot be offered as evidence to support the application. If necessary, the court may assist the minor in remedying technical defects in the application and in presenting relevant and material facts.

2.5 Ruling.

(a) ***Form of Ruling.*** The court's ruling on the application must include a signed order and written findings of fact and conclusions of law. The findings and conclusions may be included in the order. The court may use Form 2D, but it is not required to do so.

(b) ***Grounds for Granting Application.*** The court must grant the application if the minor establishes, by a preponderance of the evidence, that:

(1) the minor is mature and sufficiently well informed to make the decision to have an abortion performed without notifying either of the minor's parents, the minor's managing conservator, or the minor's legal guardian, as the case may be;

(2) notifying either of the minor's parents, the minor's managing conservator, or the minor's legal guardian, as the case may be, would not be in the minor's best interest; or

(3) notifying either of the minor's parents, the minor's managing conservator, or the minor's legal guardian, as the case may be, may lead to physical, sexual, or emotional abuse of the minor.

(c) ***Grounds for Denying Application.*** If the minor can establish none of the grounds in Rule 2.5(b) by a preponderance of the evidence, the court must deny the application. If the court, the guardian ad litem, or the attorney ad litem are unable to contact the minor before the hearing despite diligent attempts to do so, or if the minor does not attend the hearing, the court must deny the application without prejudice.

(d) ***Time for Ruling.*** The court must rule on an application as soon as possible after it is filed, subject to any postponement requested by the minor, and immediately after the hearing is concluded. Section 33.003(h), Family Code, states that a court must rule on an application by 5:00 p.m. on the second business day after the day the application is filed, or if the minor requests a postponement, after the date the minor states she is ready for the hearing, and that if the court does not rule within this time, the application is deemed to be granted.

(e) ***Notification of Right to Appeal.*** If the court denies the application, it must inform the minor of her right to appeal under Rule 3 and furnish her with the notice of appeal form, Form 3A.

Adopted Dec. 22, 1999, eff. Jan. 1, 2000. Amended Nov. 14, 2006, eff. March 1, 2007; Feb. 27, 2007, eff. March 1, 2007.

Notes and Comments

1. Section 33.003(b), Family Code, permits an application to be filed in "any county court at law, court having probate jurisdiction, or district court, including a family district court, in this state." The initial assignment of an application to a specific court in a county is made by the clerk with whom the application is filed (not by the minor). Given the diversity of needs and circumstances among Texas courts, these rules allow the courts in each county to tailor the procedures for filing, handling, and assigning applications prescribed by these rules to best meet those needs and circumstances. Chapter 74, Subchapter C, Government Code, affords the presiding judge of an administrative judicial region broad discretion to assign active judges within the region, as well as visiting judges, to hear matters pending in courts within the region. *See* Tex. Govt. Code §§ 74.054, 74.056; *see also id.*, § 74.056(b) (presiding judges may request judges from other judicial regions for assignment); § 74.057 (Chief Justice may assign judges from one judicial region to another). Section 25.0022, Government Code, provides for assignment of probate judges. Furthermore, Chapter 74, Subchapter D, Government Code, authorizes district and statutory county court judges within a county to hear matters pending in any district or statutory county court in the county. *Id.*, § 74.094(a). Finally, Section 74.121, Government Code, permits courts within a county to transfer cases among courts having jurisdiction over the case. If no local rule governs assignments, then Rule 2.1(b)(4) controls.

2. Because an application is considered filed when it is actually received by the clerk, the timing provisions relating to filing by mail of Tex. R. Civ. P. 21a are inapplicable.

3. Section 33.003(f), Family Code, provides that a guardian ad litem may be (1) a person who may consent to treatment for the minor under Sections 32.001(a)(1)–(3), Family Code; (2) a psychiatrist or an individual licensed or certified as a psychologist under the Psychologist's Licensing Act, Article 4512c, Vernon's Texas Civil Statutes; (3) an appropriate employee of the Department of Protective or

Regulatory Services; (4) a member of the clergy; or (5) another appropriate person selected by the court. The trial court may also consider appointing a qualified person requested by the minor. Although not directly applicable to these proceedings, the standards embodied in Chapter 107, Family Code, reflect legislative intent that competent and qualified persons be appointed to serve as ad litems and may provide general guidance concerning the nature of those qualifications. Appointment of an employee of the Department of Protective and Regulatory Services to serve as guardian ad litem may give rise to a conflict of interest not immediately apparent at the time since the Department may be involved with the minor's family due to an abuse or neglect investigation, or may be party to a suit affecting the parent–child relationship, or may already be serving as the child's managing conservator.

4. The duties of guardians ad litem are not susceptible of precise definition. Generally, a guardian ad litem should interview the minor and conduct any investigation the guardian believes to be appropriate, without violating Rules 1.3 and 1.4, to assist the court in arriving at an opinion whether the minor is mature and sufficiently well informed to make the decision to have an abortion performed without notification to either of her parents or a managing conservator or guardian, whether notification would not be in the best interest of the minor, or whether notification may lead to physical, sexual, or emotional abuse of the minor. In making these determinations, the following factors have been considered in other jurisdictions with similar parental notification statutes:

Whether the minor has been examined by a doctor of medicine, doctor of osteopathy, or registered nurse — who is licensed to practice in Texas —and has given that health care provider an accurate and complete statement of her medical history.

Whether the minor has been provided with information or counseling bearing on her decision to have an abortion.

Whether the minor desires further counseling.

Whether, based on the information or counseling provided to the minor, she is able to give informed consent.

Whether the minor is attending school, or is or has been employed.

Whether the minor has previously filed an application that was denied.

Whether the minor lives with her parents.

Whether the minor desires an abortion or has been threatened, intimidated or coerced into having an abortion.

Whether the pregnancy resulted from sexual assault, sexual abuse, or incest.

Whether there is a history or pattern of family violence.

Whether the minor fears for her safety.

These considerations may not be relevant in every case, are not exclusive, and may not be sufficient to discharge the guardian ad litem's responsibilities in every case. Use of these factors as a basis for civil liability or as a statement of the standard of care is contrary to their intended purpose. Nothing in this comment alters existing standards of conduct under the Texas Disciplinary Rules of Professional Conduct, the Texas Rules of Disciplinary Procedure, or the Code of Judicial Conduct.

In addition to these general guidelines, Chapter 107, Family Code, sets forth duties of guardians and attorneys ad litem appointed in suits affecting the parent–child relationship. These duties are not directly applicable to proceedings under Chapter 33, Family Code, and may be incompatible with the nature of such proceedings, but they reflect general legislative intent concerning the responsibilities of ad litems.

5. Under Rule 2.5(b), once a court concludes that an application should be granted on a single ground, it need not address other grounds. But in addressing any ground, the court should attempt to ascertain, among other factors, whether the pregnancy resulted from sexual assault, sexual abuse, or incest. The legislative history of Chapter 33, Family Code, indicates that one of the principal purposes of the statute was to screen for sexual crimes and abuse of minors so as to protect them against further victimization.

Rule 2. Proceedings in the Trial Court

Text of rule, subject to public comments received [comments period ends April 1, 2016], effective January 1, 2016. See, also, text of rule effective until January 1, 2016.

2.1 Where to File an Application; Court Assignment and Transfer; Application Form; Effect of a Nonsuit or Prior Determination.

(a) *Counties in which an application may be filed.* An application for an order under Section 33.003, Family Code, must be filed in the minor's county of residence, unless one of the following exceptions applies.

(1) *Minor's parent is a presiding judge.* If the minor's parent, managing conservator, or guardian is a presiding judge of a court described in (b)(1) in the county of the minor's residence, the application must be filed in:

(A) a contiguous county; or

(B) the county where the minor intends to obtain the abortion.

(2) *Residence in a county with a population of less than 10,000.* If the minor's county of residence has a population of less than 10,000, the application must be filed in:

(A) the minor's county of residence;

(B) a contiguous county; or

(C) the county where the minor intends to obtain the abortion.

(3) *Nonresident minor.* If the minor is not a Texas resident, the application must be filed in the county where the minor intends to obtain the abortion.

(b) *Courts in which an application may be filed; assignment and transfer.*

(1) *Courts with jurisdiction.* An application may be filed in a district court (including a family district court), a county court at law, or a court having probate jurisdiction.

(2) *Application filed with district or county clerk.* An application must be filed with either the district clerk or the county clerk, who will assign the application to a court as provided by

local rule or these rules. The clerk to whom the application is tendered cannot refuse to accept it because of any local rule or other rule or law that governs the filing and assignment of applications or cases. The clerk must accept the application and transfer it immediately to the proper clerk, advising the person tendering the application where it is being transferred.

(3) *Court assignment and transfer by local rule.* The courts in a county that have jurisdiction to hear applications may determine by local rule how applications will be assigned between or among them. A local rule must be approved by the Supreme Court under Rule 3a, Texas Rules of Civil Procedure.

(4) *Initial court assignment if no local rule.* Absent a local rule, the clerk who files an application—whether the district clerk or the county clerk—must assign it as follows:

(A) to a district court, if the active judge of the court, or a judge assigned to it, is available;

(B) if the application cannot be assigned under (A), then to a statutory county or probate court, if the active judge of the court, or a judge assigned to it, is available;

(C) if the application cannot be assigned under (A) or (B), then to the constitutional county court, if it has probate jurisdiction, and if the active judge of the court, or a judge assigned to it, is available;

(D) if the application cannot be assigned under (A), (B), or (C), then to the district court.

(5) *Judges who may hear and determine applications.* An application may be heard and determined by the active judge of the court to which the application is assigned, by any judge authorized to sit for the active judge, or by any judge who may be assigned to the court in which the application is pending. An application may not be heard or determined, or any proceedings under these rules conducted, by a master or magistrate.

(c) *Application form.* An application consists of two pages—a cover page and a separate verification page—if the minor is not represented by an attorney at the time of filing. If the minor is represented by an attorney at the time of filing, the application must include a third page, the attorney's sworn statement or declaration made under penalty of perjury.

(1) *Cover page.* The cover page may be submitted on Form 2A, but use of the form is not required. The cover page must be styled "In re Jane Doe" and must not disclose the name of the minor or any information from which the minor's identity could be derived. The cover page must state:

(A) that the minor is pregnant;

(B) that the minor is unmarried, is under 18 years of age, and has not had her disabilities removed under Chapter 31, Family Code;

(C) that the minor wishes to have an abortion without notifying or obtaining consent from either of her parents or a managing conservator or guardian, and the statutory ground or grounds on which she relies;

(D) that venue is proper in the county in which the application has been filed;

(E) whether the minor has retained an attorney, and if so, the attorney's name, email address, mailing address, and telephone number;

(F) whether the minor requests the court to appoint a particular person as her guardian ad litem; and

(G) that, concerning her current pregnancy, the minor has not previously filed an application that was denied; or

(H) if the minor has filed a previous application with respect to the current pregnancy that was denied, that this application is being filed in the same court that denied the previous application and that there has been a material change in circumstances since the time the previous application was denied.

(2) *Verification page.* The verification page may be submitted on Form 2B, but use of the form is not required. The verification page must be separate from the cover page, must be signed by the minor under oath or under penalty of perjury, and must state:

(A) the minor's full name, date of birth, physical address, mailing address, and telephone number;

(B) the name, address, telephone number, and relationship to the minor of any person the minor requests the court to appoint as her guardian ad litem;

(C) if the minor has not retained an attorney, a telephone number—whether that of the minor or someone else (such as a physician, friend, or relative)—at which the minor may be contacted immediately and confidentially until an attorney is appointed to represent her; and

(D) that all information contained in the application, including both the cover page and the verification page, is true.

(3) *Attorney's statement.* The minor's attorney must file with the application a sworn statement or unsworn declaration made under penalty of perjury that attests to the truth of the minor's claims regarding venue and prior applications.

(d) ***Time of filing.*** An application is filed when it is actually received by the district or county clerk.

(e) ***Nonsuit requires permission.*** A minor may not withdraw or nonsuit an application without permission of the court.

(f) ***Res judicata effect of prior determination.***

(1) *General rule.* A minor who has filed an application and obtained a determination by the court under Rule 2.5 may not initiate a new application proceeding with respect to the same pregnancy, and the prior determination is res judicata on the issue whether the minor may consent to an abortion without notification to, or consent of, a parent, managing conservator, or guardian.

(2) *Exception for material change in circumstances.* A minor whose application is denied may submit a new application to the court that denied the application if the minor shows that there has been a material change in circumstances since the prior application was denied.

2.2 Clerk's Duties.

(a) ***Assistance in filing.*** The clerk must give prompt assistance—in a manner designed to protect the minor's confidentiality—to persons seeking to file an application. If requested, the clerk must administer the oath for the verification page or provide a person authorized to do so. The clerk must also redact from the cover page any information identifying the minor. The clerk must ensure that both the cover page and the separate verification page are completed in full.

(b) ***Filing procedure.*** The clerk must assign the application a cause number that does not identify the assigned judge and affix it to both the cover page and the verification page. The clerk must then provide a certified copy of the verification page to the person filing the application. The clerk must file the verification page under seal in a secure place where access is limited to essential court personnel.

(c) ***Distribution.*** When an application is filed, the clerk must distribute the cover page and verification page, or a copy of them, to the appropriate court immediately. If appointment of a specific person as guardian ad litem has been requested, the clerk must also communicate the information to the appropriate court immediately.

(d) ***If judge of assigned court not available.*** The clerk must determine immediately whether the judge of the court to which the application is assigned is available to hear the application within the prescribed time period. If that judge is not available, the clerk must immediately notify the local administrative judge or judges and the presiding judge of the administrative judicial region and must send them any information requested, including the cover page and verification page.

(e) ***Notice of hearing and appointments.*** When the clerk is advised by the court of a time for the hearing or of the appointment of a guardian ad litem or an attorney ad litem, the clerk must immediately give notice—as directed in the verification page and to each appointee—of the hearing time or appointment. A court coordinator or other court personnel may give notice instead of the clerk.

(f) ***Orders.*** The clerk must provide the minor's attorney and the guardian ad litem with copies of all court orders, including findings of fact and conclusions of law.

(g) ***Certificate of court's failure to rule within time prescribed by statute.*** If the court fails to rule on an application within the time required by Section 33.003(h), Family Code, then, upon the minor's request, the clerk must immediately issue a certificate to that effect, stating that the application is deemed to be denied. The clerk may use Form 2E but is not required to do so.

2.3 Court's Duties. Upon receipt of an application from the clerk, the court must promptly:

(a) appoint a qualified person to serve as guardian ad litem for the minor applicant;

(b) unless the minor has a retained attorney, appoint an attorney ad litem for the minor, who must not be the same person appointed as guardian ad litem;

(c) set a hearing on the application; and

(d) advise the clerk of the appointments and the hearing time.

2.4 Hearing.

(a) ***Time.***

(1) *General rule.* The court must conduct a hearing in time to rule on the application by the deadline stated in Rule 2.5(f).

(2) *Minor may request postponement.* The minor may postpone the hearing by written request to the clerk. The request may be submitted on Form 2C, but use of the form is not

required. The request must either specify a date on which the minor will be ready for the hearing or state that the minor will later provide a date on which she will be ready for the hearing. Once the minor determines when she will be ready for the hearing, she must notify the clerk of that time in writing. The postponed hearing must be conducted in time for the court to rule on the application by the deadline stated in Rule 2.5(f).

(b) ***Place.*** The hearing should be held in a location, such as a judge's chambers, that will ensure confidentiality. The hearing may be held away from the courthouse.

(c) ***Persons attending.*** The hearing must be closed to the public. Only the judge, the court reporter, other essential court personnel, the minor, her attorney, her guardian ad litem, and witnesses on the minor's behalf may be present.

(d) ***Record.*** The court, the minor, the minor's attorney, or the guardian ad litem may request that the record—the clerk's record and reporter's record—be prepared. A request by the minor, the minor's attorney, or the guardian ad litem must be in writing and may be, but is not required to be, on Form 2I (if an appeal will be taken) or 2J (if an appeal will not be taken). The court reporter must provide an original and two copies of the reporter's record to the clerk. When the record has been prepared, the clerk must contact the minor, if she has requested the record; the minor's attorney; and the guardian ad litem at the telephone numbers shown on Form 2I or 2J and make it available to them. The record must be prepared and made available immediately if it has been requested for appeal or to demonstrate the past or potential abuse of the minor. When a notice of appeal is filed, the clerk must forward the record to the court of appeals in accordance with Rule 3.2(b).

(e) ***Hearing to be informal.*** The court should attempt to rule on the application without regard to technical defects in the application or the evidence. Affidavits of persons other than the minor are admissible. Statements in the application cannot be offered as evidence to support the application. If necessary, the court may assist the minor in remedying technical defects in the application and in presenting relevant and material facts.

2.5 Ruling.

(a) ***Form of ruling.*** The court's ruling on the application must include a signed order and written findings of fact and conclusions of law. The findings and conclusions may be included in the order. The court may use Form 2D, but it is not required to do so.

(b) ***Grounds for granting application.*** The court must grant the application if the minor establishes, by clear and convincing evidence:

(1) that the minor is mature and sufficiently well informed to make the decision to have an abortion performed without notice to, or consent of, a parent, managing conservator, or guardian; or

(2) that the notification or attempt to obtain consent would not be in the minor's best interest.

(c) ***The mature-and-informed inquiry.*** In determining whether the minor meets the requirements of (b)(1), the court must consider the experience, perspective, and judgment of the minor. The court may:

(1) consider all relevant factors, including:

(A) the minor's age;

(B) the minor's life experiences, such as working, traveling independently, or managing her own financial affairs; and

(C) steps taken by the minor to explore her options and the consequences of those options;

(2) inquire as to the minor's reasons for seeking an abortion;

(3) consider the degree to which the minor is informed about the state-published informational materials described by Chapter 171, Health and Safety Code; and

(4) require the minor to be evaluated by a licensed mental health counselor, who must return the evaluation to the court for review within three business days.

(d) ***The best-interest inquiry.*** In determining whether the minor meets the requirements of (b)(2), the court may inquire as to:

(1) the minor's reasons for not wanting to notify and obtain consent from a parent, managing conservator, or guardian;

(2) whether notification or the attempt to obtain consent may lead to physical or sexual abuse;

(3) whether the pregnancy was the result of sexual abuse by a parent, managing conservator, or guardian; and

(4) any history of physical or sexual abuse from a parent, managing conservator, or guardian.

(e) ***Grounds for denying the application.*** The court must deny the application if:

(1) the minor does not establish either ground in (b) by clear and convincing evidence; or

(2) the minor does not attend the hearing; and

(A) the minor had actual knowledge of the setting; or

(B) diligent attempts were made to notify the minor of the setting.

(f) ***Time for ruling.*** The court must rule on an application as soon as possible after it is filed, subject to any postponement requested by the minor, and immediately after the hearing is concluded. Section 33.003(h), Family Code, states that a court must rule on an application by 5 p.m. on the fifth business day after the day the application is filed, or if the minor requests a postponement, by 5 p.m. on the fifth business day after the date the minor states she is ready for the hearing.

(g) ***Failure to timely rule.*** If the court fails to timely rule on an application, the application is deemed to be denied.

(h) ***Notification of the right to appeal.*** If the court denies the application, it must inform the minor of her right to appeal under Rule 3 and furnish her with the notice of appeal form, Form 3A.

Adopted Dec. 22, 1999, eff. Jan. 1, 2000. Amended Nov. 14, 2006, eff. March 1, 2007; Feb. 27, 2007, eff. March 1, 2007; Dec. 29, 2015, eff. Jan. 1, 2016.

Notes and Comments

1. Section 33.003(b), Family Code, permits an application to be filed in "a county court at law, court having probate jurisdiction, or district court, including a family district court, in the minor's county of residence" or, if an exception applies, in a contiguous county or the county where the abortion would be performed. The initial assignment of an application to a specific court in a county is made by the clerk with whom the application is filed (not by the minor). Given the diversity of needs and circumstances among Texas courts, these rules allow the courts in each county to tailor the procedures for filing, handling, and assigning applications prescribed by these rules to best meet those needs and circumstances. Chapter 74, Subchapter C, Government Code, affords the presiding judge of an administrative judicial region broad discretion to assign active judges within the region, as well as visiting judges, to hear matters pending in courts within the region. *See* Tex. Govt. Code §§ 74.054, 74.056; *see also id.* § 74.056(b) (presiding judges may request judges from other judicial regions for assignment); § 74.057 (Chief Justice may assign judges from one judicial region to another). Section 25.0022, Government Code, provides for assignment of probate judges. Furthermore, Chapter 74, Subchapter D, Government Code, authorizes district and statutory county court judges within a county to hear matters pending in any district or statutory county court in the county. *Id.* § 74.094(a). Finally, Section 74.121, Government Code, permits courts within a county to transfer cases among courts having jurisdiction over the case. If no local rule governs assignments, then Rule 2.1(b)(4) controls.

2. Because an application is considered filed when it is actually received by the clerk, the timing provisions relating to filing by mail of Tex. R. Civ. P. 21a are inapplicable.

3. Section 33.003(f), Family Code, provides that a guardian ad litem may be (1) a person who may consent to treatment for the minor under Sections 32.001(a)(1)–(3), Family Code; (2) a psychiatrist or an individual licensed or certified as a psychologist under Chapter 501, Occupations Code; (3) an appropriate employee of the Department of Family and Protective Services; (4) a member of the clergy; or (5) another appropriate person selected by the court. The trial court may also consider appointing a qualified person requested by the minor. Although not directly applicable to these proceedings, the standards embodied in Chapter 107, Family Code, reflect legislative intent that competent and qualified persons be appointed to serve as ad litems and may provide general guidance concerning the nature of those qualifications. Appointment of an employee of the Department of Family and Protective Services to serve as guardian ad litem may give rise to a conflict of interest not immediately apparent at the time since the Department may be involved with the minor's family due to an abuse or neglect investigation, or may be party to a suit affecting the parent-child relationship, or may already be serving as the child's managing conservator.

4. The duties of guardians ad litem are not susceptible of precise definition. Generally, a guardian ad litem should interview the minor and conduct any investigation the guardian believes to be appropriate, without violating Rules 1.3 and 1.4, to assist the court in arriving at an opinion whether the minor is mature and sufficiently well informed to make the decision to have an abortion performed without notification to, or consent of, either of her parents or a managing conservator or guardian or whether notification or the attempt to obtain consent would not be in the best interest of the minor. Rule 2.5(c) and (d) list some nonexclusive factors outlined in Section 33.003(i–1)–(i–2), Family Code, that a court may consider in deciding whether the statutory criteria for a bypass have been met. Factors that have been considered in other jurisdictions with similar parental notification and consent statutes include:

- whether the minor has been examined by a doctor of medicine, doctor of osteopathy, or registered nurse—who is licensed to practice in Texas—and has given that health care provider an accurate and complete statement of her medical history;
- whether the minor has been provided with information or counseling bearing on her decision to have an abortion;
- whether the minor desires further counseling;
- whether, based on the information or counseling provided to the minor, she is able to give informed consent;
- whether the minor is attending school, or is or has been employed;

• whether the minor has previously filed an application that was denied;

• whether the minor lives with her parents;

• whether the minor desires an abortion or has been threatened, intimidated, or coerced into having an abortion;

• whether the pregnancy resulted from sexual assault, sexual abuse, or incest;

• whether there is a history or pattern of family violence; and

• whether the minor fears for her safety.

These considerations may not be relevant in every case, are not exclusive, and may not be sufficient to discharge the guardian ad litem's responsibilities in every case. Use of these factors as a basis for civil liability or as a statement of the standard of care is contrary to their intended purpose. Nothing in this comment alters existing standards of conduct under the Texas Disciplinary Rules of Professional Conduct, the Texas Rules of Disciplinary Procedure, or the Code of Judicial Conduct.

In addition to these general guidelines, Chapter 107, Family Code, sets forth duties of guardians and attorneys ad litem appointed in suits affecting the parent-child relationship. These duties are not directly applicable to proceedings under Chapter 33, Family Code, and may be incompatible with the confidential and expeditious nature of such proceedings, but they reflect general legislative intent concerning the responsibilities of ad litems.

5. Under Rule 2.5(b), once a court concludes that an application should be granted on a single ground, it need not address other grounds. But in addressing any ground, the court should attempt to ascertain, among other factors, whether the pregnancy resulted from sexual assault, sexual abuse, or incest. The legislative history of Chapter 33, Family Code, indicates that one of the principal purposes of the statute was to screen for sexual crimes and abuse of minors so as to protect them against further victimization.

Rule 3. Appeal from Denial of Application

Text of rule effective until January 1, 2016. See, also, text of rule, subject to public comments received [comments period ends April 1, 2016], effective January 1, 2016.

3.1 How to Appeal. To appeal the denial of an application, the minor must simultaneously file a notice of appeal with the clerk of the court that denied the application, file a copy of the notice of appeal with the clerk of the court of appeals to which an appeal is to be taken, and advise the clerk of the court of appeals by telephone that an appeal is being taken under Chapter 33, Family Code. The minor may use Form 3A but is not required to do so. The notice of appeal must:

(a) be styled "In re Jane Doe";

(b) state the number of the cause in the trial court;

(c) be addressed to a court of appeals with jurisdiction in the county in which the application was filed;

(d) state an intention to appeal; and

(e) be signed by the minor's attorney or attorney ad litem appointed by the trial court.

3.2 Clerk's Duties.

(a) ***Assistance in Filing.*** The trial court clerk must give prompt assistance — in a manner designed to protect the minor's confidentiality — to persons seeking to file an appeal. Such assistance must include assuring that the notice of appeal is addressed to the proper court of appeals and that the minor's name and identifying information are not disclosed.

(b) ***Forwarding Record to Court of Appeals.*** Upon receipt of a notice of appeal, the trial court clerk must instanter forward to the clerk of the court of appeals the notice of appeal, the clerk's record (original papers or copies) excluding the verification page, and the reporter's record. The trial court clerk must not send the record to the clerk of the court of appeals by mail but must, if feasible, deliver it by hand or transmit it by facsimile or other electronic means. If neither of these methods is feasible, then the record may be sent by overnight delivery.

(c) ***Certificate of Court's Failure to Rule Within Time Prescribed by Statute.*** If the court of appeals fails to rule on an application within the time required by Section 33.004(b), Family Code, upon the minor's request, the clerk of the court of appeals must instanter issue a certificate to that effect, stating that the trial court's order is reversed and judgment is rendered that the application is deemed by statute to be granted. The clerk may use Form 3D but is not required to do so.

3.3 Proceedings in the Court of Appeals.

(a) ***Briefing and Argument.*** A minor may request to be allowed to submit a brief and to present oral argument, but the Court may decide to rule without a brief or oral argument.

(b) ***Ruling.*** The court of appeals—sitting in a three-judge panel—must issue a judgment affirming or reversing the trial court's order denying the application. The court may use Form 3C but is not required to do so.

(c) ***Time for Ruling.*** The court of appeals must rule on an appeal as soon as possible, subject to any postponement requested by the minor. Section 33.004(b), Family Code, states that a court must rule on an appeal by 5:00 p.m. on the second business day after the notice of appeal is filed with the court that denied the application, or if the minor requests a postponement, after the date the minor states she is ready to proceed, and that if the court does not rule within this time, the appeal is deemed to be granted.

(d) *Postponement by Minor.* The minor may postpone the time of ruling by written request filed either with the trial court clerk at the time she files the notice of appeal or thereafter with the court of appeals clerk. The request may be submitted on Form 3B, but use of the form is not required. The request must either specify a date on which the minor will be ready to proceed to ruling, or state that the minor will later provide a date on which she will be ready to proceed to ruling. Once the minor determines when she will be ready to proceed to ruling, she must notify the court of appeals clerk of that date in writing.

(e) *Opinion.*

(1) *Opinion Optional.* A court of appeals may issue an opinion explaining its ruling, but it is not required to do so.

(2) *Time.* Any opinion must issue not later than:

(A) ten business days after the day on which a notice of appeal is filed in the Supreme Court, if an appeal is taken to the Supreme Court; or

(B) sixty days after the day on which the court of appeals issued its judgment, if no appeal is taken to the Supreme Court.

(3) *Confidential Transmission to Supreme Court.* When the court of appeals issues an opinion, the clerk must confidentially transmit it instanter to the Supreme Court and to the trial court.

Adopted Dec. 22, 1999, eff. Jan. 1, 2000. Amended Nov. 8, 2000, eff. March 1, 2001.

Notes and Comments

1. Chapter 33, Family Code, provides for no appeal from an order granting an application.

2. A request to postpone the ruling of the court of appeals may be used in conjunction with a request for oral argument or to submit briefing.

3. Neither Chapter 33, Family Code, nor these rules prescribes the appellate standard of review.

4. Although publication of appellate court opinions is prohibited by statute, the Supreme Court may amend these rules to address issues arising from their application and interpretation.

Rule 3. Appeal From Denial of Application

Text of rule, subject to public comments received [comments period ends April 1, 2016], effective January 1, 2016. See, also, text of rule effective until January 1, 2016.

3.1 How to Appeal. To appeal the denial of an application, the minor must file a notice of appeal with the clerk of the court that denied the application, file a copy of the notice of appeal with the clerk of the court of appeals to which an appeal is to be taken, and advise the clerk of the court of appeals by telephone that an appeal is being taken under Chapter 33, Family Code. The minor may use Form 3A but is not required to do so. The notice of appeal must:

(a) be styled "In re Jane Doe";

(b) state the number of the cause in the trial court;

(c) be addressed to a court of appeals with jurisdiction in the county in which the application was filed;

(d) state an intention to appeal; and

(e) be signed by the minor's attorney.

3.2 Clerk's Duties.

(a) *Assistance in filing.* The trial court clerk must give prompt assistance—in a manner designed to protect the minor's confidentiality—to persons seeking to file an appeal. The clerk must ensure that the notice of appeal is addressed to the proper court of appeals and that the minor's name and identifying information are not disclosed.

(b) *Forwarding record to court of appeals.* Upon receipt of a notice of appeal, the trial court clerk must immediately forward to the clerk of the court of appeals the notice of appeal, the clerk's record excluding the verification page, and the reporter's record. The trial court clerk must deliver the record to the clerk of the court of appeals by hand or send it by fax or email. The clerk must not send the record by mail.

(c) *Certificate of court's failure to rule within time prescribed by statute.* If the court of appeals fails to rule on an application within the time required by Section 33.004(b), Family Code, then, upon the minor's request, the clerk of the court of appeals must immediately issue a certificate to that effect, stating that the trial court's order is affirmed. The clerk may use Form 3D but is not required to do so.

3.3 Proceedings in the Court of Appeals.

(a) *Briefing and argument.* A minor may request to be allowed to submit a brief and to present oral argument, but the court may decide to rule without a brief or oral argument.

(b) *Ruling.* The court of appeals—sitting in a three-judge panel—must issue a judgment affirming or reversing the trial court's order denying the application. The court may use Form 3C but is not required to do so.

(c) *Time for ruling.* The court of appeals must rule on an appeal as soon as possible, subject to any postponement requested by the minor. Section 33.004(b), Family Code, states that a court must rule on an appeal by 5 p.m. on the fifth business day after the notice of appeal is filed with the court that denied the application, or if the minor requests a postponement, by 5 p.m. on the fifth business day after the date the minor states she is ready to proceed.

(d) ***Postponement by minor.*** The minor may postpone the time of ruling by written request filed either with the trial court clerk at the time she files the notice of appeal or thereafter with the court of appeals clerk. The request may be submitted on Form 3B, but use of the form is not required. The request must either specify a date on which the minor will be ready to proceed to ruling, or state that the minor will later provide a date on which she will be ready to proceed to ruling. Once the minor determines when she will be ready to proceed to ruling, she must notify the court of appeals clerk of that date in writing.

(e) ***Opinion.***

(1) *Opinion optional; must preserve confidentiality.* A court of appeals may issue an opinion explaining its ruling, but it is not required to do so. An opinion that is designated for publication or public release must be written in a way to preserve the confidentiality of the identity of the minor.

(2) *Time.* Any opinion must issue not later than:

(A) ten business days after the day on which a notice of appeal is filed in the Supreme Court, if an appeal is taken to the Supreme Court; or

(B) sixty days after the day on which the court of appeals issued its judgment, if no appeal is taken to the Supreme Court.

(3) *Transmission to Supreme Court and trial court.* When the court of appeals issues an opinion, the clerk must transmit it immediately to the Supreme Court and to the trial court. If the opinion is not designated for publication or public release, the transmission must be confidential.

(f) ***Failure to timely rule.*** If the court of appeals fails to timely rule on the appeal, the trial court's judgment is deemed to be affirmed.

Adopted Dec. 22, 1999, eff. Jan. 1, 2000. Amended Nov. 8, 2000, eff. March 1, 2001; Dec. 29, 2015, eff. Jan. 1, 2016.

Notes and Comments

1. Chapter 33, Family Code, provides for no appeal from an order granting an application.

2. A request to postpone the ruling of the court of appeals may be used in conjunction with a request for oral argument or to submit briefing.

3. Neither Chapter 33, Family Code, nor these rules prescribe the appellate standard of review.

4. The 2015 amendments to Chapter 33, Family Code, permit the court of appeals to publish an opinion "if the opinion is written in a way to preserve the confidentiality of the identity of the pregnant minor." TEX. FAM. CODE § 33.004(c–1). Any opinion that is released to the public must not only omit the minor's name and other directly identifying information but it must also describe the facts in a way that those who know the minor would not be able to recognize her.

Rule 4. Appeal to the Supreme Court

Text of rule effective until January 1, 2016. See, also, text of rule, subject to public comments received [comments period ends April 1, 2016], effective January 1, 2016.

4.1 How to Appeal to the Supreme Court. To appeal from the court of appeals to the Supreme Court, the minor must simultaneously file a notice of appeal with the Clerk of the Supreme Court, file a copy of the notice of appeal with the clerk of the court of appeals, and advise the clerk of each court by telephone that an appeal is being taken under Chapter 33, Family Code. The minor may use Form 4A but is not required to do so. The notice of appeal must:

(a) be styled "In re Jane Doe";

(b) state the number of the cause in the court of appeals;

(c) state an intention to appeal; and

(d) be signed by the minor's attorney or attorney ad litem appointed by the trial court.

4.2 Clerk's Duties.

(a) ***Assistance in Filing.*** The Clerk of the Supreme Court must give prompt assistance — in a manner designed to protect the minor's confidentiality — to persons seeking to file an appeal. Such assistance must include assuring that the notice of appeal is addressed to the Supreme Court and that the minor's name and identifying information are not disclosed.

(b) ***Forwarding Record to Supreme Court.*** Upon receipt of a notice of appeal to the Supreme Court, the clerks of the court of appeals and Supreme Court must instanter have forwarded to the Supreme Court the record that was before the court of appeals.

4.3 Proceedings in the Supreme Court. A minor may request to be allowed to submit a brief and to present oral argument, but the Court may decide to rule without a brief or oral argument. The Court must rule as soon as possible.

Adopted Dec. 22, 1999, eff. Jan. 1, 2000.

Rule 4. Appeal to the Supreme Court

Text of rule, subject to public comments received [comments period ends April 1, 2016], effective January 1, 2016. See, also, text of rule effective until January 1, 2016.

4.1 How to Appeal to the Supreme Court. To appeal from the court of appeals to the Supreme Court, the minor must file a notice of appeal with the clerk of the Supreme Court, file a copy of the notice of appeal with the clerk of the court of appeals, and advise the clerk of each court by telephone that an appeal is being taken under Chapter 33, Family Code. The minor may use Form 4A but is not required to do so. The notice of appeal must:

(a) be styled "In re Jane Doe";

(b) state the number of the cause in the court of appeals;

(c) state an intention to appeal; and

(d) be signed by the minor's attorney.

4.2 Clerk's Duties.

(a) ***Assistance in filing.*** The clerk of the Supreme Court must give prompt assistance—in a manner designed to protect the minor's confidentiality—to any person seeking to file an appeal. The clerk must ensure that the notice of appeal is addressed to the Supreme Court and that the minor's name and identifying information are not disclosed.

(b) ***Forwarding record to Supreme Court.*** Upon receipt of a notice of appeal to the Supreme Court, the clerks of the court of appeals and Supreme Court must immediately forward to the Supreme Court the record that was before the court of appeals.

4.3 Proceedings in the Supreme Court. A minor may request to be allowed to submit a brief and to present oral argument, but the Court may decide to rule without a brief or oral argument. The Court must rule as soon as possible.

Adopted Dec. 22, 1999, eff. Jan. 1, 2000. Amended by order of Dec. 29, 2015, eff. Jan. 1, 2016.

APPENDIX 1A

Text of rule effective until January 1, 2016. See, also, text of rule, subject to public comments received [comments period ends April 1, 2016], effective January 1, 2016.

INSTRUCTIONS FOR APPLYING TO THE COURT FOR A WAIVER OF PARENTAL NOTIFICATION

(Form 1A)

Your situation and the law

If you are younger than 18 and have not been legally "emancipated," you are "unemancipated," which means that you are legally under the custody or control of your parent(s), managing conservator, or guardian. (A "managing conservator" is a parent, other adult, or agency appointed by a court to have custody or control of you.)

If you are pregnant, unemancipated, and younger than 18, you cannot get an abortion in Texas unless:

· your doctor first informs your parent(s), managing conservator, or guardian at least 48 hours before you can have an abortion,

or unless

· a judge issues an order that "waives," or removes, the requirement that you must let your parent(s), managing conservator, or guardian know about your planned abortion.

How to get a waiver of parental notification

· Fill out the application

To get a court order waiving the requirement that you tell your parent(s), managing conservator, or guardian about your planned abortion, you or someone acting on your behalf must complete Forms 2A and 2B, ***Confidential Application for Waiver of Parental Notification***. Form 2A is the "Cover Page' for the Application; it requests basic information about why you are seeking the order. Form 2B is the "Verification Page," which requests information about you.

On the Verification Page, you will be asked to tell the court how you may be contacted quickly and confidentially. It is very important that you provide this information because the court may later need to contact you about your application. If you cannot be contacted, your application will be denied. You may list a phone, pager, beeper, or fax number, or other way that you can be contacted. You can but need not give your own number — instead, you can ask the court to contact you through someone who is helping you or acting on your behalf. You may also list a second person who may be contacted on your behalf.

You or someone acting on your behalf must deliver the forms to the clerk in the district court, county court-at-law, county court, or probate court to be filed. The court clerk can help you complete and file the application, and can help you get a hearing on your request. However, the clerk cannot give you legal advice or counsel you about abortion.

All of the information you put on the application is confidential. You do not have to pay a fee to file this application.

· Your hearing

The court will tell you when to come to the courthouse for your "hearing." In your hearing, you will meet with a judge to discuss your request. The court will hold your hearing within two days (not counting weekends and holidays) after you file your application.

After you file your application, the court will appoint a person to meet with you before the hearing and help the judge decide your application. The person is called a "guardian ad litem." In your application you may ask the court to appoint someone you want to be your guardian ad litem (who can be a relative, clergy, counselor, psychiatrist or psychologist, or other adult), but the court is not required to appoint this person.

You must have a lawyer with you at your hearing. You may hire your own lawyer, or you may ask the court to appoint one to represent you for free. The person appointed to be your lawyer might also be appointed to be your guardian ad litem.

· **Keeping it confidential**

Your hearing will be confidential and private. The only persons allowed to be there are you, your guardian ad litem, your lawyer, court staff, and any person whom you request to be there.

You already know that your application stays confidential. So will everything from your hearing: all testimony, documents and other evidence presented to the court, and any order given by the judge. The court will keep everything sealed. No one else can inspect the evidence.

· **The court's decision**

The court must "rule" -- issue a decision on your application — before 5:00 p.m. on the second day after the day you filed your application, not counting weekends and holidays.

If the court fails to rule within that time, it counts as an "OK" to you — it is an automatic waiver of the requirement that you inform your parent(s), managing conservator, or guardian about your planned abortion. If this happens, you can get a certificate from the court clerk that says that your request is "deemed granted," which means that your application was approved.

If the court *does* rule within the required time, the court issues an order that does one of the following four things:

(1) Approves your request because the court finds that you are mature enough and know enough to choose on your own to have an abortion;

(2) Approves your request because it is in your best interests to *not* notify your parent(s), managing conservator, or guardian before getting the abortion;

(3) Approves your request because notifying your parent(s), managing conservator, or guardian before getting the abortion may lead to physical, sexual, or emotional abuse of you; or

(4) Denies your request because the court does not find (1), (2) or (3).

If you say, or if there is evidence, that you have been or may be sexually abused, the court must treat your claim as a very serious matter and may be required to refer it to the police or other authorities for investigation.

· **Appealing the court's decision**

If the court denies your request, you may ask another court to hear your case. This request is called an "appeal," and the new court will be the Court of Appeals.

To appeal the first court's decision, have your own lawyer or your court-appointed lawyer fill out Form 3A, ***Notice of Appeal in Parental Notification Proceeding.*** The lawyer must file it with the clerk of the court that denied your request for a waiver of parental notification.

You will *not* have to go to the Court of Appeals. Instead, the Court of Appeals will review the written record and will issue a written ruling on your appeal no later than 5:00 p.m. on the second day after the day you file the *Notice of Appeal*, not counting weekends and holidays.

The Court of Appeals will provide its ruling to you, the lawyer, your guardian ad litem, or any other person designated by you to receive the ruling.

The same guardian ad litem and lawyer who helped you with your first hearing can help with your appeal.

· **Getting the forms you need**

Forms 2A and 2B, the Cover Page and Verification Page to the *Confidential Application for Waiver of Parental Notification*, and Form 3A, *Notice of Appeal in Parental Notification Proceeding,* should all be attached to these instructions.

If these forms are not attached to these instructions, you can get them from the clerk of the district, county court-at-law, county, or probate court or Court of Appeals. These forms are also available on the Texas Judiciary Internet website at www.courts.state.tx.us

FORM 1A. INSTRUCTIONS FOR APPLYING TO THE COURT FOR A WAIVER OF PARENTAL NOTIFICATION AND CONSENT

Text of form, subject to public comments received [comments period ends April 1, 2016], effective January 1, 2016. See, also, text of form effective until January 1, 2016.

Your situation and the law

If you are younger than 18 and have not been legally "emancipated," you are "unemancipated," which means that you are legally under the custody or control of your parents (or one of your parents), a managing conservator, or a guardian. (A "managing conservator" is an adult or agency appointed by a court to have custody or control of you.)

If you are pregnant, unemancipated, and younger than 18, you cannot get an abortion in Texas unless:

- your doctor informs one of your parents or your managing conservator or guardian at least 48 hours before the abortion and obtains the consent of your parent, managing conservator, or guardian; *or*
- a judge issues an order that "waives" or removes the requirement that you must let a parent or your managing conservator or guardian know about your planned abortion and obtain his or her consent to it.

How to get a waiver of parental notification and consent

Fill out the application

To get a court order waiving the requirements that you tell a parent or your managing conservator or guardian about your planned abortion and obtain his or her consent, you must complete Forms 2A and 2B, ***Confidential Application for Waiver of Parental Notification***. Form 2A is the "Cover Page" for the Application; it requests basic information about why you are seeking the order. Form 2B is the "Verification Page," which requests information about you.

On the Verification Page, you will be asked to tell the court how you may be contacted quickly and confidentially. It is very important that you provide this information because the court may later need to contact you about your application. If you cannot be contacted, your application will be denied. You may list a phone number, email address, or any other way that you can be contacted. You can but need not give your own number—instead, you can ask the court to contact you through someone who is helping you or acting on your behalf. You may also list a second person who may be contacted on your behalf.

You or someone acting on your behalf must deliver the forms to the clerk in the district court, county court at law, county court, or probate court to be filed. The court clerk can help you complete and file the application, and can help you get a hearing on your request. However, the clerk cannot give you legal advice or counsel you about abortion.

All of the information you put on the application is confidential. You do not have to pay a fee to file this application.

Your hearing

The court will tell you when to come to the courthouse for your "hearing." In your hearing, you will meet with a judge to discuss your request. The court will hold your hearing within five days (not counting weekends and holidays) after you file your application.

After you file your application, the court will appoint a person to meet with you before the hearing and help the judge decide your application. The person is called a "guardian ad litem." In your application you may ask the court to appoint someone you want to be your guardian ad litem (who can be a relative, clergy, counselor, psychiatrist or psychologist, or other adult), but the court is not required to appoint this person.

You must also have a lawyer with you at your hearing. You may hire your own lawyer, or you may ask the court to appoint one to represent you for free.

Keeping it confidential

Your hearing will be confidential and private. The only persons allowed to be there are you, your guardian ad litem, your lawyer, court staff, and any person whom you request to be there.

You already know that your application stays confidential. So will everything from your hearing: all testimony, documents and other evidence presented to the court, and any order given by the judge. The court will keep everything sealed. No one else can inspect the evidence.

The court's decision

The court must "rule"—issue a decision on your application—before 5 p.m. on the fifth day after the day you filed your application, not counting weekends and holidays.

If the court fails to rule within that time, then your request is automatically denied. You can get a certificate from the court clerk that says that your request is "deemed denied." If you choose to appeal, the certificate will be sent to the appellate court to explain what happened in your case.

If the court *does* rule within the required time, the court issues an order that does one of the following three things:

(1) approves your request because the court finds that you are mature enough and know enough to choose on your own to have an abortion;

(2) approves your request because it is in your best interests *not* to notify or to attempt to obtain the consent of your parent or your managing conservator or guardian before getting the abortion; or

(3) denies your request because the court does not find (1) or (2).

If you say, or if there is evidence, that you have been or may be sexually abused, the court must treat your claim as a very serious matter and may be required to refer it to the police or other authorities for investigation.

Appealing the court's decision

If the court denies your request, you may ask another court to hear your case. This request is called an "appeal," and the new court will be the court of appeals.

To appeal the first court's decision, have your lawyer fill out Form 3A, ***Notice of Appeal in Parental Notification Proceeding.*** The lawyer must file it with the clerk of the court that denied your request for a waiver of parental notification.

You will *not* have to go to the court of appeals in person. Instead, the court of appeals will review the written record and will issue a written ruling on your appeal no later than 5 p.m. on the fifth day after the day you file the *Notice of Appeal*, not counting weekends and holidays.

The court of appeals will provide its ruling to you, your lawyer, your guardian ad litem, or any other person designated by you to receive the ruling.

The same guardian ad litem and lawyer who helped you with your first hearing can help with your appeal.

Getting the forms you need

Forms 2A and 2B, the Cover Page and Verification Page to the *Confidential Application for Waiver of Parental Notification*, and Form 3A, *Notice of Appeal in Parental Notification Proceeding*, should all be attached to these instructions.

If these forms are not attached to these instructions, you can get them from the clerk of the district, county court at law, county, or probate court or from the clerk of the court of appeals. These forms are also available on the Texas Judiciary website at www.txcourts.gov.

Amended by order of Dec. 29, 2015, eff. Jan. 1, 2016.

APPENDIX 2A

Text of rule effective until January 1, 2016. See, also, text of rule, subject to public comments received [comments period ends April 1, 2016], effective January 1, 2016.

Attention Clerk: Please Expedite

Confidential Application for Waiver of Parental Notification: Cover Page (Form 2A)

As prescribed by the Clerk of the Supreme Court of Texas pursuant to Tex. Fam. Code § 33.003(m).

(Do not complete this section. Court staff will complete this section.)

CAUSE NO. ______________________

IN RE JANE DOE IN THE ____________________

COUNTY, TEXAS

Important: Your Application has two parts: (1) this cover sheet (Form 2A), which asks for basic information about your application; and (2) a separate verification page (Form 2B), which asks for information about you and for you to swear to the truth of everything you say in the cover sheet and verification page. You or someone acting on your behalf must complete both of these forms. If you are completing this application for a minor, remember that "I" or "my" refers to the minor rather than to you.

---

1. I ask the court for an order that allows me to have an abortion without first telling my parent(s), managing conservator, or guardian before I have an abortion. I swear or affirm that **(place a check mark in all the blanks for which you answer "yes")**:

______ I am pregnant.

______ I am unmarried and younger than 18 years of age.

______ I do not have an order from a Texas court that gives me the same legal rights and responsibilities as an adult.

2. I request this order for one of the following reasons **(place a check mark beside any that apply)**:

______ I am mature enough to decide to have an abortion without telling my parent(s), managing conservator, or guardian. I also know enough about abortion to make this decision.

Please continue to the next page.

______ Telling my parent(s), managing conservator, or guardian that I want an abortion is not in my best interest.

______ Telling my parent(s), managing conservator or guardian that I want an abortion may lead to physical or emotional abuse of me.

______ Telling my parent(s), managing conservator or guardian that I want an abortion may lead to sexual abuse of me.

3. Please check one of the following statements:

______ I **do not** have a lawyer. (The court will appoint one for you).

______ I have a lawyer, who is:

Lawyer's name: ____

Lawyer's address: ____

Lawyer's phone: ____

4. The court must appoint a "guardian ad litem" for you. A guardian ad litem meets with you before the hearing and helps the judge decide your application. Please state whether you want the court to appoint someone you know as your guardian ad litem. This person could be a relative, a member of the clergy, a counselor, a psychiatrist or psychologist, or other adult, or your lawyer. You do not have to ask the court to appoint someone you know. Keep in mind that the court may appoint the person you request, but it does not have to.

______ I am requesting that the court appoint someone I know as my guardian ad litem (you will identify this person on your verification page)

______ I am not requesting the court to appoint someone I know as my guardian ad litem. (The court will appoint someone it chooses).

5. Please state whether you have filed a Confidential Application for Waiver of Parental Notification other than this one.

______ I have filed another Confidential Application for Waiver of Parental Notification.

______ I have **not** filed another Confidential Application for Waiver of Parental Notification.

(End of Cover Page)

FORM 2A. CONFIDENTIAL APPLICATION FOR WAIVER OF PARENTAL NOTIFICATION AND CONSENT: COVER PAGE

Text of rule, subject to public comments received [comments period ends April 1, 2016], effective January 1, 2016. See, also, text of rule effective until January 1, 2016.

Attention Clerk: Please Expedite

Confidential Application for Waiver of Parental Notification and Consent: Cover Page (Form 2A)

As prescribed by the Clerk of the Supreme Court of Texas pursuant to Tex. Fam. Code § 33.003(m).

(Do not complete this section. Court staff will complete this section.)

CAUSE NO. ____________________

IN RE JANE DOE IN THE ____________________

____

____________COUNTY, TEXAS

Important: Your Application has two parts: (1) this cover sheet (Form 2A), which asks for basic information about your application; and (2) a separate verification page (Form 2B), which asks for information about you and for you to swear to the truth of everything you say in the cover sheet and verification page. You must complete both of these forms.

---

1. I ask the court for an order that allows me to have an abortion without first telling and obtaining the consent of my parent, managing conservator, or guardian. I swear or affirm that **(place a check mark in all the blanks for which you answer "yes"):**

_____I am pregnant.

_____I am unmarried and younger than 18 years of age.

_____I do not have an order from a Texas court that gives me the same legal rights and responsibilities as an adult.

2. I request this order for one of the following reasons **(place a check mark beside any that apply):**

_____I am mature enough to decide to have an abortion without telling and obtaining the consent of my parent, managing conservator, or guardian. I also know enough about abortion to make this decision.

_____Telling my parent, managing conservator, or guardian that I want an abortion and attempting to obtain his or her consent is not in my best interest.

_____Telling my parent, managing conservator, or guardian that I want an abortion may lead to physical or emotional abuse of me.

_____Telling my parent, managing conservator, or guardian that I want an abortion may lead to sexual abuse of me.

3. Please check all that apply:

______I live in the county where this application is being filed.

______My parent, managing conservator, or guardian is a presiding judge of a district court, a county court at law, or a court having probate jurisdiction in the county where I live, and **(check any that apply)**:

> ______The county where I live is contiguous to (shares a border with) this one.
>
> ______I intend to obtain the abortion in this county.

______The population of the county where I live has a population of less than 10,000, and **(check any that apply)**:

> ______The county where I live is contiguous to (shares a border with) this one.
>
> ______I intend to obtain the abortion in this county.

______I am not a Texas resident, but I intend to obtain the abortion in this county.

4. Please check one of the following statements:

______I do **not** have a lawyer. (The court will appoint one for you).

______I have a lawyer, who is:

Lawyer's name: ______________________________

Lawyer's email address: ______________________________

Lawyer's address: ______________________________

Lawyer's phone: ______________________________

5. The court must appoint a "guardian ad litem" for you. A guardian ad litem meets with you before the hearing and helps the judge decide your application. Please state whether you want the court to appoint someone you know as your guardian ad litem. This person could be a relative, a member of the clergy, a counselor, a psychiatrist or psychologist, or another adult. You do not have to ask the court to appoint someone you know. Keep in mind that the court may appoint the person you request, but it does not have to.

______I am requesting that the court appoint someone I know as my guardian ad litem. (You will identify this person on your verification page.)

______I am not requesting the court to appoint someone I know as my guardian ad litem. (The court will appoint someone it chooses.)

6. Please state whether you have filed a Confidential Application for Waiver of Parental Notification and Consent other than this one with respect to your current pregnancy.

______I have filed another Confidential Application for Waiver of Parental Notification and Consent with respect to my current pregnancy.

______I have **not** filed another Confidential Application for Waiver of Parental Notification and Consent with respect to my current pregnancy.

7. If you have filed another Confidential Application for Waiver of Parental Notification and Consent with respect to your current pregnancy, please answer the following questions. If you have not filed another Application with respect to your current pregnancy, do not answer these questions.

   What court ruled on your previous application? ______________________________

   Has there been a material change in circumstances since the time your previous application was denied? (Write "yes" or "no.") ______________________________

Amended by order of Dec. 29, 2015, eff. Jan. 1, 2016.

APPENDIX 2B

Text of rule effective until January 1, 2016. See, also, text of rule, subject to public comments received [comments period ends April 1, 2016], effective January 1, 2016.

CAUSE NO. ____________________

(Do not fill in the blank above. Court staff will fill in the blank.)

Confidential Application for Waiver of Parental Notification: Verification Page (Form 2B)

As prescribed by the Clerk of the Supreme Court of Texas pursuant to Tex. Fam. Code §33.003(m)

Important: Your Application has two parts: (1) this cover sheet (Form 2A), which asks for basic information about your application; and (2) a separate verification page (Form 2B), which asks for information about you and for you to swear to the truth of everything you say in the cover sheet and verification page. You or someone acting on your behalf must complete both of these forms. If you are completing this application for a minor, remember that "I" or "my" refers to the minor rather than to you.

---

1. If you are requesting the court to appoint someone you know as your guardian ad litem (*see* Question 4 on the Cover Sheet, Form 2A), please identify them:

   Name: ____________________ Relationship: ____________________

   Address: ______________________________ Phone: __________

2. If you do not have a lawyer, please complete the two blanks below. Tell us how the court, the lawyer appointed by the court, and the guardian ad litem appointed by the court can quickly contact you. If you cannot be contacted, your application will be denied. You can choose to be contacted by telephone, pager/beeper, or any other method by which you can be contacted immediately and confidentially. You do not have to give us your own telephone number, and you can have us contact someone else who helps you.

   ____________________ ____________________

   Person to be contacted (you or another person) Another person to be contacted (optional)

   ____________________ ____________________

   Phone/pager/beeper/fax number(s) Phone/pager/beeper/fax number(s)

Important: Please sign your name in the blank below. You must sign your name before a notary public, court clerk, or other person authorized to give oaths.

I swear or affirm that the information in my Application (both the Cover Sheet and this Verification Page) is true and correct.

____________________ ____________________

Signature of minor or other person completing this form Full name of minor printed or typed (if minor is not person completing this form)

____________________ ____________________

Name of person completing this form printed or typed Minor's date of birth

Sworn to or affirmed in my presence this __________ day of __________, ___.

____

Notary Public, Clerk or other person authorized to give oaths

FORM 2B. CONFIDENTIAL APPLICATION FOR WAIVER OF PARENTAL NOTIFICATION AND CONSENT: VERIFICATION PAGE

Text of rule, subject to public comments received [comments period ends April 1, 2016], effective January 1, 2016. See, also, text of rule effective until January 1, 2016.

CAUSE NO. ______________________________

(Do not fill in the blank above. Court staff will fill in the blank.)

Confidential Application for Waiver of Parental

Notification and Consent: Verification Page (Form 2B)

As prescribed by the Clerk of the Supreme Court of Texas pursuant to Tex. Fam. Code § 33.003(m)

Important: Your Application has two parts: (1) the cover sheet (Form 2A), which asks for basic information about your application; and (2) this verification page (Form 2B), which asks for information about you and for you to swear to the truth of everything you say in the cover sheet and verification page. You must complete both of these forms.

1. Please provide the following information.

   Your full name: ______________________________

   Your date of birth: ______________________________

   Your address (if the place you receive mail is different than the place you actually live, list both addresses): ______________________________

   Your telephone number: ______________________________

2. If you are requesting the court to appoint someone you know as your guardian ad litem (*see* Question 5 on the Cover Sheet, Form 2A), please identify them:

   Name: ______________________________

   Relationship: ______________________________

   Address: ______________________________

   Phone: ______________________________

3. If you do not have a lawyer, please complete the two blanks below. Tell us how the court, the lawyer appointed by the court, and the guardian ad litem appointed by the court can quickly contact you. If you cannot be contacted, your application will be denied. You can choose to be contacted by telephone or any other method by which you can be contacted immediately and confidentially. If you share a telephone number with another person, or there is another reason why you do not want to be contacted at the telephone number you provided above, you can have us contact someone else who helps you.

   Person to be contacted (you or another person): ______________________________

   Phone number or other contact information: ______________________________

   Another person to be contacted (optional): ______________________________

   Phone number or other contact information: ______________________________

<u>Important</u>: Please complete either Option 1 or Option 2 below. You do not have to complete both. If you complete Option 1, you must sign your name before a notary public, court clerk, or another person authorized to give oaths. If you complete Option 2, you do not have to sign your name before a notary public or any other person, but you must swear that the information in your Application is true "under penalty of perjury." "Perjury" means lying to a judge, and it is a crime. If you swear that a statement is true "under penalty of perjury," and you make the statement knowing that it is false, you could be prosecuted in criminal court.

Option 1

I swear or affirm that the information in my Application (both the Cover Sheet and this Verification Page) is true and correct.

____________________ ____________________

Signature of minor

____________________ ____________________

Name of minor printed or typed Minor's date of birth

Sworn to or affirmed in my presence this ___ day of ________, 20 ___.

____

Signature of notary public, clerk, or other person authorized to give oaths

Option 2

My name is ________ (*First*) ________ (*Middle*) ________ (*Last*), my date of birth is ________, and my address is ________ (*Street*), ________ (*City*), ________ (*State*), ________ (*Zip Code*), and ________ (*Country*). I declare under penalty of perjury that the information in my Application (both the Cover Sheet and the Verification Page) is true and correct.

Executed in ________ (*County*), State of ________, on the ________ day of ________ (*Month*), ________ (*Year*).

____

Signature of minor

Amended by order of Jan. 1, 2016, eff. Jan. 1, 2016.

APPENDIX 2C

Text of rule effective until January 1, 2016. See, also, text of rule, subject to public comments received [comments period ends April 1, 2016], effective January 1, 2016.

REQUEST TO POSTPONE TRIAL COURT HEARING IN PARENTAL NOTIFICATION PROCEEDING; DESIGNATION OF ALTERNATIVE TIME FOR HEARING (Form 2C)

CAUSE NO. ____________________

IN RE JANE DOE

IN THE ____________________

____

____________________COUNTY, TEXAS

Please check and complete any questions below that apply:

_____ I request that the court postpone its hearing on my application. The hearing currently is due to be held on or by _________ at _________ a.m./p.m.

_____ Please rule on my application by 5 p.m. on the second business day after (please state a date after which you will be ready to have the hearing): _______________. The clerk will notify you concerning the specific time of the hearing.

_____ I will contact you at a later time to determine a time for the hearing.

Attorney's Signature: ____________________

Attorney's Name, Printed: ____________________

Attorney's State Bar No.: ____________________

Attorney's Address: ____________________

Attorney's Telephone: ____________________

Attorney's Fax No.: ____________________

FORM 2C. REQUEST TO POSTPONE TRIAL COURT HEARING IN PROCEEDING TO WAIVE PARENTAL NOTIFICATION AND CONSENT; DESIGNATION OF ALTERNATIVE TIME FOR HEARING

Text of rule, subject to public comments received [comments period ends April 1, 2016], effective January 1, 2016. See, also, text of rule effective until January 1, 2016.

CAUSE NO. ____________

IN RE JANE DOE — IN THE ____________

____

____________COUNTY, TEXAS

Please check and complete any questions below that apply:

____ I request that the court postpone its hearing on my application. The hearing currently is due to be held on or by ________ at ________ a.m./p.m.

____ Please rule on my application by 5 p.m. on the fifth business day after (please state a date after which you will be ready to have a hearing) ________. The clerk will notify you concerning the specific time of the hearing.

____ I will contact you at a later time to determine a time for the hearing.

Attorney's Signature: ____________
Attorney's Name, Printed: ____________
Attorney's State Bar No.: ____________
Attorney's Address: ____________
Attorney's Telephone: ____________
Attorney's Email Address: ____________
Attorney's Fax No.: ____________

Amended by order of Jan. 1, 2016, eff. Jan. 1, 2016.

APPENDIX 2D

Text of rule effective until January 1, 2016. See, also, text of rule, subject to public comments received [comments period ends April 1, 2016], effective January 1, 2016.

JUDGMENT AND FINDINGS OF FACT AND CONCLUSIONS OF LAW ON APPLICATION IN PARENTAL NOTIFICATION PROCEEDING (Form 2D)

CAUSE NO. ____________________

IN RE JANE DOE IN THE __________________

____

____________COUNTY, TEXAS

This matter was heard on this _____ day of ___________________, _____. Based on the testimony and evidence presented, this court finds:

3. The applicant is pregnant.

4. The applicant is unmarried and under 18 years of age.

5. The applicant has not had her disabilities as a minor removed under Chapter 31 of the Texas Family Code.

6. The applicant wishes to have an abortion without her doctor notifying either of her parents, her managing conservator or guardian.

7. A preponderance of the evidence supports the following [State "yes" beside any issue for which the court finds in favor of the applicant by a preponderance of the evidence. If any one issue is decided in favor of the applicant, the court need not consider other issues]:

_____ The applicant is mature and sufficiently well informed to make the decision to have an abortion performed without notification to either of her parents, her managing conservator or guardian.

Findings of Fact/Conclusions of Law: ________________________________

____

____

____

____

____

_____ **Notifying either of the applicant's parents, managing conservator or guardian would not be in her best interest.**

Findings of Fact/Conclusions of Law: ________________________

____

____

____

____

____

_____ **Notifying either of the applicant's parents, managing conservator or guardian may lead to physical, sexual, or emotional abuse of the applicant.**

Findings of Fact/Conclusions of Law: ________________________

____

____

____

____

____

THEREFORE, IT IS ORDERED

_____ The application is GRANTED and the applicant is authorized to consent to the performance of an abortion without notifying either of her parents or a managing conservator or guardian.

______ The application is DENIED. The applicant is advised of her right to appeal under Rule 3 of the Texas Parental Notification Rules and will be furnished a Notice of Appeal form, Form 3A.

All costs shall be paid by the State of Texas pursuant to Family Code Chapter 33.

____
Judge Presiding

FORM 2D. JUDGMENT AND FINDINGS OF FACT AND CONCLUSIONS OF LAW ON APPLICATION IN PROCEEDING TO WAIVE PARENTAL NOTIFICATION AND CONSENT

Text of rule, subject to public comments received [comments period ends April 1, 2016], effective January 1, 2016. See, also, text of rule effective until January 1, 2016.

CAUSE NO. ____________________

IN RE JANE DOE IN THE ____________________

____

____________COUNTY, TEXAS

This matter was heard on this ___ day of _________, 20 ___. Based on the testimony and evidence presented, this court finds:

1. The applicant is pregnant.

2. The applicant is unmarried and under 18 years of age.

3. The applicant has not had her disabilities as a minor removed under Chapter 31 of the Texas Family Code.

4. The applicant wishes to have an abortion without her doctor notifying and obtaining the consent of either of her parents, her managing conservator, or her guardian.

5. Clear and convincing evidence supports the following: [State "yes" beside an issue for which the court finds in favor of the applicant by clear and convincing evidence. If any one issue is decided in favor of the applicant, the court need not consider the other issues.]

_____ The applicant is mature and sufficiently well informed to make the decision to have an abortion performed without notification to, or the consent of, either of her parents, her managing conservator, or her guardian.

Finding of Facts and Conclusions of Law:

____

____

____

____

____

____

_____ Notifying and attempting to obtain the consent of either of the applicant's parents, her managing conservator, or her guardian would not be in her best interest.

Findings of Facts and Conclusions of Law:

____

____

____

____

____

____

THEREFORE, IT IS ORDERED:

____The application is GRANTED and the applicant is authorized to consent to the performance of an abortion without notifying and obtaining the consent of either of her parents or a managing conservator or guardian.

____The application is DENIED. The applicant is advised of her right to appeal under Rule 3 of the Rules for a Judicial Bypass of Parental Notice and Consent Under Chapter 33 of the Family Code and will be furnished a Notice of Appeal form, Form 3A.

All costs shall be paid by the State of Texas pursuant to Family Code Chapter 33.

____

Judge Presiding

Amended by order of Jan. 1, 2016, eff. Jan. 1, 2016.

APPENDIX 2E

Text of rule effective until January 1, 2016. See, also, text of rule, subject to public comments received [comments period ends April 1, 2016], effective January 1, 2016.

CERTIFICATE OF DEEMED GRANTING OF APPLICATION IN PARENTAL NOTIFICATION PROCEEDING (Form 2E)

CAUSE NO. ____________________

IN RE JANE DOE | IN THE ______________________

____

______________COUNTY, TEXAS

This will certify that on the ______ day of ________________, _____, Jane Doe filed an application for a court order authorizing her to consent to an abortion without the parental notice required by Section 33.002, Family Code. The court did not rule on the application by 5:00 p.m. on the second business day after the day the application was filed. Accordingly, under Section 33.003(h), Family Code, the application is deemed to be GRANTED.

Signed this ________ day of ______________________, ______.

____

Judge Presiding or Clerk

FORM 2E. CERTIFICATE OF DEEMED DENIAL OF APPLICATION IN PROCEEDING TO WAIVE PARENTAL NOTIFICATION AND CONSENT

Text of rule, subject to public comments received [comments period ends April 1, 2016], effective January 1, 2016. See, also, text of rule effective until January 1, 2016.

CAUSE NO. ____________________

IN RE JANE DOE IN THE ____________________

____

________________COUNTY, TEXAS

This will certify that on the ___ day of __________, 20 ___, Jane Doe filed an application for a court order authorizing her to consent to an abortion without the parental notice and consent required by Sections 33.002 and 33.0021, Family Code. The court did not rule on the application by 5 p.m. on the fifth business day after the day the application was filed. Accordingly, under Rule 2.5(g) of the Rules for a Judicial Bypass of Parental Notice and Consent Under Chapter 33, Family Code, the application is deemed to be DENIED.

Signed this ___ day of __________, __________.

____

Judge Presiding or Clerk

Amended by order of Jan. 1, 2016, eff. Jan. 1, 2016.

APPENDIX 2F

Text of rule effective until January 1, 2016. See, also, text of rule, subject to public comments received [comments period ends April 1, 2016], effective January 1, 2016.

ORDER THAT COSTS IN PARENTAL NOTIFICATION PROCEEDING BE PAID BY STATE PURSUANT TO TEXAS FAMILY CODE §33.007 (Form 2F)

Notice: To guarantee reimbursement, this Order must be served on the Director, Fiscal Division, Texas Department of Health, within the deadlines imposed by Tex. Paren. Notif. R 1.9(b).

CAUSE NO. ____________________

IN RE JANE DOE

IN THE ____________________

____

____________________ COUNTY, TEXAS

ORDER

In this proceeding filed under Texas Family Code § 33.003, the court heard evidence on the ________ day of ________________, ______, concerning court costs. Based on the evidence presented, pursuant to Texas Family Code § 33.007, the State of Texas is ordered to pay:

1. Reasonable and necessary attorney ad litem fees and expenses of $____________________ to:

   Name: State Bar No.

   Address:

   Telephone: Federal Tax ID:

8. Reasonable and necessary guardian ad litem fees and expenses of $____________________ to:

   Name:

   Address:

   Telephone: Federal Tax ID:

9. Court reporter's fees certified by the court reporter to:

   Name:

   Address:

   Telephone: Federal Tax ID:

10. All court costs certified by the clerk.

____

Judge Presiding

FORM 2F. ORDER THAT COSTS IN PROCEEDING TO WAIVE PARENTAL NOTIFICATION AND CONSENT BE PAID BY STATE PURSUANT TO TEXAS FAMILY CODE § 33.007

Text of rule, subject to public comments received [comments period ends April 1, 2016], effective January 1, 2016. See, also, text of rule effective until January 1, 2016.

Notice: To guarantee reimbursement, this Order must be served on the Director, Fiscal Division, Texas Department of Health, within the deadlines imposed by Rule 1.9(b) of the Rules for a Judicial Bypass of Notice and Consent Under Chapter 33 of the Family Code.

CAUSE NO. ____________________

IN RE JANE DOE IN THE ____________________

____

____________________COUNTY, TEXAS

ORDER

In this proceeding filed under Texas Family Code § 33.003, the court heard evidence on the ___ day of __________, 20 ___, concerning court costs. Based on the evidence presented, pursuant to Texas Family Code § 33.007, the State of Texas is ordered to pay:

1. Reasonable and necessary attorney ad litem fees and expenses of $ ___ to:

   Name:

   State Bar No.

   Address:

   Telephone:

   Federal Tax ID:

2. Reasonable and necessary guardian ad litem fees and expenses of $ ___ to:

   Name:

   Address:

   Telephone:

   Federal Tax ID:

3. Court reporter's fees certified by the court reporter to:

   Name:

   Address:

   Telephone:

   Federal Tax ID:

4. All court costs certified by the clerk.

____

Judge Presiding

Amended by order of Jan. 1, 2016, eff. Jan. 1, 2016.

APPENDIX 2G

Text of rule effective until January 1, 2016. See, also, text of rule, subject to public comments received [comments period ends April 1, 2016], effective January 1, 2016.

CLERK'S CERTIFICATION OF COURT COSTS AND FEES AND TRANSMISSION OF ORDER FOR PAYMENT IN PARENTAL NOTIFICATION PROCEEDING (Form 2G)

Director, Fiscal Division
Texas Department of Health
1100 West 49th Street
Austin TX 78756

Re: *In re Jane Doe*

Cause No. ______________________

Court: ______________________

County: ______________________

Dear Sir or Madam:

Please find enclosed a certified copy of an Order issued on ______________________, 20____, in the referenced case. Please pay the amounts to the payees as stated in the Order.

In accordance with the Order, I certify the following fees and costs for payment as follows:

Amount: $______________________

Name of the Clerk: ______________________

Address : ______________________

Tax Identification No.: ______________________

Thank you.

Sincerely,

____

[seal] Name: ______________________

Encl: Certified copy of Order Position: ______________________

FORM 2G. CLERK'S CERTIFICATION OF COURT COSTS AND FEES AND TRANSMISSION OF ORDER FOR PAYMENT IN PROCEEDING TO WAIVE PARENTAL NOTIFICATION AND CONSENT

Text of rule, subject to public comments received [comments period ends April 1, 2016], effective January 1, 2016. See, also, text of rule effective until January 1, 2016.

Director, Fiscal Division
Texas Department of Health
1100 West 49th Street
Austin TX 78756

Re: *In re Jane Doe*

Cause No. ______________________________

Court: ______________________________

County: ______________________________

Dear Sir or Madam:

Please find enclosed a certified copy of an Order issued on ________, 20 ___, in the referenced case. Please pay the amounts to the payees as stated in the Order.

In accordance with the Order, I certify the following fees and costs for payment as follows:

Amount: $ ______________________________

Name of the Clerk: ______________________________

Address: ______________________________

Tax Identification No.: ______________________________

Thank you.

Sincerely,

____

[seal]

Name: ______________________________

Position: ______________________________

Encl.: Certified copy of Order

Amended by order of Jan. 1, 2016, eff. Jan. 1, 2016.

APPENDIX 2H

Text of rule effective until January 1, 2016. See, also, text of rule, subject to public comments received [comments period ends April 1, 2016], effective January 1, 2016.

ORDER APPOINTING INTERPRETER FOR CHAPTER 33, FAMILY CODE PROCEEDINGS (Form 2H)

CAUSE NO. ____________________

IN RE JANE DOE

IN THE ________________________

____

________________COUNTY, TEXAS

ORDER

ORDERED that for good cause, the following person is appointed an interpreter to assist the applicant in applying for relief under Chapter 33, Family Code:

Name: ____________________________ State Bar No. ______________

Address: ____

Telephone: ____________________ Federal Tax ID: __________________

Signed: this ____ day of ____________________, 20____.

____
Judge

OATH FOR INTERPRETER

I, ____________________, do swear or affirm that I am competent and well versed in the ____________________ language and shall: (1) make a true interpretation of all the proceedings to the applicant; (2) repeat verbatim all statements, questions, and answers of all persons who are a part of the proceeding, to applicant, counsel, the court, and others in the English language and in the ____________________ language, using my best skill and judgment.

I shall not: (1) participate in any manner other than as an interpreter in the decision making or adjudicative process; (2) communicate with any other person regarding the proceedings except a literal translation of questions, answers, or remarks made during the proceeding, or (3) disclose or discuss any of the proceedings with any person following entry of judgment.

____

Print Name: ____________________

Address: ____________________

____

Telephone: ____________________

SWORN TO AND SUBSCRIBED before me on ____________________, 20___

[seal] ____________________________________

FORM 2H. ORDER APPOINTING INTERPRETER FOR A PROCEEDING TO WAIVE PARENTAL NOTIFICATION AND CONSENT UNDER CHAPTER 33, FAMILY CODE

Text of rule, subject to public comments received [comments period ends April 1, 2016], effective January 1, 2016. See, also, text of rule effective until January 1, 2016.

CAUSE NO. ____________________

IN RE JANE DOE IN THE ______________________

____

__________ COUNTY, TEXAS

ORDER

ORDERED that for good cause, the following person is appointed an interpreter to assist the applicant in applying for relief under Chapter 33, Family Code:

Name: ______________________ State Bar No. ____________

Address: ______________________________________

Telephone: ______________________ Federal Tax ID: ____________

Signed: this ___ day of ________, 20 ___.

____

Judge

OATH FOR INTERPRETER

I, ________, do swear or affirm that I am competent and well versed in the ________ language and will: (1) make a true interpretation of all the proceedings to the applicant; and (2) repeat verbatim all statements, questions, and answers of all persons who are a part of the proceeding to the applicant, counsel, the court, and others in the English language and in the ________ language, using my best skill and judgment.

I will not: (1) participate in any manner other than as an interpreter in the decision making or adjudicative process; (2) communicate with any other person regarding the proceedings except a literal translation of questions, answers, or remarks made during the proceeding; or (3) disclose or discuss any of the proceedings with any person following entry of judgment.

____

Signature

____

Printed Name

____

Address

____

Telephone Number

SWORN TO AND SUBSCRIBED before me on ________, 20 ___.

[Seal]

____

Amended by order of Jan. 1, 2016, eff. Jan. 1, 2016.

APPENDIX 2I

Text of rule effective until January 1, 2016. See, also, text of rule, subject to public comments received [comments period ends April 1, 2016], effective January 1, 2016.

Form 2I: NOTICE TO CLERK AND COURT REPORTER TO PREPARE RECORDS

CAUSE NO.____________________________

IN RE JANE DOE:

This matter was heard on the _______ day of ______________, _______. The Court has issued a final judgment. **Jane Doe may desire to appeal.** Jane Doe requests the court reporter and appropriate clerk to prepare instanter a record of the trial proceedings and make it available to:

__________________________ __________________________

__________________________ __________________________

__________________________ __________________________

(Name and address of guardian ad litem) **(Name and address of minor's attorney)**

Immediately upon completion of the record, the clerk must contact both the undersigned attorney and the guardian ad litem at the following telephone numbers to advise that the record is available:

__________________________ __________________________

(Telephone number for guardian ad litem) **(Telephone number for minor's attorney)**

A copy of this notice has been given to both the appropriate clerk and court reporter and no additional request for the record of the trial proceedings is required. The filing of this document with the clerk constitutes proof that written request for preparation of the trial record was made.

Signed the _______ day of ______________, _______ at _______ [time] a.m./p.m [circle one]

____
ATTORNEY

____
GUARDIAN AD LITEM

Caution: no officials or court personnel involved in the proceedings may ever disclose to anyone outside the proceedings—including the minor's parent, managing conservator, or legal guardian—that the minor is or has ever been pregnant, or that she wants or has ever wanted an abortion, except as permitted by law.

FORM 2I. NOTICE TO CLERK AND COURT REPORTER TO PREPARE RECORDS

Text of rule, subject to public comments received [comments period ends April 1, 2016], effective January 1, 2016. See, also, text of rule effective until January 1, 2016.

CAUSE NO. ______________________________

IN RE JANE DOE:

This matter was heard on the ___ day of __________, __________. The Court has issued a final judgment. **Jane Doe may desire to appeal.** Jane Doe request the court reporter and appropriate clerk to immediately prepare a record of the trial proceedings and make it available to:

______________________________	______________________________
______________________________	______________________________
______________________________	______________________________
(Name and address of guardian ad litem)	**(Name and address of minor's attorney)**

Immediately upon completion of the record, the clerk must contact both the undersigned attorney and the guardian ad litem at the following telephone numbers to advise that the record is available:

______________________________	______________________________
(Telephone number for guardian ad litem)	**(Telephone number for minor's attorney)**

A copy of this notice has been given to both the appropriate clerk and court reporter and no additional request for the record of the trial proceedings is required. The filing of this document with the clerk constitutes proof that written request for preparation of the trial record was made.

Signed the ___ day of __________, __________ at __________ [time] a.m./p.m. [circle one]

____

ATTORNEY

____

GUARDIAN AD LITEM

Caution: no official or court personnel involved in the proceedings may ever disclose to anyone outside the proceedings—including the minor's parent, managing conservator, or legal guardian—that the minor is or has ever been pregnant, or that she wants or has ever wanted an abortion, except as permitted by law.

Amended by order of Jan. 1, 2016, eff. Jan. 1, 2016.

APPENDIX 2J

Text of rule effective until January 1, 2016. See, also, text of rule, subject to public comments received [comments period ends April 1, 2016], effective January 1, 2016.

Form 2J: NOTICE TO CLERK AND COURT REPORTER TO PREPARE RECORDS

CAUSE NO.____________________

IN RE JANE DOE:

This matter was heard on the ______ day of ______________, ______. The Court has issued a final judgment and **no appeal will be taken.** Jane Doe's attorney/guardian ad litem requests the court reporter and appropriate clerk to prepare a record of the trial proceedings and make it available to:

____________________	____________________
____________________	____________________
____________________	____________________
(Name and address of guardian ad litem)	**(Name and address of minor's attorney)**

Upon completion of the record, the clerk must contact both the undersigned attorney and the guardian ad litem at the following telephone numbers to advise that the record is available:

____________________	____________________
(Telephone number for guardian ad litem)	**(Telephone number for minor's attorney)**

A copy of this notice has been given to both the appropriate clerk and court reporter and no additional request for the record of the trial proceedings is required. The filing of this document with the clerk constitutes proof that written request for preparation of the trial record was made.

Signed the ______ day of ______________, ______ at _______ [time] a.m./p.m [circle one]

____
ATTORNEY

____
GUARDIAN AD LITEM

Caution: no officials or court personnel involved in the proceedings may ever disclose to anyone outside the proceedings—including the minor's parent, managing conservator, or legal guardian—that the minor is or has ever been pregnant, or that she wants or has ever wanted an abortion, except as permitted by law.

FORM 2J. NOTICE TO CLERK AND COURT REPORTER TO PREPARE RECORDS

Text of rule, subject to public comments received [comments period ends April 1, 2016], effective January 1, 2016. See, also, text of rule effective until January 1, 2016.

CAUSE NO. ____________________

IN RE JANE DOE:

This matter was heard on the ___ day of __________, __________. The Court has issued a final judgment and **no appeal will be taken.** Jane Doe's attorney or guardian ad litem requests the court reporter and the appropriate clerk to prepare a record of the trial proceedings and make it available to:

______________________	______________________
______________________	______________________
______________________	______________________
(Name and address of guardian ad litem)	**(Name and address of minor's attorney)**

Upon completion of the record, the clerk must contact both the undersigned attorney and the guardian ad litem at the following telephone numbers to advise that the record is available:

______________________	______________________
(Telephone number for guardian ad litem)	**(Telephone number for minor's attorney)**

A copy of this notice has been given to both the appropriate clerk and the court reporter and no additional request for the record of the trial proceedings is required. The filing of this document with the clerk constitutes proof that written request for preparation of the trial record was made.

Signed the ___ day of __________, __________ at __________ [time] a.m./p.m. [circle one]

____

ATTORNEY

____

GUARDIAN AD LITEM

Caution: no official or court personnel involved in the proceedings may ever disclose to anyone outside the proceedings—including the minor's parent, managing conservator, or legal guardian—that the minor is or has ever been pregnant, or that she wants or has ever wanted an abortion, except as permitted by law.

Amended by order of Jan. 1, 2016, eff. Jan. 1, 2016.

APPENDIX 3A

Text of rule effective until January 1, 2016. See, also, text of rule, subject to public comments received [comments period ends April 1, 2016], effective January 1, 2016.

Attention Clerk: Please Expedite

Notice of Appeal in Parental Notification Proceeding (Form 3A)

As prescribed by the Clerk of the Supreme Court of Texas pursuant to Tex. Fam. Code § 33.004(d).

CAUSE NO. ____________________

IN RE JANE DOE IN THE ________________________

____

________________COUNTY, TEXAS

(Important: Your lawyer or court-appointed lawyer should fill out the information below.)

On this _____ day of _______________, _____, notice is hereby given that Jane Doe appeals to the ________ Court of Appeals from the final order entered in the above-referenced cause denying her application for a court order authorizing her to consent to an abortion without the parental notification required by Section 33.002, Family Code.

Attorney's Signature: ________________________

Attorney's Name, Printed: ________________________

Attorney's State Bar No.: ________________________

Attorney's Address: ________________________

Attorney's Telephone: ________________________

Attorney's Fax No.: ________________________

FORM 3A. NOTICE OF APPEAL IN PROCEEDING TO WAIVE PARENTAL NOTIFICATION AND CONSENT

Text of rule, subject to public comments received [comments period ends April 1, 2016], effective January 1, 2016. See, also, text of rule effective until January 1, 2016.

Attention Clerk: Please Expedite

Notice of Appeal in Proceeding to Waive Parental Notification and Consent (Form 3A)

As prescribed by the Clerk of the Supreme Court of Texas pursuant to Tex. Fam. Code § 33.004(d).

CAUSE NO. ____________

IN RE JANE DOE IN THE ____________

____

____________COUNTY, TEXAS

Important: Your lawyer should fill out the information below.

On this ___ day of ________, 20 ___, notice is hereby given that Jane Doe appeals to the ________ Court of Appeals from the final order entered in the above-referenced cause denying her application for a court order authorizing her to consent to an abortion without the parental notification and consent required by Sections 33.002 and 33.0021, Family Code.

Attorney's Signature ____________
Attorney's Name, Printed ____________
State Bar No. ____________
Attorney's Address ____________
Attorney's Telephone ____________
Attorney's Email Address ____________
Attorney's Fax No. ____________

Amended by order of Jan. 1, 2016, eff. Jan. 1, 2016.

APPENDIX 3B

Text of rule effective until January 1, 2016. See, also, text of rule, subject to public comments received [comments period ends April 1, 2016], effective January 1, 2016.

REQUEST TO POSTPONE COURT OF APPEALS' RULING IN PARENTAL NOTIFICATION PROCEEDING; DESIGNATION OF ALTERNATIVE TIME FOR RULING (Form 3B)

CAUSE NO. ______________

IN RE JANE DOE

IN THE COURT OF APPEALS FOR THE

____________ DISTRICT OF TEXAS

AT ____________________, TEXAS

Please check and complete any questions below that apply:

______ I request that the court postpone its ruling on my appeal. The appeal currently is due to be ruled on by __________ at __________ a.m./p.m.

______ Please rule on my appeal by 5:00 p.m. on the second business day after (please state a date after which you will be ready to have the hearing): ______________________. The clerk will notify you concerning the specific time of the hearing.

______ I will contact you at a later time to determine a time for ruling on my appeal.

Attorney's Signature: ____________________________

Attorney's Name, Printed: ____________________________

Attorney's State Bar No.: ____________________________

Attorney's Address: ____________________________

Attorney's Telephone: ____________________________

Attorney's Fax No.: ____________________________

FORM 3B. REQUEST TO POSTPONE COURT OF APPEALS' RULING IN PROCEEDING TO WAIVE PARENTAL NOTIFICATION AND CONSENT; DESIGNATION OF APTERNATIVE TIME FOR RULING

Text of rule, subject to public comments received [comments period ends April 1, 2016], effective January 1, 2016. See, also, text of rule effective until January 1, 2016.

CAUSE NO. ________________

IN RE JANE DOE	IN THE COURT OF APPEALS FOR THE ________________ DISTRICT OF TEXAS AT ________________, TEXAS

Please check and complete any questions below that apply:

____ I request that the court postpone its ruling on my appeal. The appeal currently is due to be ruled on by 5 p.m. on ________________.

____ Please rule on my appeal by 5 p.m. on the fifth business day after (state a date after which you will be ready to proceed) ________________.
If the court holds oral argument, the clerk will notify you of its date and time.

____ I will contact you at a later time to determine a time for ruling on my appeal.

Attorney's Signature ________________
Attorney's Name, Printed ________________
Attorney's State Bar No. ________________
Attorney's Address ________________
Attorney's Telephone ________________
Attorney's Email Address ________________
Attorney's Fax No. ________________

Amended by order of Jan. 1, 2016, eff. Jan. 1, 2016.

APPENDIX 3C

Text of rule effective until January 1, 2016. See, also, text of rule, subject to public comments received [comments period ends April 1, 2016], effective January 1, 2016.

JUDGMENT ON APPEAL IN PARENTAL NOTIFICATION PROCEEDING (Form 3C)

CAUSE NO. ____________________

IN RE JANE DOE

IN THE COURT OF APPEALS FOR THE

__________ DISTRICT OF TEXAS

AT ____________________, TEXAS

It is ORDERED that the trial court's final order in this cause denying the minor's application for a court order authorizing her to consent to an abortion without the parental notice required by Section 33.002, Family Code, is:

________ Affirmed. The minor will be advised of her right to appeal under Rule 4 of the Texas Parental Notification Rules and furnished a Notice of Appeal form, Form 4A.

________ Reversed and the application is GRANTED.

_____ Opinion to follow.

_____ No opinion to follow.

____
Justice

Other Members of the Panel:

Justice ____________________ Justice ____________________

Date: ____________________

FORM 3C. JUDGMENT ON APPEAL IN PROCEEDING TO WAIVE PARENTAL NOTIFICATION AND CONSENT

Text of rule, subject to public comments received [comments period ends April 1, 2016], effective January 1, 2016. See, also, text of rule effective until January 1, 2016.

CAUSE NO. ______________

IN RE JANE DOE	IN THE COURT OF APPEALS FOR THE ________ DISTRICT, TEXAS AT ________, TEXAS

It is ORDERED that the trial court's final order in this cause denying the minor's application for a court order authorizing her to consent to an abortion without the parental notice and consent required by Sections 32.002 and 33.0021, Family Code, is:

____ Affirmed. The minor will be advised of her right to appeal under Rule 4 of the Rules for a Judicial Bypass of Parental Notice and Consent Under Chapter 33 of the Family Code and furnished a notice of appeal form, Form 4A.

____ Reversed and the application is GRANTED.

____ Opinion to follow.

____ No opinion to follow.

____

Justice

Other members of the panel:

Justice ________

Justice ________

Date: ______________________________

Amended by order of Jan. 1, 2016, eff. Jan. 1, 2016.

APPENDIX 3D

Text of rule effective until January 1, 2016. See, also, text of rule, subject to public comments received [comments period ends April 1, 2016], effective January 1, 2016.

CERTIFICATION OF DEEMED REVERSAL OF ORDER ON APPEAL IN PARENTAL NOTIFICATION PROCEEDING
(Form 3D)

CAUSE NO. ____________________

IN RE JANE DOE

IN THE COURT OF APPEALS FOR THE

__________ DISTRICT OF TEXAS

AT ____________________, TEXAS

This will certify that on the _______ day of ____________________, ______, Jane Doe filed her notice of appeal from an order denying her application for a court order authorizing her to consent to an abortion without the parental notice required by Section 33.002, Family Code. The court of appeals did not rule on her appeal by 5:00 p.m. on the second business day after the day the notice of appeals was filed. Accordingly, under Section 33.004(b), Family Code, the order is deemed to be REVERSED and the application is deemed to be GRANTED.

Signed this ______ day of ____________________, ______.

____
Judge Presiding or Clerk

FORM 3D. CERTIFICATION OF DEEMED AFFIRMANCE OF ORDER ON APPEAL IN PROCEEDING TO WAIVE PARENTAL NOTIFICATION AND CONSENT

Text of rule, subject to public comments received [comments period ends April 1, 2016], effective January 1, 2016. See, also, text of rule effective until January 1, 2016.

CAUSE NO. ____________

IN RE JANE DOE	IN THE COURT OF APPEALS FOR THE ____________ DISTRICT OF TEXAS AT ____________, TEXAS

This will certify that on the ___ day of ________, 20 ___, Jane Doe filed her notice of appeal from an order denying her application for a court order authorizing her to consent to an abortion without the parental notice and consent required by Sections 33.002 and 33.0021, Family Code. The court of appeals did not rule on her appeal by 5 p.m. on the fifth business day after the day the notice of appeals was filed. Accordingly, the order is deemed to be AFFIRMED.

Signed this ___ day of ________, 20 ___.

____

Judge Presiding or Clerk

Amended by order of Jan. 1, 2016, eff. Jan. 1, 2016.

APPENDIX 4A

Text of rule effective until January 1, 2016. See, also, text of rule, subject to public comments received [comments period ends April 1, 2016], effective January 1, 2016.

ATTENTION CLERK: PLEASE EXPEDITE

NOTICE OF APPEAL TO TEXAS SUPREME COURT IN PARENTAL NOTIFICATION PROCEEDING (Form 4A)

CAUSE NO. ____________

IN THE SUPREME COURT OF TEXAS

IN RE JANE DOE

On this _________ day of ______________________, _______, notice is hereby given that Jane Doe petitions the Supreme Court of Texas for review of the order entered in Cause No. ______________, in the ___________ Court of Appeals affirming the denial of her application for a court order authorizing her to consent to an abortion without the parental notice required by Section 33.002, Family Code.

Attorney's Signature: ______________________________

Attorney's Name, Printed: ______________________________

Attorney's State Bar No.: ______________________________

Attorney's Address: ______________________________

Attorney's Telephone: ______________________________

Attorney's Fax No.: ______________________________

FORM 4A. NOTICE OF APPEAL TO TEXAS SUPREME COURT IN PROCEEDING TO WAIVE PARENTAL NOTIFICATION AND CONSENT

Text of rule, subject to public comments received [comments period ends April 1, 2016], effective January 1, 2016. See, also, text of rule effective until January 1, 2016.

ATTENTION CLERK: PLEASE EXPEDITE

Notice of Appeal to the Texas Supreme Court in Proceeding to Waive Parental Notification and Consent (Form 4A)

CAUSE NO. ______________________

IN THE SUPREME COURT OF TEXAS

IN RE JANE DOE

On this ________ day of ________, 20 ___, notice is hereby given that Jane Doe petitions the Supreme Court of Texas for review of the order entered in Cause No. ________, in the ________ Court of Appeals affirming the denial of her application for a court order authorizing her to consent to an abortion without the parental notice and consent required by Sections 33.002 and 33.0021, Family Code.

Attorney's Signature ______________________
Attorney's Name, Printed ______________________
Attorney's State Bar No. ______________________
Attorney's Address ______________________
Attorney's Telephone ______________________
Attorney's Email Address ______________________
Attorney's Fax No. ______________________

Amended by order of Jan. 1, 2016, eff. Jan. 1, 2016.

RULES GOVERNING GUARDIANSHIP CERTIFICATION [REPEALED]

Repealed by Order of the Supreme Court, dated August 19, 2014, effective September 1, 2014

Rules I to XVI. Repealed by Order of the Supreme Court, dated Aug. 19, 2014, eff. Sept. 1, 2014

Historical Notes

For subject matter of former rules, see, now, Rules and Fees of the Judicial Branch Certification Commission.

STATEWIDE RULES CONCERNING THE ELECTRONIC FILING AND SERVICE OF DOCUMENTS IN PARTICIPATING JUSTICE OF THE PEACE COURTS [Repealed]

Repealed by Order of the Supreme Court, dated December 13, 2013, effective January 1, 2014

Rules 1.1 to 7.2. Repealed by Order of the Supreme Court, dated Dec. 13, 2013, eff. Jan. 1, 2014

TEXAS BOARD OF LEGAL SPECIALIZATION STANDARDS FOR ATTORNEY CERTIFICATION

Amended December 8, 2006, effective December 8, 2006

Including Amendments Received Through February 1, 2016

These Standards for Attorney Certification are established by the Texas Board of Legal Specialization after approval of the Supreme Court of Texas.

The Standards for Attorney Certification are divided into two parts.

PART I, GENERAL REQUIREMENTS: —These requirements apply to all specialty areas.

PART II, SPECIFIC AREA REQUIREMENTS: —These are specific requirements that apply to the individual specialty areas. Included are the definitions, substantial involvement, and other requirements for certification and recertification. For example, "Specific Area Requirements for Criminal Law" refers to the specific requirements for certification and recertification in criminal law.

Definitions as used in these Standards:

"TBLS" refers to the Texas Board of Legal Specialization.

"SBOT" refers to the State Bar of Texas.

"CLE" refers to continuing legal education.

"Plan" refers to the Texas Plan for Recognition and Regulation of Specialization in the Law.

"Rules" refers to the Attorney Rules and Regulations of TBLS.

"Applicant" refers to either a certification or recertification applicant unless otherwise specifically stated.

"Standards" refers to the Standards for Attorney Certification. The Standards are composed of both the General Requirements and the Specific Area Requirements.

PART I. GENERAL REQUIREMENTS

Section I. Preface

The Supreme Court of Texas has prescribed the following requirements for board certification pursuant to the recommendation of TBLS.

A. The purpose of these Standards is to recognize those attorneys having special competence in one or more of the specialty areas included in these Standards. In making the determination of special competence, TBLS will consider the following:

1. The substance and complexity of the tasks submitted to show the required substantial involvement in the specialty area;

2. The professional accomplishments of the attorney in the specialty area;

3. The skill and ability of an attorney in the specialty area;

4. The knowledge of the attorney as shown on the specialty area examination; and

5. The character and fitness of the attorney.

B. No standard shall in any way limit the right of a board certified attorney to practice in all areas of law. Any attorney, alone or in association with any other attorney, shall have the right to practice in all areas of law, even though board certified in a specific area of law.

C. No attorney shall be required to obtain board certification before practicing in any area of law. Any attorney, alone or in association with any other attorney, shall have the right to practice in any area of law, even though not board certified in that area.

D. Board certification is individual and voluntary. Requirements for and benefits derived from certification may not be fulfilled by or attributed to a law firm of which a board certified attorney is a member.
Amended by Supreme Court Order Dec. 8, 2006, eff. Dec. 8, 2006.

Section II. General Requirements

A. Membership and Practice.

1. SBOT Membership. An applicant and board certified attorney must be an active member in good standing of the SBOT.

2. Texas Office and Practice.

a. Certification Applicant. For the three years immediately preceding application, a certification applicant must have maintained a Texas office from which he or she personally conducts business an average of at least 3 days per week, until certification is achieved. Failure to meet this requirement will result in denial of application. TBLS may waive this requirement upon a showing of good cause.

b. Board Certified Attorney and Recertification Applicant. A board certified attorney and recertification applicant must continue to meet the substantial involvement requirements pertinent to the specialty area whether or not an office is maintained in Texas. For other recertification qualifications, refer to the applicable Specific Area Requirements.

B. Forms. Documents, applications, questionnaires, and examinations involved in the certification and recertification process shall be prescribed and approved by TBLS.

C. Fees. An applicant and board certified attorney shall timely pay the required fees established by TBLS.

D. Expiration of Certification. Certification shall be for a period of 5 years at the end of which time recertification shall be permitted upon the terms and conditions established by TBLS.

E. Revocation of Certification. A certificate of special competence issued by TBLS may be revoked for good cause as determined by TBLS.

F. Failure to Furnish Information and Misrepresentation. Certification or recertification may be denied, revoked, or other appropriate action taken because of an applicant's or board certified attorney's failure to furnish the information requested by TBLS or because of his or her misrepresentation of any material fact to TBLS.

G. Required Period of Law Practice. An applicant for certification shall have been engaged in the practice of law for a period of at least 5 years on a full-time basis. Years of practice need not be consecutive.

H. Definition of the Practice of Law. "Practice of law" means full-time legal work done primarily for the purpose of providing legal advice or representation. After admission to the bar of any state of the District of Columbia, service as a judge or associate judge of any court of record shall be considered practice of law. Corporate or government service, including military service, after admission to the bar of any state or the District of Columbia, shall be considered practice of law if the work done was legal in nature and primarily for the purpose of providing legal advice to, or representation of, the corporation or government agency or individuals connected therewith. TBLS may allow other legal work, such as teaching law or writing legal publications, to be combined with the part-time practice of law to satisfy this requirement.
Amended by Supreme Court Order Dec. 8, 2006, eff. Dec. 8, 2006.

Section III. Disclosure of Conduct

A. Disciplinary Sanctions.

1. At the time of filing an application, a certification applicant shall disclose whether he or she has ever been sanctioned for professional misconduct as defined in Rule 8.04 of the Texas Disciplinary Rules of Professional Conduct by any authorized disciplinary authority, including a court, and shall also disclose whether he or she has a pending investigation for professional misconduct. During the application process, the applicant has a continuing duty to promptly report to TBLS the institution of a disciplinary investigation and the receipt of a disciplin-

ary sanction as described above and to provide additional information TBLS may request on such matters.

2. A board certified attorney has a continuing duty to report any sanction for professional misconduct as defined in Rule 8.04 of the Texas Disciplinary Rules of Professional Conduct, by any authorized disciplinary authority, including a court, and shall provide additional information TBLS may request on such matters.

3. TBLS may deny certification or recertification, revoke certification, or take other appropriate action upon a finding that an applicant or board certified attorney has engaged in professional misconduct as defined above or upon notice of a pending disciplinary investigation concerning the applicant or board certified attorney. In deciding what action is appropriate, TBLS will consider the seriousness of the underlying facts included in the findings, the passage of time since the sanction, and the conduct of an applicant or board certified attorney since the findings were made.

4. Failure to disclose an investigation or sanction or the failure to respond to a request for information from TBLS on such matters will be considered a material misrepresentation and may be cause for denial, revocation, or other appropriate action by TBLS.

B. Criminal Conviction.

1. An applicant or board certified attorney shall disclose whether he or she has ever been convicted of, or given probation or fined for, a serious crime as hereinafter defined, whether the above resulted from a plea of guilty or nolo contendere or from a verdict after trial or otherwise and regardless of the pendency of an appeal. The term "serious crime" includes barratry; any felony; any lesser offense involving dishonesty, misappropriation of money or other property or conduct that adversely affects the administration of justice; and any attempt, conspiracy or solicitation of another to commit any of the foregoing crimes.

2. TBLS may deny certification or recertification, revoke certification, or take other appropriate action if an applicant or board certified attorney has been convicted, given probation or fined for a serious crime as defined in this Section.

Amended by Supreme Court order of Dec. 8, 2006, eff. Dec. 8, 2006.

Section IV. Peer Review

A. Reference Requirements.

1. An applicant shall submit a minimum of five names and addresses of persons to be contacted as references to attest to his or her competence in the specialty area. For the types of references required for each specialty area, refer to the appropriate Specific Area Requirements. These persons shall be:

a. Substantially involved in the specialty area in which the applicant is seeking certification or recertification.

b. Individuals who are not partners or associates of the applicant.

c. With respect to a certification applicant, peers with whom the applicant has had dealings in the 3 years immediately preceding application.

d. With respect to a recertification applicant, peers with whom the applicant has had dealings since certification or the most recent recertification.

2. TBLS may, at its option, request references from other attorneys and/or judges.

3. A Confidential Statement of Reference Form approved by TBLS will be submitted by TBLS directly to the selected peer and shall be returned directly to TBLS.

B. Evaluation of Peer Review Information. In evaluating peer review information on an applicant, TBLS shall consider the knowledge and experience of the references in the applicant's specialty area and the nature of the dealings between the references and the applicant.

C. Confidentiality. All Statements of Reference received by TBLS shall be confidential.

D. Denial. TBLS may deny certification or recertification based on information received through the peer review process. General information concerning the denial shall be provided to the applicant subject to the confidentiality rule.

Amended by Supreme Court order of Dec. 8, 2006, eff. Dec. 8, 2006.

Section V. Continuing Legal Education

A. CLE Requirement.

1. Certification. A certification applicant must complete 60 hours of CLE in the specialty area within the three years immediately preceding application, through December 31 of the year of application.

2. Recertification. A recertification applicant must complete 100 hours of CLE in the specialty area by December 31 of each 5th year of certification.

B. Qualifying CLE. An applicant or board certified attorney must obtain CLE credit in the specialty area in which certification or recertification is sought by the following methods:

1. Attendance at a live CLE program, including live video conferences;

2. Viewing or listening to an on-line CLE program;

3. Participating in a CLE teleconference;

4. Attendance at a showing of a CLE video;

5. Self study such as reading cases or legal periodicals, subject to the limitation of 5 hours credit each calendar year; and

6. Other activity in the specialty area, to be determined on an individual basis, such as:

a. Teaching a CLE course for attorneys or paralegals;

b. Participation as a panelist or speaking on a symposium or similar program;

c. Attendance at a lecture series or similar program sponsored by a qualified education institution or bar group;

d. Authorship of a book or article published in a professional publication or journal; and

e. Active participation in the work of a professional committee dealing with a specific problem in the specialty area.

Amended by Supreme Court order of Dec. 8, 2006, eff. Dec. 8, 2006.

Section VI. Substantial Involvement

A. Percentage of Practice Requirement in the Specialty Area.

An applicant or board certified attorney must devote a minimum required percentage of time practicing in a specialty area each year as set forth in the Specific Area Requirements unique to each specialty area.

1. A certification applicant must devote the required percentage during each year of the 3 years immediately preceding application.

2. A board certified attorney must devote the required percentage during each year of certification. Refer to the Recertification Requirements in the Specific Area Requirements.

3. Failure to meet the required percentage of practice may be grounds for denial or revocation.

B. Specific Tasks Requirements. An applicant must provide information as required by TBLS concerning specific tasks he or she has performed in the applicable specialty area. In evaluating experience, TBLS may take into consideration the nature, complexity, and duration of the tasks handled by an applicant in the specialty area.

C. Exceptions. A certification applicant is expected to meet the tasks requirements listed in the Specific Area Requirements in the specialty area. TBLS may permit exceptions for an applicant who does not meet the task requirements specified in an individual specialty area. For the substantial involvement required for each specialty area, please refer to the appropriate Specific Area Requirements.

1. Judicial Experience.

a. Certification Applicant. TBLS may permit a certification applicant to substitute judicial experience appropriate to each specialty area. In making this determination, TBLS may take into consideration the nature, complexity, and duration of the matters the certification applicant has handled in the specialty area. The judicial experience shall be at least equivalent to the Specific Area Requirements of the specialty area, and the determination of equivalency shall be in the sole discretion of TBLS.

b. Board Certified Attorney and Recertification Applicant. TBLS may permit a board certified attorney or recertification applicant who is serving as a full-time county, state or federal trial, appellate, probate, family, or bankruptcy judge (including a U.S. magistrate judge or Texas associate judge) to remain certified during his or her judicial service subject to the following conditions:

(1) A board certified attorney or recertification applicant who is affected by this provision shall continue to pay the annual fee.

(2) If a board certified attorney desires to continue certification after December 31 of the calendar year which he or she ceases to serve as a full-time judge, he or she shall timely complete the recertification process with TBLS and shall comply with the TBLS Rules. A board certified attorney whose certification was extended by reason of service as a full-time judge must satisfy all the requirements for recertification except that, for purposes of the initial recertification only, the substantial involvement requirement shall be waived and the CLE requirement shall be prorated based on the year in which the board certified attorney ceased judicial service.

2. Unusual or Exceptional Experience. TBLS may permit a certification applicant to substitute unusual or exceptional experience for one or more of the specific area requirements in the specialty area. In making this determination, TBLS may take into consideration the nature, complexity, and duration of the matters that the certification applicant has handled in the specialty area. The unusual

or exceptional experience shall at least be equivalent to the Specific Area Requirements of the specialty area, and the determination of equivalency shall be in the sole discretion of TBLS.

Amended by Supreme Court order of Dec. 8, 2006, eff. Dec. 8, 2006.

Section VII. Examination

A. Passing of an Examination. A certification applicant must pass a written examination applied uniformly to all certification applicants to demonstrate sufficient knowledge, proficiency, and expertise in the specialty area to justify the representation of special competence to the legal profession and to the public.

B. Failure of an Examination. After a certification applicant has taken and failed an examination 3 times in a specialty area, the applicant is ineligible to apply for the next 3 years' examination in that specialty area.

Amended by Supreme Court order of Dec. 8, 2006, eff. Dec. 8, 2006.

PART II. SPECIFIC AREA REQUIREMENTS

These are specific requirements that apply the [1] individual specialty area listed below. The specific requirements include the definitions, substantial involvement, reference, and other certification and recertification requirements for each specialty area. You will also need to refer to PART I, the Standards for Attorney Certification, Part I—General Requirements for requirements that apply to all specialty areas.

Section Number	Specialty Area	Area ID	Year Started
Section I	Criminal Law	CR	1975
Section II	Family Law	FM	1975
Section III	Labor and Employment Law	LB	1975
Section IV	Estate Planning and Probate Law	EP	1977
Section V	Civil Trial Law	CT	1978
Section VI	Personal Injury Trial Law	PI	1978
Section VII	Immigration and Nationality Law	IM	1979
Section VIII	Real Estate Law		
	Commercial	RC	1983
	Farm and Ranch	RF	1983
	Residential	RR	1983
Section IX	Tax Law	TX	1983
Section X	Bankruptcy Law		
	Consumer	CB	1984
	Business	BB	1988
Section XI	Oil, Gas and Mineral Law	OG	1986
Section XII	Civil Appellate Law	AP	1987
Section XIII	Administrative Law	AD	1989
Section XIV	Consumer and Commercial Law	CS	1993
Section XV	Juvenile Law	JV	2001
Section XVI	Health Law	HE	2002
Section XVII	Workers' Compensation Law	WC	2004
Section XVIII	Criminal Appellate Law	CA	2010

Amended by Supreme Court order of March 18, 2014, eff. March 18, 2014.

Section I. Criminal Law

A. **DEFINITION.** Criminal law is the practice of law dealing with, by way of definition not limitation, matters involving:

- legal aspects of pretrial release;
- examining trial, indictment, information and complaint;
- change of venue; continuance;
- severance;
- discovery;
- speedy trials;
- jeopardy;
- immunity;
- confessions;
- search and seizure;
- identification;
- competence to stand trial and culpable mental state;
- jury voir dire;
- rules of evidence—state and federal (e.g., impeachment, extraneous offenses, etc.);
- procedure and rules of evidence at punishment hearings;
- U.S. sentencing guidelines;
- law of sentences;
- legal aspects of plea bargaining and guilty pleas;
- motions for new trial;
- motions for arrest of judgment;
- appeals;
- post conviction remedies;
- probation and parole granting;
- probation and parole revocation;
- executive clemency;
- death penalty;
- other substantive criminal offenses;
- and juvenile crimes.

B. **SUBSTANTIAL INVOLVEMENT.** Applicant must show substantial involvement and special competence in Texas criminal law practice by providing such information as may be required by TBLS.

1. **Certification.**

a. Percentage of Practice Requirement. Applicant must have devoted a minimum of 25% of his or her time practicing criminal law in Texas during each year of the 3 years immediately preceding application as defined in Section I, A of the Specific Area Requirements for Criminal Law.

b. Task Requirements. Applicant shall provide information concerning Texas criminal law matters as described in the definition. In evaluating experience, TBLS may take into consideration the nature, complexity, and duration of the tasks handled by applicant in criminal law.

(1) Applicant shall list the number of Texas criminal law matters for each of the following categories that he or she has participated in during the 3 years immediately preceding application:

(a) State felony jury trials;

(b) State misdemeanor jury trials;

(c) Federal jury trials;

(d) State appeals;

(e) Federal appeals;

(f) State and federal non-jury trials;

(g) State and federal pleas of guilty;

(h) State and federal post-conviction remedies;

(i) State death penalty (trial, appeal; and/or habeas);

(j) Juvenile proceedings;

(k) Dismissals;

(*l*) Grand jury no bills;

(m) Cases decided on pre-trial motions where evidence was presented (such as motions to suppress evidence);

(n) Probation or parole revocations; and

(*o*) Other criminal law matters not listed above.

(2) Applicant shall have handled, as lead counsel, during his or her entire practice, the following minimum number of Texas criminal law cases in 3 of the following categories:

(a) 5 state felony jury trials;

(b) 10 state misdemeanor jury trials or 5 state felony jury trials in addition to those listed in Section I, B,1,b(2)(a) above;

(c) 5 federal jury trials or substantial involvement in 10 federal cases in which there was a contested issue that required the applicant to file pleadings or a memorandum of law (or both) on behalf of the client and that resulted in the granting of relief without a hearing or in an adversarial hearing with the trial court having to resolve a contested issue of law or fact. "Contested issues" could include anything from the legality of a search to the appropriateness of a sentence;

(d) Any combination of 5 state or federal appeals.

2. **Recertification.** Applicant must have devoted a minimum of 25% of his or her time practicing criminal law in Texas during each year of the 5 year period of certification as defined in Section I, A of the Specific Area Requirements for Criminal Law except as provided for in Part I–General Requirements, Section VI, C,1(b).

C. **REFERENCE REQUIREMENTS.** Applicant must submit a minimum of 5 names and addresses of persons to be contacted as references to attest to his or her competence in criminal law. These persons shall be substantially involved in criminal law and be familiar with applicant's criminal law practice.

1. **Certification.** Applicant must submit names of persons with whom he or she has had dealings involving criminal law matters within the 3 years immediately preceding application.

2. **Recertification.** Applicant must submit names of persons with whom he or she has had dealings involving criminal law matters since certification or the most recent recertification.

3. **Reference Types.** Applicant must submit the following types of references:

a. Four Texas attorneys who are substantially involved in criminal law. Applicant shall have tried a criminal law matter with or against one of these attorneys.

b. One judge of any court of record in Texas before whom applicant has appeared as an advocate in a criminal law matter.

Amended by Supreme Court order of Feb. 10, 2009, eff. Feb. 10, 2009.

Section II. Family Law

A. **DEFINITION.** Family law is the practice of law dealing with, by way of definition not limitation, matters involving:

- the Texas Family Code, Titles 1, 2, 4 or 5;
- Texas Penal Code, Chapter 25 (offenses against the family);
- the law of homestead and other exempt property; the taxation law of divorce and interspousal transaction;
- torts relevant to family law matters;
- the trial of cases arising out of the above matters; and
- appeals arising out of the above matters

B. **SUBSTANTIAL INVOLVEMENT.** Applicant must show substantial involvement and special competence in Texas family law practice by providing such information as may be required by TBLS.

1. **Certification.**

a. Percentage of Practice Requirement. Applicant must have devoted a minimum of 35% of his or her time practicing family law in Texas during each year of the 3 years immediately preceding application as defined in Section II, A of the Specific Area Requirements for Family Law.

b. Task Requirements. Applicant must provide information concerning specific tasks he or she has performed in Texas family law. In evaluating experience, TBLS may take into consideration the nature, complexity, and duration of the tasks handled by applicant.

(1) Applicant must meet each of the following 3 categories within the 3 years immediately preceding application:

(a) Participated as lead counsel for a party or child(ren) in a total of 9 contested final trials or binding arbitrations in Texas family law cases in which oral testimony was taken and in which issues were determined by a finder of fact in a court of record or in a binding arbitration, excluding default judgments, and

(i) at least 4 of the trials must have involved issues of property division, and

(ii) at least 4 trials must have involved appointment or modification of conservatorship.

(b) Participated as lead counsel for a party or child(ren) in 30 contested family law matters involving issues pertaining to Texas Family Code, Titles 1, 2, 4, or 5, handled and disposed of prior to and without the necessity of a contested final hearing or trial of the matters on the merits.

(c) Satisfied 2 of the following 3 categories:

(i) Handled the trial as lead counsel for a party or child(ren) in 2 Texas civil jury trials at the county court at law or district court level; one involving family law and submitted to the jury for decision;

(ii) Conducted the appeal of 1 Texas civil case involving family law to a Texas Court of Appeals or the Supreme Court of Texas in which briefs were filed by the applicant as lead counsel on behalf of a party or child(ren). TBLS will take into consideration the nature, complexity, and duration of a mandamus or writ of habeas corpus in determining whether it qualifies for this category; or

(iii) Represented a party or child(ren), or served as a mediator or arbitrator in a cumulative total of 25 Texas mediations, arbitrations, and/or collaborative law cases involving family law. The TBLS will take into consideration the nature, complexity, and duration of the mediations, arbitrations, and/or collaborative law cases in determining whether they qualify in this category.

2. **Recertification.** Applicant must have devoted a minimum of 35% of his or her time practicing family law in Texas during each year of the 5 year period of certification as defined in Section II, A of the Specific Area Requirements for Family Law except as provided for in Part I–General Requirements, Section VI, C,1(b).

C. **REFERENCE REQUIREMENTS.** Applicant must submit a minimum of 5 names and addresses of persons to be contacted as references to attest to his or her competence in family law. These persons must be substantially involved in family law, and be familiar with applicant's family law practice.

1. **Certification.** Applicant must submit names of persons with whom he or she has had dealings involving family law matters within the 3 years immediately preceding application.

2. **Recertification.** Applicant must submit names of persons with whom he or she has had dealings involving family law matters since certification or the most recent recertification.

3. **Reference Types.** Applicant must submit the following types of references:

a. Four Texas attorneys who practice in the applicant's geographic area and who are substantially involved in family law. Applicant must been an opposing counsel to one of these attorneys either in litigation, hearing, or negotiation of a family law matter.

b. One judge of any court of record in Texas whom applicant has appeared before as lead counsel in the trial of a family law matter.

Amended by Supreme Court order of Feb. 10, 2009, eff. Feb. 10, 2009; amended eff. Feb. 8, 2011.

Section III. Labor and Employment Law

A. **DEFINITION.** Labor and employment law is the practice of law dealing with the relationships among employers, employees or their labor organizations, except workers' compensation. It includes, by way of definition not limitation, State or Federal laws regulating or involving:

- Labor relations (National Labor Relations Act),
- Occupational Safety and Health (does not include workers' compensation or non-subscriber matters),
- Equal Employment Opportunity,

- Wage and Hour and leave matters, including FLSA, FMLA, USERRA, Texas Payday Act, and judicial review of unemployment compensation matters,
- Employment-related torts, employment contracts, and 42 U.S.C. 1983 employment litigation, and
- Whistleblowers and non–EEO retaliation.

The practice of law dealing with ERISA, bankruptcy, and administrative proceedings may, under the proper circumstances, constitute the practice of labor and employment law within the meaning of this section.

B. SUBSTANTIAL INVOLVEMENT. Applicant must show substantial involvement and special competence in labor and employment law practice by providing such information as may be required by TBLS.

1. **Certification.**

a. Percentage of Practice Requirement. Applicant must have devoted a minimum of 25% of his or her time practicing labor and employment law during each year of the 3 years immediately preceding application as defined in Section III, A of the Specific Area Requirements for Labor and Employment Law.

b. Task Requirements. Applicant must provide information as required by TBLS concerning specific tasks he or she has performed in labor and employment law. In evaluating experience, TBLS may take into consideration the nature, complexity, and duration of the tasks handled by applicant.

(1) Applicant must show that he or she has engaged directly and substantially in a broad practice of labor and employment law in at least 3 of the areas within the definition of labor and employment law as set forth in Section III, A above, one of which must be practice involving the National Labor Relations Act. Applicant must submit required information concerning such practice, the frequency of the work, the jurisdictions involved, and the nature of the issues involved.

(a) Applicant must show practice involving laws regulating or involving labor relations (National Labor Relations Act) by one of the following methods:

i. Actual experience through practice, or

ii. Completion of a minimum of 24 hours of continuing legal education (CLE) in comprehensive courses on the National Labor Relations Act, completed within the 3 years immediately preceding the application through June 1 of the year of application. The substitution of CLE in lieu of actual practice involving the National Labor Relations Act is in addition to the CLE requirement submitted to satisfy Part I–General Requirements, Section V, A,1.

(b) In addition to meeting the above requirement, applicant must show that he or she has been engaged directly and substantially in 2 additional areas within the definition of labor and employment law as set forth in Section III, A above.

(c) Applicant must show by detailed response that he or she has engaged at a significant level of responsibility in litigation in federal or state court or arbitration in at least one of the 3 areas applicant submitted to satisfy Section III, B,1,b(1)(a-b) above.

2. **Recertification.** Applicant must have devoted a minimum of 25% of his or her time practicing labor and employment law during each year of the 5 year period of certification as defined in Section III, A of the Specific Area Requirements for Labor and Employment Law except as provided for in Part I–General Requirements, Section VI, C,1(b).

C. REFERENCE REQUIREMENTS. Applicant shall submit a minimum of 5 names and addresses of persons to be contacted as references to attest to his or her competence in labor and employment law. These persons shall be substantially involved in labor and employment law, and be familiar with applicant's labor and employment law practice.

1. **Certification.** Applicant shall submit names of persons with whom he or she has had dealings involving labor and employment law matters within the 3 years immediately preceding application.

2. **Recertification.** Applicant shall submit names of persons with whom he or she has had dealings involving labor and employment law matters since certification or the most recent recertification.

3. **Reference Types.** Applicant shall submit the following types of references:

a. Four attorneys who are substantially involved in labor and employment law. Applicant shall have been involved in litigation or arbitration with or against one of these attorneys in a labor and employment law matter.

b. One of the following before whom applicant has appeared as an advocate in a labor or employment law matter:

(i) a judge of any court of record,

(ii) an arbitrator, or

(iii) an administrative law judge.

Amended by Supreme Court order of Feb. 10, 2009, eff. Feb. 10, 2009; amended eff. Feb. 8, 2011.

Section IV. Estate Planning and Probate Law

A. DEFINITIONS.

1. Estate planning and probate law is the practice of law involving the Texas Probate Code, Texas Property Code the Internal Revenue Code and other federal, state and local statutes and interpretive material in connection with matters in which issues of estate planning and probate are significant factors. The practice of estate planning and probate law includes, but is not limited to,

- consulting with clients and giving advice regarding estate planning, probate and guardianship law;
- analyzing, planning and making recommendations for the conservation and disposition of clients' estates in accordance with the clients' expressed desires, including tax effects and consequences;
- drafting legal instruments to effectuate the clients' estate plans, *(e.g., wills, trusts and other legal documents);*
- representing clients before courts which hear and decide cases involving decedent's estates and guardianships;
- representing clients by litigating contested probate and guardianship issues in trial and appellate courts;
- representing clients in cases before the Internal Revenue Service and other taxing authorities and courts with respect to proposed, completed and ongoing transactions and other matters involving tax issues which are related to estate planning and probate law; and
- representing clients in the administrative appeal and litigation of tax issues involving transfers of assets during lifetime and at death.

2. The following terms shall have the following application or meaning:

a. Prepared. Applicant personally performed the majority of the work in the matter, including its presentation (*e.g., to clients, governmental agencies, courts*), if applicable.

b. Supervised/Reviewed. Applicant was responsible to the client for (i) documents prepared by a lawyer or paralegal who is under applicant's direct supervision, or (ii) the review, prior to execution or filing, of tax returns and related documents prepared by a non-legal professional (*e.g., accountant, appraiser*).

B. SUBSTANTIAL INVOLVEMENT.

Applicant must show substantial involvement and special competence in estate planning and probate law practice by providing such information as may be required by TBLS.

1. **Certification.**

a. Percentage of Practice Requirement. Applicant must have devoted a minimum of 25% of his or her time practicing estate planning and probate law during each year of the 3 years immediately preceding application as defined in Section IV, A of the Specific Area Requirements for Estate Planning and Probate Law.

b. Task Requirements. Applicant must provide information as required by TBLS concerning specific tasks he or she has performed in estate planning and probate law. In evaluating experience, TBLS may take into consideration the nature, complexity, and duration of the tasks handled by applicant.

(1) Applicant must show sufficient involvement in a substantial portion of the activities described in **both** of the following categories within the 3 years immediately preceding application.

(a) **Estate Planning**

i. Counseled clients in estate planning, including giving advice with respect to gifts, life insurance, wills, trusts, business arrangements and agreements, and other estate planning matters.

ii. Prepared or supervised the preparation of estate planning instruments, e.g., simple and complex wills, including provisions for testamentary trusts, tax deductions and elections; revocable and irrevocable inter vivos trusts; business planning agreements; powers of attorney and other estate planning instruments.

(b) **Estate Administration and Tax Matters.** Represented clients with respect to the probate and/or administration of decedents' estates and trusts, including dependent and independent administration and muniments of title, guardianships, determinations of heirships, and will and trust litigation; prepared, reviewed, or supervised the preparation of federal gift, estate, and generation skipping transfer tax returns, Texas inheritance tax returns, and U.S. fiduciary income tax returns; and representation before the Internal Revenue Service, state taxing authorities, or the courts, in connection with such tax returns and related controversies.

2. **Recertification.** Applicant must have devoted a minimum of 25% of his or her time practicing estate planning and probate law during each year of the 5 year period of certification as defined in Section IV, A of the Specific Area Requirements for Estate Planning and Probate Law except as provided for in Part I–General Requirements, Section VI, C,1(b).

C. **REFERENCE REQUIREMENTS.** Applicant must submit a minimum of 5 names and addresses of persons to be contacted as references to attest to his or her competence in estate planning and probate law. These persons must be substantially involved in estate planning and probate law, and be familiar with applicant's estate planning and probate law practice.

1. **Certification.** Applicant must submit names of persons with whom he or she has had dealings involving estate planning and probate law matters within the 3 years immediately preceding application.

2. **Recertification.** Applicant must submit names of persons with whom he or she has had dealings involving estate planning and probate law matters since certification or the most recent recertification.

3. **Reference Types.** Applicant must submit the following types of references:

a. Four attorneys who are substantially involved in estate planning and probate law.

b. One judge, who is an attorney, before whom applicant has appeared in an estate planning and probate law matter, contested or uncontested. If there is no such judge, applicant shall submit the name of a judge of a court of record before whom he or she has appeared in an estate planning and probate matter.

Amended by Supreme Court order of Feb. 10, 2009, eff. Feb. 10, 2009.

Section V. Civil Trial Law

A. **DEFINITIONS.**

1. Civil trial law is the practice of law dealing with litigation of civil controversies in all areas of substantive law before State and Federal courts of record.

2. A trial is a contested proceeding in a court of record within the judicial branch of government which involves the submission of testimonial evidence to a court or jury in support or defense of claims for relief submitted by the parties. A trial shall be deemed to have commenced upon the initial presentation of evidence to the court or jury. For purposes of this definition, a summary judgment proceeding or any other pre-trial proceeding does not constitute a trial.

3. Lead counsel in a jury case is the role in which an attorney takes primary responsibility for the representation of the client during trial and whose activities in trial shall at a minimum include: (i) conducting jury selection, (ii) making an opening statement or making a closing argument, and (iii) conducting significant direct or cross examination of live witnesses at trial.

B. **SUBSTANTIAL INVOLVEMENT.** Applicant must show substantial involvement and special competence in Texas civil trial law practice by providing such information as may be required by TBLS.

1. **Certification.**

a. Percentage of Practice Requirement. Applicant must have devoted a minimum of 35% of his or her time practicing civil trial law in Texas during each year of the 3 years immediately preceding application as defined in Section V, A of the Specific Area Requirements for Civil Trial Law.

b. Task Requirements. Applicant must provide information as required by TBLS concerning specific tasks he or she has performed in Texas civil trial law. In evaluating experience, TBLS may take into consideration the nature, complexity, and duration of the tasks handled by applicant.

(1) Applicant must have tried during his or her practice a minimum of 20 civil trials in a court of record in Texas involving an amount in controversy in excess of $25,000 or other significant nonmonetary claims. Of these trials;

i. At least 7 shall have been jury trials conducted by applicant as lead counsel and submitted to the trier of fact in a court of record in Texas; and

ii. No more than 1/3 of the cases submitted by the applicant shall have been personal injury cases and no more than 1/3 shall have been family law cases.

2. **Recertification.** Applicant must have devoted a minimum of 35% of his or her time practicing civil trial law in Texas during each year of the 5 year period of certification as defined in Section V, A of the Specific Area Requirements for Civil Trial Law except as provided for in Part I–General Requirements, Section VI, C, 1(b).

C. **REFERENCE REQUIREMENTS.** Applicant must submit a minimum of 5 names and addresses of persons to be contacted as references to attest to his or her competence in civil trial law. These persons must be substantially involved in civil trial law, and be familiar with applicant's civil trial law practice.

1. **Certification.** Applicant must submit names of persons with whom he or she has had dealings involving civil trial law matters within the 3 years immediately preceding application.

2. **Recertification.** Applicant must submit names of persons with whom he or she has had dealings involving civil trial law matters since certification or the most recent recertification.

3. **Reference Types.** Applicant must submit the following types of references:

a. Four Texas attorneys who are substantially involved in civil trial law. Applicant must have tried a civil trial law matter with or against one of these attorneys.

b. One judge of any court of record in Texas whom applicant has appeared before as an advocate in a civil trial law matter.

Amended by Supreme Court order of Feb. 10, 2009, eff. Feb. 10, 2009; amended eff. Feb. 8, 2011.

Section VI. Personal Injury Trial Law

A. DEFINITIONS.

1. Personal injury trial law is the practice of law dealing with litigation of claims involving trauma or disability, physical or mental, to a person. It includes, by way of definition, and not limitation, litigation involving personal injury aspects of:

- automobile and other vehicular accident reparations;
- governmental claims;
- professional malpractice claims;
- products liability claims;
- statutory claims;
- insurance contract claims; or
- any negligent or intentional tort claims.

2. A trial is a contested proceeding in a court of record within the judicial branch of government which involves the submission of testimonial evidence to a court or jury in support or defense of claims for relief submitted by the parties. A trial shall be deemed to have commenced upon the initial presentation of evidence to the court or jury. For purposes of this definition, a summary judgment proceeding or any other pre-trial proceeding does not constitute a trial.

3. Lead counsel in a jury case is the role in which an attorney takes primary responsibility for the representation of the client during trial and whose activities in trial shall at a minimum include: (i) conducting jury selection, (ii) making an opening statement or making a closing argument, and (iii) conducting significant direct or cross examination of live witnesses at trial.

4. Lead counsel in a non-jury case is the role in which an attorney is primarily responsible for the representation of the client during trial and whose activities at a minimum include conducting significant direct or cross examination of live witnesses at trial.

B. SUBSTANTIAL INVOLVEMENT.

Applicant must show substantial involvement and special competence in Texas personal injury trial law practice by providing such information as may be required by TBLS.

1. **Certification.**

a. Percentage of Practice Requirement. Applicant must have devoted a minimum of 25% of his or her time practicing personal injury trial law in Texas during each year of the 3 years immediately preceding application as defined in Section VI, A of the Specific Area Requirements for Personal Injury Trial Law.

b. Task Requirements. Applicant must provide information as required by TBLS concerning specific tasks he or she has performed in Texas personal injury trial law. In evaluating experience, TBLS may take into consideration the nature, complexity, and duration of the tasks handled by applicant.

(1) Applicant must have tried during his or her entire practice, as lead counsel, at least 10 contested civil cases which were submitted to the trier of fact in a court of record in Texas. Five of the required 10 cases must have been personal injury jury trials.

(a) Five (5) of the required 10 contested cases must have been personal injury jury trials. (A personal injury jury trial does not include judicial review of decisions of the Texas Department of Insurance; Workers' Compensation Division, Texas Workers' Compensation Commission, or Industrial Accident Board.); and

(b) From the cases submitted, applicant must have devoted a minimum of 20 separate days in trial, of which 10 days must have been devoted to personal injury jury trials.

2. **Recertification.** Applicant must have devoted a minimum of 25% of his or her time practicing personal injury trial law in Texas during each year of the 5 year period of certification as defined in Section VI, A of the Specific Area Requirements for Personal Injury Trial Law except as provided for in Part I–General Requirements, Section VI, C,1(b).

C. **REFERENCE REQUIREMENTS.** Applicant must submit a minimum of 5 names and addresses of persons to be contacted as references to attest to his or her competence in personal injury trial law. These persons must be substantially involved in personal injury trial law, and be familiar with applicant's personal injury trial law practice.

1. **Certification.** Applicant must submit names of persons with whom he or she has had dealings involving personal injury trial law matters within the 3 years immediately preceding application.

2. **Recertification.** Applicant must submit names of persons with whom he or she has had dealings involving personal injury trial law matters since certification or the most recent recertification.

3. **Reference Types.** Applicant must submit the following types of references:

a. Four Texas attorneys who are substantially involved in personal injury trial law. Applicant must have tried a personal injury trial law matter with or against one of these attorneys.

b. One judge of any court of record in Texas whom applicant has appeared before as an advocate in a personal injury trial law matter.

Amended by Supreme Court order of Feb. 10, 2009, eff. Feb. 10, 2009; amended effective Feb. 8, 2011.

Section VII. Immigration and Nationality Law

(Area ID: IM / Year Started: 1979)

A. **DEFINITION.** Immigration and nationality law is the practice of law dealing with the Immigration and Nationality Act of 1952, as amended, and all successor and other laws and regulations dealing with immigration and naturalization. The practice includes, by way of definition and not limitation,

- all aspects of securing an immigrant or non-immigrant visa or other documentation to enter the United States, including all petitions and applications filed with the U. S. Department of State, the U. S. Department of Labor, the U. S. Department of Justice, the U. S. Department of Homeland Security, and the U. S. Public Health Service;
- naturalization proceedings;
- citizenship proceedings;
- asylum applications;
- removal proceedings and related applications for relief;
- bond and custody proceedings;
- rescission proceedings;
- registry proceedings;
- administrative proceedings not listed above relating to immigration and nationality law before government agencies of competent jurisdiction;
- all administrative and judicial review of the above; and
- original proceedings in immigration matters before judicial courts.

B. **SUBSTANTIAL INVOLVEMENT.** Applicant must show substantial involvement and special competence in immigration and nationality law practice by providing such information as may be required by TBLS.

1. **Certification.**

a. Percentage of Practice Requirement. Applicant must have devoted a minimum of 25% of his or her time practicing immigration and nationality law during each year of the 3 years immediately preceding application as defined in Section VII, A of the Specific Area Requirements for Immigration and Nationality Law.

b. Task Requirements. Applicant must provide information as required by TBLS concerning specific tasks he or she has performed in immigration and nationality law. In evaluating experience, TBLS may take into consideration the nature, complexity, and duration of the tasks handled by applicant.

(1) Applicant must exhibit substantial involvement and special competence in each of the following immigration and nationality law matters participated in within the 3 years immediately preceding application.

(a) Administrative Hearings. Representation of clients in at least 9 contested hearings before immigration judges involving removal or bond determination, with no more than 3 having involved only bond matters.

(b) Petitions and Applications. Representation of clients before the U.S. Department of Homeland Security and/or the U.S. Department of State in the preparation and filing of petitions and applications. A minimum of 10 petitions or applications must have been filed, at least 3 of which must have been employment based petitions.

(c) Citizenship/Naturalization. Representation of clients before the U.S. Department of Homeland Security, U.S. Department of State, and/or judicial courts in citizenship, naturalization, and/or renunciation or revocation matters.

(2) In addition to meeting Section VII, B, 1, b, (1), (a–c) above, applicant must meet two of

the following categories within the 3 years immediately preceding application.

(a) Alien Labor Certifications. Representation of employers and/or aliens before the various state employment services, U.S. Department of Labor, and U.S. Department of Homeland Security in preparation and filing of alien labor certification cases.

(b) Administrative Appeals and Advisory Opinions. Representation of clients in appeals and/or proceedings before the Board of Immigration Appeals, Administrative Appeals Office, Board of Alien Labor Certification Appeals, the U.S. Department of State Advisory Opinions office, or other administrative appellate entities with competent jurisdiction over matters related to immigration and nationality law.

(c) Review in Judicial Courts. Representation of clients in judicial matters relating to immigration and nationality law such as applications for writs of habeas corpus, mandamus, declaratory judgments, criminal matters involving the immigration law, petitions for review in judicial courts, and ancillary proceedings in judicial courts.

(d) Employer Sanctions. Representation of clients in administrative proceedings relating to employer sanction, employment discrimination, and/or document fraud matters under the Immigration Nationality Act.

(e) Deferred Inspections, Expedited Removal, Humanitarian Parole, Documentary Waiver Requests, Deferred Action Requests, Private Bills, I–9 and LCA related Audits and Proceedings, Immigration Related Database Corrections, or other administrative proceedings not listed relating to immigration and nationality matters before governmental agencies of competent jurisdiction. Representation of clients in these types of matters.

2. **Recertification.** Applicant must have devoted a minimum of 25% of his or her time practicing immigration and nationality law during each year of the 5 year period of certification as defined in Section VII, A of the Specific Area Requirements for Immigration and Nationality Law except as provided for in Part I–General Requirements, Section VI, C,1(b).

C. REFERENCE REQUIREMENTS. Applicant must submit a minimum of 5 names and addresses of persons to be contacted as references to attest to his or her competence in immigration and nationality law. These persons must be substantially involved in immigration and nationality law, and be familiar with applicant's immigration and nationality law practice.

1. **Certification.** Applicant must submit names of persons with whom he or she has had dealings involving immigration and nationality law matters within the 3 years immediately preceding application.

2. **Recertification.** Applicant must submit names of persons with whom he or she has had dealings involving immigration and nationality law matters since certification or the most recent recertification.

3. **Reference Types.** Applicant must submit the following types of references:

a. Three attorneys who are substantially involved in immigration and nationality law.

b. One of the following:

(1) An attorney with or against whom applicant has tried an immigration and nationality law matter, or

(2) An attorney from a U.S. Department of State consular office, or

(3) A U.S. Department of Homeland Security officer whom has adjudicated a matter by applicant and reviewed and/or made a decision on applicant's filing.

c. One of the following judges as described below:

(1) One judge of any court of record before whom applicant has appeared as an advocate in an immigration and nationality law case, or

(2) An immigration judge before whom applicant has appeared in an administrative hearing.

Amended by Supreme Court order of Feb. 10, 2009, eff. Feb. 10, 2009; amended eff. Feb. 8, 2011; June 2, 2015, eff. Jan. 1, 2016.

Section VIII. Real Estate Law

A. DEFINITIONS.

1. **Real Estate Law.** Real estate law is the rendering of advice and services concerning the laws applicable to land and the improvements and appurtenances (including air and subsurface estates) to land. It also includes the acquisition, transfer, development, financing and use of land; and includes without limitation, knowledge of the legal restrictions and constraints imposed privately and by local, state and federal governments upon land and the improvements to land.

2. Certification is available for the sub-categories of real estate law defined below:

a. **Residential Real Estate Law.** Legal practice including advice and services in connection with the acquisition, ownership, leasing, financing, use, transfer and disposition of residential real property.

b. **Commercial Real Estate Law.** Legal practice involving advice and services in connection with the acquisition, ownership, leasing, financing, use, transfer and disposition of real property other than residential, farm, ranch, or oil, gas and mineral property.

c. **Farm and Ranch Real Estate Law.** Legal practice involving advice and services in connection with the acquisition, ownership, financing, use, transfer and disposition of farm and ranch property, including a basic knowledge of mineral rights.

B. SUBSTANTIAL INVOLVEMENT. Applicant must show substantial involvement and special competence in Texas residential, commercial, or farm and ranch real estate law practice by providing such information as may be required by TBLS.

1. **Certification.**

a. Percentage of Involvement Requirement.

(1) Applicant must have devoted a minimum of 30% of his or her total time practicing Texas real estate law during each year of the 3 years immediately preceding application as defined in Section VIII, A,1 of the Specific Area Requirements for Real Estate Law.

(2) Applicant may seek certification in one or more sub-categories of Texas real estate law. In addition to devoting the minimum percentage of total time to Texas real estate law as indicated in Section VIII, B,1, a(1) above, applicant must have devoted the required percentage of practice to each sub-category in which certification is being sought.

(a) **Residential Real Estate Law.** Twenty (20%) percent of applicant's total time must have been devoted to the practice of Texas residential real estate law during each year of the 3 years immediately preceding application as defined in Section VIII, A,2(a) of the Specific Area Requirements for Real Estate Law.

(b) **Commercial Real Estate Law.** Twenty (20%) percent of applicant's total time must have been devoted to the practice of Texas commercial real estate law during each year of the 3 years immediately preceding application as defined in Section VIII, A,2(b) of the Specific Area Requirements for Real Estate Law.

(c) **Farm and Ranch Real Estate Law.** Ten (10%) percent of applicant's total time must have been devoted to the practice of Texas farm and ranch real estate law during each year of the 3 years immediately preceding application as defined in Section VIII, A,2(c) of the Specific Area Requirements for Real Estate Law.

b. Task Requirements. Applicant must provide information as required by TBLS concerning specific tasks he or she has performed in Texas commercial, residential or farm and ranch real estate law. In evaluating experience, TBLS may take into consideration the nature, complexity, and duration of the tasks handled by applicant.

(1) Applicant must list the number of matters handled in the categories listed below within the 3 years immediately preceding application for each sub-category of Texas real estate law (i.e., residential, commercial, or farm and ranch) in which certification is being sought:

(a) Purchase and Sale,

(b) Loan Transactions/Financing,

(c) Equity Financing,

(d) Government Agency Financing,

(e) Construction and Development,

(f) Easements, including Utility Easements,

(g) Title Searches and Examinations,

(h) Title Insurance,

(i) Condemnation Matters,

(j) Leases,

(k) Landlord/Tenant Problems,

(*l*) Foreclosures and Other Remedial Actions by Creditors,

(m) Taxation Aspects of Real Estate Transactions,

(n) Environmental and Land Use Matters,

(*o*) Oil and Gas, and Other Mineral Matters,

(p) Zoning, Restrictions, and Land Use Planning,

(q) Subdivisions,

(r) State and Federal Land Regulations,

(s) Legislation, and

(t) Other Real Estate Law Matters or Transactions.

(2) Applicant must provide a detailed explanation that would clearly demonstrate substantial involvement within the 3 years immediately preceding application for each sub-category of Texas real estate law (i.e., residential, commercial, or farm and ranch) in which certification is being sought.

(3) Applicant must submit a resume or job summary reflecting activities for at least 5 years immediately preceding application.

2. **Recertification.**

a. Applicant must have devoted a minimum of 30% of his or her time practicing Texas real estate law during each year of the 5 year period of certification as defined in Section VIII, A, 1 of the Specific Area Requirements for Real Estate Law except as provided for in Part I–General Requirements, Section VI, C.1(b).

b. Applicant may seek recertification in one or more sub-categories of Texas real estate law. In addition to devoting the minimum percentage of total time to Texas real estate law as indicated in Section VIII, B, 2,a above, applicant must have devoted the required percentage of practice to each sub-category in which recertification is being sought.

(1) **Residential Real Estate Law.** Twenty percent (20%) of applicant's total time must have been devoted to the practice of Texas residential real estate law during each year of the 5 year period of certification as defined in Section VIII, A,2(a) of the Specific Area Requirements for Real Estate Law.

(2) **Commercial Real Estate Law.** Twenty percent (20%) of applicant's total time must have been devoted to the practice of Texas commercial real estate law during each year of the 5 year period of certification as defined in Section VIII, A,2(b) of the Specific Area Requirements for Real Estate Law.

(3) **Farm and Ranch Real Estate Law.** Ten percent (10%) of applicant's total time must have been devoted to the practice of Texas farm and ranch real estate law during each year of the 5 year period of certification as defined in Section VIII, A,2(c) of the Specific Area Requirements for Real Estate Law.

C. **REFERENCE REQUIREMENTS.** Applicant must submit a minimum of 5 names and addresses of persons to be contacted as references to attest to his or her competence in the sub-category of real estate law (i.e., residential, commercial, or farm and ranch) in which applicant is seeking certification or recertification. These persons must be substantially involved in real estate law, and be familiar with applicant's real estate law practice.

1. **Certification.** Applicant must submit names of persons with whom he or she has had dealings involving real estate law (i.e., residential, commercial, or farm and ranch) matters within the 3 years immediately preceding application.

2. **Recertification.** Applicant must submit names of persons with whom he or she has had dealings involving real estate law (i.e., residential, commercial, or farm and ranch) matters since certification or the most recent recertification.

3. **Reference Types.** Applicant must submit the names of 5 Texas attorneys who are substantially involved in the sub-category of real estate law (i.e., residential, commercial, or farm and ranch) in which applicant is seeking certification or recertification.

Amended by Supreme Court order of Feb. 10, 2009, eff. Feb. 10, 2009.

Section IX. Tax Law

A. **DEFINITION.** Tax law is the practice of law involving the Internal Revenue Code and other federal, state and local tax statutes and interpretive material in connection with matters in which issues of taxation are significant factors. The practice of tax law includes, but is not limited to,

- consultations with clients and the giving of advice regarding the tax consequences of proposed, completed and ongoing transactions;
- the giving of advice regarding the reporting of transactions and other matters of taxing authorities;
- practice before the Internal Revenue Service and other taxing authorities with respect to proposed, completed and ongoing transactions and other matters; and
- the administrative appeal and litigation of tax issues.

The practice of tax law may involve special emphasis in subspecialties such as income, estate or gift tax law, international tax law, business associations tax law, oil and gas tax law, employee benefits tax law, and criminal tax law, but applicant must demonstrate a broad-based knowledge of the area of tax law.

B. **SUBSTANTIAL INVOLVEMENT.** Applicant must show substantial involvement and special competence in tax law practice by providing such information as may be required by TBLS.

1. **Certification.**

a. Percentage of Practice Requirement. Applicant must have devoted a minimum of 35% of his or her time practicing tax law during each of any 5 of the 7 years immediately preceding application as defined in Section IX, A of the Specific Area Requirements for Tax Law.

b. Task Requirements. Applicant must provide information as required by TBLS concerning specific tasks he or she has performed in tax law.

In evaluating experience, TBLS may take into consideration the nature, complexity, and duration of the tasks handled by applicant.

(1) Applicant must provide the number of matters or transactions in the following categories that he or she has handled during any 5 of the 7 years immediately preceding application:

(a) Real estate transactions,

(b) Corporate formations, liquidations and reorganizations,

(c) Corporate merger and acquisition,

(d) Corporate security offerings (debt or equity),

(e) Partnership formation and syndication,

(f) Preparation of employee benefit plans,

(g) Contested tax proceedings (including audits and investigations),

(h) Litigated proceedings (state or federal court),

(i) Ruling and determination requests,

(j) Preparation of tax returns (income, estate, gift and state),

(k) Oil and gas transactions,

(*l*) Formulation of estate plans,

(m) Formation of exempt organizations, and

(n) Other tax law matters or transactions.

(2) Applicant must provide a description of that portion of his or her practice over the past 7 years that indicates substantial involvement in the practice of tax law. Include in the description: (i) the types of matters in which tax law issues were significant (*e.g., real estate, oil and gas, corporate, partnerships, individual tax planning, international, estate planning, employee benefits, excise or state*); (ii) individual role in such matters; (iii) the types of clients represented; (iv) employment in government service; and (v) teaching tax law courses.

2. **Recertification.** Applicant must have devoted a minimum of 35% of his or her time practicing tax law during each year of the 5 year period of certification as defined in Section IX, A of the Specific Area Requirements for Tax Law except as provided for in Part I–General Requirements, Section VI, C,1(b).

C. **REFERENCE REQUIREMENTS.** Applicant must submit a minimum of 5 names and addresses of persons to be contacted as references to attest to his or her competence in tax law. These persons must be substantially involved in tax law, and be familiar with applicant's tax law practice.

1. **Certification.** Applicant must submit names of persons with whom he or she has had dealings involving tax law matters within the 3 years immediately preceding application.

2. **Recertification.** Applicant must submit names of persons with whom he or she has had dealings involving tax law matters since certification or the most recent recertification.

3. **Reference Types.** Applicant must submit the names of 5 individuals who are familiar with his or her tax law practice.

Amended by Supreme Court order of Feb. 10, 2009, eff. Feb. 10, 2009.

Section X. Bankruptcy Law

A. **DEFINITIONS.**

1. **Bankruptcy Law.** The practice of law dealing with the representation of parties in matters primarily involving the Bankruptcy Code, but also involving other aspects of debtor creditor relations as they affect or are affected by bankruptcy or insolvency.

2. Certification is available for the sub-categories of bankruptcy law defined below:

a. **Consumer Bankruptcy Law.** The practice of law dealing with the representation of non-business debtors and/or their creditors in all areas of bankruptcy. It includes primarily representation in matters involving the Bankruptcy Code, and homestead and exemption laws, and also, without limitation, all aspects of consumer debtor-creditor relations as they affect or are affected by bankruptcy.

b. **Business Bankruptcy Law.** The practice of law dealing with the representation of business debtors, their creditors, and/or trustees in all areas of bankruptcy. It includes primarily representation in matters involving the Bankruptcy Code, and also, without limitation, all aspects of business debtor-creditor relations as they affect or are affected by bankruptcy or insolvency. The term "business bankruptcy law" includes the representation of debtors, creditors, trustees, or other parties in business cases under chapters 7, 9, 11, 12 and 13 of the Bankruptcy Code.

B. **SUBSTANTIAL INVOLVEMENT.** Applicant must show substantial involvement and special competence in consumer bankruptcy law or business bankruptcy law by providing such information as may be required by TBLS.

1. **Certification.**

a. Percentage of Practice Requirement.

(1) **Bankruptcy Law.** Applicant must have devoted a minimum of 30% of his or her total time practicing bankruptcy law during each year of the 3 years immediately preceding application as defined in Section X, A,1 of the Specific Area Requirements for Bankruptcy Law.

(2) Applicant may seek certification in one or both sub-categories of bankruptcy law. In addition to devoting the minimum percentage of total time to bankruptcy law as indicated in Section X, B,1,a(1) above, applicant must have devoted the required percentage of practice to the sub-category in which certification is being sought.

(a) **Consumer Bankruptcy Law.** Twenty percent (20%) of applicant's total time must have been devoted to the practice of consumer bankruptcy law during each year of the 3 years immediately preceding application as defined in Section X, A,2,a of the Specific Area Requirements for Bankruptcy Law.

(b) **Business Bankruptcy Law.** Twenty percent (20%) of applicant's total time must have been devoted to the practice of business bankruptcy law during each year of the 3 years immediately preceding application as defined in Section X, A,2,b of the Specific Area Requirements for Bankruptcy Law.

b. Task Requirements. Applicant must provide information as required by TBLS concerning specific tasks he or she has performed in the subcategory of bankruptcy law in which certification is being sought. In evaluating experience, TBLS may take into consideration the nature, complexity, and duration of the tasks handled by applicant.

(1) **Consumer Bankruptcy Law.** Applicant must have represented debtors or creditors in contested matters and/or adversary proceedings during his or her practice as described below:

(a) Fifteen (15) contested matters and/or adversary proceedings which involved a hearing in state or federal court in connection with bankruptcy or debtor or creditor rights disputes.

(b) Eight (8) of the 15 contested matters and/or adversary proceedings must have involved the presentation of evidence in bankruptcy court (other than in support of a default judgment or a settlement agreement).

(2) **Business Bankruptcy Law.** Applicant shall have met, during his or her practice, 12 of the following categories listed below. Regardless of the categories selected, applicant must have participated in at least 8 contested matters and/or adversary proceedings which shall have involved the presentation of evidence in bankruptcy court (other than in support of a default judgment or a settlement agreement).

(a) 2 objections to discharge or determinations of dischargeability;

(b) 2 avoidance actions under the Bankruptcy Code to include any combination of the following:

- fraudulent conveyances;
- preferential transfers;
- avoidances of an unperfected or unrecorded transfer by a hypothetical bona fide purchaser or lien creditor;
- recoveries of a setoff; and
- post-petition transfers;

(c) 1 complaint for subordination;

(d) 4 modifications of automatic stay;

(e) 4 sales, use (including cash collateral) or leases of property;

(f) 3 assumptions or rejections of a lease or other executory contract;

(g) 2 post-petition extensions of secured or unsecured credit;

(h) 2 involuntary petitions;

(i) 4 contested objections to the allowance of claims;

(j) 2 contested appointments of a trustee or examiner;

(k) 3 contested conversions or dismissals;

(*l*) 3 contested turnovers of property;

(m) 1 reclamation;

(n) 2 motions for abandonment;

(*o*) 3 examinations under Rule 2004;

(p) 1 revocation of an order of confirmation of a plan under either chapters 9, 11, 12 or 13;

(q) 1 contested modification of a plan under either chapters 9, 11, 12 and 13 of a Debtor engaged in business;

(r) 5 voluntary petitions with schedules and statements of Debtors engaged in business, under chapter 7;

(s) 5 voluntary petitions, with schedules and statements, under chapters 9, 11, 12 or 13, of Debtors engaged in business;

(t) 5 confirmation hearings of plans under chapters 9, 11, 12 or 13, of a Debtor engaged in business;

(u) Preparation of 3 disclosure statements and plans of reorganization under chapter 11;

(v) 3 contested requests for allowance and/or payment of an administrative priority of claim;

(w) Preparation of 3 reorganization plans under chapters 9, 12 or 13 of a Debtor engaged in business;

(x) 2 proceedings to determine the validity, priority or extent of a lien or other interest in property of a Debtor engaged in business;

(y) 1 complaint for injunctive or declaratory relief;

(z) 3 representations of the trustee of a Debtor engaged in business;

(aa) 3 bankruptcy related adversary proceedings or contested matters of a type other than as described above, of a Debtor engaged in business;

(bb) 1 appeal from the bankruptcy court;

(cc) Representation of official committees in 2 business bankruptcy cases;

(dd) The preparation and presentation of a paper at a State Bar approved seminar or institute dealing with a business bankruptcy topic;

(ee) Service as an examiner or trustee; and

(ff) Other business bankruptcy matter(s) not described above.

2. **Recertification.**

a. **Bankruptcy Law.** Applicant must have devoted a minimum of 30% of his or her total time practicing bankruptcy law during each year of the 5 year period of certification as defined in Section X, A,1 of the Specific Area Requirements for Bankruptcy Law except as provided for in Part I–General Requirements, Section VI, C,1(b).

b. Applicant may seek recertification in one or both sub-categories of bankruptcy law. In addition to devoting the minimum percentage of total time to bankruptcy law as indicated in Section X, B,2,a(1) above, applicant must have devoted the required percentage of practice to the sub-category in which recertification is being sought.

(1) **Consumer Bankruptcy Law.** Twenty percent (20%) of applicant's total time must have been devoted to the practice of consumer bankruptcy law during each year of the 5 year period of certification as defined in Section X, A,2,a of the Specific Area Requirements for Bankruptcy Law.

(2) **Business Bankruptcy Law.** Twenty percent (20%) of applicant's total time must have been devoted to the practice of business bankruptcy law during each year of the 5 year period of certification as defined in Section X, A,2,b of the Specific Area Requirements for Bankruptcy Law.

C. **REFERENCE REQUIREMENTS.** Applicant must submit a minimum of 5 names and addresses of persons to be contacted as references to attest to his or her competence in consumer bankruptcy law or business bankruptcy law. These persons must be substantially involved in bankruptcy law, and be familiar with applicant's consumer bankruptcy law or business bankruptcy law practice.

1. **Certification.** Applicant must submit names of persons with whom he or she has had dealings involving bankruptcy law matters within the 3 years immediately preceding application.

2. **Recertification.** Applicant must submit names of persons with whom he or she has had dealings involving bankruptcy law matters since certification or the most recent recertification.

3. **Reference Types.** Applicant must submit the following types of references:

a. Four attorneys who are substantially involved in consumer bankruptcy law or business bankruptcy law. Applicant must have been an adversary against one of these attorneys in a consumer bankruptcy law or business bankruptcy law matter.

b. One judge of any bankruptcy court whom applicant has appeared before as an advocate in a consumer bankruptcy law or business bankruptcy law matter.

Amended by Supreme Court order of Feb. 10, 2009, eff. Feb. 10, 2009.

Section XI. Oil, Gas and Mineral Law

(Area ID: OG / Year Started: 1986)

A. **DEFINITION.** Oil, gas and mineral law comprises law applicable to oil, gas and other minerals and interests in oil, gas and other minerals and to the acquisition, ownership, leasing, development, transfer, disposition and financing of these substances. The practice of oil, gas and mineral law requires, without limitation,

- knowledge of land titles and surface use;
- conveyances, contracts and other documents typically used in oil, gas and other mineral transactions;
- statutes and regulations affecting oil, gas and minerals;
- litigation involving oil, gas and mineral rights; and
- the taxation of oil, gas and other minerals and of transactions concerning them.

B. **SUBSTANTIAL INVOLVEMENT.** Applicant must show substantial involvement and special competence in Texas oil, gas and mineral law practice by providing such information as may be required by TBLS.

1. **Certification.**

a. Percentage of Practice Requirement. Applicant must have devoted a minimum of 35% of his or her time practicing Texas oil, gas and mineral law during each year of the 3 years immediately preceding application as defined in Section XI, A of the Specific Area Requirements for Oil, Gas and Mineral Law. Any time during which the applicant worked as a landman will not count toward the percentage of practice requirement.

b. Task Requirements. Applicant must provide information as required by TBLS concerning specific tasks he or she has performed in Texas oil, gas and mineral law. In evaluating experience, TBLS may take into consideration the nature, complexity, and duration of the tasks handled by applicant. For the 3 years immediately preceding application:

(1) Applicant must provide the number of matters or transactions he or she has handled in the following categories:

(a) Oil, gas and mineral leases,

(b) Lease assignments,

(c) Drilling or division order title opinions,

(d) Division orders,

(e) Purchase and sales contracts for oil, gas and minerals,

(f) Lease ratifications,

(g) Pooling or unitization agreements,

(h) Farmout agreements,

(i) Drilling and service contracts,

(j) Operating agreements,

(k) Mineral or royalty deeds,

(*l*) Easements, surface use and/or damage agreement,

(m) Gathering, processing and transportation agreements,

(n) Oil, gas and mineral deeds of trust,

(*o*) Oil, gas and mineral financing transactions,

(p) Sales, purchases and trades of oil, gas and mineral properties,

(q) Lease operations disputes,

(r) Ad valorem and other tax matters,

(s) Environmental issues, agreement or claims, including those related to hydraulic fracturing,

(t) Seismic agreements and the right of oil and gas operators to conduct seismic operations,

(u) Mineral contractor liens,

(v) Issues related to royalty payment, including production valuation and the deduction of post-production costs,

(w) Issues arising out of horizontal drilling, including regulatory issues and the ownership or production,

(x) Areas of mutual interest, participation and development agreements, and

(y) Other oil, gas and mineral law matters or transactions.

(2) Applicant must provide the number of matters in which he or she has provided substantive oil, gas and mineral law representation before regulatory agencies (e.g., the Railroad Commission of Texas, the Bureau of Ocean Energy Management, the Bureau of Safety and Environmental Enforcement, the Federal Energy Regulatory Commission) along with a summary of the nature of such representation.

(3) Applicant must provide the number of matters in which he or she has provided substantive oil, gas or mineral law representation before any tribunals (e.g. trial courts, appellate courts, arbitration panels, mediations) along with a summary of the nature of such representation.

c. Additionally, applicant must submit a resume or job summary reflecting his or her activities for at least 5 years immediately preceding application.

2. **Recertification.** Applicant must have devoted a minimum of 35% of his or her time practicing Texas oil, gas, and mineral law during each year of the 5 year period of certification as defined in Section XI, A of the Specific Area Requirements for Oil, Gas and Mineral Law except as provided for in Part I–General Requirements, Section VI, C, 1(b).

C. REFERENCE REQUIREMENTS. Applicant must submit a minimum of 5 names and addresses of persons to be contacted as references to attest to his or her competence in oil, gas and mineral law. These persons must be substantially involved in oil, gas and mineral law, and be familiar with applicant's oil, gas and mineral law practice.

1. **Certification.** Applicant must submit names of persons with whom he or she has had dealings involving oil, gas and mineral law matters within the 3 years immediately preceding application.

2. **Recertification.** Applicant must submit names of persons with whom he or she has had dealings involving oil, gas and mineral law matters since certification or the most recent recertification.

3. **Reference Types.** Applicant must submit the names of 5 Texas attorneys who are substantially involved in oil, gas and mineral law.

Amended by Supreme Court order of Feb. 10, 2009, eff. Feb. 10, 2009; June 2, 2015, eff. Jan. 1, 2016.

Section XII. Civil Appellate Law

(Area ID: AP / Year Started: 1987)

A. DEFINITION. Civil appellate law is the practice of law involving proceedings brought before a civil appellate court either by appeal of a final judgment or appealable interlocutory order or by an original proceeding in the appellate court. The preparation and presentation of the court's charge and of post-trial and other dispositive motions at the trial court level shall also be considered the practice of civil appellate law. The practice of civil appellate law that qualifies for substantial involvement and special competence should generally cover multiple areas of procedure and substantive law and not be limited to any one, narrow area of law (unless substantial involvement and special competence can otherwise be shown).

Serving as a judge on a civil appellate court or as an attorney in an advisory capacity to a civil appellate court (such as a briefing or staff attorney, law clerk, or in another position which requires comparable duties) is also considered the practice of civil appellate law.

For these purposes "civil appellate courts" include the United States Supreme Court, the Federal Court of Appeals, the Texas Supreme Court, the Texas Courts of Appeals, and comparable courts of other jurisdictions.

B. SUBSTANTIAL INVOLVEMENT. Applicant must show substantial involvement and special competence in civil appellate law practice by providing such information as may be required by TBLS.

1. **Certification.**

a. Percentage of Practice Requirement. Applicant must have devoted a minimum of 25% of his or her time practicing civil appellate law during each year of the 3 years immediately preceding application as defined in Section XII, A of the Specific Area Requirements for Civil Appellate Law.

b. Task Requirements. Applicant must provide information as required by TBLS concerning specific tasks he or she has performed in civil appellate law. In evaluating experience, TBLS may take into consideration the nature, complexity, and duration of the tasks handled by applicant.

(1) Applicant must have handled all or a substantial part of at least 12 civil appellate cases during his or her practice. A case that was submitted to one appellate court and then to a higher court will be considered only one case. Civil appellate cases in which applicant filed a brief or presented oral argument, and original proceedings were filed by applicant in an appellate court (such as petition for writs of mandamus or habeas corpus) are subject to the following additional requirements:

(a) All 12 cases must have been fully briefed on the merits at the appellate level;

(b) At least 6 of the 12 cases must have been handled by applicant within the 3 years immediately preceding application;

(c) Applicant must have been lead counsel in at least 6 of the 12 cases;

(d) Applicant must have presented oral argument to an appellate court on one significant issue of substantive or procedural law in at least 4 of the 12 cases;

(e) At least 6 of the 12 cases must have involved an appeal from a final judgment or other dispositive order which included a finding on a substantive or procedural issue;

(f) In at least 5 of the 12 cases, the appellate court must have issued an opinion on the merits that dealt with at least one substantive issue; and

(g) At least 3 of the 12 cases must have involved the prosecution or defense of a petition to the highest court of the jurisdiction to review the decision of an intermediate appellate court.

(2) Service as an attorney in an advisory capacity to a civil appellate court (such as a briefing or staff attorney, law clerk, or in another position which requires comparable duties) for at least 5 years may be considered by TBLS as the equivalent of the requirements set out in Section XII, B,1,b(1)(a–g) above. Service for less than 5 years may be considered proportionally.

2. **Recertification.** Applicant must have devoted a minimum of 25% of his or her time practicing civil appellate law during each year of the 5 year period of certification as defined in Section XII, A of the Specific Area Requirements for Civil Appellate Law except as provided for in Part I–General Requirements, Section VI, C,1(b).

C. REFERENCE REQUIREMENTS. Applicant must submit a minimum of 5 names and addresses of persons to be contacted as references to attest to his or her competence in civil appellate law. These persons must be substantially involved in civil appellate law, and be familiar with applicant's civil appellate law practice.

1. **Certification.** Applicant must submit names of persons with whom he or she has had dealings involving civil appellate law matters within the 3 years immediately preceding application.

2. **Recertification.** Applicant must submit names of persons with whom he or she has had dealings involving civil appellate law matters since certification or the most recent recertification.

3. **Reference Types.** Applicant must submit the following types of references:

a. Four Texas attorneys who are substantially involved in civil appellate law. Applicant must have prosecuted a civil appellate law matter with or against one of these attorneys.

b. One judge of an appellate court in Texas before whom applicant has appeared as an advocate in a civil appellate law matter.

Amended by Supreme Court order of Feb. 10, 2009, eff. Feb. 10, 2009; June 2, 2015, eff. Jan. 1, 2016.

Section XIII. Administrative Law

A. DEFINITION. Administrative law is the practice of law dealing with the regulatory, licensing, enforcement, and adjudicative powers of local, state and federal governmental agencies. Applicant must demonstrate substantial involvement and special competence in the practice of Texas and federal administrative law, including, without limitation, representing clients before administrative agencies, practicing law within those agencies, and handling judicial proceedings involving those agencies.

B. SUBSTANTIAL INVOLVEMENT. Applicant must show substantial involvement and special competence in Texas and federal administrative law practice by providing such information as may be required by TBLS.

1. **Certification.**

a. Percentage of Practice Requirement. Applicant must have devoted a minimum of 30% of his or her time practicing Texas and federal administrative law during each year of the 3 years immediately preceding application as defined in Section XIII, A of the Specific Area Requirements for Administrative Law.

b. Task Requirements. Applicant must provide information as required by TBLS concerning specific tasks he or she has performed in Texas and federal administrative law. In evaluating experience, TBLS may take into consideration the nature, complexity, and duration of the tasks handled by applicant.

(1) **Contested Case Experience.** Applicant must show primary responsibility as a party representative, agency representative or presiding official (e.g. an administrative law judge or hearing officer) in one of the following 4 categories during his or her entire practice:

(a) Contested Cases Resolved. A total of 10 contested case hearings before Texas or federal administrative agencies of which at least:

(i) 5 cases must have been resolved after hearings on the merits were held and involved final orders issued by the agencies, and

(ii) 5 cases may have been resolved by applicant's involvement in formal alternative dispute resolution (ADR) proceedings (i.e. mediations or arbitrations), or in case preparation and presentation to an internal agency forum after active case development (such as, oral and written discovery, pre-hearing motion practice, investigation, witness preparation, and settlement conferences or negotiations).

(b) **Time in Hearing.** A minimum of 60 days in contested case hearings before Texas or federal administrative agencies, of which 15 days may be in ADR proceedings (i. e. mediations or arbitrations), or equivalent formal agency settlement procedures, involving contested cases before administrative agencies.

(c) **Judicial Review.** Ten (10) proceedings involving the judicial review of agency orders under the Texas Administrative Procedure Act or the Federal Administrative Procedure Act.

(d) **Combination of Cases.** A combination of contested case hearings and judicial review proceedings totaling 10 matters.

(2) General Administrative Law Experience. In addition to the cases required in Section XIII, B, 1, b, (1) above, applicant must meet 3 of the following categories during his or her entire practice:

(a) **Major Rulemaking Proceedings.** Substantial involvement in a major rule-making proceeding before a Texas or federal agency such as petitioning for or drafting rules.

(b) **Original Judicial Proceeding.** Primary responsibility for a party in 3 original judicial actions in Texas or federal court involving agency activities, for example, suits challenging agency rules or the prosecution or defense of suits for injunction, declaratory judgment, mandamus, or enforcement.

(c) **Uncontested Proceedings.** Primary responsibility as a hearings examiner, agency counsel, private practitioner, or presiding official (e.g. an administrative law judge or hearing officer) in 12 uncontested proceedings.

(d) **Client Counseling.** Primary responsibility for client counseling as agency counsel (either with an agency or in the attorney general's office) or as a private practitioner in 5 substantial matters dealing with, for example, the necessity of obtaining permits, the interpretation of agency requirements or statutory authority, compliance with Open Meetings or Open Records Acts; or

(e) **Additional Contested Case Hearings or Judicial Proceedings.** Primary responsibility as a party representative, agency representative, or presiding official (e.g. an administrative law judge or hearing office) in:

i. an additional 5 contested case hearings before Texas or federal administrative agencies;

ii. an additional 5 proceedings involving the judicial review of agency orders under the Texas Administrative Procedure Act or the Federal Administrative Procedure Act; or

iii. a combination of contested case hearings and judicial review proceedings totaling 5 matters.

2. **Recertification.** Applicant must have devoted a minimum of 30% of his or her time practicing Texas or federal administrative law during each year of the 5 year period of certification as defined in Section XIII, A of the Specific Area Requirements for Administrative Law except as provided for in Part I–General Requirements, Section VI, C,1(b).

C. **REFERENCE REQUIREMENTS.** Applicant must submit a minimum of 5 names and addresses of persons to be contacted as references to attest to his or her competence in administrative law. These persons must be substantially involved in administrative law, and be familiar with applicant's administrative law practice.

1. **Certification.** Applicant must submit names of persons with whom he or she has had dealings involving administrative law matters within the 3 years immediately preceding application.

2. **Recertification.** Applicant must submit names of persons with whom he or she has had dealings involving administrative law matters since certification or the most recent recertification.

3. **Reference Types.** Applicant must submit the following types of references:

a. Three Texas attorneys who are substantially involved in administrative law. Applicant shall have tried an administrative law matter with or against one of these attorneys.

b. Two of the following (present or former) before whom applicant has appeared as an advocate in an administrative law matter:

(1) A judge of any court of record in Texas, Texas Courts of Appeal, or the Texas Supreme Court.

(2) A hearing officer or hearing examiner of an administrative agency with jurisdiction in Texas.

Amended by Supreme Court order of Feb. 10, 2009, eff. Feb. 10, 2009; amended eff. Feb. 8, 2011.

Section XIV. Consumer and Commercial Law

A. DEFINITIONS.

1. Consumer and commercial law is the practice of law dealing with consumer and commercial transactions, including transactions of individual and business consumers and commercial transactions between businesses and other businesses or individuals. The practice of consumer and commercial law also includes the prosecution and defense of claims as well as business compliance. Consumer and commercial law includes, by way of example, but not limitation, matters involving,

- the Texas Deceptive Trade Practice—Consumer Protection Act;
- Title 5, Subtitle C of the Texas Insurance Code;
- the Uniform Commercial Code;
- the Texas Credit Code;
- the Texas Manufactured Housing Standards Act;
- the Texas Transportation Code, and Title 14, Subtitle A, Texas Occupations Code;
- Title 5, Chapter 59 (Self–Storage Facility Liens), Chapter 61 (Motor Vehicle Mortgagee's Lien), and Chapter 70, Sub–Chapter A (Possessory Liens), Sub–Chapter B (Liens on Vessels), Sub–

Chapter D (Aircraft Repair and Maintenance Lien), and Texas Property Code;

• laws dealing with landlord-tenant relationship;

• the Federal and Texas Fair Debt Collection Practices Act;

• the Federal Truth in Lending Act; and

• other federal and state laws dealing with sales, leases, insurance, credit, and collection activities involving consumers.

2. "Contested consumer or commercial matters" means law suits filed in a court of record in which an answer is filed and which have been resolved other than by "No Answer Default" or "Dismissal for Want of Prosecution". Applicant must have been counsel from initiation through resolution of the suit and representation completed. Contested consumer or commercial matters may also include cases involving issues of consumer or commercial law submitted to binding arbitration either before or after suit is filed, however, these will be considered on a case by case basis.

B. <u>SUBSTANTIAL INVOLVEMENT.</u> Applicant must show substantial involvement and special competence in Texas consumer and commercial law practice by providing such information as may be required by TBLS.

1. **<u>Certification.</u>**

a. <u>Percentage of Practice Requirement.</u> Applicant must have devoted a minimum of 30% of his or her time practicing Texas consumer and commercial law during each year of the 3 years preceding application as defined in Section XIV, A of the Specific Area Requirements for Consumer and Commercial Law.

b. <u>Task Requirements.</u> Applicant must provide information as required by TBLS concerning specific tasks he or she has performed in Texas consumer and commercial law. In evaluating experience, TBLS may take into consideration the nature, complexity, and duration of the tasks handled by applicant.

(1) Applicant must provide the number of hours he or she has devoted to each of the following within the 3 years immediately preceding application:

(a) Counseling of clients regarding claims and defense of claims in the area of consumer and commercial law;

(b) Representation of clients in preparation, prosecution and defense of consumer and commercial claims;

(c) Representation of clients in alternative dispute resolution procedures as defined by Tex. Civ. Prac. & Rem. Code, Chapter 154; and

(d) The advising and counseling of persons or business entities in areas involving the establishment, revision or maintenance of procedures, practices, forms or programs to comply with consumer and commercial laws.

(2) Applicant must have represented clients as lead counsel in at least 24 contested consumer or commercial matters in Texas within the 5 years immediately preceding application.

(3) In addition to matters required in Section XIV, B,1,b(2) above, applicant must have met one of the following categories within the 10 years immediately preceding application:

(a) Five (5) contested consumer or commercial law matters in which issues were submitted to the finder of fact in a court of record in Texas, with applicant having been lead counsel in at least 2 of these matters; or

(b) Five (5) binding arbitration proceedings dealing with consumer or commercial law matters in which issues were submitted to an arbitrator (or arbitration panel), tried to conclusion on presentation of oral testimony, which either (i) involved an amount in controversy in excess of $5,000, or (ii) referred the matter to arbitration by a county court at law, district court, or federal court, with applicant having been lead counsel in at least 2 of these matters; or

(c) A combination of 5 matters as described in Section XIV, B,1,b(3)(a–b) above.

2. **<u>Recertification.</u>** Applicant must have devoted a minimum of 30% of his or her time practicing Texas consumer and commercial law during each year of the 5 year period of certification as defined in Section XIV, A of the Specific Area Requirements for Consumer and Commercial Law except as provided for in Part I–General Requirements, Section VI, C,1(b).

C. <u>REFERENCE REQUIREMENTS.</u> Applicant must submit a minimum of 5 names and addresses of persons to be contacted as references to attest to his or her competence in consumer and commercial law. These persons must be substantially involved in consumer and commercial law, and be familiar with applicant's consumer and commercial law practice.

1. **<u>Certification.</u>** Applicant must submit names of persons with whom he or she has had dealings involving consumer and commercial law matters within the 3 years immediately preceding application.

2. **Recertification.** Applicant must submit names of persons with whom he or she has had dealings involving consumer and commercial law matters since certification or the most recent recertification.

3. **Reference Types.** Applicant must submit the names of 5 Texas attorneys who are substantially involved in consumer and commercial law. Applicant must have been an adversary in a consumer and commercial law matter with 2 of these attorneys.

Amended by Supreme Court order of Feb. 10, 2009, eff. Feb. 10, 2009.

Section XV. Juvenile Law

A. **DEFINITION.** Juvenile law is the practice of law dealing with judicial and administrative proceedings under Title 3 of the Texas Family Code, and other Texas statutes, including but not limited to, the Human Resource Code, the Texas Education Code, the Texas Rules of Evidence, the Texas Rules of Civil Procedure, and the Texas Code of Criminal Procedure, as they relate to juvenile proceedings. Juvenile law is the practice of law involving, by way of definition not limitation,

- detention hearings;
- probable cause determinations;
- pre-trial hearings on motions to quash and to suppress;
- jury adjudication hearings;
- non-jury trial adjudication hearings;
- disposition negotiations and proceedings;
- proceedings seeking certification (transfer) to criminal court;
- determinate sentence proceedings;
- proceedings under Chapter 55 of the Family Code involving mentally ill or mentally retarded juveniles;
- parole revocation proceedings;
- juvenile appeals;
- post-adjudication hearings and matters;
- state and federal remedies;
- proceedings for sealing or destruction of juvenile records;
- juvenile justice alternative education program placements;
- proceeding involving registration of sex offenders; and
- other proceedings dealing with the rights of juveniles including those involving school discipline, special education, alcoholic beverages, and transportation.

B. **SUBSTANTIAL INVOLVEMENT.** Applicant must show substantial involvement and special competence in Texas juvenile law practice by providing such information as may be required by TBLS.

1. **Certification.**

a. Percentage of Practice Requirement. Applicant must have devoted a minimum of 25% of his or her time practicing juvenile law in Texas during each year of the 3 years immediately preceding application as defined in Section XV, A of the Specific Area Requirements for Juvenile Law.

b. Task Requirements. Applicant must provide information as required by TBLS concerning specific tasks he or she has performed in Texas juvenile law. In evaluating experience, TBLS may take into consideration the nature, complexity, and duration of the tasks handled by applicant.

(1) Applicant must provide the number of juvenile law matters that he or she has participated within the 3 years immediately preceding application in each of the following categories:

(a) Jury adjudication hearings;

(b) Non–Jury contested adjudication hearings;

(c) Pleas of true and stipulations of evidence;

(d) Detention hearings;

(e) Dismissals and sanction level one dispositions;

(f) Cases placed on deferred prosecution;

(g) Cases decided on pre-trial motions;

(h) Disposition proceedings;

(i) Modification of disposition proceedings;

(j) Proceedings involving mentally ill or retarded children;

(k) Proceedings involving records sealing or destruction;

(*l*) Parole revocation proceedings;

(m) Certifications to criminal court;

(n) Determinate sentence proceedings;

(*o*) Release/transfer hearings under determinate sentence act;

(p) Hearings to transfer determinate sentence probation to adult probation;

(q) Proceedings representing clients subject to with removal or expulsion from school (including truancy), or special education ARD hearings;

(r) Juvenile appeals;

(s) State or federal post-adjudication procedure or remedies;

(t) Other matters involving youths' rights and the need for legal representation within the juvenile probation or correctional system.

(2) Applicant must have handled, as lead counsel or in a primary capacity, during his or her practice, Texas juvenile law cases in 3 of the following 4 categories:

(a) Three (3) jury trials (for purposes of this requirement, a case in which the jury has been empanelled will qualify).

(b) Five (5) contested non-jury trials.

(c) Appeals/Special Proceedings. Any combination of the following:

i. Three (3) appeals.

ii. Three (3) proceedings in which a juvenile is subject to removal or expulsion from school, special education ARD hearings (including truancy), or state or federal post-adjudication procedure or remedies.

(d) Certification or Determinate Sentences. Meet one of the following:

i. Three (3) certification or determinate sentence cases.

ii. Six (6) hours of approved CLE in comprehensive courses dealing with certification or determinate sentences within the 3 years immediately preceding application. The substitution of CLE in lieu of actual experience in certification or determinate sentence cases is in addition to the CLE requirement submitted to satisfy Part I–General Requirements, Section V, A,1.

2. **Recertification.** Applicant must have devoted a minimum of 25% of his or her time practicing juvenile law in Texas during each year of the 5 year period of certification as defined in Section XV, A of the Specific Area Requirements for Juvenile Law except as provided for in Part I–General Requirements, Section VI, C,1(b).

C. REFERENCE REQUIREMENTS. Applicant must submit a minimum of 5 names and addresses of persons to be contacted as references to attest to his or her competence in juvenile law. These persons must be substantially involved in juvenile law, and be familiar with applicant's juvenile law practice.

1. **Certification.** Applicant must submit names of persons with whom he or she has had dealings involving juvenile law matters within the 3 years immediately preceding application.

2. **Recertification.** Applicant must submit names of persons with whom he or she has had dealings involving juvenile law matters since certification or the most recent recertification.

3. **Reference Types.** Applicant must submit the following types of references:

a. Four Texas attorneys who are substantially involved in juvenile law. Applicant must have tried a juvenile law matter with or against one of these attorneys.

b. One judge of any court of record in Texas as described below:

(1) a judge whom applicant appeared before as an advocate in a juvenile law matter; or

(2) a judge who has personal knowledge of applicant's abilities and experience.

Amended by Supreme Court order of Feb. 10, 2009, eff. Feb. 10, 2009.

Section XVI. Health Law

(Area ID: HE / Year Started: 2002)

A. DEFINITION. Health law is the practice of law dealing with federal, state, and local law, rules and regulations, and other jurisprudence affecting the health care industry and health care patients. It primarily deals with the operational, regulatory, and transactional legal issues arising from the application of these laws, rules, and regulations to patients, health care providers, health care vendors, and entities which pay for health care services, including without limitation, the relationships among providers, payors, vendors, and patients in the health care industry; and delivery of health care services.

B. SUBSTANTIAL INVOLVEMENT. Applicant must show substantial involvement and special competence in Texas health law by providing such information as may be required by TBLS.

1. **Certification.**

a. Percentage of Practice Requirement. Applicant must have devoted a minimum of 35% of his or her time practicing health law in Texas during each year of the 3 years immediately preceding application as defined in Section XVI, A of the Specific Area Requirements for Health Law.

b. Task Requirements. Applicant must provide information as required by TBLS concerning specific tasks he or she has performed in Texas health law. In evaluating experience, TBLS may take into consideration the nature, complexity, and duration of the tasks handled by applicant.

(1) Applicant must have handled as lead counsel or in a primary capacity, several of the categories listed below in order to sufficiently demonstrate an expertise in Texas health law within the 3 years immediately preceding application by (i) counseling clients and educating

clients which may include trade associations, (ii) advising or counseling clients with respect to the establishment or modification of procedures, practices, forms, programs, or transactions to comply with laws in those areas as they relate to health law, or (iii) representing clients in preparation of claims handled through mediation, arbitration, or litigation.

(a) Health care antitrust;

(b) Fraud and abuse/referral prohibitions;

(c) Health care contract issues;

(d) Managed care and managed care organizations;

(e) Risk management/quality assurance/utilization review/patient safety;

(f) Licensure and certification;

(g) Patient rights;

(h) State licensing and federal COPs;

(i) Medical staff/professional rights;

(j) Physicians practice issues;

(k) Reimbursement and coverage (state and federal);

(l) Finance including tax/tax exemptions;

(m) Administrative proceedings;

(n) Hospital/institutional operations;

(o) Mental health;

(p) Drugs, devices, and IRBs;

(q) Business organizations, mergers and acquisitions;

(r) Labor and employment law;

(s) Health information technology, privacy, confidentiality, and the HIPAA security and privacy;

(t) Governmental entities/political subdivisions; and

(u) Long term care.

2. **Recertification.** Applicant must have devoted a minimum of 35% of his or her time practicing health law during each year of the 5 year period of certification as defined in Section XVI, A of the Specific Area Requirements for Health Law except as provided for in Part I–General Requirements, Section VI, C,1(b).

C. **REFERENCE REQUIREMENTS.** Applicant must submit a minimum of 5 names and addresses of persons to be contacted as references to attest to his or her competence in health law. These persons shall be substantially involved in health law and be familiar with applicant's health law practice.

1. **Certification.** Applicant must submit names of persons with whom he or she has had dealings involving health law matters within the 3 years immediately preceding application.

2. **Recertification.** Applicant must submit names of persons with whom he or she has had dealings involving health law matters since certification or the most recent recertification.

3. **Reference Types.** Applicant must submit 5 Texas attorneys who are substantially involved in health law.

Amended by Supreme Court order of Feb. 10, 2009, eff. Feb. 10, 2009; June 2, 2015, eff. Jan. 1, 2016.

Section XVII. Workers' Compensation Law

A. DEFINITION. Workers' compensation law is the practice of law dealing with the rights and duties of employees, employers, health care providers, and insurance carriers arising out of the Texas Workers' Compensation Act. For purposes of this certification, it also includes matters involving workers' compensation claim disputes adjudicated under the Administrative Procedure Act. This includes, without limitation, the representation of clients before the Texas Department of Insurance; Workers' Compensation Division, Texas Workers' Compensation Commission, the State Office of Administrative Hearings, and in suits for judicial review of the decisions of each of these agencies. Each attorney certified in workers' compensation law must understand income benefit payments and medical benefit payments, as well as the administrative obligations of claimants, employers, and insurance carriers. The practice of workers' compensation law requires that practitioners demonstrate a significant knowledge of the injury process, and its effect on the human body.

B. SUBSTANTIAL INVOLVEMENT. Applicant must show substantial involvement and special competence in Texas workers' compensation law practice by providing such information as may be required by TBLS.

1. Certification.

a. Percentage of Practice Requirement. Applicant must have devoted a minimum of 30% of his or her time practicing Texas workers' compensation law during each year of the 3 years immediately preceding application as defined in Section XVII, A of the Specific Area Requirements for Workers' Compensation Law.

b. Task Requirements. Applicant must provide information as required by TBLS concerning specific tasks he or she has performed in Texas workers' compensation law. In evaluating experience, TBLS may take into consideration the nature, complexity, and duration of the tasks handled by applicant.

(1) Applicant must have been lead counsel (as a party representative or agency representative) in 3 of the following 5 categories. Hearings listed in each of the categories must arise from independent administrative claims disputes and may not be listed if a proceeding involving that dispute was otherwise listed on the application. Claims with the same Division or Commission numbers cannot be repeated.

(a) Thirty-six (36) Benefit Review Conferences concluded by agreement or by the report of a Benefit Review Officer within the 3 years immediately preceding application.

(b) Thirty-six (36) Benefit Contested Case Hearings litigated to a final contested decision before the Texas Department of Insurance; Workers' Compensation Division or the Texas Workers' Compensation Commission within the 3 years immediately preceding application.

(c) Thirty-six (36) Contested Case Hearings under Chapter 413 litigated to a final contested decision before the State Office of Administrative Hearings or substantial evidence review at a trial court level within the 3 years immediately preceding application.

(d) Twenty-four (24) appeals to the Appeals Panel of the Texas Department of Insurance; Workers' Compensation Division or the Texas Workers' Compensation Commission following a decision of a Benefit Contested Case Hearing Officer within the 3 years immediately preceding application.

(e) Six (6) suits for judicial review of decisions of the Texas Department of Insurance; Workers' Compensation Division, the Texas Workers' Compensation Commission, or the Industrial Accident Board litigated to a decision within the 10 years immediately preceding application.

2. Recertification. Applicant must have devoted a minimum of 30% of his or her time practicing Texas workers' compensation law during each year of the 5 year period of certification as defined in Section XVII, A of the Specific Area Requirements for Workers' Compensation Law except as provided for in Part I–General Requirements, Section VI, C,1(b).

C. REFERENCE REQUIREMENTS. Applicant must submit a minimum of 5 names and addresses of persons to be contacted as references to attest to his or her competence in workers' compensation law. These persons must be substantially involved in workers' compensation law, and be familiar with applicant's workers' compensation law practice.

1. Certification. Applicant must submit names of persons with whom he or she has had dealings involving workers' compensation law matters within the 3 years immediately preceding application.

2. Recertification. Applicant must submit names of persons with whom he or she has had dealings involving workers' compensation law matters since certification or the most recent recertification.

3. Reference Types. Applicant must submit the following types of references:

a. Three Texas attorneys who are substantially involved in workers' compensation law. Applicant shall have tried a workers' compensation law matter with or against two of these attorneys.

b. Two of the following (present or former) before whom applicant has appeared as an advocate in a Texas workers' compensation law matter:

(i) judges of any court of record in Texas, courts of appeals in Texas, or the Supreme Court of Texas;

(ii) Benefit Contested Case Hearing Officers or Appeals Panel Judges with the Texas Department of Insurance; Workers' Compensation Division, or the Texas Workers' Compensation Commission; or

(iii) hearing examiners with the State Office of Administrative Hearings.

Amended by Supreme Court order of Feb. 10, 2009, eff. Feb. 10, 2009.

Section XVIII. Criminal Appellate Law

(Area ID: CA / Year Started: 2010)

A. DEFINITIONS.

1. Criminal appellate law is the practice of law in a criminal appellate case, which includes the following proceedings:

a. Appeal or defense of a judgment or order in a criminal law matter, or juvenile adjudication, to an appellate court;

b. Preparation of, or responding to, a petition for discretionary review or related brief to the Texas Court of Criminal Appeals;

c. Prosecution or defense of an application for an extraordinary matter, such as Petition for Writ of Mandamus or Application for Original Habeas Corpus, to the Texas Court of Criminal Appeals, a Texas Court of Appeals, United States District Court, or United States Circuit Court of Appeals, in a criminal matter;

d. Prosecution or defense of an application for post-conviction writ of habeas corpus from a misdemeanor conviction to a statutory county court exercising habeas corpus jurisdiction, or from a final felony conviction in Texas state court, either capital or non-capital;

e. Prosecution or defense of an application for habeas corpus from a final felony conviction, either capital or non-capital, in United States District Court under 28 USC § 2254, or 28 USC § 2255;

f. Prosecution or defense of an appeal to a United States Circuit Court of Appeals from the judgment of a United States District Court in an action under 28 USC § 2254 or 28 USC § 2255; or

g. Prosecution or defense of any criminal law matter at the United States Supreme Court.

2. Applicable appellate courts include the:

a. United States Supreme Court;

b. United States Circuit Courts of Appeals;

c. Texas Supreme Court exercising jurisdiction over adjudications in a juvenile case;

d. Texas Court of Criminal Appeals;

e. Texas Courts of Appeals;

f. Texas District Courts exercising post-conviction habeas corpus jurisdiction under Article V § 8, Texas Constitution, or Articles 11.07, 11.071 or 11.072, Code of Criminal Procedure;

g. United States District Courts exercising post-conviction habeas corpus jurisdiction under 28 USC § 2254 or 28 USC § 2255; and

h. Statutory Texas county courts sitting as Courts of Appeals in cases under Title II, Chapter 30, Government Code or exercising post-conviction habeas corpus jurisdiction under Article V § 16, Texas Constitution, or Article 11.072, Code of Criminal procedure.

B. SUBSTANTIAL INVOLVEMENT. Applicant must show substantial involvement and special competence in criminal appellate law practice by providing such information as may be required by TBLS.

1. **Certification.**

a. Percentage of Practice Requirement. Applicant must have devoted a minimum of 25% of his or her time practicing criminal appellate law during each year of the 3 years immediately preceding application as defined in Section XVIII, A of the Specific Area Requirements for Criminal Appellate Law.

b. Task Requirements. Applicant must provide information concerning specific tasks he or she has performed in criminal appellate law. In evaluating experience, TBLS may take into consideration the nature, complexity, and duration of the tasks handled by applicant.

(1) Applicant shall provide information regarding his or her participation in each of the following types of criminal appellate cases during his or her entire practice:

(a) Appeal or defense of a judgment or order in a criminal law matter, or juvenile adjudication, to a criminal appellate court;

(b) Preparation of, or responding to, a petition for discretionary review or related brief to the Texas Court of Criminal Appeals;

(c) Prosecution or defense of an application for an extraordinary matter, such as petition for writ of mandamus or application for original habeas corpus, to the Texas Court of Criminal Appeals, a Texas Court of Appeals, United States District Court, or United States Circuit Court of Appeals, in a criminal matter;

(d) Prosecution or defense of an application for post-conviction writ of habeas corpus from a misdemeanor conviction to a statutory county court exercising habeas corpus jurisdiction, or from a final felony conviction in Texas state court, either capital or non-capital;

(e) Prosecution or defense of an application for habeas corpus from a final felony conviction, either capital or non-capital, in United States District Court under 28 USC § 2254, or 28 USC § 2255;

(f) Prosecution or defense of an appeal to a United States Circuit Court of Appeals from the judgment of a United States District Court in an action under 28 USC § 2254 or 28 USC § 2255; and

(g) Prosecution or defense of any criminal law matter at the United States Supreme Court.

(2) *Anders* briefs shall not satisfy any task requirement.

(3) Applicant, as an attorney for a party to a criminal appellate case, shall have been listed as a signatory to and have personally performed substantial work in, drafting the pleadings or brief for that party in a minimum of 50 tasks as defined in B, 1, b, (1) (a–g) above

during his or her entire practice. Of these 50 tasks, applicant shall have:

(a) handled at least 25 tasks within the 3 years immediately preceding application; and

(b) performed a minimum of 5 oral arguments at a Court of Appeals, the Texas Court of Criminal Appeals, a United States Circuit Court of Appeals, or the United States Supreme Court during his or her entire practice.

(4) Service as an attorney in an advisory capacity to a criminal appellate court (such as a briefing or staff attorney, law clerk, or in another position which requires comparable duties) for at least 5 years may be considered by TBLS as the equivalent of the requirements set out in Section XVIII, B, 1, b, (1) (a–g) above. Service for less than 5 years may be considered proportionally.

2. **Recertification.** Applicant must have devoted a minimum of 25% of his or her time practicing criminal appellate law during each year of the 5 year period of certification as defined in Section XVIII, A of the Specific Area Requirements for Criminal Appellate Law except as provided for in Part I–General Requirements, Section VI, C, 1, (b).

C. REFERENCE REQUIREMENTS. Applicant must submit a minimum of 5 names and addresses of persons to be contacted as references to attest to his or her competence in criminal appellate law. These persons must be substantially involved in criminal appellate law, and be familiar with applicant's criminal appellate law practice.

1. **Certification.** Applicant must submit names of persons with whom he or she has had dealings involving criminal appellate law matters within the 3 years immediately preceding application.

2. **Recertification.** Applicant must submit names of persons with whom he or she has had dealings involving criminal appellate law matters since certification or the most recent recertification.

3. **Reference Types.** Applicant must submit the following types of references:

a. Four Texas attorneys who are substantially involved in criminal appellate law. Applicant must have tried a criminal appellate law matter with or against one of these attorneys.

b. One judge of any court of record in Texas whom applicant has appeared before as an advocate in a criminal appellate law matter.

(Amended by Supreme Court orders of Sept. 28, 2010, eff. Sept. 28, 2010; March 18, 2014, eff. March 18, 2014; June 2, 2015, eff. Jan. 1, 2016.)

Section XIX. Construction Law

(Area ID: CO / Year Started: 2016)

A. DEFINITION. Construction law is the practice of law dealing with the transactions and relationships among contractors, subcontractors, suppliers, owners, architects, engineers, governmental entities, insurers, sureties and lenders regarding development, design and construction on public and private projects. It includes, by way of definition, not limitation:

- knowledge of construction-related law, including applicable statutes and common law principles and doctrines;
- drafting, negotiation, and operation of construction-related contract documents and provisions, including the active management and oversight of such transactional matters;
- knowledge of procurement and project delivery systems;
- construction lending, insurance and suretyship;
- construction claim development and presentation, including, but not limited to, the analysis of mechanic's lien claims, payment and performance bond claims, construction and design defect claims, contract claims, delay and special damages claims, construction specific statutory claims (*e.g.* Prompt Pay Act, Trust Fund Act), construction accident, injury and OSHA claims, administrative claims, private labor and wage claims (related to construction), judgment collection and enforcement, tort claims arising from design and construction activities, and equitable claims arising from design and construction activities; and
- construction dispute resolution through negotiation, litigation, arbitration, administrative hearings, mediation and other forms of dispute resolution, including the active management and oversight of such dispute-related matters.

B. SUBSTANTIAL INVOLVEMENT. Applicant must show substantial involvement and special competence in Texas construction law practice by providing such information as may be required by TBLS.

1. **Certification.**

a. Percentage of Practice Requirement. Applicant must have devoted a minimum of 40% of his or her time practicing Texas construction law during each year of the 5 years immediately preceding application as defined in Section A above of the Specific Area Requirements for Construction Law.

b. Task Requirements. Applicant must provide information as required by TBLS concerning specific tasks he or she has performed in Texas construction law. In evaluating experience, TBLS may take into consideration the nature, complexity, and duration of the tasks handled by applicant.

(1) Applicant must show that he or she has engaged directly and substantially in a broad practice of Texas construction law within the 5 years immediately preceding application, and must show specific involvement in at least two (2) of the areas below for each of the 5 years preceding application:

(a) Negotiation, preparation and operation of contracts and other documents related to construction law.

(b) Experience with procurement and project delivery systems, construction lending, insurance and suretyship.

(c) Construction claim development and presentation including, but not limited to, the analysis of mechanic's lien claims, payment and performance bond claims, construction and design defect claim, contract claims, delay and special damages claims, specific statutory claims related to construction (e.g. Prompt Pay Act, Trust Fund Act), construction accident, injury and OSHA claims, administrative claims, private labor and wage claims related to construction, judgment collection and enforcement and negligence and other tort claims arising from design and construction activities.

(d) Construction dispute resolution through negotiation, litigation, arbitration, administrative hearings, mediation or other forms of dispute resolution.

(2) Applicant must show by detailed response that he or she has engaged at a primary level of responsibility for a client or employer in, or has had active management and oversight of one or more attorneys involved in, at least one of the areas applicant submitted to satisfy Section B, 1, b, (1) above.

(3) Applicant must submit a resume or job summary reflecting activities for at least five (5) years or longer immediately preceding application.

2. **Recertification.** Applicant must have devoted a minimum of 40% of his or her time practicing Texas construction law during each year of the 5 year period of certification as defined in Part II, A of the Specific Area Requirements for Construction Law except as provided for in Part I–General Requirements, Section VI, C, 1(b).

C. **REFERENCE REQUIREMENTS.** Applicant must submit a minimum of 5 names and addresses of persons to be contacted as references to attest to his or her competence in Texas construction law. These persons must be Texas attorneys who are substantially involved in construction law, and be familiar with applicant's construction law practice, and are not partners or associates of the applicant.

1. **Certification.** Applicant must submit names of persons with whom he or she has had dealings involving construction law matters within the 3 years immediately preceding application.

2. **Recertification.** Applicant must submit names of persons with whom he or she has had dealings involving construction law matters since certification or the most recent recertification.

Adopted by order of Oct. 20, 2015, eff. Jan. 1, 2016. Amended by order of Dec. 15, 2015, eff. Jan. 1, 2016.

TECHNOLOGY STANDARDS

Rule 1. Introduction

1.1 PURPOSE

Pursuant to Texas Government Code, Chapter 77, Section 77.031, this document delineates standards for the technological needs of the judicial system. This document is approved by the Judicial Committee on Information Technology (JCIT) that was created by the 74th Texas Legislature. Changes to this document are effective 90 days after adoption and publication by the JCIT.

1.2 VERSIONS

Version	Action	Release Date
1.0	Initial Draft	April 11, 2012
1.1	Added Audio/Video Standards	July 25, 2012
1.2	Added eFiling Filing Types	November 12, 2013
1.3	Added additional eFiling Types	March 21, 2014
1.4	Added standards for Additional Services; Removed Digital Signature standard (covered in rules); Various changes to other standards	October 14, 2014
2.0	Small changes to codes per county feedback	February 20, 2015
2.5	Small changes to codes per county feedback	August 14, 2015

1.3 DEFINITIONS

Attachment—any unique supporting document including exhibits and proposed orders that are not defined in Rule 21 (a) of the Texas Rules of Civil Procedure.

Digital Media—any files stored in an electronic format. This can include (but is not limited to) text, audio and video files.

Document—a pleading, plea, motion, application, request, exhibit, brief, memorandum of law, or other instrument in electronic form.

DPI—Dots per inch

Lead Document—a document as defined by Rule 21 (a) of the Texas Rules of Civil Procedure. If filing a single document, it is the lead document.

NARA—National Archives and Records Administration

NIEM—National Information Exchange Model—a partnership of the U.S. Department of Justice, the U.S. Department of Homeland Security, and the U.S. Department of Health and Human Services designed to develop, disseminate and support enterprise-wide information exchange standards and processes that can enable jurisdictions to effectively share critical information in emergency situations, as well as support the day-to-day operations of agencies throughout the nation. NIEM was adopted formally by JCIT and is promulgated in data exchanges in Texas Administrative Code, Title 1, Part 8, Chapter 177.

Electronic Court Filing (ECF) standards—a set of non-proprietary extensible markup language (XML) and Web services specifications, along with clarifying explanations and amendments to those specifications that have been added for the purpose of promoting interoperability among electronic court filing vendors and systems.

OCA—Office of Court Administration

OCR—Optical Character Recognition

PDF—Portable Document Format—for the purpose of these standards this is PDF 1.4 (ISO 19005–1:2005—Revised as ISP/NP 19005–1). This standard specifies how to use PDF for long-term preservation of electronic documents and is applicable to documents containing combinations of character, raster and vector data.

PDF Distiller—a program or application that converts files into PDF files so that the printed appearance of a document is preserved regardless of the application used to create it. This functionality is commonly seen as "Print to PDF", "Save to PDF" or "Export to PDF".

PDF Software—software that conforms to International Organization for Standardization (ISO) 32000–

1:2008. This standard specifies standards for creating (writing), reading, displaying and interacting with PDF documents.

JCIT—Judicial Committee on Information Technology

1.4 REFERENCES

- Apple QuickTime supported formats—http://support.apple.com/kb/HT3775
- NIEM—http://www.niem.gov
- OASIS LegalXML Electronic Court Filing (ECF) specifications—http://www.oasis-open.org/committees/legalxml-courtfiling/
- VLC media player supported formats—http://www.videolan.org/vlc/features.html
- Windows media player supported formats—http://support.microsoft.com/kb/316992

Amended effective March 21, 2014. Amended by Supreme Court Oct. 14, 2014, eff. Oct. 14, 2014; Feb. 20, 2015, eff. Feb. 20, 2015; Oct. 5, 2015, eff. Nov. 1, 2015.

Rule 2. System Data Exchange Standards

In accordance with Texas Administrative Code, Title 1, Part 8, Chapter 177, information exchanges that occur between the various systems (electronic filing manager, case management, document management, etc.) should occur using the current OASIS LegalXML specifications. The OASIS LegalXML specification is a subset to NIEM.

Amended effective March 21, 2014.

Rule 3. Digital Media Standards

In addition to content and formatting promulgated by the Texas Rules of Civil Procedure, Texas Code of Criminal Procedure, and Texas Rules of Appellate Procedure, the following standards apply to digital media filed electronically or scanned from source records (filed after the effective date of these standards) by the clerk.

3.1 DOCUMENTS

A. An e-filed document must be in text-searchable PDF, using fonts specified in the PDF specification, on 8.5×11 page size, with the content appropriately rotated.

B. When possible, the document should be generated directly from the originating software using a PDF distiller.

C. Prior to being filed electronically, a scanned document must have a resolution of 300 DPI. Preferably, scanned documents should be made searchable using OCR technology.

D. An e-filed document may not contain any security or feature restrictions including password protection or encryption and may not contain embedded multi-media video, audio, or programming.

E. Documents may not contain package PDF's. PDF's should not be embedded inside of another PDF. Documents may not contain embedded fonts. Each document must be a single PDF. An appellate court may require that multiple PDF documents be combined into a single PDF document and bookmarks used to separate content appropriately. The content of the document should not depend on bookmarks.

F. Any e-filed document filename should contain only alphanumeric characters that are part of the Latin1_General character set. No special characters are allowed and the length of the filename should be restricted to 50 characters.

3.2 AUDIO/VIDEO

A. The following media players are supported (specific audio/video formats can be found on each media player's website):

a. QuickTime (Apple)

b. VLC media player (VideoLAN Organization)

c. Windows media player (Microsoft)

B. When an audio/video file is natively supported by at least one media player listed in these standards, the file must not be converted into another format.

C. If an audio/video file is not natively supported by at least one media player listed in these standards, the file must be converted to another format supported by at least one media player listed. The original, any hardware requirements, and software needed to view/hear the original must be submitted as well.

D. If modifications are needed to enhance the native audio/video, a copy of the original must be made. The modified copy (submitted in addition to the original audio/video) must also be generated in a format supported by at least one media player listed in these standards.

Amended effective March 21, 2014. Amended by order of Oct. 5, 2015, eff. Nov. 1, 2015.

Rule 4. eFiling Filing Configurations

Below are the standard filing configurations to be used in the eFiling system for district, county court at law, probate, and constitutional county courts. This list of filing configurations must be accepted in each court. Courts and clerks may not add to this configuration, but may eliminate codes if not needed in a particular jurisdiction.

It is important to note that these standards only apply to the electronic filing system which is a delivery system and are NOT standards for a county case management or document management system.

4.1 CIVIL CASES

4.1.1 CASE CATEGORIES/TYPES

Case Category Code	Case Type Codes
Civil—Contract	Debt/Contract—Consumer/DTPA
	Debt/Contract—Debt/Contract
	Debt/Contract—Fraud/Misrepresentation
	Debt/Contract—Other
	Foreclosure—Home Equity–Expedited
	Foreclosure—Other
	Franchise
	Insurance
	Landlord/Tenant
	Non–Competition
	Partnership
	Other Contract
Civil—Employment	Discrimination
	Retaliation
	Termination
	Workers' Compensation
	Other Employment
Civil—Injury or Damage	Assault/Battery
	Construction
	Defamation
	Malpractice—Accounting
	Malpractice—Legal
	Malpractice—Medical
	Malpractice—Other Professional Liability
	Motor Vehicle Accident
	Premises
	Product Liability—Asbestos/Silica
	Product Liability—Other
	Other Injury or Damage
Civil—Other Civil	Administrative Appeal
	Antitrust/Unfair Competition
	Bill of Review
	Code Violations
	Communicable Disease
	Foreign Judgment
	Fraudulent Liens
	Garnishment
	Intellectual Property
	Judicial Review—Fraudulent Documents

	Lawyer Discipline
	Perpetuate Testimony
	Securities/Stock
	Tortious Interference
	Toll Road
	Transfer Structured Settlement Payment Rights
	Other Civil
Civil—Real Property	Condemnation
	Eminent Domain
	Partition
	Quiet Title
	Trespass to Try Title
	Other Property
Civil—Related to Criminal Matters	Expunction
	Judgment Nisi
	Non–Disclosure
	Occupational Driver's License
	Seizure/Forfeiture
	Sexual Predator (Health & Safety Code 841)
	Writ of Habeas Corpus—Pre-indictment
	Other
Civil—Tax	Tax Appraisal
	Tax Delinquency
	Other Tax

4.1.2 *Filing Types*

New Case	Subsequent Filings
Affidavit of Indigency	Affidavit of Indigency
Application	Amended Filing
Petition	Answer/ Response
Transfer (County Use Only)	Bond
	Counter Claim/Cross Action/Interpleader/Intervention/Third Party
	Contest
	Filing of Action other than Original
	Garnishment
	Motion (No Fee)
	Motion for Contempt
	Motion for New Trial
	Motion to Modify
	Motion to Reinstate
	Motion to Terminate Wage Withholding
	Motion to Transfer
	Notice
	Notice of Appeal
	No Fee Documents
	Proposed Order
	Request

4.2 Family/Juvenile Cases

The Title IV–D Agency (Texas Office of the Attorney General—Child Support Division) will file its documents under the "Family/Juvenile—Title IV–D (OAG Use Only)" category and use only the case and filing types that begin with "(Title IV–D OAG Use Only) for all its new and subsequent filings.

4.2.1 CASE CATEGORIES/TYPES

Case Category Code	Case Type Codes
Family/Juvenile—Marriage Relationship	Annulment with Children
	Annulment No Children
	Declare Marriage Void
	Divorce with Children
	Divorce No Children
Family/Juvenile—Other Family Law	Adult Adoption
	Register Foreign Judgment
	Garnishment
	Habeas Corpus
	Name Change
	Protective Order
	Removal of Disabilities of Minority
	Unaccompanied Alien Child
	Other
Family/Juvenile—Parent–Child Relationship	Adoption/Adoption with Termination
	Child Protection
	Child Protection (Gov. Code 24.620)
	Child Support
	Custody or Visitation
	Gestational Parenting
	Grandparent Access
	Parentage/Paternity/Voluntary Legitimation
	Termination of Parental Rights
	Other Parent–Child
Family/Juvenile—Post-judgment Actions	Enforcement
	Modification—Custody
	Modification—Other
Family/Juvenile—Title IV–D (OAG Use Only)	(Title IV–D OAG Use Only) Establishment
	(Title IV–D OAG Use Only) Paternity
	(Title IV–D OAG Use Only) Interstate—No TX Cause
	(Title IV–D OAG Use Only) Interstate—Existing TX Cause
	(Title IV–D OAG Use Only) Enforcement
	(Title IV–D OAG Use Only) Intervention
	(Title IV–D OAG Use Only) Other—Billed
	(Title IV–D OAG Use Only) Other—Not Billed
	(Title IV–D OAG Use Only) Capias/Writ
	(Title IV–D OAG Use Only) Service Documents

4.2.2 FILING TYPES

New Case	Subsequent Filings
Affidavit of Indigency	Affidavit of Indigency
Application	Amended Filing

Petition Transfer (County Use Only) (Title IV–D OAG Use Only) Establishment (Title IV–D OAG Use Only) Paternity (Title IV–D OAG Use Only) Interstate—No TX Cause (Title IV–D OAG Use Only) Interstate—Existing TX Cause (Title IV–D OAG Use Only) Enforcement (Title IV–D OAG Use Only) Intervention (Title IV–D OAG Use Only) Other—Billed (Title IV–D OAG Use Only) Other—Not Billed (Title IV–D OAG Use Only) Capias/Writ (Title IV–D OAG Use Only) Service Documents	Answer/Contest/Response/Waiver Bond Counter Claim/Cross Action/Interpleader/Intervention/Third Party Habeas Corpus (Continuing Jurisdiction) Motion (No Fee) Motion for Contempt Motion for Enforcement Motion for New Trial Motion to Modify Motion to Modify and Enforce Motion to Reinstate Motion to Revoke/Suspend/Withhold Motion to Stay Motion to Terminate Wage Withholding Motion to Transfer Notice Notice of Appeal Notice of Delinquency No Fee Documents Proposed Order Request (Title IV–D OAG Use Only) Establishment (Title IV–D OAG Use Only) Paternity (Title IV–D OAG Use Only) Interstate—No TX Cause (Title IV–D OAG Use Only) Interstate—Existing TX Cause (Title IV–D OAG Use Only) Enforcement (Title IV–D OAG Use Only) Intervention (Title IV–D OAG Use Only) Other—Billed (Title IV–D OAG Use Only) Other—Not Billed (Title IV–D OAG Use Only) Capias/Writ (Title IV–D OAG Use Only) Service Documents

4.2.3 PARTY TYPES

For each Title IV–D case type, the court will list one (1) Petitioner and two (2) Respondents as required party types.

4.3 PROBATE CASES

4.3.1 CASE CATEGORIES/TYPES

Case Category Code	Case Type Codes
Probate	Dependent Administration
	Independent Administration
	Foreign Will
	Letters Testamentary
	Muniment of Title
	Other Estate Proceedings
	Small Estate Proceedings
	Open Safety Deposit Box
Probate—Guardianship	Guardianship—Adult
	Guardianship—Minor

	Guardianship Management Trust
	Sale of Property
Probate—Other	Other Probate
	Condemnation/Eminent Domain (Bexar/Denton/Travis County Only)

4.3.2 FILING TYPES

New Case	**Subsequent Filings**
Affidavit on Indigency	Affidavit on Indigency
Application	Amended Filing
Application with Ad Litem	Annual Account
Guardianship Information	Annual Report
Letter	Answer/Response
Petition	Application for Removal
Will/Codicil	Application in an Existing Estate
Transfer (County Use Only)	Application on Sale of Personal Property
	Application on Sale of Real Property
	Bond
	Claim
	Counter Claim/Cross Action/Interpleader/Intervention/Third Party/Contest
	Final Account
	Final Report
	Inventory
	Inventory—(filed after the 90th day after the date the personal rep has qualified)
	Motion (No Fee)
	No Fee Documents
	Notice
	Oath
	Proposed Order
	Request
	Will/Codicil

4.4 MULTI-DISTRICT LITIGATION (MDL) CASES

The case categories and types below are updated upon an order from the Supreme Court creating or removing a MDL case type.

4.4.1 CASE CATEGORIES/TYPES

Case Category Code	**Case Type Codes**
Multi-District Litigation (MDL)	MDL—Asbestosis
	MDL—GM Ignition Switch
	MDL—Hailstorm
	MDL—Hurricane Ike
	MDL—Product Liability

4.4.2 FILING TYPES

New Case	**Subsequent Filings**
Affidavit of Indigency	Affidavit of Indigency
Application	Amended Filing
Petition	Answer /Response
Transfer (County Use Only)	Bond
	Counter Claim/Cross Action/Interpleader/Intervention/Third Party Contest
	Motion (No Fee)
	Motion for Contempt

Motion for Enforcement
Motion for New Trial
Motion to Modify
Motion to Reinstate
Motion to Terminate Wage Withholding
Motion to Transfer
Notice
Notice of Appeal
No Fee Documents
Proposed Order
Request

4.5 *Criminal Cases*

4.5.1 Case Categories/Types

Case Category Code	Case Type Codes
Criminal—Misdemeanor	Appeal from a Lower Court
	Misdemeanor A
	Misdemeanor B
	Misdemeanor C
	Magistrate Case
	Writ—Other
	Writ—Habeas Corpus
Criminal—Felony	Appeal from a Lower Court
	Capital Felony
	Felony Indictment
	Felony Information
	Magistrate Case
	Writ—Other
	Writ—Habeas Corpus

4.5.1 Filing Types

New Case	Subsequent Filings
	Amended Filing Affidavit Application Bond Election as to Punishment Letters Motion Motion to Revoke Probation/Adjudicate Guilt Notice Other Documents Not Listed Pleas Proposed Order Request Report/Return Sanctions Toward Effective Probation (STEP) Statement of Facts Form Warrants Writs

4.6 Other Standard System Configurations

4.6.1 AccepTAnce of Documents Tendered for Filing

A clerk must accept a document tendered for e-filing unless specifically authorized not to accept the document(s) by statute, Texas Rules of Appellate Procedure, or by the Texas Rules of Civil Procedure for the reasons listed below.

Category	Reason	Authority
Sealed Documents	Documents filed under seal or presented to court *in camera* cannot be eFiled.	TRCP 21(f)(4) TRAP 9.10
Vexatious Litigant	Filer has been found to be a vexatious litigant and has not presented an order from the local administrative judge permitting the filing.	CPRC § 11.103

4.6.2 Request for Correction

A clerk may request a filer to correct an e-filed document only for the following reasons. The request must state the reason and reference any supporting authority as follows:

Category	Reason	Authority
Insufficient Fees	Fees submitted are insufficient. Please resubmit your filing with the correct case type/filing type. *<provide short summary as to what fees were not included>*	TRCP 99(d) and Gov't Code, § 51.318(b)(7) and (8) Gov't Code § 51.317(a) Local Gov't Code § 118.052; § 118.121; or § 118.131
Insufficient Funds	Credit Card was declined. Please resubmit with a valid method of payment.	TRCP 99(d) and Gov't Code, § 51.318(b)(7) and (8) Gov't Code § 51.317(a) Local Gov't Code § 118.052; § 118.121; or § 118.131
Document Addressed to Wrong Clerk	The document is addressed to a court for which this clerk's office does not accept filings. Please correct or re-file with the appropriate clerk's office.	
Incorrect/Incomplete Information	Please resubmit using the correct • Cause number • Case Type • Case Category • Filing Code • Party names on document(s) • Attorney/Party email address(es)	
Incorrect Formatting	Please resubmit the document • By rotating the document so that the file mark will appear in the upper right corner • In text searchable PDF • Directly converted to PDF if possible. • With a 300dpi resolution • With a page size of 8.5″ × 11″ • With no embedded fonts	TRCP 21 (f)(8)
PDF Documents Combined	You have submitted multiple documents for filing in a single PDF. The file-mark will only appear on documents submitted as lead documents. Please file all lead documents as separate PDF documents.	
Illegible/Unreadable	Please resubmit in a format that is legible.	
Sensitive Data	Please resubmit with all sensitive data redacted: • DL, SSN, Passport Number, Tax ID Number, Government Issued ID	TRCP 21c (a–f) TRAP 9.10 NOTE:

	Number • Bank Account Number, Credit Card Number, Financial Account Number • Birth Date, Home Address and name of any person who was a minor when the suit was filed.	Family Code § 102.008 and § 105.006 require identification of children by name and DOB
Filer's Request	The filer requested that this filing be returned.	

4.6.3 Additional Services

A clerk may offer additional services as outlined in statute that are charged in addition to any filing fees. The following additional services are allowed to be offered in the eFiling system. A clerk may choose not to offer a particular service and eliminate it from their local configuration, however, a clerk may not add a service not shown below.

If a clerk chooses to provide additional services functionality, all of the services listed below beginning with (Title IV–D OAG Use Only) must be made available to the Title IV–D Agency. The Title IV–D Agency will use only these additional services.

Additional Service	**Statute**
Additional Plaintiffs (11–25)	Government Code 51.317 (b–1)(1)
Additional Plaintiffs (26–100)	Government Code 51.317 (b–1)(2)
Additional Plaintiffs (101–500)	Government Code 51.317 (b–1)(3)
Additional Plaintiffs (501–1000)	Government Code 51.317 (b–1)(4)
Additional Plaintiffs (1001+)	Government Code 51.317 (b–1)(5)
Adoptive Child VSU	Health and Safety Code 191.0045(d)
Adoptive Child DPW	Health and Safety Code 191.0045(d)
Authenticated Certificate	Local Government Code 118.060
Bill of Cost	Local Government Code 118.011(c) Government Code 51.319(3)
Bond Approval Fee	Government Code 51.318(b)(6)
Certificate Issuance	Local Government Code 118.060
Certificate of Name Change	Family Code 45.106(c)
Certificate of No Appeal	Local Government Code 118.060 Government Code 51.318(b)(4)
Copies—Certified	Local Government Code 118.011(3)(B) Government Code 51.318(b)(7)
Copies—Exemplified	Government Code 51.519(3)
Copies—Non–Certified	Local Government Code 118.011(3)(C) Government Code 51.318(b)(8)
Copies—Service	Rules of Civil Procedure 99(a)
Document over 25 pages after 120 days or upon approving order	Local Government Code 118.052(2)(B)(vi)
Issue Abstract of Judgment	Local Government Code 118.052(1)(C)(i) Government Code 51.318 (b)(5)
Issue Bench Warrant	Local Government Code 118.059 Government Code 51.318 (b)(2)
Issue Capias	Local Government Code 118.059 Government Code 51.318 (b)(2)
Issue Citation	Local Government Code 118.059 Government Code 51.318(b)(2)
Issue Citation—Certified Mail	Local Government Code 118.059

Additional Service	Statute
	Government Code 51.318(b)(2)
Issue Citation—Hague Convention	Texas Rules of Civil Procedure 108a.
Issue Citation—Insurance Commission	Government Code 118.131(a)
Issue Citation—Publication	Local Government Code 118.059 Government Code 51.318(b)(2)
Issue Citation—Registered Mail	Local Government Code 118.059 Government Code 51.318(b)(2)
Issue Citation—Secretary of State	Local Government Code 118.059 Government Code 405.031(a) Civil Practice and Remedies Code 17.091
Issue Citation—State Highway Commission	Government Code 118.131(a)
Issue Commission to Take Deposition	Local Government Code 118.059
Issue Expunction—Certified Mail	Code of Criminal Procedure 102.006(a)(2 and 3)
Issue Expunction—Electronic	Local Government Code 118.059 Government Code 51.318(b)(2)
Issue Letter Rogatory	Local Government Code 118.011(c) Government Code 51.319(3)
Issue Letters Testamentary, Guardianship, or Administration	Local Government Code 118.052(3)(D)
Issue Notice of Order Suspending License	Family Code 232.008(d)
Issue Order of Sale	Local Government Code 118.052(1)(C)(ii) Government Code 51.318(b)(2)
Issue Order Staying Suspended License	Family Code 232.008(d)
Issue Order Vacating Suspended License	Family Code 232.013(b)
Issue Precept/Notice	Local Government Code 118.059 Government Code 51.318(b)(2)
Issue Precept—Secretary of State	Local Government Code 118.059 Government Code 51.318(b)(2)
Issue Protective Order	Family Code 82.042
Issue Show Cause	Local Government Code 118.059
Issue SR42 (Transcript of Civil Proceedings)	Local Government Code 118.059 Texas Administrative Code
Issue Subpoena	Local Government Code 118.059 Government Code 51.318(b)(1)
Issue Summons	Code of Criminal Procedure 23.03(9)
Issue Tax Warrant	Local Government Code 118.059
Issue Temporary Restraining Order	Local Government Code 118.059
Issue Warrant	Government Code 51.318(b)(2)
Issue Writ	Local Government Code 118.059 Government Code 51.318(b)(2)
Issue Writ—Secretary of State	Government Code 51.318(b)(2)
Issue Writ of Attachment	Government Code 51.318(b)(2)
Issue Writ of Execution	Government Code 51.318(b)(2)
Issue Writ of Garnishment	Government Code 51.318(b)(2)
Issue Writ of Scire Facias	Local Government Code 118.059
Issue Writ of Sequestration	Government Code 51.318(b)(2)
Issue Writ of Withholding	Family Code 110.004
Judge Signatures	Local Government Code 118.101(11)

Additional Service	Statute
Jury Fee	Rules of Civil Procedure 216 Government Code 51.604(a)
OPR Double Recording Fee 1st Page	Local Government Code 191.007
OPR Double Recording Fee for Additional Pages	Local Government Code 191.007
OPR Recording Fee 1st Page	Local Government Code 118.013
OPR Recording Fee for Additional Pages	Local Government Code 118.013
Postage (1–5 Pages)	Civil Practice and Remedies Code 17.025
Postage (6–10 Pages)	Civil Practice and Remedies Code 17.025
Postage (11–15 Pages)	Civil Practice and Remedies Code 17.025
Postage (16–20 Pages)	Civil Practice and Remedies Code 17.025
Postage (21–25 Pages)	Civil Practice and Remedies Code 17.025
Postage (26–30 Pages)	Civil Practice and Remedies Code 17.025
Postage (31–35 Pages)	Civil Practice and Remedies Code 17.025
Postage (36–40 Pages)	Civil Practice and Remedies Code 17.025
Postage (41–45 Pages)	Civil Practice and Remedies Code 17.025
Postage (46–50 Pages)	Civil Practice and Remedies Code 17.025
Postage (51–150 Pages)	Civil Practice and Remedies Code 17.025
Postage (151–1300 Pages)	Civil Practice and Remedies Code 17.025
Postage (1300+ Pages)	Civil Practice and Remedies Code 17.025
Postage (1oz Letter to Canada/Mexico)	Civil Practice and Remedies Code 17.025
Postage (1oz Letter International)	Civil Practice and Remedies Code 17.025
Postage (Large APO/DPO/FPO Box)	Civil Practice and Remedies Code 17.025
Post Judgment—Issue Citation	Local Government Code 118.052(1)(C)(ii)
Post Judgment—Issue Citation—Certified Mail	Local Government Code 118.052(1)(C)(ii)
Post Judgment—Issue Citation—Publication	Local Government Code 118.052(1)(C)(ii)
Post Judgment—Issue Citation—Secretary of State	Local Government Code 118.052(1)(C)(ii)
Post Judgment—Issue Commission to Take Deposition	Local Government Code 118.052(1)(C)(ii)
Post Judgment—Issue Letters	Local Government Code 118.052(1)(C)(ii)
Post Judgment—Issue Order of Sale	Local Government Code 118.052(1)(C)(ii)
Post Judgment—Issue Precept/Notice	Local Government Code 118.052(1)(C)(ii)
Post Judgment—Issue Show Cause	Local Government Code 118.052(1)(C)(ii)
Post Judgment—Issue Subpoena	Local Government Code 118.052(1)(C)(ii)
Post Judgment—Issue Tax Warrant	Local Government Code 118.052(1)(C)(ii)
Post Judgment—Issue Temporary Restraining Order	Local Government Code 118.052(1)(C)(ii)
Post Judgment—Issue Writ	Local Government Code 118.052(1)(C)(ii)
Record Search	Local Government Code 118.011(c) Government Code 51.318 (b)(3)
Service—Additional Copy	Texas Rules of Civil Procedure 736.3 (c)
Service—Certified Mail	Local Government Code 118.063 Government Code 51.319(2)
Service—Certified Mail—Expedited Foreclosure	Texas Rules of Civil Procedure 736.3 (b)

Additional Service	Statute
Service—Constable—Certified Mail	Local Government Code 118.131(a)
Service—Constable—Order of Sale/Writ of Execution	Local Government Code 118.131(a)
Service—Constable—Personal Service	Local Government Code 118.131(a)
Service—Constable—Posting	Local Government Code 118.131(a)
Service—Constable—Publication	Local Government Code 118.131(a)
Service—Constable—Subpoena—More than five days	Local Government Code 118.131(a)
Service—Constable—Subpoena—Less than five days	Local Government Code 118.131(a)
Service—Constable—Tax Sale	Local Government Code 118.131(a)
Service—Constable—Writ—(Precinct)—(List writ type if applicable)[1]	Local Government Code 118.131(a)
Service—Constable—All Other	Local Government Code 118.131(a)
Service—Publication	Local Government Code 118.011(c) Government Code 51.319(3)
Service—Registered Mail	Local Government Code 118.063 Government Code 51.319(2)
Service—Sheriff—Certified Mail	Local Government Code 118.131(a)
Service—Sheriff—Order of Sale	Local Government Code 118.131(a)
Service—Sheriff—Personal Service	Local Government Code 118.131(a)
Service—Sheriff—Posting	Local Government Code 118.131(a)
Service—Sheriff—Publication	Local Government Code 118.131(a)
Service—Sheriff—Subpoena—More than five days	Local Government Code 118.131(a)
Service—Sheriff—Subpoena—Less than five days	Local Government Code 118.131(a)
Service—Sheriff—Writ—(List writ type if applicable)[2]	Local Government Code 118.131(a)
Service—Sheriff—All Other	Local Government Code 118.131(a)
(Title IV–D OAG Use Only) Citation Issuance	Family Code 231.202(1)
(Title IV–D OAG Use Only) Citation Issuance—TRCP R 106 Sub Service	Rules of Civil Procedure 106
(Title IV–D OAG Use Only) Citation Issuance—Publication	Rules of Civil Procedure 116
(Title IV–D OAG Use Only) Citation Issuance—Certified Mail	Family Code 231.202(4)(A)
(Title IV–D OAG Use Only) Precept Issuance	Family Code 231.202(1)
(Title IV–D OAG Use Only) Precept Issuance—TRCP R 106 Sub Service	Rules of Civil Procedure 106
(Title IV–D OAG Use Only) Precept Issuance—Publication	Family Code 231.202(1)
(Title IV–D OAG Use Only) Precept Issuance—Certified Mail	Family Code 231.202(4)(A)
(Title IV–D OAG Use Only) Subpoena Issuance by Clerk	Family Code 231.202(6)
(Title IV–D OAG Use Only) Service of Process through Law Enforcement	Family Code 231.202(4)(A)

Additional Service	Statute
Z–(County Use Only)—Service—Constable—(List service type)—(List precinct number)[3]	

[1] Local Government Code 118.131(a) allows a commissioners court to set fees for the services of sheriffs and constables. In instances where the commissioners court sets different amounts for different types of writs, clerks may designate the type of writ and have multiple "Service–Constable–Writ" services available.

[2] Local Government Code 118.131(a) allows a commissioners court to set fees for the services of sheriffs and constables. In instances where the commissioners court sets different amounts for different types of writs, clerks may designate the type of writ and have multiple "Service–Sheriff–Writ" services available.

[3] In some counties, clerks use additional services to route money to the appropriate general ledger accounts. In these cases, clerks can use "Z–(County Use Only)—Service—Constable" additional services to route to the appropriate account. In these cases, the services listed should be associated with an existing "Service—Constable" type of additional service that the filer would normally use.

Former Rule 5 amended effective March 21, 2014. Renumbered as Rule 4 and amended by Supreme Court Oct. 14, 2014, eff. Oct. 14, 2014. Amended by order of Feb. 20, 2015, eff. Feb. 20, 2015; Oct. 5, 2015, eff. Nov. 1, 2015.

RULES AND FEES OF THE JUDICIAL BRANCH CERTIFICATION COMMISSION

Adopted September 1, 2014

Including Amendments Received Through February 1, 2016

RULES OF THE JUDICIAL BRANCH CERTIFICATION COMMISSION

RULE 1.0. GENERAL PROVISIONS

1.1. Authority

These rules are promulgated under Section 152.101 of the Government Code.

Adopted by orders of the Supreme Court May 13, 2014, and August 19, 2014, eff. September 1, 2014.

1.2. Definitions

The following words and terms, when used in these rules, have the following meanings, unless the context clearly indicates otherwise.

(a) **Act** means the Act of May 2, 2013, 83rd Leg., R.S., ch. 42, § 1.01 (SB 966), which is codified in Chapters 151–157 of the Government Code.

(b) **Advisory board** means a board that is established by law or the Commission to advise the Commission on rules, policies, or technical matters.

(c) **Applicant** means any person seeking a certification, registration, or license from the Commission.

(d) **Certification** means a certification issued by the Commission. The term includes provisional certification.

(e) **Commission** means Texas Judicial Branch Certification Commission.

(f) **Complainant** means any person, including the Director, who has filed a complaint with the Commission against any person whose activities are subject to the Commission's jurisdiction.

(g) **Director** or **Administrative Director** means the Administrative Director of the Office of Court Administration of the Texas Judicial System, or the Director's designee.

(h) **License** means a license issued by the Commission.

(i) **Office** means the Office of Court Administration of the Texas Judicial System.

(j) **Presiding officer** means the Commission member designated by the Supreme Court under Section 152.056 of the Government Code.

(k) **Registration** means a registration issued by the Commission.

(*l*) **Regulated person** means a person who holds a certification, registration, or license issued by the Commission.

(m) **Respondent** means any person, regardless of whether the person is certified, registered, or licensed, who is charged with violating a law that establishes a regulatory program administered by the Commission, a rule adopted by the Commission, or an order issued by the Commission or the Director.

(n) **Review committee** means a committee of advisory board members appointed by the Commission to review complaints filed against a regulated person.

Adopted by orders of the Supreme Court May 13, 2014, and August 19, 2014, eff. September 1, 2014.

1.3. Program Fees

(a) Fees set by the Commission for each program are published on the Commission's website separately from these rules and must be paid as prescribed on the website. The program fees include fees for initial applications, renewals, duplicate licenses, examinations, and any other fees specific to a particular program.

(b) All program fees are nonrefundable unless stated otherwise.

Adopted by orders of the Supreme Court May 13, 2014, and August 19, 2014, eff. September 1, 2014.

1.4. Counting Time

In computing any period of time prescribed or allowed by these rules, the day of the act, event, or default after which the designated period of time begins to run is not included. The last day of the period so computed is to be included, unless it is a Saturday, Sunday, or legal holiday, in which event the period runs until the end of the next day which is not a Saturday, Sunday, or legal holiday. Saturdays, Sundays, and legal holidays must otherwise be counted for purposes of calculating time periods under these rules.

Adopted by orders of the Supreme Court May 13, 2014, and August 19, 2014, eff. September 1, 2014.

1.5. Access to Commission Records

As a judicial branch entity, the Commission is not a governmental body subject to the Public Information Act set forth in Chapter 552 of the Government Code. Public access to the Commission's records is governed either by Rule 12 of the Rules of Judicial Administration or by applicable statutory or common law. The Director is the Commission's records custodian.

Adopted by orders of the Supreme Court May 13, 2014, and August 19, 2014, eff. September 1, 2014.

RULE 2.0. POWERS, DUTIES, AND RESPONSIBILITIES

2.1. Powers and Duties of the Commission

(a) The Commission shall:

(1) administer and enforce the Act, these rules, and the standards or codes of ethics applicable to each profession regulated by the Commission;

(2) in consultation with appropriate advisory boards, develop and recommend rules to the Supreme Court;

(3) in consultation with appropriate advisory boards, develop and recommend to the Supreme Court a code of ethics for each profession regulated by the Commission;

(4) set fees in amounts reasonable and necessary to cover the costs of administering the programs or activities administered by the Commission subject to approval of the Supreme Court;

(5) in consultation with appropriate advisory boards, establish qualifications for certification, registration, and licensing; and

(6) approve curriculum for court reporter career schools and colleges and court reporter programs in technical institutes and public community colleges.

(b) The Commission may:

(1) require applicants to pass an examination and charge fees for the examination;

(2) require regulated persons to obtain continuing education and approve continuing education courses; and

(3) elect officers and appoint necessary committees.

Adopted by orders of the Supreme Court May 13, 2014, and August 19, 2014, eff. September 1, 2014.

2.2. Commission Meetings

(a) Every meeting of the Commission must be open to the public as provided by the Commission's Public Meetings Policy.

(b) A quorum for the Commission is a majority of all the members of the Commission. When a quorum is present, a motion before the Commission is carried by an affirmative vote of the majority of the Commission members present that are participating in the vote.

(c) The presiding officer may limit the number and length of comments provided on any item on the agenda.

(d) The Commission must provide the public with a reasonable opportunity to appear before the Commission and speak on any issue under the Commission's jurisdiction. A person who wishes to speak at a Commission meeting must sign in and may speak at the designated time.

(e) The presiding officer or the presiding officer's designee may grant continuances with regard to hearings and other matters before the Commission.

Adopted by orders of the Supreme Court May 13, 2014, and August 19, 2014, eff. September 1, 2014.

2.3. Powers and Duties of the Administrative Director

(a) The Administrative Director must administer and enforce the Commission's programs and policies as provided by the Act and other applicable law, including, but not limited to:

(1) processing applications for and issuing certifications, registrations, and licenses;

(2) developing procedures and forms;

(3) conducting investigations;

(4) issuing cease and desist orders as provided by Section 153.003 of the Government Code;

(5) administering exams, including administering exams in conjunction with a person with whom the Commission contracts to develop and administer examinations;

(6) maintaining records pertaining to applicants and regulated persons; and

(7) performing any other duty assigned by the Commission or specified by law.

(b) The Administrative Director must supervise the Office's provision of support to the Commission under the administrative attachment required by Section 152.103 of the Government Code. The Administrative Director may delegate the powers and duties prescribed by law or these rules to staff of the Office after providing written notice of such delegation to the Commission.

(c) The Administrative Director may bring items to the Commission's attention for its consideration, including, but not limited to, proposals for new or amended rules and agenda items for Commission meetings.

Adopted by orders of the Supreme Court May 13, 2014, and August 19, 2014, eff. September 1, 2014.

2.4. Advisory Boards

(a) Advisory boards must advise the Commission on policy and regulated persons.

(b) Each advisory board must meet at least once each year and at the call of the presiding officer.

(c) Advisory boards must assist the Commission by developing and recommending rules to the Commission and may establish subcommittees to provide this assistance.

(d) Advisory boards must perform other duties as requested by the Commission or required by law.

(e) The purpose and membership of each advisory board is detailed in the provisions of the Act for each specific program regulated by the Commission. The Commission may establish other advisory boards. The following advisory boards are created by the Act:

(1) Court Reporters Certification Advisory Board;

(2) Guardianship Certification Advisory Board;

(3) Process Server Certification Advisory Board; and

(4) Licensed Court Interpreter Advisory Board.

Adopted by orders of the Supreme Court May 13, 2014, and August 19, 2014, eff. September 1, 2014.

RULE 3.0. CERTIFICATION, REGISTRATION, AND LICENSING

3.1. Initial Applications

(a) All applications for certification, registration, and licensing must be submitted on forms published on the Commission's website and accompanied by the appropriate application fee. In appropriate circumstances, the Commission may require an applicant to submit information in addition to that called for on the application forms.

(b) An applicant must comply with submission requirements stated on the application form. Incomplete applications will not be processed.

(c) An applicant must provide the Commission with his or her Texas and national criminal history records by fingerprint search according to directions published on the Commission's website. The criminal history searches must be conducted no more than 90 days before an application is submitted.

Adopted by orders of the Supreme Court May 13, 2014, and August 19, 2014, eff. September 1, 2014.

3.2. Renewal Applications

(a) A person must not perform work requiring certification, registration, or a license under the Act with an expired certification, registration, or license.

(b) The Commission will notify a regulated person by email before the date that the person's certification, registration, or license is scheduled to expire. A regulated person's failure to receive a renewal notice from the Commission does not exempt the person from any requirement of these rules or of any other rules governing the person's profession.

(c) All certification, registration, and license renewal applications must be submitted on forms published on the Commission's website. A regulated person must comply with submission requirements stated on the renewal form. Incomplete applications will not be processed.

(d) The renewal application and all applicable fees are due 45 days prior to the expiration of the certification, registration, or license. An application is timely if it is postmarked on or before the due date. Failure to complete a renewal application at least 45 days prior to expiration may result in a lapse of certification, registration, or license.

(e) Any continuing education that is required to be fulfilled as part of the renewal application must be completed prior to the certification, registration, or license expiration date to avoid payment of a late renewal fee.

(f) Notwithstanding (b) through (e), a regulated person who fails to renew his or her certification, registration, or license in a timely manner because the person was on active duty in the United States armed forces serving outside this State is exempt from any increased renewal fee that the person would otherwise be required to pay for failing to renew in a timely manner.

(g) Notwithstanding (b) through (e):

(1) A regulated person who is a member of the state military forces or a reserve component of the armed forces of the United States, and who is ordered to active duty by the proper authority, is entitled to an extension of his or her certification, registration, or license period equal to the deployment period and an additional amount of time to complete any continuing education requirements and any other requirements related to the renewal of the person's certification, registration, or license.

(2) The individual must submit to the Director a written request, accompanied by a copy of the orders placing the person on active duty.

(3) The Director must make the extension based on information in the copy of the orders provided. The additional amount of time must be equal to the total number of months that the person serves on active duty.

(4) An individual making a request under this rule must notify the Director of any change in the length of deployment.

(5) A regulated person is exempt from any increased fee or other penalty for failing to renew the person's certification, registration, or license in a timely manner if the individual furnishes to the Commission satisfactory documentation that the individual failed to renew in a timely manner because the individual was on active duty in the United States armed forces serving outside this State.

(h) The Commission must refuse to accept a regulated person's application for renewal if the Commission receives notice of child support arrearages pursuant to Section 232.0135 of the Family Code. Upon receipt of further notice that the person has complied with Section 232.0135(b), the Commission must accept an application for renewal subject to all requirements of these rules.

Adopted by orders of the Supreme Court May 13, 2014, and August 19, 2014, eff. September 1, 2014.

3.3. Endorsement; Reciprocity

(a) The Commission may waive any prerequisite to obtaining a certification, registration, or license for an applicant after reviewing the applicant's credentials and determining that the applicant holds a certification, registration, or license issued by another jurisdiction that has certification, registration, or licensing requirements substantially equivalent to those of this State.

(b) The Commission may waive any prerequisite to obtaining a certification, registration, or license for an applicant who holds a certification, registration, or license issued by another jurisdiction with which this State has a reciprocity agreement. Subject to the approval of the Supreme Court, the Commission may make an agreement with another state to allow for certification, registration, or licensing by reciprocity.

Adopted by orders of the Supreme Court May 13, 2014, and August 19, 2014, eff. September 1, 2014.

3.4. Alternative Application Procedure for Military Spouses

(a) This rule applies to an applicant who is the spouse of a person serving on active duty as a member of the armed forces of the United States.

(b) The Commission may issue a certification, registration, or license to an applicant described under (a) who:

(1) holds a current certification, registration, or license issued by another state that has requirements that are substantially equivalent to the requirements for the certification, registration, or license; or

(2) within the five years preceding the application date, held a certification, registration, or license in this State that expired while the applicant lived in another state for at least six months.

(c) The Commission may allow an applicant who meets the requirements of (b) to demonstrate competency by alternative methods or credentials in order to meet the requirements for obtaining a particular certification, registration, or license issued by the Commission. For purposes of this Section, the standard methods of demonstrating competency are the specific exam, education, and experience required to obtain a particular certification, registration, or license.

(d) In lieu of the standard methods of demonstrating competency for a particular certification, registration, or license and based on the applicant's circumstances, the alternative methods for demonstrating competency may include any combination of the following as determined by the Commission:

(1) education;

(2) continuing education;

(3) examinations (written or skills);

(4) letters of good standing;

(5) letters of recommendation;

(6) work experience; or

(7) other methods or credentials required by the Commission.

(e) The applicant must:

(1) submit an application and proof of the requirements under this rule and for that particular certification, registration, or license on a form and in a manner prescribed by the Commission; and

(2) be subject to the same criminal history background check required of the persons applying for that particular certification, registration, or license.

(f) A person who applies for a certification, registration, or license under this rule is exempt from paying an application fee.

(g) The Director may issue a license by endorsement under this rule to an applicant who meets the requirements of (b) in the same manner set forth in Section 51.404 of the Occupations Code.

Adopted by orders of the Supreme Court May 13, 2014, and August 19, 2014, eff. September 1, 2014.

3.5. Eligibility for Persons with Criminal History

(a) An initial or renewal application may be denied, and a regulated person may be disciplined, if the person's criminal history or other information indicates that the person lacks the honesty, trustworthiness, or integrity to hold the certification, registration, or license. After consultation with the appropriate advisory boards, the Commission will develop and publish on its website guidelines for each regulatory program listing the categories of crimes that are considered to indicate that a person lacks the honesty, trustworthiness, or integrity to hold the particular certification, registration, or license. The Director will determine whether an initial or renewal application will be denied under this rule using the guidelines developed by the Commission and the factors listed in (b). If the Director denies an application, the applicant may request that the Commission reconsider the decision under Rule 3.6.

(b) In making a determination under (a), the Commission or Director may consider:

(1) the nature and seriousness of the crime;

(2) the extent to which certification, registration, or licensing might offer an opportunity to engage in further criminal activity of the same type as that in which the person previously had been involved;

(3) the relationship of the crime to the ability, capacity, or fitness required to perform the duties and discharge the responsibilities of the occupation;

(4) the extent and nature of the person's past criminal activity;

(5) the age of the person when the crime was committed;

(6) the amount of time that has elapsed since the person's last criminal activity;

(7) the conduct and work activity of the person before and after the criminal activity;

(8) evidence of the person's rehabilitation or rehabilitative effort while incarcerated or after release;

(9) proof that the applicant:

(A) maintained a record of steady employment;

(B) supported his or her dependents;

(C) maintained a record of good conduct; and

(D) paid all outstanding court costs, supervision fees, fines, and restitution ordered in any criminal case in which the applicant has been convicted; and

(10) any other evidence of the person's fitness, including, but not limited to, letters of recommendation.

(c) A person may request that the Commission, through the Director, issue a criminal history evaluation letter regarding the person's eligibility for certification or licensure under this rule.

(1) The person may request a criminal history evaluation letter if the person:

(A) is enrolled or is planning to enroll in an educational program that prepares a person for an initial certification or license or is planning to take an examination required by the Commission for an initial certification or license; and

(B) has reason to believe that the person is ineligible for certification or licensing due to a conviction or deferred adjudication for a felony or misdemeanor offense or other criminal history.

(2) The request must be in writing and must state the basis for the person's potential ineligibility. The requestor must provide the Commission with his or her criminal records pursuant to the fingerprinting requirements for the particular certification or licensing program. The Commission may request additional information from the requestor.

(3) If the Director determines that a ground for ineligibility does not exist, the Director must notify the requestor in writing of the Director's determination on each ground of potential ineligibility.

(4) If the Director determines that the requestor is ineligible, the Director must issue a letter setting out each basis for potential ineligibility and the Director's determination as to eligibility.

(5) The Director must provide notice under (c)(3) or issue a letter under (c)(4) not later than the 90th day after the date that the Commission receives the request.

(6) The Commission is not bound by the Director's determination if:

(A) the requestor fails to disclose known information that is relevant to the evaluation; or

(B) there is a change in the person's circumstances after the evaluation notice or letter is issued.

Adopted by orders of the Supreme Court May 13, 2014, and August 19, 2014, eff. September 1, 2014.

3.6. Denial of Application; Reconsideration

(a) Application Review. The Director must review each application and determine whether the applicant meets the Commission's qualifications for the particular certification, registration, or license. The Director must also determine whether the applicant meets the Commission's criminal history eligibility requirements. If a person who has applied to be a certified guardian does not clearly meet the experience or education requirements in these rules, the Director must consult with members of the Guardianship Certification Advisory Board before approving or denying the application.

(b) Denial of Application. The Director may deny an application only if the applicant fails to meet the qualifications set forth in these rules or the Commission's criminal history eligibility requirements. The Director must furnish to the applicant a written statement that succinctly states the reason for denying the application.

(c) Request for Reconsideration. Within 20 days of the date of the notice that the Director has denied an application, the applicant may request that the Commission reconsider the denial. The request must be in writing, identify each point or matter about which reconsideration is requested, and set forth the grounds for the request for reconsideration.

(d) Reconsideration Procedure. The Commission must reconsider the request at its next meeting and may allow the applicant or other witnesses to appear at the meeting and present sworn testimony. The Commission may limit the number of witnesses appearing and the time allotted for a witness's testimony.

(e) Commission Action on Request. After reconsidering a decision of the Director, the Commission may:

(1) affirm the Director's decision; or

(2) reverse the Director's decision.

(f) Final Decision. The Commission must notify the applicant in writing of its decision on reconsideration. The Commission's decision is final and may not be appealed.

Adopted by orders of the Supreme Court May 13, 2014, and August 19, 2014, eff. September 1, 2014.

3.7. Examination Security

(a) Except as provided in Rule 3.10, when an applicant must take an examination in order to obtain a certification or license, the applicant may only use methods of assistance that are available to, and authorized for, other persons taking the examination. A person who uses or provides unauthorized assistance in connection with an examination violates this rule. Conduct that violates this rule includes but is not limited to the following:

(1) obtaining or attempting to obtain from any source examination questions or answers for use by an applicant, prospective applicant, or any other person, including a person associated with a school or examination preparation course;

(2) providing or attempting to provide examination questions or answers to an applicant, prospective applicant, or any other person, including a person associated with a school or examination preparation course;

(3) presenting a falsified or fraudulent document to gain entry to an examination;

(4) presenting a falsified or fraudulent document concerning an individual's results from an examination;

(5) taking an examination for another person;

(6) as an applicant or prospective applicant, knowingly allowing another person to take an examination for the applicant or prospective applicant;

(7) while taking an examination, using any materials not authorized by the Commission or testing service for use in the examination, including but not limited to notes or study aides;

(8) bringing to the examination site or leaving the examination site with examination questions or answers obtained from the current examination or from previous examination attempts;

(9) while taking an examination, communicating with any person, other than an authorized representative of the Commission or testing service, about the examination; or

(10) for open book examinations, bringing any materials into the examination, including hand-written notes in approved reference materials, other than those materials approved by the Commission or testing service.

(b) The contents of any examination that is required for the issuance of a Commission certification or license are confidential.

(c) An applicant who cheats on an examination will be disqualified and may not take the examination again until two years have elapsed from the date of the examination at which the applicant was disqualified.

Adopted by orders of the Supreme Court May 13, 2014, and August 19, 2014, eff. September 1, 2014.

3.8. Examination Rescheduling

(a) A person may reschedule an examination to another regularly scheduled examination date at no charge if the person notifies the Commission or vendor at least two days prior to the examination and complies with the instructions of the Commission or vendor.

(b) A person who reschedules an examination under this rule may apply the examination fee paid for the cancelled examination to the rescheduled examination.

Adopted by orders of the Supreme Court May 13, 2014, and August 19, 2014, eff. September 1, 2014.

3.9. Examination Fee Refund

(a) To obtain a refund of an examination fee, a person who is unable to take the examination must:

(1) if the examination is administered by a vendor, comply with the vendor's notice and documentation requirements; or

(2) if the examination is administered by the Commission, provide written notice to the Director not less than 10 days prior to the date of the examination or provide the Director, as soon as possible, with documentation of the person's inability to take the examination because of an emergency.

(b) A person seeking a refund must apply for the refund in writing within one year of the date that the person paid the fee. The person must, upon request, provide the Office additional information necessary to process the refund.

Adopted by orders of the Supreme Court May 13, 2014, and August 19, 2014, eff. September 1, 2014.

3.10. Access to Examinations and Examination on Religious Holy Days

(a) Reasonable accommodation for examinations will be made available as required by the Americans with Disabilities Act of 1990, Public Law 101–336. Reasonable accommodation means an adjustment or modification of the standard testing conditions that ameliorates the impact of the applicant's disability without doing any of the following:

(1) fundamentally altering the nature of the examination;

(2) fundamentally altering the Commission's ability to determine through the examination whether the applicant possesses the essential eligibility requirements;

(3) compromising the validity of the examination;

(4) compromising the security of the examination; or

(5) imposing an undue burden on the Commission or on the examination vendor.

(b) If an examination is scheduled on a date that is a religious holy day, a person whose religious beliefs prevent that person from taking an examination on such date will be permitted to take the examination on an alternate date. The alternate date must be a regularly scheduled examination date unless the person's religious beliefs prevent the person from taking the examination on such date.

(c) A person who needs a reasonable accommodation for an examination or who requests to take the examination on an alternate date must notify the Director or examination vendor, as applicable, of the request at least 10 days prior to the scheduled examination.

Adopted by orders of the Supreme Court May 13, 2014, and August 19, 2014, eff. September 1, 2014.

3.11. Examination Results

(a) Unless the examination is graded or reviewed by a testing service, not later than the 30th day after the date that a person takes an examination, the Commission must notify the person of the results of the examination.

(b) If the examination is graded or reviewed by a testing service:

(1) the Commission must notify the person of the results of the examination not later than the 30th day after the date that the Commission receives the results from the testing service; and

(2) if notice of the examination results will be delayed for longer than 90 days after the examination date, the Commission must notify the person of the reason for the delay before the 90th day.

(c) If requested in writing by a person who fails an examination, the Commission must furnish the person with an analysis of the person's performance on the examination.

(d) Examination results are valid for one year from the date of the examination, unless stated otherwise in specific program statutes or rules.

Adopted by orders of the Supreme Court May 13, 2014, and August 19, 2014, eff. September 1, 2014.

3.12. Responsibilities of Regulated Persons

(a) A regulated person must comply with the rules for the program under which the person is regulated.

(b) A regulated person must respond to requests for information from the Commission or the Director pertaining to renewal of certification, registration, or licensure; complaints alleging misconduct by the regulated person; and investigative inquiries by the Commission or Director. The regulated person must respond to a request for information within the time prescribed in the request.

(c) A regulated person must provide the Commission with the person's name, business name, business address, home address, business and home telephone numbers, email address, and fax number, and must notify the Commission of any change in contact information within 30 days of the change. Failure to comply with this rule may result in disciplinary action.

(d) A regulated person who, after being certified, registered, or licensed, is convicted of any felony or misdemeanor offense must immediately notify the Commission of the conviction.

Adopted by orders of the Supreme Court May 13, 2014, and August 19, 2014, eff. September 1, 2014.

3.13. Voluntary Surrender of Certification, Registration, or License

(a) A regulated person may voluntarily surrender the person's certification, registration, or license. The surrender must be submitted to the Director on the form approved by the Commission, and the form must be completed fully. The Director may request additional information.

(b) A voluntary surrender is effective after the Director receives it, verifies that the form is complete, and changes the person's status on the Commission's website.

(c) The person must provide written notice of the voluntary surrender as required by the Director.

(d) The circumstances under which the certification, registration, or license is surrendered will be noted in the person's records with the Commission and will be taken into account if the person applies in the future. A voluntary surrender does not affect any disciplinary matters before the Commission at the time of surrender.

Adopted by orders of the Supreme Court May 13, 2014, and August 19, 2014, eff. September 1, 2014.

RULE 4.0. CONTINUING EDUCATION

4.1. Applicability

These rules establish continuing education requirements for each of the professions regulated by the Judicial Branch Certification Commission. Additional continuing education requirements may be found in the rules for each program.

Adopted by orders of the Supreme Court May 13, 2014, and August 19, 2014, eff. September 1, 2014.

4.2. Continuing Education Requirement

A regulated person must obtain the minimum number of hours of continuing education required by the rules for the person's particular program. The person must obtain the required hours within the prescribed time period.

Adopted by orders of the Supreme Court May 13, 2014, and August 19, 2014, eff. September 1, 2014.

4.3. Approval of Continuing Education Courses

(a) Continuing education courses must be approved by the Commission. A continuing education course is an organized program of learning designed to increase or maintain the skills or competence of the regulated persons for whom it is intended. A continuing education course must be developed and presented by persons with education or experience in the subject matter of the course.

(b) The provider of a continuing education course may request approval of a course. To request approval of a course, a provider must file a completed application on the appropriate form published on the Commission's website.

(1) The application must be accompanied by an outline and materials that describe the course objectives and content, describe the teaching methods to be used, identify the presenters and provide their credentials, indicate the time allotted to each segment, and provide the date and location of the program.

(2) The course must comply with the course content requirements contained in the rules for the group of regulated persons to whom it will be offered.

(c) A regulated person may request approval of a continuing education course on the appropriate form published on the Commission's website.

(1) The person may request approval prior to the date that the course will be offered or at the time the person files a renewal application.

(2) The application must be accompanied by an outline and materials that describe the course content, identify the presenters, indicate the time allotted to each segment, and provide the date and location of the program.

(3) The course must comply with the course content requirements contained in the rules for the group of regulated persons to whom it will be or has been offered.

(d) The Director may approve or deny a request for approval of a continuing education course. Upon approval, the Director will determine the number of hours of continuing education for the course.

(e) The Commission will publish on its website a list of courses that are approved as continuing education.

(f) A continuing education provider whose course has been approved must retain participant course completion records for a period of three years after completion of the course. Upon request, a provider must provide information, including attendance records, to the Commission within 10 days of the request.

(g) A regulated person must obtain a certificate of attendance or other documentation from a continuing education course provider to prove the person's attendance or completion of all continuing education activity from the provider and submit the documentation to the Commission with the person's renewal application. The person must retain a copy of the documentation for a period of three years after completion of the course.

(h) A regulated person may appeal the Director's denial of a request for approval by submitting a written appeal to the Commission within 15 days of notification of the denial. The Commission must review the denial at its next regularly scheduled meeting. The regulated person will be notified of the Commission's decision not less than 15 days after the decision.

(i) The Commission, through the Director, may request additional information from a regulated person to verify the person's compliance with continuing education requirements.

(j) If a regulated person's certification or license expires and the person is permitted under these rules to renew late, the person must comply with the continuing education requirements for the person's profession. The continuing education credit must be earned during the certification or license period preceding expiration, or within the appropriate late renewal period. Continuing education credit earned during the late renewal period may not be used to satisfy the continuing education for the person's subsequent renewal period.

(k) The following do not qualify as continuing education activities under these rules:

(1) attendance at, or participation in, professional or association business meetings, general sessions, or policy making sessions;

(2) service on a committee or council or as an officer in a professional organization;

(3) activities completed to satisfy the requirements of a disciplinary action; and

(4) any activity completed as ordered by a judicial officer.

Adopted by orders of the Supreme Court May 13, 2014, and August 19, 2014, eff. September 1, 2014.

RULE 5.0. COMMISSION ENFORCEMENT

5.1. Investigations

The Commission, through the Director, may conduct investigations as necessary to enforce the laws administered by the Commission and these rules.

Adopted by orders of the Supreme Court May 13, 2014, and August 19, 2014, eff. September 1, 2014.

5.2. Subpoenas

(a) The Commission may issue a subpoena as provided by this rule. No party, complainant, or other person may request that the Commission issue a subpoena.

(b) The Commission may request and, if necessary, compel by subpoena:

(1) the production for inspection and copying of records, documents, and other evidence relevant to the investigation of an alleged violation of the Act, a law establishing a regulatory program administered by the Commission, a rule adopted under the Act, or an order issued by the Commission or Director; and

(2) the attendance of a witness for examination under oath.

(c) A subpoena under this rule may be issued throughout this State and may be served by any disinterested person designated by the Commission or the Director.

(d) The Commission, acting through the Attorney General, may bring an action to enforce a subpoena issued under this rule against a person who fails to comply with the subpoena.

(e) Venue for an action brought under this rule is in a district court in:

(1) Travis County; or

(2) any county in which the Commission may hold a hearing.

(f) The court must order compliance with the subpoena if the court finds that good cause exists to issue the subpoena.

Adopted by orders of the Supreme Court May 13, 2014, and August 19, 2014, eff. September 1, 2014.

5.3. Cease and Desist Orders

The Director may issue a cease and desist order if the Director determines that the action is necessary to prevent a violation of:

(a) the Act;

(b) a law establishing a regulatory program administered by the Commission; or

(c) a rule adopted under the Act or order issued by the Commission or the Director.

Adopted by orders of the Supreme Court May 13, 2014, and August 19, 2014, eff. September 1, 2014.

5.4. Administrative Sanctions—Denial, Revocation, Suspension, or Refusal to Renew; Reprimand; Probation

(a) The Commission may deny, revoke, suspend, or refuse to renew a certification, registration, or license or may reprimand a regulated person:

(1) for a violation of the Act, a law establishing a regulatory program administered by the Commission, a rule adopted under the Act, or an order issued by the Commission or Director; or

(2) based on the person's criminal history or other information as authorized by these rules.

(b) If the Commission revokes a certification, registration, or license, the Commission may state the length of the revocation in its order.

(c) Suspension.

(1) The Commission may suspend a certification, registration, or license:

(A) for a designated period of time, except that a court reporter's certification may not be suspended longer than 12 months;

(B) until the regulated person corrects the deficiencies that were the grounds for suspension; or

(C) until the regulated person complies with any conditions imposed by the Commission.

(2) A person who was suspended under (c)(1)(B) or (C) must apply for reinstatement.

(3) The Commission on its own motion may conduct a hearing to inquire into a suspension and may revoke the certification, registration, or license of a regulated person if it finds that the person has not corrected the deficiencies that were the grounds for the suspension or has not complied with the conditions imposed.

(d) The Commission may place on probation a person whose certification, registration, or license is suspended. If a certification, registration, or license suspension is probated, the Commission may require the person to:

(1) report regularly to the Commission on matters that are the basis of the probation;

(2) limit practice to the areas prescribed by the Commission; or

(3) complete professional education until the person attains a degree of skill satisfactory to the Commission in those areas that are the basis for the probation.

(e) The Commission must suspend a regulated person's certification, registration, or license pursuant to the provisions of Section 232.011 of the Family Code upon receipt of a final order issued under Chapter 232 of the Family Code. Pursuant to Section 232.011, the Commission must take such action without a hearing or additional review.

Adopted by orders of the Supreme Court May 13, 2014, and August 19, 2014, eff. September 1, 2014.

5.5. Injunction

(a) The Commission may apply to a district court in any county for an injunction to restrain a violation of the Act or a rule adopted under the Act.

(b) At the request of the Commission, the Attorney General must initiate and conduct an action in a district court in the State's name to obtain an injunction under Section 153.005 of the Government Code.

(c) If the State prevails in a suit under Section 153.005, the Attorney General may recover on behalf of the State reasonable attorney's fees, court costs, and reasonable investigative costs incurred in relation to the proceeding.

(d) The Commission may also request that a court having jurisdiction over a guardian remove the guardian under Section 1203.052(b) of the Estates Code.

Adopted by orders of the Supreme Court May 13, 2014, and August 19, 2014, eff. September 1, 2014.

5.6. Administrative Penalty and Administrative Sanction

(a) The Commission may impose an administrative penalty on a person regulated under the Act who violates the Act or a rule or standard adopted or order issued under the Act.

(b) A proceeding imposing an administrative penalty may be combined with a proceeding to impose an administrative sanction otherwise imposed under the Act.

Adopted by orders of the Supreme Court May 13, 2014, and August 19, 2014, eff. September 1, 2014.

5.7. Amount of Penalty

(a) The amount of an administrative penalty may not exceed $500 for each violation. Each day that a violation continues or occurs is a separate violation for purposes of imposing a penalty.

(b) The amount of the penalty may be based on:

(1) the seriousness of the violation, including the nature, circumstances, extent, and gravity of the violation;

(2) the threat to health or safety caused by the violation;

(3) any previous violations;

(4) the amount necessary to deter a future violation;

(5) whether the violator demonstrated good faith, including, when applicable, whether the violator made good faith efforts to correct the violation; and

(6) any other matter that justice may require.

Adopted by orders of the Supreme Court May 13, 2014, and August 19, 2014, eff. September 1, 2014.

5.8. Complaint Filing and Review; Report and Notice of Violation, Penalty, and Sanction

(a) A complaint against a regulated person may be filed by a person with personal knowledge of the alleged violation or by the Commission or a court of this State.

(b) A complainant, other than the Commission or a court, must use the complaint form provided on the Commission's website. The complaint must include the name and contact information of the complainant and the respondent, describe the factual basis for any allegations, and include any necessary documentation or other supporting materials or information. The complaint must be signed by the complainant and submitted to the Commission according to the instructions on the Commission's website.

(c) Upon receipt of a properly executed complaint, the Commission must send a copy of the complaint and any attachments to the respondent and direct the respondent to submit a written answer to the complaint under penalty of perjury, within 20 days of the date of the notice. The notice will be sent to the respondent's last known address in the Commission's records. If the respondent is a provisionally certified guardian, the Commission must also send a copy of the complaint and attachments to the guardian's supervisor. The respondent may request an extension of time to file an answer, but the request must be made before the expiration of the 20–day period.

(d) The Commission must refer a properly executed complaint and the results of any investigation conducted by the Commission to a review committee established by the Commission and comprised of members of the appropriate advisory board.

(1) The review committee must hold at least one meeting to review the complaint and answer, make the initial determination on whether a violation occurred, and recommend the imposition of a penalty, a sanction, or both.

(2) The review committee may hold additional meetings to consider a complaint or seek additional information, but it has no obligation to do so. The review committee is not an investigatory body and will generally render its recommendation to the Commission based on the submissions of the complainant and the respondent and the information gathered by an Office investigation.

(3) The complainant and the respondent may attend the review committee's meetings. The chair of the review committee may limit the length of comments made to the Committee.

(4) The review committee must make its recommendation to the Commission in writing and notify the respondent of its recommendation. If the review committee requests additional information, it may allow up to 30 days to provide the additional information.

(e) The Commission must review the determination and recommendation of the review committee, accept or revise the determination and recommendation as necessary, and give the respondent written notice by certified mail of the Commission's determination on whether a violation occurred and of each recommended penalty or sanction, if any. The notice will be sent to the respondent's last known address in the Commission's records.

(f) The notice required under (e) must:

(1) include a brief summary of the alleged violation;

(2) state the amount of any recommended penalty;

(3) state any recommended sanction; and

(4) inform the respondent of the respondent's right to a hearing on the occurrence of the violation, the amount of the penalty, or the imposition of the sanction.

(g) The Director may dismiss complaints that clearly do not allege misconduct or that are not within the Commission's jurisdiction. The Director must inform the Commission of all dismissals made under this rule. A person who files a complaint that is dismissed under this rule may request in writing that the Commission reconsider the complaint.

Adopted by orders of the Supreme Court May 13, 2014, and August 19, 2014, eff. September 1, 2014.

5.9. Penalty Paid, Sanction Accepted, or Hearing Requested

(a) Not later than the 20th day after the date that the respondent receives the notice sent under Rule 5.8(e), the respondent in writing may:

(1) accept the determination of the Commission and recommended penalty or sanction; or

(2) request a hearing on the occurrence of the violation, the imposition or amount of the penalty, or the imposition of the sanction.

(b) If the respondent accepts the determination and recommended penalty or sanction or fails to respond to the notice, the Commission by order must approve the determination and impose the recommended penalty or sanction.

Adopted by orders of the Supreme Court May 13, 2014, and August 19, 2014, eff. September 1, 2014.

5.10. Notice; Hearing

(a) If the respondent requests a hearing, the Commission must give the parties written notice of the hearing that includes the time, place, legal authority, and jurisdiction under which the hearing is held and the laws and rules related to the violation.

(b) The presiding officer of the Commission may hold prehearing conferences.

(c) The respondent may appear, testify, present evidence, and respond to questions from the Commission at the hearing. The complainant may appear and may testify at the discretion of the prosecutor and the presiding officer.

(d) A party may appear by telephone or videoconference or present the testimony of a witness by telephone or videoconference according to the procedures below.

(1) A party may request to appear by telephone or to present the testimony of a witness by telephone, upon timely motion stating the reason for the request, containing the pertinent telephone number, and affirmatively stating that the proposed witness will be the same person who appears telephonically at the hearing. A party may request to appear by videoconference or to present the testimony of a witness by videoconference, upon timely motion stating the reason for the request and the city in which the party or witness will be located at the time of the proceeding. A timely motion for telephone or videoconference appearance will not be deemed granted unless granted by written order of the presiding officer.

(2) The motion is timely if it is filed no later than 10 days before the hearing. The presiding officer may grant an exception to this requirement if it clearly appears from specific facts shown in writing that compliance with the deadline was not reasonably possible and that failure to meet the deadline was not the result of the negligence of the party.

(3) All substantive and procedural rights apply to telephone and videoconference proceedings, subject only to the limitations of the physical arrangement.

(4) Documentary evidence to be offered at a telephone or videoconference proceeding must be served on all parties and filed with the Commission at least seven days before the proceeding unless the presiding officer, by written order, amends the filing deadline. If a party intends to utilize documentary evidence with a witness at a telephone or videoconference proceeding, it is the offering party's responsibility to ensure that the witness has the document.

(5) For a telephone or videoconference proceeding, the following may be considered a failure to appear and grounds for default:

(A) failure to answer the telephone or videoconference line;

(B) failure to free the line for the proceeding; and

(C) failure to be ready to proceed as scheduled.

(e) At the request of the Commission, at least one member of the applicable advisory board review committee may attend the hearing to consult with the Commission on the reasons for the advisory board review committee's recommendations under Rule 5.8(d).

(f) At the hearing, the Commission must apply the general rules of evidence applicable in a district court, except that the Commission may admit and consider any information that the Commission determines is relevant, trustworthy, and necessary for a full and fair adjudication and determination of fact or law. The Commission may establish rules for the conduct of the hearing.

(g) The Commission will deliberate and announce its decision at the conclusion of the hearing. The Commission must make findings of fact and conclusions of law and must promptly issue an order on the occurrence of the violation, the amount of any penalty imposed, and the imposition of any sanction. The Commission must serve the respondent and the complainant with a copy of the order by certified mail with return receipt requested or by certified mail with electronic return receipt.

(h) The notice of the Commission's order under (g) must include a statement of the right of the respondent to appeal the order under Section 153.058 of the Government Code.

(i) The complainant and respondent are each responsible for their own costs of preparing for and attending the hearing.

(j) If the respondent fails to appear at the hearing:

(1) upon proof that notice of the hearing was given to the respondent, the Commission may proceed in the respondent's absence; and

(2) the factual allegations in the complaint may be deemed admitted.

(k) Proof that a document was sent to a party's last known address, as shown by the Commission's records, creates a rebuttable presumption that the document was received. The addressee's failure to claim a document that was properly addressed and served is insufficient to rebut the presumption.

Adopted by orders of the Supreme Court May 13, 2014, and August 19, 2014, effective September 1, 2014.

5.11. Options Following Decision: Pay, Accept, or Appeal

Not later than the 30th day after the date that the Commission issues an order imposing an administrative penalty or sanction, the respondent must:

(a) pay the penalty or accept the sanction; or

(b) file an appeal of the Commission's order contesting the occurrence of the violation, the imposition or amount of the penalty, or the imposition of the sanction.

Adopted by orders of the Supreme Court May 13, 2014, and August 19, 2014, eff. September 1, 2014.

5.12. Collection of Penalty

(a) If the respondent does not pay the penalty and the enforcement of the penalty is not stayed, the Attorney General may sue to collect the penalty and may recover reasonable expenses, including attorney's fees, incurred in recovering the penalty.

(b) A penalty collected under these rules will be deposited in the state treasury in the general revenue fund.

Adopted by orders of the Supreme Court May 13, 2014, and August 19, 2014, eff. September 1, 2014.

5.13. Appeal

(a) A person seeking to appeal an order that imposes a penalty or sanction must submit a written appeal of the order to the General Counsel of the Office within 30 days after the Commission's order is issued. The General Counsel must promptly forward the appeal to a special committee consisting of three Administrative Regional Presiding Judges.

(b) The committee will be chosen by the Presiding Judges, but the committee must not include the Presiding Judge for the administrative region in which the appellant resided at the time of the decision. If the alleged violation involves a certified guardian, the committee must consist of two Regional Presiding Judges and the Presiding Judge of the statutory probate courts.

(c) The General Counsel must notify the Commission of the filing of an appeal and, upon request, must make the appeal materials available to the Commission or its legal representative.

(d) The appeal must contain:

(1) a copy of the notice of the Commission's order with which the appellant is dissatisfied; and

(2) a statement succinctly explaining why the appellant is dissatisfied with the Commission's decision.

(e) The Office must adopt rules or policies to ensure that any Office employee who provides clerical, administrative, or other direct support to the Commission does not communicate regarding the substance of any appeal under this rule with any other Office employee who facilitates the appeal process under this rule. The rules or policies must also provide that Office employees may communicate regarding nonsubstantive aspects of appeals, such as to ensure the completeness and accuracy of appeal materials to be forwarded to the special committee.

(f) Upon receiving notice of an appeal of a disciplinary action imposing a penalty or sanction, the Commission must provide to the General Counsel, and the General Counsel must submit to the special committee, electronic or paper copies of the complaint and any original attachments, any written answer timely submitted by the appellant, notice of the Commission's decision imposing a penalty or sanction, and any other documents or written evidence considered by the Commission pertaining to the decision complained of on appeal. The Commission must provide a copy of these items to an appellant upon request, and may charge costs for such copies as set forth in Rule 12.7 of the Rules of Judicial Administration.

(g) Absent approval by the special committee, submission of materials other than those described in (f) is prohibited. The special committee may, in its sole discretion, allow an appellant to submit additional written materials relating to the appeal. Otherwise, only the written materials described in (f) will be considered. A request to submit additional materials must clearly identify the additional materials for which inclusion is requested.

(h) The special committee must consider the appeal under an abuse of discretion standard of review for all issues except issues involving questions of law. The standard of review for issues involving questions of law is de novo. Under either standard, the burden is on the appellant to establish that the Commission's decision was erroneous.

(i) The special committee may consider the appeal without a hearing and may conduct its deliberations by any appropriate means. The special committee may, in its sole discretion, conduct a hearing and allow testimony from the appellant or any other person with knowledge of the underlying facts relating to the disciplinary action complained of.

(j) The special committee may confer in writing with a certification, registration, or license holder who is in the same profession as the appellant if the special committee provides to the appellant:

(1) notice of the special committee's request for information; and

(2) a copy of the certification, registration, or license holder's response.

(k) If the special committee sustains the finding that a violation occurred, the special committee may:

(1) uphold or reduce the amount of any penalty and order the appellant to pay the full or reduced amount of the penalty; and

(2) uphold or reduce any sanction and order the imposition of the sanction.

(*l*) If the special committee does not sustain the finding that a violation occurred, the special committee must order that a penalty is not owed and that a sanction may not be imposed.

(m) If the appellant paid the penalty and if the amount of the penalty is reduced or the penalty is not upheld by the special committee, the special committee must order that the appropriate amount plus accrued interest be remitted to the appellant not later than the 30th day after the date the judgment of the special committee becomes final. The interest accrues at the rate charged on loans to depository institutions by the New York Federal Reserve Bank. The interest must be paid for the period beginning on the date the penalty is paid and ending on the date the penalty is remitted.

(n) The special committee must notify the Commission and appellant in writing of its decision. No rehearing or further appeal is allowed.

Adopted by orders of the Supreme Court May 13, 2014, and August 19, 2014, eff. September 1, 2014.

5.14. Disposition by Agreement

(a) Any disciplinary matter may be disposed of by agreement, unless precluded by law. The agreement must be in writing and may be in the form of a stipulation, a settlement agreement, or a consent order.

(b) The Commission may designate its presiding officer or the Director to adopt or reject an agreement.

(c) The agreement must:

(1) include proposed findings of fact and conclusions of law; and

(2) be signed by all parties to the agreement and their representatives.

(d) Upon receipt of the agreement, the Commission or the Director may:

(1) adopt the agreement and issue a final order;

(2) reject the agreement and remand the disciplinary matter for a hearing before the Commission;

(3) reject the agreement and order further investigation by the Director; or

(4) take such other action as the Commission or the Director find just.

Adopted by orders of the Supreme Court May 13, 2014, and August 19, 2014, eff. September 1, 2014.

5.15. Alternative Dispute Resolution

(a) In addition to the procedures under Rule 5.14, the Commission encourages the resolution and early settlement of all contested disciplinary matters through voluntary settlement procedures.

(b) At any time after the filing of a complaint against a regulated person, the Director may initiate a settlement conference on the Director's own motion or at the request of any party. Settlement conferences are voluntary.

(c) The complainant and the respondent are the parties in a settlement conference. The Commission (through one or more Commission members, Office staff, or counsel) may also participate as a party in a settlement conference at the sole option of the presiding officer.

(d) A settlement conference may be used to reach agreement about all or a portion of the ultimate issues in a disciplinary matter or to reach agreement about how to handle disputed matters. The parties may use a mediator for a settlement conference or conduct the settlement conference without a mediator.

(e) The complainant and the respondent may not bind the Commission to any resolution of a disciplinary matter pending before the Commission. The presiding officer may appoint one or more Commission members or staff to attend the settlement conference. The Commission representative must participate in the proceedings in an effort to resolve the dispute within the parameters of any instructions received from the Commission.

(f) In the event a settlement of some or all of the disputed issues is reached during the settlement conference, the Commission must review the terms of the settlement at the next regularly scheduled Commission meeting. The Commission may accept the settlement terms, reject the settlement terms and restore all proceedings on the disciplinary matter to the status quo as it existed immediately prior to the settlement conference, or refer the matter for further negotiation.

(g) The parties may agree to retain a mediator to assist with the settlement conference.

(1) The parties must notify the presiding officer in writing of their agreement to retain a mediator. That notice must include the name, address, and telephone number of the mediator selected; a statement that the parties have entered into an agreement with the mediator as to rate and method of his or her compensation; and an affirmation that the mediator is qualified to serve.

(2) Upon receipt of a properly filed notice under (1), the presiding officer will enter an order referring the case to the mediator.

(h) If the parties do not agree to a mediator, the presiding officer may appoint an individual to serve as mediator in the settlement conference.

(i) An individual appointed to serve as a mediator under (g) or (h) must meet the qualifications set forth in the Civil Practice and Remedies Code Section 154.052. Pursuant to Section 154.052(c) of the Code, an individual who has served as a judge in Texas may be appointed to serve as a mediator.

(j) The Commission will not pay any fees or costs associated with a settlement conference unless good cause is shown and the Commission and Office agree to do so prior to the settlement conference.

(k) All communications in the settlement conference between or among the parties, and between each party and mediator, if any, are confidential under the same terms as provided in Section 154.053 of the Civil Practice and Remedies Code. Information shared with the mediator in separate meetings will not be given to any other party unless the party sharing the information explicitly gives the mediator permission to do so. Material provided to the mediator is not required to be provided to the other parties and will not be filed or become a record in the disciplinary proceedings. Notes taken during the settlement conference by the parties and the mediator must be destroyed at the end of the process.

(*l*) Any agreement reached by the parties will be reduced to writing and signed by the parties before the end of the settlement conference. These writings may be informal in nature. The parties may agree that the written agreement remain confidential if there is no requirement of law to the contrary. Any part of the agreement that may affect the disposition of the disciplinary proceeding (such as agreements concerning relevant facts) must be filed in the record of the disciplinary proceeding.

(m) If the parties use a mediator for the settlement conference, the mediator must maintain confidentiality in accordance with Section 2009.054 of the Government Code. The mediator may not communicate to the Commission matters discussed with the parties in the settlement conference. The mediator will report to the Commission in writing whether the settlement conference resulted in a settlement of the matter in dispute, or other stipulations or matters that the parties agreed be reported.

(n) Required Filings. The following documents must be filed with the Commission: any request for the appointment of a mediator, any objection to the referral of the matter to a settlement conference, any objection to the appointment of a mediator, any notice required to be given, any settlement agreement, any report prepared by the mediator, and any similar documents as may become necessary or appropriate in the course of the settlement conference.

Adopted by orders of the Supreme Court May 13, 2014, and August 19, 2014, eff. September 1, 2014.

RULE 6.0. COURT REPORTERS CERTIFICATION AND SHORTHAND REPORTING FIRMS REGISTRATION

6.1. Definitions

(a) **Advisory Board** means the Court Reporters Certification Advisory Board.

(b) **Certification** means a certification issued by the Supreme Court of Texas on the Commission's recommendation.

(c) **Code of Professional Conduct** means the Code of Professional Conduct for Certified Shorthand Reporters and Court Reporting Firms approved by the Supreme Court of Texas.

(d) **Court reporter** and **shorthand reporter** mean a person who engages in shorthand reporting.

(e) **Court reporting** and **shorthand reporting** mean the practice of shorthand reporting for use in litigation in the courts of this State by making a verbatim record of an oral court proceeding, deposition, or proceeding before a grand jury, referee, or court commissioner using written symbols in shorthand, machine shorthand, or oral stenography.

(f) Court reporting firm, shorthand reporting firm, and **affiliate office** mean an entity wholly or partly in the business of providing court reporting or other related services in this State. A court reporting firm, shorthand reporting firm, or affiliate office is considered to be providing court reporting or other related services in this State if:

(1) any act that constitutes a court reporting service or shorthand reporting service occurs wholly or partly in this State;

(2) the firm or affiliate office recruits a resident of this State through an intermediary located inside or outside of this State to provide court reporting services, shorthand reporting services, or other related services in this State; or

(3) the firm or affiliate office contracts with a resident of this State by mail or otherwise and either party is to perform court reporting services, shorthand reporting services, or other related services wholly or partly in this State.

(g) **Official court reporter** means the shorthand reporter appointed by a judge under Section 52.041 of the Government Code as the official court reporter for a particular court.

(h) **Registration** means a registration issued by the Commission.

(i) **RPR** means the Registered Professional Reporter certification issued by the National Court Reporters Association.

(j) **Uniform Format Manual** means the manual approved by the Supreme Court of Texas that governs the form of official reporters' records and freelance transcriptions.

Adopted by orders of the Supreme Court May 13, 2014, and August 19, 2014, eff. September 1, 2014.

6.2. Requirement of Certification or Registration

(a) A person may not engage in shorthand reporting in this State or be appointed as an official court reporter or deputy court reporter unless that person is certified as a shorthand reporter by the Supreme Court of Texas.

(1) A certification must be for one or more of the following methods of shorthand reporting:

(A) written shorthand;

(B) machine shorthand;

(C) oral stenography; or

(D) any other method of shorthand reporting authorized by the Supreme Court.

(2) A person may not assume or use the title or designation "court recorder," "court reporter" or "shorthand reporter," or any abbreviation, title, designation, words, letters, sign, card, or device tending to indicate that the person is a court reporter or shorthand reporter, unless the person is certified as a shorthand reporter by the Supreme Court of Texas. Nothing in this rule must be construed to either sanction or prohibit the use of electronic court recording equipment operated by a noncertified court reporter pursuant and according to rules adopted or approved by the Supreme Court of Texas.

(b) A court reporting firm and its affiliate offices must register with the Commission. Unless a firm and its affiliate offices are registered with the Commission, the firm must not:

(1) use the title or designation "court recording firm," "court reporting firm," or "shorthand reporting firm" or any abbreviation, title, designation, words, letters, sign, card, or device tending to indicate that the firm is a court reporting firm or shorthand reporting firm; or

(2) offer services as a court reporting firm or shorthand reporting firm, unless the firm and its affiliate offices are registered with the Commission.

(c) A certification or registration expires at 12:01 a.m. on January 1 following the second anniversary of the date on which it was issued unless the certification or registration is renewed before that time pursuant to Rule 6.3(d)(1). Thereafter, the certification or registration expires at 12:01 a.m. on each second January 1 unless renewed.

(d) These rules do not apply to:

(1) a party to the litigation involved, the party's attorney, or a full-time employee of either; or

(2) court reporting services performed outside of this State by a shorthand reporter who is not certified in this State for use in a court proceeding in this State, provided that the work resulting from those services is produced and billed wholly outside of this State.

(e) Subject to the requirements of Rule 6.4(d) and (e), nothing in these rules should be construed to prohibit the employment of a noncertified shorthand reporter until a certified shorthand reporter is available in the judicial district where services of a shorthand reporter are desired.

(f) To qualify for certification, a person must:

(1) satisfy the requirements of Section 3.0 of these rules;

(2) pass an examination as required by the Commission in one or more of the methods of shorthand reporting authorized by Rule 6.2(a)(1); and

(3) be a high school graduate or possess the GED equivalent.

(g) Examination procedures.

(1) To take an examination, an applicant for certification must file the required forms and pay the required fees according to the deadlines established by the Commission.

(2) Prior to or simultaneously with the submission of an applicant's application to take Part A of the examination, the applicant must submit a statement of proficiency.

(A) The statement of proficiency must be on the form provided by the Commission and must contain the certification of a court reporting school instructor.

(B) If the applicant attended and learned court reporting skills at a court reporting school, the statement of proficiency must be countersigned by the appropriate administrative officer of the school.

(C) The person making the certification required in (A) must certify that the applicant has satisfactorily passed at the rate of 95% accuracy at least two tests on new material of each of the following:

(i) five minutes of two-voice dictation of questions and answers given at 225 words per minute;

(ii) five minutes of dictation of a jury charge given at 200 words per minute; and

(iii) five minutes of dictation of selected literary material given at 180 words per minute.

(D) The tests required by (C) must be administered and graded by the person who certifies the applicant's statement of proficiency and must be taken by the method of shorthand reporting for which the applicant has applied for examination. The two tests must have been taken and passed no more than one year apart.

(E) The applicant may not be deemed eligible to take an examination until the Commission receives the statement of proficiency.

(F) If the Commission has on file a valid statement of proficiency for an applicant, the applicant is not required to file a new statement of proficiency. A statement of proficiency is valid for one year from the date of the last proficiency test described in (C) and must be valid on the date of the examination for which the applicant has applied.

(G) In lieu of the statement of proficiency, an applicant who is certified as an RPR or pursuant to a national examination that the Commission determines is of equivalent or greater degree of difficulty than the RPR examination may submit a letter from the certifying organization.

(H) The letter submitted under (G) must:

(i) be an original on the certifying organization's letterhead;

(ii) state the certification that the applicant has attained and the date the certification expires; and

(iii) attest that the applicant has passed the exam for the certification and is currently certified and in good standing.

(I) The national certification must be valid on the date of the Texas examination for which the applicant has applied.

(J) The letter submitted under (G) is valid until the next expiration date of the applicant's national certification.

(h) Each examination will be given in two parts to be designated Part A and Part B.

(1) Part A component.

(A) Part A will be composed of five minutes of two-voice dictation of questions and answers given at 225 words per minute, five minutes of dictation of a jury charge given at 200 words per minute, and five minutes of dictation of selected literary material given at 180 words per minute.

(B) Each applicant must personally take down the test and must reduce the takedown to writing.

(C) The minimum passing grade on each section of Part A is 95% accuracy. An error will be charged for:

(i) each wrong word;

(ii) each omitted word;

(iii) each added word not dictated;

(iv) each contraction where read as two words;

(v) two words where read as a contraction;

(vi) each misplaced word;

(vii) each misplaced period that materially alters the sense of a group of words or a sentence;

(viii) each misspelled word;

(ix) each plural or singular if the opposite was dictated; and

(x) each wrong number.

(D) Applicants may use a dictionary during Part A.

(E) Applicants will be allowed three hours to complete the transcription of Part A of the test. If time permits, an applicant may review his or her transcript but may use only the original takedown from which the transcript was prepared to review the transcript.

(2) Part B component.

(A) Part B of the test must consist of objective questions touching on elementary aspects of court reporting, spelling, and grammar and Texas rules and procedure.

(B) Applicants may not use a dictionary during Part B.

(C) The minimum passing grade on Part B is 75%.

(3) Notwithstanding Rule 3.11(d), an applicant who passes Part A or Part B of the examination but fails the other part will not be required to be reexamined on the part that the applicant passed.

(i) An applicant who fails an examination may request that the examination be regraded by sending a written request to the Commission office within 20 days of the date of notice that the applicant has failed the examination. If the examination is regraded, the Commission will inform the applicant of the results of the regrading. Upon receipt of the regrading results, the applicant may request a personal review of the examination with a member of the advisory board. The request for a personal review must be in writing and filed within twenty days of the notice of regrading results.

(j) The Commission must certify to the Supreme Court of Texas the names of applicants who have completed all application requirements and are determined on examination to be qualified in professional shorthand reporting. In its certification, the Commission must specify the method or methods of reporting used by each successful applicant in taking the examination.

(k) A person certified under Chapter 52 of the Government Code prior to September 1, 1983, may retain a general certification authorizing the person to use any method of shorthand reporting authorized in Rule 6.2(a)(1), provided that the person keeps the certification in continuous effect.

(*l*) To register, a court reporting firm or affiliate office must pay all required fees and register on a form provided by the Commission. The registration form must state whether any officers, directors, or managerial employees of the firm or affiliate office have been finally convicted of a felony or misdemeanor other than a minor traffic offense or juvenile offense.

(m) The Commission may:

(1) refuse to certify to the Supreme Court the application of a person who was finally convicted of an offense that directly relates to the duties and responsibilities of a certified court reporter as determined using the factors listed in Rule 3.5; or

(2) refuse to register a court reporting firm or affiliate office if an officer, director, or managerial employee of the firm or affiliate office was finally convicted of a felony or misdemeanor that directly relates to providing court reporting services as determined using the factors listed in Rule 3.5.

Adopted by orders of the Supreme Court May 13, 2014, and August 19, 2014, eff. September 1, 2014.

6.3. Renewal of Certification or Registration

(a) Notwithstanding Rule 3.2(b), not later than the 30th day before the date a court reporter's or court reporting firm's certification or registration is scheduled to expire, the Commission will notify the reporter or firm of the impending expiration at the reporter's or firm's last known address according to the Commission's records. Failure to receive the notice does not exempt a court reporter or a court reporting firm from any requirements of these rules.

(b) Nonrenewal due to student loan default.

(1) The Commission must not renew the certification of a certified shorthand reporter who is designated to be in default on loans guaranteed by the Texas Guaranteed Student Loan Corporation (TGSLC) under Section 57.491(c) of the Education Code unless the reporter presents to the Board a certificate issued by TGSLC certifying that:

(A) the reporter has entered a repayment agreement on the defaulted loan; or

(B) the reporter is not in default on a loan guaranteed by TGSLC.

(2) The Commission must not renew the certification of a certified shorthand reporter who is designated to be in default on a repayment agreement with TGSLC under Section 57.491(g) of the Education Code unless the reporter presents to the Commission a certificate issued by TGSLC certifying that:

(A) the reporter has entered another repayment agreement on the defaulted loan; or

(B) the reporter is not in default on a loan guaranteed by TGSLC or on a repayment agreement.

(3) The Commission must provide a certified shorthand reporter an opportunity for a hearing under the procedures set out in Rule 5.10 prior to taking action concerning nonrenewal of certification for default on a student loan.

(c) To qualify for renewal of certification or registration, a certified court reporter, court reporting firm, or affiliate office must pay all required fees, submit all required forms, and comply with renewal procedures. In addition, certified court reporters must comply with the Commission's continuing education requirements in Rules 4.1–4.3 and 6.6. An application for renewal must state:

(1) if the applicant is a court reporter, whether the applicant has been finally convicted of a criminal offense other than a minor traffic offense since the reporter's last certification;

(2) if the applicant is a court reporting firm or affiliate office, whether an officer, director, or managerial employee has been finally convicted of a criminal offense other than a minor traffic offense since the firm's or affiliate office's last registration; and

(3) if the applicant is a court reporter, whether the applicant has ever been the subject of a disciplinary action by a licensing authority in another jurisdiction requiring certification, registration, or licensure to provide court reporting services, and whether the applicant is the subject of a pending disciplinary action before the Commission, including actions in which the Commission imposed a sanction that has not been completed.

(d) Renewal before and after expiration.

(1) A person who is otherwise eligible to renew a certification or registration may renew an unexpired certification or registration by paying the required renewal fee and submitting the required forms to the Commission before the expiration of the certification or registration.

(2) A person whose certification or registration has expired may not engage in activities that require a certification or registration until the certification or registration has been renewed.

(3) A person whose certification or registration has been expired for less than one year may renew the certification or registration by paying to the Commission the appropriate renewal fee.

(4) A person whose certification or registration has been expired for one year or more may not renew the certification or registration. The person may obtain a new certification or registration by complying with the requirements and procedures for obtaining an original certification or registration, including the examination requirements.

(5) A person who was certified as a court reporter in this State, moved to another state, and is currently certified and has been in practice in the other state for the two years preceding the date of application may obtain a new certification without reexamination if the person:

(A) submits appropriate renewal forms and documentation showing that the person has complied with the continuing education requirements in the Commission's rules;

(B) pays the appropriate renewal fee;

(C) submits documentation from the other state indicating that the person is currently licensed, has been licensed for the two years immediately preceding the application for renewal in Texas, and is in good standing; and

(D) submits documentation from the person's employer showing that the person has been working for at least two consecutive years prior to the date of application in Texas.

(6) The documentation required under (d)(5)(D) must include the beginning date of the person's employment and must be original, notarized, and on the employer's letterhead. If the person has been employed by more than one employer during the two-year period, the person must submit documentation from each employer showing the beginning and ending date of the person's employment.

Adopted by orders of the Supreme Court May 13, 2014, and August 19, 2014, eff. September 1, 2014.

6.4. Responsibilities of Certified Court Reporters

(a) A certified court reporter is entitled to use the title "Certified Shorthand Reporter" or the abbreviation "CSR." A certified shorthand reporter may administer oaths to witnesses anywhere in this State.

(b) The transcription of any proceeding and any other document certified by a certified shorthand reporter for use in litigation in the courts of this State must contain a signed certification in the form required by the Uniform Format Manual.

(c) A certification of a transcript of a court proceeding by an official court reporter must contain a signed certificate in the form required by the Uniform Format Manual.

(d) A noncertified shorthand reporter may report an oral deposition only if:

(1) the noncertified reporter delivers an affidavit to the parties or to their counsel present at the deposition stating that a certified shorthand reporter is not available; or

(2) the parties or their counsel stipulate on the record at the beginning of the deposition that a certified shorthand reporter is not available.

(e) A noncertified shorthand reporter who is employed when a certified shorthand reporter is not available must include with the certification of a transcription of a court proceeding an affidavit that no certified shorthand reporter was available to perform the duties of the court reporter.

(f) Official court reporters, deputy court reporters, and substitute court reporters must comply with the Act, Chapter 52 of the Government Code, and all applicable provisions of the Texas Rules of Appellate Procedure in conducting of the business of their offices.

Adopted by orders of the Supreme Court May 13, 2014, and August 19, 2014, eff. September 1, 2014.

6.5. Enforcement

(a) After notice and an opportunity for a hearing under Rule 5.10, the Commission must reprimand, assess a reasonable fine against, or suspend, revoke, or refuse to renew a shorthand reporter's certification for:

(1) fraud or corruption;

(2) dishonesty;

(3) willful or negligent violation or failure of duty;

(4) incompetence;

(5) fraud or misrepresentation in obtaining certification;

(6) a final conviction of an offense that directly relates to the duties and responsibilities of a certified shorthand reporter, as determined using the factors listed in Rule 3.5;

(7) engaging in the practice of shorthand reporting using a method for which the reporter is not certified or while certification is suspended;

(8) unprofessional conduct, including but not limited to:

(A) failing to deliver a transcript or statement of facts to a client or court in a timely manner as determined by statute, court order, or agreement;

(B) producing an inaccurate transcript or statement of facts;

(C) producing an incomplete transcript or statement of facts except upon order of a court, agreement of the parties, or request of a party;

(D) failing to disclose as soon as practical to the parties or their attorneys existing or past financial, business, professional, family, or social relationships, including contracts for court reporting services, that might reasonably create an appearance of partiality;

(E) advertising or representing falsely the qualifications of a certified shorthand reporter or that an unlicensed individual is a certified shorthand reporter;

(F) failing to charge all parties or their attorneys to an action the same price for an original transcript or statement of facts and failing to charge all parties or their attorneys the same price for a copy of a transcript or statement of facts or for like services performed in an action;

(G) failing to disclose in writing to all parties or their attorneys upon request at any time an itemization of all rates and charges to all parties or their attorneys;

(H) reporting any proceeding if the reporter is related to a party or their attorney within the second degree by affinity or consanguinity unless:

(i) as soon as practicable, the reporter discloses the relationship in writing to all parties and the court; and

(ii) either

A. no objection to the use of the reporter on the grounds of the relationship is made by any party or the court within a reasonable period after the disclosure; or

B. the court enters an order finding that, under the circumstances, the relationship does not create an appearance of partiality and that good cause exists to permit use of the reporter;

(I) reporting a proceeding if the reporter is financially interested in the action or is associated with a firm that is financially interested in the action;

(J) failing to notify all parties or their attorneys of a request for a transcript or statement of facts, or any part thereof, in sufficient time for copies to be prepared and delivered simultaneously with the original;

(K) going "off the record" during a deposition when not agreed to by all parties or their attorneys unless ordered to do so by the court;

(L) giving, directly or indirectly, benefiting from, or being employed as a result of any gift, incentive, reward, or anything of value to attorneys, clients, or their representatives or agents, except for nominal items that do not exceed $100 in the aggregate per recipient per year;

(M) charging for a copy at a rate more than one-third the per page cost of the original and first copy; and

(N) failing to comply with the requirements of the Uniform Format Manual for Texas Court Reporters;

(9) entering into or providing services under a prohibited contract described by Section 154.115 of the Government Code;

(10) committing any other act that violates Chapter 154 of the Government Code, a rule adopted under the Act, or a provision of the Code of Professional Conduct; or

(11) other sufficient cause.

(b) In this rule, an officer, director, or managerial employee of a shorthand reporting firm or affiliate office will be referred to as "a principal." After notice and an opportunity for a hearing under Rule 5.10, the Commission may reprimand, assess a reasonable fine against, or suspend, revoke, or refuse to renew the registration of a shorthand reporting firm or affiliate office for:

(1) fraud or corruption;

(2) dishonesty;

(3) conduct on the part of a principal if the principal orders, encourages, or permits conduct that the principal knows or should have known violates this chapter;

(4) failure of a principal to take reasonable remedial action to avoid or mitigate the consequences of conduct by a person who the principal knows or should have known violated this chapter and over whom the principal has direct supervisory authority;

(5) fraud or misrepresentation in obtaining registration;

(6) a final conviction of a principal of a felony or misdemeanor that directly relates to providing court reporting services, as determined under Rule 3.5;

(7) engaging the services of a reporter that the shorthand reporting firm or affiliate office knew or should have known was using a method for which the reporter is not certified;

(8) knowingly providing court reporting services while the shorthand reporting firm's or affiliate office's registration is suspended or engaging the services of a shorthand reporter whose certification was suspended if a principal knew or should have known of the suspension;

(9) unprofessional conduct, including a pattern of giving (directly or indirectly), benefiting from, or being employed as a result of giving any gift, incentive, reward, or anything of value to attorneys, clients, or their representatives or agents, except for nominal items that do not exceed $100 in the aggregate for each recipient each year—provided, however, that nothing in this rule should be construed to define providing value-added business services, including long-term volume discounts, such as the pricing of products and services, as prohibited gifts, incentives, or rewards;

(10) entering into or providing services under a prohibited contract described by Section 154.115 of the Government Code;

(11) committing any other act that violates Chapter 154 of the Government Code, a rule adopted under the Act, or a provision of the Code of Professional Conduct; or

(12) other sufficient cause.

(c) When a certified shorthand reporter or court reporting firm reports an alleged violation to the Commission pursuant to the reporting obligation in the Code of Professional Conduct, the information must be provided in writing and must be signed by the person providing the information and accompanied by pertinent documentation, if any.

Adopted by orders of the Supreme Court May 13, 2014, and August 19, 2014, eff. September 1, 2014.

6.6. Continuing Education

(a) A certified court reporter must complete at least 10 hours of approved continuing education during each certification period. The 10 hours must include a minimum of 2.5 hours in ethics, Texas rules, or both.

(b) The required hours must be earned prior to the expiration of the certified court reporter's certification period.

(c) Notwithstanding Rule 4.3(c)(1), a certified court reporter must submit requests for approval of continuing education by September 30 of the year that the reporter's certification expires.

(d) Continuing education may be earned by:

(1) verified attendance or participation in an approved program, activity, or course;

(2) verified personal preparation of educational presentations pertaining to the profession of court reporting or serving as an instructor, speaker, or panel member at an approved continuing education course; or

(3) writing articles pertaining to the court reporting profession that are published in a state or nationally recognized professional journal of court reporting or law—provided, however, that no more

than 2.5 hours may be earned under this category during any one certification period.

(e) Credit earned under (d)(2) will be awarded as follows:

(1) for participation as an instructor in an approved continuing education program, the number of hours approved for attendees of the presentation; and

(2) for preparation time, up to 2.5 hours.

(f) A court reporter may earn preparation and teaching credit for instructing an approved continuing education course only one time per certification period.

(g) An article submitted under (d)(3) must be approved by the Director to receive continuing education credit. Credit will not be allowed for the same article published in more than one publication.

(h) All courses must be relevant to the needs of court reporters and the reporting service needs of users and must:

(1) contribute to the advancement, extension, and enhancement of the professional skills and knowledge of the individual in the practice of shorthand reporting;

(2) include at least one subject that is directly related to the court reporter's ability to produce accurate and timely transcripts, such as:

(A) English, including grammar, linguistics, and transcript styles;

(B) medicine, including terminology, techniques, and concepts likely to be encountered during litigation;

(C) the legal system, including litigation procedures and substantive presentations on various specialties within the law;

(D) technology-related subjects, including terminology and concepts likely to be encountered during litigation (e.g., accident reconstruction) and technological developments in the field of court reporting (e.g., computer technology);

(E) transcript preparation; or

(F) business management, including financial issues, personnel issues, and time management.

(i) In addition to the activities listed in Rule 4.3(k), the following do not qualify as continuing education activities for certified court reporters under these rules:

(1) entertainment and recreation;

(2) tours or visiting exhibits;

(3) any function for which the court reporter receives remuneration as part of his or her regular employment;

(4) courses that emphasize nonverbal skills (e.g., golf, tennis, dancing, basket-weaving, CPR or first aid courses, floral design, etc.);

(5) any activity completed before the first renewal period for which the renewal applicant is required to obtain continuing education; and

(6) reading books or articles or submitting book reviews, article reviews, or tests (including those books and accompanying tests that are part of the approved reading list of the National Court Reporters Association).

Adopted by orders of the Supreme Court May 13, 2014, and August 19, 2014, eff. September 1, 2014.

RULE 7.0. GUARDIANSHIP CERTIFICATION

7.1. Definitions

(a) **Certified guardian** means a person who is certified by the Commission to provide guardianship services in this State.

(b) **Corporate fiduciary** has the meaning assigned by Section 1002.007 of the Estates Code.

(c) **Engaged in the business of providing guardianship services** means to perform, offer to perform, or advertise the performance of guardianship services for compensation.

(d) **Guardian** has the meaning assigned by Section 1002.012 of the Estates Code.

(e) **Guardianship program** means a local, county, or regional program that provides guardianship and related services to an incapacitated person or other person who needs assistance in making decisions concerning the person's own welfare or financial affairs.

(f) **Guardianship services** means conducting, performing, or administering the duties and powers prescribed by the Estates Code or under a court order in a guardianship matter.

(g) **Incapacitated person** has the meaning assigned by Section 1002.017 of the Estates Code.

(h) **Minimum Standards for Guardianship Services** means the Minimum Standards for Guardianship Services promulgated under Section 155.101 of the Government Code.

(i) **Private professional guardian** means a person, other than an attorney or a corporate fiduciary, who is engaged in the business of providing guardianship services.

(j) **Provisionally certified guardian** means a person who has received provisional certification to provide guardianship services in this State from the Commission.

(k) **Supervisor** means a certified guardian who has notified the Commission that he or she will be responsible for overseeing an applicant for provisional certification.

(*l*) **Volunteer** means a person who renders guardianship services on behalf of a guardianship program or on behalf of the Department of Aging and Disability Services and who does not receive compensation that exceeds the authorized expenses that the person incurs in performing those services.

(m) **Ward** has the meaning assigned by Section 1002.030 of the Estates Code.

Adopted by orders of the Supreme Court May 13, 2014, and August 19, 2014, eff. September 1, 2014.

7.2. Requirement of Certification

(a) To provide guardianship services in this State, the following individuals must be certified by the Commission:

(1) an individual who is a private professional guardian;

(2) an individual who will provide those services to a ward of a private professional guardian on the guardian's behalf;

(3) an individual, other than a volunteer, who will provide those services, or other services under Section 161.114, Human Resources Code, to a ward of a guardianship program or the Department of Aging and Disability Services on the program's or department's behalf; and

(4) a person who at any time supervises direct providers of guardianship services, unless the person is exempt under Section 155.001(6) of the Government Code.

(b) To be eligible for certification, a person must:

(1) satisfy the requirements of Section 3.0 of these rules;

(2) be at least 21 years of age;

(3) be a high school graduate or possess the GED equivalent;

(4) have two years of relevant work experience related to guardianship or have met the following education or training requirements:

(A) a minimum of a bachelor's degree conferred by a college or university accredited by an organization recognized by the Texas Higher Education Coordinating Board in a field related to guardianship; or

(B) completion of a course curriculum or training specifically related to guardianship approved by the Commission;

(5) successfully pass, after no more than four exam attempts, an examination approved by the Commission that covers Texas law and procedure related to guardianship and any other examination required and approved by the Commission testing knowledge of guardianship issues;

(6) attest under penalty of perjury whether he or she has ever been adjudged guilty of, or entered a plea of guilty or no contest in return for a grant of deferred adjudication with respect to, any felony or misdemeanor offense, which will be considered using the factors listed in Rule 3.5; and

(7) attest under penalty of perjury whether he or she:

(A) has ever been relieved of responsibilities as a guardian or fiduciary by a court, employer, or client for actions involving fraud, moral turpitude, misrepresentation, material omission, misappropriation, theft, assault, battery, abuse, neglect, breach of trust, breach of fiduciary duty, or conversion;

(B) has ever been found civilly liable or settled a claim in an action, including but not limited to a surcharge action, that involved allegations of fraud, misrepresentation, material omission, misappropriation, theft, assault, battery, abuse, neglect, breach of trust, breach of fiduciary duty, or conversion on the applicant's part;

(C) has ever been denied certification or had his or her certification revoked or suspended in Texas or any other jurisdiction that requires certification, registration, or licensure to provide guardianship services; or

(D) has ever surrendered his or her certification in Texas or any other jurisdiction that requires certification, registration, or licensure to provide guardianship certification.

(c) If any of the circumstances described in (b)(6) or (7) exist, the applicant must describe the circumstances with particularity and provide any related documentation requested by the Commission.

(d) Examination.

(1) An individual who has failed the exam four times is not eligible for certification unless the individual petitions the Commission in writing for permission to take the exam again. The petition must set out in detail all facts that support the request, demonstrate that the individual has completed all other requirements for certification except

for passing the exam, and demonstrate that no other impediments to certification exist.

(2) The Commission must consider the petition at its next regularly scheduled meeting and determine, without a formal hearing, whether permission to take the exam again will be granted or denied. The Commission may impose conditions to granting permission, including requiring the petitioner to provide additional information or complete specified continuing education prior to taking the exam again. If an individual fails or refuses to strictly and completely comply with the conditions specified by the Commission, permission to take the exam again will be denied.

(3) An individual may petition the Commission only one time for permission to take the exam following four unsuccessful attempts. An individual who is granted permission to take the exam again and who fails the exam again is not eligible for certification. If the Commission denies permission to take the exam again, the individual is not eligible for certification.

(4) The decision of the Commission is final and is not subject to appeal, reconsideration, or any further action.

(e) Notwithstanding Rule 7.2(a), an individual who must be certified but does not meet the requirements for certification under Rule 7.2(b) may provide guardianship services in this State if the person obtains provisional certification pursuant to Rule 7.4.

(f) Notwithstanding any other provision of these rules:

(1) pursuant to Section 1104.253 of the Estates Code, a family member or friend of an incapacitated person is not required to be certified under these rules to serve as the person's guardian; and

(2) an employee of the United States Veterans Administration appointed to serve as a guardian for an incapacitated person under Section 1002.017(3) of the Estates Code is not required to be certified under these rules to serve as the person's guardian.

(g) Upon certification, the certified guardian will be issued a certificate, which will be valid for two years from the date of issuance. New certificates will be issued for successive two-year periods upon timely and satisfactory completion of the renewal process.

(h) A certified guardian may use the designation "TxCG" to indicate that the guardian is certified by the Commission. Provisionally certified guardians may not use such designation.

Adopted by orders of the Supreme Court May 13, 2014, and August 19, 2014, eff. September 1, 2014.

7.3. Responsibilities of Certified Guardians; Reporting Requirements

(a) Standards and Rules. A certified guardian must comply with these rules and with the Minimum Standards for the Provision of Guardianship Services adopted by the Commission.

(b) Notice to Commission. A certified guardian must immediately notify the Commission if:

(1) the guardian is indicted for, formally charged with, adjudged guilty of, or enters a plea of no contest in return for a grant of deferred adjudication with respect to any felony or misdemeanor offense;

(2) any proceeding listed in Rule 7.2(b)(7) is initiated;

(3) events or circumstances would require any changes to the attestation required by Rule 7.2(b)(7); or

(4) the guardian is removed as a guardian under Chapter 1203 of the Estates Code.

(c) Notice from Commission. If the Commission receives notice of any of the items in (b) in any manner other than from the certified guardian, the Director will contact the certified guardian regarding the notice by first class mail. Notice from the Director on behalf of the Commission is deemed given when sent to the certified guardian at the last home address on file in the Commission's records.

(d) Documents filed with court. Each document prepared by or on behalf of a certified guardian and filed with a court must include the certified guardian's certification number.

(e) Not later than January 31 of each year, each guardianship program must provide to the Commission the following information for the preceding year:

(1) the number of wards served by the guardianship program reported by county in which the application to create a guardianship for the ward was filed, and the total number of wards served by the guardianship program;

(2) the name, business address, and business telephone number of each individual employed by or volunteering or contracting with the guardianship program to provide guardianship services to a ward or proposed ward of the program;

(3) the name of each county in which an individual described in (2) provides or is authorized to provide guardianship services;

(4) the total amount of money received from the State of Texas for the provision of guardianship services; and

(5) the amount of money received from any other public source, including a county or the federal government, for the provision of guardianship services, reported by source, and the total amount of money received from those public sources.

(f) Not later than January 31 of each year, each private professional guardian must provide to the Commission the following information for the preceding year:

(1) the number of wards served by the private professional guardian reported by county in which the application to create a guardianship for a ward was filed and the total number of wards served by the private professional guardian, including the name of each ward and the docket number and court having jurisdiction of the guardianship;

(2) the aggregate fair market value of the property of all wards that was managed by the private professional guardian;

(3) the name, business address, and business telephone number of each individual who provided guardianship services to a ward of a private professional guardian on behalf of the private professional guardian;

(4) the total amount of money received from the State of Texas for the provision of guardianship services;

(5) the amount of money received from any other public source, including a county or the federal government, for the provision of guardianship services, reported by source, and the total amount of money received from those public sources;

(6) whether the private professional guardian was removed as a guardian by the court or resigned as a guardian in a particular case, and, if so, a description of the circumstances causing the removal or resignation, the style of the suit, the docket number, and the court having jurisdiction over the proceeding;

(7) reaffirmation of Rule 7.2(b)(6) and (7); and

(8) a copy of the private professional guardian's application for a certificate of registration with each county clerk required by Section 1104.302 of the Estates Code.

(g) Not later than January 31 of each year, the Department of Aging and Disability Services Guardianship Program must provide to the Commission a statement containing:

(1) the name, address, and telephone number of each department employee who is or will be providing guardianship services to a ward or proposed ward on behalf of the department; and

(2) the name of each county in which each employee named in (1) is providing or is authorized to provide those services.

(h) Information that must be submitted under (e), (f), and (g) must be submitted on appropriate forms and in the manner determined by the Commission.

Adopted by orders of the Supreme Court May 13, 2014, and August 19, 2014, eff. September 1, 2014.

7.4. Provisional Certification

(a) Application for provisional certification. An individual who does not meet the requirements for certification in Rule 7.2(b)(4) and (5) may apply for provisional certification in writing on the forms provided by the Commission. An applicant for provisional certification must identify the applicant's supervisor on the application form. The supervisor must sign the application form.

(b) Requirements for provisional certification. To be eligible for provisional certification, an applicant must meet all requirements in Rule 7.2(b)(1)–(3), (b)(6)–(7), and (c). Provisional certification expires on the second anniversary of the date the certificate is issued.

(c) Responsibilities of provisionally certified guardian.

(1) A provisionally certified guardian may provide guardianship services in this State only under the supervision of a certified guardian supervisor. In order to maintain provisional certification, a provisionally certified guardian must have a certified guardian supervisor, even if the provisionally certified guardian is not currently providing guardianship services.

(2) A provisionally certified guardian must comply with these rules and with the Minimum Standards for Guardianship Services.

(3) Notice to Commission. A provisionally certified guardian must immediately notify the Commission if:

(A) the provisionally certified guardian obtains a different supervisor or is without a supervisor;

(B) the provisionally certified guardian is indicted for, formally charged with, adjudged guilty of, or enters a plea of no contest in return for a grant of deferred adjudication with respect to any felony or misdemeanor offense;

(C) any proceeding listed in Rule 7.2(b)(7) is initiated;

(D) events or circumstances would require any changes to the attestation required by Rule 7.2(b)(7); or

(E) the provisionally certified guardian is removed as a guardian under Chapter 1203 of the Estates Code.

(4) Documents filed with court. Each document prepared by or on behalf of a provisionally certified guardian and filed with a court must include the provisionally certified guardian's certification number and the name and certification number of his or her supervisor.

(5) A provisionally certified guardian must comply with the continuing education requirements in Rules 4.1–4.3 and 7.7. A provisionally certified guardian, when he or she meets the qualifications for certification, must submit documentation as described in Rule 4.3(g) with his or her application for certification.

(d) Responsibilities of supervisor.

(1) A supervisor must:

(A) assume primary responsibility for guiding the provisionally certified guardian's work and for supervising, generally and directly, as necessary, the quality of the provisionally certified guardian's work;

(B) meet with each provisionally certified guardian at least once every two weeks, with at least one of these meetings being face-to-face each month;

(C) assist the provisionally certified guardian in activities to the extent that the supervisor considers it necessary and appropriate;

(D) ensure that the provisionally certified guardian is familiar with the provisions of these rules and the Minimum Standards for Guardianship Services; and

(E) monitor the provisionally certified guardian's compliance with these rules and the Minimum Standards for Guardianship Services.

(2) A supervisor may not supervise more provisionally certified guardians than a reasonably prudent supervisor operating under substantially similar circumstances would supervise at one time.

(3) A supervisor whose certification expires, is revoked, or is suspended, or who voluntarily surrenders his or her certification, may not continue as a supervisor and must notify all provisionally certified guardians under that person's supervision that the person may not continue as a supervisor.

(4) A supervisor must immediately notify the Commission, or cause notice to be sent to the Commission, if the supervisor ceases to supervise a provisionally certified guardian.

(5) A supervisor may not:

(A) be related within the second degree by affinity (marriage) or within the third degree by consanguinity (blood or adoption) to a person whom he or she is supervising; or

(B) be an employee of or under the employment supervision of a person whom he or she is supervising.

(e) Notice from Commission. If the Commission receives notice from the supervisor under (d)(4), or receives notice of any of the items in (c)(3) in any manner other than from the provisionally certified guardian, the Director, on behalf of the Commission, will contact the provisionally certified guardian regarding the notification by first class mail. Notice from the Director on behalf of the Commission is deemed given when sent to the provisionally certified guardian at the last home address on file in the Commission's records.

(f) Prohibition on representation as a certified guardian. The supervisor and provisionally certified guardian may not state, represent, or imply that the provisionally certified guardian is a certified guardian.

(g) Expiration of provisional certification.

(1) A provisionally certified guardian may be provisionally certified for only one two-year period unless a waiver is approved by the Commission. For a provisionally certified guardian, a waiver may only be granted by the Commission before the expiration of the two-year period. For a formerly certified guardian whose certification expired or was surrendered unrelated to discipline, the Commission may grant a new provisional certification to allow the individual to work while pursuing certification again. It is the responsibility of the provisionally certified guardian to contact the Director regarding any questions or concerns about the expiration of provisional certification, requirements for full certification, or requesting a waiver.

(A) To request a waiver from the Commission, the provisionally certified guardian must send a written request to the Director. The request must include the reasons for seeking the waiver, the time period of the extension, and verification of attendance at Commission-approved continuing education during the provisional certification period. The provisionally certified guardian may include information in support of his or her request for a waiver, such as a letter of support from the designated guardian supervisor. If the provisionally certified guardian has not yet passed the required exam or completed required continuing education, the provisionally certified guardian must include in a request for a waiver the details of his or her plan for completion of these requirements and the amount of time necessary to do so.

(B) The Commission will consider the request at a regularly scheduled Commission meeting. The request must be received by the Director not less than 30 days prior to the next scheduled meeting of the Commission. If a request for waiver is not received in time to be heard at a regularly scheduled meeting before the provisional certification expires, the request will not be considered.

(2) Upon expiration of a provisionally certified guardian's certification, the guardian must immediately provide written notice of the expiration to each court in which the guardian has been appointed pursuant to Section 1101.151 or Section 1101.152 of the Estates Code and, if the guardian provides guardianship services on behalf of the Department of Aging and Disability Services or a guardianship program, to each of those organizations on whose behalf the guardian provides guardianship services.

(h) If a provisionally certified guardian applies to be a certified guardian within one year of obtaining provisional certification, the applicant need not submit a new criminal history record.

Adopted by orders of the Supreme Court May 13, 2014, and August 19, 2014, eff. September 1, 2014.

7.5. Renewal of Certification

(a) A renewal application and all applicable fees are due 45 days prior to the expiration of the certification. An application is timely if it is postmarked on or before the due date. Failure to complete a renewal application at least 45 days prior to expiration may result in a lapse of certification.

(b) To be eligible for renewal, the certified guardian must:

(1) pay all required fees;

(2) apply within the required time;

(3) comply with Rule 7.2(b)(6)–(7); and

(4) meet the continuing education requirements in Rules 4.1–4.3 and 7.7.

Adopted by orders of the Supreme Court May 13, 2014, and August 19, 2014, eff. September 1, 2014.

7.6. Enforcement

(a) After notice and an opportunity for a hearing under Rule 5.10, the Commission may deny, suspend, or revoke certification or provisional certification; issue a public or private reprimand; or impose other disciplinary action, if the applicant, certified guardian, or provisionally certified guardian has:

(1) failed to comply with any rule applicable to certified guardians or provisionally certified guardians;

(2) failed to comply with any of the Minimum Standards for the Provision of Guardianship Services;

(3) failed to pay any applicable fee established by the Commission;

(4) failed to meet the requirements for certification, provisional certification, or renewal established by the Commission;

(5) falsely represented or misstated any material fact to the Commission;

(6) been adjudged guilty of or entered a plea of guilty or no contest in return for a grant of deferred adjudication to any felony or misdemeanor offense, and the factors listed in Rule 3.5 weigh in favor of disciplinary action;

(7) been found civilly liable or settled a claim in an action, including but not limited to a surcharge action, that involved fraud, misrepresentation, material omission, misappropriation, theft, assault, battery, abuse, neglect, breach of trust, breach of fiduciary duty, or conversion;

(8) been relieved of responsibilities as a guardian or fiduciary by a court, employer, or client for actions involving fraud, moral turpitude, misrepresentation, material omission, misappropriation, theft, assault, battery, abuse, neglect, breach of trust, breach of fiduciary duty, or conversion;

(9) been found liable in a subrogation action by an insurance or bonding agent or in a subrogation action brought by an interested party;

(10) failed to notify the Commission of a violation of any of the provisions set forth in Rule 7.2(b)(6)–(7); or

(11) engaged in conduct that poses a substantial threat to the well-being of a ward or the ward's estate.

(b) The Commission may suspend or revoke certification or provisional certification if the certificate was granted:

(1) contrary to these rules and the requirements for certification or provisional certification; or

(2) to an individual who is not eligible to acquire a certificate or provisional certificate or who has made any false representations or misstatement of material fact to the Commission.

(c) If the respondent in a complaint or enforcement proceeding is a provisionally certified guardian, all notices sent to the respondent under Rule 5.10 will be copied to his or her designated certified guardian supervisor.

Adopted by orders of the Supreme Court May 13, 2014, and August 19, 2014, eff. September 1, 2014.

7.7. Continuing Education

(a) A certified guardian must complete at least 12 hours of approved continuing education during each certification period. The 12 hours must include a minimum of two hours of ethics and one hour of legislative update. In this rule, the term "certified guardian" includes a provisionally certified guardian.

(b) The required hours must be earned prior to the expiration of the certified guardian's certification period.

(c) A certified guardian may carry forward for the following certification period not more than four regular continuing education hours, not including ethics or legislative update hours, which were earned in excess of the 12 hours used to satisfy the continuing education requirements of the immediately previous certification period. Ethics hours and legislative update hours may not be carried forward from one certification period to another certification period even if the hours were earned in excess of the minimum requirements for ethics and legislative update hours.

(d) A continuing education activity for a certified guardian must be an organized program of learning dealing with matters that are directly related to the guardianship profession, the services guardians provide, and the legal process involved in guardianship proceedings. A continuing education activity should increase participants' understanding of the Texas judicial system, the responsibilities of a certified guardian, and the certified guardian's impact on the judicial process and the public.

(e) Continuing education activities for certified guardians must include one or more of the following subjects:

(1) guardianships;

(2) trust administration;

(3) powers of attorney;

(4) mental or physical health or geriatric health;

(5) ethics for guardians, including cooperation with lawyers, judges, and fellow guardians and courtesy to all litigants;

(6) Texas statutes, rules, and case law relevant to the guardianship profession;

(7) the role and responsibilities of the certified guardian under the Estates Code, rules adopted by the Supreme Court relating to guardianship certification, and the Minimum Standards for the Provision of Guardianship Services adopted by the Commission; and

(8) management issues, including financial planning and accounting.

(f) A certified guardian may request up to six hours of continuing education credit during each two-year certification period for teaching courses, speaking at seminars, or authoring books or articles related to the subject matter specified in (e). The certified guardian must submit an application for teaching credit on a form provided by the Commission. Credit for preparation and presentation may be provided on the basis of hour-for-hour credit for each hour spent preparing the article or book or making the presentation.

Adopted by orders of the Supreme Court May 13, 2014, and August 19, 2014, eff. September 1, 2014.

RULE 8.0. PROCESS SERVER CERTIFICATION

8.1. Definitions

Certified process server means a person who is certified by the Commission to serve process statewide.

Adopted by orders of the Supreme Court May 13, 2014, and August 19, 2014, eff. September 1, 2014.

8.2. Initial Certification Requirement

(a) A person seeking statewide certification to serve process must file with the Commission an application, sworn or under penalty of perjury, in the form prescribed by the Commission.

(b) An application must comply with the requirements of Rule 3.1 and also contain a statement indicating whether the applicant has ever been convicted of a felony or of a misdemeanor involving moral turpitude. The Commission or Director may deny certification to an applicant convicted of a felony or of a misdemeanor involving moral turpitude. If an applicant's criminal history reflects that the applicant was charged with a felony or a misdemeanor involving moral turpitude and the charges resulted in an outcome other than acquittal or conviction (such as pretrial diversion, probation, deferred adjudication, community supervision, or similar result), the Commission or Director may consider the applicant's criminal history using the factors listed in Rule 3.5 in determining whether the application should be granted.

(c) The application must include a certificate from the director of a civil process service course, approved by the Commission for certification in every state court, stating that the applicant has completed the approved course within the prior year for initial certification. The applicant bears the burden of establishing that he or she has completed within the prior year a course approved by the Commission for certification in every state court.

(d) Applications will be reviewed and either approved or rejected for good cause stated. In appropriate circumstances, the Commission or Director may approve applications on a conditional or probationary basis.

(e) Certification is effective for three years from the last day of the month that the certification issues, unless it is revoked or suspended under these rules.

Adopted by orders of the Supreme Court May 13, 2014, and August 19, 2014, eff. September 1, 2014.

8.3. Renewal of Certification

(a) To renew a certification, a process server must timely submit to the Commission a renewal application, including a current criminal history statement and all applicable fees, and complete the continuing education requirements in Rules 4.1–4.3 and 8.5.

(b) The renewal application and all applicable fees are due 45 days prior to the expiration of the certification. An application is timely if it is postmarked on or before the due date. Failure to complete a renewal application at least 45 days prior to expiration may result in a lapse of certification.

(c) A certified process server whose certification expires between September 1, 2014 and August 31, 2017 must, before renewing the certification, provide the Commission with his or her Texas and national criminal history records by having his or her fingerprints submitted according to directions published on the Commission's website. The Texas and national criminal history searches must be conducted no earlier than 90 days preceding the date the renewal application is submitted.

Adopted by orders of the Supreme Court May 13, 2014, and August 19, 2014, eff. September 1, 2014.

8.4. Enforcement

After notice and hearing under Rule 5.10, the Commission may revoke, suspend, or refuse to renew any certification issued under Rule 8.2; issue a letter of reprimand to a certified process server; or impose an administrative penalty on a certified process server for:

(a) conviction of a felony offense or of a misdemeanor offense involving moral turpitude, as determined using Rule 3.5; or

(b) other good cause as determined by the Commission.

Adopted by orders of the Supreme Court May 13, 2014, and August 19, 2014, eff. September 1, 2014.

8.5. Continuing Education

(a) To renew certification, a certified process server must establish that all required continuing education has been completed. Rules 4.1–4.3 supplement this rule and establish additional requirements for continuing education.

(b) A certified process server must complete at least 12 hours of approved continuing education during the process server's three-year certification period. For process servers who are already certified on the effective date of these rules, the three-year requirement begins with the process server's next three-year certification period.

(c) A continuing education activity for a certified process server must be an organized program of learning dealing with matters that are directly related to service of process. A continuing education activity should increase participants' understanding of the Texas judicial system, the responsibilities of a certified process server, and the certified process server's impact on the judicial process and the public.

Adopted by orders of the Supreme Court May 13, 2014, and August 19, 2014, eff. September 1, 2014.

RULE 9.0. LICENSED COURT INTERPRETERS

9.1. Definitions

(a) A **Basic Designation** permits the interpreter to interpret court proceedings in justice courts and municipal courts that are not municipal courts of record, other than a proceeding before the court in which the judge is acting as a magistrate.

(b) **Dishonorable** means lacking in integrity, indicating an intent to deceive or take unfair advantage of another person, or bringing disrepute to the profession of court interpretation.

(c) **Licensed court interpreter** means a person who is licensed by the Commission to interpret court proceedings for an individual who can hear but who does not comprehend English or communicate in English.

(d) A **Master Designation** permits the interpreter to interpret court proceedings in all courts in this State, including justice courts and municipal courts.

(e) **Unethical** means conduct that does not conform to generally accepted standards of conduct for professional court interpreters.

Adopted by orders of the Supreme Court May 13, 2014, and August 19, 2014, eff. September 1, 2014.

9.2. Licensing Requirement

(a) The Commission must issue a court interpreter license to a person who:

(1) satisfies the requirements of Section 3.0 of these rules;

(2) prior to filing an application with the Commission, satisfactorily completes a Commission-approved orientation course of at least six hours;

(3) satisfies the examination requirements of Rule 9.3; and

(4) completes all requirements, including satisfying the examination requirements within one year of the date of the application.

(b) A license issued under this rule is valid for one year from the date of issuance and must have a language endorsement for each language that the applicant will interpret.

Adopted by orders of the Supreme Court May 13, 2014, and August 19, 2014, eff. September 1, 2014.

9.3. Examination

(a) Each applicant must pass all parts of a Commission approved language examination for each language that the applicant will interpret.

(b) An applicant must pass the written examination with a score of at least 80%.

(c) An applicant must pass all three parts of the oral examination according to the following:

(1) An applicant scoring at least 60% on each part of the oral examination is eligible for a Basic Designation license.

(2) An applicant scoring at least 70% on each part of the oral examination is eligible for a Master Designation license.

(d) An applicant taking an examination must comply with the Commission's examination requirements under Rules 3.7–3.9.

(e) An applicant who fails an examination may apply for reexamination at a scheduled examination held at least six months after the date the individual failed the original examination.

Adopted by orders of the Supreme Court May 13, 2014, and August 19, 2014, eff. September 1, 2014.

9.4. Renewal

(a) To renew a license, a court interpreter must timely submit to the Commission a renewal application and all applicable fees and complete the continuing education requirements in Rules 4.1–4.3 and 9.7.

(b) The renewal application and all applicable fees are due 45 days prior to the expiration of the license. An application is timely if it is postmarked on or before the due date. A licensed court interpreter's failure to receive a renewal notice from the Commission does not exempt the interpreter from any requirements of these rules or of other rules governing the profession.

(c) A person whose license has been expired for one year or less may renew the license by paying to the Commission the appropriate renewal fee for late renewals.

(d) A licensed court interpreter whose license expires between September 1, 2014 and August 31, 2015 must, before renewing the license, provide the Commission with his or her Texas and national criminal history records by having his or her fingerprints submitted according to directions published on the Commission's website. The Texas and national criminal history searches must be conducted no earlier than 90 days preceding the date the renewal application is submitted.

Adopted by orders of the Supreme Court May 13, 2014, and August 19, 2014, eff. September 1, 2014.

9.5. Responsibilities of Licensed Court Interpreters

(a) A licensed court interpreter must include his or her name and license number on all official correspondence and on all contracts and invoices for court interpreter services.

(b) A licensed court interpreter must present his or her court interpreter license upon the request of a court or an officer of the court.

Adopted by orders of the Supreme Court May 13, 2014, and August 19, 2014, eff. September 1, 2014.

9.6. Enforcement

(a) After notice and an opportunity for a hearing under Rule 5.10, the Commission may deny, revoke, suspend, or refuse to renew a license or reprimand a licensed court interpreter on finding that the person:

(1) made a material misstatement in an application for a license;

(2) disregarded or violated Chapter 157 of the Government Code, or a rule adopted under Chapter 157;

(3) engaged in dishonorable or unethical conduct likely to deceive, defraud, or harm the public or a person for whom the interpreter interprets; or

(4) was finally convicted of a crime that indicates the person lacks the honesty, trustworthiness, or integrity to hold the license, as determined using Rule 3.5.

(b) The Commission may reissue a license to an individual whose license has been revoked if the individual applies in writing to the Commission and shows good cause to justify reissuance of the license.

(c) The Commission may assess an administrative penalty under Chapter 153 of the Government Code against a person who violates Chapter 157 of the Code or a rule adopted under that chapter.

Adopted by orders of the Supreme Court May 13, 2014, and August 19, 2014, eff. September 1, 2014.

9.7. Continuing Education

(a) To renew a license, a licensed court interpreter must complete eight hours of approved continuing education in courses approved by the Commission, including two hours of instruction in ethics.

(b) Except as provided by (c), the continuing education hours must have been completed within the term of the current license, in the case of a timely renewal. For a late renewal, the continuing education hours must have been completed within the one year period immediately prior to the date of renewal.

(c) A licensed court interpreter may carry forward to the next certification period up to four continuing education hours, but ethics credit may not be carried forward.

(d) A licensed court interpreter may not receive continuing education credit for attending the same course more than once within the same license period.

(e) Notwithstanding Rule 4.3(g), a licensed court interpreter must retain a copy of the certificate of completion for a course for one year after the date of completion. In conducting any inspection or investigation of the licensed court interpreter, the Commission may examine the licensed court interpreter's records to determine compliance with this requirement.

(f) To be approved, a continuing education course must be dedicated to instruction in one or more of the following topics:

(1) law and rules affecting the practice of a licensed court interpreter;

(2) ethics;

(3) practice topics, such as etiquette, modes, vocabulary, technology, transcription, translation, grammar and spelling, and voice training; or

(4) business practices.

Adopted by orders of the Supreme Court May 13, 2014, and August 19, 2014, eff. September 1, 2014.

FEES OF THE JUDICIAL BRANCH CERTIFICATION COMMISSION

Certified Court Reporters and Court Reporting Firms

(a) Applicants for Certification and Certified Reporters.

(1) Certification Application Fee. Each applicant must submit a certification fee of $85 with the completed application.

(2) Examination Fee. Each applicant who is taking the certification examination must submit an examination fee of $75 for Part B, $125 for Part A, or $190 for Parts A and B combined by the date established by the Commission.

(3) Examination Late Fee. The late fee that must be paid by an applicant whose application to take the examination is late according to the deadlines established by the Commission is $25.

(4) Renewal Fee (Before Expiration of Certification). Each certified court reporter must submit a renewal fee of $200 on or before the expiration date of the certification. If this fee is not timely paid, the certification will expire pursuant to Rule 6.3.

(5) Renewal Fee (Expired for Ninety Days or Less). A person whose certification has been expired for 90 days or less may renew the certification by paying a renewal fee of $300.

(6) Renewal Fee (Expired More than Ninety Days but Less than One Year). A person whose certification has been expired for more than 90 days but less than one year may renew the certification by paying a renewal fee of $400.

(7) Recertification Fee (Moved to Another State). A person who was certified in this State, moved to another state, and is currently certified and has been in practice in the other state for the two years preceding the date of application may obtain a new certification without reexamination by paying a fee of $400.

(8) Subscription Fee. With each fee required by (a)(4)–(7), a person must pay an additional, subscription fee of $10 to fund a common Internet licensing system pursuant to Section 2054.2591 of the Government Code.

(9) Regrading Fee. A person who requests that an examination be regraded must pay a regrading fee of $35.

(10) Replacement Fees. A person who requests a replacement for the person's certificate must pay a fee of $15. A person who requests a replacement for the person's ID card must pay a fee of $5.

(b) Court Reporting Firms.

(1) Registration Fee. Each registrant must submit a registration fee of $200 along with the completed registration form.

(2) Renewal Fee (Before Expiration of Registration). Each registered court reporting firm and affiliate office must submit a renewal fee of $200 on or before the expiration date of the registration. If this fee is not timely paid, the registration will expire pursuant to Rule 6.3.

(3) Renewal Fee (Expired for Ninety Days or Less). A firm whose registration has been expired for 90 days or less may renew the registration by paying a renewal fee of $300.

(4) Renewal Fee (Expired More than Ninety Days but Less than One Year). A firm whose registration has been expired for more than 90 days but less than one year may renew the registration by paying a renewal fee of $400.

(5) Replacement Fee. A firm that requests a replacement registration certificate must pay a fee of $15.

(6) Subscription Fee. With each fee required by (b)(2)–(4), a person must pay an additional, subscription fee of $12 to fund a common Internet licensing system pursuant to Section 2054.2591 of the Government Code.

Adopted by orders of the Supreme Court May 13, 2014, and August 19, 2014, eff. September 1, 2014.

Certified Guardians

(a) Application fee—$25 (An employee of the Texas Department of Aging and Disability Services who is applying for certification to provide guardianship services to a ward of the Department is exempt from payment of this fee.)

(b) Exam fee (initial)—$175 (This fee must be paid separately from all other fees by the date established in the exam schedule.)

(c) Exam fee (retake)—$175 (This fee must be paid separately from all other fees by the date established in the exam schedule.)

(d) Renewal fee—$25 (An employee of the Texas Department of Aging and Disability Services who is applying for renewal of certification to provide guardianship services to a ward of the Department is exempt from payment of this fee.)

(e) Late fee—$75

(f) Replacement fee—$5

Adopted by orders of the Supreme Court May 13, 2014, and August 19, 2014, eff. September 1, 2014.

Certified Process Servers

(a) Application fee—$225

(b) Renewal fee—$225

(c) Late fee (for late renewals, in addition to renewal fee)—$110

(d) Subscription fee to accompany each initial or renewal application, to fund participation in a common Internet licensing system under Section 2054.2591 of the Government Code—$5

(e) Replacement fee—$5

Adopted by orders of the Supreme Court May 13, 2014, and August 19, 2014, eff. September 1, 2014.

Licensed Court Interpreters

(a) Application fee—$75

(b) Renewal application fee—$50

(c) Upgrade to Master application fee—$25

(d) Additional endorsement fee—$25

(e) Replacement license fee—$5

(f) Written examination fee—$100

(g) Oral examination fee—$300

(h) Renewal Fee (Expired for Ninety Days or Less). A person whose license has been expired for 90 days or less may renew the certification by paying a renewal fee of $75.

(i) Renewal Fee (Expired More than Ninety Days but Less Than One Year). A person whose license has been expired for more than 90 days but less than one year may renew the certification by paying a renewal fee of $100.

Adopted by orders of the Supreme Court May 13, 2014, and August 19, 2014, eff. September 1, 2014.

THE TEXAS LAWYER'S CREED—A MANDATE FOR PROFESSIONALISM

Adopted November 7, 1989

Reaffirmed March 26, 2013

Including Amendments Received Through February 1, 2016

ORDER OF ADOPTION

The conduct of a lawyer should be characterized at all times by honesty, candor, and fairness. In fulfilling his or her primary duty to a client, a lawyer must be ever mindful of the profession's broader duty to the legal system.

The Supreme Court of Texas and the Court of Criminal Appeals are committed to eliminating a practice in our State by a minority of lawyers of abusive tactics which have surfaced in many parts of our country. We believe such tactics are a disservice to our citizens, harmful to clients, and demeaning to our profession.

The abusive tactics range from lack of civility to outright hostility and obstructionism. Such behavior does not serve justice but tends to delay and often deny justice. The lawyers who use abusive tactics instead of being part of the solution have become part of the problem.

The desire for respect and confidence by lawyers from the public should provide the members of our profession with the necessary incentive to attain the highest degree of ethical and professional conduct. These rules are primarily aspirational. Compliance with the rules depends primarily upon understanding and voluntary compliance, secondarily upon re-enforcement by peer pressure and public opinion, and finally when necessary by enforcement by the courts through their inherent powers and rules already in existence.

These standards are not a set of rules that lawyers can use and abuse to incite ancillary litigation or arguments over whether or not they have been observed.

We must always be mindful that the practice of law is a profession. As members of a learned art we pursue a common calling in the spirit of public service. We have a proud tradition. Throughout the history of our nation, the members of our citizenry have looked to the ranks of our profession for leadership and guidance. Let us now as a profession each rededicate ourselves to practice law so we can restore public confidence in our profession, faithfully serve our clients, and fulfill our responsibility to the legal system.

The Supreme Court of Texas and the Court of Criminal Appeals hereby promulgate and adopt "The Texas Lawyer's Creed—A Mandate for Professionalism" as attached hereto and made a part hereof.

In Chambers, this 7th day of November, 1989.

THE TEXAS LAWYER'S CREED—A MANDATE FOR PROFESSIONALISM

I am a lawyer. I am entrusted by the People of Texas to preserve and improve our legal system. I am licensed by the Supreme Court of Texas. I must therefore abide by the Texas Disciplinary Rules of Professional Conduct, but I know that professionalism requires more than merely avoiding the violation of laws and rules. I am committed to this creed for no other reason than it is right.

I. OUR LEGAL SYSTEM

A lawyer owes to the administration of justice personal dignity, integrity, and independence. A lawyer should always adhere to the highest principles of professionalism.

1. I am passionately proud of my profession. Therefore, "My word is my bond."

2. I am responsible to assure that all persons have access to competent representation regardless of wealth or position in life.

3. I commit myself to an adequate and effective pro bono program.

4. I am obligated to educate my clients, the public, and other lawyers regarding the spirit and letter of this Creed.

5. I will always be conscious of my duty to the judicial system.

II. LAWYER TO CLIENT

A lawyer owes to a client allegiance, learning, skill, and industry. A lawyer shall employ all appropriate means to protect and advance the client's legitimate rights, claims, and objectives. A lawyer shall not be deterred by any real or imagined fear of judicial disfavor or public unpopularity, nor be influenced by mere self-interest.

1. I will advise my client of the contents of this Creed when undertaking representation.

2. I will endeavor to achieve my client's lawful objectives in legal transactions and in litigation as quickly and economically as possible.

3. I will be loyal and committed to my client's lawful objectives, but I will not permit that loyalty and commitment to interfere with my duty to provide objective and independent advice.

4. I will advise my client that civility and courtesy are expected and are not a sign of weakness.

5. I will advise my client of proper and expected behavior.

6. I will treat adverse parties and witnesses with fairness and due consideration. A client has no right to demand that I abuse anyone or indulge in any offensive conduct.

7. I will advise my client that we will not pursue conduct which is intended primarily to harass or drain the financial resources of the opposing party.

8. I will advise my client that we will not pursue tactics which are intended primarily for delay.

9. I will advise my client that we will not pursue any course of action which is without merit.

10. I will advise my client that I reserve the right to determine whether to grant accommodations to opposing counsel in all matters that do not adversely affect my client's lawful objectives. A client has no right to instruct me to refuse reasonable requests made by other counsel.

11. I will advise my client regarding the availability of mediation, arbitration, and other alternative methods of resolving and settling disputes.

III. LAWYER TO LAWYER

A lawyer owes to opposing counsel, in the conduct of legal transactions and the pursuit of litigation, courtesy, candor, cooperation, and scrupulous observance of all agreements and mutual understandings. Ill feelings between clients shall not influence a lawyer's conduct, attitude, or demeanor toward opposing counsel. A lawyer shall not engage in unprofessional conduct in retaliation against other unprofessional conduct.

1. I will be courteous, civil, and prompt in oral and written communications.

2. I will not quarrel over matters of form or style, but I will concentrate on matters of substance.

3. I will identify for other counsel or parties all changes I have made in documents submitted for review.

4. I will attempt to prepare documents which correctly reflect the agreement of the parties. I will not include provisions which have not been agreed upon or omit provisions which are necessary to reflect the agreement of the parties.

5. I will notify opposing counsel, and, if appropriate, the Court or other persons, as soon as practicable, when hearings, depositions, meetings, conferences or closings are cancelled.

6. I will agree to reasonable requests for extensions of time and for waiver of procedural formalities, provided legitimate objectives of my client will not be adversely affected.

7. I will not serve motions or pleadings in any manner that unfairly limits another party's opportunity to respond.

8. I will attempt to resolve by agreement my objections to matters contained in pleadings and discovery requests and responses.

9. I can disagree without being disagreeable. I recognize that effective representation does not require antagonistic or obnoxious behavior. I will neither encourage nor knowingly permit my client or anyone under my control to do anything which would be unethical or improper if done by me.

10. I will not, without good cause, attribute bad motives or unethical conduct to opposing counsel nor bring the profession into disrepute by unfounded accusations of impropriety. I will avoid disparaging personal remarks or acrimony towards opposing counsel, parties and witnesses. I will not be influenced by any ill feeling between clients. I will abstain from any allusion to personal peculiarities or idiosyncrasies of opposing counsel.

11. I will not take advantage, by causing any default or dismissal to be rendered, when I know the identity of an opposing counsel, without first inquiring about that counsel's intention to proceed.

12. I will promptly submit orders to the Court. I will deliver copies to opposing counsel before or contemporaneously with submission to the Court. I will promptly approve the form of orders which accurately reflect the substance of the rulings of the Court.

13. I will not attempt to gain an unfair advantage by sending the Court or its staff correspondence or copies of correspondence.

14. I will not arbitrarily schedule a deposition, court appearance, or hearing until a good faith effort has been made to schedule it by agreement.

15. I will readily stipulate to undisputed facts in order to avoid needless costs or inconvenience for any party.

16. I will refrain from excessive and abusive discovery.

17. I will comply with all reasonable discovery requests. I will not resist discovery requests which are not objectionable. I will not make objections nor give instructions to a witness for the purpose of delaying or obstructing the discovery process. I will encourage witnesses to respond to all deposition questions which are reasonably understandable. I will neither encourage nor permit my witness to quibble about words where their meaning is reasonably clear.

18. I will not seek Court intervention to obtain discovery which is clearly improper and not discoverable.

19. I will not seek sanctions or disqualification unless it is necessary for protection of my client's lawful objectives or is fully justified by the circumstances.

IV. LAWYER AND JUDGE

Lawyers and judges owe each other respect, diligence, candor, punctuality, and protection against unjust and improper criticism and attack. Lawyers and judges are equally responsible to protect the dignity and independence of the Court and the profession.

1. I will always recognize that the position of judge is the symbol of both the judicial system and administration of justice. I will refrain from conduct that degrades this symbol.

2. I will conduct myself in Court in a professional manner and demonstrate my respect for the Court and the law.

3. I will treat counsel, opposing parties, the Court, and members of the Court staff with courtesy and civility.

4. I will be punctual.

5. I will not engage in any conduct which offends the dignity and decorum of proceedings.

6. I will not knowingly misrepresent, mischaracterize, misquote or miscite facts or authorities to gain an advantage.

7. I will respect the rulings of the Court.

8. I will give the issues in controversy deliberate, impartial and studied analysis and consideration.

9. I will be considerate of the time constraints and pressures imposed upon the Court, Court staff and counsel in efforts to administer justice and resolve disputes.

Adopted by Supreme Court and Court of Criminal Appeals Nov. 7, 1989. Reaffirmed by Supreme Court March 26, 2013.